THE

MAYAN

LANGUAGES

The Mayan Languages presents a comprehensive survey of the language family associated with the Classic Mayan civilization (AD 200–900), a family whose individual languages are still spoken today by at least six million indigenous Maya in Mexico, Guatemala, Belize, and Honduras. This unique resource is an ideal reference for advanced undergraduate and postgraduate students of Mayan languages and linguistics. Written by a team of experts in the field, *The Mayan Languages* presents in-depth accounts of the linguistic features that characterize the thirty-one languages of the family, their historical evolution, and the social context in which they are spoken.

The Mayan Languages:

- provides detailed grammatical sketches of approximately a third of the Mayan languages, representing most of the branches of the family;
- includes a section on the historical development of the family, as well as an entirely new sketch of the grammar of "Classic Maya" as represented in the hieroglyphic script;
- provides detailed state-of-the-art discussions of the principal advances in grammatical analysis of Mayan languages;
- includes ample discussion of the use of the languages in social, conversational, and poetic contexts.

Consisting of topical chapters on the history, sociolinguistics, phonology, morphology, syntax, semantics, discourse structure, and acquisition of the Mayan languages, this book will be a resource for researchers and other readers with an interest in historical linguistics, linguistic anthropology, language acquisition, and linguistic typology.

Judith Aissen is Professor Emeritus of Linguistics at the University of California, Santa Cruz.

Nora C. England is Dallas TACA Centennial Professor in the Humanities and Professor of Linguistics at the University of Texas at Austin. She is also Director of the Center for Indigenous Languages of Latin America at the University of Texas at Austin.

Roberto Zavala Maldonado is Researcher and Professor at the Centro de Investigaciones y Estudios Superiores en Antropología Social (CIESAS) in Mexico. He was also Joint-Director of the Project for the Documentation of Languages of Meso-America.

ROUTLEDGE LANGUAGE FAMILY SERIES

Each volume in this series contains an in-depth account of the members of some of the world's most important language families. Written by experts in each language, these accessible accounts provide detailed linguistic analysis and description. The contents are carefully structured to cover the natural system of classification: phonology, morphology, syntax, lexis, semantics, dialectology, and sociolinguistics.

Every volume contains extensive bibliographies for each language, a detailed index and tables, and maps and examples from the languages to demonstrate the linguistic features being described. The consistent format allows comparative study, not only between the languages in each volume, but also across all the volumes in the series.

The Mayan Languages
Edited by Judith Aissen, Nora C. England & Roberto Zavala Maldonado

The Austronesian Languages of
Asia and Madagascar
Edited by Nikolaus Himmelmann & Sander Adelaar

The Bantu Languages
Edited by Derek Nurse & Gérard Philippson

The Celtic Languages,
2nd Edition
Edited by Martin J. Ball & Nicole Müller

The Dravidian Languages, 2nd Edition
Edited by Sanford B. Steever

The Germanic Languages
Edited by Ekkehard Konig & Johan van der Auwera

The Indo-Aryan Languages
Edited by George Cardona & Dhanesh K. Jain

The Indo-European Languages,
2nd Edition
Edited by Mate Kapović

The Iranian Languages
Edited by Gernot Windfuhr

The Languages of Japan and Korea
Edited by Nicolas Tranter

The Khoesan Languages
Edited by Rainer Vossen

The Mongolic Languages
Edited by Juha Janhunan

The Munda Languages
Edited by Gregory D.S. Anderson

The Oceanic Languages
Edited by John Lynch, Malcolm Ross & Terry Crowley

The Romance Languages
Edited by Martin Harris & Nigel Vincent

The Semitic Languages
Edited by Robert Hetzron

The Sino-Tibetan Languages,
2nd Edition
Edited by Graham Thurgood & Randy J. Lapolla

The Slavonic Languages
Edited by Bernard Comrie & Greville G. Corbett

The Tai-Kadai Languages
Edited by Anthony Diller

The Turkic Languages
Edited by Éva Csató & Lars Johanson

The Uralic Languages
Edited by Daniel Abondolo

THE

MAYAN

LANGUAGES

Edited by
Judith Aissen, Nora C. England, and
Roberto Zavala Maldonado

Routledge
Taylor & Francis Group

LONDON AND NEW YORK

First published 2017 by Routledge

2 Park Square, Milton Park, Abingdon, Oxfordshire OX14 4RN

52 Vanderbilt Avenue, New York, NY 10017

Routledge is an imprint of the Taylor & Francis Group, an informa business

First issued in paperback 2019

Copyrgight © 2017 selection and editorial matter Judith Aissen, Nora C. England and Roberto Zavala Maldonado; individual chapters, the contributors.

The right of Judith Aissen, Nora C. England and Roberto Zavala Maldonado to be identified as the authors of the editorial material, and of the authors for their individual chapters has been asserted by them in accordance with sections 77 and 78 of the Copyright, Designs and Patents Act 1988.

All rights reserved. No part of this book may be reprinted or reproduced or utilised in any form or by any electronic, mechanical, or other means, now known or hereafter invented, including photocopying and recording, or in any information storage or retrieval system, without permission in writing from the publishers.

Notice:
Product or corporate names may be trademarks or registered trademarks, and are used only for identification and explanation without intent to infringe.

British Library Cataloguing-in-Publication Data
A catalogue record for this book is available from the British Library

Library of Congress Cataloging-in-Publication Data
Names: Aissen, Judith, 1948– editor. | England, Nora C., editor. | Zavala, Roberto, editor.
Title: The Mayan languages / edited by Judith L. Aissen, Nora C. England, and Roberto Zavala Maldonado.
Description: New York : Routledge/Taylor & Francis Group, [2017] | Series: Routledge language family series
Identifiers: LCCN 2016049735 | ISBN 9780415738026 (hardback)
Subjects: LCSH: Mayan languages. | Mayan languages—History. | Mayan languages—Social aspects. | Indians of Mexico—Languages—History. | Mexico—Civilization. | Mexico—Languages—History. | Historical linguistics—Mexico.
Classification: LCC PM3961 .M39 2017 | DDC 497/.415—dc23
LC record available at https://lccn.loc.gov/2016049735

ISBN: 978-0-415-73802-6 (hbk)
ISBN: 978-0-367-86913-7 (pbk)

Typeset in Times New Roman
by Apex CoVantage, LLC

CONTENTS

ABBREVIATIONS

1	first person
2	second person
3	third person
A	set A
ABIL	abilitative
ABS	absolutive
ABST	abstract noun
ACT	active
ADMIR	admirative
ADV	adverb(ial)
AF	agent focus
AFF	affect word
AFFIRM	affirmative
AFV	affective verb
AGT	agent
AGTV	agentive
ANIM	animate
ANTIC	anticausative
AP	antipassive
APPL	applicative
ART	article
ASP	aspect
ASPL	aspectless
ASSUR	assurative
ATT	attenuator
ATTR	attributive
AUG	augmentative
AUX	auxiliary
B	set B
BEN	benefactive
CAUS	causative
CEL	celerative
CFP	clause final particle
CIS	completive intransitive status
CL	clitic
CLF	classifier
COM	comitative
COMP	complementizer
CON	connective
COND	conditional

COP	copula
CP	completive
CTS	completive transitive status
D	deictic
DAT	dative
DCM	discourse continuity marker
DEB	debitive
DEF	definite
DEIC	deictic
DEM	demonstrative
DEP	dependent
DER	derivation, derived
DET	determiner
DIM	diminutive
DIR	directional
DIS	dependent intransitive status
DISP	dispositional
DIST	distributive
DM	dependency marker
D.NML	nominal suffix for derived transitives
DS	directional suffix
DST	distal
DTR	detransitive
DTS	dependent transitive status
DTV	derived transitive
DUB	dubitative
DUR	durative
EMPH	emphasis, emphatic
ENC	enclitic
EP	epenthetic
ERG	ergative
EVID	evidential
EXCL	exclusive
EXCLAM	exclamatory
EXH	exhortative
EXIST	existential
EXPL	expletive
EXPR	expressive
F	feminine
FOC	focus
FOR	formal
FS	final suffix
FUT	future
GEN	generic
HAB	habitual
HESIT	hesitation
HUM	human
I	intransitive
ICP	incompletive

IIS	incompletive intransitive status
IMP	imperative
IMPIS	imperative intransitive status
IMPTS	imperative transitive status
INAL	inalienable
INAN	inanimate
INCH	inchoative
INCL	inclusive
IND	indicative
INDEP	independent
INDF	indefinite
INF	infinitive
INST	instrument(al)
INTR	intransitivizer
INTS	intensifier
INV	inverse
IOPR	indirect object pronoun
IPFV	imperfective
IPRF	imperfect
IRR	irrealis
IS	intransitive status
ITR	iterative
ITS	incompletive transitive status
ITV	intransitive verb suffix
IV	intransitive verb
LOC	locative
M	masculine
MAL	malefactive
MEAS	measure word
MOD	modal
MOV	movement element
MP	marked possession
N	noun
NEG	negative
NF	nonfinite
NML	nominal
NMLZ	nominalizer
NT	neutral aspect
NUM	numeral
OBL	oblique
OBLIG	obligative
ONOM	onomatopoeic
OPT	optative
ORD	ordinal
OST	ostensive
PAR	particle
PART	partitive
PAT	patient
PF	phrase final

PFV	perfective
PL	plural
PN	proper noun
POS	positional (predicate)
POSS	possessive
POT	potential
PRED	predicative (derivation)
PREP	preposition
PRF	perfect
PROG	progressive
PRON	pronoun
PROSP	prospective aspect
PROX	proximate, proximal
PST	past
PSV	passive
PTCP	participle
PURP	purpose(ive)
Q	interrogative particle/pronoun
QUOT	quotative
REDUP	reduplicant
REL	relative clause, relativizer
RELAL	relational
REP	reportative
REPET	repetitive
RES	result state
RN	relational noun
RR	reflexive/reciprocal
SAP	speech act participant
SD	syntactic dependence
SG	singular
SOC	sociative
SS	status suffix
STAT	stative
SUB	subordinator
SUBJ	subjunctive
SUF	suffix
T	transitive
TCM	temporal cohesion marker
TERM	terminative
THV	thematic vowel
TOP	topic marker
TR	transitive, transitivizer
TS	transitive status
TV	transitive verb suffix
UNPOSS	unpossessed
VN	verbal noun
VRBZ	verbalizer

CONTRIBUTORS

Judith Aissen is Professor Emeritus of Linguistics at the University of California Santa Cruz.

Scott AnderBois is Assistant Professor of Cognitive, Linguistic, and Psychological Sciences at Brown University.

Brandon O. Baird is Assistant Professor of Spanish and Linguistics at Middlebury College.

Rusty Barrett is Associate Professor of English at the University of Kentucky.

Jürgen Bohnemeyer is Associate Professor of Linguistics at the State University of New York at Buffalo.

Lyle Campbell is Professor of Linguistics at the University of Hawai'i at Mānoa.

Telma A. Can Pixabaj is a researcher at the Centro de Investigaciones Multidisciplinarias sobre Chiapas y la Frontera Sur, CIMSUR-UNAM.

Jessica Coon is Associate Professor of Linguistics at McGill University.

Alejandro Curiel Ramírez del Prado is an independent scholar.

Nora C. England is Professor of Linguistics at the University of Texas at Austin.

John B. Haviland is Distinguished Professor of Anthropology at the University of California San Diego.

Robert Henderson is Assistant Professor of Linguistics at the University of Arizona.

Charles Andrew Hofling is Professor Emeritus of Anthropology at Southern Illinois University Carbondale.

Terrence Kaufman is Emeritus Professor of Anthropology and Linguistics of the University of Pittsburgh; currently director of the Institute for the Documentation of the Languages of Meso-America (IDLMA), El Cerrito, California.

Danny Law is Assistant Professor of Linguistics at the University of Texas at Austin.

Pedro Mateo Pedro is Assistant Research Professor at the University of Maryland Language Science Center and Professor in the Faculty of Education, Universidad del Valle de Guatemala, Altiplano.

Eladio Mateo Toledo is Professor and Senior Researcher of Linguistics at the Centro de Investigaciones y Estudios Superiores en Antropología Social (CIESAS).

Barbara Pfeiler is Professor and Senior Researcher of Linguistics at the Universidad Nacional Autónoma de México, Mérida, Yucatán, Mexico.

Gilles Polian is Professor and Senior Researcher of Linguistics at the Centro de Investigaciones y Estudios Superiores en Antropología Social (CIESAS).

Clifton Pye is Associate Professor of Linguistics at the University of Kansas.

Sergio Romero is Assistant Professor of Spanish and Portuguese and of Latin American Studies at the University of Texas at Austin.

David Stuart is Professor of Art and Art History at the University of Texas at Austin.

Roberto Zavala Maldonado is Professor and Senior Researcher of Linguistics at the Centro de Investigaciones y Estudios Superiores en Antropología Social (CIESAS).

CHAPTER 1

INTRODUCTION

Judith Aissen, Nora C. England, and Roberto Zavala Maldonado

This is a book about the Mayan languages. No such comprehensive work has been published in English, so this is a first for a relatively well-known language family. There are more or less thirty extant Mayan languages spoken in Guatemala, Mexico, and Belize (in this volume see Law for a map of the contemporary languages, Campbell for an overview of Mayan historical and comparative linguistics, and Campbell or Kaufman for family relationships). They range between very small (under thirty speakers, for instance Itzaj) to quite large (close to a million speakers, for instance K'iche'). While the Mayan family is among the most robust in Latin America, there are signs of language shift, with some children in at least some communities not learning to speak the language of their forebears. Most of the languages, however, have speakers in most age groups and most are used in daily activities to varying extents (see Haviland, this volume, on Mayan conversation and interaction and Romero, this volume, on social factors in language variation).

In what follows, we introduce the chapters in this volume via a sketch of the history of research on Mayan languages (§1), and an outline of some of the main features of the languages (§2). Sections 3 and 4 present variant spellings of the language names and the orthographies which are used in linguistic research on Mayan.

1 HISTORY OF LINGUISTIC RESEARCH

Although Mayan linguistics has its roots in the dictionaries and grammars written by Spaniards in the sixteenth and seventeenth centuries, a new burst of research began in the mid-twentieth century. The beginnings were mostly at the University of Chicago, where Manuel J. Andrade in the 1930s and Norman McQuown starting in the 1950s were pivotal figures in Mayan linguistics. Both were leaders in the use of technology in linguistic research – Andrade pioneered the use of audio technology in the field and McQuown the use of mainframe computers for language documentation. Both contributed greatly to the language archives at Chicago with their own material on Mayan and other Mesoamerican languages, fueling future research there for many years. McQuown was founding director of the archive and taught many students who went on to make their own contributions, including Terrence Kaufman (as an undergraduate), Christopher Day (PhD 1967; see Day 1973), Nicholas A. Hopkins (1967), John Attinasi (PhD 1973), Louanna Furbee (PhD 1974; see Furbee 1976b), Judith M. Maxwell (1982), and Thomas C. Smith-Stark (1983). The Harvard Chiapas Project, although established to train anthropologists, produced several who devoted themselves to language: Robert M. Laughlin (PhD 1963), Victoria Bricker (PhD 1968; see Bricker 1973), and John Haviland (PhD 1972). Two linguists who specialized in Mayan languages also graduated from Harvard: John Robertson (PhD 1974; see Robertson 1980), and Colette Grinevald (Craig) (PhD 1975; see Craig 1977).

In the early period, represented mostly by the Chicago linguists (McQuown was then known as the "father" of Mayan linguistics) and a few others, the approach was primarily historical and descriptive, concentrating on articulatory phonology, morphology, dialectology, lexicon, and lexicography. Great advances were made in the history of Mayan languages (Campbell, this volume) and continue to be made today (Kaufman, Law, and Law and Stuart, this volume). Historical knowledge about the Mayan family of languages has been said to approach that of Indo-European, even though there are few documents to rely on. Early dissertations provided some of the first modern linguistic grammars or grammatical sketches of Mayan languages (e.g., Kaufman 1963; Day 1967; Fought 1967; Hopkins 1967; Canger 1969); two of these were later published (Kaufman 1971; Day 1973). Lyle Campbell began his work in the sixties and received his PhD in 1971, later publishing the results of his studies of K'ichean linguistic prehistory (1977). Louanna Furbee further added to Mayan text collections by editing three issues of the IJAL *Native American Text Series* devoted to Mayan languages (1976a, 1979, 1980). Robert Laughlin, while always protesting that he was *not* a linguist, nevertheless published the first truly full-length dictionary of a Mayan language (Tsotsil; 1975), followed by two volumes of texts (1977, 1980) and a colonial dictionary of Tsotsil (Laughlin and Haviland 1988).

Another group that was active in the Mayan area was SIL International (Wycliffe Bible Translators), principally in the sixties and seventies. Among their scholarly publications, all listed at SIL International, are dictionaries, grammatical works or descriptions, and texts.

The study of grammar expanded greatly in the seventies, partly as a result of the establishment of the Proyecto Lingüístico Francisco Marroquín (PLFM) by Kaufman and others. The PLFM gave the opportunity to twelve young linguists (Glenn Ayres, Linda Brown, Karen Dakin, Margaret Datz, Jon Dayley, Nora England, Tom Larsen, Judith Maxwell, Linda Munson, William Norman, Robin Quizar, Stephen Stewart) to work on Mayan languages and direct the preparation of dictionaries by speakers of Mam, K'iche', Kaqchikel, Tz'utujil, Ixil, Akateko, Q'anjob'al, Q'eqchi', Poqomchi', Chuj, Ch'orti', Awakatek, and Popti'. Many of these linguists wrote dissertations on the languages of the groups they were in charge of, usually grammars, and some of these were published (Stewart 1980; England 1983; Dayley 1985; Ayres 1991). Others, like Larsen 1988, while never published, became and remain standard grammatical references. Besides the PLFM linguists, a number of others also began their work in the seventies, often leading to publications in the seventies and eighties. The work by these linguists includes John Robertson's dissertation on verbal agreement in Mayan (1980), John Haviland's grammar of Tsotsil (1981), Laura Martin's dissertation on positionals in Q'anjob'al (1977), Robin Quizar (1979) on word order, James Mondloch on K'iche' voice (1981), John Du Bois on Sakapulek grammar (1981), and Thom Smith-Stark on Poqomam phonology and morphology (1983). Work on syntax began to mature in the seventies. Many of the grammars produced in this period had more substantial syntax sections than did earlier ones. There was active research in the comparative syntax of Mayan (Norman and Campbell 1978); typological work, documented in a number of influential papers by Thom Smith-Stark (Smith-Stark 1978 was the most important of these); and in formal syntax, e.g., Colette Grinevald Craig (1977), Frank Trechsel (1981), Ava Berinstein (1985), and Judith Aissen (1987). (See England and Baird, Polian, Zavala Maldonado, and Aissen, this volume, for information about grammar in Mayan languages, as well as the overviews in Bennett (2016), Coon (2016), Henderson (2016), and England (2017).)

Some of the signs that Mayan linguistics was consolidating as a field in the 1970s and 1980s were the production of a large bibliography (Campbell et al. 1978), the appearance of several collections of articles (McClaran 1976; England 1978; Martin 1979), the IJAL text collection mentioned earlier, a series of *Talleres* (workshops) which were held alternately in Mexico and Guatemala during the late seventies and early eighties, and even a fairly short-lived journal (*The Journal of Mayan Linguistics*). In addition, a few publications in this period and a little later appeared in Spanish (Kaufman 1972; Haviland 1981; England and Elliott 1990; Ayres 1991), foreshadowing a time when publication in Spanish would become more common as scholarship began to be directed toward and to be produced by speakers of Mayan languages.

The study of Mayan hieroglyphs has a long history, which we will not cover here except to note that in the seventies there were a number of important breakthroughs, many having to do with the structure of the language used in the hieroglyphs. It was discovered that the writing was in many instances "phonetic" (actually syllabic), that the glyphs represented actual spoken language, and that the writing often combined logograms with syllabograms. All of this was a result of a collective effort on the part of archaeologists, art historians, epigraphers, and linguists (such as Floyd Lounsbury at Yale). See Law and Stuart, this volume, for the results of this collective initiative with regard to knowledge about the structure of the language represented by the glyphs.

The 1980s saw several other developments. One was the vicious civil war that erupted in Guatemala (1978–1984), effectively blocking any outside research for the duration and in fact blocking any new research by foreign scholars for many years. In spite of this, linguists continued to work on the material they had already collected and many advances were made (also see Barrett, this volume, for examples of Mayan war-related rhetoric). In terms of theoretical contributions, besides those already mentioned in syntax, significant work began to appear on discourse. This included dissertations by Margaret Datz (1980), Jill Brody (1982), and Charles Andrew Hofling (1982), the last two under the direction of Marshall Durbin at Washington University. John Du Bois did ground-breaking work on ergativity and discourse (see Aissen, this volume, on information structure). And then, at the very end of the decade (1988–89), the PLFM sponsored two more training sessions for speakers of thirteen different Mayan languages, which led directly to the establishment of OKMA in 1990.

OKMA (Oxlajuuj Keej Maya' Ajtz'iib') was a linguistic research group that flourished for nineteen years and produced an extensive list of publications, including pedagogical grammars, standardizing grammars, reference grammars, dialect studies, studies of derivation, readers for children, and dictionaries. All were written by native speakers of Mayan languages and were produced in Spanish (or Maya in the case of the readers). Of particular interest are the reference grammars, which established a new standard of grammar writing for Mayan languages (García Ixmatá 1997; García Matzar and Rodríguez Guaján 1997; López Ixcoy 1997; Pérez and Jiménez 1997; Santos Nicolás and Benito Pérez 1998; Can Pixabaj 2007, Mó Isém 2007; Pérez Vail 2007). Three of the grammars, those of Can Pixabaj, Mó Isém, and Pérez Vail, were the first reference grammars to be written by Mayas about languages they did not themselves speak natively.

Studies of space were carried out in the nineties, sponsored by the Max Planck Institute in Nijmegen, and involved scholars such as John Haviland, Lourdes de León, Penelope Brown, Eve Danziger, and Jürgen Bohnemeyer. (See Bohnemeyer, this volume, for a summary of some of that work and its later elaboration in his MesoSpace project.) Grammar writing continued, for instance with Zavala Maldonado (1992). A notable achievement in the nineties was the publication by Hofling of a full set of materials – grammar, dictionary, and texts – on Itzaj (Hofling 1991, 2000; Hofling and Tesucún 1997). In no other Mayan language has this triple set of publications by the same author been achieved. (See Hofling, this volume, for a sketch of the Yucatecan languages.)

An astonishing achievement carried out mostly through the nineties was the creation by Florentino Ajpacajá Tum of a *monolingual* K'iche' dictionary with over 20,000 entries

(Ajpacajá Tum 2001). Ajpacajá Tum learned about dictionary making at the PLFM, where he was in the first group to be trained (1972–1974). He came back to dictionary making on his own initiative after translating the Catholic Missal into K'iche' for the parish of Santa Catarina Ixtahuacán, and realizing that there was a significant amount of highly specialized vocabulary that even he, by then an elder, did not know. He set out to find that vocabulary and collected it in his dictionary, the first *full-length* monolingual dictionary of a Mayan language and a dictionary on the order of Laughlin's dictionary of Tsotsil (1975), the *Diccionario Maya Cordemex* (Barrera Vásquez 1980), and Hofling's Itzaj dictionary (1997).

One of the main developments after 2000 involved the upgrading of the CIESAS (Centro de Investigaciones y Estudios Superiores en Antropología Social, Mexico) graduate programs in linguistics. This resulted in the production of many excellent MA theses written by Mayas about their own languages (principally from Mexico, but several from Guatemala as well). CIESAS has just granted its first PhDs to Mayas, to Margarita Martínez Pérez (2016) and José del Carmen Osorio May (2016). Moreover, several Mayas have earned their doctorates in linguistics in the United States: Eladio Mateo Toledo (2008), Pedro Mateo Pedro (2010), Juan Jesús Vázquez Álvarez (2011), and Telma Can Pixabaj (2015). The topics that have been covered in these theses and dissertations have been quite diverse, with many treating advanced topics in morphosyntax and syntax. Studies of acquisition restarted in 1980 with Clifton Pye's dissertation (1980) and gained significant ground after 2000 with later work by Pye and by Lourdes de León (2005), Pedro Mateo Pedro (2010), Barbara Pfeiler, and Margarita Martínez Pérez (see Pye, Pfeiler, and Mateo, this volume). A new grammar of Tseltal (Polian 2013) set a new high standard for grammar writing. (See the grammar sketches, this volume, for condensed versions of Mayan grammars.)

The last decade has also seen a significant expansion of work in formal and descriptive linguistics. Questions of morphosyntax have dominated research in Mayan linguistics for many decades and continue to command attention, but work is currently emerging in phonetics, phonology, pragmatics, and semantics. A new conference, FAMLi (Form and Analysis in Mayan Linguistics, previously Formal Approaches to Mayan Linguistics), initiated biennial meetings in 2010 and has published several proceedings volumes (Shklovsky et al. 2011; Clemens et al. 2012). On these developments, see in this volume England and Baird, AnderBois, and Henderson, as well as the papers in Bennett (2016), Coon (2016), and Henderson (2016), which complement this volume.

A substantial body of research on Mayan languages has also been produced in the areas of linguistic anthropology, cognitive linguistics, and sociolinguistics. John Haviland's work on Tsotsil speech interaction has spanned a long period from the seventies until the present. (See his chapter, this volume, for a guide to work on conversational interaction in Mayan.) The relation between language and mind are central themes in the work of John Lucy (1992a, b), Eve Danziger (2001), Paul Kockelman (2010), and Olivier LeGuen. Topics addressed in the work on the relationship between language and mind include the role of language in the construction of time and space, in the classification of objects and quantities, and in the social construction of identity and emotions. The encoding of spatial relations has been central to the work of William Hanks (1990) and Jürgen Bohnemeyer (see Bohnemeyer, this volume). Work on the sociolinguistics of Mayan-speaking communities has lagged somewhat but has begun to be addressed (see Romero, this volume). Recent work on the role of language in the socialization of children has been carried out by Lourdes de León (2005) and Margarita Martínez Pérez (2016), both working in Tsotsil communities. Another area, one that has received attention in the work of Bricker (1973), Hanks (2010), Garcia (2012), and Romero, is the relationship between language and religion. Hanks and Romero have been interested in how Catholic doctrine has shaped Mayan languages. Bricker has worked on humor in Mayan ritual and religious observance, and García has looked at language in newly introduced postwar Mayan ritual. Finally, there have been a number of contributions to the study of Mayan poetics (e.g., Gossen 1974; Hull and Carrasco 2012); see Barrett, this volume).

2 TYPOLOGICAL CHARACTERISTICS OF MAYAN LANGUAGES

Phonologically, Mayan languages are characterized by a series of voiceless stops matched by a series of glottalized stops. In the glottalized series, the bilabial stop is implosive for all languages. A few languages (or dialects of languages) may also have an implosive uvular stop, and a very few languages may additionally have an implosive alveolar stop (but only if they also have an implosive uvular stop). The implosives vary between voiced and voiceless or partially voiceless. They also vary in the strength of the implosion. All other glottalized stops are ejective. Affricates are also voiceless and are paired with ejective counterparts. Fricatives are voiceless. The voiced consonants include nasals, liquids, and glides. The two laryngeals ([h] and [ʔ]) at times behave like independent consonants and at other times seem to be features of vowels (not all languages have *h*). Mayan languages have five canonical vowels, the majority of them having phonemic vowel length, and a few languages have added a sixth canonical vowel (a central mid or high vowel) to the basic inventory. Three Mayan languages have developed distinctive tone from certain combinations of vowels and *h* or glottal stop. (See England and Baird, and Campbell, this volume, for phonology and phonetics; also Bennett (2016).)

Mayan languages are basically agglutinative. They have both prefixes and suffixes, and a few have a limited number of infixes as well (always either glottal stop or *h*). Derivational affixes are almost entirely suffixes, while inflectional affixes are either prefixes or suffixes, with more prefixes than suffixes. Clitics, both proclitics and especially enclitics, are common. Mayan languages are head marking. Verbs mark the person and number of subjects and objects. They may also mark aspect and may carry suffixes that distinguish the type of verb and its status (dependent or independent). Non-verbal predicates index their subjects. Possessed nouns take prefixes that index their possessors, and almost all words (called *relational nouns*) that introduce oblique participants, including most locatives, take prefixes that index the participant or complement. In addition to the basic inflectional morphology, verbs in many languages co-occur with several kinds of 'directionals' – clitics or affixes derived from motion verbs that convey direction, trajectory, or aspect.

Mayan languages are morphologically ergative. Person markers belong to two different sets, called set A and set B in the Mayan literature. Set A markers index the subjects of transitive verbs, the possessors of nouns, and the complements of relational nouns. Set B markers index the subjects of intransitive verbs and non-verbal predicates as well as the objects of transitive verbs. Many Mayan languages are split-ergative, meaning that there are conditions when the alignment of affixes is not ergative. Under these conditions, set A is used for indexing the subjects of intransitive verbs as well as transitive verbs, usually resulting in nominative-accusative alignment. The circumstances that provoke split ergativity in the languages that have it are either aspect (mostly lowland languages and some that have been in contact with the lowlands) or certain types of subordinate clauses (Mamean and Q'anjob'alan languages). Other languages (K'ichean (except Poqom) and Tseltalan) do not have split ergativity. (See Polian, this volume, on morphology, and Zavala, this volume, on alignment.)

Among the major word classes that can be defined for Mayan languages are the usual nouns, verbs, adjectives, and adverbs, but there are two word classes that are special to the family. One is *positionals*, formed on a very large set of roots that must take a derivational affix to form words, either positional predicates or verbs (intransitive or transitive). Positional roots refer to position, form, constitution, or "attitude" of an object, and are basically stative. The other characteristically Mayan class of words has been referred to as *affect* or *expressive* words. They include both words that refer to sounds or actions (and possibly actions with their characteristic sounds) and predicates either derived from the words in this category or derived from verb roots through special affixes that create affect/expressive verbs from ordinary roots. Affect/expressive words function as adverbs or secondary predicates, while the derived forms function as predicates (see Polian, this volume, on morphology). Some of the languages have very rich morphology connected to affect/expressive words or positionals, much of which is related to pluractionality (see Henderson, this volume). In addition to these, some Mayan languages have numeral classifiers (two types), noun classifiers (two types), or genitive classifiers and may have other types of categorizing devices as well (for discussion of some of these, see Polian, this volume, on morphology, as well as individual grammar sketches). Finally, it should be noted that changes in word class in Mayan languages are always accomplished through derivational affixes, with the exception of some ambivalent roots (roots that belong to two classes simultaneously; languages differ as to whether they have few or many such ambivalent roots). There is essentially no conversion.

Verbs in Mayan languages are marked for aspect. The set of aspect markers may at times be combined with categories of time or mood, but the languages are basically not tensed languages. Time is indicated in clauses by temporal adverbs or is deduced from the temporal context of prior clauses or from default temporal interpretations of aspect markers. There may be an aspect marker that includes temporal information such as 'limited to the past' or 'related to an event established by the discourse as occurring at a particular time.' Aspect markers always precede prefixed person markers on the verb. Set A markers always precede the verb stem and follow aspect markers; in some languages set B markers follow the verb stem and in others they precede the stem, coming between aspect and set A (some languages have both patterns for the position of set B). Therefore the order of these elements on an intransitive verb can be either ASP-stem-SET B or ASP-SET B-stem, while on a transitive verb it is either ASP-SET A-stem-SET B or ASP-SET B-SET A-stem.

Mayan languages are verb initial. A small group (Mamean and Q'anjob'alan languages) has rigid basic VAO (VSO) order, but the rest have a either a very flexible basic VOA (VOS) order which permits VAO (VSO) as well, or a more rigid VOA (VOS) order that does not permit VAO (VSO) (England 1991). More generally, Mayan languages are *head*-initial: they are prepositional, not postpositional; a possessed noun precedes its possessor; complementizers precede the clauses they introduce. While the languages can be characterized as verb initial, many sentences are *not* verb initial, because there are two positions before the verb that are reserved for topicalization (clause initial) or focus (before the verb) (see Aissen, this volume, on information structure). Thus many utterances have at least one (and sometimes two) arguments before the verb. AVO (SVO) is an especially common order among the flexible order languages. As in other head-marking languages, pronouns, being indexed on the head, do not in general occur unless they are topicalized or focused. It is therefore common for clauses to have one or no lexical arguments (see Du Bois 1987; Aissen, this volume, on information structure).

The voice systems of Mayan languages are fairly rich (Dayley 1983; Coon 2016), indicated morphologically by a suffix on the verb. Most languages have more than one passive, usually one or more plain syntactic passives and possibly one or several passives that add some element of meaning such as completion of the event or intentionality of the agent. In addition, there are several different antipassives, including an absolutive antipassive (with either no patient or an oblique patient), in some languages an object incorporation antipassive, and in some languages an agent focus antipassive in which the verb agrees with the agent and the patient is oblique. Passives and antipassives clearly decrease the valency of the verb. There is also an agent focus construction whose valency is less clear (see below). Some languages have a productive causative which increases valency. See individual language sketches in this volume for details.

Many languages also have an applicative construction which adds a third argument to a transitive verb. Except for Huastec, the applicative is formed with the suffix -b'e. In Western Mayan, b'e forms a Goal applicative, with the third argument interpreted as recipient, benefactive, malefactive, etc. (see Polian, this volume, on Tseltalan, and Coon, this volume, on Chol). The added argument is treated syntactically like the object of a transitive clause, and is indexed by set B markers (the 'secundative' alignment of Malchukov et al. 2010). Some Eastern Mayan languages have an applicative with the same suffix, but the third argument is interpreted as instrument (although there are lexical remnants of a former use of this suffix with functions similar to those that have been noted for Western languages). Interestingly, the instrumental applicative is used only when that argument is focused, questioned, or relativized. In some languages, the applicative instrument argument is treated like the object of a transitive and is indexed by set B markers; in others, it remains syntactically more peripheral (see Dayley 1985 on Tz'utujil and Can, this volume, on K'iche').

In languages without a Goal applicative, the third argument of a ditransitive verb is treated as an oblique (the 'indirective' alignment of Malchukov et al. 2010). There is yet another way to express a recipient argument, sometimes called a proleptic (anticipatory) strategy. This involves a simple transitive clause in which the recipient is coded as possessor (genitive) of the theme object. Thus 'John gave Mary's book.' is understood as 'John gave Mary a book.' Depending on the verb semantics, there may be some ambiguity in interpretation, but it is usually more common to interpret the genitive as recipient than possessor. A fourth way to form ditransitive constructions, found principally in Tojol-ab'al, is a serial verb construction (Curiel, this volume).

Morphological ergativity extends to syntactic ergativity in a number of Mayan languages. The phenomenon that reflects syntactic ergativity most clearly involves extraction. In some languages transitive subjects cannot be extracted (e.g., for purposes of focus, interrogation, relativization) while intransitive subjects and transitive objects can be. The usual way to extract the agent argument in these languages is to use an agent focus construction. There are two agent focus constructions. One is syntactically antipassive: the patient is oblique and the verb agrees with the agent argument. The other shares properties with the antipassive but the patient is a direct argument of the verb, not oblique. This construction has two direct arguments (agent, patient), but the verb is morphologically intransitive. Languages vary in their patterns of agreement, with some permitting agreement only with the patient and some with either agent or patient, as determined by a person hierarchy. There is a sizeable literature on Mayan agent focus. (See Stiebels 2006; also Aissen, this volume, on information structure.)

In addition to the fact that all Mayan languages are morphologically ergative and some are syntactically ergative as well, there are several languages that have a kind of "split intransitivity" with agentive and non-agentive intransitives treated differently (for example, see Coon, this volume, on Chol). And finally, in a number of languages the distribution of voice structures is sensitive to salience hierarchies (person, animacy, topi-cality). In general, active transitive verbs are used when the subject (agent) is higher than the object (patient) on the relevant hierarchy, but a marked construction (usually passive or antipassive) is used when the patient is higher than the agent (see Zavala, this volume, on alignment).

Mayan languages have several types of complex predicates. The best known of these is the secondary predicate. The types that have been found in the family include depictives, resultatives, and end-of-state constructions. The principal work on complex predicates is by Mateo Toledo (2008, this volume).

Complement clauses in Mayan differ as to whether they are finite on non-finite. The finite ones further differ as to whether they are introduced by a complementizer or not, while the non-finite ones may be aspectless or infinitive (see Aissen, this volume, on complement clauses). Many complex structures in Mayan languages have been identified as the source of auxiliary constructions in which the matrix verb grammaticalizes as an auxiliary and the embedded verb functions as a lexical verb. Relative clauses differ as to whether they have a relativizer or relative pronoun or not, and as to whether they are headed or headless. Headed relative clauses follow the head in most languages, but Chol and Chontal have prenominal relatives as well (a result of language contact). Adverbial clauses are of several types and are usually finite but dependent and have a subordinator that corresponds to their type and introduces the dependency. One type that is found all over the family is the motion-cum-purpose type. These clauses vary in the degree of inte-gration between the motion verb and its dependent. (See the individual grammar sketches for examples of complex clause structures.)

3 LANGUAGES

For language relationships see Kaufman, this volume, or Campbell, this volume. The names of Mayan languages have been spelled in several ways over time; we mostly use the spellings of the Academia de Lenguas Mayas de Guatemala (ALMG) for Guatema-lan languages and the spellings of INALI (Instituto Nacional de Lenguas Indígenas) for Mexican languages. Because the spellings have varied, we present a list with the current spellings, older Spanish-based spellings, and other variants. In Spanish-speaking coun-tries all of the language names that end in *tek/tec* would have a final *o* as well.

Language Names		
Current	*Older (if different)*	*Additional Variants*
Achi	Achí	
Akatek	Acatec	
Awakatek	Aguacatec	
Chicomuseltec	Chicomuceltec	Kabil
Chontal (de Tabasco)		Yokot'an
Chuj		
Ch'ol/Chol		
Ch'olti'	Choltí	Cholti'
Ch'orti'	Chortí	
Huastec		Wastek, Teenek
Itzaj	Itzá	
Ixil		Ixhil

Language Names

Current	Older (if different)	Additional Variants
Kaqchikel	Cakchiquel	
K'iche'	Quiché	K'ichee'
Lacandón		Lakantun
Mam		
Mocho' (+Tuzantec)	Mochó, Motozintlec	Cotoque, Kotoke (for both varieties)
Mopan	Mopán	
Poqomam	Pocomam	Pokomam
Poqomchi'	Pocomchí	Pokomchi'
Popti'	Jacaltec	Jakaltek
Q'anjob'al	Kanjobal	
Q'eqchi'	Kekchí	
Sakapultek	Sacapultec	
Sipakapense	Sipacapense	Sipacapeño, Sipakapenyo
Tojol-ab'al	Tojolabal	Tojolab'al
Tseltal	Tzeltal	
Tsotsil	Tzotzil	
Tz'utujil	Tzutujil	Tzutuhil, Tz'utujiil
Tektitek	Teco	Teko, (Cakchiquel *sic*)
Uspantek	Uspantec	
Yucatec Maya		Maya, Yucatec

4 ALPHABET

There have been a number of practical alphabets for writing Mayan languages since the arrival of the Spaniards. Today there is general agreement on most of the conventions for writing the different languages. Much of the agreement can be attributed to the Academia de Lenguas Mayas de Guatemala (ALMG), which in 1987 attempted to establish a single alphabet for the Mayan languages of Guatemala. It also promoted certain alphabetic conventions that have been embraced more widely, such as using the grapheme <k> for the velar stop instead of the Spanish-based <c/qu>. The alphabetic symbols in use today are arranged in Tables 1.1 and 1.2, with IPA equivalents in brackets. The graphemes represent phonemes, so the IPA symbols are chosen to represent that phoneme, but not all of its allophonic variations. If there is more than one grapheme for a particular phoneme, the variants are separated with a slash, and the variation is explained below.

Variation in the graphemes

'/ʔ/7   These are different ways in which the authors represent the glottal stop. Although the glottal stop is different from glottalized consonants, the ALMG and INALI have chosen to represent the glottal stop with the same symbol that indicates glottalization on consonants, the apostrophe <'>. Two of the authors have maintained the difference by using either <ʔ> (Polian) or <7> (Kaufman) for glottal stop. Haviland also creates a difference by using a curved apostrophe <'> for glottal stop but a straight apostrophe <'> after a consonant to indicate glottalization.

b'/b   In some Mayan languages the bilabial implosive has weakened to the extent that it is a phonetic [b]. However, some write the bilabial

TABLE 1.1 CONSONANTS

p [p]		t [t]	ty [tʲ]		ky [kʲ]	k [k]	q [q]	ʼ/ʔ/7 [ʔ]
pʼ [pʼ]		tʼ [tʼ]	tyʼ [tʲʼ]		kyʼ [kʲʼ]	kʼ [kʼ]	qʼ [qʼ]	
bʼ/b [ɓ/b]								
		tz/ts [ts]	ch [tʃ]	tx [tʂ]				
		tzʼ/tsʼ [tsʼ]	chʼ [tʃʼ]	txʼ [tʂʼ]				
	th [θ]	s [s]	x/xh/ẍ [ʃ]	x [ʂ]		j [x/h]	j [χ]	h [h]
m [m]		n [n]	ñ [ɲ]			nh/ng [ŋ]		
		l [l]						
		r [ɾ]						
w/v [w]				y [j]				

TABLE 1.2 VOWELS

	Short			Long			Lax	
i	ä	u	ii		uu	ï		ü
e		o	ee		oo	ë		ö
	a			aa			ä	
			‘Glottalized’, ‘broken’, or ‘rearticulated’					
			iʼi		uʼu			
			eʼe		oʼo			
				aʼa				

implisive as <b> even though it is still implosive, so the writing is not a very good guide to the phonetics. The <b> grapheme is used in the Mexican languages Tsotsil, Tseltal, Chol, Chontal, Yucatec, and Huastec.

tz/ts	<ts> is used in the Mexican languages Tojol-abal, Tseltal, Tsotsil, Chol, Chontal, and Yucatec.
tzʼ/tsʼ	The same distribution as tz/ts.
th	Only occurs in Huastec.
x/xh/ẍ	Those languages that have retroflex fricatives use <x> for the retroflex and <xh> for the postalveolar fricative. Those that do not have retroflexes use <x> for the postalveolar fricative. It should be noted that the Comunidad Lingüística Mam of the ALMG uses <ẍ> for the postalveolar fricative. However, this symbol is not at all practical and we do not use it here; we use <xh>.
j	This grapheme represents /χ/ for most languages that have maintained the uvulars, /x/ for most others, but /h/ for a few that do not have a velar or uvular fricative.
h	This usually represents /h/, but in Qʼanjobʼal it represents the absence of a glottal stop before a vowel.
nh/ng	The velar nasal is represented by <nh> in Chuj and Poptiʼ, but by <ng> in Mochoʼ. These are the only languages that have this sound.
w/v	Speakers of Ixil, Tseltal, and Tsotsil prefer writing <v> for the structural /w/, presumably because it is more often pronounced as a voiced fricative [β, v] than a bilabial approximant.
Tone:	ʹindicates high tone, but also indicates high/falling tone in Uspantek; ʻindicates low tone.

V'V   The so-called glottalized, broken, or rearticulated vowels, although they may come from or represent some vowel (either long or short) plus glottal stop, are usually written V'V in the languages where this rearticulation occurs because that is what people hear. It is regarded as too abstract to write them as VV' or V'. These vowels are used in Yucatec, Itzaj, Mopan, Lacandón, and Teko, although they are not always described using this terminology but instead are simply described as a short vowel followed by a glottal stop and possibly another identical vowel. In Yucatec they are often counted as an addition to the vowel inventory.

The official alphabets of the ALMG do not accommodate all dialect variation, since their aim is to standardize. Symbols that have been used for some of the variation include, for instance, <tch, tch', sh> for the apico-postalveolar series in Todos Santos Mam, or <ie> and <uo/ua> for the diphthongs in Atitlán Tz'utujil, Santa María Kaqchikel, San Luís Poqomam, and Santa Cruz Poqomchi'. It should also be mentioned that there is considerable tension between the opposing ideas of "unification" – writing structurally similar or historically identical sounds the same way even if their pronunciations are different – and "local identity" – writing sounds that have a different local pronunciation differently from the structurally similar sounds in other places. Sometimes one tendency dominates and sometimes the other. The use of <v> for /w/ in Ixil, Tsotsil, and Tseltal responds to local identity issues, as does the use of <ts> instead of <tz> for the alveolar affricate in a number of Mexican languages, and the use of <ẍ> instead of <xh> for the postalveolar fricative in Mam. The use of <b'> for [wʔ, mʔ] in Poqomam and Poqomchi', on the other hand, is a response to unification issues, as does the use of <w> for all the pronunciations of /w/ in different dialects of Kaqchikel ([w, β, b, v, w̥, f]).

All of the chapters except Chapters 3 (Mayan History and Comparison) and 7 (Phonology and Phonetics) use the practical orthography described here except when phonetics is being discussed.

REFERENCES

Aissen, Judith. 1987. *Tzotzil clause structure*. Dordrecht: Reidel.

Aissen, Judith. 2017. "Correlates of ergativity in Mayan." In *OUP handbook of ergativity*, ed. by Jessica Coon, Diane Massam, and Lisa Travis. Oxford: Oxford University Press.

Ajpacajá Tum, Florentino Pedro. 2001. *K'ichee' choltziij*. Guatemala City: Cholsamaj.

Ayres, Glenn. 1991. *La gramática ixil*. La Antigua, Guatemala: Centro de Investigaciones Regionales de Mesoamérica.

Barrera Vásquez, Alfredo. 1980. *Diccionario Maya Cordemex*. Mérida, Yucatán, México: Ediciones Cordemex.

Bennett, Ryan. 2016. "Mayan phonology." *Language and Linguistic Compass* 10: 469–514.

Berinstein, Ava. 1985. *Evidence for multiattachment in K'ekchi Mayan*. New York: Garland.

Bricker, Victoria Reifler. 1973. *Ritual humor in highland Chiapas*. Austin: University of Texas Press.

Brody, M. Jill. 1982. "Discourse processes of highlighting in Tojolabal Maya morphosyntax." PhD diss., Washington University.

Campbell, Lyle. 1977. *Quichean linguistic prehistory*. Berkeley: University of California Press.

Campbell, Lyle, Pierre Ventur, Russell Stewart, and Brant Gardner. 1978. *Bibliography of Mayan languages and linguistics* (Institute for Mesoamerican Studies, 3). Albany: State University of New York.

Canger, Una Rasmussen.1969. "Analysis in outline of Mam a Mayan language." PhD dissertation, University of California, Berkeley.

Can Pixabaj, Telma. 2007. *Jkemiik Yoloj li Uspanteko: Gramática Uspanteka*. Guatemala: Oxlajuuj Keej Maya' Ajtz'iib' and Editorial Cholsamaj.

Can Pixabaj, Telma. 2015. "Complement and purpose clauses in K'iche'." PhD diss., University of Texas, Austin.

Clemens, Lauren Eby, Robert Henderson, and Pedro Mateo Pedro, eds. 2012. *Proceedings of FAMLi 2: Formal approaches to Mayan linguistics*. Cambridge: MIT Working Papers in Linguistics, vol. 74.

Coon, Jessica. 2016. "Mayan morphosyntax." *Language and Linguistic Compass* 10: 515–50.

Craig, Colette G. 1977. *The structure of Jacaltec*. Austin: University of Texas Press.

Danziger, Eve. 2001. *Relatively speaking: Language, thought, and kinship among the Mopan Maya*. Oxford Studies in Anthropological Linguistics. Oxford: Oxford University Press.

Datz, Margaret Dickeman. 1980. "Jacaltec syntactic structures and the demands of discourse." PhD diss., University of Colorado.

Day, Christopher. 1967. "The Jacalec language." PhD dissertation, University of Chicago.

Day, Christopher. 1973. *The Jacaltec language*. Bloomington: Indiana University Publications.

Dayley, Jon P. 1983. "Voice and Ergativity in Mayan Languages." In *Studies in Mesoamerican Linguistics*, ed. by Alice Schlichter, Wallace Chafe and Leanne Hinton (*Reports from the Survey of California and Other Indian Languages*, 4), 2–119. Berkeley. First published 1981 in *Journal of Mayan Linguistics*, 2, 2: 3–82.

Dayley, Jon P. 1985. *Tzutujil grammar*. University of California Publications in Linguistics, vol. 107.

De León, Lourdes. 2005. *La llegada del alma: Lenguaje, infancia y socialización entre los mayas de Zinacantán*. Mexico City: Centro de Investigaciones y Estudios Superiores en Antropología Social, Instituto Nacional de Antropología e Historia, and Consejo Nacional de Culturas y Artes.

Du Bois, John W. 1981. "The Sacapultec language." PhD diss., Berkeley.

Du Bois, John W. 1987. "The discourse basis of ergativity." *Language* 63: 805–55.

England, Nora C., ed. 1978. *Papers in Mayan linguistics*. Columbia: University of Missouri.

England, Nora C. 1983. *A grammar of Mam, a Mayan language*. Austin: University of Texas Press.

England, Nora C. 1991. "Changes in basic word order in Mayan languages." *International Journal of American Linguistics* 57: 446–86.

England, Nora C. 2017. "Mayan languages." In *Oxford research encyclopedia of linguistics*. Oxford: Oxford University Press. doi: http://dx.doi.org/10.1093/acrefore/9780199384655.013.60

England, Nora C., and Stephen R. Elliott, eds. 1990. *Lecturas Sobre la Lingüística Maya*. Guatemala: Centro de Investigaciones Regionales de Mesoamérica.

Fought, John. 1967. "Chortí (Mayan): phonology, morphophonemics and morphology." PhD dissertation, Yale university.

Furbee, Louanna, ed. 1976a. *Mayan texts I. Native American texts series*, vol. 1, no. 1. Chicago: University of Chicago Press.

Furbee [-Losee], Louanna. 1976b. *The correct language, Tojolabal: A grammar with ethnographic notes*. New York: Garland.

Furbee, Louanna, ed. 1979. *Mayan texts II, Native American texts series* (Monograph No. 3). Chicago: University of Chicago Press.

Furbee, Louanna, ed. 1980. *Mayan texts III, Native American texts series* (Monograph No. 5). Chicago: University of Chicago Press.

Garcia, María Luz. 2012. "Discourse, social cohesion and the politics of historical memory in the Ixhil Maya region of Guatemala." PhD diss., University of Texas, Austin.

García Matzar, Pedro (Lolmay), and José Obispo Rodríguez Guaján (Pakal). 1997. *Rukemik ri Kaqchikel Chi': Gramática Kaqchikel*. Guatemala: Editorial Cholsamaj.

García Ixmatá, Pablo (Ajpub'). 1997. *Rukeemiik ja Tz'utujiil Chii': Gramática Tz'utujiil*. Guatemala: Editorial Cholsamaj.

Gossen, Gary H. 1974. *Chamulas in the world of the Sun*. Cambridge: Harvard University Press.

Hanks, William F. 1990. *Referential practice: language and lived space among the Maya*. Chicago: University of Chicago Press.

Hanks, William T. 2010. *Converting words: Maya in the age of the cross*. Berkeley: University of California Press.

Haviland, John B. 1981. *Sk'op Sotz'leb: El Tzotzil de San Lorenzo Zinacantan*. México: UNAM.

Henderson, Robert. 2016. "Mayan semantics." *Language and Linguistic Compass* 10: 551–88.

Hofling, Charles A. 1982. "Itza Maya morphosyntax from a discourse perspective." PhD diss., Washington University.

Hofling, Charles A. 1991. *Itzá Maya texts, with a grammatical overview*. Salt Lake City: University of Utah Press.

Hofling, Charles A. 2000. *Itzaj Maya grammar*. Salt Lake City: University of Utah Press.

Hofling, Charles A., and Félix Fernando Tesucún. 1997. *Itzaj Maya-Spanish-English dictionary: Diccionario maya itzaj-español-inglés*. Salt Lake City: University of Utah Press.

Hopkins, Nicholas A. 1967. "The Chuj language." PhD diss., University of Chicago.

Hull, Kerry, and Michael Carrasco. 2012. *Parallel worlds: Genre, discourse, and poetics in contemporary, colonial, and Classic period Maya literature*. Boulder: University of Colorado Press.

Kaufman, Terrence Scott. 1963. "Tzeltal grammar." PhD dissertation, University of California, Berkeley.

Kaufman, Terrence. 1971. *Tzeltal phonology and morphology*. Berkeley: University of California Publications in Linguistics, No. 61.

Kaufman, Terrence. 1972. *El Proto-Tzeltal-Tzotzil: Fonología comparada y diccionario reconstruido*. México: UNAM.

Kockelman, Paul. 2010. *Language, culture, and mind: Natural constructions and social kinds*. Cambridge: Cambridge University Press.

Larsen, Thomas Walter. 1988. "Manifestations of ergativity in Quiché grammar." PhD diss., University of California, Berkeley.

Laughlin, Robert M. 1975. *The great Tzotzil dictionary of San Lorenzo Zinacantan* (Smithsonian Contributions to Anthropology 19). Washington, DC: Smithsonian Institution Press.

Laughlin, Robert M. 1977. *Of cabbages and kings: Tales from Zinacantan*. Smithsonian Contributions to Anthropology 23. Washington, DC: Smithsonian Institution Press.

Laughlin, Robert M. 1980. *Of shoes and ships and sealing wax: Sundries from Zinacantan* (Smithsonian Contributions to Anthropology 25). Washington, DC: Smithsonian Institution Press.

Laughlin, Robert M., and John B. Haviland. 1988. *The great Tzotzil dictionary of Santo Domingo Zinacantan; with grammatical analysis and historical commentary*. 3 vols (Smithsonian Contributions to Anthropology 31). Washington, DC: Smithsonian Institution Press.

López Ixcoy, Candelaria Dominga (Saqijix). 1997. *Ri Ukemiik ri K'ichee' Chii': Gramática K'ichee'*. Guatemala: Editorial Cholsamaj.

Lucy, John A. 1992a. *Language diversity and thought* (Studies in the Social and Cultural Foundations of Language, 12). Cambridge: Cambridge University Press.

Lucy, John A. 1992b. *Grammatical categories and cognition* (Studies in the Social and Cultural Foundation of Language, 13). Cambridge: Cambridge University Press.

Malchukov, Andrej, Martin Haspelmath, and Bernard Comrie. 2010. "Ditransitive constructions: A typological overview." In *Studies in ditransitive constructions: A comparative handbook*, ed. by Andrej Malchukov, Martin Haspelmath, and Bernard Comrie, 1–64. Berlin: Mouton de Gruyter.

McClaran, Marlys, ed. 1976. *Mayan linguistics, volume one*. Los Angeles: University of California, American Indian Studies Center.

Martin, Laura. 1977. "Positional roots in Kanjobal (Mayan)." PhD diss., University of Florida.

Martin, Laura, ed. 1979. *Papers in Mayan linguistics*. Columbia: Lucas Brothers.

Martínez Pérez, Margarita. 2016. "*Xchanel-xchanubtasel*: Lenguaje, acción y enseñanza en actividades valoradas entre los mayas de San Juan Chamula." PhD diss., Centro de Investigaciones y Estudios Superiores en Antropología Social.

Mateo Pedro, Pedro. 2010. "The acquisition of verb inflection morphology in Q'anjob'al Maya: A longitudinal study." PhD diss., University of Kansas.

Mateo Toledo, Eladio. 2008. "The family of complex predicates in Q'anjob'al (Maya); their syntax and meaning." PhD diss., University of Texas, Austin.

Maxwell, Judith. 1982. "How to talk to people who talk funny: the Chuj (Maya) solution." PhD diss., University of Chicago.

Mó Isém, Romelia. 2007. *Rikemiik li Tujaal Tziij: Gramática Sakapulteka*. Guatemala: Oxlajuuj Keej Maya' Ajtz'iib' and Editorial Cholsamaj.

Mondloch, James L. 1981. "Voice in Quiche Maya." PhD diss., The University at Albany, SUNY.

Norman, William M., and Lyle Campbell. 1978. "Toward a Proto-Mayan Syntax: A Comparative Perspective on Grammar." In *Papers in Mayan Linguistics*, ed. by Nora C. England, 136–56. Columbia, MO: University of Missouri.

Osorio May, José del Carmen. 2016. "Temas de la sintaxis del yokot'an de Tecoluta, Nacajuca, Tabasco." PhD dissertation, Centro de Investigaciones y Estudios Superiores en Antropología Social, México.

Pérez, Eduardo (B'aayil), and Odilio Jiménez (Ajb'ee). 1997. *Ttxoolil Qyool Mam: Gramática Mam*. Guatemala: Editorial Cholsamaj.

Pérez Vail, José Reginaldo. 2007. *Xtxolil Yool B'a'aj: Gramática Tektiteka*. Guatemala: Oxlajuuj Keej Maya' Ajtz'iib' and Editorial Cholsamaj.

Polian, Gilles. 2013. *Gramática del tseltal de Oxchuc*. Tomos I y II. México: Centro de Investigaciones y Estudios Superiores en Antropología Social.

Pye, Clifton. 1980. "The acquisition of grammatical morphemes in Quiche Mayan." PhD diss., University of Pittsburgh.

Quizar, Stephanie (Robin). 1979. "Comparative word order in Mayan." PhD diss., University of Colorado, Boulder.

Robertson, John. 1980. *The structure of pronoun incorporation in the Mayan verbal complex*. New York: Garland.

Santos Nicolás, José Francisco (Pala's), and José Gonzalo Benito Pérez (Waykan). 1998. *Rukorb'aal Poqom Q'orb'al: Gramática Poqom (Poqomam)*. Guatemala: Cholsamaj.

Shklovsky, Kirill, Pedro Mateo Pedro, and Jessica Coon, eds. 2011. *Proceedings of formal approaches to Mayan linguistics I*. Cambridge: MIT Working Papers in Linguistics, vol. 63.

Smith-Stark, Thomas. 1978. "The Mayan antipassive: some facts and fictions." In *Papers in Mayan linguistics*, ed. by Nora C. England, 169–87. Columbia: University of Missouri.

Smith-Stark, Thomas. 1983. "Jilotepeque Pocomam phonology and morphology." PhD diss., University of Chicago.

Stewart, Stephen O. 1980. *Gramática Kekchí*. Guatemala: Editorial Académica Centroamericana.

Stiebels, Barbara. 2006. "Agent focus in Mayan languages." *Natural Language and Linguistic Theory* 24: 501–70.

Trechsel, Frank. 1981. "A categorial treatment of Quichean (Mayan) ergativity." PhD diss., University of Texas, Austin.

Vázquez Álvarez, Juan Jesús. 2011. "A grammar of Chol, a Mayan language." PhD diss., University of Texas, Austin.

Zavala Maldonado, Roberto. 1992. *El Kanjobal de San Miguel Acatán*. México: Universidad Nacional Autónoma de México.

PART 1

LANGUAGE DEVELOPMENT, HISTORY, AND CHANGE

CHAPTER 2

MAYAN LANGUAGE ACQUISITION

Clifton Pye, Barbara Pfeiler, and Pedro Mateo Pedro

1 THE CONTRIBUTIONS OF MAYAN LANGUAGE ACQUISITION RESEARCH

Research on the acquisition of the Mayan languages has a 45-year history, beginning in the late sixties with Brian Stross's (1969) study of Tseltal child language and continuing into the seventies with Stephen H. Straight's (1976) study of Yucatec children's phonology and Pye's (1979) study of K'iche' children's inflectional morphology. In the nineties, Penelope Brown, Lourdes de León, and Barbara Pfeiler began longitudinal studies documenting the acquisition of Tseltal, Tsotsil, and Yucatec respectively. Pye initiated new longitudinal studies documenting the acquisition of Ch'ol, Mam, and Q'anjob'al in 2005; Pfeiler began a longitudinal study of Huastec in 2010; and Pedro Mateo Pedro started a longitudinal study of Chuj in 2011.

The acquisition studies of Brown, de León, Mateo Pedro, Pfeiler, and Pye all employed a longitudinal design. The investigators visited three or more two-year-old children being raised in monolingual households at least twice a month for periods of from nine months to three years. The recordings document the interactions between children and their families in typical Mayan domestic settings.

The longitudinal studies provide a complete picture of how the grammars of individual children develop over time. The small number of children in longitudinal studies invariably raises the issue of whether the language of these children is representative of all children acquiring the language. Our research is not unique in this respect, and seminal contributions to acquisition research on other languages have relied on longitudinal observations of one to three children, e.g. Taine (1877), Brown (1973), Bittner et al. (2003). Ultimately, it is necessary to account for the linguistic development of each child regardless of how representative this child's acquisition might be.

Research on Mayan language acquisition contributes to the understanding of the language acquisition process in two key respects. Mayan acquisition research shows how children acquire typologically unusual features such as glottalized consonants, relational nouns, an ergative system of agreement for subjects and objects, theme-specific verbs, and absolute spatial reference systems. The polysynthetic nature of the Mayan verb complex is also distinctive in that it licenses the frequent omission of both subjects and objects. Topic and focus phrases have defined preverbal positions that contrast with the unmarked positions of subject, object, locative, and instrumental phrases.

Mayan acquisition research is also significant for demonstrating what can be gained by comparing the acquisition of historically related languages in a systematic fashion. Mayan languages exhibit substantial variation on common Mayan themes. At the same time, comparing data from multiple children acquiring multiple languages introduces a level of complexity that is qualitatively different from that seen in studies of one or two languages. It is not easy to display, let alone interpret, data from three children from each of nine languages. Our chapter provides examples of how we approach this problem.

The previous longitudinal studies of different Mayan languages led Brown, de León, Pfeiler, and Pye to a joint investigation of inflectional development in Tseltal, Tsotsil, Yucatec, and K'iche'. This collaboration enabled us to recognize the significant role that the contexts of use play in Mayan language acquisition (Brown et al. 2013). Pye recognized that the comparative method of historical linguistics can be applied to research on language acquisition by focusing on the acquisition of the contexts of use (Pye et al. 2007, 2013; Pye and Pfeiler 2014; Pye 2017). This method employs the term 'contexts of use' to refer to the contexts in which each element is used in a language. For example, languages with prototypical ergative alignment systems use ergative person markers to cross-reference the subjects of transitive verbs. Transitive verbs provide a context of use that identifies ergative markers as such. Yucatec and Ch'ol, unlike K'iche' and Q'anjob'al, extend the ergative person markers to cross-reference the subjects of intransitive verbs in the incompletive aspect (Larsen and Norman 1979). The extension of ergative person markers in Yucatec and Ch'ol to intransitive verbs gives them contexts of use that differ from the contexts where Q'anjob'al and K'iche' use ergative markers.

This variation shows that the contexts of use are a contingent feature of each language that results from its unique linguistic history. The sounds, lexical categories, ergative and absolutive person markers, and status and applicative suffixes, to name a few of the features that we present in this chapter, have inherited similar forms from Proto-Mayan but vary in their contexts of use in the modern Mayan languages. Our chapter illustrates the effects that variation in the contexts of use has on the acquisition of common Mayan linguistic elements.

The comparative approach that we employ in this chapter has significant theoretical implications. Detecting universal aspects of language acquisition remains a central focus of acquisition research. Comparing language acquisition results within the Mayan language family controls for such major environmental factors as cultural and socioeconomic differences. The challenge is to detect the needle of common acquisition processes amidst a haystack of surface variation. Investigating the acquisition of related languages significantly shrinks the size of the haystack that we have to sift through, but does not eliminate the surface variation altogether. This chapter documents the progress made to date in the search for significant generalizations across a wide range of Mayan features.

We use the IPA in the examples in our chapter with two exceptions. We use <'> rather than <?> for the glottal stop. We sometimes cite examples that use the standardized writing systems for individual Mayan languages. In these cases, we supply the IPA form in brackets. Asterisks indicate omitted morphemes in the children's examples.

2 MAYAN CARETAKER SPEECH

Mayan children are typically raised in extended families that include grandparents, aunts, and uncles. Mayan infants experience a polyadic conversational context with many participants, and as a result Mayan children hear more language directed to other speakers than to themselves. The polyadic interaction between Mayan speakers includes the babies as speakers and listeners (de León 2000, 2005; Pfeiler 2007). Tsotsil mothers interpret the baby's gestures and non-linguistic expressions in culturally specific manners (de León 2000, 2005). Another striking finding is the use of evidentials to report and to prompt the children's speech in Tsotsil (de León 2005), Yucatec (Pfeiler 2007), and Tojolabal (Curiel 2016).

The language that caretakers address to infants and toddlers differs significantly from language to language in terms of sounds, words, and pitch (Snow and Ferguson 1977). Larsen (1949) published an early study of the sounds and words in Huastec babytalk. K'iche' babytalk also contains distinctive words and sounds (Pye 1986). Bernstein and Pye (1984) found that K'iche' mothers used a lower pitch when speaking to children than to adults. In contrast, Tsotsil mothers do not lower their pitch when speaking to children (de León 2000, 2005; Martínez Pérez 2013). Repetition is also an important component of speech to K'iche' children (Pye 1986). However, Brown (1998b) reports that repetition is used in speech to both adults and children in Tseltal rather than constituting a feature that is specific to child-directed speech. Q'anjob'al, Mam, and Yucatec adults use special admonitive negation forms *ta*, *qa'*, and *bik* respectively to warn children not to do something. Research on child-directed speech suggests major differences between Mayan and European languages and needs more documentation in Mayan languages.

3 LEXICAL DEVELOPMENT

Lexical development is of theoretical interest because of claims that cognitive development restricts the categories of words that children produce (cf. Gentner and Boroditsky 2001; Hao et al. 2015). Cognitive hypotheses predict an overall similarity in the structure of children's lexicons to the extent that children follow a common course of cognitive development. Cognitive hypotheses do not predict variation in lexical development across languages.

Lexical development illustrates the variation on a theme to be found in the speech of Mayan children. Although the adult languages have most lexical categories in common, they use them in different contexts. For example, the existential verb in K'iche' (k'oo-l-ik, exist-positional-status$_{IV}$, 'exist, have') belongs to the same positional class of words as the positional roots tak'-al-ik (stand-positional-status$_{IV}$, 'stand') and sep-el-ik (kneel-positional-status$_{IV}$, 'kneel like a woman'). The existentials in Mam (at) and Q'anjob'al (ay) do not take verbal or positional affixes, and thus constitute their own unique lexical category within these languages. Such differences reflect the structure of the lexicon in the individual languages and can be examined by counting the words that belong to each lexical category in each language.

There are also differences between the Mayan languages in the degree to which lexical roots can be used as either nouns or verbs, or as intransitive verbs or transitive verbs. K'iche' has relatively few polyvalent roots, whereas Yucatec has a set of "action nouns" that can be used as either nouns or verbs (Lois and Vapnarsky 2006). Adult Yucatec speakers use action nouns most frequently as verbs, and Yucatec children first use the action nouns as verbs. The children use the verb stems with an inflection, but do not inflect the noun stems (Pfeiler 2006). We have not yet explored the acquisition of polyvalent roots in other Mayan languages.

Children's early words reflect key features of the adult grammars. Rather than imposing some type of universal conceptual categories on their language, children adopt the specific lexical types that occur in the adult language. K'iche' children produce the locative proadverb particle *wi*(*h*) when a locative or instrumental phrase appears in the preverbal focus position. Children acquiring Huastec produce a copula verb. Mam children use intransitive verbs to express events with an agent and patient. Ch'ol and Mam children extend existential negation to negate verbs.

Studies of lexical development have documented different patterns of lexical development in Mayan languages. Brown (1998a) and de León (2001b) analyzed the speech of two children acquiring Tseltal (Brown) and two children acquiring Tsotsil (de León). They found that children acquiring these languages produced more verb types than noun types. De León (2007) reported a similar result for a child acquiring Ch'ol.

Brown (1998a) attributed the Tseltal results to the "verb-friendly" nature of Mayan languages. Verbs can stand alone as complete sentences in Mayan languages, which decreases the use of noun phrases. However, the verb-friendly nature of Mayan languages does not result in the production of more verb types among all children acquiring Mayan languages. Children acquiring K'iche' produce more noun types than verb types (Pye 1992). The differences between the lexicons of children acquiring different Mayan languages show that neither cognitive development nor frequent verb use account for lexical acquisition.

To illustrate the lexical differences between the languages, we compared the lexical types produced by one two-year-old speaker for five Mayan languages. All of the children produced odd sounds, exclamations, and uninterpretable syllables, which we counted in an "other" category. We counted words with different affixes as different lexical types in accordance with the hypothesis that two-year-old speakers do not productively control derivational and inflectional processes, e.g. the Mam existential *at* and its negative form *nti'*. As shown in Table 2.1, the children produced many examples of nouns and verbs, in addition to adjectives, adverbs, demonstratives, determiners, and grammatical particles of various kinds.

Table 2.1 shows that children acquiring Huastec and Ch'ol produced high numbers of verb types, whereas the children acquiring Q'anjob'al, Mam, and K'iche' produce more noun types than verb types. The Ch'ol result replicates the finding in de León's (2007) study. One surprising result is that children acquiring Huastec and Ch'ol produce more transitive verb types than intransitive verb types, whereas the children acquiring Mam and K'iche' produce more intransitive verb types than transitive verb types. The difference is particularly striking for Mam, where the adult grammar employs intransitive constructions for many propositions expressed by transitive verbs in the other Mayan languages.

Another surprise is that the data in Table 2.1 show significant differences between the languages in the children's production of relational nouns. We will discuss the production of relational nouns in the section on the acquisition of the applicative construction. The applicative construction eliminates a frequent context of use for relational nouns in

TABLE 2.1 CHILDREN'S LEXICAL TYPES IN FIVE MAYAN LANGUAGES

	Huastec 2;4.9		Ch'ol 2;1.30		Q'anjob'al 2;0		Mam 2;0.2		K'iche' 2;1.17	
	n	%	*n*	%	*n*	%	*n*	%	*n*	%
Intransitive verbs	22	11.0 %	39	13.9 %	6	8.6 %	39	13.6 %	8	6.8 %
Transitive verbs	50	25.0 %	65	23.2 %	12	17.1 %	21	7.3 %	7	5.9 %
Existential	3	1.5 %	10	3.6 %	1	1.4 %	6	2.1 %	1	0.8 %
Common nouns	41	20.5 %	45	16.1 %	37	52.9 %	76	26.6 %	31	26.3 %
Proper nouns	7	3.5 %	12	4.3 %	4	5.7 %	26	9.1 %	4	3.4 %
Pronouns	2	1.0 %	3	1.1 %			4	1.4 %	3	2.5 %
Relational nouns	4	2.0 %	2	0.7 %	3	4.3 %	15	5.2 %	1	0.8 %
Demonstratives	11	5.5 %	22	7.9 %	3	4.3 %	10	3.5 %	3	2.5 %
Adjectives	4	2.0 %	5	1.8 %			8	2.8 %	7	5.9 %
Other	56	28.0 %	77	27.4 %	4	5.7 %	81	28.4 %	53	44.9 %
Total	200		280		70		286		118	

Ch'ol, Tseltal, and Tsotsil. Even where the adult languages use relational nouns to express oblique arguments, as in K'iche', the children show a marked delay in their production. The use of relational noun phrases in Mam is clearly more productive, and their use by Mam children to express oblique arguments shows that the structure is not beyond the capacity of two-year-olds in the right circumstances (1).

MAM
(1) Mam two-year-old use of relational noun phrase
    ku' pe tu'n.   (WEN 2;0.2)
    = maa   pa   kub'   kape   t-u'n-a
    PROX   cut   down coffee A2-by-ENC
    'You recently cut the coffee.' (lit. 'The coffee (was) cut down by you.')

The language-specific use of common Mayan elements that we find in Mayan children's utterances demonstrates one example of variation on the Mayan core.

4 SEMANTIC DEVELOPMENT

The acquisition of lexical meaning requires children to determine the appropriate contexts of use for each word. Children sometimes use words in non-adult contexts. Stross's (1969) dissertation research was an important early contribution in this domain. Stross took Tenejapa Tseltal children along a plant trail and invited them to identify plants in their natural setting. Stross collected data from twenty-five children between the ages of four and thirteen.

Stross found that children under five years of age overextended some plant names to related species and underextended other plant names. The children substituted general terms such as *te'* 'tree' for specific names. Stross (103–4) reports that a two-and-a-half year old girl correctly identified a type of guava tree that was growing close to her house, but could not name the same type of tree if it was growing in another location. Stross found that part of the variation in the names that the children produce reflected variation in adult naming. He also found that sometimes the children could name a plant after being told how the plant was used. Three children were able to identify a use for a plant, but could not name it (108). Stross's observations agree with the findings of later studies on semantic development in English (Anglin 1977), but demonstrate a sophisticated methodological advance over studies that rely upon picture naming tasks.

The theme-specific meanings of Mayan verbs provide an interesting domain in which investigators have explored semantic development. For example, Tseltal has different theme-specific verbs for 'eat tortilla-like things', 'eat meat-like things', 'eat soft things', 'eat crunchy things', and 'eat sugarcane'. Two-year-old Tseltal children produce theme-specific verbs for eating, carrying, breaking, putting something down, or tipping something over (Brown 2008). Two-year-old K'iche' children produce theme-specific breaking verbs, but overextend the verbs beyond the adult contexts of use (Pye et al. 1996). For example, K'iche' children use the verb *-t'oqopiix* 'break string, rope, etc.' in place of the verb *-q'upiix* 'break something hard' in reference to breaking a stick. The K'iche' results extend Stross's observations on the overextension of plant names to the verb domain. Taken together, these studies demonstrate ways in which children acquiring Mayan languages display a productive use of semantic features that differ from those of their parents.

Another interesting semantic topic, the development of spatial reference, was documented for Tseltal (Brown 1994, 2001; Brown and Levinson 2000), and Tsotsil (de León 1994, 2001a). Tseltal and Tsotsil speakers live in mountainous terrain with an upslope direction in a predominantly southerly direction and a downslope direction in a predominantly northerly direction. The words for 'up' and 'down' in Tseltal and Tsotsil have been extended to denote southern and northern directions on horizontal surfaces such as those inside a house. Children acquiring Tseltal and Tsotsil display an early and productive use of the horizontal uses of 'up' and 'down' that is basic to these languages. Several of Brown's examples for children acquiring Tseltal refer to play with toy cars inside the house.

5 PHONOLOGICAL DEVELOPMENT

The phonology of Mayan languages features a primary contrast between plain and ejective consonants. A voicing contrast only appears in Mayan languages as a result of incorporating Spanish loan words. Stephen H. Straight's study of Yucatec children's phonology (1976) and Pye, Ingram, and List's study of K'iche' children's phonology (1987) are the main sources of information on phonological development in Mayan languages. Straight asked Yucatec children to imitate a list of Yucatec words and reported their accuracy in producing consonantal contrasts in word-initial and final positions.

Pye et al. extracted a composite phonology from five K'iche' children that they compared with a composite phonology based on data from fifteen children acquiring English. The composite phonologies for both languages represent a basic set of word-initial consonants that a majority of two-year-old children in both languages produce. The comparison of the K'iche' and English composite phonologies is shown in Table 2.2. The parentheses indicate that the children produced the sounds in a limited number of words.

These composite phonologies show that children acquiring K'iche' and English typically produce nasal stops, voiceless stops, and the glide /w/. The differences between the two groups of children include the fact that English children produce a series of voiced stops, while K'iche' children produce the voiceless velar fricative /x/. These differences can be traced to the presence of these consonants in one language and their absence in the other. However, this explanation does not extend to the children's use of the affricate /tʃ/ and the liquid /l/, which occur in both English and K'iche'.

Pye et al. used these similarities and differences to test two theories of phonological development. Differences in the frequency of use of the consonants in English and K'iche' explain why children acquiring English produce voiced stops and K'iche' children produce the velar fricative. However, consonant frequencies in the adult languages do not offer a full explanation for the consonants that children produce. The fricative

TABLE 2.2 COMPOSITE INITIAL CONSONANT INVENTORIES IN K'ICHE' AND ENGLISH

K'iche'					English			
(m)	n				(m)	n		
(ɓ)					b	d	(g)	
p	t	tʃ	k	ʔ	p	t	k	
			x		(f)	(s)		h
w					w			
	l							

TABLE 2.3 COMPOSITE CHILD PHONOLOGIES FOR FIVE MAYAN LANGUAGES

	Nasals			Stops			Ejectives		Fricatives		Glides	Glides
Yucatec	m+	n	p+	t+	k	tʃ	ɓ	(ʃ)		h	l+	w	(j)
Ch'ol	m+	ɲ	p	c		tʃ+	ɓ			h+	l	w	j
Q'anjob'al	m+	n	p	t+	k+	tʃ+		(ʃ)	x	h+	l	w	j
Mam	m	n+	p	t+	k+	tʃ+					l	w	j
K'iche'	m	n	p	t+	k+	tʃ+	ɓ		x		l+	w+	(j)

/s/ is frequent in K'iche', and yet children acquiring K'iche' typically substitute [ʃ] for [s]. Pye et al. concluded that the number of lexical contrasts that use each sound, i.e. the number of lexical types, rather than the token frequencies of consonants explains the different consonants that English and K'iche'-speaking children produce in their early words.

Motor theories of children's phonological development tie the consonants that children produce to their developing articulatory abilities (Locke 1983; MacNeilage and Davis 1990). A motor theory of articulatory development predicts that children acquiring all languages will be initially restricted to the production of sounds that they can produce with immature articulatory gestures. Such theories do not explain why children acquiring K'iche' can produce /tʃ/ and /l/ but children acquiring English cannot. Pye et al. concluded that the structure of the adult phonology as evidenced by the number of lexical contrasts is an additional factor in children's phonological development.

Recently we extended the K'iche' study by extracting the child phonologies for Yucatec, Ch'ol, Q'anjob'al, and Mam (Pfeiler et al. 2008). We analyzed the phonologies of three to five children acquiring each language and compared the results to the K'iche' data. We extracted composite phonologies for the children in each language following the procedures of the earlier K'iche' study. Table 2.3 compares the composite child phonologies for these five Mayan languages. The parentheses in the table indicate consonants that the children used in a limited number of words, while the plus signs indicate consonants that the children used in a high number of words, cf. Pye et al. (1987).

These results augment the original observations made for K'iche' in Pye et al. (1987) and show that initial consonant production differs significantly from that of other languages (cf. Cook 2006; Ingram 1989; Van Severen et al. 2013). Mayan children generally produce a full set of nasals, plain stops, and glides. In all five of these Mayan languages, children regularly produce /tʃ/ and /l/ as initial consonants. Their production of ejective consonants and fricatives is more variable.

Looking across Table 2.3, we find characteristic features that distinguish the child phonologies of one Mayan language from the others. Children acquiring Yucatec and Ch'ol do not produce an initial /x/. Children acquiring Mam and K'iche' do not produce an initial /h/. Children acquiring Ch'ol produce /ɲ/ and /c/. These results provide direct evidence that children's initial consonant production is not solely the result of developing motor control, but reflect the properties of the adult phonology as filtered through the children's early lexicons. The children's sounds, like their words, exhibit variation on a common Mayan theme.

6 MORPHOLOGICAL DEVELOPMENT

The rich inflectional system of the Mayan verb complex has significant implications for our understanding of morphological development. Children acquiring the Romance and

Germanic languages are limited to the production of verbs with or without an inflectional suffix, whereas children acquiring Mayan languages can produce verbs with different combinations of inflections (a minimum of three morphological contrasts in each of five positions results in 3^5 or 243 distinct morpheme combinations). The complex morphology of Mayan verbs makes them ideal for investigating whether children initially produce a default form of the verb complex, e.g. a non-finite form, as well as investigating the productivity of children's developing morpheme combinations. The children's morphological development provides another example of variation on a common Mayan theme.

Inflectional templates for transitive verbs in the indicative mood for eight Mayan languages are shown in (2). Huastec is the only one of these languages that marks aspect by means of a suffix rather than a prefix. Mayan status suffixes encode the combination of transitivity, aspect, mood, and derivational status. The status suffixes also mark phrasal position in Q'anjob'al and K'iche'. The status suffixes vary across the Mayan languages to the extent that they mark different combinations of transitivity, mood, etc. The parentheses in (2) indicate the languages in which the status suffix also marks phrasal position. The brackets for Huastec reflect its use of a portmanteau system of agreement marking in which a single marker indicates combinations of subjects and objects on transitive predicates.

(2)   Indicative transitive verb templates in eight Mayan languages
     a. Tseltal   Aspect-Set A-Stem-Status-Set B
     b. Yucatec   Aspect-Set A-Adverb-Stem-Status-Set B
     c. Ch'ol   Aspect-Adverb-Set A-Adverb-Stem-Status-Set B
     d. Tsotsil   Aspect-Set B1-Set A-Stem-Status-Set B2
     e. Q'anjob'al   Aspect-Set B-Set A-Adverb-Stem-(Status)
     f. Mam   Aspect-Set B-Movement-Set A-Stem-Enclitic
     g. K'iche'   Aspect-Set B-Movement-Set A-Stem-(Status)
     h. Huastec   [Set B/Set A]-Adverb-Stem-Status-Aspect

Mayan languages have an ergative system of agreement marking. The Set A (ergative) markers cross-reference the subjects of transitive verbs and nominal possessors. Set B (absolutive) markers cross-reference the subjects of non-transitive predicates and the objects of transitive verbs. The Set B person markers follow the verb stem in Yucatec, Ch'ol, and Tseltal. They follow the aspect marker in Q'anjob'al, Mam, and K'iche'. They occur in either position in Tsotsil depending primarily on the presence or absence of the preverbal aspect marker.

Person marking in the individual Mayan languages diverges from this general alignment pattern to different extents (see Zavala, this volume, on alignment). Huastec uses a portmanteau system of agreement marking on transitive predicates. Yucatec, Ch'ol, Q'anjob'al, and Mam extend the use of the Set A markers to cross-reference the subjects of intransitive verbs in specific contexts. Mam also extends the Set A markers to cross-reference the objects of transitive verbs. Mam adds an enclitic to mark the contrast between third and non-third persons. Huastec, Yucatec, and Ch'ol use auxiliary verbs to express movement much like English, e.g. "I am going to see you."

The verb complexes also differ across the Mayan languages in the degree to which they incorporate adverbial modifiers. K'iche' and Mam incorporate movement verbs that follow the Set B markers. The incorporated movement verbs are infrequent in K'iche', but obligatory on all but three transitive verbs in Mam. Huastec, Yucatec, and Ch'ol incorporate adverbs immediately preceding the verb root. Ch'ol also incorporates adverbial clitics immediately after the aspect marker.

6.1 Mayan status suffixes

The Mayan status suffixes provide crucial information on productivity in Mayan children's inflectional development. Two-year-old Mayan children generally produce the status suffixes with a remarkable degree of success (Pye 1983; Pfeiler 2003; Mateo Pedro 2015). The children continue to produce the status suffixes in many of their obligatory contexts, as they grow older. Examples of the two-year-old children's production of K'iche' and Yucatec status suffixes are shown in (3).

K'ICHE' and YUCATEC
(3) Two-year-old production of status suffixes

	Intransitive Verb		Transitive Verb	
a. K'iche'	TIY (2;1)	Adult	LIN (2;0)	Adult
	loq	= tʃ-at-el-oq	ntʃapu	= k-Ø-in-tʃap-oh
		IMP-B2-leave-DEP.I		ICP-B3-A1-grab-TV
	'Leave!'	'Leave!'	'I will grab it.'	'I will grab it.'

b. Yucatec	ARM (2;0)	Adult	SAN (2;0)	Adult
	káhak	= sáan kah-ak-Ø	kaʃtik	= k-u kaʃt-ik-Ø
		while begin-DEP.I-B3		ICP-A3 find-NMLZ.TV-B3
	'It began a while ago.'	'It began a while ago.'	'She finds it.'	'She finds it.'

While K'iche' and Yucatec preserve a number of cognate status suffix forms, they have undergone historical changes that broaden the use of cognate forms in one language and narrow their use in the other language. For example, Yucatec extended the nominalized forms (/-ik/, /-Vl/) to incompletive and progressive contexts resulting in an increase in both the contexts of use and the frequency of nominalized verbs in Yucatec (Bricker 1981). Yucatec now restricts the indicative forms (/-ah/, /-ih/) to mark only the completive aspect. The nominalized suffixes are highly restricted in K'iche' since K'iche' speakers only use nominalized forms in a small set of complement clauses and idiomatic expressions (Mondloch 1981; Larsen 1988). K'iche' lacks a distinct imperative form, while Yucatec has a distinct imperative form for intransitive verbs (/-en/), which contrasts with the subjunctive form (/-Vk/) that is also used in imperative contexts. We contrast the status suffixes and their contexts of use for K'iche' and Yucatec in Table 2.4.

TABLE 2.4 K'ICHE' AND YUCATEC STATUS SUFFIXES AND THEIR CONTEXTS OF USE (PARENTHESES INDICATE USE IN CLAUSE-FINAL CONTEXTS)

Context	Transitive suffixes			Intransitive suffixes	
	K'iche'		Yucatec	K'iche'	Yucatec
	Root	Derived			
COMPLETIVE	(-oh)	-VVj	-ah	(-ik)	(-ih)
INCOMPLETIVE	(-oh)	-VVj	-ik	(-ik)	-Vl
PROGRESSIVE	(-oh)	-VVj	-ik	(-ik)	-Vl
WANT	(-oh)	-VVj	-ik	(-ik)	-Vl
GO	-V'	-VVj	-ik	a/(-oq)	-Vl
SUBJUNCTIVE	-V'	-VVj	(-eh)	a/(-oq)	-Vk
IMPERATIVE	-V'	-VVj	(-eh)	a/(-oq)	-Vk/-en
PERFECT	-Vm	-Vm	-m-ah	-inaq	-a'an

Pye and Pfeiler (2014) compared the acquisition of status suffixes in Yucatec and K'iche'. Our analysis of the adult speech showed that 56 percent to 77 percent of K'iche' verbs and 77 percent to 89 percent of Yucatec verbs addressed to children appear with only a single suffix. Only 6 percent to 15 percent of the Yucatec verbs appeared with more than two suffixes in the adult speech. The K'iche' and Yucatec children also have different production profiles. The two-year-old K'iche' children produced status suffixes with great accuracy, while the two-year-old Yucatec children had relative difficulty producing the indicative status suffix on intransitive verbs. We also found that two-year-old K'iche' children produce multiple verbs with different endings in accord with the adult grammar, while even three-year-old children acquiring Yucatec produce most verbs with a single status suffix. This difference suggests that whereas K'iche' children are using the status suffixes productively, Yucatec children rely upon a lexical strategy that generates verbs with suffixes as frozen forms.

These results show an effect of the contexts of use. The indicative forms have restricted contexts of use in Yucatec, and the Yucatec children produce the indicative verb suffixes less frequently than the K'iche' children. K'iche' makes extensive use of a suffix for derived transitive verbs, and the K'iche' children produce this suffix in the great majority of its obligatory contexts.

The adult input frequencies are not correlated with the overall frequency of production in the children and do not explain the language-specific differences between children acquiring K'iche' and Yucatec. Both of the two-year-old Yucatec children had difficulty producing the indicative and imperative status suffixes on intransitive verbs, but not on transitive verbs. The frequency of the adult status suffix production does not account for this difference. While both adults produced few tokens of the imperative suffix on intransitive verbs, they also produced few tokens of the dependent suffix on intransitive verbs. The Yucatec children had no difficulty producing the dependent suffix, but had greater difficulty producing the indicative suffix on intransitive verbs.

Pye (1983) noted that the positional constraint on the use of some status suffixes in K'iche' requires children to acquire two forms of each verb: one with the status suffix in phrase-final position and one without the status suffix in phrase-medial position. K'iche' speakers insert these status suffixes at the end of phonological phrases, thus marking phrase boundaries with stressed syllables. While children acquiring K'iche' sometimes produce status suffixes in phrase-medial position, they demonstrate a statistically significant difference in their production of status suffixes in the two positions (Pye 1983). This accomplishment shows that K'iche' children know at least two syllables in verbs even though they sometimes only produce one syllable in different contexts.

One question to come out of this research is how far the results extend to children acquiring the other Mayan languages. Pye et al. (2007) made a start toward answering this question by examining the forms of intransitive and transitive verbs that two-year-old children produced in five Mayan languages. Pye et al. found that differences in the children's verb inflections reflect differences in the morphological structure of the adult languages. Verbs in Yucatec, Huastec, Ch'ol, Q'anjob'al, and K'iche' typically appear in the adult languages with status suffixes. The verbs in Huastec have suffixes that indicate transitivity and aspect. In comparison with these languages, verbs in Tseltal, Tsotsil, and Mam are often produced in adult speech without status suffixes.

We found that while children acquiring K'iche' and Yucatec frequently produce the status suffixes on verbs (Pye and Pfeiler 2014), children acquiring Tseltal and Tsotsil frequently produce the verb roots (Brown 1997; de León 1999). The examples in (4) illustrate this difference.

K'ICHE' (Pye and Pfeiler 2014:396) and TSELTAL (Brown 1997:47)
(4) Children's verb productions
(a) TIY (2;1)   K'iche' Adult
     loq!   = *tʃ-*at-el-oq
                              IMP-B2-leave-DEP.I
     'Leave!'   'Leave!'

(b) X'anton (2;1–2;2)   Tseltal Adult
     t'uʃ   = *ja *x-ts'us
                              ICP A1-shut
     'I shut it.'   'I shut it.'

The example in (4a) was produced by a K'iche' child who was two years and one month old and shows a typical example of K'iche' children's verb forms. TIY omits the imperative prefix /tʃ-/ and the second person absolutive marker /at-/ but includes the final consonant of the verb root and the dependent intransitive status suffix. Brown (1997) provides the example in (4b) from a Tseltal child who produces only the verb root. X'anton omits the incompletive aspect marker and the first person ergative prefix.

Tables 2.5 and 2.6 add data for two-year-old children acquiring Huastec, Ch'ol, and Mam to the data published in Pye et al. (2007). The Stem + Set B column in Table 2.5 groups together the Absolutive + Stem productions in Huastec, Q'anjob'al, Mam, and

TABLE 2.5 INTRANSITIVE VERB FORMS

Language	Stem		Stem + Status		Stem + Set B		Other	
	n	%	n	%	n	%	n	%
Huastec	3	42.9%	3	42.9%			1	14.3%
Yucatec	14	36.8%	16	42.1%	8	21.1%		
Ch'ol	32	50%	27	42.2%	1	1.6%	4	6.3%
Tseltal	62	78.5%	8	10.1%	9	11.4%		
Tsotsil	17	89.5%	2	10.5%				
Q'anjob'al	7	87.5%	1	12.5%				
Mam	61	89.7%			4	5.9%	3	4.4%
K'iche'	10	52.6%	9	47.4%				

TABLE 2.6 TRANSITIVE VERB FORMS

Language	Stem		Stem + Status		Set A + Stem		Set A + Stem + Status		Other	
	n	%	n	%	n	%	n	%	n	%
Huastec	9	12.2%	25	33.8%	6	8.1%	30	40.5%	4	5.4%
Yucatec	2	6.1%	29	87.9%					2	6.1%
Ch'ol	49	38.6%	60	47.2%	6	4.7%	10	7.9%	2	1.6%
Tzeltal	54	59.3%	11	12.1%	3	3.3%			23	25.3%
Tzotzil	18	69.2%	4	15.4%	4	15.4%				
Q'anjob'al	12	60%	8	40%						
Mam	41	73.2%			10	17.9%			5	8.9%
K'iche'	1	6.7%	14	93.3%						

K'iche' with the Stem + Absolutive productions in Yucatec, Ch'ol, Tseltal, and Tsotsil. Table 2.6 shows that the children acquiring Huastec, Yucatec, Ch'ol, and K'iche' produced around 42 percent of their intransitive verbs with a suffix. The two-year-old children acquiring Tseltal, Tsotsil, Q'anjob'al, and Mam produced approximately 85 percent of their intransitive verbs as bare stems. Table 2.6 shows a similar pattern occurred in the children's transitive verb forms.

The results show that children acquiring Mayan languages frequently produce the final syllables in words. Pye et al. (2007) proposed a right-edge advantage for Mayan children's verb morphology to describe the children's syllable final verb production. The right-edge advantage in Mayan languages is due to the way in which prosody interacts with the presence or absence of a status suffix in utterance-final position. Mayan languages generally stress the final syllable in an utterance. We found that the variation in the forms of the children's first verbs across the Mayan languages can be accounted for by the right-edge advantage. Thanks to these results we have a better understanding of how a single principle leads to dramatic differences in the forms of children's verb forms.

These findings characterize the language that the children produce and not the language they comprehend. The children produce stressed syllables rather than morphemes. Many of the children's syllables contain status suffixes that encode contrasts of transitivity, mood, and derivational status. The semantic and syntactic complexity of the status suffixes does not impede the children's production of status suffixes. The children evidently have full access to the functional projections for the status suffixes, but not the verb roots in some cases.

6.2 The applicative construction

The right-edge advantage also accounts for the early acquisition of derivational morphology in Mayan languages. Derivational morphemes are usually attached after the verb root although some Mayan languages mark one of the passive voices with an infix. These derivations have different degrees of productivity in the adult languages, which lead to different frequencies of use in speech to Mayan children. The applicative derivational suffix offers further insight into how the right-edge advantage extends to morphological domains beyond verb inflection.

Many Mayan languages have an applicative derivation that adds a form of the Proto-Mayan *-b'e suffix to the verb stem (Mora-Marín 2003). The Eastern Mayan languages, including K'iche', use the applicative suffix to focus an instrument or locative phrase. The instrument or locative phrase appears in the preverbal focus position and the applicative suffix is added to the verb. An example of the K'iche' applicative construction is shown in (5).

K'ICHE' (Dayley 1981:28)
(5) tʃ'iitʃ   ʃ-ø-in-sok-b'ee-x   aw-eetʃ   .
    machete CP-B3-A1-wound-APPL-DTV   A2-of
    'It was a machete that I wounded you with.'

The Eastern Mayan languages use relational noun phrases to express instrument and locative phrases that are not in focus. Larsen (1988) reported a great deal of dialect variation in K'iche' in the use of the applicative construction, and Dayley (1985) documents a number of different constructions in Tz'utujil used to focus instrument phrases, only one of which is the applicative. Norman (1978) discusses the different properties and distribution of the applicative among the K'ichean languages. These studies indicate that the instrumental applicative in Eastern Mayan is unstable.

In contrast to the situation in the east, the Greater Tseltalan languages have a more productive and stable applicative derivation that is obligatory for goal arguments including dative, benefactive, malefactive, and patient possessors. The Greater Tseltalan languages, in contrast to the Eastern Mayan and Q'anjob'alan languages, cannot use relational noun phrases to express goals. As a result of these different contexts of use, the applicative suffix is more frequent and productive in the Greater Tseltalan languages than in the Eastern Mayan languages. In order to acquire the applicative suffix, Mayan children must determine the contexts in which the applicative derivation is used in contrast to the contexts in which the relational noun phrase is appropriate.

Although the applicative verbs in K'iche' and Tseltal have similar structures, there are obvious differences in the K'iche' and Tseltal children's use of applicatives. The most obvious difference is in the ages of the children; the Tseltal children begin using verbs with applicative suffixes almost a full year before the K'iche' children (6).

TSELTAL (Brown 2007:133)
(6) Lus (2;0)   Tseltal Adult
     poʃben alus   = *ja *s-poʃ-be-n   alus
                          ICP A3-steal-APPL-B1   alux
     'Alux steals it from me.' 'Alux steals it from me.'

A second difference occurs in the verbs that the children used with the applicative. The K'iche' children confined their use of the applicative suffix to the verbs *-ets'a* 'play' and *-tʃ'aw* 'talk' (Pye 2007). The Tseltal children use the applicative with a wider array of verbs (Brown 2007). K'iche' verbs with meanings like the Tseltal verbs *-ak'* 'give/put' and *-poʃ* 'steal' occur more frequently in K'iche' conversations than the K'iche' verbs *-ets'a* and *-tʃ'aw*, so Tseltal children have many more occasions in which they can use applicatives than K'iche' children. The applicative data provides a clear demonstration of the effect that the contexts of use has on children's language production.

Brown (2007) mentions that the children acquiring Tseltal occasionally omit the applicative suffix. Brown (1997) provides the example in (7).

TSELTAL (Brown 1997:47)
(7) X'anton (2;2)   Tseltal Adult
     ti'at w-akan   = *la *s-ti'-*be-at   w-akan
                          CP   A3-bite-APPL-B2   A2-foot
     'It bit your foot.'   'It bit your foot.'

In this example X'anton managed to produce the second person absolutive pronominal suffix with the verb while omitting the intervening applicative suffix. The omission of the applicative suffix would change the grammatical status of the person suffix in the adult grammar from indirect object (a possessor in this example) to direct object (i.e. 'bit you' instead of 'bit your'). This is most likely a simple case of omission rather than a difference between the child and adult grammars.

Instead of using the applicative construction, K'iche' children use relational nouns to express dative objects (8). The K'iche' children frequently omit the preposition *tʃi*, but produce the possessed relational noun to indicate the dative object.

K'ICHE' (Pye 2007:669)
(8) TIY (2;2)   K'iche' Adult
     m ja qeh.   = m *tʃ-ø-*a-ja'   *tʃi-q-ee.
                             m IMP-B3-A2-give   to-A1PL-POS
         'Give it to us.'   'Give it to us.'

The K'iche' children's omission of prepositions in K'iche' produces a result that is similar to the Tseltal example in (7). In (8) TIY omits the preposition *tʃi*, which in the adult grammar would change the indirect object to direct object status (i.e. 'give ours' instead of 'give to us'). Contextual evidence suggests this is also a case of omission rather than evidence of a difference between the child and adult grammars. K'iche' children omit the preposition over a long period. They only produced the preposition *tʃi* in a third to a half of its obligatory contexts at three years of age.

We can extend the right-edge advantage to the children's production of relational noun phrases as in the case of TIY's utterance. Assuming that relational noun phrases constitute a prosodic domain that is a miniature version of the verb complex, we predict that children acquiring Mayan languages with relational noun phrases like the one in (8) will tend to omit the preceding preposition but preserve the relational noun. Thus, even though goal phrases are expressed by applicative suffixes in Tseltal and relational noun phrases in K'iche', the right-edge advantage applies to both domains.

The acquisition data show that the right-edge advantage does not completely explain the form of the children's verbs. Tseltal children omit the applicative suffix, but still produce the appropriate absolutive marker. K'iche' children do not produce applicative verb forms until much later even though the form is identical to that in Tseltal. The evidence shows that the context of use interacts with the right-edge advantage to determine the parts of the verb complex that Mayan children produce.

6.3 Acquisition of the left edge

The right-edge advantage explains why children acquiring Mayan languages favor the production of verb-final syllables, but it does not account for how the full verb complex develops in children's speech. Among the issues to investigate in this regard is whether Mayan children produce the Set B markers that follow the verb stem before the Set B markers that precede the verb stem. We are also interested in the degree to which the children's production of the Set A and Set B markers preceding the verb stem are produced in conjunction with the preceding aspect markers or independently of the aspect markers. All of these issues bear on the main question of the degree to which prosodic structure determines how the verb complex develops in each language.

A comparison of how children acquire the Set B (absolutive) markers in Yucatec, Tseltal, Tsotsil, and K'iche' revealed significant differences in the children's production of these morphemes (Brown et al. 2013). While the Set B markers occur before the verb stem in K'iche', they are verb suffixes in the other three languages. Children acquire the Set B markers earlier in Yucatec and Tseltal than in Tsotsil and K'iche'. Tsotsil is a special case because it places some Set B markers before the verb stem and some after the verb stem. Children acquiring Tsotsil produce the Set B suffixes at higher frequencies than the Set B markers before the verb stem. These results extend the right-edge advantage to account for the early production of Set B markers in the Mayan languages.

6.4 Acquisition of ergative alignment

The acquisition of the ergative alignment system in Mayan languages is complicated. All Mayan languages place the ergative markers before the verb stem, but some languages, e.g. Huastec, Yucatec, and Ch'ol, allow some adverbs to occur between the ergative markers and the verb stem (Pye and Pfeiler 2017). The ergative markers also display different degrees of phonetic merger with the aspectual clitics that precede them.

The Set A and Set B markers have different contexts of use across the Mayan languages. K'iche' marks person on verbs in the imperative mood in contrast with Yucatec, Ch'ol, Tseltal, and Q'anjob'al. Many of the languages extend the Set A markers to intransitive verbs in contexts that differ from one language to the next (Larsen and Norman 1979). Examples of extended ergative marking for three Mayan languages are shown in (9). The first intransitive verb -ooq' 'cry' in the Mam example (9a) is in the progressive aspect, and yet it has the third person plural absolutive person marker *tʃi*, whereas the Q'anjob'al and Yucatec intransitive verbs in (9b) and (9c) have ergative prefixes.

Mam (England 1983:259), Q'anjob'al, and Yucatec
(9) Intransitive verbs with extended ergative marking

    a. Mam   Adverbial Context
       n-tʃi ooq'   t-poon   ky-tʂuu'
       PROG-B3PL cry A3-arrive A3PL-mother
       'They were crying when their mother arrived.'

    b. Q'anjob'al   Progressive Context
       lanan   ha-waj-i.
       PROG   A2-sleep-ITV
       'You are sleeping.'

    c. Yucatec   Progressive Context
       táan   a   wen-el.
       PROG A2   sleep-NMLZ.I
       'You are sleeping.'

Children not only have to acquire the forms of the Set A and Set B markers, but also determine their specific contexts of use in each language. We expect to find cases of undergeneralization or overgeneralization if the children formulate rules for the Set A markers that are either too restrictive or too general. Children might selectively omit the person markers in contexts they have not heard before.

We can appeal to the right-edge advantage to explain the differences we observe in the children's production of the Set A person markers. The Set A markers precede the verb root in all of the Mayan languages. Most Mayan languages have two allomorphs of the Set A markers; one is used before vowel-initial verb stems and the other is used before consonant-initial verb stems. The right-edge advantage predicts that children will produce the Set A allomorphs that are part of the syllable containing the verb root (i.e. the vowel-initial allomorphs) earlier than the Set A allomorphs that form a separate syllable that precedes the verb root (i.e. the consonant-initial allomorphs). Brown et al. (2013) report this result for children acquiring Yucatec, Tseltal, Tsotsil, and K'iche'. Mateo Pedro (2015) reports the same result for children acquiring Q'anjob'al.

K'iche' children gradually increase their production of the agreement markers between two and three-and-a-half years of age (Pye 1990). The K'iche' children produced very

TABLE 2.7 EXTENDED ERGATIVE CONTEXTS IN MAM, Q'ANJOB'AL, AND YUCATEC

	Adverbial		Aspectual		
Language	Time	Manner	Desiderative	Progressive	Incompletive
Mam	Extended	Extended	Extended		
Q'anjob'al		Extended		Extended	
Yucatec		Extended	Extended	Extended	Extended

few cases of Set B markers for the subject of transitive verbs and Set A markers for the subject of intransitive verbs. These data show that K'iche' children had successfully generalized the use of the ergative markers to the contexts of use licensed in K'iche'.

Children acquiring Huastec, Yucatec, Ch'ol, and K'iche' produce the Set A markers at different rates in the different languages (Pye and Pfeiler 2017). This observation suggests that Mayan children do not acquire the preconsonantal Set A allomorphs in a uniform manner despite similarities in form and structural position of the Set A markers across the Mayan languages. Rather, the Set A markers in different Mayan languages pose distinct challenges to children acquiring them. This difference is most readily seen by investigating how Mayan children acquire the contexts in which the adult languages extend Set A (ergative) markers to intransitive verbs, as shown in (9) above. Table 2.7 shows some contexts of extended Set A marking in Yucatec, Q'anjob'al, and Mam.

As was the case for the status suffixes, we observe an interplay between the contexts of use for a linguistic feature and its frequency of use in the adult language. Mam and Q'anjob'al adults use intransitive verbs far more frequently in indicative contexts than in aspectless contexts, and thus children acquiring Mam and Q'anjob'al hear relatively few intransitive verbs with Set A cross-reference markers (Pye et al. 2013). Yucatec children, on the other hand, hear equal numbers of intransitive verbs in indicative and aspectless contexts, and therefore have robust evidence that their language extends Set A (ergative) markers to intransitive verbs. We analyzed whether this difference in the frequency of use led to a greater use of extended ergative marking in children acquiring Yucatec.

The examples in (10) show that children acquiring all three of these languages produce early instances of intransitive verbs in extended Set A contexts. The Mam child WEN and the Q'anjob'al child XHIM produced Set A markers on the intransitive verbs in (10a) and (10b) respectively. The Yucatec child ARM omits the Set A marker in (10c). We count the example in (10c) as Set A omission rather than the overextension of the third person Set B zero marker because we do not find Set B overextensions for other persons (Pye 1990).

MAM, Q'ANJOB'AL, and YUCATEC (Pye et al. 2013:322)
(10) Children's extended ergative use
a. WEN (2;0.25)   Mam Adult
     taaʃ xhunt kuun.   = *i   t-axs   xunt   q-u'n.
                                              so   A3-return   one   A1PL-by
     'So that another returns by us.'   'So that another returns by us.'

b. XHIM (2;9)   Q'anjob'al Adult
     lan hamulnaxil tom.   = lan   ha-mulnax-il   dom
                                              PROG   A2-work-NMLZ   Dominga
     'Dominga you are working.'   'Dominga you are working.'

c. ARM (2;0.15)   Yucatec Adult
    ok peek'.   = *táan   *uy-ok-*ol   peek'
                                       PROG   A3-enter-NMLZ.I dog
    'The dog is coming in.'   'The dog is coming in.'

The children's use of the Set A markers to cross-reference the subject of intransitive verbs shows that they distinguish between the indicative and extended ergative contexts as well as between intransitive and transitive verbs. There are no examples of a Set A marked intransitive subject in indicative or imperative contexts. The children recognize at least one context for extended ergativity even though they do not always produce the Set A marker in that context.

The frequency with which the children produced Set A markers in extended ergative contexts had no relation to the number of such sentences the adult speakers produced. The adult speaker of Yucatec produced many utterances in extended ergative contexts, while the Yucatec child ARM only produced the Set A marker on 14 percent of intransitive verbs. Meanwhile, the Q'anjob'al adult produced very few verbs in extended ergative contexts, but all three Q'anjob'al children produced Set A markers on a high proportion of their intransitive verbs. The Mam children display a lower frequency of use than the Q'anjob'al children even though the adult speaker produced a greater number of intransitive verbs in extended ergative contexts.

The Mayan person markers provide yet another illustration of the ways in which the individual Mayan languages have produced a variation on a common theme. Children confront unique problems in acquiring the person markers in each Mayan language. The children's morpheme production is unrelated to the frequency of use in the adult languages, but exhibits a sophisticated understanding of the unique contexts of use in each language. The acquisition results show that children can acquire inflections in rare contexts as easily as they do in frequent contexts. While the children frequently omit the person markers, they do not overgeneralize their use.

7 SYNTACTIC DEVELOPMENT

The acquisition of syntax in Mayan languages has received relatively little attention due to the prominence of the verb morphology. A few studies have investigated different aspects of syntactic development in Mayan languages especially as the syntax interacts with the verb morphology. The research on applicatives and extended ergativity that we discussed in the previous section are examples of this research. Most syntactic research to date has only analyzed acquisition data from individual Mayan languages (e.g. Pye and Quixtan Poz 1988, 1989). In this section we discuss Mayan children's use of argument omission and pronouns.

Like most Mayan languages, K'iche' has variable word orders. It has an unmarked word order of verb-object-subject, but topicalized noun phrases appear in the sentence-initial position and focused noun phrases occur in preverbal position (Aissen 1992 and Chapter 11, this volume). The relative order of the subject and object is also affected by their animacy and definiteness features (England 1991). The cross-reference markers for subject and object on verbs and possessed nouns license the omission of these arguments. Adult speakers produce very few sentences with both subjects and objects in informal contexts where much information can be inferred from the discourse context (Du Bois 1987).

Like adults, K'iche' children do not produce many sentences that contain overt subjects and objects. Two K'iche' children, TIY and CAR, produced a majority of their transitive sentences with a VSO word order. The child CHA produced a majority of transitive sentences with a VOS word order (Pye 1992).

The vast majority of the children's sentences contained just a predicate or a predicate and a single argument. TIY, for example, produced a total of nine sentences that contained both a subject and an object. She produced twenty-six sentences with a verb (either transitive or intransitive) and a subject and 112 sentences with a verb and a direct object. She omitted the subject in 92 percent of her utterances and the direct object in 67 percent. Brown (1998a) analyzed the arguments that two-year-old Tseltal children produced. She found that the children omitted the subjects of transitive verbs in 84 percent of their utterances and the direct objects of transitive verbs in 60 percent. Mateo Pedro (2015:158) reports that Q'anjob'al children omitted the subjects in between 80 and 90 percent of their utterances with transitive verbs and the direct objects in between 45 and 60 percent. Brown and Mateo Pedro's results are very close to the results for K'iche', and support the idea that the conditions for the use of overt arguments are similar in K'iche', Q'anjob'al, and Tseltal.

Almost all of the lexical subjects that the K'iche' children produced were independent pronouns. The pronouns and agreement markers for the subject emerge in parallel in the K'iche' children's speech. The K'iche' children used the pronouns for emphasis rather than as substitutes for the agreement markers. The children's subject pronouns followed the verb rather than appearing in the sentence-initial topic or preverbal focus positions. The children's use of independent pronouns follows the adult pattern of use. The example in (11) shows an interchange between TIY and her older sister SEP. SEP initiates the exchange about TIY's hand and TIY responds by emphasizing that SEP is the one who gave her hand. TIY's utterance has a verb-subject-object word order that is expected with a pronominal agent.

K'ICHE'
(11) TIY's (2;10.5) pronoun use

SEP	K'iche' Adult		
ajakom aq'ab' e'.	= a-ja'-om	a-q'ab'	e'.
	A2-give-PRF	A2-hand	there
'You have given your hand there.'	'You have given your hand there.'		
TIY (2;10.5)	K'iche' Adult		
jakom at e lee q'ab' e.	= *a-ja'-om	at	lee	*a-q'ab' e'
	A2-give- PRF	PRON	the	A2-hand there
'YOU have given your hand there.'	'YOU have given your hand there.'		

There is an interesting difference between the use of lexical and pronominal arguments in K'iche' and Tseltal. Whereas the K'iche' children favored the use of pronominal subjects, the Tseltal children favored the use of lexical subjects. Pronouns in Tseltal contain the focus particle *ja'* (= [xa']) and are used in the preverbal focus position in adult speech. They occur after the verb in a topic construction headed by *te* (Polian 2013:144). Brown observed that Tseltal children use focus pronouns like *ja'at* (= [xa'at]) 'you' in the postverbal position where they do not occur in adult speech (12). These examples show that Tseltal children exhibit a K'iche'-like usage of pronouns for emphasis rather than the Tseltal use of the pronouns for focus. This usage marks a major difference between the child and adult grammars of Tseltal.

TSELTAL (Brown 1998a:136)
(12) Children's use of focus pronouns

Child Form	Adult Target	English translation
mal xa'at	= la a'-mal	'You spilled it.'
utʃa xa'at	= utʃa'	'You drink it!'
tes xa'at	= ja x-tes-at	'I comb you.'

Mateo Pedro (2015:79) reports that children acquiring Q'anjob'al produced pronominal forms both before and after the verb. One of the examples that Mateo Pedro reports contains a focused form that the child produced after the verb rather than in the preverbal focus position (13). This example shows that Q'anjob'al children use pronouns for focus, but do not produce the pronouns in the preverbal focus position of the adult grammar.

Q'ANJOB'AL (Mateo Pedro 2015:79)
(13) Child's use of focus pronoun

Xhim (2;4)		Q'anjob'al Adult			
toχ ajin a wewe.	=	ajin	q-in	toq	b'aj wewe.
		PRON POT-B1		go.POT to	Huehuetenango
'I will go to Huehuetenango.'		'I will go to Huehuetenango.'			

8 CONCLUSION

This chapter describes a few features of Mayan child languages. Two-year-old speakers of any language produce incomplete versions of words and sentences. Child language provides a unique variant of the adult language that needs to be described on its own terms. We are beginning to understand the linguistic elements that Mayan children produce or omit in specific languages, and have started to paint a picture of the variation that exists within and between different Mayan child languages.

Common features in the adult Mayan languages are the basis of the common features in the children's languages. Mayan children acquire the existential verbs and relational nouns of the adult languages. They produce the plain stops, affricates, nasals, glides, and one liquid of the adult phonologies. Mayan children acquire the theme-specific Mayan verbs, and absolute spatial language of the adult languages. Mayan children latch onto the roots of verbs, but add the status suffixes that typify the adult languages. Like adult speakers, Mayan children frequently omit the subjects and objects from sentences and will use pronouns to the extent that they are used in the adult languages.

We are fortunate to have comparative acquisition data from so many Mayan languages. The comparative data is essential to show both the overall similarities between the children's grammars as well as the ways in which differences emerge in the children's language. We point to a right-edge advantage that leads Tseltal, Tsotsil, and Mam children to produce many bare verb roots, while children acquiring Huastec, Ch'ol, Yucatec, K'iche', and Q'anjob'al produce verbs with status suffixes. All Mayan children produce ergative agreement markers by the age of 2;0, and they all demonstrate an awareness of the language-specific contexts for their use. Acquisition data from languages in all of the branches of the Mayan language family strengthens our understanding of the diversity to be found in the children's grammars.

Mayan languages have linguistic features such as ejective stops, a verb complex, ergative agreement, and focus constructions that are not addressed in current acquisition theories. Discussing the implications that the Mayan results have for each acquisition theory would take us beyond the available space and would distract attention from our primary goal of describing the language of Mayan children. We leave it as an exercise for readers to work out the ways in which Mayan child grammars reveal the limitations of current acquisition theories (cf. Brown 1998a; Pye 1983, 2001, 2017).

One significant development that emerges from our collaborative research is a better appreciation of the ways in which Mayan language acquisition differs from the processes of historical change that led to the linguistic diversity seen across the Mayan language family. Although language change is often attributed to the failings of children, no one has compared historical changes with the language that children actually produce. We are in a position for the first time to compare historical processes with acquisition processes and determine any potential connections between the two. While there are some similarities, such as the omission of uvular stops and aspectual prefixes, there are many differences (Pye 2009). Overall, Mayan children display a remarkable ability to pick up the peculiarities of each language; we find no evidence that children acquiring K'iche', for example, ever adopt the contexts of extended ergativity seen in Mam or Q'anjob'al.

Although we have learned much about the paths that Mayan children follow in their language development, there is a lot of work that remains. We do not have acquisition data for the many endangered Mayan languages. Sadly, it may be too late to document the acquisition of Chontal, Itza, and Lacandon. We also recognize the need to return what we have learned about the acquisition of the languages to the Mayan communities so that bilingual teachers in the schools are better prepared to understand the sophisticated language of Mayan children. We are clearly far from the end of our journey.

ACKNOWLEDGMENTS

Our colleagues on the Mayan Language Acquisition Project have provided numerous insights into the workings of their languages, which have furthered our understanding of Mayan language acquisition. Data collection for K'iche' was supported by grants from the Organization of American States and the Wenner Gren Foundation to the first author. Data collection for Ch'ol, Mam, and Q'anjob'al was funded by grants from the National Science Foundation (BCS-0613120 and BCS-0515120) and the University of Kansas. Data collection for Huastec and Yucatec was funded by the Consejo Nacional de Ciencia y Tecnología of Mexico (CB105596, CB4639-H, and CB27893-H) and from the Programa de Apoyo a Proyectos de Investigación e Innovación Tecnológica-Universidad Nacional Autónoma de México (IN401207) to the second author. Pfeiler and Pye each received Fulbright scholar awards in 2015 that supported further collaboration for work on this chapter. All of these projects would not have been possible without the aid and support of the children's families as well as the efforts of the team of Huastec investigators: Leonarda Hernández Gutiérrez, Magdalena Martínez Enríquez, Alicia Hernández Martínez, and Andrés Cruz Cruz; the Yucatec investigators: Neifi Vermont Vermont, Andrés Dzib Dzib, and Adiel Mena Keb; the Ch'ol investigators: Pedro Gutiérrez Sánchez, Asunción López Pérez, and Melba del Carmen Martínez Pérez; the K'iche' investigators: Augustin Huix Huix, Pedro Quixtan Poz, Emilio Quiej Huix, and Santos Quiej Huix; the Mam investigators: Ana Elizabeth López Ramirez, Juana Isabel López Morales, Sheny Ortíz García, and Luis Hernandez López Ramirez; and the Q'anjob'al investigators: Flora García, Diego Martínez Esteban, Francisco Pedro Mateo, Pedro Martínez Esteban, Efraín Ramón de León, Basilio Luin Bernabé, and Basilio Sebastian Basilio.

We also thank the editors of this volume for suggestions that have substantially improved our initial drafts. We are responsible for any remaining errors.

REFERENCES

Aissen, Judith. 1992. "Topic and focus in Mayan." *Language* 68: 43–80.

Anglin, Jeremy M. 1977. *Word, object, and conceptual development*. New York: Norton.

Bernstein Ratner, Nan, and Clifton Pye. 1984. "Higher pitch in BT is not universal: Acoustic evidence from Quiché Mayan." *The Journal of Child Language* 11: 515–22.

Bittner, Dagmar, Wolfgang U. Dressler, and Marianne Kilani-Schoch, eds. 2003. *Development of verb inflection in first language acquisition: A cross-linguistic perspective*. Berlin: Mouton de Gruyter.

Bricker, Victoria R. 1981. "The source of the ergative split in Yucatec Maya." *Journal of Mayan Linguistics* 2: 83–127.

Brown, Penelope. 1994. "The INs and ONs of Tzeltal locative expressions: The semantics of static descriptions of location." *Linguistics* 32: 743–90.

Brown, Penelope. 1997. "Isolating the CVC root in Tzeltal Mayan: A study of children's first verbs." In *Proceedings of the 28th annual child language research forum*, ed. by Eve V. Clark, 41–52. Stanford: CSLI/University of Chicago Press.

Brown, Penelope. 1998a. "Children's first verbs in Tzeltal: Evidence for an early verb category." *Linguistics* 36: 713–53.

Brown, Penelope. 1998b. "Conversational structure and language acquisition: The role of repetition in Tzeltal adult and child speech." *Journal of Linguistic Anthropology* 8: 197–221.

Brown, Penelope. 2001. "Learning to talk about motion UP and DOWN in Tzeltal: Is there a language-specific bias for verb learning?" In *Language acquisition and conceptual development*, ed. by Melissa Bowerman and Stephen C. Levinson, 512–43. Cambridge: Cambridge University Press.

Brown, Penelope. 2007. "Culture-specific influences on semantic development: Acquiring the Tzeltal 'benefactive' construction." In *Learning indigenous languages: Child language acquisition in Mesoamerica*, ed. by Barbara Pfeiler, 119–54. Berlin: Mouton de Gruyter.

Brown, Penelope. 2008. "Verb specificity and argument realization in Tzeltal child language." In *Crosslinguistic perspectives on argument structure: Implications for language acquisition*, ed. by Melissa Bowerman and Penelope Brown, 167–89. Mahwah: Lawrence Erlbaum.

Brown, Penelope, and Stephen C. Levinson. 2000. "Frames of spatial reference and their acquisition in Tenejapan Tzeltal." In *Culture, thought, and development*, ed. by L. Nucci, G. Saxe, and E. Turiel, 167–97. Mahwah: Lawrence Erlbaum.

Brown, Penelope, Barbara Pfeiler, Lourdes de León, and Clifton Pye. 2013. "The acquisition of agreement in four Mayan languages." In *The acquisition of ergativity*, ed. by Edith L. Bavin and Sabine Stoll, 271–306. Amsterdam: John Benjamins.

Brown, Roger. 1973. *A first language: The early stages*. Cambridge: Harvard University Press.

Cook, Eung-Do. 2006. "The patterns of consonantal acquisition and change in Chipewyan (Děne Suliné)." *International Journal of American Linguistics* 72: 236–63.

Curiel, Alejandro. 2016. "Estructura narrativa y evidencialidad en tojolabal." PhD diss., Universidad Nacional Autónoma de México.

Dayley, John. 1981. "Voice and ergativity in Mayan languages." *Journal of Mayan Linguistics* 2: 3–82.

Dayley, John. 1985. *Tzutujil grammar*. Berkeley: University of California Press.

Du Bois, John W. 1987. "The discourse basis of ergativity." *Language* 63: 805–55.

England, Nora C. 1983. *A grammar of Mam, a Mayan language*. Austin: The University of Texas Press.

England, Nora C. 1991. "Changes in basic word order in Mayan languages." *International Journal of American Linguistics* 57: 446–86.

Gentner, Deidre, and Lera Boroditsky. 2001. "Individuation, relativity, and early word learning." In *Language acquisition and conceptual development*, ed. by M. Bowerman and S. Levinson, 215–56. Cambridge: Cambridge University Press.

Hao, Meiling, Youyi Liu, Hua Shu, Ailing Xing, Ying Jiang, and Ping Li. 2015. "Developmental changes in the early child lexicon in Mandarin Chinese." *Journal of Child Language* 42: 505–37.

Ingram, David. 1989. *First language acquisition: Method, description and explanation*. Cambridge: Cambridge University Press.

Larsen, Kay. 1949. "Huasteco baby talk." *El México Antiguo* 7: 295–98.

Larsen, Thomas W. 1988. "Manifestations of ergativity in Quiché grammar." PhD diss., University of California.

Larsen, Thomas W., and William M. Norman. 1979. "Correlates of ergativity in Mayan grammar." In *Ergativity: Towards a theory of grammatical relations*, ed. by F. Plank, 347–70. New York: Academic Press.

de León, Lourdes. 1994. "Exploration in the acquisition of geocentric location by Tzotzil children." *Linguistics* 32: 857–84.

de León, Lourdes. 1999. "Verb roots and caregiver speech in early Tzotzil acquisition." In *Cognition and function in language*, ed. by Barbara A. Fox, Dan Jurafsky, and Laura A. Michaelis, 99–119. Stanford: Stanford University Center for Language and Information.

de León, Lourdes. 2000. "The emergent participant: Interactive patterns of socialization of Tzotzil (Mayan) children." *Journal of Linguistic Anthropology* 8: 131–61.

de León, Lourdes. 2001a. "Finding the richest path: Language and cognition in the acquisition of verticality in Tzotzil (Mayan)." In *Language acquisition and conceptual development*, ed. by Melissa Bowerman and Stephen Levinson, 544–65. Cambridge: Cambridge University Press.

de León, Lourdes. 2001b. "Why Tzotzil (Mayan) children prefer verbs: The role of linguistic and cultural factors over cognitive determinants." In *Proceedings of the 8th conference of the international association for the study of child language*, ed. by Margareta Almgren, Adoni Barrena, Maria-Jose Ezeizabarrena, Itziar Idiazabal, and Brian MacWhinney, 947–69. Somerville: Cascadilla Press.

de León, Lourdes. 2005. *La llegada del alma: Lenguaje, infancia y socialización entre los mayas de Zinacantán*. México: Centro de Investigaciones y Estudios Superiores en Antropología Social, Instituto Nacional de Antropología e Historia.

de León, Lourdes. 2007. "A preliminary view at Ch'ol (Mayan) early lexicon: The role of language and cultural context." In *Learning indigenous languages: Child language acquisition in Mesoamerica*, ed. by Barbara Pfeiler, 85–102. Berlin: Mouton de Gruyter.

Locke, John L. 1983. *Phonological acquisition and change*. New York: Academic Press.

Lois, Ximena, and Valentina Vapnarsky. 2006. "Root indeterminacy and polyvalence in Yukatekan Mayan languages." In *Lexical categories and root classes in Amerindian languages*, ed. by Ximena Lois, and Valentina Vapnarksy, 69–116. Frankfurt: Peter Lang Verlag.

MacNeilage, Peter F., and Barbara L. Davis. 1990. "Acquisition of speech production: Frames, then content." In *Attention and performance 13: Motor representation and control*, ed. by M. Jeannerod, 453–75. Hillsdale: Erlbaum.

Martínez Pérez, Margarita. 2013. "Los rasgos del habla dirigida a niños en el tsotsil huixteco: un estudio en tres hogares." In *Nuevos Senderos en el Estudio de la Adquisición de Lenguas Mesoamericanas. Estructuras, Narrativa y Socialización*, ed. by Lourdes de León Pasquel, 83–120. México: Centro de Investigaciones y Estudios Superiores en Antropología Social.

Mateo Pedro, Pedro. 2015. *The acquisition of inflection in Q'anjob'al Maya*. Amsterdam: John Benjamins.

Mondloch, James L. 1981. "Voice in Quiché-Maya." PhD diss., State University of New York.

Mora-Marín, David F. 2003. "Historical reconstruction of Mayan applicative and antidative constructions." *International Journal of American Linguistics* 69: 186–228.

Norman, William M. 1978. "Advancement Rules and Syntactic Change: the Loss of Instrumental Voice in Mayan." *Berkeley Linguistic Society* 4: 258–76.

Pfeiler, Barbara. 2003. "Early acquisition of the verbal complex in Yucatec Maya." In *Development of verb inflection in first language acquisition*, ed. by Dagmar Bittner, Wolfgang U. Dressler, and Marianne Kilani-Schoch, 379–99. Berlin: Mouton de Gruyter.

Pfeiler, Barbara. 2006. "Polyvalence in the acquisition of early lexicon in Yucatec Maya." In *Lexical categories and root classes in Amerinidian languages*, ed. by Ximena Lois and Valentina Vapnarsky, 319–41. Frankfurt: Peter Lang Verlag.

Pfeiler, Barbara. 2007. "'Lo oye, lo repite y lo piensa'. The contribution of prompting to the socialization and language acquisition in Yukatek Maya toddler." In *Learning indigenous languages: Child language acquisition in Mesoamerica*, ed. by Barbara Pfeiler, 183–202. Berlin: Mouton de Gruyter.

Pfeiler, Barbara, C. Pye, P. Mateo, A. E. López, and P. Gutiérrez. 2008. "Adquisición de consonantes iniciales en cinco lenguas mayas: un análisis fonológico." In *Memorias del IX Encuentro Internacional de Lingüística en el Noroeste*, ed. by Rosa María Ortiz Ciscomani, 73–89. Hermosillo: Universidad de Sonora.

Polian, Gilles. 2013. *Gramática del Tseltal de Oxchuc*. México, D. F.: CIESAS.

Pye, Clifton. 1979. "The Acquisition of Quiché (Mayan)." *Current Anthropology* 20: 459–60.

Pye, Clifton. 1983. "Mayan telegraphese: Intonational determinants of inflectional development in Quiché Mayan." *Language* 59: 583–604.

Pye, Clifton. 1986. "Quiché Mayan speech to children." *The Journal of Child Language* 13: 85–100.

Pye, Clifton. 1990. "The acquisition of ergative languages." *Linguistics* 28: 1291–330.

Pye, Clifton. 1992. "The Acquisition of K'iche' (Maya)." In *The crosslinguistic study of language acquisition*, vol. 3, ed. by Dan Isaac Slobin, 221–308. Hillsdale: Erlbaum.

Pye, Clifton. 2001. "The acquisition of finiteness in K'iche' Maya." In *Proceedings of the 25th annual Boston university conference on language development*, ed. by Anna H.-J. Do, Laura Domínguez, and Aimee Johansen, 645–56. Somerville: Cascadilla Press.

Pye, Clifton. 2007. "The genetic matrix of Mayan three-place predicates and their acquisition in K'iche' Mayan." *Linguistics* 45: 653–82.

Pye, Clifton. 2009. "Cycles of complementation in the Mayan languages." In *Cyclical change*, ed. by Elly van Gelderen, 265–84. Amsterdam: John Benjamins.

Pye, Clifton. 2017. *The comparative method of language acquisition research*. Chicago: University of Chicago Press.

Pye, Clifton, David Ingram, and Helen List. 1987. "A comparison of initial consonant acquisition in English and Quiché." In *Children's language*, vol. 6, ed. by Keith Nelson, and Anne van Kleeck, 175–90. Hillsdale: Erlbaum.

Pye, C., D. F. Loeb, and Y. Y. Pao. 1996. "The Acquisition of Breaking and Cutting." In *The Proceedings of the Twenty-seventh Annual Child Language Research Forum*, ed. by Eve V. Clark, 227–236. Stanford: Center for the Study of Language and Information.

Pye, Clifton, and Barbara Pfeiler. 2014. "The comparative method of language acquisition research: A Mayan case study." *Journal of Child Language* 41: 382–415.

Pye, Clifton, and Barbara Pfeiler. 2017. "A comparative study of the acquisition of nominative and ergative agreement in European and Mayan languages." In *The Oxford handbook of ergativity*, ed. by Diane Massam, Jessica Coon, and Lisa Travis, 665–89. Oxford: Oxford University Press.

Pye, Clifton, Barbara Pfeiler, Lourdes de León, Penelope Brown, and Pedro Mateo Pedro. 2007. "Roots or edges? Explaining variation in children's early verb forms across five Mayan languages." In *Learning Indigenous languages: Child language acquisition in Mesoamerica*, ed. by Barbara Pfeiler, 15–47. Berlin: Mouton de Gruyter.

Pye, Clifton, Barbara Pfeiler, and Pedro Mateo Pedro. 2013. "The acquisition of extended ergativity in Mam, Q'anjob'al and Yucatec." In *The acquisition of ergativity*, ed. by Edith Bavin and Sabine Stoll, 307–35. Amsterdam: John Benjamins.

Pye, Clifton, and Pedro Quixtan Poz. 1988. "Precocious passives (and antipassives) in Quiché Mayan." In *Papers and reports on child language development*, vol. 27, ed. by Eve V. Clark, 71–80. Stanford.

Pye, Clifton, and Pedro Quixtan Poz. 1989. "Why functionalism won't function: The acquisition of passives and antipassives in K'iche' Mayan." *Working Papers in Language Development*, 4, 39–53. The Child Language Program, University of Kansas.

Snow, Catherine, and Charles Ferguson, eds. 1977. *Talking to children*. New York: Cambridge University Press.

Straight, Stephen H. 1976. *The acquisition of Maya phonology: Variation in Yucatec child language*. New York: Garland.

Stross, Brian. 1969. "Aspects of language acquisition by Tzeltal children." PhD dissertation, University of California, Berkeley.

Taine, Hippolyte. 1877. "The acquisition of language by children." *Mind* 2: 252–9.

Van Severen, Lieve, Joris J. M. Gillis, Inge Molemans, Renate van den Berg, Sven de Maeyer, and Steven Gillis. 2013. "The relation between order of acquisition, segmental frequency and function: the case of word-initial consonants in Dutch." *Journal of Child Language* 40: 703–40.

CHAPTER 3

MAYAN HISTORY AND COMPARISON

Lyle Campbell

1 INTRODUCTION

The intention of this chapter is to present an overview of Mayan historical and comparative linguistics and to point to areas where further investigation and fresh thinking may prove rewarding. While each language has its own complex history, due to space limitations I concentrate on aspects of Mayan reconstruction and linguistic changes relevant to the family as a whole.[1]

2 BACKGROUND

Relationships among Mayan languages were recognized already in Spanish colonial sources. For example, Francisco Ximénez (1702:1) had a clear understanding of the family relationship among many of the Mayan languages, Tzotzil [Tsotsil], Zendal [Tseltal], Chanabal [Tojolabal], Coxoh, Mame [Mam], Lacandón, Peten [Itzaj], Q'aq'chiquel [Kaqchikel], Q'aq'chi [Q'eqchi'], and Poq'omchi, [Poqomchi']. He remarked that for the languages to be related in this way was no miracle, since that kind of relationship is seen in the "daughters of Latin" (the Romance languages). Lorenzo Hervás y Panduro (1800:304) in his catalogue of the world's languages reported that "the languages *Maya* [Yucatec Maya], *Cakchi* [Q'eqchi'], *Poconchi* [Poqomchi'], *Cakchiquil* [Kaqchikel] and *Pocoman* [Poqomam] are related"; his evidence included number words, many other words, and "not a little of their grammatical structure." Some highlights in the history of Mayan comparison and reconstruction were Karl Hermann Berendts's (1876) collection of materials and classification; Otto Stoll's (1884, 1885) classification, comparative word lists, and postulation of sound correspondences and some regular sound changes; Charles-Félix-Hyacinthe Gouhier Comte de Charencey's (1870, 1872) classification and sound correspondences; Alfred Kroeber's (1939) classification and his confirmation of the close connection between Huastec and Chicomuseltec; and Abraham M. Halpern's (1942) set of sound correspondences and the first real reconstruction of several Proto-Mayan sounds. (Proto-Mayan is henceforth abbreviated PM.) Often Norman McQuown (1955, 1956) is credited as founder of modern Mayan comparative linguistics. Several PM phonemes postulated by McQuown were eliminated in later refinements (see Kaufman 1964, 1969, 1976, 1990; Campbell 1977:89–90, 97–101, 1988:6–12; Kaufman and Norman 1984; Kaufman with Justeson 2003; see below). The view of PM reconstruction in Campbell and Kaufman (1985) still represents the consensus view, for the most part.

The documentation of Mayan languages has increased dramatically since the 1980s, with dictionaries and grammars now available for most of the languages. This has greatly facilitated comparison and reconstruction, and provides a rich and needed foundation for Mayan historical linguistic advances yet to come.

3 CLASSIFICATION

There are some thirty Mayan languages. The most widely accepted classification of the family is given in Table 3.1 (degree of indentation corresponds to degree of relatedness).

Note that the spelling of the names of Mayan languages in Guatemala follows recommendations of the Academia de Lenguas Mayas de Guatemala (http://www.almg.org.gt/), and those in Mexico the spellings of INALI (2009).

The only extinct Mayan languages are Chicomuseltec and Choltí, though some others are highly endangered, for example Itzaj (Itzá) and Mocho' (Motozintleco). Sometimes the language of Maya hieroglyphic writing is also listed as extinct, although it probably did not disappear, but rather was the ancestor to one or more of the modern Ch'olan

TABLE 3.1 CLASSIFICATION OF THE MAYAN LANGUAGES

Huastecan
        Huastec, Chicomuseltec
Core Mayan (Central Mayan)
        Yucatecan
                Maya (Yucatec Maya), Lacandón
                Itzaj (Itzá, Itza'), Mopan
        Western Mayan
            Cholan-Tseltalan
                Cholan
                      Ch'ol, Chontal (Yokot'an)
                      Choltí (extinct), Ch'orti'
                Tseltalan
                      Tseltal, Tsotsil
            Greater Q'anjob'alan (Q'anjob'alan-Chujean)
                Q'anjob'alan
                      Q'anjob'al, Akatek, Jakaltek (Popti')
                      Mocho' (Motozintlec) (with Tuzantec)
                Chuj-Tojolabal
                      Chuj, Tojolabal (Tojol-ab'al)
    K'ichean-Mamean (Eastern Mayan)
        K'ichean
                Q'eqchi'
                Uspantek
                Poqom
                      Poqomam, Poqomchi'
                Central K'ichean (K'ichean Proper)
                      K'iche'
                      Kaqchikel, Tz'utujil
                      Sakapultek
                      Sipakapense
        Mamean
                Mam, Tektitek (Teko)
                Awakatek, Ixil

languages into which it evolved (much as Latin did not become extinct but evolved into modern Romance languages). Coxoh, much talked about in colonial sources from Chiapas, may be another extinct Mayan language, though Campbell and Gardner (1988) argue that it was probably a dialect of Tseltal. Newly discovered Mayan languages have been added to the family since 1965: Akatek, Sakapultek, Sipakapense, and Tektitek (Teko) (Kaufman 1969, 1975). Sometimes Achi and Chalchiteko are listed as additional Mayan languages, though here Achi is considered a variety of K'iche' and Chalchiteko a variety of Awakatek, not distinct languages, though recognized as distinct ethnic entities in Guatemala. Finally, it has never been resolved whether Tuzantec is a dialect of Mocho' or a separate language. Whatever its status, it is sufficiently different from Mocho' to merit investigation. Unfortunately, both Mocho' and Tuzantec are critically endangered.

The most generally accepted view of the Mayan subgrouping is presented in Table 3.1. The groupings Huastecan, Yucatecan, Ch'olan-Tseltalan, Greater Q'anjob'alan, and Eastern Mayan (Mamean-K'ichean) are clear and for the most part uncontroversial. Opinions have differed about whether Tojolabal belongs to Greater Q'anjob'alan or to Ch'olan-Tseltalan (Law 2014 for a survey of opinions). The most generally accepted view holds that the Huastecan branch was the first to separate from the rest of the family. Next, Yucatecan branched off, and later the remaining Core Mayan groups separated into distinct branches. It has generally been accepted that Ch'olan-Tseltalan and Greater Q'anjob'alan belong together in a single branch (sometimes called Western Mayan), though this has never been completely confirmed. K'ichean and Mamean (Eastern Mayan) clearly belong together in a single branch. (See Campbell and Kaufman 1985; Kaufman 1990, this volume).

Any uncertainties about aspects of Mayan subgrouping may be due to some scholars' confusion over some diffused characteristics among Mayan languages, making it difficult to distinguish shared innovations (the only reliable evidence of subgrouping) from changes shared due to diffusion across language boundaries, as for example, borrowing in the Greater Lowland Mayan Linguistic Area and in the Huehuetenango diffusion area (see §8). For example, because Huastecan shares several sound changes with Ch'olan-Tseltalan and with Yucatecan, it was sometimes thought these groups should be classified together in a single subgroup (see for instance Campbell 1977:100–1; Robertson 1977, 1992; Law 2014). Nevertheless, Huastecan grammar and lexicon are so different from the other Mayan languages, it seems highly probable that it has indeed been split away from them for a considerable time. This means that several of the similarities it shares with Ch'olan-Tseltalan and Yucatecan, including some shared sound changes, must be due to language contact after Huastecan had separated from the others or to independent parallel developments. For example, it is clear from several of the seemingly shared sound changes in several of the languages that they were not shared innovations but rather took place independently at distinct times in slightly varying phonological environments in different branches of the family (see Justeson et al. 1985).

Comparative work dedicated to individual subgroups has made significant contributions to Mayan historical linguistics generally, for example, for Ch'olan Kaufman and Norman (1984), for K'ichean Campbell (1977), for Huastecan Norcliffe (2003), for Tseltalan Kaufman (1972), and for Yucatecan Fisher (1973). A serious reconstruction of the Greater Q'anjob'alan subgroup is much needed and would no doubt clarify subgrouping issues, particularly that of disputed Tojolabal and uncertain broader connections with Ch'olan-Tseltalan, and would help to determine which traits are due to areal diffusion and whether some potential cognates are actually loanwords instead.

4 RECONSTRUCTION

As mentioned, many take Norman McQuown's (1955, 1956) reconstruction of PM phonemes as the point of departure for modern Mayan comparative linguistics. Kaufman
(1964, 1969, 1976) refined this reconstruction in several ways, for example, by showing
that McQuown's tonal contrast did not belong to PM, that PM had no labialized velars
and no complete series of palatalized sounds, and that *b' (imploded b) should replace
McQuown's *p' (see below in this section for discussion of these). Campbell (1977:89)
refined the reconstruction further by showing that PM distinguished *r from *y, and that
*ə could be eliminated (see below). These refinements resulted in the phonemic inventory
of PM given in Table 3.2 (see Campbell and Kaufman 1985).

Most Mayan morphemes are monosyllabic, and PM had the possible syllable shapes
(canonical forms) *CVC*, *CV:C*, *CVC₁C₂*, and *CV₁ʔV₁C*, where in *CVC₁C₂* the C_1 of the
consonant cluster was limited to *h*, *ʔ*, or a fricative *s*, *š*, or *x*. In each of these, the initial
consonant is in fact optional. That is, traditionally Mayanists have followed Terrence
Kaufman's canonical shapes, which have initial *C* under the belief that those that might
appear to be vowel-initial instead began with a glottal stop as their onset. However, since
Proto-Mayan has a different set of possessive and ergative pronominal markers that
attach to vowel-initial roots distinct from the set that attaches to consonant-initial forms,
it is clear that not all Mayan morphemes should be considered consonant-initial, that PM
also had vowel-initial morphemes. Thus, in the conventional canonical forms, the first
C should be understood as optional, as *(C)VC*, *(C)V:C*, *(C)VC₁C₂*, and *(C)V₁ʔV₁C*. Note
that Kaufman sometimes interprets *CV₁ʔV₁C* as equivalent to *CV: ʔC*.[2]

While this reconstruction is accepted by most scholars, the phonetic nature of some
of the sounds has not gone without question, and future research ought to investigate
the phonetic content of these as well as that of some other sounds that have not received
attention. For example, it seems secure that PM *b' was imploded ([ɓ]) (possibly with a
voiceless allophone syllable finally) – its reflexes are imploded in most of the languages.
Nevertheless, some scholars expect symmetry and so would reconstruct it as a voiceless
and ejective *p' to match the other consonants of the glottalic series (*t', *tʸ', *ts, *č',
*k', *q'), which are assumed to be ejective. However, it is not unusual for languages
to have a glottalic series which combines some implosive sounds together with some
ejective sounds, and if glottalic series have any implosive sounds, these tend to favor the
labial position, i.e. the bilabial implosive ([ɓ]) (see Greenberg 1970; Campbell 1973a),
making PM with an imploded *b* not at all unusual.

Although PM is typically reconstructed with only a single imploded sound in its glottalic
series, labial *b'*, some Mayan languages underwent a conditioned sound change which

TABLE 3.2 PROTO-MAYAN PHONEMES

p	t	tʸ	ts	č	k	q	ʔ
b'	t'	tʸ'	ts'	č'	k'	q'	
	l						
	r						
m	n				ŋ		
	s			š	x		
w				y			h

i		e	a	o	u

V: (vowel length)

created an ejective *p'* in addition to *b'* (cf. Campbell 1977:38, 115–16, 1996; Kaufman and Norman 1984:85; Law 2014; Wichmann 2006b). This began in Ch'olan-Tseltalan and Yucatecan, and then diffused to Poqomam and dialects of Poqomchi'. Different scholars have suggested different conditioning environments for the change (see Campbell 1996; Kaufman and Norman 1984; Wichmann 2006b). Campbell (1996) postulated that the change appeared to affect original **b'* in words which had an apical consonant, and then the new sound, *p'*, was extended by onomatopoeia (and sound symbolism) to additional words that did not have that environment. That does not, however, account for all cases. Wichmann (2006b:51), in contrast, concludes: "**p* and **b'* optionally become *p'* in CVC roots unless the other consonant is a voiceless bilabial stop, a glottalized stop or a voiced consonant (other than *l*)." His opinion, however, that "sound changes can be spontaneous," with its seeming suggestion that sound changes need not be regular (p.51), will be disputed.

The **q'*, on the other hand, has not received any particular attention and is generally thought to have been a voiceless ejective uvular stop in PM. However, its phonetic character may profit from closer consideration. In most of the K'ichean and Mamean languages, syllable-initial /q'/ is phonetically a voiceless imploded uvular stop (and imploded in other positions as well in several of the languages), [qˤ] (see, for example, Pinkerton 1986; England 1983). Based on the number of languages in which this sound is imploded, it is possible – I would say probable – that PM **q'* was also imploded (phonetically [qˤ]).

This imploded uvular goes against Greenberg's (1970) original proposed implicational universal, that in the glottalic series the presence of an imploded sound at any point of articulation further back in the mouth implies that the members of the series at points of articulations further towards the front of the mouth should also be imploded (for example, the presence of /ɗ/ implies /ɓ/ (and not /p'/), though the presence of /ɓ/ does not imply anything for sounds further back in the mouth, so the language could have either /t'/ or /ɗ/). The imploded uvular in the glottalic series of these Mayan languages has forced this proposed implicational universal to be revised (Campbell 1973a). Also, until the facts of the voiceless imploded uvular stop in K'ichean languages became known, it was hypothesized that all imploded sounds must be voiced; this claim had to be abandoned.

There has been occasional curiosity about the phonetic nature of PM **ŋ* and its non-nasal reflexes in some subgroups (cf. Fox 1978). Nevertheless, there seems to be little basis for serious doubt that it was a velar nasal in PM. The reconstruction is based on the sound correspondence: *h/w/y* in Huastecan;[3] *n* in Yucatecan, Ch'olan-Tseltalan, and a few of the Greater Q'anjob'alan languages; *ŋ* in the rest of the Greater Q'anjob'alan languages; and something like but different from *x* in Eastern Mayan languages (details below). Those with *n* underwent the change **ŋ > n*. There really is no plausible alternative reconstruction for **ŋ*, since there are straightforward sound correspondences that support the reconstruction of **w*, **h*, **n*, and **x*, the other sounds encountered in reflexes of **ŋ* in some of the languages. Nevertheless, curiosity leads us to wonder what might have been in the phonetic makeup of this sound or in its reflexes in Huastecan and Eastern Mayan languages – which are at opposite geographical extremes of the Mayan family – that could lead it to lose its nasality and to become a voiceless fricative in Eastern Mayan and *w/h/y* in Huastecan (under different conditions). These are not common phonological changes.

There is verification of the change **ŋ > n* both in the comparative evidence and in loanwords from Ch'olan in some Q'anjob'alan languages from the time before Ch'olan had changed its *ŋ* to *n*. For example, Mocho' *čo:ŋ* 'to sell' was borrowed from Ch'olan, which has **čon* (cf. Proto-Mayan **ko:ŋ*), after Ch'olan had undergone the change **k > č* but before it had changed **ŋ > n* (compare native Mocho' *koŋob'* 'market', which preserves original sounds, **koŋ* 'to sell' + *-Vb'* 'instrument, place of') (Kaufman 1976).

The relationship between the reflexes of PM *ŋ and PM *x in K'ichean has implications for the phonetic makeup of PM *x. The reflex of PM *x is x in all the K'ichean languages; the reflex of PM *ŋ is also x in K'ichean languages with the exceptions of Q'eqchi', where it is h, and Uspantek, where it is also x but is distinct from the reflex of PM *x in that a vowel preceding x from PM *ŋ has falling tone, but a vowel before x from PM *x does not. Since the two correspondences sets contrast, it is necessary to reconstruct two separate sounds in Proto-K'ichean (PK) – both cannot be *x. I proposed that the one from PM *ŋ should be reconstructed as something more fronted than the one from PM *x; I argued that PM *ŋ > PK *x (velar) and PM *x > PK *χ (uvular), and that what has been reconstructed as PK *x probably was phonetically uvular, making *χ a better symbol to represent it (Campbell 1977, 2013:184). What is written as x (<j> in practical orthography) in all Eastern Mayan languages is phonetically [χ] (a voiceless uvular fricative). Since Eastern Mayan and some Greater Q'anjob'alan languages contrasted uvular and velar stops, as did PM, it is not implausible that K'ichean languages once also contrasted uvular and velar fricatives, as seems to be supported by the difference in the K'ichean reflexes of conventionally reconstructed PM *x and PM *ŋ, and by extension, that conventionally reconstructed PM *x phonetically was actually *χ, as are its reflexes in Eastern Mayan and some Greater Q'anjob'alan languages. It might seem odd to assume PM had *χ (uvular) but no corresponding *x (velar), but this situation is not so uncommon. Castilian Spanish (various Peninsular dialects), for example, has only χ with no corresponding x. Perhaps a motivation for the shift of PM *ŋ to Eastern Mayan *x was to fill in the missing gap for the velar fricative x in the presence of uvular χ (though later the *x from *ŋ and the *χ merged in all Eastern Mayan languages except Q'eqchi' and Uspantek). In short, I propose that PM had *ŋ and *χ, and no *x, a situation which may have contributed to *ŋ losing its nasality and becoming x in some of the languages.

The sounds *t̯ʸ and *t̯ʸ' are unusual within the PM system, and the sound correspondences upon which they are based have complicated reflexes, as seen in Table 3.3 (sets (4a) and (4b)), where they are compared with other similar sounds.

Note that the Huastecan reflexes of these sounds are not as straightforward as those of some of the other subfamilies, as seen in the comparisons in Table 3.4.

Clearly there has been considerable shifting among these sounds in Huastecan from PM times.

We may wonder if it is possible to eliminate *t̯ʸ and *t̯ʸ' from PM, given that neither shows up as such in any Mayan language and, though we reconstruct four distinct sounds, *t, *ts, *č, and *t̯ʸ (and their glottalized counterparts), no language in any of the subgroups shows more than three different contrasts for the four correspondences

TABLE 3.3 SOUND CORRESPONDENCES RELATED TO *t̯ʸ and *t̯ʸ'

	Huastecan	Yucatecan†	Gr-Tseltalan	Gr-Q'anjob'alan	Mamean	K'ichean	PM
(1a)	t	t/č	t	t	č	t	*t
(1b)	t'	t'/č'	t'	t'	t'	t'	*t'
(2a)	t	ts	ts	ts	ts	ts	*ts
(2b)	t'	ts'	ts'	ts'	ts'	ts'	*ts'
(3a)	č	č	č	č	č	č	*č
(3b)	č'	č'	č'	č'	č'	č'	*č'
(4a)	t	t/č	t	č	ts	č	*t̯ʸ
(4b)	t'	t'/č'	t'	č'	č'	č'	*t̯ʸ'

†Note that in Yucatecan, *t and *t̯ʸ merged to t (and *t', *t̯ʸ' > t'); then t (from both sources) > č word-finally and before front vowels (also t' from both earlier sounds > č' in this same environment).

TABLE 3.4 SOME HUASTECAN CORRESPONDENCES

	Veracruz Huastec	San Luis Potosí Huastec	Chontla Huastec	Chicomuseltec	Proto-Huastecan	PM
(1a)	ts	č	t̪	č	*t̪	**t
(1b)	ts'	č'	t̪'	č'	*t̪'	**t'
(2a)	t	t	t	t	*t	**ts
(2b)	t'	t'	t'	t'	*t'	**ts'
(3a)	č	ts		č	*č	**č
(3b)	č'	ts'		č'	*č'	**č'
(4a)	t	t	t	t	*t	**tʸ
(4b)	t'	t'	t'	t'	*t'	**tʸ'
(5a)	č	ts	č	č	*č	**k
(5b)	č'	ts'	č'	č'	*č'	**k'

(adapted from Norcliffe 2003; see also Kaufman 1985)

sets. Yucatecan and Ch'olan-Tseltalan lack evidence that *tʸ and *tʸ' might ever have been distinct from *t and *t'; K'ichean and Greater Q'anjob'alan show no indication that they ever contrasted with *č and *č'. We might wonder whether it is possible to reduce the number of PM sounds by showing that *tʸ and *tʸ' can be derived from some other PM sounds in some conditioning environment. Or at least we might think it should be possible to find a phonetically more plausible reconstruction to represent these sounds. However, no convincing solution has suggested itself that would allow us either to combine these with other sounds (conditioned in some environment) or to come up with a more phonetically plausible reconstruction. Alternative reconstructions involving *ts or *č (and their glottalized counterparts) do not seem possible, since these logical candidates are already taken up, reconstructed to represent the sounds of other correspondence sets (as in sets (2) and (3) of Table 3.3) which contrast with these.

Nevertheless, a more plausible reconstruction would be satisfying. The likely phonetic nature of *tʸ and *tʸ' in PM is not clear from the sounds in the correspondence sets upon which they are based – sometimes the reconstruction has been characterized as palatalized alveolar stops, sometimes as dental stops in contrast with alveolar or some other more backed articulation. It is suspicious that no other sounds in the dental-alveolar(-alveopalatal) region share a palatalized or front/back contrast such as that between *t and *tʸ. Nevertheless, Huastecan with its retroflexed *ṭ (and *ṭ') from PM *t (and *t') and its *t (and *t') from PM *tʸ (and *tʸ', respectively) suggests that a PM contrast in terms of some more anterior t-like sound contrasting with some more posterior one may be in the right direction. In fact, a reconstruction with PM *ṭ (and *ṭ') (retroflex stops) replacing *t (and *t') and with *t (and *t') replacing *tʸ and *tʸ' might be more appealing – at least it has the slight advantage that sounds equivalent to the reconstructed ones actually occur somewhere, if only in the Chontla dialect of Huastec. Still, a dental/alveolar vs. retroflex contrast is no less suspicious than a palatalized (or dental) vs. alveolar contrast when it affects no sounds in series other than the stops.

In particular, the Mamean reflexes of *tʸ and *tʸ' align differently from those of other subgroups. The sound correspondences in Table 3.3 become clearer when the Mamean chain shift is taken into account:

$$*č > ç$$
$$*t > č$$
$$*r > t$$

For example, Mamean *č* of set (1a) (Table 3.3) comes from an earlier **t* and thus matches the *t* correspondences in other subgroups, making the reconstruction of **t* clearer. We might ask, though, why an *r* would shift to a *t*. Neither *r* > *t* nor *č* > *č̣* (retroflex) is a natural nor expected change.[4] If the sequence of changes was a pull chain, why would *č* > *č̣*, leaving a gap into which *t* was pulled (*t* > *č*), leaving a gap for *t* into which *r* was pulled (*r* > *t*)? A change from an ordinary *č* to a retroflex *č̣* is highly unusual and not at all expected. However, if the language came to lack *t* (because it changed to *č* to fill the gap left by **č* > *č̣*), that might have been some motivation for the unusual **r* > *t* change.

Some scholars are skeptical of the existence of push chains; many oppose teleological explanations in linguistics and thus object to reliance on the need or intention to maintain phonological distinctions on which push chains are assumed to depend. Nevertheless, the existence of push chains is an empirical matter, and there is solid empirical evidence that some chain shifts were indeed push chains. For example, in the vowel shift in New Zealand English, historical documentation confirms that the stages in the shift took place in a push chain. First, the "trap" vowel (the vowel in words like *trap*) raised, impinging on the space of the "dress" vowel; second, as a consequence the "dress" vowel raised; and, third, this raised "dress" vowel crowded the "kit" vowel, which in reaction centralized (towards barred "i"). This historically attested sequence of shifts allowed the vowels to avoid merger and to maintain their phonemic contrasts from the vowels that shifted into their space. (See Gordon et al. 2004, especially pp. 264–5, for details.)

Conventionally, PM is reconstructed with contrastive vowel length, five long vowels matched by five short ones: *i*, *e*, *a*, *o*, *u*, and V: (vowel length). The question can be asked, was this opposition phonetically one of a pure length difference and nothing else, or was there possibly a vowel-quality distinction involved (in addition to the length difference or instead of it)? In a majority of the Mayan languages that maintain the contrast, the "short" vowels are typically also more open or slightly lower than their "long" counterparts, except that "short" /a/ is phonetically [ə] or schwa-like. Whether the contrast originally was one of pure length and nothing else, or whether it involved also a vowel-quality difference, might be of no particular significance, involving merely notational variants of the same thing. However, phonetically the opposition does involve a vowel-quality difference between the "long" and matching "short" vowels (a close/open contrast, a tense/lax contrast in some of the languages, for example in most K'ichean languages). This suggests that perhaps the opposition involved phonetically a vowel-quality distinction in PM as well. Viewing the contrast this way could have some satisfying implications. In most of the languages that have the contrast, what is represented as short /a/ is phonetically [ə] and long /aː/ is [a]. Most of the Mayan languages (and dialects of languages) which have lost the "length" contrast nevertheless maintain the opposition in the low vowels, between the conventionally rendered /aː/ and /a/, the latter as *ə* (except in certain environments, e.g. before *h* or *ʔ*, where it is *a*) (see Campbell 1977:89–90). If PM had had solely a straightforward length contrast, there would be no strong phonetic motivation for why the contrast traditionally represented as /aː/ vs. /a/ should not have been lost along with the loss of the length contrast in the other vowels in those languages. Rather, it appears that PM also had a vowel-quality difference between the vowels traditionally reconstructed as "long" vs. "short" rather than merely a pure length contrast, and this helps make clear why phonetic *ə* (or something *ə*-like) shows up as the counterpart to *a* in so many of the languages, even in those that otherwise lost the length opposition – the distinction between *ə* and *a* is phonetically more salient, more distinct, than that, say, between /i/ and /ɪ/, or between /u/ and /ʊ/. Thus, while it was correct to eliminate PM **ə* from the PM inventory as reconstructed earlier, perhaps we should resuscitate PM *[ə] phonetically as the "short" counterpart to "long" *a, as part of the overall vowel opposition in PM which contrasted "long" (phonetically higher, closer, or tenser) vowels with "short" vowels (phonetically lower, more open, laxer). Terrence Kaufman (personal communication, about this paper) does not believe that a tense/lax opposition is sufficient to describe the phonetic character of the vowel distinctions in question, though he accepts that in most of the languages, the "length" opposition involves also a quality distinction between vowels of the opposing sets. I propose, as a hypothesis for further testing, that the PM length contrast involved a vowel-quality difference between conventionally reconstructed long and short vowels in addition to or instead of a pure length-only contrast.

McQuown (1956) had postulated a tonal contrast for PM. Only four Mayan languages have tone: Yucatec Maya, Lacandón, Uspantek, and Mocho' – and they belong to three different subbranches of the family.[5] Tonal contrasts in these languages developed from segmental phonology involving vowels followed by laryngeals (h or ʔ) and from long vowels, though the changes involved are not the same in each language. In Yucatec Maya, $*V{:}C > \acute{V}C$ (long vowel gave low tone), and $*VhC > \grave{V}C$ and $*VʔC > \grave{V}_1ʔV_1C$ – high tones when laryngeals were involved. In Uspantek, in word-final syllables only, low tone (i.e. falling) developed from $*VhC > \acute{V}{:}C$; $*VʔC > \acute{V}{:}C$ when the C was a stop or affricate; word-final $Vʔ > \acute{V}$; and $*Vŋ > \acute{V}{:}x$; otherwise, long vowels in final syllables have high tone, $*V{:} > \grave{V}{:}$ (Campbell 1977:38, 89). In Mocho', PM $*VʔC$ and $*VhC$ developed an echo vowel, becoming $V_1ʔV_1C$ and V_1hV_1C respectively, and then $V_1ʔV_1C > \acute{V}{:}C$ with falling pitch. (See Palosaari 2011:95–106 for details.) The fact that the laryngeals produce high (rising) tone in Yucatec Maya but low (falling) tone in the other languages has implications for general claims about tonogenesis (see Palosaari 2011).

5 LEXICAL RECONSTRUCTION

Kaufman with Justeson's (2003) 1,505-page Mayan etymological dictionary, with over 3,000 etymologies, is a particularly important and valuable contribution to Mayan linguistics – something which nearly all other language families of the Americas lack. This is a rich, ripe resource, available to be exploited for contributions to Mesoamerican prehistory, Mayan linguistic prehistory, Mayan epigraphy, and much more. It follows and provides further support for the now most generally accepted classification of the languages and reconstruction of the phonology (as described above). (See Kaufman, this volume, for discussion of PM lexical items.)

6 PM MORPHOSYNTAX

We should expect much more to be discovered in the future about PM morphosyntax and particularly about the history of the grammar of the various subgroups and individual languages. Nevertheless, the study of Mayan historical syntax is considerably in advance of that of most other language families in the Americas and, it is safe to say, also of most of those of the rest of the world. Studies include England (1991) on word order, Kaufman and Norman (1984) on Ch'olan morphology, Mora-Marín (2003) on reconstruction of applicative and antidative constructions, Norman (1978) on "instrumental voice," Norman and Campbell (1978) about PM syntax generally, Robertson (1992) on tense/aspect/mood/voice in verbs, and especially Kaufman's (2002) detailed treatment of Mayan morphosyntax. These studies reveal that PM was an ergative language, with associated antipassive constructions. In Mayan languages, transitive verbs bear ergative markers that cross-reference their subjects; these ergative markers are equivalent in form to the possessive pronominal prefixes that nouns bear. The subjects of intransitive verbs and the objects of transitive verbs both bear absolutive cross-referencing markers, which are distinct from the ergative ones. It is argued that PM had VOS (Verb-Object-Subject) basic word order when the subject was higher than the object on the "animacy" hierarchy (where 'human' is highest, 'animate' next highest, and 'inanimate' lowest), but had VSO word order when subject and object were equal in animacy. PM nominal possession was of the form, for example, [her-house the woman] for 'the woman's house'. PM also had relational nouns for locative functions, i.e. possessed noun root in construction, for example the equivalent of [his-head] for 'on him' and [your-stomach] for 'in you'. (For a much more complete reconstruction of PM morphosyntax, see Kaufman 2002).

7 CONTRIBUTIONS FROM WRITTEN SOURCES

Several Mayan languages have abundant written attestations beginning shortly after earliest Spanish contact. There is extensive room for continued investigation of these sources to find out about changes in Mayan languages, though there have been a number of contributions to understanding several changes in Mayan languages based on the linguistic study of these documents (see Campbell 1973b, 1974, 1977, 1988, 1990, 2013; Kaufman 1980, for some examples). The findings from these investigations have served (1) to document former contrasts now lost and sound changes that have taken place; (2) to refine some reconstructions of PM phonology; (3) to distinguish diffused changes from legitimate shared innovations, and to clarify evidence for subgrouping; (4) to uncover and explain grammatical changes; (5) to identify ancient extinct languages with scarce attestation (Coxoh, for example); (6) to determine the relative age of changes; and (7) to aid deciphering Mayan hieroglyphic writing, to use Mayan historical linguistics to understand Mayan epigraphy, and to use findings in the writing system to study changes in the languages. For example, Campbell (1973b, 1977) showed that the change in Poqomam, Poqomchi', and Q'eqchi' of *ts* to *s* took place in relatively recent times, based on earlier colonial attestations. Campbell (1974, 1977) examined older sources to show that the change of *k* and *k'* to *ky* and *k'y* respectively when the next consonant after an intervening non-round vowel was a uvular (*q*, *q'*, *χ*) had diffused across dialects of several K'ichean languages. Similarly, Yucatec Maya older written sources reveal that the language contrasted *h* and *x*, though these have merged to *h* in modern Yucatec Maya (Campbell 1990). Huastecan sources reveal that modern Huastec labialized velars k^w and $k^{w'}$ developed from earlier sequences of velar stop (*k* or *k'*) followed by a round vowel (*u* or *o*) followed by a glide (*w*, *y*, *h*, *ʔ*) followed by a vowel (Kaufman 1980; Campbell 1990). Campbell and Gardner (1988) identified Coxoh as an extinct dialect of Tseltal based on scant lexical attestations in colonial sources. Campbell (1990) traced the development in Kaqchikel morphology from aspect to tense markers.

In recent years many studies, too numerous to survey adequately here, have applied findings of Mayan historical linguistics to the interpretation of the language (languages) in which the Maya hieroglyphic texts are written and to examining the Maya script for what it can reveal about changes in Mayan languages. A few examples include Campbell (1984, 1990, 2013), Justeson and Campbell (1984, 1997), Houston et al. (2000), Wichmann (2006a, 2006b), Law (2013a, 2014), and the papers in Wichmann (2004), among many others. They show that the language of the Maya script is definitely Ch'olan (though opinions vary about details of which Ch'olan language(s) may have been involved). For example, Campbell (1984) argued that attestations in Maya hieroglyphic writing demonstrate that the changes in Ch'olan of **k > č* and *e: > i* took place at a time before the texts were written, establishing a *terminus ante quem* for these changes. Almost certainly much stands to be gained in future historical linguistic work involving Maya hieroglyphic writing.

8 LANGUAGE CONTACT

Very significant for Mayan historical linguistics is the study of language contact, what Mayan languages have received from others, what they have contributed to others, and diffusion among Mayan languages themselves – both loanwords and structural influences. See, for example, Kaufman 1964, 1976, 1980, this volume; Campbell 1973b, 1977, 1997b; Campbell and Kaufman 1976; Justeson et al. 1985; Campbell et al. 1986; Barrett 1996, 2002; Kaufman and Justeson 2009; Law 2009, 2013a, 2013b, 2014, this volume; Wichmann and Hull 2009, etc. Opinions differ concerning the identification of some borrowings; for example, Wichmann and Brown (2003) include as loans numerous cases that many other linguists would not accept based on standard criteria for loanword identification. Mayan languages participate in the Greater Lowland Mayan Linguistic Area (Justeson et al. 1985; Law 2014; Kaufman, this volume), in the Huehuetenango diffusion area (a.k.a. the Huehuetenango Sphere, involving Mamean and Greater Q'anjob'alan languages except Tojolabal and Mocho') (Kaufman 1974, 2002, this volume; Barrett 2002), and in the broader Mesoamerican Linguistic Area (Campbell et al. 1986). As Law (2014:31) points out, changes shared among languages of the Lowland Mayan Linguistic Area include phonological borrowings, diffusion of specific sound changes, direct borrowing of several bound morphemes, and much convergence or borrowing of syntactic patterns and morphosyntactic structures. Law (2014:175) identifies features shared through contact among two or more languages in the lowlands that range from diffused phonological innovations (phonemic mergers, sound changes and even new phonemic contrasts), to syntactic and semantic patterns (the loss of the agent focus antipassive, the development of an inclusive/exclusive distinction in person marking, aspect-based split ergativity), to the direct replication of actual morphological forms, linguistic 'matter' (several person markers, voice and aspect suffixes, auxiliaries, plural markers, numeral classifiers), etc.

These linguistic areas/diffusion zones all deserve more attention, and it is in particular in the study of diffusion among Mayan languages that we can hope to untangle some of the remaining issues involving subgrouping and whether certain shared changes happened independently or are due to diffusion.

9 PROPOSALS OF REMOTE RELATIVES OF MAYAN LANGUAGES

Numerous proposals of distant genetic relationships have attempted to link Mayan with other families, for example with Araucanian (Mapudungun) (Stark 1970), "Amerind" (Greenberg 1987), Arawakan, Chipaya-Uru, Hokan, Hokan-Siouan, Huave, Lenca, Mixe-Zoquean, Paezan, Penutian, Tarascan, Totonacan, and Yunga, among others. Suffice it to say, most of these have been discredited. For most, the evidence presented is insufficient to eliminate accident or diffusion as possible explanations, and often either flawed methods or inappropriate application of appropriate procedures were involved, resulting in proposals that fail to reach a level of reasonable plausibility (see Campbell 1997a; Campbell and Poser 2008). The proposal that initially seemed suggestive to join Mayan with Chipaya-Uru (Olson 1964, 1965), to which Yunga was added (Stark 1972), has not held up under examination (Campbell 1973c). The so-called Macro-Mayan hypothesis, actually a series of interrelated hypotheses, would link Mayan with Mixe-Zoquean and Totonacan, sometimes also with Huave (see Radin 1924; McQuown 1942, 1956; Brown and Witkowski 1979, among others). The evidence presented was insufficient to support the claimed connections. The only proposal of an external kinship between Mayan and some other family so far which seems to have a chance of holding up is with Mixe-Zoquean. Though the proposal seemed plausible, earlier work on the topic failed to show that borrowing and accidental similarity could not have accounted for the evidence presented on the proposal's behalf (see, for example, Brown and Witkowski 1979). However, David Mora-Marín's (2016) recent investigation, utilizing careful methods, makes this proposal of genetic relatedness much more plausible. Attempts to find other remote relatives of Mayan will no doubt continue. It is impossible to anticipate how successful they may be, but it is unlikely that striking breakthroughs are in store, and proposals that do not follow careful, appropriate methods will surely not hold up to scrutiny.

10 PM LINGUISTIC PREHISTORY

Studies of Mayan linguistic prehistory have reached numerous rich conclusions (see in particular Kaufman 1976, this volume). Kaufman (1976) had hypothesized that PM was spoken in the Cuchumatanes Mountains of Guatemala, around Soloma, c.2200–4200 BP, where speakers exploited both highland and lowland ecological zones. He has revised that now to locate the PM homeland around Uspantán (Kaufman, this volume). Reconstructed vocabulary shows PM speakers to have been highly successful agriculturalists, with the maize complex at the core of a full range of Mesoamerican cultigens. The reconstructed vocabulary of PM reveals a culture characterized by various Mesoamerican cultigens and domestic animals, the maize complex, various Mesoamerican and Mayan items of material culture, aspects of commerce, its own ritual and religion, and social organization. (See Kaufman, this volume, for a full description of the lexical items that reflect these cultural domains.)

A brief summary of Mayan diversification follows (for a fuller account, see Kaufman 1976, this volume.). The glottochronological dates associated with these various events are Kaufman's; many dispute the accuracy of glottochronology, but at least the dates can be taken as reflecting a general relative chronology. PM diversified around 4,200 years ago, ultimately occupying the areas of the present-day languages, when Huastecan separated from the rest of the family, leaving the highlands, going down the Usumacinta River. Yucatecan split off from the remaining body of Mayan next, c.3900 BP, then moved down into the lowlands c.3500 BP. Eastern Mayan branched off from the main remaining body of Mayan next at c.3600 BP, and then branched into Greater K'ichean and Mamean c.3400 BP. Both Greater K'ichean and Mamean began to diversify internally at around 2600 BP. Kaufman hypothesizes that Ch'olan-Tseltalan (Greater Tseltalan) and Greater Q'anjob'alal belong to a single branch, labeled Western Mayan, which broke up c.3000 BP. Ch'olan-Tseltalan (Greater Tseltalan), in his view, moved down into the lowlands after 3000 BP. Each of these, Ch'olan-Tseltalan (Greater Tseltalan) and Greater Q'anjob'alal, began diversifying at c.2100 years ago. Tseltalan speakers moved to the Chiapas highlands from the Mayan lowlands c.2200 BP. The Lowland Mayan Linguistic Area was formed during the Classic Maya period, contributing many loanwords both within the Mayan family and to neighboring non-Mayan languages and diffused structural traits (Justeson et al. 1985). The K'ichean groups expanded into eastern and southern Guatemala quite late, after 1200 AD. Much of eastern Guatemala below the Motagua River was occupied by Xinkan speakers, though Poqomam groups invaded their territory after the conquest of the Rabinal Valley by the Rabinal lineage of the K'iche' had displaced the Poqomam, separating them from their Poqomchi' relatives around 1250 AD. (See Campbell 1988, 1997b).

A persistent question is, how did closely related Huastec (in Veracruz and San Luis Potosí) and Chicomuseltec (in Chiapas) come to be separated by such a distance, and when did that happen? Ideas include: (1) Huastecan migrated north after separating from the rest of the Mayan family, later diversified, and Chicomuseltec then migrated back to be next to other Mayan languages; (2) Huastecan stayed near the other Mayan languages, diversified, and then Huastec went north and Chicomuseltec stayed behind; (3) Huastecan went partway between current Huastec territory and the rest of the Mayan area, split up there, and then Huastec continued on north to its present location while Chicomuseltec migrated back to its location next to other Mayan languages. Whatever the truth, it is clear that Huastecan was in contact with languages of the Maya lowlands, since both Huastecan languages share several sound changes and some morphological similarities due to contact with these languages (see Norcliffe 2003; Law 2014). For example, the Huastec word *tak'in* 'silver, money, precious metal', has received commentary, since it seems clearly borrowed from a lowland Mayan language. It is analyzable, composed of pieces that in PM would be *$ta\mathclose{?}$* 'excrement' + *$q'i\mathord{:}\eta$* 'sun, day', a Mesoamerican calque, as in Nahuatl *teo:kwitlatl* 'gold, precious metal' (*teo:-* 'god' + *kwitlatl* 'excrement'). However, Huastecan has *k'ih* 'day', not *k'in*, which is the form Ch'olan-Tseltalan and Yucatecan have. This thus is a borrowing from one of those languages into Huastecan, after Huastecan had changed *η to *h* in this position (see Norcliffe 2003; cf. Campbell 1988:211; Kaufman 1980). Huastecan shares with lowland Mayan languages (Ch'olan-Tseltalan and Yucatecan) and some Greater Q'anjob'alan languages the changes: *$r > y$, *$q > $*k (and *$q' > $*k'), and *$k > č$ (and *$k' > č'$). However, because the complicated conditioning environments for the changes *$k > č$ and *$k' > č'$ in Ch'olan-Tseltalan languages (see Kaufman and Norman 1984) are different from in Huastecan, this change (or at least aspects of the change) had to have happened independently in these different subgroups, thus this particular change is not compelling evidence of later contact among the languages of these subgroups.

These kinds of evidence of Huastecan contact with lowland Mayan languages would seem to favor a view of Huastecan being nearer other Mayan languages before diversifying, with Huastec then later migrating north. With a location closer to the body of Mayan languages, the coincidence of Chicomuseltec ending up where it did is less surprising, and does not need an explanation of how it got exactly there that a surprising back migration from present-day Huastec territory would require.

Kaufman (this volume, Kaufman and Justeson 2009:68, 70–2) argues that there are six loans from pre-proto-Huastecan into languages of central and northeastern Mexico that provide evidence that Huastecan phonology differed little from PM when it arrived in or near its ethnohistorically known location, that is, supporting the view that Huastecan went north early, and then only later Chicomuseltec separated and ended up in Chiapas next to other Mayan languages. It is unlikely that most linguists will find these cases convincing, though unfortunately, there is insufficient space here for the evaluation they deserve. Briefly, one is Yemé *xat* 'how many?' < pM *xar* 'how many?' (Huastec *xay*). But why would a language borrow a word meaning 'how much?', and /t/ is not compelling evidence of /r/ in an assumed donor language, especially not just a single example with *t* thought to connect with *r*. It is quite possible that accidental similarity provides stronger possible explanation for this case. Another involves 'to walk' in Tarascan, but verbs are rarely borrowed, especially not ones with common meanings, and Tarascan is not especially close to Huastec geographically. Another involves 'bat' in Proto-Oto-Pamean, a word not often borrowed anywhere. Other examples putatively reflect Huastec(an) before the change of *k(') > č(') (or a corresponding sound). However, Yemé *kamaw* 'to die', similar to PM *kam* 'to die' (Huastec *čem, čam*) is probably just an accidental phonetic similarity; a verb meaning 'to die' is hardly ever borrowed. Tarascan *khamé-ri* 'bitter' (cf. PM *k'ah* 'bitter') also is an unlikely loan, and together with *kapárhi* 'bumblebee' (cf. PM *ka:b'* 'bee, honey') is probably accidentally similar; what accounts for the extra sounds in these Tarascan forms that do not match sounds of Mayan words? In face of the evidence of later contacts with languages of the Mayan lowlands, the case for Huastecan being in Huastec territory early and then Chicomuseltec coming back later seems less likely.

There are very few cases such as the *tak'in* 'precious metal' one of later loans from other Mayan languages into Huastecan. John Justeson (personal communication) points out that there was arguably Mayan presence in the epi-Classic period in central Mexico at Cacaxtla and Xochicalco, and that Chontal were known travelers, so that Huastecan could have gotten Mayan loans long after Huastec was in its present location.

NOTES

1 I thank John Justeson and Terrence Kaufman for valuable comments on an earlier version of this paper. They do not, however, agree with everything presented here.

   The spelling of the names of Mayan languages in Guatemala follows recommendations of the Academia de Lenguas Mayas de Guatemala (http://www.almg.org.gt/), and those in Mexico the spellings of INALI (2009) (in anglicized versions).

   The phonetic symbols employed here are those common to Mayanists and Americanist scholars. Their IPA equivalents where different are:

Americanist	IPA
tʸ	tʲ
č	tʃ
b'	ɓ
t'	tʔ
tʸ'	tʲʔ
ṭ	ṭ
ṭ'	ṭʔ
ts'	tsʔ
č'	tʃʔ
k'	kʔ
q'	qʔ
š	ʃ
y	j

2 Kaufman (2015) has a different analysis and presents arguments in favor of an original and underlying morpheme-initial glottal stop and against vowel-initial forms. While all the cases he points out indeed point to initial glottal stops, I believe that in all (or nearly all), the insertion of a phonetic glottal stop before vowel-initial morphemes can be predicted from context when morphemes come together. This is an important issue, however, and deserves careful consideration.

3 PM *ŋ underwent several conditioned changes in Huastecan; the exact conditions for the Huastecan reflexes are complicated:

*ŋ > w /#__ (sometimes Ø, conditions yet to be determined)
*ŋ > h /__# (and *ŋ> w / u, o __#, though with some variation)
*ŋ > y / aʔ__# (Norcliffe 2003:74–7).

4 Some have speculated that a change of r > d followed by d > t might not seem unnatural; however, creation of a voiced stop d in a system that has no other voiced stops would be highly unlikely.

5 Formerly, the Tsotsil of San Bartolomé de los Llanos (a.k.a. Carranza Tsotsil) had been reported also to have a tonal contrast; however, Herrera Zendejas (2013) argues convincingly that it does not have phonemically contrastive tone, but rather that a vowel before a glottalized consonant becomes predictably laryngealized and has a falling pitch.

REFERENCES

Barrett, Rusty. 1996. "The effects of k'ichean/mamean contact in Sipakapense." *Berkeley Linguistics Society* 22: 25–36.

Barrett, Rusty. 2002. "The Huehuetenango Sprachbund and Mayan language standardization in Guatemala." In *Proceedings of the 38th Chicago linguistics society: The panels*, ed. by Mary Andronis, Erin Debenport, Anne Pycha, and Keiko Yoshimura, 309–18. Chicago: Chicago Linguistics Society.

Berendts, Carl Hermann. 1876. "Remarks on the centres of ancient civilization in Central America and their geographical distribution." *Bulletin of the American Geographical Society* 1875–1875: 3–14.

Brown, Cecil H., and Stanley R. Witkowski. 1979. "Aspects of the phonological history of Mayan-Zoquean." *International Journal of American Linguistics* 45: 34–47.

Campbell, Lyle. 1973a. "On glottalic consonants." *International Journal of American Linguistics* 39: 44–6.

Campbell, Lyle. 1973b. "The philological documentation of a variable rule in the history of Pokom and Kekchi." *International Journal of American Linguistics* 39: 133–4.

Campbell, Lyle. 1973c. "Distant genetic relationships and the Maya-Chipaya hypothesis." *Anthropological Linguistics* 15: 113–35.

Campbell, Lyle. 1974. "Quichean palatalized velars." *International Journal of American Linguistics* 40: 132–4.

Campbell, Lyle. 1977. *Quichean linguistic prehistory* (University of California Publications in Linguistics, 81). Berkeley: University of California Press.

Campbell, Lyle. 1984. "The implications of Mayan historical linguistics for glyphic research." In *Phoneticism in Mayan hieroglyphic writing*, ed. by John Justeson and Lyle Campbell, 1–16. (Institute for Mesoamerican Studies, Publication 9). Albany: SUNY Albany.

Campbell, Lyle. 1988. *The linguistics of Southeast Chiapas* (Papers of the New World Archaeological Foundation, 51). Provo: New World Archaeological Foundation.

Campbell, Lyle. 1990. "Philological studies and Mayan languages." In *Historical linguistics and philology*, ed. by Jacek Fisiak, 87–105. Berlin: Mouton de Gruyter.

Campbell, Lyle. 1996. "On sound change and challenges to regularity." In *The comparative method reviewed: regularity and irregularity in language change*, ed. by Mark Durie and Malcolm Ross, 72–89. Oxford: Oxford University Press.

Campbell, Lyle. 1997a. *American Indian languages: the historical linguistics of Native America*. Oxford: Oxford University Press.

Campbell, Lyle. 1997b. "The linguistic prehistory of Guatemala." In *Papers in honor of William Bright*, ed. by Jane Hill, P. J. Mistry, and Lyle Campbell, 183–92. Berlin: Mouton de Gruyter.

Campbell, Lyle. 2013. *Historical linguistics: an introduction*. 3rd edition. Edinburgh: Edinburgh University Press, and Cambridge: MIT Press.

Campbell, Lyle, and Brant Gardner. 1988. "Coxoh." In *The linguistics of southeast Chiapas, Mexico*, ed. by Lyle Campbell, 315–38. (Papers of the New World Archaeological Foundation, 50). Provo: New World Archaeological Foundation.

Campbell, Lyle, and Terrence Kaufman. 1976. "A linguistic look at the Olmecs." *American Antiquity* 41: 80–9.

Campbell, Lyle, and Terrence Kaufman. 1985. "Mayan linguistics: where are we now?" *Annual Review of Anthropology* 14: 187–98.

Campbell, Lyle, Terrence Kaufman, and Thomas Smith-Stark. 1986. "Mesoamerica as a linguistic area." *Language* 62: 530–70.

Campbell, Lyle, and William J. Poser. 2008. *Language classification: history and method*. Cambridge: Cambridge University Press.

Charencey, Charles-Félix-Hyacinthe Gouhier comte de. 1870. *Notice sur quelques familles de langues du Mexique*. Havre: Imprimerie Lepellatier.

Charencey, Charles-Félix-Hyacinthe Gouhier comte de. 1872. *Recherches sur les lois phonètique dans les idiomes de la famille mamehuastèque*. Paris: Maisonneuve.

England, Nora C. 1983. *A grammar of Mam, a Mayan language*. Austin: University of Texas Press.

England, Nora C. 1991. "Changes in basic word order in Mayan languages." *International Journal of American Linguistics* 57: 446–86.

Fisher, William M. 1973. "Towards the reconstruction of Proto-Yucatecan." PhD diss., University of Chicago.

Fox, James A. 1978. "Proto-Mayan accent, morpheme structure conditions, and velar innovations." PhD diss., University of Chicago.

Gordon, Elizabeth, Lyle Campbell, Jennifer Hay, Margaret Maclagan, Andrea Sudbury, and Peter Trudgill. 2004. *New Zealand English: its origins and evolution*. Cambridge: Cambridge University Press.

Greenberg, Joseph H. 1970. "Some generalizations concerning glottalic consonants, especially implosives." *International Journal of American Linguistics* 36: 123–45.

Greenberg, Joseph H. 1987. *Language in the Americas*. Palo Alto: Stanford University Press.

Halpern, Abraham M. 1942. "A theory of Maya ts-sounds." *Notes in Middle American Archaeology and Ethnology* 13: 51–62. Carnegie Institute of Washington.

Herrera Zendejas, Esther. 2013. "Patrón acentual, F0 y consonantes laríngeas en el tsotsil de Venustiano Carranza." Paper presented at the Congreso de Idiomas Indígenas de Latinoamérica VI, University of Texas, Austin, October 24, 2013.

Hervás y Panduro, Lorenzo. 1800–05. *Catálogo de las lenguas de las naciones conocidas y numeracion, division, y clases de estas segun la diversidad de sus idiomas y dialectos*. Madrid: Administraciondel Real Arbitrio de Beneficiencia. (See also: 1784–87. *Catalogo delle lingue conosciute e notizia della loro affinità e diversità.*)

Houston, Stephen D., John S. Robertson, and David Stuart. 2000. "The language of classic Maya inscriptions." *Current Anthropology* 41: 321–56.

INALI. 2009. *Catálogo de las lenguas indígenas nacionales: variantes lingüísticas de México con sus autodenominaciones y referencias geoestadísticas*. Mexico: Instituto Nacional de Lenguas Indígenas (INALI).

Justeson, John, and Lyle Campbell. 1984. *Phoneticism in Mayan hieroglyphic writing.* (Institute for Mesoamerican Studies, Publication 9.) Albany: SUNY Albany, Institute for Mesoamerican Studies/Austin: University of Texas Press.

Justeson, John, and Lyle Campbell. 1997. "The linguistic background of Maya hieroglyphic writing: arguments against a 'Highland Mayan' role." In *The language of Mayan hieroglyphs*, ed. by Martha J. Macri and Anabel Ford, 41–67. San Francisco: Pre-Columbian Art Research Institute.

Justeson, John, William Norman, Lyle Campbell, and Terrence Kaufman. 1985. *The foreign impact of lowland Mayan languages and script.* (Middle American Research Institute, publication 53.) New Orleans: Tulane University.

Kaufman, Terrence. 1964. "Materiales lingüísticos para el estudio de las relaciones internas y externas de la familia de idiomas Mayanos." In *Desarrollo Cultural de los Mayas*, ed. by Evon Vogt, 81–136. Mexico: Universidad Nacional Autónoma de México.

Kaufman, Terrence. 1969. "Teco – a new Mayan language." *International Journal of American Linguistics* 35: 154–74.

Kaufman, Terrence. 1972. *El Proto-Tzeltal-Tzotzil: Fonología comparada y diccionario reconstruido* (Cuaderno 5). Mexico: Centro de Estudios Mayas.

Kaufman, Terrence. 1974. *Idiomas de Mesoamérica.* Guatemala: Seminario de Integracion Social.

Kaufman, Terrence. 1975. "New Mayan languages in Guatemala: Sacapultec, Sipacapa, and others." *Mayan Linguistics* 1: 67–89.

Kaufman, Terrence. 1976. "Archaeological and linguistic correlations in Mayaland and associated areas of Meso-America." *World Archaeology* 8: 101–18.

Kaufman, Terrence. 1980. "Pre-Columbian borrowing involving Huastec." In *American Indian and Indo-European studies: papers in honor of Madison S. Beeler*, ed. by Kathryn Klar, Margaret Langdon, and Shirley Silver, 101–12. (Trends in Linguistics, Studies and Monographs 16). The Hague: Mouton.

Kaufman, Terrence. 1985. "Aspects of Huastec dialectology and historical phonology." *International Journal of American Linguistics* 51: 473–6.

Kaufman, Terrence. 1990. "Algunos Rasgos Estructurales de los Idiomas Mayances con Referencia Especial al K'iche'." In *Lecturas sobre la Lingüística Maya*, ed. by Nora C. England and Stephen R. Elliott, 59–114. Antigua Guatemala: CIRMA.

Kaufman, Terrence. 2002. "Reconstructing Mayan morphology and syntax." University of Pittsburgh, unpublished manuscript.

Kaufman, Terrence. 2015. "Initial glottal stop in Mayan languages." University of Pittsburgh, unpublished paper.

Kaufman, Terrence, with John Justeson. 2003. *A preliminary Mayan etymological dictionary.* www.famsi.org/reports/01051/pmed.pdf.

Kaufman, Terrence, and John Justeson. 2009. "Historical linguistics and pre-Columbian Mesoamerica." *Ancient Mesoamerica* 20: 221–31.

Kaufman, Terrence, and William Norman. 1984. "An outline of Proto-Cholan phonology, morphology, and vocabulary." In *Phoneticism in Maya hieroglyphic writing*, ed. by John S. Justeson and Lyle Campbell, 77–166. (Institute for Mesoamerican Studies, Publication 9). Albany: State University of New York.

Kroeber, Alfred L. 1939. "Classification of the Mayan languages." In *Cultural and natural areas of native North America*, by Alfred L. Kroeber, 112–5. Berkeley: University of California Press.

Law, Danny. 2009. "Pronominal borrowing among the Maya." *Diachronica* 26: 214–52.

Law, Danny. 2013a. "Mayan historical linguistics in a new age." *Language and Linguistics Compass* 7: 141–56.

Law, Danny. 2013b. "Inherited similarity and contact-induced change in Mayan languages." *Journal of Language Contact* 6: 271–99.

Law, Danny. 2014. *Language contact, inherited similarity and social difference: the story of linguistic interaction in the Maya lowlands.* Amsterdam: John Benjamins.

McQuown, Norman A. 1942. "Una posible síntesis lingüística macro-mayance." *Mayas y Olmecas* 2: 37–8. Tuxtla Gutiérrez: Sociedad Mexicana de Antropología, Reunión de Mesa Redonda sobre problemas antropológicos de México y Centro América.

McQuown, Norman. A. 1955. "The indigenous languages of Latin America." *American Anthropologist* 57: 501–69.

McQuown, Norman. A. 1956. "The classification of the Mayan languages." *International Journal of American Linguistics* 22: 191–5.

Mora-Marín, David F. 2003. "Historical reconstruction of Mayan applicative and antidative constructions." *International Journal of American Linguistics* 69: 186–228.

Mora-Marín, David F. 2016. "Testing Proto-Mayan-MijeSokean hypothesis." *International Journal of American Linguistics* 82: 125–80.

Norcliffe, Elizabeth. 2003. "The reconstruction of Proto-Huastecan." MA thesis, University of Canterbury, Christchurch, New Zealand. http://hdl.handle.net/10092/3442.

Norman, William. 1978. "Advancement rules and syntactic change: the loss of instrumental voice in Mayan." *Berkeley Linguistics Society* 4: 458–76.

Norman, William M., and Lyle Campbell. 1978. "Toward a Proto-Mayan syntax: a comparative perspective on grammar." In *Papers in Mayan linguistics*, ed. by Nora C. England, 136–56. (Studies in Mayan Linguistics, 2, Miscellaneous Publications in Anthropology, 6). Columbia: Museum of Anthropology, University of Missouri.

Olson, Ronald D. 1964. "Mayan affinities with Chipaya of Bolivia I: correspondences." *International Journal of American Linguistics* 30: 313–24.

Olson, Ronald D. 1965. "Mayan affinities with Chipaya of Bolivia II: cognates." *International Journal of American Linguistics* 31: 29–38.

Palosaari, Naomi Elizabeth. 2011. "Topics in mocho phonology and morphology." PhD diss., University of Utah.

Pinkerton, S. 1986. "Quichean (Mayan) glottalized and non-glottalized stops: a phonetic study with implications for phonological universals." In *Experimental Phonology*, ed. by John J. Ohala and J. J. Jaeger, 125–39. Orlando, FL: Academic Press.

Radin, Paul. 1924. "The relationship of Maya to Zoque-Huave." *Journal de la Société des Américanistes de Paris* 16: 317–24.

Robertson, John S. 1977. "A proposed revision in Mayan subgrouping." *International Journal of American Linguistics* 43: 105–20.

Robertson, John S. 1992. *The history of tense/aspect/mood/voice in the Mayan verbal complex.* Austin: University of Texas Press.

Stark, Louisa R. 1970. "Mayan affinities with Araucanian." *Chicago Linguistic Society* 6: 57–69.

Stark, Louisa R. 1972. "Maya-Yunga-Chipayan: a new linguistic alignment." *International Journal of American Linguistics* 38: 119–35.

Stoll, Otto. 1884. *Zur Ethnographie der Republik Guatemala.* Zürich: Orell Füssli. (Spanish translation: 1958 *Etnografía de Guatemala.* [Publicación 8]. Guatemala: Seminario de Integración Social Guatemalteca.)

Stoll, Otto. 1885. "Supplementary remarks to the grammar of the Cakchiquel language, ed. by Daniel G. Brinton." *Proceedings of the American Philosophical Society* 22: 255–68.

Wichmann, Søren, ed. 2004. *The linguistics of Maya writing*. Salt Lake City: University of Utah Press.

Wichmann, Søren. 2006a. "Mayan historical linguistics and epigraphy: A new synthesis." *Annual Review of Anthropology* 35: 279–94.

Wichmann, Søren. 2006b. "A new look at linguistic interaction in the lowlands as a background for the study of Maya Codices." In *Sacred books, sacred languages: two thousand years of ritual and religious Maya literature*, ed. by Rogelio Valencia Rivera and Geneviève Le Fort, 45–64. (Acta Mesoamericana, 18). Markt Schwaben: Anton Saurwein.

Wichmann, Søren, and Cecil H. Brown. 2003. "Contact among some Mayan languages: inferences from loanwords." *Anthropological Linguistics* 45: 57–93.

Wichmann, Søren, and Kerry Hull. 2009. "Loanwords in Q'eqchi', a Mayan language of Guatemala." In *Loanwords in the world's languages: a comparative handbook*, ed. by Martin Haspelmath and Uri Tadmor, 873–96. Berlin: Mouton de Gruyter.

Ximénez, Francisco. c.1702. *Arte de las tres lenguas cakchiquel, quiche y tzutuhil*. (Published in 1993 as: *Arte de las tres lenguas kaqchiquel, k'iche' y tz'utujil* [Biblioteca Guatemala, 31]. Guatemala: Academia de Geografía e Historia de Guatemala.)

CHAPTER 4

ASPECTS OF THE LEXICON OF PROTO-MAYAN AND ITS EARLIEST DESCENDANTS

Terrence Kaufman

1 INTRODUCTION

The aim of the present study is to investigate the content and structure of lexical material that can be reconstructed to proto-Mayan and some of its earlier direct descendants. Our main interest is: What did proto-Mayans definitely know and talk about? Knowing this helps us identify the area where proto-Mayans lived (cf. the work on proto-culture and homelands that has been produced by students of the Indo-European languages (e.g., Schrader 1883; Childe 1926; Dumézil 1958; Benveniste 1973; Gamkrelidze and Ivanov 1984; Mallory 1989)). It might also help us profile the culture of proto-Mayans in comparison/contrast to contemporaneous non-Mayan cultures. We know a lot about present-day Mayan-speaking populations; we have varying amounts of documentation about Mayan-speaking populations since 1519; some Mayans produced written records between 200 BCE and 1700 CE that reflect only a tiny part of their cultural knowledge. (The vast extent of epigraphic, iconographic, ceramic, and architectural material that has survived the years and been found by present-day investigators makes the study of Mayan antiquities a rich and rewarding undertaking.)

It is important not simply to project what we know about contemporary Mayan societies back in to the distant past. Our projections about the distant past must be based on rich comparative data, and when there is something we don't know, we need to acknowledge it. Maybe we'll know it later on down the line.

Though Mayan linguistic studies achieved an impressive level of maturity during the early 1960s, and have maintained and beefed up that maturity, there is plenty of work, both documentary and comparative, that remains to be done. What can be presented here is a sizable set of terms that can be reconstructed to proto-Mayan (pM), Southern Mayan (SM), Central Mayan (CM), Eastern Mayan (EM), and Western Mayan (WM) (these terms are defined below in §4).

In addition, there is a sizable body of diffused lexical material shared by Ch'olan and Yukatekan ("Lowland") or by Ch'olan, Tzeltalan, and Yukatekan ("Greater Lowland") where the actual point from which a particular item was diffused can usually not be reliably established. This material is usually considered to be diffused because Yukatekan + Greater Tzeltalan is not a node on the Mayan family tree. However, there are two ways that something shared between Yukatekan and part of the rest of the family could be part of Southern Mayan genetically: (a) if Eastern Mayan innovated, leaving Yu+WM reflecting what SM had; or (b) if Western Mayan innovated, leaving Yu+EM reflecting what SM had.

There is a moderate amount of Mije-Sokean influence on certain subsets of Mayan languages; there is some Totonakan influence; there is some Sapoteko influence. These influences will not be especially focused on here (for a full discussion see Kaufman 2001–2016ms). A few cases where Mije-Sokean influence covered almost the whole Mayan family are mentioned below.

Mayan languages have elaborate derivational morphology and compounding strategies. Productive patterns can have been deployed independently in individual languages or subgroups to produce lexical items that look like they could be cognate, but are not necessarily cognate. It would be useful to expound the patterns that are (or have been) productive and able to produce ambiguous data, but time and space allotment do not permit this. Generally speaking, the data presented here are not compounds or phrasal lexemes, which are productively creatable in Mayan languages, but there is a certain number of denominal verbs, and nominalizations based on verbs; none of the ones I present seemed to me likely to be later parallel productive innovations, but readers may come to their own conclusions.

2 ARCHEOLOGICAL FRAMEWORK FOR MESO-AMERICA

The archeological phases of Meso-America are conventionally grouped into several periods (period names and chronologies are based on Evans 2012):

1   The Archaic (4000–2000 BCE) – in which plant domestication took place and early agriculture began;
2   A Formative or Pre-Classic period (2000 BCE–250 CE) – at the beginning of which ceramics, highly productive agriculture, public buildings and clearly marked regional differentiation of culture patterns all make their appearance; by the middle Formative, writing and the Meso-American calendar were invented;
3   The Proto-, Full, and Post-Classic (250 CE–1500 CE). Here irrigation and state systems appear.

The time frame of the data discussed is from 2200 to 200 BCE, a period of 2,000 years, quite a chunk of time.

3 BACKGROUND TO THE PRESENT WORK

Mayan languages occupy about one-third of the territory of Meso-America (see Figure 4.1). There are thirty Mayan languages. Two are dead and poorly documented, but Mayan languages are overall rather well documented. Serious documentation began in earnest around 1958, with the Chicago Project, though Norman A. McQuown did extensive documentation of Western. Wasteko before that. For an orientation to research by me that feeds into the expositions and assertions in the present study, see the PMED (Kaufman with Justeson 2003:7–17).

Over the years, beginning in 1960, I created a slip file with Mayan cognate sets. In the late 1990s I created a WordPerfect file with Mayan etymological data; after 2002 I added the OKMA (Cu Cab et al. 2003) data to it. In 2003, with the computational help of John Justeson, I handed over to FAMSI for posting on their website a "Preliminary Mayan Etymological Dictionary" (PMED), with over 3,040 entries. This

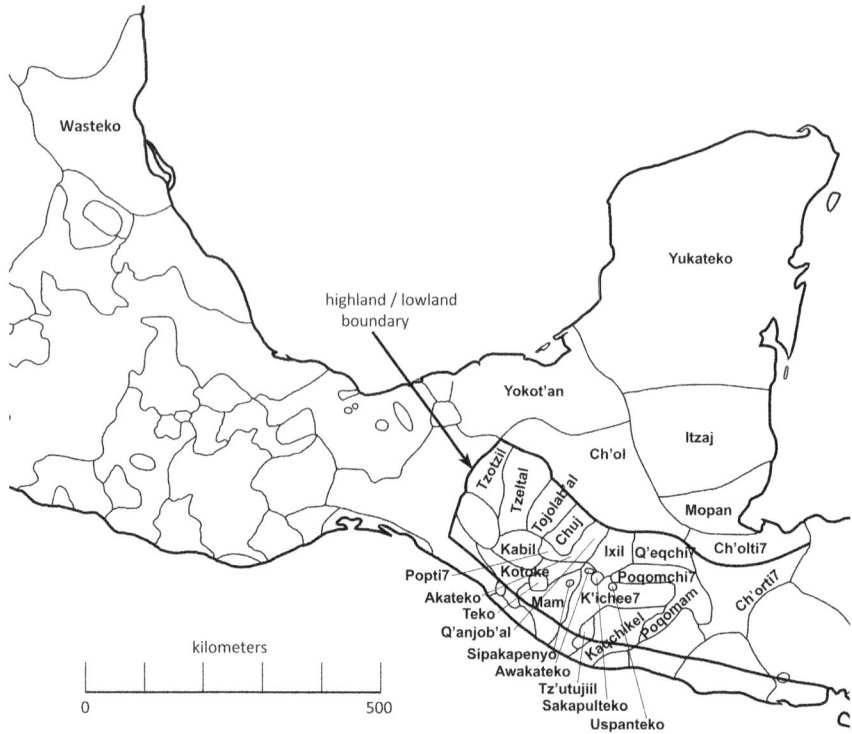

FIGURE 4.1 GEOGRAPHIC DISTRIBUTION OF MAYAN LANGUAGES CA. 1500 CE. (Lakantun did not come into existence until after the 1520s when some speakers of Yukateko fled to Ch'ol territory to avoid *reducción* by the Spanish.)

contains whatever data I had gathered and had databased before that time. There is a good deal of data that I have collected that is not yet databased. When added to the PMED it will, to a moderate degree, increase its bulk, its coverage, and its accuracy. It is difficult to project the number of new etymologies that will be added, but there will be a respectable number. (It should be pointed out that the PMED does have some errors in it, due to my failing to purge certain proposed etymologies of lexemes from specific individual languages that simply do not belong, though they are phonologically comparable.)

In sum, the data analyzed in the present work constitute a reliable, representative, and extensive sample of what will eventually be known of the vocabulary of proto-Mayan, Southern Mayan, and Central Mayan. It is not complete, but it is far more than a good start.

There is one type of data that has so far not entered into established etymologies in a principled way – sound symbolic morphemes. Descriptively, this is a rich topic, but I failed to relate to it in a focused way till the mid-1980s, when I was working on Wasteko and Huasteca Nawa. Because of my personal trajectory in language documentation,

Wasteko was the last Mayan language I worked on. There are dedicated derivational processes that use symbolic morphemes. I did discover this in 1960, and wrote it up in my Tzeltal Grammar (dissertation 1963, publication 1971), and named a category of "affect roots" (coded F). Any Mayan language will have at least 300 symbolic/affect roots, and 750–1,000 symbolic lexemes.

The reason reconstructed symbolic morphemes gave not been collected together is that most Mayanists in their lexical compilations have not identified symbolic roots as such. Most have not tried to elicit them (they will have gotten some by the way), and so their lexical databases are insufficient in this regard. I should note that Nora England, as research director of OKMA (1990–2009), commissioned reference grammars of several Guatemalan Mayan languages that were written by her trainees, and were to cover sound symbolism ("affect words"). Most of those grammars (PQM: Santos Nicolás and Benito Pérez 1998, KAQ: García Matzar and Rodríguez Guaján 1997, TZU: Cholotio and García Ixmatá 1998, SAK: Mó Isém 2007, USP: Can Pixabaj 2007, MAM: Rojas Ramírez et al. 1993, TEK: Pérez Vail 2007) make a worthy attempt at describing the morphosyntax of symbolic roots; a few of them (QEQ: Tzul and Tzinmaj Cacao 2001, KCH: López Ixcoy 1997, MAM: Pérez and Jiménez 1997, TZU: García Ixmatá 1997) pay only lip service and cite four to eight examples only. In any case, affect/symbolic roots should be numerous in any dictionary, and explicitly assigned to the appropriate morphosyntactic class.

Had there been appropriately focused field work on each of the otherwise well-documented Mayan languages, a sizable number of symbolic roots would be projectable to early stages of Mayan – however, because of the big gaps in the lexical documentation, I cannot offer a plausible/likely number of reconstructed symbolic roots for Mayan, but at least 100 might not be a bad guess. Another factor that is present in Meso-America is that certain symbolic root shapes, with specific meanings, are shared by languages that are genetically unrelated to one another – thus instantiating diffusion, another whole research topic worthy of pursuit. Diffusion of symbolic morphemes almost never involves Spanish; Spanish is poor in symbolic morphemes.

I have included most of the entries from the PMED that show identifiable sound symbolism, a paltry subset of reality, in §6.32.

4 SKETCH OF MAYAN DIVERSIFICATION

4.1 The chronological aspect of Mayan diversification

Figures 4.2a and 4.2b present a classification for the thirty languages of the Mayan family, along with estimated dates associated with its diversification.

Together they represent the following diversification model:

[1] Wastekan splits off from pMayan, leaving SMayan [2200 BCE]
[2] Yukatekan splits off from SMayan, leaving CMayan [1900 BCE]
[3] Eastern separates from Western [1600 BCE]

I say this this way because there is a list of innovations shared by Eastern; while there are two or three unique Western developments, in general Western can be viewed as the last remaining set of Mayan languages that did not innovate away from something else. Whether the separation of EM from the rest of CM involved population movement by

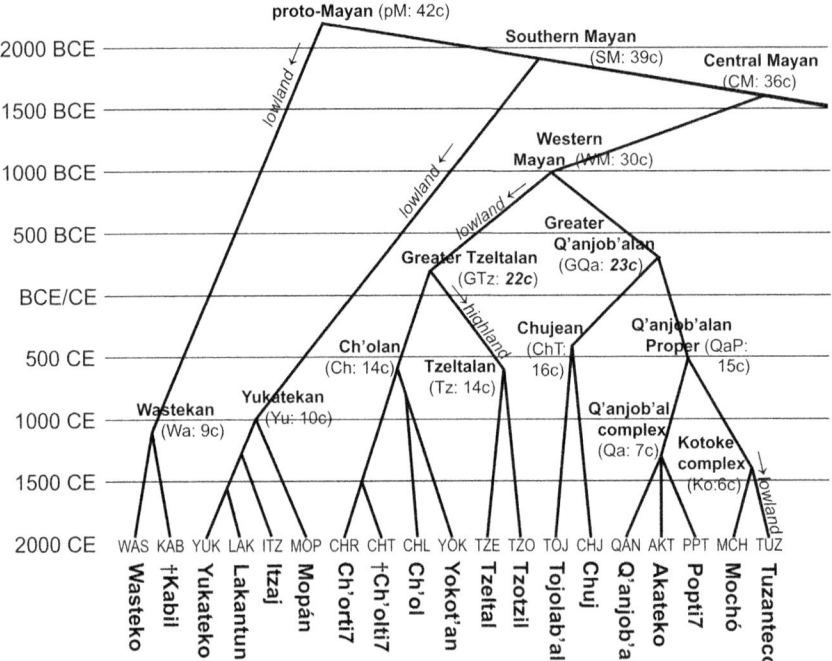

FIGURE 4.2A DIVERSIFICATION OF MAYAN LANGUAGES: WASTEKAN, YUKATEKAN, AND
WESTERN MAYAN SUBGROUPS

pEM or simply diversification without movement seems an imponderable to me, given
the kinds of inferences the data allow us to draw.

[4a] Eastern [1400 BCE] => Greater K'ichee7an, Greater Mamean
        Greater K'ichee7an [600 BCE] =>
            K'ichee7an Proper + Uspanteko [till 500 CE],
            Poqom + Q'eqchi7 [till 500 CE]
        Greater Mamean [600 BCE] =>
            Mamean Proper [till 500 CE]
            Ixilan [till 600 CE]

[4b] Western [1000 BCE] => Greater Tzeltalan, Greater Q'anjob'alan
        Greater Q'anjob'alan [ca. 100 BCE
            adjusted to 300 BCE)] =>
            Q'anjob'alan Proper [till 500 CE]
            Chujean [till 400 CE]

My glottochronological estimate is that Greater Q'anjob'alan broke up twenty-one
centuries ago (Kaufman 1974:85). However, a shift of *k > ch (but not of *k' to ch') took
place in common Chujean, therefore after Greater Q'anjob'alan diversification, under
the same conditions as in Greater Tzeltalan. The Greater Tzeltalan shift was completed
at least slightly before the breakup of that subgroup around 200 BCE (see below), so the
breakup of Greater Q'anjob'alan must be pushed back to at least 300 BCE. Justeson (p.c.

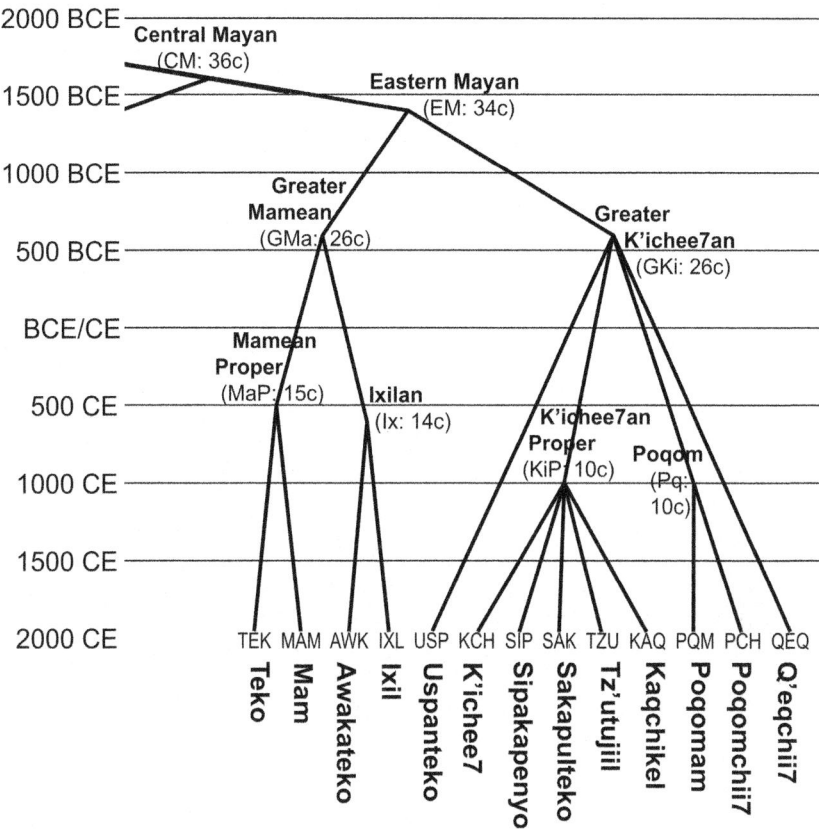

FIGURE 4.2B DIVERSIFICATION OF MAYAN LANGUAGES: EASTERN MAYAN SUBGROUP

2016) calculates that there is a 55 percent chance of getting departures in glottochronological estimates this large at this time depth by chance alone.

> Greater Tzeltalan [100 CE
>   (adjusted to 200 BCE)] =>
>   Tzeltalan Proper [till 600 CE]
>   Ch'olan [till 600 CE]

The diversification of the Greater Tzeltalan languages is fixed rather precisely at around 200 BCE by a correlation between a complex pattern of lexical diffusion with archeological evidence for the timing of the breakup of Greater Tzeltalan into separate regions (Kaufman and Justeson 2007:200, 2008:86–7). Justeson (p.c., 2016) calculates a 52 percent chance of getting departures in glottochronological estimates this large at this time depth by chance alone. See Figure 4.4. for geographical distributions of Mayan language groups around 750 BCE and 250 CE.

In this study lexical data characteristic of pMayan, SMayan, CMayan, EMayan, and WMayan are presented and analyzed; anything lower on the diversification chain is rarely dealt with.

Since Wastekan is the first to break off, interesting Wastekan data that might be archaisms are discussed. Given the low number of confirmed cognates between Wastekan and the rest of Mayan, it would be foolhardy to suggest that only what is shared by Wastekan and at least one other Mayan language is reliably to be credited to proto-Mayan. On the other hand, only statistical reasoning can be brought to bear on the number of well-distributed etyma that happen to be missing from Wasteko. (Of the non-inherited lexical material in Wasteko, only a small number can be traced to other known languages of Mexico – Mije-Sokean, Nawa, Sapoteko, Yokot'an (itself Mayan) for the most part. The languages that used to be spoken in Mexico north of Wasteko have mostly disappeared without adequate documentation, and languages of that type may have been spoken even further south when Wasteko moved into its known locations around 4,000 years ago and Meso-America as a culture zone was still under formation; evidence for their presence is suggested by Mayan-looking vocabulary in Yemé and Pajalat [Kaufman and Justeson 2008:70–2]):

> Two loans from Mayan into languages of Northern Mexico and six into languages of Central Mexico show a very early stage of phonological development: Pajalat [t] for Mayan *r, which shifted to y in attested Wasteko and Ch'olan [but not in concert], k for Mayan *k, which shifted to ch in attested Wasteko and Ch'olan [but not in concert]; nh for Mayan *nh, which shifted to w, y, j, or 7 in Wasteko and to n in Ch'olan. Since we have no reason to assume any other Mayans in Northern Meso-America except Wastekans [by 1800 BCE] and Ch'olans [700–900 CE], the phonology under discussion must reflect pre-Wastekan, and the location of pre-Wastekan must have included the Basin of Mexico for at least some period of time.
>
> Quoted from Kaufman 2001–2016:103–4, with some adjustments in wording. (See §5 for an explanation of the phonological symbols used here and throughout.)

pMayan?	CMexico	NMexico
*jar 'how many?'		Pajalat jat 'how many?'
*kam 'to die'		Yemé #kamaw 'to kill'
*kam 'to die'	Tarasko khamá- 'to be finished/used_up'	
*ka:b' 'bee; honey'	Tarasko kapárhi 'bumblebee'	
*k'ah 'bitter'	Tarasko khamé-ri 'bitter'	
*kem 'to weave'	Nawa ke:ml- 'to wear clothes'	
*xanh 'to walk'	Tarasko xanhára-ni 'to walk'; xanhá-ri 'road'	
*so7tz' 'bat'	pOto-Pamean *tzoatz7 'bat'	
*7ahq'ol 'up; on'	Nawa ahko 'up'; ahko.l-li 'shoulder, upper arm'	

This provides additional evidence that Wastekan shifted Mayan *k, *k' to ch, ch' independently of the similar (but limited) shift in Greater Tzeltalan.

The reflexes of the proto-Mayan word for 'bat' in Oto-Pamean are consistent with the early Mayan pronunciation *so7tz', but not with Ch'olan *su(:)tz' or Wasteko thut'. Early Mayan **so7tz'** 'bat' => proto-Oto-Pamean *tzoa-tz7 'bat' [Bartholomew #533] => Matlatzinka xi7=sotz7i [HLH] (earlier xi7=tzotz7i) 'bat' <= earlier [xi7= tzotz7] ({xi7} means 'leaf-shaped').

Quoted from Kaufman 2001–2016:103–4, with some adjustments in wording.

Generally speaking, the bulk of our inferences about the vocabulary of early Mayan is going to be based on etymologies that can be characterized as Southern Mayan. (This is somewhat parallel to how Indo-Europeanists deal with Anatolian: no one wants to accept that only what Anatolian shares with the rest of IE is all that we have to work with in characterizing the lexicon or morphology of pIE – even though an occasional scholar may adopt such a point of view to see how far it leads.)

4.1.2 Labels for subgroupings in Mayan

Proto-Mayan: anything found in Wasteko and any other Mayan language(s), apart from loans from Ch'olan (probably specifically YOK) in epiClassic Central Mexico. Since there are somewhat fewer than 300 Wasteko roots with cognates elsewhere in Mayan, this does not give a good sample of what the real vocabulary of pM was.

To be categorized as Southern Mayan, an etymon must have a reflex in at least one Yukatekan language, one Western Mayan language, and one Eastern Mayan language, where diffusion from the Mayan Lowlands is not the probable explanation. Most of these items are good candidates for pM; they simply do not survive in Was. As discussed above, a particular etymon found in Yukatekan and either Western Mayan or Eastern Mayan might properly belong to Southern Mayan if Eastern Mayan or Western Mayan has innovated away from what Southern Mayan had, and the observed distribution of apparent cognates was probably not the result of diffusion involving Yukatekan.

To be categorized as Central Mayan, an etymon must have a reflex in at least one Eastern Mayan and one Western Mayan language, and if the etymon is not widespread in one (or both) branches, there is no evidence for borrowing involving statable subsets of each branch's languages.

Yukatekan, as opposed to Wastekan, has a rather large number of cognates with Central Mayan languages. Since Central Mayan split into Eastern and Western only 300 years after Southern split into Yukatekan and Central and since most of the basic vocabulary shared by EM and WM is also found in Yu, what can be assigned to Central Mayan is most of the time not going to be very different from what Southern Mayan had.

To be categorized as Eastern Mayan, an etymon must have a reflex in at least one GK'ichee7an and one GMamean language, where borrowing could not be the explanation.

To be categorized as Western Mayan, an etymon must have a reflex in at least one GQ'anjob'alan and one GTzeltalan language, where borrowing could not be the explanation.

Eastern Mayan and Western Mayan reconstructions will only be presented when for a particular lexical meaning virtually all Eastern Mayan or Western Mayan languages have innovated a term.

Within the area where Mayan languages are spoken, there are several diffusion zones, within which lexical material is shared across subgroup boundaries:

[a] LL (Lowland): Yu + Ch;
[b] GLL (Greater Lowland): Yu + GTz (Ch + Tz);
[c] diffusion outside (Greater) Lowland, mostly from Ch'olan into Q'anjob'alan, Ixil, Uspanteko, Q'eqchi7;
[d] Hue (Huehuetenango): Mamean Proper + Q'anjob'alan Proper.

There is one important imponderable: we know that there has been diffusion among the Mayan languages. Some diffused items are recognizable because of the particular phonological history of the source of the diffusion. In cases where there was diffusion, and the source of the diffusion, and the borrowing languages, did not, or could not, undergo any sound change, such diffusion would not be detectable, except sometimes by a very

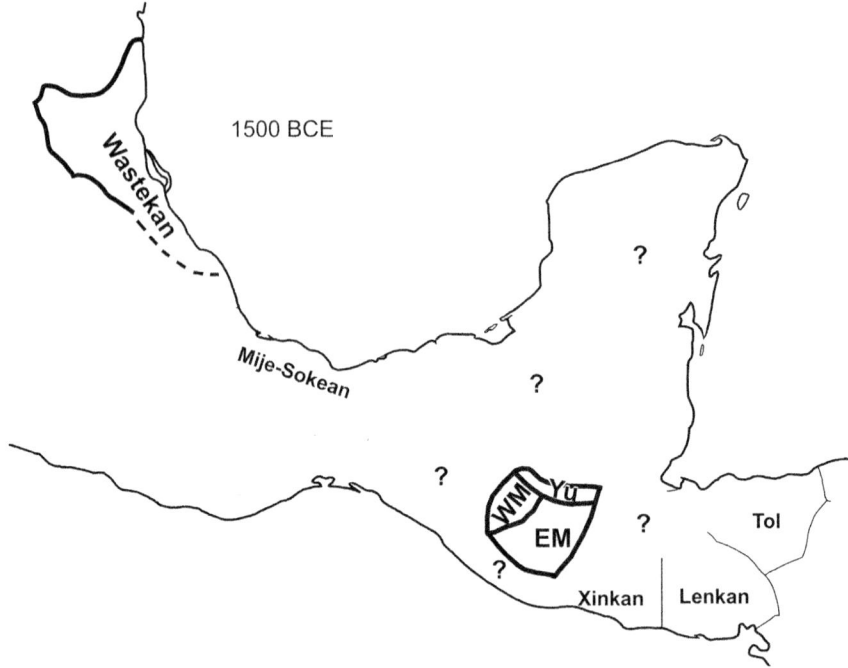

FIGURE 4.3 APPROXIMATE GEOGRAPHIC DISTRIBUTION OF MAYAN LANGUAGE GROUPS CA. 1500 BCE, ALONG WITH LOCATIONS OF NON-MAYAN GROUPS MENTIONED IN THE TEXT.

limited geographical distribution, when (a) they fit into one of the diffusion spheres established by the cases where sound changes permit the recognition of borrowing, or when (b) they are found only among neighboring languages.

Sounds that are completely stable in Mayan are *p, *b', *ty', *s, *x, *7, *m, *n, *l, *w, *y; short *i, *e, *o, *u. Sounds that undergo change in individual Mayan languages include *t, *t', *ty, *tz, *tz', *ch, *ch', *k, *k', *q, *q', *j, *h, *nh, *r, *a, and long vowels. See §5. (Some details of Wastekan have been glossed over, because it was out of contact with other Mayan languages for millennia.)

4.2 Geographical movements associated with the diversification of Mayan

My current view about Mayan diversification differs in a few details from that presented forty years ago (Kaufman 1976a). Where I do not contradict that article here, I still believe what I said there.

The proto-Mayan homeland must have been in a highland zone.

> "Besides having a considerable number of terms for plants and animals of cold country or Highlands, proto-Mayan also has terms for exclusive hot country or lowland plants and animals – e.g. *7ahiin 'cayman'; *map 'cohune palm'; *7inuup 'silk-cotton tree'; *tz'iin 'cassava'."
>
> Kaufman 1976a:105.

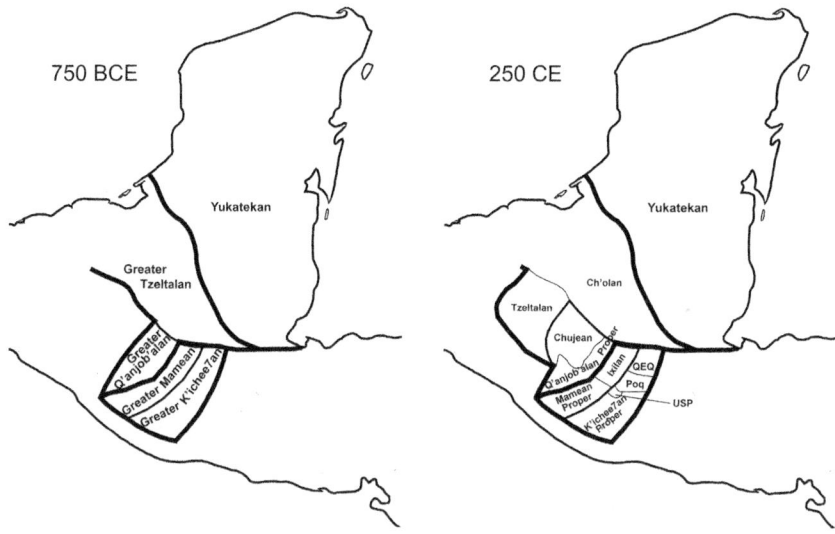

FIGURE 4.4 APPROXIMATE GEOGRAPHIC DISTRIBUTIONS OF MAYAN LANGUAGE GROUPS (A) CA. 750 BCE AND (B) CA. 250 CE.

At present,

> [I]n the Mayan area at least, there are exclusively lowland peoples who are ignorant of any of the flora or fauna found only in the highland zone; there are, however, no primarily highland peoples ignorant of salient flora and fauna of the lowland zone. Since proto-Mayan vocabulary conforms to the latter specification, I suppose proto-Mayan was spoken in a highland zone bordering on the Lowlands.
>
> Kaufman 1976a:105.

Two other traits of highland peoples/environment are (a) no reconstructible names for different kinds of fish, (b) names for fresh-water crabs, but not salt-water crabs or other seafood. Both EM and much of WM is located in the Guatemalan Highlands; archeologically, the Mayan population in the Lowlands to the north was intrusive back to at least 800 BCE (see below).

> Proto-Mayan names for other domesticated plants do not point to any particular area or epoch within Meso-America.
>
> Kaufman 1976a:105.

I still take the proto-Mayan homeland to be in Northern Highland Guatemala, but the area around Soloma (cf. Kaufman 1976a:104) is too high and cold to have been a desirable area to settle in when there was a small population and no competition for land occupancy. The area around Uspantán is warmer and less broken. At the time when agriculture was becoming the mode of subsistence, and the population was not yet large, people would have chosen to live in an area with a milder climate and leveler topography. The area around Uspantán fits those requirements.

After the Wastekans moved out of the Highlands and down the Usumacinta, the remaining Mayans, who I call Southern Mayans, percolated around in the Highlands, and between about 1900 and 1600 BCE broke up into three groups: first Yukatecan versus Central Mayan around 1900 BCE, then Eastern Mayan versus Western Mayan around 1600 BCE.

When Yukatekan broke off from Central Mayan, it did not do so by moving into the Lowlands. The timing of the earliest Mayan occupation in the northern Lowlands is debated by archeologists, but there seems to be general agreement that it took place between about 1200 and 800 BCE (Hammond 2000; Stanton and Ardren 2005). So Yukatekan stayed in the Highlands for several hundred years before leaving for the Lowlands.

When Wastekans, and later, Yukatekans, moved into the Lowlands there were already people there, speaking unknown non-Mayan languages. Archeologically, the area is known to have been inhabited during the Archaic period, and there were sedentary groups in the northern and southern Lowlands from about 1200 BCE that archeologists generally are not willing to identify as Mayan.

All the languages that moved into the Lowlands lost the Mayan phonemes *r, *nh, and *q, but not necessarily all at the same time. These sounds are rare in Meso-America. Xinkan, Lenkan, and Tol, on the southern edge of Mayan territory (see Figure 4.3), have phonemic rosters that lack these sounds, but have glottalized plosives like Mayan, and languages typologically like one or more of them may have been spoken in the lowland areas that Mayans moved into. I have seen no lexical evidence to support a specific identification for the substratum language(s). Some of the distinctively Yukatekan and Lowland (Yu+Ch) vocabulary might be owing to one or more of these substratum languages, and the 4–6 plausible lexical overlaps between Yukatekan and Wasteko might be attributable to such a substratum, since Wastekan, Yukatekan, and Greater Tzeltalan most likely all moved through the Southern Mayan Lowlands in arriving at their known destinations.

Wastekan did not merge *q with /k/ until after Totonako borrowed some words from Wastekan after 1000 CE; and Tarasko borrowed <xanhá-ra-ni> 'caminar'; <xanhá-ri> 'camino' from pre-Wasteko *xanh 'to walk', before Wasteko eventually changed it to xe7 (Kaufman and Justeson 2008:71,72). Assumptions and arguments that these changes were part of a common ancestry of Wastekan with Western Mayan or Greater Tzeltalan, or of interactions of Wastekans with such groups in Southern Mayan territory, are fallacious (contra Fox 1978:92–100; Campbell 1979:931–4, this volume; Robertson 1993; Robertson and Houston 2003; for more detail see Kaufman and Justeson 2008:70–3). For example, most of the supposed common innovations proposed by Fox, Robertson, and Campbell have demonstrably developed independently in different branches at different times.

Eastern Mayan separated from Western Mayan and expanded eastward, and Western Mayan separated from Eastern Mayan and expanded westward, but this all happened in the northern Guatemalan Highlands.

Eastern Mayan began to diversify around 1400 BCE, Western Mayan began to diversify around 1000 BCE.

Western Mayan diversified into Greater Tzeltalan and Greater Q'anjob'alan. Greater Tzeltalan moved down into the Lowlands sometime after 1000 BCE, and this is plausibly the basis for the breakup of WM. By 600 BCE inhabitants of the Lowlands are "readily identifiable" as Mayan (Chase and Chase 2012:256), and probably a couple of centuries earlier given evidence for the sharing of cultural features between sites in northern Yucatan and the southern Lowlands between 800 and 400 BCE (Stanton and Ardren 2005). However, some scholars feel that not all Greater Tzeltalans left the Guatemalan Highlands. David Mora-Marín (2005), and some others working on, but not really deciphering, Kaminaljuyú Stela 10, think that that writing system is expressing a Ch'olan language, which has been taken to entail that some Greater Tzeltalans continued to occupy part of the Guatemalan Highlands. I find the facts presented as evidence to be unconvincing (not necessarily wrong). Greater Q'anjob'alan was left in the Huehuetenango Highlands.

When Greater Tzeltalans moved into the Lowlands, they came into contact with Yukatekan. While some Yukatekans may have stayed put, and mingled with, or gotten assimilated by, the GTzeltalans, some had already moved further north, where they maintained their distinctive identity.

The chronological diversification of GTz and interaction between GTz and Yu is as follows:

WM begins to diversify around 1000 BCE.

By about 800 BCE, GTz moves into the Lowlands and comes into contact with Yukatekan; Lowland Mayan civilization emerges.

Starting around 200 BCE (Kaufman and Justeson 2007:199–200), Tzeltalans moved out of the western Mayan Lowlands into the Chiapas Highlands, and GTz was split into Ch'olan and Tzeltalan.

This left the Ch'olans in the Southern Mayan Lowlands. The contact situation between Ch'olan and Yukatekan resulted in a great deal of shared vocabulary between Ch'olan and Yukatekan: when we can tell, we see that most (probably about 75 percent) originated in Ch'olan, and some (approximately) 25 percent originated in Yukatekan (Justeson et al. 1985:19). This diffusion zone is called the Lowland Zone. The epigraphic Mayan language is Ch'olan, not Yukatekan.

Tzeltalans also participate in Lowland Mayan civilization; hieroglyphic texts in Tzeltalan territory are written in Ch'olan; some of the lexical diffusion between Yukatekan and Ch'olan goes into and maybe from Tzeltalan.

At some point after 800 CE (the "Maya collapse") in the Yukatekan-speaking area, Epigraphic Mayan texts show occasional Yukatekan lexical items; in some cases, whole texts may have been composed in Yukatekan.

A great deal of vocabulary is shared between Tzeltalan, Ch'olan, and Yukatekan. Some of it was diffused before GTz broke up into pCh and pTz, and some later, after pTz had moved into the Chiapas Highlands. Mayan civilization in the Lowlands was in especially close contact with Tzeltalans in highland Chiapas. This diffusion zone is called the Greater Lowland Zone. Since Ch'olan and Tzeltalan together make up the Greater Tzeltalan branch of the family, some of the GLL vocabulary will have originated in pGTz and been in play before 200 BCE (when GTz broke up) and borrowed by Yukatekan any time after 1000 BCE (when GTz came into existence).

Eastern Mayan broke up into Greater Mamean and Greater K'ichee7an around 1400 BCE. Greater Mamean gradually spread in a SW direction, and Greater K'ichee7an expanded to the south and east. When Greater Mamean spread, it made contact with Q'anjob'alan proper languages, and to a lesser degree with Chujean and Kotoke languages. The results of this language contact are seen in the Huehuetenango Sphere (cf. Kaufman 2015ms:passim; cf. England 1991:455ff; Danny Law 2014:26, 42, 50, 51; Kaufman 1974:85, 1990:86).

Other language contact situations within the Mayan area have had noticeable consequences, but not to the extent of Lowland, Greater Lowland, or Huehuetenango. Ixil has loans from both K'ichee7 and Ch'olan; Q'eqchi7 and Poqom have Ch'olan loans; Q'anjob'alan Proper languages have Ch'olan loans. And so on.

4.3 Swadesh list in proto-Mayan

As an exercise that can indirectly reveal the degree of diversification within Mayan, Table 4.1 presents reconstructions that correspond to the glosses on the Swadesh 100-word lexicostatistical list. For the record, every proto-Mayan phoneme is instantiated in this list. The rarest phoneme, *ty', is exemplified twice.

TABLE 4.1 COMPARATIVE MAYAN 100-WORD SWADESH LIST. Unmarked reconstructions may be taken to be proto-Mayan; anything that does not pass the distribution tests for proto-Mayan is labelled by the subgroup it belongs to.

Swadesh List	
*7iin	1. I // yo
*7at	2. you (sg., pl.) // tú, Usted, Ustedes
*7o7nh	3. we (incl., excl.) // nosotros
CM *yo; CM *wa	4. this // este
SM *tye; SM *la ~ *le	5. that // ese, aquel
SM *b'a	6. what? // qué?
LL+WM *mak	7. who? // quién?
*ma	8. not // no (es)
CM *juun.iil	9. all // todo(s)
*ya..	10. many // muchos
*juun	11. one // uno
*ka7-ib'	12. two // dos
CM *nim	13. big // grande
SM *najt	14. long // largo
SM *ty'iin	15. small // chico, pequeño
*7ix	16. woman // mujer, hembra
*xiib'	17. man // hombre, varón
*winaq	18. person, folk // gente, cristiano
*kar	19. fish // pescado, pez
*tz'ikin	20. bird // pájaro, ave
CM *tz'i7	21. dog // perro, chucho
*7uk'	22. louse // piojo
*tyee7	23. tree // palo, árbol
*b'aq; *7iiyaanh	24. seed // semilla de cualquier planta (no de maíz, no para sembrar)
*xaq	25. leaf // hoja
*7ib'	26. root // raíz
EM+ *7i7nh	27. bark // cáscara, corteza
CM *tz'uhuum	28. skin // piel, pellejo, cutis
CM *ti7.b'ej, ERG+ ti7	29. flesh, meat // carne
*kik'	30. blood // sangre
*b'aaq	31. bone // hueso
???	32. egg // huevo, blanquillo
???	33. grease, rendered fat // grasa (no manteca, no sebo)
*7uuk'aa7	34. horn // cuerno, cacho
*nheeh	35. tail // cola, rabo
SM *xiik'	36. feather, pinion // pluma (grande de alas)
*wi7	37. hair (of head) // cabello, pelo
SM *jo7l	38. head // cabeza
*xikin	39. ear // oreja, oído
*Haty	40. eye // ojo
*nhii7	41. nose // nariz
*tyii7	42. mouth // boca
*7eeh	43. tooth // diente
*7a7q'	44. tongue // lengua
*7iSk'aq	45. (finger)(toe)nail // uña

*7aqan	46. foot // pie
EM *ty'ehk	47. knee // rodilla
*q'ab'	48. hand // mano
*paam	49. belly, stomach // barriga, panza, estómago
*nuuq'	50. neck // cuello, pescuezo
*7iim	51. breasts // chiches, tetas
???	52. heart // corazón
SM *seh..	53. liver // hígado
*7uk'	54. to drink it // beberlo, tomarlo
*wa7	55. to eat it // comer (en general)
*ti7	56. to bite it // morderlo
*7il	57. to see it // verlo
CM *7ab'i(r)	58. to hear it // oirlo
SM *na7	59. to know it // saberlo
*war	60. to sleep // dormir
*kam	61. to die // morir
*kam.isa	62. to kill, slay it // matarlo
*nuhx	63. to swim // nadar
EM *xik.a-:n	64. to fly // volar
*xanh	65. to walk // andar, caminar
*tyaal	66. to come // venir
SM *koy P	67. to lie, lying // estar acostado, echado, tirado
???	68. to sit, sitting, seated // sentarse
CM *wa7 P	69. to stand, standing // estar parado
*ye7	70. to give it // dar, regalar
SM *Hal	71. to say it // decir
*q'inh	72. sun // sol
*7iik'	73. moon // luna
SM *eeq'	74. star // estrella, lucero
*Ha7	75. water // agua
*nhab'	76. rain // lluvia
SM *toonh	77. stone, rock // piedra
*pooq	78. sand // arena; polvo // dust
*ch'ohch'	79. earth, dirt, soil // tierra
*tyoq	80. cloud // nube
EM *sib'	81. smoke // humo
*q'ahq'	82. fire // fuego, lumbre
*tya7nh	83. ashes // ceniza
???	84. to burn // arder
*b'eeh	85. path, road // camino
*witz	86. mountain // cerro
*kaq	87. red // rojo, colorado
*ra7x	88. green // verde
*q'an	89. yellow // amarillo
*saq	90. white // blanco
*7ejq'	91. black // negro
*7aHq'ab'	92. night // noche
*tiqaw	93. hot // caliente (del día, sol)
SM *ke7h	94. cold // frío, helado (del día)
CM *nohj	95. to get full // llenarse
SM *7utz	96. good // bueno
SM *7a(a)k'	97. new // nuevo
SM *wol P	98. round (like a ball) // boludo, redondo
SM *tyaq	99. dry // seco
*b'ih	100. name // nombre

It should be noted that for the following glosses there is so much lack of uniformity across the family that the evidence does not point with any weight to a probable pM form: *egg*, *grease*, *heart*, *sitting*, *to burn*. The remaining ninety-five forms cited here either were the pM forms, or quite plausibly may have been the pM form, having no widespread competitors. If one wanted to do statistical counts measuring the lexical conservatism of individual languages, only ninety-five glosses could be used.

5 THE SOUNDS OF PROTO-MAYAN

Here, in summary form, are the symbols used by me to represent reconstructed Mayan morphemes. A somewhat expanded set of ASCII symbols has been used by the PLFM to write Mayan languages, and by the PDLMA to write Mayan, Mije-Sokean, Totonakan, Nawa, Sapotekan, and Southern Oto-Pamean languages. The PLFM orthography was made official in Guatemala in 1987, with one deviation: <7> was ill-advisedly replaced by <'>, requiring /p7 t7 tz7 ch7 tx7 k7 q7/ to be spelled <p-' t-' tz-' ch-' tx-' k-' q-'>, where the hyphen has no other motivation.

Consonants

p	t	ty	tz	ch	k	q	7
b'	t'	ty'	tz'	ch'	k'	q'	
			s	x		j	h
m	n				nh		
	l						
	r						
w			y				

Vowels

i		u
e		o
	a	

vowel length /:/ (orthographically, long vowels are written double)

C = an undetermined consonant
V = an undetermined vowel
.. dots appear where the sounds of the language stop agreeing with each other (this point is not necessarily the end of a morpheme, but it probably is)

Syllable types

CVC
CV:C
CV7C
CVhC
CVSC, where S = s x j

Morphophonemes

*H is /h/ word-initially, but deleted after ERG proclitics, as is *7. It is found in under ten roots, for example *Ha7 'water', *Ho7 'five', *Haty 'eye', *Hal 'to say it', *Huul 'to arrive', *Ha7b' 'year'.

Morphophonemic rules

//V:// => /V/ in non-final syllables
//V7// => /V:/ in non-final syllables

Other cover symbols

*abc a reconstruction based on regular sound correspondences
#abc a projected ancestral form where some of the sounds in individual languages
    show sound symbolic effects or that the item is diffused
T: has /t/ in languages that change *t to /ch/
K: has /k/ in languages that change *k to /ch/
R: has /r/ in languages that have /r/ only in symbolic morphemes
L: has /l/ or its reflex in languages where GKi has /r/
MA = Meso-America or Meso-American
pM = proto-Mayan
pMS = proto-Mije-Sokean

Codes for morpheme types and morpheme boundaries

=abc abc=	postpound, prepound
.abc abc.	derivation
>abc abc>	class shifter
- abc abc-	inflection
+abc abc+	clitic

6 RECONSTRUCTED MAYAN LEXICAL DATA PRESENTED HERE

Several semantic domains are analyzed. When their content can be used to draw inferences about Mayan habitat or culture, these inferences are developed.
  Semantic basis of selection of items for presentation in this work:

Any items unique to Mayan or that help to define the homeland. This is not a long list,
    because most of what is reconstructible is characteristic of all human existence, or
    is found generally in Meso-America.
Items that name categories that are particularly salient in Mayan discourse and word-cre-
    ation practices, and reveal the classification systems of certain semantic domains,
    even though they may not be unique to the Mayan region. Colors, sensations, types
    of eating, breakdowns of plant and animal taxonomies, kinship, social structure, and
    counting/numeration all have peculiar if not always unique Mayan configurations.
All plant and animal names that can be reconstructed for pM, SM, or CM will be pre-
    sented, in spite of the fact that most of them are not decisive in helping to pinpoint
    the homeland. An effort has been made to find the scientific names of the plant and
    animal terms presented here.

The reconstructed lexemes are grouped into thirty-three domains, with discussion where
warranted. In general it can be said that when an expected term like 'elder sibling' is missing from a domain in the list below, the item is unstable, having been frequently replaced
by neologisms, or the original term has partly been displaced by a loan-word, usually one
of Mije-Sokean origin – in any case the available data does not allow the projection of a
pM or pSM or pCM form.

Universals of human experience, most verbs, and most body parts are not listed unless they have a characteristic Mayan or Meso-American twist.

Note: every discrepancy in the spelling of a reconstruction between this document and anything I have published before is to be taken as a correction.

Animal and plant names

Ethnobiological research since the early 1960s has established that within any Meso-American community (and communities around the world) there is a shared taxonomy for animal names and another one for plant names into which all known animal and plant names are fit. A primary feature of these taxonomies is the presence of labels for primary life-forms below the "kingdom" category of *animal* or *plant*. For plants there are major life-forms "tree", "vine", "herb", "grass", and "palm", as well as minor life-forms "maize", "pineapple-bromeliad-agave", and others. Mushrooms, mosses, and algae are not considered to be plants. For animals, primary life-forms include "mammals", "birds", "fishes", "snakes", "bugs". Among "bugs" there are subsidiary categories like "ants", "wasps and bees", "blood-suckers". (As it turns out, kingdoms and major life-forms are not all necessarily named; their existence can be revealed through sorting exercises carried out by an investigator with speakers.) I have collected plant and animal taxonomies (including all obtainable plant and animal names) for all of the languages of Latin America that I have done documentation work on since 1960, in many cases for more than one dialect of the same language. I have not, however, carried out ethnobiological research according to the collection and interviewing regimen worked out by Brent Berlin and co-workers starting in the early 1960s.

Groupings cited in square brackets are those recognized in virtually all present-day taxonomic systems: they may be named or unnamed, but the names have not been stable enough over time to be associated with reconstructed terms.

6.1 Animals

pM (WAS+WM) *nooq' 'animal'
        EM *chikop 'animal'
SM *7aalaq' 'domestic animal'//'animal doméstico'
        [GLL+QEQ; since QEQ has /q'/, it can't be a loan from a GLL language]

major life-form *mammals*: [no reconstructible term]
[every Mayan language has more than 50 mammal names]

[primates]
    SM *b'a7tz' 'howler monkey'//'zarahuato' (Alouatta)
    SM (WM+Yu?) *maax 'spider monkey'//'mono araña' [diffused] (Ateles) [The Mam-Awk form /(x=)maaxh/ was borrowed from a language that doesn't retroflex original *x; since /xh/ in Mam-Awk is the outcome for syllable-final *y, Tek has reinterpreted Mam-Awk /x=maaxh/ as Tek #x=may. On the other hand, QaP has /max/ with retroflexed *x as if an inherited form. In consequence, the form *maax could be taken as WM+Yu diffused by various paths into EM, and the GMamean forms as borrowed from a GTz language, but not from a neighboring Qa language.]

EM k'ooy 'long-tailed monkey; howler monkey'//'mico, mono; zarahuato' [This term applies to both the above types of monkey.]

[ruminants]
SM *tixl 'mountain cow, tapir'//'danta' (Tapirus)
pM *kehj 'white-tailed deer'//'venado de cola blanca' (Odocoileus virginianus)

[carnivores]
pM *saq=b'iin 'weasel'//'comadreja' (Mustela)
CM *tz'i7 'dog'//'perro' (Canis familiaris)
From Sapoteko *pe7kku 'dog'
Wasteko borrows pik'o7
and Yukatekan borrows *pe:k';
Sapoteko *pe7kku <= *kwe7kku is in turn borrowed
from pMS *7uku, with Sapoteko animate classifier *kwe+ tacked on at the beginning.
pM (WAS+GQa,+LL as day name) *7o(7)q 'coyote' (Canis latrans)
EM xo7jb' 'coyote' (Canis latrans)
SM *pahar 'skunk' (Conepatus leuconotus/semistriatus)
pM *koj 'cougar'//"león" (Puma concolor)
pM *b'ahlam 'jaguar'//"tigre" (Panthera onca)

[rodents]
SM *ku7k 'squirrel'//'ardilla' (Sciurus)
pM *ha(h)laaw 'agouti'//'serete' (Dasyprocta)
pM *b'a7h 'gopher'//'(tal)tuza' (Geomys)
EM *7imul 'rabbit'//'conejo' (Sylvilagus)
GLL *t'u7l 'rabbit'//'conejo' (Sylvilagus)
[pCh *t'uhl in Kaufman and Norman 1984:550 is wrong.]
SM *ch'o7h 'mouse'//'ratón' (Mus)
pM *sootz' 'bat'//'murciélago (Chiroptera)

[odd critters]
SM *7ib' 'nine-banded armadillo' (Dasypus novemcinctus)

pM (Wa+EM) *huhty' 'possum'//'tlacuache' (Didelphis)
WM+LL *7uch 'possum'//'tlacuache' (Didelphis)

Most of the foregoing mammal categories are depicted and spelled in Mayan hieroglyphs.

major life-form *birds*: pM *tz'ikin 'bird'//'pájaro'
SM *tu7x 'female bird; vulva'//'pájaro hembra; vulva'
SM *(7aj=)tzoo7 'male bird'//'pájaro varón/macho'

[the average Mayan language has more than 100 bird names]

[turkey]
EM *7ak' 'turkey'//'guajolote' (Meleagris gallopavo)
[meaning mostly shifted to 'chicken']
CM (EM+QaP+Ch) *7ak'.aach 'wild turkey'//'pavo de monte'
(Meleagris gallopavo) [meaning mostly shifted to 'turkey']

[Note: *7ak' may originally have had a wider distribution, since *7ak'.aach is based on it. In WM it would have been displaced by the Sokean borrowing *tu7nuk, or else by an extension of *7ak'.aach to mean 'domestic turkey'.]
  pM (WAS+WM) *palach 'tom turkey'//'guajolote varón'

[large carnivorous birds]
  pM *t'iiw or *t'ihw 'hawk'//'gavilán' (Accipiter),
         and maybe 'águila'//'eagle' (Harpia harpyja)
       CM *xi(h)k 'hawk'//'gavilán' (Accipiter)

  CM #liK.liK 'sparrow hawk, kestrel'//'gavilancillo' (Falco sparverius)
[forms like this are widespread in Meso-America; pM *k would have shifted to /ch/ in GTz, but in fact /k/ is found there.]
  'buzzard' has many widespread names:
  SM (EM+Yu) *k'uty 'buzzard, vulture'//'zopilote' (Cathartes sp)
    WM *hos 'buzzard, vulture'//'zopilote' (Cathartes sp)
    WM *7us.. 'buzzard, vulture'//'zopilote' (Cathartes sp)
    WM *xulem 'buzzard, vulture'//'zopilote' (Cathartes sp)

  SM *7ikiin '(barn) owl'//'tecolote, búho' (Bubo)
    (~ EM 7ix+ kiin)

    CM #tuhKuL 'horned owl'//'tecolote, búho' (Bubo virginianus) [diffused; extra-
      Mayan parallels found]
  pM *xooch' 'screech owl'//'lechuza' (Tyto alba)

[nighthawk, whippoorwill//tapacamino (Chordeiles sp, Caprimulgus) would go with large carnivorous birds, but the term is unstable; the most widespread form, GLL *pu7juy, is borrowed from pMS *pu7juyu.]

  SM (LL+WM) *q'a7aw 'boat-tailed grackle'//'zanate' (Quiscalus)
  pM #ty'oK 'boat-tailed grackle'//'zanate' (Quiscalus) [diffused; symbolic]

  pM *jooj 'crow; raven'//'cuervo' (Corvus) [in the Highlands]; 'heron'//'garza'
    (Ardea) [in the Lowlands]
Ravens are found only in the Highlands; herons are found only in the Lowlands. By acquiring a new application in the Lowlands, the term *jooj was not lost. The Xinka lowlanders on the Pacific side borrowed Mayan *jooj as joja 'heron'.

  CM *(7ix=)muukuur 'turtle-dove'//'tortolita'(Streptopelia?)
  CM *(7ix=)pumuuy 'wild dove'//'paloma silvestre' (Columba)

  pM (WAS+GKi) #KuyuC 'parrot'//'perico' [diffused; cf. Totonako /quyu(:)t 'parrot']

  SM (LL+WM) *ty'e(e)l 'parrot, parakeet'//'loro, perico, chocoyo, cotorra'
    (Psittaciformes)
    EM *k'e(e)l 'parrot, parakeet'//'loro, perico, chocoyo, cotorra' (Psittaciformes)
  [the GTz, i.e. TZO, form could come from either *ty'el or *k'el]
  [forms like #kili are found in several non-Mayan Meso-American languages, making us suspect that *k' may be an older pronunciaion. In any case, diffusion is in play.]

SM *moo7 'macaw'//'guacamaya' (Ara)
  CM *kaqiix 'macaw' ("red x")//'guacamaya' (Ara)

SM *ty'ejeC 'woodpecker; mockingbird'//'pájaro carpintero; cenzontle' (Picidae; Mimus)
  [cf. proto-Mije-Sokean *tzeje 'woodpecker']

CM *q'u7q' 'quetzal' (Pharomachrus)
CM *xeew 'bluebird'//'pájaro azul' (Sialia mexicana)

SM *tz'uunu7n 'hummingbird'//'chupaflor' (Trochilus)

[Note: inasmuch as only about 20 bird names are projectable back to early Mayan, we may note that bird names have been less stable through time than mammal names.]

[reptiles]:
turtles
  pM *peetz or *peety 'turtle'//'tortuga' [Wa+Mam] (Testudo)
    CM *kok 'turtle'//'tortuga' [diffused] (Testudo)
    LL+WM *7ahk 'turtle'//'tortuga' (Testudo)

snakes
  pM *kaan 'snake'; [CM] 'cramp'//'culebra; calambre'
  pM *so7ty 'rattle(snake)'//'(víbora de) cascabel' (Crotalus)

[every Mayan language has quite a few snake names, mostly descriptive compounds]

[lizards]
  pM *7ohkoC 'lizard'//'lagartija' (Lacertilia)
  pM *7ahiin 'cayman'//'lagarto, caimán' (Caiman)
  CM *7oohan 'iguana' (Iguana)
    WM *7ina=tam 'iguana' (Iguana)
    LL *huuj 'iguana' (Iguana)

[batrachians]
  pM *woo7 'toad'//'sapo' (Bufo)
    SM *peq 'toad'//'sapo' (Bufo)

  SM *7amooch 'frog'//'rana' (Rana)

fishes
  SM *kar 'fish'//'pescado, pez'
    CM *kar.a ~ *kar.i (vt) 'to fish it'//'pescarlo'
  CM *mutz'utz' 'little fish'//'pescadito'
[different kinds of fish are rare in the Mayan Highlands, but in the Lowlands there may be around 15 named fishes]

[shelled creatures]
  SM *t'oot' 'snail'//'caracol' (Gastropoda)
    CM *puur 'snail'//'caracol' (Gastropoda)

CM (EM+GQ)*tap 'fresh-water crab'//'cangrejo' (Brachyura)
    GLL+QEQ *ya7x 'fresh-water crab'//'cangrejo' (Brachyura)

bugs:
["bugs" (insects, arachnids, and "worms") are biologically rampant in Meso-America,
    and any Mayan language has at least 200 named creatures of this type]

[bood-suckers]
    CM *poty' 'bedbug'//'chinche' (Cimex)

    pM *siip 'tick'//'garrapata' (Ixodida)

    pM *7uk' 'head louse'//'piojo de cabeza' (Pediculus humanus capitis)
    CM *u+tzaa7 7uk' 'nit'//'liendre' ("its-shit-of louse")
    CM *saq 7uk' '(body) louse'//'piojo (del cuerpo)' (Pediculus humanus humanus)

    pM *k'aq 'flea'//'pulga' (Pulex; Ctenocephalides)
    pM *7ook-VC k'aq 'chigger'//'nigua' (Tunga penetrans) (literally "enter-ing flea")
        [WAS+WM]

    CM *jut 'grub'//'gusano'; 'chigger'//'nigua' (Tunga penetrans)

pM *siina7nh 'scorpion'//'alacrán' (Scorpio)

[bees & wasps]
    SM *hoonon 'wasp//avispa (Vespidae); bumblebee//abejorro' (Bombus)
    CM *7ahqaanh 'wasp('s nest)'
        [a similar-sounding pSokean form *7okɨwVC is reflected in WAS, TZE, and
            TOJ]
    SM *kaab' 'honey(-bee)'//'abeja, colmena' (Apis)
    SM *(7ix=)kab' 'beeswax'

[flies]
    SM *7us 'gnat'//'mosquito' (Culex); 'fly'//'mosca' (Diptera)
    pM *ha7h 'green fly'//'mosca verde'; 'fly grub'//'gusano de mosca'
    SM *xe7n 'mosquito'//'zancudo' (Anopheles)

[crickets, grasshoppers, locusts/cicadas]
    SM *chiil.. 'cricket'//'grillo' (Gryllidae); 'grasshopper'//'saltamontes' (Caelifera)
    CM *lool 'cricket'//'grillo' (Gryllidae); 'locust, cicada'//'chicharra, cigarra'
        (Cicadidae); 'grasshopper'//'saltamontes, chapulín' (Caelifera)
    SM *sahk' 'grasshopper'//'saltamontes, chafpulín' (Caelifera); 'locust,
        cicada'//'chicharra, cigarra' (Cicadidae)

pM *sanik 'ant'//'hormiga' (Formica)
    EM+GQan *ch'eken 'leaf-cutter ant'//'zompopo' (Atta, Acromyrmex)

SM *pehpen 'butterfly'//'mariposa' (Rhopalocera)
SM *kuhka7y 'lightning bug, firefly'//'luciérnaga' (Lampyridae)
    [diffused]

SM (LL+WM) *luqum 'earth-worm'//'lombriz' (Lumbricina)

pM *7am 'spider'//'araña' (Araneae) [// pMS *7a:mu]

[given that only about 25 reconstructed 'bug' names can be cited, the names of bugs have not been very stable over time]

6.2 Plants

pM *b'aq' 'seed, pip, pit'

CM *nahq' 'pit, kernel'

SM *soj (Yu+MCH+KCH) 'plant blight; dead leaves; flaky bark of gumbolimbo'// 'plaga, argenio; broza; palo jiote'

major life-form *trees*: pM *tyee7 'tree'//'árbol'

CM *sanik tyee7 'onion cordia, Spanish elm'//'laurel blanco' (Cordia alliodora) [literally "ant tree"]

pM *b'aty 'cork tree'//'jonote, corcho, balsa' (Heliocarpus appendiculatus)

CM *piit 'elephant ear'//'conacaste, guanacast(l)e' (Enterolobium cyclocarpum)

pM *7aqit 'pricklenut'//'guácima' (Guazuma ulmifolia)

SM *7aajaaw=tyee7 'white sapote, Mexican apple'//'matasano' (Casimiroa edulis) [literally "lord tree"]

pM *ha7as 'marmalade fruit'//'zapote mamey' (Pouteria sapota/mammosa) [LL+WM(+WAS?)]

EM+GQan *//tu7l.ul// ?'marmalade fruit'//'zapote mamey'(Pouteria mammosa); 'sapodilla plum'//'zapotillo, chicozapote' (Manilkara achras)

SM *muuy 'sapodilla, naseberry'//'chicozapote, zapotillo' (Manilkara zapota)

CM *k'iwex 'soursop'//'anona' (Annona muricata)

pM (Wa+Yu+QEQ) *7ab'a(l) 'hogplum'//'jocote' (Spondias spp.)

pM (Wa+EM) *q'iinom 'hogplum'//'jocote' (Spondias spp.)
    CM (MCH+POQ+QEQ) *rum 'hogplum'//'jocote' (Spondias spp.)
    WM *po7om 'hogplum'//'jocote' (Spondias spp.)

pM *(7i)kaq' 'guava'//'guayaba' (Psidium)
    [replaced by Sokean loan < *patajaC in LL+WM]

Yuk and Itz have a different form from #patah, suggesting independent borrowing. #patah is also found in some GKi languages, successfully displacing the native form.

pM *7oonh 'avocado'//'aguacate' (Persea americana)

CM *tzitz 'Nectandra'//'aguacatillo' (Nectandra)

pM *7ajx ~ *7ojx 'breadnut'//'ramón, ojite, ujushte' (Brosimum alicastrum)

   SM *7ix.i.7m=tyee7 'breadnut'//'ramón' Brosimum alicastrum)
[This second term is literally "shelled maize tree"; it is not clear if there is a single tree
or plant to which this term originally applied, or if the term was independently created
several times. But the identification as 'ramón' in both TZE and KAQ suggests that this
was an innovation that replaced *7ojx ~ *7ajx]

   pM #KaKaw 'cacao' (Theobroma cacao) [borrowed from pMS *kakawa or later
      developments within MS into individual Mayan languages or recent group
      ancestors. In GTz + Chujean it postdates the shift *k > ch, ca. 200 BCE.]
   CM *peeq 'wild cacao'//'pataxte' (Theobroma cacao) [this may have meant
      'undifferentiated cacao' before the introduction of #KaKaw]

SM *tz'iin 'sweet cassava'//'yuca' (Manihot esculenta)
pM (WAS+WM) *tz'iin tyee7 'sweet cassava'//'yuca' (Manihot esculenta) [literally
   "cassava tree": in MA folk taxonomy, cassava is a tree]

pM *toq'oor 'willow'//'saúz, sauce' (Salix)

SM *tyaj 'pine'//'pino, ocote' (Pinus)
CM *k'isiis 'cypress'//'ciprés' (Cupressus spp.)
SM (LL+WM) *k'uh=tyee7 'tropical cedar'//'cedro' (Cedrela odorata) [lit. "god tree"]

   pM *kaqaaj 'gumbolimbo'//'palo mulato, palo (de) jiote' (Bursera spp.) [probably
      contains the root *kaq 'red']

CM *jih 'oak'//'encino, roble' (Quercus spp.)

pM *hu7nh 'Ficus'//'amate' (Ficus spp)
   'bark paper'//'papel de corteza de amate';
   'book'//'libro' [Ficus bark paper, and "books" and ornaments made from it may
      date to the Late Formative, ca 300 BCE]

SM *k'uxub' 'annatto'//'achiote' (Bixa orellana)
   CM *ho7ox 'annatto'//'achiote' (Bixa orellana)

pM *7inuup 'silk-cotton tree'//'ceiba, pochote' (Ceiba pentandra)

minor life-form **palms**: pM *7apak' 'palm(-tree)'//'palma' (Arecaceae)
   SM *xa7nh 'palm'//'palma' (Arecaceae)
   pM *map 'cohune palm'//'palma de coyol' (Orbignya cohune)
   SM *k'iib' 'parlor palm'//'pacaya' (Chamaedorea elegans)

   major life-form **vines**: SM *7a7q' 'vine'
      CM *quul 'vine, creeper'

pM *kenaq' 'beans'//'frijol' (Phaseolus vulgaris)
pM *we7t' 'type of bean' [WAS+Tz]

SM *k'uhm ~ *k'uum 'pumpkin'//'ayote, calabaza amarilla' (Cucurbita pepo pepo)
   SM *sakiil 'pumpkin seed'//'pepita de ayote'
CM (EM+GQ) *muukun 'summer squash'//'ayote de tierra fría, güicoy' (Cucurbita pepo)
GLL *tzohl 'calabaza chata verde' (Cucurbita pepo)
CM (EM+GQ) *q'ohq' 'winter squash'//'chilacayote, tzílaca' (Cucurbita ficifolia)

pM *ch'imaah ~ *ch'umaah 'chayote'//'chayote, güisquil' (Sechium edule)

pM *tz'usub' 'grape'//'uva' (Vitis sp.)

pM *lah 'nettle'//'chichicaste, ortiga' (Urera baccifera)

CM *ty'up.aq 'soaproot, soapberry'//'amole, jabón de monte, jaboncillo' (Sapindus saponaria)

CM *pixp 'tomato'//'tomate, jitomate' (Solanum lycopersicum)
   EM+ *7ix=kooyaa7 'tomato'//'tomate, jitomate' (Solanum lycopersicum)
     [borrowed from Mije-Sokean: pMS *ko:ya:7]

pM *7iis 'sweet potato'//'camote' (Ipomoea batatas)

major life-form *herbs*: CM *tz'u7l 'herb'//'hierba'
   CM *7iityaaj 'pot-herbs, greens'//'verdura, hierba, quelites'

pM *tees or *tzees 'pigweed'//'bledo' (Amaranthus sp.)

SM (GQ+GM) *ch'a7b'i7n 'rattlepod'//'chipilín' (Crotalaria)

pM *7iik 'chili pepper'//'chile' (Capsicum)

pM *mahy ~ *ma7y 'tobacco'//'tabaco' (Nicotiana tabacum) [diffused, with extra-Mayan parallels]
   GLL *k'uhtz 'tobacco'//'tabaco'

CM *siik' 'cigar'//'puro'
   EM+GQ *siik'.i ~ *siik'.a (vt) 'to smoke it'//'fumarlo'

CM *tzihb' 'fern'//'helecho, palmita' (Pteridium)

CM *tuhs 'marigold'//'flor de muerto' (Tagetes electa)

SM *su7n 'sunflower'//'girasol, mirasol' (Tithonia rotundifolia) [KiP is from *su7un; Yu, TUZ, GM could be from either *su7un or *su7n]

WM *muuh 'American black nightshade'//'yerbamora' (Solanum americanum)
EM *7iimu7ut [idem]

(In Mayaland the leaves, but not the berries, of this plant are widely eaten, boiled as greens.)

For 'goosefoot'//'epazote' (Chenopodium ambrosioides) there is no term reconstructible to EM or WM; all terms relate to lower-level groupings; yet goosefoot is one of the oldest domesticated plants in MA.

major life-form **grasses**: SM *7aaq 'grass; thatching'
    CM *k'im 'straw'//'paja'

    pM (WAS+TZE+MCH) *toom 'kind of grass'

    CM *puuj 'cattail'//'tule' (Typha)

    CM *7aaj 'reed'//'(caña de) carrizo' (Phragmites australis)

    pM (WAS+Tz) *chanhib' or *kanhib' 'bamboo'//'otate, bambú' (Bambusa, Arundinaria)

minor life-form **maize**:
    pM *tz'utuj 'corn tassel'//'flor de milpa' [cf. pSokean *tzutu7 'corn spike'//'espiga de maíz']
    pM *7ajn 'roasting ear'//'elote'
    pM *nhal 'maize ear'//'mazorca'
    CM *hi7h 'young maize ear'//'jilote'
    pM *b'aqal 'corncob'//'olote' [WAS+Yu+WM]
        EM *b'aql.aq ~ *b'ajl.aq 'corncob'//'olote'
    [These forms are possibly based on *b'aaq 'bone']

minor life-form "**pineapples**" (no common term for this category)
    WM+ *pajk' 'pineapple'//'piña' (Ananas comosus) [This plant originated in lowland South America, but reached Meso-America in pre-Columbian times.]

    CM *pehtaq(') 'prickly pear'//'nopal, tuna' (Opuntia)
        pM (WAS+Yu) *paq'aC 'prickly pear'//'nopal, tuna' (Opuntia)

    pM *kiih 'century plant (fiber)'//'maguey; cáñamo, ixtle' (Agave)
        CM *saq=kiih 'century plant'//'maguey'(Agave) [lit. "white century-plant"]
    CM *7eek'   'bromelia'//'pie de gallo, tecolúmate' (Bromelia)

non-plant life-form **fungus**
    CM (EM+GQ) *q'uux 'moss'//'musgo'

    CM *q'an=tzuhh 'type of mushroom' (lit. "yellow bottlegourd")

6.3 Agriculture

    pM *7iiyaanh 'seed [for planting]'//'semilla'
    [Extended forms like *7iynh.a(H)C with varying final C are found in several low-level subgroups]

pM *7aw (vt) 'to plant/sow it'//'sembrarlo'
   CM *7aw.b'.al 'planting stick'//'coa'
      CM *7aw.al 'planting'//'siembra'

pM (WAS+Toj) *7alVj 'cornfield'//'milpa'
   CM (TZE+QEQ) *k'al 'cornfield'//'milpa'

CM *7aq'iin 'weeding corn'//'limpia'

pM *7ix (vt) 'to shell maize'//'desgranar maíz'
pM *7ix.i (vt) [idem]

SM *7ix.i.7m 'maize kernels on or off the cob'//'maíz en grano; maíz desgranado'
[the pM form cited in Kaufman and Norman 1984 is wrong.]
   CM *7ix.i.7m.a (vt) 'to shell [dry] corn'//'desgranar maíz seco'

[Maize planting, harvesting, and processing seem to have been in place in proto-Mayan times; whether everyone was a full-time farmer, or not, is not entailed by the reconstructible terms.]

6.4 Food preparation

SM *k'il (vt) 'to toast it, roast it'//'tostarlo, dorarlo'
   EM *k'il.i (vt) [idem]

CM (EM+GQ) *b'ol (vt) 'to broil it'//'asarlo'

SM *q'ut (vt) 'to mash (chili, tomato) in mortar with pestle'//'machacarlo (chile, tomate) en molcajete'

SM *puty' (vt) 'to crush, squash (chili, tomato)'// 'machacarlo, destriparlo (chile, tomate, olote cocido)'

pM *kee7.e (vt) 'to grind it'//'molerlo'
LL+WM *juch' (vt) 'to grind it'
[This is probably borrowed from pMS *j@tz 'to grind it']

Throughout Meso-America, when leached maize (nixtamal) is ground into maize dough (masa) on a quern (metate) with a muller (mano), this is done in three steps: the first grinding is called *quebrantar*; the second grinding is called *repasar*; the third grinding is called *afinar*. Every Mayan language has a distinct lexeme for each of these meanings, but on the pM, SM, or CM level no terms are reconstructible for *quebrantar* (first pass), *repasar* (second pass), or *afinar* (third pass). This correlates with the archeological record. Rosenswig (2006) shows that, in southern Meso-America, maize was exploited and ground at a much increased rate starting around 1000 BCE. The size of maize cobs had doubled, consumption of fermented maize including stalks was replaced by increased consumption of maize kernels, and the use of querns and mullers increased. It is plausibly in this era that the multistage grinding process and its vocabulary developed; this would support the dating of the breakup for pM, SM, and CM to before 1000 BCE, when the basics of maize consumption and processing were in place and the breakup of EM and WM occurred around or after that date.

"It is noteworthy that there are no proto-Mayan words for comal (clay griddle) or torti-lla" (Kaufman 1976a:105). In southern Meso-America before about 900 CE clay griddles (comales) were not used and tortillas were not eaten. All present-day Mayan languages have words for these things, but the terms used cannot be reconstructed to the pM or SM level, and certain widespread apparent cognates must be neologisms that have spread by diffusion, or old words with reassigned meanings that have also spread by diffusion. In several languages the word for griddle is based on a borrowing from Mije-Sokean.

6.5 Foods

SM *maatz' 'corn gruel'//'atole'

SM *7uul 'corn gruel'//'atole' [from Sokean; pSo *7unu < pre-pSo *7u:nu]. The vowel length in Mayan suggests that it was borrowed from a pre-proto-Sokean form *7u:nu from before Sokean lost pMS vowel length (this phenomenon is attested in other Mayan lexical borrowings from Sokean). The fact that Mayan has /l/ in this word might reflect an earlier existence of phonetic [l] (of unclear phonemic status) in pMS; cf. the WM borrowed word for 'turkey'.

SM (YUK+EM) *saq=Ha7 'corn gruel'//'atole'

pM *q'oor 'corn dough'//'masa' [EM +'atole']

CM *b'uuch 'leached maize, hominy'//'nixtamal'

pM *k'aj 'pinole'

6.6 Hunger and types of eating

pM *wa7.ij(-aal) 'hunger'//'hambre'
   [probably related to *wa7 'to eat']

CM *wa7 (vi) 'to eat in general'//'comer'
   WM *we7 (vi) [idem]

pM *ti7 (vt) 'to bite it; eat meat/mushrooms'//'morderlo, comer carne/hongos'
   CM *ti7.b'ej, ERG+ti7 'meat'//'carne'
      WM *b'aq'.et 'meat, flesh'//'carne'

SM *k'ux (vt) 'to eat crunchy things'//'comer cosas tostadas, crujientes'
   SM (EM+Yu) *k'uux 'roasting ear'//'elote'

CM *lo7 (vt) 'to eat soft things, fruit, eggs'//'comer cosas suaves, frutas, huevos'

pM *7uk' (vt) 'to drink it'//'beberlo, tomarlo'

6.7 Sensations: smells and taste

pM *tyu7h 'stinking'//'hediondo, apestoso'

pM *ki7 'sweet'//'dulce'

pM *k'ah 'bitter; gall'//'amargo; hiel amarga'

pM *7a7tz'aam 'salt'//'sal'

SM (LL+WM) *paaj ~ *pa7j 'sour'//'agrio, ácido'
  EM *ch'am 'sour'//'agrio, ácido'

6.8 Sickness

pM *ra7h or *raah 'painful; spicy hot'//'doloroso, que duele; picante'

CM *yaaj 'sick(ness), wound, sore, suffering'//'enfermo, enfermedad, herida, llaga, sufrimiento'

pM *maal 'swelling'//'hinchazón'

pM *saal 'mange'//'sarna'

CM *meem 'dumb'//'mudo'
  WM *7umaa7 'dumb'//'mudo' (from Mije-Sokean)

SM (LL+WM) *7ahnh 'medicinal herb'//'hierba medicinal'

CM *tz'ak 'medicine'//'medicina, remedio' [cf. pMS *tzok]
  CM *7aj=tz'aak 'curer'//'curandero'

CM (Hue) *kuun 'curing power'//'poder del curandero'
  EM *7aj=kuun 'curer'//'curandero'

6.9 Colors

pM *saq 'white'//'blanco'

pM *ra7x 'grue [undifferentiated green and blue]; unripe'//'verde, azul; no maduro'

pM *7ejq' 'black'//'negro'

pM *q'an 'yellow; ripe'//'amarillo; maduro'

pM *kaq 'red'//'rojo, colorado'

This is the complete set of basic color terms.

6.10 Movement: direction

pM (WAS+GLL) *7ehm (vi) 'to go down'//'bajar(se)'

NO 'to GO UP' can be reconstructed

pM *tya(a)-l (vi) 'to come'//'venir'
  [morphologically complex]
  *tyaal is reconstructed from WAS, Yu, maybe Tz.

*tyal is reconstructed from Ch, maybe Tz, Poqom, QEQ. WAS has a variant /tsi7/, and GMameam has only /tzaaj/
   < *tya(a)- + *-(:)j or *-(:)nh]

SM *beh.i-:n ~ *b'ihn (vi) 'to go, travel, walk'//'ir, viajar, andar, caminar'
   GK *b'eh (vi) 'to go away, travel, walk'//'irse, viajar, andar, caminar'
   [many EM lgs have reflexes of both *b'eh.i-:n ~ *b'ihn and *b'eh] which
      are lexically distinct; the pM word *b'eeh 'road' seems related to these
      verbs.]

CM *xi7 (vi) 'to go away'//'irse'
CM (EM+GQ) *7oonh (vi) 'to go away'//'irse'

pM *Huul (vi) 'to arrive here'//'llegar aquí'
   pM *Huulaa7 'visitor, guest'//'huésped, visita'

EM+ *7apo-:n (vi) 'to arrive elsewhere'//'llegar en otra parte' [This has the
   appearance of an antipassive, but there is no known tv that it could be
   based on.]

pM *q'ot (vi) 'to make a circuit, to walk around the outside edge'//'caminar al
   rededor' [WAS+QEQ];
   'to arrive elsewhere'//'llegar en otra parte'[GLL]

SM *q'ahx (vi) 'to pass by, cross over'//'pasar, cruzar'
   CM *7ik' ~ *7ek' (vi) 'to pass by, cross over'//'pasar, cruzar'

pM *7eel (vi) 'to go out'//'salir'
   GLL *loq' (vi) 'to go out'//'salir'

pM *7ook (vi) 'to go in'//'entrar'
   SM *7ook.E.b'(.aal) 'entry, way in'//'entrada'
   pM *7ok.esa (vt) 'to put it in'//'meterlo'

SM *sut (vt) 'to turn it'//'darle vuelta, voltearlo'
   SM *suht (vi) 'to return, go back'//'volver, regresar'

6.11 Movement: manner

CM *nuhx (vi) 'to swim'//'nadar'

CM *nhihk (vi) 'earth to quake'//'temblar la tierra'

pM *xanh (vi) 'to walk'//'caminar, andar'
   SM *xanh.ab' 'sandal'//'huarache, sandalia'

EM *7ahn, WM *7ahnh (vi) 'to run'//'correr'
CM *7ahn(h).im.aj (vi) 'to run (away), flee'//'correr, huirse'

6.12 Property, exchange, and commerce

[None of the reconstructible terms for exchange of goods entails the use of money.]

> CM *7eleq' 'theft'//'robo'
>> CM *7elVq'.a (vt)'to steal it'//'robarlo'
>> CM *7elVq'.oom 'thief'//'ladrón'

> SM *majaan 'loan, something borrowed'//'préstamo'

> pM *jal (vt) 'to exchange it'//'hacerle cambio'
>> SM *k'ex (vt) 'to exchange it'//'hacerle cambio'

> SM *toj (vt) 'to pay it'//'pagarlo'

> CM *k'aas 'debt'//'deuda'
>> GLL *b'et 'debt'//'deuda'

> pM *k'aay 'sale'//'venta'
> pM *k'aay.i (vt) 'to sell it'//'venderlo'
>> GLL *konh (vt) 'to sell it'//'venderlo' [GQa forms that seem to reflect pM *ch are borrowings from Ch'olan.]

NB: there is no pM or SM term for 'to buy', but *man is a candidate for CM if EM innovated away from it. In the absence of a monetary economy, terms that later mean 'to sell' might earlier have meant 'to give in exchange for something of equal value', and terms that later mean 'to buy' might have meant 'to accept from its owner something for which you have given him/her something of equal value'.

> CM (LL+WM) *man (vt) 'to buy it'//'comprarlo'
>> EM+ *loq' (vt) 'to buy it'//'comprarlo'

> SM *k'iwik 'market'//'mercado, plaza'
> [No necessary implication of use of money in exchange of goods.]

> SM *mahtaan 'gift'//'regalo'
>> CM *siih 'gift'//'regalo'

> CM *7aq' 'to put it'//'ponerlo' means 'to give it to him or her'//'dárselo' when combined with the applicative suffix {.b'e} in languages – e.g. all Ch'olan languages and therefore Epigraphic Mayan – that preserve {.b'e}. In languages that lack {.b'e}, 7aq' can mean 'to give'. GK languages lack *7aq'.

> CM *ye7 (=> ya7 in KiP) 'to give it, to put it'//'darlo, ponerlo'. pCh *ye7 means 'to take it in the hand'//'agarrarlo' [CHL] and 'to show it'//'mostrarlo' [YOK]. pCh *ye7.b'e means 'to give it to him/her'//'dárselo'. MCH and pCh also have *7aq'.

6.13 Social organization

CM *7aamaaq' 'town'//'pueblo'

pM *b'ih 'name'//'nombre'

CM *b'eh.oom 'rich person'//'rico, adinerado'
  EM *q'iinoom 'rich person'//'rico, adinerado'

pM *7aajaaw 'lord, boss'//'señor, jefe'

CM *pataan 'tribute, service'//'tributo, servicio'
  [what you give to or do for a ruler or a community because you owe it to them by
      virtue of your being of lower status]
  [trabajo (CHT,CHR), mecapal (Kp), and milpa (MCH) are shifted/extended
      meanings]

pM *7ab'.aat 'servant, messenger, errand-boy'//'mensajero, mandadero, mozo'
  [cf. pCeltic *ambi=ag.to-s 'one who has been sent around']
  [based on the transitive verb *7ab' 'to send him', surviving only in Wasteko, as
      /7aba7/]
SM *taq (vt) 'to send him, order him'//'enviarlo, mandarlo, obligarlo'

CM *muun 'slave'//'esclavo'
  [The term 'slave' refers to one in a state of servitude, where the master decides
      what work the slave will do; after Spaniards introduced the concept of 'work',
      the root √mun was adapted to create terms for 'work' and 'community service']

GK+GQ *k'ul 'enemy'//'enemigo, contrario'
  GLL *naq 'enemy'//'enemigo, contrario'

The reconstructible terms that relate to social organization indicate settled village life
('town') and social stratification where not every person has the same rights ('lord',
'slave', 'tribute'), or amount of property ('rich man').

6.14 Kinship and types of people

pM *winaq 'person; man'//'gente; hombre'

pM *7ix 'female//'hembra'

pM 7ix= [classifying prepound] 'female; relatively smaller or weaker thing or being'
  [not necessarily animate]//'hembra; ser o cosa relativamente más pequeño o
  menos fuerte' [no necesariamente animado]

CM *7ix.oq 'female; woman'//'hembra; mujer'

pM *7aj= [classifying prepound] 'male; relatively larger or stronger animate
  being'//'varón, macho; ser animado relativamente más grande o más fuerte'

SM *xiib' 'male'//'varón, macho'

While several studies have been devoted to the analysis of colonial Yukateko kinship, no comprehensive study of Mayan kinship with an aim to reconstruct its earliest stages/ state as a system has come to my attention. Consequently, I have no predecessors to defer to or to argue against. In any case, I do not offer suggestions about the pMayan system; I simply present the reconstructible terms in a logical order.

females
    pM *naa7 'mother'//'madre'
        CM *naan 'mother'//'madre'
        EM+Qa *chuuch 'mother'//'madre'

    CM *chuchu7 'step-mother'//'madrasta'

    pM *7aal 'woman's offspring'//'hijo/hija de mujer'
        CM *7aal.a (vt) 'to give birth to him/her'//'dar a luz a él/ella'

    pM (WAS+LL+KOT) *miim 'grandmother'//'abuela'
        [Meaning shifts to 'mother' in several descendant languages.]
        SM (LL+WM) *chiich 'grandmother'//'abuela'
        CM (EM+Tz) *yaah 'grandmother'//'abuela'

    pM *7i7h 'woman's grandchild'//'nieto/nieta de mujer'

males
    GLL *yuum 'father; lord'//'padre; señor' [borrowed from pSokean *yumi 'lord, boss']
    SM #TaaT 'father'//'padre' [diffused]

    pM *maam 'grandfather; man's grandchild'//'abuelo; nieto/nieta de hombre'

    pM *7ikaan 'MoBr'//'hermano de la madre'

    CM (EM+GQ) *k'aajol 'man's son'//'hijo de hombre'
        WM *nity'an 'man's son'//'hijo de hombre'

    pM *7ikaaq' 'nephew'//'sobrino'

siblings
    EM *7atz 'same sex elder sibling'//'hermano/hermana mayor del mismo sexo'
        [borrowed from pSokean *7atzi 'elder male kinsman']
    LL *saku7n 'same sex elder sibling'//'hermano/hermana mayor del mismo sexo'

    CM *7ichl.al 'elder brother'//'hermano mayor'

GLL *kiik 'man's elder sister'//'hermano mayor de varón'

    EM+Qa *7aanaab' 'man's sister'//'hermana de varón'
    SM (Yu+WM+GM) *7ihtz'iin 'same sex younger sibling'//'hermano/hermana menor del mismo sexo'
    SM (Yu+Ch+GK) *tyaaq' 'same sex younger sibling'//'hermano/hermana menor del mismo sexo'

SM *xib'.aal 'woman's brother'//'hermano de hembra'
   [based on *xiib' 'male']

spouse
   SM (LL+WM) *7anat 'wife; older woman'//'esposa; viej(it)a'
      [> Yu 7ataan, > Tz 7antz]
      EM *ERG+ixq.eel 'wife'//'esposa'
        [an easy innovation meaning "one's woman part"]
   SM (YUK+Ki) *7ix=nhaah.iil 'wife'//'esposa'
      [an easy innovation meaning "female dwelling thing"]

   SM (Yu+GQ+GM) *7iitaam 'old man; man; husband'//'viejo; hombre; marido'

in-laws
   pM *mu7 'cross-sex sibling-in-law'//'cuñado/cuñada del sexo opuesto'

   CM *7ix=na7m 'man's sister-in-law'//'cuñada de varón'

   pM *jawan 'woman's sibling-in-law'//'cuñado/cuñada de hembra'

   pM (Wa+Yu+Tz+Mam) *b'aal 'man's brother-in-law'//'cuñado de varón'
      CM (GQ+EM) *b'aal.uk 'man's brother-in-law'//'cuñado de varón'

   pM *nhii7 'man's father-in-law; man's son-in-law'//'suegro de hombre; yerno de
      hombre'

   pM *7al7iib' 'woman's parent-in-law; daughter-in-law'//'suegro/suegra de mujer;
      nuera'

young ones
   LL+GQ *7unee7 'baby'//'criatura, nene'
      [borrowed from pSokean *7une7 'baby']
      EM *nee7 'baby'//'criatura, nene' [resembles pSokean but may have an
        independent origin]

6.15 Body parts as/and object parts

   SM *r+eeh 'its (sharp) edge'//'su filo' *ITS FRONT.TOOTH

   SM *u+tyii7 'its edge'//'su orilla' *ITS MOUTH

   SM *u+tyii7 nhaah 'door'//'puerta' *ITS-MOUTH of-HOUSE, "house's mouth"

   SM *r+iit 'its bottom'//'su fondo' *ITS ARSE

   pM *u+xikin 'its corner'//'su esquina' *ITS EAR

   pM *tya+ u+b'aah 'on top of it'//'encima de ello' *AT ITS HEAD

   pM *u+wi7 'its tip'//'su punta' *ITS HEAD/HAIR

SM *tya+ u+Haty 'in front of it'//'en frente de ello' *AT ITS FACE/EYE

pM *r+aqan 'handle; stalk'//'cabo, mango; tallo' *ITS LEG/FOOT

SM *r+ooq 'handle'//'cabo, mango' *ITS LEG/FOOT

pM *r+ahlaanh 'under it'//'debajo de ello' *ITS UNDERNEATHNESS

pM *xuk 'corner, side'//'esquina, lado'

[The metaphorical extension of human body-part names for the parts of
inanimate objects is a characteristic of all Mayan and many other Meso-American
languages.]

SM *r+Ha7-aal (ERG+)Haty 'tear(s)'//'lágrima(s)' *ITS-WATER of-FACE/EYE,
"face's water"

CM *u+q'ab' tyee7 'branch(es)'//'rama(s)' *ITS-ARM of-TREE, "tree's arm"

6.16 Earth and sky

pM *kab' 'earth'//'tierra'
    SM *ch'o7ch' 'earth'//'tierra'

CM *malaaj 'sea-coast'//'la costa del Pacífico' [areal?] [Mayans living in the
Highlands are familiar with the Pacific coast because of seasonal harvesting
activities that some participate in. This term is the only one shared among two or
more languages.]

SM *taq'aanh 'field, plain, flat place'//'campo, llano,
        planada'

SM *najb' 'lake, sea'//'lago, laguna, mar'

SM *witz 'mountain, hill'//'cerro'

pM *ka7nh 'sky'//'cielo'

6.17 Weather

pM *kahoq 'thunder'//'trueno'
    (EM+GQ) #kaayu(m)pa7 'lightning'//'relámpago';
        'thunder'//'rayo'
        [from Soke *keyo-pa 'it flashes']

pM *nhab' 'rain'//'lluvia'

CM *tahiiw 'frost'//'helada' [only exists above 6,000 feet]

SM *b'aty 'hail'//'granizo'
  EM+GQ *saq=b'aty 'hail'//'granizo'

pM *7i7q' 'wind'//'viento', 'air'//'aire'

6.18 Time

SM *ha7b' 'year'//'año'

pM *7iik' 'moon'//'luna'

SM (GLL+QEQ) *7eeq' 'star'//'estrella'
  EM *ch'umiil 'star'//'estrella'

pM *q'iinh 'sun, day, time, festival'//'sol, día, tiempo, fiesta'

SM (EM+LL) *7aj=q'iinh 'day-keeper, calendar priest'//'sacerdote Maya'

SM *tya+ q'iinh 'during the day'//'durante el día, de día'

CM *7eew.ii(r) 'yesterday'//'ayer'

CM *7oonh.eer 'before, a long time ago'//'antes, hace mucho tiempo'

The Meso-American 260-day calendar probably came into existence among the Olmecs, and started spreading to other areas between 1000 and 600 BCE; see §6.31.

6.19 Numbers

For a discussion of the structure of numerical expressions in Mayan, see Kaufman (2015ms:§B4, 1986, 1990).

pM *jar-ub' 'how much?, how many?'//'¿cuánto?, ¿cuántos?'

SM *b'ah 'first'//'primero'
  CM *nah 'first'//'primero'

[Note: bear in mind the Mayan rule that underlying long vowels are shortened in non-final syllables.]

pM *juun 'one'//'uno'
  CM *ju(n).juun 'each one'//'cada uno'
  CM *juun=ha7b'.eer 'one year ago'//'hace un año'

pM *ka7-ib' [sic] 'two'//'dos'
  SM *u+ka7b' '2nd'//'segundo'
  SM *ka7b'.eej 'day after tomorrow'//'pasado mañana'
  SM *ka7b'.ej.eer 'day before yesterday'//'antier'

pM *7oox-ib' /7oxib'/ [sic] 'three'//'tres'

SM *r+oox '3rd'//'tercero'
CM *7oox.eej 'in three days'//'en tres días'
CM *7oox.ej.eer 'three days ago'//'hace tres días'

pM *kaanh-ib' /kanhib'/ [sic] 'four'//'cuatro'
CM *u+kaanh '4th'//'cuarto'
CM *koonh.eej 'in 4 days'//'en 4 días'
CM *koonh.ej.eer '4 days ago'//'hace 4 días'

pM *Ho7-oob' '5'
SM *r+Hoo7 /ro:7/ '5th'

pM *waqaq-iib' '6'

pM *huuq-uub' /huquub'/ '7'

pM *waqxaq-iib' '8'

pM *b'eleenh-eeb' /b'elenheeb'/ '9'

pM *lajuunh-eeb' /lajunheeb'/ '10'

CM *juun=lajuunh /junlajuunh/ '11'

CM *kab'=lajuunh '12'
WM *laj=ka7/b' '12'

CM *7oox=lajuunh /7oxlajuunh/ '13'

CM *kaanh=lajuunh /kanhlajuunh/ '14'

CM *Ho7=lajuunh '15'

CM *waqaq=lajuunh '16'

CM *huuq=lajuunh /huqlajuunh/ '17'

CM *waqxaq=lajuunh '18'

CM *b'eleenh=lajuunh /b'elenhlajuunh/ '19'

pM *=winaq 'x20'

SM *=k'ahl 'x20'

pM *jun=winaq '20'
CM *jun=k'ahl '20'

CM *lajuunh u+ka7=winaq '30'

CM *ka7=winaq '40'

CM *ka7=k'ahl '40'

CM *lajuunh r+oox=k'ahl /.. roxk'ahl/ '50'

CM *7oox=k'ahl /7oxk'ahl/ '60'

pM *Ho7=winaq '100'
   pM *Ho7=k'ahl '100'

CM *waqaq=k'ahl '120'

CM *waqxaq=k'ahl '160'

CM *lajuunh=k'ahl /lajunhk'ahl/ '200'

6.20 Counting and measurement

pM *7aj (vt) 'to count it'//'contarlo(s)'

CM *7eht 'measuring cord'//'cuerda para medir'
SM *r+eht.aal 'mark, sign, foot-print'//'seña, huella'
   CM *7eht.a (vt) 'to measure it'//'medirlo'

pM *k'ut.u(u)b' 'fore-finger; hand-span'//'dedo índice; cuarta'

pM *k'ut (vt) 'to point at it, show it', which is the basis of *k'ut.u(u)b', is currently
   found only in EM, but it must have been present in pM and lost as a verb in the
   languages that currently lack a reflex of it. WAS has a nominalized reflex of pM
   *k'ut, /tx'uuty/ 'hand-span'.

6.21 Fire

pM *q'ahq' 'fire'//'fuego, lumbre'
   EM *q'a7q' 'fire'//'fuego, lumbre'

EM *sib' 'smoke'//'humo'
   LL *b'utz' 'smoke'//'humo'

pM *tya7nh 'ashes; quicklime'//'ceniza(s); cal'
   EM *chuun 'quicklime'//'cal'

pM *sii7 'firewood'//'leña'

6.22 Entertainment and ceremony

CM *7aala7s 'toy'//'juguete'

pM *b'ix 'dancing'//'baile'

CM *b'ity (vi) 'to sing'//'cantar'

pM *waj.b' 'musical instrument'//'instrumento músico'

pM *suub' 'flute, whistle'//'chirimía, flauta, pito'

CM *xaaq(-i) tyaj 'pine needles'//'juncia, hoja de pino'

6.23 Magic

pM *laab' 'enchantment, witching'//'encanto, brujería'

SM *poom 'copal incense'//'copal' (Bursera bipinnata, Bursera tomentosa)
[from pMS *po:mʉ7]

pM *war (vi) 'to sleep'//'dormir'
    CM *war.ib' ~ *war.ub' 'bed, sleeping-quarters'//'cama, dormitorio'

SM *wa(h)r 'animal spirit_companion/counterpart; shape-shifter'//'contraparte
    animal, tonal; nahual'
    [probably based on the root √war 'to sleep']

6.24 Clothing and adornment

SM *tyiinh 'cotton'//'algodón' (Gossypium)

SM *tuhx 'cottonseed'//'semilla de algodón'

SM *nooq' 'cotton (thread); clothing'//'(hilo de) algodón; ropa'

CM *tuhx=nooq' 'cotton'//'algodón'

SM *pet.eht 'spindlewhorl'//'malacate, huso'

SM *tz'is (vt) 'to sew it'//'coserlo, costurarlo'
    pM *tz'is.Vb' 'needle'//'aguja'
    CM *b'aaq 'needle'//'aguja' *BONE

pM *kem (vt) 'to weave it'//'tejerlo' [Though currently found only in EM, it has
    been borrowed into languages of Central Mexico, presumably from the ancestor
    of Wasteko as it made its way north to its long-time historical location, or after it
    established itself there and started influencing its new neighbors.]
    WM *jal (vt) 'to weave it'//'tejerlo'

CM *xih.ab' 'comb'//'peine'

pM *weex 'men's pants [with long legs, short legs, or no legs]'//'calzón'

SM *q'uu7 'nest; blanket'//'nido; cobija, chamarra'

SM *b'uhq 'clothing'//'ropa'

SM *k'ooj 'mask'//'máscara' [diffused]

pM *7uuh 'bead; necklace'//'perla, cuenta; collar, gargantilla'

SM *b'on (vt) 'to paint it, dye it'//'pintarlo, teñirlo'

SM *tz'ihb' "writing"//"escritura"
CM *tz'ihb'.a (vt) "to write it"//"ecribirlo"
["writing" cannot be the original meaning of this term, because writing emerged
in MA around 600 to 500 BCE (La Venta Stela 500 BCE; San José Mogote before
550 BCE). In some languages the reflex of *tz'ihb' also means 'stripes woven into
cloth', and that may reflect the term's original application.]

In 1519 Meso-America, cotton clothing was worn only by the privileged classes; the
unprivileged classes wore clothing made of agave fiber (pM *kiih) (Ludden 1997:esp.
11–14).

6.25 Materials

SM (Yu+WM) *toonh 'stone'//'piedra'
EM *7a7b'aj 'stone'//'piedra'

pM *tyaah 'obsidian'//'obsidiana'

SM *tyooq' 'flint'//'pedernal'

pM *k'aj/haanh/m (*j ~ *h, *nh ~ *m) 'string, cord, rope;
vine'//'cuerda, pita, lazo; bejuco'

6.26 Tools

pM *kaa7 'quern'//'metate, piedra de moler'

SM *u+q'ab' kaa7 'muller'//'mano de metate, mano de piedra'

CM *7aq'een 'wooden platform for quern support'//'tabla de molendero'

SM *hu7x 'whetstone'//'piedra de afilar' [Stone tools are sharpened with other types
of stone.]

CM *7ikaj 'axe'//'hacha'

pM *7ehb' (WAS+LL+QEQ) 'ladder'//'escalera'
EM *yooch 'ladder'//'escalera'
[Meso-American ladders are made by cutting notches in which to step in a log
that is then leaned up against the surface to be scaled.]

CM *lem 'mirror'//'espejo'

6.27 Containers

SM *chiim 'net bag; shoulder bag'//'red, matate; morral, bolsa'

CM *ty'u7uy 'bag'//'bolsa'

CM *xu7uk 'basket with handles'//'canasta con argollas/agarrador'

pM *mul (WAS+GK) 'water jug'//'cántaro'; 'water gourd'// 'tecomate'; 'gourd
dipper'//'jícara'

CM *q'i(h)b' 'water jar'//'cántaro, tinaja'

pM *la(a)q 'bowl'//'escudilla, plato hondo'

pM *tzuhh 'water gourd'//'tecomate'
[Note: The reconstruction *tzuhh does not violate the phonotactic
constraints of proto-Mayan; inasmuch as monosyllables can have the shape
*CVh, *CV:h, *CV7h, and *CVhC they can also have the shape *CVhh.
In any case the reconstruction offered is the one required by the sound
correspondences.]

SM *johm 'gourd dipper'//'guacal, jícara'

#tzimah 'gourd dipper or bowl'//'guacal, jícara'
[looks like pM but is a loan from pMS *tzima7. Since the sound correspondences
are not completely regular the data point to several borrowings after Mayan
diversified.]

CM *jukuub' 'dugout; trough'//'canoa; batea, comedero'

SM *tyem 'canoe, raft'//'canoa, balsa'

6.28 Furniture

SM *pohp 'mat'//'petate'

pM *ch'aaq 'bed; rack'//'cama; tapesco'

CM *7aab' 'hammock'//'hamaca' [introduced after 1300 CE]
*"There seems to be a Central Mayan word for hammock (*7a:b') but the word
may either have meant something else originally, or managed to spread after the
introduction of hammocks around 1300 CE"* (Kaufman 1976a:105). From Wikipedia
"hammock": '[H]ammocks . . . were not part of Classic era Maya civilization; they
were said to have arrived in the Yucatán from the Caribbean fewer than two centuries
before the Spanish conquest.']

SM *teem 'seat, bench'//'asiento, banco'
   CM *q'ahnh 'seat, bench'//'asiento, banco'

6.29 Structures

pM *7atyooty or *7atyuuty 'house; container'//'casa; recipiente'
SM *nhaah 'house; dwelling'//'casa; domicilio'

[*7atyooty and *nhaah are not synonyms, though they partially overlap. Both
are found in Yu, QaP, and GKi. In these languages the reflex of *nhaah is usually
not possessed. Other languages have only one of the two.]

SM *paat 'shack, hut'//'choza, jacal'

CM *q'aH.. 'bridge'//'puente'
   [*q'a7j(a).. GTz, GQa, GMa; *q'a7aam Kp; *q'ah QEQ]

pM *b'eeh 'road'//'camino' cf. *b'eh 'to go'

6.30 Miscellaneous

CM *7ar 'being there, existing'//'que está, que hay'

CM *laaj 'to come to an end'//'acabarse, terminarse'

CM *7ihq(atz) 'load'//'carga'
CM *7ihq.a (vt) 'to carry it'//'cargarlo'
   LL+WM *kuch (vt) 'to carry it'//'cargarlo'

CM *7ojtyaq.i (vt) 'to recognize it'//'conocerlo'

pM *watyik'/b' 'dream'//'sueño'

6.31 Day names of the Meso-American 260-day calendar

as manifested in Mayan languages [Kaufman 1988–1989ms].
   For the era addressed in this chapter – from proto-Mayan to the break-ups of WM and
EM – comparative Mayan linguistics provides more detailed data on the development
and diffusion of the Meso-American 260-day calendar than about any other early Mayan
cultural practices. Space restrictions make it impossible to develop this topic here; some
major results are presented in summary.
   In Kaufman 1988–2016 I postulate [passim] that the orginal set of twenty Meso-
American day names had the following meanings:

   1. CAYMAN, 2. WIND, 3. NIGHT, 4. IGUANA, 5. SNAKE, 6. DEATH, 7. DEER,
   8. RABBIT, 9. WATER, 10. COYOTE, 11. (HOWLER) MONKEY, 12. TOOTH,
   13. REED, 14. JAGUAR, 15. EAGLE, 16. (TURKEY) BUZZARD, 17. EARTH-
   QUAKE, 18. FLINT, 19. STORM, 20. MACAW.

In non-Mayan language groups of Meso-America, almost all day names are ordinary lexical items that agree closely with these meanings. Upon its adoption by Mayans, there was
considerable innovation in this system, far more than in any other linguistic or cultural group.

Two partly overlapping day-name systems, shown in Tables 4.2a and 4.2b, can be reconstructed for early stages of Mayan linguistic history.

A WM system can be reconstructed that is basically equivalent to what is found in Greater Q'anjob'alan languages. Justeson (p.c.) observed that departures in the Greater Tzeltalan subgroup of WM are largely restricted to names shared with Yukatekan; they reflect innovations and diffusion among (G)LL languages. The WM system takes us back at least to the breakup of WM around 600 BCE, and possibly earlier.

Note the 10 Western Mayan innovations from the general MA system: 2 NIGHT > WOT.ANH, 4 *IGUANA > K'ANA7, 5 SNAKE > 7AB'AQ, 6 DEATH > TYOX, 8 *RABBIT > LANHB'AT, 9 *WATER > MULUC, 10 DOG > COYOTE, 13 REED >

TABLE 4.2A RECONSTRUCTED MAYAN DAY NAMES. Day names are numbered according to the generally prevailing order in which they were cited in colonial sources. The names in caps are the glosses reconstructed by Kaufman (1988–89ms., 2001–2016ms.) for the original Meso-American day-name system. In the right column are the Mayan forms, with glosses when determinable, that can be projected to Southern Mayan (SM), Central Mayan (CM), Western Mayan (WM), Lowland Mayan (LL), Greater Lowland Mayan (GLL), and Eastern Mayan (EM).

Reconstructible Mayan Day Names

1. CAYMAN	SM *7iimox '?'	11. MONKEY	CM *b'a7tz' 'howler monkey' (< SM)
2. WIND	SM *7i7q' 'wind' (< pM)	12. TOOTH	EM *7eeh 'tooth' (< pM)
3. NIGHT	EM+Yuk *7a(h)q'ab'.a(a)l 'night' (< pM) WM *wot.anh 'a god name'	13. REED	LL+WM *b'e7n '?' EM *7aaj 'reed' (< SM)
4. IGUANA	WM+Yuk *k'an. '?' EM k'aat 'burning; net'	14. JAGUAR	SM *hi7ix '?'
5. SNAKE	EM+LL *kaan 'snake' (< pM)	15. EAGLE	CM *tz'ikin 'bird' (< pM) LL #men '?'
6. DEATH	EM+Yuk *kam.eeh 'dying' [only as a day name] (<pM *kam 'to die') WM *tyox '?'	16. BUZZARD	EM *7aj=maq '?' WM+Yuk *kab' 'wax' (< SM)
7. DEER	SM *kehj 'deer' LL #manik' '?' [see discussion below]	17. EARTHQUAKE	EM no7oj '?' LL+WM *kab' 'earth' (< pM)
8. RABBIT	LL+WM *lanhb'at '?' EM *q'an.iil ~ *q'an.eel '?'	18. FLINT	CM *tinhahx '?' LL *7eHtz'na(X)b' '?' [*H = *: or *7]
9. WATER	LL+WM *muluC 'water jug/ jar/gourd' (< pM); EM *tohj 'payment'?	19. STORM	SM *kahoq 'thunder' (< pM)
10. COYOTE	EM *tz'i7 'dog' (< SM); GLL #7ok (< pM *7o7q 'coyote')	20. MACAW	LL+WM *7aajaaw 'lord' (an expanded/derived form 7ajw.aal is found in GTz and MCH) (< pM) EM *(juun) 7aj=pujb' '(one) blowgunner'

TABLE 4.2B CONTRASTING WESTERN AND EASTERN MAYAN DAY-NAME SYSTEMS.

Differences in Mayan day-name systems largely follow the division between the two branches of Central Mayan. A small proportion of day-name vocabulary has diffused within Western Mayan, but the system as a whole plausibly existed in proto-WM. There is much greater and probably later diffusion within Eastern Mayan, but the Eastern Mayan system as presented is not questionable; see text.

The Western and Eastern Mayan day-name systems

WESTERN MAYAN		EASTERN MAYAN
1 **7iimox** [god]	=	1 **7iimox** [god]
2 **7i7q'** 'wind'	=	2 **7i7q'** 'wind'
3 **wot.anh** [god]		3 **7ahq'ab',aal** 'night'
4 **k'ana7** [god]		4 **k'aat** 'burning; net'
5 **7ab'aq** [god]		5 **kaan** 'snake'
6 **tyox** [god]		6 **kam.eeh** 'dying'?
7 **kehj** 'deer'	=	7 **kehj** 'deer'
8 **lanhb'at** [god]		8 **q'anEEl** '?'
9 **muluC** 'water jar'		9 **tohj** 'payment'
10 **7o7q** 'coyote'		10 **tz'i7** 'dog'
11 **b'a7tz'** 'howler monkey'	=	11 **b'a7tz'** 'howler monkey'
12 **?7ehub'** '?'		12 **7eeh** 'tooth'
13 **b'e7n** [god]		13 **7aaj** 'reed'
14 **hi7ix** [god]	=	14 **hi7ix** [god]
15 **tz'ikin** 'bird'	=	15 **tz'ikin** 'bird'
16 **kab'.in** 'wax'		16 **7aj=maq** '?' [god]
17 **kab'** 'earth'		17 **no7oj** '?' [god]
18 **tinhahx** [god]	=	18 **tinhahx** [god]
19 **kahoq** 'storm'	=	19 **kahoq** 'storm'
20 **7aajaaw** 'lord'		20 **7aj=puhb'** 'blowgunner'

B'E7N, 16 *BUZZARD > WAX, 20 *MACAW > LORD. 1 CAYMAN > *7IIMOX, 14 JAGUAR > *HI7IX and 15 EAGLE > BIRD are pan-Mayan.

Quoted from Kaufman 1988–2016:162–3.

Eastern Mayan languages share a number of unique cognate terms; these reflect numerous innovations from the general MA day-name vocabulary:

Note the 7 Eastern Mayan innovations 4 *IGUANA > BURNING, 8 *RABBIT > YELLOWNESS/RIPENESS/BELOVEDNESS/FATNESS, 10 WATER > *TOHJ, 15 EAGLE > BIRD, *16 BUZZARD > *7AJ=MAQ, 17 QUAKE > *NO7OJ, 20 *MACAW > BLOWGUNNER. 1 CAYMAN > *7IIMOX, 14 JAGUAR > *HI7IX and 15 EAGLE > BIRD are pan-Mayan.

This system is obviously ancient. Three Mam-Awakateko day names that are candidates for pre-proto-Mamean origins: are *k'ach BURNING (< *IGUANA), *chooj PAYMENT (< *WATER), and *chi7j '?' (< *FLINT) show a shift of earlier *t to Greater Mamean *ch, which could be as early as 600 BCE, or a few centuries later. The agreement among EM day names is based in part on later diffusion among EM languages. The Sakapulteko names seem to have been borrowed whole hog from K'ichee7. Several Ixil names are borrowings from K'ichee7. In Mam-Awakateko, the word *kameey DEATH seems to show a shift of earlier *h to *y, something that characterizes Kaqchikel and Tz'utujiil, and Mam-Awakateko *7iiq' WIND should be 7i7q'* if it were a native word.

Thus it seems as if the Eastern Mayan calendrical names could be of common Greater K'ichee7an (before 600 BCE) origin, diffused to the other Eastern Mayan languages."

Since we have already adopted the position that the MA day-name system was adopted in Mayan languages only after WM and EM had become different from each other, we can see that four day names – *7iimox, *hi7ix, and *tinhahx, which have no known meaning other than the names of days 1, 14, and 18, and *tz'ikin 'bird' rather than 'eagle' for day 15 – are found in both the WM and EM systems, and suggest diffusion.

Significantly, in the Mayan adoption of the MA calendar about half of the day names were replaced by specialized vocabulary with no known referent except the day itself. It can safely be said that most Meso-American day-name lists do not have such a high proportion of uninterpretable terms as any Mayan list taken at random. This must mean something, but what it does mean is not yet clear. The Eastern Mayan list has only five such items (Cayman, Rabbit, Jaguar, Earthquake, Flint), but this is 25 percent of the list, and still outside the range of uninterpretable terms in the typical non-Mayan MA day-name list. At this moment these uninterpretable terms can not be traced to any non-Mayan language, though such an effort might pan out in the future.

I suspect that most of these terms were names of gods associated with the corresponding day. This is suggested by the WM day name *wot.anh, the name of the third day, usually 'night' in other calendars; it is also attested as the name of a god <votan> in colonial sources dealing with Western Mayan communities. Unfortunately, pre-Columbian god names are especially poorly reported for the Western Mayan region.

My current working hypothesis (Kaufman MS) is that each day name refers to a particular episode in myths that were at least partially shared throughout MA – and that the day names that are god names refer to gods that participated in the story/episode called up by the day name. The best example I have so far of a shared myth is day 20, which refers to the story of how two enchanted boys (the "young lords") mortally wounded the demigod Seven Macaw in the jaw with a blow-gun pellet. Some languages name this day 'macaw' [Misteko], some call it 'blow-gunner' [EM], some call it 'lord' [LL+WM]; some call it 'flower' [Nawa], for reasons I cannot fathom so far. The first three terms refer to parts of a visual representation of the blow-gun incident, of which at least one instance has been documented outside Mayaland, for example, in a mural from the Mixteca.

It is obvious that there is no, and never was a, single Mayan day-name system. The calendar was adopted by Mayans, and probably invented by non-Mayans, after the Mayan languages had already diversified into Wa, Yu, WM, and EM branches; distinct though similar systems of day names were adopted in the various groups from outside sources that have not yet been identified, but in some cases plausibly from one Mayan group to another. What we can reconstruct about how non-Mayan peoples contribute to the systems we find in play in the ethnohistorical record, and in epigraphic Mayan texts, is mostly a task for the future.

6.32 A smattering of symbolic morphemes

Those that got registered in the PMED

GK+Qa #Lep 'lightning'//'relámpago'

GK+GQ #Lup 'to fly'//'volar'

CM #t'uL 'drop'//'gota'

CM *b'ul 'frothy, bubbling'//'espuma; borbotear'

EM+Qa #joR 'snoring'//'ronquido'

EM #Tool.V (vt) 'to roll it'//'rodarlo'

EM+ #Toq (vi) 'to break in half'//'quebrarse en dos'

EM+GQ *mee7 'sheep'//'carnero'. The referent cannot be pre-Columbian.

pM *chiC.chiC 'rattle'//'chinchín'

pM *hat'is ~ *hat'ix ~ *hach'ix, etc. 'sneezing'//'estornudar'
    CM #hat'is
    EM+Hue #hat'ix
    GK #(h)ach'ix-am
    GLL #ha7=tzihaam

CM *ty'iw 'to peep (as a chick)'//'piar'

7 CONCLUSION AND ADMONITIONS

How can the material in this chapter be used apart from the way I have used it? The short answer is that you should refer to Kaufman with Justeson (2003), because that is where virtually all the data is that I have used in the reconstructions cited here, plus a good deal more. As stated, most reconstructible verbs and body-part names have been left out of this study, because they do not reveal anything characteristic about the proto-Mayan habitat or culture. Admittedly, the fact that 'hand' may include 'forearm' is not merely a boring factoid, but it is hardly unique or characteristic of Mayan. Indeed, one could undertake a study of just the body-part and body-product terms of Mayan and make an interesting contribution to the literature. A study of terms relating to the evaluation of behavior would be interesting. A study of kinds of speaking would be rewarding.

As for the data that I have presented here, more inferences could be squeezed out of the data than what I have tried to do. I would urge the interested scholar with: *While considering all the available relevant data, do not overinterpret it*. For one thing, the data are not complete, and the results of a reconstruction are never complete. When you perceive a problem that cannot be solved without more relevant data, *go out and get that data*, and if that data is not to be had, be resigned to the fact that some problems cannot be solved, and some questions should not be asked. In the meantime, do not jump to conclusions.

Another issue I urge my readers to consider: *steer clear of reductionism;* do not claim that sets of entities that share some striking features are in fact the same entity – when they are not the same. Examine all the available data, and do not jump to conclusions. A problem that you cannot solve today may be elegantly solved by somebody else tomorrow or the day after.

An earlier version of this study was presented at the 15th Spring Workshop on Theory and Method in Linguistic Reconstruction, 14–16 March 2014, Linguistics Department, University of Michigan, Ann Arbor.

ACKNOWLEDGMENTS

John Justeson produced the figures in consultation with me. I thank him for feedback on the content of this chapter. He has pointed out cases where I could make things clearer, and pointed out relevant facts that I forgot to mention, and at least one fact that I was unaware of. His input was especially helpful on the discussion of the Mayan day names.

REFERENCES

1. General bibliography

Benveniste, Émile. 1973. *Indo-European language and society*. Index by Jean Lallot. Translated by Elizabeth Palmer. Miami: University of Miami Press.

Campbell, Lyle. 1979. "Middle American languages." In *The languages of native America: historical and comparative assessment*, ed. by Lyle Campbell and Marianne, 902–1000. Austin: University of Texas Press.

Can Pixabaj, Telma Angelina. 2007. *Jkemiik Yoloj li Uspanteko: Gramática Uspanteka*. Guatemala City: OKMA and Cholsamaj.

Chase, Diane Z., and Arlen F. Chase. 2012. "Complex societies in the Southern Maya lowlands: their development and florescence in the archaeological record." In *Oxford handbook of Mesoamerican archaeology*, ed. by Deborah Nichols and Christopher A. Pool, 255–67. New York: Oxford University Press.

Childe, V. Gordon. 1926. *The Aryans: A study of Indo-European origins*. London: Kegan Paul.

Cholotio, Andrés, and Pablo García Ixmatá. 1998. *Gramática descriptiva del idioma Tzutujil*. Antigua Guatemala: Proyecto Lingüístico Francisco Marroquín.

Cu Cab, Carlos Humbero, Juan Carlos Sacba Caal, Juventino Pérez Alonzo, María Beatriz Par Sapóm, Marina Magdalena Ajcac Cruz, Matilde Eustaquio Caal Ical, Nikte' María Juliana Sis Iboy, Pakal José Obispo Rodríguez Guaján, Saqijix Candelaria López Ixcoy, Teodoro Cirilo Ixcoy Herrera, Walter Rolando Pérez Morales, Waykan José Gonzalo and Benito Pérez. 2003. *Maya'choltzij: Vocabulario comparativo de los idiomas Mayas de Guatemala*. Guatemala City: OKMA and Cholsamaj.

Dumézil, Georges. 1958. *L'Idéologie tripartite des Indo-Européens*. Brussels: Latomus.

England, Nora. 1991. "Changes in basic word order in Mayan languages." *International Journal of American Linguistics* 57: 446–86.

Evans, Susan Toby. 2012. "Time and space boundaries: chronologies and regions in Mesoamerica." In *Oxford handbook of Mesoamerican archaeology*, ed. by Deborah Nichols and Christopher A. Pool, 114–26. Oxford: Oxford University Press.

Fox, James A. 1978. "Proto-Mayan accent, morpheme structure constraints, and velar innovations." PhD diss., University of Chicago.

Gamkrelidze, Thomas V., and Vjačeslav Ivanov. 1984. *Indo-European and the Indo-Europeans: a reconstruction and historical analysis of a proto-language and proto-culture. Part I: The text. Part II: Bibliography, indexes*. Preface by Roman Jakobson. Translated by Johanna Nichols (Trends in Linguistics. Studies and Monographs [TiLSM] 80). Berlin: De Gruyter Mouton.

García Ixmatá, Pablo. 1997. *Rukeemik ja Tz'utujiil Chii': Gramática Tz'utujiil*. Guatemala City: Cholsamaj.

García Matzar, Pedro, and José Obispo Rodríguez Guaján. 1997. *Rukemik ri Kaqchikel chi': Gramática Kaqchikel*. Guatmala City: Cholsamaj.

Hammond, Norman. 2000. "The Maya lowlands: pioneer farmers to merchant princes." In *The Cambridge history of the native peoples of the Americas. Volume II: Mesoamerica, part 1*, ed. by Richard E. W. Adams, 197–249. Cambridge: Cambridge University Press.

Justeson, John, William Norman, Lyle Campbell, and Terrence Kaufman. 1985. *The foreign impact on lowland Mayan language and script*. New Orleans: Middle American Research Institute of Tulane University.

Kaufman, Terrence. 1964. "Materiales lingüísticos para el estudio de las relaciones internas y externas de la familia de idiomas mayanos." In *Desarrollo Cultural de los Mayas*, ed. by Evon Z Vogt, 81–136. Mexico City: UNAM Seminario de Cultura Maya. Reprinted 1971.

Kaufman, Terrence. 1969a. "Some recent hypotheses on Mayan diversification." *Working Paper no. 26a*, Language-Behavior Research Laboratory, University of California, Berkeley.

Kaufman, Terrence. 1969b. "Teco – a new Mayan language." *IJAL* 35: 154–74.

Kaufman, Terrence. 1970. "Posición del tzeltal y del tzotzil en la familia lingüística mayance." In *Ensayos de Antropología en la Zona Central de Chiapas*, ed. by Norman McQuown and Julian Pitt-Rivers, 171–84. Mexico: Instituto Nacional Indigenista.

Kaufman, Terrence. 1971. *Tzeltal phonology and morphology*. Berkeley: University of California Publications in Linguistics No. 61.

Kaufman, Terrence. 1972. *El Proto-Tzeltal-Tzotzil: Fonología Comparada y Diccionario reconstruído* (Centro de Estudios Mayas Cuaderno 5). Mexico: UNAM Centro de Estudios Mayas.

Kaufman, Terrence. 1974. *Idiomas de Mesoamérica* (Seminario de Integración Social Guatemalteca, Publicación 33). Guatemala City: Ministerio de Educación.

Kaufman, Terrence. 1976a. "Archaeological and linguistic correlations in Mayaland and associated areas of Meso-America." *World Archaeology* 8: 101–18.

Kaufman, Terrence. 1976b. "New Mayan languages in Guatemala; Sacapultec, Sipacapa, and others." In *Mayan linguistics*, vol. 1, ed. by Marlys McClaran, 67–89. Los Angeles: UCLA American Indian Studies Center.

Kaufman, Terrence. 1979. "Pre-Columbian borrowing in and out of Huastec." In *American Indian and Indoeuropean studies: papers in honor of Madison S. Beeler*, ed. by Kathryn Klar, Margaret Langdon, and Shirley Silver, 101–12. Berlin: De Gruyter Mouton.

Kaufman, Terrence. 1985. "Aspects of Huastec dialectology and historical phonology." *International Journal of American Linguistics* 51: 473–6.

Kaufman, Terrence. 1990. "Algunos Rasgos Estructurales de los Idiomas Mayances con Referencia Especial al K'iche'." In *Lecturas sobre la Lingüística Maya*, ed. by Nora C. England and Stephen R. Elliott, 59–114. Antigua Guatemala: Centro de Investigaciones Regionales de Mesoamérica (CIRMA).

Kaufman, Terrence. 1994. "Symbolism and change in the sound system of Huastec." In *Sound symbolism*, ed. by Leanne Hinton, Johanna Nichols, and John J. Ohala, 63–75. Cambridge: Cambridge University Press.

Kaufman, Terrence, and Lyle Campbell. 1985. "Mayan linguistics: where are we now?" *Annual Review of Anthropology* 14: 187–98.

Kaufman, Terrence, with John Justeson. 2003. *A preliminary Mayan etymological dictionary*. www.famsi.org; www.albany.edu/pdlma.

Kaufman, Terrence, and John Justeson. 2007. "The history of the word for Cacao in ancient Mesoamerica." *Ancient Mesoamerica* 18: 193–237.

Kaufman, Terrence, and John Justeson. 2008. "The Epi-Olmec language and its neighbors." In *Classic-period cultural currents in Southern and Central Veracurz*, ed. by Philip J. Arnold and Christopher A. Pool, 55–84. Washington, DC: Dumbarton Oaks.

Kaufman, Terrence, and William Norman. 1984. "An outline of proto-Cholan phonology, morphology, and vocabulary." In *Phoneticism in Mayan hieroglyphic writing*, ed. by Lyle Campbell and John Justeson, 77–166. (Publication No. 9, Institute for Mesoamerican Studies). SUNY, The University at Albany.

Law, Danny. 2014. *Language contact, inherited similarity and social difference: The story of linguistic interaction in the Maya lowlands*. Amsterdam: Benjamins.

López Ixcoy, Candelaria Dominga. 1997. *Ri ukemiik ri K'ichee' Chii': Gramática K'ichee'*. Guatemala City: Cholsamaj.

Ludden, Andrea. 1997. *Aztec garments: From birth to fulfilment*. http://lasa.international .pitt.edu/LASA97/ludden.pdf

Mallory, J. P. 1989. *In search of the Indo-Europeans: language, archaeology and myth*. London: Thames & Hudson.

Mó Isém, Romelia. 2007. *Rikemik li Tujaal Tziij: Gramática Sakapulteka*. Guatemala City: OKMA and Cholsamaj.

Mora-Marín, David F. 2005. "Kaminaljuyu Stela 10: script classification and linguistic affiliation." *Ancient Mesoamerica* 16: 63–87.

Pérez, Eduardo, and Odilio Jiménez. 1997. *Ttxoolil qyool Mam: Gramática Mam*. Guatemala City: Cholsamaj.

Pérez Vail, José Reginaldo. 2007. *Xtxolil Yool B'a'aj: Gramática Tektiteka*. Guatemala City: OKMA and Cholsamaj.

Robertson, John S. 1993. "The origins and development of the Huastec pronouns." *International Journal of American Linguistics* 59: 294–314.

Robertson, John, and Stephen Houston. 2003. "El problema del Wasteko: Una perspetiva lingüística y arqueológica." In *XVI Simposio de Investigaciones Arqueológicas en Guatemala, 2002*, ed. by J. P. Laporte, B. Arroyo, H. Escobedao and H. Mejía, 714–24. Guatemala City: Museo Nacional de Arqueología y Etnología.

Rojas Ramírez, Maximiliano, Hilario Ramírez López, and Eva Ramírez Jiménez. 1993. *Gramática del idioma Mam*. La Antigua Guatemala: Proyecto Lingüístico Francisco Marroquín.

Rosenswig, Robert M. 2006. "Sedentism and food production in early complex societies of the Soconusco, Mexico." *World Archaeology* 38: 329–54.

Santos Nicolás, José Francico, and José González Benito Pérez. 1998. *Rukorb'aal Poqom q'orb'al: Gramática Poqom/Poqomam*. Guatemala City: Cholsamaj.

Schrader, Otto. 1883. *Sprachvergleichung und Urgeschichte: Linguistisch-historische Beiträge zur Erforschung des indogermanischen Altertums*, 1st edition. Jena: H. Costenoble 1883, 2nd edition. 1890, 3rd edition. 1906.

Stanton, Travis W., and Tracy Ardren. 2005. "The middle formative of Yucatán in context: the view from Yaxuná." *Ancient Mesoamerica* 16: 213–28.

Tzul, Julio Alberto, and Alfonso Tzinmaj Cacao. 2001. *Gramátical del idioma Q'eqchi'*. La Antigua Guatemala: Proyecto Lingüístico Francisco Marroquín.

2. Unpublished manuscripts by Terrence Kaufman

Kaufman, Terrence. 1974ms. *Ixil Dictionary*, computer printout. Irvine: University of California.

Kaufman, Terrence. 1974ms. "Some issues, substantive and otherwise, in the classifi-cation of the Mayan languages." Paper given at the annual meetings of the American Anthropological Association, 1974.

Kaufman, Terrence. 1978ms. "The current state of Mayan comparative phonology." Paper given at Third Mayan Workshop, Cobán, 5+ pp.

Kaufman, Terrence. 1984ms. "Cross-currents of grammatical innovation in the Mayan languages, with especial reference to Tojolabal." Paper given at The Language of Writ-ing in the Mayan Region, University of Chicago.

Kaufman, Terrence. 1986ms. "Some structural traits of the Mayan languages, with espe-cial reference to K'ichee7," Published in Spanish translation as Kaufman, Terrence. 1990. "Algunos Rasgos Estructurales de los Idiomas Mayances con Referencia Espe-cial al K'iche'." In *Lecturas sobre la Linguistica Maya*, ed. by Nora C. England and Stephen R. Elliott, 59–114. Antigua Guatemala: CIRMA.

Kaufman, Terrence. 1986–89ms. "Mayan comparative studies." Unpublished manuscript.

Kaufman, Terrence. 1988–89ms. "The day-names of the Meso-American calendar." Pre-sented at Santa Barbara conference on Mayan writing, February 1989.

Kaufman, Terrence. 1990ms. "Some preliminary hypotheses on the structure of the NP in proto-Mayan." Presented at Third Spring Workshop on Theory and Method in Lin-guistic Reconstruction, 6–8 April 1990, Pittsburgh, Pennsylvania. Also presented at Symposium "Current Issues in Mayan Linguistics." Kentucky Foreign Language Con-ference, Lexington. April 1990.

Kaufman, Terrence. 2001ms. "Language contact in preclassic Meso-America and the lan-guages of Teotihuacán." Paper delivered at the annual meetings of the Society for Amer-ican Archaeology, New Orleans, 19 April 2001. An expanded version was presented in two 2-hour sessions at the Third Morris Swadesh Colloquium, UNAM-IIA, August 29, 2001. PDLMA. www.albany.edu/pdlma. The content of this paper was also delivered in a 6-hour session at CIESAS in San Cristóbal de Las Casas on July 17, 2002.

Kaufman, Terrence. 2001–2016ms. *Olmecs, teotihuacaners, and toltecs: language his-tory and language contact in Meso-America.*

Kaufman, Terrence. 2014. *Mayan comparative studies: the noun phrase.*

Kaufman, Terrence. 2015. *Mayan comparative studies [combined file].* PDLMA. http://www.albany.edu/ims/Kaufman-Mayan%20Comparative%20Studies.pdf

Kaufman, Terrence, and Brent Berlin. 1962. *Tzeltal-Tzotzil linguistic acculturation.*

3. Lexical databases by Terrence Kaufman

Kaufman, Terrence. Mochó lexical database. 5600+ items. Based on field work conducted in Summer 1967, Fall 1967, and Summer 1968. Databased in ShoeBox.

Kaufman, Terrence. Tuzanteco lexical database. 4800+ items. Based on field work con-ducted in Fall 1967 and Summer 1968. Databased in ShoeBox.

Kaufman, Terrence. Ixil lexical database. 8000+ items. Based on field work conducted in Fall 1968, Summer 1969, and Summer 1970. Databased in ShoeBox.

Kaufman, Terrence. Chamula Tzotzil lexical database. 3700+ items. Based on field work conducted in Winter-Spring-Summer 1960, Summer 1961, and Summer 1962. Data-based in ShoeBox.

4. Terrence Kaufman questionnaires

Kaufman, Terrence. 1962. *Mayan Vocabulary Survey*, revised 1964. Has 1436 glosses plus about 100 grammatical and phonological questions – specifically about Mayan languages. Has been used by several Mayanists.

Kaufman, Terrence. 1970. *Mayan Dialect Survey (Cuestionario Lingüístico para la Investigación de Variaciones Dialectales en las Lenguas Mayances de Guatemala)*, revised 1971. Devised to collect diagnostic data for dialect classification in Mayan languages. Has about 600 glosses, including all in Swadesh (100-word), Mayers (*Languages of Guatemala*), Stoll (*Ethnographie der Guatemala*), and Sapper (*Das Nördliche Mittel-Amerika*) as well as glosses of known diagnostic value for distinguishing dialects in Mayan languages. Includes complete noun and verb paradigms as well as relational nouns, question words, equational nouns, and other grammatical phenomena typical of Mayan languages. Used by PLFM and several other Mayanists.

Kaufman, Terrence. 1970. *Kaufman's Basic Concept List on Historical Principles*, revised 1973. Based on a keypunched collation of all obtainable "diagnostic lists" (about 25) and the glosses in all comparative linguistic studies involving at least three languages and between 200 and 750 reconstructed forms (about 35). The list at an early stage had about 2500 glosses and 200–300 morphosyntactic points; now pared down to about 700 items. Useable world-wide.

Kaufman, Terrence. 1983. *Huastec dialect survey questionnaire*, ca 1200 lexical queries and ca 200 grammatical queries. Applied in 18 towns Summer 1983 and Summer 1984. A shortened version was applied with two additional speakers from each town in Summer 1986 and Summer 1987.

CHAPTER 5

LANGUAGE CONTACTS WITH(IN) MAYAN

Danny Law

1 INTRODUCTION

It is increasingly clear that the history of Mayan languages is one of almost constant vigorous, and at times turbulent, linguistic exchange. The outcomes of that history have varied according to the languages involved and the sociohistorical context of the linguistic contact. Documented linguistic outcomes include not only borrowed lexical items, but also the direct transfer of grammatical morphology, phonological innovations, and morphosyntactic and semantic patterns. The following sections briefly discuss colonial and post-colonial contact with Spanish and contact with non-Mayan indigenous languages, Mixe-Zoquean in particular, but also at a more superficial level Nahuan, Totonacan, and Oto-Manguean. Then, the chapter reviews changes due to contact among Mayan languages, particularly in the Huehuetenango and lowland Mayan spheres of linguistic interaction, followed by a discussion of contact and genetic relationships for Tojol-ab'al and Huastec. The chapter concludes with a discussion of what the observed linguistic outcomes and ethnographic, historical, and archaeological evidence might tell us about the possible mechanisms through which language contact molded the shape of Mayan languages.

2 CONTACT WITH SPANISH

After nearly half a millennium of colonial contact with Spanish, it is unsurprising that Mayan languages have been affected. The reverse is also true: local varieties of Spanish often at least partially reflect influence from local indigenous languages, though it is not always easy in practice to distinguish that influence from non-standard forms derived from Spanish archaisms or from L2 acquisition errors not due to a Mayan L1 interference.

2.1 Mayan influence on regional Spanish

Lexical borrowings from Mayan languages into Spanish can be found, varying from region to region. These are primarily nouns and some adjectives (Escobar 2013), though Yucatec Spanish has reportedly borrowed the diminutive particle *chan* from Yucatec Maya (Suárez Molina 1945). Lexical borrowings from Mayan into local varieties of Spanish are often only minimally accommodated phonologically, so borrowed words often do not follow the phonotactic restrictions of native Spanish words (Lope Blanch 1987). Other forms of phonological interference typical of adult language shift are also common in local varieties of Spanish, such as the adoption of Mayan prosodic features (Michnowicz and Barnes 2013), articulation of segments with Mayan-like place and manner (for example, the articulation of /ɲ/ as a nasal-glide sequence /nj/; Yager 1982), and Mayan-like allophonic variation (no fricativization of voiced stops intervocalically, merging of /f/ and /p/ word-initially, deletion of intervocalic velar fricatives, word-final nasals realized as bilabials in Yucatec Spanish, weakening or deletion of unstressed vowels, and insertion of word-initial glottal stops; see Lope Blanch 1987; Michnowicz 2012, 2015 for more discussion).

Some instances of structural transfer from Mayan languages to local Spanish varieties have also been proposed, including the loss of gender and number distinctions in unstressed person clitics (García Tesoro 2006; García Tesoro 2010), redundant possessive pronouns in structures such as *su carro de Juan* 'his car of John', and the maintenance, and possible increase in frequency, of old Spanish indefinite article + possessive structures (*un mi amigo, una mi tacita de café*) (Martin 1978, 1985; Company Company 2005). In most of the cases of structural change in local Spanish varieties, it is difficult to establish whether the feature is due to L1 interference (also referred to as substratum influence) or to so-called 'interlanguage' features that are the result of imperfect acquisition of a target L2 language.

2.2 Spanish influence on Mayan

The linguistic influence of Spanish on Mayan is similar in type, though higher in degree. It is primarily lexical but there is evidence that Spanish has influenced the shape of Mayan languages at other linguistic levels as well. Most Mayan languages have borrowed a fairly large number of nouns from Spanish. Spanish verbs are frequently used in Mayan languages, but as infinitive forms in a light verb construction with a matrix 'to do' verb. Romero (2006:152–3) noted for K'iche' that infinitive verbs from Spanish were rarely phonologically accommodated, suggesting that most uses of these forms are code switches. Wichmann and Hull (2009) surveyed lexical borrowing in Q'eqchi' and found that roughly 10 percent of their lexical corpus consisted of loanwords from Spanish, and all but one of those were nouns. In fact, they report, nearly 20 percent of Q'eqchi' nouns in their corpus had been borrowed from Spanish.

In light of the severity of Spanish colonial and postcolonial political and cultural oppression in Latin America in general, non-lexical (structural or grammatical) influence from Spanish on Mayan languages appears rather modest, and fairly recent. Studies of language acquisition (Pye 2013), and sociolinguistics (Romero 2006) have shown that even in communities with extensive Spanish presence and ongoing language shift, syntactic or structural influence from Spanish is low. In some communities, the degree of Spanish grammatical influence is becoming even lower due to hyperdifferentiation deriving from ideologies of linguistic and ethnic difference and resistance to Spanish influence (Barrett 2008). Nevertheless, structural influence from Spanish has been observed. Mayan languages have adopted numerous discourse particles, conjunctions, complementizers, and the like from Spanish, including *pero, porque, entonces, pues, o*, and *y* (Brody 1987). These were once considered grammatical morphemes, and more resistant to borrowing, but subsequent research has shown them to be very commonly shared through contact around the world (Matras 2007). Additionally, a variety of syntactic features in Mayan languages have been argued in the literature to be calques of Spanish structures. The development of periphrastic passives (Montgomery-Anderson 2010), the grammaticalization of 'to go' verbs to refer to future events, and perhaps the apparently recent, independent development of definite articles and noun-adjective word order in some Mayan languages may be the result of Spanish influence. Such cases are hard to prove with any degree of confidence, however. These changes all follow cross-linguistically well-trodden paths of grammaticalization, and the pervasive presence of Spanish removes the possibility of clues based on the geographical distribution of such innovations.

3 CONTACT WITH OTHER INDIGENOUS LANGUAGES

While Spanish contact is certainly an important part of the history of language contact in the Mayan language family, the linguistic traces of contact with other indigenous languages of the Americas, and with other Mayan languages, are a rich area for investigation into the pre-Columbian and colonial history of the Mayan family. Mayan contacts with other indigenous families, inferred primarily from loanwords, have been used as evidence of historical relationship between Mayan speakers and most of their pre-Columbian neighbors, including Xinkan, Lenkan, Totonacan, Oto-Manguean (particularly Zapotecan and perhaps Chiapaneco), Nahuan, and Mixe-Zoquean. The Mayan family is part of the so-called Mesoamerican linguistic area. Campbell et al. (1986) defined this area with five features that they argued have roughly the same geographical distribution: similar nominal possession strategy, the use of relational nouns, a (historically) vigesimal numeral system, non-verb-final basic word order (and lack of switch reference), and a variety of semantic calques. However, none of these features are found universally in the languages of the region, and most are found outside of the region as well. It might be more accurate to say that within the region, the proposed "Mesoamerican" linguistic features are found more frequently than they are outside of the region. In fact, the most widely distributed of these features within Mesoamerica is the vigesimal numeral system, which one might argue to be as much technological (i.e. learned through instruction) as linguistic. The extent to which the Mesoamerican linguistic area (and indeed, linguistic areas in general) reflects some common underlying historical cause or mechanism of change is the subject of ongoing debate, but it is very likely that the defining features of the Mesoamerican linguistic area, to the extent that they accurately capture the linguistic lay of the land, reflect a long history of cultural exchange. A great deal of new data has become available since this pioneering work on Mesoamerica as a linguistic area, and reanalysis of patterns of linguistic similarity would doubtless refine our picture of the complex linguistic history of the region. In particular, more research on historical contact between specific Mayan and non-Mayan indigenous languages, rather than the simple mapping of the geographical distribution of linguistic features, is needed to begin to trace the development of these large-scale linguistic patterns and their historical origins.

Seemingly at odds with the fame of Mesoamerican linguistic interaction is the assertion that Mesoamerican languages, including Mayan, generally manifest cross-linguistically low levels of lexical borrowing (Kaufman and Justeson 2009:222). Nevertheless, several authors have identified a fairly sizeable body of loanwords both in and from Mayan languages (Campbell and Kaufman 1976; Justeson et al. 1985). Campbell and Kaufman (1976) use fifty widespread lexical borrowings that they attribute to Mixe-Zoquean as evidence that the Olmec civilization conducted its affairs in Mixe-Zoquean. The early date for loanwords that a link with the Olmec civilization would require has been contested (Wichmann 1999), as has the Mixe-Zoquean origin of some of the proposed loans, but it is nevertheless clear that Mixe-Zoquean speakers have had a substantial impact on Mesoamerican languages, and particularly on Mayan. In addition to several lexical borrowings, apparently from different times, it has been argued that some Mayan languages have imported grammatical material from Mixe-Zoquean languages, including the Mixe-Zoquean third person ergative *'i-, which appears to have been borrowed into Chol and Ixil, and more speculatively, pre-Awakatek and pre-Q'eqchi', and the Chiapas Zoque ergative case marker *= 'is*, which appears to be the source of the third person ergative *s-*, *'is-*, and *x-* in Q'anjob'alan and Tseltalan languages (Kaufman and Justeson 2009:222). In addition, a prenominal relative clause-marking enclitic *=bä* in Chol appears to have been borrowed from Zoquean (Martinez 2007:179), and an iterative reduplicated root plus the suffix *-na* in Chontal and Chol for affect verbs is borrowed from Zoquean *ROOT.ROOT-na:y'* (Kaufman and Justeson 2009:222).

Zavala (2000, 2002) looks at syntactic similarities between Mixe-Zoquean and Mayan languages and argues that grammatical influence goes in both directions. For example, several Cholan-Tseltalan and Q'anjob'alan languages, as well as several Mixe-Zoquean languages, have auxiliary verbs of motion and aspect that Zavala argues were copied from Mayan into Mixe-Zoquean languages. On the other hand, a distinctive pattern of incorporated secondary predicates found in Chol and Huastec, spoken on either side of the Mixe-Zoquean geographical range, is clearly borrowed from Mixe-Zoquean into these two Mayan languages.

In some cases, the direction of borrowing is unclear or contested. Another syntactic similarity between many Mayan and Mixe-Zoquean languages, the grammaticalization of verbs of motion as directional complements to main verbs, is clearly areally shared. It is found in all Mixe-Zoquean languages and many Mayan languages, excluding Huastecan, Chontal, Cholti and Ch'orti', Q'eqchi', and Yucatecan. Kaufman and Justeson (2009:222) assert that this feature was "probably the result of influence on Mayans by Mije-Sokeans." While they do not enumerate arguments to support this, one argument in favor of this direction of influence is that the feature is found throughout the Mixe-Zoquean family, but is missing in two branches of Mayan (Yucatecan and Huastecan) and several individual languages in other branches. This distribution within the Mayan family suggests that it is a comparatively recent areal feature among Mayan languages. Zavala (2002:181–3), however, presents evidence that the direction of influence was more likely to be from Mayan to Mixe-Zoquean. Mixe-Zoquean directionals are generally formally identical to the lexical verbs from which they originated and only provide directional movement meanings, while directionals in Mayan languages frequently show considerable phonological reduction and, in some cases, have become grammaticalized as aspect markers, both of which suggest more time in the process of grammaticalization. In addition, directionals in Mayan are more productive: in many Mayan languages, more than one directional may be used in a phrase, and directionals can occur with many different predicate types, while in Mixe-Zoquean, only one directional is allowed per clause, and they can only occur with verbal predicates. Zavala (2002:183) also notes that they are much more frequent in Mayan speech than in Mixe-Zoquean. Given the scale of observed grammatical and lexical interaction between Mayan and Mixe-Zoquean, based on essentially exploratory research, it is likely that additional systematic investigation of Mixe-Zoquean and lowland Mayan languages, particularly, will yield evidence of additional contact features.

Nahuan languages have also been argued to have had a significant linguistic impact on Mayan languages, though to my knowledge, all clear examples of Nahuan influence on Mayan are lexical borrowings. Campbell (1977:103–9) gives seventy-four lexical borrowings from Gulf Coast Nahua into K'iche'an languages. Justeson et al. (1985:25) give eighteen Nahua loanwords in Yucatecan. These are generally attributed either to postclassic Toltec or to colonial influence. Postclassic hieroglyphic texts also provide evidence of Nahuan influence in the names of deities in the codices (Macri and Looper 2003), also the result of Toltec influence. More controversially, words attested in Classic period (AD 300–800) texts have been interpreted as Nahuan loans, including *ko'haw* 'helmet', *y-ohl* 'erg3-heart' *pata(n)* 'tribute', *iyuwal* '?' (Macri and Looper 2003), and *witik* '?' (Macri 2005). Perhaps the most controversial is the claim that *kakaw*, attested throughout Meso-america and in hieroglyphic texts from the Early Classic on, is of Nahuan, rather than Mixe-Zoquean, origin. Such claimed loanwords have been taken as evidence of a Nahuan affiliation with the early central Mexican power of Teotihuacan (Macri and Looper 2003), and, perhaps even support for a central Mexican homeland for proto-Uto-Aztecan (Dakin and Wichmann 2000). However, a Nahuan origin for these terms is, in all cases, prob-lematic, and for at least some of the terms has been thoroughly refuted (Kaufman and Justeson 2007). Other more minor contacts are suggested by small numbers of lexical borrowings from Totonacan and Zapotec and possibly other Oto-Manguean languages, though apparently only at fairly superficial levels.

4 CONTACT AMONG MAYAN LANGUAGES

For most of their history, Mayan languages have been in contact with one another, and it is perhaps not surprising that some of the most extensive forms of contact-induced change in Mayan languages are the result of contact with other Mayan languages. This diffusion of linguistic forms is partly facilitated by structural similarities between donor and recipient languages because they are related (Law 2013a). That same fact of relat-edness also represents a methodological complication. It does not prevent us from iden-tifying all effects of contact between related languages, but it almost certainly obscures some of those effects so that, for example, rates of lexical borrowings between related languages may well have been much higher than we are able to determine after the fact. In spite of this, the impact of areally shared innovations is discernible, particularly in two major spheres of linguistic interaction: One is centered in the area of Huehuetenango in Highland Guatemala, and involves some Mamean, K'iche'an, and Q'anjob'alan lan-guages. The other is centered in the Maya lowlands, involving principally the Ch'olan and Yucatecan languages, as well as Tseltalan, Q'anjob'alan, Poqomam and Poqomchi', Q'eqchi', Ixil, and, by some accounts (Law 2013b) Huastecan as well. That Q'anjob'alan languages and varieties of Ixil participate in both spheres of interaction makes these languages particularly significant and interesting as the meeting point of contact zones. Future research on the history of contact in Q'anjob'alan and Ixil will doubtless provide great insight into patterns of historical interaction among the family as a whole.

4.1 Huehuetenango contact zone

The areal innovations that are evident in the Huehuetenango sphere of linguistic inter-action appear to be strikingly recent, and, in some cases, still spreading. Areally shared features in the region are phonological, morphological, and syntactic. Campbell (1974, 1977) described dialectal variation across several languages, with a focus on K'iche'an, and showed that several sound changes were spreading to geographically adjacent vari-eties, regardless of language boundaries. These sound changes include the innovation of retroflex affricates (both plain and ejective) and fricative phonemes and palatalization in a variety of conditions (both assimilatory, preceding high vowels, and dissimilatory, pre-ceding low vowels and uvular stops – for more details, see Campbell 1974, 1977). Barrett (2002), the most detailed exploration of the Huehuetenango contact zone to date, notes, in addition to these sound changes, that many languages around Huehuetenango have inno-vated noun classifier systems. Syntactically, Huehuetenango languages have innovated a VSO basic word order and possibly split ergativity in dependent and aspectless clauses, though the latter may in fact be a retention of proto-Mayan. It is worth noting that none of these features share a common distribution, and likely represent independent if overlapping historical processes. For example, Barrett argues, on the basis of the distribution of each feature across languages and dialects of languages in the region, that Mam, or Mamean more generally, was the source of the retroflex consonants, palatalization, and VSO word order, while Q'anjob'alan appears to have been the source of noun classifiers, and K'iche'an is the likely origin of the incorporated preverbal absolutive. The study of contact in the Huehuetenango zone is still only preliminary. Additional systematic work that considers shared similarities among these languages in the context of the entire family is needed, and will very likely yield numerous additional examples of areal phenomena involving Q'anjob'alan, Mamean, and K'iche'an.

4.2 Lowland contact zone

Lowland Mayan language contact has received somewhat more attention than highland language contact. Because the linguistic geography of the lowlands was more dramatically altered during the postclassic and colonial period than the highlands, there is less evidence of ongoing diffusion of areally shared innovation for lowland languages, but the impact of contact in the region is no less clear. It seems likely that many of the innovations were shared somewhat earlier than the areal innovations discussed above for the highlands. As with the Huehuetenango contact zone, the Maya lowlands have been involved in several areally diffused sound changes, shared morphosyntactic innovations, lexical borrowing and, on a slightly smaller scale, even the copying of bound grammatical morphology across language boundaries. Justeson et al. (1985) distinguish between core "lowland Mayan" linguistic features, which they define as unique to Cholan and Yucatecan languages, and an additional layer of "Greater Lowland Mayan" features, that are found in Q'anjob'alan or Tseltalan, as well as Cholan and Yucatecan. Law (2014) recasts this division slightly as a lowland core and periphery, noting that some areal innovations appear to involve languages around the edges of the lowlands (the periphery), specifically excluding Eastern Cholan, while others are mostly restricted to contact between Yucatecan and Eastern Cholan (the core). In fact, as with the Huehuetenango area, the geographical distribution of virtually every lowland areal feature is different, though they often overlap with one another

One of the distinctive features of lowland Mayan languages is the unique vocabulary associated with these languages. As noted above, the true extent of lexical borrowing might be difficult to assess. Several studies of lowland Mayan loanwords (Justeson et al. 1985; Kaufman with Justeson 2003; Wichmann and Brown 2003; Wichmann and Hull 2009) have identified some ninety lexical items that are unique to Cholan and Yucatecan languages, and an additional hundred that are also shared with Q'anjob'alan or Tseltalan. It is likely that Cholan languages are the source for much of the shared lexicon, although it is not always possible to ascertain directionality (Justeson et al. 1985:17). Even with peripheral participants in the lowland contact zone, the lexical influence of Cholan is high, though again, relatedness is an obstacle to getting reliable data. Traditionally, loanwords from related languages are identified on the basis of sound changes that affected one language, but not another, and then identifying words that underwent the sound change in the language that did not go through that sound change. This means in practice loanwords can only be identified confidently if (1) the word has sounds in the appropriate context to undergo a distinguishing sound change, and (2) the word can be reconstructed to an earlier stage in the family without the sound change. Since most lowland languages only have one or two clear sounds changes that would distinguish them from others, and since lexical innovations are likely to be borrowed and not identifiable as loanwords by these criteria, this method does not provide a clear picture of lexical borrowing in the region. Wichmann and Brown (2003) use a method based on distributional criteria, in addition to phonological innovations, to look at lexical borrowing in Q'eqchi', Ixil, and Chicomucelltec. They identified 70 percent of Q'eqchi' loanwords from other Mayan languages, and 40 percent of Ixil loanwords from other Mayan languages, as being from Cholan. Based on the minimal data available for Chicomucelltec, they found that it had fairly minor influence from Cholan, but showed several lexical borrowings from neighboring Tseltalan and Q'anjob'alan languages. While these findings are interesting in their own right, it should be emphasized that because of the differences in methods, what is considered a loanword in these studies is somewhat different from what is considered a loanword according to the stricter traditional approach.

Regardless of the method used, it seems that a surprisingly high proportion of identifiable lowland Mayan loanwords are verbs. Wichmann and Hull (2009) report that half of the loanwords from Cholan and Yucatecan are verbs, all of which are directly incorporated into the recipient language as verbs (as noted above in §2.2, loanwords from Spanish are overwhelmingly nouns). In Justeson et al.'s (1985:11) list of seventy-two lowland lexemes, thirty-three (46 percent) are verbs. The apparent ease with which verbs were areally shared is likely due to the fact that the verbal template for the languages involved and the phonological shape of verbs in the relevant languages were very similar, requiring little if any accommodation (Law 2013a).

Contact has also left a substantial imprint on lowland Mayan phonology. As with the Huehuetenango contact zone, several sound changes have applied to some, but not all, of more than one subgroup. In some cases, the innovation is even found in some, but not all, dialects of individual languages; — evidence of recent diffusion. In several cases, these phonological innovations extend substantially beyond the boundaries of the lowlands, at times involving languages from all but one or two subgroups of the family. Areally shared sound changes that involve lowland languages include an innovative contrast between /b'/ and /p'/ (Justeson et al. 1985; Wichmann 2006), a shift of *r to /y/ and *ŋ to /n/ (Justeson et al. 1985:12), the shift of *ty to /t/, the merging of *j and *h, the loss of contrastive vowel length (Law 2014), and the shift of *k(') to /ch(')/ and *q(') to /k(')/ (Law et al. 2014).

Convergence in the morphosyntax of lowland Mayan languages due to contact is also substantial. Most research on this has focused on the grammar surrounding person marking, aspect, and the verbal complex. Comparative research into other areas of the structure of lowland Mayan languages will undoubtedly reveal further instances of areally shared structural innovations. Lowland Mayan aspect-based split ergativity is clearly an areal feature (Justeson et al. 1985). The use of set A person markers and an incompletive suffix based on the historically nominalizing -*Vl* suffix is shared by Yucatecan, Chol, and Chontal. Ch'orti', Poqomchi', and Ixil all suspend the usual ergative pattern of person marking in the incompletive aspect. In Ch'orti' and Ixil, incompletive verb forms do not use a historically nominalizing suffix, while the incompletive verb form of Poqomchi' uses -*ik*, a suffix functionally equivalent to -*Vl* in lowland languages, but not cognate (Law 2014). An accusative marking pattern is apparent in Cholti only in the progressive, and there is no evidence of split ergativity in the language of the hieroglyphs, so this innovation cannot even be reconstructed for proto-Cholan (Law et al. 2006).

Alignment patterns are far from the only way in which person marking in lowland languages has been shaped by contact. Eastern Cholan and Yucatecan languages have almost identical morphological forms for person marking (Law 2009). Some of the similarity is common inheritance, but a great deal involves idiosyncratic changes to individual morphemes. Several languages along the northwestern edge of the lowlands and continuing into the Cuchumatanes have developed inclusive/exclusive distinctions in first person plural, using internal morphological material. In addition, lowland languages, as well as Ixil, have converged in innovating a consistently post-verbal placement of the set B clitic (Law 2009).

Other grammatical borrowings include a plural -*oob*' suffix, a stative positional -*tahl* (Justeson et al. 1985), the loss of obligatory verbal derivation for focused agents, a dramatic expansion of numeral classifiers, the use of *wal* and positionals meaning 'to stand' to mark the progressive aspect, the borrowing of Classic Mayan -*oom* into the colonial Yucatec religious register, and the borrowing of *ti=* as a marker of completive aspect from Yucatec into Chol (Law 2014).

4.3 Huastec and the lowlands

A recurring question in the history of the Mayan family is where Huastec and its extinct close relative Chicomuceltec fit with respect to the other subgroups. Based on the substantial divergence between Huastecan and other Mayan languages, it is widely believed that Huastecan forms a separate branch of the Mayan family tree, and was the first linguistic community to separate from proto-Mayan (Swadesh 1953:226; McQuown 1964:69; Kaufman 1976). The existence of several potential loanwords from Huastec and into Huastec from languages near the present-day Huasteca (Kaufman 1980; Kaufman and Justeson 2008) is plausibly further evidence, not only of an early separation of Huastec from proto-Mayan but also of a significant amount of time spent in its present location. For example, Kaufman and Justeson (2008) identify several loanwords from Huastec into the extinct and fragmentarily attested languages Yemé and Pajalat, which were spoken to the north of the Huasteca. Among these borrowings, they highlight Yemé <jat> 'How many?.' They argue that this word was borrowed from Huastec when it still had the proto-Mayan form *jar, which has since changed to *jay*. This one loanword suggests that Huastec was far enough north to interact with Yemé speakers at a point when it maintained proto-Mayan /r/.

Another line of evidence from lexical borrowing that supports Kaufman's proposed early departure from the Maya region is the presence of several loans from Huastec in Kaufman's reconstruction of proto-Oto-Pamean. Oto-Pamean is a linguistically diverse family, suggesting several millennia of differentiation at least since the proto-language was spoken. Kaufman and Justeson mention specifically *mu*' 'cross-sex sibling-in-law' from proto-Mayan *mu*' and *tzoa-tz*' 'bat' argued to be from proto-Mayan *so'tz*' 'bat'. They note that loans from proto-Oto-Pamean into Huastec can also be identified, though they do not give the details.

While suggestive, using relatively few loanwords to triangulate the ancient location of proto-Huastecan speakers is not without problems. Individual loanwords can often enter languages through surprising and circuitous routes, so individual loans without clear history provide only threads of evidence, which can at times be contradictory (for example, the presence of a clear borrowing in Huastec from lowland Mayan languages, *tak'in* 'gold', is problematic for Kaufman's account in the other direction). The weight of those loanwords needs to be inferred in the context of other historical evidence. The strength of Kaufman and Justeson's inferences in this case depends on two problematic assumptions that they make about Ancient Mesoamerican linguistic history: (1) They note that lexical borrowing seems to be fairly uncommon across different language families in Mesoamerica. Based on this, they assume that any lexical borrowing indicates intensive contact, much as is assumed elsewhere for the borrowing of grammatical morphology. This is not impossible, but as it conflicts with current understanding of what is typical for lexical borrowing (Haspelmath and Tadmoor 2009), it begs more extensively argued support. (2) They assume that languages have mostly stayed in place over time. This last is partly inferred from the patterns they highlight in lexical borrowings, but is also used to strengthen the weight of those borrowings. This is somewhat circular. It also conflicts with what we know about the more recent history of the region, where movement of people across the landscape of Mesoamerica has been extensive.

To complicate the picture further, linguistic evidence beyond loanwords seems to support a different picture of Huastecan development, one that did not involve a complete lack of contact between Huastecan and other Mayan languages since proto-Mayan times. Huastec shares several innovative morphological and phonological features with Cholan-Tseltalan languages. Campbell (1988:211) notes that Huastec shares several sound changes with Cholan-Tseltalan languages (and others), including *r>y, *q>k, t'>t, and *k>ch, and that Huastec is like Cholan and other lowland and Western Mayan languages in marking plurality for person with a separate enclitic morpheme, unlike the suppletive person markers that marked plural person in Eastern Mayan languages and proto-Mayan. Robertson (1992) and Robertson and Houston (2003) highlight that both Huastec and Tseltalan had reflexes of the proto-Mayan passive *-at as a passive of derived transitives, and an innovative passive -ey as a passive for root transitives, a -Vl suffix on incompletive intransitive verbs, as well as possible similarities at an earlier stage in pronominal development, with respect to the position of set B absolutive markers. The incorporated secondary predicate mentioned above as being shared by Huastec and Chol, because of contact, in both cases, with Mixe-Zoque is another linguistic parallel, though one with a more obvious source. Robertson (1992) and Robertson and Houston (2003) suggest that these similarities are evidence of close genetic relationship. Campbell (1988:211) notes that they could be due to either shared inheritance or contact. Under Kaufman's model, these features would presumably have arisen independently by chance.

Work on language contact in the Maya lowlands (Law 2014) provides some additional support for the idea that Huastec shares innovative features with lowland languages because of contact, rather than inheritance or chance. The majority of the features that Huastec shares with Cholan-Tseltalan, including all of the sound changes, are features identified, without reference to Huastec, as lowland areal innovations. If Huastec shares these features with Cholan-Tseltalan through contact, it is not necessary to group Huastecan with Cholan-Tseltalan genetically, but such an account also suggests that the history of Huastecan must allow for a mechanism for intensive contact between Huastecan and the Maya lowlands, either by positing that Huastec speakers emigrated to the Huasteca in the postclassic, rather than the early preclassic, or that there was continuous and substantial communication between the Huasteca and the lowlands throughout Huastecan history, possible through continuous trade or more extended ranges for those languages in the postclassic (Law 2013b, 2017).

4.4 Tojol-ab'al

Another debate about linguistic affiliation in the Mayan family also has language contact at its heart: the question of the relationship of Tojol-ab'al to the rest of the family. Both grammar and lexicon in Tojol-ab'al share innovative forms with Q'anjob'alan and with

Tseltalan. For example, first and second person markers, inclusive and exclusive, the irrealis suffix, imperative, the comitative preposition *sok*, the agentive relational noun -*u'un*, phrase-final distal and topic clitics, plural for nouns, and the loss of the agent focus structure are all innovations in Tojol-ab'al that are shared with Tseltal. The stative positional suffix -*an*, the potential enclitic *oj*=, the dubitative mood particle *ama*, progressive marker *wan*, the plural for humans -*e'*, and the general preposition *b'ay* are all innovative features that Tojol-ab'al shares with Chuj (Law 2017). In terms of phonological innovations, Tojol-ab'al, like Chuj, changed *k to /ch/ in certain contexts, but retained its glottalized counterpart /k'/. Like Tseltal (and unlike Chuj), Tojol-ab'al shifted pM *ŋ to /n/, and pM glottal *h to velar /x/. Given the number of areally shared sound changes in the region, none of these are particularly telling. Lexically, the same pattern holds: Tojol-ab'al shares 65 percent of its basic vocabulary with Tseltal and 69 percent with Chuj. In an extended lexicon of around 1,300 words, Tojol-ab'al is a little more like Tseltal: 41 percent versus 28 percent similarity with Chuj (Law and Adell 2015). Confronted with this mixture, opinions vary as to whether Tojol-ab'al is best considered a Q'anjob'alan language with substantial influence from Tseltalan (Kaufman 1974; Schumann 1981, 1983; Campbell and Kaufman 1985; Dakin 1988) or a Tseltalan language that has been substantially influenced by the Q'anjob'alan language Chuj (Robertson 1977; Campbell 1988).

Law (2011, 2017) argues that the mixture of Chujean and Tseltalan linguistic features, at all levels, is substantial enough to call into question any claim to a traditional line of descent from one or the other language. This would qualify Tojol-ab'al as a unique type of contact language; one that, like a mixed language, did not undergo the dramatic restructuring of a creole, but that, unlike prototypical mixed languages, is not consistent about which donor language contributed material to which part of the grammar. Instead, Tojol-ab'al appears to have thoroughly intermixed forms from both contributing languages throughout its grammar and lexicon, typical of cases of dialect mixing and code switching involving related languages.

5 CONCLUSION: PROCESSES AND MOTORS OF CHANGE

This brief overview has highlighted the pervasive impact of language contact in the history of Mayan languages. Contact among Mayan languages is now known to have been truly substantial, though much more work is needed, particularly on the Huehuetenango contact zone and on the complex history of the Q'anjob'alan subgroup, as well as features of syntax and morphology in lowland languages beyond person marking and aspect. There are new and tantalizing hints that the influence on Mayan languages from other indigenous language families, particularly Mixe-Zoquean, has also been profound.

Mayan languages provide an intriguing contrast between the types of linguistic influence seen from other Mayan languages (and perhaps Mixe-Zoquean), and the type of linguistic effects that Spanish has had. It is certainly the case that Spanish grammatical influence can be seen in some Mayan languages at a structural level with basic word order, discourse particles, and perhaps contact-induced grammaticalizations, particularly in communities that are experiencing rapid shift to Spanish. Overall, however, there appears to be widespread and long-standing resistance by speakers of most Mayan languages to Spanish influence beyond the lexicon. Even within the lexicon, the lexical categories that are borrowed and the way in which new material is incorporated into recipient Mayan languages is markedly different, and seemingly much less invasive, than effects of contact from other indigenous languages. This is undoubtedly due, in part, to the typological distance between Spanish and Mayan languages on the one hand, and the facilitating effect of shared inherited similarity in cases of contact with related Mayan languages, on the other. A long history of minimal integration between indigenous and ladino communities may also play a role. However, as Barrett (2008) suggests in a study of Sipakapense language use, another important component of the resistance to Spanish influence is ideological, with speakers asserting and reinforcing a perceived hyperdistinction between Spanish and Mayan. This may well hold true in the opposite direction as well. Cross-linguistically high levels of grammatical borrowing across Mayan languages can be attributed in part to ideologies of sameness: a sense of common origin, reinforced by inherited similarity in language, regardless of the mutual intelligibility of languages involved (Law 2013a, 2014:ch. 9).

The patterns of contact among Mayan language that have been identified to date are surprising in their variety. While there seem to be two general linguistic 'epicenters' of language contact – the lowlands and Huehuetenango – few of the isoglosses of individual areal features bundle tidily, and the overall amount of overlap for each isogloss is fairly low. For example, Law (2014) compared the distribution of six areally shared lowland phonological innovations and found that Chol, Chontal, and Cholti all shared all six of the innovations (unsurprising, since participation of a Cholan language in an areally shared sound change was a defining trait of a 'lowland' areal feature), but Yucatecan languages shared no more phonological innovations with Cholan than did Q'anjob'alan languages, in spite of the fact that Yucatecan and Cholan are generally characterized as the core languages of the lowland language area (Figure 5.1).

The idiosyncrasies of individual isoglosses suggest a confluence of historical pressures and mechanisms, all giving rise to these contact zones, rather than such areas emerging in a particular historical moment or through a specific sociopolitical force. For both the Huehuetenango sphere of linguistic interaction and the Maya lowlands, we can identify clear political entities that maintained political and social power for a substantial period of time: the Mam kingdom with its center in Saqulew for the highlands (Barrett 2002), and the Classic Maya civilization for the lowlands. The lowland Cholan language of hieroglyphic inscription clearly enjoyed regional favor as the language of elite scribal practice, and the relative status that this Cholan language and its speakers would have exercised is undeniable (Houston et al. 2000). Yet, as clear as these candidates are for a driving, generative force for the creation of two contact areas, the details, in both cases, seem to suggest that these sociopolitical entities are only indirectly relevant at best. In Huehuetenango, many of the changes that have been noted appear to still be in the process of spreading, and affect different dialects of participating languages to different degrees, suggesting shallowness of time depth for the spread of the innovation. A political entity that was supplanted more than half a millennium ago by the K'iche', and subsequently by the Spanish, seems a poor fit to explain these ongoing and very recent processes of diffusion.

In the lowlands, the evidence of hieroglyphic texts show that relatively few of the most striking lowland areal features are present in the language of the hieroglyphs. Until the Late Classic, the language of the hieroglyphs maintains a phonemic contrast in vowel length and maintains the /h/ /x/ distinction. The /k/ to /ch/ sound change is only variably realized, and by implication /q/ may not have shifted to /k/, though this distinction is not documented orthographically (Law et al. 2014). Split ergativity based on aspect is unattested in hieroglyphic texts, numeral classifiers are optional, and ergative prevocalic person markers in hieroglyphic texts retain the archaic forms (*w-*, *y*, *k-*) rather than the innovative forms shared by Cholti, Chorti, and Yucatecan (*inw-*, *uy-* and *kaw-* (*kiw-* in Mopan).

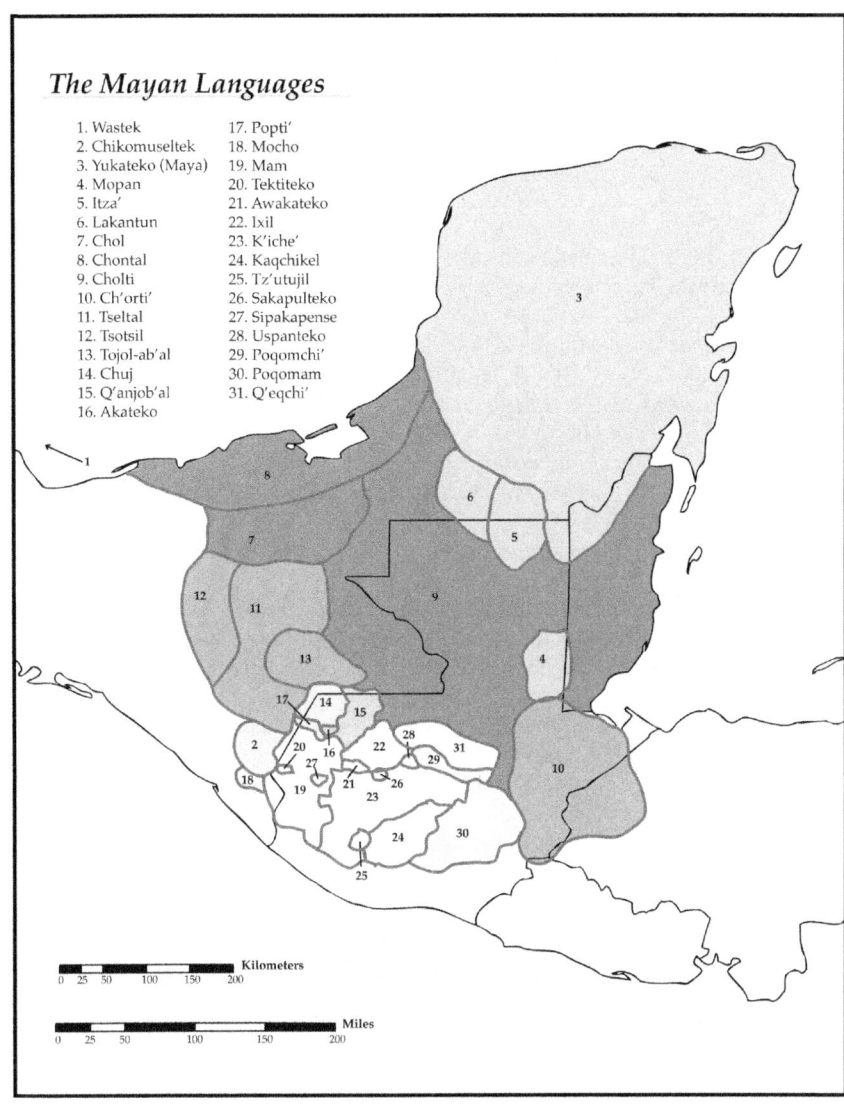

The Mayan Languages

1. Wastek
2. Chikomuseltek
3. Yukateko (Maya)
4. Mopan
5. Itza'
6. Lakantun
7. Chol
8. Chontal
9. Cholti
10. Ch'orti'
11. Tseltal
12. Tsotsil
13. Tojol-ab'al
14. Chuj
15. Q'anjob'al
16. Akateko

17. Popti'
18. Mocho
19. Mam
20. Tektiteko
21. Awakateko
22. Ixil
23. K'iche'
24. Kaqchikel
25. Tz'utujil
26. Sakapulteko
27. Sipakapense
28. Uspanteko
29. Poqomchi'
30. Poqomam
31. Q'eqchi'

FIGURE 5.1 MAP OF THE MAYAN LANGUAGES. OVERLAPPING ISOGLOSSES: DARKER GRAY = MORE AREAL INNOVATIONS, LIGHTER = FEWER AREAL INNOVATIONS

Furthermore, several extensive morphosyntactic changes, including the innovation of an inclusive/exclusive contrast, the innovation of distinct plural enclitics for first and second person, and the innovation of aspect-based split ergativity from nominalizations, affected most of the lowland languages except for Eastern Cholan, including the language of the hieroglyphs, and its close relatives, Cholti and Ch'orti'. All of this suggests that the extensive contact-induced changes of the Maya lowlands postdate the height of Classic Maya power, much as the ongoing changes in the Huehuetenango contact zone seem to postdate the end of the Mam kingdom. In both cases, we find support for the hypothesis that it is not the unilateral and asymmetrical social relations of dynasts that have spurred the greater part of Mayan language contact, but the multilateral and more socially balanced social relations that arise in political and social upheaval, or that are orthogonal to asymmetrical state power relations.

REFERENCES

Barrett, Rusty. 2002. "The Huehuetenango Sprachbund and Mayan language standardization in Guatemala." In *Proceedings of the 38th Chicago linguistics society: the panels,* ed. by Mary Andronis, Erin Debenport, Anne Pycha, and Keiko Yoshimura, 309–18. Chicago: Chicago Linguistics Society.

Barrett, Rusty. 2008. "Linguistic differentiation and Mayan language revitalization in Guatemala." *Journal of Sociolinguistics* 12: 275–305.

Brody, Jill. 1987. "Particles borrowed from Spanish as discourse markers in Mayan languages." *Anthropological Linguistics* 29: 507–21.

Campbell, Lyle. 1974. "Quichean palatalized velars." *International Journal of American Linguistics* 40: 132–4.

Campbell, Lyle. 1977. *Quichean linguistic prehistory*. Berkeley: University of California Press.

Campbell, Lyle. 1988. *The linguistics of Southeast Chiapas, Mexico* (Papers of the New World Archaeological Foundation, 50). Provo: New World Archaeological Foundation.

Campbell, Lyle, and Terrence Kaufman. 1976. "A linguistic look at the Olmecs." *American Antiquity* 41: 80–9.

Campbell, Lyle, and Terrence Kaufman. 1985. "Mayan linguistics: Where are we now?" *Annual Review of Anthropology* 14: 187–98.

Campbell, Lyle, Terrence Kaufman, and Thomas C. Smith-Stark. 1986. "Mesoamerica as a linguistic area." *Language* 62: 530–70.

Company Company, Concepción. 2005. "Frequency of use and language contact in syntax: the indefinite article + possessive in American Spanish." *Spanish in Context 2*: 131–56.

Dakin, Karen. 1988. "Las Lenguas Kanjobalanas: Polémicas clasificatorias." In *Studia Humanitatis: Homenaje a Rubén Bonifaz Nuño*, ed. by Aurora Ocampo, 111–33. México: Universidad Nacional Autónoma de México.

Dakin, Karen, and Søren Wichmann. 2000. "Cacao and chocolate: a Uto-Aztecan perspective." *Ancient Mesoamerica* 11: 55–75.

Escobar, Ana María. 2013. "Spanish in contact with Amerindian languages." In *The handbook of hispanic linguistics*, ed. by José Ignacio Hualde, Antxon Olarrea, and Erin O'Rourke, 65–88. Hoboken: Wiley-Blackwell.

Garcia Tesoro, Ana Isabel. 2006. "Language contact in Guatemala: Changes in the Spanish atonic pronominal system through contact with the Mayan language Tzutujil." *Tópicos del Seminario* 15: 11–71.

Garcia Tesoro, Ana Isabel. 2010. "Spanish in contact with Tzutujil in Guatemala: changes in the third-person unstressed pronoun system." *Revista Internacional de Lingüística Iberoamericana 8*: 133–56.

Haspelmath, Martin, and Uri Tadmoor, eds. 2009. *Loanwords in the world's languages: a comparative handbook*. Berlin: De Gruyter Mouton.

Houston, Stephen, John Robertson, and David Stuart. 2000. "The language of classic Maya inscriptions." *Current Anthropology* 41: 321–56.

Justeson, John S., William M. Norman, Lyle Campbell and Terrence Kaufman. 1985. *The foreign impact on lowland Mayan language and script.* New Orleans: Middle American Research Institute, Tulane University.

Kaufman, Terrence. 1974. *Idiomas de Mesoamerica.* Guatemala City, Guatemala: Ministerio de Educación.

Kaufman, Terrence. 1976. "Archaeological and linguistic correlations in Mayaland and associated areas of Meso-America." *World Archaeology* 8: 101–18.

Kaufman, Terrence. 1980. "Pre-Columbian borrowing involving Huastec." In *American Indian and Indo-European studies: papers in honor of Madison S. Beeler,* ed. by Kathryn Klar, Margaret Langdon, and Shirley Silver, 101–12. (Trends in Linguistics, Studies and Monographs, 16). The Hague: Mouton.

Kaufman, Terrence, with John Justeson. 2003. *A preliminary Mayan etymological dictionary.* Foundation for the Advancement of Mesoamerican Studies. http://www.famsi.org/reports/01050/index.html. Last accessed 3 June 2013.

Kaufman, Terrence, and John Justeson. 2007. "The history of the word for cacao in ancient Mesoamerica." *Ancient Mesoamerica* 18: 193–237.

Kaufman, Terrence, and John Justeson. 2008. "The Epi-Olmec language and its neighbors." In *Classic-period cultural currents in Southern and Central Veracruz,* ed. by Philip Arnold III and Christopher Pool, 55–83. Cambridge: Harvard University Press.

Kaufman, Terrence, and John Justeson. 2009. "Historical linguistics and pre-Columbian Mesoamerica." *Ancient Mesoamerica* 20: 221–31.

Law, Danny. 2009. "Pronominal borrowing among the Maya." *Diachronica* 26: 214–52.

Law, Danny. 2011. "Linguistic inheritance, social difference, and the last two thousand years of contact among lowland Mayan languages." PhD diss., University of Texas, Austin.

Law, Danny. 2013a. "Inherited similarity and contact-induced change in Mayan languages." *Journal of Language Contact* 6: 271–99.

Law, Danny. 2013b. "Parallel development and the case of Wastek." Invited Talk, Linguistics Colloquium Series, The University of Texas at Austin, February 8, 2013.

Law, Danny. 2014. *Language contact, inherited similarity and social difference: The story of linguistic interaction in the Maya Lowlands* (Current Issues in Linguistic Theory Series). Amsterdam: John Benjamins.

Law, Danny. 2017. "Language mixing and the case of Tojol-b'al." *Diachronica* 34: 40–78.

Law, Danny, and Eric Adell. 2015. "Similitud léxica y la historia del Tojol-ab'al." Paper presented at the Congreso de Idiomas indígenas de Latinoamerica VII, Austin, TX. Oct. 29, 2015.

Law, Danny, John Robertson, and Stephen Houston. 2006. "Split ergativity in the history of the Cholan branch of the Mayan language family." *International Journal of American Linguistics* 72: 415–50.

Law, Danny, John Robertson, Stephen Houston, Marc Zender, and David Stuart. 2014. "Areal shifts in classic Maya phonology." *Ancient Mesoamerica* 25: 357–66.

Lope Blanch, Juan M. 1987. *Estudios sobre el español de Yucatán.* Mexico City, Mexico: Universidad Autónoma de México.

Macri, Martha. 2005. "Nahua loan words from the early classic period: Words for cacao preparation on a Río Azul ceramic vessel." *Ancient Mesoamerica* 16: 321–6.

Macri, Martha, and Matthew Looper. 2003. "Nahua in ancient Mesoamerica: Evidence from Maya inscriptions." *Ancient Mesoamerica* 14: 285–97.

McQuown, Norman A. 1964. "Los orígenes y la diferenciación de los mayas según se infiere del estudio comparativo de las lenguas mayanas." In *Desarrollo cultural de los mayas*, ed. by Evon Z. Vogt and Alberto Ruz Lhuillier, 49–76. Mexico City: Universidad Nacional Autónoma de México, Facultad de Filosofía y Letras, Seminario de Cultura Maya.

Martin, Laura. 1978. "Mayan influence in Guatemalan Spanish: a research outline and test case." In *Papers in Mayan linguistics*, ed. by Nora C. England, 106–26. Columbia: University of Missouri Press.

Martin, Laura. 1985. "Una mi tacita de café: The Indefinite Article in Guatemalan Spanish." *Hispania* 68(2): 383–7.

Martínez Cruz, Victoriano. 2007. "Los adjetivos y conceptos de propiedad en chol." MA thesis, Centro de Investigaciones y Estudios Superiores en Antropología Social, México.

Matras, Yaron. 2007. "The borrowability of structural categories." In *Grammatical borrowing in cross-linguistic perspective*, ed. by Yaron Matras and Jeanette Sakel, 31–73. Berlin: Mouton de Gruyter.

Michnowicz, Jim. 2012. "The standardization of Yucatan Spanish: Family case studies in Izamal and Mérida." In *Selected proceedings of the hispanic linguistics symposium 2010*, ed. by Kimberly Geeslin and Manuel Díaz-Campos, 102–15. Somerville: Cascadilla Proceedings Project.

Michnowicz, Jim. 2015. "Maya-Spanish contact in Yucatan, Mexico: context and sociolinguistic implications." In *New perspectives on hispanic contact linguistics in the Americas*, ed. by S. Sessarego and M. González Rivera, 21–42. Madrid: Iberoamericana/Vervuert.

Michnowicz, Jim, and Hilary Barnes. 2013. "A sociolinguistic analysis of pre-nuclear peak alignment in Yucatan Spanish." In *Selected proceedings of the 15th Hispanic Linguistics Symposium*, ed. by C. Howe, S.E. Blackwell and M. Lubbers Quesada, 22–235. Somerville: Cascadilla Proceedings Project.

Montgomery-Anderson, Brad. 2010. "Grammaticalization through language contact: the periphrastic passive in Chontal Mayan." *Journal of Language Contact* 3: 84–100.

Pye, Clifton L. 2013. "A tale of two mam children: Contact-induced language change in Mayan child language." *International Journal of American Linguistics* 79: 555–75.

Robertson, John. 1977. "A proposed revision in Mayan subgrouping." *International Journal of American Linguistics* 43: 105–20.

Robertson, John. 1992. *The history of tense/aspect/mood/voice in the Mayan verbal complex*. Austin: University of Texas Press.

Robertson, John, and Stephen Houston. 2003. "El problema del Wasteko: Una perspectiva lingüística y arqueológica." In *XVI simposio de investigaciones arqueológicas en Guatemala*, ed. by Juan Pedro Laporte, Bárbara Arroyo, Héctor Escobedo, and Héctor Mejía, 723–33. Guatemala: Ministerio de Cultura y Deportes.

Romero, Sergio F. 2006. "Sociolinguistic variation and linguistic history in Mayan: The case of K'ichee'." PhD diss., University of Pennsylvania.

Schumann G., Otto. 1981. "La Relación Lingüística Chuj-Tojolabal." In *Los Legítimos Hombres: Aproximación antropológica al grupo Tojolabal*, ed. by Mario Humberto Ruz, 129–69. Mexico: Centro de Estudios Mayas, Universidad Nacional Autónoma de México.

Schumann G., Otto. 1983. "Algunos Aspectos de la Relación Chuj-Tojolabal." In *Antropología e Historia de los Mixe-Zoques y Mayas: Homenaje a Frans Blom*, ed. by Lorenzo Ochoa and Thomas A. Lee Jr., 355–63. Mexico: Universidad Autónoma de México.

Suárez Molina, Víctor M. 1945. El español que se habla en Yucatán: Apuntamientos filológicos. Mérida, Mexico: La universidad de Yucatán.

Swadesh, Morris. 1953. "The Language of the Archaeological Huastecs." *Notes on Middle American Archaelogy and Ethnology* 4: 223–7.

Wichmann, Søren. 1999. "A conservative look at diffusion involving Mixe-Zoquean languages." In *Archaeology and Language II: Archaeological Data and Linguistic Hypotheses*, ed. by Blench, Roger and Matthew Spriggs, 297–323. London: Routledge.

Wichmann, Søren. 2006. "Mayan historical linguistics and epigraphy: A new synthesis." *Annual Review of Anthropology* 35: 279–94.

Wichmann, Søren, and Cecil H. Brown. 2003. "Contact among some Mayan Languages: Inferences from loanwords." *Anthropological Linguistics* 45: 57–93.

Wichmann, Søren, and Kerry Hull. 2009. "Loanwords in Q'eqchi', a Mayan language of Guatemala." In *Loanwords in the world's languages: a comparative handbook*, ed. by Martin Haspelmath and Uri Tadmor, 873–96. Berlin and New York: Mouton de Gruyter.

Yager, Kent. 1982. "Estudio del cuadro consontántico del español de Mérida, Yucatán con consideraciones de posible influencia maya." MA thesis, University of California: Santa Barbara.

Zavala, Roberto. 2000. "Olutec motion verbs: Grammaticalization under Mayan contact." Berkeley Linguistics Society 26: 139–51.

Zavala, Roberto. 2002. "Calcos sintácticos en algunos complejos verbales Mayas y Mixe-Zoques." *Pueblos y Fronteras* 4: 169–87.

CHAPTER 6

CLASSIC MAYAN
An overview of language in ancient hieroglyphic script

Danny Law and David Stuart

1 INTRODUCTION

This essay provides an overview of the language attested in ancient Maya hieroglyphic writing, or what we choose to call Classic Mayan.[1] The writing system was in use for nearly two thousand years, beginning in what archaeologists call the Late Preclassic period (ca. 300 B.C.) and lasting until the time of European conquest and domination. In this period the hieroglyphic script was used throughout the region we traditionally know as the "Lowland Maya area," concentrated mostly in the lowlands of what is today Guatemala, Belize, southern Mexico (Yucatan, Campeche, Quintana Roo, Chiapas, and Tabasco) and parts of western Honduras. Thousands of ancient texts survive on stone monuments, various portable objects such as ceramics, and in three (possibly four) screen-fold books dating to the later stages of the script's history. These mostly record religious and historical information, although the styles and genres of such texts varied considerably over time and space. Remarkably, virtually all of the extant hieroglyphic texts seem to represent a single "prestige" language that, even at the time of its use, may have been highly formalized and even archaic in some of its features (Macri and Ford 1997; Houston et al. 2000). With the decipherment of the script in the 1980s and '90s, specialists soon realized that many of the basic phonological, morphological, and syntactic features of this language are represented in great detail by the ancient writing system. These are now the subject of considerable study, debate, and discussion. However, as the following sections attest, in spite of a variety of confounding factors and interpretive obstacles, there is a great deal that we can say about the linguistics of ancient Maya writing

2 HISTORY OF DECIPHERMENT AND LINGUISTIC ANALYSIS

The decipherment of Maya hieroglyphic writing resulted from the efforts of numerous scholars working for more than a century (Kelley 1962; Coe 1992; G. Stuart 1992). Its intellectual roots can be traced to early studies of hieroglyphs recorded in Bishop Diego de Landa's sixteenth-century *Relación de las Cosas de Yucatan*, published in 1864, which included the so-called "alphabet" of signs as well as illustrations of day and month hieroglyphs. These studies led to the identification of a handful of word signs or *logograms*, but the true nature of the ancient writing system as a whole would remain unknown for nearly a century. Most of the research before the 1930s focused on the calendar and its structure, but some conceptual progress in the decipherment was also being made. While many assumed that the hieroglyphs captured only ideas, and not actually linguistic forms, as early as the 1870s some scholars had noted evidence of a phonetic (syllabic) component to ancient Maya script. However, these early insights, built upon fundamental misunderstandings, produced little firm progress in decipherment, and doubts soon emerged over the true extent of phoneticism in the glyphs. An emerging "German School" led by Eduard Seler was harsh in its rejection of phoneticism and laid the groundwork for a debate that would intensify over the ensuing decades. Later studies by Cyrus Thomas and Benjamin Lee Whorf proposed different phonetic solutions – Thomas in particular had important insights that anticipated work by Knorosov by half a century. But these were still flawed and were once again widely and easily critiqued. By mid-twentieth century the script remained poorly understood, apart from a few widely accepted logographic readings and a fairly detailed understanding of the calendar and its mechanisms (Thompson 1950).

In the 1950s, the Russian linguist Yuri Knorosov proposed a syllabic reading for a number of hieroglyphs in the codices, essentially expanding upon various tentative proposals made earlier by Brinton, Thomas, and others. His insights proved key to a wider decipherment of syllabic signs, yet his understanding of the script as a whole remained incomplete and flawed (over two-thirds of Knorosov's proposed readings proved incorrect). Nevertheless, by the 1960s there was little doubt that some signs represented CV syllables that could be strung together to spell words and spoken forms. David Kelley and Floyd Lounsbury were instrumental in refining and expanding on Knorosov's methods (Kelley 1976). It was in these years that other epigraphic work that focused on Classic monuments discerned elements of written history and identified "event glyphs" such as birth and accession as well as personal names and titles (Berlin 1958; Proskouriakoff 1960). By the 1970s and early 1980s, epigraphic work increasingly fused the refined phonetic approach with larger historical analysis of texts and narratives, leading to progressively more sophisticated linguistic approaches to the ancient script (Schele 1982; Justeson and Campbell 1984; Bricker 1986).

Despite this steady progress, the complexity of the system's orthography and visual canons were not adequately understood until the late 1980s. One key development was the recognition that logograms and syllabograms (see §3) could assume multiple forms, or allographs. The identification of rigid substitution sets, sometimes involving up to ten or more signs, soon came to be essential to the decipherment (Stuart 1987, 1990). The wide informal dissemination of drawings and photographs of inscriptions via photocopiers, as well the formal publications of the Corpus of Maya Hieroglyphic Inscriptions program, facilitated the collaborative involvement of numerous scholars. Starting in the early 1980s, lexical decipherments (as opposed to vague semantic glosses) progressed at a rapid pace and continued through the 1990s.

Over the last several decades, as the decipherment has steadily matured, the study of hieroglyphs has naturally become a subfield of Mayan linguistics. Today many of the pressing issues in Maya epigraphic research focus on the wealth of linguistic data now available from the ancient texts. A good deal of this research strives to understand linguistic patterns in light of the long and complex history of Mayan languages and their interactions.

A basic question that has often been asked since the early days of decipherment is: What language are the hieroglyphic inscriptions most closely related to? The phonetic decipherments of the late 1980s and 1990s revealed distinctive linguistic features that persuasively placed the language of Classic period texts in the Cholan subgroup of the Mayan family (Campbell 1984; Houston et al. 2000). Phonological features of Cholan lexemes are widely documented in the inscriptions, as in the widespread use of /ch/ as a reflex of proto-Mayan /*k/, seen in **chi-ji** for *chij*, 'deer', a form that appears in no other Mayan family but Ch'olan and Tseltalan (< proto-Mayan **kehj*). The weight of the Cholan evidence is undeniable, yet recently there has emerged suggestive evidence in inflectional verb morphology that, within Cholan, Ch'orti and its ancestral language Cholti are the closest relatives of the language of the Classic inscriptions (Houston et al. 2000). Interestingly, the use of Cholan forms is apparent throughout the lowlands, even as far as sites in northern Yucatan.

3 THE NATURE OF THE WRITING SYSTEM

All Maya hieroglyphic signs represent word signs (logograms) or syllables (syllabograms). There are no "ideograms" in Maya script, despite some early claims, so that every graphic unit of the script conveys linguistic information. Logograms conform to CVC or CVCVC roots (as will be discussed, phonemically VC roots appear to have a phonetic glottal stop in the onset when word-initial). Syllabograms represent CV sequences (including ?V) and can be strung together to spell a number of different roots and derivational affixes. Some conventions for syllabic spellings could signal different qualities (aspiration, glottalization) of the vowel or syllable nucleus as well as vowel length.

Logograms and syllabic signs are combined into glyph blocks. The visual arrangement of sign groups into "blocks" is fairly consistent over time and space. While words can be written across several glyph blocks, a single glyph block rarely contains incomplete portions of two different morphemes. A single glyph block is often designed to contain multiple words and even one or more complete predicates, and the grouping of these larger constituents in more complex glyph blocks suggests scribes' awareness of and attention to syntactic and grammatical categories. Visual design and format also appear to have been important considerations in the layout of glyph blocks. Example (1) shows how three glyphs blocks composed of both logograms and syllables conform to a verb, a prepositional phrase, and a personal name of the subject:

(1)   **CHUM[mu]** **ti** **AJAW**   **AJAW**

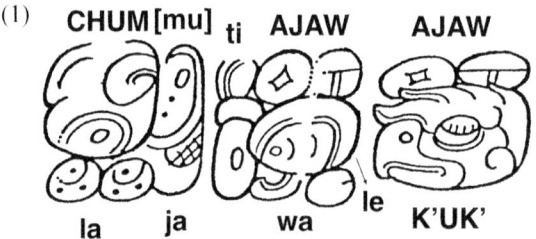

la   **ja**   **wa**   **le**   **K'UK'**

CHUM-la-ja ti-AJAW-wa-le K'UK'-AJAW[2]
chum-l-aj-Ø   ti   ajaw-l-e(l)   k'uk'   ajaw
sit-POS-INTR-B3   PREP   king-vl.vl   PN
'K'uk' Ajaw sits in kingship (accedes to the throne).' {La Corona Panel 2}

On the other extreme, we find texts where each glyph block contains only one sign, as in the passage in (2), from the dedicatory inscription of a ceramic vessel, which consists of four glyphs blocks, each composed of a single syllabogram, to spell the possessed nominal form *u-tz'ihb'aal* 'Its writing'.

(2)   **u**   **tz'i**   **b'a**   **li**

u tz'i b'a li
u-tz'ihb'-aal
A3-write-vl
'Its text' {Ceramic Vessel, Robicsek 1978:Plate 108}

Within glyph blocks, signs typically appear in a left-to-right and top-to-bottom arrangement, with one "main sign" often spatially dominant. Scribes exhibited considerable leeway in arranging these elements and employing allographs, to the extent that spellings of the very same word or expression might look nothing like one another. Figure 6.1 shows several variant spellings of the same term given in example (2), *tz'ihb'* 'writing/painting'.

Scribes could write basic lexical roots as logograms, as syllables, or as combinations of these two categories. Where syllables accompany logograms, they mostly serve as *phonetic complements*, reinforcing or cueing their lexical values. Figure 6.2 gives several examples of the word *usiij* 'vulture'. The logogram **USIIJ** is a recognizable image of the bird's head in profile. This by itself can convey the word *usiij* in various settings, yet on its surface the sign's phonetic value may seem ambiguous, as other terms for "vulture" (*k'uuch*, for example) might be thought to be indicated with a vulture head logogram. This ambiguity is resolved through the addition of the phonetic complements **u**, **si**, and **ja**

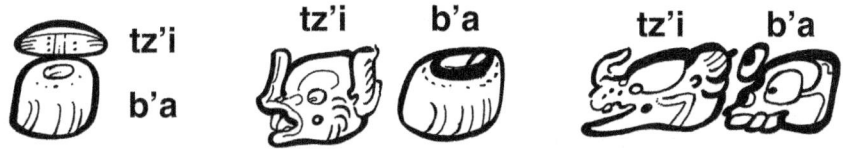

FIGURE 6.1 THREE EXAMPLES OF *TZ'IHB'*

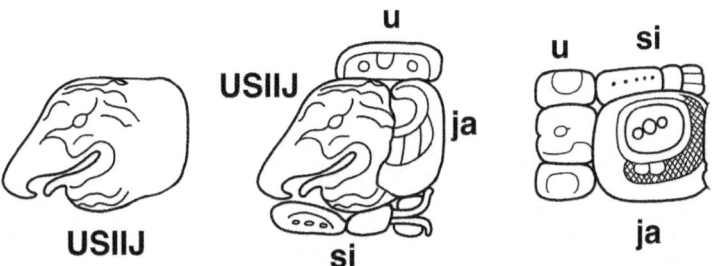

FIGURE 6.2 VARIANT SPELLINGS OF *USIIJ* 'VULTURE'

FIGURE 6.3 SYNHARMONIC SPELLINGS: *CH'OK* 'YOUTH', *LAKAM* 'BANNER', *KUTZ* 'TURKEY'

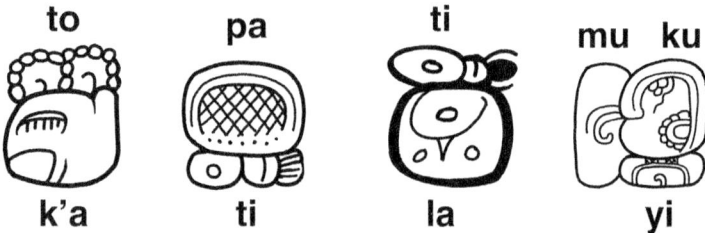

FIGURE 6.4 DISHARMONIC SPELLINGS: *TOOK'* 'FLINT KNIFE', *PAAT* 'BACK, BEHIND', *TIHL* 'TAPIR', *MUKUUY* 'DOVE'

in the combination **u-USIIJ-si-ja**. Finally, the word may be written purely phonetically with three syllables **u-si-ja**.[3]

Because syllabic signs represent both a consonant and a vowel, and most words in Classic Mayan end in a consonant, spellings using CV syllable signs often involve a final syllabic sign with an unpronounced vowel. The vowel used in this position can be synharmonic (matching the last vowel of the word) or disharmonic. The former class was first recognized by Knorosov (1954) in his initial work with spellings in the late codices, whereas disharmonic spellings were defined much later, initially by one of the authors (Stuart) and developed in collaboration with others (Houston et al. 1998). These spelling patterns suggest that the repetition of a vowel across two sequential CV signs (CV_1-CV_1) tends to point to a short internal vowel of the spelled root. This is also true when a CV syllable serves as a phonetic complement on a CVC logogram with the same vowel. Figure 6.3 provides examples of this pattern.

Disharmonic spellings tend to mark "complex" syllable nuclei that are either a long vowel (CVVC) or include an internal /h/ (CVhC) or glottal stop (CV'C) (Houston et al. 1998). One example is the disharmonic combination **u-si-ja** cited above, which apparently cues a long vowel in *usiij* 'vulture'. Other examples of disharmonic spellings are shown in Figure 6.4.

It is unclear whether the exact vowel used for disharmonic spellings could have distinguished orthographically between the three types of "complex" vowels, or whether this distinction was underspecified in the orthography. At present, the determination of which complex vowel was intended in a given disharmonic spelling is largely based on comparative evidence from other Mayan languages. Toward the end of the Late Classic, after AD 700, we find an increasing use of synharmonic spellings where disharmonic ones had long been the norm. This may be due to the loss of contrastive vowel length in the spoken language. In example (3a) a disharmonic complement **ki** agrees with the reconstructible long vowel in *-ook* 'leg'. The same word written in a Late Classic temple in Copan (3b) is spelled synharmonically **yo-ko**.

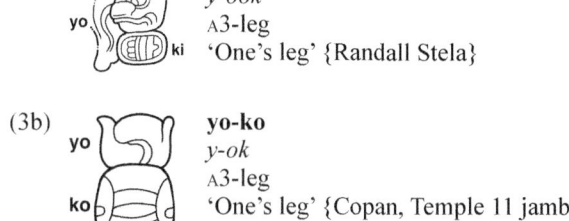

(3a)　OOK　　**yo-OOK-ki**
　　yo　　　　*y-ook*
　　　　ki　　A3-leg
　　　　　　'One's leg' {Randall Stela}

(3b)　yo　　**yo-ko**
　　ko　　　*y-ok*
　　　　　　A3-leg
　　　　　　'One's leg' {Copan, Temple 11 jamb}

At the very least, such examples appear to reflect the writing system's capacity to represent changes in phonology, if not consistently nor necessarily in "real time." It should be stressed that, like the conventions of most writing systems, these spelling "rules" were often contravened, whether by accident or design, but they do seem to be discernable tendencies that reflected scribes' sensitivities to the details of language.

4 THE LANGUAGE: TYPOLOGICAL OVERVIEW AND BASIC SYNTAX

4.1 Typological overview

The language recorded in the Classic script displays some regional and temporal variation. It is clear, however, that the corpus of texts, with a couple of possible isolated exceptions, records a single, remarkably uniform language. That language is consistent in many ways with other Mayan languages. It has a fairly small phonemic inventory, which includes contrastive distinctions in ejective versus plain stop consonants, but not between voiced and voiceless consonants (a possible three-way contrast in bilabials b'-p'-p was likely implosive vs. ejective vs. voiceless). Glottal and velar points of articulation were contrastive for stops and fricatives and vowel length was also contrastive.

Classic Mayan was a head-marking language. It was morphologically fairly agglutinative, with most words consisting of multiple clearly delimitable morphemes, and relatively little irregularity or suppletion. The language displayed ergative alignment in the morphology of person marking, as well as syntactically in focus constructions. Two separate paradigms of person markers were deployed, one of which (set A) marked the agent of transitive verbs, as well as possession in noun phrases (including the specialized set of relational nouns), while the other (set B) marked the object of transitive verbs and the single argument of intransitive verbs and stative predicates. While closely related languages, including Chol and Chontal, restrict this ergative alignment pattern to clauses in completive aspect, the language of Maya hieroglyphs shows no evidence of split ergativity.

4.2 Basic syntax

Classic Mayan was a predicate-initial language. A variety of word types could be used as predicates, including intransitive verbs, transitive verbs, and, in stative constructions, nouns. In intransitive clauses (4) and statives (5a and 5b), the subject followed the predicate.

(4)

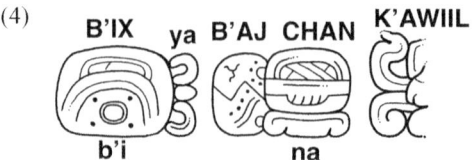

b'i-B'IX-ya B'AJ-CHAN-na [K'AWIIL-la]
b'ix-Ø =iiy   B'aj(laj) Chan K'awiil
go-B3=PST   PN
'(since) B'ajlaj Chan K'awiil went.' {Dos Pilas HS 4}

(5a)

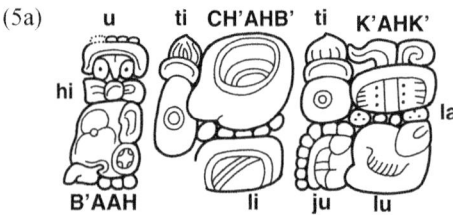

u-B'AAH-hi TI-CH'AHB'-li TI K'AHK'-la ju-lu
u-b'aah-Ø   ti   ch'ahb'-il   ti   k'ahk'-al   jul
A3-head-B3   PREP   penance-vl   PREP   fire-vl   spear
'His image is in [the act of] *ch'ahb* with a fiery spear.' {Yaxchilan L 24}

(5b)

YAX-TZUTZ-CHAN-na u-K'AB'A'-b'a-a u-LAKAM-TUUN-ni
Yax Tzutz Chan-Ø   u-k'ab'a'   u-lakam-tuun
PN-B3   A3-name   A3-large-stone
'Yax Tzutz Chan is the name of his stela.' {Copan St F}

Intransitive verbs of motion could express location syntactically by placing a location immediately following the predicate, without any preposition or relational noun, and preceding any overt subjects (6).

(6)

HUL-li ?-HA' B'AJ-CHAN-na K'AWIIL-la
hul-i-Ø   ?-ha'   B'ajl(aj)   Chan K'awiil

arrive-B3   ?-water   (TOPONYM)   PN
'Bajlaj Chan K'awiil arrives at ?-Ha' (Dos Pilas).' {Dos Pilas HS 2}

The basic word order for transitive clauses was verb-object-subject (7). Oblique arguments could be expressed in prepositional phrases and as the object of relational nouns. Deviations from a verb-initial basic word order are attested for cases of topic or focus of an argument, including OVS (8) and SVO (9). At present, we know of no clear examples where both object and subject have been fronted.

(7)

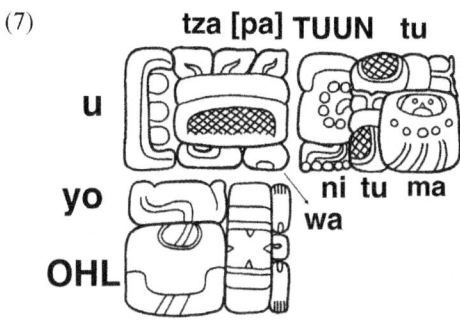

u-(tz'a-pa)-wa TUUN-ni tu-tu-ma yo-OHL-K'INICH
V   O   S
[u-tz'ap-aw-Ø]   [tuun]   [tutuum yohl k'inich]
A3-plant-TR-B3   stone   PN
'Tutuum Yohl K'inich plants the stone.' {Quirigua St C}

(8)

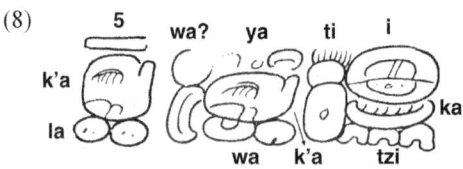

5-k'a-la wa?-ya-k'a-wa ti-i-ka-tzi
O   V   S
[ho' k'al]   wa   [y-ak'-aw-Ø]   [Ø]   ti   ikatz
5   k'al   ?   A3s-give-TR-B3   PREP tribute
'Five-score, he ? gives as tribute.' {Naranjo St 32}

(9)

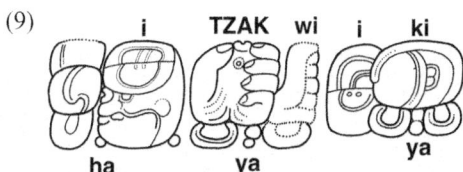

ha-i TZ'AK-wi-ya i-ki-ya
S   V   O
[haa'-Ø]   [tzak-w-Ø =iiy]   [ikiiy]
FOC-B3   grasp-AP-B3=PST   Ikiiy
'He (was the one who) conjured Ikiiy (a deity).' {La Corona Element 11}

The SVO example (9) involves what is referred to as an agent focus construction. The agent, in these cases expressed with the focus particle (and null third person marking) *haa'-Ø*, is located outside of the verb phrase in preverbal focus position and the main verb is reduced in valence through a suffix, either -V*w* or -V*n* (perhaps depending on the syllabic structure or morphology of the stem – Zender 2010:13, n. 13). In most examples of the agent focus both agent and patient are third person, so it is not clear whether the single remaining agreement on the verb (a zero-marked 'absolutive') agrees with the agent or the patient.

While the agent focus is clearly parallel to the structure found in other Mayan languages, other basic features of Classic Mayan syntax are perhaps the least understood aspect of Classic Maya grammar at present. It is increasingly apparent that coordinated and dependent clauses are pervasive in the hieroglyphic corpus, a fact that reinforces the need for further study on this topic. The body of Classic Mayan texts is a rich resource to examine basic clause types and the relationships between them since many texts that express very similar information differ precisely in terms of how the various elements of the text fit together syntactically. Given the present state of knowledge in the field, however, we limit our comments here to brief observations about two types of syntactic relations: coordinated clauses and relative clauses.

4.3 Clause coordination

Two clauses of the same type may be coordinated by juxtaposition. There are no overt markers or morphological changes to the clauses involved. Example (10) shows coordination between two possessed noun phrases *u took'* 'their flint (weapons)' and *u pakal* 'their shields' that jointly function as the subject of an undeciphered intransitive verb that refers to military defeat.

(10)

?-yi u-TOOK'-u-PAKAL
?-i-Ø   u-took'   u-pakal
?-INTR-B3   A3-flint knife   A3-shield
'His flint and shield (military might) was vanquished.' {Tonina M 91}

Another poetic commentary on warfare (example 11) exemplifies coordinated verbal phrases, *nahb'aj* 'to pool' and *witzaj* 'to heap up', along with their respective subjects *u ch'ich'el* 'their blood' and *u-jol-il* 'their skulls'.

(11)

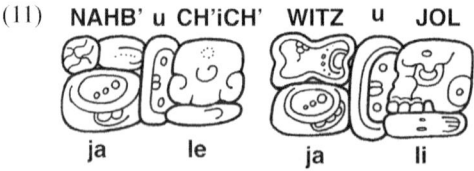

NAHB'-ja-u-CH'ICH'-le WITZ-ja-u-JOL-li
nahb'-aj-Ø   u-ch'ich'-el   witz-aj-Ø   u-jol-il

pool-INTR-B3   A3-blood-vl   hill-INTR-B3   A3-skull-vl
'Their blood pools and their skulls pile up (lit. "get hilled").' {Dos Pilas HS 2
west Step 3}

Example (12) also illustrates clausal coordination between two matrix clauses in a parallel
couplet. In this case, both verbs share a single, fronted third person plural agent *haa'oob'*
'they', as well as the prepositional phrase *ti tahnlam* 'at the half period' (of a calendric cycle)'.

(12)

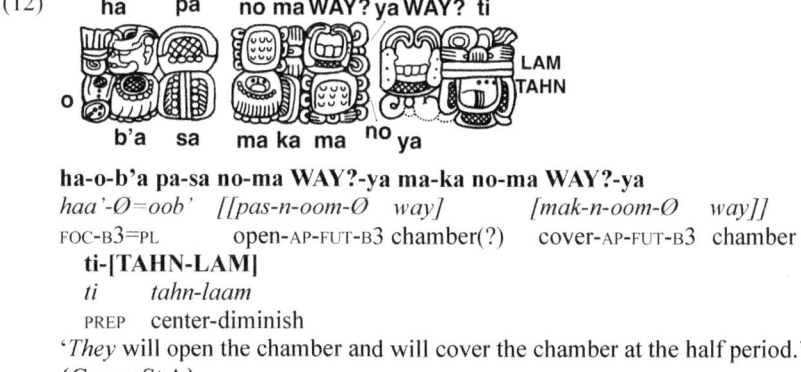

ha   pa   no ma WAY? ya WAY? ti
LAM
TAHN
b'a   sa   ma ka ma   no ya

ha-o-b'a pa-sa no-ma WAY?-ya ma-ka no-ma WAY?-ya
haa'-Ø=oob'   [[pas-n-oom-Ø   way]   [mak-n-oom-Ø   way]]
FOC-B3=PL   open-AP-FUT-B3 chamber(?)   cover-AP-FUT-B3   chamber
ti-[TAHN-LAM]
ti   tahn-laam
PREP   center-diminish
'*They* will open the chamber and will cover the chamber at the half period.'
{Copan St A}

4.4 Relative clauses

While not discussed in the literature, relative clauses appear to be a frequent structure in
Classic Mayan discourse. However, relative clauses do not appear to be morphologically
marked in most cases, but are indicated through juxtaposition. They frequently occur
with the past deictic marker *=iiy*, which appears to be limited to dependent clauses that
are intransitive or stative. Agent relative clauses use an agent focus structure with *haa'*
acting as a relative pronoun (13). We are not presently aware of examples of an object
relative clause, though these would likely be unmarked and therefore difficult in practice
to distinguish from an adjacent independent clause. Relative clauses immediately follow
the head noun that they modify.

(13)   u KAB   u CHAN nu AJAN? na TZAK wi 18 u B'AAH

ji   ya ti \ TI'   ha [i]   ya   CHAN nu
K'AHK'
u-KAB'-ji-ya u-CHAN-nu-ti-TI'-K'AHK'-AJAN?-na ha-i
u-kab'-j=iiy   u-chana'n   ti'-k'ahk'-ajan   haa'-Ø
A3-earth-DER=PST   A3-captor   PN   FOC-B3
    TZAK-wi-ya 18-u-B'AAH CHAN-nu
    tzak-w-Ø=iiy   waxak-lajuun   u-b'aah chana'n
    conjure-AP-B3=PST   PN
'. . . overseen by the captor of Ti' K'ahk' Ajan, who conjured Waxaklajuun Ub'aah
Chana'n.' {Copan St 6}

Because Classic Mayan has a null copula and third person absolutive is also null, it is
impossible to distinguish between stative relative clauses and a nominal apposition (14)

(14) **ITZAMNAAJ?**   u   ?   a   ?

B'AHLAM   nu   **CHAN**   ki

ITZAMNAAJ?-B'AHLAM u-CHAN-nu-? a-?-ki
Itzamnaaj B'ahlam   u-chana'n(-Ø)   a-?-k
PN   A3-captor(-B3)   PN
'Itzamnaaj B'ahlam, the captor of A. . . k.'
OR
'Itzamnaaj B'ahlam, *who is* the captor of A. . . k.' {Yaxchilan St 12}

5 PHONOLOGY

Writing systems are unavoidably imperfect representations of speech sounds and ancient scripts present especially difficult challenges in the study of the phonology of ancient languages. Maya hieroglyphic writing is certainly no exception. Through the script's carefully devised system of phonemic representation we can attain some sense, however imperfect, of how scribes understood and even analyzed the sound system in their own language. Overall the hieroglyphic script has proven to be surprisingly attuned to minute diachronic and diatopic variation, and, in some cases, synchronic phonological processes.

5.1 Syllable structure

The shape of syllables in Classic Mayan is simple, overall. CVC syllables predominate, particularly with roots (see Figure 6.5).

Some noun roots, as well as words involving -VC suffixes or CV- prefixes (such as the third person ergative prefix *u-*, which is phonetically CV [ʔu]) may have one or more CV syllables in the first syllable of the word.

K'IN

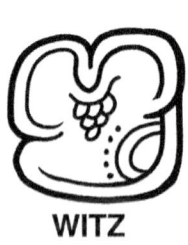

WITZ   **HAAB'**   ni

FIGURE 6.5 CVC WORDS: *WITZ* 'HILL', *HAAB* 'YEAR, SEASON', *K'IN* 'SUN, DAY'

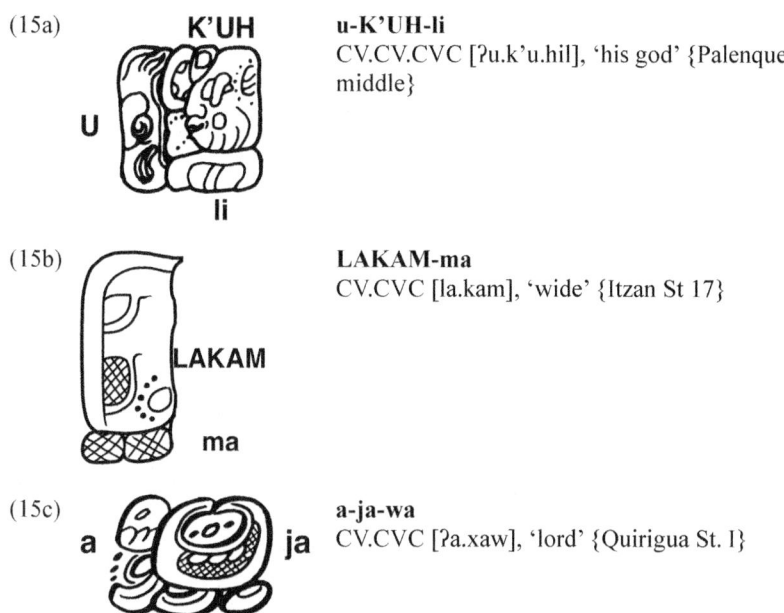

(15a)

K'UH

u-K'UH-li
CV.CV.CVC [ʔu.k'u.hil], 'his god' {Palenque TI, middle}

U

li

(15b)

LAKAM

LAKAM-ma
CV.CVC [la.kam], 'wide' {Itzan St 17}

ma

(15c)

a   **ja**

a-ja-wa
CV.CVC [ʔa.xaw], 'lord' {Quirigua St. I}

wa

Words involving single-vowel suffixes may also consist of only CV syllables

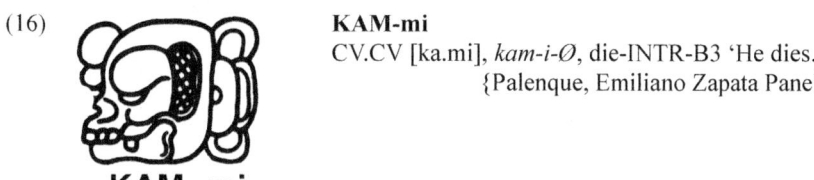

(16)

KAM-mi
CV.CV [ka.mi], *kam-i-Ø*, die-INTR-B3 'He dies.'
{Palenque, Emiliano Zapata Panel}

KAM   mi

5.2 Phonemic inventory

The phonemic inventory of Classic Mayan is presented in Tables 6.1 and 6.2. The phonemic system is fairly simple, with around 21 consonant phonemes and 10 vowel phonemes, including long and short vowels (distinguished according to disharmonic spelling conventions noted above). Phonemes in Tables 6.1 and 6.2 and text transcriptions use the standard alphabet developed and endorsed by the Academia de Lenguas Mayas de Guatemala (ALMG). Where these symbols differ from the IPA standard, we have included IPA symbol in parentheses for clarification.

Like many Mayan languages, Classic Mayan had a phonemic contrast between pulmonic egressive stops and affricates and glottalized, ejective ones. Among bilabial stops there might have been a three-way contrast between the plain (pulmonic egressive) stop, a 'glottalized' ejective, and an implosive (IPA /ɓ/). However, the presence of the bilabial ejective /p'/ is not clear in the glyphic corpus. No lexeme with this phoneme has been firmly deciphered, and historical-comparative evidence is somewhat ambiguous as to whether or not the phoneme would have existed. (see Wichmann 2006; Law 2014:42–4, Campbell, this volume, for discussion on this issue).

TABLE 6.1 CONSONANT INVENTORY

	Bilabial	Alveolar	Alveopalatal	Palatal	Velar	Glottal
Stops						
Plain	p b' (ɓ)	t			k	' (ʔ)
Ejective	p'?	t'			k'	
Affricates						
Plain		tz (ts)	ch (tʃ)			
Ejective		tz' (ts')	ch'(tʃ')			
Fricatives		s	x (ʃ)		j (x)	h
Resonants						
Nasal	m	n				
Lateral		l				
Glide	w			y (j)		

TABLE 6.2 VOWEL INVENTORY

i		u	ii (i:)		uu (u:)
e		o	ee (e:)		oo (o:)
	a			aa (a:)	

The script represented a contrast between the velar and glottal fricatives (Grube 2004), something that escaped the notice of researchers until the 1990s. Apart from the consonant inventory, the 10 vowel phonemes show a contrast between short (V) and long vowels (VV), as discussed previously in terms of spelling conventions in the hieroglyphic script.

The glottal consonants, /h/ and /'/, are phonotactically slightly different from other consonants in the language. Based on comparative evidence, it seems that both could appear between a vowel and the consonant of a syllable coda, perhaps, based on how they were treated in spelling conventions, as part of the syllable nucleus and not as a coda consonant cluster. If they are a consonant cluster, no other such consonant clusters are attested in the language. If they are part of the syllable nucleus, no other consonants occur in this syllabic position.

In addition, the glottal stop, but not the glottal fricative, appears not to have been phonemic word-initially. All syllables are phonetically consonant-initial. Stems that begin with glottal stop, however, only maintain that glottal stop word-initially. When they appear with a prefix, like the ergative pronouns, the glottal stop is lost.

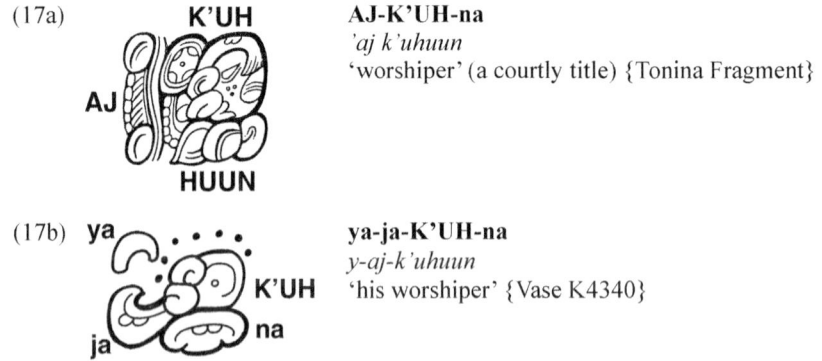

(17a) **K'UH** / **AJ** / **HUUN**
AJ-K'UH-na
'aj k'uhuun
'worshiper' (a courtly title) {Tonina Fragment}

(17b) **ya** / **ja** / **K'UH** / **na**
ya-ja-K'UH-na
y-aj-k'uhuun
'his worshiper' {Vase K4340}

For this reason it appears that word-initial glottal stops are not phonemically contrastive.

5.3 Phonological rules and processes

While there were doubtless many phonological processes that occurred in the spoken version of Classic Mayan, the phonemic nature of its written representation means that those processes are prone to be "undone" in the written record. However, there are several spellings that suggest general processes of epenthesis and deletion. Here, we discuss three of these that occur with varying degrees of frequency.

5.3.1 Syncope

Perhaps the most widespread phonological process attested in the glyphs is the deletion of underlying vowels in a tri-syllabic word. When a sequence of segments of the form CVCVCVC occurs as a single word, the second vowel, the nucleus of the second syllable, is elided to form two CVC syllables (see Stuart 1987).

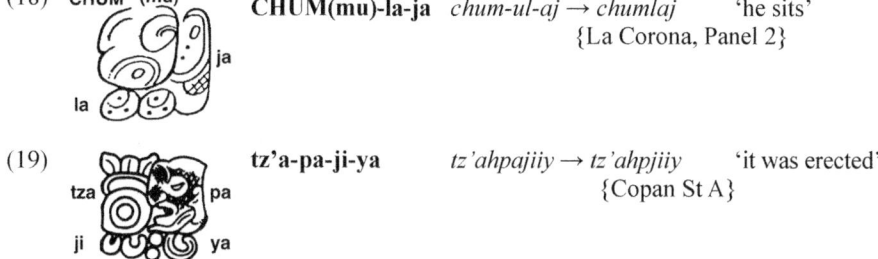

(18) CHUM (mu)   **CHUM(mu)-la-ja**   *chum-ul-aj* → *chumlaj*   'he sits'
la ja   {La Corona, Panel 2}

(19)   **tz'a-pa-ji-ya**   *tz'ahpajiiy* → *tz'ahpjiiy*   'it was erected'
tza pa   {Copan St A}
ji ya

In certain derived nouns we see a similar process at work.

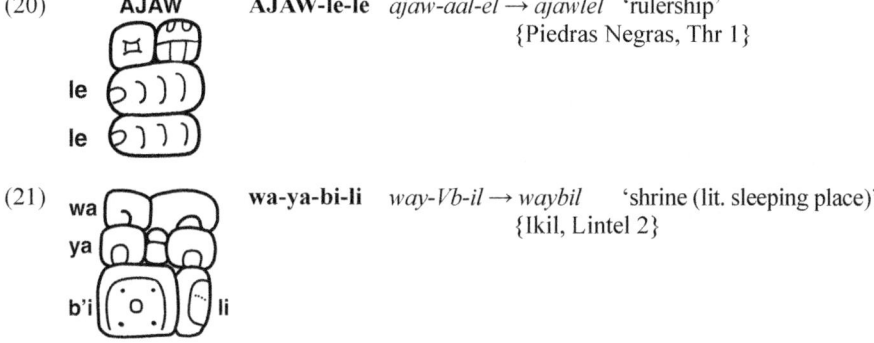

(20)   AJAW   **AJAW-le-le**   *ajaw-aal-el* → *ajawlel*   'rulership'
le   {Piedras Negras, Thr 1}
le

(21) wa   **wa-ya-bi-li**   *way-Vb-il* → *waybil*   'shrine (lit. sleeping place)'
ya   {Ikil, Lintel 2}
b'i li

This vowel elision is only evident in the script because of the obvious spelling contrast between two-syllable words and three-syllable derived forms of those same words. The contrast between passivized root transitives (with -*h*-. . .-*aj*) and the same form with the adverbial enclitic -*iiy* is a good example of this. When the clitic is not present, in syllabically spelled forms, the /a/ of the intransitive suffix -*aj* is represented: **jo-ch'a-ja** *johch'aj* 'it is drilled'. However, when the past tense suffix is there, the syllable used to spell out the root will match the vowel of the root: **jo-ch'o-ji-ya**, *johch'jiiy* '[since] it was drilled'. This is common practice for silent vowels in phonetic complements. When it is not pronounced, the vowel of a syllabic sign frequently agrees with the preceding vowel.

5.3.2 Adjacent vowels: VV → V'V, V', V

As with many other Mayan languages, Classic Mayan had a particular aversion to V-V sequences. However, the shape of morphemes, some being VC and some CV, makes it very possible to achieve sequences in which two vowels are underlyingly adjacent. In one such context, the ergative prefixes, this "clash of the vowels" is avoided because of the existence of a distinct set of ergative prefixes specifically for vowel-initial stems. In other cases, it is clear from historical reconstruction or internal analysis that a particular example involves underlying adjacent vowels, but the spelling conventions are poorly understood, or simply do not specify the exact phonological form, leaving us uncertain how the conflict was resolved. There are some clues in the glyphic data, however, that illuminate, at least partially, some of the strategies used to resolve V-V sequences.

One interesting example is the complex prepositional phrase 'to him/her', usually spelled **tu-B'AAH** *t-u-b'aah*. This involves three underlying morphemes: the preposition *ti* or *ta*, an ergative pronoun *u* and the noun *b'aah* 'head/self': *ti(~ta)-u-b'aah*. This leaves the adjacent vowels *i(~a)-u* in the underlying form. In the most common form of this expression, the first vowel was simply elided: *t-u-b'aah* (23c). Two other strategies are also attested, however. In a couple of rare occurrences, including the Early Classic Tikal Stela 4 (23a), the insertion of a glottal stop, with both vowels maintained, appears to have been used (*ta-'u-b'aah*). In the Palenque area, a kind of intermediate strategy is attested with the spelling **tu-'u-b'aah** for *tu'b'aah*, in which a glottal stop is inserted and the vowel of the preposition deleted (23b).

(22a) **ta   u**

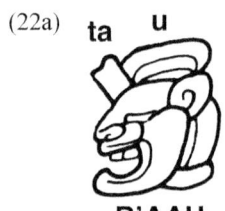

B'AAH

ta-'u-B'AAH
ta   'u-b'aah
PREP   A3-head
'On his head/self' {Tikal St 4}

(22b) **tu   u**

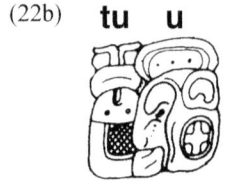

B'AAH

tu-'u-B'AAH
t-u'-b'aah
PREP-A3-head/self
'On his head/self' {Palenque Tab Sun}

(22c) **tu**

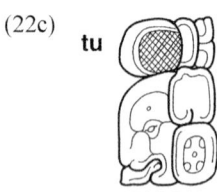

B'AAH

tu-B'AAH
t-u-b'aah
PREP-A3-head/self
'On his head/self' {Chinikiha Pan 1}

5.3.3 Coda deletion: CVC-CVC → CV-CVC (optionally, when C is n, l, y, w, j, or h)

Certain consonants are more susceptible than others to deletion. In some cases, particularly when immediately followed by a consonant-initial syllable, the coda consonants n, l, y, w, j, or h were optionally not written. We interpret this as evidence of coda deletion of sonorants and velar and glottal fricatives. These are not very common in the script, but known examples include:

(23)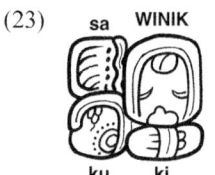

sa-ku-WINIK-ki
saku(n) winik
'older brother' {Palenque Palace Tab}

(24)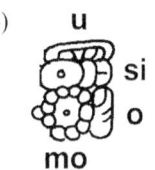

u-si-mo-'o
usi(ij) mo'
'vulture macaw (dance)' {Yaxchilan area lintel}

These seem to occur in cases of compound nouns when the first noun is bisyllabic. However, in practice, it is difficult to distinguish spellings that indicate a deleted consonant in the phonetic realization of a word from under-spellings, which also occur, and which are presumed to be orthographic abbreviations that do not indicate anything about the pronunciation of the represented form.

6 MORPHOLOGY AND WORD CLASSES

The hieroglyphic corpus attests a range of inflectional and derivational morphemes as well as a variety of clause types and syntactic structures. Several morphological facts of the language, as discussed next, can lead to a great deal of potential ambiguity of interpretation of specific texts. However, continuing linguistic and decipherment work has the potential to shed greater light on such grammatically ambiguous passages.

6.1 Person marking

The two sets of person markers found in the Classic corpus (ergative and absolutive) are presented in Table 6.3. Here and throughout, a question mark (?) indicates that the morpheme identification is uncertain, or not widely accepted in the field. An asterisk (*) indicates that the form is unattested and therefore is a hypothetical reconstruction using standard procedures of the comparative method.

By far the most common forms are those in the third person, as shown by the ubiquitous presence of the *u-* and *y-* prefixes in the script, marking either possession or the

TABLE 6.3 SET A AND SET B PERSON MARKERS

	Set A (ergative) Person Markers				Set B (absolutive) Person Markers	
	Singular		Plural		Singular	Plural
	_C	_V	_C	_V		
1	ni-	w-	?ka-	?k-	-een	?-o'n
2	a-	aw-	?i-	*iiw-	?-at/ ?-eet	*-eex
3	u-	y-	u-	y-	-∅	-∅

agents of transitive verbs. While non-third person forms are also attested, they are often difficult to interpret (see Law et al. 2014 for more discussion of non-third person forms). Among the absolutive (set B) markers, the second person absolutive -*at* is fairly clearly attested with the syllable /ta/. There is some question, however, as to whether the vowel of the suffix is the more conservative /a/ or if it reflects the innovative /ee/ vowel found in the modern Ch'olan languages. The two known examples of a possible first person plural suffix -*o'n* both involve roots that are not known, or are unclear contextually, so it is not firmly established that these are, in fact, set B person markers. The proposed examples of first person plural markers for set A are likewise somewhat controversial. No occurrence of the second person plural (reconstructable as *-eex* for the set B markers and *ii- ~ *iiw- for set A) has yet been uncontroversially identified.

(25)  **wi**
a **na**
ke **na**

a-wi-na ke-na
a-winak-een
A2SG-servant-B1SG
'I am your servant.' {Piedras Negras L 3 caption}

The ergative set is used in transitive verb phrases to reference the subject and on nouns to reference the possessor. If overt and not just pronominal, the possessor follows the possessed nouns. Because of this, if a noun phrase with a possessive marker is used, one can occasionally see a sequence of two consecutive ergative markers. All examples of this involve honorific titles or status terms that use an embedded possessive structure, such as the term *yajawte'* (lit. "lord of the tree"):

(26)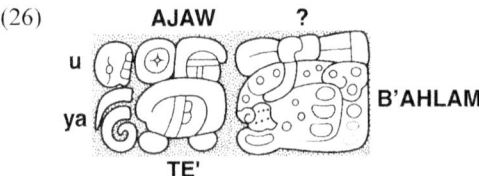

u-ya-AJAW-TE' ?-B'AHLAM
u-y-ajaw-te'   ?-b'ahlam
A3-A3-lord-tree PN
'(he is) the lord-of-the-tree of ? B'ahlam.' {Yaxchilan L 35}

Example 26 has two distinct, nested possessive markers, with distinct referents *te'* 'tree', the possessor of *ajaw* 'lord', and *? B'ahlam*, the possessor of *y-ajaw-te'* 'lord of the tree'. This contrasts with unpossessed examples of the same title, which have only the ergative marker that agrees with the title-internal possessor *te'* 'tree':

(27)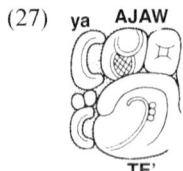

ya-AJAW-TE'
y-ajaw-te'
A3-lord-tree
'(he is) the lord-of-the-tree.' {Yaxchilan HS3, Step 4}

6.2 Plural agreement

As noted above, plurality was indicated obligatorily for first and second person plural person marking (at least for the forms that are attested). Plurality for nouns and third person plural verb agreement was optional and limited to plurality of animates, or possibly only humans and supernatural beings. Example 28 shows a case in which a clearly plural referent takes agreement that is unmarked for plural. In it, the oven, *chitinil*, is possessed by three supernatural beings, but the possessive marker *u-* is unmarked for number.

(28)

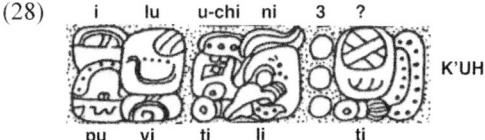

u-chi-ti-ni-li 3-?-ti K'UH
u-chitin-il ux-?t k'uh
A3-oven-vl three-? god
'The oven of the three ? gods.' {Palenque Temple of the Cross}

The main optional plural marker is an enclitic *=oob'*. The following examples show use of the plural enclitic *=oob'* on a nominal form (29), the third person independent pronoun (30), and on both intransitive (31) and transitive (32) verbs.

(29)

TZAK-K'AWIIL-OOB'?
tzak-k'awiil=oob'?
conjure-K'awiil=PL
'conjure-k'awiils (supernatural being).' {Yaxchilan L 39}

(30)

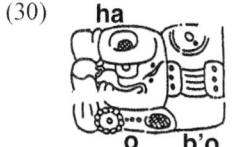

ha-'o-b'o
ha'-Ø=ob (Note loss of vowel length, cf. *haa'-oob*)
FOC-B3-PL
'they' {Copan T 11 jamb}

(31)

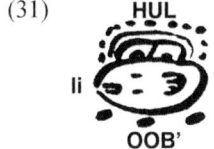

HUL-li-OOB'
hul-i-Ø=oob'
arrive-INTR-B3=PL
'They arrive.' {Naj Tunich Drawing 52}

(32)

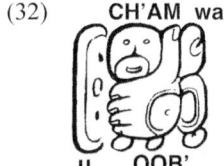

u-CH'AM-wa-OOB'
u-ch'am-aw-Ø=oob'
A3-receive-TR-B3-PL
'He receives them.' {Palenque TXIX platform}

In addition to the plural enclitic *=oob'*, multiplicity could be indicated with a enclitic *=taak* (33). Examples of *=taak* are also all animate, and based on cognate forms in modern Chol and Tseltal, it is likely that it indicates collective or distributive, rather than strictly plural.

(33)

4-TE'-ch'o-ko-TAAK
chan-te' ch'ok=taak
four-CLF: generic youth=PL
'the four youths' {Copan St I}

**4
TE'
ko
ch'o
TAAK**

6.3 Root and word classes

There are several classes of roots that are discernible in the glyphic corpus and that agree
generally with the root classes found in other Mayan languages. Root classes include
intransitive verbs, transitive verbs, positionals, nouns, prepositions, and numbers. Tentative identification of some affect roots has also been proposed (Zender 2010). Verbs,
positionals, and possibly affect words cannot be used alone as stems. Nouns, prepositions, and numbers can. All root classes except for prepositions can occur, depending on
morphological derivation and syntactic position, as a variety of word types, including at
least intransitive verbs, transitive verbs, nouns, adjectives, and adverbs. Here, we provide
a brief overview of the distribution and distinguishing characteristics of each of these
major root classes.

6.3.1 Transitives

Intransitive, transitive, and positional roots communicate events and states and are almost
entirely of the form CVC (some of these are ?VC; as noted previously, the phonemic
status of syllable-initial glottal stop is questionable). Transitive roots refer to actions with
two core arguments. They must carry morphological marking in order to be used in a
verb phrase. When used in transitive clauses they take a vowel harmonic suffix -V_1w that
is consistently written with the syllabic sign **wa** (34). The vowel harmonic nature of this
root is evident in phonetic spellings of roots. When the syllabic signs spell out the final
consonant of the root, these always use a vowel that matches the vowel of the root (35).

(34)

u-CHOK-wa-ch'a-ji K'AWIIL-CHAN-na-K'INICH
u-chok-ow-Ø   ch'aaj   k'awiil chan k'inich
A3-throw-TR-B3   incense PN
'K'awiil Chan K'inich casts incense.' {Seibal HS Tab 3}

(35)

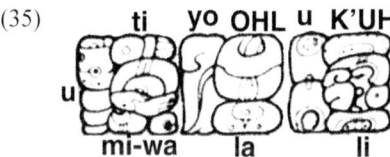

u-ti-mi-wa yo-OHL-la u-K'UH-li
u-tim-iw-Ø   y-ohl   u-k'uh-il
A3-incline-TR-B3   A3-heart   A3-god-vl
'He pleases his gods.' {Palenque TI west}

In transitive clauses, the subject is indicated on the verb with the ergative (set A) person markers and the object is referenced with the absolutive (set B) markers. The third person absolutive marker is -Ø, and no clear examples of transitive verbs with first or second person absolutive markers have been identified (though non-third person marking for the subject of a transitive verb does exist), so in the attested corpus, transitive verbs only have overt marking for the ergative. This means that, in terms of person marking, transitive phrases and possessed noun phrases are identical, with context and affixation distinguishing the two.

While derivation is widespread in Maya hieroglyphic texts (a topic that is illustrated in most of the subsections of §6.3), derivational morphemes that yield transitive words are uncommon. Only three possible transitivizing suffixes have been proposed to exist in the corpus of inscriptions: a transitive suffix for positional roots, discussed in §6.3.2; a possible causative transitive -se/-es (or -esa); and a transitivizing suffix -V that varies between -i and -a, both of which are infrequent and their existence is debatable.

6.3.2 Positionals

Positionals are another root class that cannot occur without suffixation. They typically have stative or inchoative meanings (depending on suffixation) related to orientation or form. They are readily identifiable through a suite of morphemes that are unique to this root class. Most hieroglyphic attestations of positional roots are intransitive verb phrases. Positional roots are derived as intransitive verbs with one of two suffixes, -laj and -wani. There does not appear to be a functional difference between the two. There are both geographical and temporal patterns of variation for these two suffixes (-wani appears to be a late and western innovation) but there are examples of the use of both forms within a single site and even a single text in the same grammatical context, so the variation must have also been stylistically motivated. Other positional morphology includes the stative -Vil, a possible positional transitive suffix -bu ~ -Vb, and a possible nominal/gerundive -taal, though in this case, the sole example of the suffix is not grammatically clear.

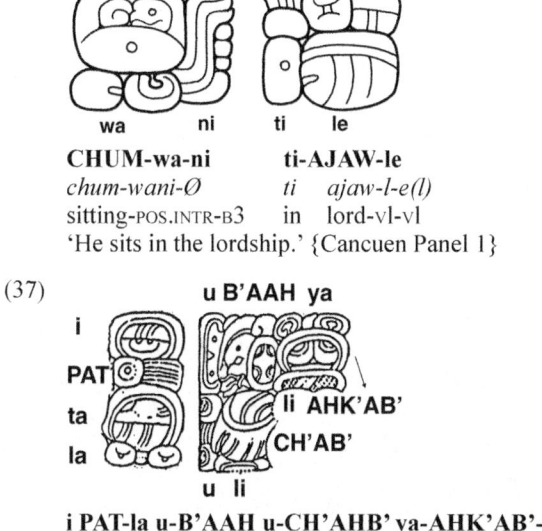

(36) CHUM (mu)   AJAW

wa   ni   ti   le

CHUM-wa-ni   **ti-AJAW-le**
chum-wani-Ø   *ti*   *ajaw-l-e(l)*
sitting-POS.INTR-B3   in   lord-vl-vl
'He sits in the lordship.' {Cancuen Panel 1}

(37)   u B'AAH ya

i
PAT   li AHK'AB'
ta   CH'AB'
la

u   li

i PAT'-la u-B'AAH u-CH'AHB' ya-AHK'AB'-li
i   *pat-al-Ø*   *u-b'aah   u-ch'ahb'   y-ahk'ab'-aal*

then   form-POS.Vl-B3   A3-head   A3-penance   A3-night-Vl
'Now the embodiment of his *ch'ahb*, his *ak'ab* is formed.' {Copan St I}

(38)   u TZ'AK   u   pa   ?

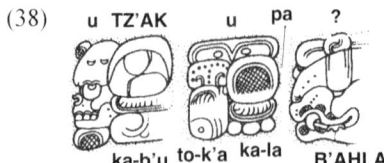

ka-b'u to-k'a ka-la   **B'AHLAM**

u-TZ'AK-ka-b'u u-to-k'a-pa-ka-la [?-B'AHLAM]
u-tz'ak-(V)b'u   u-took'-pakal   ? b'ahlam
A3-complete-TR   A3-flint-shield   PN
'He completes the war of ? Bahlam (a predecessor).' {Yaxchilan, L46}

(39)   **B'AAH   CHUM (mu)**

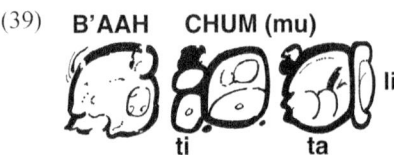

ti   ta   li

B'AAH ti-CHUM ta-li
b'aah-Ø   ti   chum-taal
head-B3   PREP   sitting-POS?
'His person [is] in [the act of] sitting.' {Ceramic vessel, Kerr 2784}

Aside from the morphology unique to positionals, the only derivational process that appears to affect positionals is nominalization, which is discussed in §6.3.4.2 below.

6.3.3 *Intransitives*

Single argument predicates, both stative and verbal (intransitive), are very frequent in hieroglyphic texts and there is an appropriately developed set of resources attested in the corpus that derive intransitive verbs and nominalizations, as well as a large set of intransitive roots.

6.3.3.1 Intransitive roots

Intransitive roots seem not to occur without overt morphological adornment, though this is ambiguous in some examples spelled logographically. In intransitive verb phrases, root intransitives (and some derived intransitives) have a suffix *-i*. This is generally spelled using a syllabic sign Ci where the consonant reflects the final C of the root. In example (40) the intransitive root *tal* 'to arrive' is marked as an intransitive verb stem with the suffix *-i*.

(40)

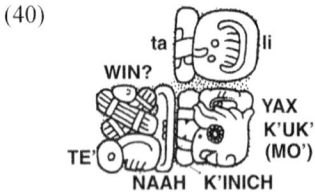

ta   li
WIN?
YAX
K'UK'
(MO')
TE'
NAAH K'INICH

ta-li WIIN?-TE'-NAAH K'INICH-YAX-[K'UK'-MO']
tal-i-Ø   wiin(?)-te'-naah K'inich Yax K'uk' Mo'

come-INTR-B3   ?-tree-house   PN
'K'inich Yax K'uk' Mo' comes from the "? House" (a ceremonial structure),'
{Copan Alt Q}

An overt syllabic spelling of the suffix is usually present even when the root is spelled logographically (41). However, there are examples of an intransitive root spelled logographically without any syllabic complementation (42). The variation does not appear to be conditioned linguistically and it seems reasonable to assume that in such cases, the *-i* suffix would have been pronounced.

(41)

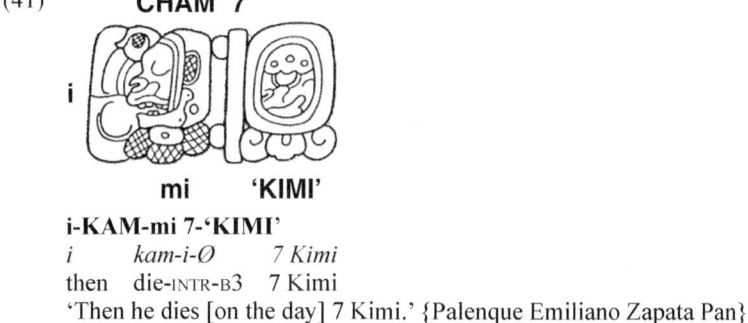

CHAM 7

i

mi   **'KIMI'**

i-KAM-mi 7-'KIMI'
i   kam-i-Ø   7 Kimi
then   die-INTR-B3   7 Kimi
'Then he dies [on the day] 7 Kimi.' {Palenque Emiliano Zapata Pan}

(42)   **CHAM   ?**

KAM ?
kam(-i)-Ø   ?
die-INTR-B3   ?(god name)
'The ?(god) dies.' {Tikal MT 29}

As these examples show, intransitive verb stems obligatorily inflect with absolutive (set B) person markers. There are currently no clear known examples of an intransitive verb with first or second person inflection. Because the marker of third person absolutive is null, all examples of intransitive verb phrases in the glyphic corpus lack overt person marking. It is unclear if the *-i* marker of root intransitives would have been used with first and second person absolutive markers or not (in Cholti it remains, in Chol and Chontal it is elided). New texts and analyses may yet clarify this.

Intransitivizing derivational and valence-changing morphology is exceptionally well represented in the glyphic corpus. The majority of verbal predicates in the hieroglyphic corpus are intransitive. Many of these are either root intransitives or passive forms (<*h*>. . .-*aj*, -*naj*). There are also frequent examples of two antipassive suffixes (-*Vw* and -*Vn*), a mediopassive or inchoative suffix (-*V¹y*) and noun-intransitivizing suffix -*aj* or -*iij*.

6.3.3.2 Passive

Passive voice phrases in hieroglyphic texts require a suffix, which is *-aj* for transitive roots and *-naj* for derived transitive stems. Comparative evidence suggests that the full form of the passive for root transitives also had an infixed <h> following the vowel of the root. This is not indicated orthographically, however.

(43)

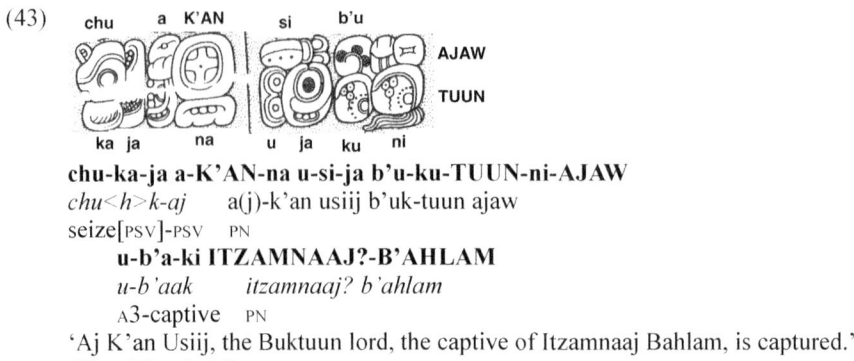

chu-ka-ja a-K'AN-na u-si-ja b'u-ku-TUUN-ni-AJAW
chu<h>k-aj   a(j)-k'an usiij b'uk-tuun ajaw
seize[PSV]-PSV   PN

    u-b'a-ki ITZAMNAAJ?-B'AHLAM
    u-b'aak   *itzamnaaj? b'ahlam*
    A3-captive   PN

'Aj K'an Usiij, the Buktuun lord, the captive of Itzamnaaj Bahlam, is captured.'
{Yaxchilan L 46}

Derived transitives take the suffix *-naj* in the passive voice. It is unclear if these forms are derived first into a transitive verb with the *-V* transitivizing suffix mentioned above, or if they are simply intransitive verbs derived from a noun. It does appear, however, that the associated argument is semantically the patient.

(44)

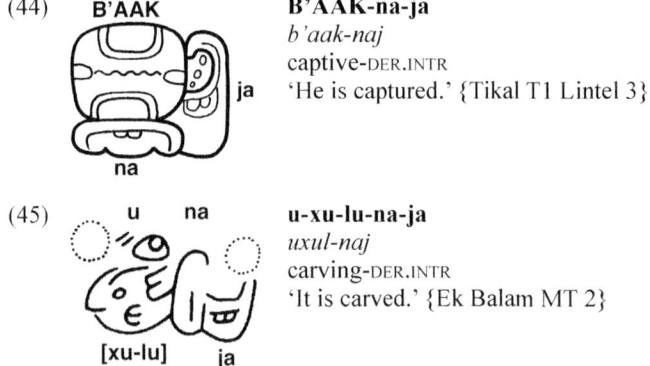

B'AAK-na-ja
b'aak-naj
captive-DER.INTR
'He is captured.' {Tikal T1 Lintel 3}

(45)

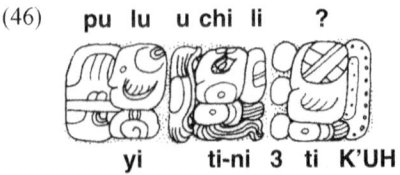

u-xu-lu-na-ja
uxul-naj
carving-DER.INTR
'It is carved.' {Ek Balam MT 2}

6.3.3.3 Inchoative *-V₁y(i)*

Another suffix that is occasionally found on root transitives in intransitive verbal contexts is the vowel harmonic suffix $-V_1y$. This is always indicated orthographically with the syllabic sign **-yi** and it is unclear whether or not the /i/ of the syllable was also pronounced, possibly to represent the same thematic marker of intransitives found on root intransitives.

The $-V_1y$ suffix can attach to transitive roots in contexts where the <h>. . .-*aj* passive can also occur. When the $-V_1y$ suffix is used on transitive roots, the single remaining argument is the semantic patient of the verb.

(46)

pu-lu-yi u-chi-ti-ni-li 3-?-ti K'UH
pul-uy-i-Ø   *u-chitin-il*   *ux-?*   *k'uh*
burn-MP-INTR-B3   A3-oven-vl   three-?   god
'The three gods are fired in his oven.' {Palenque Temple of the Foliated Cross}

This form is often described as a 'mediopassive', although the precise semantic and structural difference between *<h>. . .-aj* and *-V₁y* for transitive roots is not entirely clear. The agent of transitive verbs with *-V₁y* can be expressed obliquely with *u-kab-j-iiy*.

(47)

TZUTZ-yi u-11-WINIKHAAB' u-KAB'[ji]-ya K'INICH JAN PAKAL
tzutz-uy-Ø   *u-b'uluk-winikhaab'*   *u-kab'-j=iiy*   *k'inich janahb'pakal*
finish-MP-B3   A3-eleven-k'atun   A3-earth-DER=PST   PN
'The eleventh k'atun is finished under the authority of K'inich Janahb' Pakal.' {Palenque Tab 96}

Unlike the *<h>. . .-aj* passive, however, the *-V₁y* suffix is also found frequently on a sub-set of intransitive roots, specifically those that have inchoative or change-of-state meanings.

(48)

ju-b'u-yi u-TOK'-PAKAL yi-ICH'AHK K'AHK' K'UH
jub'-uy-i-Ø   *u-tok'-pakal*   *y-ich'ahk*   *k'ahk'*   *k'uh(-ul)*
fall-MP-INTR-B3   A3-flint-shield   A3-claw   fire   god(-vl)
     ka-KAN AJAW
     kan(ul?)   *ajaw*
     snake   lord

'The armaments of Yich'ahk K'ahk', the Holy Kanul Lord, fall.' {Tikal T1, L3}

(49)

LOK'-yi
lok'-oy-i-Ø
exit-MP-INTR-B3
'He leaves.' {Dos Pilas HS2)

6.3.3.4 Antipassive

There are also several examples of transitive roots in what have traditionally been called antipassive structures, though, as mentioned previously, they do not always involve the demotion of the object. These use one of two suffixes, *-Vw(i)* and *-Vn(i)*. Those two suffixes are found in several different structures: the previously discussed agent focus (50), in which the agent of the transitive verb is removed from the verb phrase, for-mally intransitivizing the verb, and placed before the verb in focus position; and the object-incorporating antipassive, in which both agent and patient of the verb remain in situ, but the object becomes a generic, rather than specific, referent; these can include nouns with a variety of modifiers (51), and the verb is formally intransitive, only inflected with one (absolutive) person marker (52). We have been unable to identify any textual examples of what might be considered a true (absolutive) 'antipassive' structure, in which any reference to an object is entirely removed from the phrase.

(50)

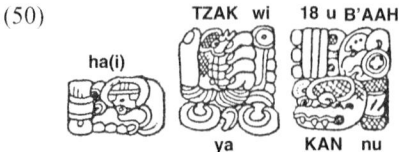

ha-i TZAK-wi-ya 18-u-B'AAH CHAN-nu
haa'-Ø   tzak-w-Ø=iiy   waxak-lajuun u-b'aah chan
FOC-B3   conjure-AP-B3=PST   PN
'He conjured the eighteen-heads-serpent (a war deity).' {Copan St 6}

(51)

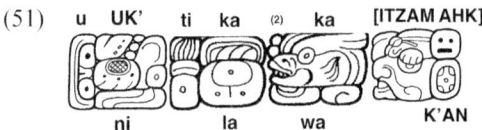

u-k'u-ni ti-ka-la ka²-wa ITZAM K'AN AHK
uk'-n-i-Ø   tikal   kakaw   itzam k'an ahk
drink-AP-INTR-B3 hot?   cocoa   PN
'Itzam k'an Ahk drinks hot? cocoa.' {Piedras Negras Panel 3}

(52)

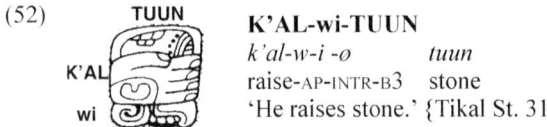

K'AL-wi-TUUN
k'al-w-i -ø   tuun
raise-AP-INTR-B3   stone
'He raises stone.' {Tikal St. 31}

The difference in distribution between *-Vw* and *-Vn* is currently unclear. There are no known examples of the same stem occurring with both, so it is possible that the difference is lexically or phonologically determined (Zender 2010:13, n. 13).

6.3.3.5 Noun > Intransitive

In addition to productive valency-altering morphology that creates intransitive verbs from transitive verbs, there is also a very productive set of derivational suffixes that derive intransitive verbs from nouns, including nominalized verbs. This is done with either *-aj* or possibly *-iij*, which may be considered allomorphs of a single productive suffix. Note the contrasts in 53 and 54 of nouns and the verbs derived from them.

(53a)

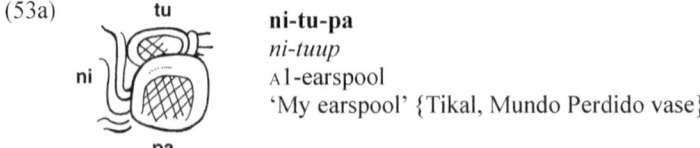

ni-tu-pa
ni-tuup
A1-earspool
'My earspool' {Tikal, Mundo Perdido vase}

(53b)

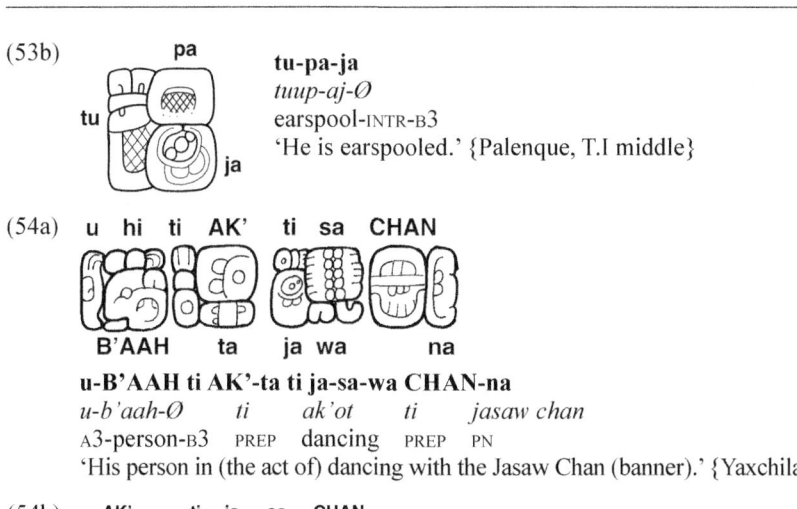

pa

tu

ja

tu-pa-ja
tuup-aj-Ø
earspool-INTR-B3
'He is earspooled.' {Palenque, T.I middle}

(54a) u hi ti AK' ti sa CHAN

B'AAH ta ja wa na

u-B'AAH ti AK'-ta ti ja-sa-wa CHAN-na
u-b'aah-Ø   ti   ak'ot   ti   jasaw chan
A3-person-B3 PREP dancing PREP PN
'His person in (the act of) dancing with the Jasaw Chan (banner).' {Yaxchilan, L 33}

(54b)   AK'   ti ja sa CHAN

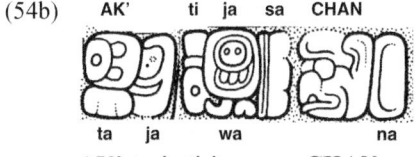

ta   ja   wa   na

AK'-ta-ja ti-ja-sa-wa CHAN-na
ak'(o)t-aj-Ø   ti   jasaw chan
dancing-INTR-B3 PREP PN
'He dances with the Jasaw Chan (banner).' {Yaxchilan L 9}

In some of these examples the suffix derives a verb from a compound noun consisting of a verb and an object (if it is transitive) or a location (if an intransitive verb of motion), a productive nominalization strategy that is discussed in §6.3.4.2.2 below. For nominalizations from transitive verbs, this structure can be somewhat ambiguous with the passive form – both have a clear object and the passive and intransitivizing suffixes are both spelled with the syllabic sign **ja**. However, the underlying structure is quite different, since in the passive form, the semantic patient fills the single argument position for the verb phrase, while in the case of intransitivized compound nouns, the single argument is the semantic agent of the verb. Thus, in examples such as 55, below, the single argument of the verb is recorded as the Tikal king *Sihyaj Chan K'awiil*, and not the semantic patient of the verb, *hu'n*, as would be expected for a passive construction.

(55a)   HU'N   SIH [K'AWIIL]

K'AL

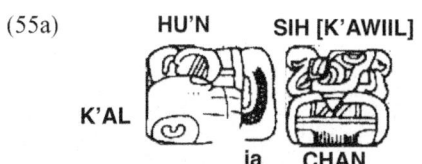

ja   CHAN

K'AL-HU'N-ja sihyaj chan k'awiil
k'al-hu'n-aj-Ø   Sihyaj Chan K'awiil
raise-paper-INTR PN
'Sihyaj Chan K'awiil crown-raises.' {Tikal St 31}

(55b)

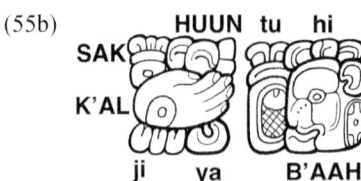

K'AL-ji-ya SAK-HU'N tu-B'AAH
k'a<h>l-j-Ø=iiy   sak-hu'n   t-u-b'aah
raise[PSV]-PSV-B3=PST white-paper PREP-A3-person
'The white paper (diadem) is raised onto his head.' {Palenque Palace Tab}

(56)

OCH
i   **OCH-B'IH-ja**
i   och-b'ih-aj-Ø
then   enter-road-INTR-B3
'Then he road-enters (dies).' {Palenque Palace Tab}

b'i

6.3.4 Nouns

6.3.4.1 Underived nouns and derivations

Underived nouns can occur as arguments in a verb phrase, a modifier, an adjunct, or as the head of a stative predicate. Nominal roots are slightly more varied in terms of their phonological shape, and include CVCVC (e.g. *kakaw* 'cacao beans') and CVCCVC (*ko'haw* 'helmet') roots, as well as the more common CVC (*witz*). Nouns generally refer to things, places, and ideas. Unlike verbs and positionals, most nouns do not require morphological derivation, though a subclass of nouns must be possessed unless derived. For these words, the morpheme used to derive unpossessed forms is the *-Vl* suffix, though the vowel for this can vary from word to word, and some words take a suffix *-is* or *-aas*, though it is unclear if this is simply lexically determined or if there is a semantic difference in the morphemes used:

(57a)   **u CH'AHB'**

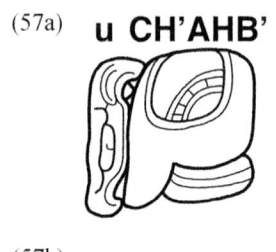

U-CH'AHB'
u-ch'ahb'
A3-penance
'his penance' {Palenque TS}

(57b)   **CH'AHB'**

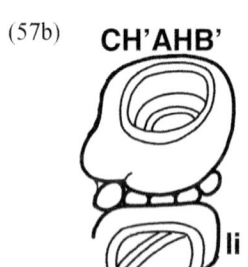

CH'AHB'-li
ch'ahb'-il
penance-vl
'penance' {Yaxchilan L 24}

(58a)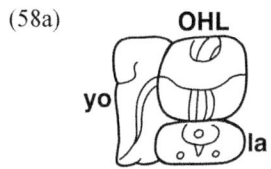

yo-OHL-la
y-ohl
A3-heart
'its heart, center' {Palenque TI middle}

(58b)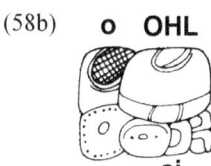

OHL-la-si
ohl-is
heart-ABS
'heart'{Palenque Palace Tab}

Other nouns are not generally possessed and require derivation, usually with the abstracting *-V(V)l* suffix, when they are possessed. This suffix is consistently spelled with the syllabic sign **li**, but there is some evidence that the suffix may have two allomorphs that are mostly phonologically conditioned, *-il* for CVC stems (59) and *-aal* for non-CVC stems (60). Exceptions to this appear to be lexically determined.

(59a)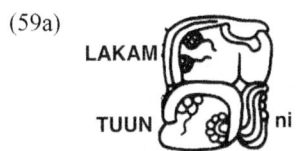

LAKAM-TUUN-ni
lakam-tuun
banner stone
'stela' {Copan St. A}

(59b)

U-LAKAM-TUUN-ni-li
u lakam-tuun-il
A3-banner-stone-Vl
'his stela'

(60a)

i	TZAK-ja	K'AWIIL-la	U-KAB'=ya 4-TE'	ch'o-ko
i	*tza\<h\>k-aj-Ø*	*k'awiil*	*u-kab'=iiy 4-te'*	*ch'ok*
then	conjure[PSV]-PSV-B3	k'awiil	A3-earth=? 4-CLF:GEN	youth

'Then K'awiil is conjured under the authority of the four youths.'{Copan St I}

(60b)

U-TZAK-wa U-K'AWIIL(wi)-la-li
u-tzak-aw-Ø   *u-k'awiil-aal*
A3-conjure-trans-B3   A3-K'awiil-vl
'He conjures his K'awiil.' {Yaxchilan, L 25}

Another suffix, *-el*, which derives attached or inherently associated body parts, is attested for the words *b'aakel* (one's bone) and *ch'ich'el* (one's blood).

(61)

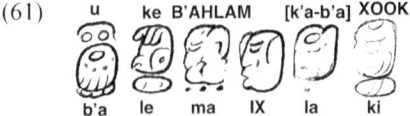

u **ke B'AHLAM** [k'a-b'a] **XOOK**

b'a le ma IX la ki

u-b'a ke-le B'AHLAM-ma IX (k'a-b'a)-la XOOK-ki
u-b'aak-el   *b'ahlam*   *Ix K'ab'al Xook*
A3-bone-INAL   jaguar   PN
'the jaguar bone of Lady K'abal Xook' {Yaxchilan, carved bone}

6.3.4.2 Nominalization

Many nouns in the hieroglyphic corpus are derived from other root and word classes. Derivational suffixes are attested that derive nouns from verbs, adjectives, positionals, and other nouns. Nominalization strategies include bare-root nominalization, probably involving either lengthening or aspiration of the root vowel, object incorporation, gerundive or infinitive *-Vl* (*-el* for intransitive roots), instrumental *-ib'*, *-Vb'*, and the agentive *-oom*, *-n-oom*.

6.3.4.2.1 BARE-ROOT NOMINALIZATION

Transitive verb roots occasionally appear in nominal contexts as bare logographs. This appears to have involved either vowel lengthening or infixation of <h> between the vowel and the coda consonant. This may be indicated in rare examples with phonetic complementation, suggesting a disharmonic spelling (63), but most examples are simply spelled with a bare logogram for the verb root. Frequently, these nominalizations are also possessed and have the possessive suffix *-il* or *-uul*, discussed above. *Muuk* 'tomb', a nominalization of the transitive root *muk* 'to bury', is the most commonly attested of these. Examples 62–65 illustrate this nominalization strategy.

(62)

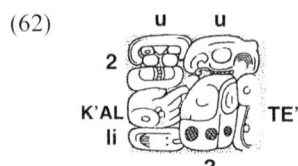

u u
2
K'AL   TE'
li
?

u-2-K'AL-li u-?-te'
u-cha'-k'al-il   *u-?-te'*
A3-two-raise-vl   A3-?-tree
'the second raising of the ? tree' {Tonina M 141}

(63)

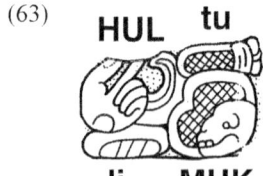

HUL **tu**

li **MUK**

HUL-li tu-MUUK
hul-i-Ø   *t-u-muuk*
arrive-INTR   PREP-A3-bury[NMLZ]
'He arrived at his tomb.' {Tonina area Zapata panel}

(64)

u pa **OTOOT**

li si yo ti

u-pa-si-li yo-OTOOT-ti
u-paas-il   *y-otoot*
A3-open[NMLZ]-vl   A3-dwelling
'the door (opening) of her house' {Yaxchilan L 23}

(65)
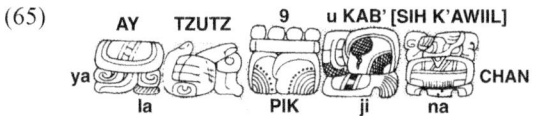

AY-ya-la TZUUTZ 9-PIK u-KAB'-ji SIHYAJ-CHAN-K'AWIIL
ayal   tzuutz   b'olon-pik   u-kab'-ij   Sihyaj Chan K'awiil
EXIST   finish[NMLZ]   nine-baktun   A3-earth-DER   PN
'There was the 9 baktun finishing under Sihyaj Chan K'awiil.' {Tikal St 31}

6.3.4.2.2 OBJECT INCORPORATION
Perhaps the most frequent nominalization strategy attested in the hieroglyphs is argument incorporation nominalization, in which a verbal stem and a (generic) noun phrase are joined to form a compound noun. For transitive stems, the incorporated noun is always the semantic patient of the action.

(66)
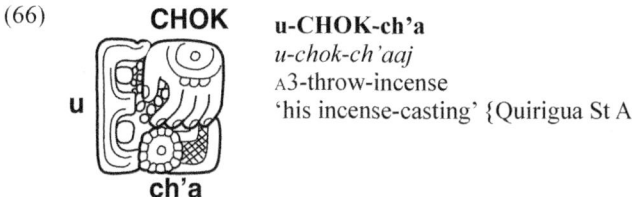

u-CHOK-ch'a
u-chok-ch'aaj
A3-throw-incense
'his incense-casting' {Quirigua St A}

(67)
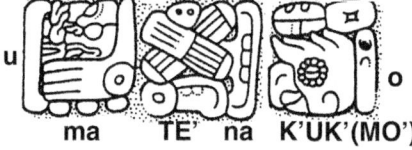

u-CH'AM-ma-K'AWIIL WIIN?-TE'-NAAH (K'UK'-MO')-'o-AJAW
u-ch'am-k'awiil-Ø   wiinte'-naah   k'uk-mo' ajaw
A3-grasp-k'awiil-B3   Wiinte'-building   PN
'K'uk' Mo' Ajaw's k'awiil-taking (is) at Wiinte' Naah.' {Copan Alt Q}

(68)
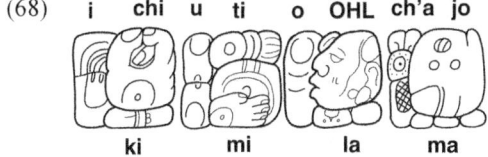

i   chi-ki u-ti-mi-'o-OHL-la   ch'a-jo-ma
i   chik   u-tim-ohl   ch'ajoom
Then   ?   A3-please-heart   *ch'ajoom* (royal title)
'Then may the *ch'ajoom's* heart-pleasing happen.' {Palenque TI west}

(69)
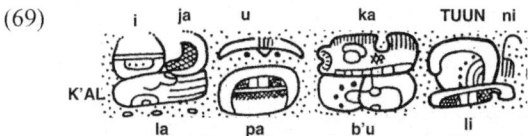

i-K'AL-la-ja u-pa ka-b'u TUUN-ni-li

i   k'a<h>l-aj   u-pak-b'u-tuun-il
then   wrap[PSV]-PSV   A3-face.down-POS.TR-stone-VI
'Then his laid-face-down-stone is wrapped.' {Kansas City Lintel}

Intransitive verbs of motion may have an argument incorporated, in which case it may be a destination (70) or a subject (71). Many examples are with the root *och* 'to enter'.

(70)

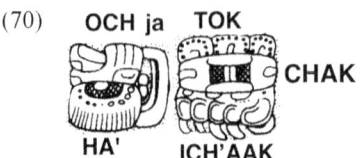

OCH-HA'-ja CHAK-TOK-ICH'AAK
och.ha'-aj-Ø   chak-tok-ich'aak
enter.water-INTR-B3   PN
'Chak Tok Ich'aak water-enters (dies).' {Tikal St 31}

(71)

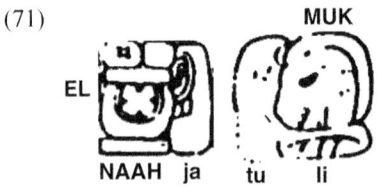

EL-NAAH-ja u-MUK-li
el-naah-aj-Ø   *u-muuk-il*
rise-house-INTR-B3   A3-bury[NMLZ]-VI
'His tomb is dedicated.'   {Piedras Negras Panel 4}

Positional roots without verbalizing morphology may also be nominalized through noun incorporation. With positional roots, the meanings are less transparent, but they are traditionally interpreted as nominalizations of events, rather than states.

(72)

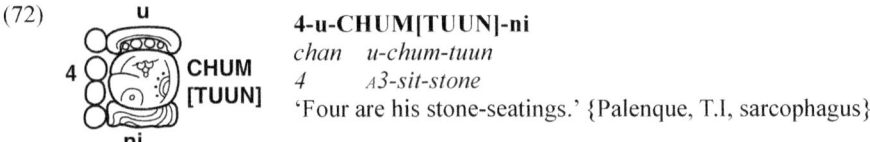

4-u-CHUM[TUUN]-ni
chan   u-chum-tuun
4   A3-sit-stone
'Four are his stone-seatings.' {Palenque, T.I, sarcophagus}

(73)

CHUM-mu YAX-K'IN
chum-yax-k'in
sit-new-sun
'Yaxk'in (a month) seating' {Leiden Plaque}

In all cases of incorporation nominalization, the resulting noun can be possessed, derived with the abstract/partitive -*Vl* suffix, or derived into an intransitive verb with the suffix -*aj*, as mentioned in the previous section.

6.3.4.2.3 -*Vl* NOMINALIZATION

Occasionally we find examples of verbal gerunds or infinitives that are derived from verbs through a -*Vl* suffix. Intransitive verbs appear to be derived with the suffix -*el* or -*al*. It is unclear what determines the vowel, but it could be that root intransitives and CVC passive stems take -*el* (74) while derived intransitives and non-CVC passives mostly take the suffix -*al* (75):

(74)   i chi na i   u   ti mi   je   a OHL

ki   la   la

i-chi na-i-ki u ti-mi je-la a-OHL-la

i	*chi*	*na'ik*	*u-ti<h>m-j-eel*	*a(w)-ohl*
then	go?	OPT	A3-please[PSV]-PSV-vl	A2SG-heart

'Then, may the pleasing of your heart take place.' {Palenque TI west}

(75)   T'AB'? yu   wa-ja   u   TUUN

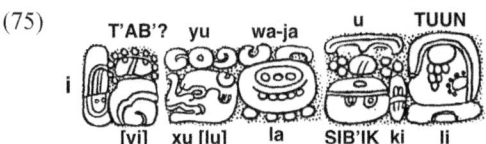

[yi] xu [lu]   la   SIB'IK ki   li

i-T'AB'?[yi] yu-xu-lu-wa-ja-la u-SIB'IK-ki TUUN-li

i	*t'ab'-ay-i*	*y-uxul-waj-al*	*u-sib'ik tuun-il*
then	ascend-MP-INTR	A3-carving-AP-Vl	A3-soot stone-Vl

'Then the carving of the soot stone (altar) rises.'{Copan Altar Z}

6.3.4.2.4 INSTRUMENTAL: -*IB'*

Another frequently attested nominalization is the instrumental suffix, which derives a noun meaning 'instrument that facilitates action X' from root and derived verbs and positionals. This suffix has several allomorphs. One is the suffix -*ib'*, which may vary with -*Vb'* with some roots. Comparison with Ch'orti' suggests that the suffix -*ib'* was accompanied by an infixed <h>, as with the passive voice. This is the form used for CVC verb roots, both transitive and intransitive. The suffix -*nib'* is attested in a few cases for non-CVC stems and -*lib'* appears to be the instrumental nominalizer form for positionals.

(76)   yu

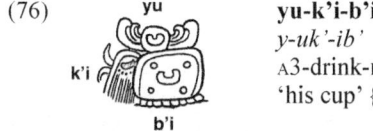

k'i

b'i

yu-k'i-b'i
y-uk'-ib'
A3-drink-INST
'his cup' {Vase, K1398}

(77)   WAY [b'i]

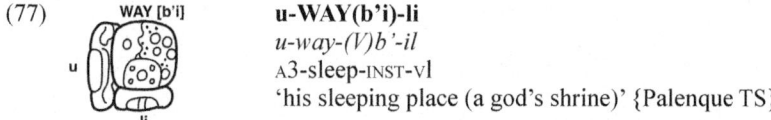

u

li

u-WAY(b'i)-li
u-way-(V)b'-il
A3-sleep-INST-vl
'his sleeping place (a god's shrine)' {Palenque TS}

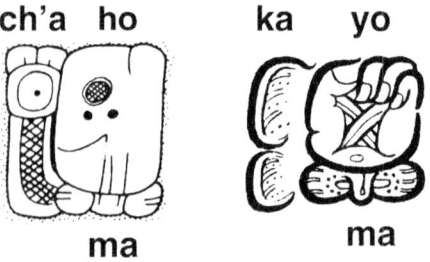

ch'a   ho   ka   yo

ma   ma

FIGURE 6.6 *-OOM* AGENTIVES

6.3.4.2.5 AGENTIVE *-OOM*

A final nominalizing suffix is the agentive *-oom*. This is used to derive nouns with the meaning 'the doer of action X'. This suffix appears to be homophonous with a future or potential suffix *-oom*, but they have different, if potentially overlapping, distributions. The agentive suffix is attested mainly with other nouns, such as *ch'aaj* 'incense', *kay* 'fish' and *k'ay* 'song/singing' (see Figure 6.6). The potential aspectual suffix *-oom* only attaches to intransitive verb stems, as is discussed in the next section.

6.3.5 Adjectives

A small root class of adjectives is identifiable in the glyphic corpus. It can be difficult to distinguish root adjectives and root nouns in practice since both can be attributive and predicative. Adjectives, however, do not appear as arguments without derivation. Color, quantity, and quality are the most common adjectival meanings.

(78)   mi   o   pa ta   YAL   tz'u tz'i

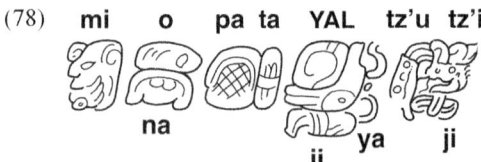

na   ya   ji
              ji

mi-o-na pa-ta YAL-ji-ya tz'u-tz'i-ji
mi   oon-Ø   pata(an)   y-ahl-j=iiy   tz'utz'ij
?DUB   much   tribute   A3-say-DER=PST   coati
' "Is there not much tribute?", said the coati.' {Ceramic Vessel, K8076}

(79)   IK'   chi   AJAW

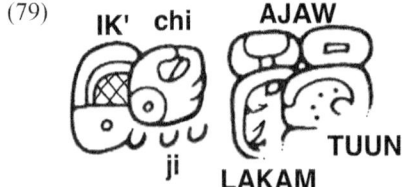

ji   TUUN
         LAKAM

IK'-chi-ji LAKAM-TUUN-AJAW
Ik'   chij   lakam   tuun ajaw-Ø
black   deer   banner   stone lord-B3
'It is black deer, the lord of Lakam Tuun.' {Yaxchilan HS 2, step 7}

FIGURE 6.7 ATTRIBUTIVE -*VL* NOUNS

(80)  **u-SAK-HU'N-la**
U-sak-hu'n-al
A3-white-paper-vl
'his white paper (headband)'
{Palenque Tablet of Inscriptions, Center Panel}

(81) **CHAK u-pa**

CHAK u-pa-ka-la K'INICH
chak-Ø   u-pakal   K'inich
red-B3   A3-shield   PN
'Great (lit. red) is the shield of K'inich.' {Palenque Notre Dame Panel
[Schele and Miller 1986:82]}

Nouns can also be used as modifiers without derivation, or can be derived with an attributive -*Vl* suffix, which is distinguishable from the abstract and possessed noun -*Vl* by being vowel harmonic for most words, and in being consistently a short vowel (see Figure 6.7).

6.3.6 Prepositions and relational nouns

There are two prepositions in the hieroglyphic corpus, the general-purpose preposition *ti ~ ta* and the preposition *tahn* 'within', which appears to be a grammaticalized reduction of the relational noun u-tahn 'its chest'. The preposition *tahn* generally appears in locative expression referring to interior spaces, such as caves.

(82)  **TAHN-na CH'E'N-na**
tahn   ch'e'n
within   cave
'within the cave/town' {Palenque, T. XIX}

The preposition *ti ~ta* (the form varies somewhat temporally, regionally, and stylistically) can introduce a variety of different types of oblique arguments. It is most commonly used for locative expressions (83), and metaphorical extensions to placement in states or within events (84, 85 – *ti ch'ahb'il*) as well as in time (86). However, it is also attested with instrumental (85 – *ti k'ahk'al jul*), and recipient/benefactive (87).

(83)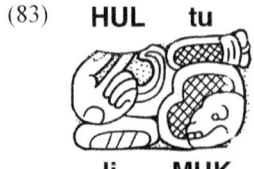

HUL-li tu-MUUK
hul-i-Ø   *t-u-muuk*
arrive-INTR-B3   PREP-A3-bury[NMLZ]
'He arrived at his tomb.' {Tonina Zapata panel}

(84)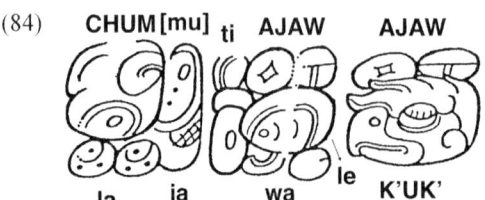

CHUM-la-ja ti-AJAW-wa-le K'UK'-AJAW
chum-l-aj-Ø   *ti*   *ajaw-l-e(l)*   *k'uk'*   *ajaw*
sit-POS-INTR-B3   PREP   king-VI.VI   PN
'K'uk' Ajaw sits in kingship (accedes to the throne).' {La Corona Pan 2}

(85)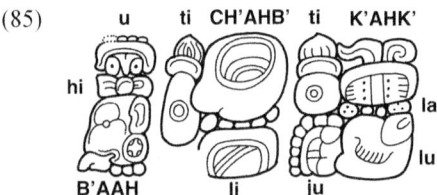

u-B'AAH ti-CH'AHB'-li ti K'AHK'-la ju-lu
u-b'aah-Ø   *ti*   *ch'ahb'-il*   *ti*   *k'ahk'-al*   *jul*
A3-person-B3   PREP   penance-VI   PREP   fire-VI   spear
'His person (is) in (the act of) penance with a fiery spear.' {Yaxchilan L 24}

(86)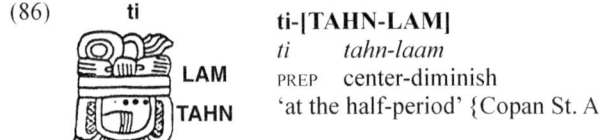

ti-[TAHN-LAM]
ti   *tahn-laam*
PREP   center-diminish
'at the half-period' {Copan St. A}

(87)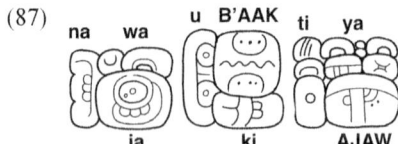

na-wa-ja u-B'AAK-ki ti -ya-AJAW-wa
na<h>w-aj   *u-b'aak*   *ti*   *y-ajaw*
display[PSV]-PSV   A3-captive   PREP   A3-lord
'The captive is displayed to his lord.' {Yaxchilan area lintel, Kimbell Art Museum}

6.3.6.1 Locative meanings without prepositions

For stative predicates and intransitive verbs of motion, location referenced with top-onymns can be expressed without the use of a preposition. In most cases, the noun phrase naming the location is placed immediately following the predicate and before any overt subjects (88) However, in other cases, the location can occur following the core grammatical arguments as well (89).

(88)

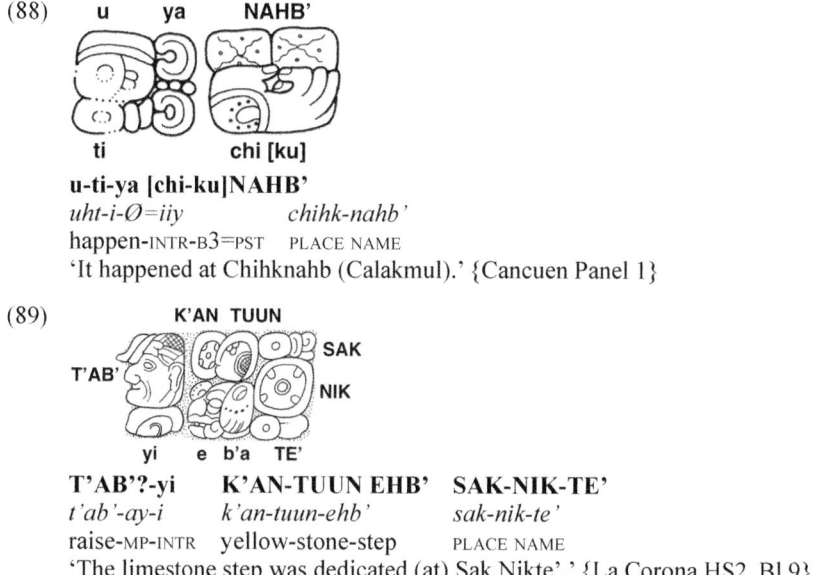

u ya NAHB'

ti chi [ku]

u-ti-ya [chi-ku]NAHB'
uht-i-Ø=iiy   *chihk-nahb'*
happen-INTR-B3=PST   PLACE NAME
'It happened at Chihknahb (Calakmul).' {Cancuen Panel 1}

(89)

K'AN TUUN

T'AB'   SAK

NIK

yi   e b'a TE'

T'AB'?-yi   **K'AN-TUUN EHB'**   **SAK-NIK-TE'**
t'ab'-ay-i   *k'an-tuun-ehb'*   *sak-nik-te'*
raise-MP-INTR   yellow-stone-step   PLACE NAME
'The limestone step was dedicated (at) Sak Nikte'.' {La Corona HS2, Bl 9}

6.3.6.2 Relational Nouns

More precise locations, as well as grammatical relations, were specified by relational nouns, which are formally possessed nouns, mostly body parts. Alone, these are functionally and semantically versatile. They can function both to introduce oblique clauses and as core arguments, and they generally retain their literal body-part meaning as well.

(90)

NAL

wi

a

chi

a-wi-chi-NAL
aw-ichnal
A2SG-presence
'before you' {Tikal Burial 196 vase, K8008}

(91)

u

TI'

HU'N

na

u-TI'-HU'N-na
u-ti'hu'n
A3-lip-book
'the margin of the book(?)' {Tonina M 140}

More unambiguously locative phrases are often introduced with a combination of the general preposition *ti ~ ta*. In such cases, the preposition heads the prepositional phrase and the relational noun is the formal head of the preposition's complement.

(92)

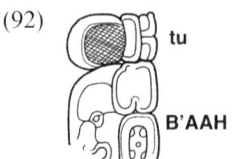

tu
B'AAH

tu-B'AAH
t-u-b'aah
PREP-A3-self
'to him' {Chinikiha Pan 1}

(93)

tu   pa

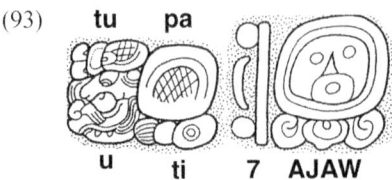

u   ti   7   AJAW

tu-u-pa-ti 7-AJAW(day sign)
t-u'-paat   huk   Ajaw
PREP-A3-back   seven   Ajaw (Day Name)
'after (the day) 7 Ajaw'. {Emiliano Zapata Panel}

Many of the non-locative functions of prepositions in English are more commonly performed in Classic Mayan by an innovative and apparently open derivational class of relational nouns that form a separate system from the set of locative relational nouns based on body parts. The general pattern is an ergative marker followed by a noun or verb root that has been derived with a -*Vj* suffix of unclear form, always written with the syllable **ji**.

By far the most common of these, in keeping with the thematic content of most inscriptions, is **u-KAB'-ji**, which is used to express obliquely the argument that has or had institutional authority for a particular action. This is often used to express the agent of a passive verb (94), though the noun phrase associated with *ukab'ji* (as we analyze it) need not have actually performed the action, or even been present when it occurred. In example 95, the event is the half-completion of a period of time. The participant referenced by the *u-kab'ji* phrase in this case was clearly not physically completing the cycle, but rather had institutional oversight for the action.

(94)   LAM ja   K'AWIIL u   KAB' 4 IXIK

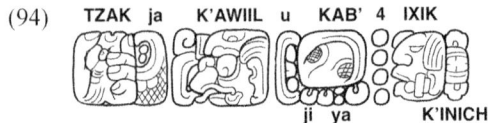

ji ya   K'INICH

TZ'AK-ja K'AWIIL u-KAB'-ji-ya 4-IXIK-K'INICH
tza<h>k-aj   *k'awiil u-kab'-j=iiy*   *chan ixik k'inich*
conjure[PSV]-PSV   k'awiil A3-earth-DER=PST   PN
'K'awiil was conjured by Chan Ixik K'inich.' {Yaxchilan, St 32}

(95)   LAM ja   1   CHAN   KAB'   u   KAB' MAM   ?   [SIH K'AWIIL]

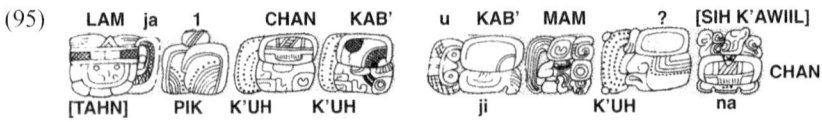

                                                          CHAN
[TAHN]   PIK   K'UH   K'UH   ji   K'UH   na

(TAHN)LAM-ja 1-PIK CHAN-K'UH
tahn-la<h>m-aj   *juun-pik*   *chan(al)* *k'uh*
middle-diminish[PSV]-PSV   one-eight.thousand   sky   god

KAB'-K'UH . . . U-KAB'-ji MAM K'UH-? SIH-CHAN-na-K'AWIIL

kab'(al)k'uh . . . u-kab'-ji   *mam*   *k'uh(-ul) ?*

earth   god. . .   A3-earth-DER   ancestor   god(-vl) ?

    Sihyaj Chan K'awiil

    PN

'The eight thousand Sky Gods (and) Earth Gods are partially diminished . . . overseen by the Ancestor Sihyaj Chan K'awiil.' {Tikal St. 31}

In rare cases, these phrases seem to function as core arguments of a main verb.

(96)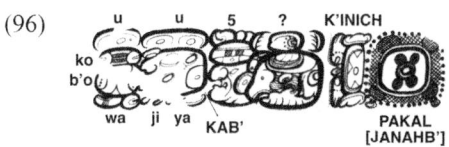

u-ko-b'o-wa u-KAB'-ji-ya 5-?-AJAW

u-kob'-Vw   *u-kab'-j=iiy*   *jo'*   *?*   *ajaw*

A3-perpetuate?-TR   A3-earth-DER=PST   five   k'atun   lord

    K'INICH-(JANAHB'?-PAKAL)

    K'inich Janahb' Pakal

    PN

'He (K'inich K'uk' Bahlam) perpetuates(?) the ritual oversight of K'inich Janab Pakal, the five-k'atun (score years) lord.' {Palenque 96 glyphs}

A fairly large set of this type of phrase exists, all the examples of which are used to introduce additional arguments associated with an event, and to specify the semantic relation that those arguments have with the event (see Figure 6.8).

It is unclear whether these phrases are transitive verbs or possessed nouns (MacLeod 2004; Robertson et al. 2004:284–6), but it is clear that they functionally fulfill a role similar to non-locative/spatial relational nouns in other Mayan languages (some of which are also transparently derived from transitive verbal roots). However, the fact that this appears to be an open and productive derivational class is unique among Mayan languages.

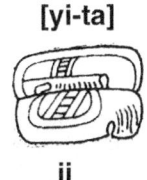

FIGURE 6.8 ATTESTED DERIVED RELATIONAL NOUNS, AND FUNCTION IN SENTENCE: *YITAJI* 'COMITATIVE' (TIKAL, ST 31), *UMEK'JI* 'ENCOMPASSED BY' (TAB 96 GLYPHS, COP. ST. A), *UPAATIJ* 'AFTER' (LA CORONA PANEL 2), *YALAJI* 'QUOTATIVE' (K8008 HUMMINGBIRD POT)

6.2.7 Numbers

Classic Mayan made use of a vigesimal (base-20) system of numerals. Pronunciation for most number terms is presumed from comparative data, although a few direct phonetic spellings mostly agree with those reconstructions. For example, the ending **-na** on spellings incorporating "one" (*juun*) agrees with the long vowel of the word (ex. **LAJUUN-na**, for *lajuun* 'ten'). Some late-period (post-800 CE) scribes in Yucatan took pains to write Yukatekan pronunciations over Classic Mayan forms, as in the phonetic spellings of **o-xo** for "three" (*ux* being the probable Classic Mayan form) and **ka-na** for "four" (instead of *chan*).

For higher numbers, two words for 20, *winik* or *win(ik)al* (the word for 'person' as well, owing to a human being's twenty digits) and *k'al*, are attested, as is *pik* for 8,000 (see example 95, above). It is important to note that the numeration of days and years operated somewhat differently than the straight base-20 system for other counted objects (see Stuart 2012).

Classic Mayan had optional numeral classifiers. The most generic and frequent of these was *-te'*, occurring in varied contexts in reference to people, time periods, and objects.

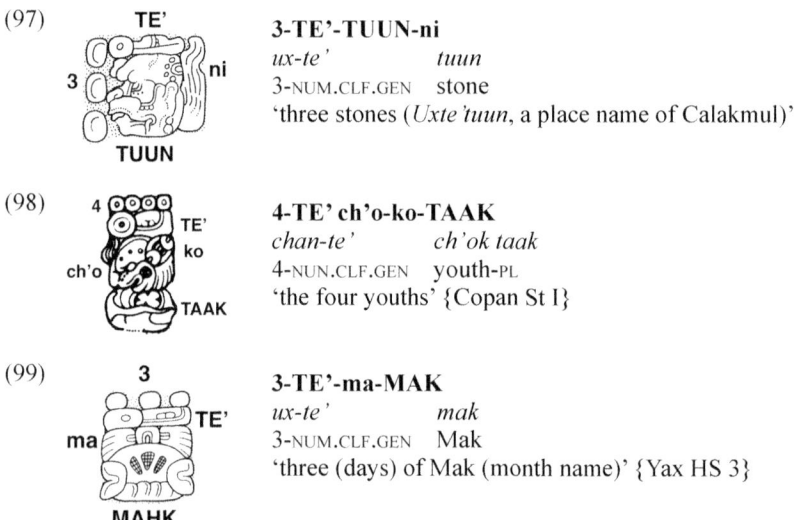

(97)   **3-TE'-TUUN-ni**
ux-te'   *tuun*
3-NUM.CLF.GEN   stone
'three stones (*Uxte 'tuun*, a place name of Calakmul)'

(98)   **4-TE' ch'o-ko-TAAK**
chan-te'   *ch'ok taak*
4-NUN.CLF.GEN   youth-PL
'the four youths' {Copan St I}

(99)   **3-TE'-ma-MAK**
ux-te'   *mak*
3-NUM.CLF.GEN   Mak
'three (days) of Mak (month name)' {Yax HS 3}

Other numeral classifiers and measure words are attested, apparently with far more specific scopes of reference: the rare classifier *-tikil* seems restricted to the counting of people. Still other terms are used in counts or measures of distance, such as *-nab* or *-nahb'* 'handspan'.

Ordinal numbers can be expressed by adding a non-referential third person ergative prefix to the number, as in *u-juun-* for "first" or *u-ho'lajuun-* for "fifteenth." These can also be accompanied by a suffix *-tal* added to the number (100), though many examples that appear to be ordinal in nature lack this addition (101). It is often unclear in texts whether a given example of this structure is in fact ordinal, or if it is actually a possessed cardinal number ("his/her 7 . . .").

(100)

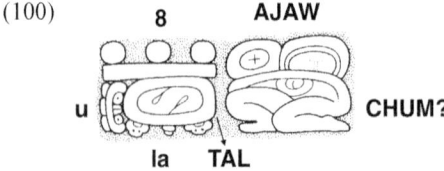

u-8-TAL-la CHUM?-AJAW
u-waxak-tal   chum?-ajaw
A3-eight-ORD   seating-lord
'the eighth lord-seating' {Yaxchilan L. 37}

(101)

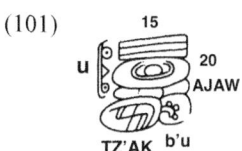

u-15–20-TZ'AK-b'u-AJAW example
u-ho'lajuun-winik-tz'ak-b'u   ajaw
a3-fifteen-twenty-fulfill-POS.TR   lord
'the thirty-fifth fulfilling lord' {Naranjo Altar 1}

The cardinal and ordinal forms of 'one' were suppletive, and there are two attested forms used for the ordinal 'first': *naah* (102) and *yax* (103).

(102)

HUL-li u-NAAH-TAL-la IX-ka-KAN-AJAW SAK NIKTE'
hul-i-Ø=iiy   u-naah-tal   ix-kan(-ul)   ajaw   saknikte'
arrive-INTR-B3=PST   A3-first-ORD   F-snake(-vl)   lord   PLACE
'The first Kanul princess arrived at Saknikte'.' {La Corona Pan 6}

(103)

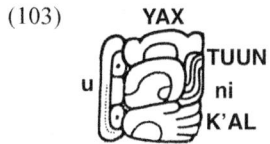

u-YAX-K'AL-TUUN-ni
u yax-k'al-tuun
A3-first-raise-stone
'his first stone-raising' {Piedras Negras St. 6}

Numbers can also be incorporated into the verb. In these cases, the number immediately precedes the verb:

(104)

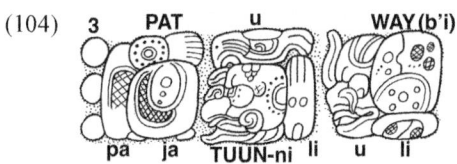

3-pa-PAT-ja u-TUUN-ni-li u-WAY-b'i-li
ux   pa<h>t-aj-Ø   u-tuun-il   u-way-b'-il
three   form[PSV]-PSV-B3   A3-stone-vl   A3-sleep-INST-vl
'Thrice are constructed their shrines.' {La Corona Pan 1}

(105)

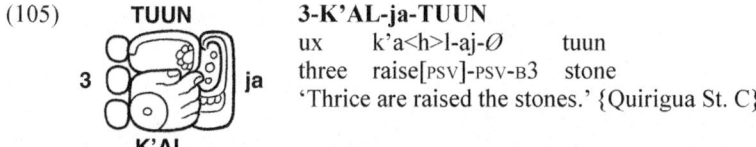

3-K'AL-ja-TUUN
ux   k'a<h>l-aj-Ø   tuun
three   raise[PSV]-PSV-B3   stone
'Thrice are raised the stones.' {Quirigua St. C}

7 ASPECT AND MOOD

7.1 Aspect and temporal reference

Aspect, or at least temporal reference, in hieroglyphic texts has been a topic of great debate among epigraphers. In a textual corpus with a clear emphasis on dates and temporal relationships between events, overt temporal and aspectual grammatical marking are largely absent. Calendrical information accompanying most texts often provides explicit information about the temporal relationships between clauses in a text. However, it has long been noted that, unlike many Mayan languages, finite verb phrases in the glyphic corpus do not carry any aspectual prefixes or preverbal particles. Some have interpreted this as evidence that hieroglyphic texts exclusively record clauses in completive aspects, which in some other Mayan languages are unmarked. This is still a hypothesis that merits investigation. In the authors' opinions, however, it is unlikely that in such a large body of texts, even one with a historical slant, incompletive aspect would be utterly absent, and one of the authors (Law 2016) has argued, based on comparative evidence, that the language of Maya hieroglyphs did not distinguish completive and incompletive aspects in finite clauses.

There are several clitics or suffixes that are clearly related to time reference and aspect, though the precise meaning and function of these morphemes is not always clear. Perhaps the most frequently attested of these is the enclitic *=iiy*. This has been analyzed as completive aspect marker, a past tense suffix (Robertson et al. 2004), and a past temporal deictic enclitic (Wald 2007). Ongoing work by Law suggests that, in additional to temporal and discursive functions, details of the distribution of this marker are dependent on valence (transitive verb phrases do not appear in contexts with *=iiy*) and syntactic relations between clauses (*=iiy* seems to occur only in temporal adverbial clauses and relative clauses, and perhaps other dependent clauses). A clearer analysis of this morpheme will require additional investigation.

A slightly less problematic aspectual morpheme is the intransitive future or potential suffix *-oom*, mentioned previously. This suffix only attaches to intransitive stems, including intransitive roots, passive verbs, and antipassives. The most common occurrences are with the intransitive verb *uht* 'to happen' (*uht-oom*) and with the passivized transitive root *tzu<h>tz-aj* 'was finished':

(106)

u-to(ma) 4-AJAW 13-YAX-SIHOOM
uht-oo(m)-Ø   chan   Ajaw   uxlajuun   Yaxsihoom
happen-POT-B3   four   Ajaw   thirteen   Yax(Month)
    TZUTZ-jo-ma u-15-WINIKHAAB'
    tzu<h>tz-(a)j-oom-Ø   u-ho'lajuun   winikhaab'
    finish[PSV]-PSV-POT-B3   A3-fifteen   k'atun
'4 Ajaw 13 Yax shall happen, the 15th K'atun shall be finished.' {Copan St. A}

Some examples of this suffix occur on transitive roots that have been intransitivized with the so-called antipassive suffix *-Vn*.

(107)

ha-'o-b'a-pa-sa no-ma-WAY-ya-ma-ka-no-ma WAY-ya
haa'-oob' *pas-n-oom-Ø*   *way*   *mak-n-oom-Ø*   *way*
3.FOC-PL   open-AP-POT-B3   ?   close-AP-POT -B3   ?
'*They* shall cover ?, and open ?.' {Copan St. A}

All of the examples of *-oom* occur with intransitive verb phrases that refer to specific future dates in the calendar or events associated with specific future dates. Because of this association with the predictable workings of the calendar, it may be that this suffix communicated an idea of inevitability – the assuredness of calendric stations – for the events in question. See Law (2014:111–15) for a historical account of this suffix in Classic Mayan.

7.1 Negation

Finally, some instances of negation are attested in the glyphic corpus. Negation is accomplished by an independent negation particle that precedes the verb phrase. The general negative morpheme is *ma*, but *machaj* and *mi* are also used, with functions that appear related to negation. In general, *ma* seems to appear mostly to negate verbal predicates (108), whereas *machaj* negates non-verbal predicates, or is possibly the head of a non-verbal predicate (109). *Mi* is less frequent and less clear in its distribution, but may be a dubitative marker, rather than negation per se (110).

(108)

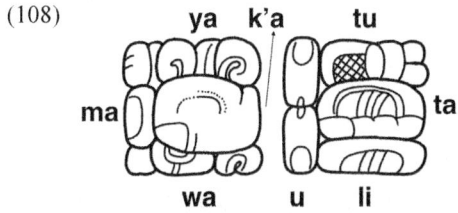

ma-ya-k'a-wa u-tu-ta-li
ma   *y-ak'-aw-Ø*   *u-tut-aal*
NEG   A3-give-TR-B3   A3-?-VI
'He did not give their *tutaal* (to the gods).' {Palenque, TI east}

(109)

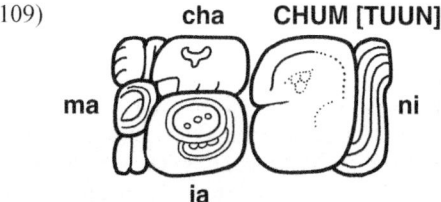

ma-cha-ja CHUM-TUUN-ni
machaj-Ø   *chum-tuun*
NEG-B3   sit-stone
'It is not a stone-seating.' {Palenque TI, east}

(110)   **mi   o   pa ta   YAL   tz'u tz'i**

na   **ji**   **ya**   **ji**

mi-o-na pa-ta YAL-ji-ya tz'u-tz'i-ji

mi	*oon-Ø*	*pata(an)*	*y-ahl-j=iiy*	*tz'utz'ij*
?DUB	much	tribute	A3-say-DER=PST	coati

' "Is there not much tribute?", said the coati.' {Ceramic Vessel, K8076}

8 CONCLUSIONS

The preceding discussion has illustrated both the viability of linguistic research on Classic Mayan as well as the obstacles that the study of an ancient written language entails. One obstacle in the linguistic analysis of Classic Mayan involves the mechanics of the hieroglyphic script, and the inevitable partiality with which a written system can encode the complexity of human language. We hope this chapter has shown that, although some linguistic information is inevitably lost when a language is written down, there is still ample space for linguistic insight, even with respect to phonology. Continued decipherments, refined understanding of orthographic conventions and regional and temporal variation will allow opportunities to enhance our understanding of the phonology and morphology of the language even further. Perhaps the greatest untapped reservoir of grammatical information lies in the syntax of the language. Our admittedly superficial treatment here of syntactic structure is the most comprehensive on the topic to date, to our knowledge. This, coupled with the fact that syntactic ordering phenomena are not obscured by spelling conventions, as is the case with phonology, means that this topic is ripe for more detailed exploration.

From this brief grammatical overview, the fruit of at least three decades of collaboration and scholarship from a host of epigraphers, archaeologists, art historians, and linguists, it is apparent that the language of Maya hieroglyphic inscriptions has much in common with other Mayan languages. However, there is increasing evidence that it has some characteristics that are unique innovations, including, for example, what appears to be an open derivational class of grammatical relational nouns and the apparent lack of obligatory overt aspectual marking (this is still debated, although it should be noted that Ch'olti' and Ch'orti' share this feature at least in transitive clauses). The fact that not all features of Classic Mayan would find parallels in other Mayan languages is to be expected for a natural language, but does present one of numerous methodological difficulties as we move forward. Many grammatical analyses of glyphic texts were only accepted among epigraphers once they had been shown to conform to structures attested in some other Mayan language. At the same time, a full contrastive analysis of grammatical structure, with examples of all of the relevant paradigmatic and structural oppositions, is unlikely for perhaps most of the grammatical features of the language – the lack of attested examples of the second person plural and the fact that all finite verb phrases in the corpus have third person absolutives are telling examples of this. The reality of such accidental gaps in the record justifies, or at least excuses, a greater reliance on comparative-historical data than would normally make sense for synchronic linguistic description. However, such a historical perspective risks missing those features that make this language truly unique.

NOTES

1 The space and format of this chapter do not allow for a comprehensive bibliography of published work on this topic, but the grammatical study of Maya hieroglyphics has developed over decades of close collaboration and independent insights of dozens of epigraphers, art historians, archaeologists and linguists. We would like to acknowledge the central role that this international community of scholars has played in discovering and refining many of the insights that we summarize here. We would particularly like to thank Stephen Houston, Marc Zender, Nikolai Grube, and Alfonso Lacadena for many stimulating discussions of hieroglyphic grammar over the years. Most of the images for the numerous grammatical examples were drawn by David Stuart, but we have also adapted portions of drawings by Linda Schele, Ian Graham, Nikolai Grube, Nicholas Carter, and Alexandre Safronov.

2 Standard conventions for transliterating Maya hieroglyphs in Roman script (Stuart 1985) indicate logographic signs with all-capital letters and syllabic signs with lower-case letters. All glyphs within a glyph block are connected with hyphens, and spaces indicate a new glyph block.

3 As an aside, it is interesting to note that this word is attested in modern Ch'orti' as *usij* (Martinez et al. 1996:241), but is otherwise only attested in Q'anjob'alan languages (Kaufman 2003).

REFERENCES

Berlin, Heinrich. 1958. "El glifo 'emblema' en las inscripciones Mayas." *Journal de la Société des Americanistes* 47: 111–19.

Bricker, Victoria R. 1986. *A grammar of Mayan hieroglyphs*. New Orleans: Middle American Research Institute, Tulane University.

Campbell, Lyle. 1984. "The implications of Mayan historical linguistics for glyphic research." In *Phoneticism in Mayan hieroglyphic writing*, ed. by John Justeson and Lyle Campbell, 1–16. (Institute for Mesoamerican Studies, Publication 9). Albany: SUNY.

Coe, Michael D. 1992. *Breaking the Maya code*. New York: Thames and Hudson.

Grube, Nikolai. 2004. "The orthographic distinction between velar and glottal spirants in Maya hieroglyphic writing." In *The linguistics of Maya writing*, ed. by Søren Wichmann, 61–81. Salt Lake City: University of Utah Press.

Houston, Stephen, John S. Robertson, and David Stuart. 2000. "The language of classic Maya inscriptions." *Current Anthropology* 41: 321–56.

Houston, Stephen, David Stuart, and John S. Robertson. 1998. "Disharmony in Maya hieroglyphic writing: linguistic change and continuity." In *Anatomía de una civilización: Aproximaciones interdisciplinarias a la cultura maya,* ed. by Andrés Ciudad Ruíz, Y. Fernández Marquénez, J. Miguel García Campillo, J. Iglesias Ponce de León, Alfonso Lacadena García-Gallo and L. T. Sanz Castro, 275–96. Madrid: Sociedad Española de Estudios Mayas.

Justeson, John, and Lyle Campbell, eds. 1984. *Phoneticism in Mayan hieroglyphic writing* (Institute for Mesoamerican Studies, Publication 9). Albany: SUNY.

Kaufman, Terrence, with the assistance of John Justeson. 2003. *A preliminary Mayan etymological dictionary*. http://www.famsi.org/reports/01051/index.html.

Kelley, David H. 1962. "A history of the decipherment of Maya script." *Anthropological Linguistics* 4: 1–48.

Kelley, David. 1976. *Deciphering the Maya script*. Austin: University of Texas Press.

Knorosov, Yuri. 1954. *La antigua escritura de los pueblos de America Central*. Mexico City: Fondo de Cultura Popular.

Law, Danny. 2014. *Language contact, inherited similarity and social difference: The story of linguistic interaction in the Maya lowlands* (Current Issues in Linguistic Theory Series). Amsterdam: John Benjamins.

Law, Danny. 2016. "The (Re)Invention of Incompletive Aspect in Cholan." Invited talk, The 2016 Maya Meetings. University of Texas at Austin, Austin, Texas. January 15, 2016.

MacLeod, Barbara. 2004. "A world in a grain of sand: Transitive perfect verbs in the classic Maya script." In *The linguistics of Maya writing*, ed. by Søren Wichmann, 291–325. Salt Lake City: University of Utah Press.

Macri, Martha J., and Anabel Ford, eds. 1997. *The language of Maya hieroglyphs*. San Francisco: Pre-Columbian Art Research Institute.

Martínez, Vitalino Pérez, Federico García, Felipe Martínez, and Jeremías López. 1996. *Diccionario del Idioma Ch'orti'*. Antigua, Guatemala: Proyecto Lingüístico Francisco Marroquín.

Proskouriakoff, Tatiana. 1960. "Historical implications of a pattern of dates at Piedras Negras, Guatemala." *American Antiquity* 25: 454–75.

Robertson, John S., Stephen Houston, and David Stuart. 2004. "Tense and aspect in Maya hieroglyphic script." In *The linguistics of Maya writing*, ed. by Søren Wichmann, 259–89. Salt Lake City: University of Utah Press.

Robicsek, Francis. 1978. *The smoking Gods: Tabacco in Maya art, history and religion*. Norman: University of Oklahoma Press.

Schele, Linda. 1982. *Maya glyphs: the verbs*. Austin: University of Texas Press.

Schele, Linda, and Mary Ellen Miller 1986. *The blood of kings: dynasty and ritual in Maya art*. Fort Worth: Kinbell Art Museum.

Stuart, David. 1987. *Ten phonetic syllables*. Research Reports on Ancient Maya Writing 14. Washington, DC: Center for Maya Research.

Stuart, David. 1990. *A new carved panel from the Palenque area*. Research Reports on Ancient Maya Writing 32. Washington, DC: Center for Maya Research.

Stuart, David. 2012. "The varieties of ancient Maya numeration and value." In *The construction of value in the ancient world*, ed. by John K. Papadopoulos and Gary Urton, 497–515. Los Angeles: Cotsen Institute of Archaeology, UCLA.

Stuart, George. 1985. "A guide to the style and content of the series." *RRAMW* 15: 7–12.

Stuart, George. 1992. "Quest for decipherment: A historical and biographical survey of Maya hieroglyphic investigation." In *New theories on the ancient Maya*, ed. by Elin C. Danien and Robert J. Sharer, 1–63. Philadelphia: University of Pennsylvania, University Museum.

Thompson, J. Eric S. 1950. *Maya hieroglyphic writing: An introduction*. Washington, DC: Carnegie Institution of Washington.

Wald, Robert Francis. 2007. "The verbal complex in classic-period Maya hieroglyphic inscriptions: Its implications for language identification and change." PhD diss., University of Texas at Austin.

Wichmann, Søren. 2006. "Mayan historical linguistics and epigraphy: A new synthesis." *Annual Review of Anthropology* 35: 279–94.

Zender, Marc. 2010. "Baj 'Hammer' and related affective verbs in Classic Mayan." *The PARI Journal* 11: 1–16.

PART 2

GRAMMAR

CHAPTER 7

PHONOLOGY AND PHONETICS

Nora C. England and Brandon O. Baird

1 PHONOLOGY

The phonology of Mayan languages is well known both descriptively and historically. To begin the discussion of the sound systems of Mayan languages, it is useful to consider the sound inventory that has been reconstructed for Proto-Mayan (Campbell and Kaufman 1985:190; Campbell, this volume, slightly modified in terms of placement of *h and *χ). International Phonetic Alphabet symbols are used here and elsewhere in this chapter. The practical orthography is described in Chapter 1.

Consonants									Vowels	
p	t	tʲ	ts	tʃ	k	q	ʔ		i	u
ɓ	t'	tʲ'	ts'	tʃ'	k'	q'			e	o
	s			ʃ		χ	h		a	
m	n				ŋ				+ vowel length	
	l									
	r									
w			j							

As can be seen, Proto-Mayan had a series of voiceless pulmonic stops and affricates matched by a series of glottalized stops (ejective or implosive) and affricates (ejective), the glottal stop, a set of voiceless fricatives, several nasals, and a set of four sonorants. It had five canonical vowels plus vowel length. Although Mayan languages have gone through a number of changes in their sound systems, these general characteristics still apply to most of them.

The major changes have involved reducing the consonant inventory through loss of the postalveolar palatalized stops (all languages) or the uvular stops (all non-Eastern languages except the Q'anjob'alan group, where the loss is underway but not complete), or through loss of the velar nasal (most languages except Chuj, Popti', and Mocho'), loss of *r (all non-K'ichean languages except in borrowings and affect words), or *h (most K'ichean except Poqom; Mamean, Q'anjob'alan). Change has also resulted in increasing the consonant inventory by adding a series of retroflex affricates and fricatives (Mamean and some Q'anjob'alan languages), a series of palatal stops (distinctively in Mamean languages, phonetically in some K'ichean languages), or adding *p' in contrast with *ɓ (most Cholan languages, all Yucatecan languages, Tseltal, Tsotsil, Poqomam, some Poqomchi'). The vowel inventory has been reduced by eliminating vowel length (Western languages except Mocho', although one or two of them have reintroduced long vowels, usually through the loss of *h between identical vowels). The number of vowels has also been increased by adding a higher central vowel (Mopan, Itzaj, Lacandon, Chol, and Chontal). In addition, some languages have developed tone contrasts (Yucatec, Lacandon, Uspantek, possibly one dialect of Tsotsil and Mocho').

Individual languages have also suffered changes in phonotactics. For instance, Proto-Mayan root shapes were quite restricted (CVC, CV:C, CVʔC, CV:ʔC or CVʔV₁C, CVhC, CVs/ʃ/xC according to Kaufman 1976), and syllable structure was equally restricted, with CV(C) the prevalent pattern. Contemporary languages, however, may show a number of other possibilities. With regard to root shapes these may include different vowel configurations or additional consonant clusters. Contemporary syllable shapes may include other consonant clusters in onset or coda position or no consonant in these positions. While most languages do not allow vowel sequences and either insert an epenthetic consonant or delete one of the vowels when this occurs due to particular combinations of morphemes, a very few (such as Ixil and Q'anjob'al) do permit adjacent vowels.

There are a few changes that are restricted to one or very few languages. Examples are the loss of *ts (but not /ts'/) in Poqomam and some dialects of Poqomchi', the change of *s → θ in Huastec, the pharyngealization of /q'/ in Achi, the palatalization of [t] and [n] in Chol, the addition of an apico-postalveolar affricate/fricative set in Mam of Todos Santos in addition to the retroflex set, the diphthongization of long *e and long *o (*e: → ie, *o: → uo~ua) in single noncontiguous dialects of Tz'utujil, Kaqchikel, Poqomam, and Poqomchi', the change of the pronunciation of /ɓ/ to [wʔ] in onset position and [mʔ] in coda position in Poqomam and two dialects of Poqomchi', the "hardening" of the approximants in Q'eqchi' (/w/ → [ᵏw] and /j/ → [ʲj]), or the change from a length contrast to a tense/lax distinction in the vowels of all dialects of Kaqchikel and one dialect of K'iche', plus the reduction of the vowel inventory to nine or six vowels in most dialects of Kaqchikel.

Some of the changes are not apparent in the sound inventory of a language, due to a series of shifts that leaves the original sound in place but in different words. For instance, in Mam, *tʃ → ts̺, *t → tʃ, and *r → t (Kaufman 1976:107; Campbell, this volume). The language therefore still has /t/ and /tʃ/, but coming from different source words. It also still has /r/, due to its use in affect words and Spanish borrowings, so the inventory of sounds in this area has only changed through the addition of the retroflex affricate /ts̺/ and no sounds have been completely lost.

1.1 Consonants

All Mayan languages have the stops /p, t, k/ and the affricates /ts, tʃ/, except Poqomam and some dialects of Poqomchi', which have converted /ts/ to /s/. The uvular /q/ is found in all Eastern languages and in Q'anjob'alan languages, but is in the process of disappearing in the latter group. In general /q/ merged with /k/ but in Q'anjob'alan languages it is merging with /x/. The stops are usually released with aspiration in coda position; /q/ in this position may be affricated instead of aspirated. In K'iche', for example, the following example shows a /t/ with aspiration in coda position, but /q/ is affricated (López Ixcoy 1997:21–2).

K'ICHE'

	Onset position		**Coda position**	
/t/	[ti.ˈkoʔn]	'crop'	[poʔtʰ]	'women's blouse'
	[pa.ˈtan]	'tumpline'	[tiʔtʰ.ˈkiːɬ]	'anger'
/q/	[qu.ˈlaːχ]	'neck'	[ʔuːqˣ]	'wrapped skirt'
	[ʔe.ˈqaʔn]	'burden'	[saqˣ.ˈsoχ]	'whitish'

In some languages, such as Q'anjob'al and Akatek, there is no release of the stops word-finally before a significant pause, although the same words will be released with or without aspiration if the speaker continues with no pause. Thus the following are all possible pronunciations of the same word (Raymundo González et al. 2000:26–7):

Q'ANJOB'AL/AKATEK

[ʔiˈnat] ~ [ʔiˈnat^{h}] ~ [ʔiˈnat˺] 'seed'

Several of the K'ichean languages palatalize the velar stops in one or more of the following contexts: before (a short) /a/ plus a uvular consonant, before /i/, before /e/, after /i/ and /e/. The first context is clearly the least expected and is an instance of dissimilation, while the other contexts are the more usual assimilation to the following or preceding high or mid front vowel. Poqomam of Palin has palatalization in all of the possible contexts (Santos Nicolás and Benito Pérez 1998:10–11):

POQOMAM (PALÍN)

[k^{j}ik^{j}']	'blood'
[k^{j}eˈʔik^{j}]	'grind, e.g. corn'
[w^{ʔ}iːk^{j}]	'blow'
[tʃ'eːk^{j}]	'knee'
[k^{j}aq^{h}]	'red'
[k^{j}aˈχam^{ʔ}]	'four'

In Mam, Teko, and Awakatek palatalization began the same way, but the palatal stops have become separate phonemes, principally because the third person plural ergative marker, originally *k*-, has palatalized and is used before all vowels, as in the following examples.

MAM (IXTAHUACÁN)

[ˈk^{j}aːts'an]	'their salt'
[k^{j}eːtʃ]	'their measure of land (Sp. *cuerda*)'
[k^{j}iːtʃ]	'their chili pepper'
[k^{j}oːʔʂ]	'their achiote (annatto)'
[ˈk^{j}uʔχal]	'their identification papers, their land title'

All pulmonic stops and affricates have a corresponding glottalized pair. The bilabial glottalized stop is almost always implosive but the implosion may be very weak, which in some Western languages has led to it becoming or approximating a plain voiced stop (for instance in Tseltal it is [b], Polian 2013:82). A number of languages now have a contrast between a voiceless and voiced bilabial glottalized consonant (/p'/ vs. /ɓ/ (or /b/)). This contrast exists in Chol and Chontal, in all Yucatecan languages, and in Tseltal, Tsotsil, Poqomam, and some Poqomchi'.

YUCATEC (Bricker et al. 1998)

[ɓòːl]	'blunt, dull'	[pòːl]	'head, chief'	[p'òːl]	'swell, inflate'

The uvular glottalized stop varies between implosive and ejective; the alveolar glottalized stop is implosive in a very few languages (e.g., Tz'utujil, some dialects of Mam, and a few others). All other glottalized stops and affricates are ejective. If a glottalized stop is implosive it tends to be voiced in onset position, but this is not universal. It is almost always voiceless in coda position.

Fricatives are always voiceless while sonorants are voiced. In some languages (e.g., K'ichean proper) all the non-nasal sonorants devoice in coda position. The devoicing may result in notable fricativization as well. The pronunciation of /w/ varies substantially in different languages; some of the possibilities are [w, v, β, b] and the voiceless [w?, f, p] in coda position. Q'eqchi' devoices or partially devoices nasals in coda position (Stewart 1980:9), but such nasal devoicing is not common in other languages. Examples of the non-nasal sonorants in Kaqchikel follow.

KAQCHIKEL (García Matzar and Rodríguez Guaján 1997:16–17)

	Onset position		Coda position	
/l/	[liqˠ]	'plate'	[χiɬ]	'ear of dried corn'
	[ʔa.ˈlaʔ]	'young man'	[ʃkˈoɬ.ˈmaʔç]	'it was rolling'
/r/	[ɾiʃ]	'green'	[kiɾ̥]	'fish'
	[pi.ˈɾom]	'split'	[paɾ̥.ˈkɪç]	'yucca (Spanish bayonet)'
/w/	[wi.ˈniqˠ]	'people'	[ʔu.ˈtiw̥]~[ʔu.ˈtif]	'coyote'
	[wa.ˈweʔ]~[va.ˈveʔ]	'here'	[tew̥.ˈtɔχ]	'somewhat cold'
/j/	[jaʔ]	'water'	[moç]	'blind'
	[ʃkˈo.ˈjɪɾ̥]	's/he got thin'	[kˈaç.ˈkˈɔχ]	'somewhat bitter'

The glottal stop is somewhat anomalous, in that it behaves both like a consonant and a vowel feature. By and large it is treated like a consonant, but sometimes some manifestations of glottal stop are treated like vowel features. The strongest argument for treating glottal stop like a consonant is that it can fill the consonant position in roots that are restricted to a CVC shape. Most Mayan languages restrict transitive verb roots and positional roots to this shape, as did Proto-Mayan, and the glottal stop can fill either of the consonant positions (although not very frequently). For instance, the following examples are from Mam.

MAM (IXTAHUACÁN) (Maldonado Andrés et al. 1986)

waʔ-	'standing'	positional root
ʔaw-	'plant'	transitive root
seʔ-	'do'	transitive root
ʔutʃ-	'quiet: crying baby'	positional root

However, glottal stop can also appear after vowels when other consonants are not possible, such as in the shape CVʔC. For instance, intransitive and noun roots in Mam can have this shape. The only other consonant that is permitted as the first consonant in root final clusters in Mam is /n/, and not in all classes (England 1983:93–6). Examples with CVʔC are:

tseʔj-	'burn'	intransitive root
tʃˈiʔʃ	'thorn'	noun root

Furthermore, in Mam at least, glottal stop has some other characteristics of being a vowel feature. For instance, there are several suffixes with glottal stops in which the glottal stop migrates to follow a long vowel in the stem. One of these suffixes is -ʔn, which forms transitive participles and the transitive stem form that is used whenever there is a directional. If the stem has a long vowel followed by any sonorant, the glottal stop migrates to the vowel (England 1983:125):

ˈsχoːma-   'undress'   +   -ʔn   >   ˈsχoːʔman-

Proto-Mayan root shapes, as detailed by Kaufman 1976, besides CVʔC or CVːʔC, could also have the forms CVhC or CVs/ʃ/xC. The following examples show these shapes (Kaufman and Norman 1984; Kaufman 1990):

*ahl 'heavy'	*ism 'beard'	*piʃp 'tomato'	*naxt 'far'

These forms have been less stable than CVʔC (although the last has not been entirely stable either) and have disappeared in many languages. *CVhC has often gone to CVːC or simply CVC, while other consonant clusters have often been simplified or have been broken up through inserting a vowel. In K'iche' (Kaufman 1990:66) *CVhC has become CVːC and the other clusters have generally lost the last consonant. Thus the K'iche' forms for the preceding words are:

K'ICHE'

[ʔaːɬ] 'heavy'	[ʔis] 'hair'	[piʃ] 'tomato'	[naχ] 'far'

1.2 Vowels

The majority of the Mayan languages have ten vowels: five short vowels in the canonical positions for five-vowel systems (/i, e, a, o, u/) plus five long vowels in the same positions. All of the Eastern languages except Kaqchikel and two dialects of K'iche' have long and short vowels, as does Mocho' of the Western division and all Yucatecan and Huastecan languages. Several Western languages, such as Akatek and some dialects of Tseltal, are reintroducing long vowels, but these come from different sources. For instance, in Akatek the long vowels come principally from historical *CVxC or *CVʔC sequences (Raymundo González et al. 2000:47):

Akatek	Q'anjob'al		Akatek	Chuj	
[noːˈnaχ]	[noxˈnaqˣ]	'full'	[tʃˈeːn]	[k'eʔn]	'rock'
[taːˈnaχ]	[taxˈnaqˣ]	'ripe'	[taːn]	[taʔn]	'mineral lime'

Kaqchikel has shifted to a tense/lax vowel system and additionally has reduced the vowel inventory to nine or six vowels. The lax vowels are generally lower than the tense vowels, except for lax /a/, which is usually either a high or mid central vowel. Nine-vowel dialects of Kaqchikel have resulted from a collapse of the distinction between lax /e/ and lax /a/, while six-vowel dialects have resulted from a collapse of the distinction between tense and lax vowels for all vowel qualities except /a/. Further, the distinction between tense and lax vowels only occurs in final syllables, where tense vowels correspond to historical long vowels and lax vowels correspond to historical short vowels. (This is parallel to the distinction between short and long vowels being maintained only in final syllables in most dialects of K'iche'.) In non-final syllables all vowels are tense. Kaqchikel of Sololá reportedly maintains ten vowels, at least for some speakers, five tense and five lax (see §2.2 regarding the phonetics of the Sololá vowels). Examples of the nine Kaqchikel vowels are:

KAQCHIKEL

Lax vowels			**Tense vowels**		
/ɨ/	[ʔɨχ]	'green corn'	/a/	[ʔaχ]	'cane field'
			/e/	[mem]	'mute'
/ɪ/	[k'ɪʃ]	'shame'	/i/	[k'iʃ]	'chayote'
/ɔ/	[rɔχ]	'we'	/o/	[roχ]	'his/her avocado'
/ʊ/	[ʃuˈtʊkʰ]	's/he stirred it'	/u/	[ʃtukʰ]	'it was stirred'

The Chichicastenango and Chiché dialect of K'iche' also makes a distinction between tense and lax rather than long and short vowels and has ten vowels, while the dialect of K'iche' spoken in Cantel and parts of Totonicapán has only six vowels, five tense and a lax /a/. The Western languages Chol and Chontal are also six-vowel languages, with a high central vowel as well as the low central vowel /a/. In all of the six-vowel languages the high central vowel usually corresponds historically to a short /a/ while the low central vowel corresponds to a long /a/ (Kaufman and Norman 1984:85–6, for details of the correspondences in Cholan).

In other languages the distinction between long and short vowels may or may not be accompanied by a change in vowel quality. For instance, in Mam short vowels except /a/ are typically lower and laxer than long vowels, while in K'iche' short vowels are usually (see §2.2.) of the same quality as long vowels. (Examples from England 1983 for Mam and from Telma Can Pixabaj for K'iche', reproduced from England 2001. Note that Santa Lucía Utatlán permits long vowels in non-word-final position, which not all dialects of K'iche' do.)

MAM (IXTAHUACÁN)

Short vowels				**Long vowels**		
/a/	[ˈʔawal]	'crop'		/a:/	[ʔaˈwa:l]	'farmer'
/e/	[ɓetʃ]	'sprout'		/e:/	[ɓe:tʃ]	'flower'
/i/	[ʔitʃˤ]	'mouse'		/i:/	[ʔi:tʃˤ]	'chili pepper'
/o/	[tʃˤɔkʰ]	'grackle'		/o:/	[tʃˤo:kʰ]	'plow'
/u/	[ʔʊs]	'fly'		/u:/	[ʔu:ts]	'cradle'

K'ICHE' (SANTA LUCÍA UTATLÁN)

Short vowels				**Long vowels**		
/a/	[tʃaχ]	'pine'		/a:/	[tʃa:χ]	'ashes'
/e/	[ʃumeˈso]	's/he swept it'		/e:/	[ʃme:ˈsikʰ]	'it was swept'
/i/	[k'iʃ]	'shame'		/i:/	[k'i:ʃ]	'thorn'
/o/	[ʔoχ]	'we'		/o:/	[ʔo:χ]	'avocado'
/u/	[ʃutʃuˈpo]	's/he turned it off'		/u:/	[ʃtʃu:ˈpikʰ]	'it was turned off'

The length of long vowels may also differ from language to language. Thus some dialects of K'iche' have long vowels that are only slightly longer than short vowels, while Q'eqchi' has long vowels that are much longer than short vowels, and Mam long vowels are longer than in K'iche' but not as long as in Q'eqchi'. Frazier (2009) shows that all types of Yucatec long vowels are approximately twice as long as short vowels.

All of the Western languages except Mocho' lost the distinction between long and short vowels and are five-vowel or six-vowel languages (unless they later reintroduced vowel length distinctions, as in Akatek). Examples from Q'anjob'al (de Diego Antonio et al. 1996):

Q'ANJOB'AL

/a/	[ʔax]	'cane'	[ʔaxan]	'green corn'
/e/	[mem]	'mute, dumb'		
/i/	[k'iʃ]	'thorn'	[k'iˈʃaw]	'shame'
/o/	[ʔon]	'avocado'	[on-]	'we (set B prefix)'
/u/	[ʔun]	'paper, book'		

The Yucatecan languages Mopan, Itzaj, and Lacandon also have a high central vowel in addition to the five canonical short and long vowels, giving them eleven vowels. An example of the contrast between this vowel and short and long *a* in Itzaj follows (Hofling and Tesucún 2000:5).

ITZAJ
    [k'iʃ] 'tie'   [k'aʃ] 'knot'   [k'aːʃ] 'forest'

A few languages permit vowel sequences. All dialects of Ixil do, although usually in different words. The examples that follow show (1) a vowel sequence in a verb form from Nebaj due to a Set B marker suffixed to a vowel terminal verb stem, (2) a vowel sequence in a root in Cotzal, and (3) a vowel sequence in a complex group of enclitics in Chajul (note the root is the same as that of Cotzal, but it has a long vowel instead of a vowel sequence) (words taken from Poma S. et al. 1996).

IXIL
  1 [ʔaćaluin]   'you hug me'   (Nebaj)
  2 [ṣiakʰ]   'child'   (Cotzal)
  3 [ṣaːkʰ ʔinćae]   'they are children' (Chajul)

1.3 Stress

Mayan languages have four stress patterns, all of which are predictable. They are (Kaufman 1990:67):

1   Stress on heavy syllables (e.g., Huastec, Northern Mam, Yucatecan)
2   Final syllable stress (e.g., K'iche', Achi, Kaqchikel, Tz'utujil, Sipakapense, Saka-pultek, Uspantek (but interacts with tone), Q'eqchi', Poqomam, Poqomchi', Western Mam, Mocho', Chol)
3   Penultimate stress (e.g., Southern Mam, Ixil, Chontal)
4   First syllable lexical stress, last syllable phrasal stress (e.g., Q'anjob'al, Akatek, Popti', Tsotsil, Tseltal, Itzaj, Mopan).

Kaufman further states that he believes that Proto-Mayan stress was of the first type and very similar to Huastec. According to Larsen and Pike (1949) and Edmonson (1988) Huastec stress falls on the last long vowel of the word and if there are no long vowels, it falls on the first short vowel, with some further complications if the word is phrase-final. It may be that Southeastern Huastec has a different stress rule (Kondić 2012). While the principal conditioning element in defining the heavy syllable is vowel length, in Northern Mam there is a hierarchy of heaviness starting with long vowels as the heaviest syllable, then vowel plus glottal stop, then vowel plus consonant (England 1983). The last heaviest syllable is stressed.
    Examples of heavy syllable stress.

MAM (Maldonado Andrés et al. 1986)
Heaviest – long V:	[koˈleːtʰ]	'defend'	[ˈkoːlatʰ]	'abandon'
Heavy – last Vʔ:	[puʔˈlaʔ]	'dipper'	[ˈlaʔχatʰ]	'cheat'
Less heavy – closed syllable:	[ʔoχˈlaɓ]	'rest'	[ˈʔoχtṣa]	'long ago'
Vː vs. Vʔ:	[tquʔqaˈniːl]	'the burned one'		

Examples of initial lexical stress and final phrase stress in Q'anjob'al follow (Mateo Toledo 1999:62). Note that lexical items in isolation take phrasal stress (i.e., final).

Q'ANJOB'AL

    [po'qoq]   'powder'
    [wi'naq]   'man'
    [Maş 'stentoq cham 'winaq ix Mi'kin.]   'The man pushed Mikin.'

1.4 Tone

Several Mayan languages have developed contrastive tone. The best known of these is Yucatec, but Southern Lacandon and Uspantek also have contrastive tone, one dialect of Tsotsil may have contrastive tone, and Mocho' has been analyzed as having contrastive tone. In addition phonetic pitch differences are found in a number of dialects of Mam, Teko, and Tuzantec. Tone comes from two sources – sequences of vowel + *h, or sequences of vowel + glottal stop.

According to Frazier (2009:19), Yucatec Maya has the following vowel shapes:

v	SHORT	[tʃak] 'red'	(short, unmarked for tone, modal voice)
v̀v	LOW TONE	[tʃà:k] 'boil'	(long, low tone, modal voice)
v́v	HIGH TONE	[tʃá:k] 'rain'	(long, high tone, modal voice)
v́v̰	GLOTTALIZED	[tʃáa̰k] 'starch'	(long, high tone followed by creaky voice)

Campbell (1977:89) characterizes Frazier's 'glottalized' shape as $\acute{V}?V_1$, which Frazier (2009:20–1) says is a possible, but rare, pronunciation of this shape. Campbell further says that vowel length is predictable from tone – all vowels with tone are long except this particular shape, where the vowel is short, and all vowels with no tone are also short. Since Frazier characterizes this shape as having a long vowel (plus creaky voice), the predictability of vowel length is even simpler from her perspective – all vowels marked for tone are long, while unmarked vowels are short. Campbell gives the Proto-Mayan sources for Yucatec tones as follows:

*CV:C	>	$C\grave{V}$:C
*CV?C	>	$C\acute{V}_1?V_1C$
*CVhC	>	$C\acute{V}$:C
*CVhCVC	>	$C\acute{V}$:CVC

Examples of each of the four vowel shapes follow (Bricker et al. 1998:xv). The first column gives the Proto-Mayan source shape.

*CVC	CVC	[katʃ]	'split, fracture'
*CV:C	$C\grave{V}$:C	[kà:tʃ]	'fragment'
*CVhC	$C\acute{V}$:C	[ká:tʃ]	'split slowly'
*CV?C	$C\acute{V}?V_1C$	[ká?atʃ]	'be split, fractured'

Yucatec scholars generally agree on the vowel shapes presented by Frazier, and usually refer to 'glottalized' or 'broken' vowels as one of those shapes. They may represent it as $\acute{V}_1?V_1$ (e.g., Bricker et al. 1998:xiii). Most scholars who work on other Mayan languages usually refer to vowel plus glottal stop sequences instead of 'glottalized' or 'broken' vowels. Phonetic work on this topic is just beginning to be done (see §2.1.), and the question that remains is whether this shape is best analyzed as an allophone of a vowel plus glottal stop sequence, or as a separate phonemic vowel type. This issue is somewhat independent of whether the shape is accompanied by distinctive tone or not, although it should be noted that in many of the languages that have this $V_1?V_1$ sequence it is usually accompanied by some pitch difference. It may be that the resolution of this question will be different for different languages.

Southern Lacandon also has high tone contrasts on long vowels only, in which high tone derives from *VhC in Proto-Mayan (Bergqvist 2008:65). Other long vowels have low (neutral) tones, while short vowels have no tone contrasts. Examples of the three-way contrast on the verb 'to chop' follow (Bergqvist 2008:66).

LACANDÓN

[kuɓuhik]	'he chops it (with an axe)'
[kuɓúːhur]	'it was chopped'
[kuɓuːh]	'he (axe-)chops (things)'

Uspantek has been described as having descending tone in contrast with neutral tone on long vowels in the final syllable, while high tone is found in contrast with neutral tone on short vowels in the penultimate syllable (Kaufman 1975:100–2; Can Pixabaj 2007:39–49). (Note that Kaufman and other sources disagree about whether penultimate vowels with high tone can be long or not; Kaufman says they can.) According to Campbell (1977:38), descending tone derives from *CV?C, *CV?VC, or *CVhC[STOP/AFFRICATE] sequences, or from vowels before Uspantek [χ] that derives from Proto-K'ichean *x, which in turn derives from Proto-Mayan *ŋ. He does not offer an explanation of the derivation of high tone in penultimate syllables, which he treats as stress and says is not yet understood. Examples of Uspantek words with high or descending tone and with neutral tone follow (from Can Pixabaj 2007).

USPANTEK

High or descending tone		Neutral tone	
[ʔínqʼaɓ]	'my hands'	[ʔintʃʼeːkʰ]	'my knee'
[ʔínkar]	'my fish'	[ʔinkaːɓ̰]	'my honey'
[ʔíʃim]	'corn'	[ʔikim]	'below'
[ʃoχʔélikʰ]	'we went out'	[tʃakuneːl]	'worker'
[kʼájɓel]	'market'	[saqwetʃ]	'potato'
[wûːχ]	'book, paper'	[keːχ]	'deer'
[sîːpʰ]	'gift'	[siːpʰ]	'tick'
[ʔinkʼâːχ]	'my flour'	[ʔinkʼaːtʰ]	'my net'
[qaχâːɓ̰]	'our rain'	[ʔintʃʼaːɓ̰]	'my arrow'

Bennett and Henderson (2013) offer yet another analysis of tone in Uspantek. They say (2013:591) that Uspantek has "a single H tone that is restricted to the penultimate mora of the word." The perceived descending tone in final syllables, according to them, results from high tone being assigned to the penultimate mora and then falling through the last mora. If the last syllable is light, then a high tone occurs on the penultimate syllable. They go on to explain penultimate stress and tone on short vowels by saying that default stress is word-final, but since tone and stress must occur on the same syllable, and tone is not always on the final syllable, stress must sometimes shift to the penultimate syllable. Some words bear lexical tone, but certain segments block or condition tone. Finally, some functional morphemes introduce a high tone that may not appear on the morpheme itself. Lexical tone is not predictable (although the blocking of lexical tone may be) but morphological tone is predictable. The analysis that Bennett and Henderson offer depends on and refines the analysis by Can Pixabaj (2007, cited by Bennett and Henderson as 2006) of which words and morphemes bear tone. Tone and its interaction with stress in Uspantek ends up being far more complex than in the other Mayan languages that have tone or pitch differences, largely because it is associated with both lexical items and functional morphology, can be blocked or conditioned by certain segments, and is also connected to stress.

The Tsotsil of San Bartolo, formerly called San Bartolomé de los Llanos and now officially named Venustiano Carranza, also has been said to have tone. In this dialect of Tsotsil a contrastive low tone comes from the loss of *h before a consonant, according to Kaufman (1972:84–5), for instance:

TSOTSIL (SAN BARTOLO)

| *tʃ'uhm | > | [tʃ'ùm] | 'ayote squash' |
| *pohp | > | [pòp] | 'straw mat' |

In addition, syllables alternate low and high tones, starting with high tone. If there is a sequence of *hC or CC between the vowels of two syllables, the first will have low tone instead of high tone, and then the tones will alternate, as in the following (Kaufman 1972:85).

| *tʃikin | > | [(ʃ)tʃíkìn] | 'ear' |
| *ɓankil | > | [ɓànkíl] | 'older brother' |

Several minimal pairs for tone are offered by Sarles (1966:28). These are all polysyllabic; Sarles says that monosyllables with different underlying tones are not pronounced differently in isolation by most speakers.

| [ʔòlíl] | 'half, mid, middle' | [ʔólìl] | 'child' |
| [hák'bètík] | 'we ask you (sg)' | [hàk'bétìk] | 'we are asked (they ask us)' |

However, Herrera Zendejas has more recently (2013) argued that apparent tonal contrasts in San Bartolo Tsotsil result from laryngealization and falling pitch on a vowel that precedes a glottalized consonant. She finds that some of the words for which Kaufman reconstructs a vowel followed by *h do not actually have a falling F_0; in [pop] 'straw mat' she shows that the F_0 in fact rises. She further shows that falling pitch results from the presence of a glottalized consonant in the word, for instance [ʔitʃ'] 'louse' has falling pitch while [ʔitʃ] 'chili' does not. Glottalized consonants are neutralized before other consonants but maintain the effects of laryngealization and falling pitch on the previous vowel. Thus [ʃik'] 'feather' shows the characteristic falling pitch and laryngealization on the vowel, and those effects are maintained in the compound [ʃikmit] 'bird feather' although the glottalization of the [k] has been neutralized.

Mocho' and the dialects of Teko and Mam spoken along the Chiapas-Huehuetenango border have either low or high pitch as a development from *V(:)ʔ(C) sequences. The main question with regard to these phenomena is whether the pitch changes should be analyzed as phonemic tone contrasts or allophonic variations of Vʔ(C) sequences. They have most recently been analyzed as phonemic tone contrasts in Mocho' (Palosaari 2011). However, Martin (1984) analyzed these contrasts as allophonic variations that were close to becoming phonemic distinctions. According to Palosaari (2011:85), Mocho' has low tone that is restricted to long vowels in stressed syllables in nouns and that contrasts with plain long vowels and short vowels. The historical source for low tone is *VʔC sequences. Examples of the contrasts follow (Palosaari 2011:39).

MOCHO'

[ʔìːs]	'lazy person'	[ʔiːs]	'potato'	[ʔis=kʲaq]	'(finger)nail'
[kàːŋ]	'sky'	[kaːŋ]	'four'	[k'aŋ]	'loud'

Martin, however, takes the closely related Tuzantec data into account as well, and says that those words that have a falling pitch in her data (Palosaari's low tone) have a vowel-glottal stop-copy vowel sequence in Tuzantán. An example follows:

'sky'   Motozintla: [kâːŋ]   Tuzantán: [káʔàŋ]

Martin concludes that an analysis that can cover both Mocho' and Tuzantec data is preferable to one that only covers Mocho'. She therefore proposes that the underlying form for phonetic rising pitch on a long vowel is a long vowel and that the underlying form for phonetic falling pitch on a long vowel is a Vʔ sequence.

Mam of Ixtahuacán has a long vowel with falling pitch as the correlate of the sequence V:ʔ. In this case there is no reason to analyze this as phonemic tone, but rather as an allophone of glottal stop. The following example shows a glottal stop after a short vowel, which is then converted to falling pitch with no glottal closure when the vowel is lengthened. The vowels in question, whether long or short, have creaky voice that comes from the presence of a glottal.

MAM (IXTAHUACÁN)

/aʔ/   [ʔa̰ʔ]   'water'   /waːʔya/   [wa̰ːya]   'my water'

Teko in both Mazapa and Tectitán associates pitch changes with glottal stop, but the details are different in the two towns. In general, certain shapes are realized as a vowel plus glottal stop, while others are realized as a VʔV₁ where the two vowels have opposing pitches. The patterns are:

TEKO

		Tectitán	**Mazapa**	
VʔC	>	[VʔC]	[V̀ʔV́C]	
VC'	>	[VC']	[V̀ʔV́C']	(stressed syllable; C' = ejective/implosive)
Vʔ#	>	[V́ʔV̀#]	[V̀ʔV́#]	
V:ʔC	>	[V̀ʔV́:C]	[V̀ʔV́:C]	
V:ʔ#	>	[V:ʔ#]	[V:ʔ#]	

Examples follow. Mam (Ixtahuacán) is added to show the source of some of the copy vowels.

TEKO, MAM

		Tectitán	**Mazapa**	**Mam (Ixtahuacán)**	
V	[a]	[sanikʰ]	[saniṯʲ]	[snikʲ]	'ant'
VʔC	[òʔó] (M)	[ʔoʔṣ]	[ʔòʔóṣ]	[ʔoʔṣ]	'achiote (annatto)'
VC'	[àʔá] (M)	[χaɓ]	[χàʔáɓ]	[χ6aːl]	'rain'
Vʔ#	[áʔà] (T)	[ʔáʔà]	[ʔàʔá]	[ʔa̰ʔ]	'water'
V:	[aː]	[ʔaːɠ]	[ʔaːɠ]	[ʔaːɠ]	'vine'
V:C#	[àʔáː]	[ntsàʔáːχ]	[ntsàʔáːχ]	[ntsâʔχa]	'my ashes'
V:ʔ#	[aːʔ]	[waːʔ]	[waːʔ]	[wâːya]	'my water'

Clearly, further investigation of pitch in the languages that are close to the Chiapas-Huehuetenango border is needed. All of the towns where Northern Mam is spoken should be sampled, as well as those where Teko is spoken, plus both Mocho' and Tuzantec, and finally the southernmost varieties of Tsotsil. Teko in Mazapa, Mocho', and Tuzantec are all moribund. None of these languages/dialects are in contact with Yucatec, Lacandon, or Uspantek, but they all probably had contact with each other (except possibly Tsotsil) and they all show different details of the development of pitch from vowel plus glottal stop or /h/.

Tone contrasts are obviously recent in Mayan languages, and are still emerging in some of them but are entirely absent in the majority. Tone has usually developed from long vowels plus a glottal consonant (/ʔ, h/), but in some languages it has also developed from short vowels plus a glottal.

1.5 Phonotactics

Mayan languages differ considerably in their phonotactic characteristics, chiefly as a result of changes they have undergone. The most conservative patterns are that the majority of syllables are CVC, CVʔC, CVhC, or CV, there are few consonant clusters and none above two consonants, and there are no vowel sequences. However, some languages such as Mam and the K'iche' of Chichicastenango have rules that drop vowels in non-stressed syllables, resulting in longer and more frequent consonant clusters. Others such as Ixil, Q'anjob'al, and Tseltal of Oxchuc have eliminated some intervocalic consonants and now permit adjacent vowels. Words never begin with vowels (apparent vowel-initial words all have glottal onsets), except in Q'anjob'al, Akatek, Tseltal, and Tojol-abal, where the absence of a glottal onset contrasts with its presence, as in the following example in Q'anjob'al:

Q'ANJOB'AL
     [ʔon]   'avocado'   [on]   'your avocado'

K'iche' is in general quite conservative phonotactically. The following portion of a text in K'iche' shows a few consonant clusters, one in the word ʃkiɓiχ that results from joining the morphemes ʃ- and ki-, another in rqataːt that comes from vowel dropping, another in the word tʃkop that results from vowel dropping, and the last in kikamsaːχ from joining the morphemes kam- and -saː. There are no vowel sequences. The syllable shapes that are found are CV, CVː, CCV, CVC, CVːC, and CCVC. The text fragment is from Nahualá (Can Pixabaj 2004:219).

K'ICHE'
    1 'Komo ʃki'ɓiχ rqa'taːt qa'naːn, na'ɓe kaː'noq:
       'Thus as our forebears said before:'

    2 Na ki'ɓan ta k'aʃ tʃe le k'atʃeʔ'laχ,
       'Don't do damage to the mountain,'

    3 na ki'ɓan ta k'aʃ tʃe χo sin tʃkop,
       'don't do damage to an animal,'

    4 q'iχi'ra na
       'let it still develop'

5 k'a te ri? kikam'sa:χ.
   'then you kill it.'

Other languages, although they may have longer and somewhat more frequent consonant clusters or may permit vowel sequences, will look quite similar to K'iche' in their overall structures. However, even some dialects of K'iche' (for instance, Chichicastenango) and the closely related Tz'utujil may have fairly long consonant clusters (Dayley 1985:46 for Tz'utujil). A more audible difference among languages has to do with the basic phonology. Chol, for instance, sounds to speakers of other languages like it has a lot of palatals (because of the palatalization of /t/ and /n/) and a preponderance of the high mid vowel, Mam sounds like it is full of retroflexed sounds, while Yucatec is perceived as sing-song (because of tone), and Achi is distinctive because of its pharyngeal pronunciation of what is a glottalized uvular in other languages.

2 PHONETICS

Although the descriptive phonology of Mayan languages is relatively well documented, there is a considerable gap in the literature concerning their phonetic analysis. The following subsections review some of the acoustic, aerodynamic, and auditory studies of Mayan languages, the majority of which have been carried out within the last decade. Although the greater part of these phonetic studies has dealt with Yucatec, there is a growing number of studies on other Mayan languages, particularly those spoken in Guatemala. Nonetheless, phonetics remains one of the most understudied aspects of Mayan languages, and, consequently, a fertile field for future research as experimental phonetic data is needed in order to corroborate the different phonological claims that have been set forth in the literature.

2.1 Consonants

The majority of the phonetic analyses of consonants in Mayan languages have examined differences between pulmonic and ejective or implosive (glottalized) stops. Aerodynamic work on Kaqchikel, K'iche', Poqomchi', Q'eqchi', and Tz'utujil (Pinkerton 1986), and, more recently, Q'anjob'al (Shosted 2011) has demonstrated that /q'/ varies between ejective and implosive in different languages, and even in different dialects of the same language. In Pinkerton's study, she found evidence for an ejective /q'/ in Carchá Q'eqchi' and San Cristóbal Poqomchi', for an implosive /q'/ in Kaqchikel, K'iche', Tz'utujil, Tactic Poqomchi', and Chamelco Q'eqchi', and for both an ejective and implosive in Cobán Q'eqchi'. Shosted (2011) showed that Q'anjob'al also has an implosive /q'/, and, in a perception task, that differences between the glottalized /k', q'/ were more robust than between the pulmonic /k, q/ in Q'anjob'al. Furthermore, Shosted's work demonstrates that in Q'anjob'al, /k'/ and /q'/ are acoustically distinct in the context of front vowels, but that this distinction degrades as the vowels become more back.

In Tz'utujil, Bennett (2010) used acoustic data to corroborate previous claims of the allophonic realization of aspirated pulmonic stops before consonants and word-finally and of the allophonic variation of ejectives as implosives pre-vocalically. In this analysis, Bennett proposes that these allophonic stop alternations in Tz'utujil are driven by the need to preserve paradigmatic place of laryngeal states, i.e., the aspiration of pulmonic stops before consonants and word-finally enhances the phonetic contrast with ejectives in exactly the contexts where the two might be most confused. However, as Bennett readily admits, such a hypothesis needs to be tested via perceptual studies.

In Yucatec, Frazier (2009, 2011) noted dialect differences in the bilabial implosive /ɓ/. In western dialects (Mérida, Santa Elena), normal characteristics were reported: a greater than average lowering of the larynx and an increase in amplitude until the burst. However, in eastern dialects (Sisbicchén, Xocén, and Yax Che), there were signs of pre-nasalization, especially among males, and there was no steady increase in amplitude until the burst. She concludes by stating that an aerodynamic study is needed before more conclusive statements can be made about /ɓ/ in Yucatec. It is of note that while studies on the bilabial implosive in non-Mayan languages have generally found that it is correlated with a high pitch (F_0), acoustic data in Q'anjob'al (Shosted 2011), Tz'utujil (Bennett 2010), and Yucatec (Frazier 2009, 2011) have all shown it to be a tone-depressing consonant, or that it is correlated with a lower F_0.

Work on fricatives in Mayan languages is less extensive. Léonard et al. (2009) analyzed the durational and spectral features of the posterior fricatives /x/ and /h/ in Tseltal and found that they have merged in some dialects. Preliminary work by Shosted (2014) on Q'anjob'al using electropalatography (EPG) and MRI images (static) has shown that the fricative [ʂ] may indeed be a true retroflex, articulated with a pronounced upward curling of the tongue tip. As Bennett (2016a) points out, Hamann (2003) suggests that subapical fricatives are not found in any language and Q'anjob'al may be the first documentary proof of such a sound.

The glottal stop in Mayan languages has recently begun to receive attention, particularly its relationship with the surrounding vowels, which, depending on the language, may be /Vʔ/ or /VʔV/, the latter being classified as a 'rearticulated', 'glottal', 'broken' or even 'echo' vowel. In Yucatec, it is generally agreed that /VʔV/ is a vowel shape and several studies have demonstrated that the realization of a full glottal stop is rare and that it is canonically produced as a long vowel with modal voice interrupted by creaky voice, or [VV̰] (Frazier 2009, 2011; Avelino et al. 2011). In Frazier (2009, 2011), it was found that implosives, obstruents, and sonorants were more likely to be followed by a vowel with glottalization (either creaky voice or a full glottal stop) than ejectives and glottal stops. However, there was also significant between-speaker variation in her study. Frazier (2013:10) concludes that "[g]iven such variation, we are in need of more data before speculating on the degree of dialect/gender/age-specific variations in the production of glottalization."

Following Frazier's (2009) methodology, the glottal stop has also been acoustically analyzed in K'iche' (Baird 2011) and Q'anjob'al (Baird and Francisco Pascual 2012); however, as /VʔV/ is not considered a vowel shape in either language, both analyses examined sequences of /Vʔ/. In K'iche', it was found that the phonetic realization of /Vʔ/ varied according to the following phoneme – a full glottal stop was more frequently maintained before vowels and in word-final position whereas realizations as [VʔV] and [VV̰] were much more common before consonants. On the other hand, the phonetic realization of /Vʔ/ in Q'anjob'al was canonically reduced to creaky voice, or [VV̰], in all but word-final position regardless of the location of the word within a larger phrase and only one example of [VʔV] was found. These between-language differences were attributed to the phonological differences between the languages: Q'anjob'al phonology permits adjacent vowels whereas K'iche' phonology does not. Thus, when the /Vʔ/ sequence is followed by a vowel, a full glottal stop was generally maintained in K'iche' in order to separate the two vowel phonemes while the same sequence was predominately realized as creaky voice in Q'anjob'al because the vowels could be adjacent. As in Yucatec,

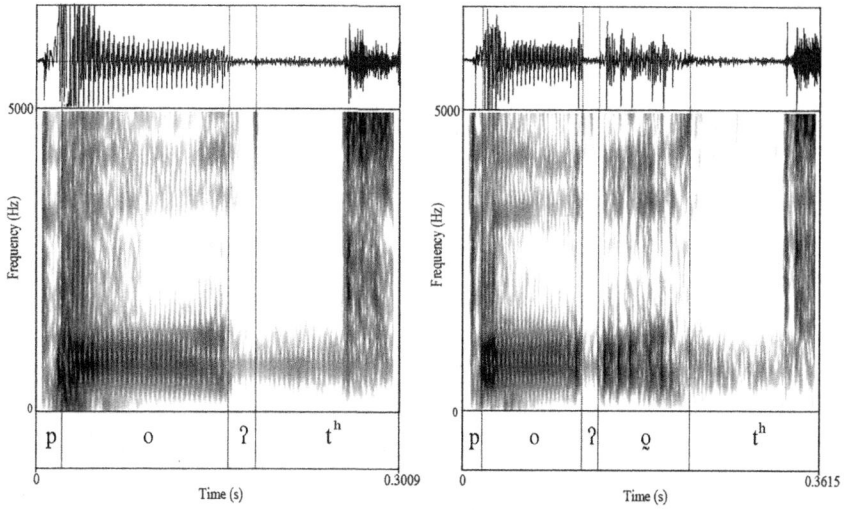

FIGURE 7.1 SPECTROGRAMS OF PHONETIC REALIZATIONS OF /POʔT/ 'WOMEN'S BLOUSE'
AS BOTH [POʔTʰ] AND [POʔO̯Tʰ] BY THE SAME SPEAKER OF K'ICHE'

(adapted from Baird 2011:45)

variation in the phonetic realizations of the glottal stop in both K'iche' and Q'anjob'al
was prevalent in the phonological environments that permitted different realizations, as
seen in Figure 7.1: realizations of /poʔt/ 'women's blouse' as [poʔtʰ] and [poʔo̯tʰ] by the
same female speaker of K'iche' during the same task. Again, future work is needed to
more fully understand these variations.

2.2 Vowels

As detailed in §1 above, Proto-Mayan has been reconstructed as having ten vowels in
five points of articulation with a contrast in duration, and different languages have gone
through different processes that have resulted in five-, six-, nine-, and ten-vowel systems,
some of which maintain contrasts in duration, vowel quality, and/or tone. Experimental
work on different aspects of the vowel systems in Mayan languages is limited to studies in Q'anjob'al (Shosted 2011), Yucatec (Frazier 2009), Kaqchikel (Bennett 2016b),
K'iche' (Baird 2010, 2016), and Tsotsil (Herrera Zendejas 2013). While Shosted's (2011)
study on Q'anjob'al was primarily focused on stops, he noted that both [i] and [e] demonstrate a dramatic drop in F_2 when followed by uvulars, while F_1 rises. According to Herrera Zendeja's (2013) acoustic work on San Bartolo Tsotsil, although it has a five-vowel
system without phonemic vowel length, the five vowels are actually /i, e, a, o, ɨ/.

In Yucatec, Frazier (2009) demonstrates that although the long vowels (High, Low,
and Glottalized) are always longer than the short vowel, there are two distinct patterns
of vowel length: one in western dialects (Mérida and Santa Elena) and another in eastern
dialects (Sisbicchén, Xocén, and Yax Che). In western dialects, long vowels were all
approximately the same length, whereas in eastern dialects, High tone vowels were longer
than all other vowels. Additionally, each vowel shape retained its canonical realization

in word-final position and differences in vowel length were not as robust in non-final position, i.e. short vowels were longer and long vowels were shorter. Vowel quality was not analyzed in this study.

Based on corpus data, Bennett (2016b) analyzed the Sololá dialect of Kaqchikel, which is claimed to have a ten-vowel system with a tense-lax distinction (Majzul et al. 2000). In his analysis, Bennett found that lax vowels tend to be more centralized than their tense counterparts and that there were no differences in duration between tense and lax vowel pairs. However, his preliminary data also demonstrate that /i, ɪ/ may be merging in this dialect and that allophonic variants of the lax central vowel include [a, ɨ, ɯ].

In Baird (2010, 2016), the vowels of stressed, word-final syllables in several dialects of K'iche' were analyzed – three that are said to maintain phonemic vowel length, Almolonga, Nahualá, and Zunil, and one that does not, Cantel (López Ixcoy 1994). The analyses of both duration and vowel quality revealed that Nahualá maintains a ten-vowel system and that differences between short and long vowel pairs are primarily seen in duration although there are some differences in vowel quality and that Cantel does indeed have a reduced, six-vowel system where short /a/ has become the sixth mid-vowel, interpreted as /ɐ/. When compared to the other dialects, the high vowels were more centralized in Cantel. The data from Almolonga and Zunil reveal a possible intermediate stage of development of the vowel systems. In both dialects, there were no differences in either vowel quality or duration between the short and long /e/, suggesting that Almolonga and Zunil now have nine-vowel systems that are, in several aspects, similar to the nine-vowel systems in several dialects of Kaqchikel reported in §1.2. Vowel plots demonstrating vowel quality in Nahualá and Cantel are presented in Figures 7.2 and 7.3.

2.3 Stress

Among linguists (phoneticians in particular), stress in Yucatec is somewhat controversial and still not fully understood. Bricker et al. (1998) state that there is a default stress pattern in Yucatec, in which stress falls on the final syllable if a word has no long vowels, whereas if one long vowel is present the stress falls on that syllable, and if two long vowels are present it falls on the first long vowel. In contrast, Krämer (2001) proposes that stress in Yucatec is quantity sensitive and, since all final syllables end in a consonant in Yucatec, final syllables must bear stress and that initial syllables also attract stress. Thus, stress is assigned to initial and final syllables in a phrase, as well as to any heavy (bimoriac) syllables intervening between them. Gussenhoven and Teeuw (2008) state that Yucatec has three long syllables, Long High, Long Low, and Glottalized, which are stressed, as well as a word-initial short syllable. Thus, tone or glottalization features are what attract stress, rather than length, and words with only short vowels have initial, rather than final, stress.

In a production study involving stress in both Spanish loan words and native Yucatec words, Kidder (2013) notes a prosodic change in three syllable Spanish loan words in which the first and third syllables lengthen, while the second syllable shortens. However, the same was not true of Yucatec words as no strong pattern for stress placement cued by duration or pitch emerged from her data. The results of her analysis show that the only reliable pattern found for stressed syllables in Yucatec was in words that contained a High, Low, or Glottalized vowel; those vowels were significantly longer than short or neutral vowels. Words without any long vowels did not reveal any pattern of prominence. In a follow-up perception task involving native speaker intuitions, the speakers most often identified the syllables containing High, Low, or Glottalized vowels as being

Nahualá K'iche' Vowels

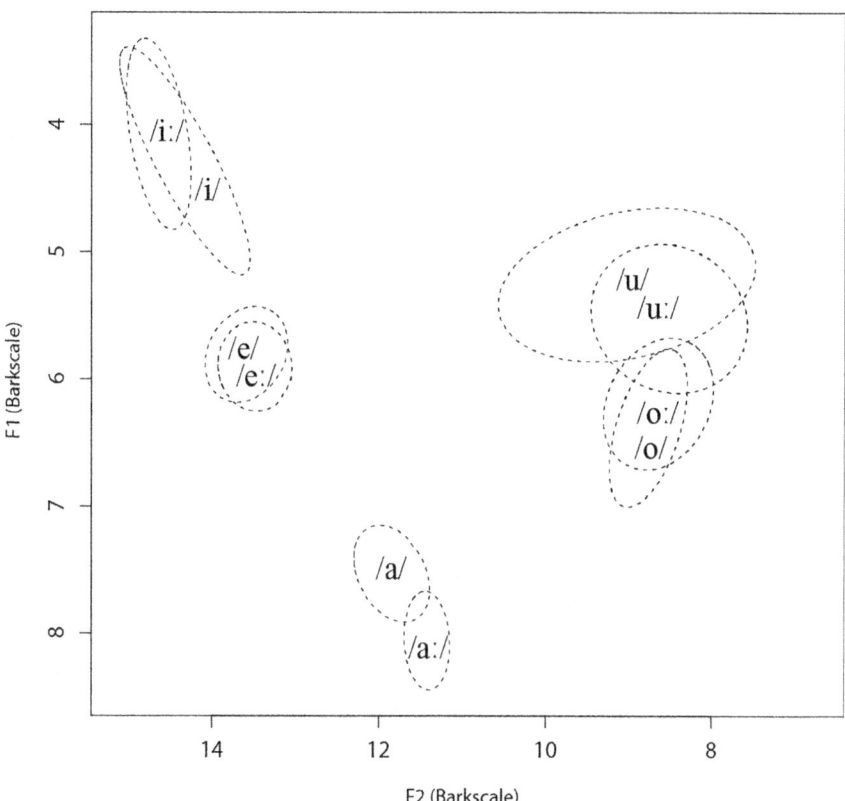

FIGURE 7.2 VOWEL PLOTS DEMONSTRATING K'ICHE' VOWEL QUALITY IN THE DIALECT
OF NAHUALÁ

(adapted from Baird 2016)

the strongest, although the effect was not significant. Although Bricker et al. (1998), Krämer (2001), and Gussenhoven and Teeuw (2008) all posited that either tones, glottalized vowels, or initial or heavy syllables might be the bearers of stress, the data collected by Kidder (2013) suggest that only tones and glottalized vowels are consistently longer in duration than other vowels and that they do not receive any additional word level prominence. Kidder concludes that there are two possible accounts concerning stress in Yucatec: (i) metrical stress exists in Yucatec, but is signaled neither by pitch nor duration, and is instead signaled by an as yet undiscerned phonetic cue, or (ii) metrical stress does not exist in Yucatec.

Experimental work on stress in Q'eqchi' by Berinstein (1979) indicates that speakers acoustically marked stressed syllables containing both long and short vowels with a significantly higher pitch and intensity, but not a longer duration, than unstressed syllables. She proposed that peak height and intensity are conditioned by stress in Q'eqchi', not the number of syllables or phonemic length (moras). In a follow-up perception study of stress

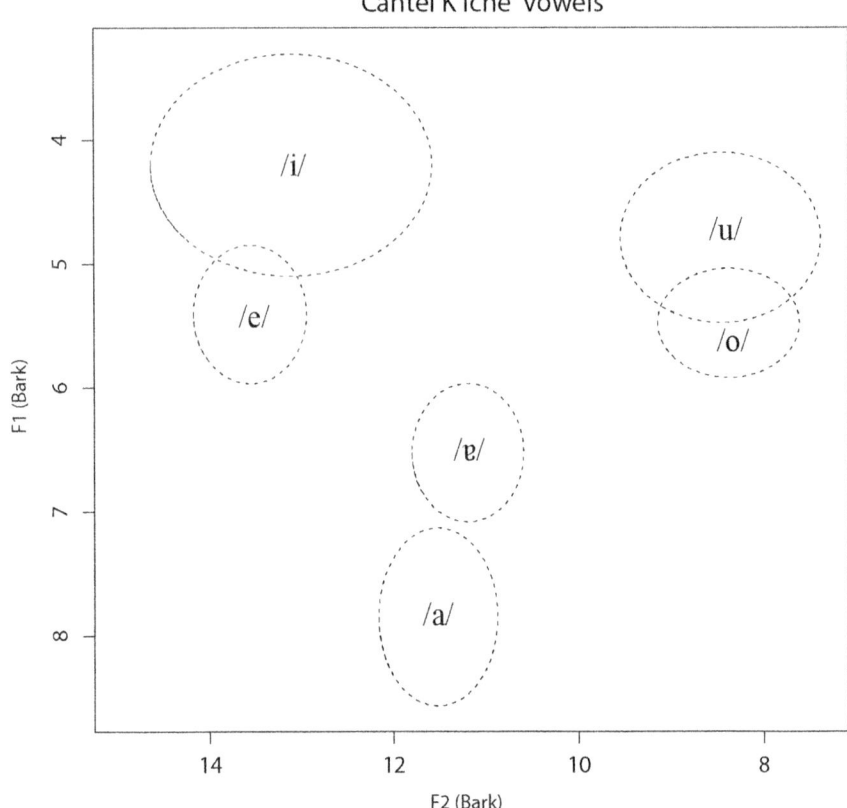

FIGURE 7.3 VOWEL PLOTS DEMONSTRATING K'ICHE' VOWEL QUALITY IN THE DIALECT
                OF CANTEL

(adapted from Baird 2016)

involving speakers of Q'eqchi' and Kaqchikel, the data revealed that Kaqchikel speakers
used duration as a perceptual cue of stress while Q'eqchi' speakers did not. Berinstein
concluded that phonological differences between the languages affect the acoustic realization and auditory perception of stress – Q'eqchi' maintains phonemic vowel length and
uses differences in duration to contrast between short and long vowels whereas Kaqchikel
has lost phonemic vowel length and no longer needs to use duration to contrast short and
long vowels. Consequently, duration has been repurposed in Kaqchikel as an acoustic and
auditory cue of stress while in Q'eqchi' it has not.

Baird (2015) examined the acoustic correlates of stress in three dialects of K'iche':
Cantel, Nahualá, and Zunil. In a comparison of word-final stressed syllables with long
vowels, word-final stressed syllables with short vowels, and non-final unstressed syllables, which are claimed to also be short vowels in the literature, the stressed syllables in
all three dialects had a significantly higher pitch than the unstressed syllables. Differences
in intensity or vowel reduction in unstressed syllables were not, however, demonstrated.

(Only words with the vowels /oː, o/ were analyzed for stress in Baird (2015), since this was the only vowel pair that did not demonstrate significant differences in vowel quality in any of the three dialects and did demonstrate a significant difference in vowel length in Nahualá and Zunil.) Similar to Berinstein (1979), the results also revealed dialect differences in the use of duration to mark stress. In Nahualá and Zunil, which maintain phonemic vowel length, word-final long vowels were significantly longer than both word-final short vowels and non-final unstressed vowels. As there were no significant differences in duration between word-final short vowels and non-final unstressed vowels, it was determined that non-final unstressed vowels in these dialects of K'iche' are indeed short vowels. However, in Cantel, which no longer employs phonemic vowel length, there were no differences in duration between word-final long and short vowels and both were significantly longer than non-final unstressed vowels. The data was further analyzed according to position within the utterance, phrase-final vs. phrase-medial, and evidence of declination, or downsloping, of the pitch contour throughout the phrase, was found in all three dialects as the phrase-final syllables had a significantly lower pitch than the phrase-medial syllables. However, only in the Cantel dialect did the phrase-final syllables demonstrate significant word-final lengthening. Thus, following the proposal of Berinstein (1979), it was concluded that a higher pitch is the most consistent acoustic correlate of stress in K'iche' while the use of duration to mark stress depends on the phonological structure of the dialect, specifically, the presence or absence of phonemic vowel length.

2.4 Tone

The tonal system of Yucatec was first described by Pike (1946). Fisher (1976) provides some of the first graphs of pitch contours that indeed demonstrate that there is a High tone, that final syllables are distinguished by a falling pitch, and that non-final syllables are distinguished by a rising pitch. However, Fisher presents no numerical or statistical analysis of these contours.

Recent experimental work has increased our knowledge of tones in Yucatec. For example, Kügler and Skopeteas (2006) and Kügler et al. (2007) demonstrate that Low tone is realized as a low level pitch, whereas High tone is realized as a rise in pitch. Gussenhoven and Teeuw's (2008) experimental data confirms that only long vowels are marked with tones and that unstressed syllables (non-initial short syllables in content words and syllables in function words) are incapable of bearing tones. Within their proposal, the lexical representation of Long High includes an H-tone, and Glottalized vowels also have an H-tone linked to the first mora, which was also found in Frazier (2009, 2013) and Avelino et al. (2011). However, they propose an L-insertion rule that places an L-tone between H-tones, provided that at least one toneless syllable or mora intervenes. Finally, they state that the string of tones is realized straightforwardly, except for a lowering effect that H-tones have on subsequent tones.

According to Frazier (2009, 2011), tone may be a dialect feature of Yucatec as experimental data reveals that in western dialects (Mérida, Santa Elena), each vowel shape is associated with a unique tonal contour while no tonal contrast is produced in eastern dialects (Sisbicchén, Xocén, and Yax Che). In a perception task (Frazier 2009), listeners were able to perform at better than chance at distinguishing between High tone vowels and Glottalized vowels. Perception generally mirrored production: participants from the western dialects used both initial pitch and glottalization as perceptual cues whereas most participants from the eastern dialects (except Yax Che) did not use initial pitch as a perceptual cue.

Furthermore, in western dialects Frazier (2013) demonstrates that the high tone associated with the first mora of glottalized vowels canonically occurs at the beginning of the vowel and that creaky voice occurs near the end (98 percent of the time in her data). Based on the concept of phasing (Silverman 1997), which states that it is common in laryngeally complex languages that tone and non-modal phonation are not simultaneously produced, but rather are phased with respect to each other, Frazier proposes that Yucatec is a minimally laryngeally complex language because the tonal system is not complex and the use of non-modal phonation is restricted to glottalized vowels. Yucatec therefore has one phasing pattern: tone followed by creak. Glottalized vowels were produced with high pitch even when they were not produced with glottalization, thus, the high pitch of the glottalized vowels cannot be solely conditioned by the following creaky voice, as pitch (as seen in the perception study in the previous paragraph) is an important cue to this vowel shape.

Finally, while tone in Yucatec is contrastive on a lexical level, it has also been described in grammatical studies as being used in the expression of voice inflection paradigms in transitive verbs where the tones of grammatical voices override the underlying tones of the verb root (Orie and Bricker 2000): active voice maintains the underlying tone of the verb root, antipassive voice is marked by Low tone, middle voice is marked by High tone, and passive voice is marked by a Rearticulated or Glottalized vowel. In an acoustic study of the Peto dialect of Yucatec, Avelino et al. (2011) found results that indicate, contrary to these previous descriptions, that most voice categories are not marked by tone-phonation features and that the underlying tone of the verb root is commonly maintained throughout the different grammatical voices. Exceptions were the underlying Low tone in passive voice, which was marked by a Glottalized vowel, and male speakers, who marked middle voice with High tone and antipassive with low tone.

2.5 Intonation

Within the Autosegmental-Metrical model of intonation (Liberman 1975; Pierrehumbert 1980; Ladd 1996), different languages have been analyzed and Tones and Break Indices (ToBI) transcription systems have been proposed for Q'eqchi' (Berinstein 1991; Wagner 2014) and K'iche' (Nielsen 2005). Although Nielsen described K'iche' as an edge language with stress-driven language pitch accents, it should be noted that this analysis was based on one speaker analyzed during a field methods course at UCLA and her problematic claim of lexical stress in K'iche' is based on the observation that some enclitics do not receive stress (as detailed in Henderson 2012) and that some recent Spanish loanwords in K'iche' can keep their non-final stress pattern. Burdin et al. (2015) classify K'iche' as a head-edge language.

Nielsen (2005) also noted that Yes/No questions in K'iche', which are syntactically marked by the question marker *la*, end with a rising intonation, or boundary tone, while statements end with a falling boundary tone. This was analyzed via a production and perception study in the Cantel dialect by Baird (2010). The production study confirmed that Yes/No questions are canonically produced with rising boundary tones and statements are produced with falling boundary tones; however, *la* was rarely used to mark Yes/No questions. In a follow-up perception study, phrases with rising boundary tones were perceived as Yes/No questions and phrases with falling boundary tones were perceived as statements, regardless of the presence of the Yes/No question-marking word *la*. Consequently, the data suggest that there appears to be a loss of meaning and lack of use to the *la* question marker in Cantel K'iche' and that intonation alone is used to mark Yes/No questions.

Apart from these studies, the majority of the studies on the intonational systems of Mayan languages have analyzed the prosodic prominence, if any, given to a focused or topicalized constituent. However, as detailed in Aissen, this volume, on information structure, topic and focus are often marked via changes in word order in Mayan languages, and typically consist of moving the constituent to a pre-verbal position, although in some languages in situ focus, i.e., no changes in word order, is possible (Velleman 2014).

Studies on different varieties of Yucatec have generally come to the same conclusion, that neither a topicalized nor a focused constituent receives any prosodic emphasis and that both are marked solely through syntactic means (Gussenhoven 2006; Kügler and Skopeteas 2006, 2007; Kügler et al. 2007; Gussenhoven and Teeuw 2008; Avelino 2011). Kügler et al. (2007) found that topicalized constituents are accompanied by a salient tonal event, an H-tone associated with the right edge of the topic phrase, but that this tone is associated with the topic suffix – e' and cannot be used independently of the suffix in order to indicate topicalization. There were some minor differences reported among these studies. For example, Kügler et al. (2007) found that L-tones are realized as Low in topic and focus whereas Avelino (2011) found that L-tones could be modified in the phonetic implementation that is overridden by intonational melodies.

In the K'iche' dialect of Santa María Tzejá, Ixcán, Yasavul (2013) analyzed the difference between pre-verbal focus and contrastive-topic constituents and only found significant acoustic differences between the two in terms of range of the pitch rise, which only demonstrated a mean difference of 6 Hz. As Yasavul states, this may not be enough of a perceptual difference for listeners. However, it should be noted that the data in this study was elicited by recordings of non-native speakers and only analyzed prosodic emphasis on non-K'iche' words: Spanish proper names with non-final stress patterns such as María. An additional study in this dialect by Burdin et al. (2015) examined phrasing and duration of nouns, adjectives, and noun phrases as cues to focus. Their results demonstrate that while both nouns and adjectives were longer when they were followed by a prosodic break, there were no significant effects of focus condition on word duration in the Santa María Tzejá, Ixcán dialect of K'iche'.

Broad and contrastive focus constituents in intransitive sentences were compared in the K'iche' dialects of Nahualá and Cantel in Baird (2014) in both naturalistic and controlled production tasks with native speakers. In contrast to the previous studies described in this section, the results revealed that a contrastive focus constituent was significantly more marked than a broad focus constituent in several acoustic aspects. The most common acoustic strategy of contrastive focus marking was an earlier alignment of intonational events, i.e., an earlier valley, or start of the pitch contour rise, and an earlier occurrence of the pitch peak. A greater pitch rise was also used among the speakers, though it revealed a considerable amount of between-speaker variation as females marked contrastive focus with a greater rise than males. Additionally, it was the only acoustic cue of contrastive focus marking that was correlated with bilingual language dominance: Spanish-dominant bilinguals tended to mark contrastive focus in K'iche' with a greater overall pitch rise than K'iche'-dominant bilinguals. The use of greater duration to mark a contrastive focus constituent was also used, but, similar to the findings on stress in Baird (2014), its use was dialectal: similar to the speakers from Santa María Tzejá, Ixcán examined in Burdin et al. (2015), K'iche' speakers from Nahualá, with phonemic vowel length, did not use a longer duration to mark contrastive focus whereas speakers from Cantel, without phonemic vowel length, did use a longer duration. Finally, as reported in Velleman (2014), in situ contrastive focus marking in K'iche' is possible with subjects of intransitive verbs and objects of transitive verbs. The results of Baird (2014) reveal that speakers who marked subjects of intransitive verbs for contrastive focus both syntactically and in situ interchangeably marked in situ contrastive focus to a greater prosodic degree than the syntactically marked contrastive focus constituent and that both contrastive focus constituents were marked more than a non-contrastive (broad) focus constituent. It was concluded that the in situ contrastive focus constituent was marked to a greater degree than the syntactically marked contrastive focus constituent because a greater emphasis on the constituent would be the only cue of focus in the in situ structure. Examples of pitch contours of broad and syntactically marked contrastive focus phrases are presented in Figure 7.4 and of broad and in situ contrastive focus phrases are presented in Figure 7.5.

No phonetic studies of pauses have been made, but Can Pixabaj and England (2011) suggest that the *possibility* of a pause can distinguish fronted topicalized constituents from fronted focus constructions in K'iche' (although Yasavul 2013 claims that he found no support for this in an experimental task done in part with non-native speakers). This is another area where further experimental and phonetic studies would be useful.

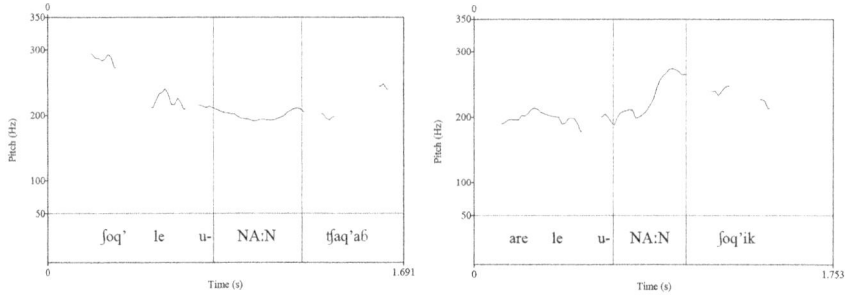

FIGURE 7.4 K'ICHE' PITCH TRACKS OF THE BROAD FOCUS *XOQ'LE UNAAN CHAQ'AB'* 'HIS/ HER MOTHER CRIED AT NIGHT' AND THE SYNTACTICALLY MARKED CONTRASTIVE FOCUS *ARE LE UNAAN XOQ'IK* 'IT WAS HIS/HER MOTHER THAT CRIED' AS PRODUCED BY A FEMALE SPEAKER FROM NAHUALÁ. THE SYLLABLE BEING MARKED FOR CONTRASTIVE FOCUS IS *NAAN*.

(from data presented in Baird 2014)

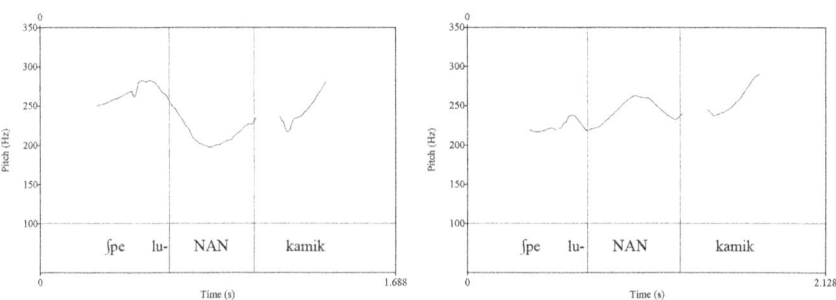

FIGURE 7.5 K'ICHE' PITCH TRACKS OF THE BROAD AND IN SITU CONTRASTIVE FOCUS *XPE LUNAN KAMIK* 'HIS/HER MOTHER CAME TODAY' AS PRODUCED BY A FEMALE SPEAKER FROM CANTEL. THE SYLLABLE BEING MARKED FOR CONTRASTIVE FOCUS IS *NAN*, WHICH DOES NOT HAVE A LONG VOWEL IN THE CANTEL DIALECT.

(from data presented in Baird 2014)

REFERENCES

Avelino, Heriberto. 2011. "Intonational patterns of topic and focus constructions in Yucatec Maya." In *New perspectives in Mayan linguistics*, ed. by Heriberto Avelino, 56–79. Newcastle upon Tyne: Cambridge Scholars Publishing.

Avelino, Heriberto, Eurie Shin, and Sam Tilsen. 2011. "The phonetics of laryngealization in Yucatec Maya." In *New perspectives in Mayan linguistics*, ed. by Heriberto Avelino, 1–20. Newcastle upon Tyne: Cambridge Scholars Publishing.

Baird, Brandon O. 2010. "The phonological systems of Spanish-K'ichee' (Mayan) bilinguals: cases of linguistic convergence and mutual language influences." MA thesis, University of Texas, Austin.

Baird, Brandon O. 2011. "Phonetic and phonological realizations of 'broken glottal' vowels in K'ichee'." In *Proceedings of formal approaches to Mayan linguistics I*, ed. by Kiril Shklovsky, Pedro Mateo Pedro, and Jessica Coon, 39–49. Cambridge: MITWPL 63.

Baird, Brandon O. 2014. "An acoustic analysis of contrastive focus marking in Spanish-K'ichee' (Mayan) bilingual intonation." PhD diss., University of Texas, Austin.

Baird, Brandon O. 2015. "Acoustic correlates of stress in K'ichee': a preliminary analysis." In *Proceedings of formal approaches to Mayan linguistics (FAMLi) II*, ed. by Lauren Eby Clemens, Robert Henderson, and Pedro Mateo Pedro, 21–34. Cambridge: MITWPL 74.

Baird, Brandon O. 2016. "Dialectal evolution of the vowel systems of K'ichee': An experimental approach." Poster presented at 3rd Workshop on Sound Change, Salamanca, Spain, March 4, 2016.

Baird, Brandon O., and Adán Francisco Pascual. 2012. "Realizaciones fonéticas de /Vʔ/ en Q'anjob'al (Maya)." In *Proceedings of CILLA V*. Austin: University of Texas. http://www.ailla.utexas.org/site/cilla5/Baird_Pascual_CILLA_V.pdf

Bennett, Ryan. 2010. "Contrast and laryngeal states in Tz'utujil." In *The UCSC linguistics research center 2010 laboratory report*, ed. by Grant McGuire, 93–120. Santa Cruz: UCSC.

Bennett, Ryan. 2016a. "Mayan phonology." *Language and Linguistic Compass* 10: 469–514.

Bennett, Ryan. 2016b. "La tensión vocálica en el kaqchikel de Sololá, Guatemala: un estudio preliminar." In *Las Actas del Seminario Phonologica*, Colegio de México.

Bennett, Ryan, and Robert Henderson. 2013. "Accent in Uspanteko." *Natural Language and Linguistic Theory* 31(3): 589–645.

Bergqvist, Jan Henrik Göran. 2008. "Temporal reference in Lacandon Maya: speaker- and event-perspectives." PhD diss., School of Oriental and African Studies, University of London.

Berinstein, Ava. 1979. "A cross-linguistic study on the perception and production of stress." *UCLA Working Papers in Phonetics* 47.

Berinstein, Ava. 1991. "The role of intonation in K'ekchi Mayan discourse." In *Texas linguistic forum* 32, ed. By Cynthia McLemore, 1–19. Austin: Department of Linguistics and the Center for Cognitive Science, The University of Texas.

Bricker, Victoria, Eleuterio Poʔot Yah and Ofelia Dzul de Poʔot. 1998. *A dictionary of the Maya language as Spoken in Hocobá, Yucatán*. Salt Lake City: University of Utah Press.

Burdin, Rachel Steindel, Sara Phillips-Bourass, Rory Turnbull, Murat Yasavul, Cynthia Clopper, and Judith Tonhauser. 2015. "Variation in the prosody of focus in head-and head/edge-prominence languages." *Lingua* 165b: 254–76.

Campbell, Lyle. 1977. *Quichean linguistic prehistory*. Berkeley: University of California Press.

Campbell, Lyle, and Terrence Kaufman. 1985. "Mayan linguistics: Where are we now?" *Annual Review of Anthropology* 14: 187–98.

Can Pixabaj, Telma. 2004. "La topicalización en K'ichee': Una perspectiva discursiva." *Licenciatura* thesis, Universidad Rafael Landívar, Guatemala.

Can Pixabaj, Telma Angelina. 2007. *Jkemiik yoloj li Uspanteko: Gramática Uspanteka*. Guatemala: Cholsamaj and Oxlajuuj Keej Maya' Ajtz'iib'.

Can Pixabaj, Telma, and Nora C. England. 2011. "Nominal topic and focus in K'ichee'." In *Representing language: essays in honor of Judith Aissen*, ed. by Rodrigo Gutiérrez-Bravo, Line Mikkelsen, and Eric Potsdam, 15–30. California Digital Library eScholarship Repository. Linguistic Research Center, University of California, Santa Cruz. http://escholarship.org/uc/item/0vf4s9tk, or http://escholarship.org/uc/lrc_aissen

Dayley, Jon P. 1985. *Tzutujil grammar* (University of California Publications in Linguistics, vol. 107). Los Angeles and Berkeley: University of California Press.

de Diego Antonio, Diego, Francisco Pascual, Nicolás de Nicolás Pedro, Carmelino Fernando González, and Santiago Juan Matias. 1996. *Diccionario del idioma Q'anjob'al*. La Antigua Guatemala: Proyecto Lingüístico Francisco Marroquín.

Edmonson, Barbara Wedemeyer. 1988. "A descriptive grammar of Huastec (Potosino Dialect)." PhD diss., Tulane.

England, Nora C. 1983. *A grammar of Mam, a Mayan language*. Austin: University of Texas Press.

England, Nora C. 2001. *Introducción a la gramática de los idiomas mayas*. Guatemala: Cholsamaj.

Fisher, William M. 1976. "On tonal features in the Yucatan dialects." In *Mayan linguistics* 1, ed. by Marlys McClaran, 29–43. Los Angeles: University of California Los Angeles American Indian Studies Center.

Frazier, Melissa. 2009. "The production and perception of pitch and glottalization in Yucatec Maya." PhD diss., University of North Carolina, Chapel Hill.

Frazier, Melissa. 2011. "Tonal dialects and consonant-pitch interaction in Yucatec Maya." In *New perspectives in Mayan linguistics*, ed. by Heriberto Avelino, 21–55. Newcastle upon Tyne: Cambridge Scholars Publishing.

Frazier, Melissa. 2013. "The phonetics of Yucatec Maya and the typology of laryngeal complexity." *Language Typology and Universals* 66: 7–21.

García Matzar, Pedro (Lolmay), and José Obispo Rodríguez Guaján (Pakal). 1997. *Rukemik ri Kaqchikel chi': Gramática Kaqchikel*. Guatemala: Cholsamaj.

Gendrot, Cédric, Jean Léo Léonard, and Gilles Polian. 2009. "Correlación laringovelar y variación dialectal del tseltal (Maya occidental, Chiapas, México)." *Estudis Romànics* 311–29.

Gussenhoven, Carlos. 2006. "Yucatec Maya tones in sentence perspective." Poster presented at LabPhon 10, Paris 29 June–1 July 2006. http://www.let.ru.nl/gep/carlos/yucatec_maya_poster.pdf

Gussenhoven, Carlos, and Renske Teeuw. 2008. "A moraic and a syllable H-tone in Yucatec Maya." In *Fonología instrumental: Patrones fónicos y variación*, ed. by Esther Herrera Zendejas and Pedro Martín Butragueño, 49–71. Mexico City: Colegio de México.

Hamann, Silke. 2003. "The phonetics and phonology of retroflexes." PhD diss., Utrecht University.

Henderson, Robert. 2012. "Morphological alternations at the intonational phrase edge: the case of K'ichee'." *Natural Language and Linguistic Theory* 30: 741–89.

Herrera Zendejas, Esther. 2013. "Patrón acentual, F_0 y consonantes laríngeas en el tsotsil de Venustiano Carranza." Paper presented at the Congreso de Idiomas Indígenas de Latinoamérica VI, University of Texas, Austin, October 24, 2013.

Hofling, Charles Andrew, with Félix Fernando Tesucún. 2000. *Itzaj Maya grammar.* Salt Lake City: University of Utah Press.

Kaufman, Terrence. 1972. *El Proto-Tzeltal-Tzotzil: Fonología comparada y diccionario reconstruido.* Mexico: UNAM.

Kaufman, Terrence. 1975. *Proyecto de alfabetos y ortografías para escribir las lenguas mayances.* La Antigua Guatemala: Proyecto Lingüístico Francisco Marroquín.

Kaufman, Terrence. 1976. "Archaeological and linguistic correlations in Mayaland and associated areas of Meso-America." *World Archaeology* 8: 101–18.

Kaufman, Terrence. 1990. "Algunos rasgos estructurales de los idiomas Mayances con referencia especial al K'iche'." In *Lecturas sobre la lingüística Maya,* ed. by Nora C. England and Stephen R. Elliott, 59–114. La Antigua Guatemala: Centro de Investigaciones Regionales de Mesoamérica.

Kaufman, Terrence S., and William M. Norman. 1984. "An outline of Proto-Cholan phonology, morphology, and vocabulary." In *Phoneticism in Mayan hieroglyphic writing,* ed. by John S. Justeson and Lyle Campbell, 77–166. (Institute for Mesoamerican Studies, 9). Albany: State University of New York.

Kidder, Emily. 2013. "Prominence in Yucatec Maya: The role of stress in Yucatec Maya words." PhD diss., The University of Arizona.

Kondić, Snježana. 2012. "A grammar of South Eastern Huastec, a Maya language from Mexico." PhD diss., University of Sydney and Université Lyon 2 Lumière.

Krämer, Martin. 2001. "Yucatec Maya vowel alternations – Harmony as syntagmatic identity." *Zietschrift für Sprachwissenschaft* 20: 175–217.

Kügler, Frank, and Stavros Skopeteas. 2006. "Interaction of lexical tone and information structure in Yucatec Maya." In *TAL 2006 – International Symposium on Tonal Aspects of Languages,* Rochelle, France: 380–8.

Kügler, Frank, and Stavros Skopeteas. 2007. "On the universality of prosodic reflexes of contrast: the case of Yucatec Maya." In *Proceedings of the XVI. International Congress of Phonetic Sciences,* Saarbrücken, Germany, 4–10 August 2007: 1025–28.

Kügler, Frank, Stavros Skopeteas, and Elisabeth Verhoeven. 2007. "Encoding information structure in Yucatec Maya: On the interplay of prosody and syntax." *Interdisciplinary Studies on Information Structure* 8: 187–208.

Ladd, D. Robert. 1996. *Intonational phonology.* Cambridge: Cambridge University Press.

Larsen, Raymond, and Eunice Victoria Pike. 1949. "Huasteco intonation and phonemes." *Language* 25: 268–77.

Léonard, Jean, Cédric Gendrot, and Gilles Polian. 2009. "Correlación laringovelar y variación dialectal del tseltal (Maya occidental, Chiapas, México)". *Estudis Romànics,* Hemeroteca Científica Catalana 2009, 311–329.

Liberman, Mark. 1975. "The Intonational System of English." PhD dissertation, MIT.

López Ixcoy, Candelaria Dominga (Saqijix). 1994. *Las vocales en K'ichee'.* Antigua, Guatemala: Oxlajuuj Keej Maya' Ajtz'iib'.

López Ixcoy, Candelaria Dominga (Saqijix). 1997. *Ri ukemiik ri K'ichee'chii': Gramática K'ichee'.* Guatemala: Cholsamaj.

Majzul, Filiberto Patal, Pedro Oscar García Matzar, and Carmelina Espantzay Serech. 2000. *Rujunamaxik ri Kaqchikel chi': variación dialectal en Kaqchikel.* Ciudad de Guatemala, Guatemala: Cholsamaj.

Maldonado Andrés, Juan, Juan Ordóñez Domingo, and Juan Ortiz Domingo. 1986. *Diccionario Mam*. Guatemala: Centro de Reproducciones de la Universidad Rafael Landívar.

Martin, Laura. 1984. "The emergence of phonemic tone in Mocho (Mayan)." Paper presented at the American Anthropological Association Meetings, Denver.

Mateo Toledo, Eladio. 1999. La cuestión Akateko-Q'anjob'al, una comparación gramatical. Thesis, licenciatura, Universidad Mariano Gálvez.

Nielsen, Kuniko. 2005. "Kiche intonation." *UCLA Working Papers in Phonetics* 104: 45–60.

Orie, Olankie Ola, and Victoria Bricker. 2000. "Placeless and historical laryngeals in Yucatec Maya." *International Journal of American Linguistics* 66: 283–317.

Palosaari, Naomi Elizabeth. 2011. "Topics in mocho phonology and morphology." PhD diss., University of Utah.

Pierrehumbert, Janet. B. 1980. *The phonetics and phonology of English intonation*. New York: Garland Press.

Pike, Kenneth L. 1946. "Phonemic pitch in Maya." *International Journal of American Linguistics* 12: 82–8.

Pinkerton, Sandra. 1986. "Quichean (Mayan) glottalized and nonglottalized stops: A phonetic study with implications for phonological universals." In *Experimental phonology*, ed. by J. J. Ohala and J. J. Jaeger, 125–39. Orlando: Academic Press.

Polian, Gilles. 2013. *Gramática del tseltal de Oxchuc* (Publicaciones de la Casa Chata). Mexico: Centro de Investigaciones y Estudios Superiores en Antropología Social.

Poma S., Maximiliano, Tabita J. T. de la Cruz, Manuel Caba Caba, María Marcos Brito, Domingo Solís Marcos, and Nicolás A. Cedillo. 1996. *Gramática del Idioma Ixil*. La Antigua Guatemala: Proyecto Lingüístico Francisco Marroquín.

Raymundo González, Sonia, Adán Francisco Pascual, Pedro Mateo Pedro, Eladio Mateo Toledo. 2000. *Sk'exkixhtaqil yallay Koq'anej: Variación dialectal en Q'anjob'al*. Guatemala: Cholsamaj.

Santos Nicolás, José Francisco (Pala's), and José Gonzalo Benito Péres (Waykan). 1998. *Rukorb'aal Poqom q'orb'al: Gramática Poqom (Poqomam)*. Guatemala: Cholsamaj.

Sarles, Harvey B. 1966. "A descriptive grammar of the Tzotzil language as spoken in San Bartolomé de los Llanos, Chiapas, México." PhD diss., University of Chicago.

Shosted, Ryan K. 2011. "Towards a glottalic theory of Mayan." In *New perspectives in Mayan linguistics*, ed. by Heriberto Avelino, 80–113. Newcastle upon Tyne: Cambrige Scholars Publishing.

Shosted, Ryan K. 2014. "Retroflexion in Q'anjob'al obstruents." Paper presented at Workshop on the Sound Systems of Mexico and Central America, Yale University, April 4–6 2014.

Silverman, Daniel. 1997. *Phasing and recoverability*. New York: Garland.

Stewart, Stephen. 1980. *Gramática kekchí*. Guatemala: Editorial Académica Centro Americana.

Velleman, Leah B. 2014. "On optional focus movement in K'ichee'." In *Proceedings of formal approaches to Mayan linguistics (FAMLi) II*, ed. By Lauren Eby Clemens, Robert Henderson, and Pedro Mateo Pedro, 107–18. Cambridge: MITWPL 74.

Wagner, Karl Olaw Christian. 2014. "An intonational description of Mayan Q'eqchi'." MA thesis, Brigham Young University.

Yasavul, Murat. 2013. "Prosody of focus and contrastive topic in K'iche'." *Ohio State University Working Papers in Linguistics* 60: 129–60.

CHAPTER 8

MORPHOLOGY

Gilles Polian

1 INTRODUCTION

Mayan languages are rich in morphology, both inflectional and derivational. They are synthetic, as they tend to aggregate several morphemes in words, especially verbs, and their morphology is mainly of the agglutinating type, i.e. consisting of roots and affixes easily segmentable, although non-concatenative morphological patterns also exist, like vowel alternation or reduplication. Inflectional morphology is particularly regular. For instance, verbal conjugations have almost no irregularity: most Mayan languages lack verbal inflection classes.[1] Finally, Mayan constructions strongly tend to be head-marked (Nichols 1986): syntactic relations are morphologically marked only on the syntactic head and not on the dependent constituent.

This chapter is divided in two broad sections. In §2, I review the main morphological patterns present in the family: affixation, non-concatenative morphology, and compounding. In §3, I present the word classes and their typical morphology, both inflectional and derivational.

2 MORPHOLOGICAL PATTERNS

The main morphological patterns observed in Mayan languages are synthetized in (1). Infixation and vowel/tone alternations are restricted to a few languages; other patterns are general to the whole family.

(1) a. Concatenative: • Affixation: – Suffixation
                                         – Prefixation
                                         – Infixation
                          • Compounding

     b. Non-concatenative: • Reduplication (total, partial, duplifixation)
                             • Conversion
                             • Vowel alternation (lengthening/shortening, quality changes)
                             • Tone alternation

The next sections review these patterns one by one.

2.1 Affixation

Most morphological processes consist of suffixation. Prefixes are few and mainly inflectional, some of them of high text frequency, especially person and TAM markers, as in (2).

KAQCHIKEL
(2) **xk- at- ki-** tzuq -u²
      POT- B2SG- A3PL- feed -SS:T.DEP
      'Let them feed you.' (adapted from García Matzar and Rodríguez Guaján 1997:187)

This example illustrates the case of a finite transitive verb. As in many other languages, Mayan verbs are the word class in which most morphological complexity is concentrated (see §3.1 below). (2) shows argument indexing of both subject and object in a head-marking fashion (argument affixes are obligatory, contrary to argument NPs), with the markers traditionally described as belonging to "Set A" (ergative/possessive) and "Set B" (absolutive) respectively. It also displays a CVC root, *tzuq* 'to feed', which is overwhelmingly the most common type of phonological shape for lexical roots (especially for verbs).

Affixes vary in their possible phonological patterns depending on the language: prefixes are limited to a (C)(V)(C)- pattern, i.e. they consist of a consonant (rarely two, as *xk-* 'POT' in (2)) or one vowel, that may be followed and/or preceded by a consonant. Suffixes are more varied and can be bisyllabic, but many Mayan languages seem especially to favor a -VC pattern for suffixes, as in *-u²* 'status suffix for dependent transitives' in (2) (see §3.1 below on this kind of suffix).

Infixation is mainly restricted to the pattern CV<h>C (or CV<j>C when /h/ has merged with /j/), that is, it only applies to CVC roots. It has been reconstructed for Proto-Mayan (Kaufman and Norman 1984:109), but is only maintained in languages of the Cholan-Tseltalan (Chol, Ch'orti', Tseltal) and K'ichean (Poqom, Tz'utujil) branches, where it derives numeral classifiers (see §3.6) and intransitive stems from transitive and positional roots (see §3.4). For example in Jilotepequeño Poqomam (Smith-Stark 1983:144): *rap* (positional root) 'long and thin' > *ra<h>p* 'numeral classifier for long and thin things' and *k'at* (transitive root) 'burn something' > *k'a<h>t* (intransitive stem) 'burn'. Other derivations may involve both an <h> infix and a derivational suffix.

In some cases, the loss of this infix has been compensated by the emergence of a contrastive tone, e.g. Yucatec (Justeson 1986; Hofling, this volume; see also §2.3.1 below). A CV<²>C infixation is also reported for Mam (England 1983:54) and for Chontal (Osorio May 2005:43), in the latter case as a minor allomorph of <j> infixation.

Controversies exist for some languages regarding the status of person markers either as affixes or as clitics, see for example the discussion in Larsen (1988:153ff), where this author argues in favor of a clitic analysis of absolutive (Set B) markers in K'ichee', *contra* Mondloch (1978) and Dayley (1981). For Set A markers, they are more consistently analyzed as prefixes, but for example they are claimed to be clitics in Yucatec by Lehmann (1998:34).

2.2 Vowel variation in suffixes

A very common phenomenon in the family is for suffixal vowels to be variable or to drop in certain circumstances. The variation may be predictable, arbitrary or something in between. It is predictable when it involves regular processes of assimilation or dissimilation. I comment first on the former, which corresponds to vowel harmony: the variable vowel replicates the preceding vowel, generally the root vowel. For instance, the suffix which derives positionals (see §3.4) in Cholan-Tseltalan languages and in K'ichee' is -Vl (Ch'orti' -Vr), e.g. Chontal *ch'a* 'to lie down' > *ch'a-al* 'lying', *ch'ox* 'to squat' > *ch'ox-ol* 'squatting', etc. (Osorio May 2005:71). The same occurs in Yucatecan with several -VC suffixes: -Vl~-Vr, status suffix for intransitive verbs in incompletive, -Vb'~-V² for instrumental nouns, etc. (see Hofling, this volume); also in Mam with -Vj, which derives measure words (England 1983:46); and many other suffixes across the family.

Vowel harmony may concern only certain vowels. For example, the transitive dependent status suffix -V$^?$ in most languages of the K'ichean and Q'anjob'alan groups is -a$^?$ when the root vowel is /a, e, i/, but assimilates with back vowels (/o, u/) to -o$^?$ and -u$^?$ respectively (see (2) for an illustration of the -u$^?$ allomorph). Even more restricted is the transitive plain status suffix -V, which presents itself basically as -o. Harmony is then triggered only by a preceding /u/ (Robertson 1992:62). This phenomenon is shown in K'ichee' in (3) (from Larsen 1988:231, 233).

K'ICHEE'

(3) Vowel harmony in transitive status suffixes

a. Dependent {*cha-* 'IMP'}		b. Plain {*x-* 'PFV', *in-* 'A1SG'}	
cha-b'an-a$^?$	'do it!'	x-in-b'an-o	'I did it'
cha-k'ex-a$^?$	'change it!'	x-in-k'ex-o	'I changed it'
cha-miq'-a$^?$	'heat it'	x-in-miq'-o	'I heated it'
cha-koj-o$^?$	'use it!'	x-in-koj-o	'I used it'
cha-pus-u$^?$	'slit it!'	x-in-pus-u	'I slit it'

Other suffixes display similar kinds of assimilative conditionings, with exceptions in some cases. For instance in Chol, the status suffix -V for root transitive verbs in the perfective aspect harmonizes with the root vowel except with /a/, in which case, it is unpredictably -a or -ä (Vázquez Alvarez 2011:92ff). This kind of partial harmony with particular suffixes is quite common throughout the family.

The opposition of two sets of vowels /a, e, i/ versus /o, u/, which can be stated in terms of "back versus non-back" or "rounded versus non-rounded", is also frequently involved in a dissimilative phenomenon (or "disharmony"): some suffixal vowels display an alternation between /u/ and /i/, taking the opposite backness/roundedness value of the preceding vowel: it is /u/ if preceded by /a, e, i/, but /i/ if preceded by /o, u/.[2] This applies for example to the iterative suffix -Vlan in Tseltal: *maj* 'hit' > *maj-ulan, lek'* 'lick' > *lek'-ulan, tij* 'move' > *tij-ulan, boj* 'cut' > *boj-ilan, yuk'* 'shake' > *yuk'-ilan*. The same phenomenon appears in different suffixes throughout the family: Yucatec -k$\acute{V}$Vn and Mopan -kVn causative (Hofling, this volume), Mam -pVV transitivizer (England 1983:48), Ixil -Vx attenuative adjective (Ayres 1991:48) and -V transitivizer (ibid., p.58).

The conditioning of the variable vowel of a suffix may also be only partial, ranging from cases that appear as imperfect harmony/disharmony to cases where apparently there are little more than mere tendencies, i.e. where some gaps emerge in the combinatorial grid between the suffixal vowel and the root vowel. For instance, Edmonson (1988:154ff) presents the distribution of the transitive status suffix -Vy in Huastec as in Table 8.1.

TABLE 8.1 PARTIAL CONDITIONING OF -VY SUFFIX IN HUASTEC

Root Vowel	-ay	-ey	-iy	-oy	-uy
a	+	−	+	−	+
e	(+)	+	−	+	−
i	(+)	−	+	+	−
o	−	−	+	+	−
u	(+)	−	+	−	+

Key: +: well attested; (+): few cases; -: unattested

Some tendencies can be observed: (1) the allomorph with least restrictions is -*iy*, the one most constrained is -*ey*; (2) no allomorph is compatible with all root vowels; (3) vowel harmony seems to play some role here, as all suffixal vowels present cases of identity with the root vowel.[3]

This kind of pattern is commonly found in other languages, e.g. with the suffix -Vl of marked possession in Tseltal (Polian 2013:438) or -Vñ~-V, derived transitive status suffix in Chol (Vázquez Álvarez 2011:97), among others.

Finally, it is not uncommon for suffixal vowels to drop when more suffixes are added to the word. For instance in Huastec Edmonson (1988:102) states that "the vowels of the (. . .) root intransitive thematic suffixes are routinely deleted when a vowel-initial inflectional suffix is added": *bix-om* 'dance' > *bix-m-a:tz*{dance-AP-PFV} 'danced'.[4] However, this phenomenon is not exclusive of suffixes and may be part of a general tendency to drop short unstressed vowels in certain contexts, including root vowels (see England 1983:43 on this phenomenon in Mam and Dayley 1985:45–7 on Tz'utujil). For example, a syncope phenomenon is documented, whereby the vowel of the second syllable of stems of more than two syllables is elided (e.g. in Cholan, Kaufman and Norman 1984:86; in Tseltal, Polian 2013:112ff).

2.3 Non-concatenative morphology

2.3.1 Vowel and tone alternations

We know since Smith (1976:58) that "Mayan languages show a substantial amount of vowel alternations in their morphophonology", which generally concern either length or quality. Yucatec is probably the language where these alternations, combined with tone and state of glottis alternations, have been put to the greatest use for inflectional morphology, as they have come to be the regular exponents for voice with root transitives. As illustrated in (4), basic transitive roots, used directly as active stems, display a short vowel, whereas rearticulation ($V^{\prime}V$), length with high tone ($\acute{V}V$) and length with low tone ($\grave{V}V$) form the agentive passive, agentless passive and antipassive, respectively.

YUCATEC
(4) Vowel alternations and voice (Bricker et al. 1998:333)
{*k-* 'IPFV', *in* 'A1SG', *u* 'A3SG', *p'eh* 'chip', *-ik/-el* 'SS'}

a. active form	CVC	k-in	**p'eh**-ik	'I chip it'
b. agentive passive	CV$^{\prime}$VC	k-u	**p'e'eh**-el	'it is chipped (by s.o.)'
c. agentless passive/middle voice	C$\acute{V}$VC	k-u	**p'éeh**-el	'it gets chipped'
d. antipassive	C$\grave{V}$VC	k-in	**p'èeh**	'I chip'

Similarly, K'ichee' uses lengthening (CVC>CV:C) as the regular passive marking for transitive roots (López Ixcoy 1997:45). This lengthening corresponds originally to the <h> infixation (Campbell 1977), which is maintained as such in Tz'utujil. In Poqomam, lengthening, as an alternative to <h> infixation, forms inchoative ("versive") stems from positional roots (Smith-Stark 1983:376), among other derivations. Several cases of derivational lengthening are also reported for Huastec (Edmonson 1988:106ff). In Mam, lengthening functions as a transitivizing device for positional and affect roots, e.g. *mok'* (positional root) 'crouched' > *mook'* (transitive stem) 'to crouch (it)' (England 1983:102).

Beyond verbs, length alternations are common in nouns, linked to possession. This phenomenon has been attributed to Proto-Mayan by Smith (1976). For example in K'ichee' the final syllable of nouns is lengthened with possession: *kinaq'* 'bean' > *nu-kinaaq'* 'my bean' (López Ixcoy 1997:44). Huastec also displays many cases of lengthening or shortening with possession, with or without additional suffixes to the noun: lengthening (like K'ichee') in *nuk'* 'neck' > *ʔu nuːk'* 'my neck', or shortening in *haːwʔ* 'dried leaves' > *ʔin hawʔ-liːl* 'its dried leaves' (Edmonson 1988:107 and 362, respectively). This last example, which corresponds to a change of length of the root vowel when a suffix is added, is very common in Mayan languages that maintain length contrast, and may be more phonological in nature or may have been morphologized (associated to specific derivations) to different degrees. A purely phonological case for instance would be Ixtahuacán Mam, where a phonological constraint bans more than one long vowel in a word. This leads to shortening when a suffix with a long vowel is added: *q'uulan* 'warm' > *t-q'ulan-iil* '(its) warmth' (England 1983:51, where *-iil* is a nominalizer and *t-* is 'A3SG').

Concerning vowel quality alternations, most of those are the evolution of previous short-long alternations. For example, Itzaj has /ä~a/ alternations where Yucatec displays /a~aː/, as a result of the regular evolution where short /a/ gives /ä/ and long /aː/ gives /a/. Similarly, where K'ichee' has the already mentioned length alternation with possession *tz'iʔ* 'dog' > *nu-tz'iiʔ* 'my dog', Palín Poqomam (K'ichean) has *tz'eʔ* > *nu-tz'iiʔ* (Benito Pérez, p.c.), where short /i/ evolved to /e/ before a glottal stop, yielding an /e~iː/ alternation. In two other K'ichean languages, some length alternations have evolved into monophthongal/diphthongal alternations, as a result of the diphthongization of previous long /eː/ and /oː/ (as /ie/ and /uo/ respectively in Santiago Tz'utujil, Dayley 1983:27, and /ie/ and /ua/ respectively in Jilotepequeño Poqomam, Smith-Stark 1983:100). The same kind of phenomenon has also given rise to a derivational /a>o/ mutation in Tsotsil, where some verbal and positional CaC roots derive a CoC noun or a numeral classifier stem, e.g. *maj* 'hit' (transitive) > *moj* '(*n* number of) blows' (numeral classifier) (see Polian, this volume).

A few instances of vowel mutation have emerged for other reasons than length and its offspring. A case is Q'anjob'al. In this language, the normal exponent of 'A2SG' with stems starting with *ʔV* is the dropping of the initial glottal stop, e.g. *ʔon* 'avocado' > *on* 'your avocado' (orthographically *on>hon*). Additionally, Santa Eulalia and Barillas dialects present a lowering of initial high vowels (/i>e/ and /u>o/) with 'A2SG', e.g. *ʔun* 'paper' > *on* 'your paper' (Raymundo González et al. 2000).

2.3.2 Reduplication

Reduplication is common and varied in all Mayan languages, and typically covers meanings like distributivity, iteration, emphasis or attenuation. On the one hand, reduplication can concern complete words, independently of syllabicity. For example adjectival emphasis is indicated in Itzaj by full reduplication, as *b'ek'ech-b'ek'ech* {thin-REDUP} 'very thin' (Hofling and Tesucún 2000:173). On the other hand, many reduplicative patterns take as input only CVC roots, be it total ($C_1V_1C_2$-$C_1V_1C_2$) or partial reduplication ($C_1V_1C_2$-V_1C_2, C_1V_1-$C_1V_1C_2$, etc.), and derivational patterns frequently combine particular reduplications and affixes. For example, the "diffusive" (attenuative/distributive) derivation for CVC adjectives in Tseltal requires total reduplication plus a suffix *-tik*: *k'an* 'yellow' > *k'an-k'an-tik* 'yellowish'.

Linking elements between reduplicants are not rare. For instance Yucatec has two distributive derivations for expressive words (Le Guen 2014): $C_1V_1C_2$-$\mathbf{V_1}$-$C_1V_1C_2$ (close distribution) and $C_1V_1C_2$-*en*-$C_1V_1C_2$ (loose distribution), e.g. *k'om-o-k'om* 'with holes (tightly distributed)' and *k'om-en-k'om* 'with holes (here and there)' (from *k'om* 'to warp, to depress, to hollow').

Duplifixes are particularly common, that is, combinations of fixed and reduplicative segments (Haspelmath 2002:24), where the fixed segments do not correspond to independently existing affixes. For example some Ixil duplifixes are the following (Ayres 1991:25–6): -V₁x 'passive'[5] (*b'an* 'do' > *b'an-ax* 'be done', *chi'* 'bite' > *chi'-ix* 'be bitten', etc.), -C₁o 'diffusive' (*saq* 'white' > *saq-so* 'whitish', *q'es* 'old' > *q'es-q'o* 'oldish', etc.) and -V₁'C₂an 'transitive iterative' (*q'os* 'hit' > *q'os-o'san* 'hit several times', *txeq'* 'hammer' > *txeq'-e'q'an* 'hammer several times', etc.).

2.3.3 Conversion

Derivation is generally overtly marked in Mayan languages. Cases of covert derivation, or "conversion", are limited, and in most instances emerge through the erosion of a previous affix, especially of the Proto-Mayan infix *<h>. The loss of this infix as a detransitivizer (passivizer or anticausitivizer) created several cases of transitive>intransitive conversion, e.g. in Tsotsil, Poqomam (Smith-Stark 1983:330) and in some dialects of K'ichee'. Other K'ichee' dialects mark passive for root transitives with vowel length, as an evolution of the infix (see §2.4.1 above), but in dialects like Cantel that lost length with all vowels but /a/ all transitive roots with vowels other than /a/ become passive by conversion (Larsen 1988:252). In all these cases, aspect and/or person inflection maintain the distinction between the root transitive and the converted intransitive, e.g. in Tsotsil *i-Ø-s-mak* {PFV-B3-A3-close} 's/he closed it' > *i-Ø-mak* {PFV-B3-close} 'it got closed'.

There are also cases of particular roots and stems that function directly as members of different classes, especially as noun and adjective, noun and verb, or transitive verb and positional. Those cases are better treated as polycategoriality than conversion, as no directionality of derivation is self-evident.

2.4 Compounding

Compounding is especially productive in noun formation in Mayan languages. Verbal and adjectival compounds do exist, but are somehow more restricted to particular languages and to fewer patterns. The most common compounding patterns are presented from §2.4.1 to §2.4.5.

2.4.1 Modifier-head nominal compounds

The prenominal position of the modifier in these compounds is reminiscent of the fact that attributive adjectives also tend to be prenominal in the family. The modifier here can be a noun, an adjective (it may be hard to distinguish attribution and compounding in A+N groups), a positional root or more rarely a verbal root. Examples:

- Yucatec: *nik-te'* {flower-tree (N+N)} 'frangipani (kind of tree with flowers)' (Hofling, this volume).
- K'ichee': *saq-wach* {white-face (A+N)} 'potato' (López Ixcoy 1997:104).
- Tseltal: *mak-te'* {close-stick (T+N)} 'fence, corral'.

2.4.2 Modifier-head verbal compounds

Yucatecan and Cholan-Tseltalan languages allow the incorporation of adverbial modifiers before the verbal stem, as in Itzaj *k-u-jan-tal* {IPFV-A3-quickly-come} 's/he comes quickly' (Hofling and Tesucún 2000:83). Those incorporated modifiers are typically adverbs, adjectives or positional roots.

2.4.3 Head-possessor nominal compounds

In all Mayan languages, the possessed noun precedes the possessor NP and bears a Set A prefix indexing the possessor ('her-house the woman' = 'the woman's house'). Particular possessive constructions may have lexicalized meanings, e.g. 'its hand/arm (of the) tree' for 'branch' (in K'ichee' *u-q'ab' chee'*, López Ixcoy 1997:105), but these should be considered syntactic phrases rather than compounds, insofar as they show no sign of fusion.[6] Such phrases may be reanalyzed as unitary nouns, e.g. in K'ichee' *xaq-chaj* {leave-pine} 'pine needles' (Larsen 1988:122); note that the A3 possessive prefix has disappeared, and that the compound as a whole can receive another possessor: *nu-xaq-chaaj* {*nu-* 'A1SG', with final lengthening marking possessed status} 'my pine needles'.

2.4.4 Transitive verb-object verbal and nominal compounds

Various kinds of combinations between a transitive root or stem and a noun corresponding to the verb's notional object exist in Mayan languages. The most productive pattern corresponds to noun incorporation, where the compound typically describes habitual human activities like tortilla-making, corn-sowing or wood-chopping. Object-incorporating compounds vary in terms of category, according to the construction, the language, and/or to the particular analysis, between (1) (finite) intransitive verb stems, (2) non-finite intransitive stems (infinitives) and (3) nouns. A finite incorporating verb in Q'anjob'al is illustrated in (5) (in boldface): the verb takes a special suffix (*-wi*), glossed as a kind of antipassive because it signals a morphological intransitivization of the verb where only the agent is pronominally indexed (with Set B). The incorporated noun immediately follows as a bare stem with generic meaning.

Q'ANJOB'AL
(5) Y-et   **ch'-Ø-uqte-wi**   **no**   heb'.
     A3SG-when   IPFV-B3SG-chase-AP   animal   they
     '[That is how they order things] when they hunt'. [adapted from Mateo Toledo 2008:72]

The non-finite incorporating verb is shown boldfaced in (6) in the same language, as complement of a motion verb. A different suffix between the verb and the incorporated noun is involved (*-oj*) and the verb bears no person or TAM inflection.

Q'ANJOB'AL
(6) Max-in   toj   **tzok'-oj**   si'
     PFV-B1SG   go   cut-INF   firewood
     'I went to cut firewood.' [adapted from Mateo Toledo 2008:263]

All Mayan languages seem to have non-finite incorporating forms as in (6), but not all have the finite ones as in (5) (the clearest cases are in Eastern Mayan, Q'anjob'alan and Yucatecan). Non-finite forms are categorially close to nouns. Unsurprisingly, some of those T-N (transitive verb + noun) compounds become more nominal by acquiring nominal features. For instance, Hofling and Tesucún (2000) observes that Itzaj T-N compounds are basically verbal but that some of them can derive nominal uses, e.g. *paay-chi²* {lend-mouth} 'pray' (as a verb) or 'prayer' (as a noun) (*ibid.*, p.80 and 127). Note that no intervening suffix is required here for the incorporation.

Other kinds of nominal T-N compounds are agentive nouns and instrument nouns, generally involving specialized suffixes on the transitive stem, for instance in K'ichee' *b'an-ol-sii²* {make-AGT.NML-firewood} 'lumberjack' and *pis-b'al-wa* {wrap-INST-tortilla} 'napkin for wrapping tortillas' respectively (López Ixcoy 1997:105). Noun classifier prefixes (see §3.2 below) may also be required on those compounds in some languages, as in Itzaj *²aj-kon-b'äk'* {M-sell-meat} 'meat seller' (Hofling and Tesucún 2000:128).

Finally, in some cases the incorporated noun is in an instrumental relation with the preceding transitive stem, rather than being its notional object. For example in Itzaj: *chach-k'ä(ä)²* {grab-hand} 'grab with hand' (Hofling and Tesucún 2000:80).

2.4.5 Coordinate compounds

Several Mayan languages, at least from the K'ichean and Tseltalan branches, have nominal coordinate compounds of the kind of 'father-mother' for 'parents' (Wälchli 2005). The two nominal stems of those compounds typically display a loose degree of fusion, as some affixes may intervene between them. For example possessive prefixes are generally repeated on both stems, as in K'ichee' *qa-ti²t qa-maam* {A1PL-grandmother A1PL-grandfather} 'our grandparents' (López Ixcoy 1997).

Coordinate compounds of other categories (verbal, adjectival) are rarer. Verbal coordinate compounds in Tseltal display also the property of splitting their affixes into shared (one for the whole compound) and separated (repeated on both stems), as in (7). Here, the personal absolutive suffix *-on* is shared and the imperfective prefix *x-* is separated (the preverbal imperfective auxiliary *ya* is also shared). See Polian (2013) for more details.

TSELTAL
(7) Ya   x-we²   x-²uch'-on.
    IPFV   IPFV-eat IPFV-drink-B1SG
    'I eat and drink (I have a complete meal).'

2.4.6 Adjectival compounds

The most productive reported pattern for forming adjectival compounds in Mayan languages concerns color terms, where one of the five basic color terms ('black', 'white', 'red', 'blue/green' and 'yellow') is combined with another CVC root (verbal, positional, adjectival or unidentified), plus a particular suffix (*-e²en* in Yucatec, Bricker 1999, *-an* in Tsotsil/Tseltal), e.g. in Yucatec *²éek'-kum-e²en* {black-swell-SUF} 'puffy black, deep purple (sky dark with clouds)' (Bricker 1999:287), where *kum* is a positional root. As this example shows, those compounds typically have a very specific meaning, which covers brightness, texture, size, etc.

3 ROOT AND WORD CLASSES

In what follows, I give a non-exhaustive overview of the inflectional and derivational profile of the main root and word classes found in Mayan languages, excluding from the discussion uninflected words and particles, like prepositions or demonstratives. The categories presented appear in (8).

(8) Major lexical classes

- Transitive and intransitive verbs (roots and stems clearly distinguished morphologically), §3.1
- Nouns (roots and stems), §3.2.
- Adjectives (roots and stems), §3.3.
- Positionals (a category of roots and of derived stems whose class ascription is problematic), §3.4.
- Affects/expressives (terminological variation; defines a morphological domain either associated with other word classes or belonging to its own class), §3.5.
- Numerals (and associated morphemes, e.g. numeral classifiers), §3.6.
- Adverbs, §3.7.
- Non-verbal predicates (controversial status), §3.8.

In phonological terms, the dominant root form in the family is CVC. I assume, as do many other Mayanists (see Kaufman 2015), that orthographic VC roots actually begin with a non-represented glottal stop /ʔ/; note this is a controversial issue.[7] All transitive and positional roots are exclusively CVC. Other root types are more diverse; common alternative syllabic patterns are CV:C, CV{h/j}C, CV.CVC and CVC.CVC.

Stems are defined as the forms to which inflectional material, e.g., person or TAM morphemes, can be directly added. They can be radical (inflectible bare roots) or derived (roots plus derivative material). The roots that are not directly inflectible (i.e. that do not constitute stems by themselves) may be difficult to classify lexically, as the classificatory evidence is only indirect, i.e. through their associated derived stems. Many positional roots (§3.4) fall under this case. It has been proposed for the Yucatecan languages that many roots are not categorially determined, see Lois and Vapnarsky (2003, 2006); I will not discuss this issue here.

3.1 Verbs

Verbs can be identified in all Mayan languages as the only words that combine with a set of specific morphemes, which includes some the following: TAM markers, indicators of transitivity and of syntactic dependency, voice-changing morphemes and grammaticalized motion auxiliaries. Person marking in many cases is not specific to verbs, as it is shared with non-verbal predicates (Set B markers) and nouns (Set A markers, indicating possessors). Nevertheless, divergent specialization of person morphology has occurred in several languages. For example, prefixed absolutive markers in Tsotsil and Ch'orti' are exclusively verbal, whereas suffixed absolutive markers are used both on verbs and non-verbal predicates.[8] Such divergences often correlate (at least in their genesis) with the presence versus absence of TAM prefixes.

A salient feature of Mayan verbs is that the morphology typically distinguishes transitive and intransitive verbs, both through person marking – transitive verbs normally take ergative markers – and, sometimes, by the use of different allomorphs of TAM categories. Further, for derived verbs, transitivizing and intransitivizing suffixes are often clearly distinguished. For example in Tseltal many roots derive a pair of an intransitive and a transitive verb; in most cases, the intransitivizer ends in /j/, while the transitivizer ends in /n/ or /y/, e.g. *k'op* 'word, speech' > *k'op-oj* 'to speak, to talk' (intransitive), *k'op-on* 'to talk to s.o.' (transitive). Thus, it is rare for a Mayan verb not to have its transitivity made explicit by its inflectional and/or derivational morphology.

TAM categories always include a basic perfective-imperfective opposition (alternatively called completive-incompletive). Other categories frequently found in the TAM systems are: progressive, irrealis/potential/future (terminological variation), perfect,[9] imperative and exhortative. Their morphological expression is generally either a prefix (sometimes analyzed as a proclitic), a suffix or a preverbal auxiliary. These three possibilities are illustrated by Akatek data (Zavala 1992):

AKATEK

(9) a. TAM prefix
     x- 'perfective':   *x-ach-wey-i*
                               PFV-B2SG-sleep-SS:1.IND
                               'you slept'

     b. TAM suffix
     -an 'intr. imperative': *wey-an*
                               sleep-IMP
                               'sleep!'

     c. Preverbal auxiliary
     lalan 'progressive':   ***lalan** a-wey-i*
                               PROG A2SG-sleep-SS:1.IND
                               'you are sleeping'[10]

The suffix *-i* in (9a) and (9c) is known as "thematic suffix" or "status marker/suffix". Most Mayan languages display on their verbs this kind of suffix,[11] inherited from Proto-Mayan (Robertson 1992:61), which generally conflates information about transitivity – transitive versus intransitive – and information about mood/syntactic status: indicative (or "plain", "declarative", etc.) versus subjunctive (or "optative") or independent versus dependent. Some elements analyzed as status suffixes also mark aspect as well as the fact that the verb is morphologically derived, rather than radical. Status suffixes for root transitives in K'ichee' are illustrated in (3) above.

For instance, the *-i* of Akatek in (9) explicitly marks the verb as intransitive and indicative, and contrasts with -V(ʔ) for transitives (Zavala 1992:64). Both suffixes are exclusively phrase-final, meaning that they drop if anything follows within their clause, be it another satellite of the verb or any other constituent. This morphoprosodic condition exists for several elements analyzed as status suffixes, at least in Q'anjob'alan and K'ichean languages. Note that there is no general agreement among authors about what counts or not as a status suffix in every Mayan language.

A complex relation exists between some status suffixes and derivational suffixes, as some derivational suffixes have been diachronically reanalyzed as part of the normal inflection of verbs. Several cases of this kind are observable in Cholan languages. For instance, Chol has a suffix *-Vñ* (*-V* in perfective) which is commonly analyzed as a status suffix for derived transitive verbs, as in *way-is-añ* {sleep-CAUS-SS} 'to make somebody sleep'.[12] Now, this suffix also functions as a transitivizing suffix, as in *ixim* 'corn' > *ixm-añ* 'to shell corn' (Vázquez Alvarez 2011:98). So this is a case of a derivational suffix that has spread into the verbal inflectional morphology domain (this is clear also from a comparative point of view).[13] Huastec is another language where status suffixes display a double identity as normal (obligatory) verbal inflectional material and as verbalizers.

Complexity in the verbal domain in Cholan and Yucatecan languages also stems from the fact that nouns, especially nominalized forms of verbs, have been recruited for renovating the imperfective aspect. This was first described for Yucatec by Bricker (1981). In Chol, the current imperfective for intransitive verbs is illustrated in (10a). This construction originally emerged as 'my arrival occurs' or something similar, where the matrix predicate *mi* took as its subject a possessed nominalized form of the verb with suffix *-el*. The suffix *-el* now apparently contrasts with the intransitive status suffix *-i*, which has been restricted to perfective aspect, (10b). Incidentally, a split-ergative pattern was created (see Vázquez 2011).

CHOL
(10) a. Imperfective: mi   k-jul-**el**
                      IPFV A1-arrive-SUF
                      'I arrive.'

     b. Perfective: tyi   jul-**i**-y-oñ
                      PFV   arrive-SS:I.IND-EP-B1SG
                      'I arrived.'

So in (10a), *-el* occupies the slot and function of a status suffix, although it still works as a canonical nominalizer in other cases. Another possible analysis, as argued by Coon (2013), is that *-el* is still a bona fide nominalizer here rather than a verbal status suffix, and that the construction must still be interpreted as 'my arrival occurs'.

In their inventory of detransitivizing voices, all Mayan language present at least an antipassive, which eliminates the patient or demotes it to oblique status, and one or several passives. As Kaufman and Norman (1984:107) express it, "Mayan languages typically have several different ways of forming passives; these are distinguished according to the type of transitive stem involved, whether or not the agent of the action may be expressed, whether the action of the verb is marked as successful, possible, or sudden, as well as according to other features". For instance, K'ichee' distinguishes the simple passive, marked by vowel lengthening (root transitives) or suffix *-x* (derived transitives), from the completive passive, marked by suffix *-(V)taj* (Larsen 1988:250–5), which emphasizes the telicity of the event (e.g. 'finished being Ved' versus simply 'being Ved').

Other common voice categories are the agent focus (Stiebels 2006; analyzed in some cases as an inverse voice by Aissen 1999 and Zavala, this volume), necessary in order to focus, interrogate or relativize the agent in K'ichean, Mamean, Q'anjob'alan and Yucatecan;[14] a benefactive or instrumental applicative, reconstructed as *-b'e* for Proto-Mayan, with reflexes in Eastern and Western branches (Mora-Marín 2003); an "object-incorporating" voice (see (5) above), present according to Robertson (1992:57) in Mam, Q'anjob'alan, Q'eqchi' and Yucatecan, and a kind of anticausative voice, often described as "medio-passive" or "middle voice" (see for example (4c) for Yucatec). For an exhaustive survey of voice in Mayan languages, see Dayley (1981).

The incorporation of motion verbs into the verbal complex is also a recurrent grammatical feature. In all Mayan languages, a closed set of basic intransitive motion verbs (frequently along with some phasal verbs), as 'go', 'come', 'go up', 'go down', etc., get grammaticalized as preverbal auxiliaries in a motion-cum-purpose kind of construction (Zavala 1993). In K'ichean and Mamean, this process has led to the integration of motion verb roots into the prefixal domain, between absolutive and ergative personal prefixes, as in Poqomam *?oo* 'go' in (11). In Mamean these have been further grammaticalized as directionals (Zavala 1993).

POQOMAM
(11) x-ah-**?oo**-r-il-a?
     PFV-B1PL-**go**-A3SG-see-SS:T.DEP
     'he went to see us' [Santos Nicolás and Benito Pérez (1998:197)]

In most Mayan languages, more or less the same set of motion verbs give rise to a distinct grammaticalized category, that of directionals ('to come' > 'hither', etc.) (see England 1976 for Mam, Mateo Toledo 2004 for Q'anjob'al, Haviland 1993 for Tsotsil).

Infinitives are proposed for several Mayan languages (see the studies on non-finite structures in several Mayan languages in Palancar and Zavala 2013). Their relation to action nominalizations is complex, as some forms display a mixed verbal-nominal behavior. For example, Larsen (1988:395ff) shows that K'ichee' nominalized verbs, which he calls "action nominalizations", may either head ordinary noun phrases or appear as non-finite verbs in complement clauses, with different properties in each case (see also Can Pixabaj 2015).

Mayan languages typically possess the following verbalizations (only the most productive patterns are mentioned):

- Causative: most Mayan language show a causative (transitivizer) suffix which originally involved an /s/ (Smith 1976:57), e.g. K'ichee' -isa, Mam -sa(a), Yucatecan -(e)s(a), Huastec -θ, etc. It applies at least to intransitive stems, and often also to adjectives, but normally not to transitive stems. For example in K'ichee' kam 'to die' > kam-isa 'to kill' (Larsen 1988:195).
- Positional verbs: some of the most regular derivational patterns in Mayan languages concern positional roots, which produce, in particular, pairs of a causative and an inchoative stem with the meaning "{cause/get into} some particular state (position, shape, etc.)", see §3.4 below.
- Iteratives and distributives: affixes that modulate the aspectual profile of the verb, e.g., pluractionals, are common. Those combine with verbal stems or function as verbalizers (see Henderson 2012 and this volume on pluractionality in Mayan). Expressive (or "affective") morphology, which produces verbs and other kinds of words (see §3.5), typically marks pluractionality, along with emphasis. "Celeritives", which mark the action as "sudden, unexpected or happening instantaneously" (Kaufman and Norman 1984:109), belong to the same broad domain. An example could be the -V*la²* suffix in K'ichee', which according to Larsen (1988:248) adds the meaning 'quickly, rapidly' or is interpreted as a repetitive, e.g. x-∅-uu-sik'-*ila²* {PFV-B3SG-A3SG-pick.up-CEL} 's/he picked it (various ones) up ~ s/he picked it up repeatedly'.
- Inchoative (or "versive"): nouns and adjectives derive corresponding change of state intransitive verbs ('to become x'). Some languages use the same suffix for both word classes (e.g. Tseltal -ub), others display two different suffixes (e.g. Tojol-ab'al: -b' for nouns, -ax for adjectives, Gómez Cruz 2010).
- Other denominal verbs: pairs of a transitive verb and a related agentive intransitive verb commonly derive from nouns denoting the action or its product, as in K'ichee' b'iix 'song' > b'ix-o- 'to sing (it)' (Larsen 1988:133). This last form is transitive, and the corresponding intransitive verb is formed through the antipassive: b'ix-o-n- 'to sing'. This derivational chain *noun > transitive > intransitive (antipassive)* is very common in Eastern Mayan. "Usative" transitivization of nouns, i.e. with the meaning "to use {the noun} on something" (often described as "applicative"), is widespread, e.g. in Mam a² 'water' > a²-la 'to water something' (England 1983:103). This kind of transitivization may also mean "to consider/treat/use as an instance of . . . ", e.g. in Tseltal me² 'mother' > me²-in 'to consider/treat as one's own mother' or si² 'firewood' > si²-in 'to use as firewood'.

3.2 Nouns

Nouns in Mayan languages inflect for possession in several ways: the possessor is indexed by a Set A prefix, and either non-possession or marked status of possession can be indicated by additional suffixes (see below). Some nouns also inflect for plural, and some languages maintain (either productively or as frozen forms) one or both Proto-Mayan nominal gender prefixes. Finally, when they function as non-verbal predicates nouns also take a Set B absolutive marker indexing the subject.

Possession is the main inflectional issue that specifically affects Mayan nouns and justifies the establishment of possessive noun classes. The following criteria are the most common for this classification:

a. Presence/absence of a particular suffix when possessed.
b. Presence/absence of a particular suffix when non-possessed (frequently described as the "absolute" use; the corresponding suffix is sometimes called "absolutive", although this leads to confusion with absolutive person markers).[15]
c. Possibility/impossibility of being possessed.
d. Possibility/impossibility of being non-possessed.
e. Other formal changes under possession (lengthening, tonal change, suppletive forms etc.).
f. Presence of a possessive classifier when possessed (Yucatecan, Mam and Teko).

For example, Lehmann (1998:48), in an important study for understanding the phenomenon of possession in Mayan languages, proposes six subclasses for Yucatec, grouped in three major classes (Table 8.2).

All Mayan languages lend themselves to similar classifications, although the exact number of classes, along with their corresponding defining properties, varies according to the author and the language, generally ranging between two and seven. For instance, all Mayan languages have a special suffix used typically for kin and body-part terms when non-possessed ("absolute use") similar to Yucatec -*tsil*: K'ichean -V*Vj*~-*axeel*, Mam -*b'aj* ~ -*j*, Cholan-Tseltalan -*Vl*, Huastec -*lek*, etc. For example in Yucatec, *sukuʔn* 'elder brother' cannot be used as a bare stem: it must appear possessed, as *in sukuʔn* {*in* 'A1SG'} 'my elder brother' or else be made absolute, as *sukuʔn-tsil* 'elder brother'.

The existence of possessed forms marked with an additional suffix – corresponding to the alienable nouns in their "possessible convertible" subclass in Table 8.2 – is

TABLE 8.2 POSSESSIVE NOUN CLASSES IN YUCATEC

Class	Subclass	Absolute use	Possessed use	Semantic classes
neutral		N	N	diverse
inalienable	inabsoluble	–	N	parts of wholes
	absoluble	N-*tsil*		kin
alienable	impossessible	N	–	persons, configurations of nature
	possessible convertible		N-*il/-el*	most
	classifiable		possessive classifier + N	objects of cultural sphere

(Lehmann 1998)

also general to the family, typically with a -V(V)l suffix. This phenomenon is diversely described as "abstract noun formation", "relationalization" (Lehmann 1985, 1998:54), "abnormal possession" (Dayley 1985) or "marked possession" (Polian 2013). Some authors analyze it as orthogonal to the phenomenon of possessive noun classes, rather than part of it, as many nouns can take this additional suffix independently of their class. Dayley (1985:146) describes it for Tz'utujil in the following terms:

> Abnormal possession deviates from the prototypical ownership situation in some way. Thus, when an inanimate object or an animal has something that would normally be owned only by a human, then the possessed noun is marked with -VVl as abnormal. Or when a human possesses something that is normally alienable, but possesses it in an inalienable way, then the possessed noun is marked with -VVl as abnormal.

Thus, 'my wood', as in (12a), is a prototypical case of possession, whereas 'the bean's stick (stake)', as in (12b), is non-prototypical, because of the inanimate possessor, and thus requires the additional -VVl suffix (-aal in this case, the vowel is lexically determined and can be any of the five vowels).

TZ'UTUJIL
(12) a. *nuu-chee²*
         A1SG-wood/stick
         'my wood'

      b. *r-chee²-aal*   *ja*   *kinaq'*
         A3SG-wood/stick-SUF   ART   bean
         'the bean's stick (stake)' [Dayley 1985:146]

Marked/abnormal possession in many cases resembles a derivational pattern: it is to some extent both semantically and morphologically unpredictable (more or less so according to each particular case and to each language). Furthermore, it can be seen as a particular case of a more general derivational pattern which produces what is generally termed in Mayan grammars "abstract nouns" from nouns, adjectives, positionals (or positional roots) and sometimes also from verbs. Abstract nouns are of the inalienable type (they require possessor) and they typically denote an abstract property of some entity. With adjectives and positionals, they derive the corresponding quality noun (like -*ness* in English) and when possible with verbs it is a kind of nominalization. For example the same Tz'utujil suffix -VVl mentioned in the previous paragraph nominalizes adjectives, as *q'eq* 'black' > *r-q'eq-aal* 'its blackness' (Dayley 1985:185), where *r-* is the possessive A3SG prefix (any other grammatical person could be possessor if relevant: 'my blackness', etc.).[16]

Plural is unevenly grammaticalized with nouns across the family. In a language like Tseltal, all non-possessed nouns can be pluralized through the suffix -*etik*; this is optional with non-human referents and non-specific human referents, but obligatory with specific human referents. In contrast, Mam has a plural clitic *qa* for nouns which is always optional, including with specific human referents. For example in (13) the plural person marking on the verb (*chi* 'B3PL') is enough to establish the plurality of the subject, and thus the plural clitic is not necessary, though possible. Compare with the same sentence in Tseltal in (14): the plural suffix -*etik* is obligatory here, whereas it is the plural marking -*ik* on the verb that is optional.

MAM
(13) ma   chi   beet   (qa=)xuʔj
    PROX B3PL walk (PL=)woman
    'The women walked.' [adapted from England 1983:145]

TSELTAL
(14) behen-Ø(-ik)   te   ʔants*(-etik)=e
    walk-B3-PL   ART woman-PL=DET
    'The women walked.'

In some languages, one finds nominal plural morphemes with exclusive human reference, e.g. *-e'* in Tojol-ab'al (Gómez Cruz 2010).

Most Mayan languages maintain some reflex(es) of the two Proto-Mayan gender prefixes *ʔaj-* 'masculine' and *ʔix-* feminine. As a derivational device, at least one of them (generally *ʔaj-*) survives in all languages but Huastec, producing demonyms from toponyms, e.g. in Akatek *ʔaa-soloma* 'person from Soloma' (Zavala 1992:41). In most of those languages, it also derives a person-denoting noun, typically an agentive noun, from nominal or adjectival stems, e.g. in Ixil *tz'ib'* 'writing' > *ah-tz'ib'* 'writer' (Ayres 1991:33). In Yucatecan and Cholan-Tseltalan languages, reflexes of both prefixes appear with personal names and with some animal and plant names, as a kind of nominal class prefix (see Arcos López 2009 on Chol) and as a device which contributes to the semantic specificity of some expressions, for example with adjective+noun combinations (see in particular Lois 1998 on Itzaj).

Deverbal nouns are abundant. Besides action nouns (which are alternatively analyzed as "infinitives" by some authors, see previous section), the most common types are agent nouns – e.g. in Huastec with suffix *-Vm*: *tzemθ-aʔ-* 'to kill' > *tzemθ-om* 'killer, butcher' (Edmonson 1988:110) – and a kind of noun that is either an instrument or a location, frequently with a suffix involving a /b(')/. For example in Ixil (Ayres 1991:53): *b'ix* (intransitive) 'to dance' > *b'ix-ab'al~b'ix-eb'al* 'money paid for dancing' (instrument) or 'dance hall' (location).

A subclass of nouns present in all Mayan languages is that of relational nouns. Those are obligatorily possessed forms of nominal origin – some may even show relics of nominal morphology – which function as syntactic relators, in particular as adpositions and subordinators. For example the relational noun *umaal* in K'ichee' introduces an agent, which is indexed through the possessive prefix: *w-umaal* 'by me', *aw-umaal* 'by you', *r-umaal* by 'him/her/it', etc. (López Ixcoy 1997:234).

3.3 Adjectives

Adjectives are generally recognized as making up a word class of their own in the different Mayan languages, and includes words denoting color, size and physical properties. Adjectives tend to be of the 'nouny' type, as they usually share more morphological features with nouns than with verbs. In particular, they take none of the special verbal morphology described in the previous section, such as TAM markers. Moreover, there usually are several morphemes that combine equally well with nouns and with adjectives, such as inchoative verbalizers or suffixes that derive an abstract noun (see previous section). Adjectives and nouns also share the property of functioning directly as non-verbal predicates.

A typical derivation for Mayan adjectives is an "attenuative" or "diffusive" suffix such as -Coj~-Cuj in K'ichee': *kaq* 'red' > *kaq-koj* 'reddish' or *piim* 'thick' > *pim-poj* 'somewhat thick' (Larsen 1988:144; see §2.3.2 for this kind of partial reduplication).

The main problem in describing the adjectival class in each language is to establish its boundaries with participles and other 'adjectivoid' words (cross-linguistically a very common difficulty), such as perfect participles and positionals (see next section). Several studies deal with this issue in quite different ways. Martínez Cruz (2007) establishes a medium-sized (less than 100 items) adjectival class in Chol by defining them as those words that function directly (without additional morphology) as prenominal attributive modifiers. This excludes all participles, which require the relative clause clitic marker =*bä* – a loan from Zoque – to modify a noun. This criterion only works for Chol (and Chontal), as other Mayan languages lack this kind of marker. Thus, England (2004) on Mam and Gómez Cruz (2010) on Tojol-ab'al must rely on a variety of morphological and morphosyntactic properties to distinguish adjectives. As is often the case when using a set of heterogeneous criteria, Gómez Cruz (2010) finds a resulting continuum between canonical adjectives and non-canonical ones, such as participles.

Perfect forms of verbs in most cases appear as a kind of participle and are categorially akin to non-verbal predicates (especially to adjectives). For example Akatek has intransitive participles in -*naj* (*kam* 'to die' > *kam-naj* 'dead') and passive participles from transitive stems in -*b'il* (*man* 'to buy' > *man-b'il* 'bought') (Zavala 1992:108). However, some authors analyze perfect forms as members of the verbal TAM paradigms because of their systematicity.

Other derived adjectives are based on positional roots and noun stems. For example Tseltal derives proprietive ('having N') denominal adjectives, which are used exclusively as prenominal modifiers, e.g. *'ich* 'chili' >*'ich-il* 'with chili', as in *'ich-il mats'* 'dough with chili'.

3.4 Positionals

All Mayan languages possess a class of derived words traditionally called "positionals" because they semantically codify notions of position ('seated'), spatial arrangement ('piled up'), shape ('round') or other physical properties ('small', 'withered', 'wet', etc.). They may also mean 'for some entity in the referred position/shape/etc., to be in some place'. In some languages several hundred of them have been registered. Their particular morphosyntactic properties in some languages justify (at least for some authors) assigning them to a word class of their own (Martin 1977; Kaufman 2015 on Q'anjob'al), whereas for others they are a kind of adjective (Haviland 1994 on Tsotsil), or a participle (Edmonson 1988 on Huastec, Polian 2013 on Tseltal). Some authors (e.g. Larsen 1988) prefer instead to place them under a vague characterization as "stative predicates" (which is terminologically rather problematic, see §3.8 below). Depending on the language, they may show categorial affinity either to intransitive verbs or to adjectives, or to both at the same time, as is shown below.

The identification of positionals is firstly morphological: they are positionals because they are formed on a CVC root, called positional root, with the relevant suffix: -Vl (harmonic vowel) in Cholan-Tseltalan, -V:l in Huastec, -*an* in Q'anjob'alan, -Vkbal in Yucatec, -Vl~-Vn in K'ichee', etc. For example in Huastec: *chin-i:l* 'extended and rigid', *mo'-o:l* 'thrown down', *kex-e:l* 'widened', etc. (Edmonson 1988:176).

Canonical positional roots exist only through derived stems (positional words), which means that they never appear underived. All Mayan languages also display a number of positional roots that are polycategorial, as they also function directly as members of other root classes, mainly as transitive roots, and to a lesser extent as intransitive, nominal and adjectival roots. In Q'anjob'al, Mam or K'ichee', exclusively positional roots outnumber polycategorial ones (see Martin 1977 on Q'anjob'al), whereas in Tseltal and Tsotsil, more than a half of positional roots are also basically transitive (see Haviland 1994; Polian, this volume).[17]

Positional roots are associated with a rich and specialized derivational morphology. Besides deriving the stems that are simply described as "positionals" here, this morphology also typically produces distributive positional stems, nouns and several verb forms. The positional verbs especially include a causative (transitive) and an inchoative (intransitive) verb, which mean respectively 'to put into such a position/shape/etc.' and 'to get/be put into such a position/shape/etc.' (or alternatively, 'for some entity in the referred position/shape/etc., to put it/come to be in some place'). A specific designation for those verbs proposed by Kaufman (2015) is "depositive" for the transitive and "assumptive" for the intransitive.

The main syntactic function of positionals (as a word class, not as a root class) is as predicates. They are generally like other non-verbal predicates in not taking verbal TAM markers, but in some languages they display several features proper of intransitive verbs. This is illustrated with the positional *t'uy-ul* 'seated' in K'ichee' in (15): they take the phrase-final *-ik* status suffix of independent intransitive verbs, (15a), and they can appear inflected with the following categories, which are otherwise exclusively verbal: imperative, (15b), perfect participle, (15c), the action nominalization (or infinitive), (15d), and they appear in the construction with motion auxiliary, (15e).

(15) Verbal features on positionals in K'ichee' (from Larsen 1988:292)

    a. Status suffix: *t'uy-ul-ik*   'seated'
                      sit-POS-SS:I.IND

    b. Imperative: *ch-at-t'uy-ul-oq*   'sit (down)!'
                      IMP-B2SG-sit-POS-SS:I.DEP

    c. Perfect: *t'uy-ul-inaq*   's/he has sat (down)'
                      sit-POS-PRF

    d. Nominalization   *t'uy-ul-eem*   'sitting (down)'
                      sit-POS-NMLZ

    e. With motion aux.   *x-in-e'-t'uy-ul-oq*   'I went to sit (down)'
                      PFV-B1SG-go-sit-POS-SS:I.DEP

Thus, positional stems in K'ichee' are categorially very close to intransitive verbs. Nevertheless, a positional stem as *t'uy-ul* cannot inflect for perfective or imperfective aspects, which would be **x-at-t'uy-ul-ik* {PFV-B2SG-sit-POS-SS:I.IND} (intended: 'you sat down'), for instance. Instead of the latter, a proper verbalization of the root must be used (see below).

Positionals in some languages also display a categorial affinity to adjectives, which manifests itself in the fact that many of them can function as prenominal attributive modifiers, as in Tojol-ab'al (Gómez Cruz 2010), e.g. *tek'-an taj* {stand-POS pine} 'standing pine'. This function may be secondary in terms of corpus frequency with respect to the predicative one, but the same is probably also true of most adjectives. Another adjectival feature is the fact that they derive (or are associated with) abstract nouns denoting the corresponding abstract property. For example, from the same Tojol-ab'al positional *tek'-an* 'standing' derives the abstract noun *s-tek'-an-al* 'its standing position' (*ibid.* p.144) through the suffix *-al* (as other abstract nouns, it must be possessed, here by the *s-* 'A3'). The case of Tojol-ab'al is interesting because positionals in this language are at the same time close to adjectives and to intransitive verbs: *tek'-an* may also be conjugated as a regular intransitive verb, e.g. *wa x-tek'-an-i-Ø* {IPFV IPFV-stand-POS-SS:I. IND-B3SG} 's/he stands up', here with the regular intransitive inflection for imperfective aspect.

3.5 Affects/expressives

Mayan languages use special roots and/or derivations to add expressivity to speech. Those often have a sound symbolic element, either motivated, as in onomatopoeia, or conventional, as in association of certain kinds of phonemes with some semantic content (Hinton, Nichols and Ohala 1994). They may correspond to what is known as "ideophones" in African linguistics (Voeltz and Kilian-Hatz 2001), expressives in Asian, Austronesian, etc., linguistics (Diffloth 1972, 1976; Tufveson 2007) and mimetics in Japanese (Kita 1997). Many Mayanists have called them "affect (roots/words/verbs)" since Kaufman (1971). Some recent studies use the term "expressives" instead (Pérez González 2012; Polian 2013; Le Guen 2014), for the sake of terminological uniformity with linguists from outside of Mesoamerica. I follow this last trend here.

Expressives in Mayan can come as inflected and/or uninflected words depending on the language. Uninflected expressives appear as adverbs or secondary predicates modifying the main predicate, as *ni'm* in (16) from Mam. By default, they are accompanied by a light verb like 'to do', as in (17) in K'ichee', as they cannot function as main predicates. This is typical of ideophones in many languages (see Voeltz and Kilian-Hatz 2001). In this last example, the expressive is introduced by a preposition. Uninflected expressives appears frequently with reduplication. They can be radical or derived.

MAM
(16) **ni'm**   x-tz'-eel-x   xjaal   t-u'n   cheej
      EXPR   DEP.PROX-B3SG-go.out-DIR person A3SG-RN horse
      'Umph! the horse pushed the man.' [adapted from England 1983:85]

K'ICHEE'
(17) chi **puuq'** x-Ø-u-b'an   ri   ak'aal pa   ri   ja'
      PREP EXPR PFV-B3SG-A3SG-do DEM boy   PREP DEM water
      'The boy splashed through the water.' (lit. 'The boy did *splash!* in the water')
      [adapted from López Ixcoy 1997:170]

Inflected expressives may function as main predicates. They are typically words derived from expressive roots or from roots of other categories (mainly positional or transitive) with a dedicated expressive morphology which often includes reduplication (especially duplifixes). In some languages, they are a kind of verb and differ from other verbs only through their expressive semantic and their dedicated derivational morphology. This is the case of K'ichee' (Baronti 2001), as in (18), where the expressive verb *pun-upup* is derived from the root *pun* trough the expressive duplifix *-V₁C₁V₁C₁*. Note that its inflection is that of a normal intransitive verb (perfective prefix *x-*).

K'ICHEE'

(18) x-Ø-pun-upup   chwa   q'iij   saaq
      PFV-B3SG-to.fall.suddenly-EXPR.INTR RN   earth   light
'He was born prematurely.' [Baronti 2001:78]

Inflected expressives may also make up their own word class, distinct from verbs. This is the case in Tseltal and Tsotsil (see Polian, this volume). In some cases, they are analyzed as a kind of defective verb, e.g. with aspectual restrictions, as in Jilotepequeño Poqomam (Smith-Stark 1983).

3.6 Numerals and classifiers

Most Mayan languages are classifier languages and have sets of classifiers that are used, obligatorily or optionally, in quantifying constructions, especially with numerals,[18] a situation that has been reconstructed for Proto-Mayan (Smith 1976:54). Some languages lost their numeral classifier systems, like Mam and Huastec, and so use numeral roots directly as cardinal numeral words, e.g. *ajaj oox tx'yaan saq* {DEM three dog white} 'those three white dogs' (Mam, England 1983:149). In the other languages, numeral roots are used compounded or suffixed with classificatory morphemes, although there are some exceptions (some numeral roots that appear alone). For instance, to count animals in Tsotsil one uses the classifier *kot*, e.g. *ox-kot ts'i'* {three-NUM.CLF:animal dog} 'three dogs'; some other common classifiers in Tsotsil are *vo?* for human beings, *p'ej* for small round things and *ch'ix* for long things. The numeral root *ox* 'three' never appears alone; a default suffix *-ib* must be used if no specific classifier is selected: *ox-ib*.

Canonical sortal numeral classifiers, i.e. which are obligatorily used under the relevant conditions, like those of Tsotsil, are reported in Western Mayan and Yucatecan languages, along with Poqomam (Eastern Mayan). Most of those classifiers denote a shape or configuration and are based on positional roots through an original infix <h> (maintained in Chol, Tseltal and Poqomam; see Berlin 1968 for an exhaustive study of numeral classifiers in Tseltal). Some Chol examples appear in (19).

CHOL

(19) Examples of sortal numeral classifiers (Arcos López 2009)

Positional root		Classifier	Applied to . . . (non-exhaustive)
bil	'standing and rigid'	*bi<j>l*	'standing poles', 'needles', 'banana trees'
kits'	'long'	*ki<j>ts'*	'ropes', 'threads', 'hanging hair'
koty	'on all fours'	*ko<j>ty*	'animals', 'tables', 'cars'

Action numeral classifiers are very similar to sortal numeral classifiers, but they specify an action, as 'blow', 'knot', etc., rather than a concrete entity. Some numeral classifiers can be used indifferently as sortal or action classifiers, for instance in Tseltal *pa<h>k* from the transitive root *pak* 'to fold', e.g. *ox-pa<h>k* {three-fold<NUM.CLF>} 'three folded (fabrics)' [sortal interpretation] or 'three acts of folding' [action interpretation].

In Akatek (Q'anjob'alan), Zavala (2000) distinguishes two sets of numeral classifiers. One involves a closed set of three suffixes (*-wan* 'human', *-k'on* 'animal' and *-eb'* 'inanimate'), one of which is obligatorily present with numerals. The other involves an open set of classifier words, which are formally positionals (with suffix *-an*, see §3.4), such as *k'it-an* 'objects separated from each other', *jen-an* 'two-dimensional extended objects', etc. Classifiers of the second type are more loosely bound to the numeral (they normally appear after one of the classifier suffixes, and only exceptionally replace it) and their use is optional (and rather infrequent).

Another kind of numeral classifier, different from sortal ones, are mensuratives, which are used for counting portions or containers of mass nouns or of aggregates, such as '*n* handspans/bottles/piles/pieces/loads of . . . '. They usually appear in the same slot as sortal classifiers, but they may show some differences with the latter; see Zavala (2000) for the demonstration of this difference in Akatek. Mensurative classifiers are different from measure words, which are formally nouns used in apposition to numeral expressions and which exist in all Mayan languages. For example in Huastec *hun ya²ub ²i ²at'em* {one fistful PART salt} 'one fistful of salt' (Edmonson 1988:431).

For Eastern Mayan languages, grammarians have been reluctant to use the term "numeral classifier" and have preferred to talk about "enumeratives" (e.g. Dayley 1985:164 on Tz'utujil; Larsen 1988:125 on K'ichee'; Ayres 1991:55 on Ixil), but the difference is probably more terminological than substantive. Their function is similar, namely "to restrict the scope of meaning of the following noun or specify its form, shape, condition, or position" (Dayley 1985:165). They are allegedly different from numeral classifiers because they are never obligatory, but in this they are not different from the second kind of numeral classifiers in Akatek commented on above. As numeral classifiers, they can be sortal, they can be mensurative, or they can classify actions. An example of a mensurative enumerative in K'ichee' is *k'ulaaj* for 'pairs', as in *ox-k'ulaaj xajaab'* {three-pair sandal} 'three pairs of sandals' (Larsen 1988:126). This enumerative derives from the positional root *k'ul* 'married' through the suffix -*aaj*, which is a productive derivational pattern for enumeratives in K'ichee'. When no enumerative is present, default suffixes must be used with most numeral roots, e.g. in K'ichee' *ox-ib'* 'three' (the same in Tsotsil, cf. the beginning of the section).

Beyond classifiers, numerals display some specific morphology. First, they have corresponding distributive forms, which involve either reduplication or a special suffix. For example in Tektiteko *jun* 'one' > *junjun* 'one by one', *kab'* 'two' > *ka-kab'* 'two by two', etc. From 'five' on, the suffix -*chaq* is needed: *jweb'-chaq* 'five by five' (Pérez Vail 2007). Next, they derive ordinals through possession in the third person singular, with or without an additional suffix.[19] The ordinal 'first' might be an exception, as it is generally a suppletive form. The noun ordinally qualified may function as the syntactic possessor of the ordinal. For example in Itzaj *u-ka²-p'eel ²ak'ä²* {A3SG-two-NUM.CLF:inanimate night} 'the second night' (Hofling and Tesucún 2000:141). In this case, the ordinal does not bear an additional suffix but still requires a numeral classifier, as do all cardinal numerals in Itzaj.

3.7 Adverbs

Many words are used adverbially in Mayan languages, some of them exclusively so, but generally without a specifically adverbial morphology. Adjectives commonly develop adverbial uses (e.g. 'good' for 'well'), and some nouns and verb forms also do. For example in Tseltal the noun *ahnimal* 'race, hurry', derived from the intransitive verb *ahn* 'to run away, to flee', may be used adverbially as 'quick'. Thus, when adverbs show some morphology, it is typically nominal or adjectival morphology: for example, some adverbs derive abstract nouns, as most adjectives do. Expressive words ("affect words", see §3.5) also cover part of the functional domain served by adverbs in other languages.

Adverbial derivation in most Mayan languages is restricted to suffixes that derive (non-productively) time adverbs measuring distance from now to some point in the past or in the future. They combine with some numeral roots – e.g. in Tsotsil *cha²-ej* 'in two days', *chab-je* 'two days ago' (*cha²~chab* 'two') – and with a few other roots, as in Tsotsil *vol-je* 'yesterday (the root *vol* has no clear meaning) or in Ixil *jun-aab'* 'in one year' (*jun* 'one' + *yaab'* 'year', Ayres 1991:68).

3.8 Non-verbal/stative predicates

Nouns, adjectives and numerals may generally be used predicatively in Mayan languages. In this function, they denote a (temporary or permanent) state and bear an absolutive (Set B) personal marker indexing the subject, but no TAM marker, as those are restricted to verbs. This is illustrated in (20) with an adjective and a numeral in Q'anjob'al. As such, they all constitute potential (stative) non-verbal predicates, as this is one of the syntactic functions that members of those word classes can normally fulfill ("normally", as there may be some exceptions). But this does not constitute "non-verbal predicates" (or "stative predicates") as a word class.

Q'ANJOB'AL
(20) Jelan/ka-wan   hex.
      smart/two-NUM.CLF:human   B2PL
      'You all are smart/two people.' [Mateo Toledo 2008:62]

Things get complicated as one finds in Mayan languages many non-verbal words whose only possible function is as predicates, but that are neither clearly nouns, adjectives or numerals. This is the case for positionals in some languages (see §3.4). Many Mayanists are then tempted to describe those words as "non-verbal predicates" (or "stative predicates") as the name of a word class, or at least as a convenient shortcut expression which roughly corresponds to "a kind of word which is not a verb and which is typically used predicatively (with a stative interpretation), but whose word-class assignation still needs to be figured out". For example, Larsen (1988:288) comments on the formation of the positional form with -Vl suffix in K'ichee' in the following terms: "The suffix -Vl derives a non-verbal stative predicate meaning 'to be in the state denoted by the root' (. . .) ".The drawback of this kind of formulation, frequent in Mayan grammars, is that it creates a confusion between syntactic function ("predicate"), semantics ("stative") and lexical classification. Some authors, like Bohnemeyer (2002:153–66), solve this terminological issue by establishing a "stative predicates proper" class, which is part of the broader class of "stative predicates", where nouns and adjectives also belong.

Some authors ascribe only a residual group of words to a class of "non-verbal predicates". For instance, Zavala (1992:97) uses this category only for three Akatek items: the focus marker *ja²*, the existential copula *²ey* and the transitory state copula *e(ey)*. The cognate items cause classification problems in all Mayan languages. In any case, more work needs to be done on these classificatory issues.

NOTES

1 Huastec is an exception with its idiosyncratic system of status suffixes (Edmonson 1988).

2 Some cases of "front versus non-front" opposition also exist, e.g. -VVb' plural in K'ichee' (-*iib'* after /a, o, u/, -*aab'* after /e, i/; López Ixcoy 1997:101).

3 See Edmonson (1988:74ff) for a general survey of this kind of phenomenon in Huastec.

4 Huastec data from Edmonson (1988) were changed to match current practice in Mayan orthography.

5 Note that reduplication of the root vowel in a duplifix can also be viewed as vowel harmony, see §2.3.

6 Dayley (1985:188) assumes a category of "phrasal compounds" for cases of low fusion between compound members in Tz'utujil.

7 Some authors treat this initial glottal stop as phonetic, e.g. Larsen (1988:54) for K'ichee'. In all Mayan languages, this glottal stop drops when a Set A prefix is added (and also in other contexts in some languages), although there are exceptions, see for example Lehmann (1998:35) and Polian (2013:135).

8 Other cases include Mam, which has developed partially different Set B sets for verbs and non-verbal predicates (England 1983), and the A1sg marker in K'ichee', which displays different allomorphs as transitive subject and as possessor on nouns (Larsen 1988:213).

9 Some authors do not include perfect in the TAM inventory because of the participial character of perfect forms (i.e., they are more akin to non-verbal predicates, see §3.3), e.g. Zavala (1992) on Akatek. Other authors include perfect forms as members of the TAM systems despite of their participial status.

10 *Lalan* auxiliary triggers split ergativity, this is why the subject of *wey* 'sleep' is marked by a Set A (ergative) prefix rather by an absolutive one (Set B)

11 Tseltal, Tsotsil and Mam have lost most of the original status suffixes of Proto-Mayan.

12 Although this suffix also appears with some root transitive verbs, which indicates that this is more probably a case of different verbal inflectional classes, partially overlapping with a root/derived condition.

13 See also Kaufman and Norman (1984:105), who show that several status suffixes for intransitive verbs of Cholan languages originate from intransitivizing suffixes, which were reanalyzed as part of the normal inflection of intransitive verbs.

14 Agent focus forms are morphologically intransitive and bear only a Set B (absolutive) affix, which indexes the patient or the agent, depending on the language.

15 The need of a term like "absolute" instead of "non-possessed" stems from the fact some absolute stems can be further used as new possessible stems. For example in Huastec *'in xeke:l* {A3 leave} 'its leaves (of a tree)' requires the suffix *-lek* when non-possessed: *xekl-lek* 'leaf' (with vowel reduction). This last form can be possessed if suffixed with *-il* ("marked possession" pattern, see below), as *'u xekl-le:k-il* {A1 leave-ABSOL-SUF} 'my leaves (for wrapping tamales)' (Edmonson 1988:374; see also Lehmann 1998:55 for Yucatec).

16 As Kaufman (2015) highlights it, abstract nouns can also be interpreted as "part possession". That is, they can also denote parts of an entity with the corresponding property. For example, the same Tz'utujil form *r-q'eq-aal* 'its blackness' could also mean 'its black part'.

17 Polycategoriality is dispensable here if "positionality" is viewed as a morphological rather than a lexical phenomenon. This would mean that a transitive root (or intransitive, etc.) that derives positional forms may be said to be properly a (monocategorial) transitive root which appears to be compatible with positional derivative morphology, rather than a polycategorial transitive-positional root. As a consequence, positional roots would be reduced to a default category, made up of those roots which associate

with positional morphology but which cannot be assigned to another lexical category, because they do not function directly as inflectible stems. This position makes sense for those Mayan languages like Tseltal in which allegedly polycategorial positional roots are the majority.

18 Additionally, Q'anjob'alan and Mamean languages have noun classifier systems. This phenomenon will not be discussed here. See Zavala (2000) for a complete description of all the classificatory devices in Akatek.

19 Ordinals in Huastec may appear without possessors, see Edmonson (1988:419).

REFERENCES

Aissen, Judith. 1999. "Agent focus and inverse in Tzotzil." *Language* 75: 451–85.

Arcos Lopez, Nicolás. 2009. "Los clasificadóres numerales y las clases nominales en ch'ol." MA thesis, CIESAS.

Ayres, Glenn. 1991. *La Gramatica Ixil*. Guatemala: Centro de Investigaciones Regionales de Mesoamerica.

Baronti, D. S. 2001. "Sound symbolism use in affect verbs in Santa Catarina Ixtahuacán." PhD diss., University of California at Davis, California.

Berlin, Brent. 1968. *Tzeltal numeral classifiers: a study in ethnographic semantics*. The Hague: Mouton.

Bohnemeyer, Jürgen. 2002. *The grammar of time reference in Yukatek Maya*. Munich: LINCOM.

Bricker, Victoria R. 1981. "The source of the ergative split in Yucatec Maya." *Journal of Mayan Linguistics* 2: 83–127.

Bricker, Victoria R. 1999. "Color and texture in the Maya language of Yucatan." *Anthropological Linguistics* 41: 283–307.

Bricker, Victoria R., Eleuterio Po'ot Yah, and Ofelia Dzul de Po'ot. 1998. *A dictionary of the Maya language as spoken in Hocabá, Yucatán*. Salt Lake City: The University of Utah Press.

Campbell, Lyle. 1977. *Quichean linguistic prehistory*. vol. 81. Berkeley: University of California Press.

Can Pixabaj, Telma Angelina. 2015. "Complement and purpose clauses in K'iche'." PhD diss., University of Texas, Austin.

Coon, Jessica. 2013. *Aspects of split ergativity*. Oxford: Oxford University Press.

Dayley, Jon. 1981. "Voice and ergativity in Mayan languages." *Journal of Mayan Linguistics* 2: 6–82.

Dayley, Jon. 1985. *Tzutujil grammar*. Berkeley/Los Angeles/London: University of California Press.

Diffloth, G. 1972. "Notes on expressives meaning." Chicago Linguistic Society 8: 439–47.

Diffloth, G. 1976. "Expressives in Semai." In *Austroasiatic studies*, ed. by P. C. Jenner, L. C. Thompson, and S. Starosta, 249–64. Honolulu: University press of Hawaii.

Edmonson, Barbara Wedemeyer. 1988. "A descriptive grammar of Huastec (Potosino dialect)." PhD diss., Tulane University.

England, Nora C. 1976. "Mam directionals and verb semantics." In *Mayan linguistics I*, ed. by Marlys McClaran, 201–11. Los Angeles: University of California American Indian Studies Center.

England, Nora C. 1983. *A grammar of Mam, a Mayan language*. Austin: University of Texas Press.

England, Nora C. 2004. "Adjectives in Mam." In *Adjective classes: a cross-linguistic typology,* ed. by R.M.W. Dixon and Alexandra Y. Aikhenvald, 125–46. Oxford: Oxford University Press.

García Mátzar, Pedro Lolmay, and José Obispo Rodríguez Guaján Pakal. 1997. *Rukemik ri Kaqchikel Chi': Gramática Kaqchikel.* Guatemala: Cholsamaj.

Gómez Cruz, José. 2010. "Adjetivos en tojol-ab'al." MA thesis, CIESAS, México.

Haspelmath, Martin. 2002. *Understanding morphology.* London: Arnold.

Haviland, John. 1993. "The syntax of Tzotzil auxiliaries and directionnals: the grammaticalization of 'motion'." *Berkeley Linguistics Society* 19: 35–49.

Haviland, John. 1994. "'Te xa setel xulem' [The buzzards were circling]: categories of verbal roots in (Zinacantec) Tzotzil." *Linguistics* 32: 691–741.

Henderson, Robert. 2012. "Ways of pluralizing events." PhD diss., University of California Santa Cruz.

Hinton, Leanne, Johanna Nichols, and John J. Ohala, ed. 1994. *Sound symbolism.* Cambridge: Cambridge University Press.

Hofling, Charles Andrew, and Félix Fernando Tesucún. 2000. *Itzaj Maya grammar.* Salt Lake City: The University of Utah Press.

Justeson, John S. 1986. "Yucatecan phonological history." Unpublished manuscript.

Kaufman, Terrence. 1971. *Tzeltal phonology and morphology.* Berkeley/Los Angeles: University of California Publications.

Kaufman, Terrence. 2015. *Mayan comparative studies* [with the help of Will Norman on verb morphology]. Unpublished manuscript (under continuous updating by the author).

Kaufman, Terrence, and William Norman. 1984. "An outline of proto-cholan phonology, morphology and vocabulary." In *Phoneticism in Mayan hieroglyphic writing,* ed. by John Justeson and Lyle Campbell, 77–166. Albany: Institute for Mesoamerican Studies.

Kita, Sotaro. 1997. "Two-dimensional semantic analysis of Japanese mimetics." *Linguistics* 35: 379–415.

Larsen, Thomas W. 1988. "Manifestations of ergativity in Quiché grammar." PhD diss., University of California, Berkeley.

Le Guen, Olivier. 2014. "Expressive morphology in Yucatec Maya." In *Patterns in Mesoamerican morphology,* ed. by Jean-Léo Léonard and Alain Khim, 178–211. Paris: Michel Houdiard.

Lehmann, Christian. 1985. "On grammatical relationality." *Folia Linguistica* 19: 67–109.

Lehmann, Christian. 1998. *Possession in Yucatec Maya.* Newcastle: Lincom.

Lois, Ximena. 1998. "Gender markers as "rigid determiners" of the Itzaj Maya world." *International Journal of American Linguistics* 64: 224–82.

Lois, Ximena, and Valentina Vapnarsky. 2003. *Polyvalence of lexical roots in Yukatekan Mayan languages.* Munich: LINCOM.

Lois, Ximena, and Valentina Vapnarsky, eds. 2006. *Lexical categories and root classes in Amerindian languages.* Bern: Peter Lang.

López Ixcoy, Candelaria Dominga. 1997. *Ri Ukemiik ri K'ichee' Chii': Gramática K'ichee'.* Guatemala: Cholsamaj.

Martin, Laura Ellen. 1977. *"Positional roots in kanjobal."* PhD diss., University of Florida.

Martínez Cruz, Victoriano. 2007. "Los adjetivos y conceptos de propiedad en chol." MA thesis, CIESAS, México.

Mateo Toledo, Eladio. 2004. "Directional markers in Q'anjob'al (Maya); their syntax and interaction with aspectual information." MA thesis, University of Texas, Austin.

Mateo Toledo, Eladio. 2008. "The family of complex predicates in Q'anjob'al (Maya); their syntax and meaning." PhD diss., University of Texas, Austin.

Mondloch, James L. 1978. "Disambiguating subjects and objects in Quiché." *Journal of Mayan Linguistics* 1: 3–19.

Mora-Marín, David F. 2003. "Historical Reconstruction of Mayan Applicative and Antidative Constructions." *International Journal of American Linguistics* 69: 186–228.

Nichols, Johanna. 1986. "Head-marking and dependent-marking grammar." *Language* 62: 56–119.

Osorio May, José del Carmen. 2005. "Análisis de la Morfología Verbal del Yokot'an, 'Chontal' del Poblado de Tecoluta, Nacajuca, Tabasco." MA thesis, CIESAS, México.

Palancar, Enrique, and Roberto Zavala, eds. 2013. *Clases léxicas, posesión y cláusulas complejas en lenguas de Mesoamérica*. Mexico: CIESAS.

Pérez González, Jaime. 2012. "Predicados expresivos e ideófonos en tseltal." MA thesis CIESAS, Mexico.

Pérez Vail, José R. 2007. *Xtxolil Yool B'a'aj: Gramática Tektiteka*. Guatemala: Cholsamaj.

Polian, Gilles. 2013. *Gramática del tseltal de Oxchuc*. Mexico: CIESAS.

Raymundo González, Sonia, Adán Francisco Pascual, Pedro Mateo Pedro, and Eladio Mateo Toledo. 2000. *Sk'exkixhtaqil Yallay Koq'anej: Variación Dialectal en Q'anjob'al*. Guatemala: Cholsamaj.

Robertson, John. 1992. *The history of tense/aspect/mood/voice in the Mayan verbal complex*. Austin: University of Texas Press.

Santos Nicolás, José Francisco Pala's, and Waykan José Gonzalo Benito. 1998. *Rukorb'aal Poqom Q'orbal: Gramática Poqom*. Guatemala: Cholsamaj.

Smith, Thomas C. 1976. "Some hypotheses on syntactic and morphological aspects of Proto-Mayan (*PM)." In *Mayan linguistics volume I*, ed. by Marlys McClaran, 44–66. Los Angeles: American Indian Studies Center, University of California at Los Angeles.

Smith-Stark, Thomas. 1983. "Jilotepequeño Pocomam phonology and morphology." PhD diss., University of Chicago.

Stiebels, Barbara. 2006. "Agent focus in Mayan languages." *Natural Language and Linguistic Theory* 24: 501–70.

Tufvesson, Sylvia. 2007. "Expressives." In *Field manual volume 10*, ed. by Asifa Majid, 53–8. Nijmegen: Max Planck Institute for Psycholinguistics.

Vázquez Alvarez, Juan Jesús. 2011. "A grammar of Chol, a Mayan language." PhD diss., University of Texas, Austin.

Voeltz, Erhard, and Christa Kilian-Hatz. 2001. *Ideophones*. Amsterdam: John Benjamins.

Wälchli, Bernhard. 2005. Co-compounds and natural coordination. Oxford: Oxford University Press.

Zavala, Roberto. 1992. *El Kanjobal de San Miguel Acatán*. México: Universidad Nacional Autónoma de México.

Zavala, Roberto. 1993. "Clause integration with verbs of motion in Mayan languages." MA diss., University of Oregon, Eugene.

Zavala, Roberto. 2000. "Multiple classifier systems in Akatek (Mayan)." In *Systems of nominal classification*, ed. by Gunter Senft, 114–46. Cambridge: Cambridge University Press.

CHAPTER 9

ALIGNMENT PATTERNS

Roberto Zavala Maldonado

1 INTRODUCTION

Alignment refers to the way core arguments are distinguished from one another by the morphosyntax. In Mayan, morphological alignment involves two sets of cross-reference markers which are attached to the head of the clause, i.e., the predicate (in one language there are three sets). These mark the main syntactic functions: S (intransitive subject), O (transitive object) and A (transitive agent). Different patterns of alignment emerge, depending on how the two sets of markers map onto the three syntactic functions. These are introduced below and discussed in detail in §§2–5 and §7.

All members of the Mayan family exhibit an ergative alignment pattern in which S and O are treated alike, whereas A is treated differently (Dixon (1979) and Dixon (1994)). Within Mesoamerican languages, Mayan languages were the first group of languages that were recognized as showing an ergative alignment pattern. In addition to Mayan languages, all Mixe-Zoquean (Wichmann 1995; Zavala 2007; Faarlund 2012) and Chinantecan languages (Foris 2000) exhibit an ergative system.

Ergative alignment in Mayan involves pronominal markers on predicates. Since all the languages of the family are head-marking, these do not require the presence of external NPs. These markers, which provide information about person, number and syntactic function, have traditionally been referred to by Mayanists as belonging to Sets A and B (and C in one language, Ch'orti'), according to their form and function. The morphemes called Set A function as "ergative" but also as "possessor" and sometimes as "nominative", Set B functions as "absolutive" and sometimes as "accusative", whereas the third set, Set C, functions as "nominative in incompletive aspect". I will follow tradition and use the labels A, B, and C when discussing the pronominal cross-reference markers. As illustration consider the examples in (1) from Akatek, where the second-person singular marker from Set B *ach-* signals both the S of an intransitive verb, (1a), and the O of a transitive verb, (1b), while *aw-*, second-person singular from Set A, signals the A of a transitive verb, (1c).

AKATEK
(1) a. tol   chi-**ach**-kam eyman
      so   ICP-**B2SG**-die quickly
      'So you die quickly.'

  b. chi-**ach**-w-a'   ok jun aab'il y-ul   te'
     ICP-**B2SG**-A1SG-put DIR one year A3-in wood
     'I will put you in jail for one year.'

  c. maa   in-**aw**-etne
     NEG.CP B1SG-**A2SG**-deceive
     'You didn't deceive me.'

As in other ergative languages, the ergative cross-referencing pattern found in Mayan does not occur in all grammatical conditions. A great number of these languages make use of alternative alignment patterns triggered by aspect (Yukatekan, Cholan, Poqomam, Poqomchi', Ch'orti'), clausal dependency (Q'anjob'alan, Mamean), inherent features of arguments (Mocho'), and inherent features of the predicate (Chol, Chontal, Poqomchi', Mopan). The non-ergative patterns that have been attested within the family are accusative (§3) (Mocho', Yukatekan, Cholan, Poqomam, Poqomchi', Q'anjob'alan), tripartite (§4) (Ch'orti'), neutral (§5) (Mam), inverse (§7) (Huastec, Cajolá Mam), and agentive (§6) (Chol, Chontal, Poqomchi', Mopan). The non-ergative patterns found in Mayan have been treated as different cases of split ergativity in which the unmarked pattern is always ergative, whereas the marked patterns are the non-ergative ones.

Since the beginning of the research on ergativity in Mayan, one important question that has been raised is whether the morphological ergative pattern attested in all languages of the family has deep consequences in various complex structures resulting in syntactic rules governed by an ergative pattern, or whether the ergative alignment constitutes only a surface morphological phenomena without any significant consequences in the syntactic rules that govern the formation of clauses. A second important question that has been raised is whether the grammatical processes triggered by the ergative pattern are also shared by other languages with ergative syntax (Larsen and Norman 1979; England 1983a, 1983b). A third area of research has investigated the diachronic paths that resulted in the different split alignment patterns found in Mayan (Larsen and Norman 1979; Robertson 1980; Bricker 1981; England 1983a, 1983b; Kaufman 1990; Coon 2010, 2012, inter alia). And finally, the seminal work by Du Bois (1987) on the distribution of new and given information in Sakapultek discourse, has been very influential for investigating the relation between discourse patterns and grammar (cf. England and Martin (2003), and Hofling (2003)). Du Bois has argued that Sakapultek, as well as many other languages of the world, share a preferred argument structure (PAS) pattern according to which new information tends to be introduced through an NP in S or O functions whereas the A function is reserved for given information. Du Bois considers that the PAS pattern constitutes the basis for the ergative grammatical alignment in Mayan and elsewhere. This hypothesis has been recently challenged by Martínez (2012) and Vázquez and Zavala (2013) who have argued that, at least in Tsotsil and Chol, the distribution of information in discourse does not follow an ergative pattern, but instead an agentive pattern in which new information is distributed predominantly in O and S_o functions, while both the A and the S_A functions pattern alike in terms of being reserved for conveying given information (see Aissen, this volume, on information structure).

The distinctive features of the various alignment patterns and their distribution among the languages of the family are discussed in the following sections.

2 THE ERGATIVE PATTERN

All Mayan languages show an ergative alignment pattern to encode core grammatical relations on predicates. In K'iche', for instance, subjects of both intransitive verbs (2a) and non-verbal predicates (2b), as well as objects of transitive verbs (2c), are marked with Set B markers, while agents of transitive verbs are cross-referenced with Set A markers on the verb, as in (3).

K'ICHE'
(2) a. x-**at**-war-ik
      CP-**B2SG**-sleep-IS
      'You slept.' (Larsen 1990:319)

b. **at**=   achih=chik
   B2SG=   man=now
   'You are now a man.' (Velleman 2014:34)

c. achi   x-**at**-w-il-o
   man   CP-**B2SG**-A1SG-see-TS
   'I saw you as a man.' (Can Pixabaj 2015:64)

(3) la   x-Ø-**a**-tij   k'u   le   wa
    Q   CP-B3SG-**A2SG**-eat   PAR   DET food
    'Did you eat the food?' (Can Pixabaj 2015:155)

In K'iche' and the rest of the Mayan languages, Set A markers are also used to encode the possessor on nouns (4a), and complements of relational nouns – functional words that head obliques and adjuncts (4b).

K'ICHE'
(4) a. x-Ø-u-rayi-j   le   **a**-naan   x-Ø-u-tij   ichaaj
       CP-B3SG-A3SG-desire-ACT   DET **A2SG**-mother CP-B3SG-A3SG-eat greens
       'Your mother wanted to eat greens.' (Can Pixabaj 2015:158)

   b. Ø   k'ax   u-keem-ik   le   paas   **aw**-umaal
      B3SG   bad   A3SG-weave.PSV-VN   DET belt   **A2SG**-RN
      'It is hard for you to weave the belt.' (Can Pixabaj 2015:121)

The ergative alignment pattern found in K'iche' has been reconstructed for Proto-Mayan. In the reconstructed language, similar to K'iche', there are two subparadigms of Set A markers, one that precedes vowel-initial stems and one that precedes consonant-initial stems. On the other hand, there is only one paradigm of Set B markers, as shown in Table 9.1. In some languages, Set B markers are clitics that precede or follow the predicate (for a summary of the facts see Dayley 1990:388).

As in many other ergative systems, the morphologically unmarked relation is the absolutive. Among the pronominal markers on the predicates, the only one that is unmarked in Mayan is the third-person absolutive.

In Mayan languages, the ergative pattern not only structures the cross-referencing morphology, but is also found in the organization of some grammatical processes. Some languages show syntactic constraints on ergative arguments in the formation of focus, relative clauses, and information interrogatives, and others on control in subordinate

TABLE 9.1 PROTO-MAYA ERGATIVE AND ABSOLUTIVE MARKERS

Person	Set A (ergative) _V _C		Set B (absolutive)
1SG	*inw-	*in-	*iin
2SG	*aaw-	*a-	*at
3SG	*r-	*u-	*Ø
1PL	*q-	*q-	*o'nh
2PL	*eer-	*iw-	*ix
3PL	*k-	*k-	*eb'

(Kaufman 1990:71–2)

clauses. In Ixtahuacán Mam, for instance, the syntactic rules that operate in the formation of focus, relative clauses and information interrogatives are unconstrained on S and O arguments, (5a) and (5b), but not on A arguments, where a distinctive agent focus (AF) construction must be used (5c). The AF construction in Mam behaves as a canonical anti-passive with demoted O. It exhibits an AF suffix on the verb, -*n*, and marks the semantic agent as intransitive subject, making this argument accessible to the formation of focus constructions in the same way as the absolutive arguments S and O. Thus, in Dixon's terms (Dixon 1979, 1994), the formation of focus, relatives and information interrogatives operates on an S/O pivot in Mam.

IXTAHUACÁN MAM
(5) a. xiinaq   x-tz-uul
       man   PROX.DEP-B3SG-arrive.here
       '*The man* arrived here.' (England 1983a: 4)

   b. qa-cheej   x-chi   kub'   t-tzyu-'n   xiinaq
      PL-horse   PROX.DEP-B3PL   DIR   A3SG-grab-DS   man
      'The man grabbed *the horses*.' (England 1983a: 4)

   b. xiinaq   x-Ø-kub'   tzyuu-**n**   t-e   qa-cheej
      man   PROX.DEP-**B3SG**-DIR   grab-**AF**   A3SG-RN:PAT   PL-horse
      '*The man* grabbed the horses.' (England 1983a: 5)

Similar restrictions to form unmarked focus, relative clauses and information interrogatives with transitive agents exist in Yucatec, Tsotsil, and languages of the Q'anjob'alan, Mamean and K'ichean branches (Dayley 1981, 1990; Stiebels 2006). The Mayan AF construction always involves detransivization of the verb. In addition to the AF type that expresses the patient as oblique and the agent as absolutive subject, there is a second main type that expresses the patient as a direct argument coded in the verb with Set B whereas the agent in focus is left unmarked by person markers on the verb. In Q'anjob'al, for instance, the extraction of S, (6a), and O, (6b), are unmarked, but the extraction of the A, (6c), requires the presence of the AF marker -*on* on the verb, which detransitivizes the verb. Unlike Mam, which demotes the patient to oblique status, in Q'anjob'al, the patient is maintained as the only argument marked on the verb by Set B.

Q'ANJOB'AL
(6) a. man=Ø=aq   jun   q'in   tu   hoq-Ø='ok-oq
       NEG=B3=NEG   one   celebration that POT-B3=enter-IRR
       'There is not going to be any celebration.' (Pascual 2007:29)

   b. y-uj=tol   a=Ø   jun   a'-ej   tu   ch-Ø-y-uk'   heb'
      A3-because=that   FOC=B3 one   water-UNPOSS   that ICP-B3-A3-drink   3PL
      'Because it is that water that they drink.' (Pascual 2007:29)

   c. k'am tzet   x-**ach**=xib'te-**n**-i
      NEG something   CP-**B2SG**=frighten-**AF**-IS
      'Didn't anything frighten you?' (Pascual 2007:30)

Only some Mamean and K'ichean languages use the AF construction without regard to the grammatical person of agent and patient. In Q'eqchi, for instance, both the agent in focus and the oblique patient may be expressed with a NP referring to either a speech act participant (SAP) or a third person.

Q'EQCHI'
(7) a. ani   na-Ø-il-o-k   q-e   (laao)   **3:1**
        who   ICP-**B3SG**-see-AF-IS   A1PL-DAT   we
        'Who takes care of us?' (Berinstein 1985:152)

    b. lain   x-**in**-sak'-o-k   **r**-e   **1:3**
        I   CP-**B1SG**-hit-AF-IS   A3SG-DAT
        'I am the one who will listen to him.' (Berinstein 1985:183)

    b. lain   t-**in**-a'bi-**n**-q   **aku**-e   **1:2**
        I   FUT-**B1SG**-listen-AF-IS   A2SG-DAT
        'I am the one who will listen to you.' (Berinstein 1998:220)

    In contrast, other languages use the AF construction only when a third person low ranking in animacy or topicality A acts on a third person high ranking in animacy or topicality O (Tsotsil) (Aissen 1999), or a third-person A acts on an O with no restriction on person (Q'anjob'alan). The Tsotsil pair of examples in (8) shows that agent extraction is allowed when the extracted A is higher in animacy than the O, (8a), whereas the marked construction is required when the O is higher in animacy than the A, (8b). The Q'anjob'al examples in (9a) and (9b) show that the AF construction is required when the A in focus is third person independently of the person of the O; in contrast, (9c) shows that when the agent refers to a SAP, the verb is not detransitivized by -*on* since it takes person markers for both A and O.

TSOTSIL
(8) a. buch'u   s-pas   mantal   **A3 anim:O3 inan**
        who   A3-make   order
        'Who's giving the orders?' (Aissen 1999:459)

    b. k'usuk   nox   tij-**on**-uk   li   j-malal-e   **A3 inan:O3 anim**
        whatever just awaken-AF-IRR   DET   A1-husband-ENC
        'Just anything wakes my husband.' (Aissen 1999:464)

Q'ANJOB'AL
(9) a. ti   tol   a=ø   jun   ix   ti   ch-**in**='etne-**n**-i   **A3:O1**
        this that   FOC=B3 one   woman   this ICP-B1SG=deceive-AF-IS
        'It is in this way that this woman deceives me.' (Pascual 2007:40)

    b. a=Ø   jun   witz   tu   ch-Ø=kol-**on**   heb'   anima   tu'   **A3:O3**
        FOC=B3 one   mountain   that   ICP-B3=help-AF   3PL   people that
        'It is the mountain which helps those people.' (Pascual 2007:48)

    c. a=in   hoq-**ex**=**in**-tayne-j   **A1:O2**
        FOC=B1SG   POT-B2PL=A1SG-take_care-TS
        'I am the one who is going to take care of you all.' (Pascual 2007:41)

    In languages such as Awakatek and several K'ichean languages (K'iche', Tz'utujil, Sakapultek and Sipakapense), the Set B marker on the AF verb does not refer consistently to the semantic agent or patient, but to the most prominent argument in a person hierarchy (1>2>3PL>3SG) independent of its core syntactic role. Thus, for instance, in the combination 2:3, the person coded by Set B in the AF construction is second-person A, but in the combination 3:2, the person coded by Set B is the second-person O, as illustrated in (10) from K'iche'.

K'ICHE'

(10) a. aree   ri   at   x-**at**-ch'ay-ow   ri   achii   **2:3**
        FOC   DET   you   CP-**B2SG**-hit-AF   DET   man
        'You are the one who hit the man.' (Larsen 1988:503)

    b. jachin   x-**at**-ch'ay-ow-ik   **3:2**
        FOC   CP-**B2SG**-hit-AF-IS
        'Who hit you?' (Larsen 1988:506)

Given the restriction on extraction of A, it has been claimed that languages such as Mam and Q'eqchi are syntactically ergative. The same claim cannot be made for other Mayan languages due to mixed constraints on extraction of A and to the fact that in the AF construction the surface S is not always the underlying A (Larsen 1987; Aissen 1999; Stiebels 2006).

Mam also shows an ergative pattern in the way control operates in infinitival subordinate clauses (England 1983a:7). Motion-cum-purpose clauses and complement structures with causative verbs require absolutive controllers (S, O) in the matrix clause and S controlees in the embedded clause. When the controlee is an underlying agent of a transitive verb it is expressed as a syntactic S while the underlying O is expressed as oblique (11a) or as an incorporated noun (11c), i.e. it loses its syntactic object properties. Thus, Mam requires S/O controllers.

IXTAHUACÁN MAM

(11) a. o   **chi**   e'x   xjaal   [laq'oo-l   t-ee]
        CP.INDEP   **B3PL**   go   person   buy-NF   A3SG-RN:PAT
        'The people went to buy it.' (England 1983b: 299)

    b. ma   **chin**-x   aaj-a   [b'eeta-l]
        PROX.INDEP   **B1SG**-DIR   return=1SG   walk-INF
        'I went to walk.' (England 1983b: 299)

    c. ma   **tz'**-ok   n-q'o-'n-a   [tx'eema-l   sii']
        PROX.INDEP   **B2SG**-DIR   A1SG-give-DS=1SG/2SG   cut-INF   firewood
        'I made you cut wood.' (England 1983b: 300)

A third syntactic ergative pattern found in some Mayan languages has been discussed for K'iche' (Velleman 2014) and Yucatec (Verhoeven and Skopeteas 2015). In these two languages, foci in situ are accessible only for O and S, but impossible for A. As an illustration consider the following examples from K'iche'. In (12a), the focused NP in O function appears in situ when the clause is the response to the question 'What does Maria want to eat?', whereas in (12b), the NP in S function also follows the verb in response to the question 'Which of them is going to eat?'.

K'ICHE'
(12) a. aree   k-Ø-u-tij   [le   ichaj]$_{FOC}$ le   al   Mari'y.
        FOC   ICP-B3SG-A3SG-eat:TR   DET   vegetable   DET   miss   María
        'María will eat [the vegetables]$_{FOC}$.' (Velleman 2014:186)

      b. aree   ka-Ø-wa'   [le   al   Mari'y]$_{FOC}$.
        FOC   ICP-B3SG-eat:INTR   DET   miss   María
        '[María]$_{FOC}$ will eat.' (Velleman 2014:186)

In contrast, in the answer to the question 'Who is going to eat the vegetables?', which is a context that induces focus on the A argument, K'iche' disallows focus in situ, (13a), and instead the marked AF construction with extraction is required, (13b).

K'ICHE'
(13) a. * aree   k-Ø-u-tij   le   ichaj   [le   al   Mari'y]$_{FOC}$
          FOC   ICP-B3SG-A3SG-eat:TR   DET   vegetable   DET   miss   María
          '[María]$_{FOC}$ will eat the vegetables.' (Velleman 2014:186)

      b. aree   [le   al   Mari'y]$_{FOC}$ k-Ø-tij-ow   le   ichaj
        FOC   DET   miss   María   ICP-B3SG-eat-AF   DET   vegetable
        '[María]$_{FOC}$ will eat the vegetables.' (Velleman 2014:224)

Thus, in K'iche' and Yucatec, S and O can be foci in situ or be extracted without further morphological marking, whereas the interpretation of A as focus requires a marked extraction construction. This shows that both languages follow a syntactic ergative pattern in the formation of focus (see Aissen, this volume, on information structure).

3 SPLIT ERGATIVITY: THE ACCUSATIVE PATTERN

As is common in ergative systems, many Mayan languages are not consistently ergative, but instantiate a different alignment pattern under certain conditions (Dixon 1979:79–98). The conditions which induce argument-marking splits in Mayan are also common to other ergative languages: aspect distinctions, clausal dependency, inherent features of arguments, and inherent features of the verb. In Mayan, all of these types of splits involve the extension of the ergative (Set A) morpheme that marks the A in the unmarked conditions to S in the marked structural conditions. This is what Dixon (1979:78, 1994:63–7) referred to as "extended ergativity" since the same sets of markers occurring in the ergative pattern, which is the unmarked pattern, are also used in the neutral, agentive and accusative patterns, the marked patterns. Thus in the patterns of extended ergativity, no additional sets of morphemes are dedicated exclusively to mark dependent objects vs. independent objects, agentive intransitive subjects vs. non-agentive intransitive subjects, or nominative vs. accusative arguments.

Split ergativity motivated by aspectual distinctions occurs in Yucatecan, Cholan and Poqom languages. Yucatecan and Cholan languages follow an ergative pattern in completive aspect (Set B marks S and O, whereas Set A marks A), but follow an accusative pattern in the incompletive aspect (Set B marks O, whereas Set A marks A and S). The aspectual split is illustrated with examples from Itzaj. In completive aspect, the second-person A, (14a), patterns differently from the second-person S, (14b), and O, (14c).

ITZAJ
(14) a. t-**aw**-il-aj-Ø
         CP-**a2sg**-see-TS.CP-B3
         'You saw it.' (Hofling 2000:36)

     b. tal-**eech**
         come-**B2SG**
         'You came.' (Hofling 2000:37)

     c. t-uy-il-aj-**ech**
         CP-A3-see-TS.CP-**B2SG**
         'He saw you.' (Hofling 2000:37)

In contrast, in incompletive aspect, both A, (15a), and S, (15b), receive the same marker, whereas O, (15c), patterns differently, resulting in an accusative alignment.

ITZAJ
(15) a. k-**aw**-il-ik-Ø
         ICP-**A2SG**-see-TS.ICP-B3
         'You see it.' (Hofling 2000:36)

     b. k-**a**-wen-el
         ICP-**A2SG**-sleep-IS.ICP
         'You sleep.' (Hofling 2000:45)

     c. k-uy-il-ik-**ech**
         ICP-A3-see-TS.ICP-**B2SG**
         'He sees you.' (Hofling 2000:37)

Historical evidence suggests that Chol and Chontal borrowed the accusative marking pattern induced by aspect through contact with Yucatecan languages. Proto-Yucatecan shows a very similar split system, and this is not attested in the Tseltalan subgroup (Tseltal and Tsotsil) which, together with Cholan, forms Greater Tseltalan (Kaufman and Norman 1984:90; Law et al. 2006). In Chol, for instance, in the incompletive aspect, both A and S are cross-referenced with Set A markers, whereas the primary object (henceforth PO) is marked with a member of the paradigm of Set B, as in (16).

CHOL
(16) a. mi   **k**-äk'-eñ-Ø   tyak'iñ
         ICP   **A1**-give;APPL-TS.DEP-B3   money
         'I give him money.'

     b. ba'   mi   **k**-sujty-e(1)=loñ   maja
         where   ICP   **A1**-return-NMLZ=PL1EXCL   DIR:go
         '. . . to the place where we go back.'

     c. jiñi   mi   i-xik'-**oñ**-o'=la
         3PRON   ICP   A3-order-**B1**-PL3=1PL.INCL
         'They order us.' (Gutiérrez and Zavala 2005)

In completive aspect, Chol, like Itzaj, follows an ergative pattern where Set A cross-references the A, whereas Set B cross-references PO and S:

CHOL
(17) a. ixku   wa'l=i   bajche' tyi **aw**-il-ä-ø
        instead   now=ENC   how   CP   **A2SG**-see-TS-B3
        '[. . .] and now, how did you see it?'

   b. ibi   li   k-amigo   tyi i-päy-ä-y-**ety**   maja
      QUOT   DET   A1SG-friend   CP   A3SG-call-TS-EP-**B2SG**   DIR:away
      'My friend took you.'

   c. tyi majl-i-y-**ety**   tyi kaskada
      CP   go-IS-EP-**B2SG**   PREP waterfall
      'You went to the waterfall.' (Gutiérrez and Zavala 2005)

Similarly, both Poqomam and Poqomchi show the accusative alignment pattern in the potential and progressive aspects, as shown in the following examples of both languages in the potential aspect.

POQOMAM
(18) a. k-in-**a**-to'-om
        ICP-B1SG-**A2SG**-help-POT.TR
        'You will help me.' (Courtesy of José Francisco Santos Nicolás)

   b. n-**a**-wur-a
      POT-**A2SG**-sleep-IS
      'You will sleep.' (Santos and Benito 1998:183)

   c. **ti**-ni-to'-om
      B2SG-A1SG-help-POT.TR
      'I will help you.' (Courtesy of José Francisco Santos Nicolás)

POQOMCHI'
(19) a. na=k-iin   **aw**-il-om
        POT=ENC-B1SG   **A2SG**-see-POT.TR
        'You are going to take care of me.' (Mó Isém 2006:174)

   b. n-**aw**-el-ih
      POT-**A2SG**-leave-IS
      'You are going to leave.' (Mó Isém 2006:176)

   c. na=k-**aat**   w-il-om
      POT=ENC-**B2SG**   A1SG-see-POT.TR
      'I will take care of you.' (Mó Isém 2006:174)

Several authors (Comrie 1978; Larsen and Norman 1979; Robertson 1980; Bricker 1981; Kaufman 1990; Coon 2010, 2012, inter alia) have argued that the accusative pattern linked to incompletive (imperfective), potential and progressive aspect in Yucatecan, Cholan and Poqom languages arose diachronically from biclausal structures that included a matrix verb with a nominalized intransitive verb functioning as complement. In all of these languages, the suffixes following the intransitive stem have been analyzed synchronically or diachronically as nominalizers, suggesting that the subordinated verbs are to be treated as possessed nouns whose possessor expresses the subject of the embedded nominalized verb (see especially Robertson 1980; Bricker 1981; Kaufman 1990). Comparative and synchronic facts have linked the grammaticalized aspect markers which trigger split ergativity in these languages to formerly phasal, positional or other types of matrix predicates requiring intransitive nominalized complements. In sum, historically, the Set A marker that appears on the lexical intransitive verb marked the possessor of a nominalized embedded verb.

Recently, Coon (2010, 2012) has argued that Chol does not exhibit a split in the behavior of person marking conditioned by aspect. According to her analysis, the incompletive and progressive markers still function as matrix intransitive predicates, while the Set A on the nominalized embedded verb should still be analyzed as a nominal possessor marker, instead of a subject marker. Thus, under Coon's analysis, the incompletive marker of examples like (20) is a matrix predicate that shows third-person agreement (Set B) cross-referencing a possessed nominal phrase, where the prefix *a-* functions as second-person possessor instead of a clausal subject.

CHOL
(20) mi-Ø$_i$ [a-wäy-el]$_i$
      ICP-B3   A2SG-sleep-NMLZ
      'You sleep' (lit., ~ 'Your sleeping occurs'). (Coon 2010:216)

In Coon's view, all verbal forms in Chol, independent of aspect, show an ergative cross-referencing pattern and there is no need to recognize a split-ergative pattern. Also, in Coon's treatment of the facts, both intransitive and transitive verbs following imperfective markers are nominalizations, even though, unlike intransitive nominalizations, transitive verbs, such as *a-mek'-oñ*, in (21), do not have an overt nominalizer. Moreover, unlike true intransitive nominalizations that combine with determiners and adjectives and function as complements of a preposition, transitive forms such as *a-mek'-oñ* do not present these properties making the analysis of transitive forms as true nominalizations unconvincing.

CHOL
(21) mi-Ø$_i$ [a-mek'-oñ]$_i$
      ICP-B3   A2SG-hug-B2SG
      'You hug me.' (Coon 2010:216)

Languages of the Q'anjob'alan branch spoken in the Huehuetenango area (Q'anjob'al (Francisco Pascual 2007; Mateo Toledo 2013), Jakaltek (Craig 1977), Akatek (Zavala 1992) and Chuj (Buenrostro Díaz 2013)) and the Mamean languages Awakatek (Larsen 1981) exhibit an argument-marking split in aspectless dependent clauses. For Q'anjob'al, Francisco Pascual (2007) found seven different syntactic constructions where dependent clauses follow an accusative marking pattern: (a) aspectless complement clauses, (b) purpose clauses, (c) coordinate clauses, (d) clauses with preverbal depictive secondary predicates, e) preverbal resultative secondary predicates, (f) preverbal manner adverbs, (g) preverbal aspect/modal auxiliaries. Dependent clauses have many properties that set them apart from other subordinate structures. The verb in a dependent clause is fully marked for person but does not bear an aspect marker. Further, when the dependent verb is transitive, it takes a dependent suffix cognate with the AF marker *-on*. The examples in (22) from Q'anjob'al illustrate the ergative pattern for marking third-person core arguments of independent clauses, whereas the examples in (23) show the accusative pattern in aspectless complement clauses.

Q'ANJOB'AL

(22) a. a=Ø=ton   no'   ti'   ch-Ø=y-il   heb'   hin=mam
FOC=B3=DEM   PRON:animal   PROX   ICP-**B3**=**A3**-see   PL3   A1SG=father
          w=ichmam
          A1SG=grandfather
       'It is this animal that my grandparents see.' (Francisco Pascual 2007:175)

b. asan   xin   tolto=k'al   q-Ø='ok   y=iqatz   ch'en   kamyon   ti
only   then   still=DUR   POT-**B3**=enter   A3-load   CLF   truck   PROX
       'Well, the truck-load is still going to get in.' (Francisco Pascual 2007:196)

Q'ANJOB'AL

(23) a. x-Ø=tzaqay   [**Ø**=**y**-il-on   s-masanil]
CP-B3=be.able   **B3**=**A3**-see-SD   A3-everything
       'He was able to see everything.' (Francisco Pascual 2007:90)

b. asta=k'al   hoq-Ø=y-al   [y-ok   mojanil   tu']
until=DUR   POT-B3=A3-say   A3-enter   marriage   DST
       'Until he says that the marriage ceremony can be celebrated.' (Francisco Pascual 2007:90)

The following examples from Awakatek illustrate the split triggered by the presence of an adverb preceding the dependent clause. The second-person A, (24a), and S (24b), show the same marker, whereas O, (24c), is marked differently.

AWAKATEK

(24) a. ye   **aw**-il-ool   Ø
when   A2SG-see-ACT.INF   B3SG
       'When you saw him.' (Larsen 1981:137)

b. ye   **aw**-uul-e'n
when   A2SG-arrive.here-NMLZ
       'When you arrived.' (Larsen 1981:136)

c. ye   t-il-ool   **axh**
when   A3SG-see-ACT.INF   **PRON.2SG**
       'When he saw you.' (Larsen 1981:137)

Comrie (1978:377–8) and others have considered that the dependency-based split in Mayan resulted from nominalizations in a way similar to the aspect-based split, where the Set A marker originally marked a nominal possessor. Examples such as (24b) from Awakatek support this hypothesis since the verb overtly bears a nominalizer. However, the nominalization hypothesis is unsuitable for explaining the accusative pattern in Q'anjob'alan languages since none of these languages make use of overt nominalizers in the dependent structures that provoke a split.

Mocho' is the only Mayan language that exhibits a type of split ergativity governed by lexical features of the argument where the highest-ranking participants follow the accusative pattern and the lowest-ranking participants follow the ergative pattern (Larsen and Norman 1979:352; Dixon 1994:83–94). SAPs are marked on the verb according to an accusative alignment: both S and A referring to SAPs are cross-referenced on verbs by Set A prefixes in all aspect and syntactic contexts, whereas an O referring to an SAP is always marked with Set B suffixes (25).

MOCHO'
(25) a. eewi   **ii**-wa'-i   bweno
      yesterday   **A1SG**-eat-IS   well
      'Yesterday, I ate well.' (Martin 1998:203)

     b. k-**ii**-patzbe'-Ø   eeqan
       POT-**A1SG**-deceive-B3   tomorrow
       'I will lie (to him) tomorrow.' (Martin 1998:204)

     c. naabaa   ch-aa-patzbe'-**qin**
       only   ICP-A2SG-deceive-**B1SG**
       'You're just lying to me.' (Martin 1998:204)

Ergative alignment is found when the arguments refer to third persons. In this context, S and O are marked with Set B, while A is marked with Set A, as it is common in the rest of the family (26).

MOCHO'
(26) a. **Ø**-ook-i   ch-antiil-oq   oso
      B3-enter-IS   A3-wife-IRR   bear
      'She became the bear's (so-called) wife.' (Martin 1998:202)

     b. **ch**-ik'-a-**Ø**   noonh   ch-antiil-e'
       A3-carry-TS-**B3**   DIR:going   A3-wife-PL
       'They took their wives.' (Martin 1998:208)

Thus, Mocho' is unique among the Mayan languages since split marking is based on the semantic features of the core arguments.

4 THE TRIPARTITE PATTERN

Ch'orti' is the only Mayan language that exhibits three sets of pronominal markers and makes use of two alignment patterns triggered by an aspectual distinction. The three sets are shown in Table 9.2.

TABLE 9.2 THE THREE SETS OF PRONOMINAL MARKERS OF CH'ORTI'

Person	Set A	Set B	Set C
1SG	in-/ni-	-en	in-
2SG	a-	-et	i-
3SG	u-	-Ø	a-
1PL	ka-	-on	ka-
2PL	i-	-ox	ix-
3PL	u-...-ob'	-ob'	a-...-ob'

(Quizar 1979)

In completive aspect Ch'orti' shares with the rest of the Mayan languages the ergative pattern whereby Set A marks A, (27a), while Set B marks S, (27c), and O, (27b). Non-verbal predicates, as in (27d), mark their subject with Set B in all conditions.

CH'ORTI'

(27) a. **in**-ira-Ø   e   winik
       A1SG-see-B3SG   DET   man
       'I saw the man.' (Quizar 1979:43)

    b. e   winik   u-ira-**en**
       DET   man   A3SG-see-**B1SG**
       'The man saw me.' (Quizar 1979:44)

    c. k'axi-**en**   ta   ch'en
       fall-**B1SG**   PREP   hole
       'I fell into the hole.' (Quizar 1979:44)

    d. pakar-**en**
       upside.down-**B1SG**
       'I am upside down.' (Quizar 1979:45)

On the other hand, in the incompletive aspect, Chorti' follows a tripartite marking pattern whereby Set A marks A, (28a), Set B marks O, (28a), and a third set, Set C, marks S, (28b).

CH'ORTI'

(28) a. **u**-kohk-o-Ø
       A3SG-wait for-SS-**B3SG**
       'He waits for him.' (Quizar and Knowles-Berry 1988:79)

    b. **a**-k'ot-oy
       C3SG-arrive-SS
       'He arrives.' (Quizar and Knowles-Berry 1988:79)

Notice that in completive aspect the marker coding S follows the predicate, (27c), while in incompletive aspect, the marker coding S precedes the predicate, (28c). Thus, the order of morphemes also signals a different alignment pattern: in completive aspect the marker signaling S and O follows the verb and the marker signaling A precedes it, in incompletive aspect the markers for A and S precede the verb whereas the marker for O follows it. This is sketched as follows:

Alignment type signaled by order of person markers in Ch'orti':

Completive aspect	A (Ergative)	– V– O (Absolute)
		V – S (Absolute)
Incompletive aspect	A (Nominative)	– V – O (Accusative)
	S (Nominative)	– V

5 THE NEUTRAL PATTERN

Mamean languages show an ergative alignment pattern in finite independent clauses, as shown in the examples in (29) from Ixtahuacán Mam (England 1983b) where

O and S are cross-referenced on the verb with Set B, while the A is marked with Set A.

IXTAHUACÁN MAM
(29) a. ma   tz'=etz   **n**-tzyu-'n=a
        PROX B2SG=DIR A1SG-grab-DS=1SG/2SG
        'I grabbed you.' (England 2013:119)

   b. ma   **chin**=etz t-tzyu-'n=a
        PROX **B1SG**=DIR A2PL-grab-DS=2SG/1SG
        'You grabbed me.' (England 2013:119)

   c. ma   **chin** b'eet=a
        PROX **B1SG** walk=1SG
        'I walked.' (England 1983a: 2)

In addition to the unmarked ergative pattern, Mam exhibits a neutral alignment system in which all core arguments (O, A and S) are marked with Set A in the contexts of aspectless dependent clauses (following a group of temporal subordinators and adverbs, as well as aspectless purpose, result and stative relative clauses) (England 1983b: 247). The following examples from Ixtahuacán and Cajolá Mam illustrate the neutral pattern. In (30a) and (31a) both third-person A and O are marked with Set A, the same set that indexes S in examples (30b) and (31b).

IXTAHUACÁN MAM
(30) a. ok   **t**-ku'-x   **ky**-awa-'n   xjaal   kjo'n
        when:POT A3SG-DIR-DIR A3PL-plant-DS person cornfield
        'When the people plant the cornfield.' (England 1983b: 259)

   b. ela   t=b'aj   meq't   n-Ø-xi'   t-waa-'n   xjaal
        when A3SG=DIR be.heated ICP-B3SG-DIR A3SG-eat-DS person
        'When it was heated, the person ate it.' (England 1983a: 10)

CAJOLÁ MAM
(31) a. teej   **t**-tzaj   **t**-na-'n
        when A3SG-DIR A3SG-remember-DS
        'When she evoked him.'

   b. o'kx   **t**-uul-t   klemensya
        then A3SG-come-again Clemencia
        'And then Clemencia came.' (Pérez Vail 2014:27)

This pattern, which England (1983b: 257–64) describes as a case of "spreading ergativity", appears only in the Mamean languages Mam, Teko (Pérez Vail 2007), and Awakatek. England (1983a) uses comparative data from Awakatek and Ixil to explain the neutral alignment system in Mam as an overgeneralization of an original accusative split system occurring in dependent clauses still attested in Ixil. In Ixil Set A marks only S and A in dependent clauses, while O is marked with Set B in all conditions, similar to the conditions discussed in the Q'anjob'al examples in (23). In Mam, most transitive verbs require a grammaticalized intransitive motion verb functioning as directional which precedes the lexical transitive verb. Probably due to the effect of clause union (Zavala 1993:136–51), O is marked on the directional. It is likely that in dependent clauses, Set A spread from marking only S of lexical intransitive verbs (the pattern attested in Ixil) to marking O on the directional which was originally an intransitive verb. Thus, the basic intransitive and transitive verb structures of dependent clauses of Mam gave rise to the patterns schematized in (32).

(32) a. Dependent intransitive verb: S(Set A)-IV
     b. Dependent transitive verb: O(Set A)-directional   A(Set A)-TV

From cases such as (32b), Mam extended the neutral marking by analogy to the few cases where transitive verbs appear without a preceding directional, as in (33).

IXTAHUACÁN MAM
(33) ok   qo   tzaalaj-al   ok   **t-q-il**   u'j   t-e
     POT B1PL   be happy-POT   when   A3SG-A1PL-see   book   A2SG-RN/pos
     yool   t-e   I'tzal
     word   A3SG-RN/POS   Ixtahuacán
     'We will be happy when we see the Ixtahuacán dictionary.' (England 1983b: 260)

In contrast, Awakatek restricted the neutral pattern to transitive verbs with preverbal directionals, (34a) and (34b), but maintained the ergative pattern when the transitive verb had postverbal directionals or no directional at all, (34c).

AWAKATEK
(34) a. ye   **a**-b'een-e'n   **w**-uky'-aal
        DET A2SG-go-NMLZ   A1SG-carry-INF
        'When I carried you off,. . .' (Larsen 1981:141)

     b. ye   **aw**-uul-e'n
        DET A2PL-arrive.here-NMLZ
        'When you arrived. . .' (Larsen 1981:125)

     c. ye   t-il-ool   **axh**
        DET A3SG-see-INF   B2SG
        'When he saw you.' (Larsen 1981:125)

Thus, Awakatek shows a complex system that England interprets as midway between Ixil and Mam and that, she suggests, may be taken as a model of how the present-day Mam neutral system evolved, as sketched in Table 9.3.

TABLE 9.3 THE SPREAD OF ERGATIVE MARKER TO CONVEY S AND O OF DEPENDENT CLAUSES IN MAMEAN LANGUAGES

Language	Set A	Set B	Contexts in dependent clauses
Ixil	S/A	O	All
Awakatek	S/A	O	With postverbal directionals or no directional
	S/A/O		With preverbal directionals
Mam, Teko	S/A/O		All

6 THE AGENTIVE PATTERN

In addition to the ergative and accusative patterns conditioned by incompletive aspect, a number of languages exhibit an agentive alignment pattern motivated by the semantic role of the single argument of intransitive predicates. These are Mopan (Danziger 1996), one of the four Yucatecan languages; Chol and Chontal, both languages of the Western Cholan subgroup (Vázquez Álvarez 2002; Gutiérrez Sánchez 2004; Osorio May 2005, 2016); and Poqomchi', one of the ten K'ichean languages. Intransitive predicates in these languages enter into two different syntactic constructions. In the first one, as is common with intransitive verbs of any type within the majority of the Mayan languages, the subject is marked directly on the lexical verb in completive aspect with Set B (35a), whereas in the second construction, the notional subject of the intransitive predicate is marked in all conditions on a light-verb with Set A, as in (35b). The second construction is a complex structure headed by a transitive light-verb whose syntactic subject is marked with Set A and its object is marked with Set B cross-referencing an agentive nominalized intransitive verb.

CHONTAL

(35) a. t'ëb-Ø-on   të   te'
     ascend-PFV-B1   PREP   tree
     'I went up on top of the tree.' (Osorio May 2016:49)

   b. kë-che-n-Ø   ts'e'n-e
     A1-do-TS.ICP.DER-B3   laugh-NMLZ
     'I laugh.' (Osorio May 2016:56)

The different way the subject is marked within the particular construction, as ergative or as absolutive, indicates the nature of the involvement of the single participant of the event portrayed. When the notional subject is a volitional entity, it is coded as the subject of a transitive light-verb with Set A, in contrast, if it refers to a non-volitional or an affected entity, S is coded with Set B on the lexical verb.

In Chol and Chontal, non-verbal predicates and non-agentive intransitive verbs in completive mark their subject with Set B, the same set that marks primary objects (PO) of transitive verbs under all conditions. For instance, in the Chol example in (36a), the first-person suffix -oñ marks the PO of the clause headed by the transitive verb *pijty* 'wait' and the S of the clause headed by the intransitive verb *chäm* 'die'. The same marker indicates the subject of the non-verbal predicate *wiñik* 'be a man' in (36b).

CHOL

(36) a. y-om-Ø=äx=tyo   mi a-pijty-añ-**oñ**=la   ba'-ora
     A3-want-B3=AFFIRM=still ICP A2-wait-SS.DTV-**B1SG**=PL when-time
     mi ta'=x   chäm-i-y-**oñ**
     Q   CP=AFFIRM die-IS-EP-**B1SG**
     'It would be good if you keep waiting for me until I have died.'

   b. wiñik-**oñ**
     man-**B1SG**
     'I am a man.'

Chol verbs that mark S with Set B in completive aspect include eventuality predicates that convey: change of location, change of state, inchoative, and phase verbs, such as the ones shown in Table 9.4 (Gutiérrez Sánchez 2004).

TABLE 9.4 EXAMPLES OF NON-AGENTIVE INTRANSITIVE VERBS

Change of location

och 'enter'	*ju'b* 'descend'	*jul* 'arrive here'
k'äjk 'ascend, go up'	*k'ax* 'cross'	*k'oty* 'arrive there'
lets 'ascend'	*majl* 'go'	*ñijk* 'move'
säjl 'cross'	*sajp* 'descend'	*tyäl* 'come'

Change of state

ujp' 'collapse, crumble'	*bajk'* 'be wrapped'	*bäjl* 'set the sun'
bijty' 'get a fright, startle'	*bo'y* 'get bored'	*bul* 'come off'
ch'ojy 'wake up'	*ch'ujy* 'get up'	*chäm* 'die'
chijp 'get loose'	*jäjl* 'slip'	*jejm* 'collapse'
jojch 'fell' 'be born (birds)'	*jojm* 'pile up'	*jujp'* 'get fat'
k'ajl 'come unstuck'	*kijts'* 'break up'	*kol* 'grow'
lejm 'burn'	*lijk'* 'get tired'	*mäjk* 'get cloudy'
ñajay 'forget'	*p'ojl* 'breed'	*pajay* 'die'
päjk 'get dirty'	*pojm* 'blister'	*sijty* 'fall'
sojk 'get crazy'	*sujp'* 'immerse'	*ty'ujy* 'drip'
tyäjts' 'slip'	*tyejch* 'get up, wake up'	*tyojp'* 'be born'
xejw 'get tipped over'	*xijty'* 'surrender'	*xujl* 'break'
yäjl 'fell'	*jux-k'iy* 'slip'	*jits'-kuy* 'faint'

Inchoative (noun/adjective + inchoative suffix)

säk-an 'become white'	*tsäts-an* 'become hard'	*wiñik-iy-el* 'become a man'

Phase and modal verbs

ujtyl 'finish'	*joloñ* 'finish'	*jil* 'finish'
säjl 'finish'	*ñijl* 'begin'	*kaj* 'begin'
kel 'begin'	*mejl* 'be able'	

Unlike non-agentive verbs, agentive intransitive predicates do not mark S with Set B. Predicates such as *troñ* 'work' and *ch'uj* 'pray', among others, whose notional subject refers to a volitional agent, enter into the transitive light-verb construction in order to receive inflectional morphology. In this construction, the transitive light-verb *cha'l* 'to do' bears the morphological information that conveys aspect, person, and status suffixes, while a nominalized form of the verb functions as object of the light-verb. The notional subject of the intransitive predicate is marked on the transitive light-verb with Set A, irrespective of aspect, (37a) and (37b). Agentive verbs cannot appear directly inflected by a Set B marker, as shown by the ill-formed structure in (37c).

CHOL

(37) a. bajche' tyi **k-cha'l-e-Ø**   troñ-el   tyi   montañaj-tyak
    since   CP   **A1-do-**TS.CP.DEP **-**B3   work-NMLZ   PREP   mountain-PL
    'Since I worked in the mountains.'

   b. mi   **i-cha'-añ-Ø**   ch'uj-el
    ICP   **A3-do-**TS.ICP.DEP-B3   pray-NMLZ
    'He prays.'

   c. *tyi   troñ-i-y-**oñ**
    CP   work-IS-EP-**B1SG**
    Intended reading: 'I worked.'

Chol agentive predicative stems are of two types: (i) stems that receive an overt nominalizer when occurring in the light-verb construction, and (ii) bare stems without

TABLE 9.5 EXAMPLES OF AGENTIVE PREDICATE STEMS

Agentive stems with overt nominalizer

ajñ-el 'run'	*tse'ñ-al* 'laugh'	*k'äñ-ol* 'cook'
ñuxej-el 'swim'	*si'-bal* 'cut firewood'	*p'olm-al* 'sell'
oj-bal 'cough'	*tsojty-el* 'crawl'	*misej-el* 'sweep'
ñaj-al 'dream'	*oñ-el* 'scream'	*juch'-bal* 'grind'

Action nouns

ja'tsijñ 'sneeze'	*woj* 'bark'	*lojk* 'fart'
bots 'sprout'	*tsijb* 'write'	*ts'ak* 'cure'
lojk 'boil'	*xej* 'vomit'	*ch'uyu'b* 'whistle'
ñojk' 'snore'	*tyis* 'fart'	*loty* 'deceive'
soñ 'dance'	*chu'* 'suck'	*jula'* 'visit'

morphological derivation. The predicative stems of the last type may express simultaneously the semantics associated with canonical nouns or verbs and for this reason they are known in the Mayan literature as verbal nouns or action nouns (Larsen and Norman 1979:356, Kaufman 1990:103–4). Illustrative examples of each type of agentive stem appear in Table 9.5.

Chol exhibits the features common in languages of the agentive type (Mithun 1991:511). Various groups of Chol intransitive verbs exhibit both non-agentive and agentive behavior. The difference in behavior correlates with a change in meaning. A verb with an agentive subject takes Set A and participates in the light-verb construction, whereas the same verb with a non-agentive subject takes Set B and does not participate in the light-verb construction; this is what Dixon (1994:78–82) called the fluid-S pattern. In (38a) the event of jumping is portrayed as an unplanned action caused by the existence of bugs under the referent, whereas in (38b), expressed through the light-verb construction, the event is portrayed as a volitional act.

CHOL

(38) a. tyi lujty'-i-y-**oñ**
      CP jump-IS-EP-**B1**
      'I jumped around.' (because some ants bit me)

    b. tyi **k**-cha'l-e-Ø   lujty'-el
      CP **A1**-do-TS.CP.DEP-B3 jump-NMLZ
      'I jumped around.' (I was playing with a rope).

The use of different constructions with some predicates distinguishes inanimate subjects, which are always non-volitional, from human subjects, in cases when they perform an action with control and volition. With inanimate subjects the intransitive construction is used, whereas with human subjects the light-verb construction is used instead (39).

CHOL

(39) a. tyi lets-i-Ø   i-tyojol
      CP ascend-IS-**B3** A3-price
      'The price went up.'

    b. tyi **i**-cha'l-e-Ø   lets-el
      CP **A3**-do-TS.CP.DEP-B3 ascend-NMLZ
      'He climbed (on the ladder).'

In Chol, many positional stems behave as both non-agentive and agentive predicates. With some roots the change of construction conveys a change of state undergone by the subject, (40a), versus an activity performed in a specific position by a volitional subject, (40b) and (40c).

CHOL
(40) a. tyi   wa'-le-y-**oñ**
      CP   stand-POS.SS.CP-EP-**B1**
      'I stood up.'

    b. tyi   k-cha'l-e-Ø   wa'-tyäl
        CP   A1-do-TS.CP.DEP-B3   stand-NMLZ.POS
        'I urinated.' (Male speaker)

    c. tyi   k-cha'l-e-Ø   tsuty-tyäl
        CP   A1SG-do-TS.CP.DEP-B3   crouch.down-NMLZ.POS
        'I urinated.' (Female speaker)

Like positionals, a group of derived ideophonic roots forming verbal bases enter into both constructions. The subject of the agentive construction has control over the action, whereas the subject of the non-agentive construction is affected by the action (41).

CHOL
(41) a. tyi   pär-pär-ñi-y-**oñ**
      CP   ONOM-REDUP-AFF-EP-**B1SG**
      'I was shivering.'

    b. tyi   k-cha'l-e-Ø   pär-pär-ñi-y-el
        CP   A1SG-do-TS.CP.DEP-B3   ONOM-REDUP-AFF-EP-NMLZ
        'I moved producing the noise of "pärpär".'

Poqomchi' (K'ichean) is another language where the argument-marking pattern divides intransitive predicates into two subclasses. Similar to Western Cholan languages, non-agentive verbs in Poqomchi' mark their subjects with Set B, (42), while agentive predicates obligatorily appear in a nominalized form functioning as the object of a light-verb construction. In Poqomchi', a major group of non-agentive verbs refers to events that encode change of state and change of location.

POQOMCHI'
(42) a. x-Ø-kim-ik   i   kixlaan
        CP-B3SG-die-IS   DET   chicken
        'The chicken died.'

    b. x-in-q'uht-ik   pan   johtik
        CP-B1SG-get.tired-IS   PREP   ascend
        'I got tired going uphill.'

Unlike non-agentive intransitive verbs, agentive stems cannot mark their subject with Set B (absolutive) on the lexical predicate, (42a). Within the light-verb construction, the notional subject is coded with Set A in all contexts. Poqomchi', unlike the Western Cholan languages, requires that the nominalized agentive stem in object position be marked with a possessor coreferential with the Set A marker on the light-verb, (43b) and (43c).

POQOMCHI'
(43) a. * x-Ø-**ab'ix**-ik
          CP-B3SG-**plant**-IS
          Intended reading: 'He planted.'

      b. x-Ø-**i**-b'an   **r**-ab'iix
          CP-B3SG-**A3SG**-do   A3-corn.field
          'He planted.'

      c. x-Ø-**in**-b'an   **n**-se'-eel
          CP-B3SG-**A1SG**-do   A1-laugh-NMLZ
          'I laughed.'

A set of intransitive verbs in Poqomchi' enters into both constructions. The light-verb construction is used when the S refers to a volitional agent that controls the action, while the same verb occurring in the intransitive construction refers to actions performed by a less controlling subject affected by the action (44).

POQOMCHI'
(44) a. x-Ø-oq'-ik
          CP-B3SG-cry-IS
          'He cried.' (Context: chopping onion, being a baby, being angry or happy)

      b. x-Ø-i-b'an   r-oq'-iim
          CP-B3SG-A3SG-do   A3SG-cry-NMLZ
          'He cried.' (Context: He acts as if he is sad, or he enjoys crying.)

Until recently the only Mayan language that had been reported to have an agentive system was Mopan (Danziger 1996). As in other Yucatecan languages, Mopan transitive verbs mark the ergative argument with Set A and the absolutive argument with Set B, (45).

MOPAN
(45)   ko'ox   **in**-wichn-es-Ø-**ech**
          HORTATIVE   **A1**SG-bathe-CAUS-TR.SUBJ-**B2SG**
          'Let's go and I'll bathe you.' (Danziger 1996:384)

Recall that Yucatecan languages exhibit an aspect-based split that results in an accusative alignment. Unlike other Yucatecan languages, only non-agentive intransitive verbs exhibit an aspect-based split in Mopan. This class of verbs marks its S with Set B in completive aspect (46a), but with Set A in incompletive aspect, (46b).

MOPAN
(46) a. nak'-Ø-**ij**   t-u-wich   tunich
          ascend-CP-**B3**   PREP-A3-face   stone
          'He climbed up onto a stone.' (Danziger 1996:392)

b. walak-oo'   **u**-nak'-äl
   HAB-B3PL   A3-ascend-NMLZ
   'They always climb up.' (Danziger 1996:392)

In contrast, intransitive agentive predicates mark their single argument with Set A under all conditions, independently of aspect. Unlike non-agentive verbs, agentive predicates in Mopan require that all aspectual distinctions be conveyed by higher predicates taking as complement the nominal form of the agentive predicate whose possessor refers to the single argument performing the event with volition and control. Completive aspect is expressed through the phase verb *job'* 'finish' or the light-verb *uch* 'occur', while incompletive aspect is conveyed with the grammaticalized durative auxiliary *tan*, as shown in the pair of examples in (47).

MOPAN
(47) a. job'-Ø-ij   **u**-xej   a   tz'ub'
        finish-CP-B3   A3-vomit   DET   boy
        'The boy finished vomiting.' (Danziger 1996:395)

   b. uch-Ø-ij   **in**-lox
      occur-CP-B3   A1SG-fight
      'I fought.' (Danziger 1996:393)

   c. a   tz'ub'-u   jab'ix   tan   **u**-yawat
      DET   child-FOC   like   DUR   A3-yell
      'The child, seems like he's yelling.' (Danziger 1996:393)

There are two features that make Mopan different from Poqomchi'. First, the Mopan light-verb is intransitive while that of Poqomchi' is transitive, and second, the matrix verb in Mopan does not bear a coreferential person marker with the possessor of the agentive predicate as Poqomchi' does.

To sum up, within the Mayan family, Chol, Tabasco Chontal, Mopan and Poqomchi' are the only four languages that developed an agentive alignment pattern employing the two original sets of pronominal markers and the use of the light-verb construction in which the agentive predicates function as nouns (action nouns or nominalizations). The coding pattern for distinguishing non-agentive from agentive verbs is very similar in the two Western Cholan languages, being more elaborated in Chol than in Tabasco Chontal, with more items within the agentive class, and with more verbs showing fluid subject. Within Western Cholan, the semantic motivation for using one construction over the other to mark the S is still very transparent, which indicates that the system is an innovation traced back not even to proto-Cholan, but only to proto-Western Cholan. The development of agentive alignment in Mopan may have arisen as a result of contact with Western Cholan languages, although the synchronic manifestation of the pattern in Mopan differs in terms of the light-verb involved in the construction, and the constituent within the light-verb construction where the agentive subject is overtly marked. Western Cholan languages mark the agentive argument on the transitive light-verb and not on the nominalized agentive stem, while Mopan exhibits a complex inventory of light-verbs, all of them intransitives, and marks the logical subject as possessor of the agentive stem.

Poqomchi' also borrowed the agentive alignment pattern from Western Cholan languages. This claim is based on the assumption that such a parallel manifestation of an agentive pattern could not have been a coincidental independent development. The alignment patterns within Chol, Tabasco Chontal and Poqomchi' share several features. In addition to the ergative pattern, these three languages exhibit an aspectual split with non-agentive verbs whereby S is marked with Set B only in the completive aspect, while Set A is required in the incompletive aspect. Also, the three languages use the light-verb construction headed by a light-verb meaning 'do' in which the agentive stem behaves as a regular noun in O function. In addition, all three languages show semantic alternations with a large set of verbs based on volitionality and control. In all of them the predicates that encode change of location, change of state, and inchoatives are treated as members of the paradigm of non-agentive verbs, while activity predicates are treated as agentive predicates.

However there are also some differences with respect to the way the agentive pattern operates in each of the three languages. Poqomchi', unlike Western Cholan languages, has a very small set of purely agentive verbs. In addition, in Poqomchi', agentive stems that function as objects of the light-verb are expressed as possessed nouns, whereas in Western Cholan they occur as non-possessed nouns. In Poqomchi', unlike Western Cholan, some activity verbs that convey meanings such as 'snore', 'deceive', 'bother', 'bark', and 'cough' are treated as non-agentive verbs. In Western Cholan, ideophones and positionals are treated as both agentive and non-agentive and occur in both constructions, whereas in Poqomchi' they are treated as non-agentive stems only. The fact that no other K'ichean language exhibits an agentive alignment pattern supports the assumption that Poqomchi' acquired the agentive alignment pattern through contact from Western Cholan.

7 THE INVERSE PATTERN

Direct vs. inverse alignment is involved when the morphosyntactic realization of a clause is determined by the relative rank of A and O on some dimension like person, animacy, or topicality. In the 'direct' construction, A outranks O on the relevant dimension; in the 'inverse' construction, O outranks A. The direct construction is unmarked, whereas the inverse is marked. There are only two languages in the Mayan family in which the opposition is determined by person: Huastec (Zavala 1994) and Cajolá Mam (Pérez Vail 2014). In all the others, the opposition is found only with third-person coarguments and is determined by factors like animacy, definiteness, and topicality. Following Algonquian tradition, the higher third person is referred to here as the *proximate* and the lower third person as the *obviative*. Further, except for Huastec, the opposition between direct and inverse in Mayan is realized *syntactically* through the choice of construction, with direct clauses realized as active transitives and inverse clauses realized as non-transitives of some type. In Huastec, the opposition based on the person hierarchy is realized *morphologically* through the form of agreement.

The five contexts that motivate different marking patterns in inverse languages are sketched in (48).

(48)		*A*		*O*
	(a) Direct	(SAP	:	3)
	(b) Inverse	(3	:	SAP)
	(c) Local	(SAP	:	SAP)
	(d) 3:3 Direct	(3 [PROX]:		3[OBV])
	(e) 3:3 Inverse	(3 [OBV] :		3[PROX])

Huastec exhibits a morphological inverse system in contexts (a) and (b), i.e., when one of the coarguments is first or second person (a SAP). Huastec, like other Mayan languages, has two different sets of person markers. Set B signals the S of intransitive verbs, (49a), and the PO of transitive verbs, (49c), whereas Set A signals the A, (49b). When one of the coarguments of the transitive verb is a SAP the language shows a hierarchical agreement system since the verb takes only one overt person marker referring to either the A or the PO. The verb bears an ergative marker when the A outranks the PO in the person hierarchy, (49b). On the other hand, the verb bears the absolutive marker when the PO outranks the A within the same hierarchy, (49c). The person hierarchy that operates in Huastec is: 1>2>3. The morpheme *ti-* in (49c) signals that the SAP coincides with the PO.

HUASTEC
(49) a. **in**   ul-tz-itz
      B1SG arrive.here-CP-already
      'I already arrived.'

    b. jee' **u**   chi'-th-aal   u   lojoobil
       here A1SG come-CAUS-ICP A1SG hoe
       'Here, I brought my hoe.'

    c. ani yab ø che'-nek u   aamu ti-k-**in**   pijch-iy
       and NEG B3 come-PFV A1SG boss INV-DEP-**B1SG** feed-TS
       'My boss has not come to feed me.'

Table 9.6 shows the agreement morpheme used for all combinations of A and PO. The paradigm of ergative proclitics (Set A) appears in the column at the extreme right of Table 9.6. The Set B morphemes and their allomorphs appear at the bottom of Table 9.6. The morpheme *ti-* (or *t-*) is analyzed as in inverse marker that appears whenever the O is a SAP. Thus, it appears in canonical inverse constructions (3:SAP) and in local constructions (SAP:SAP). Huastec is a language that has assimilated the local combinations within the same system of non-local combinations, a pattern that has been attested in other inverse languages. Cross-linguistically in inverse languages, local configurations can follow two major patterns. In the first pattern, local configurations are treated as a different subsystem that does not follow the regular direct or inverse marking model. In the second pattern, local configurations are members of the regular direct and inverse alternations that include a third person and a SAP. Huastec belongs to the second group of languages since it has assimilated both local configurations (1:2 and 2:1) as inverse constructions with an overt inverse marker. The local combinations observed in Table 9.6 show some irregularities that can be explained historically as analogical changes when

TABLE 9.6 PRONOMINAL PROCLITICS IN POTOSINO HUASTEC

POA		1SG	1PL	2SG	2PL	3 SET A (Ergative)
	1SG			*t-u*	*t-(ix-)u*	*u*
	1PL			*t-u*	*t-(ix-)u*	*i*
	2SG	*t-in*	*t-u*			*a*
	2PL	*t-in*	*t-u*			*a*
	3	*t-in*	*t-u*	*t-i*	*t-i*	*in*
SET B (Absolutive)		*in*	*u*	*it*	*ix/it*	*Ø/u*

compared to the more regular and conservative system observed in colonial Huastec (see Zavala 1994 for more discussion).

See below for the realization of clauses in Huastec in which both arguments are third person.

The person hierarchy is also relevant to the realization of clauses in Cajolá Mam, but the opposition is expressed through the choice of syntactic construction. In this language an active transitive clause is used to convey situations in which the A is a SAP and the O is third person. In both examples in (50), the SAP is coded with Set A, while the O is coded with Set B on the verb.

CAJOLÁ MAM

(50) a. n-**chi**   b'aj-x   **n**-k'le-'n=e'   txqan   wiir
ICP-**B3PL**   DIR-DIR   **A1SG**-carry-DS=1SG   many   child
'I take the group of children away.' (Pérez Vail 2014:46)

    b. ma   Ø=**t**-il=a   Wa'n
PROX   **B3SG=A2SG**-see=2SG   John
'You saw John.' (Pérez Vail 2014:1)

In contrast, a marked intransitive construction has to be used when the notional A is third person and the notional O is a SAP. In (51a), an intransitive structure is used where the notional O referring to first person is coded as S, and the notional A appears as an oblique headed by a relational noun. The ungrammatical example in (51b) shows that the active transitive construction is banned under these conditions.

CAJOLÁ MAM

(51) a. Ø=**in**-tza   chq'o-'n=e'   **t**-u'n=pe=tzun   qtzan
CP=**B1SG**-DIR   send-DS=1SG   **A3SG**-RN:by=ANAPHORIC=SO   deceased
    n-liib'=e'   qya
    A1SG-mother.in.law=1SG   woman
'I was sent off by my mother-in-law.'

    b. *Ø=**in**-tza   **t**-chq'o-'n=e'   qtzan   n-liib'=e'
CP=**B1SG**-DIR   **A3SG**-send-DS=1SG   deceased   A1SG-mother.in.law=1SG
    qya
    woman
Intended reading: 'My deceased mother-in-law sent me off.' (Pérez Vail 2014:3)

In addition to the passive with oblique agent, (51a), Cajolá Mam employs two other alternative constructions to convey situations with third-person agents acting on SAP patients. Both of these are marked constructions given that they are structurally intransitive but semantically transitive. The first is an antipassive construction with oblique patient, (52), and the second is an intransitive type of clause headed by an underived intransitive verb whose subject refers to the patient, followed by an oblique phrase expressing the agent, as illustrated in the examples in (53).

CAJOLÁ MAM

(52) a. Ø=tza   yooli=n=te   xhnuula   **w**-ee=ye'
B3SG=DIR   speak=AP=DET   lady   **A1SG**-RN:DAT=1SG
'The lady called me.' (Pérez Vail 2014:150)

b. ma   Ø=wuuli-n   Wa'n   **t**-ee=ya
   PROX **B3SG**=scold-AP John **A2SG**-RN:at=2SG
   'John scolded you.' (Pérez Vail 2014:144)

CAJOLÁ MAM
(53) a. in=a'   **n-qo**   kim=te'   **t-u'n**
    ICP=EMPH ICP-**B1PL** die=EMPH **A3SG**-RN:by
    'It (the catholic mass) kills us.' (Lit. 'We die by it') (Pérez Vail 2014:151)

b. ma   Ø=b'o'lj=a   **t-u'n**
   PROX **B2SG**=spoil=2SG **A3SG**-RN:by
   'He spoiled you.' (Lit. 'You got spoiled by it.') (Pérez Vail 2014:145)

DeLancey (1981) has argued, based on a cross-linguistic survey, that the ranking of a SAP and third person in inverse languages is determined by a universal hierarchy (SAP > 3rd), while the ranking of first and second persons is determined on a language-particular basis. In Cajolá Mam, the active transitive construction is disallowed when the agent is third person and the patient is a SAP. However when both coarguments are *local* participants (both SAPs), there are no restrictions in using the active, (54), or the various marked intransitive constructions to convey either 1:2 or 2:1 situations, as illustrated by the passive and antipassive constructions in (55). Thus, in Cajolá Mam, first and second person occupy the same position in the person hierarchy and for this reason local configurations are part of a different subsystem that does not follow the obligatory direct or inverse marking model.

CAJOLÁ MAM
(54) a. ok   **chin**   x-e'l   **t**-k'le-'n=a
    POT **B1SG** go-POT **A2SG**-take-DS=2SG
    'You will take me.'

b. ok   **k**-x-e'l   **n**-k'le-'n=a
    POT **B2SG**-DIR-POT **A1SG**-take-DS=2SG
    'I will take you.' (Pérez Vail 2014:153)

CAJOLÁ MAM
(55) a. ma   **tz'**-il-wi=ya   **w**-u'n=e'
    PROX **B2SG**-see-PSV=2SG **A1SG**-RN:by=1SG
    'I saw you./You were seen by me.' (Pérez Vail 2014:154)

b. in   Ø=yooli-n=a   **w**-i'j=e'
   ICP **B2SG**=speak-AP=2SG **A1SG**-RN:about=1SG
   'You talk about me.' (Pérez Vail 2014:154)

In Cajolá Mam, the unmarked/marked opposition in clauses that have one SAP argument is also found when both arguments are third person. The transitive active (direct) construction occurs when the third-person A outranks the third-person O in animacy or topicality. In contrast, the marked (inverse) construction occurs when the third-person notional O is higher in animacy or topicality than the third-person notional A. In the Algonquianist tradition, the NPs that pattern with SAPs are referred to as *proximates*, whereas the NPs that pattern with non-SAPs are referred to as *obviatives*. Therefore, in the person hierarchy of Algonquian languages, proximates are more prominent than obviatives. The fact that the same situation can be expressed using the direct or the inverse patterns has led some authors (Givón 1994) to treat inverse systems as a mechanism whose basic function is related to voice, in such a way that the direct construction is used when the A is more topical than the O, whereas the inverse construction is used when the O is more topical than the A. The inverse and direct patterns with two third-person arguments are sketched in (56).

(56)   **A**   **O**
      Direct   3/PROX   3'/OBV
      Inverse   3'/OBV   3/PROX

Cajolá Mam uses the same morphosyntax to convey the inverse/direct opposition when both participants are third person as the one used when one participant is a SAP. Languages of this type are said to have an *integrated inverse system* (Gildea 1994). In Cajolá Mam, unlike Algonquian languages, there is no morphological marking of obviation on NPs. However, the terminology used by Algonquianists to refer to high-ranked third-person vs. low-ranked third-person NPs will be maintained when talking about third-person NPs, since the distinction between proximates and obviatives is as relevant in Cajolá Mam as it is in Algonquian.

Aissen (1997, 1999) has shown that the principles which govern obviation in Algonquian are shared by Tsotsil, and some other languages that lack explicit markers indicating their status as obviatives or proximates. In these languages, as in Algonquian, it is possible to observe the effects of obviation in a specific set of syntactic contexts where, due to the semantic and pragmatic properties of the coarguments involved, the construction has to be coded in active transitive form or in some non-transitive form. The syntactic contexts that trigger the obligatory use of inverse in Algonquian are the same as those that trigger the use of non-transitive clauses in Tsotsil and many other Mayan languages. Although in several cases the proximate or obviative status of the coarguments involved in a transitive clause depends on pragmatic factors related to topicality, there are two grammatical contexts within Algonquian languages in which the obviation status of the coarguments is completely syntacticized. That is, under specific conditions, a clause will follow only one of the two patterns: direct or inverse. A clause follows the direct pattern when the A is animate and the O inanimate. In (57), the transitive verb bears the morphological trappings of the direct marking pattern, i.e. the verb marks the high-ranking participant of the clause with an ergative person prefix since a high-ranking A (a human) acts on a low-ranking O (an animal).

CAJOLÁ MAM
(57) ma   Ø=t-il   xjaal   wixh
     PROX   B3SG=A3SG-see   person   cat
     'The person saw the cat.' (Pérez Vail 2014:182)

The situations portrayed in (58a) and (58b) are coded obligatorily with marked intransitive constructions (antipassive and passive with oblique agent), since the agent is a low-ranking NP (animal) acting on a high-ranking NP (human) expressing the patient. This type of situation cannot be coded using the active transitive structure, as shown by the ungrammatical example in (58c).

CAJOLÁ MAM

(58) a. ma Ø=tooki-n waakx **t**-e k'waal
   PROX **B3SG**=attack-AP cow **A3SG**-RN:to child
   'The cow charged at the child.' (Pérez Vail 2014:180)

 b. ma **tz'**-il-wi xjaal **t**-u'n wixh
   PROX **B3SG**-see-PSV person **A3SG**-RN:by cat
   'The person was seen by the cat.' (Pérez Vail 2014:187)

 c. *ma tz'-ok t-tooki-'n waakx k'waal
   PROX B3SG-DIR A3SG-attack-DS cow child
   Intended reading: 'The cow charged at the child.' (Pérez Vail 2014:180)

The realization of clauses with certain coreference relations involving possessors is also governed by obviation. When A is coreferential with the possessor of O, the clause can only be realized in the unmarked active form, as shown in (59).

CAJOLÁ MAM

(59) ma Ø=t-yo qya t-chmiil
  PROX B3SG=A3SG-wait woman A3SG-husband
  'The woman$_i$ waited for her$_i$ husband.' (Pérez Vail 2014:199)

A non-active clause is required in the opposite context, when the notional O is coreferential with the possessor of the subject. Under these conditions, the clause obligatorily follows the inverse pattern. The propositional content of (60) in Cajolá Mam cannot be conveyed by a direct clause.

CAJOLÁ MAM

(60) ma tz'-il-wi qya t-u'n t-chmiil
  PROX B3SG-see-PSV woman A3SG-RN:by A3SG-husband
  'The woman$_i$ was seen by her$_i$ husband.' (Pérez Vail 2014:200)

These restrictions are based in the fact that the possessor is always more prominent (proximate) than the possessed (obviative) and this status is shared with the coreferential argument (see discussion in Aissen 1997, 1999).

We saw above for Huastec that when the direct-inverse opposition is determined by person, it is expressed morphologically: when one argument is a SAP, agreement is hierarchical. When both arguments are third person, the opposition is expressed syntactically, as in Cajolá Mam. Huastec uses a passive construction when an obviative A acts on a proximate O, i.e., in the context where Cajolá Mam uses the non-active constructions triggered by obviation. The Huastec direct/active construction occurs obligatorily when the possessor of the O is coreferential with the A, as in (61).

HUASTEC

(61) **in** k'exeen-a' in kumpaale
  A3 tease-TS A3 friend
  i. 'He$_i$ was teasing his$_i$ friend.'
  ii. *'His$_i$ friend was teasing him$_i$'

The opposite configuration, in which the possessor of the A is coreferential with the PO, is obligatorily expressed using the passive construction with an oblique agent, as in (62).

HUASTEC

(62) taam   Ø   ool-chi-**n**-al-itz   an   ka'ap+neel k'al in   miim
     then   **B3** offer-APPL-**PSV**-ICP-already DET food   PREP A3 mother
     '[the boy is playing again] and he is being offered food by his mother.'

In sum, the Huastec passive with oblique agent construction is the equivalent of the Cajolá Mam non-active clause types occurring when the possessor of the subject is coreferential with the PO. However, while Cajolá Mam expresses the direct/inverse opposition with all persons through the choice of syntactic construction, Huastec expresses it morphologically when one argument of a transitive verb is a SAP, but syntactically when both are third person. Thus whereas Cajolá Mam exhibits an integrated inverse system, Huastec exhibits a split system.

Huastec differs from Cajolá Mam in that animacy is not relevant to determining the relative rank of third persons. This means that either active or passive constructions can be used to convey an event that includes a human agent and an inanimate patient or an inanimate agent and a human patient. However, a factor that does play a role for marking obviation in Huastec, similar to Cajolá Mam, is definiteness. Noun phrases in Huastec are ranked in a definiteness hierarchy. Clauses with definite agents acting on indefinite patients are obligatorily coded as active/direct, (63a), in contrast, clauses with an indefinite agent acting on a definite patient are obligatorily coded as passive, (63b).

HUASTEC

(63) a. juun   i   inik   **in**   tzu'-uw   a   kwaan
        one   INDF   man   **A3**   see-TS   HUM   John
        'Juan saw a man.'

   b. taam   ti   Ø   kal+een+ch-**at**   k'al   juun i kwee' chik
      then   CL   **B3**   assault-**PSV**.CP   PREP   one INDF thief PL
      'Then he was assaulted by some thieves.'

Unlike Cajolá Mam and Huastec, which exhibit a direct/inverse opposition both in cases in which one of the coarguments of a transitive clause is a SAP as well as when both coarguments are third person, there are languages within the family that only exhibit a direct/inverse opposition when both coarguments are third person. Pure obviation systems have been studied for the following Mayan languages: Tsotsil (Aissen 1997, 1999), Tseltal (Polian 2013), Tojolab'al (Curiel 2007), Q'anjob'al (Francisco Pascual 2007), Akatek (Zavala 1997; Zavala 2007) and Chol (Zavala 2007; Vázquez Álvarez 2011). These languages show a transitive/non-transitive alternation triggered by obviation but do not exhibit a direct vs. inverse alternation when a SAP is involved in a transitive clause. The passive construction used when A is obviative and O is proximate is a morphosyntactic device shared by all Mayan languages in which the grammar is sensitive to obviation. The passive construction is used when the A is inanimate and the O animate, (64), when the A is indefinite and the O definite, (65), and when the possessor of the A is coreferential with the O, (66).

CHOL
(64) mu'=ba   i-tyaj-ty-ä-tyak   tyi   chäme   li   la'=(a-)wakax=i
     ICP=Q   A3-find-PSV-NMLZ-PL   PREP   illness   DET   2PL=A2-cow=ENC
     'Did your cow get sick (sometimes)?' (Vázquez 2011:352)

TOJOLAB'AL
(65) ti   'il-j-i-Ø='a   y-uj   kristyano jumasa'
     there   see-PSV-IS-B3=DST   A3-by   people   PL
     'He was seen by people there.' (Curiel 2007:107)

TSELTAL
(66) Pero   ya   x-tal   il-ot-ok-Ø   y-u'un   te   y-ijts'in=e.
     but   ICP ICP.INTR-come   see-PSV-IRR-B3   A3-RN   DET   A3-brother=DET
     'But her little brother comes to see her.' (Polian 2013:256)

In addition to the passive construction, Tsotsil (Aissen 1999), Q'anjob'al (Francisco Pascual 2007) and Akatek (Zavala 2007) also make use of the agent focus construction to convey situations with obviative A's and proximate O's when A is extracted. In these languages the AF construction alternates with the passive when the A is inanimate and the O animate, (67), when the A is indefinite and the O definite, (68), and when the possessor of the A is coreferential with the O, (69).

Q'ANJOB'AL
(67) a=ø=k'al=ab'   xiwilal   tu   Ø=aq'-on   kam   ix
     EMPH=B3=DUR=REP   fear   that B3=do-AF   die   PRON:she
     'They say that the fear killed her.' (Francisco Pascual 2007:73)

TSOTSIL
(68) Mu   xa   buch'u   x-Ø-mak'lan-on
     NEG CLF who   NT-B3-feed-AF
     'There's no one to support him.' (Aissen 1999:457)

AKATEK
(69) ja'   naj   s-mam   naj   unin x-Ø-ii-on   toj   naj
     EMPH   N.CLF   A3-father   N.CLF boy   CP-B3-carry-AF   DIR:go   PRON:he
     'Hisᵢ father took the boyᵢ' (Zavala 2007:300)

In sum, Mayan languages have three of the four types of inverse and obviative systems known cross-linguistically (Gildea 1994). Listed in (i)–(iv) below, these are based on the following contexts:

(a)	Direct	(SAP	: 3)
(b)	Inverse	(3	: SAP)
(c)	Local	(SAP	: SAP)
(d)	3:3 Direct	(3 [PROX]:	3[OBV])
(e)	3:3 Inverse	(3 [OBV] :	3[PROX])

  (i) *inverse alignment*: a morphosyntactic opposition exists only for SAP:3 and
       3:SAP.
  (ii) *pure obviation system*: a morphosyntactic opposition exists only for 3[PROX]:
       3[OBV] vs. 3[OBV]: 3[PROX].

(iii) *integrated inverse system*: the same morphosyntactic opposition marks SAP:3 vs. 3:SAP and 3[PROX]: 3[OBV] vs. 3[OBV]: 3[PROX]

(iv) *split inverse system*: different morphosyntactic oppositions mark SAP:3 vs. 3:SAP and 3[PROX]: 3[OBV] vs. 3[OBV]: 3[PROX].

Out of these four systems, Mayan languages exhibit the last three types. Cajolá Mam exhibits an integrated inverse system in which the direct (active) vs. inverse (non-active) alternation is attested in clauses that include a SAP and also in clauses in which both coarguments are third-person participants. Huastec has a split inverse system that is expressed through agreement when a SAP is involved and an active vs. passive opposition triggered by obviation. Tsotsil, Tseltal, Tojolab'al, Q'anjob'al, Akatek and Chol, among others, exhibit a pure obviation system that use the active vs. non-active alternations triggered by obviation but do not exhibit an inverse vs. direct alternation when a SAP is involved in a transitive clause. The effects of obviation have been observed in a specific set of syntactic contexts that were first investigated by Aissen (1997, 1999). These contexts have been used as structural diagnostics for determining the languages in which obviation plays a crucial role. Further study on the pragmatics of different structures involving two participants has to be done in Mayan in order to shed light on other marked devices for encoding the "inverse" pragmatic function, namely the mechanisms used by languages to render an event in which O is treated as proximate and A as obviative.

8 CONCLUSION

The alignment patterns shown in Mayan languages have prompted extensive work both in describing the patterns found in individual languages, and in comparing the patterns found in the family and their specific diachronic developments. There has been significant work in distinguishing the ergative as a primary unmarked pattern from different secondary marked patterns, as well as the conditions that trigger the various types of splits and their historical sources. In addition to the ergative morphology, both early and recent work has established that in some languages, a set of grammatical phenomena operate according to ergative syntactic rules, but there is still more work to be done on this front. Research on discourse concerning the distribution of given and new information in Sakapultek and other Mayan languages has inspired important work that links ergative morphology to a "universal" discourse pattern where new discourse referents are introduced as absolutive arguments not as ergatives (Du Bois 1987). Recent work on Tsotsil and Chol has demonstrated that the distribution of new and given discourse referents does not align with morphological ergativity given that in these two Mayan languages, and probably in many others, the flow of information follows not an ergative pattern but an agentive one. New discourse referents are realized as O and S_O but not as A or S_A. Finally, the comparison of the patterns found in Mayan with patterns found in other language families has prompted the discoveries of unknown alignment systems such as the different types of inverse, agentive, and obviation systems found in a great number of Mayan languages of the different branches. The agenda for future research on Mayan alignment patterns needs to investigate the manifestation and diachronic development of the various split marking patterns, the effect of language contact in the development of non-ergative patterns, the exact morphosyntactic contexts that trigger the accusative pattern under dependency in the Huehuetenango area, the distribution of new and given discourse referents in languages of different branches taking in consideration factors such as agentivity and volitionality, and the relevance of obviation in the different languages of the family.

REFERENCES

Aissen, Judith. 1997. "On the syntax of obviation." *Language* 73: 705–50.

Aissen, Judith. 1999. "Agent focus and inverse in Tzotzil." *Language* 75: 451–85.

Berinstein, Ava. 1985. *Evidence for multiattachment in K'ekchi Mayan.* New York: Garland.

Berinstein, Ava. 1998. "Antipassive and 2–3 retreat in K'ekchi Mayan: Two constructions with the same verbal reflex." In *Studies in American Indian languages: description and theory*, ed. by Leanne Hinton and Pamela Munro, 212–22. Berkeley: University of California Press.

Bricker, Victoria R. 1981. "The source of the ergative split in Yucatec Maya." *Journal of Mayan Linguistics* 2: 83–127.

Buenrostro Díaz, Cristina. 2013. "La voz en Chuj de San Mateo Ixtatán." PhD diss., El Colegio de México, México, D.F.

Can Pixabaj, Telma Angelina. 2015. "Complement and purpose clauses in K'iche'." PhD diss., The University of Texas, Austin.

Comrie, Bernard. 1978. "Ergativity." In *Syntactic typology*, ed. by Winfred P. Lehmann, 329–94. Austin: University of Texas.

Coon, Jessica. 2010. "Rethinking split ergativity in Chol." *International Journal of American Linguistics* 76: 207–53.

Coon, Jessica. 2012. "Split ergativity and transitivity in Chol." *Lingua* 122: 241–56.

Craig, Colette. 1977. *The structure of Jacaltec.* Austin: University of Texas Press.

Curiel Ramírez Del Prado, Alejandro. 2007. "Estructura de la información, enclíticos y configuración sintáctica en tojol'ab'al." MA thesis, CIESAS, México.

Danziger, Eve. 1996. "Split intransitivity and active-inactive patterning in Mopan Maya." *International Journal of American Linguistics* 62: 379–414.

Dayley, Jon P. 1981. "Voice and ergativity in Mayan languages." *Journal of Mayan Linguistics* 2: 3–82.

Dayley, Jon P. 1990. "Voz y Ergatividad en Idiomas Mayas." In *Lecturas sobre la Lingüística Maya*, ed. by Nora C. England and Stephen Elliot, 335–98. Guatemala: CIRMA.

DeLancey, Scott. 1981. "An interpretation of split ergativity." *Language* 57: 626–57.

Dixon, Robert M. W. 1979. "Ergativity." *Language* 55: 59–138.

Dixon, Robert M. W. 1994. *Ergativity.* Cambridge: Cambridge University Press.

Du Bois, John. 1987. "The discourse basis of ergativity." *Language* 63: 805–55.

England, Nora C. 1983a. "Ergativity in Mamean (Mayan) languages." *International Journal of American Linguistics* 49: 1–19.

England, Nora C. 1983b. *A grammar of Mam, a Mayan language.* Austin: University of Texas Press.

England, Nora C. 2013. "Marking aspect and mood and inferring time in Mam (Mayan)." *Berkeley Linguistics Society* 33: 119–40.

England, Nora C., and Laura Martin. 2003. "Issues in the comparative argument structure analysis in Mayan narratives." In *Preferred argument structure: grammar as architecture for function*, ed. by John W. Du Bois, Lorraine E. Kumpf, and William J. Ashby, 131–57. Amsterdam/Philadelphia: John Benjamins.

Faarlund, Jan Terje. 2012. *A grammar of Chiapas Zoque.* Oxford: Oxford University Press.

Foris, David Paul. 2000. *A grammar of Sochiapan Chinantec.* Arlington: SIL International.

Francisco Pascual, Adán. 2007. "Transitividad y dependencia sintáctica y discursiva en Q'anjob'al." MA thesis, CIESAS, México.

Gildea, Spike. 1994. "Semantic and pragmatic inverse — 'inverse alignment' and 'inverse voice' — in Carib of Surinam." In *Voice and inversion. Typological studies in language*, vol 30, ed. by T. Givón, 187–230. Amsterdam: John Benjamins.

Givón, Talmy. 1994. "The pragmatics of de-transitive voice." In *Voice and inversion*, ed. by Talmy Givón, 3–44. Amsterdam: John Benjamins.

Gutiérrez Sánchez, Pedro. 2004. "Las clases de verbos intransitivos y el alineamiento agentivo en el chol de Tila, Chiapas." MA thesis, CIESAS, México.

Gutiérrez Sanchez, Pedro, and Roberto Zavala. 2005. "Chol and Chontal: two Mayan languages of the agentive type." Paper presented at The Typology of Stative-Active Languages, Max Planck Institute for Evolutionary Anthropology, Leipzig, Germany.

Hofling, Charles Andrew. 2000. *Itzaj Maya grammar*. Salt Lake City: Utah University Press.

Hofling, Charles Andrew. 2003. "Tracking the deer: nominal reference, parallelism and preferred argument structure in Itzaj Maya narrative genres." In *Preferred argument structure. Grammar as architecture for function*, ed. by John DuBois, Lorraine Kumpf, and William Ashby, 385–410. Amsterdam/Philadelphia: John Benjamins.

Kaufman, Terrence. 1990. "Algunos rasgos estructurales de los idiomas mayances con referencia especial al K'iche'." In *Lecturas sobre la Lingüística Maya*, ed. by Nora England and Stephen Elliot, 59–114. Guatemala: CIRMA.

Kaufman, Terrence, and William M. Norman. 1984. "An outline of proto-Cholan phonology, morphology and vocabulary." In *Phoneticism in Mayan hieroglyphic writing*, ed. by John S. Justeson and Lyle Campbell, 77–166. Albany: Institute for Mesoamerican Studies, State University of New York.

Larsen, Thomas W. 1981. "Functional correlates of ergativity in Aguacatec." *Berkeley Linguistics Society* 7: 136–53.

Larsen, Thomas W. 1987. "The syntactic status of ergativity in Quiché." *Lingua* 71: 33–59.

Larsen, Thomas W. 1988. "Manifestations of ergativity in Quiché grammar." PhD diss., University of California, Berkeley.

Larsen, Thomas W. 1990. "Notas sobre ergatividad en la gramática Maya." In *Lecturas sobre la lingüística Maya*, ed. by Nora C. England and Stephen R. Elliott, 319–34. Antigua, Guatemala: CIRMA.

Larsen, Thomas W., and William M. Norman. 1979. "Correlates of ergativity in Mayan grammar." In *Ergativity: Toward a theory of grammatical relations*, ed. by Frans Plank, 347–70. London: Academic Press.

Law, Danny, John Robertson, and Stephen Houston. 2006. "Split ergativity in the history of the Ch'olan branch of the Mayan language family." *International Journal of American Linguistics* 72: 415–50.

Martin, Laura. 1998. "Irrealis constructions in Mocho (Mayan)." *Anthropological Linguistics* 40: 198–213.

Martínez, Rosendo. 2012. "Las manifestaciones sintácticas, semánticas y discursivas de la agentividad en el tsotsil de Huixtán, Chiapas." MA thesis, CIESAS, Mexico D.F.

Mateo Toledo, Eladio. 2013. "Cláusulas sin aspecto e infinitivas en q'anjob'al." In *Clases léxicas, posesión y cláusulas complejas en lenguas de Mesoamérica*, ed. by Enrique Palancar and Roberto Zavala Maldonado, 247–76. México, D.F.:CIESAS.

Mithun Marianne. 1991. "Active-agentive case marking and its motivation." *Language* 67: 510–46.

Mó Isém, Romelia. 2006. "Fonología y Morfología del Poqomchi' Occidental." *Licenciatura* thesis, Universidad Rafael Landívar, Guatemala.

Osorio May, José del Carmen. 2005. "La morfología verbal en el yokot'an 'chontal' de Tecoluta, Nacajuca, Tabasco." MA thesis. México: CIESAS.

Osorio May, José del Carmen. 2016. "Temas de la sintaxis del yokot'an de Tecoluta, Nacajuca, Tabasco." PhD diss. México: CIESAS.

Pérez Vail, José Reginaldo. 2007. *Xtxolil yool B'a'aj: Gramátia tektiteka*. Guatemala City: Cholsamaj and OKMA.

Pérez Vail, José Reginaldo. 2014. "La inversion y obviación en mam de Cajolá." M.A. thesis, CIESAS, México.

Polian, Gilles. 2013. *Gramática del tseltal de Oxchuc*. México City: CIESAS.

Quizar, Robin. 1979. "Comparative word order in Mayan." PhD diss., University of Colorado, Boulder.

Quizar, Robin, and Susan M. Knowles-Berry. 1988. "Ergativity in the Cholan languages." *International Journal of American Linguistics* 54: 73–95.

Robertson, John S. 1980. *The structure of pronoun incorporation in the Mayan verbal complex*. New York: Garland Publications.

Santos Nicolás, José Francisco, and José Gonzalo Benito Pérez. 1998. *Rukorb'aal Poqom Q'orb'al. Gramática Poqom (Poqomam)*. Guatemala: Cholsamaj.

Stiebels, Barbara. 2006. "Agent focus in Mayan languages." *Natural Language and Linguistic Theory* 24: 501–70.

Vázquez Álvarez, Juan Jesús. 2002. "Morfología del verbo de la lengua chol de Tila, Chiapas." MA thesis, CIESAS, México.

Vásquez Álvarez, Juan Jesús. 2011. "A grammar of Chol, a Mayan language." PhD diss., The University of Texas, Austin.

Vázquez, Juan Jesús, and Roberto Zavala. 2013. "La estructura argumental preferida en chol, una lengua agentiva." In *Memorias del VI Congreso de Idiomas Indígenas de Latinoamérica*, 24–6 de octubre de 2013, UT Austin.

Velleman, Leah Bridges. 2014. "Focus and movement in a variety of K'ichee'." PhD diss., The University of Texas, Austin.

Verhoeven, Elisabeth, and Stavros Skopeteas. 2015. "Licencing focus constructions in Yucatec Maya." *International Journal of American Linguistics* 81: 1–40.

Wichmann, Søren. 1995. *The relationship among the Mixe-Zoquean languages of Mexico*. Salt Lake City: University of Utah Press.

Zavala, Roberto. 1992. *El Kanjobal de San Miguel Acatán*. México: UNAM.

Zavala, Roberto. 1993. "Clause integration with verbs of motion in Mayan languages." MA thesis, University of Oregon, Eugene.

Zavala, Roberto. 1994. "Inverse alignment in Huastec." *Función* 15/16: 27–81.

Zavala, Roberto. 1997. "Functional analysis of Akatek voice constructions." *International Journal of American Linguistics* 63: 439–74.

Zavala, Roberto. 2007. "Inversion and obviation in Mesoamerica." In *Linguistische Berichte Sonderheft* 14, ed. by Peter K. Austin and Andrew Simpson, 267–306. Hamburg: Helmut Buske Verlag.

CHAPTER 10

COMPLEMENT CLAUSES

Judith Aissen

1 INTRODUCTION

1.1 Scope of the chapter

Complement clauses are clauses which function as arguments of higher predicates. Within the broader domain of complex structures, they are distinct from clauses which function as adjuncts (adverbial clauses and relative clauses) or as conjuncts. They are also distinct from monoclausal structures with multiple predicates, as in serialization and secondary predication. None of these are discussed here. Higher predicates sometimes become grammaticized as auxiliary verbs and TAM markers, but I assume that once they are grammaticized, we are no longer in the domain of complementation.[1]

Many grammars of Mayan languages include a description and classification of complement clause types, with examples of the kinds of predicates which select each type. A number of works have focused especially on issues related to complementation. These include Craig (1977), a pioneering study, half of which is devoted to the syntax of complementation in Jakaltek; Berinstein (1985), which examines the very interesting interaction of agent focus constructions with complementation in Q'eqchi'; Kockelman (2003), a study of the classification of complement-taking predicates in Q'eqchi'; Verhoeven (2007), which provides a very detailed view of complementation in Yucatec Maya from a typological perspective; and Can Pixabaj (2015), an in-depth study of complementation in K'iche'. These works all contain material which is relevant not only to the language in question, but also to the Mayan family more widely and to the phenomenon of complementation in general.

This chapter identifies four basic complement structures in Mayan. They can mostly be distinguished by their surface properties, but a little less obvious on the surface is the fact that they are also structurally distinct. We take here a syntactic approach to the inventory of complement types, identifying them with different clause 'sizes'. Section 1.2 is a brief introduction to the four types and §2 sketches the structural assumptions that underlie the rest of the chapter. Properties of each of the four types are discussed in §3, with examples from various Mayan languages. Of interest here is the existence of two types of non-finite clause, one which corresponds to an infinitive, with no TAM marking and no agreement with the subject, and one which carries no TAM marking but does agree with the subject. Also important are restrictions, found throughout Mayan, on transitive infinitives. Once the formal properties of complement clause types are established, we turn in §4 to the way they are distributed in several languages and more generally to some of the factors which determine that distribution. Section 5 discusses cross-clausal interactions of the sort known as CONTROL, RAISING, and CLAUSE UNION, showing that these are found with both of the non-finite structures mentioned above, i.e., with infinitival structures, as is common, but also with complement structures that register subject agreement.

1.2 Background

Clausal complementation in Mayan generally follows typological patterns documented in works like Givón (2001) and Noonan (2007). Cross-linguistically, it is common for complement clauses to come in several forms which, loosely speaking, differ from one another in how closely they resemble independent clauses. English, for example, has an inventory of four subordinate clause types, called *indicative, subjunctive, infinitive,* and *gerund*:

(1) a. We saw [(that) he had stopped].
     b. We advised [that he not leave].
     c. We hoped [to leave].
     d. We stopped [singing].

Indicative complements are identical to independent clauses (except for the presence of the complementizer), (1a). The subjunctive complement in (1b) is also sentence-like in that it retains all of its arguments. However, it differs from the indicative in that the verb lacks the full range of inflectional possibilities. The distinction between present and past is neutralized, and 'leave' is the only possible form of the verb in (1b) regardless of the person and number of the subject or the tense of the main verb. The complement in (1c) is an infinitival clause. I follow Noonan (2007) in taking the absence of a canonically marked subject as the defining feature of an infinitival clause. (1d) is a gerundive complement.

Fundamental in the syntax of complement clauses is the distinction between *reduced* and *non-reduced* clauses. In English, only indicative clauses are non-reduced; all the others are, in one or more respects, reduced. The choice of complement clause type is determined by the embedding predicate (the complement-taking predicate (CTP), in Noonan's terminology), and by the semantic relation between the CTP and the complement clause. The choice of complement clause type is not arbitrary. In general, the more reduced the complement clause, the more semantically dependent it is on the embedding clause. Dependence holds principally along two dimensions: temporal and referential. We discuss these issues in §4.

In Mayan, subordinate clauses fall into two classes, *finite* and *non-finite*. Finite clauses are headed by verbs which inflect for aspect (or perhaps in some cases, tense), non-finite clauses are headed by verbs which do not. Finite complements are of two types: those which are introduced by a complementizer (COMP+*finite*) and those which are not (*simple finite*). These do not differ inflectionally, but they are distinguished on syntactic grounds and are selected by different sets of CTPs. Non-finite complements are also of two types: *aspectless* and *infinitival*. Aspectless verbs inflect for the person and number (='phi' (φ)) features of the subject (and object) while infinitives do not. The distribution of inflectional features is summarized in Table 10.1. The marking of φ features of the object is constrained in infinitives (see §3.4.1).

TABLE 10.1 INFLECTIONAL PROPERTIES OF COMPLEMENT TYPES

	Aspect	*Features of subject*	*Features of object*
COMP+finite	√	√	√
simple finite	√	√	√
non-finite aspectless		√	√
non-finite infinitive			(√)

Each of these complement types occurs in a larger syntactic context, and I will propose that each is associated with a particular level in the clausal hierarchy, §2.

Tsotsil is a language which has all four complement types, distinguishable by the presence or absence of certain (partly language-particular) morphosyntactic features. COMP+finite complements are introduced by a complementizer and have all the features of independent clauses. Further, they occur extraposed, yielding VSO order when the COMP+finite complement is O, as in (2) (unmarked order in Tsotsil is VOS). (The boundaries of complement clauses are marked by brackets throughout.)

TSOTSIL

(2) l-y-il   ti   s-me'   un-e   [ti   muk'=bu   ta   s-sa'   y-ajnil
    CP-A3-see   DET   A3-mother PAR-ENC   COMP   never   ICP   A3-seek   A3-wife
    ti   s-krem   un-e].
    DET   A3-son   PAR-ENC
    'His mother saw that her son was never going to find a wife.' {Laughlin 1977:55}

Simple finite clauses in Tsotsil are similar in that the verb is fully inflected with aspect and person markers. They are different in that they lack a complementizer and are not extraposed. Hence when such a complement is O, the order is VOS, as in (3).

TSOTSIL

(3) Mu   s-k'an   [ch-k-uch'-be-tik]   li   yajval=balamil-e.
    NEG   A3-want   ICP-A1-drink-APPL-1PL.INCL   DET   lord=earth-ENC
    'The Earth Lord didn't want us to drink it.' {Laughlin 1977:155}

Aspectless clauses lack morphological aspect marking but retain person marking for all arguments of the complement predicate (here, the object, being 3rd person singular, is not overtly marked):

TSOTSIL

(4) K'u=yu'un   mu   x-av-ak'   [k-uch'   vo']-e?
    why   NEG   NT-A2-let   A1-drink   water-ENC
    'Why don't you let me drink water?' {Laughlin 1977:45}

Infinitives lack both morphological aspect marking and person marking for the complement subject:

TSOTSIL

(5) Vo'on-e   mu   j-k'an   [mil-el].
    1SG-ENC   NEG   A1-want   kill-PSV/INF
    'Me, I didn't want to be killed.' {Laughlin 1977:139}

Some Mayan languages have all four types, some do not. The K'ichean languages, for example, have two types of finite complements and a well-developed category of infinitives. However, they lack aspectless complements. On the other hand, Jakaltek and Yucatec make rich use of aspectless forms and, although they have infinitives, these are quite restricted, as we will see below.

2 A LAYERED APPROACH TO CLAUSE STRUCTURE

An assumption common to all theories of syntax is that clauses have a layered, hierarchical structure. What the primitive elements of clause structure are, how the various levels are labelled, what relations among elements are possible, and how clause structure is represented vary considerably. But there is agreement that it is necessary to distinguish a predicative core, which contains the predicate and its arguments, and that this core can be embedded within a larger unit containing elements like tense and mood, and that this clausal unit can be further embedded within a yet larger element which is associated with the illocutionary force of the sentence.

Given this layered conception of clause structure, it is tempting to identify complement types which vary in their degree of reduction with particular layers in the hierarchical structure of the clause. COMP+finite clauses, which are syntactically like independent clauses, correspond to a high layer in the hierarchy, something like 'sentence'; simple finite complements contain a specification for TAM categories and correspond to something like 'clause'; complements which contain the predicate and its arguments, but lack TAM marking, correspond (minimally) to the predicative core.

Following Aissen (1992), I will adopt a phrase structure analysis of clause structure (Figure 10.1) which recognizes (at least) three levels in the verbal projection: VP, headed by the verb (= predicative core); IP, headed by a specification of aspect (=clause); and CP, headed by complementizer (=sentence).

The presence of aspect marking in a clause entails that the structure is at least as large as IP; if it contains in addition a complementizer, it must be a CP. The absence of aspect suggests a structure smaller than IP. Each of these phrases can contain additional elements. Important for our purposes are the location of focus, negation, and fronted interrogative pronouns. I assume that fronted interrogative (WH) pronouns are located within CP and that fronted foci are located within IP (Figure 10.2).

Negation is located between IP and CP, as shown in Figure 10.3. Negation may itself head a phrase (i.e., NEGP), but this is ignored here. What is important is that

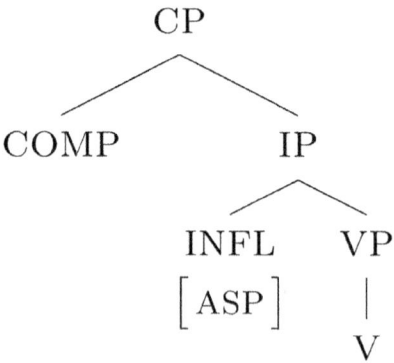

FIGURE 10.1 CLAUSE STRUCTURE

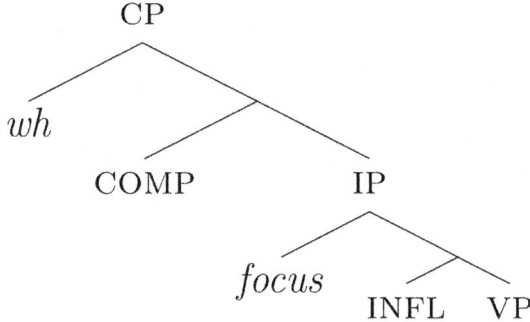

FIGURE 10.2 THE POSITION OF FRONTED INTERROGATIVES AND FOCI

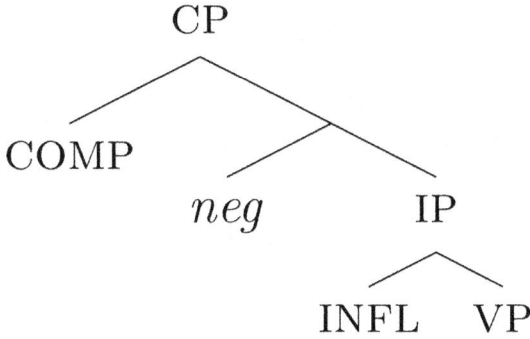

FIGURE 10.3 THE POSITION OF NEGATION

there is a structural position for negation within a CP complement, but not an IP complement.

We can now identify particular complement types with different projections, as per (6). A similar approach is taken to Yucatec in Gutiérrez Bravo (2010), to K'iche' in Can Pixabaj (2015), and to Q'anjob'al in Mateo Toledo (this volume).

(6) a. COMP+finite complements are CPs
    b. Simple finite complements are IPs
    c. Aspectless complements and infinitives are smaller than IP, i.e., VPs (possibly plus additional structure)

With this general understanding in place, we can consider in more detail the properties of the various complement types in Mayan.

3 COMPLEMENT TYPES

3.1 COMP+finite

3.1.1 Declaratives

The proposal that COMP+finite complements are CPs predicts that they can contain all the elements found in an independent clause. Thus, they will contain the predicative core:

TSOTSIL
(7) S-na'-oj || [ti   ch'abal   x-ch'amal-e].
    A3-know-PRF   COMP   NEG.exist   A3-child-ENC
    'He knew that he did not have a child.' {Laughlin 1977:42}

They will mark aspect and display the full range of voice alternations:

TSOTSIL
(8) Ja'   ch-na'-e || [ti   x-ti'-at   ta   chon   un-e].
    FOC   ICP-know-PSV   COMP   NT-bite-PSV   PREP   animal   PAR-ENC
    'It was known that he would be eaten by the animals.' {Laughlin 1977:81}

They will admit sentential negation:

TSOTSIL
(9) I-y-il   ti   s-me'   un-e || [ti   muk'=bu   ta   s-sa'   y-ajnil
    CP-A3-see   DET   A3-mother   PAR-ENC   COMP   never   ICP   A3-seek   A3-wife
    ti   s-krem   un-e].
    DET   A3-son   PAR-ENC
    'His mother saw that her son was never going to find a wife.' {Laughlin 1977:55}

A feature of COMP+finite complements in Mayan is that they do not occupy the same position as a corresponding non-clausal argument, but occur at the right periphery of the matrix clause. In an otherwise VOS language, a CP complement functioning as O follows S, as in (2). In VSO languages, the normal position for (any) O is already to the right of the subject, so surface order may not visibly change when O is a finite clause. However, the right-edge position of CP complements is visible in ditransitive clauses. In Jakaltek, for example, the usual order in ditransitives is [V S O IO], (10a). But if O is a CP complement, it occurs after the IO, not before it. Thus (10b) shows [V S IO O] order.

JAKALTEK
(10) a. X-[y]-a'   ix   te'   hum   w-et   an.
      CP-A3-give   PRON.F   CLF   book   A1SG-DAT   EXCL
      'She gave the book to me.' {Craig 1977:9}

    b. X-[y]-al   naj   tet   anma   yul   parke   ewi ||
      CP-A3-say   PRON.M   to   people   in   park   yesterday
      [chubil   chim   huluj   naj   presidente   konhob].
      COMP   may   come   DET   president   village
      'He said to people yesterday in the park that the president may come to the village.' {Craig 1977:248}

Note that the complement shifts all the way to the right in (10b), following not only matrix arguments, but also matrix adjuncts.

There is a prosodic correlate of clausal extraposition: an extraposed complement constitutes its own intonational phrase, separate from the intonational phrase corresponding to the matrix (the prosodic break is represented by ||). In a some languages, this break can be diagnosed by the presence of particles and enclitics which are restricted to the right edge of an intonational phrase (Aissen 1992; Henderson 2012). These include the Tsotsil particle *un* (meaningless) and the definite enclitic *e*, as in (2), and the Jakaltek 1st person exclusive clitic *an*, as in (11). The presence of these elements *before* the finite complement signals an intonational phrase break at that point. Thus while there is no visible reordering of constituents in an example like (11), the break marked by the clitic *an* provides evidence that there is extraposition (Craig 1977:276ff).

JAKALTEK
(11) X-[y]-al   hin   mam   an || [chubil   x-kam   no'   cheh].
     CP-A3-say   A1SG   father EXCL   COMP   CP-die   DET   horse
     'My father said that the horse died.' {Craig 1977:236}

There are several languages where complements to verbs of communication and propositional attitude are finite, but systematically lack an overt complementizer. Yucatec Maya is one. Complements in examples like (12) have been analyzed in different ways:[2]

YUCATEC {Gutiérrez Bravo 2010}
(12) T-u   y-a'al-aj   [ts'o'ok   u   chu'uk-ul   tumen   u   yiik'al
     CP-A3   EP-say-CTS   TERM   A3   catch.PSV-IIS by   A3   odor
         le   muulo'ob-a'].
         DET   pyramid-ENC
     'He said that he had already been caught by the bad smell of the pyramid.'

Bohnemeyer (2002) and Verhoeven (2007) analyze them as syntactically independent of the matrix ('juxtaposed' or 'paratactic'), though semantically dependent.[3] For them, the absence of the complementizer follows then from the fact that they are independent clauses. Gutiérrez Bravo (2010) takes the complement in examples like (12) to be syntactically embedded, but analyzes it as an IP not a CP, hence lacking a position for the complementizer. A third possibility is that they are CP complements, but lack a pronounced complementizer.

Complements to the same CTPs in Poqomam (K'ichean) also lack an overt complementizer, but these complements obligatorily shift to the left (Santos Nicolás and Benito Pérez (1998:433ff).

POQOMAM
(13) [X-u-loq'   la   uuq   laa'   nu-tuut]   x-u-q'or   ma'   Lu'.
     CP-A3SG-buy   DET   cloth DEM   A1SG-mother   CP-A3SG-say   CLF   Lu'
     'Lu' said that my mother bought this length of cloth.'

Examples like (13) might involve fronting of the complement clause (cf. Ross's (1973) analysis of English examples like *He left, they said* in terms of Slifting) or they might involve a parenthetical (cf. Reinhart 1983).[4] Whether a complementizer is present or not, the fact seems to be that Poqomam does not permit complements to verbs of communication and knowledge to remain in situ (in VOS order) nor does it permit extraposition (giving VSO order). The closest that one can get then to the English translation is apparently via the construction in (13).

COMP+S complements typically correspond to what would be expressed in indicative (realis) mood in a language like Spanish. Some languages have several declarative complementizers, indicating different degrees of epistemic commitment on the part of the speaker towards the truth of the proposition expressed by the complement. Jakaltek is such a language. The complementizer *chubil* indicates a high level of epistemic commitment, while *tato* (= *ta-to* 'COND-still') indicates a lower level (Craig 1977). Per Craig, (14a), with *chubil*, is appropriate because the source of the information is an authority who is in a position to have reliable information, while (14b) involves a less reliable source.

JAKALTEK

(14) a. X-[y]-al   naj   alkal   [chubil   ch-ul-uj   naj   presidente].
        CP-A3-say   DET   alcalde   COMP   ICP-arrive-FUT   DET   president
        'The alcalde said that the president is going to come.'

     b. X-[y]-al   naj   [tato   ch-ul-uj   naj   presidente].
        CP-A3-say   PRON.M COMP ICP-arrive-FUT   DET   president
        'He said that the president is going to come.' {Craig 1977:268}

CP complements are sometimes also used to express irrealis modalities, corresponding to what would be expressed by the subjunctive in Romance. This construction is frequently found when there is disjoint reference between the matrix and complement subjects, alternating with a 'smaller' complement type when there is coreference; see §4 for related discussion). In Jakaltek, the non-assertive complementizer *tato* (see (14b)) also introduces complements to desideratives and anti-desideratives.

JAKALTEK

(15) a. Ay   w-al-a'   [(tato)   ch-ach   way-i].
        EXIST   A1SG-say-FUT   COMP   ICP-B2SG sleep-SS
        'I would like for you to sleep.' {Craig 1977:234}

     b. Ch-in   xiw   [tato   ch-ach   ayk'ay-oj   swi'   te'   nhah].
        CP-B1SG   fear   COMP ICP-B2SG fall-FUT   its.head CLF   house
        'I am afraid you will fall from the roof.' {Craig 1977:235}

In Tz'utujil, the declarative complementizer *chi* is also used to introduce the complement to desideratives and some other modals:

TZ'UTUJIL

(16) a. N-r-aajo'   [chi n-war-i].
        ICP-A3SG-want   COMP ICP-sleep-SS
        'He wants her/him to sleep.' {Dayley 1985:392}

     b. Rajwaxiik   [(chi)   n-in-b'e].
        necessary   COMP   ICP-B1SG-go
        'It is necessary that I go.' {Dayley 1985:397}

Interestingly, the presence of the complementizer in irrealis contexts is variable in both Jakaltek and Tz'utujil (note the parentheses). More research is needed in order to know whether the complementizer is truly optional in these cases or whether its absence signals a structurally smaller complement, i.e., the simple finite type discussed in §3.2.

3.1.2 Interrogative complements

Certain CTPs select finite interrogative complements, for example, verbs corresponding to 'ask, tell, know'. Within the class of interrogative complements, there are two subtypes, corresponding to two types of questions – alternative and information. Thus the complement in (17a) corresponds to the alternative question in (17b):

TSOTSIL
(17) a. S-jak'-be   la   un,   [mi   kom   ti   x-ch'ul=tot-e].
      A3-ask-APPL   CL   PAR   Q   remain   DET   A3-godfather-ENC
      'He$_i$ asked if his$_i$ godfather was left behind.' {Laughlin 1977:366}

    b. Mi   kom   ti   j-ch'ul=tot-e?
      Q   stay   DET   A1-godfather-ENC
      'Did my godfather remain?'

and the complement in (18a) corresponds to the information question in (18b).

(18) a. L-a-s-jak'-be   [bu   j-na-tikotik   bu   j-lumal-tikotik,
      CP-B2-A3-ask-APPL   where   A1-house-1PL.EXCL   where   A1-land-1PL.EXCL
        k'usi   bat-em   j-pas-tikotik].
        what   go-PRF   A1-do-1PL.EXCL
      'He asked you where our home was, where our country was, what we had come to do.' {Laughlin 1980:106}

    b. Bu   j-na-tikotik?
      where   A1-house-1PL.EXCL
      'Where are our houses?'

Interrogative complements are CPs. The particle *mi* that occurs in both (17a, b) can be analyzed as an interrogative complementizer. In (17a), it introduces an interrogative complement; in (17b), it conveys the illocutionary force of the utterance. If it is a complementizer, then the complement in (17a) must be a CP. In line with Figure 10.2, I assume that fronted interrogative expressions, as in (18a,b), move to a high position in CP.

These examples show that the interrogative clauses can stand alone, with the illocutionary force of questions. Hence they raise the question whether in (17a, 18a) those clauses might be paratactic to the matrix, e.g., 'he asked him [something]; "did his god-father remain?"', rather than subordinate.

A paratactic analysis is problematic for languages in which main clause questions and interrogative complements are not identical. In Tz'utujil, main clause alternative questions are optionally introduced by *la*, while complement alternative interrogatives are obligatorily introduced by *wi*:

TZ'UTUJIL
(19) a. La   n-at-war-i?
      Q   ICP-B2SG-sleep-SS
      'Are you going to sleep?' {Dayley et al. 1996:226}

b. Jaa'   k'axa-n   ch-we   [wi   n-in-b'e].
   PRON.3   ask-AF   DAT-1SG COMP   ICP-B1SG-go
   'He was the one who asked me if I was going.' {Dayley et al. 1996:205}

In Yucatec, too, there are differences between main clause questions and complement interrogatives. Both are signaled by *wáah*, but the position of *wáah* is different in the two cases (it occurs clause-initially when it introduces a complement clause, while in polar questions, it encliticizes to a 'highlighted' constituent (Bohnemeyer 2002:109)).

The Tsotsil examples in (17a, 18a) themselves raise a different kind of problem for the paratactic analysis. In both, the interrogative clause represents discourse. Under the paratactic analysis, it represents direct discourse, under the subordinate analysis, indirect discourse.

What is key here is that deixis works differently in direct and indirect discourse – this is reflected by the fact that the italicized pronouns in Table 10.2 are not constant across the two discourse types. In direct discourse, deixis is relativized to the *reported* speech situation. Hence 1st person refers to the *reported* speaker (the matrix subject of verbs of communication). In indirect discourse, deixis references the speech situation itself, with 1st person referring to the speaker of the utterance. In the Tsotsil examples, the distribution of person is correctly predicted by the subordinate, indirect discourse analysis. Reference to the matrix subject in (17a) does not use the 1st person, while reference to the utterance speaker in (18a) does.

In summary, COMP+finite complements correspond to full, independent sentences and are analyzed here as CPs. They can contain all the elements found in CP (e.g., negation, aspect marking, person marking). CP complements come into two varieties: declarative and interrogative, determined by the CTP. The declarative type obligatorily extraposes in most Mayan languages and constitutes an intonational phrase separate from the matrix.

3.2 Simple finite complements

I use the term 'simple finite' to refer to a complement which is sentence-like in that the verb is finite and all arguments are expressed. In these respects, simple finite clauses are like COMP+finite ones. They differ in that the former are not introduced by a complementizer, cf. (20) from Tsotsil.

TSOTSIL
(20) l-y-a'i   [i-t'om   li   vits-e].
     CP-A3-hear   CP-explode   DET   mountain-ENC
     'He heard the mountain explode.' {TEXT}

TABLE 10.2 DIRECT AND INDIRECT DISCOURSE COMPARED

Ex.	Direct discourse	Indirect discourse
(17)	He asked him, "Was *my* godfather left behind?"	He_i asked him [whether *his*_i god-father was left behind].
(18)	He asked you, "Where is *their* house?"	He asked you [where *our* house was].

Since the complement in (20) can stand alone perfectly well as an independent sentence and it is not introduced by a complementizer, a paratactic analysis should again be considered (*he heard it, the mountain exploded*). However, in Tsotsil, when the arguments are instantiated by full nominals, word order (VOS) shows that the object complement is embedded within the matrix, not juxtaposed to it (see also (3) above).

TSOTSIL

(21) I-y-il   [i-tal   li   ants]   li   jun   vinik   li   xulem   to   ox.
     CP-A3-see CP-come DET woman DET a   man   DET buzzard CL   CL
     'The man who had been a buzzard saw the woman come in.' {Laughlin 1977:152}

(22) Mu   [x]-s-k'an   [x-lok']   i   ch'ul-vo'   ta=jmek-e.
     NEG NT-A3-want   NT-end   DET holy-water   ever-ENC
     'The holy rain didn't want to let up at all.' {Laughlin 1977:137}

Simple finite complements then are not introduced by a complementizer and in Tsotsil, they do not extrapose. In addition, they do not constitute prosodically independent phrases. (21) suggests this, albeit imperfectly in its cited form. All three instances of the determiner *li* license the phrase-final enclitic *-e*, but the only position in which it can potentially appear is at the very end of the sentence.

In Tsotsil, simple finite complements are selected by desideratives (22) (also (23) below) modals (24), and verbs of direct perception (20) and (21). A feature which unifies these is temporal dependency: the situation denoted by the complement is either future-oriented with respect to that of the matrix verb (as with desideratives), has no temporal reference (as with modals like *xu'* 'can'), or it is co-temporaneous with that of the matrix (as with verbs of direct perception). Morphologically, the aspect marked on the complement verb usually matches that of the matrix, perhaps a form of agreement. (23) shows both matrix and complement verb in incompletive aspect:

TSOTSIL

(23) ti=mi yu'un   ta   s-k'an   [ta   x-chik'-ik   li   s-na-ik-e]
     if   because ICP A3-want ICP A3-burn-PL DET A3-house-PL-ENC
     'If they want to burn their house . . . ' {Laughlin 1980:43}

(24) shows both verbs in 'neutral' aspect, an aspectual category in Tsotsil which neutralizes the distinction between completive and incompletive and is often found in the scope of negation and modals (see also (22)).

TSOTSIL

(24) Mi   x-[y]-u'   [x-i-jelav]?
     Q   NT-A3-can NT-B1-pass.by
     'Can I pass by?' {Laughlin 1977:72}

(20) and (21), complements to verbs of direct perception, show perfective aspect on both matrix and complement verb.

Other languages which require a distinction between COMP+S and simple finite complements include Tseltal and Poqomam. (25) and (26) both have a clausal complement which occurs in situ (VOS) and lacks a complementizer. (Compare (26) with (13), also from

Poqomam, where the complement cannot remain in situ. This difference is determined by the matrix CTP.)

TSELTAL
(25) Ma   s-k'an   [x-lok'-at   bel]   te   Xun-e.
     NEG   A3-want   ICP-leave-B2   DIR   DET   John-ENC
     'John doesn't want you to leave.' {Polian 2013a:821}

POQOMAM
(26) X-u-reej   [x-u-tik   ab'iix]   la   sa   imaas.
     CP-A3SG-want   CP-A3SG-plant   cornfield   DET   DIM   gentleman
     'The gentleman wanted to seed his cornfield.' {Santos Nicolás and Benito Pérez
     1998:436}

The systematic absence of a complementizer in these examples suggests that simple finites correspond to a structure which is smaller than CP. Since they include aspect, which, by hypothesis, is associated with INFL, they must be at least as big as an IP. Given the assumptions made earlier about where various other elements sit (see Figure 10.2), this analysis makes predictions about the elements which are possible within a simple finite complement. If preverbal focus is within IP then preverbal focus should be possible within such a complement. Where the relevant facts have been documented (Tsotsil, Tseltal), this prediction is borne out. We illustrate here with Tseltal.

TSELTAL
(27) Ja'   xan=ix   j-k'an   [jo'on   xan=ix   x-jajch'-on   bel   at'el].
     FOC   more=now   A1-want   FOC.1SG   more=now   ICP-begin-B1   DIR   work
     'I just wanted to begin working myself.' {Polian 2013a:821}

Further, if negation is located outside of IP and simple finite complements are IPs, negation should be impossible. Again, where the facts have been documented (Tsotsil, Tseltal), this is correct. If the complement is to be negated, it is necessary to introduce the complementizer, a visible cue that the complement is a CP and 'big' enough to include negation.

TSELTAL
(28) a. ?? Ya j-k'an   [ma   x-ch'ay   ta   aw-ot'an-ik].
            ICP A1-want   NEG   ICP-lose   PREP   A2-heart-PL

     b. Ya   j-k'an   [te   ma   x-ch'ay   ta   aw-ot'an-ik].
        ICP   A1-want   COMP   NEG   ICP-lose   PREP   A2-heart-PL
        'I want you all not to forget.' {Polian 2013a:821}

Some of the CTPs which select simple finite complements also select COMP+finite ones. In some cases, this choice reflects different senses of the verb and its relation to the complement. In Tsotsil, for example, when a verb of direct perception denotes the apprehension of an event, it takes a simple finite complement, as in (20, 21). But it can also denote the apprehension of a fact, in which case it behaves like a verb of cognition and selects a CP complement, one which is introduced by a complementizer and is extraposed (see (2)).

In the languages cited above, simple finite complements occur in situ. But in several K'ichean languages, they occur in clause-final position. Larsen (1988:390) discusses examples like those in (29a, b) which lack a complementizer, but reorder to the right and occasion a prosodic break (though how large a break is currently unknown):

K'ICHE'
(29) a. K-w-aaj   k-in-b'ee-k.
     ICP-A1SG-want   ICP-B1SG-go-SS
     'I want to go.'

   b. Ka-r-aj   ri   achii k-in-u-ch'ay-o.
      ICP-A3SG-want   DET   man   ICP-B1SG-A3SG-hit-SS
      'The man wants to hit me.'

The lengthened vowel on the matrix verb in (29a) signals the right edge of a prosodic constituent and the VSO order in (29b) is the result of reordering (the order with a non-clausal object is typically VOS).[5] Can Pixabaj (2015) shows that such complements do not permit internal negation nor focus fronting and further that they show both temporal and referential dependence on the matrix clause. In all these respects, they conform to simple finite complements.

    Similar examples are found in Tz'utujil, also K'ichean:

TZ'UTUJIL
(30) a. La   n-aw-aaj   [n-at-b'e]?
     Q   ICP-A2SG-want   ICP-B2SG-go
     'Do you want to go?' {Dayley et al. 1996:5}

   b. Najiin-i   [n-in-wa'-i].
      PROG-SS   ICP-B1SG-eat-SS
      'I am eating.' {Dayley 1985:392}

    The long vowel on the matrix verb in (30a) and the status suffix on the main predicate in (30b) indicate that these verbs are followed by a prosodic break (again, how large is not clear). In both K'iche' and Tz'utujil, this construction is found with desideratives and some other prospective verbs (e.g., 'think about x-ing').

3.3 Aspectless complements

As the label suggests, the verb which heads an aspectless clause does not mark aspect. However it does index the φ features of its arguments (see Table 10.1). Aspectless complements play a relatively small role in some languages, e.g., Tsotsil, and the category does not exist in K'ichean. But in Mamean, Q'anjob'alan, and Yucatecan, they play a central role (see §4.4).

    In (31a, b), from Tsotsil, the causative verb *ak'* 'let, have' takes an aspectless complement.

TSOTSIL
(31) a. Mu   x-[y]-ak'   [vay-ik-on].
     NEG   NT-A3-let   sleep-SS-B1
     'She doesn't let me sleep.' {Laughlin 1977:56}

   b. K'u=yu'un mu   x-av-ak'   [k-uch'   vo']-e?
      why   NEG   NT-A2-let   A1-drink   water-ENC
      'Why don't you let me drink water?' {Laughlin 1977:45}

These examples involve temporal dependency since the temporal reference of the complement cannot be earlier than that of the matrix verb.

In Tsotsil, agreement on aspectless forms is like that of aspect-bearing verbs: intransitives index the subject with Set B markers (31a), while transitives index the subject with Set A (31b).[6] However, Tsotsil is unusual within Mayan in preserving a fully ergative agreement system on aspectless verbs. In many languages of the family, some or all aspectless forms are associated with so-called 'extended ergativity' (a form of split ergativity), (see Zavala, this volume). In extended ergativity, intransitive subjects (as in 32a) are marked with Set A markers, like subjects of transitives (32b), rather than with Set B.

JAKALTEK (Craig 1977:240, 237)
(32) a. K'ul   [ku-tiyoxl-i   tet   anma].
         good   A1PL-greet-SS   OBL   people
         'It is good to greet people.'

    b. Yilal   [ku-kuy-ni   abxubal].
         necessary   A1PL-learn-DEP   Jakaltek
         'It is absolutely necessary that we learn Jakaltek.'

This pattern of agreement is summarized in Table 10.3.

Extended ergativity may arise in several ways. One, associated with lowland languages (Cholan, Yucatecan, Poqom (K'ichean)), involves nominalization of complement clauses (Robertson 1976; Norman and Campbell 1978; Dayley 1981; Coon 2013). In this case, the fact that intransitive subjects are indexed by Set A, rather than Set B, reflects their status (current or historic) as possessors (but see Kaufman 1990:86ff for a more complex view of the relation between possessors and extended ergativity). In Q'anjob'alan and Mamean, aspectless forms with an extended ergative pattern are also triggered by the presence of certain preverbal elements and do not, at least not obviously, involve nominalization or complementation.[7]

Under the earlier proposal that aspectless complements correspond to a small constituent, something smaller than IP, we expect various elements that occur higher in the structure to be impossible. Craig (1977:243) shows, for example, that aspectless clauses in Jakaltek do not admit internal negation. To negate such a complement, speakers use a CP complement, as CPs provide the structural space for negation, (33c). The complement in (33c) is introduced by a complementizer, contains aspect, and the intransitive subject is indexed by Set B, not Set A, cf. (33a).

JAKALTEK
(33) a. K'ul   [j-uk'-i].
         good   A1PL-drink-SS
         'It is good to drink.'

TABLE 10.3 EXTENDED ERGATIVITY

	Intransitive	Transitive
subject	A	A
object	–	B

b. * K'ul   [mach/mat   j-uk'-i].
    good   NEG   A1PL-drink-SS
    ('It is good not to drink.')

c. K'ul   [ta(to)   mach   ch-onh   uk'-i].
    good   COMP   NEG   ICP-B1PL   drink-SS
    'It is good that we do not drink.'

Polian (2013a:823) shows that aspectless complements in Tseltal do not permit internal foci (or negation). The aspectless complement in (34) contrasts with the simple finite one in (27).

TSELTAL

(34) a. Ma   la   y-ak'   [j-k'opon-at].
    NEG   CP   A3-let   A1-speak.to-B2SG
    'He didn't let ME speak to you.'

b. *Ma   la   y-ak'   [jo'on   j-k'opon-at].
    NEG   CP   A3-let   FOC.B1SG   A1-speak.to-B2SG
    ('He didn't let me speak to you.')

The properties and distribution of aspectless clauses shed interesting light on the structure of clauses headed by non-verbal predicates in Mayan. Although non-verbal predicates do not mark aspect, the clauses they head do *not* pattern like aspectless clauses, but rather like finite ones. Mateo Toledo (2011:172; this volume) shows for Q'anjob'al that a non-verbal clause can be selected by a CTP like *oche* 'want' that takes COMP+finite complements (35a), but not by one like *aq'le* 'try' that selects only aspectless complements (35b).

Q'ANJOB'AL

(35) a. Chi   w-oche-j   [tol   watx'-il   anima   hex].
    ICP   A1SG-want-SS   COMP   good-ABS   people   B2PL
    'I want you to be good people.'

b. *Max   w-aq'le-j   [(tol)   niman   hin].
    CP   A1SG-try-SS   COMP   big   B1SG
    ('I tried to be a big person.')

Further, he shows that clauses headed by non-verbal predicates permit the same range of pre-predicate elements as verbal predicates in finite clauses (e.g., negation, focus). Hence, the complement types selected by particular CTPs must be characterized in terms of their syntactic structure, not in terms of morphological marking per se. See also Craig (1977:237ff) and Bohnemeyer (2002:93) on the non-occurrence of non-verbal predicates in aspectless clauses in Yucatec and Jakaltek, respectively.

3.4 Infinitival clauses

Infinitives are non-finite verbs which lacks normal expression of the subject. For Mayan, this means that the verb will lack either Set A or Set B marking, depending on transitivity and/or other factors that enter into subject marking. Typologically, clauses headed by infinitives are frequently found in complement function, where the interpretation of the subject is determined by (i.e., 'controlled by') some argument of the matrix clause. All Mayan languages appear to have infinitives and, as expected, they frequently head complement clauses. The pair in (36) illustrates infinitive clauses based on intransitive and transitive verbs in Tz'utujil (Dayley 1985:393).

TZ'UTUJIL

(36) a. X-qaa-maj   [wa'-iim].
        CP-A1PL-begin   eat-INF
        'We began to eat.'

    b. X-qaa-maj   [choy-oj   chee'].
        CP-A1PL-begin   cut-INF   tree
        'We began to cut trees.'

In both cases, the infinitive is formed by suffixation (the form of the suffix depends on the transitivity of the stem and, in the case of transitives, on whether the verb is a root transitive or a derived transitive),[8] and in both, the infinitive clause functions as object of the transitive phasal verb *maj* 'begin'. The subject of the infinitive does not inflect on the infinitive. Here, its interpretation is determined by the matrix subject.

A feature of infinitival complements in many Mayan languages is that they are themselves case-marked like nominal arguments. In (36a, b), the complement is a direct argument because the matrix verb is transitive and takes its clausal argument as direct object. In (37a, b), also from Tz'utujil, where the matrix predicate is intransitive, the situation is different. In this case, the infinitival complement must be introduced by a preposition. With the argument structure of the intransitive saturated by the matrix subject, the additional infinitival argument must be marked as oblique.

TZ'UTUJIL

(37) a. N-in-tajin   [chi   b'ijn-eem].
        ICP-B1SG-PROG   PREP   walk-INF
        'I am walking.' (I am in the act of walking)

    b. N-oq-tajin   [chi   b'an-oj   way].
        ICP-1PL-PROG   PREP   make-INF   tortilla
        'We are making tortillas.' {Dayley 1985:394}

3.4.1 Transitivity-based restrictions on infinitives

The most interesting feature of infinitives in Mayan is that every language of the family shows significant restrictions on infinitives based on transitive stems (see Polian 2013b and Coon et al. 2014 for related observations). In most languages, infinitives based on transitive stems cannot take full direct objects. Thus the fact that the objects in (36b, 37b) are bare nouns (*chee'* 'tree', *way* 'tortilla') is not accidental – replacing them with the definite *ja chee'*/*ja way* 'the tree'/'the tortilla' results in ungrammaticality.

From a family-wide perspective, infinitives based on transitive stems show the range of behaviors typologically associated with *antipassive* verbs. Depending on the language, the notional object may be morphologically incorporated, it may be 'pseudo incorporated' (in the sense of Massam 2001, i.e., bare), or it may be demoted to oblique status. In languages where transitive infinitives take only bare objects, a gap is created, and languages use different strategies to fill it. Most languages resort to aspectless clauses to express what cannot be expressed in an infinitival clause. A few have innovated an infinitive which can take a full direct object; these constructions are themselves subject to restrictions or are morphologically more complex than the more basic transitive infinitive. Our primary goal here to document this phenomenon, not to explain it, but in closing we will consider briefly why transitive infinitives might be restricted.

Yucatec has intransitive infinitives, but not transitive ones (Bohnemeyer 2002; Gutiérrez Bravo 2002). Thus contexts which permit an infinitive when the complement is intransitive (38a), take an aspectless form when the complement is transitive (38b) (Verhoeven (2007) refers to this as the 'split pattern'). Note the agreement with the subject in (38b) (A1s) and its absence in (38a). Note also that infinitives have INCOMPLETIVE status suffixes, while transitive aspectless forms *in the split pattern* take DEPENDENT (also known as SUBJUNCTIVE) status suffixes (which may be ø, as in (38b)).

YUCATEC

(38) a. Tèen-e' k-in   bin [kul-tal tu   xùul le   bèeh-o'].
     me-TOP ICP-A1SG go   sit-POS.IIS at   end   DET way-ENC
     'Me, I'll go sit(ting) down at the end of the road.'

   b. Chéen h   tàal-en   [in   xíimbat-ech].
     just   CP come-B1SG A1SG walk:APPL-B2SG
     'I only came to visit you.' {Bohnemeyer 2002:99}

However, Yucatec is one of the few Mayan languages which has morphological incorporation and a verb which has incorporated its object can then function as an infinitive (Bohnemeyer 2002:126, Gutiérrez Bravo 2002):

YUCATEC

(39) Le   nohoch máak-o' bih-a'a-n   [ts'on-kéeh].
    DET big   man-ENC go-PTCP-PRF hunt deer
    'The gentleman has gone to hunt deer.' {Gutiérrez Bravo 2002:14}

An infinitive can be derived from a transitive stem in Yucatec then, but only if the object is incorporated first.

Jakaltek and other Q'anjob'alan languages have infinitives of transitive stems, but the object must be bare, i.e., undetermined, as in (40a), from Craig (1977); see also Zavala (1992:315) on Akatek, and Mateo Toledo (2013) on Q'anjob'al. If the object is not bare, Jakaltek resorts to an aspectless complement, identifiable by subject agreement on the verb (40b).

JAKALTEK

(40) a. Ch-in   to [il-o' qinh].
      ICP-B1SG go see-INF fiesta
      'I am going to see the fiesta.' {Craig 1977:245}

   b. Xk-in   to [w-il-a'   naj].
     CP-B1SG go A1SG-see-FUT PRON.M
     'I went to see him.' {Craig 1977:238}

Mam is like Tz'utujil and Jakaltek in that it permits a transitive infinitive if the object lacks a determiner and is interpreted as non-specific, (41a). If it is specific, though, it must be presented as oblique, (41b) (England 2013:286–7).

MAM
(41) a. Ma   tz'=ok   n-q'o-'n=a   [tx'eema-l sii'].
          PROX B3S=DIR   A1SG-give-DEP=1SG   cut-INF   firewood
          'I had him cut firewood.'

      b. O   chi   e'x   xjaal   [laq'oo-l   t-ee].
          CP B3PL go   people   buy-INF   A3SG-DAT
          'The people went to buy it.'

If the oblique in (41b) is omitted, the complement verb is interpreted as objectless (= 'the people went to buy'). Demotion is a feature of antipassive in Mam (in simple clauses and agent focus), so its appearance in non-finite clauses is in line with other patterns in the language.

The pervasiveness of these restrictions indicates that transitive infinitives in Mayan lack the capacity to license a full-fledged direct object. We could describe this in terms of 'low transitivity' or in terms of a process of obligatory detransitivization (antipassivization) or in terms of abstract Case. In Case terms, transitive infinitives lack the capacity to license Case on their objects. The fact that undetermined/non-specific noun phrases are possible in most languages is because these do not require Case (Baker 1988; Massam 2001).

At least two subgroups have innovated a transitive infinitive which is capable of taking a determined direct object – K'ichean and Tseltalan. In K'iche' and Tz'utujil (both K'ichean) for example, the 'simple' transitive infinitive is formed on the transitive stem by suffixation of -oj (root transitives) or -n (derived transitives), and permits only an undetermined/non-specific object. However, both languages have a second form which permits a full, determined direct object. This form is inflected with Set A markers, so I will refer to it as the 'inflected infinitive'. The inflected infinitive also has two allomorphs, depending on whether the stem is a root or derived transitive. In Tz'utujil, root transitives form the inflected infinitive with the infix <j> plus the suffix -iik:

TZ'UTUJIL
(42) X-qaa-maj   [r-cho<j>y-iik   (ja   chee')].
      CP-A1PL-begin   A3SG-cut<PSV>-INF   DET   tree
      'We began to cut it (the tree).' {Dayley 1985:393}

Derived transitives form it with the suffix -x plus the same suffix -iik.

TZ'UTUJIL
(43) X-in-kajb'a'   [ki-kamsa-x-iik   ja   k'aq].
      CP-A1SG-stop   A3PL-kill-PSV-INF DET   flea
      'I stopped killing the fleas.' {Dayley 1985:401}

TABLE 10.4 INFLECTED INFINITIVE IN TZ'UTUJIL

root transitives	<j>	-iik
derived transitives	-x	-iik

Although the complement verbs in (42), (43) carry a Set A marker, it is clear from its φ features that it does not index the subject of the infinitive, but the object. The subject of (43), for example, is 1st person singular, while the Set A marker on the inflected infinitive is 3rd plural, like its object. The subject is not indexed, but is controlled by the subject of the matrix. Hence these forms are infinitives.

Interestingly, the inflected infinitive in K'iche' and Tz'utujil is based on the passive. The evidence for this is morphological: the allomorphy of the inflected infinitive is identical to that of the passive. Monosyllabic root transitives form the passive with the infix *(j)*, derived transitives with the suffix -*x* (compare Table 10.4).

TZ'UTUJIL
(44) a. X-cho<j>y-i   ja   nim   chee'.
        CP-cut<PSV>-SS   DET big   tree
        'The big tree was cut.' {Dayley 1985:197}

     b. Jar   iib'ooy   x-kamsa-x-i.
        DET   armadillo   CP-kill-PSV-SS
        'The armadillo was killed.' {Dayley 1985:341}

Obviously this raises the question whether the non-finite clauses in (42) and (43) are really transitive, as assumed above. Evidence that they are, and in particular, that they are not passive, comes from the possibility of a reflexive in the complement (see Larsen (1988:444) and Can Pixabaj (2015) on this construction in K'iche'):[9]

TZ'UTUJIL
(45) X-in-b'e   [chi   [r]-qo'ma-x-ik   w-ii'].
     CP-B1SG-go   PREP A3SG-cure-PSV-INF   A3SG-RR
     'I am going to cure myself.' {ELIC}

Reflexive clauses cannot be passivized, hence the non-finite complement in (45) must be active. The reflexive is the object of the complement verb, and is bound by the subject of the complement, which is itself controlled by the matrix subject. (Note that the object is indexed on the infinitive via Set A3 but that prefix is always deleted after *chi* (Dayley 1985:35).) These forms raise a number of questions. One is why the passive serves as the base for the transitive infinitive in Tz'utujil and the other K'ichean languages. Another is why the object is indexed by Set A markers, rather than by the Set B markers that otherwise index objects. A likely explanation is that these constructions are nominalizations and have access only to the case licensing found in nominals. I.e., the object is inflected as the possessor of the nominalized verb. We have already seen evidence that uninflected infinitival clauses are nominalized in K'ichean, namely they are case-marked exactly like non-clausal nominals. The same is true of the inflected infinitive: the clause is unmarked when it functions as second argument of a transitive predicate, (46a), but oblique when it functions as second argument of an intransitive predicate, (46b).

TZ'UTUJIL
(46) a. X-qaa-maj   [r-cho<j>y-iik].
        CP-A1PL-begin A3SG-cut<PSV>-INF
        'We began to cut it.' {Dayley 1985:393}

b. X-in-pit   ch   [a-tz'e<j>t-iik].
    CP-B1SG-come PREP A2SG-see<PSV>-INF
    'I came to see you.' {Dayley 1985:383}

A transitive infinitive with the capacity to govern a determined direct object has also emerged in Tseltalan. Polian (2013a, b) provide descriptions of this phenomenon in Tseltal which we will draw on here. Tseltal uses the suffix *-el* to derive a variety of non-finite verbs. Among them are infinitives based on intransitive stems, both active and passive.

TSELTAL
(47) a. Ya   j-xi'   [nux-el].
         ICP   A1-fear   swim-INF
         'I am afraid of swimming.'

     b. Ya   j-k'an   [il-el].
         ICP   A1-want   see-INF.PSV
         'I want to be seen.' {Polian 2013b:364}

The complement in (47a) is an active intransitive; the one in (47b) is passive. In neither case is the infinitive inflected; in both, its subject is understood to be controlled by the matrix subject. Tseltal also derives an infinitive based on a transitive stem which is interpreted as active. In this case, the infinitive is inflected:

TSELTAL
(48) Ya   j-xi'   [y-ut-el   te   Xun=e].
     ICP   A1-fear   A3-scold-INF   DET   John=ENC
     'I am afraid of scolding John.' {Polian 2013b:370}

(48) looks entirely parallel to (46a) in Tz'utujil: the Set A marker on the infinitive clearly does not index the subject (which is 1st person), but looks like it indexes the object (which is 3rd). Further, the infinitive itself is plausibly derived (at least historically) from a passive non-finite form (cf. (47b)).

However, Polian (2013b) shows that the Set A marker on the infinitive does not in fact index the object. The evidence is that in contrast to Tz'utujil (and other K'ichean languages), the Set A marker can only be A3. It cannot be A1 or A2:

TSELTAL
(49) *Ya   j-xi'   [aw-ut-el].
      ICP   A1-fear   A2-scold-INF
      ('I am afraid of scolding you.') {Polian 2013b:370}

Since 1st and 2nd person arguments must be morphologically indexed on the head, speakers must use a different construction to express the intended sense of (49), either a finite clause, an aspectless one, or a different infinitival structure, depending on the dialect (Polian 2013b and p.c.). Further, Polian shows that the impossibility of (49) does not reflect a person-based restriction, for neither can the transitive infinitive take the 3rd person plural suffix which routinely occurs with Set A prefixes to index a plural participant.

TSELTAL
(50) *Ya j-xi'   [y-ut-el-ik].
     ICP   A1-fear   A3-scold-INF-PL
     ('I am afraid of scolding them.') {Polian 2013b:371}

Since plural marking is optional in Tseltal, the intended reading can be expressed in this construction, but the form *y-ut-el* (A3-scold-INF), without the plural suffix, must be used.

In short, the A3 marker found in examples like (48) does not index the object of the clause. How should it be analyzed then? Polian suggests that it registers the presence of an agent. Another way perhaps to put it is that it registers the transitivity of the complement and in that way parallels transitivity markers that occur widely in other languages (see also Shklovsky 2012).

While Mayan languages have infinitives then, transitive infinitives are systematically restricted. In most languages, infinitives based on transitive stems cannot grammatically govern a direct object but involve various strategies of detransitivization (incorporation of the object, restriction to bare objects ('pseudo-incorporation'), or demotion of the object to oblique). Most languages use aspectless clauses in place of the infinitive to express a full nominal object. A few families have innovated a transitive infinitive which can govern a full-fledged direct object, but in at least one of them (Tseltalan), these forms too are restricted to 3rd person objects – objects which do not require overt indexation on the head. Table 10.5 summarizes the distribution of the infinitive in the languages we have discussed, languages which represent five subfamilies. In all five, intransitive infinitives are formed productively and without restrictions.

Clearly a very important question is how to understand the systematic absence of fully transitive infinitives. Explaining this phenomenon would require making more theoretical assumptions than are appropriate in this chapter. However, one approach would be to adopt the idea that Case licensing of objects requires functional structure above the VP (and below IP). Then we could base an explanation for the deficiency of transitive infinitives in terms of the larger structure containing infinitives, i.e., as a consequence of the absence of the structural apparatus which is required to license Case on objects. See Coon (2013) for an analysis which develops this approach in connection with Chol.

3.4.2 Purposive adjuncts

The reader may have noticed that a number of the examples of infinitives cited in the previous section involve intransitive verbs of motion, i.e., *go, come*. These are not usually

TABLE 10.5 RESTRICTIONS ON TRANSITIVE INFINITIVES

	Infinitive based on transitive stem	Remedy
Yucatec	only possible with incorporation	aspectless clause
Jakaltek	only possible with bare non-specific object	aspectless clause
Mam	only possible with non-specific object	demotion
Tz'utujil	uninflected infinitive possible only with bare non-specific object	inflected infinitive
Tseltal	inflected infinitive possible only with 3rd person object	various

regarded as CTPs, but in a number of Mayan languages they provide one of the most frequent contexts for infinitives. Examples from several languages are given in (51).

(51) JAKALTEK
　　a. Ch-in　　　to　[il-o'　　qinh].
　　　ICP-B1SG　go　see-INF　fiesta
　　　'I am going to see the fiesta.' {Craig 1977:245}

　　MAM
　　b. O　chi　e'x　xjaal　　[laq'oo-l　t-ee].
　　　CP　B3PL　go　people　buy-INF　A3SG-DAT
　　　'The people went to buy it.' {England 2013:286}

　　TZ'UTUJIL
　　c. Inin　chaaq'a'　x-in-pit　　　　[pa　ya'aan-eem].
　　　1SG　at.night　CP-B1SG-come　PREP　water-INF
　　　'I came to water at night.' {Dayley 1985:381}

Here the infinitival clause is interpreted with purposive semantics, with its subject controlled by the matrix subject. Whether the infinitival clause should be classified as an
adjunct or a complement (i.e., argument) is unclear; the answer depends on whether verbs
of motion like *go* include a purposive argument in Mayan (see Can Pixabaj 2015 for some
discussion of this issue in K'iche').

　　The use of infinitives in purpose clauses is typologically common (Schmidtke-Bode
2009). Haspelmath (1989) has suggested that the infinitives spread, through grammaticization, from clauses with purposive semantics to complements (without purposive
semantics). We will see in §4 that the distribution of infinitives in some Mayan languages
provides support for this scenario.

4   DISTRIBUTION OF COMPLEMENT TYPES

4.1 Introduction

With this description of the formal properties of the four complement types, we can turn
to their distribution in particular languages. Typological work on complementation has
shown that choice of complement type is not arbitrary, but depends on the matrix predicate
and its relation to the complement. As mentioned at the outset, complements which are
semantically dependent on the matrix are likely to be syntactically reduced – this is what
Givón (2001:Ch.12) calls an iconic relation between the form of a complement clause and
its relation to the matrix. This can be conceived in terms of 'event compression' (Givón
2001), where events are characterized (in part) by their temporal setting and the participants
involved. When the temporal setting and the participants of matrix and complement are
entirely independent, the events denoted by the two clauses are clearly distinct.

　　This is mirrored in complement choice. Of the CTPs identified, for example, in Givón
(2001) and Noonan (2007), there are three which impose no temporal or referential
restrictions on the complement: verbs of communication (e.g., *say, tell, ask, wonder*),
verbs of propositional attitude (e.g., *think, believe*), and verbs of knowledge (e.g., *know,
regret, realize, remember, forget*). Cross-linguistically, if a language has CP complements, they will be selected by verbs of these classes. Mayan is no exception: languages
with a COMP+finite type complement use it in these contexts. In addition to providing the

structural space for TAM marking and realization of all arguments, the complementizer clearly marks the two clauses as separate, as does their prosody.

For other classes of CTP, the complement generally does not show full independence from the matrix, but is subject – for varying reasons – either to temporal constraints and/or to referential ones. DESIDERATIVE and MANIPULATIVE CTPs impose a future orientation on their complements; in the case of verbs of DIRECT PERCEPTION, there must be temporal overlap between the events denoted by the two clauses; and MODALS and PHASALS do not denote events distinct from those denoted by the complement, hence there can be no temporal independence. With respect to referential (in)dependence, full referential independence between the two clauses is possible for desideratives and verbs of direct perception (*I want you to go*; *I saw you fall*), but not with the other classes. Hence to varying degrees, these CTP classes determine dependent complements and select reduced complement types. Below we discuss some of the specific motivations which underlie the distribution of complement choice in Mayan languages.

4.2 Availability

An overriding factor is availability. If a language lacks a complement type, then obviously no predicate can select it. The K'ichean languages lack aspectless forms, so predicates which take reduced complements must choose between infinitives and simple finite clauses. Table 10.6 shows the distribution of complement types in Tz'utujil (this is based on Dayley 1985 and is surely incomplete, as Dayley's grammar does not aim to be a systematic study of the properties of all CTP verbs; note that there is no information on the complements of direct perception verbs).

Restrictions on infinitives also determine the choice of complement type. We saw earlier that transitive infinitives in many Mayan languages limit the type of object they accept and as a consequence are simply not available when the object is a full, determined nominal. For example, CTPs which in Jakaltek and Yucatec take infinitives when the complement is intransitive take aspectless complements when the complement is transitive and has a determined object (Jakaltek) or an unincorporated one (Yucatec).

4.3 Grammaticization

Craig (1977:244) observes that infinitives are selected in Jakaltek (only) by 'verbs of desire, verbs of movement, and causative verbs' (a similar restriction holds in Yucatec) (Table 10.7).

TABLE 10.6 DISTRIBUTION OF COMPLEMENT TYPES IN TZ'UTUJIL

Verb class	COMP+finite	Simple finite	Infinitive
utterance	x		
propositional attitude	x		
knowledge/factive	x		
desiderative	x	x	x [less usual]
manipulative			x
motion			x
modal	x	x	x [less usual]
phasal			x
direct perception			

TABLE 10.7 DISTRIBUTION OF COMPLEMENT TYPES IN JAKALTEK

Verb class	COMP+finite	Simple finite	Aspectless	Infinitive
utterance	x			
propositional attitude	x			
knowledge/factive	x			
desiderative	x	x?	x	x
manipulative			x	x [caus]
motion w/ purpose			x	x
modal			x	
phasal			x	
direct perception			x	

These three verb classes are a natural class, as they are the CTPs which impose a future orientation on their complements.[10] This recalls Haspelmath's (1989) proposal that infinitives in complement function develop, through grammaticization, from verb forms with purposive semantics. In Haspelmath's account, the first step in the grammaticization process is extension from purpose clauses to the complements of CTPs which are future-oriented (or 'prospective') (i.e., desideratives and manipulatives/causatives), with extension to the complements of other CTPs occurring later. We saw in §3.4.2 that infinitives occur in many Mayan languages (including Jakaltek and Yucatec) with intransitive verbs of motion to express purpose. If this grammaticization process is the source of infinitives in Mayan, then Jakaltek and Yucatec have taken only the initial step, while the K'ichean languages, which distribute infinitives more widely (cf. Table 10.6) have taken the process further.

4.4 Event compression

The contexts which license more reduced complements in Mayan (simple finite complements, aspectless and infinitival complements) are characterized by referential and/or temporal dependencies between the two clauses.

The role of referential dependence is obvious with infinitives since infinitives lack a syntactically realized subject and depend on the matrix to provide an interpretation. How this is accomplished is discussed in §5, where we show that aspectless forms also sometimes enforce referential dependence. Referential dependence also plays a role in the choice between simple finite and COMP+finite complements. This seems to be common with desideratives which allow coreference between the complement and matrix subject, but do not require it. In several languages, desideratives and verbs of fearing (anti-desideratives) select both COMP+finite and simple finite complements, with the choice conditioned by referential dependency. In (52a, b) from Tsotsil, coreference is expressed by a reduced complement (plain finite), while disjoint reference is expressed by an unreduced one (COMP+finite).[11] Note also that aspect 'matches' in the simple finite complement, (52a), but not in the COMP+finite one, (52b).

TSOTSIL

(52) a. Mu   [x]-s-k'an   [x-bat].
        NEG   NT-A3-want   NT-go
        'She/he doesn't want to go.'

b. Mu   [x]-s-k'an   [ti   ch-bat].
   NEG NT-A3-want   COMP ICP-go
   'She/he doesn't want him/her to go.' {Haviland 1981:355}

Dayley (1985:398) observes that there is a set of verbs in Tz'utujil (which includes desideratives) which usually select simple finite complements when the subjects of the two clauses are the same (53a), but COMP+finite complements when they are different (53b).

TZ'UTUJIL
(53) a. Ja   Ta   Mari'y cheqe n-uu-na'   r-ii'   [chi n-b'e Aa   Xwaan].
        DET CLF Mary   only   ICP-A3SG-feel A3SG-RR COMP ICP-go CLF John
        'Maria is anxious about John going.'

    b. Cheqe n-uu-na'   r-ii'   [n-b'e].
       only   ICP-A3SG-feel A3SG-RR ICP-go
       'She is anxious about going.' {Dayley 1985:404}

Temporal dependence is structurally enforced in both infinitival and aspectless complements, neither of which marks aspect. Plain finite complements too often involve temporal dependence (see Can Pixabaj 2015, for example, on K'iche').

To close this section, we discuss some of the factors which determine complement selection in Yucatec. This discussion is based on Verhoeven (2007), which should be consulted, as what is described below is necessarily very partial.

We mentioned independent finite declarative complements in Yucatec earlier, (12). These are referentially and temporally independent of the matrix clause. They are selected by verbs of knowledge, of propositional attitude, and 'commentative' verbs which take factive complements (e.g., corresponding to 'be glad that, regret', etc.). As noted above (see (12)), there is disagreement as to their syntactic analysis and whether they are embedded or not. We will not try to resolve this here.

There are four types of dependent complements in Yucatec, each of which shows temporal dependence on the matrix. Each of the four types is associated with a particular STATUS, shown in parentheses (IS = incompletive status; DS= dependent status). Status is marked by a suffix, which may be ø (Hofling, this volume). The four types are shown in Figure 10.4. One of these, Type 1, is regarded as clausal in the Yucatecan literature and corresponds here to a plain S complement; the others are called 'verbal cores' (Bohnemeyer 2002 and Verhoeven 2007) and correspond here to VP complements.

The choice of complement type depends primarily on three factors: whether the subject of the complement is referentially dependent on an argument in the matrix; whether the complement is irrealis or realis, and whether the complement is transitive or intransitive (Bohnemeyer 2002; Verhoeven 2007)

The most general complement type is Type 2 ('incompletive core'), which is headed by an aspectless verb with INCOMPLETIVE status morphology. It is associated with realis modality, and is not referentially dependent on the matrix clause (though coreference is not precluded, see (54)). This type, which can be based on both transitive and intransitive stems, forms the complement to verbs of direct perception (54), phasals (55), some causatives, and some verbs which express an attitude towards a proposition or situation (see 58a below).

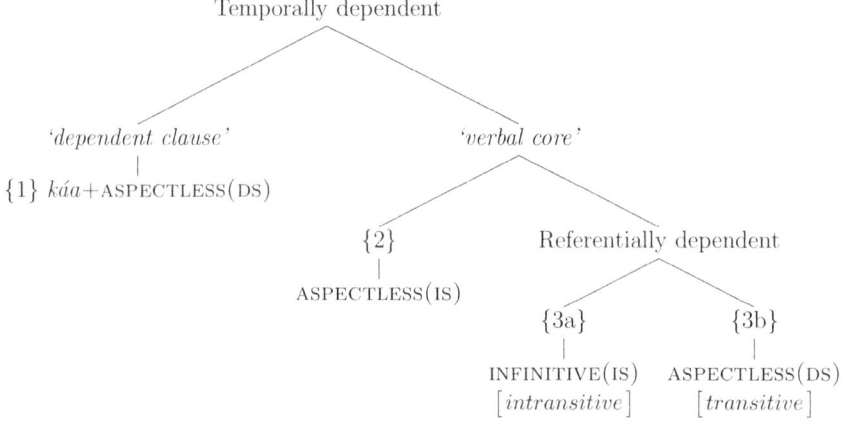

FIGURE 10.4 DEPENDENT COMPLEMENTS IN YUCATEC

YUCATEC (intransitive complement)
(54) T-u   y-il-ah   [in   tàal].
     CP-A3   EP-see-CTS   1SG   come.IIS
     'He saw me coming.' {Verhoeven 2007:294}

YUCATEC (transitive complement)
(55) Tíin   kah-ik   [in   meyah-t-ik   in   kòol].
     PROG.1SG begin-ITS 1SG   work-TR-ITS   1SG   milpa
     'I am starting to make my milpa.' {Verhoeven 2007:130}

More restricted is the infinitive , Type 3a. It is of course referentially dependent on the matrix and is found with CTPs which impose a 'prospective' orientation on the complement (future-oriented desideratives, verbs of motion, some causatives) as well with some habitual CTPs ('know how to', 'used to'). As described above, infinitives are formed only on intransitive stems, (56a), and take INCOMPLETIVE status morphology. Its transitive counterpart, Type 3b, is formed on an aspectless verb with DEPENDENT status, (56b).

YUCATEC
(56) a. In   k'áat   [na'k-al   teh   che'-o'].
        1SG   wish   climb-IIS   DEF:LOC   tree-D2
        'I want to climb on the tree.'

     b. In   k'áat   [in   kan   màaya'].
        1SG   wish   1SG   learn.DTS   Maya
        'I want to learn Maya.' {Verhoeven 2007:137}

Pairs like (56a, b) illustrate the 'split' pattern of Verhoeven.

The final type, Type 1, consists of the element *káa* plus an aspectless verb phrase, whose head can be either transitive or intransitive and with DEPENDENT status morphology.

Although *káa* is often referred to as a complementizer, Gutiérrez Bravo (2015:72n) suggests that it occupies the same structural position as (the many) aspect markers in Yucatec (Bohnemeyer 2002). Like *káa*, all of these combine with aspectless VPs in various statuses. It thus makes sense on structural grounds to treat *káa* as a mood marker in INFL (see Figure 10.1). If this is correct, *káa* clauses are IPs, i.e., simple S complements.

káa clauses correspond roughly to subjunctive complements in Romance languages and are associated with irrealis modality and disjoint reference. On the one hand, they contrast with Type 3 with respect to referentiality: a set of desiderative verbs which select Type 3 when the complement subject is controlled by the matrix subject (56), select a *káa* clause complement when it is not, (57).

YUCATEC
(57) In   k'áat   [káa   wen-ek-ech].
      1SG   wish   KAA   sleep-DIS-B2SG
      'I want you to sleep.' {Verhoeven 2007:132}

On the other hand, *káa* clauses are associated with irrealis, and contrast on this dimension with Type 2 complements. For example, with some predicates of what Verhoeven calls 'emotional or evaluative attitude', a Type 2 complement is interpreted as referring to an actual or likely situation (58a), but a *káa* clause complement to a hypothetical one.

YUCATEC
(58) a. Uts   t-in   t'àan   [u   k'áax-al   ha'].
          good   LOC-A1SG speech   A3   rain-IIS   water
          'I like that it is raining/I like it to rain.'

      b. Uts   t-in   t'àan   [káa   k'áax-ak   ha'].
          good   LOC-A1SG speech   KAA   rain-DIS   water
          'I would like if/that it will rain/rained.' {Verhoeven 2007:309}

The distribution of complement types in Yucatec is thus sensitive in complex ways to temporal dependence, referential dependence, mood (realis vs. irrealis), epistemic commitment, and transitivity, and to the way these interact with the meanings of particular CTPs. It seems likely that complement choice in all or most Mayan languages has similar complexities, ones which will become evident with further research.

5 ARGUMENT SHARING IN NON-FINITE CLAUSES

We close this chapter by discussing more systematically the identification of the subject in non-finite clauses. This is an important issue in infinitival clauses, since they lack specified subjects. Hence a value for the subject must be supplied external to the clause, e.g., by Control. Control however is not the only mechanism which achieves this: Raising and Clause Union are other constructions which occur in Mayan and which involve infinitives lacking specified subjects. Interestingly, all three of these constructions – Control, Raising, and Clause Union – are found not only with infinitival complements, but also with aspectless complements. Thus both types of non-finite clause in Mayan permit the cross-clausal interactions that are involved in these constructions. We will start first with Control, then move to Raising, and finally to Clause Union, discussing in turn both infinitival constructions and aspectless ones.

5.1 Control

Control is involved in examples like (59), where the complement subject is interpreted as coreferential with the matrix subject.

JAKALTEK
(59) Ch-[y]-oche   naj   [kanhalw-oj].
      ICP-A3-like   PRON.M   dance-INF
      'He likes to dance.' {Craig 1977:311}

(59) involves what Stiebels (2007) calls *structural* control, i.e., identification of the complement subject with the matrix subject is structurally enforced by the absence of the complement subject. But obligatory coreference between complement subject and a matrix argument can be found even when the complement subject is syntactically present, e.g., as evidenced by indexing on the complement verb.

JAKALTEK
(60) a. Ch-[y]-oche   ix   [s-watx'e-'   s-ba].
          ICP-A3SG-like   PRON.F   A3-make-IRR   A3-RR
          'She likes to arrange herself.' {Craig 1977:238}

      b. Ch-in   s-chej   naj   [hin   kol-o'   ix].
          ICP-B1SG   A3-order   PRON.M   A1SG   help-IRR   PRON.F
          'He orders me to help her.' {Craig 1977:242}

These examples have aspectless complements, not infinitival ones, but still require coreference between the complement subject and a matrix argument (the subject in (60a), the object in (60b)) (Craig 1977:239). They involve what Stiebels calls *inherent* control, i.e., coreference is enforced lexico-semantically, not structurally. Given the structural features of Mayan infinitives that we have documented here – in particular, the limited availability of transitive infinitives – it is not surprising that inherent control would play a significant role in Mayan complementation. In Jakaltek, infinitival constructions cannot be used in cases like (60a, b), but the required coreference between complement subject and matrix subject or object is still enforced by the CTP.

5.2 Raising

Raising refers to constructions in which an argument (typically the subject) of the complement is realized as a syntactic argument of the matrix verb, even though it (ostensibly) bears no semantic role in the matrix. Raising often results in a surface structure which is identical to that of Control, as in the English pair:

(61) a. John wants [to be happy].   Control
      b. John seems [to be happy].   Raising

In (61a), *John* has semantic roles in both the matrix clause and the complement (=*John₁ wants that he₁ be happy*), while in (61b), *John* has a semantic role only in the complement clause (= *It seems that John is happy*). Nonetheless, *John* clearly has a syntactic role in the matrix of (61b), i.e., it is the matrix subject. Hence, we say that *John* raises into the matrix.

A battery of tests have been developed to distinguish Control and Raising in English and other languages (Davies and Dubinsky 2004), but with a few exceptions (Craig 1977; Verhoeven 2007), these have not been applied to the Mayan cases. In Mayan, the chief evidence in favor of raising analyses has been the co-existence of pairs like (61b) (*John seems to be happy*) and its paraphrase *It seems that John is happy*, which are presumed to be synonymous. In Mayan, the best candidates for such pairs are found with complement-taking aspectual predicates.

Consider the expression of progressive aspect in K'iche'. The progressive 'auxiliary' *tajin* occurs in two structures.[12] The two structures distribute the features of aspect and person differently. In the first, both the progressive and the lexical verb ('eat') inflect for aspect, but only the lexical verb inflects for person. In this case, *tajin* can be analyzed as an intransitive CTP which selects a simple finite clause as its sole argument, something like 'my eating is happening'. Since the clausal argument is 3rd person, there is no overt marking on the matrix CTP.

K'ICHE'
(62) Ka-tajin [k-in-wa'-ik].
     ICP-PROG   ICP-B1SG-eat-SS
     'I am eating.' {López Ixcoy 1997:175}

In the second structure, the progressive inflects for both aspect and person, while the lexical verb is in infinitival form.

K'ICHE'
(63) K-in-tajin   [pa tz'ib'an-ik].
     ICP-B1SG-PROG   PREP write-SS
     'I am writing.' {López Ixcoy 1997:177}

Assuming that the argument structure of (63) is like that of (62), the subject of the complement clause must raise into the matrix, where it is indexed on the matrix verb.

Evidence that the 1st person does become grammatical subject of *tajin* in (63) (and is not simply indexed there for morphological reasons) comes from the obligatory presence of the preposition (*pa*) which introduces the infinitive. Once the complement subject raises to the matrix, the argument structure of the matrix is saturated and the complement clause must function as an oblique, flagged by a preposition. Thus, the surface grammatical relations in (62) and (63) are clearly different.

Raising in K'iche' results in an infinitival form, where the (raised) subject is not indexed on the complement verb. But aspectless forms appear in the same position in other languages. Polian (2013b:362) cites the pair in (64) from Tseltal (these parallel (62) and (63), respectively).

TSELTAL
(64) a. Yakal [j-tsak-bel-at].
        PROG   A1-grab-NF.TR-B2SG
        'I am grabbing you.'

     b. Yakal-on   [ta   j-tsak-bel-at].
        PROG-B1SG   PREP   A1-grab-NF.TR-B2SG
        'I am grabbing you.'

Yakal is a CTP which selects an aspectless clause in Tseltal (note the subject agreement in the complement in both (64a, b)). In (64a), that clause is its sole argument. In (64b), *yakal* is indexed with features of the complement subject (1SG), suggesting that the complement subject has raised to become subject of the matrix. Again, the presence of the preposition in (64b) shows that the 1st person is matrix subject, and the clausal complement an oblique argument.[13]

To a limited degree then, Raising, like Control, appears to be possible both with infinitival complements and with aspectless ones.

5.3 Clause Union

Clause Union is another construction in which nominals which bear semantic relations in the complement become syntactic arguments of the matrix verb. In several Mayan languages, Clause Union is triggered by the basic causative verb and shows a pattern of derived grammatical relations which is attested in other languages: when the complement is intransitive, its subject becomes direct object of the matrix; when the complement is transitive, both arguments become arguments of the matrix, with the details determined by factors not relevant here.

What *is* relevant here is that Clause Union in Mayan can involve an infinitival complement, as in Jakaltek (65), where the complement subject is indexed only on the main verb. But it can also involve an aspectless complement, as in Tsotsil (66), where the subject is indexed both on the complement verb and on the matrix. See Craig (1977) and Aissen (1987) for details.

JAKALTEK
(65) Ch-ach   w-a'   [xew-oj].
      ICP-B2SG   A1SG-CAUS   rest-INF
      'I make you rest.' {Craig 1977:362}

TSOTSIL
(66) L-i-y-ak'   [ak'otaj-ik-on].
      CP-B1-A3-CAUS   dance-SS-B1SG
      'He let me dance'. {Aissen 1987:215}

In sum, some of the cross-clausal interactions which are limited in many European languages to structures with infinitival complements, occur in structures with aspectless complements in Mayan. Many of the traditional accounts of these constructions take the unavailability of case or agreement in the complement to be central to the analysis. Since aspectless verbs in Mayan which figure in Raising, Control, and Clause Union *do* have person marking (though not aspect marking), they suggest that such accounts cannot be the whole story.

6 SUMMARY

Table 10.8 summarizes some of the properties discussed here in connection with the four complement types. The properties above the line characterize more independent complements, the ones below the line more dependent complements.

Table 10.8 shows that COMP+finite complements exhibit all the properties associated with independent complements, and none of those associated with dependent ones. The

TABLE 10.8 PROPERTIES OF COMPLEMENT TYPES

	COMP+*finite*	*Simple finite*	*Aspectless*	*Infinitive*
aspect	y	y	n	n
subject agreement	y	y	y	n
object agreement	y	y	y	restricted
internal negation	y	n	n	n
internal focus	y	n	n	n
extraposition	y	n/y	n	n
prosodic independence	y	n/y?	n	n
aspect agreement	n	y	n/a	n/a
host raising	n	?	y	y
host control	n	?	y	y
host clause union	n	n?	y	y

non-finite types largely lack the properties associated with independent complements (argument agreement in aspectless clauses being the exception), but exhibit the properties associated with dependent complements. The classification of these three types, at least with respect to these properties, is generally clear.

Less clear is the simple finite type, which is more heterogeneous across the family and, judging from published descriptions, subject to variation within individual languages. Further, for some of the properties listed here, the facts have not been documented. What does seem clear is that simple finite clauses are intermediate between the most independent complement type (COMP+finite) and the non-finite types, and are generally found in semantically dependent (e.g., irrealis) contexts. More research on the properties of this type in particular languages is needed to clarify their analysis. It is quite possible that in the end, it will be necessary to recognize several subtypes.

NOTES

1 Relevant work on some of the topics *not* discussed here includes Mateo Toledo 2008 on complex predicates in Q'anjob'al; Gutiérrez Bravo 2015 on relative clauses in Yucatec; Aissen and Zavala 2010, which includes several papers on secondary predication in Mayan languages; Zavala 1993 on the grammaticalization of verbs of motion in Mayan; and Robertson 1976, Bohnemeyer 2002, and Coon 2013, among others, on the analysis of aspect markers as complement-taking predicates.

2 In glossing Yucatec examples, I retain the spelling of original sources, but have aimed to regularize the glosses. Following Hofling (this volume), I use ICP (INCOMPLETIVE) and CP (COMPLETIVE) for preverbal aspect markers and the following abbreviations for status suffixes: IIS/ITS (incomplete intransitive/transitive status), CIS/CTS (completive intransitive/transitive status), DIS/DTS (dependent intransitive/transitive status).

3 These authors take the optional presence of the enclitic *-e'* separating the complement from the main clause as evidence for the juxtaposition analysis:

YUCATEC
(i) Tíin   tukl-ik-e'   [yan   u   k'áax-al   ha'].
     PROG:A1SG   think-ITS-ENC   DEB   A3SG   rain-IIS   water
     'I am thinking that it will rain.' {Verhoeven 2007:125}

If *e'* occurs only clause-finally, as these works assume, then the complement appears to be external to the matrix. However, AnderBois (2016) shows structures with *e'* that do not involve complementation, but a topic-comment structure, roughly 'according to what I think, it will rain'.

4 Descriptions of related phenomena in other Mayan languages include Craig (1977:259ff.) on 'inversion' in Jakaltek and Zavala (1992:307) on Akatek.

5 There may be some dialect variation in this area. López Ixcoy (1997:430) cites analogous examples with both vos and vso order.

6 However, in Tsotsil, the allomorphy of Set B is sensitive to whether the verb carries an aspect prefix (or particle). Aspectless forms always determine Set B suffixes, while aspect-bearing forms (almost) always determine Set B prefixes.

7 Aspectless forms figure in the grammatical aspect system of a number of languages. These are cases in which intransitive CTPs which selected aspectless complements have come to function as grammatical aspect markers. See Robertson (1976), Bohnemeyer (2002), and Coon (2013) for discussion.

8 The transitive infinitive is formed with -*oj* (for monosyllabic (root) transitives) and -*n* (for bisyllabic (derived) transitives) (Dayley 1985).

9 The infinitive suffix -*iik* retains its long vowel sentence-finally and before a definite noun phrase; otherwise it undergoes a regular process of vowel shortening.

10 In fact, these verb classes also take aspectless complements (see Table 10.7) and when they do, they require a suffix (V') on the complement verb which Day (1973) and Craig (1977) identify as a future suffix.

11 The dependent complement is possible though without coreference – at least in Tsotsil and Tseltal – when the complement subject is 1st or 2nd person (see (3), Tsotsil, and (25), Tseltal).

12 López Ixcoy (1997) reports that there is a third structure in which *tajin* is not inflected at all.

13 Craig (1977:Ch.10) argued for a Raising ('Promotion') analysis for certain Jakaltek constructions involving higher phasal verbs. Thus she took (i), where the matrix verb agrees with the complement subject, to be derived from (ii), where it does not.

JAKALTEK (Craig 1977:290, 289)
(i)   Xk-ach   ichi   [ha-munlayi].
      CP-B2SG   begin   A2SG-work
      'You began to work.'
(ii) X-'ichi   [ha-munlayi.]
      CP-begin   A2SG-work
      'You began to work.'

However, the Raising analysis is dubious. There is evidence that (ii) is rather an auxiliary construction (R. Zavala, p.c.); further, some of Craig's original discussion suggests that (i) really involves (inherent) Control, not Raising. In particular, the subject in the (i) structure must be animate. This is expected if what is involved is Control; it is not at all expected if it is Raising. Still puzzling is the fact that an imperative cannot be formed from the (i) structure (Craig 1977:294).

REFERENCES

Aissen, Judith. 1987. *Tzotzil clause structure*. Dordrecht: Reidel.
Aissen, Judith. 1992. "Topic and focus in Mayan." *Language* 63: 43–80.

Aissen, Judith, and Roberto Zavala, ed. 2010. *La predicación secundaria en las lenguas de meso-américa*. Mexico City: CIESAS.

AnderBois, Scott. 2016. "Semantics and pragmatics of (not)-at-issueness in Yucatec Maya attitude reports." *Semantics & Pragmatics* 9(19): 1–50.

Baker, Mark. 1988. *Incorporation*. Chicago: University of Chicago Press.

Berinstein, Ava. 1985. *Evidence for multiattachment in K'ekchi Mayan*. New York: Garland Publishing.

Bohnemeyer, Jürgen. 2002. *The grammar of time reference in Yukatek Maya*. Munich: LINCOM.

Can Pixabaj, Telma Angelina. 2015. "Complement and purpose clauses in K'iche'." PhD diss., University of Texas.

Coon, Jessica. 2013. *Aspects of split ergativity*. Oxford: Oxford University Press.

Coon, Jessica, Pedro Mateo Pedro, and Omer Preminger. 2014. The role of Case in A-Bar extraction asymmetries: Evidence from Mayan. *Linguistic Variation* 14: 179–242.

Craig, Colette. 1977. *The structure of Jacaltec*. Austin: University of Texas Press.

Davies, William, and Stanley Dubinsky. 2004. *The grammar of raising and control*. Oxford: *Blackwell*.

Day, Christopher. 1973. *The Jacaltec language*. Bloomington: Indiana University Publications *(Language Science Monographs, 12)*.

Dayley, Jon P. 1981. "Voice and ergativity in Mayan languages." *Journal of Mayan Linguistics* 2: 3–82.

Dayley, Jon P. 1985. *Tz'utujil grammar*. Berkeley: University of California Press.

Dayley, Juan Felipe, Francisco Pérez Mendoza, and Miguel Hernández Mendoza. 1996. *Diccionario Tz'utujil*. La Antigua, Guatemala: Proyecto Lingüístico Francisco Marroquín.

England, Nora. 2013. "Cláusulas con flexión reducida en mam." In *Clases léxicas, posesión y cláusulas complejas en lenguas de Mesoamérica*, ed. by Enrique L. Palancar and Roberto Zavala, 277–303. Mexico City: CIESAS.

Givón, Talmy. 2001. *Syntax: An introduction*. Amsterdam: John Benjamins.

Gutiérrez Bravo, Rodrigo. 2002. "Formas verbales incorporadas transitivas en maya yucateco." In *Del cora al maya yucateco: Estudios lingüísticos sobre algunas lenguas indígenas mexicanas*, ed. by Paulette Levy, 131–78. México City: UNAM.

Gutiérrez Bravo, Rodrigo. 2010. "Los complementos oracionales en maya yucateco." *Lingüística Mexicana* 5: 5–31.

Gutiérrez Bravo, Rodrigo. 2015. Las cláusulas relativas en maya yucateco (Estudios de Lingüística, 22). México City: El Colegio de México.

Haspelmath, Martin. 1989. "From purposive to infinitive – A universal path of grammaticization." *Folia Linguistica Historica* X(1–2): 287–310.

Haviland, John. 1981. Sk'op sotz'leb: el tzotzil de San Lorenzo Zinacantán. Mexico City: UNAM.

Henderson, Robert. 2012. "Morphological alternations at the intonational phrase edge: the case of K'ichee'." *Natural Language & Linguistic Theory* 30: 741–87.

Kaufman, Terrence. 1990. "Algunos rasgos estructurales de los idiomas mayances con referencia especial al k'iche'." In *Lecturas sobre la lingüística maya*, ed. by Nora C. England and Stephen R. Elliott, 59–114. Antigua Guatemala: CIRMA.

Kockelman, Paul. 2003. "The interclausal relations hierarchy in Q'eqchi' Maya." *International Journal of American Linguistics* 69: 25–48.

Larsen, Thomas. 1988. "Manifestations of ergativity in Quiché grammar." PhD diss., University of California, Berkeley.

Laughlin, Robert. 1977. *Of cabbages and kings*. Washington, DC: Smithsonian Institution Press.

Laughlin, Robert. 1980. *Of shoes and ships and sealing wax*. Washington, DC: Smithsonian Institution Press.

López Ixcoy, Candelaria Dominga. 1997. *Gramática K'ichee'*. Guatemala City: Cholsamaj.

Massam, Diane. 2001. "Pseudo noun incorporation in Niuean." *Natural Language & Linguistic Theory* 19: 153–97.

Mateo Toledo, B'alam. 2008. "The family of complex predicates in Q'anjob'al Maya: their syntax and meaning." PhD diss., University of Texas.

Mateo Toledo, B'alam. 2011. "The finiteness of nonverbal predicates in Q'anjob'al (Maya)." In *New perspectives in Mayan linguistics,* ed. by Heriberto Avelino, 160–82. Newcastle upon Tyne: Cambridge Scholars Publishing.

Mateo Toledo, B'alam. 2013. "Cláusulas sin aspecto e infinitivas en q'anjob'al." In *Clases léxicas, posesión y cláusulas complejas en lenguas de Mesoamérica*, ed. by Enrique L. Palancar and Roberto Zavala, 247–76. Mexico City: CIESAS.

Noonan, Michael. 2007. "Complementation." In *Language typology and syntactic description*, vol. 2, ed. by Timothy Shopen, 52–150. Cambridge: Cambridge University Press.

Norman, William M., and Lyle Campbell. 1978. "Towards a proto-Mayan syntax: a comparative perspective on grammar." In *Papers in Mayan linguistics*, ed. by Nora C. England, 136–56. Columbia: University of Missouri.

Polian, Gilles. 2013a. *Gramática del tseltal de Oxchuc*. Mexico City: CIESAS.

Polian, Gilles. 2013b. "Infinitivos transitivos: innovaciones del tseltal en la familia maya." In *Clases léxicas, posesión y cláusulas complejas en lenguas de Mesoamérica*, ed. by Enrique L. Palancar and Roberto Zavala, 339–80. Mexico City: CIESAS.

Reinhart, Tanya. 1983. "Point of view in language – the use of parentheticals." In *Essays on deixis*, ed. by Gisa Rauh, 169–94. Tübingen: Gunter Narr Verlag.

Robertson, John. 1976. "The structure of pronoun incorporation in the Mayan verbal complex." PhD diss., Harvard University.

Ross, John Robert. 1973. "Slifting." In *The formal analysis of natural languages*, ed. by Maurice Gross, Morris Halle, and Marcel Paul Schützenberger, 133–69. The Hague: Mouton.

Santos Nicolás, José Francisco, and José Gonzalo Benito Pérez. 1998. *Rukorb'aal Poqom Q'orb'al (Gramática Poqom)*. Guatemala City: Cholsamaj.

Schmidtke-Bode, Karsten. 2009. *A typology of purpose clauses*. Amsterdam: John Benjamins.

Shklovsky, Kirill. 2012. "Person-case effects in Tseltal." *The Linguistic Review* 29: 439–90.

Stiebels, Barbara. 2007. "Towards a typology of complement control." In *Studies in complement control, ZAS Papers in Linguistics* 47: 1–80. Berlin: ZAS.

Verhoeven, Elisabeth. 2007. *Experiential constructions in Yucatec Maya: A typologically based analysis of a functional domain in a Mayan language*. Amsterdam: John Benjamins.

Zavala, Roberto. 1992. *El kanjobal de San Miguel Acatán*. Mexico City: Universidad Nacional Autónoma de México.

Zavala, Roberto. 1993. "Clause integration with verbs of motion in Mayan languages." MA thesis, University of Oregon.

CHAPTER 11

INFORMATION STRUCTURE IN MAYAN*

Judith Aissen

1 INTRODUCTION

The study of INFORMATION STRUCTURE in Mayan has proceeded in tandem with the study of morphology and syntax. This is hardly surprising, given the range of morphosyntactic devices that are harnessed by the various languages to encode information structure relations. Such devices include word order, voice, and agreement, as well as specialized syntactic constructions and morphology. A sensitivity to the status of elements in the 'flow' of information has thus been an unavoidable correlate of basic grammatical description. Our goal here is to survey the present understanding of information structure in Mayan and to identify some major gaps in what we know.

'Information' refers to what we learn about individuals and situations. The status of a fact with respect to informativity is inherently dynamic: what is 'new' information at one moment is likely to be 'old' information in the next. Factors which play a role in how informativity determines linguistic form include the distinction between 'given' and 'new' discourse referents, the identification of the individual about whom information is provided (the 'topic'), and the identification of what information in a message is new (the 'focus') (Krifka 2008). The discussion that follows will therefore be organized around these three notions and their complements:

(1) a. GIVEN (discourse referents) vs. NEW (discourse referents)
    b. FOCUS vs. BACKGROUND
    c. TOPIC vs. COMMENT

The information structural status of an element at a particular point in time is determined against the background of the current DISCOURSE CONTEXT. Following many others, I take the discourse context to include the discourse participants, minimally the speaker and the addressees, as well as what is called the COMMON GROUND (CG). The CG is the set of propositions which the discourse participants have agreed to mutually accept. These propositions can be taken for granted as the discourse moves forward, they are 'presupposed'. The CG also contains a set of 'given' discourse referents, those referents that have already been introduced into the discourse, or that are known to be familiar to speaker and addressee. Some of these referents are more salient than others, e.g., by virtue of recency of mention or for some inherent reason.

I assume that the goal of discourse is 'to discover the way things are', to update the CG, typically by adding propositions to the CG. Questions, both explicit and implicit, play a key role in determining the direction in which the CG develops. An assertion which is proffered by the speaker and accepted by the addressee updates the CG.

Sections 2–5 discuss what is currently known about information structure in Mayan. We start in §2 with Du Bois's important work on the encoding of given and new discourse referents and with recent refinements to his account. Section 3 briefly surveys early approaches to the study of topic and focus in Mayan. Section 4 establishes pragmatic and morphosyntactic properties of various focus constructions in Mayan, distinguishing information focus from contrastive focus. In §5, two distinct topic constructions (internal and external) are identified on structural grounds; pragmatic differences are shown to correlate with their syntactic differences.

2 GIVEN VS. NEW

Du Bois (1987) showed that there is a significant correlation between the GIVENNESS status of discourse referents (GIVEN vs. NEW) and grammatical function. Based on a corpus of unplanned speech in Sakapultek (Mayan), he proposed that new discourse referents are introduced as O or S (also as oblique), while A is reserved for reference to discourse referents which are already part of the discourse context, i.e., are GIVEN. This is the theory of PREFERRED ARGUMENT STRUCTURE. In the common situation then where the speaker wishes to refer to a new discourse referent as agent, she is likely to first introduce that referent as S of an intransitive verb, often one which is low in semantic content, e.g., an existential or a verb of motion, followed by a transitive clause in which the referent functions as A.[1]

SAKAPULTEK
(2) a. X-aq'an   jun   achenh . . .   chu'   ch'ee',
       CP-ascend   a   man   atop   tree
       'A man climbed up a tree.'

  b. x-a-r- . . . -ch'up-o'   nik'yaj   peeras.
     CP-MOV-A3- . . . -pick-SS   some   pears
     'he went and picked some pears.' (Du Bois 1987:813)

Table 11.1 shows the distribution of new and non-new mentions for each of the three core argument positions in Du Bois's corpus.

Thus, while S + O are associated with both new and non-new mentions, A is associated almost exclusively with non-new mentions. England and Martin (2003) present similar statistics for four further Mayan languages (Mam, Mocho, Tektiteko, and Q'anjob'al). Based on the Sakalpultek data, Du Bois proposes a constraint he calls 'Avoid New A'.

Although Du Bois does not distinguish *types* of intransitive verbs in his statistics, his discussion (p. 836) distinguishes intransitive verbs whose use is *pragmatically* motivated (by virtue of the capacity to introduce a new discourse referent as S) from ones whose use is *semantically* motivated (by virtue of semantic content). He does not flesh out this distinction, but does say that it is different from the intransitive split associated with volitionality and control (Mithun 1991). However, in recent work on Tsotsil and Chol, Martínez (2012)

TABLE 11.1 DISTRIBUTION OF NEW VS. NON-NEW IN SAKAPULTEK

	New	Non-new	Total	% New
A	6	181	187	3.2
S+O	100	328	428	23.3

and Vázquez and Zavala (2013) have argued, in essence, that this split in discourse function *is* sensitive to agentivity. Distinguishing agentive subjects (S_A) from non-agentive ones (S_O), their proposal is that new discourse referents are introduced as O and S_O, with A and S_A functions restricted to discourse referents already in the CG, i.e., given.[2]

Table 11.2, constructed from data in Vázquez and Zavala (2013), shows the distribution of new and non-new mentions for the Chol corpus.[3] It is directly comparable to the Sakapultek data in Table 11.1 and the ratio of new to non-new mentions is similar. However, Vázquez and Zavala (2013), tease the category S+O apart into three relations: S_A, S_O, and O.[4] When these relations are distinguished, as shown in Table 11.3, a different picture emerges. The distribution of non-new and new for A is close in the two languages (new referents account for only about 3 percent of As in both), but the profiles of S_A and S_O are quite different. The percentage of new S_A is nearly identical to that of A, with both relations almost exclusively reserved for given discourse referents. New discourse referents are introduced much more frequently in other grammatical relations: S_O, O, and oblique.

It is reasonable to ask whether the distinct roles that S_A and S_O play in Chol information structure is related to the fact that the two relations are also distinguished morphosyntactically (see fn. 4 and references). More work on a wider range of languages is needed to be certain, but the fact that Tsotsil shows a similar split between S_A and S_O but does not distinguish them in the morphosyntax (Martínez 2012) suggests that the theory of Preferred Argument Structure needs to make a more fine-grained distinction between types of intransitive S.

The packaging of given and new discourse referents in Mayan has repercussions elsewhere in the grammars of these languages, especially in the choice of voice and in the morphosyntax of focus. The connection to voice is clear: the dispreference for new As means that active transitive clauses will be avoided when A is indefinite; some alternative mode of expression, e.g., passive, will be used instead. Such a constraint has been observed in various languages (see England 1991).

Further, in the partition of a sentence into topic-comment and focus-background, A and O each have default information structure statuses: the default status of A is as topic (not focus); the default status of O is as part of the comment, hence not topic but possibly focus.

(3) A_{Topic} [. . . O . . .] $_{Comment}$

TABLE 11.2 DISTRIBUTION OF NEW VS. NON-NEW IN CHOL

	New	Non-new	Total	%New
A	17	640	657	2.6
S+O	454	2087	2541	17.9

TABLE 11.3 DISTRIBUTION OF NEW VS. NON-NEW IN CHOL

	New	Non-new	Total	%New
A	17	640	657	2.6
S_A	3	100	103	2.9
S_O	271	1465	1736	15.6
O	180	522	702	26
Oblique	173	261	434	40

These considerations probably motivate the existence in many Mayan languages of special morphosyntactic apparatus when A is focused (see §4.4.1 below).

3   PREVIOUS WORK ON TOPIC AND FOCUS

Since at least the 1970s, observations concerning the grammatical encoding of topic and focus are found in the Mayan literature, primarily as part of broader descriptions. In addition, there have been at least two large-scale studies devoted to information structure in particular Mayan languages – Datz (1980) on Jakaltek and Brody (1982) on Tojolab'al.

Early work on topic and focus was couched in terms of word order, conceived as a linear ordering of S, O, and V. Durbin and Ojeda (1978), for example, observe that all six orders of the three elements are possible in Yucatec Maya, but that different orders are associated with different discourse functions of S and O (some orders are also subject to morphological restrictions). They note, for example, that APV (SOV) requires that the first NP be [+specific] and that the second (if determinerless) be focused:

YUCATEC
(4) Le wíinik=o'   j-chakmo'ol   k-u-kíins-ik.
    DET man=ENC   CLF-jaguar   ICP-A3-kill-SS
    'That man kills jaguars (not other animals).' (Durbin and Ojeda 1978:72)

A similar approach is taken in Dayley (1985:304) for Tz'utujil, where it is reported that five of the six orders are possible. Again, different orders are associated with particular discourse functions of S and O and some are subject to morphological restrictions.

Initial steps towards a more syntactically articulated proposal were taken in Norman (1977), which proposed that *topics* occupied sentence-initial position, while *foci* occurred preverbally. These two 'positions' are linearly indistinguishable when only a single constituent precedes the verb, but may be distinguished in the presence of other elements, e.g., negation. This approach was further developed in Aissen (1992) and grounded in a theory of phrase structure that recognized various levels of clausal-structure (see §5.2 below). This analysis identified three distinct positions for topic and focus: one for (preverbal) focus and two for (preverbal) topic. The distinctions between these structural positions and their associated pragmatic differences are discussed in §5.2-§5.3.

A methodological note: since *topic* and *focus* are information structure relations, verifying that a linguistic element in an utterance is *topic* or *focus* requires access to the context in which that utterance occurs. Therefore, wherever possible, examples given below are cited along with the relevant discourse context. In the absence of context, e.g., in (4), from Yucatec, we are forced to rely on translations which approximate the pragmatic sense of the original.

4   FOCUS

4.1   New information focus

The notion of 'focus' is usually introduced through question and answer pairs. In the Tsotsil dialogue in (5), the FOCUS is that element in the answer which corresponds to the interrogative expression in the question, namely *Muk'ta Jok* (the focused element is indicated by F (subscript); the corresponding material in the English translation is shown in small caps).

TSOTSIL

(5) a. Bu   l-a-'ay?
      where   CP-B2-go
      'Where did you go?'

    b. L-i-'ay   ta   Muk'ta Jok'$_F$.
      CP-B1-go to   Muk'ta Jok'
      'I went to MUK'TA JOK'.' (Laughlin 1977:118)

The remainder of the answer corresponds to what is presupposed in the question (*you went somewhere*) and is the BACKGROUND. The focus in the answer to a simple information question is variously called *information focus, new information focus, rheme,* and *non-contrastive focus*. The information focus in (5b) remains in situ, i.e., it occurs in the same position as a corresponding non-focused constituent. The dialogue in (6) (between a child and parent) shows that the same is true for an argument focus.

TSOTSIL

(6) Q: K'usi   ta   j-lajes   ta   ch'ivit   tana?
      what   ICP   A1-eat in   market now
      'What am I going to eat in the market?'

    A: Ta j-lo'-tik   manko$_F$ ta   j-ti'-tik   ch'ich'$_F$.
      ICP A1-eat-1PL.INCL mango ICP A1-eat-1PL.INCL blood
      'We'll eat MANGO, we'll eat [boiled] BLOOD.' {TEXT}

New information focus has not been much discussed in the Mayan literature, probably because it does not involve any syntactic or morphological changes (nor has a role for intonational marking been identified in most of the languages, either for new information focus or contrastive focus, see below, §4.5). However recent work of Velleman (2014) and Verhoeven and Skopeteas (2015) has identified a constraint on in situ focus which had not been previously known. They argue that in Yucatec and K'ichee', the subject of a transitive clause (A) which remains in situ cannot be felicitously interpreted as new information focus. In K'ichee', for example, Velleman (p. 186) cites the contrast between an in situ O (7) and an in situ A (8) (# indicates infelicity).

K'ICHEE'

(7) a. What does María want to eat?

    b. Aree k-u-tij   le   ichaj$_F$ le   al   Mari'y.
      FOC   ICP-A3SG-eat DET vegetable DET CLF María
      ' María will eat THE VEGETABLES.'

K'ICHEE'

(8) a. Who is going to eat the vegetables?

    b. #Aree k-u-tij   le   ichaj   le   al   Mari'y$_F$.
      FOC   ICP-A3SG-eat DET vegetable DET CLF María
      Intended: 'MARÍA will eat the vegetables.'

One might think that this contrast follows from Du Bois's 'Avoid New A' constraint (§2). But it does not. Du Bois's constraint concerns the realization of new *discourse referents*,

not new *information*. What is new in an 'information focus' is not the discourse referent itself, but the relation of the discourse referent to a proposition. For example, in the
interchange, 'who left?', 'John left', *John* is new information focus, but need not refer
to a new discourse referent. Further, the constraint on an in situ information focus A is
not as general as the 'Avoid New A' constraint. While all Mayan languages are probably
subject to some version of 'Avoid New A', only some restrict a new information focus A.
For example, Tseltal does not (see discussion in §4.4.1 below, especially (40b)). Velleman
(2014) argues that the constraint on an in situ information focus A is in fact found only
in those languages which require special agent focus morphology for *moved* foci. We
will return to this question in §4.4.1 after discussing contrastive focus and agent focus
morphology.

4.2 Contrastive focus pragmatics

What *has* been discussed a great deal in the Mayan literature is CONTRASTIVE focus, as this
does involve special morphology and syntax. Consider for example, the exchange in (9)
from Tsotsil:

TSOTSIL
(9) a. Q: "What are you doing?"

    b. A: "Ta   j-ts'un,   ta   j-ts'un   ton,   ta   j-ts'un   te'."
          ICP A1-plant ICP A1-plant rock ICP A1-plant tree
        'I'm planting, I'm planting rocks, I'm planting trees.'

    c. Narrator:
        Pero chobtik$_F$ ts-ts'un   un.
        but   corn   ICP.A3-plant PAR
        'But it was CORN that he was planting.' (Laughlin 1977:334)

The first two clauses (9a, b) report a dialogue, followed in (9c) by the narrator's comment. In (9c), *chobtik* 'corn' is focused and occurs not in the canonical post-verbal position but before the verb. (I assume for now that the focus moves to its surface position,
but discuss an alternative analysis in §4.3.3.)

An important question is why focus would move when it can remain in situ. Work on
a range of languages has observed that a moved ('ex situ') focus is often explicitly contrastive in a way that an unmoved focus is not (Kiss 1998; Vallduví and Vilkuna 1998;
Hartmann and Zimmermann 2007). This has also been noted for many Mayan languages,
including Tz'utujil (Dayley 1985:324–5), Q'eqchi' (Berinstein 1985:93), K'ichee' (López
Ixcoy 1997:380), Yucatec Maya (Gutiérrez-Bravo and Monforte 2011; Gutiérrez-Bravo
2015) and Tseltal (Polian 2013:774). In (9c), *chobtik* 'corn' contrasts with *ton* 'rock,
stone' and *te'* 'tree' in the previous utterance, (9b). Not only does the narrator assert that
he was planting corn, but, at the same time, he rejects the assertions of the immediately
preceding utterances, *he was planting rocks, he was planting trees.*

To make sense of this, I will assume, following Rooth (1992), that the interpretation
of a sentence S which contains a focus F involves reference to a set of ALTERNATIVE propositions that differ from S only in the value of F. For (6), that set of alternatives might
include *we'll eat tortillas, we'll eat meat*, etc., as well as the proffered answer, *we'll eat
mango, we'll eat [boiled] blood.* See AnderBois (this volume) for further discussion of
alternative sets.

In answers to non-contrastive wh-questions, the other members of this alternative set are not evoked, cf. (5), (6). In answering, the speaker simply offers a proposition as true. However, in (9b), the alternative propositions are made explicit and (9c) not only offers an alternative as true (*they planted corn*), it also rejects all of the earlier alternatives (*they planted stones, they planted trees*). It is the contrastive nature of the focus in (9c) that licenses its preverbal position.

Different contexts give rise to specific types of contrastive focus readings (so-called 'selective', 'corrective', 'exhaustive', etc., see Dik et al. (1981) for an overview). (10) illustrates one more context which licenses preverbal focus in Tsotsil – the unexpected-ness of the focus (for a similar observation in Tseltal, see Polian 2013:777).

TSOTSIL

(10) a. Something had landed at the foot of the tree. They went to look. There was a straw mat. Something was rolled up inside the straw mat. "Hell, what could it be? Let's go, let's untie the straw mat," the two men said to each other. They untied it. You know what –

b. Tseb   san-antrex_F   la   te   s-ta-ik   un.
   girl   San-Andrés   CL   there   A3-find-PL   PAR
   'It was A SAN ANDRÉS GIRL that they found there.' (Laughlin 1977:69)

(10b) provides the answer to an explicit question (*hell, what could it be?*). In this case, no alternative has been made explicit, but because the value of the focus (girl from San Andrés) is *unexpected*, (10b) nonetheless has a marked relation to the set of focus-evoked alternatives. We can understand 'unexpectedness' in terms of the set of alternatives that focus evokes: assuming that this set includes only *culturally* appropriate *alternative propositions*, a proposition with an unexpected focus, like (10b), would not be a member of that set.

4.3 Contrastive focus constructions

The term 'contrastive focus' is used here in a pragmatic sense, not a syntactic one, i.e., it refers to a particular relation to the discourse, not to any particular syntactic position or construction.

There are various syntactic constructions that can be used to express contrastive focus in Mayan: the FOCUS can be structured as a non-verbal predicate with the BACKGROUND presented in a headless relative which functions as its subject (§4.3.1); it can remain in situ and be flagged by a clause-initial focus particle (§4.3.2). It can also be realized in preverbal position, as in the Tsotsil examples (9)–(10). The structure of such examples is discussed in §4.3.3; I will conclude that at least some foci move to their surface position.

In many Mayan languages, focus constructions involve a functional element which also functions in the language as a demonstrative and/or a copula. One of the difficulties in analyzing the syntax of focus in Mayan lies in distinguishing these various functions. Where the analysis of this multifunctional element is at issue, I will refer to it (and gloss it) simply as 'F'.

4.3.1 Focus-as-predicate

The focus can function as (non-verbal) predicate of its own clause, taking a headless relative clause as subject. Examples from several languages are shown in (11)–(13).

YUCATEC
(11) Tèech_F   [le   k=u   bin   tak   Yaxley=o'].
     2SG   DET   IPFV=A3   go   as.far.as   Yaxley=D2
     'You are the one that is going up to Yaxley.'
     (lit: 'the (one who is) going up to Yaxley is YOU') (Verhoeven and Skopeteas 2015)

TSELTAL
(12) Tsa'-tuluk'_F   [te   ya   a-lo']   cabrón.
     shit-turkey   DET   ICP   A2-eat   bastard
     'It's TURKEY SHIT that you're eating, asshole.'
     (lit: 'that (which) you're eating is TURKEY SHIT') (Polian 2013:776)

K'ICHEE'
(13) Aree   la'_F   [le   x-in-kowin-ik   x-in-b'i-ij].
     COP   DEM   DET   CP-B1SG-be.able-SS   CP-A1SG-say-SS
     'THAT's what I could say.' (lit: 'that (which) I could say is THAT') (Velleman 2014:116)

The headless relative presents the presupposed BACKGROUND against which the FOCUS is new information. Thus, (11) presupposes that there is someone going up to Yaxley and asserts that that individual is the addressee; (12) presupposes that there is something you are eating and asserts that it is turkey shit, etc. These examples exhibit the usual PREDICATE–SUBJECT order in Mayan. They differ from typical intransitive verbal clauses only in that the predicate is non-verbal and the subject is not headed by a noun. It is clear though from the presence of the determiners and complementizers that the post-focal material is nominal and functions as subject. The construction is thus built out of familiar pieces and therefore does not constitute a special 'focus construction'. Note that in some cases, the focus is 'supported' by an instance of F, which I assume functions as copula here, e.g., (13) (see below for further discussion).

4.3.2 In situ focus with focus particle

In several languages, including at least Tsotsil, Tseltal, and Tojolab'al, a contrastive focus can remain in situ and be flagged by F. In all three languages, F has the form *ja'*.[5]

The key feature of (14)–(17) is that the contrastive focus is in its base position and separated from F (= *ja'*). Context is provided, where available, to make clear that we are indeed dealing with *contrastive* focus.

TSOTSIL
(14) a. Context: He hadn't worked at all –

     b. ja'   i[i]-'abtej   taj   antz_F   un=e.
        FOC   CP-work   DEM   woman   PAR=ENC
        'It was THAT WOMAN who worked.' (Laughlin 1977:390)

TSOTSIL
(15) a. Context: They (the Zinacantecos) didn't win –

     b. ja'   i-kuch   yu'un   i   soktometik_F.
        FOC   CP-prevail   by   DET   Chiapanecos
        'It was THE CHIAPANECOS that won.' (Laughlin 1977:358)

TSELTAL

(16) Ja'=me   ya   x-chon   te   k'ankujk'=e $_F$.
FOC=CL   ICP   A3-sell   DET   Cancuc=ENC
'It was THE CANCUQUEROS who sold it.' (Polian 2013:773)

TOJOLAB'AL

(17) Ja'   y-a'-a-y-i'   tak'in   ja=j-tat=i $_F$.
FOC   A3-give-TV-A3-DAT   money   DET=A1-father=ENC
'It was MY FATHER to whom he gave the money.' *or* 'It was MONEY that he gave my father.' (Curiel, this volume)

It is clear from the word order in (14)–(17) that the focus is not the predicate and therefore that F does not function here as a copula. I assume it is a focus marker (FOC).

Note that when the focus remains in situ, the FOCUS and BACKGROUND are not structurally partitioned in surface structure. This distinguishes this construction from other contrastive focus constructions. A related fact is that the 'scope' of the focus particle in this construction is ambiguous. In (18), either the subject or the object can be interpreted as focus; the same is true in Tseltal (Polian 2013:774) and in Tojolab'al (see 17).

TSOTSIL

(18) Ja'   i-s-mil   Antun   li   Xun=e.
FOC   CP-A3-kill   Antonio   DET   Juan=ENC
'It was JUAN who killed Antonio.' *or* 'It was ANTONIO who Juan killed.' (Haviland 1981:244)

4.3.3 Moved focus

Let us return now to examples like Tsotsil (9)–(10) with a preverbal NP focus. These are the ones most frequently discussed in the Mayan literature. (10) is repeated below as (19) along with examples from several other languages.

TSOTSIL

(19) Tseb   san-antrex $_F$ la   te   s-ta-ik   un.
girl   san-andrés   CL   there   A3-find-PL   PAR
'It was A SAN ANDRÉS GIRL that they found there.' (Laughlin 1977:69)

YUCATEC

(20) Tèech $_F$ k=a   bin   tak   Yaxley.
2SG   IPFV=A2   go   as.far.as   Yaxley
'YOU are going up to Yaxley.' (Verhoeven and Skopeteas 2015)

TSELTAL

(21) J-yame' $_F$ la   x-ch'ites-on,   j-mam $_F$ la   x-ch'ites=on   awil.
A1-grandmother   CP   A3-raise-B1SG   A1-grandfather   CP   A3-raise-B1SG   EVID
'It was MY GRANDMOTHER who raised me, it was MY GRANDFATHER who raised me.' (Polian 2013:776)

I assumed earlier that these are derived by movement (as in Aissen 1992). In the movement analysis, these examples involve a single clause, with the focus moving from its base position to a position high in the clause. However, a different analysis has often been assumed in passing and is explicitly argued for in Tonhauser (2003). This alternative takes examples like (19)–(21) to be instances of the focus-as-predicate construction (§4.3.1). Unlike the examples seen earlier, the purported headless relative carries no apparatus (i.e., determiners, complementizers) that identify it as a nominal or as a subordinate clause. The two alternative structures are shown schematically in Figure 11.1.

One difference between the two analyses concerns the relation between the focus and the following clause. In the right-hand structure, the focus originates in the following clause and moves to its surface position (as represented by the indices, *t* marks the position from which the focus moves). In the left-hand structure, the focus is never part of the following clause. Rather it is linked semantically to a (covert) operator which moves as part of the syntax of relative clauses (this movement accounts for various morphosyntactic effects related to movement, e.g., agent focus morphology).

Two problems have been noted for the left-hand focus-as-predicate analysis. First, the posited headless relative subject does not *look like* a nominal, as it carries none of the trappings of a nominal constituent, i.e., no determiner or complementizer. Rather, the post-focal constituents in (19)–(21) look clausal, as expected under the alternative movement analysis. The key question is whether a clause – with no determiner or complementizer – can function as a nominal argument in syntactic contexts outside of focus. Velleman (2014) argues in connection with K'ichee' that it cannot, and concludes that the predicate-as-focus analysis is not correct. This question needs careful examination in the various languages.

Further, in an experimental study of focus constructions in Yucatec, Verhoeven and Skopeteas (2015) compared agreement in examples like (22a, b). (22a) is clearly the focus-as-predicate construction, with a headless relative as subject. At issue is the analysis of (22b) where the post-focal material is 'bare', lacking a determiner or subordinator.

YUCATEC

(22) a. Tèech$_F$ [*le*   k=u   bin   tak   Yaxley=o'].
         2SG   DET IPFV=A3 go   as.far.as Yaxley=D2
         'YOU are the one that is going up to Yaxley.'
         (lit: 'the (one who is) going up to Yaxley is YOU.')

     b. Tèech$_F$ k=a   bin   tak   Yaxley.
         2SG   IPFV=A2   go   as.far.as Yaxley
         'YOU are going up to Yaxley.'

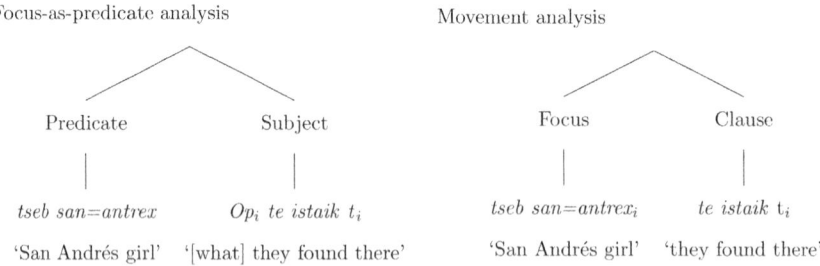

Focus-as-predicate analysis   Movement analysis

Predicate   Subject   Focus   Clause

tseb san=antrex   Op$_i$ *te istaik t$_i$*   *tseb san=antrex$_i$*   *te istaik* t$_i$

'San Andrés girl' '[what] they found there'   'San Andrés girl' 'they found there'

FIGURE 11.1 ALTERNATIVE ANALYSES FOR PREVERBAL FOCUS

In both, the focus is a 2nd person pronoun which corresponds to subject of the post-focal clause, but the agreement facts are different. In (22b), agreement on the verb must match the focus in person (2nd person), while in (22a), it need not (it shows 3rd person agreement).[6] Verhoeven and Skopeteas (2015) conclude that the preverbal focus in the bare construction originates within the following clause, where it determines agreement, and moves to its surface position. In (22a), on the other hand, agreement is not with the focus (which is the predicate of its clause), but with the covert operator that can be 3rd person. Velleman (2014:109ff) makes a similar argument for K'ichee'.

Nonetheless, there are also compelling reasons related to the realization of NP and DP foci to think that the focus-as-predicate analysis may be correct for nominal foci. In a number of languages, an NP focus requires no special 'support', while a DP focus (a focused nominal with determiner) does. In Tsotsil, for example, NP focus does not require *ja'* while DP focus does. Example (23) shows two parallel clauses, one with a DP focus (supported) and one with an NP focus (not supported).

TSOTSIL
(23) Ja'   [taj   chauk]$_F$ i-'abtej   un=e,   chauk$_F$ i-'abtej.
    FOC   DET   thunderbolt   CP-work   PAR=ENC   thunderbolt   CP-work
    'It was THAT THUNDERBOLT who [went to] work. THUNDERBOLT worked.' (Laughlin 1977:405)

Example (24) from Tseltal shows an example of DP focus in context (this example involves elision of the presupposed material).

TSELTAL
(24) a. Mach'a   ts'in   te   yak   nuts-aw=e?
      who   then   DET   PROG   chase-AP=ENC
      'Who is the one that is chasing?'

   b. Ja'   [te   cheb   mamaletik=e]$_F$.
      FOC   DET   two   elders=ENC
      'It's THE TWO OLDER MEN.' [i.e., (the ones who are chasing) are THE TWO OLDER MEN.] (Polian 2013:454)

This restriction on DP foci is mirrored by a restriction on DP *predicates* (where no focus is involved). In all Mayan languages, a NP can be inflected directly with Set B markers and function as predicate, (25).

(25) a. TSOTSIL
      Tzeb-on   to.
      girl-B1SG   still
      'I am still a girl.' (i.e., unmarried)

   b. TSELTAL
      Winik-at   ix.
      man-B2SG   CL
      'You were already a man.'

But in many Mayan languages, a DP cannot function as predicate without the 'support' of an additional element which is often identical to the focus marker. In Tsotsil and Tseltal, it is *ja'*, the same element that occurs in focus constructions.

TSOTSIL
(26) a. Ja'   li   sonso   indio-on=e.
         COP   DET   foolish   Indian-B1SG=ENC
         '[Since] I'm the stupid Indian.' (Laughlin 1977:38)
     b. *Li sonso indio-on-e.

TSELTAL
(27) a. Ja'=me   te   j-chinam-tik=e . . .
         COP=CL   DET   A1-brain-1PL.INCL=ENC
         '[As for white pozol], it is our brain.' (Polian 2013:452)

     b. *Te   poxtaywanej-on=e.
         DET   doctor-B1SG=ENC
         not: 'I am the doctor.' (Polian 2013:449)

Since these examples do not involve focus, *ja'* is not a focus marker here, but a copula. The copula is needed to 'shift' the DP from its canonical function (that of argument) to a non-canonical one (predicate). (Note that clauses with DP predicates are identificational clauses, clauses in which the referents of two DPS are identified.)

Clearly, the restriction on DP foci would follow if NP/DP foci *were* NP/DP predicates. It remains unclear though how to reconcile this with the agreement facts reported for Yucatec (see (22)), facts which favor the movement analysis. In arguing for focus movement, Verhoeven and Skopeteas address the question why a DP cannot be directly focused in Yucatec. They suggest that DP focus is blocked because the output is mistakable for a relative clause. However, since structural ambiguity does not generally cause derivations to 'crash', it is unclear why it should do so in this case. A worthwhile first step would be to investigate whether other languages show contrasts in agreement like those documented above for Yucatec.

If nominal foci are best analyzed as predicates, it is important to ask whether *all* clause-initial foci should be analyzed as predicates. The predicate analysis is plausible for NPS and DPS because they can function as predicates (the latter usually with the support of a copula). But there are other phrase types which cannot function as predicates but can be preverbal focus. The clearest cases are PP's. In Tsotsil, for example, a PP cannot function as predicate. To predicate a location of some entity, a deictic adverb *te* 'there' or *li'* 'here') functions as predicate and the PP modifies the adverb, as in (28a). But a PP can function on its own as contrastive focus, (28b):

TSOTSIL
(28) a. *(Te)   ta   Soktom   i   kampana=e,
         there   in   Chiapa   DET   bell=ENC
         'The bells were there in Chiapa.' (Laughlin 1977:100)

     b. [Ta   s-ba   me   l-av-ajnil]_F   ch-a-muy=e,   mu   me   ta   jol
         P   A3-top   CL   DET-A2-wife   ICP-B2-climb=ENC NEG   CL   on   top
         na-uk.
         house-IRR
         'It's ON TOP OF YOUR WIFE that you should climb, not onto the rafters.' (Laughlin 1977:56)

(The larger context of (28b) shows clearly that we are dealing with contrastive focus.)

In K'ichee' too, a PP predicate requires the stage-level copula *k'o* (29a), but a PP can be contrastive focus without it (29b).[7,8]

K'ICHEE'

(29) a. Le   nu-taat   *(k'o)   pa   le   ab'iix.
        DET   A1SG-father   COP   P   DET   cornfield
        'My father is in the milpa.'

    b. La   [pa   ch'aat]_F   t'uy-ul   wi?
       Q   PREP bed   sit-POS   CL
       'Is it ON THE BED that s/he is seated?' (López Ixcoy 1997:308)

I conclude then that while preverbal NP and DP foci may be predicates (with headless relative subjects), a preverbal PP focus must move to its surface position.

We saw earlier that F can be used as a focus marker in some languages, marking an in situ contrastive focus. It can also mark a moved focus (I cite examples here with PP focus since these are clearly moved):

TSOTSIL

(30) a. the elders came back by horse, as for the soldiers . . .
        ja'   [ta   y-ok]_F   la   tal-ik   un.
        FOC   PREP A3-foot   CL   come-PL   PAR
        'They came back ON FOOT.' (Laughlin 1977:62)

    b. my comadre . . .
       ja'   [ta   avyon]_F   i-bat, . . .
       FOC   PREP airplane   CP-go
       'My comadre went BY PLANE [we went by car].' (Laughlin 1980:91)

Since *ja'* does not occur with PP predicates (other elements do), it cannot be a copula here, but must instead be a focus marker. Hence (30a.b) are instances of a hybrid focus construction, one involving both fronting of the focus *and* flagging with a focus marker.

4.3.4 Summary

We have identified three distinct constructions in Mayan for the expression of contrastive focus, plus a fourth hybrid construction:

• focus-as-predicate construction (§4.3.1)

TSELTAL (=12)

(31) Tsa'-tuluk'_F   [*te*   ya   a-lo']   cabrón.
     shit-turkey   DET   ICP   A2-eat   bastard
     'It's TURKEY SHIT that you're eating, asshole.'
     (lit: 'that (which) you're eating is TURKEY SHIT')

• moved focus without focus marker (§4.3.3)

K'ICHEE' (=29b)

(32) La   pa   ch'aat_F   t'uy-ul wi?
     Q   PREP   bed   sit-POS CL
     'Is it ON THE BED that s/he is seated?' (López Ixcoy 1997:308)

• moved focus with clause-initial focus marker (§4.3.3)

TSOTSIL (=30b)
(33) Ja' [ta   avyon]$_F$ i-bat, li   vo'otik=e   [ta   karo]$_F$
     FOC PREP airplane CP-go DET 1PL.INCL=ENC PREP car
     l-i-bat-tik.
     CP-B1-go-1PL.INCL
     'She went BY PLANE, we went BY CAR. (Laughlin 1980:91)

• in situ focus, with clause-initial focus marker (§4.3.2)

TOJOLAB'AL (=17)
(34) Ja' y-a'-a-y-i'   tak'in   ja=j-tat=i.
     FOC A3-give-TV-A3-DAT money   DET=A1-father=ENC
     'It was MY FATHER to whom he gave the money.' *or* 'It was MONEY that he gave
     my father.'

   In his discussion of contrastive focus constructions in Tseltal, Polian (2013:773ff)
suggests that these constructions are associated with different degrees of contrast,
e.g., that the moved focus and focus-as-predicate constructions indicate a greater
degree of contrast than does an in situ focus (with focus particle). This seems plausible since the 'stronger' constructions are the ones which structurally partition focus
and background (cf., English where cleft constructions convey a stronger degree of
focal contrast than does intonation alone). It is an interesting question how Polian's
suggestion can be verified for Tseltal, and whether it can be verified for other Mayan
languages.

4.4 Focus morphosyntax

4.4.1 Agent focus

One of the most studied topics in Mayan grammar is the special morphosyntax
associated with focus of the 'agent', i.e., the argument corresponding to the subject of a transitive clause (A). Such morphosyntax is not found in all Mayan languages, but is common in Eastern Mayan (K'ichean and Mamean), and is found also
in Q'anjob'alan and in a few other languages (e.g., Zinacantec dialect of Tsotsil,
Yucatec Mayan) (see Stiebels 2006 for a survey). The examples in (35)–(36) from
Jakaltek illustrate this morphosyntax. (35) shows a simple transitive clause without
focus. The verb is transitive and agrees with A through the usual ergative (Set A)
agreement.

JAKALTEK
(35) X-[y]-il   naj   ix.
     CP-A3-see PRON.3SG.M PRON.3SG.F
     'he saw her' (Craig 1977:211)

(36a, b) show focus of O and A, respectively. In (36a), the verb form does not change,
but in (36b), it obligatorily carries the suffix *-ni* (historically derived from *-n* plus the
intransitive status suffix *-i*). This suffix induces detransitivization of the verb and loss of
the ergative (Set A) marker.

JAKALTEK

(36) a. Ha'   ix_F   x-[y]-il   naj.
       FOC   PRON.3SG.F   CP-A3-see   PRON.3SG.M
       'It was HER who he saw.'

    b. Ha'   naj_F   x-'il-ni   ix.
       FOC   PRON.3SG.M   CP-see-AF   PRON.3SG.F
       'It was HIM who saw her.' (Craig 1977:212–3)

Although this morphosyntax is often called AGENT FOCUS (AF), it is not peculiar to focus of A per se. It is associated with a syntactic operation of fronting ('extraction') which is common to interrogatives, relative clauses, focus, and certain indefinite constructions. There is a great deal of variation in the details of AF constructions across the family – their morphology, distribution, and agreement patterns (see Stiebels (2006) and Coon et al. (2014) for recent perspectives and Aissen (2017) for discussion). What is relevant here is that AF morphology provides visible means to distinguish preverbal focus and topic. When the preverbal constituent is A, AF morphology indicates that it is focus while its absence (usually) indicates that it is topic. We will appeal to this below.

As noted earlier, recent work on K'ichee' and Yucatec has observed a correlation between the possibility of in situ focus and the use of AF morphology under focus movement. In both languages, focus movement of A requires AF morphology.[9] Also in both languages, while in situ focus is in general possible, it is *not* possible with the subject of a transitive clause, (8). In effect, a focused A can only occur *ex situ* – where it triggers AF morphology; it cannot remain in situ where it would occur without that morphology.

It is possible that the co-occurrence of these phenomena in K'ichee' and Yucatec is coincidental, i.e., that the correlation is not significant. However, Velleman (2014) presents convincing evidence that the correlation is genuine. She observes that there are 'exceptional' contexts in K'ichee' where agent extraction does *not* permit agent focus morphology and shows that in the same contexts, a focused agent may remain in situ. Two such contexts are reflexive and extended reflexive clauses (Mondloch 1981). (37a, b) show that the agent is extracted in reflexive and extended reflexive clauses without special morphology (Velleman 2014:153, 155):

K'ICHEE'

(37) a. ri   alah   [ri   x-u-xi'-j   r-iib']
       DET boy   DET CP-A3SG-scare-SS   A3SG-RR
       'the boy who scared himself'

    b. Jachin   x-u-sok   r-aqan?
       who   CP-A3SG-hurt   A3SG-leg
       'Who_i hurt his_i leg?'

(38)–(39) show that the agent in a reflexive or extended reflexive clause may be focused in situ (Velleman 2014:226).

K'ICHEE'

(38) a. Who got scared?

    b. Aree   x-u-xi'-j   r-iib'   le   a   Xwaan_F.
       FOC   CP-A3SG-scare-SS   A3SG-RR   DET CLF   Juan
       'JUAN got scared.' (lit. 'scared himself')

(39) a. Who hurt his leg?

    b. X-u-sok   r-aqan   le   a   Xwaan$_F$.
       CP-A3SG-wound   A3SG-leg   DET   CLF   Juan
       'JUAN hurt his leg.'

Following the same reasoning, Velleman suggests that in those languages which do not require (or use) special AF morphology, the agent may be focused in situ. Tseltal, for example, does not use special morphology when a focused agent is displaced, (40a), and it permits a focused agent to remain in situ, (40b) (Polian 2013:775, 773).

TSELTAL
(40) a. Ants$_F$ =me   ya   s-pas.
       woman=CL   ICP   A3-do
       'It is A WOMAN who does it (i.e., it is WOMEN's work).'

    b. Ja'=me   ya   x-chon   te   k'ankujk'=e$_F$.
       FOC=CL   ICP   A3-sell   DET   Cancuc-DET
       'It was THE CANCUQUEROS who sold it.' {TEXT}

The suggestion that there is a link between constraints on AF morphology and constraints on in situ focus – both within individual languages and across the family – is very interesting and calls for explanation. Velleman (2014) discusses several possible accounts and surely more will be forthcoming. On the empirical side, the generalization should be tested, controlling carefully for contexts which license in situ focus and for the distinction between information focus and contrastive focus.

4.4.2 Oblique focus

A number of Eastern Mayan languages register the focus (more generally, the extraction) of oblique constituents, especially instrumentals. In the K'ichean languages as well as in Ixil (Mamean), the applicative suffix -b'e is associated with extraction of instruments. Interestingly, this morphosyntax *only* occurs under extraction of instruments, parallel to the use of AF morphology *only* when A is extracted.[10] I offer just one example here from Tz'utujil (Dayley 1985:355).

TZ'UTUJIL
(41) Machat$_F$ x-a-choy-b'e-j   chee'.
      machete   CP-A2SG-cut-APPL-SS   tree
      'It was a MACHETE that you cut wood with.'

The instrumental applicative in Eastern Mayan is unstable, as it shows significant variation with respect to both its properties (e.g., whether it is actually an applicative and if so, which object is primary, which secondary) and its distribution. Norman (1978) discusses differences among several K'ichean languages; Larsen (1988) documents dialect variation in K'ichee'; Dayley (1985) documents multiple constructions in Tz'utujil used to extract instruments, only one of which is the applicative. Ayres (1983) discusses analogous variation in Ixil (Mamean).

4.5 Conclusion

The realization of FOCUS in Mayan involves morphological devices (e.g., special morphology for AGENT and OBLIQUE focus), dedicated syntactic positions for moved foci, and lexical resources (focus markers like *ja'*).Factors which determine how focus is realized, i.e., the distribution of these various grammatical devices, include the pragmatic distinction between *information focus* and *contrastive focus*, the category of the focus (e.g., DP vs. NP vs. PP), and the grammatical relation of the focus (e.g., A (external argument) vs. S and O). There is a good deal of variation in how these factors play out in the grammars of individual languages and many details remain to be filled in.

A notable gap in our knowledge is the extent to which intonation marks focus in Mayan, whether new information focus or contrastive focus. Relevant work exists for Yucatec Maya, where the consensus so far is that intonation plays no role (see Kügler et al. 2007 among others). On the other hand, Baird (2014) concludes that it plays some role in the speech of bilingual K'ichee'-Spanish speakers, at least in some dialects. Clearly there is a great need for work on this question in the various languages.

5 TOPIC

5.1 Introduction

Although the notions *topic* and *focus* are often taken to be complementary, they belong to different dimensions of information structure. In the context of the question in (42a), the reply in (42b) can be partitioned along two different dimensions (the topic is marked with T (subscript)).

(42) a. Where is Mary driving tomorrow?
   b. Mary$_T$ is driving to Prague$_F$ tomorrow.
      i. Focus-Background: Mary is driving to PRAGUE$_F$ tomorrow.
      ii. Topic-Comment: Mary$_T$ [is driving to Prague tomorrow]$_{COMMENT}$.

From the perspective of *informativity*, 'Prague' in (42b) is the point of greatest informativity, as the rest of the sentence is presupposed, i.e., the proposition *Mary is going somewhere tomorrow* is already in the common ground. This corresponds to a partitioning of the sentence into FOCUS and BACKGROUND (42b.i). The other dimension has to do with *the entity being talked about* and what is said about that entity. On this dimension, (42b.ii), the answer is partitioned into TOPIC (Mary) and COMMENT (the rest of the sentence). There are relations between these two partitionings: the focus is part of the comment and the topic is part of the background. But the two dimensions are distinct.

It is clear enough that Mary is the topic in (42b). But anyone who has ever tried to identify the topic in sentences of naturally occurring speech knows how difficult this can be. Various properties correlate statistically with topic-hood and are therefore helpful in identifying the topic: definiteness (because topics are usually already part of the common ground), human (because we tend to talk about humans), persistence (because we tend to continue to talk about the same entity). Further, because a continuing topic (one which is identical to the topic of the immediately preceding discourse) is highly accessible, continuing topics tend to be realized by a minimal referential expression, i.e., unstressed pronouns or ø in languages where unstressed pronouns are not pronounced. And finally, certain grammatical functions are associated with topicality, in particular subject (within a clause) and possessor (within a nominal). Some of these correlates have been used as the basis of definitions of topic (or equivalent notions), e.g., in the work of Givón (1983) also in Centering Theory (Walker et al. 1998; Beaver 2004) and in experimental work on Mayan (Verhoeven and Skopeteas 2015). However, *none* of these properties provides a sufficient or necessary condition for topic. Hence identification of the topic is made much easier if the language has some formal signal of TOPIC – COMMENT structure, morphological or syntactic.

Fortunately, for our purposes, many Mayan languages do have special syntax associated with this partition, one in which the topic precedes the comment. Since most Mayan languages are predicate-initial, preverbal positioning of an argument (or adjunct) may be a sign then that it is a topic. A complicating factor is that displaced foci also occur in a preverbal position (§4.2). However, there are various grammatical differences which distinguish topics and foci and these, along with discourse context, usually allow unambiguous identification.

Although a number of Mayan languages have preverbal topic constructions, the constructions are not uniform. In Aissen (1992), I identified two distinct constructions, differentiated primarily by their structural properties, calling them 'internal' and 'external'. This account is discussed in §5.2.[11] I also speculated that the two constructions have different pragmatic functions, with one specialized for signaling a topic switch and one for continuing topics. Although there is some truth in this, this picture is incomplete, §5.3.

I will suggest here that the two types differ in their core functions: internal topics are fundamentally 'aboutness' topics which furthermore require a predicate-argument relation between the topic and comment, while external topics are fundamentally 'frame-setting'. This approach takes the notion 'topic' to be a *prototype* with different topic constructions conforming to various degrees to the prototype (Jacobs 2001). Jacobs proposes four topic properties: separation (structural separation of topic and comment) 'aboutness' (also called 'addressation'), predication (the requirement that the topic function as an argument of the predicate (=comment), and frame-setting (see below). While internal and external topics share the first property (separation), they have different relations to the other three. Section 5.4 closes with a discussion of CONTRASTIVE TOPICS, which are related in interesting ways to topics and foci.

5.2 External and internal topic: syntax

Most Mayan languages are assumed to have a 'basic' or underlying verb-initial word order. However, many also have an alternative order in which one constituent, generally definite and often the subject, precedes the verb. This alternation is illustrated for Tsotsil by (43)–(44). (43) introduces a man into the discourse context. The noun phrase *jun vinik* is indefinite and occurs in post-verbal position. This is, in fact, the only possible position for (non-partitive) indefinite subjects.

TSOTSIL
(43) I-vay   la   ta   be   jun   vinik   ta   yak'ol Bik'it Nich.
     cp-sleep CL   PREP path   a   man   PREP above B.   N.
     'A man slept by the trail above Bik'it Nich.' (Laughlin 1977:54)

(44) (from a different narrative) also contains reference to a man. In this case, the man had been introduced into the discourse several sentences earlier (as a post-verbal indefinite). After several sentences about other protagonists, the narrative turns back to the man

with (44). The referring expression, *ti vinik* is now preverbal (the double-bar here and below indicates an intonational phrase boundary):

TSOTSIL

(44) A   ti   vinik   un=e_T ‖   mu   to   ox   la   x-'och   svayel   un.

A	ti	vinik	un=e$_T$ ‖	mu	to	ox	la	x-'och	svayel	un.
TOP	DET	man	PAR=ENC	NEG	CL	CL	CL	ASP-enter	his.sleep	PAR

'The man, he hadn't fallen asleep.' (Laughlin 1977:49)

The preverbal nominal has many of the properties associated with topics: it is definite, it is human-referring, and the referent persists into subsequent discourse. Hence I assume this is a topic construction and that *ti vinik* in (44) is a topic. Note that in addition to their preverbal position, topics in Tsotsil may be 'flagged' by the particle *a* as in (44).

Tz'utujil also has alternations in word order which are determined by discourse context. Dayley (1985) characterizes PREDICATE–SUBJECT order as the more basic, used always '(1) when the existence of the subject is not presupposed and (2) when the subject is presupposed but is being introduced into the conversation' [p. 302]. Under both conditions, the referent is not part of the CG.

TZ'UTUJIL

(45) a. X-pi   jun   aachi   Xelaju'.

X-pi	jun	aachi	Xelaju'.
CP-come	one	man	Quetzaltenango

'A man came from Quetzaltenango.'

    b. Aj-nawala'   ja   w-xaayiil.

Aj-nawala'	ja	w-xaayiil.
one.of-Nahualá	DET	A1SG-wife

'My wife is from Nahualá.' (Dayley 1985:302)

On the other hand, intransitive clauses show SUBJECT–PREDICATE order 'when the subject is the topic of the discourse in general' and 'generally, when the subject is given information' [p. 302], i.e., when the subject *is* part of the CG.

TZ'UTUJIL

(46) Ja   nuu-chaaq'_T   x-ajnamaj-i ja   toq   laj   x-ch'e<j>y-i.

Ja	nuu-chaaq'$_T$	x-ajnamaj-i ja	toq	laj	x-ch'e<j>y-i.
DET	A1SG-little.brother	CP-flee-SS	DET when	IRR	CP-hit<PSV>-SS

'My little brother fled when he was going to be beaten.' (Dayley 1985:303)

The construction in (46) clearly also qualifies as topic construction.

In both Tsotsil and Tz'utujil, the topic is structurally separated from the comment, one of the properties that Jacobs associates with topics. Further, in both languages, the topic occurs high in the clause and therefore precedes sentential operators like negation (for Tsotsil, see (44)).

TZ'UTUJIL

(47) Ja   ch'ooy_T   ma   x-uu-tij   ta   ja   kéeso.

Ja	ch'ooy$_T$	ma	x-uu-tij	ta	ja	kéeso.
DET	rat	NEG	CP-A3SG-eat	IRR	DET	cheese

'The rat didn't eat the cheese.' (Dayley 1985:321)

(See Aissen (1992) for evidence that topics of both types also precede the polar interrogative marker.)

Despite these similarities (a preverbal, structurally high position), there are significant structural differences between Tsotsil and Tz'utujil topics which concern the tightness of the connection between topic and comment. Tsotsil topics are only loosely connected to what follows, while Tz'utujil topics are much more tightly integrated. I will refer to these two types then as 'external' and 'internal' topics, anticipating the structural distinction drawn below. It appears that Mayan languages generally use either the external or the internal type as their 'basic' topic construction. Languages with an external construction include Tsotsil, Tseltal, Tojolab'al, Q'anjob'al, Jakaltek, and Yucatec. Languages with an internal construction include Tz'utujil, K'ichee', Q'eqchi', and probably other K'ichean languages.

The hallmark of an external topic then is its loose connection to the comment. Prosodically the external topic is separated from what follows by an intonational phrase break (iP), represented here by ‖. For Tsotsil, evidence of this boundary are the enclitics *un* and *e* which occur only at the right edge of an *iP* (Aissen 1992), see (44). This break can be (and often is) marked by an audible pause, similar to the pause between utterances, and the right edge of the topic is marked by a boundary tone. For Jakaltek, parallel evidence comes from the distribution of the exclusive clitic *an* (EXCL) which marks the presence of a 1st person singular or plural exclusive and occurs only at the right edge of an *iP*, as in (48) (Day 1973; Craig 1977; Aissen 1992, 2000).

JAKALTEK
(48) W-uxhtaj$_i$ an$_T$ ‖ s-loq   ho'$_i$ no' cheh   k'ej'inh tu'.
     A1SG-brother EXCL   A3s-buy PRON   CLF horse black   DEM
     'My brother, he bought that black horse.' (Craig 1977:280)

The syntactic connection between the external topic and the following 'comment' is also loose. For one thing, the topic need not correspond to any argument position in the following clause (though of course it can). That is, the external topic can be a 'hanging topic'.

YUCATEC
(49) Ch'íich'-o'b-e'$_T$ chen   x-k'òok'-o'b   u   k'ahóol.
     bird-PL-D3   only   F-nightingale-PL A3   know
     'As concerns birds, he only knows nightingales.' (Skopeteas and Verhoeven 2009)

TSELTAL
(50) Te   beel   Jobel=e$_T$, a-kuch-oj   te   a-may=-e.
     DET   travel S.C.=ENC   A2-carry-PF DET   A2-tobacco=ENC
     'For the trip to San Cristobal, you carried your tobacco.' (Polian 2013:770)

And even when it is coreferential with an argument in the following clause, that argument can be expressed by overt lexical material. This is particularly clear in Jakaltek (and probably other Q'anjob'alan languages), which has overt pronouns and where the topic *must* be resumed by a (classifier-derived) pronoun if one exists for the referent in question (Craig 1977:12; Datz 1980:149ff). In (48), that pronoun is *ho'*. The presence of the pronoun suggests that the external topic does not *move* to its surface position, as movement usually leaves a gap. The relation between a topic and a coreferential element in the 'comment' appears instead to be like the anaphoric relation that holds between a pronoun and its antecedent. Both prosodically and syntactically then, the relation between the external topic and comment resembles that of closely linked but independent sentences.

The topics of Tz'utujil are more tightly connected to the clause that follows than the external topics of Tsotsil and Jakaltek. On the prosodic side, Tz'utujil topics do not occasion an *iP* break, though it is possible that the topic corresponds to a smaller prosodic constituent (e.g., a phonological phrase); this calls for further investigation.[12]

On the syntactic side, the topic must fill a variable in the argument structure associated with the topic, i.e., Tz'utujil does not permit hanging topics:

TZ'UTUJIL
(51) *Ja   frúuta$_T$ qas   ki'   ja   máango.
      DET   fruit   very sweet DET   mango
      'As for fruit, mango is very sweet.' {ELIC}

Structurally then, internal and external topics are both separated from the comment (i.e., the pragmatic partition is paralleled by a structural one), but the nature of the separation is different. In Aissen (1992), I analyzed the structure of internal and external topic, as well as focus, in terms of the same basic clause structure presented in Chapter 10 [*Complement clauses*], one which contains (at least) two functional projections above VP. I proposed that the focus occupies the Specifier of IP, and that the internal topic of Tz'utujil occupies Specifier of CP. External topics, on the other hand, are adjoined to the CP node. Intervening between both topic positions and the focus position are positions for adverbs and for negation (these are probably distinct, but are not distinguished here).

Figure 11.2 shows both topics sitting in structurally high positions and accounts for their 'preverbal' position as well as for their position relative to negation, (44), (47). It also predicts, correctly, that topics of either type will precede the focus.

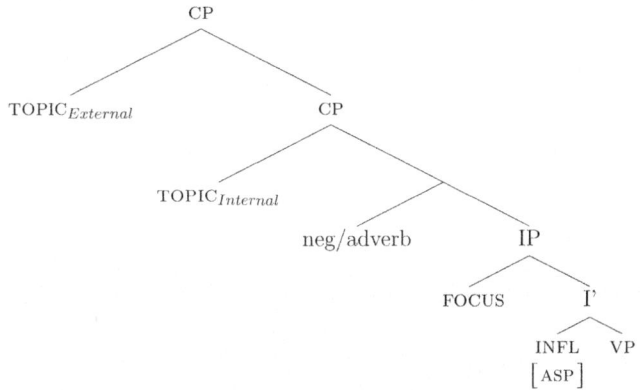

FIGURE 11.2 STRUCTURAL POSITIONS FOR TOPIC AND FOCUS IN MAYAN

TSOTSIL (external topic)

(52) A   ti   prove tseb=e$_T$ sovra$_F$ ch-'ak'-b-at.
    TOP   DET   poor   girl=ENC   leftover   ICP-give-APPL-PSV
    'It was LEFTOVERS that the poor girl was given.' (Laughlin 1977:204)

TZ'UTUJIL (internal topic)

(53) a. Ja   tzyaq$_T$ ch'ooyaa'$_F$ x-ee-tij-ow-i.
       DET   clothes   rats   CP-A3PL-eat-AF-SS
       'RATS were the ones who ate the clothes.' (Dayley 1985:309)

    b. Ja   gáarsa$_T$ cheqe   ch'uu'$_F$ n-ee-ruu-tij.
       DET   heron   only   fish   ICP-B3PL-A3SG-eat
       'It's only FISH that the heron eats.' (Dayley 1985:308)

Note that in (53a) the subject is focus (with an AF verb), while in (53b), it is topic (no AF verb).

At the same time, Figure 11.2 positions internal and external topics differently, so provides a way to account for the differences noted above. Internal topics are structurally more integrated into the clause than are external topics, and this is reflected both semantically and prosodically. It also accounts for further differences to be discussed below. Before turning to those differences, there is one question we should address, namely whether the position associated with the internal topic in (46)–(47) and (53) is really a topic position, or whether it is simply a preverbal *subject* position. In Tz'utujil, it is clear that non-subjects *can* occupy the same position (Aissen 1999). Non-subject topics arise especially in inactive intransitive clauses, when the *possessor* of the subject functions as topic. Such examples occur most frequently with the copula verb *k'o(oli)*, which functions both as an existential and as a verb of possession. In the following examples, the *grammatical* subject is the post-verbal noun phrase (the possessum). The possessor of the grammatical subject occurs in the preverbal topic position. Agreement in (54a, b) makes the *grammatical* relations clear: the verb agrees with its subject (the possessum); the preverbal topic is indexed as possessor on the possessum.

TZ'UTUJIL

(54) a. Ja   winaq$_T$ k'o   ki-paq.
       DET   people   EXIST   A3PL-money
       'The people have money.' (lit: the people's money exists)

    b. Inin$_T$ ee   k'o   w-ach'aalaal   pa   taq'aaj.
       1SG   B3PL   EXIST   A1SG-relatives   on   coast
       'I have relatives on the coast.' (lit: relatives of mine exist on the coast)

If the preverbal possessor in (54a, b) occupies the same position as the preverbal subject in (46)–(47) and (53), then it should precede focus as well as negation. Indeed, it does:

TZ'UTUJIL

(55) a. Ja   n-ata'$_T$ xa   r-ek'$_F$ ee   k'ooli.
       DET   A1SG-father   only   A3SG-chicken   B3PL   EXIST
       'My father has only chickens.'

b. Inin_T   ma   k'o   ta   n-paq.
   1SG   NEG   EXIST   IRR   A1SG-money
   'I don't have any money.'

Table 11.4 summarizes the differences between the two types of topic discussed to this point.

5.3 Internal and external topic: pragmatics

Internal topics have the property which has been called 'aboutness': the comment must be 'about' the topic in the sense that it adds a proposition to the CG which increases what we know about the topic. An influential conception of 'aboutness' topic was introduced in Reinhart (1981 (=Reinhart 1982)). Reinhart proposed that new information is not entered into the CG in an unstructured manner, but is associated with particular entities which are (usually) already in the CG. She analogized these entities to file-cards. A proposition which is *about* an entity is entered on the file card corresponding to that entity. The 'topic' then functions as an instruction to the hearer, directing him or her to the file card which should be updated; it is a kind of 'address' at which the new information is to be located. A core function associated then with the internal topic of Tz'utujil is addressation. Furthermore, it is not enough that the comment be 'about' the topic: the topic must correspond to an argument in the comment (=predicate), i.e., the internal topic cannot be a hanging topic. Thus, a second core function of the internal topic construction of Tz'utujil is predication (see the related analysis of Tz'utujil topics in terms of their logical subject-predicate relation (Aissen 1999)).

Although the external topic construction can involve predication, the fact that it permits hanging topics shows that this is not required. Whether it always involves addressation is unclear; determining this requires a more careful characterization of that relation than is possible here. However, a core function of this construction is what has been called 'frame-setting' (Jacobs 2001) or 'scene-setting': a 'scene-setting' topic provides a spatial, temporal or individual framework within which the main predication holds' (Chafe 1976:50–1). The same position which is reserved for 'topics' in languages with external topics can also be filled by a variety of adverbial phrases and clauses. (56), from Tsotsil, contains two 'scene-setting' phrases, both temporal, while (57), from Tseltal, shows a conditional clause. These provide restrictions on the 'worlds' within which the truth of the comment is evaluated, restricting the assertion in (56) to the time of the Flood, and that in (57) to hypothetical worlds in which certain events occur. See Datz (1980:136) and Bohnemeyer (2002:135ff) for the same point in Yucatec and Jakaltek, two other languages with external topics.

TABLE 11.4 INTERNAL VS. EXTERNAL TOPIC

	Internal topic	External topic
Prosody	no iP break	iP break
Hanging topic	no	yes
Resumption	no	yes (where applicable)

TSOTSIL

(56) [A   ti   vo'ne   la=e]_T,   [a   la   ti   k'alal   i-noj   li   balamil=e]_T,. . . .

TOP   DET   ago   CL=ENC   TOP   CL   DET   when   CP-fill   DET   earth=ENC

'Long ago, when the world was flooded, . . . ' (Laughlin 1977:254)

TSELTAL

(57) [Te   me   la=to   aw-ich'   tel   a-chon   molino   le'=to=e]_T,   ma

DET   if   CP=CL   A2-bring   DIR   A2-sell   mill   here=CL=ENC   NEG

x-ch'am=ix.

ICP-be.sold=CL

'If you still brought mills to sell here, they would not be sold now.' (Polian 2013:772)

These examples show again that predication is not required, and perhaps not addressation either. When the topic refers to an individual, the construction generally does involve both predication and 'aboutnesss' (addressation), but these are not necessary properties of the construction.

It is hardly surprising that the syntactic and pragmatic properties of internal and external topics align as they do. The syntactic position for internal topics is an argument position in the sense that it is filled by elements which must be linked to arguments in the clause either by movement or binding. The position occupied by external topics is, in contrast, a position for adjuncts and adverbial modifiers.

With this in place, we can return to the question of how internal and external topic relate to the functions of signaling a change in topic or a continuing topic. External topics are the primary resource in languages like Tsotsil and Jakaltek to indicate a topic shift, i.e., to signal that the topic of the current sentence is different from the topic of the immediately preceding discourse (on Jakaltek, see Datz 1980:149ff). The larger context of (44) (from Laughlin 1977:49) will illustrate. It occurs in a narrative about a wedding night. The man and woman are introduced at the outset, then the narrative describes the sleeping arrangements which included the girl's parents and a number of drunk petitioners (58a). The narrative turns back to the groom with (58b), and then continues as in (58c), where the continuing topic is realized as a null pronoun.

TSOTSIL

(58) a. There was a Chamulan. He had just been married. It was on a day like today. They entered the house, it seems, because those people don't have weddings. They marry at the house entrance. Then they went. They went to bed. And they joined each other in bed. [The groom's] father and mother slept there together with them still. The petitioners got drunk – the relatives of the boy's parents. The woman's relatives slept there still too, because it was the first night that they accompanied each other.

   b. A   ti   vinik   un=e_T,   mu   to   ox   la   x-'och   svayel   un.

   TOP   DET   man   PAR=ENC   NEG   CL   CL   CL   ASP-enter   his.sleep   PAR

   'The man, he hadn't fallen asleep.'

   c. He [ø] went and slipped inside the skirt with that wife of his.

However, indicating a change in topic is not an exclusive property of external topics. In languages like Tz'utujil and K'ichee', the *internal* topic construction is used to signal a topic switch. The following excerpt, from a K'ichee' narrative (Norman 1976:40–1), involves two protagonists, a man and an alligator. Both are introduced as indefinites in post-verbal position (59a,c). The man is the initial topic (59b), but as the narrative continues, there are three topic switches (lines d, g, and h). Each switch is marked by fronting the new topic into preverbal position. In each case, the local topic persists (albeit briefly) as topic into the subsequent sentence, where it is signaled by a null pronoun (ø). Only the lines with switch topics are given in the original K'ichee'. ('S' here covers both intransitive S and transitive A; material corresponding to S and V is italicized)).

K'ICHEE'

(59) a. VS   It is said that *there was a man*, who left here . . .

    b. VS   It is said that *that man*, *was taking a walk* beside the ocean.

    c. VS   Suddenly (there) *came an alligator*, out of the ocean.

    d. SV   *Rii ayiin*   *x-u-biq'*   b'i rii jun achih.
           DET alligator CP-A3SG-swallow DIR DET one man.
           The alligator, swallowed the one man.

    e. V   He, [ø] returned into the ocean,

    f. V   he, [ø] went down to the bottom of the ocean.

    g. SV   *Rii achih ka-r-il-oh* . . .
           DET man ICP-A3SG-see-ss
           The man, sees [that it got very dark inside the alligator. "Where am I?"
           he, [ø] says.]

    h. SV   *Raayiin*   *x-el* chi apan chuchi' lee maar,
           DET.alligator CP-go.out P DIR   its.edge DET ocean
           The alligator went out at the edge of the ocean . . .

With respect to indicating a *continuing* topic, the situation is somewhat different. The signal of a continuing topic is usually a minimal referring expression (Givón 1983; Ariel 1990; Gundel et al. 1993). In most Mayan languages, this will be a null pronominal, as in (59) from K'ichee' and (58c) from Tsotsil. There is no reason to think that a continuing topic is expressed through the external topic construction, as adjoined topics are entirely optional. On the other hand, it is plausible that the null pronoun associated with a continuing topic might well occupy the internal topic position. This is the intuition of Dayley (1985) who regards 'sentences with v – p order without an overt agent noun phrase [as] alternate attenuated forms of a – v – p sentences' [p.306]). Translated into a framework which recognizes null pronouns as syntactically potent elements, this would imply that examples like (60b) have the same structure as (60a), but with the position of the internal topic occupied by a phonologically null pronoun which refers to a continuing topic.

TZ'UTUJIL

(60) a. Ja ch'ooyaa', x-kee-tij   ja   tzyaq.
        DET rats   CP-A3PL-eat DET clothes
        'The rats ate the clothes.'

    b. ø,   x-kee-tij   ja   tzyaq.
        PRON CP-A3PL-eat DET clothes
        'They ate the clothes.' (Dayley 1985:306)

In conclusion, the internal and external topic constructions overlap somewhat in their functions: both provide the basic mechanism for indicating a change in topic. However,

TABLE 11.5 PROPERTIES OF INTERNAL AND EXTERNAL TOPICS
           IN MAYAN

	Internal	External
Separation	√	√
Predication	√	(√)
Addressation	√	(√)
Frame-setting		√

while the internal topic construction may be involved in signaling a continuing topic, there is no reason to think that the external topic plays a similar role. The more basic distinction between internal and external topic can be characterized in terms of the properties that Jacobs (2001) associates with the prototypical topics. While both involve a structural separation between topic and comment, internal topics obligatorily involve PREDICATION and ABOUTNESS, while external topics obligatorily involve FRAME-SETTING. When the external topic refers to an individual, it will usually involve aboutness and predication, indicated here as optional properties (Table 11.5).

5.4 Contrastive topic

A further function associated with both external and internal topics in Mayan is presentation of a CONTRASTIVE TOPIC. To illustrate this relation, consider the excerpt in (61) from Tsotsil. The first clause provides the context; the second and third each contains a contrastive topic.

TSOTSIL
(61) a. 'There was a couple, recently married.'

  b. A   ti   vinik=e$_{CT}$ tax-lok'   ech'el, tax-bat, tax-xanav.
      TOP DET   man=ENC   ICP-leave going   ICP-go   ICP-travel
      'As for the man$_{CT}$ he left, he went, he travelled.'

  c. A   ti   ants=e$_{CT}$ jun   yo'on   tax-kom.
      TOP DET   woman=ENC   one   heart   ICP-stay
      'As for the woman$_{CT}$ she stayed home happy.' (Laughlin 1977:67)

The phrases corresponding to 'the man' and 'the woman' are topics in their respective utterances, but they also contrast with one another. In characterizing CONTRASTIVE TOPIC, I follow Büring (2003) who develops an account in terms of *questions*. In the context of this example, (61a) raises an implicit question: *what about the couple?* This in turn raises sub-questions: *what about the man, what happened to him/what did he do?*, and *what about the woman?* The answer proceeds sub-question by sub-question, first considering the man (61b) and then the woman (61c). Each response consists of a pair, associating with each member of the couple what he or she did. The members of the set that organize the reply (the man, the woman) are CONTRASTIVE TOPICS, the other value is the focus. In these examples, the focus corresponds to the entire predicate phrase.

  Contrastive topics also occur with narrow focus, as in (62). Here an explicit question induces the construction, asking of a group which piece of chicken each member wants to eat.

CHAMULAN TSOTSIL

(62) a. Bu ch-a-k'an   ch-a-ti'-ik=e?
         Q   ICP-A2-want   ICP-A2-eat-PL=ENC
         'Which [piece of chicken] do you (pl) want to eat?'

     b. Vu'un=e$_{CT}$ ja'   ta   j-k'an   j-ti'   li'=e$_F$,
        1SG=ENC   FOC   ICP   A1-want   A1-eat   DEM=ENC
        'I want to eat this.'

     c. vo'ot=e$_{CT}$ chika ja'   ch-a-ti'   li'=e$_F$,
        you=ENC   girl   FOC   ICP-A2-eat   DEM=ENC
        'You, girl, are going to eat this,'

     d. Marta=e$_{CT}$ ja'   li'=e$_F$.
        Martha=ENC   FOC   DEM=ENC
        'Martha, this.' {TEXT}

The answer is broken down, person by person: me, you, and a third person, Martha.

The contrastive topics occur in external topic position (with the final enclitic =e that indicates the edge of an intonational phrase); the focus within each answer occurs in situ associated with the focus particle *ja'* (see §4.2) (deictic gestures accompany this utterance).

Contrastive topics share properties both with foci and with (non-contrastive) topics. They are like contrastive foci in that they evoke sets of alternatives. But they are like aboutness topics in that they organize the reply, specifying who the information in the comment is about.

In languages with an internal topic construction, contrastive topics can be realized as internal. In their discussion of K'ichee' topics, Can Pixabaj and England (2011) cite (63).

K'ICHEE'

(63) a. Ri   al   Ixchel$_{CT}$ x-u-tzak   kinaq',
        DET CLF Ixchel   CP-A3SG-cook   beans
        'Ixchel$_{CT}$ cooked beans,'

     b. ri   al   Ixkik'$_{CT}$ x-u-k'ili-j   iik,
        DET CLF Ixkik'   CP-A3SG-toast-SS   chile
        'Ixkik'$_{CT}$ toasted chilis,'

     c. are   k'u   ri   al   Nikte'$_{CT}$,   x-u-lej   ri   wa.
        EMPH PAR   DET   CLF   Nikte'   CP-A3SG-make.tortilla   DET   tortilla
        'while Nikte'$_{CT}$ made tortillas.'

The subject of each clause is a contrastive topic, with the entire predicate phrase being the associated focus. Like other topics in K'ichee', the contrastive topic is separated from what follows by a pause (see fn. 12). According to Can Pixabaj and England, the last element in a set of contrastive topics is marked by *are k'u (are* is the particle (or copula) which marks DP foci in K'ichee' so is associated with contrast).

It appears then that Mayan languages tend to use their 'basic' topic construction for contrastive topics: languages with an external topic realize the contrastive topic as external, while languages with an internal topic realize it as internal. Further research may reveal other options, including special options for signaling the final contrastive topic in a list.

6 CONCLUSION

Mayan languages – both individually and as a group – provide rich ground for the investigation of information structure. With some exceptions, work on information structure has tended to approach it from the perspective of morphology and, especially, syntax, seeking pragmatic correlates with overt categories. This is not surprising since all the key notions (given and new, topic, and focus) are marked in various ways in Mayan, implicating prosody, morphology, and syntax. The structural encoding of these relations makes it possible to identify these functions relatively easily and to investigate the way they relate linguistic form and discourse function.

But as a consequence, certain generalizations have remained obscured until recently. For example, in the area of PREFERRED ARGUMENT STRUCTURE, i.e., the mapping from GIVEN and NEW to grammatical function, the 'standard' account associates GIVEN and NEW with the categories ABSOLUTIVE and ERGATIVE, which are of course morphologically salient in Mayan. However recent work has shown that the given-new distinction aligns not with the morphosyntax, but with notions more closely related to the semantics of volitionality and agency (§2). Similarly, most work on focus in Mayan has concerned preverbal contrastive focus, as these cases involve visible dislocation and often special (e.g., agent focus) morphology. In fact, there has been a tendency to equate 'focus' with a particular syntactic construction, rather than with a particular discourse status. Only recently has work emerged on in situ focus – whether involving new information focus or contrastive focus (§4). This work has revealed unexpected restrictions on in situ focus which relate it to the morphosyntax of moved (contrastive) focus. In the study of TOPIC constructions, the most serious work, again, has focused on the *syntax* of topic constructions with the consequence that a study of the discourse properties of these constructions has been slighted (a notable exception is Datz (1980)). A related fact is that there has been very little direct work on the phenomenon of CONTRASTIVE TOPIC, a relation which tends to be encoded no differently from other kinds of topic in these languages (§5).

This chapter attempts to start from the categories of information structure themselves, to explicate the relations of topic and focus sufficiently that one could ask how various types of focus and various types of topic are linguistically encoded (if indeed they are). Enough is now known about the grammars of most Mayan languages that these questions can be fruitfully addressed.

NOTES

* I would like to thank Scott AnderBois for his very helpful comments on an earlier draft of this chapter. Needless to say, he is not responsible for anything said here.
1 The orthography has been changed in some examples to conform with current standards. Glosses and translations have generally been retained from the original source.
2 Cf. Durie (1988, 2003) for similar claims about Achenese.
3 Vázquez and Zavala (2013) do not give the data in the form shown in Tables 11.2 and 11.3. These were constructed from the data they provide in their Table 5 (lexical new mentions) and Table 6 (all mentions). Any errors of interpretation are mine.
4 Chol distinguishes these two relations in the morphosyntax, requiring use of a light verb to express subjects of agentive intransitives (Gutiérrez Sánchez 2004; Coon

2013; Vázquez and Zavala 2013); see also Zavala Maldonado, this volume, on alignment.

5 *ja'* functions also as a copula (see below) and as a demonstrative. Polian (2013) speculates that the original function of *ja'* was demonstrative, and that it developed later into a focus marker.

6 Per Skopeteas and Verhoeven, both 3rd person and 2nd person agreement are possible in (22a), while only matching (2nd person) agreement is possible in (22b).

7 Many thanks to Telma Can for discussion of these examples.

8 In K'ichee', a fronted PP must be 'resumed' by the verbal clitic *wi*.

9 Yucatec does not have an AF morpheme per se. The AF construction is characterized by the absence of otherwise expected morphology (the Set A marker and the status suffix).

10 The cognate dative-benefactive applicative in the Tseltalan languages is not restricted in this way.

11 See Can Pixabaj and England (2011) and Gutierrez-Bravo (2011) for discussion of issues which arise in extending the account to K'ichee' and Yucatec.

12 Can Pixabaj and England (2011) report that K'ichee' topics, which otherwise resemble those of Tz'utujil, are separated in main clauses (but not in embedded ones) by pause from what follows. Whether this pause marks an *iP* break, or a smaller prosodic boundary, is unclear at present. It is not uncommon for a preverbal subject to be separated by a prosodic break from the following predicate, a break usually associated with a phonological phrase, not an *iP*.

REFERENCES

Aissen, Judith. 1992. "Topic and focus in Mayan." *Language* 63: 43–80.

Aissen, Judith. 1999. "External possessor and logical subject in Tz'utujil." In *External possession*, ed. by Doris Payne and Immanuel Barshi, 167–93. Amsterdam: John Benjamins.

Aissen, Judith. 2000. "Prosodic conditions on anaphora and clitics in Jakaltek." In *The syntax of verb initial languages*, ed. by Andrew Carnie and Eithne Guilfoyle, 185–200. Oxford: Oxford University Press.

Aissen, Judith. 2017. "Correlates of ergativity in Mayan." *In OUP handbook of ergativity*, ed. by Jessica Coon, Diane Massam, and Lisa Travis. Oxford: Oxford University Press.

Ariel, Mira. 1990. *Accessing NP antecedents*. London: Routledge.

Ayres, Glenn. 1983. "The antipassive "voice" in Ixil." *International Journal of American Linguistics* 49: 20–45.

Baird, Brandon. 2014. "An acoustic analysis of contrastive focus marking in Spanish-K'ichee' (Mayan) bilingual intonation." PhD diss., University of Texas.

Beaver, David. 2004. "The optimization of discourse anaphora." *Linguistics and Philosophy* 27: 3–56.

Berinstein, Ava. 1985. *Evidence for multiattachment in K'ekchi Mayan*. New York: Garland.

Bohnemeyer, Jürgen. 2002. *The grammar of time reference in Yukatek Maya*. Munich: LINCOM.

Brody, Jill. 1982. "Discourse processes of highlighting in Tojolabal Maya morphosyntax." PhD diss., Washington University.

Büring, Daniel. 2003. "On D-trees, beans, and B-accents." *Linguistics and Philosophy* 26: 511–45.

Can Pixabaj, Telma, and Nora England. 2011. "Nominal topic and focus in K'ichee'." In *Representing language: Essays in honor of Judith Aissen*, ed. by Rodrigo Gutiérrez-Bravo, Line Mikkelsen, and Eric Potsdam, 15–30. Santa Cruz: Linguistics Research Center, University of California, Santa Cruz.

Chafe, Wallace. 1976. "Givenness, contrastiveness, definiteness, subjects, topics, and point of view." In *Subject and topic*, ed. by Charles Li, 25–55. New York: Academic Press.

Coon, Jessica. 2013. *Aspects of split ergativity*. Oxford: Oxford University Press.

Coon, Jessica, Pedro Mateo Pedro, and Omer Preminger. 2014. "The role of case in A-bar extraction asymmetries: Evidence from Mayan." *Linguistic Variation* 14: 179–242.

Craig, Colette. 1977. *The structure of Jacaltec*. Austin: University of Texas Press.

Datz, Margaret J. Dickeman. 1980. "Jacaltec syntactic structure and the demands of discourse." PhD diss., University of Colorado.

Day, Christopher. 1973. *The Jacaltec language*. Language Science Monographs. Bloomington, IN: Indiana University.

Dayley, Jon P. 1985. *Tz'utujil grammar*. Berkeley: University of California Press.

Dik, Simon, Maria Hoffmann, Jan R. de Jong, Djiang Sie Ing, Harry Stroomer, and Lourens de Vries. 1981. "On the typology of focus phenomena." In *Perspectives on functional grammar*, ed. by Teun Hoekstra, Harry van der Hulst, and Michael Moortgat, 41–74. Dordrecht: Foris.

Du Bois, John W. 1987. "The discourse basis of ergativity." *Language* 63: 805–55.

Durbin, Marshall, and Fernando Ojeda. 1978. "Basic word order in Yucatec Maya." In *Papers in Mayan linguistics*, ed. by Nora England, 69–77. Columbia: Department of Anthropology, University of Missouri.

Durie, Mark. 1988. "Preferred argument structure in an active language: Arguments against the category 'intransitive subject'." *Lingua* 74: 1–25.

Durie, Mark. 2003. "New light on information pressure: Information conduits, "escape valves", and role alignment stretching." In *Preferred argument structure: Grammar as architecture for function*, ed. by John W. DuBois, Lorraine E. Kumpf, and William J. Ashby, 159–96. Amsterdam/Philadelphia: John Benjamins.

England, Nora. 1991. "Changes in basic word order in Mayan languages." *International Journal of American Linguistics* 57: 446–86.

England, Nora, and Laura Martin. 2003. "Issues in the comparative argument structure analysis in Mayan narratives." In *Preferred argument structure. Grammar as architecture for function*, ed. by John Du Bois, Lorraine Kumpf, and William Ashby, 131–57. Amsterdam/Philadelphia: John Benjamins.

Givón, Talmy. 1983. "Introduction." In *Topic continuity in discourse*, ed. by Talmy Givon, 5–41. Amsterdam: John Benjamins.

Gundel, Jeanette, Nancy Hedberg, and Ron Zacharski. 1993. "Cognitive status and the form of referring expressions in discourse." *Language* 69: 274–307.

Gutiérrez-Bravo, Rodrigo. 2011. "External and internal topics in Yucatec Maya." In *Representing language: Essays in honor of Judith Aissen*, ed. by Rodrigo Gutiérrez Bravo, Line Mikkelsen, and Eric Potsdam, 105–19. Santa Cruz: Linguistics Research Center, University of California, Santa Cruz.

Gutiérrez-Bravo, Rodrigo. 2015. *Las clausulas relativas en maya yucateco*. Mexico D.F.: El Colegio de México.

Gutiérrez-Bravo, Rodrigo, and Jorge Monforte y Madera. 2011. "Focus, agent focus and relative clauses in Yucatec Maya." In *New perspectives in Mayan linguistics*, ed. by Heriberto Avelino, 257–74. Cambridge: Cambridge Scholars Publishing.

Gutiérrez Sanchez, Pedro. 2004. "Las clases de verbos intransitivos y el alineamiento agentivo en el chol de Tila, Chiapas." MA thesis, CIESAS.

Hartmann, Katharina, and Malte Zimmermann. 2007. "In place – out of place? Focus in Hausa." In *On information structure, meaning and form*, ed. by Kerstin Schwabe and Susanne Winkler, 365–403. Amsterdam/Philadelphia: John Benjamins.

Haviland, John. 1981. Sk'op sotz'leb: el tzotzil de San Lorenzo Zinacantán. México, D.F.: UNAM.

Jacobs, Joachim. 2001. "The dimensions of topic-comment." *Linguistics* 39: 641–81.

Kiss, E. Katalin. 1998. "Identificational focus versus information focus." *Language* 74: 245–73.

Krifka, Manfred. 2008. "Basic notions of information structure." *Acta Linguistica Hungarica* 55: 243–76.

Kügler, Frank, Stavros Skopeteas, and Elisabeth Verhoeven. 2007. "Encoding information structure in Yucatec Maya: On the interplay of prosody and syntax." *Interdisciplinary Studies on Information Structure* 8: 187–208.

Larsen, Thomas. 1988. "Manifestations of ergativity in Quiche grammar." PhD diss., University of California, Berkeley.

Laughlin, Robert. 1977. *Of cabbages and kings*. Washington, DC: Smithsonian Institution Press.

Laughlin, Robert. 1980. *Of shoes and ships and sealing wax*. Washington, DC: Smithsonian Institution Press.

López Ixcoy, Candelaria Dominga. 1997. *Gramatica K'ichee'*. Guatemala City: Cholsamaj.

Martínez, Rosendo. 2012. "Las manifestaciones sintácticas, semánticas y discursivas de la agentividad en el tsotsil de Huixtán, Chiapas." MA thesis, CIESAS, México D.F.

Mithun, Marianne. 1991. "Active/agentive case marking and its motivations." *Language* 67: 510–46.

Mondloch, James. 1981. "Voice in Quiche-Maya." PhD diss., SUNY, Albany.

Norman, William. 1976. "Quiche text." In *Native American texts series: Mayan texts 1*, ed. by Louanna Furbee-Losee, 40–60. Chicago: University of Chicago Press.

Norman, William. 1977. "Topic and focus in Mayan." Paper presented at Mayan Workshop II. San Cristóbal de las Casas, Chiapas, México.

Norman, William. 1978. "Advancement rules and syntactic change: the loss of instrumental voice in Mayan." *Berkeley Linguistics Society* 4: 458–76.

Polian, Gilles. 2013. *Gramática del tseltal de Oxchuc*. México, D.F: CIESAS.

Reinhart, Tanya. 1981. "Pragmatics and linguistics: an analysis of sentence topics." *Philosophica* 27: 53–94.

Reinhart, Tanya. 1982. *Pragmatics and linguistics: an analysis of sentence topics*. Bloomington: Indiana University Linguistics Club.

Rooth, Mats. 1992. "A theory of focus interpretation." *Natural Language Semantics* 1: 75–116.

Skopeteas, Stavros, and Elisabeth Verhoeven. 2009. "Distinctness effects on VOS order: Evidence from Yucatec Maya." In *New perspectives on Mayan linguistics*, ed. by Heriberto Avelino, Jessica Coon, and Elisabeth Norcliffe, 157–74. MIT Working Papers in Linguistics.

Stiebels, Barbara. 2006. "Agent focus in Mayan languages." *Natural Language & Linguistic Theory* 24: 501–70.

Tonhauser, Judith. 2003. "F-constructions in Yucatec Maya." In *Proceedings of SULA 2*, ed. by Jan Anderssen, Paula Menendez-Benito, and Adam Werle, 203–23. Amherst: Graduate Linguistic Student Association of the University of Massachusetts.

Vallduví, Enric, and Maria Vilkuna. 1998. "On rheme and kontrast." In *Syntax and semantics 29: The limits of syntax*, ed. by Peter Culicover and Louise McNally, 79–108. San Diego: Academic Press.

Vázquez, Juan Jesús, and Roberto Zavala. 2013. "La estructura argumental preferida en chol, una lengua agentiva." In *Memorias del VI Congreso de Idiomas Indígenas de Latinoamérica, 24–6 de octubre de 2013*, Universidad de Texas en Austin. http://www.ailla.utexas.org/site/events.html.

Velleman, Leah. 2014. "Focus and movement in a variety of K'ichee'." PhD diss., University of Texas.

Verhoeven, Elisabeth, and Stavros Skopeteas. 2015. "Licensing focus constructions in Yucatec Maya." *International Journal of American Linguistics* 81: 1–40.

Walker, Marilyn, Aravind Joshi, and Ellen Prince, ed. 1998. *Centering theory in discourse*. Oxford: Clarendon Press.

PART 3

SEMANTICS

CHAPTER 12

ORGANIZATION OF SPACE

Jürgen Bohnemeyer

1 INTRODUCTION: THE REPRESENTATION OF SPACE IN LANGUAGE

This chapter surveys the state of the art of research on the representation of space in Mayan languages. It is organized around the classification of spatial concepts depicted in Figure 12.1. This classification is treated here as an 'etic grid', a set of mutually (partially) independent properties applicable to the crosslinguistic and crosscultural exploration of the overarching conceptual domain on a trial-and-revise basis (cf. Moore et al. 2015). It is valid for all languages that have been studied to date (so far as I know); but that does not mean that it is valid for all languages, nor that it is not biased toward better-studied languages.

This classification starts from an ontological distinction among four conceptual classes: places, individuals, states, and dynamic concepts, i.e., representations of processes, activities, and state changes. States are further subdivided into 'individual-level' and 'stage-level' states. According to the proposal by Carlson (1977), the former concern individuals per se, whereas the latter are properties of certain stages of their history. In other words, individual-level properties are inherent and essential, whereas stage-level properties are variable without the variation affecting the identity of the individual.

This chapter focuses on stage-level and dynamic properties of spatial representations. The stage-level spatial properties of an individual are its location, orientation, and what I will call its 'disposition', following Bohnemeyer and Brown (2007) and others. From the perspective of English and Spanish – and from that of many other languages – disposition is a wastebasket category, with only the postures of higher animals (along with their metaphoric extensions to other kinds of individuals) providing something of a coherent core. However, the Mayan languages treat postures on a par with a much larger category of properties, many of which apply primarily or exclusively to inanimate referents. At the same time, this larger dispositional category is set apart from other spatial properties (though not without areas of gradual transition). Dispositional properties include the distribution and configuration of parts of the individual (e.g., 'piled up', 'stacked', 'spread out') and its force-dynamic (Talmy 2000a: 409–70) affordances given its interactions with the environment (e.g., 'contained', 'wedged in', 'stuck').

Locative representations may be 'topological' (Piaget and Inhelder 1956), i.e., perspective-free, or may involve a 'spatial frame of reference' (e.g., Carlson-Radvansky and Irwin 1993; Levelt 1996; Levinson 1996). Reference frames are axis systems used to define regions and directions in space. Orientation descriptions are arguably by necessity frame-dependent as well (Bohnemeyer 2003; Bohnemeyer and O'Meara 2012).

Representations of the motion of a given individual (the 'figure' in the terminology of Talmy 2000a&b) have been argued to specify two kinds of information: the 'path' and 'manner' of the event (Talmy 2000b: 21–146). Path information concerns properties of the trajectory of the event. Jackendoff (1983:161–87) distinguishes three types of path

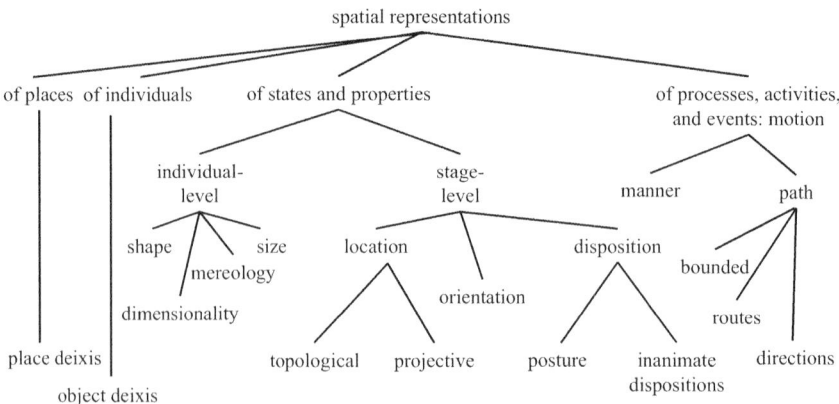

FIGURE 12.1 A CLASSIFICATION OF SPATIAL CONCEPTS

concepts: 'bounded path' concepts specify the beginning and/or endpoint of the trajectory, 'routes' refer to places traversed in between, and 'directions' orient the trajectory. Like locations, bounded paths and routes may be represented in topological or frame-dependent terms, whereas directions, like orientations, are inherently frame-dependent. Manner is a complementary category to path in a way that is quite reminiscent of how dispositional information complements locative and orientation information in the stative domain (Belloro et al. 2008). Manners are activities or processes of the figure that are cotemporaneous with the motion and may or may not be causing it. Some manners may also be conceptualized as trajectory shapes, taking the trajectory as an abstract object (e.g., 'zigzag', 'spiral', 'careen'; cf. van der Zee 2000).

2 STAGE-LEVEL STATES

2.1 Location

2.1.1 Topological relations

Place functions (Jackendoff 1983:161–70; 'localizers' in Kracht 2002) designate regions of space with respect to a reference entity or 'ground' in locative and motion descriptions. Following Piaget and Inhelder 1956, 'projective' and 'topological' place functions may be distinguished. The former, but not the latter, return regions defined in some reference frame (see below). Frame-independent or non-perspectival place functions define regions in terms of properties such as inclusion in the ground, overlap with the ground, attachment to the ground, contact with the ground, proximity to the ground, and distance from the ground.

Among Mayan languages, the expression of topological place functions has been studied in Mam (England 1978), Tseltal (Brown 1994; Bohnemeyer and Brown 2007), Tsotsil (de León 1992), Yokot'an (or Tabasco Chontal; Delgado Galvan 2013), and Yucatec (Goldap 1992; Lehmann 1992; Bohnemeyer and Stolz 2006; Bohnemeyer and Brown 2007).

A typologically unusual feature of the expression of topological place functions in Mayan languages is the general sparseness of prepositions in these languages (Kaufman 1990:78). Many Mayan languages have only a single preposition, which occurs with adverbials and obliques nearly without semantic restrictions. An example is the preposition *ta* of Tseltal. Yucatec has a counterpart (and possible cognate), *ti'*, and in addition a variety of relational nouns that appear to be in various stages of grammaticalization en route to prepositions. As far as spatial representations are concerned, these include *ich* 'eye', 'face', 'fruit', which occurs as the head of adverbials and obliques without possessive marking, expressing meanings of inclusion and containment.

Example (1) illustrates a 'ground phrase' (the phrase expressing the place function) headed by *ti'* (which in this case is reduced to *t-* or amalgamated in portmanteau with the cross-reference marker *u=* indexing the possessor). The complement is a possessed nominal meaning 'its bone', in this case referring to the antlers of a stag, who is the anaphorically represented possessor. The figure is a boy who climbed into the antlers mistaking them for a bush. This topological relation – inclusion in the spatial envelope of the antlers – is merely conveyed by stereotype implicature, a generalized conversational implicature licensed by Grice's second Quantity maxim ('Do not make your contribution more informative than is required'; Atlas and Levinson 1981). A comparison with (2) makes this abundantly clear. In (2), a ground phrase headed by *ti'* is understood as referring to a support configuration. Clearly, this difference in interpretation is not reflected in the form of the ground phrase.

YUCATEC
(1) *Ti'=yàan   le=pàal   t-u=bak'=o'.*
     PREP=EXIST;B3SG DET=child PREP-A3=bone=CFP
     'There the boy was in [the deer's] antlers.'

(2) *Ti'=wa'l-un-wa'l-o'b   te=lu'm=o'.*
     PREP=REDUP-DISP.PL-stand-B3PL   PREP:DET=ground=CFP
     'There [the bottles] are standing one by one on the ground.'

To provide specific topological information, expressions of various lexical categories can be employed. Example (3) illustrates the relational noun *iknal*, which designates a region of space defined by proximity to a stationary ground whose horizontal extension in a plane that contains the figure is construed as negligible, not unlike English *at*:

YUCATEC
(3) *Le=trisìikulo=o',   yàan   hun-p'éel   k'e'k'en   y=iknal.*
     DEF=tricycle=CFP   EXIST;B3SG   one-CLF.INAN   pig   A3=at
     'The tricycle, there's a pig by it.'

As illustrated, *iknal* may head the ground phrase itself without support by *ti'*. (Note that the possessor of *iknal*, the nominal referring to the tricycle, is left-dislocated in (3).) The ground phrase is thus in this case a possessed nominal rather than a prepositional phrase.

Proximity may also be expressed using the stative predicate *nàats'* 'be near',[1] which frequently co-occurs with *iknal*, as in (4):[2]

YUCATEC
(4) *Nàats'   t-inw=iknal=e'   yàan   hun-túul   máak=i'.*
     near;B3SG PREP-A1SG=at=TOP   EXIST;B3SG   one-CLF.ANIM   person= CFP
     'Near by me, there is a person.'

It has been hypothesized that Mayan languages use dispositional predicates to express topological information (Brown 1994; Grinevald 2006). This hypothesis is addressed in §2.1.3.

2.1.2 Projective relations and reference frames

Reference frames are systems of axes used to interpret linguistic and non-linguistic representations of the location, motion, and orientation of entities. They are constituted by an origin and one or more (semi-)axes. In representations of location/motion, the origin is a reference point, most commonly a reference entity or 'ground'. The axes are defined with respect to a contextual index, the 'anchor'. Psychologists are accustomed to classifying frames on the basis of the identity of the anchor in terms of 'egocentric' vs. 'allocentric' frames. As it turns out, however, this classification does not capture the variation in frame use across languages: egocentric and allocentric frames are used in all languages, but certain subtypes are not. These subtypes differ by the operations involved in deriving the axes. Thus, all egocentric frames are anchored to the body of an observer,[3] but only 'relative' frames involve projection (geometrically, translation or reflection) of the observer's body axes onto a distinct ground (as in 'The ball is to the left of the chair' uttered with respect to the configuration in Figure 12.2 below). In small-scale horizontal space, speakers of Dutch, English, and Japanese use relative frames and to some extent 'intrinsic' (object-centered) frames derived from the ground itself (as in 'The ball is to the right of the chair' uttered with respect to the configuration in Figure 12.2), but not 'geocentric' frames derived from the environment (e.g., 'The ball is west/upriver of the chair'). In contrast, speakers of Tenejapan Tseltal and many other languages use intrinsic and geocentric frames, but not relative ones.

Among Mayan languages, there are published accounts of reference frame use in Mopan (Danziger 1996, 1999, 2001, 2011); Tseltal (Brown and Levinson 1993, 2000, 2009; Levinson and Brown 1994; Levinson 1996, 2003; Brown 2006; Polian and Bohnemeyer 2011); Tsotsil (de León 1991, 1994); and Yucatec (Bohnemeyer and Stolz 2006; Bohnemeyer 2011; Le Guen 2011). Relative frames play a marginal role in all of the languages except for Yucatec, and even there they do not dominate, not even in small-scale space.

Whether there is an overall preference for geocentric or intrinsic frames in small-scale space seems to be highly variable. Danziger reports Mopan speakers to use exclusively intrinsic frames in small-scale space. Brown and Levinson famously found Tseltal speakers in the hamlet of Majosik', Chiapas, to prefer geocentric frames of the type that Levinson (1996) termed 'absolute'. These are abstracted from a concrete, mountain-slope-based 'up(hill)'/'down(hill)'/'across'-system (an example of what the members of the MesoSpace collective of researchers (see below) have called a 'geomorphic' system; cf. Bohnemeyer et al. (2015), Polian and Bohnemeyer (2011), O'Meara and Pérez Báez (2011)). They are abstracted in the sense that a member of this speech community will theoretically use the same 'up(hill)', 'down(hill)', or 'across' term for labeling a given direction regardless of the location of the reference point or ground, much the same way cardinal direction terms are used in other languages. Tenejapa, for example, is uphill from Majosik'. But speakers from Majosik' would continue to refer to this direction as *ajk'ol* 'up(hill)' even beyond Tenejapa and on the other side of the mountain, in places that might be construed as being downhill from Majosik' in terms of the physical terrain. This contrasts with de León's description of the use of slope-based reference frames in Zinacantán Tsotsil, which attests to only the concrete, geomorphic use.

Polian and Bohnemeyer (2011) studied the use of reference frames in three other Tseltal communities (Ch'ajkoma, Mesbilja', and Tenejapa (Lum in Tseltal)), using methods similar to those of Brown and Levinson. They found a rather different picture. Speakers in all three communities preferred intrinsic frames for locative descriptions and frames based on local landmarks for orientation descriptions. An example of a landmark-based description is (5). It locates a ball (the figure) with respect to a chair (the ground), using the local cemetery as anchor:

TSELTAL
(5) *Jich p'ekel bel ta stojol **mukinal** i pelota-i.*
    thus lying DIR PREP toward cemetery the ball-CLF
    'The ball is placed toward the cemetery [with respect to the chair].'

Descriptions based on the 'up(hill)'/'down(hill)' system and descriptions employing sunset/sunrise-based terms played a large secondary role in Ch'ajkoma and Mesbilja', but were largely absent in Tenejapa. Polian and Bohnemeyer explain this striking inter-community variation with differences in the local terrain: the mountain slope offers a much more salient and unambiguous anchor in Majosik' than in the other three communities.

Yucatec differs from the other three Mayan languages in which frame use has been studied to date in that it shows a considerably greater incidence of relative frames. Three independent studies (Bohnemeyer and Stolz 2006; Bohnemeyer 2011; Le Guen 2011) have coincided in this finding. By hypothesis, the long history of more intensive contact with Spanish may be the crucial factor explaining this distribution. Bohnemeyer (2011) observes that there seem to be no restrictions on the use of all major frame types in small-scale space in this language. Consider (6), a description of the image reproduced in Figure 12.2, which combines an intrinsic, a relative, and an absolute description:

YUCATEC
(6) *T-u=tséel$_{INT}$, te=x-ts'íik$_{REL}$ te-estée-le=chik'in$_{ABS}$=o',*
    PREP-A3=side PREP:DEF=F-left PREP:DEF-HESIT-DEF=west=CFP
    hun-p'éel bòola yàan=i', ch'uy-k'ah-a'n (. . .).
    one-CLF.INAN ball EXIST;B3SG=CFP hang-ANTIC-RES;B3SG
    '**On the (chair's) side, on the left in the, uh, the west**, there is a ball, it is suspended (. . .).'

The one restriction on frame use that all three studies have reported is a gender pattern: the cardinal direction terms are used almost exclusively by male speakers. Bohnemeyer (2011) suggests that this distribution may be accounted for in terms of occupational differences. Cardinal directions are primarily employed in male-dominated arenas of language use, such as horticulture, the construction of houses, and certain religious practices. Support for the role of topography and language contact as factors shaping practices of reference frame use comes from a recent multi-population study (Bohnemeyer et al. 2015).

2.1.3 Locative predication

Locative predication semantically involves a relation between an entity – the theme/figure – and a place (a region of space), such that it is asserted that, or questioned whether (etc.), the region of space immediately occupied by the figure and delimited by its spatial envelope is included in this place. This place may, but need not, be determined with

FIGURE 12.2 BALL AND CHAIR

respect to a second entity. The examples in (7) illustrate some of the options: the place may be denoted by a toponym (7a), specified deictically/indexically (7b), defined in terms of some state of affairs involving it (7c), or described with respect to a referential ground (7d):[4]

(7) The book is . . .
    a. . . . in Buffalo
    b. . . . over there
    c. . . . wherever you put it
    d. . . . on the table

Let us call the expression of the place at which the figure is located the **ground phrase** and the nominal that describes the ground object – if there is one – the **ground descriptor**. If the ground phrase is headed by an adposition or relational noun, it dominates the ground descriptor, which is the complement of the adposition or the possessor of the relational noun. But if the 'place function' (the conceptual function that maps the ground entity into the place; cf. §2.3, 2.1) is expressed by a case marker, as in Finnish, ground phrase and ground descriptor are constituted by the same string.

Syntactically, a locative predication involves an expression referring to the figure and a locative predicate. The latter in turn consists minimally of the ground phrase and a head. Typological research has found there to be systematic variation across languages both in the range of expressions that head locative predicates – and the conditions under which they are possible or preferred as locative predicators – and in the make.-up of the ground phrase.

The typology of 'basic locative predications' (Ameka and Levinson 2007) has two orthogonal dimensions: (i) the type of head that speakers of a given language or linguistic variety prefer to describe what crosslinguistic research suggests is the *prototype* of locative predications: an easily movable inanimate figure located in non-attached fashion with respect to a larger and less mobile ground; and (ii) the semantic extension of the 'basic locative predication' (BLC) of a given language so defined.

One hallmark of the 'grammar of space' of Mayan languages is the common occurrence of dispositional predicates (cf. §2.3) as heads of locative predicates. Consider for illustration again the Tseltal example (5), repeated in (8):

TSELTAL
(8) *Jich* **p'ek-el** *bel ta stojol mukinal i pelota-i.*
    thus lie-DISP;B3 DIR PREP toward cemetery the ball-CLF
    'The ball is placed (lit. 'is lying') toward the cemetery [with respect to the chair].'

The head of the locative predicate, glossed here as 'lying', uniquely describes the configuration between an object that lacks a dominant axis – in this case, a ball – and an implicit ground that supports it. Another example is the Yucatec description in (2), repeated in (9):

YUCATEC
(9) *Ti'=***wa'l-un-wa'l-o'b**   *te=lu'm=o'*
    PREP=**REDUP-DISP.PL-stand**-B3PL   PREP:DEF=ground=CFP
    'There [the bottles] are standing one by one on the ground'

This utterance describes a group of bottles on the ground. The root *wa'l* denotes a 'standing' disposition, meaning in this case that the figure has a dominant longest axis and is supported on one end of this axis. The use of posture verbs with meanings such as 'sit', 'stand', and 'lie' in locative descriptions is familiar from languages around the world, including from some European languages, such as Dutch and German. Dispositions include postures, but are not confined to them. They can be characterized in first approximation as any stage-level spatial property of an entity other than its location. The common presence of dispositionals in linguistic descriptions of location (and motion; cf. §3.1) in Mayan languages confounds Landau and Jackendoff's (1993) generalization that such representations are more sensitive to the properties of the ground than to those of the figure.

Bohnemeyer and Brown (2007) show that both Tseltal and Yucatec use the following range of predicators to form equivalents of English locative predications: (i) a function word that heads locative, existential, and possessive predications without imposing any selection restrictions on the theme/figure other than requiring it to be an individual; (ii) a stative predicate form of a dispositional root; (iii) a stative resultative predicate form of a verb root; (iv) a possessive predication; (v) a dynamic verb form. However, for the crosslinguistically prototypical locative scenes – a smaller, easily movable figure located in non-attached fashion with respect to larger, more stationary, and inanimate ground (Wilkins 1999; Levinson and Wilkins 2006a) – Tseltal speakers prefer a stative dispositional predicate, whereas Yucatec speakers prefer the "generic" locative/existential/possessive predicator (*yàan*, illustrated in (11), and also several examples above). The contrast is exemplified by (10) and (11), elicited as descriptions of the same stimulus – the first picture of the Topological Relations Picture Series (Bowerman and Pederson 1992, ms.) – by a Tseltal (10) and Yucatec (11) speaker, respectively:

TSELTAL

(10) *Pach-al* .... *ta   ba   mexa   te   ala   baso.*
     placed.upright.bowlshaped.container-DISP;B3   PREP   top   table   DEF   DIM   cup
     'The cup is upright on the table.' (Brown 2006:245)

YUCATEC

(11) *Le=lìuch=o',   ti'   yàan   y=óok'ol   le =mesa=o'.*
     DEF=cup=CFP   there   EXIST;B3   A3=on   DEF=table=CFP
     'The cup, it's there on the table.'

Thus, the two languages use the same resources for the expression of locative predication, but have different pragmatic preferences in terms of which construction is the
default for which function. In terms of the typology of 'basic locative predications' proposed by Ameka and Levinson (2007), based on Wilkins (1998, 1999) (cf. Levinson and
Wilkins 2006a, b), Tseltal is a Type-III language. Its speakers prefer to select one of a
large number of lexical dispositional predicators to head locative predicates. In contrast,
Yucatec is a Type-I language, which by default uses a uniform locative predicator. In
such a language, dispositional information enters the locative predication only when the
figure's disposition is pragmatically at issue. Situated in between these two types are
languages such as Dutch whose default locative predicators are a small set of posture
verbs, which are chosen on the basis of geometrical properties of the figure and thus have
a classificatory function.

What are we to make of the typological difference between Tseltal and Yucatec?
Brown 1994 and Grinevald 2006 (drawing partly on Jakaltek data) hypothesize that there
is a tradeoff between the information encoded in the head of the locative predicate and
in the head of the ground phrase, which is a generic preposition in Tseltal. However,
Bohnemeyer and Brown 2007 cast doubt on this conjecture, showing that the generic
preposition is reinforced by a meronym in Tseltal even more frequently than in Yucatec.
Bohnemeyer and Brown consider a number of plausible alternative explanations. Assuming that the Type-III strategy is the conservative one among Mayan languages – which of
course cannot be taken for granted – Yucatec may have shifted to Type I due to its history
of more intense contact with Spanish, which is likewise a Type-I language. Not mutually
exclusive with this hypothesis is an account under which the shift from Type III to Type
I is part of a larger pattern of typological change.

Delgado Galvan (2013) applies the design of Bohnemeyer and Brown (2007) to
Yokot'an (Chontal de Tabasco) and finds that this language, like Yucatec, instantiates
Ameka and Levinson's Type I. However, the dispositional system seems to be richer
than in Yucatec, more like the Tseltal one, and dispositionals appear to be used more
frequently in discourse. Delgado Galvan argues that meronyms are used more frequently
in locative predications involving the "generic" locative predicators than in dispositional
predications, which she suggests supports the complementarity hypothesis. However, it
is not clear that the frequency difference in her data is significant.

2.2 Orientation

Strategies for orientating entities have been studied in Tseltal (Brown 2006; Polian
and Bohnemeyer 2012) and Yucatec (Bohnemeyer and Stolz 2006; Bohnemeyer 2011;
Bohnemeyer and O'Meara 2011). The truth conditions of orientation descriptions can
be captured in the framework developed in Bohnemeyer and O'Meara (2012) and

Bohnemeyer (2011) in terms of an alignment of a suitable axis of the figure with an axis of a reference frame, and thus ultimately with an axis of the anchor from which the frame is derived. In Tseltal and Yucatec, the default axis of an object for the purpose of orienting it is the front axis. In (12), the front of a chair is selected explicitly by saying that the seat of the chair is 'turned west':

YUCATEC
(12) *(. . .) le=pàarte tu'x   k-u=kutal   máak=o',*
            DEF=part where;B3SG IPFV-A3=sit:INCH.ICP person=CFP
     ***chik'in   súut-ul** (. . .)*
     west;B3SG   turn\ANTIC-ICP;B3SG
     '(. . .) the part where one sits, it's **turned west** (. . .)'

Orientation can also be expressed by selecting an axis of the figure and treating it as a vector that is pointing toward a landmark. This is illustrated by the Tseltal example (13):

TSELTAL
(13) Li'   ay   tal   y=elaw   ta   ba   ay-otik=i.
     here   EXIST;B3   DIR   A3=face PREP where EXIST-B1PL=CFP
     'It [the chair] is facing toward here where we are (lit. Its face is where we are).'
     (Polian and Bohnemeyer 2011:878)

Bohnemeyer and O'Meara (2012) suggest that this strategy can be considered as implicitly likewise constituting a reference frame on the basis of the single (half) axis pointing toward the landmark. They also suggest, based on a comparison of data from Yucatec and Seri (isolate; Sonora), that orientation descriptions may be more likely to use geocentric frames compared to locative and motion descriptions. An earlier study pointing toward the same pattern is Terrill and Burenhult 2008.

2.3 Posture and disposition

Dispositional roots (usually called *positional* roots in the Mayan literature) are morphemes that lexicalize complex spatial configurations and may produce verb stems, stative predicate forms, classifiers, and other lexical categories with the appropriate derivational morphology. Distinctions that enter the conceptualization of dispositions include support/suspension (e.g., 'sit', 'stand', 'lie', 'kneel', 'lean', 'hang', 'droop', 'dangle', 'be mounted on top of something'); blockage of motion (e.g., 'be stuck to something', 'be stuck between two things'); orientation in the gravitational field (e.g., 'lie face up', 'lie face down', 'lie on side', 'be tilted at an angle'); and configurations of parts of an object with respect to one another (e.g., 'be scattered', 'be spread out', 'be in a pile', 'be lined up in a row', 'be bulging', 'be bent', 'be twisted', 'be coiled up').

Mayan dispositionals combine a number of typologically remarkable traits:

- They constitute a lexical category of their own, the members of which produce stative predicates, inchoative intransitive verbs, causative transitive verbs, and numeral classifiers through various derivational operations, some (though not all) of which are unique to dispositional roots.
- They categorize properties that are for the most part not lexicalized at all in many other languages in a highly specific manner. Thus, 152 and 267 dispositional roots

have been identified, respectively, in Yucatec and Tenejapa Tseltal (Bohnemeyer and Brown 2007; cf. also Sántiz Gómez (2010) for Oxchuc Tseltal). Tsotsil is said to have 273 (Laughlin 1975; Haviland 1994). Arcos Lopez (2009:39–52) lists 140 numeral classifiers in Ch'ol, 132 of which are morphologically derived from dispositional roots. For some highland languages such as Q'anjob'al (Martin 1977; Mateo Toledo 2004) and K'ichee' and Motosintlek (Kaufman 1990), the number of dispositional roots has been estimated to be as high as 600–700.

- Lastly, they are frequently used in locative descriptions, in a function that has been compared to that of manner verbs in motion descriptions (Brown 2000; Belloro et al. 2008). In some of the languages, they in fact represent the default choice for the heads of locative predicates (cf. §2.1.3).

Example (14), repeated from (12) above, illustrates two Yucatec dispositionals: the posture root *kul* 'sit' appears in an inchoative verb form. In contrast, the root *pek* appears in a special stative predicate form reserved to dispositionals. *Pek* is the default support root for inanimate objects that lack a unique dominant axis, but is also used with animate referents that are unconscious or (in the case of toddlers) sick.

YUCATEC
(14) *(. . .)*   *te'l*   *tu'x*   *k-u=***kutal**   *máak=o',*   *te=lu'm=o',*
          there   where   IPFV-A3=**sit:INCH.ICP**   person=CFP   PREP:DEF=earth=CFP
          hun-p'éel   *bòola*   **pek-ekbal**   *hach*
          one-CLF.INAN   ball   **lie.as.if.dropped-DISP;B3SG**   really
          tu=tu'k'=o'.
          PREP;A3=corner=CFP
    '(. . .) there where one **sits**, on (lit. with respect to) the ground, a ball is **lying**, right at its corner.'

An apparent Tseltal cognate of *pek* is *p'ek* in (5) above. Example (15) features *pek* as part of a causative verb stem:

YUCATEC
(15) *(. . .) eh,*   *yan*   *a=ch'a'-ik*   *hun-p'éel*   *chan=che'*   *wolis*
      HESIT   OBLIG   A2=take-ICP;B3SG   one-CLF.INAN   DIM=wood   round;B3SG
      *a=***pek-kunt-eh** *(. . .).*
      A2= **lie.as.if.dropped-CAUS-SUBJ;B3SG**
      '(. . .) uh, you have to take a little piece of wood that's round, in order to **lay** it **down** (. . .).'

Brown (2000) draws attention to the use of dispositionals in Tseltal motion event descriptions. This is discussed in the following section.

3 MOTION

3.1 Manner of motion

Manner of motion must be considered an understudied domain, both as concerns the conceptualizations involved and in terms of its linguistic representation, and both in Mayan languages and elsewhere.

Manners of motion are activities in the sense of Vendler's (1957) classification. Activities play a typologically somewhat unusual role in the Mayan lexicon, since many of them are lexicalized as nouns in Mayan languages or as roots that have both nominal and verbal uses without either one requiring overt derivational morphology (so-called 'action nouns' (Kaufman 1990) or 'verbo-nominals' (Lois and Vapnarsky 2003)).

Talmy's (2000b) typology of 'lexicalization patterns' distinguishes a variety of approaches to combining manner and path information in motion event descriptions. 'Verb-framed' descriptions express path information in the main verb root, whereas 'satellite-framed' descriptions express it exclusively outside the main verb root (in adpositions, case markers, or 'satellites', i.e., co-predicative adverbs or particles), leaving the main verb root free to encode manner information provided the syntax of the language permits location change descriptions to be headed by manner verbs (Narasimhan 2003).[5] Path-conflating and manner-conflating verbs also form serial verb constructions in many languages, in which there is no unique main verb. This type of construction has been argued to instantiate neither the verb-framed nor the satellite-framed type, but a third option (Ameka and Essegbey 2001; Zlatev and Yangklang 2004). Individual languages instantiate any of these patterns to the exclusion of the others or mix multiple of them.

Of these three construction types identified by Talmy, some Mayan languages' motion event descriptions instantiate exclusively the verb-framed type, albeit with a number of twists to be commented on below. These languages (i) have a set of verb roots that lexicalize notions of location change and thus resemble path-conflating verbs with meanings such as 'enter'/'exit', 'come'/'go', and 'ascend'/'descend' (but see below); and they (ii) lack any expression of path functions outside these verb roots, thus rendering combinations of manner main verbs with satellites or oblique phrases expressing path impossible. This type of Mayan language is exemplified by Yucatec. Examples (16a) and (16b) illustrate two ways of combining manner and location change verbs in Yucatec sentences. In (16a), the main verb *em* 'descend' expresses location change. The manner verb *xíiknal* 'fly', 'flutter' appears in a gerund-like form, which for verbs of its class – verbo-nominals or action nouns – is morphologically unmarked. This gerund heads a projection that is embedded into the verb phrase as an adverbial modifier.

YUCATEC

(16) a. *Le=ch'íich'=o' h-èem   u=xíiknal te=che'=o'.*
    DEF=bird=CFP   PFV-descend;B3SG   A3=fly   PREP:DEF=wood=CFP
    'The bird, it **flew down** from the tree [lit. it descended from the tree flying].'

  b. *Le=ch'íich'=o' xíiknal-il   h-úuch   uy=èem-el*
    DEF=bird=CFP   A3=fly-RELAL;B3SG   PFV-happen;B3SG   A3=descend;B3SG
    te=che'=o'.
    PREP:DEF=wood=CFP
    'The bird, it **FLEW down from** the tree [lit. in a flying manner is how it descended].'

  c. *Le=ch'íich'=o' túun   xíiknal y=óok'ol le=che'=o'.*
    DEF=bird=CFP   PROG:A3   fly   A3=on   DEF=wood=CFP
    'The bird, it is/was **flying** above the tree.'

In contrast, in (16b), the manner verb appears in the syntactically higher position. However, this sentence has a cleft-like structure, instantiating a special manner focus construction (cf. Bohnemeyer 2002:123–5), which in perfective aspect requires the support of the light verb *úuch* 'happen'. Since manner and path (or rather location change; see below) are not expressed in the same clause in (16b), this structure does not represent an exception to the generalization that the verb-framed type of description is without competition in Yucatec. And indeed, when a manner verb is combined with a ground phrase without the support of a location change verb, as in (16c), the ground phrase can only be understood as referring to the place at which the manner activity takes place, not to a place that marks the beginning or endpoint of a motion path or some space traversed in between (but not all of these).

It seems likely that all Mayan languages have constructions similar to the one illustrated in (16a). However, the following Tseltal example has no parallels in Yucatec:

TSELTAL
(17) *Ya* *x-**ben***   ***jelaw-el***   *mut*   *ta*   *ch'ajan* *tak'in.*
     ICP IPFV-walk;3A   cross-DIR   bird   PREP   cord   metal
     'The bird **walks across** the electric wire.' (Brown 2006:253)

As in (16b), the manner verb – in this case, *ben* 'walk' – is the highest up in the syntactic tree in (17). However, (17) is not a focus construction, and there is no reason to think that it is biclausal. The location change verb *jelaw* 'cross' appears in a special non-finite verb form, which is similar to the gerund form of the manner verb in (16a) (which with location change verbs is marked by a – *Vl* suffix in Yucatec; cf. *èem-el* 'descend-ing' in (20) and *na'k-al* 'ascend-ing' in (21) below). This form of location change verbs is known as the **directional** form in Mayan linguistics. Thus, a location change verb projection is embedded as a modifier or copredicate in a verb phrase headed by a manner verb in (17). As Brown (2006:251–3) observes, this instantiates satellite framing. Tseltal therefore exhibits a 'split system of conflation', as Talmy (2000b:64–5) puts it.

Whether or not Yucatec can be said to have directionals as well is somewhat unclear. This issue is discussed in §3.2. However, even if it does, these are not used in combination with manner main verbs. Thus, there are no satellite-framed motion descriptions and in this sense, no satellites in this language.

It is uncertain how widespread the Tseltal-style split system is in the Mayan language family. A plausible conjecture is that its presence in a given language correlates with the productivity of directionals in that language. Outside Tseltal, productive directional systems have been attested at least in the sister language Tsotsil (Haviland 1991; Aissen 1994), in Mam (England 1978), and in three Q'anjob'alan languages: Akatek (Zavala 1993, 1994), Jakaltek/Popti' (Grinevald in press), and Q'anjob'al (Mateo Toledo 2004). On the other hand, Yucatec is to my knowledge the only Mayan language for which the absence of a productive directional system has been explicitly stated.

Brown (2000) shows that motion descriptions in Tseltal often represent the figure's disposition (cf. §4.3) and suggests that disposition might play a role in how Tseltal speakers communicate motion information that pragmatically overlaps with that of manner in better-studied satellite-framing languages. Example (18) illustrates the use of dispositionals in Tseltal motion descriptions:

TSELTAL
(18) ***Xoj-ol***   ***mo-el***   *s-jol*   *ta*   *ala*   *plastiko.*
     inserted.tightly-DISP;B3   ascend-DIR   A3-head   PREP   DIM   plastic
     'His [the dog's] head is inserted tightly upwards into the little plastic thing.' (Brown 2000:69)

3.2 Path

As mentioned in the previous section, all Mayan languages have a set of location change verb roots, and in many – perhaps most – Mayan languages, these roots produce 'directional' forms, which can be embedded into a verb phrase seemingly functioning as Talmyan 'satellites'. Despite these fundamentals, there are a number of typological properties that make the expression of path functions in Mayan less straightforward than it might appear as first. First of all, unlike in European languages, ground phrases are completely path-neutral. They merely designate the regions of space in which the beginning or endpoint of the motion event (or some place in between) is located. This is illustrated by the Yucatec examples in (19):

YUCATEC
(19) a. *Le=kàaro=o'   ti'=yàan*   ***ich***   ***le=kàaha=o'***.
        DEF=cart=CFP   PREP=EXIST;B3SG   in   DET=box=CFP
        'The [toy] car, it is in the box.'

   b. *Le=kàaro=o'   h-òok*   ***ich***   ***le=kàaha=o'***.
        DEF=cart=CFP   PFV-enter;B3SG   in   DEF=box=CFP
        'The [toy] car, it entered (lit. in) the box.'

   c. *Le=kàaro=o'   h-hóok'*   ***ich***   ***le=kàaha=o'***.
        DEF=cart=CFP   PFV-exit;B3SG   in   DEF=box=CFP
        'The [toy] car, it exited (lit. in) the box.'

These examples feature the same ground phrase *ich le kàahao'* 'in the box' in the role of locative (19a), illative/goal (19b), and elative/source (19c). This behavior generalizes to all ground phrases and all path functions (Bohnemeyer and Stolz 2006; Bohnemeyer 2007, 2010; Bohnemeyer et al. 2007). Complete absence of locative and path distinctions from the ground phrase has also been attested for Jakaltek (Grinevald 2006, in press) and Tseltal (Bohnemeyer et al. 2007). Bohnemeyer et al. 2007 consider this a more radical type of verb-framing, unattested in the languages examined in (Talmy 2000b), all of which have ground phrases the form of which is at least somewhat sensitive to the path function.

Grinevald (2006, in press) hypothesizes that path-neutral ground phrases correlate with the occurrence of directionals. *Prima facie*, counterevidence against this hypothesis comes from Yucatec, which has exclusively path-neutral ground phrases, but arguably lacks directionals. If one considers, with Talmy (2000b: 65–6), the satellite-like use of path verb forms to be the hallmark of a directional system, then Yucatec lacks directionals and therefore falsifies Grinevald's hypothesis. The following examples illustrate the construction that comes closest to directional constructions in Yucatec (compare with the Tseltal examples (17) and (18) above):

YUCATEC
(20) *K-u=ka'=tàal*   *uy=èem-el=e'*.
      IPFV-A3=REPET=come;ICP   A3=descend-ICP=CFP
      'It comes descending again (i.e., it descends towards the speaker or listener).'

(21) *K-u=máan*   *na'k-al*   *y=óok'ol*   *le=mehen*   *búut'un=o'*
      IPFV-A3=pass;ICP   ascend-ICP   A3=top   DEF=small   hill=CFP
      'It passes ascending over the small hill'

Both examples feature a dependent use of a location change verb – *èem* 'descend' in (20) and *na'k* 'ascend' in (21) – in a non-finite – *Vl* form that appears to be a cognate of the suffix used to form directionals in Tseltal. However, in both instances, the main verb is a location change verb as well – *tàal* 'come' in (20) and *máan* 'pass' in (21). Combinations of dependent location change verbs with manner verbs are unattested and speakers reject them during elicitation.

I have been referring to the Yucatec equivalents of what are commonly called 'path verbs' or 'verbs of inherently directed motion' (Levin 1993) as 'location change verbs'. This otherwise awkward terminological choice is conditioned by the evidence presented in Bohnemeyer (2010, 2013) to the effect that these verbs are semantically compatible with scenarios in which the ground rather than the figure moves or in which a certain spatial configuration between figure or ground comes about or is dissolved as a result of the figure or the ground disappearing and subsequently reemerging at a different location (teleportation or "beaming"). This compatibility suggests that these verbs do not actually lexicalize the translational motion of the figure along a path defined with respect to the ground, but merely change of location of the figure vis-à-vis the ground.

Insensitivity to figure motion is not restricted to 'enter' and 'exit' in Yucatec. It can be shown for *òok* 'enter' and *hóok'* 'exit', but also for *na'k* 'ascend', *èem* 'descend', *líik'* 'rise', *lúub* 'fall', and *máan* 'pass', though not for *bin* 'go', *tàal* 'come', *luk'* 'leave', *k'uch* 'arrive', and *u'l* 'return (to deictic center)'. Together, these 12 roots constitute the set of location change verb roots in Yucatec; only clauses that contain one of these roots in the main verb position can be used to describe location change events in this language. The set differentiates in terms of the region of space selected with respect to the ground and in terms of whether the figure occupies this region in the beginning of the event, at the end of it, or in between. As an illustration of the lack of entailment of figure motion, consider Figure 12.3. It features the first and last frame of a short animated video clip in which a plank slides underneath a stationary ball. (The third object, a cylinder, is shown to facilitate identification of the ball as stationary.) This is one out of a series of 96 such animations created by Levinson (2001) for the crosslinguistic study of the semantics of motion event descriptions.

When asked whether this clip can truthfully be described by saying that the ball went up the plank, as in (22), most Yucatec speakers will deny this, as would speakers of English. However, when asked to correct a description such as (22) so that it becomes acceptable as a description of the scenario in the clip, speakers will produce responses such as the one in (23):

YUCATEC
(22) **H-na'k**   *le=chan   kanìika   y=óok'ol   le=tàabla=o'*
     PFV-ascend;B3SG   DEF=DIM   marble   A3=on   DEF=plank=CFP
     'The little marble, it **went up** the plank'

FIGURE 12.3 FIRST AND LAST FRAME OF "FIGURE_GROUND 14" (LEVINSON 2001; ©STEPHEN C. LEVINSON; REPRODUCED WITH PERMISSION)

(23) *Le=chan   tàabla=o'   h=péek-nah-ih,*
  DEF=DIM plank=CFP PFV=move-CP-B3SG

  káa=h-na'k   *le=chan   kanìika*
  CON=PFV-ascend;B3SG DEF=DIM marble

  y=éetel   che'   te'l   y=óokol=o'.
  A3=with wood there A3=on=CFP

'The little plank, it moved, and the little marble and the tree **ascended** there on top.'

The difference between these two descriptions is that (23) states explicitly that it was the plank that moved. As Bohnemeyer (2010) argues, this blocks a stereotype implicature (Atlas and Levinson 1981) triggered otherwise by (22) according to which it is the ball that moves, since translational motion of a figure is the stereotypical cause of location change of the figure in the experience of Yucatec speakers as much as in that of English speakers. Without this stereotype implicature being blocked or canceled, (22) seems to be considered misleading as a description of the event in Figure 12.3.

Why are some of the location change verbs compatible with non-figure-motion scenarios, whereas others are not? At least a partial possible explanation appears to be that the spatial region conceptualized as part of the source or target state of the event is defined with respect to a stationary ground in many or all cases in which non-figure-motion scenarios are excluded.

In combination with the path-neutrality of the ground phrase, the insensitivity of the location change verbs to figure motion suggests that Yucatec does not express translational motion at all, but instead represents motion purely in terms of change of location. Either the figure is specified to be located in a certain place at the source state of the event, and the target state negates this, or it is conversely the target state that is positively specified and the source state described as the absence of the target state. Levinson and Wilkins (2006b:527–37) suggest that the picture sketched here for Yucatec may well extend to Tseltal as well.[6]

Further important properties of the representation of motion in language that cannot receive adequate attention here due to space limitations are the expression of perlative or 'route' path functions that characterize neither the beginning nor the end point of the path, but some point or segment in between; the expression of 'directional' path functions, which characterize the direction in or away from which the figure is headed at a given moment; the composition of complex path functions that refer to multiple grounds; and the metaphoric use of path functions in representations of non-motion state of affairs ('fictive motion'; Talmy 2000a:99–175). These are addressed for Yucatec in Bohnemeyer (2010, 2013). Bohnemeyer et al. (2007) discuss path composition in a sample of languages that includes Tseltal and Yucatec.

4 SUMMARY AND CONCLUSIONS

Let us review some of the typologically most noteworthy traits of the representation of space in Mayan languages – especially traits that confound previously proposed generalizations:

- There is widespread use of geocentric reference frames in small-scale space complementing the use of intrinsic frames, which typically involves meronyms. In contrast, the use of relative frames seems more restricted in most populations, but varies from language to language and also from speaker to speaker, with the frequency of use of Spanish as a second language being an important predictor of the frequency of use of relative frames (cf. §2.1.2).

- Mayan languages have very large sets of dispositional roots, which lexicalize stage-level spatial properties other than location. While dispositions include the postures of animate beings, many dispositionals select for inanimate referents. In many languages, dispositional roots represent a lexical category *sui generis* (cf. §2.3).
- Dispositionals are commonly used as heads of locative predicates and as constituents of motion descriptions (cf. §3.1), confounding the generalization proposed by Landau and Jackendoff (1993) according to which locative and motion descriptions convey more information about the ground than about the figure (cf. §2.1.3). In some – though not in all – Mayan languages, dispositionals are in fact the prototypical locative predicators.
- 'Radical' verb-framing (Bohnemeyer et al. 2007): The 'ground phrases' that reference places and direction vectors in locative and motion descriptions do not express locative and path functions at all (cf. §3.1).
- Verbs that lexicalize location change with respect to a ground seem to not entail or presuppose translational motion of the figure with respect to the ground. In this sense, path may not be verbally encoded at all in some Mayan languages (cf. §5.1).

It must be stressed that most of these properties have only been attested in a few Mayan languages so far – most commonly, in Tseltal and/or Yucatec. Future research must clarify how widespread these properties are in the language family. It is my hope that the synopsis of the verbal representation of space in this chapter will contribute toward closing these gaps.

NOTES

1 *Nàats'* is a stative predicate rather than an adjective. That is to say, it does not occur as a prenominal modifier, the position of attributes in Yucatec. This distinction is discussed in Bohnemeyer (2002: Ch5). The same holds for its inverse *náach* 'be far away'.

2 In (4), the entire ground phrase is left-dislocated. The clause-final clitic particle =*i'* anaphorically represents the place denoted by the ground phrase.

3 What defines the perspective of egocentric representations is the observer, which is prototypically the cognizer or speaker. The cognizer or speaker can assume the perspective of another person, such as that of the addressee in discourse; to what extent such representations should be treated as egocentric is controversial. Intrinsic descriptions with 3rd-person grounds (e.g., *The ball is on her left*) are not egocentric except perhaps in case they involve a generic observer, as in *When one enters, the reception is on one's left*.

4 In Yucatec at least, there appears to be a fifth option: there are a number of nouns that appear to be inherently place-denoting (or to have place-denoting readings), but that refer to *kinds* of places, unlike toponyms. Examples include *ka'n* 'sky', *lu'm* 'earth', 'ground', and *k'áax* 'bush'. These nouns project ground phrases without the help of a preposition or meronym (part-whole term), a property they share with toponyms.

5 An important exception to this generalization are path specifications that do not entail location change. These may be compatible with manner verbs even in languages that are otherwise exclusively verb-framed (Aske 1989).

6 However, the discussion of the relevant phenomena in Bohnemeyer and Stolz (2006) and Levinson and Wilkins (2006b) seems somewhat dated in several respects. For instance, both chapters maintain that location change as conceptualized in the relevant Mayan verb roots is instantaneous. A more accurate way of stating the underlying observation here is that these verbs do not presuppose the space-time isomorphism of translational motion.

REFERENCES

Aissen, Judith. 1994. "Tzotzil auxiliaries." In *Space in Mayan languages,* ed. by Stephen C. Levinson and John B. Haviland. Special issue of *Linguistics* 32: 657–90.

Ameka, Felix K., and James Essegbey. 2001. "The expression of complex translational motion events in three verb-serializing languages." In *Annual report 2001*, ed. by Ann Kelly and Alissa Melinger, 94–7. Nijmegen: Max Planck Institute for Psycholinguistics.

Ameka, Felix K., and Stephen C. Levinson. 2007. "Introduction – the typology and semantics of locative predicates: Posturals, positionals and other beasts." *Linguistics* 45: 847–72.

Arcos Lopez, Nicolás. 2009. "Los classificadores numerals y las clases nominales en ch'ol." MA thesis, Centro de Investigaciones y Estudios Superiores en Antropologia Social.

Aske, Jon. 1989. "Path predicates in English and Spanish: a closer look." Berkeley Linguistics Society 15: 1–14.

Atlas, Jay David, and Stephen C. Levinson. 1981. "It-clefts, informativeness, and logical form: Radical pragmatics (revised standard version)." In *Radical pragmatics,* ed. by Peter Cole, 1–61. New York: Academic Press.

Belloro, Valeria, Jürgen Bohnemeyer, Dedre Gentner, and Kathleen Braun. 2008. "Thinking-for-speaking: evidencia a partir de la codificación de disposiciones espaciales en español y yucateco." In *Memoria del IX Encuentro Internacional De Lingüística En El Noroeste*, vol. 2, ed. by Zarina Estrada Fernández, Ana Lidia Munguía Duarte, and Rosa María Ortiz Ciccomani, 175–90. Hermosillo: Editorial UniSon.

Bohnemeyer, Jürgen. 2002. *The grammar of time reference in Yukatek Maya*. Munich: LINCOM.

Bohnemeyer, Jürgen. 2003. "The unique vector constraint: The impact of direction changes on the linguistic segmentation of motion events." In *Representing direction in language and space,* ed. by Emile van der Zee and Jon Slack, 86–110. Oxford: Oxford University Press.

Bohnemeyer, Jürgen. 2007. "The pitfalls of getting from here to there: Bootstrapping the syntax and semantics of motion event expressions in Yucatec Maya." In *Cross-linguistic perspectives on argument structure: implications for learnability*, ed. by Melissa Bowerman and Penelope Brown, 49–68. Mahwah: Lawrence Erlbaum.

Bohnemeyer, Jürgen. 2010. "The language-specificity of conceptual structure: path, fictive motion, and time relations." In *Words and the mind: How words capture human experience,* ed. by Barbara Malt and Phillip Wolff, 111–37. Oxford: Oxford University Press.

Bohnemeyer, Jürgen. 2011. "Spatial frames of reference in Yucatec: Referential promiscuity and task-specificity." *Language Sciences* 33: 892–914.

Bohnemeyer, Jürgen. 2013. "The language-specificity of conceptual structure: Taking stock." *International Journal of Cognitive Linguistics* 4: 65–88.

Bohnemeyer, Jürgen, and Penelope Brown. 2007. "Standing divided: dispositionals and locative predications in two Mayan languages." *Linguistics* 45: 1105–51.

Bohnemeyer, Jürgen, Katherine T. Donelson, Randi E. Moore, Elena Benedicto, Alyson Eggleston, Carolyn K. O'Meara, Gabriela Pérez Báez, Alejandra Capistrán Garza, Néstor Hernández Green, María de Jesús Selene Hernández Gómez, Samuel Herrera Castro, Enrique Palancar, Gilles Polian, and Rodrigo Romero Méndez. 2015. "The contact diffusion of linguistic practices: reference frames in Mesoamerica." *Language Dynamics and Change* 5: 169–201.

Bohnemeyer, Jürgen, Nick J. Enfield, James Essegbey, Iraide Ibarretxe-Antuñano, Sotaro Kita, Friederike Lüpke, and Felix K. Ameka. 2007. "Principles of event segmentation in language: the case of motion events." *Language* 83: 495–532.

Bohnemeyer, Jürgen, and Carolyn K. O'Meara. 2012. "Vectors and frames of reference: Evidence from Seri and Yucatec." In *Space and time across languages and cultures*, ed. by Luna Filipović and Katarzyna M. Jaszczolt, 217–49. Amsterdam: John Benjamins.

Bohnemeyer, Jürgen, and Christel Stolz, 2006. "Spatial reference in Yukatek Maya: a survey." In *Grammars of space*, ed. by Stephen C. Levinson and David P. Wilkins, 273–310. Cambridge: Cambridge University Press.

Bowerman, Melissa, and Eric Pederson. 1992. "Topological relations picture series." In *Space stimuli kit 1.2: November 1992*, ed. by Stephen C. Levinson, 51. Nijmegen: Max Planck Institute for Psycholinguistics.

Bowerman, Melissa, and Eric Pedersen. Ms. "Cross-linguistic perspectives on topological spatial relationships." Manuscript, Max Planck Institute for Psycholinguistics.

Brown, Penelope. 1994. "The INs and ONs of Tzeltal locative expressions: the semantics of static descriptions of location." In *Space in Mayan languages*, ed. by Stephen C. Levinson and John B. Haviland. Special issue of *Linguistics* 32: 743–90.

Brown, Penelope. 2000. "'He descended legs-upwards': Position and motion in Tzeltal frog stories." In *Proceedings of the 30th Stanford child language research forum*, ed. by Eve V. Clark, 67–75. Stanford: CSLI.

Brown, Penelope. 2006. "A sketch of the grammar of space in Tzeltal." In *Grammars of space,* ed. by Stephen C. Levinson and David P. Wilkins, 230–72. Cambridge: Cambridge University Press.

Brown, Penelope, and Stephen C. Levinson. 1993. "'Uphill' and 'downhill' in Tzeltal." *Journal of Linguistic Anthropology* 3: 46–74.

Brown, Penelope, and Stephen C. Levinson. 2000. "Frames of spatial reference and their acquisition in Tenejapan Tzeltal." In *Culture, thought and development*, ed. by Larry Nucci, Geoffrey Saxe, and Elliot Turiel, 167–97. Mahwah: Erlbaum.

Brown, Penelope, and Stephen C. Levinson. 2009. "Language as mind tools: learning how to think through speaking." In *Crosslinguistic approaches to the psychology of language,* ed. by Jianzheng Guo, Elena V. M. Lieven, Nancy Budwig, Susan Ervin-Tripp, Keiko Nakamura, and Seyda Ozcaliskan, 451–63. New York: Taylor & Francis Group.

Carlson, Gregory N. 1977. "Reference to kinds in English." PhD diss., University of Massachusetts, Amherst.

Carlson-Radvansky, Laura A., and David A. Irwin. 1993. "Frames of reference in vision and language: where is above?" *Cognition* 46: 223–44.

Danziger, Eve. 1996. "Parts and their counter-parts: social and spatial relationships in Mopan Maya." *Journal of the Royal Anthropological Institute (NS), Incorporating MAN* 2: 67–82.

Danziger, Eve. 1999. "Language, space and sociolect: cognitive correlates of gendered speech in Mopan Maya." In *Language diversity and cognitive representations*, ed. by Catherine Fuchs and Stéphane Robert, 85–106. Amsterdam: Benjamins.

Danziger, Eve. 2001. "Cross-cultural studies in language and thought: is there a meta-language?" In *The psychology of cultural experience*, ed. by Carmella C. Moore and Holly F. Mathews, 199–222. Cambridge: Cambridge University Press.

Danziger, Eve. 2011. "Distinguishing three-dimensional forms from their mirror-images: Whorfian results from users of intrinsic frames of linguistic reference." *Language Sciences* 33: 853–67.

de León, Lourdes. 1991. *Space games in Tzotzil: Creating a context for spatial reference* (Cognitive Anthropology Research Group Working Paper 4). Nijmegen: Max-Planck Institute for Psycholinguistics.

de León, Lourdes. 1992. "Body parts and Location in Tzotzil: Ongoing grammaticalization." *Zeitschrift für Phonetik, Sprachwissenschaft und Kommunikationsforschung* 45: 570–89.

de León, Lourdes. 1994. "Exploration of the acquisition of location and trajectory in Tzotzil." *Linguistics* 32: 857–84.

Delgado Galvan, Amanda. 2013. "Topological expressions in Yokot'an (Chontal de Tabasco), Nacajuca dialect." MA thesis, Leiden University.

England, Nora C. 1978. "Space as a Mam grammatical theme." In *Papers in Mayan linguistics,* ed. by Nora C. England, 225–38. Columbia: University of Missouri, Department of Anthropology.

Goldap, C. 1992. "Morphology and semantics of Yucatec space relators." *Zeitschrift für Phonetik, Sprachwissenschaft und Kommunikationsforschung* 45: 612–25.

Grinevald, Colette. 2006. "The expression of static location in typological perspective." In *Space in languages: Linguistic systems and cognitive categories,* ed. by Maya Hickmann and Stéphane Robert, 29–58. Amsterdam: John Benjamins.

Grinevald, Colette. In press. "Directionals do it because prepositions don't: Path in motion and location in Popti' (Mayan)." In *Variation and change in adpositions of movement,* ed. by H. Cuykens, W. De Mulder, M. Goyens, and T. Mortelmans. Amsterdam: Benjamins.

Haviland, John B. 1991. *The grammaticalization of motion (and time) in Tzotzil* (Cognitive Anthropology Research Group Working Paper 2). Nijmegen: Max-Planck Institute for Psycholinguistics.

Haviland, John B. 1994. "'Te xa setel xulem' (The buzzards were circling): Categories of verbal roots in (Zinacantec) Tzotzil." *Linguistics* 32: 691–742.

Jackendoff, Ray. 1983. *Semantics and cognition.* Cambridge: MIT Press.

Kaufman, Terrence. 1990. "Algunos rasgos estructurales de los idiomas Mayances." In *Lecturas Sobre la Lingüística Maya,* ed. by Nora C. England and Stephen R. Elliott, 59–114. La Antigua: Centro de Investigaciones Regionales de Mesoamérica.

Kracht, Marcus. 2002. "On the semantics of locatives." *Linguistics and Philosophy* 25: 157–232.

Landau, Barbara, and Ray Jackendoff. 1993. "'What' and 'where' in spatial language and spatial cognition." *Behavioral and Brain Sciences* 16: 217–65.

Laughlin, Robert M. 1975. *The great Tzotzil dictionary of San Lorenzo Zinacantan.* Washington, DC: Smithsonian Institution Press.

Le Guen, Olivier. 2011. "Handling frames of reference: the co-dependence of speech and gesture in spatial language and cognition among the Yucatec Mayas." *Cognitive Science* 35: 905–38.

Lehmann, Christian. 1992. "Yukatekische lokale Relatoren in typologischer Perspektive." *Zeitschrift für Phonetik, Sprachwissenschaft und Kommunikationsforschung* 45: 626–41.

Levelt, Willem J. M. 1996. "Perspective taking and ellipsis in spatial descriptions." In *Language and space,* ed. by Paul Bloom, Mary A. Peterson, Lynn Nadel, and Merrill F. Garrett, 77–107. Cambridge: MIT Press.

Levin, Beth. 1993. *English verb classes and alternations.* Chicago: University of Chicago Press.

Levinson, Stephen C. 1996. "Frames of reference and Molyneux's question: Crosslinguistic evidence." In *Language and space,* ed. by Paul Bloom, Mary A. Peterson, Lynn Nadel, and Merrill F. Garrett, 109–69. Cambridge: MIT Press.

Levinson, Stephen C. 2001. "Motion verb stimulus, version 2." In *'Manual' for the field season 2001,* ed. by Stephen C. Levinson and Nick J. Enfield, 9–13. Nijmegen: Max Planck Institute for Psycholinguistics.

Levinson, Stephen C. 2003. *Space in language and cognition.* Cambridge: Cambridge University Press.

Levinson, Stephen C., and Penelope Brown. 1994. "Immanuel Kant among the Tenejapans: Anthropology as empirical philosophy." *Ethos* 22: 3–41.

Levinson, Stephen C., and David P. Wilkins. 2006a. "The background to the study of the language of space." In *Grammars of space,* ed. by Stephen C. Levinson and David P. Wilkins, 1–23. Cambridge: Cambridge University Press.

Levinson, Stephen C., and David P. Wilkins. 2006b. "Patterns in the data: Toward a semantic typology of spatial description." In *Grammars of space,* ed. by Stephen C. Levinson and David P. Wilkins, 514–77. Cambridge: Cambridge University Press.

Lois, Ximena, and Valentina Vapnarsky. 2003. *Polyvalence of lexical roots in Yukatekan Mayan languages.* Munich: LINCOM.

Martin, Laura E. 1977. "Positional roots in Kanjobal (Mayan)." PhD diss., University of Florida.

Mateo Toledo, Eladio. 2004. "Directional markers in Q'anjob'al (Maya): Their syntax and interaction with aspectual information." MA thesis, University of Texas, Austin.

Moore, Randi E., Katherine T. Donelson, Alyson Eggleston, and Jürgen Bohnemeyer. 2015. "Semantic typology: new approaches to crosslinguistic variation in language and cognition." *Linguistics Vanguard* 1: 189–200.

Narasimhan, Bhuvana. 2003. "Motion events and the lexicon: the case of Hindi." *Lingua* 113: 123–60.

O'Meara, Carolyn K., and Gabriela Pérez Báez. 2011. "Frames of reference in Mesoamerican languages." *Language Sciences* 33: 837–52.

Piaget, Jean, and Inhelder, Bärbel. 1956. *The child's conception of space.* London: Routledge.

Polian, Gilles, and Jürgen Bohnemeyer. 2011. "Uniformity and variation in Tseltal reference frame use." *Language Sciences* 33: 868–91.

Sántiz Gómez, Roberto. 2010. "Raíces posicionales en tseltal de Oxchuc." MA thesis, Centro de Investigaciones y Estudios Superiores en Antropología Social.

Talmy, Leonard. 2000a. *Toward a cognitive semantics. Volume I: Concept structuring systems.* Cambridge: MIT Press.

Talmy, Leonard. 2000b. *Toward a cognitive semantics. Volume II: Typology and process in concept structuring.* Cambridge: MIT Press.

Terrill, Angela, and Niclas Burenhult. 2008. "Orientation as a strategy of spatial reference." *Studies in Language* 32: 93–116.

Van der Zee, Emile. 2000. "Curvature representation in the lexical interface." In *Cognitive interfaces: Constraints on linking cognitive information,* ed. by Emile van der Zee and Urko Nikanne, 143–82. Oxford: Oxford University Press.

Vendler, Zeno. 1957. "Verbs and times." *The Philosophical Review LXVI*: 143–60.

Wilkins, David. P. 1998. "The semantic extension of basic locative constructions cross-linguistically." In *Annual report 1998*, ed. by Sotaro Kita and Laura Walsh Dickey, 55–61. Nijmegen: MPI for Psycholinguistics.

Wilkins, David. P. 1999. "The verbal component in basic locative constructions." In *Annual report 1999*, ed. by Veerle van Geenhoven and Natasha Warner, 61–71. Nijmegen: Max Planck Institute for Psycholinguistics.

Zavala, Roberto. 1993. "Clause integration with verbs of motion in Mayan languages." MA thesis, University of Oregon.

Zavala, Roberto. 1994. "Se les está moviendo el tapete: Gramaticalización de verbos de movimiento en akateko." In *Memorias del II Encuentro de Lingüística en el Noroeste*, vol. II, ed. by Zarina Estrada Fernández, 101–44. Hermosillo: Universidad de Sonora.

Zlatev, Jordan, and Peerapat Yangklang. 2004. "A third way to travel: The place of Thai in motion event typology." In *Relating events in narrative: Typological and contextual perspectives*, ed. by Sven Strømqvist and Ludo Verhoeven, 159–90. Mahwah: Lawrence Erlbaum.

CHAPTER 13

FOCUS, INTERROGATION, AND INDEFINITES

Scott AnderBois

1 INTRODUCTION

In many languages, there are certain words, morphemes, or constructions which occur only (or at least primarily) in matrix or embedded questions and are therefore called *interrogative*. There are also, however, linguistic elements which are not interrogative, yet play crucial roles in question formation. Chief among these are disjunctions, focus, and wh-words, which are used as indefinites in various environments.

In Mayan languages, wh-questions appear to consist solely of these elements (the picture for polar questions is more variable and we mostly set it aside in what follows) as in (1) from Tsotsil. The indefinite wh-word, *buch'u* 'someone/who', fills the preverbal focus position – indicated here with brackets and subscript []$_F$. In (2) and (3), we see that either focus or an indefinite wh-word alone fails to produce a question interpretation.

TSOTSIL (Aissen 1996:451)
(1) [Buch'u]$_F$ s-pas   mantal?
      someone/who A3-do   order
      'Who's giving the orders?'

TSOTSIL (Aissen 1999:456)
(2) [Vo'on]$_F$ i-j-maj.
      me   CP-A1-hit
      'It was me that hit him.'

TSOTSIL (Aissen 1999:457)
(3) Oy   much'u   ch-a-s-sa'.
      exists someone/who   ICP-B2-A3-seek
      'Someone is looking for you.'

For the semanticist, then, the primary puzzle that arises is the following: What is the meaning of the focus construction in (2) and the wh-word in (3) such that their combination, (1), produces a question meaning? This puzzle, which appears to arise quite consistently across Mayan languages, has three subparts to it: the semantics of focus, §3, the semantics of indefinite wh-words, §4, and the *compositional* principles for putting the two together, §5. Section 2 provides brief background on formal theories of the semantics of questions, focus, and indefinites cross-linguistically.

2 SEMANTIC BACKGROUND

2.1 Questions

The framework we assume here is that of *possible worlds semantics*, where a possible world is a complete description of a way the world might be or might have been. Classically in this framework, the meaning of a declarative sentence is conceived of as the set of possible worlds in which the sentence is true. To take a simple example, then, a sentence like "John ran" is true in all and only the possible worlds where the real world individual that "John" refers to is a member of the set of real world individuals who were running at a given time.

(4) [[John ran]] = "that John ran" = $\{w': \text{John ran in } w'\}$

While such an approach is sensible for assertions, it immediately runs into difficulty when we apply it to the meanings of *questions*, since (matrix) questions are intuitively neither true nor false. Therefore, semanticists have instead treated the meanings of questions as sets of alternatives corresponding with varying degrees of abstraction to its possible answers. These individual alternatives, then, can either be true or false, allowing us to apply the framework of possible worlds to question meanings. Here we adopt the approach of Hamblin (1973), in which a simple example like "Who ran?" is assigned a meaning as in (5a), or a bit more formally (5b):

(5) a. [[Who ran?]] = {"that John ran", "that Ana ran", "that Lucía ran", . . .}
   b. [[Who ran?]] = $\{\{w': \text{John ran in } w'\}, \{w': \text{Ana ran in } w'\}, \{w': \text{Lucía ran in } w'\}, \ldots\}$

So, while this allows us to use the same basic formal tools to talk about assertions and questions, questions are assigned meanings which are of a different type than assertions. (4) has a set of possible worlds as its meaning; (5) has a set *of sets* of possible worlds as its meaning. For languages which have morphosyntactic elements unique to interrogatives, we can plausibly attribute this difference in type to the semantic effect of these elements. For Mayan languages, however, as we have seen in (1) for Tsotsil, there is no such element overtly present. We therefore face a choice: we can either posit covert interrogative elements (e.g. Aissen (1996)'s interrogative complementizer, C[+WH]) or we can examine the elements we do see (focus and indefinite wh-words) to see if we have been too hasty in positing such a fundamental difference between questions and assertions in the first place (or, of course, some combination of these two).

2.2 Focus

As we discuss in detail in §3, the term "focus" has been used to refer to a variety of different forms and pragmatic notions both within Mayanist literature and cross-linguistically. One use of the term, espoused by Rooth (1985, 1992), Roberts (2012), Beaver and Clark (2008), Büring (2012), and many others is to refer to elements that make reference to a salient set of alternative propositions as part of their meaning. We regard a sentence with a focused element of this sort, then, as having *two* semantic values: its ordinary semantic value – $[[. . .]]^{o}$ – and its focus semantic value – $[[. . .]]^{f}$. The latter is computed by substituting alternatives of the same semantic type as the focused element and allowing them to combine one-by-one (i.e. in *pointwise* fashion) with the other elements in the sentence.

A simple sentence like (6a), then, has the ordinary semantic value in (6b) and has as its focus semantic value the set of alternative propositions in (6c) that can be formed by substituting in other individuals in place of the meaning of the focused element, Mary.

(6) a. José saw [Mary]$_F$
   b. $[[(6a)]]^\circ$ = "that José saw Mary"
   c. $[[(6a)]]^f$ = {"that José saw Mary", "that José saw Ana", "that José saw Lucía", . . .}

In a simple sentence like (6a), the focus semantic value serves only to indicate that the speaker takes the set of alternatives in the focus semantic value to be part of contextually salient background of the conversation.[1] It does not play any role in determining the truth-conditions of the sentence, that is to say, its ordinary semantic value. In more complex sentences, however, focus semantic values can influence ordinary semantic values, as in the case of sentences like (7) which contain a focus-sensitive operators like English *only*.

   a'. José only saw [Mary]$_F$.

Here, the ordinary semantic value can only be computed by reference to the focus semantic value. To a rough approximation, (6a') conveys the meaning of (6b), but also that none of the other alternative propositions in (6c) are true. Furthermore, we can see that focus is what plays the crucial role by noting that changing the focus in (6a') – "José only [saw]$_F$ Mary" – changes the truth-conditional meaning of the sentence (i.e. that José saw Mary, but did not, say, talk to her).

Note that even in cases like (6a') where focus does influence truth-conditions, it still also has the pragmatic effect noted in (6). That is, as von Fintel (1994) points out, an example like (6a') is only felicitous in contexts where the alternative set in (6c) is previously salient. Closely related to this is the observation that both (6a) and (6a') indicate that it is background information that there is some alternative or other in (6c) which is true – i.e. that José saw someone – though there is active debate over whether this implication has the same properties as true *presuppositions* (e.g. Cohen (1999), Geurts and van der Sandt (2004), Abusch (2009)).

2.3 Indefinites

Traditionally, indefinites like English *someone* in (7a) are treated as contributing ordinary truth-conditional content, as seen in (7b), akin to a proper name like John in (4). However, as the paraphrase in (7b) makes clear, there is nonetheless a clear sense in which the contribution of an indefinite is quite different. Therefore, just as questions and focus made use of sets of alternatives, it is easy to reconceive of the meaning of an indefinite along similar lines (e.g. Kratzer and Shimoyama (2002), Groenendijk and Roelofsen (2009)). One way to think of this, parallel to the Roothian account of focus we have just sketched is to adopt a third semantic value, call it the inquisitive semantic value – $[[. . .]]^i$ – and allow this value to influence to the ordinary semantic value as in (7b').

(7) a.   José saw someone.
   b. $[[(7a)]]^{\circ}$ = "that there is some x or other (such that x is a person) which makes the sentence 'José saw x true'"
   b'. $[[(7a)]]^{\circ}$ = "that there is some alternative in $[[(7a)]]^{i}$ which is true"
   c. $[[(7a)]]^{i}$ = {"that José saw Mary", "that José saw Ana", "that José saw Lucía", . . .}

While this way of formalizing things looks in some ways like the mirror image of the Roothian focus semantics, the level of complexity represented by $[[. . .]]^{i}$ is not actually needed in this case. This is because the operation that we used to incorporate the inquisitive semantic value into the ordinary one, existential closure, is plausibly a default operation, so general that it can be built into the semantic system itself, rather than being attributed to a particular element in the sentence. More concretely, we can tweak the picture in (7) by instead taking ordinary semantic values – for all sentences – to be sets of alternatives (often singleton sets) and define sentences to be true – again, for all sentences – if and only if there is some true alternative or other in $[[. . .]]^{\circ}$.

   d. $[[(7a)]]^{\circ}$ = {"that José saw Mary", "that José saw Ana", "that José saw Lucía", . . .}

Thus far, then, we have seen that from a theoretical perspective, both focus and indefinites plausibly evoke sets of propositional alternatives. Given this, it seems plausible that the alternatives found in questions in Mayan languages such as (1), arise compositionally either from focus or from the indefinite wh-word. With this brief theoretical background in place, we now turn to examine focus and indefinites in Mayan languages in more detail.

3 FOCUS IN MAYAN

3.1 Form vs. meaning

As mentioned above, the term "focus" has been used cross-linguistically as well as within Mayanist literature to refer to several distinct, yet related, properties. In the first place, the term "focus" is often used to refer to a particular *syntactic* construction whether or not focus semantics/pragmatics is present in any sense.

While Mayan languages at least typically have verb-initial basic word orders (with VOS being more common), the literature has long recognized two kinds of preverbal positions: topic and focus (Aissen (1992) and others cite Norman (1977) as being the earliest proponent of such a view). While these names both of course reflect semantic/pragmatic properties typical of the two positions, the terms are often applied to the construction whether or not the semantic/pragmatic function is present.

For example, in (8) we see a variety of different examples which all involve the focus construction. An example like (8a) is clearly an example of focus semantics and/or pragmatics in some sense (see §3.2). The issue of whether/how questions like (8b) involve focus is of course central to our current discussion. The head noun *ixq* 'woman' in a relative clause like (8c), however, does not intuitively seem to be focused in any sense, nor are there clear semantic or typological reasons to think relative clauses ought to involve focus (pace Tonhauser (2003a)). Finally, for negative and free choice quantifiers in certain languages, (8d–8e), it is unclear whether focus semantics/pragmatics are involved without more detailed compositional semantic analysis.

Q'EQCHI' (Berinstein 1985:150)
(8) a. li k'anti'   x-Ø-lop-o-k   r-e   li   winq.
       the snake   PFV-B3-bite-AF-SS A3-DAT the   man
       'It was the snake that bit the man.'

Q'EQCHI' (Dayley 1981:20)
    b. ani   x-Ø-a-sak'?
       who   PFV-B3-A2SG-hit
       'Who did you hit?'

Q'EQCHI' (Berinstein 1985:167, modified)
    c. x-Ø-kam   li   ixq   li   x-r-il   li   winq.
       PFV-B3-die the   woman   that PFV-A3-see   the   man
       'The woman that the man saw died.'

YUCATEC (Monforte et al. 2010:51)
    d. K-u   jook'-ol te'   ich le   bolquete-o', mix ba'al k-u   y-il-ik.
       IPFV-A3 exit-SS   there in   the truck-DISTAL NEG thing IPFV-A3 EP-see-SS
       'Leaving the truck, he didn't see anything.'

TSOTSIL (Aissen 1999:464)
    e. K'us-uk   nox   tij-on-uk   li   j-malal-e.
       what-IRR just shake-AF-IRR the   A1-husband-ENC
       'Just anything wakes my husband.'

There are, then, a diverse range of different constructions which make use of the morphosyntactic position commonly referred to as the "focus" position in Mayanist literature. Not all of these cases necessarily involve focus in any semantic/pragmatic sense, while for others this remains unclear. In the case of questions, however, there is a clear semantic connection with focus (§2) as well as strong cross-linguistic evidence that focus plays a key role in question formation (Haida (2008) and references therein). Additionally, it is robustly true that questions and focus cannot co-occur in the same clause regardless of their relative order, as seen in (9).

YUCATEC (Tonhauser 2003b:116)
(9) a. *Ba'ax   María   t-u   jant-aj
        something/what María PFV-A3 eat-SS
        Intended: 'What did María eat?'

YUCATEC {ELIC}
    b. *María   ba'ax   t-u   jant-aj
       María something/what PFV-A3 eat-SS
       Intended: 'What did María eat?'

Therefore, it seems quite plausible that wh-questions are an instance not only of a focus construction in terms of their form, but also in terms of their semantics, i.e. that the semantics of focus plays a compositional role in question formation.

3.2 Two kinds of focus

We have just seen that the term "focus" in the Mayanist literature has been used both to refer to a particular set of forms as well as to the semantic and/or pragmatic properties associated with certain uses of this form. We turn now to the question of what exactly these semantic/pragmatic properties are, where again, there has been much debate both within Mayan languages and more generally. See Can Pixabaj and England (2011), Shklovsky (2012), and Velleman (2014) for recent detailed discussions, and Aissen (this volume) for a recent overview of information structure in Mayan languages.

While some authors have assumed a unified notion of focus, recent decades have seen an emerging consensus that two related but separate notions are grammatically relevant. É. Kiss (1998), who traces this distinction back to Halliday (1967), calls these two notions IDENTIFICATIONAL FOCUS and INFORMATION FOCUS. Whereas she regards information focus as being new (i.e. not presupposed) information, she ascribes to identificational focus the more specific definition in (10).

(10) **The function of identificational focus:** An identificational focus represents a subset of the set of contextually or situationally given elements for which the predicate phrase can potentially hold; it is identified as the exhaustive subset of this set for which the predicate phrase actually holds. (É. Kiss, 1998)

Therefore, while arguably every declarative sentence has an information focus, not every sentence has an identificational focus. We set aside here the issue of exhaustivity, since the question of whether/how exhaustivity is semantically encoded in Hungarian[2] (É. Kiss's main empirical focus) has itself been a matter of active debate (e.g. É. Kiss (2010), Onea and Beaver (2010), Balogh (2013)) and this issue has been little explored for Mayan languages (though Aissen (1992:50) does claim that preverbal focus Tsotsil is exhaustive).

One crucial aspect of this definition is that the notion of "contextually or situationally given elements" is quite broad, encompassing, as É. Kiss notes, both contrastive and non-contrastive uses. While the notion of "contrast" relevant here has been notoriously difficult to pin down with precision, we follow Büring (2012) and assume that contrastive uses are ones where specific alternatives in the set have been mentioned in prior discourse.

For Mayan languages, it has been argued by various authors that the preverbal focus position, similar to Hungarian, has both contrastive and non-contrastive uses (this is likely true of all Mayan languages). One fairly clear indication of this comes from K'ichee', where Can Pixabaj and England (2011) argue that preverbal foci marked with the particle *are* as in (11) do show a more limited distribution, being restricted to contrastive uses only.

K'ICHE' (Can Pixabaj and England 2011:21)
(11) Are   ri   achi   x-ø-war   kan-oq.
      EMPH   DET   man   CP-B3SG-sleep   DIR:remaining-SS
      'It was the man who stayed sleeping.'

Another question which has arisen in recent works on focus in Mayan languages is whether there are also postverbal foci (Kügler et al. (2007) for Yucatec, Shklovsky (2012) and Polian (2013) for Tseltal, Velleman (2014) for K'iche' and more generally). These authors all show that in at least some cases, answers to explicit or implicit questions may occur postverbally, as in (12), with no preverbal focus present.

K'ICHE' (Velleman 2014:210)
(12) **Context:** What do the people here eat?

Nima	k-onojel,	ka-ki-tij	le	lej.
mostly	A3PL-all	ICP-A3PL-eat	DET	tortilla

'Basically everyone eats tortillas.'

While such data appear to be quite widespread,[3] this should not be taken as an indication that identificational focus is present in such examples. First, recalling the parallel with Hungarian, É. Kiss (1998) shows that postverbal information foci in Hungarian can serve as felicitous answers provided that the answer is interpreted non-exhaustively. For the example in (12), world knowledge suggests that the postverbal phrase *le lej* 'tortillas' is to be interpreted non-exhaustively (we leave evaluation of the broader claim to future work since it requires more careful work on exhaustivity more generally). Second, as discussed in §2.2, one of the main motivations for an alternative-based semantics for focus is the existence of focus-sensitive elements like English *only*. At present, there is no evidence that such operators interact with postverbal foci (and in any case, Beaver and Clark (2008) argue that many focus-sensitive elements in English are only optionally focus-sensitive). Therefore, we tentatively conclude that while such cases may act as information foci, they do not encode identificational focus.

Since wh-words in questions across Mayan languages can only occur in the preverbal focus position, we conclude that these require identificational focus and therefore that an alternative-based analysis along the lines of that sketched in §2.2 is appropriate for the preverbal focus position itself. At the same time, as we have seen, there is evidence that individual Mayan languages may differ in their expression of related notions like information focus and contrastive focus.

4 WH-WORDS IN MAYAN

4.1 History of wh-words

One of the most striking observations about wh-words across Mayan languages is their instability, i.e. the lack of cognates across languages and even dialects of the same language. Whereas much of the lexicon of Proto Mayan has been reconstructed on the basis of large cognate sets (e.g. Kaufman and Justeson (2003)), wh-words are a systematic exception, as noted by Idiatov (2011). For example, in (13), we see a sampling of the word 'who' across languages from different branches of the family.[4]

(13)	*hita'*	HUASTEC	(Edmonson 1988:529)
	máax	YUCATEC	(Bricker and Po'ot Yah 1998:191)
	majchki	CH'OL	(Vázquez Álvarez 2011:151)
	chi	CH'ORTI'	(Pérez Martínez 1994:82)
	buch'u	TSOTSIL	(Haviland 1981:40)
	machunk'a	TOJOLAB'AL	(Brody 1982:239)
	maktxel	Q'ANJOB'AL	(Mateo Toledo 2008:76)
	k'on	MOCHO'	(Palosaari 2011:157)
	alkyee	MAM	(England 1983:250)
	jab'il	IXIL	(Ayres 1991:184)
	neen	USPANTEK	(Can Pixabaj 2007:142)

achike	KAQCHIKEL	(Patal Majzul et al. 2000:89)
jachinaq	K'ICHE'	(Larsen 1988:122)
qa'keh	POQOMAM	(Santos Nicolás and Benito Pérez 1998:216)
ani	Q'EQCHI'	(Dayley 1981:29)

Beyond the lack of cognates even across closely related languages (esp. true for Eastern Mayan in the case of *who*), we see clear signs of recent morphological complexity. Two recurring patterns in particular are potentially relevant here. First, wh-words sometimes show clear connections with semantically 'bleached' nouns with related general meanings like person, thing, etc. (e.g. *máak* 'person' in Yucatec, *achi* 'man' in K'iche'), as discussed by Tonhauser (2003b). Second, they sometimes show clear relationships with morphemes encoding or relating to focus in some way (e.g. *ha'* in Huastec, *ix* in Yucatec, *ja'* in K'iche'). These correspondences are inconsistent enough that we do not take them to be synchronically decomposable in these ways (e.g. *ix* is not synchronically productive in Yucatec), but these historical connections may well nonetheless inform our semantic investigation (and hopefully the opposite is true as well).

4.2 Semantics of wh-words

While there are many cases of diachronic connections between wh-words and semantically 'bleached' nouns, there is also a far more consistent synchronic connection between wh-words and indefinites of various kinds. Cross-linguistically, this pattern, which has been dubbed the "interrogative-indefinite affinity," is extremely common in the world's languages (see Haspelmath (1997), Bhat (2000), Haida (2008)).

Within Mayan languages, we see this affinity quite straightforwardly realized. Indefinites can be formed from wh-words, often with additional morphology present as in (14). The details of how such indefinites are formed are quite variable across and within Mayan languages (e.g. Are they fronted? Do they require irrealis marking?), though this variation is little understood at present.

TSOTSIL (Haviland 1981:40)
(14) a. **Context:** Who is on the top of the hill?
      Muk'   buch'u   tey.
      NEG.EXIST who   there
      'There's no one there.'

TSELTAL (Polian 2007:22)
    b. Bay-uk=nax   ø-bajt-ø.
        where-IRR=FOC CP.I-go-B3
        'He went wherever (all over).'

YUCATEC (Tonhauser 2003b:110)
    c. In   k'áat bin wa tu'ux.
        A1   wish go   or   where
        'I want to go somewhere'

YUCATEC (Monforte et al. 2010:207)
    d. Yaan máax-e', yaan k-u   y-a'al-ik-e': ...
        EXIST who-TOP exist IMP-A3 EP-say-SS-TOP
        'Some people say: ... '

One important note here is that in some of these cases (e.g. (14a), (14d)), wh-words are likely best analyzed as relative pronouns in free relative constructions, rather than indefinites per se. Regardless, however, the function of the wh-word is ultimately indefinite in nature in these cases, and there clearly exist many cases, such as (14b, c), for which a free relative analysis is clearly not tenable.

5 QUESTIONS IN MAYAN

As we have described in some detail, then, content questions in Mayan languages are consistently composed of an indefinite wh-word occurring in the preverbal focus position, as in (15). Here, the wh-word *máax* "who" is focused as indicated both by its preverbal position as well as the agent focus (AF) form of the verb (unlike other Mayan languages, AF in Yucatec is indicated solely by the *lack* of Set A agreement and transitive status suffix, with no AF suffix present).

YUCATEC (AnderBois 2012:351)
(15) [Máax]$_F$ uk'   le   sa'-o'?
      someone/who   drink.AF   DET   atole-DISTAL
      'Who drank the atole?'

Given the semantic parallels between indefinites, focus, and questions that we have just seen, we now ask the question of how these parts are combined to produce a question meaning. Two main approaches to this compositional question have been proposed both within Mayan languages and cross-linguistically: one where focus introduces question alternatives, and one where indefinites play this role. We focus here on Yucatec, since this issue has been explored in some depth under both approaches by Tonhauser (2003b) and AnderBois (2012) respectively.

5.1 Focus as alternative generator

As we have seen in §2.2, focus not only has a clear morphosyntactic connection with questions cross-linguistically, but also a clear semantic connection since both involve sets of alternative propositions in some way. Recent works have fleshed out how this composition could work in a variety of different unrelated languages: Beck (2006) for Korean and German and Cable (2010) for Tlingit (though both authors draw on data from a variety of other languages as well).

The basic approach these authors take is to assume that wh-words themselves are lexically specified as lacking an ordinary semantic value. Instead, they claim that wh-words themselves only have a focus semantic value as in (16).

(16) a. $[[máax]]^\circ$ = undefined
      b. $[[máax]]^f$ = {José, María, Lucía, . . .}
      c. $[[máax\ uk'le\ sa'o']]^\circ$ = undefined
      d. $[[máax\ uk'le\ sa'o']]^f$ = {"that José drank the atole", "that María drank the atole", "that Lucía drank the atole", . . .}

While the composition thus far does produce the appropriate set of alternatives (i.e. the one in (16d)), we still do not have any ordinary semantic value. The final step then, is to propose a Q operator which combines with (16d), converting the focus semantic value into an ordinary semantic value, as in (17). In essence, then, the Q operator these authors propose is a focus-sensitive operator: like *only* it makes conventional reference to the focus semantic value. However, the Q operator is a special kind of focus-sensitive operator since unlike other such elements, it does not also make reference to the ordinary semantic value.

(17) [[Q [*máax uk'le sa'o'.* . .]]° = {"that José drank the atole", "that María drank the atole", "that Lucía drank the atole", . . .}

Empirically, Cable (2010) argues for such a semantics on the basis of elements like Japanese *ka* and Tlingit *sá*, which he claims overtly instantiate the Q-particle in these languages.[5] Diachronically, the "focus particles" discussed in §4.1 found in wh-words in some languages (Huastec *ha'*, Yucatec *ix* and K'iche' *ja'*) provide superficially plausible candidates in Mayan. However, while these elements are particles which play a role in question formation, they appear to differ crucially from Beck and Cable's Q-particles since, according to available descriptions of these elements, they also occur in focus constructions outside of questions.

Synchronically, however, modern Mayan languages have no Q-particle present overtly. Therefore, it would seem that an approach where focus is the generator of question alternatives must posit a covert Q operator. While such an approach is not necessarily untenable (e.g. Beck and Cable both propose covert operators of this sort for English), it does not move us any further towards a compositional account of questions in Mayan languages. Moreover, since the account assigns no ordinary semantic value to wh-words, it is not clear how the interrogative-indefinite affinity is to be captured on such an approach. To conclude, then, we have argued that while an account based on focus alternatives may be appropriate for other languages,[6] this approach does not in fact appear to resolve the compositional puzzle for Mayan languages (at least synchronically).

5.2 Wh-words as alternative generator

Rather than focus providing the interrogative alternatives, then, we turn now to consider the other approach, on which it is the indefinite semantics of the wh-word that introduces the question's alternatives. On this approach, developed in detail by AnderBois (2012), focus semantic values play no crucial role. Instead, as discussed in §2.3, the ordinary semantic value of the wh-word introduces a set of alternatives, as in (18a), which composes with the rest of the clause to form a set of propositional alternatives, (18b).

(18) a. [[*máax*]]° = {José, María, Lucía, . . .}
      b. [[*máax uk'le sa'o'*]]° = {"that José drank the atole", "that María drank the atole", "that Lucía drank the atole", . . .}

Recent work in inquisitive semantics (e.g. Groenendijk and Roelofsen (2009), AnderBois (2012), Ciardelli et al. (2013), AnderBois (2014)) uses such representations to capture the intuition that indefinites (as well as disjunctions) typically make two contributions to the discourse. First, they provide the truth-conditional information that there is some alternative or other which is true. Second, they make salient in subsequent discourse the issue of which alternative(s) are true. By hypothesis, wh-words such as *máax* 'who' in (15) contribute indefinite semantics, and therefore introduce both components to the sentence's meaning.

Where questions differ from corresponding indefinites, then, is that questions have the wh-word or phrase in the preverbal identificational focus position. AnderBois (2012) argues that the role of focus is to presuppose the information that there is some *x* or other for which the main predication holds, as in (18c).

(18) c. **Focus presupposition of (15):** {"that someone or other drank the atole"}

Relative to the focus background in (18c), then, (18b) is no longer informative. It serves only to highlight the different possible alternatives which together comprise the logical space. Under this approach, no covert morphosyntax needs to be posited. Instead, it is indefinite wh-words which contribute question-like alternatives in all their uses plus the focus presupposition, which effectively isolates this 'inquisitive' contribution, producing the desired interrogative interpretation.

One area that the approach in this section does not address are the historical considerations touched on in §4.1. Whereas Tonhauser (2003b) attempted to make use of such facts within the formal semantic account, there is no obvious place for such decomposition in the present approach. Instead, the question becomes how indefinite wh-words arose historically across all their uses, interrogative or not. We leave this issue to future work, but given the lack of synchronic productivity in wh-word formation discussed above, we hope to have made the case that this issue is separate from the compositional question on which we focus here.

6 CONCLUSIONS

In this chapter, we have investigated the semantic composition of content questions in Mayan languages. Whereas many languages make use of question-specific morphosyntax, wh-questions in Mayan languages consist of indefinite wh-words and a preverbal focus position, both of which occur separately outside of questions. We have considered two leading approaches to this compositional problem: one in which focus is the nexus of alternatives, and one in which indefinite wh-words play this role. While some quite thorny diachronic issues remain unresolved on either view, we have argued that only the indefinite-based approach resolves this compositional puzzle without the need to posit covert interrogative morphology.

While we have focused exclusively on wh-questions here, it is worth noting that AnderBois (2012) shows that, given the deep semantic parallels between indefinites and disjunctions, the indefinite-based approach can be readily extended to polar questions (with or without preverbal foci) and alternative-question uses of focused disjunctions, at least for Yucatec. We leave more detailed investigation of these other types of questions to future work since the facts regarding these are both more variable and less well documented. For example, unlike Yucatec, many Mayan languages either lack a disjunctive coordinator or else have recently borrowed the Spanish *o*. However, we hope to have given good reason to think that such compositional issues are in principle resolvable and that doing so can shed light both on the structure and history of Mayan languages and on the formal semantics of these component constructions cross-linguistically.

NOTES

1 This description hopefully makes clear the connection between focus in the alternative-evoking sense we intend here and focus in sense of *new information*. We revisit this connection in §3 when we look specifically at focus in Mayan languages.

2 Like Mayan languages, Hungarian has an immediately preverbal (identificational) focus position, and it is here that wh-words occur in wh-questions. Note that, in line with the discussion in §3.1, relative clauses in Hungarian demonstrably do not make use of this position.

3 Velleman (2014) shows for K'iche' that transitive subjects systematically do not allow for this possibility and suggests that this is so for some other Mayan languages, including at least Yucatec. Velleman analyzes this as a reflex of the topical status of postverbal transitive subjects, an assumption we adopt here as well.

4 Beyond the variation shown here, for some languages there is known to be significant dialectal variation (e.g. Par Sapon and Can Pixabaj (2000), p. 95's work on K'iche'). One further parameter of variation is that in some cases (e.g. Kaqchikel, Uspanteko) the word cited here applies not only to animates, but to inanimates as well, similar to English 'what'.

5 One crucial point to be noted here is that Cable (2010)'s proposal has the Q-particle combining directly with the wh-phrase itself, rather than the entire question radical. In order to simplify the presentation here, we set aside this detail in our formulas, despite its relevance for the discussion of compositionality.

6 See AnderBois (2012:377–9) for theoretical arguments against even this position.

REFERENCES

Abusch, Dorit. 2009. "Presupposition triggering from alternatives." *Journal of Semantics* 27: 37–80.

Aissen, Judith. 1992. "Topic and focus in Mayan." *Language* 63: 43–80.

Aissen, Judith. 1996. "Pied-piping, abstract agreement, and functional projections in Tzotzil." *Natural Language and Linguistic Theory* 14: 447–91.

Aissen, Judith. 1999. "Agent focus and inverse in Tzotzil." *Language* 75: 451–85.

AnderBois, Scott. 2012. "Focus and uninformativity in Yucatec Maya questions." *Natural Language Semantics* 20: 349–90.

AnderBois, Scott. 2014. "The semantics of sluicing: beyond truth conditions." *Language* 90: 887–926.

Ayres, Glenn. 1991. *La gramática Ixil*. Guatemala: Centro de investigaciones regionales.

Balogh, Kata. 2013. "Hungarian pre-verbal focus and exhaustivity." *New Frontiers in Artificial Intelligence, Lecture Notes in Computer Science No. 7856:*1–16.

Beaver, David, and Brady Clark. 2008. *Sense and sensitivity: how focus determines meaning*. Oxford: Blackwell.

Beck, Sigrid. 2006. "Intervention effects follow from focus interpretation." *Natural Language Semantics* 12: 1–56.

Berinstein, Ava. 1985. *Evidence for multiattachment in K'ekchi Mayan*. New York: Garland Publishing.

Bhat, D.N.S. 2000. "The interrogative-indefinite puzzle." *Linguistic Typology* 4: 365–400.

Bricker, Victoria, Eleuterio Po'ot Yah, and Ofelia Dzul de Po'ot. 1998. *A dictionary of the Maya language: as spoken in Hocabá, Yucatán*. Salt Lake City: University of Utah Press.

Brody, Jill. 1982. "Discourse processes of highlighting in Tojolabal Maya morphosyntax." PhD diss., Washington University.

Büring, Daniel. 2012. "Focus and intonation." In Routledge companion to the philosophy of language, ed. By Gillian Russelland Delia Graff Fara, 103–15. London, Routledge.

Cable, Seth. 2010. *The grammar of Q: Q-particles, Wh-movement and pied-piping*. Oxford: Oxford University Press.

Can Pixabaj, Telma. 2007. *Jkemiik Yoloj li Uspanteko: Gramática Uspanteka.* Guatemala: OKMA and Cholsamaj.

Can Pixabaj, Telma, and Nora England. 2011. "Nominal topic and focus in K'ichee'." In *Representing language: essays in honor of Judith Aissen, ed. R.* Gutiérrez-Bravo, L. Mikkelsen, and E. Potsdam, 15–38. Linguistics Research Center, UC Santa Cruz.

Ciardelli, Ivano, and Jeroen Groenendijk, and Floris Roelofsen. 2013. "Inquisitive semantics: a new notion of meaning." *Language and Linguistics Compass* 7(9): 459–76.

Cohen, Ariel. 1999. "How are alternatives computed?" *Journal of Semantics* 16: 43–65.

Dayley, Jon. 1981. "Voice and ergativity in Mayan languages." *Studies in Mesoamerican Languages* 4: 5–119. Survey of California and Other Indian Languages.

Edmonson, Barbara. 1988. "A descriptive grammar of Huastec (Potosino dialect)." PhD diss., Tulane University.

England, Nora. 1983. *A grammar of Mam, a Mayan language.* Austin: University of Texas Press.

Fintel, Kai von. 1994. "Restrictions on quantifier domains." PhD diss., University of Massachusetts.

Geurts, Bart, and Rob van der Sandt. 2004. "Interpreting focus." *Theoretical Linguistics* 30: 1–44.

Groenendijk, Jeroen, and Floris Roelofsen. 2009. "Inquisitive semantics and pragmatics." In Proceedings of SPR 09, ed. by Jesus Larrazabal and Larraitz Zubeldia, 41–72. San Sebastián, Basque Country: Universidad del País Vasco.

Haida, Andreas. 2008. "The indefiniteness and focusing of wh-words." PhD diss., Humboldt University.

Halliday, M. A. K. 1967. "Notes on transitivity and theme in English II." *Journal of Linguistics* 3: 199–244.

Hamblin, Charles L. 1973. "Questions in Montague English." *Foundations of Language* 10: 41–53.

Haspelmath, Martin. 1997. *Indefinite pronouns.* Oxford, Oxford University Press.

Haviland, John. 1981. *Sk'op sotz'leb: el tzotzil de San Lorenzo Zinacantán.* México: UNAM.

Idiatov, Dmitry. 2011. "The instability of Eastern Mayan interrogative pronominals: interrogative pronominals as complex constructions." Presentation at 20th International Conference on Historical Linguistics. http://webh01.ua.ac.be/dmitry.idiatov/talks/2011_ICHL_Mayan_slides_Idiatov.pdf. Last accessed 24 August 2014.

Kaufman, Terrence, and John Justeson. 2003. *A preliminary Mayan etymological dictionary.* Foundation for the Advancement of Mesoamerican Studies. http://www.famsi.org/reports/01050/index.html.

Kiss, Katalin É. 1998. "Identificational focus versus information focus." *Language* 74: 245–73.

Kiss, Katalin É. 2010. "Structural focus and exhaustivity." In *Information structure: theoretical, typological and experimental perspectives,* ed. by Malte Zimmermann and Caroline Féry, 64–88. New York, Oxford University Press.

Kratzer, Angelika, and Junko Shimoyama. 2002. "Indeterminate pronouns: the view from Japanese." *Proceedings of the Third Tokyo Conference on Psycholinguistics* 1–25.

Kügler, Frank, Stavros Skopeteas, and Elisabeth Verhoeven. 2007. "Encoding information structure in Yucatec Maya: on the interplay of prosody and syntax." In Ishihar, S., Jannedy, S., and Schwarz. A. *ISIS* 8: 187–208.

Larsen, Thomas. 1988. "Manifestations of ergativity in Quiché grammar." PhD diss., University of California, Berkeley.

Mateo Toledo, Eladio (B'alam). 2008. "The family of complex predicates in Q'anjob'al (Maya); their syntax and meaning." PhD diss., University of Texas, Austin.

Monforte, Jorge, Lázaro Dzul, and Rodrigo Gutiérrez-Bravo. 2010. *Narraciones mayas*. México: INALI.

Norman, William. 1977. "Topic and focus in Mayan." Presentation at the Mayan Workshop II, San Cristobal de las Casas, Chiapas.

Onea, Edgar, and David Beaver. 2010. "Hungarian focus is not exhausted." *Proceedings of Semantics and Linguistic Theory (SALT) 19*: 342–59.

Palosaari, Naomi. 2011. "Topics in Mocho' phonology and morphology." PhD diss., University of Utah.

Par Sapón, Beatriz, and Telma Can Pixabaj. 2000. *Variación dialectal en K'ichee'*. Guatemala: Cholmasaj.

Patal Majzul, Filiberto, Pedro Oscar Garcia Matzar (Lolmay), and Carmelina Espantzay Serech (Ixchel). 2000. *Rujunamaxik ri Kaqchikel Chi': Variación dialectal en Kaqchikel*. Guatemala: Cholsamaj.

Pérez Martínez, Vitalino. 1994. Gramática del Idioma Ch'orti'. La Antigua, Guatemala: Proyecto Lingüístico Francisco Marroquín.

Polian, Gilles. 2007. "El sufijo -*uk* y la diversificación de la modalidad *irrealis* en tseltal." In *Proceedings of the conference on indigenous languages of Latin America III*. Austin, University of Texas. http://www.ailla.utexas.org/site/cilla3/Polian_CILLA_III.pdf.

Polian, Gilles. 2013. *Gramática del Tseltal de Oxchuc*. México: CIESAS/Publicaciones de la Casa Chata.

Roberts, Craige. 2012 (1996–1998). "Information structure in discourse: towards an integrated formal theory of pragmatics." *Semantics and Pragmatics* 5(6): 1–69.

Rooth, Mats. 1985. "Association with focus." PhD diss., University of Massachusetts.

Rooth, Mats. 1992. "A theory of focus interpretation." *Natural Language Semantics* 1: 75–116.

Santos Nicolás, José Francisco (Pala's), and José Gonzalo Benito Pérez (Waykan). 1998. *Rukorb aal Poqom Q'orb'al: Gramática Poqom (Poqomam)*. Guatemala: Cholmasaj.

Shklovsky, Kirill. 2012. "Tseltal clause structure." PhD diss., MIT.

Tonhauser, Judith. 2003a. "F-constructions in Yucatec Maya." In Proceedings of *semantics of *understudied *languages of the Americas (SULA) 2, ed. by Jan Anderssen, Paula Menéndez-Benito, and Adam Werle, 203–23. Amherst: GLSA.

Tonhauser, Judith. 2003b. "On the syntax and semantics of content questions in Yucatec Maya." In *Proceedings of the 6th workshop on American Indian languages (WAIL)*, ed. by Juan Castillo, 106–22. Santa Barbara: Santa Barbara Papers in Linguistics.

Vázquez-Álvarez, Juan Jesús. 2011. "A grammar of Chol, a Mayan language." PhD diss., University of Texas.

Velleman, Leah Bridges. 2014. "Focus and movement in a variety of K'ichee'." PhD diss., University of Texas.

CHAPTER 14

PLURACTIONALITY IN MAYAN

Robert Henderson

1 INTRODUCTION

The term "pluractional" originates in Newman 1980 to describe a particular class of derived verb stems in Chadic languages that had up until that point been called "intensive". The descriptive intuition that underlies their renaming is that these stems uniformly denote plural actions. For instance, reduplicating the initial syllable of the Hausa verb *nèemí* 'seek' generates a new stem *nàn-nèemí* meaning 'to seek all over' or 'to seek a lot' (Newman 2012:ex.1b). Under both translations, though, it is clear that the verb stem no longer denotes simple atomic events of seeking. While invented for Chadic languages, Newman's notion of pluractionality has proved to be fruitful. Pluractional derivations have subsequently come to be found across the world's languages, though perhaps especially so in the indigenous languages of Africa and the Americas (Mithun 1988; Wood 2007). One of the primary goals of this chapter is to show that Mayan languages are no exception, and that some are, in fact, particularly rich in pluractional morphology.

The chapter is organized around two case studies that explore the pluractional systems of two distantly related Mayan languages, Kaqchikel and Tseltal. Both languages have a variety of pluractional derivations, which will allow us to see the typological breadth of pluractionality in Mayan. The Kaqchikel case study focuses on the well-known distinction between event-internal and event-external pluractionality. The Tseltal case study focuses on a second locus of variation in pluractional meaning that partially crosscuts the event-internal/event-external distinction, namely how the plurality of events is structured in time. Finally, Mayan pluractionality raises a series of questions, both about Mayan languages and pluractionality more generally. The final section considers these questions and suggests areas for future research.

2 BRIEF TYPOLOGICAL BACKGROUND

The definition of pluractionality merely requires that pluractional verbs denote plural events. Nothing is said about the number of events that constitute that plurality, their relationships to one another in time and space, their participants, or whether they sum to an event that has an identity greater than the sum of its parts. Previous typological surveys, most prominently Cusic 1981 and Wood 2007, have shown that there are pluractionals that denote events that vary along all of these dimensions, and more importantly, that the variation is not random. Instead, pluractionals fall into common types, which cluster depending on the properties of the event pluralities that they denote. The most salient split, and the one that will most concern us in §3, is the contrast between event-internal and event-external pluractionality. Intuitively, event-internal pluractionals denote plural events that have the character of a single event. It is as if the repetitions that compose the plurality take place internal to an event that is conceived of as a single happening. In contrast, event-external pluractionals denote plural events whose repetitions are more easily individuable as separate happenings. The difference is perhaps best illustrated with an example, like the Yurok pluractional affixes in (1)–(2), which have traditionally been called the repetitive and the iterative (Garrett 2001).

YUROK (Wood 2007:153, ex. 11)
(1) **Tekw**tek'weses   ku   popsew!
    REPET.cut.IMP   DET   bread
    'Slice up the bread!'

(Wood 2007:147, ex. 5c)
(2) Kipun   kwegeskwes-ek
    winter   have.a.cold.ITR-1SG
    'In the winter time I have a cold.'

The repetitive, shown in (1), instantiates event-internal pluractionality, while the iterative in (2) is an event-external pluractional derivation. The event described in (1) necessarily involves the repetitions of a plurality of subphases of an event. That is, producing bread that is sliced necessitates cutting the bread multiple times, and each cutting event is clearly a subphase of the slicing event they sum to. While English has a single lexical item "slice (up)", which denotes events of plural character, Yurok derives a verb of similar meaning from one meaning "to cut" using an event-internal pluractional affix. In contrast, the event-external pluractional event described in (2) clearly presents a plurality of events that happen independently. They occur in different times and places, and do not, as subphases do, sum to a new event of singular character. A large body of crosslinguistic work on the contrast between pluractional verbs that appear more like (1) and those that appear more like (2) has produced a list of parameters that situate a given pluractional on the event-internal/event-external continuum following Wood 2007:87.

(3) THE EVENT-INTERNAL/EXTERNAL CONTINUUM
     a. ASPECTUAL SELECTION
         Event-internal pluractionals are preferentially formed from verb stems that would otherwise be semelfactives or achievements. Event-external pluractionals are aspectually promiscuous and can be formed from verbs stems that belong to a variety of aktionsart classes.

     b. CONTIGUITY
         The repetitions that form an event-internal pluractional event are preferentially contiguous in time and space. In contrast, event-external pluractionals do not place strict requirements on the temporal or spatial distance between the events that compose the plural events they denote.

     c. GENERICITY
         This feature is closely related to the previous one, though they do not completely overlap. The generalization is that event-internal pluractionals never allow habitual readings, while event-external pluractionals often do.

d. CARDINALITY

Pluractional verbs denote plural events. This general requirement takes no stand on the number of events that compose the plurality. The event-internal/event-external distinction makes the plurality requirement precise. In particular, event-internal pluractionals generally require plural events with large cardinalities, while event-external pluractionals can often be satisfied by events of simple plurality, i.e., two or more events.

e. SHARED TELOS

Event-internal pluractional verbs usually require that all of the events in the plurality share the same theme argument or progress toward a shared goal or result. In contrast, event-external pluractionals do not have this requirement.

f. BASE-PREDICATE ENTAILMENTS

A sentence with an event-internal pluractional often fails to entail a minimally different sentence without the pluractional morphology. In contrast, event-external pluractional sentences often entail a corresponding sentence without the pluractional morphology.

While a given pluractional might not pattern in every way like a canonical event-internal or event-external pluractional, typological work has shown that pluractionals cluster around these two poles. Given the prominent place that the event-internal/event-external distinction has played in the previous literature, the following case studies will be organized around this core contrast, allowing Mayan pluractionality to be placed in its crosslinguistic context. First, I will show that Kaqchikel has two pluractionals that differ precisely along the criteria detailed above. Then, turning to Tseltal, I will discuss variation across three different event-internal pluractionals in that language with respect to the temporal profile of the plural events they denote. Importantly, this kind of variation within a category of pluractionality is also attested in other languages with rich pluractional systems.

3 KAQCHIKEL CASE STUDY: THE INTERNAL/EXTERNAL DISTINCTION

Pluractionality is a category that has not been traditionally talked about in grammars of Mayan languages, though this is changing in more recent work (e.g., Polian 2013:349–60). We are thus in the same situation as Newman in his classic work on Hausa. Following his lead, I will identify pluractional verb stems as those which, in contrast to their underived forms, cannot describe single-event scenarios. While candidate pluractionals can be identified with this notional criterion, they are confirmed as such through truth-value judgments in a context. For instance, after touching a cup only once, speakers of Kaqchikel judge example (4) to be false and example (5) to be true, a difference that can only be attributed to the suffix -la', which can therefore be called a pluractional affix (see Henderson 2012 for an analysis of -la'). Note that I call the morphology that derives pluractional verbs "pluractional affixes" or "pluractional morphology", and retain the word "pluractional" to refer to (classes of) verb stems that have the relevant semantic properties.

KAQCHIKEL

(4) X-Ø-in-chap-**ala'**   ri   xara.
CP-B3SG-A1SG-handle-la'   DET   cup
'I touched the cup all over.' {ELIC}

(5) X-Ø-in-chap   ri   xara.
CP-B3SG-A1SG-handle   DET   cup
'I touched the cup.' {ELIC}

This section focuses on the two pluractional affixes in Kaqchikel discussed in Henderson 2012. It will be shown that one is an event-internal pluractional, while the other is an event-external pluractional, demonstrating that even within a single Mayan language we can find the two core types of pluractionality. The first kind of pluractional is illustrated by the attested near-minimal pair in (6). Morphologically, the pluractional verb stem is formed by reduplicating the verb root's initial consonant (C_1) along with /a'/. Note that a copied vowel comes along with a copied consonant in example (6a). This vowel is not written in the glosses because one finds attested examples without this vowel, which is mostly likely present for purely phonological reasons.

(Cojtí et al.1998:58)
(6) a. Ri   ajch'olöy   wakx,   n-Ø-u-chuq'-ij   ru-qül   ri   wakx
      the   butcher   cow   ICP-B3SG-A3SG-pierce-SS   A3SG-neck   the   cow
                  r-ichin   ni-Ø-käm.
                  A3SG-reason   ICP-B3SG-die
      'The cow-butcher pierces the cow's neck to kill it.'

    b. Ri   ajch'olonel   n-Ø-u-chuq'-**ucha'**   ru-qül   ri   mama'   wakx
       the   butcher   ICP-B3SG-A3SG-pierce-C_1a'   A3SG-neck   the   big   cow
       'The butcher keeps stabbing at the big cow's neck.'

Example (6a), which does not have pluractional morphology, can be used to faithfully describe a scenario in which the butcher kills the cow with a single piercing. In contrast, example (6b) cannot describe a scenario with a single blow. The pluractional affix derives a verbal stem that can only be satisfied by events of repeatedly stabbing the cow. Henderson 2012 shows that -C_1a' derives event-internal pluractionals according to the crosslinguistically established criteria.

First, as expected of event-internal pluractional morphology, -C_1a' preferentially derives pluractional stems from semelfactive verbs. This is illustrated in (7)–(9).

(7) X-Ø-u-k'oj-**ok'a'**   ru-chi'   ri   jay.
CP-B3SG-A3SG-knock-C_1a'   A3SG-mouth   the   building
'He kept knocking at the door.' {ELIC}

(Cojtí et al. 1998:371)
(8) Jun   xti   moy   r-onojel   q'ij   n-Ø-u-tzin-**itza'**   ri   ru-q'ojon
    a   little   blind   A3SG-all   day   ICP-B3SG-A3SG-sound(music)-C_1a'   the   A3SG-guitar
       pa   k'ayb'äl.
       PREP market
    'A blind person strums his guitar all day in the market.'

(9) X-Ø-u-t'in-**it'a'**   ri   kem.
    CP-B3SG-A3SG-hammer(weft)-**C₁a'** the   weaving
    'He kept hammering the weft of the weaving.' {ELIC}

Previous authors, noting that semelfactive predicates in English have uncoerced repetitive atelic uses, have drawn attention to the fact that atelic events are inherently repeatable
(Rothstein 2004). This repetition is exactly what -C₁a' requires. Verbs of other aktionsart
classes denote events that differ in one of three ways: (i) they can be temporally extended,
like activities, (ii) they can have linguistically relevant result states, like achievements,
or (iii) they can be temporally extended and have result states, like accomplishments. For
non-semelfactive predicates, -C₁a' requires aspectual coercion. This establishes its preference for targeting semelfactive verbs, as a purported event-internal pluractional should.
For instance, with achievement verbs, like those in (10)–(11), the events fail to naturally
culminate, allowing for repetition.

(10) X-Ø-in-ch'ar-**ach'a'**   ri   tros.
    CP-B3SG-A1SG-split-**C₁a'** the   stump
    'I kept chopping at the stump.' {ELIC}
    SPEAKER COMMENT: It's like if your axe is really dull.

(11) X-Ø-u-yuch'-**uya'**   ri   su't.
    CP-B3SG-A3SG-fold-**C₁a'** the   wrap
    'She kept folding over the wrap.' {ELIC}
    SPEAKER COMMENT: Like if you can't get it lined up even.

To demonstrate that -C₁a' bans culminations, note that when the base predicate is an
achievement, as in (12)–(13), a pluractional sentence fails to entail its non-pluractional
counterpart. This follows naturally if the second clauses in (12)–(13) denote events that
culminate, while the pluractional verbs in the first clauses have been coerced into semelfactives, which denote non-culminating events. The failure of entailment is explicitly
contrasted with examples like (14), where the base stem *k'oj* 'knock' is also semelfactive.

(12) X-Ø-in-ch'ar-**ach'a'**   ri   tros,   po   man x-Ø-ch'ar   ta.
    CP-B3SG-A1SG-split-**C₁a'** the   stump, but NEG CP-B3SG-split.PSV IRR
    'I kept chopping at the stump, but it didn't split.' {ELIC}

(13) X-Ø-u-tzuy-**utza'**,   po   man x-Ø-tzuy-e'   ta.
    CP-B3SG-A3SG-sit-**C₁a'**, but NEG CP-B3SG-sit-INTR IRR
    'She kept sitting up and down on it, but she didn't sit.' {ELIC}

(14) #X-Ø-u-k'oj-**ok'a'**   ru-chi   ri   jay,   po   man
    CP-B3SG-A3SG-knock-**C₁a'** A3SG-mouth the building, but NEG
        x-Ø-u-k'oj-ij   ta.
        CP-B3SG-A3SG-knock-SS   IRR
    #'She kept knocking on the door, but she didn't knock on it.' {ELIC}

Note that examples (12)–(13) not only show that -C₁a' preferentially targets semelfactives, but that C₁a'-derived verb stems also behave like event-internal pluractionals
relative to the final criterion, namely sentences with event-internal pluractional verbs do
not necessarily entail minimally different non-pluractional sentences.

Activities similarly require coercion. In particular, while such predicates can usually describe events that take place over extended stretches of time and space, -C_1a' requires the repetition of the shortest events that might fall in the denotation of the underived verbal predicate.

(15) X-Ø-u-sir-**isa'**   ri   koloch'.
      CP-B3SG-A3SG-roll-**C_1a'** the ball
      'He kept rolling the ball (back and forth in place).' {ELIC}

(16) X-Ø-u-chok-**ocha'**   ri   ch'ich'.
      CP-B3SG-A3SG-push-**C_1a'** ri car
      'He kept pushing on the car.' {ELIC}
      SPEAKER COMMENT: It's like it's stuck and keeps rocking back into place.

Finally, accomplishments verbs, like *b'än* 'build' or *tz'ib'aj* 'write', are usually only infelicitously derived by -C_1a'. This is expected if -C_1a' derives event-internal pluractionals. Event-internal pluractionals are often built on semelfactives crosslinguistically, but accomplishments have a lexical semantics that is the most radically different from semelfactives. If any verbs should resist coercion, it would be these.

C_1a'-derived verbs also pattern with event-internal pluractionals crosslinguistically by denoting events whose atomic parts are nearly contiguous in both time and space. The following examples illustrate this point in a controlled manner, but even the naturally occurring examples in (6b) and (8) describe scenarios that could only involve contiguous repetitions.

(17) Suppose Juan knocks on the door once every 10 seconds for 10 minutes.
      #A   Xwan   x-Ø-u-k'oj-**ok'a'**   ru-chi'   ri   jay.
      CLF   Juan   CP-B3SG-A3SG-knock-**C_1a'** A3SG-mouth the door
      'Juan kept knocking at the door.' {ELIC}
      SPEAKER COMMENT: No, it has to be continuous [seguido].

(18) Suppose Juan has a rash on his arm and every once in a while it itches so he scratches it.
      #A   Xwan   x-Ø-u-roch-**ora'**   r-aq'a.
      CLF   Juan   CP-B3SG-A3SG-scratch-**C_1a'** A3SG-hand
      'Juan kept scratching his arm.' {ELIC}
      SPEAKER COMMENT: No, it would be like this [scratches vigorously back and forth on her arm].

(19) Suppose you see Juan every day and he gives you a dirty look.
      #A   Xwan   x-i-ru-tz'et-**etz'a'**.
      CLF   Juan   CP-B1SG-A3SG-look.at-**C_1a'**
      'Juan keeps looking at me.' {ELIC}
      SPEAKER COMMENT: No, it would have to be like this [speaker turns his head a bit and shoots a glance over and over].

The contexts in (17)–(19) set up scenarios where the amount of time between events, the downtime, varies. In particular, we look at downtimes ranging from 10 seconds to days. Speakers' comments make it clear that -C_1a' cannot be used, especially when they act out contrary scenarios in which -C_1a' would be appropriate. They always use rapid, almost frantic, contiguous repetitions. It should not be surprising then that verbs derived by -C_1a', like event-internal pluractionals more generally, do not have habitual readings either.

The fourth property of event-internal pluractionals is that they denote events with large cardinalities. Examples (20)–(22) show that $C1a$'-derived predicates, as expected, require many repetitions.

(20) Suppose Juan looks over at you twice.
    #A   Xwan   x-i-ru-tz'et-**etz'a'**.
    CLF   Juan   CP-B1SG-A3SG-look.at-C_1**a'**
    'Juan keeps looking at me.' {ELIC}

(21) Suppose Juan taps the table 4 or 5 times.
    #A   Xwan   x-Ø-u-chap-**acha'**   ri   ch'atäl.
    CLF   Juan   CP-B3SG-A3SG-handle-C_1**a'**   the   table
    'Juan keeps touching the table.' {ELIC}

(22) Suppose Juan taps the table 15 or 20 times.
    A   Xwan   x-Ø-u-chap-**acha'**   ri   ch'atäl.
    CLF   Juan   CP-B3SG-A3SG-handle-C_1**a'**   the   table
    'Juan keeps touching the table.' {ELIC}

Finally, it is possible to show that the event pluralities denoted by C_1a'-derived verb stems require a shared arguments, and thus behave like event-internal pluractional verbs in accordance with property (3e). In particular, it is impossible to distribute parts of one of these events over parts of a participant. For instance, example (23) has no reading where each of the individuals in the denotation of the plural subject participates in a single pluractional subevent. The most salient reading of (23) has each of the people repeatedly glancing at me. Similarly, example (24) cannot be use to characterize the presented scenario. Instead, its most natural reading is one in which each of the wraps participates in its own pluractional event, namely one in which the subject rapidly touches it.

(23) Suppose there is a large group of people across the street and they each turn and glance at
    me once.
    #X-i-ki-tz'et-**etz'a'**.
    CP-B1SG-A3PL-look.at-C_1**a'**
    'They kept glancing at me.' {ELIC}

(24) Suppose there is large number of wraps on the table and someone touches each of them
    once in rapid succession.
    #X-e-ru-chap-**acha'**   ri   su't.
    CP-B3PL-A3SG-handle-C_1**a'**   the   wrap
    'He kept touching the wraps.' {ELIC}

By resisting the distribution of pluractional subevents over different participants, C_1a'-derived stems clearly behave like event-internal pluractionals crosslinguistically, which usually denote plural events that must have a shared object or progress toward the same goal. For instance, we can think of the pluractional verb stem in (23) as characterizing a complex event in which the agent shoots many little glances at a theme. Crucially, the theme and the agent must be the same across each of those events, which gives the pluractional event the character of a single event. The same is true for (23), which shows that a plural event satisfying the verb stem must have the same theme, and so once again has the character of a single event.

The previous data establish that -C$_1a$' derives canonical event-internal pluractional verbs, possessing all of the relevant properties. Turning now to the pluractional derivation exemplified in (25), we find a Kaqchikel event-external pluractional derivation contrasting with -C$_1a$' with respect to most of the previous properties. Example (25) shows that this pluractional stem is derived by the suffix -*löj*. It is pluractional because while the positional root *ch'ot* is deals with semantic notions of individuated objects falling, like teeth or grains, the pluractional form requires this process to happen repeatedly, which is captured in the translation by the verb scatter. The goal now is to show that *löj*-pluractionals are event-external pluractionals. Note that, once again, I will not be representing copy vowels in the gloss, like the second vowel in -*ch'otolöj*, because one can find many examples in which no such vowel is present.

(Cojtí et al. 1998:76)
(25) La   jun   wakx   ni-Ø-ch'ot-**olöj**   kan   r-achäq   pa   b'ëy.
     that one   cow   ICP-B3SG-fall.grains-**löj**   DIR   A3SG-feces   PREP street
     'That cow has its feces scattered in the street.'

First, like event-external pluractionals crosslinguistically, -*löj* can target predicates of all eventive aktionsart classes. In example (26) it targets an activity, in example (27) it targets an achievement, and in example (32) it targets an accomplishment. These were the kind of verb stems that -C$_1a$' could not derive without coercion, but we see not such coercion with -*löj*. Only stative predicates are ungrammatical with -*löj*, which makes sense if they do not denote events, and thus a fortiori cannot denote plural events.

Examples (26)–(28) provides further evidence that -*löj* is an event-external pluractional. Like similar morphemes crosslinguistically, the amount of downtime between repeated events is variable and can be quite large. We also see that, unlike -C1a', pluractionals derived by -*löj* can have habitual readings.

(26) X-i-b'iyin-**ilöj**.
     CP-B1SG-walk-**löj**
     'I kept having to walk.' {ELIC}
     SPEAKER COMMENT: Like if you have fields all over the place and you had to do work
                      at every one.

(27) (Ojër kan)   x-i-ch'ar-**alöj**.
     (before)   CP-B1SG-split.wood-**löj**
     'I used to split wood.' {ELIC}
     SPEAKER COMMENT: Like as a profession.

(28) (Ojër)   x-Ø-b'ixan-**ilöj**.
     (before)   CP-B3SG-sing-**löj**
     'He used to sing.' {ELIC}
     SPEAKER COMMENT: Like in a choir.

Incompletive *löj*-marked verbs have similar readings, and not surprisingly, these readings are more salient than with verbs in completive aspect.

(29) La   achin   la'   n-Ø-xub'an-**alöj**.
     that   man   there   ICP-B3SG-whistle-**löj**
     'That man is always whistling.' {ELIC}

(30) La   jun   achin   la'   n-Ø-chan-**alöj**   pa   r-ochoch.
     that   a   man   there   ICP-B3SG-naked-**löj** PREP   A3SG-house
     'That man is always naked around his house.' {ELIC}
     SPEAKER COMMENT: Like a neighbor who is always working naked in his patio and he
                      doesn't realize you can see him.

Finally, pluractionals derived by *-löj* exhibit the property of event-external pluractionality characterized by (3e). The plural events they denote need not share an object or
progress toward a shared goal. The naturally occurring example in (31) illustrates the
point. The stem *-ajmajlöj* is clearly interpreted distributively, but no one person participates in a plural event. The same is true in examples (32)–(34). None of the houses in
(32) have to be built more than once. The same could be said for eggs and takings in (33)
and people and deaths in (34). What these examples show is that the pluractional event
can be split into parts and distributed over different participants, which is exactly what is
impossible with C$_1a$'-derived pluractionals.

(Hendrick Krueger 1986:152, ex. 205)
(31) Y-e'-ajmaj-**löj**.
     ICP-B3PL-flee-**löj**
     'They go fleeing, one after another.'

(32) X-Ø-b'an-**alöj**   ri   jay.
     CP-B3SG-do.PSV-**löj**   the   house
     'The houses were built over time.' {ELIC}

(33) X-Ø-tz'am-**alöj**   ri   säqmolo'.
     CP-B3SG-take.PSV-**löj** the   eggs
     'The eggs were taken over time.' {ELIC}
     SPEAKER COMMENT: It's like you're selling eggs at the market and they were sold a
                      few at a time all afternoon until gone.

(34) X-e-kam-**alöj**.
     CP-B3PL-die-**löj**
     'They died over time.' {ELIC}
     SPEAKER COMMENT: Could be used to describe how people die during a plague.

It is clear that *löj*-derived pluractionals contrast with C$_1a$'-derived pluractionals on
almost all of the properties discussed. It only fails on one, namely the cardinality constraint. While event-external pluractionals crosslinguistically can be predicated of events
with high cardinality, it is often the case that they accept plural events of low cardinality.
This is not the case for *-löj*. For instance, speakers reject example like (33) in situations
where only two or three eggs were taken. While partially overlapping with event-internal
pluractionals in this way, *-löj* is still identifiable as an event-external pluractional derivation. Its semantic properties cluster around that of that cross-linguistically stable type.
    This section has provided a detailed description of the semantics of two different
pluractionals in Kaqchikel, illustrating that the language instantiates the two cross-
linguistically common types of pluractionality. While the survey thus reveals some of

the observed variation in Mayan pluractionality, Kaqchikel actually has many additional pluractional affixes, like the distributive event-external distributive marker *-la'* discussed in Henderson 2012, 2014, and mostly saliently, those like (35)–(36) which derive verb stems from ideophonic roots. In example (35) the reduplication of the root's rhyme derives a pluractional intransitive verb from the ideophonic root *b'ït'*. In example (36), reduplication of the root-initial consonant supports the affixation of *-öt*, deriving a pluractional intransitive verb from the ideophonic root *qitz'*.

(35) *b'ït'* 'the sound of cloth tearing'

Yalan	ni-Ø-b'it'**it'**		ri	kej	ch-u-xe'		ri	r-ejqa'n.
very	ICP-B3SG-fart.repeatedly		the	horse	PREP-A3SG-under		the	A3SG-burden

'The horse farted a lot under its burden.' {ELIC}

(Cojtí et al. 1998:250)

(36) *qitz'* 'squeak produced by chairs, beds, or loose cargo'

Ri ch'ich'	ch'at	yalan	ni-qitz'**iqöt**		taq	y-a-wär
the metal	bed	very	ICP-Ø-B3SG-squeak.repeatedly		when	ICP-B2SG-sleep

ch-u-wäch
PREP-A3SG-front

'The metal bed squeaks a lot when you sleep in it.'

While the semantic properties of these two derivations is currently unexplored, it is clear that there is a connection between pluractionals and ideophones. The next section, which focuses on Tseltal, explores this connection in more depth. In particular, Pérez González 2012 shows that expressive morphemes in Tseltal, many of which derive verb stems from ideophonic roots into, have pluractional semantics. These morphemes can thus be classified as pluractional affixes like those discussed in this section in Kaqchikel. Moreover, we will see that while many of these pluractional affixes are described as deriving event-internal pluractionals, the plural events they denote have different temporal profiles. While this kind of variation within a kind of pluractionality has not been documented for Kaqchikel, it is an attested feature of some languages with rich pluractional morphology.

3 TSELTAL CASE STUDY: STRUCTURING REPETITIONS IN TIME

The Kaqchikel case study has shown that Mayan languages instantiate the event-internal/event-external pluractional distinction. The goal of this section is to explore variation within these categories. For instance, two pluractionals that are grouped together under the previous section's diagnostics might still differ along other aspects of their meaning. Collins 2001 provides an example of this through his discussion of an event-internal pluractional in ‡Hoan (Kx'a) that requires the distribution of the plurality of events over multiple spatial locations, which is not the case for event-internal pluractional discussed in Kaqchikel. Another common point of variation within a class of pluractionals concerns the temporal structure of the plural events they denote. For instance, Van Geenhoven 2004 discusses a series of pluractionals in Kalaallisut which do not differ with respect to the event-internal/event-external distinction, but instead each pluractional affix structures, in fine-grained ways, how the repeated events are situated in time. We see precisely this phenomenon in Tseltal.

First, though, I want to briefly illustrate the contrast between event-internal and event-external pluractionals in Tseltal. Pérez González 2012 describes five suffixes in Tseltal (i.e., *-C₁on*, *-<j>awet*, *-Vnaj*, *-lajan*, and *-kVnaj*) that derive expressive predicates, but which also clearly have pluractional semantics. Moreover, Pérez González 2012 describes a split among these pluractional derivations that corresponds to the event-internal/event-external distinction. For instance, -C$_i$on is described as requiring the repetition of subevents of an event (which would correspond to subphases in the terminology used here), while -$<j>$awet involves repeated independent events. This corresponds to the distinction between event-internal and event-external pluractionality, which is reinforced in the following minimal pair.

TSELTAL (Pérez González 2012:217, ex.17)
(37) X-kot-**kon**-Ø=ix   te   alal=e
      NT-on.fours-C$_i$on-B3SG=already   DET   baby=ENC
      'The baby already crawls.'

(Pérez González 2012:217, ex.18)
(38) X-ko<**j**>t-**awet**-Ø=ix   te   alal=e
      NT-on.fours-**awet**-B3SG=already   DET   baby=ENC
      'The baby already gets up and sits down.'

As Pérez González 2012 notes, in example (37) a sequence of events of getting onto all fours is summed and presented as single event, namely an event of crawling. In contrast, example (38) presents each event of getting onto all fours as independent events which do not sum to something greater than its parts.

Additionally, the proposed event-internal pluractional -C$_i$on contrasts with other pluractionals in Tseltal with respect to tests that distinguish the two varieties of pluractionality. For instance, Pérez González (2012) describes the events that satisfy C$_i$on-marked predicates as occurring on a single occasion. In contrast, there are Tseltal pluractionals, like -Vlay, described by Polian (2013:350–1), which allow the repetitions to take place across longer periods of time, during an evening or across multiple days.

(Polian 2013:351, ex.10)
(39) Way-**ulay**-on   s-jun-al   ajk'bal.
      sleep-**Vlay**-B1[CP]   A3-one-ABST   night
      'I was sleeping and waking up all night.'

(Polian 2013:350, ex.7)
(40) Jay-eb=kati   k'aal   ya   x-jalaj-Ø   aw-u'un   ts'in   te   ya
      how.many-NUM=ADMIR   day   ICP   ICP-be.late-B3SG   A2-RN   well   DET   ICP
      a-ch'in-lo'-**ilay**-Ø?
      A2-DIM-eat-**Vlay**-B3SG
      'How many days will you go on eating it little by little.'

Some examples with -Vlay even appear to have a habitual reading, which is a core property of event-external pluractionality.

(Polian 2013:350, ex.6)
(41) Ya y-uts'in-**la**-on-ik.
      ICP A3-molestar-**Vlay**-B1-PL
      'They bother me all the time.'

These observations support a contrast between event-internal and event-external pluractionals in Tseltal. The former, exemplified by -C1on, involve repetitions of subphases of a single event on a single occasion, while the latter, exemplified by -Vlay, involves the repetition of independent events. Having illustrated an event-internal/event-external contrast in Tseltal, we can now focus on variation within these categories.

Pérez González 2012 describes three suffixes, -C1*on*, -V*naj*, and -*lajan*, as all involving the repetitions of subevents, that is, as event-internal pluractionals. They differ, though, crucially, in the temporal structure of those repetitions. For instance, -C1*on*, which we have already encountered, only requires sequential repetitions.

(Pérez González 2012:219, ex.23)
(42) X-k'oj-**k'on**-Ø   a   x-koy-Ø   ta   s-ol.
     NT-sound.obj.hitting-**C₁on**-B3SG   ICP   ICP-arrive-B3SG   PREP   A3SG-head
     'It went k'oj every little bit on his head.'

Pérez González 2012 shows that speakers judge (42) to be true in a situation where balls fall one by one from a shelf on to an individual's head. Thus, each knocking sound is kept separate, but there are apparently few constraints placed on the amount of downtime in between knocks. In contrast, the minimally different example (43) shows that -*lajan* imposes different constraints on the downtime between repetitions.

(Pérez González 2012:219, ex.24)
(43) X-k'oj-**lajan**-Ø   a   x-koy-Ø   ta   s-ol.
     NT-sound.obj.hitting-**lajan**-B3SG   ICP   ICP-arrive-B3SG   PREP   A3SG-head
     'It went k'oj in a chaotic manner on his head.'

– *lajan* requires chaotic repetitions, which Pérez González 2012 describes as both rapid and without predictable amounts of downtime between each event in the event-plurality. For instance, speakers say that (43) would be better used to characterize a scenario in which many balls come streaming off a shelf in waves knocking someone in the head.

Finally, Pérez González 2012 describes a form of event-internal pluractionality that imposes more structure on the downtime between repetitions than either two of the previous pluractionals. As shown in (44), -V*naj* actually requires periodic repetitions. That is, the amount of downtime between each event is fixed and equal.

(Pérez González 2012:222, ex.27)
(44) X-k'oj-**inaj**-Ø   ta   s-ol.
     NT-sound.obj.hitting-**inaj**-B3SG   PREP   A3SG-head
     'It sounded *k'oj* hitting his head.'

Supporting the requirement for periodicity is the fact that -V*naj* has an additional non-trivial visual component. When encountering an example like (44), speakers imagine the sound being produced by an oscillating object, for example, a ball that is bouncing up and down on a person's head at a constant rate. This example rounds out three subtypes of event-internal pluractionality in Tseltal, which differ in terms of how the downtime between repetitions is structured. The first affix, -C₁*on*, requires pauses; -*lajan* requires rapid aperiodic pauses; and -V*naj* requires periodic pauses. Tseltal, then, instantiates a kind of typologically attested variation within its event-internal pluractionals based on how the repeated events are spaced in time relative to each other.

Finally, the distinction between different types of verbal pluractionality-based structured down- time is actually recapitulated within Tseltal's system of ideophones. The core observation is that while the pluractional suffixes illustrated above apply to ideophonic roots, as well as verbal roots, ideophones can additionally undergo full reduplication, yielding a pluractional effect. Strikingly, the number of reduplications conditions the type of downtime required, allowing classes of reduplicated ideophones to be paired with classes of pluractional verb stems. The primary contrast is between ideophonic roots that have been reduplicated two times and those that have been reduplicated three times. Pérez González 2012 shows that when reduplicated twice, as in (45), the resulting stems have the same temporal profile as C1*on*-derived pluractionals. Here the speaker uses a twice-reduplicated ideophone *tat'umt'um* (which itself has a partially reduplicated base), to characterize an event that is otherwise described in the same clause by a C1*on*-derived pluractional verb. In particular, (45) describes a scenario where the wood is hit, generating a drum sound, repeatedly, but with pauses.

(Pérez González 2012:241, ex.60)
(45) Tat'umt'um-tat'umt'um   x-i-Ø,   s-tsan-tson-Ø.
      drum.sound-REDUP   NT-say-B3SG   NT-wood.sound-EXPR-B3SG
      'The hits to the wood went tat'umt'um, tat'umt'um repeatedly.'

In contrast, when reduplicated three times, the result is an ideophone that has the temporal profile of a *lajan*-derived pluractional. In fact, the following naturally occurring example shows a speaker equating the *lajan*-pluractional with the triple-reduplicated ideophone.

(Pérez González 2012:243, ex.62)
(46) Ja'-Ø   x-chak'-**lajan**-Ø   te   bay   chak'-chak'-chak'
      FOC-B3SG NT-sound.horse.hooves-**lajan**-B3SG DET where sound.metal-REDUP-REDUP
             x-chi-Ø=e, ma-uk.
             NT-say-B3SG=ENC NEG-IRR
      'The trotting of horses sounds *chak* when it goes *chakchakchak*, right?'

Just as with -*lajan*, a triple-reduplicated ideophone requires repetitions that recur quickly and in a chaotic manner. The data in (45)–(46) reinforce the generalization that frequency is a category that is pervasively grammaticized in Tseltal pluractionality. Pluractional forms are found in both the verbal and ideophonic domains with different morphology, but with similar semantic effects, in particular with respect to the temporal structure of the plural events they characterize.

To summarize, not only does Tseltal, like Kaqchikel, distinguish event-internal and event-external pluractionality, but the language has a variety of event-internal pluractionals. The variation we see across these pluractionals is similar to what is found in some other languages with rich pluractional systems, where two forms might require event-internal repetitions, but these repetitions must have different temporal profiles. Finally, while the pluractionals discussed in this section were selected because they illustrate an important kind of variation within the event-internal/event-external distinction, which has provided a framework for this chapter, as with Kaqchikel, there are other kind of pluractionals in Tseltal. Tseltal has multiple productive pluractionals derivations with distributive semantics (Polian 2013:353–60). For instance, -*tilay* affixes to both transitive and intransitive verbs. With transitive verbs like *il* 'see' in (47), it targets the object for a distributive interpretation. With intransitives, as in (48), there is distribution over an implicit spatial argument.

(Polian 2013:354, ex.16)
(47) Ya   jk-il-**tilay**-ex.
      ICP A1-ver-DIST-B2PL
      'I saw you all one by one.'

(Polian 2013:355, ex.23)
(48) Le   ya   x-'och-**tilay**-Ø   te   karo=e.
     there   ICP   ICP-enter-**DIST**-B3SG   DET   car=ENC
     'That's where the car goes in (via multiple roads).'

This is similar to the reading we get in (4) with the Kaqchikel pluractional -*la'*, which Henderson 2014 has argued is a distributive pluractional, though in (4), unlike in (48), the spatial distribution is constrained by the spatial extent of an argument. While exploring distributive pluractionals across the Mayan family must wait for future work, this observation indicates that similarities in the pluractional systems of Mayan languages may extend beyond the categories I have focused on here, namely the event-internal/event-external distinction.

4 CONCLUSIONS

Pluractionality in Mayan languages is currently under-documented. Even when a stem can be identified as a pluractional, there usually is not enough data to place it within its broader typological context. The goal for this chapter, then, was to provide an initial view of pluractionality in Mayan by examining pluractionals in two distantly related Mayan languages for which more extensive data exists.

One primary conclusion is that some Mayan languages are rich in pluractional derivations, and that this property is not restricted to one branch of the family. In a survey of 47 languages (which happened not to include any Mayan languages), Wood 2007 found that only six had more than two pluractional derivations. Strikingly, both Kaqchikel and Tseltal fit into the category of languages where pluractionality is highly coded, having many more than three such derivations. This is not true in every language in the family, though. For instance, England 1983:107 reports only one verbal derivation in Mam that could be treated as a marker of verbal plurality, namely the repetitive -*najee'*. While not all Mayan have rich pluractional morphology, the fact that some do makes Mayan languages a good testing ground for the study of pluractionality itself. The reason is that when analyzing crosslinguistic variation in pluractional semantics, it is often difficult to match up categories and run semantic tests across languages. With Mayan languages, though, this problem can be mitigated since one finds closely related languages with large numbers of pluractional derivations. This makes it is possible to look at variation in pluractional semantics across a single language or a group of closely related languages. This is what has been done in this chapter as a kind of proof of concept. What was found is that Mayan languages instantiate types of pluractionality familiar from typological work. Kaqchikel clearly exhibits a split between event-internal and event-external pluractionality. Furthermore, within those categories we also find the kinds of variation we expect. Tseltal, for instance, has a large number of event-internal pluractionals that differ in terms of how the downtime between repetitions is structured. In this way, Tseltal is similar to previously analyzed languages like Kalaallisut (Van Geenhoven 2004).

Finally, while the focus of this chapter has been to place Mayan pluractionality in its crosslinguistic context, Mayan languages have a great deal to give back to the understanding of pluractionality in general. A persistent question in the literature is whether pluractionality is related to other categories. Is it a kind of aspect? Is it a species of plurality akin to that which we find in the nominal domain? Mayan languages provide a unique perspective on these questions that has not yet been fully explored. In particular, the discussion of pluractionality in Tseltal shows its close connection to ideophone roots. Not only is there specialized reduplicative morphology for deriving pluractional ideophones, but its semantic properties can be correlated with those of bona fide verbal pluractionals. Similarly, the Kaqchikel examples in (43)–(44) belie a close connection between pluractionality and ideophones. This means that any theory of pluractionality will be constrained by facts about ideophones because it must be general enough to make sense of both pluractional verbs and pluractionality ideophones. For instance, if one thinks that pluractionality is a species of aspect, it must make sense to talk about aspect in the ideophone domain, and any resulting theory would need to explain why we observe pluractional aspect in ideophones but maybe not other kinds of aspect. Similarly, if one believes pluractionality is a kind of plural reference to events, it must make sense to talk about ideophones as being event-denoting in some way. Exploring this connection between pluractionality and ideophones in more detail, both more widely across the Mayan family and other languages, should be a major avenue for future work.

REFERENCES

Cojtí, Narciso, Martín Chacach, and Marcos Cali. 1998. *Diccionario Kaqchikel*. Guatemala: Cholsamaj.

Collins, Chris. 2001. "Aspects of plurality in ‡Hoan." *Language* 77: 456–76.

Cusic, David. 1981. "*Verbal plurality and aspect*." PhD diss., Stanford University.

England, Nora. 1983. *A grammar of Mam, a Mayan language*. Austin: University of Texas Press.

Garrett, Andrew. 2001. "Reduplication and infixation in Yurok: morphology, semantics, and diachrony." *International Journal of American Linguistics* 67: 264–312.

Henderson, Robert. 2012. "*Ways of pluralizing events*." PhD diss., University of California, Santa Cruz.

Henderson, Robert. 2014. "Dependent indefinites and their post-suppositions." *Semantics and Pragmatics* 7: 1–67.

Hendrick Krueger, Roberta A. 1986. "*The verbal category system of Cakchiquel Mayan*." PhD diss., University of Chicago.

Mithun, Marianne. 1988. "Lexical categories and the evolution of number marking." In *Theoretical morphology*, ed. by Michael Hammond and Michael Noonan, 211–34. New York: Academic Press.

Newman, Paul. 1980. *The classification of Chadic within Afroasiatic*. Leiden: Universitaire Pers Leiden.

Newman, Paul. 2012. "Pluractional verbs: An overview." In *Verbal plurality and distributivity*, ed. by Patricia Cabredo Hofherr and Brenda Laca, 185–210. Berlin: Walter de Gruyter.

Pérez González, Jaime. 2012. "*Predicados expresivos e ideófonos en tseltal*." MA thesis, CIESAS.

Polian, Gilles. 2013. *Gramática del tseltal de Oxchuc, Volume 1*. Mexico D.F.: Publicaciones de la Casa Chata.

Rothstein, Susan. 2004. *Structuring events: A study in the semantics of lexical aspect*. Oxford: Blackwell.

Van Geenhoven, Veerle. 2004. "For-adverbials, frequentative aspect, and pluractionality." *Natural Language Semantics* 12: 135–90.

Wood, Esther Jane. 2007. "*The semantic typology of pluractionality*." PhD diss., University of California, Berkeley.

PART 4

LANGUAGE IN CONTEXT

CHAPTER 15

THE LABYRINTH
OF DIVERSITY
The sociolinguistics of Mayan languages

Sergio Romero

1 WHERE ARE WE IN MAYA SOCIOLINGUISTICS?[1]

In order to be as inclusive as possible, I chose an ecumenical definition of Mayan socio-linguistics: the study of the interrelationship between language variation and social life among the Maya. From this vantage point, the literature is substantial, although uneven in quality, theoretical framework and regional focus.

The rubric "sociolinguistic" encompasses different scholarly traditions and methods studying the relationship between language variation and society. First, variationist soci-olinguistics focuses on the effects of society on language, concentrating on naturally occurring speech or – in variationist parlance- linguistic variables in relation to rele-vant social and cultural constraints influencing their particular realizations (Labov 1994). Variationists use substantial corpora involving large numbers of speakers, sociolinguis-tic interviews and/or recordings of naturally occurring speech. The goal is to identify, describe and explain social patterns of linguistic variation with the help of statistical tools. The object of study is the speech community rather than the grammar or commu-nicative competence of particular "consultants" (e.g. DeChicchis 1989; Romero 2006, 2009, 2012a, 2015b).

In contrast, research in the tradition of sociology of language, or the study of the effects of language on society, while much more prolific in Mayan studies than variationist soci-olinguistics, usually does not examine actual speech. Based on the seminal work of schol-ars like Joshua Fishman, it focuses on questions of language shift and bilingualism with a descriptive or diagnostic perspective based on surveys (Fishman 1972), e.g. in the work of Stross (1973), Collins (1988, 2005), Crossley (1989). Lewis (2001), Whiteside (2007). In the Mayan area such studies have often been carried out in Spanish by researchers not fluent in the languages they study.

In more traditional sociolinguistic disciplines such as dialectology, the study of dialect differentiation as a function of both geographic and social factors, and which embraced variationist methods decades ago, Mayanists have preferred traditional survey methods (Chambers and Trudgill 1980). The boundaries between dialect areas are usually defined in categorical rather than quantitative terms and phonology and lexicon are privileged over syntax and discourse as diagnostics (e.g. Campbell 1973, 1974, 1977; Godfrey and Collins 1987; Becker Richards and Cahuec 1994; Par Sapón and Can Pixabaj 2000; Caz Cho 2007). Rarely are dialect boundaries analyzed in quantitative rather than categorical terms (Leonard and Tuyuc Sucuc 2009; Romero 2009, 2015b).

Considerable work on stylistic variation has been done, some of which is outstanding in theoretical scope and depth of ethnographic analysis. Most of it, however, has been done by linguistic anthropologists and is partly covered elsewhere in this volume.

Another area of much active publication is language revitalization. Stimulated by the rise of the Maya movement in Guatemala, scholars have published many studies examining the goals and impact of linguistic revitalization in various Mayan languages, especially in Guatemala. Maya intellectuals have also published books and articles documenting the marginalization of Mayan languages in Guatemalan and Mexico (e.g. Cojtí 1995, 2006; England 1996, 2003; Maxwell 1996; Jiménez 1997; Choi 2003, 2011; French 2010; Berkley 2001).

Finally, some studies of language contact have examined questions of historical linguistics from a sociolinguistic perspective. This work includes both the comparative study of structural and lexical borrowing as well as research on code switching between Mayan languages and Spanish or English (e.g. Pfeiler 1988, 2014; Brody 1987, 1995; Furbee 2000; Wichmann 2003; Romero 2006; Law 2014).

Regarding regional scope, the sociolinguistic literature is rather uneven. On the one hand, there are few published studies on languages with relatively small speaker populations such as Ixil, Awakatek, Q'anjob'al, Poqom, Uspantek, Ch'ol and Wastek. On the other, research on major languages such as K'iche', Q'eqchi', Kaqchikel and Yucatec is substantial but not always representative of their great regional diversity. There are few systematic studies of the cultural and sociopolitical roles of regional variation in Mayan languages. An uneven coverage and the lack of appropriate typologies to theorize and classify the diversity of sociolinguistic situations in the Maya area are two of the most urgent gaps in Mayan sociolinguistics.

In the next section, I summarize what we know about the interrelationship of structural change in Mayan languages and the social life of the Maya based on the contributions of variationist sociolinguistics; subsequent sections discuss other approaches to the study of Mayan languages and social life

2 SOCIETY AND LANGUAGE VARIATION IN MAYAN

Although few scholars have approached the study of Mayan languages from a variationist perspective, variationists have made important contributions to the field. In particular, they have documented the role of social meaning, discourse and ethnicity as forces driving the diversification of Mayan languages. Joseph DeChicchis's work on Q'eqchi' is perhaps the first formally variationist study of a Mayan language (DeChicchis 1989). Q'eqchi' is the Mayan language with the largest territorial expansion in Guatemala. Today there are substantial Q'eqchi'-speaking populations in the departments of Baja and Alta Verapaz, Izabal, Quiché and Petén as well as in Toledo District, Belize. DeChicchis's dissertation comparatively examines a sample of phonological, morphological and syntactic variables and their social distribution. Over two years in the mid-eighties he performed systematic surveys and sociolinguistic interviews in various communities across the wide Q'eqchi' geography. DeChicchis was the first sociolinguist to examine the Q'eqchi' pattern of variation across national boundaries, comparing data from Petén, Guatemala, and Toledo District, Belize. He identified San Pedro Carchá, Guatemala, as the source of the expanding affricate allophone of /t/ and noted a number of innovations in Belizean varieties including an ongoing reinterpretation of the distant past as a narrative marker (DeChicchis 1989). He was also the first Mayanist to identify changes in progress based on quantitative differences between speakers. Although somewhat lacking in detail, his analysis of aspect and tense markers in Belize pioneered the use of quantitative methods for the study of verbal morphology in Mayan (DeChicchis 1989). DeChicchis's work suggests possible diachronic trajectories for the diversification of aspect marking, which shows substantial variation in Mayan. Cobán Q'eqchi' – the most studied Q'eqchi' dialect- has two different completive forms, sometimes labeled as "recent" and "distant past" markers in the literature (Haeserijn 1966; Tzul and Tzimaj Cacao 1997; Stewart 1980:58–62). In contrast, other K'iche'an languages, such as Kaqchikel and K'iche', have only one incompletive marker (see Table 15.1).

Table 15.1 shows that whereas Cobán Q'eqchi' has different recent /x-/ and distant /k-/ forms, K'iche' and Kaqchikel do not make the same distinction morphologically. Comparing data from his own interviews in Belize and Cobán as well as seventeenth- and eighteenth-century doctrinal texts, DeChicchis suggests, first, that /k-/ has been reinterpreted in Belize as a habituative marker, and, second, that /x-/ is becoming the sole completive marker, which DeChicchis calls "past tense". According to DeChicchis, /k-/ preserves its original completive role in a very small number of contexts. The habituative innovation is probably the result of contact and dialect leveling among migrants speaking different Q'eqchi' varieties in Belize and pushes the Q'eqchi' verbal paradigm in the direction of its sister K'iche'an languages (see Table 15.1) (DeChicchis 1989:75–98). DeChicchis's work complements the research of historical linguists who have documented the diachronic evolution of aspect in Mayan, identifying precise discourse contexts and social scenarios where the reinterpretation and diversification of aspect markers occurred (Bricker 1981; Robertson 1992; Bohnemeyer 2002).

Variationists have also contributed to clarify the relation between the emergence and diffusion of linguistic innovations and their social role. Sergio Romero's research on K'ichee', for example, examines phonological, lexical and syntactic variation, its sociocultural meaning and pragmatic role. Focusing on the Santa Maria Chiquimula (MAR) and Nahualá varieties, Romero identifies various changes in progress and examines the discourse roles of various sociolinguistic stereotypes, indices that are overt topic of metalinguistic discourse (Labov 1994:78; Romero 2006, 2009, 2012a, 2015b). The intervocalic allophony of /l/, for example, is an innovation of MAR in which the fricative allophone [ð] acts as an ethnic marker explicitly referenced as such by Chiquimulas – natives of Santa María Chiquimula- themselves. Specifically, /l/ is variably realized as [ð] in the following intervocalic environments: a_a, o_o and i_a (see Table 15.2) (Romero 2009).

TABLE 15.1 SOME EXAMPLES OF INCOMPLETIVE MARKING IN K'ICHE'AN LANGUAGES

Aspect	Cobán Q'eqchi'	K'iche'	Kaqchikel
Recent	xinb'atzun	xinetz'anik	xinetz'an
	x-in-b'atzun	x-in-etz'an-ik	x-in-etz'an
	RPST-ABS1SG-play	CP-ABS1SG-play-PF	CP-ABS1SG-play
	'I played'	'I played'	'I played'
Distant	kinb'atzun		
	k-in-b'atzun		
	DPST-ABS1SG -play		
	'I played'		

(DPST Distant Past; RPST Recent Past)

TABLE 15.2 EXAMPLES OF INTERVOCALIC ALLOPHONY OF /L/ IN MAR

Liquid	Fricative	Gloss
ala	aða	'boy'
xinalaxik	xinaðaxik	'I was born'
je na la'	jenða'	'thus'
utz b'a la'	utz b'a ða	'That's fine.'
jolom	joðom	'head'
tz'olom	tz'oðom	'wood plank'
chila'	chiða'	'over there'
ucholajil	uchoðajil	'its way'
loq'olaj	loq'oðaj	'holy'

(Stress usually falls on the last syllable in K'iche')
(Romero 2009:285)

Phonetically, this is a case of variable assibilation of intervocalic /l/, a rare phenomenon cross-linguistically (Levy 1979; Starks and Ballard 2005). The quantitative pattern of variation strongly suggests that it is a change in progress in MAR. The fricative allophone is significantly more frequent in the speech of women and men under thirty years old. The higher frequency among women mirrors a local division of labor in cultural reproduction in which women are expected to be the primary carriers and transmitters of the emblems of traditional culture such as the traditional outfit and local dialect (Romero 2006, 2009, 2015b). Fricative /l/ is construed as a sociolinguistic stereotype both by Chiquimulas and by residents of neighboring townships such as Momostenango and San Antonio Ilotenango (see Figure 15.1). The social role of idiosyncratic innovations is a powerful force for the diffusion of language changes among the highland Maya.

The interaction between social meaning and linguistic innovation may also be seen in the emergence of Lowland Q'eqchi' (LQ), a distinctive variety acting as a regional marker for second-generation migrants in the lowlands of Alta Verapaz and Petén, Guatemala (Romero 2012b). Structurally, LQ is a Western dialect lacking the phonological and lexical stereotypes associated with highland Q'eqchi' townships. Highland stereotypes include the trilled articulation of /r/, which is emblematic of Cobán, and the unrounded articulation of /k/ in kiib' "two", a stereotype of San Juan Chamelco[2] (Becker Richards and Cahuec 1994; Romero 2012b). LQ is an ethnic and a generational register indexing a positive stance vis-à-vis lowland migrant society and a stereotype of second-generation migrants. The former continue to speak as highlanders, the latter avoid highland "accents". The leveling of highland varieties in LQ therefore responded to social rather than internal structural factors as it targeted salient ethnolinguistic stereotypes (Romero 2012b).

Not every ongoing change in Mayan is directly related to social deixis or ethnic boundary work,[3] however. K'iche', for example, has undergone a series of profound changes in the syntax of negative clauses, which do not seem to be acting as sociolinguistic markers or stereotypes. First, negation marking went from simplex to bipartite; second, in some dialects, such as MAR, an idiosyncratic form of negative concord emerged in the last century (Dahl 1979; Romero 2012a, 2015a). The changes began in the middle of the sixteenth century and are reflected in the substantial corpus of K'iche' manuscripts produced

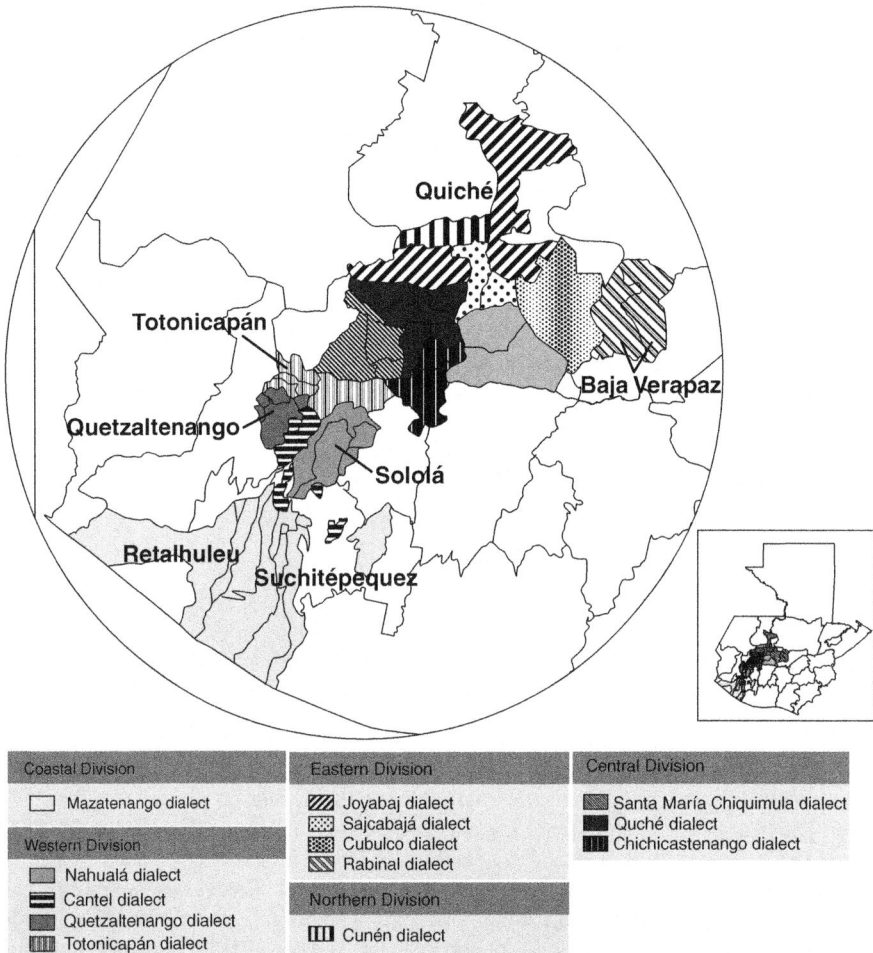

FIGURE 15.1 MAP OF DIALECT GEOGRAPHY OF K'ICHE' MAYAN

in the sixteenth and seventeenth centuries. Romero (2012a) succinctly summarizes this diachronic progression as a Mayan version of the process known in historical linguistics as Jespersen's Cycle. In Jespersen's Cycle a negator preceding the predicate head is grammaticalized as an optional marker after a nominal form variably used for emphasis, and is reinterpreted as the sole required negator (van der Auwera 2009).

COLONIAL K'ICHE' (16th century) (Anonymous 1701–1703:3r)
(1) Mak'u xutzinik xech'awik.
    mak'u x-utzin-ik   x-e-ch'aw-ik
    NEG   CP-succeed-PF   CP-ABS3PL-speak-PF
    'They did not succeed in speaking!'

MODERN K'ICHE'
(2) (Man) ajtij   ta   le   Te'k.
    Man ajtij   ta   le   Te'k
    NEG1 teacher NEG2 DET Diego
    'Diego is not a teacher'.

In colonial K'iche' the solo negator was the form *man* preceding the predicate head as in (1); in Modern K'iche', however, negation is bipartite with an optional negative marker preceding the predicate head and the actual negator following it. Whereas *man*, or its regional variant *na*, acts as an optional marker in (2), *ta* is the required negator following the nominal head *ajtij* "teacher". This chain of syntactic changes was the result of the cumulative transformation of emphasis in negation, leading to the progressive abandonment of particular forms of unmarked negation and the transformation of the emphatic form into the default negative construction (Romero 2012a).

Syntactic change in Mayan can be the result of contact with other languages as well. For example, the emergence of negative concord in some K'iche' dialects seems to be the consequence of contact with Spanish. In MAR, additional copies of the negator *ta* appear in every clause boundary to the right of the predicate head.

(3) (Manuel, 25 years old, Santa María Chiquimula)
    Le tixob'al, xqaj   ta chi   nuwach   taj.
    Le   tixob'al, x-Ø-qaj   ta   chi   nu-wach   taj.
    DET   school   CP-ABS3SG-fall   NEG2   LOC   ERG1SG-face   NEG2
    'School, I didn't like it'.

In (3), in addition to the negator *ta* in its normal collocation after the predicate head *xqaj*, the reader will notice an additional copy after the prepositional phrase *chi nuwach*. Semantically there is only one negation in the clause: the two negators do not cancel each other. The pattern is similar to that of Spanish double negatives, in which optional negative polarity items (NPIs) such as *nada* "nothing" or *nunca* "never" optionally appear to the right of the predicate head. For example, in *Yo no se nada* "I don't know anything", the NPI *nada* "nothing" appears to the right of the verb in addition to the standard negator *no* preceding it. This apparent syntactic convergence led Romero (2015a) to suggest that the emergence of negative concord in MAR was a reinterpretation of the syntax of negation triggered by contact with Spanish. Indeed, many MAR speakers are Spanish bilinguals who engage in K'iche'-Spanish code switching (Romero 2006, 2015b). Double and triple negatives are significantly more frequent in the younger age groups, precisely those with more contact with Spanish. Unlike the allophony of intervocalic /l/, however, negative concord does not seem to be an ethnolinguistic stereotype (Romero 2015b). This shows again that structural changes in Mayan are not necessarily related to ethnic identification, although the changes in discourse patterns that enable them are socially motivated. MAR is the only documented case of negative concord in Mayan (Romero 2015a). Syntactic changes motivated by contact do not necessarily presuppose a defective knowledge of the relevant Mayan language but a confluence of bilinguals' cognitive strategies seeking to maximize the efficiency of syntactic processing as well as the emerging sociolinguistic value of word order alternations (Satterfield and Barrett 2004).

Variationist research shows that social factors are crucial motivators of structural change in Mayan languages. Innovations are used to mark emerging social distinctions in Maya communities. Structural changes are often substantial and sometimes respond to contact with other languages. Variationist research highlights Mayan as a dynamic and innovative linguistic family that contrasts with the caricature of immobility and static tradition often attached to Maya peoples.

3 LANGUAGE VITALITY AND SHIFT

Mirroring social scientists' interest in the process of modernization in Maya communities in the last century, substantial research has been done on the impact of bilingualism on the use of Mayan languages (Stross 1973; Crossley 1989; García Hernández 1989; Peñalosa 1989; Langan 1990; Brown 1991; Menchú and Telón de Xulú 1993; Richards and Richards 1998; Lewis 2001; Güemez Pineda 2007). This work is fundamentally sociological in method and relies on community surveys in which speakers are asked to assess their competence in their native language and in Spanish. In some cases, these methods are complemented with observations of speaker interactions in particular contexts such as homes and markets (Knowles-Berry 1987; Brown 1991; Lewis 2001; Choi 2003; Collins 2005; Maddox 2010).

In vitality, geographic extension and number of speakers Mayan languages show substantial differences. Whereas Mam, K'iche', Kaqchikel and Yucatec Maya, for example, boast hundreds of thousands of speakers, Itzaj has only a handful of elderly speakers left (Collins 1988; Hofling 1996; Sullivan 2000; Richards 2003). Some Mayan languages, such as K'iche' and Kaqchikel are spoken by diverse congeries of ethnic groups in large and equally diverse territories, others are spoken only in small geographic spaces by a relatively small, ethnically homogeneous population. This is the case for Sakapultek and Sipakapense in the departments of Quiché and San Marcos, Guatemala, respectively (Becker Richards and Cahuec 1994; Barrett 1999; Richards 2003; Shoaps 2009a, b).

Mayan languages are not recognized as co-official by national governments and are often stigmatized by the non-Maya. They are generally absent from national state institutions, universities and businesses and their public use is limited to the local community, regional markets, traditional institutions and/or the household. Even in spaces where Mayan languages were dominant only a few decades ago, such as weekly plaza markets, they often co-exist with Spanish (Crossley 1989; García Hernández 1989; Brown 1991; Brody 1995; Cojtí 1995; Jiménez 1997; Pfeiler 1999; Sullivan 2000; Briceño 2002; England 2003; Collins 2005; Choi 2011; French 2010).

Spanish fluency has rapidly expanded in the last sixty years and Spanish has become the primary language of many Maya, especially in urban areas and among high school and college graduates. Language shift is widespread in metropolitan areas such as Guatemala City or Quetzaltenango (Brown 1991; Menchú and Telón de Xulú 1993; Bastos and Camus 1995; Lewis 2001; French 2010). Spanish fluency is not uniform in Maya communities, however. Men generally show higher proficiency than women. They are expected to travel for work outside their communities and often benefit from better educational opportunities. In contrast, women are expected to do reproductive work at home and generally have a more restricted access to schools and universities. With fewer opportunities to learn and practice, it is not surprising than they are generally less Spanish proficient than men. This unequal access to Spanish is mirrored also in higher levels of Mayan language monolingualism among women, especially in rural areas (Rosenbaum 1993; Asturias de Barrios 1994; Richards 2003).

Language shift looms larger in urban than in rural settings. In large towns many residents have only a passive knowledge of the local Mayan language and children are often raised in Spanish by parents concerned that knowledge of their native language might interfere with the acquisition of Spanish, the language of social mobility and prestige. It is not uncommon for children, however, to learn the local language from grandparents and other older relatives despite parental qualms. Language shift is especially noticeable in large commercial, industrial and tourism hubs, towns near major highways and in areas with large non-indigenous migrant populations such as Quetzaltenango in the western highlands of Guatemala, Escuintla on the southern piedmont of Guatemala, and in cities in Yucatan as well on the eastern seaboard of the peninsula (Re Cruz 1996; Sullivan 2000; Grandin 2000; Lewis 2001; French 2010; Pfeiler 2014). However, there is evidence that the impact of language shift may sometimes be exaggerated in the literature. Reliance on surveys in Spanish and speaker self-reports, rather than long-term ethnographic observation of actually occurring linguistic interactions, sometimes compromises scholars' ability to understand the social and discursive roles of Mayan languages in bilingual communities. Ethnographic research has falsified some alarmist claims of imminent language shift as in Marc Maddox's and Walter Little's research on Kaqchikel in San Antonio Aguascalientes, Guatemala, which showed contra Brown (1991) that Kaqchikel is still a vital language and an important economic resource in this community of weavers and itinerant merchants (Little 2009; Maddox 2010). Colloquial interaction in many Maya communities increasingly involves hybrid repertoires. Code switching and intensive borrowing from Spanish are common in the speech of many native speakers (Brody 1987, 1995; Bolle 2000; Furbee 2000; Collins 2005; Romero 2015b). Maya and Spanish language ideologies cast a positive eye on purist linguistic performance and frown upon hybrid speech, stigmatizing code switching and the use of Spanish loanwords despite their ubiquity. This sometimes leads to self-reports that denigrate the speaker's competence in the local language (Maxwell 1996; Berkley 2001; French 2010; Romero 2015b).

Finally, schools have generally had a deleterious effect on Mayan languages. Until recently Maya children were discouraged if not punished for speaking their native language in school. Mayan languages were not only excluded from the classroom but also actively stigmatized by teachers, who were usually not indigenous. Until intercultural bilingual education programs were introduced in the 1990s in Guatemala, bilingual education was transitional: its explicit goal was the development of literacy skills that could later be transferred to Spanish. It did not seek to promote literacy and the creation of systematic educational programs in Mayan languages but saw itself as a pedagogical strategy to develop Spanish proficiency. As a result, very few Maya are literate in their native language and many regard writing in Mayan languages as intrinsically more difficult than writing in Spanish (Richards and Richards 1996a; Jiménez 1997; Cojtí 2006; French 2010).

The introduction of intercultural bilingual educations programs in primary and secondary schools in the mid-1990s was one of the major successes of the Maya movement in Guatemala (Jiménez 1997; Bastos and Camus 2003b; England 2003; Cojtí 2006; French 2010). Also, the creation of the *K'ulb'il Yol Twitz Paxil* (Academia de Lenguas Mayas de Guatemala (ALMG)) led to the adoption of a unified alphabet for the Mayan languages spoken in Guatemala. It also stimulated the development of pan-dialectal, standardized varieties to be used in writing (Richards 1989; England 1996; Maxwell 1996; Jiménez 1997). The adoption of standardized forms, however, has met with some local resistance. In K'iche', for example, local varieties act as ethnolinguistic markers and speakers sometimes perceive standardized pronunciations as strange and claim that they do not accurately represent local speech. The local branches of the Academy of Mayan languages – known as "linguistic communities" – play a central role in educating speakers in the value of pan-dialectal forms. They also provide a venue for the expansion of literacy and for the publication of texts in and on Mayan languages (Romero 2015b). In

Mexico, writers' workshops in Chiapas and Yucatan play a similar role. In fact, scores of books of different genres including novels, poetry and narrative have been published in Tseltal, Tsotsil, Chol and Yucatec Maya. Intercultural bilingual education, however, has not yet been able to reverse the marginalization of Mayan languages as it is still marred by the lack of infrastructure, pedagogical resources and trained teachers (Richards and Richards 1996a; Berkley 2001; England 2003; French 2010; Romero 2015b).

4 LIVELIHOOD, MIGRATIONS, AND LANGUAGE SHIFT

The social dislocation provoked by rapid economic change has had a negative impact on the vitality of Mayan languages. For example, despite a large number of speakers, Yucatec Maya is undergoing rapid language shift (Pfeiler 1999; Sullivan 2000; Briceño 2002). Many children are no longer socialized in Yucatec in urban areas of the states of Yucatan, Campeche and Quintana Roo. The negative impact of the tourism industry is especially dire in eastern Yucatan and Quintana Roo, culturally and linguistically conservative areas, which became overnight the hub of the so-called Maya Riviera[4] and its massive tourism influx. In towns catering to tourists along the coast Yucatec Maya is rarely transmitted to children (Pfeiler 1988; Re Cruz 1996; Sullivan 2000; Hofling 2004; Güemez Pineda 2007).

Nevertheless, despite the marginalization and the lack of substantial government support for bilingual education in both Mexico and Guatemala, most Mayan languages continue to be used as primary languages in their communities. Hundreds of thousands of Maya children are socialized in the local language rather than in Spanish. As of 2015, only two Mayan languages are completely extinct: Chicomuceltec, formerly spoken in the state of Chiapas, Mexico, whose last speakers died in the 1970s, and Cholti', which became extinct in the late eighteenth century (Campbell and Canger 1978; Robertson, Law and Haertel 2010). Also, Itzaj, spoken in the township of San José Petén on the shores of Lake Petén Itzá in the department of Petén, Guatemala, is seriously threatened. The last remaining fluent speakers are elderly and the language is no longer taught to children despite irregular classroom instruction offered at local schools (Hofling 1996). Mochó, spoken in Chiapas, is also in a critical situation with fifteen and eleven fluent speakers left in each of its two regional varieties (Jaime Pérez González, Pers. Comm.: 2015). Not all Mayan languages are in such dire straits, however. In contrast to Itzaj, Q'eqchi' is actually expanding in territory and number of speakers. Massive migrations from the Q'eqchi' heartland in Alta Verapaz since the late nineteenth century to the lowlands of the departments of Quiché, Izabal and Petén have led to a spectacular increase of the territory inhabited by the Q'eqchi'. The expansion included Toledo District in Belize, where Q'eqchi' speakers from San Pedro Carchá, Guatemala, started to migrate in the late nineteenth century. Q'eqchi' has become a regional lingua franca in Baja and Alta Verapaz in north-central Guatemala, where both *ladinos* and Poqomchis often speak it as a second language (Romero 2012b). In townships such as Tucurú and Senahú in Alta Verapaz where Poqomchi' used to be the primary language, Q'eqchi' has all but displaced it (King 1974; Schwartz 1990; Kahn 2006; Grandia 2009; Romero 2012b).

In the last four decades hundreds of thousands of Maya have moved to the United States where many remain as either legal immigrants or undocumented workers. The majority have established themselves near friends and relatives, forming populous congregations in cities across North America. Thousands of Yucatec, Akatek, Q'anjob'al and K'iche' speakers have moved to Los Angeles, Florida and Providence, for example (Burns 1993; Whiteside 2006; Foxen 2007). Mayan languages continue to be spoken by migrants and are sometimes heard in radio broadcasts and social events in places as diverse as Los Angeles, New York and Houston, Texas. Many Maya with only marginal knowledge of Spanish, the language of the Latin American immigrant worker economy, become fluent in the United States. It is unclear what the linguistic consequences of this massive migration are, however, but it seems that it does not necessarily change speaker attitudes about Mayan languages. Maya migrants incorporate English to their linguistic repertoire in addition to Spanish, but continue to speak and teach Mayan languages to their children after they return home. Maya children socialized in the United States, however, often have only a passive knowledge of their parents' language, as is often the case with the children of first generation migrants in the United States (Peñalosa 1989; Burns 1993; Foxen 2007; Whiteside 2007; Falla 2008).

5 REGIONAL VARIATION AND DIALECTOLOGY

Mayan languages boast a surprising degree of regional variation in lexicon, phonology, morphology and syntax. Dialectal differences are such that they sometimes interfere with mutual intelligibility between speakers. This is unexpected; however, given that intense contact between neighboring areas and long distance trade have been the rule in the Maya world, not the exception, according to archaeologists and historians. The Maya highlands seem to falsify the claim that geographic isolation is a necessary condition for substantial dialect diversification. Two social factors seem crucial in the diversification of Mayan languages: First, the lack of standardized forms imposed by the state before and after the Spanish invasion favors the unimpeded diffusion of local innovations. Standardized forms have only recently been introduced in schools and have not yet modified language practices in substantial ways. Second, regional differences act as ethnic stereotypes marking the speech of distinct townships and ethnic groups. The majority of the highland Maya, for example, are descendants of ancient confederations of lineages called *amaq'*, each with a distinct history and identity going back hundreds if not thousands of years. Regional linguistic stereotypes embody this long history and social identifications (Carmack 1981; Becker Richards and Richards 1987; Jones 1998; Van Akkeren 2000; Romero 2012b, 2015b).

Not all regional differences are the result of local innovation, however. Language contact also plays an important role. For example, K'iche' loanwords act as lexical stereotypes distinguishing the Nebaj and Cotzal Ixil varieties. Core kin terms, for example, are K'iche' etyma in Cotzal as can be seen in Table 15.3.

What distinguishes the loanwords in Table 15.3 from other words in the Ixil lexicon is their role as sociolinguistic stereotypes in Cotzal. Nebaj has borrowed extensively from K'iche' as well; however, in contrast with Cotzal, most K'iche' loanwords there go unrecognized as such.[5] Cotzal seems to have been in close contact with K'iche' speakers as early as the Early post-Classic (900–1250 CE). Archaeological sites such as Vicaveval, northeast of the Cotzal township seat, show architectural features emblematic of the K'iche' such as fortified constructions rather than the open plazas prevalent in the rest of Ixil country. The Ixil at large were conquered by K'iq'ab', who led the expansion of the K'iche' confederacy, prior to 1475. Lists of tributaries from the seventeenth and eighteenth centuries attest to K'iche'an lineage names in Cotzal but not in other Ixil towns (Colby and Van den Berghe 1969; Durocher 2002; Van Akkeren 2005:41, 71–6).

Another example of regional differences likely due to differential language contact is the split between Western and Eastern Q'eqchi'. It has been suggested that the phonological contrasts between them may be the result of recent contact with Ch'olan languages

TABLE 15.3 SOME K'ICHE' LOANWORDS IN IXIL

Nebaj Ixil (Cedillo Chel and Ramírez 1999)	Cotzal Ixil (PRECMI 1995)	K'iche'	Gloss
tx'utx'	naan	naan	'mother'
b'aal	taat	taat	'father'
ixqeel	ixoj	ixoq	'wife'
q'eena'j	po't	po't	'huipil' (traditional blouse)
chik	uuq	uuq	'corte' (traditional skirt)

TABLE 15.4 SOUND DIFFERENCES BETWEEN WESTERN AND EASTERN Q'EQCHI'

Western	Eastern
w > kᵘ/_ V	w
y >tʸ/_ V	y
t	/t/ > ʧ.ts/_ V
ɓ	/ɓ/ > ∅/_ #

(Becker and Cahuec 1994)

in areas where Eastern Q'eqchi' is predominant today (Thompson 1930; Becker Richards and Cahuec 1994).

As can be seen in Table 15.4, the semi-consonantal segments /w/ and /y/ underwent fortition to [kᵘ] and [tʸ] in Western Q'eqchi'; while the occlusive /t/ is palatalized to [ʧ] before vowels in eastern dialects. The latter is probably the result of contact with Ch'ol, which was spoken until the late eighteenth century in areas where Eastern Q'eqchi' is spoken today (Thompson 1930; Van Akkeren 2012). In fact, in Modern Ch'ol palatalization continues to be a common phonological process (Vázquez Álvarez 2011), although it seemed lacking in colonial Ch'olti', which was presumably more closely related to the variety with which Q'eqchi' must have been in contact (Robertson et al. 2010).

The diachronic diffusion of palatalization of word-initial /k/ in K'iche', documented by Lyle Campbell, was another change triggered by language contact. The source seems to have been Mam, spoken in western Guatemala. In Western K'iche' velar consonants such as /k/ are palatalized before non-low vowels as in kej [kʸe:x] "deer" and kaib' [kʸe:ɓ] "two" (Campbell 1977, 1974). Campbell notes that manuscripts written in K'iche' in the sixteenth century do not distinguish palatalized from non-palatalized consonants, but those from the seventeenth century do, leading him to suggest that palatalization started in the late sixteenth century. Its subsequent eastward diffusion was probably helped by migrations in the wake of the Spanish conquest (Campbell 1974). In Achi, closely related to K'iche' and spoken in central Guatemala, the palatalized variety is incipient today (Diego Alburez, personal communication: 2012). Neither Poqomchi' nor Q'eqchi', both of which are spoken north of the Achi area in the neighboring department of Alta Verapaz, show similar palatalization patterns (Campbell 1974).

Most dialectology studies in Mayan focus on documenting variation in particular languages and in identifying dialect areas based on appropriate diagnostics (Campbell 1973, 1974, 1977; Godfrey and Collins 1987; Cojtí and López 1990; Becker Richards and Cahuec 1994; Pfeiler 1999, Par Sapón and Can Pixabaj 2000; Patal Majtzul, García Matzar, and Espantzay Serech 2000; Pérezl, García Jiménez, and Jiménez 2000; Caz

Cho 2007). Cahuec and Richards's work on Q'eqchi', for example, identifies two dialect areas – Eastern and Western – based on four phonological correspondences and a number of lexical differences (see Table 15.4) (Becker Richards and Cahuec 1994). In Yucatan, Barbara Pfeiler's excellent dialect surveys and the publications of several native speaker linguists have identified a series of east-west isoglosses in phonology and lexicon, as well as several localized innovations in syntax (Pfeiler 1999; Briceño 2002; Pfeiler and Hofling 2006). Pfeiler and Hofling (2006) also document a number of idiomatic expressions, which act as regional markers (see Table 15.5).

Pfeiler and Hofling (2006) is not a quantitative study but succeeds in showing consistent differences between the two areas. Interestingly, the geographic distribution of the diagnostics seems to match speakers' metalinguistic expectations. The variants listed in Table 15.5 are not mutually exclusive, however; both are often found in any particular community. This suggests that dialect boundaries are not categorical but quantitative, forming gradual continua. Specific areas may differ in the frequency with which each of the alternatives is chosen.

Not every language has received equal attention in Mayan dialectology. As is often the case in Mayan linguistics, the four languages with the largest number of speakers in Guatemala (K'ichee', Mam, Kaqchikel and Q'eqchi') as well as Yucatec Maya in Mexico have the lion's share (Campbell 1973, 1974, 1977; Collins 1988; DeChicchis 1989; Cojtí and López 1990; England 1990; Kaufman 1990; Becker Richards and Cahuec 1994; Par Sapón and Can Pixabaj 2000; Patal Majtzul et al. 2000; Pérez et al. 2000; Briceño 2002; Pfeiler and Hofling 2006; Romero 2006, 2009, 2012b; Caz Cho 2007). Several recent publications by native speaker linguists, however, have contributed enormously to identify the phonological, morphological and syntactic variables involved in regional variation in Popti', Q'anjob'al, Mam, Kaqchikel, K'iche' and Q'eqchi'. These works are often the first to document syntactic variation systematically, providing numerous examples of non-canonical word order in clauses and sentences and laying the groundwork for a more systematic study of discourse, style and syntactic variation in Mayan (England 1987, 1989, 1990, 1991; Malchic Nicolás et al. 2000; Raymundo González et al. 2000; Ross Montejo and Delgado Rojas 2000). Nora England's work on Mam (e.g. 1989, 1990), in particular, is seminal in the study of syntactic variation in Mayan. She documents several syntactic variables, including the complex patterns of variation in the negation of non-NP predicates, in which different dialects treat different types or moods in different ways. There is substantial variation in aspect/mood marking as well. Unlike the Ostuncalco and Tacaná dialects, Ixtahuacán lumps futures and imperatives, for example. Fronting shows quite substantial variation in Mam too. For example, in Ixtahuacán and Ostuncalco fronted objects are preceded by the particle *aa* without further modifications of the sentence (see (4) (England 1989:294–7)).

TABLE 15.5 SOME IDIOMATIC AND LEXICAL DIFFERENCES BETWEEN WESTERN AND EASTERN YUCATEC

Western	Eastern	Gloss
ma'alob'	*uts*	'good'
uts tin chi'	*ki'tin chi'*	'I like its flavor!'
uts tin xikin	*uts tin wu'uyik*	'I like how it sounds!'
xe'ek'/xa'ak'a'an	*xa'ak'a'an*	'mixed'
uyotoch/unahil	*unahil*	'her/his home'
b'ix ab'eel?	*b'ix yanikech?*	'How are you?'

(Pfeiler and Hofling 2006:32–6)

MAM OSTUNCALCO (England 1989:296)

(4) Basic sentence

Ø-Ø-t-tzuy	Jwan	Peegr
CP-ABS3SG-ERG3SG-grab	Juan	Pedro

'Juan grabbed Pedro'.

Object extracted for focus

a	Peegr Ø-Ø-t-tzuy	Jwan
DEM	Pedro CP-ABS3SG-ERG3SG-grab	Juan

'Juan grabbed Pedro'.

In Tacaná, however, the particle *aa* does not exist. Instead, the relational noun/– *e*/ is cliticized to the object (see (5)).

MAM TACANÁ (England 1989:296)

(5) Basic sentence:

Ø-Ø-ku t-pa'-o-'n	Peegr xhoq'
CP-ABS3SG-DIR ERG3SG-break-THV-DIR	Pedro water.jar

'Pedro broke the water jar'.

Object extracted for focus:

xhoq'= t-e	Ø-Ø-ku t-pa'-o-'n	Peegr
water.jar=3S-RN	CP-ABS3SG-DIR ERG3SG-break-THV-DIR	Pedro

'Pedro broke the water jar'.

In Ostuncalco object focus marking (4) is analytic, having an independent particle preceding the preposed object; in Tacaná (5), in contrast, we have a synthetic strategy in which the enclitic/– e/ attaches to the object head *xhoq'= t* "the water jar". These examples show the intricate and complex pattern of syntactic variation in Mam and highlight the substantial structural diversity of many Mayan languages.

Some scholars have analyzed dialectal variation in multilingual contact areas. Julia Becker Richards's seminal work (1985) examines phonetic variation in Lake Atitlán, an area of intense contact among three different K'iche'an languages: Kaqchikel, Tz'utujil and K'ichee'. Focusing on the phonetic realization of stressed /a/, she shows that Lake Atitlán is a linguistic transition area: stressed /a/ is realized as [e] east of the lake and as [a] to the west. The fronting of stressed /a/ started in Patzún (Kaqchikel) and is spreading westwards into Kaqchikel, Tz'utujil and K'iche' territories. She also reports evidence of "fudging" with [æ] as an intermediate phonetic realization of /a/ in San Pablo La Laguna (Becker Richards 1985). Becker Richards argues that despite structural differences among the Tz'utujil, Kaqchikel and K'iche' languages, the particular varieties spoken around Lake Atitlán show substantial phonetic convergence and high levels of mutual intelligibility as a result of hundreds of years of contact (Becker Richards 1985; Becker Richards and Richards 1987).

Mayan dialectology is moving from a descriptive to a social footing taking cognizance of the social role and history of distinctive regional forms. Nevertheless, more research is needed at the micro-local level to document village stereotypes and how they relate to ancient kin groups and lineages (Stevenson 1990; Romero 2006). Emerging differences between nearby settlements is often concurrent with conflict or secessionist tendencies within townships (Romero 2015b). Also, more work is needed to identify typologies of dialect variation in Mayan. Structurally and socially, the scope and social history of new dialect formation is heterogeneous. The complexity of regional variation in K'ichee', Kaqchikel or Ixil, or the relatively superficial differences between Western and Eastern Yucatec, for example, respond to uniquely distinct social histories and diversification processes. A better understanding of the patterns of dialectal variation across the Maya area will contribute enormously to reconstruct the history of the linguistic family.

6 REVITALIZATION

Language shift and revitalization of Mayan languages have attracted scholarly and activist attention in the last thirty years. Triggered by the rise of the Maya movement in Guatemala, this work documents the experiences of marginalization endured by speakers of Mayan languages in Mexico and Guatemala, as well as their struggle to defend language rights and revitalization (Richards 1993; Cojtí 1995; England 1996, 2003; Maxwell 1996; Richards and Richards 1996a, 1996b, 1998; Jiménez 1997; Nelson 1999; Bastos and Camus 2003a; French 2010).

The Spanish colonial administration, the Guatemalan and Mexican states, the Catholic Church and other Christian denominations have used Mayan languages as vehicles for legitimation and proselytism. Soon after the Spanish conquest started in 1523, the Mendicant friars charged with the conversion of the Maya in cooperation with Maya associates produced scores of pastoral texts in Mayan languages including catechisms, doctrines and compilations of homilies, grammars and dictionaries. They introduced Spanish-based orthographies to write Mayan languages, which eventually led to the appearance of autonomous and diverse alphabetic writing traditions (Carmack 1973; Bricker and Miram 2002; Hanks 2010; Van Akkeren 2010; Sparks 2014; Sachse 2016; Romero 2015a). The pre-Hispanic Maya had a sophisticated logo-syllabic writing system. Unfortunately, it was actively persecuted by the Spanish and was abandoned not many decades after the conquest. Scores of colonial manuscripts in Mayan languages written in the Spanish-based orthography survived the inquisitorial zeal of Franciscans and Dominicans, however. Alphabetic writing endured as social practice in some languages until the early twentieth century as in Yucatec and Q'eqchi' (Carmack 1973; Bricker 1989; Romero 2014). In most Mayan languages, however, writing decreased dramatically in the early nineteenth century but did not altogether disappear. This was partly a consequence of the collapse of the Spanish empire and its accompanying *república de indios* – the system of laws and regulations that provided a measure of protection and autonomy to indigenous communities- and partly the result of the diffusion of Spanish as language of government after independence from Spain (Romero 2014, 2015b). From the 1930s there was a revival of interest when evangelical missionaries started an ambitious program to translate the Bible and other Christian literature into every Mayan language. Missionary linguists associated with Wycliffe Bible Translators (WBT), an organization created with the millennial goal of translating the gospel into every language spoken on earth, introduced a modified version of the colonial orthography to translate and publish in Mayan languages. William Cameron Townsend, founder of WBT, did fieldwork in Guatemala in the 1930s and established the Summer Institute of Linguistics (SIL; the academic arm of the WBT) in Mexico in the 1940s. The Guatemalan government was very interested in SIL's work and President Juan José Arévalo personally met the linguists and local collaborators translating the Bible into K'iche' and Mam in 1945 (Romero 2015b). The first *Congreso Lingüístico Nacional* "National Linguistic Congress", organized by the *Instituto Indigenista Nacional* (IIN) was held in 1949 and its alphabet was officially adopted in 1950, remaining in use until the late 1980s. SIL was established in Guatemala in 1952, becoming official advisors to the IIN (Marroquín 1972; Casey 1979; Richards and Richards 1996b; French 2010).

With the rise of the Maya movement in Guatemala in the 1980's, language revitalization gained central stage. For Maya activists, language rights and control over language planning became strategic goals. A new unified alphabet was adopted by the nascent Academy of Mayan Languages of Guatemala in 1987, and gained official recognition in the same year (López Raquec 1989; Richards and Richards 1996b). The unified alphabet avoided the inconsistencies of Spanish orthography and, more importantly, was the consensual product of discussions in which only Maya could cast votes. The ALMG was founded in 1990 with the mandate of protecting language rights and promoting the use of Mayan languages (England 1996).

Scholars have examined the language ideologies and ecumenical strategies used by language activists to arrive at standardized forms acceptable to all speakers of a particular language (Maxwell 1996; Warren 1997; Nelson 1999; French 2010). These include the adoption of the most common variants as standard, the avoidance of Spanish loanwords, the reintroduction of archaic words and the creation of neologisms. There is quantitative evidence that some speakers are indeed beginning to follow these norms in speech. Barrett (2008), for example, shows that some Sipakapense youth are using fewer Spanish loanwords than their parents and grandparents. Even though Sipakapense has not benefited from the work of language activists as much as Kaqchikel or K'iche', it seems that the rise of the Maya movement is encouraging Sipakapense speakers to avoid unnecessary Spanish loanwords.

Standardization efforts, however, have met with resistance where speakers object to standardized forms that do not reflect local speech (Romero 2015b). Such resistance is not simply false consciousness or a misunderstanding of the strategic goals of the Maya movement. It embodies local power struggles, regional conflicts and established indexical practices (Hofling 1996; Romero 2015b). Anthony Berkley's ethnographic research on Yucatec Maya, for example, shows that writing is embedded in particular social landscapes where it interacts with local constructions of ethnicity, gender and power. The positive or negative evaluation of narratives produced in writing workshops in Yucatán, for example, depends on language ideologies that legitimize the works of elder men and place women at a disadvantage, especially those young and unmarried (Berkley 2001). Sergio Romero has critiqued the presupposition that language boundaries defined in terms of mutual intelligibility necessarily overlap with ethnic boundaries. Focusing on the K'iche', he argues that highland Maya language groups are often multiethnic and mutual intelligibility does not entail mutual ethnic identification and solidarity. Local varieties act as ethnic markers playing a host of indexical roles in discourse and are deeply embedded in regional linguistic economies and ethnoscapes. Regional "accents" are dense historic and cultural precipitates inseparable from local representations of ethnicity. Language policies that do not take the social role of dialectal differences into account are likely to face stiff local opposition (Romero 2012b, 2015b).

7 THE FUTURE

Although the study of Mayan sociolinguistics is still incipient, it is also full of promise and potential for new findings and innovative theoretical contributions. I do not doubt that further research in this field will enhance an already solid empirical base and substantially improve the quality of knowledge about Mayan languages and linguistics. It will clarify the relation between language and social history among the Maya and will provide tools for the study of the enormous diversity in the Mayan family.

NOTES

1   I use the unified alphabet used in Guatemala to transcribe texts in Mayan languages except for Yucatec Maya, where I use the orthography used in the source.
2   The rounded form [kʷiɓ] is the most common cross-dialectally.
3   Boundary work references semiotic practices, including speech, used to mark culturally important groups.
4   In the 1930s many descendants of the Cruzob' in eastern Quintana Roo were monolingual Yucatec speakers and most residents had almost no contact with Spanish. See Villa Rojas 1978.
5   In my fieldwork in the summer of 2015, I identified more than twenty-five K'iche' loanwords in Nebaj.

REFERENCES

Anonymous. 1701–1703. Popol Vuh. *Ayer collection*. Newberry Library.
Asturias de Barrios, Linda. 1994. "Mano de hombre, mano de mujer." PhD diss., State University of New York, Albany.
Barrett, Rusty. 1999. "A grammar of Sipakapense Maya." PhD diss., University of Texas, Austin.
Barrett, Rusty. 2008. "Linguistic differentiation and Mayan language revitalization in Guatemala." *Journal of Sociolinguistics* 12:275–305.
Bastos, Santiago, and Manuela Camus. 1995. Los mayas de la capital : un estudio sobre identidad étnica y mundo urbano. Guatemala City: FLACSO.
Bastos, Santiago, and Manuela Camus. 2003a. *El movimiento maya en perspectiva*. Guatemala City: FLACSO.
Bastos, Santiago, and Manuela Camus. 2003b. *Entre el mecapal y el cielo: Desarrollo del movimiento maya en Guatemala*. Guatemala City: Cholsamaj.
Becker Richards, Julia. 1985. "Vowel variability in a linguistic transition zone." *International Journal of American Linguistics* 51: 549–53.
Becker Richards, Julia, and Eleuterio Cahuec. 1994. "La variación sociolingüística en el idioma Q'eqchi'." *Boletín de Lingüística* 8: 1–13.
Becker Richards, Julia, and Michael Richards. 1987. "Percepciones de inteligibilidad mutua entre las variantes dialectales de la cuenca del lago de Atitlan." *Winak* 2: 205–22.
Berkley, Anthony. 2001. "Respecting Maya language revitalization." *Linguistics and Education* 12: 345–66.
Bohnemeyer, Jurgen. 2002. *The grammar of time reference in Yucatec Maya*. Berlin: LINCOM.
Bolle, David. 2000. "Notas sobre los conflictos y contactos linguisticos en el maya yucateco, el español en la zona de Rio Hondo." *Estudios de cultura maya* 21: 217–30.
Briceño, Fidencio. 2002. "Lengua e identidad entre los mayas de la península de Yucatán." *Los investigadores de la cultura maya* 10: 370–9.
Bricker, Victoria. 1981. "The source of the ergative split in Yucatec Maya." *Journal of Mayan Linguistics* 2: 83–127.
Bricker, Victoria. 1989. "The last gasp of hyeroglyphic writing in the books of Chilam Balam of Chumayel and Chan Kan." In *Word and image in Maya culture*, ed. by Willaim Hanks and Don Rice, 39–50. Salt Lake City: University of Utah Press.

Bricker, Victoria, and Helga Maria Miram. 2002. *An encounter of two worlds: The book of Chilam Balam of Kaua*. New Orleans: Tulane University Press.

Brody, Jill. 1987. "Particles borrowed from Spanish as discourse markers in Mayan languages." *Anthropological Linguistics* 29: 507–21.

Brody, Jill. 1995. "Lending the unborrowable: Spanish discourse markers in indigenous languages." In *Spanish in four continents: Studies of language contact and bilingualism*, ed. by Carmen Silva-Corvalan, 132–47. Washington, DC: Georgetown University Press.

Brown, Robert McKenna. 1991. "Language maintenance and shift in four Kaqchikel Maya towns." PhD diss., Tulane University.

Burns, Alan. 1993. *Maya in exile: Guatemalans in Florida*. Philadephia: Temple University Press.

Campbell, Lyle. 1973. "The philological documentation of a variable rule in the history of Pokom and Kekchi." *International Journal of American Linguistics* 39: 133–4.

Campbell, Lyle. 1974. "Quichean palatalized velars." *International Journal of American Linguistics* 40: 132–4.

Campbell, Lyle. 1977. *Quichean linguistic prehistory*. Berkeley: University of California Press.

Campbell, Lyle, and Una Canger. 1978. "Chicomuceltec's last throes." *International Journal of American Linguistics* 44: 228–30.

Carmack, Robert. 1973. *Quichean civilization: The ethnohistoric, ethnographic and archaeological sources*. Berkeley: University of California Press.

Carmack, Robert. 1981. *The Quiche Maya of Utatlan: the evolution of a highland Maya kingdom*. Norman: University of Okhlahoma Press.

Casey, David. 1979. "Indigenismo: the Guatemalan experience." PhD diss., University of Kansas.

Caz Cho, Sergio. 2007. *Variacion dialectal en Q'eqchi'*. Guatemala City: Cholsamaj.

Cedillo Chel, Antonio, and Juan Ramírez. 1999. *Diccionario del idioma Ixil de Santa María Nebaj*. Antigua Guatemala: Proyecto Lingüístico Francisco Marroquín.

Chambers, J. K., and Peter Trudgill. 1980. *Dialectology*. Cambridge: Cambridge University Press.

Choi, Jinsook. 2003. "Language choice and language ideology in a bilingual Mayan community: the politics of identity in Guatemala." PhD diss., The University at Albany, SUNY.

Choi, Jinsook. 2011. "El uso de los dos idiomas en Momostenango." In *La comunidad K'iche'-Maya de Santiago Momostenango: Su historia, cultura, lengua y arte*, ed. by Humberto Ak'abal and Robert Carmack, 115–40. Guatemala City: Nawal Wuj.

Cojti, Demetrio. 1995. Ub'aniik ri una'ooj uchomab'aal ri Maya' tinamit: Configuracion del pensamiento politico del Pueblo Maya (2da. parte). Guatemala City: Cholsamaj.

Cojti, Demetrio. 2006. Runa'oj ri Maya' Amaq': Configuracion del pensamiento politico del Pueblo Maya. Guatemala City: Cholsamaj.

Cojtí, Narciso, and Margarita López. 1990. "Variación dialectal del idioma kaqchikel." In *Lecturas sobre la lingüística maya*, ed. by Nora C. England and Stephen R. Elliott, 193–220. Antigua Guatemala: CIRMA.

Colby, Benjamin, and Pierre Van den Berghe. 1969. *Ixil country: A plural society in highland Guatemala*. Berkeley: University of California Press.

Collins, Wesley. 1988. "Un resumen sobre una encuesta dialectal en el area mam de Guatemala." *Winak* 4: 144–58.

Collins, Wesley. 2005. "Code-switching avoidance as a strategy for Mam (Maya) linguistic revitalization." *International Journal of American Linguistics* 71: 239–76.

Crossley, Charissa. 1989. "El uso del idioma k'iche' en los hogares de Chuixchimal, Totonicapán." *Winak* 5: 3–33.

Dahl, Östen. 1979. "Typology of sentence negation." *Language* 17: 79–106.

DeChicchis, Joseph. 1989. "Q'eqchi' variation in Guatemala and Belize." PhD diss., University of Pennsylvania.

Durocher, Bettina. 2002. *Los dos derechos de la tierra: La cuestion agraria en el pais ixil*. Guatemala City: FLACSO, MINUGUA, CONTIERRA.

England, Nora. 1987. "Variation in Mayan narrative." *Anthropological Linguistics* 29: 522–32.

England, Nora. 1989. "Comparing Mam (Mayan) clause structures: Subordinate versus main clauses." *International Journal of American Linguistics* 55: 283–308.

England, Nora. 1990. "El mam: Semejanzas y diferencias regionales." In *Lecturas sobre la lingüística maya*, ed. by Nora C. England and Stephen R. Elliott, 221–52. Antigua Guatemala: CIRMA.

England, Nora. 1991. "Changes in basic word order in Mayan languages." *International Journal of American Linguistics* 57: 446–86.

England, Nora. 1996. "The role of language standardization in revitalization." In *Maya cultural activism in Guatemala*, ed. by Edward Fischer and Robert McKenna Brown, 178–94. Austin: University of Texas Press.

England, Nora. 2003. "Mayan language revival and revitalization politics: Linguists and linguistic ideologies." *American Anthropologist* 105: 733–43.

Falla, Ricardo. 2008. *Migración transnacional retornada: juventud indígena de Zacualpa, Guatemala*. Guatemala City: Editorial Universitaria.

Fishman, Joshua. 1972. *The sociology of language; an interdisciplinary social science approach to language in society*. Rowley: Newbury House.

Foxen, Patricia. 2007. *In search of providence: Transnational Maya identities*. Nashville: Vanderbilt University.

French, Brigittine. 2010. *Maya ethnolinguistic identity: Violence, modernity and cultural rights in highland Guatemala*. Tucson: University of Arizona Press.

Furbee, Louanna. 2000. "Prestige, power and potential for language shift: The intrusion of Spanish into Tojolabal Maya." *Studies in Slavic and General Linguistics* 28: 99–103.

García Hernández, Abraham. 1989. "El uso e importancia del idioma k'iche' en el municipio de Cantel." *Winak* 5: 34–47.

Godfrey, Thomas James, and Wesley Collins. 1987. *Una encuesta dialectal en el área mam de Guatemala*. Guatemala City: ILV.

Grandia, Liza. 2009. Tz'aptz'ooqeb: El despojo recurrente del pueblo Q'eqchi'. Guatemala City: AVANCSO.

Grandin, Greg. 2000. *The blood of Guatemala: A history of race and nation*. Durham: Duke University Press.

Güemez Pineda, Miguel. 2007. "Indigenous language, culture and human rights in Yucatan." *Kroeber Anthropological Society Papers* 96: 39–54.

Haeserijn, Esteban. 1966. *Ensayo de la gramática del k'ekchi*. Purulhá, Baja Verapaz: Suquinay.

Hanks, William. 2010. *Converting words: Maya in the age of the cross*. Berkeley: University of California Press.

Hofling, Charles Andrew. 1996. "Indigenous linguistic revitalization and outsider interaction: The Itzaj Maya case." *Human Organization* 55: 108–16.

Hofling, Charles Andrew. 2004. "Language and cultural contacts among Yukatekan Mayans." *Collegicum Antropologicum* 28(Suppl 1): 241–8.

Jiménez, Odilio. 1997. "Tension entre idiomas: Situacion actual de los idiomas mayas y el español en Guatemala." Paper given at the meetings of the Latin American Studies Association, Guadalajara, Mexico.

Jones, Grant. 1998. *The conquest of the last Maya kingdom.* Stanford: Stanford University Press.

Kahn, Hillary. 2006. *Seeing and being seen: The Q'eqchi' Maya of Livingston, Guatemala and beyond.* Austin: University of Texas Press.

Kaufman, Terence. 1990. "Algunos rasgos estructurales de los Idiomas Mayances con referencia especial al K'ichee'." In *Lecturas sobre la lingüística Maya,* ed. by Nora C. England and Stephen R. Elliott, 59–114. Guatemala: CIRMA.

King, Arden. 1974. Coban and the Verapaz: History and cultural process in Northern Guatemala. New Orleans: Middle American Research Institute.

Knowles-Berry, Susan. 1987. "Linguistic decay in Chontal Mayan: The speech of semi-speakers." *Anthropological Lingusitics* 29: 332–41.

Labov, William. 1994. *Principles of language change vol. 1. Internal factors.* Cambridge: Blackwell Publishers.

Langan, Katherine. 1990. "Language proficincy use and attitude in Santo Tomás Chichicastenango: a study of language competition." PhD diss., Georgetown University.

Law, Danny. 2014. *Language contact, inherited similarity and social difference: The story of linguistic interaction in the Maya lowlands.* Philaldephia: John Benjamins.

Leonard, Jean Leo, and Cecilio Tuyuc Sucuc. 2009. "A sociolinguistic sketch of vowel shifts in Kaqchikel." In *Variation in indigenous minority language,* ed. by James Stanford and Dennis Preston, 173–227. Amsterdam/Philadelphia: John Benjamims.

Levy, R. 1979. "The phonological history of the Bugotu-Nggelic languages and its implications for Eastern Oceanic." *Oceanic Linguistics* 18: 1–31.

Lewis, M. Paul. 2001. *K'iche': A study in the sociology of language.* Dallas: SIL International.

Little, Walter. 2009. "Language choice among Maya handicraft vendors in an international tourism marketplace." In *Imagining globalization,* ed. by Ho Hon Leung and Matthew Hendley, 85–106. New York: Palgrave Macmillan.

López Raquec, Margarita. 1989. *Acerca de los alfabetos para escribir los idiomas Mayas de Guatemala.* Guatemala City: Ministerio de Cultura y Deportes.

Maddox, Marc. 2010. "Chwa'q chik iwonojel: Language shift, affect, ideology and intergenerational language use patterns iin the Quinizilapa Valley of Highland Guatemala." PhD diss., Tulane University.

Malchic Nicolás, Manuel Bernardo, Romelia Mó Isém, and Augusto Tul Rax. 2000. *Variación dialectal en Poqom.* Guatemala City: Cholsamaj.

Marroquín, Alejandro. 1972. "Panorama del indigenismo guatemalteco." *América Indígena* 32: 291–304.

Maxwell, Judith. 1996. "Prescriptive grammar and Kaqchikel revitalization." In *Maya cultural activism in Guatemala,* ed. by Edward Fischer and Robert McKenna Brown, 195–207. Austin: University of Texas Press.

Menchú, Rafael Vicente, and María Alicia Telón de Xulú. 1993. "Actitudes de los padres de familia, mayahablantes e hispanohablantes hacia la educación bilingüe para todos en Totonicapán y Patzún." *Winak* 9: 5–59.

Nelson, Dianne. 1999. *A finger in the wound: body politics in quincentennial Guatemala.* Berkeley: University of California Press.

Par Sapón, María, and Telma Can Pixabaj. 2000. *Variación dialectal en K'iche'.* Guatemala City: Cholsamaj.

Patal Majtzul, Filiberto, Pedro Garcia Matzar, and Carmelina Espantzay Serech. 2000. *Variación dialectal en Kaqchikel*. Guatemala City: Cholsamaj.

Peñalosa, Fernando. 1989. "La situación sociolingüística de los q'anjob'ales en Los Angeles." *Winak* 5: 162–75.

Pérez, Eduardo, Zoyla Blanca Luz García Jiménez, and Odilio Jiménez. 2000. *Variación dialectal en Mam*. Guatemala City: Cholsamaj.

Pfeiler, Barbara. 1988. "Yucatán: El uso de dos lenguas en contacto." *Estudios de cultura maya* XVII: 423–43.

Pfeiler, Barbara. 1999. "Situación sociolingüística de Yucatán." In *Atlas de procesos territoriales de Yucatán*, ed. by José Lugo Hup and Maria Teresa Arizaga, 269–99. Mexico City: PROESA.

Pfeiler, Barbara. 2014. "Maya and Spanish in Yucatan: An example of continuity and change." In *Iberian imperialism and language evolution in Latin America*, ed. by Salikoko Mufwene, 205–24. Chicago: University of Chicago Press.

Pfeiler, Barbara, and Charles Andrew Hofling. 2006. "Apuntes sobre la variacion dialectal en el maya yucateco." *Península* 1: 27–44.

PRECMI. 1995. *Aq'b'al Elu'l Yol Vatzsaj. Diccionario Ixil*. Guatemala City: Cholsamaj.

Raymundo González, Sonia, Adán Francisco Pascual, Pedro Mateo Pedro, and Eladio Mateo Toledo. 2000. *Variación dialectal en Q'anjob'al*. Guatemala City: Cholsamaj.

Re Cruz, Alicia. 1996. "The thousand and one faces of Cancún." *Urban Anthropology and Studies of Cultural Systems and World Economic Development* 25: 283–310.

Richards, Julia. 1989. "Mayan language planning for bilingual education in Guatemala." *International Journal for the Sociology of Language* 77: 93–115.

Richards, Julia. 1993. "The first congress of Mayan languages (1949)." In *The earliest stage of language planning: The "first congress" phenomenon*, ed. by Joshua Fishman, 199–217. Berlin: Mouton de Gruyter.

Richards, Julia, and Michael Richards. 1996a. "Maya education: A historical and contemporary analysis of Mayan language education policy." In *Maya cultural activism in Guatemala*, ed. by Edward F. Fischer and R. McKenna Brown, 208–21. Austin: University of Texas Press.

Richards, Julia, and Michael Richards. 1996b. "Mayan language literacy in Guatemala: A socio-historical overview." In *Indigenous literacies in the Americas: Language planning from the bottom up*, ed. by Nancy Hornberger, 189–212. Berlin/New York: Walter de Gruyter and Co.

Richards, Julia, and Michael Richards. 1998. "Persistencia del idioma kaqchikel de 1524 a la actualidad." *Mesoamérica* 35: 27–48.

Richards, Michael. 2003. *Atlas lingüístico de Guatemala*. Guatemala City: Serviprensa.

Robertson, John. 1992. *The history of tense/aspect/mood/voice in the Mayan verbal complex* Austin: University of Texas Press.

Robertson, John, Danny Law, and Robbie Haertel. 2010. *Colonial Cholti': The seventeenth-century Morán manuscript*. Norman: University of Oklahoma Press.

Romero, Sergio. 2006. "Sociolinguistic variation and linguistic history in Mayan: the case of K'iche'." PhD diss., University of Pennsylvania.

Romero, Sergio. 2009. "Phonological markedness, regional identity, and gender in Mayan: The fricativization of intervocalic /l/ in K'iche'." In *Variation in indigenous minority languages*, ed. by James Stanford and Dennis Preston, 281–98. Amsterdam/Philadelphia: Benjamins.

Romero, Sergio. 2012a. "A Maya version of Jespersen's cycle: The diachronic evolution of negative markers in K'iche' Maya." *International Journal of American Linguistics* 78: 77–96.

Romero, Sergio. 2012b. "'They don't get speak our language right': Language standard-ization, power and migration among the Q'eqchi' Maya." *Journal of Linguistic Anthro-pology* 22: 21–41.

Romero, Sergio. 2014. "'¡Cuánto sufrir! Solo la fe de indio me ha mantenido firme. . .': Jorge Ubico y el indigenismo del presbítero Celso Narciso Teletor." *Mesoamérica* 56: 1–23.

Romero, Sergio. 2015a. "The emergence of of double and triple negation in K'ichee' Mayan: A variationist perspective." *Language Variation and Change* 27: 187–201.

Romero, Sergio. 2015b. *Language and ethnicity among the K'ichee' Maya*. Salt Lake City: University of Utah Press.

Rosenbaum, Brenda. 1993. *With our heads bowed: the dynamics of gender in a Maya community*. Albany: Institute for Mesoamerican Studies, University at Albany, State University of New York.

Ross Montejo, Antonio Benicio, and Edna Patricia Delgado Rojas. 2000. *Variación dia-lectal en Popti'*. Guatemala City: Cholsamaj.

Sachse, Frauke. 2016. "The Expression of Christian Concepts in Colonial K'iche' Mis-sionary Texts." In *La transmisión de conceptos cristianos a las lenguas amerindias: Estudios sobre textos y contextos en la época colonial*, ed. by Sabine Dedenbach-Salazar Sáenz, 93–116. St. Augustin, Germany: Anthropos.

Satterfield, Teresa, and Rusty Barrett. 2004. "Generation gap: explaining new and emerg-ing word-order phenomena in Mayan-Spanish bilinguals." Paper given at First Interna-tional Symposium about Bilingualism in Latin America, Buenos Aires.

Schwartz, Norman. 1990. *Forest society: A social history of Peten, Guatemala*. Philadel-phia: University of Pennsylvania Press.

Shoaps, Robin. 2009a. "Moral irony and moral personhood in Sakapultek discourse and culture." In *Stance: Sociolinguistic perspectives*, ed. by Alexandra Jaffe, 92–118. Oxford: Oxford University Press.

Shoaps, Robin. 2009b. "Ritual and (im)moral voices: Locating the Testament of Judas in Sakapultek communicative ecology." *American Ethnologist* 36: 459–77.

Sparks, Garry. 2014. "The use of Mayan scripture in the Americas' first Christian theol-ogy." *Numen* 61: 396–429.

Starks, Donna, and Ellaine Ballard. 2005. "Woods Cree /ð/: An unusual type of sonorant." *International Journal of American Linguistics* 71: 102–15.

Stevenson, Paul. 1990. *Santa María Cauqué: un caso de mezcla de los idiomas cak-chiquel y quiché*. Guatemala City: Instituto Lingüístico de Verano.

Stewart, Steven. 1980. *Gramática kekchí*. Guatemala City: Editorial Académica Centroamericana.

Stross, Brian. 1973. "El contexto sociocultural en la adquisición de la lengua tzeltal." *Estudios de Cultura Maya* 9: 257–301.

Sullivan, Paul. 2000. "The Yucatec Maya." In *Supplement to the handbook of middle American Indians, volume 6. Ethnology*, ed. by John Monagham and Barbara Edmon-son, 207–23. Austin: University of Texas Press.

Thompson, J. Eric S. 1930. *Ethnology of the Mayas of southern and central British hon-duras*. Chicago: Field Museum of Natural History.

Tzul, Julio Alberto, and Alfonso Tzimaj Cacao. 1997. *Gramática del idioma Q'eqchi'*. Antigua Guatemala: Proyecto Lingüístico Francisco Marroquín.

Van Akkeren, Ruud. 2000. *The place of the lord's daughter. Rab'inal, its ethnohistory, its dance-drama*. Leiden: Center for Non-Western Studies, University of Leiden.

Van Akkeren, Ruud. 2005. *Ixil, Lugar del Jaguar: Historia y cosmovisión ixil*. Guatemala City: GTZ-Serviprensa.

Van Akkeren, Ruud. 2010. "Fray Domingo de Vico: Maestro de Autores Indígenas." *Revista de Estudios Mayas* 2(7): 1–61.

Van Akkeren, Ruud. 2012. *Xib'alb'a y el nacimiento del nuevo sol*. Guatemala City: Editorial Piedrasanta.

van der Auwera, Johan. 2009. "The Jespersen cycles." In *Cyclical change*, ed. by Elly van Gelderen, 35–71. Philadelphia: John Benjamins.

Vázquez Álvarez, Juan Jesús. 2011. "A grammar of Chol, a Mayan language." PhD diss., University of Texas, Austin.

Villa Rojas, Alfonso. 1978. *Los elegidos de Dios. Etnografía de los mayas de Quintana Roo*. Mexico City: Instituto Nacional Indigenista.

Warren, Kay. 1997. *Indigenous movements and their critics: Pan-Maya activism in Guatemala*. Princeton: Princeton University Press.

Whiteside, Anna. 2006. "Research on transnational Yucatec Maya-speakers negotiating multilingual California." *Journal of Applied Linguistics* 3: 103–12.

Whiteside, Anna. 2007. "'Transnational' Yucatecans and language practices in San Francisco, California: Results from a participatory research survey." *Kroeber Anthropology Society Papers* 96: 55–73.

Wichmann, Søren. 2003. "Contact among some Mayan languages: Inferences from loanwords source." *Anthropological Linguistics* 45: 57–93.

CHAPTER 16

MAYAN CONVERSATION AND INTERACTION

John B. Haviland

1 INTRODUCTION

When I first came to Zinacantán, early in the summer of 1966, I had been schooled in basic Tsotsil grammar and etiquette as part of preparation for fieldwork in highland Chiapas. This linguistic orientation went along with other sorts of training: practicing for involuntary bouts of heavy drinking, learning to take "fieldnotes" on ritual by attending my first Catholic Mass, and enrolling in a "field medicine" course in which I learned dosages for antibiotics, how to stave off dehydration, perform CPR, temporarily fill teeth, and ultimately pull them out with just pliers and a screwdriver. The elements of Zinacantec Tsotsil my first teachers imparted to me were roughly parallel to carpenter's tools for performing oral surgery: they hardly began to prepare me for my immediate project (studying "traditional" Zinacantec stringed instrument music), let alone for the topic I ultimately pursued (quotidian gossip) in this Mayan community. Over the course of my first summer in Zinacantán I gained basic competence in conversational Tsotsil and enough novice skills at interacting with Zinacantecs to be able to feign humanity in at least some situations. I had, however, learned a more fundamental anthropological lesson: if you can't converse with people in the ordinary circumstances of life, you don't know the relevant language(s) well enough.

My interest in conversation and interaction in Mayan languages thus grew not from theory but from personal need. I was simply very bad at interacting with Tsotsil speakers. Subsequently, I think everything I tried to learn about Tsotsil derived from the desire to address my woeful inadequacy as a conversational partner.

There are two apparently competing strands in recent work on conversation and interaction, and this chapter on such research with Mayan languages reflects my own view of how to balance their opposing motives. On the one hand, recent proposals about a human interactional substrate that underlies quite different conversational traditions, or "talk in interaction" (Schegloff 2006), presume quite general, flexible, and widely shared mechanisms. On the other, my own experience – that learning to talk appropriately in unfamiliar circumstances is maddeningly difficult – suggests that the particularities of conversation and interaction from one circumstance to another may vary both widely and deeply. Mayan conversation and interaction have contributed a surprising amount to recent debates, and one aim of this chapter is to urge Mayanists to expand this contribution with further comparative work, emphasizing both distinct "cultural" styles as well as possible commonalities across the regions where Mayan languages are spoken.

2 INTERACTION

In early ethnography in Zinacantán notions of interaction were variously employed to characterize interpersonal relations, as part of the fundamental research on demography and ethnography in the Harvard Chiapas Project. Francesca Cancian (1964), for example, wrote about "the quantity and quality of interaction" in Zinacantec families – by which she meant "patterns of affection, dominance and interaction rate among household members" (p. 542). She based her coding scheme, derived from contemporary studies of small groups, on sequences of action involving both spoken Tsotsil and associated behaviors (for instance, a child's whining and being responded to, first with verbal "affection" from his mother, and then by being given something). At around the same time, to give a quite different example, T. Berry Brazelton (1972) was observing Zinacantec births and evaluating mother-child "interactions" through the cheerfully ethnocentric lens of his famous Cambridge (Massachusetts) pediatric practice. Brazelton and his colleagues monitored twelve infants of various ages from one to nine months and documented "mother-child interactions" over four-hour periods, annotating such "mothering activities" as "glances at infant's face," "number of times of talking to infant," "number of breast feedings," and "minutes held in *rebozo*." As "infant activities" Brazelton included minutes awake, "vocalizations," or "mouthing" of hands, and so on. In an explicit comparison with "mother-child patterns in our own culture," Brazelton remarks, among other things, that "mothers rarely attempted to elicit social responses from their infants by looking at their faces or talking to them. Even during feedings when the mother would preen the baby, her glances were perfunctory and without expectation of response" (1972:102).

Both these examples of early Chiapas ethnography derived from specific concerns with the quality and quantity of what Goffman (1957) called the "communion of reciprocally sustained involvement" (p. 49) between different social entities, conceived either as individuals (a mother and her child) or as relevantly defined social categories (parents and children, siblings, adults, and so on). Recent work on interaction has concentrated less on specific kinds of interactants and the resultant properties of their interaction, and more on general principles which enable and constrain different sorts of mutual human involvement – shared attention and attunement, reciprocal engagement, coordination, joint action or commitment to action, and intersecting moral stances (see Clark 1996; Enfield et al. 2014, for recent treatments).

Starting with mother-child interactions – the central raw material for both Cancian and Brazelton – has a compelling motive: if one of the hallmarks of our species is the protracted dependence of human infants on their caregivers, something must guarantee that particular locus of "sustained involvement"; and babies must be fed, whether in the Zinacantec or the Harvard Square manner. In much the same way, recent proposals about a shared interactional substrate for human sociality (Levinson [2006] postulates a human "interaction engine") anticipate quite specific interactional mechanisms, to be found wherever humans are, although inflected in locally specific ways. (Such inflections will, of course, themselves require interactional transmission.) There is an immediate link to conversation, in that human sociality finds what has been called its "primordial site" (Schegloff 1996) in conversational interchanges. Indeed, a strong motivation for the resulting program of research has been the conviction that many properties of ordinary conversation, often identified originally through close scrutiny of American English telephone calls, have remarkably close parallels in quite unrelated languages, circumstances, and communicative traditions.

Levinson's leading example derives from a short paper by the pioneers of conversation analysis (Sacks and Schegloff 1979) who proposed two usually coordinated but occasionally competing principles for initial references to persons in conversation (one calling for a formulation adequate to the mutual recognition of the person referred to, the other for a "minimal" referring expression which supplies no more information than required – both principles obviously calling for some calculations about speaker and hearer's mutual knowledge). Levinson argues that similar principles seem to apply to conversational exchanges in quite different and unrelated languages on which he has worked. Such a perspective both narrows and broadens earlier research on "interaction" by focusing it squarely on conversational interaction, but opening it up to the manifold circumstances in which such interaction occurs and to the seemingly limitless purposes it serves in social life. Mayan languages have, perhaps accidentally, played a central part in this program of research. A subsequent collection of studies (Enfield and Stivers 2007) explores Levinson's hypothesis by examining conversational references to person in nine languages, three of which happen to be Mayan (Tseltal, Tsotsil, and Yucatec – see Brown 2007, Hanks 2007, and Haviland 2007). Similarly, three out of the four chapters in the "Culture and sociality" section of Enfield and Levinson (2006) are about Mayan languages, adding Mopan to the mix (Danziger 2006).

Note that the study of conversation implies an empirical reach that extends beyond the normal Boasian triad of grammar, vocabulary, and text. Indeed, recent studies of conversation rely on technology – audio and video recording – that makes possible corpora of iconic representations of naturally occurring linguistic interaction simply not available to linguists in the days of Boas and Sapir. Furthermore, current standards of transcription call into serious doubt earlier textual representations of many of the conversational genres of central interest to anthropology: not only interviews and "traditional narratives" (whose interactive provenance is frequently excised entirely from text collections), but also oratory, prayer, scolding, insults, and jokes (frequently rendered monologically in text despite their deep embeddedness in multi-party performances), or even audio recorded "natural" conversational exchanges (which can only serve as pale mnemonics of the corporeal and spatially extended interactions of which they were originally a part). Given the ubiquity of cameras – found on the cell phones in most Indian pockets in present-day Chiapas, for example – slightly less limited representations of talk are accessible now to most fieldworkers, although managing the resulting volume of digital recordings remains a challenge. Videorecording conversation opens to analytical attention those aspects of human interaction which are visible but not audible, notably sign, gesture, orientation, gaze, and how interactants deploy themselves (and their body parts) in space.

3 CONVERSATION IN MAYAN

Many linguists have pointed out the massive use of conversation and "quoted" dialogue in Mayan narrative, suggesting that the organization of conversation is centrally important to the analysis of any large textual corpus. (See, for example, Laughlin 1977; Burns 1980). But for which Mayan languages do we have information about conversation? Despite more than half a century of modern research on Mayan languages, surprisingly little work has been done on the ordinary contexts of their use in daily life.

Research from Chiapas in the 1960s and early 1970s produced monumental textual studies of particular marked speech genres in Tsotsil, including discourses of marriage (Laughlin 1963; J. Collier 1968), insults (Bricker 1973b), jokes and ritual humor (Bricker

1973a, 1980), proverbs (Gossen 1973), legal discourse (J. Collier 1973), dreams (Laughlin 1976), verbal dueling (Gossen 1976), folktales (Laughlin 1977), and gossip (Haviland 1977a&b). Indeed, this early era produced some of the classic taxonomic studies of speech genres as ethnolinguistic categories in the "ethnography of speaking" tradition (Bricker 1974; Gossen 1971, 1974a, b), deriving from Tsotsil terminology for kinds of speech. Gossen's influential handbook article on Tsotsil literature (Gossen 1985) also developed in some detail the kinds of linguistic parallelism found in Tsotsil, and reported throughout the Mayan area and more widely in Mesoamerica.

A second wave of research, partly building on the first, uncovered some of the central features of ordinary talk in a slightly wider range of Mayan languages. In no particular order, here are some of the important contributors and languages involved, emphasizing research on interaction and conversation rather than other topics.

In Tenejapa, Penelope Brown launched a series of detailed conversational studies of Tseltal which continue to the present and which set the standard for ethnographic perspicacity, contextual embedding, transcriptional detail, and theoretical currency. After her dissertation on gender and interaction (Brown 1979), to cite only a few, she has incorporated conversational materials into studies of politeness (Brown 1980, 1990), irony (Brown 1995), repetition, especially its possible role in language acquisition (Brown 1998), and – as part of recent detailed cross-linguistic studies pursuing the "interaction engine" idea – detailed analyses of both person reference (Brown 2007) and question-answer sequences in Tseltal conversation (Brown 2010).

Jill Brody has described notable conversational features in Tojolab'al, particularly the prevalence of what she calls "repetition" (Brody 1986, 1994) and "indirection," especially in women's speech (Brody 1991, 1993, 1996). She has also analyzed discourse particles, derived from conversational as well as monologic and broadcast sources (Brody 1987, 2000a, b).

William Hanks has delved deeply into Yucatec conversation as part of his wider studies of both the modern and the colonial languages, concentrating on how language is simultaneously situated in physical and social surrounds (Hanks 1990, 1992, 1993, 1996b). In particular, his detailed work on divinatory practices by a Yucatec shaman, with whom he had a long and close apprenticeship, locate generic particularities in a wider range of interactional practices (Hanks 1984, 1996a, 2006, 2007).

My own work on Zinacantec Tsotsil began with a quintessentially conversational activity: gossiping about one's neighbors (Haviland 1977a, b, 1998). It moved on to teasing and arguing (Haviland 1986, 1987, 1996, 1997, 2005b, 2010), with excursions into prayer and other highly structured genres in Zinacantec ritual that often leak into quotidian interaction (Haviland 1994, 2000b, 2009), along with other more general conversational mechanisms (Haviland 2007). The work on gossip naturally led to issues of certainty, evidence, responsibility, and information flow as marked in talk (Haviland and Haviland 1982, 1983; Haviland 1988a, 1989, 2002, 2005c). Shifting from always carrying around an audio recorder to routinely inflicting video cameras on my Zinacantec companions, I also embarked on the study of gesture in interaction (Haviland 2000a, 2003, 2005a).

Since the early efflorescence of work on spontaneous talk, a number of younger researchers, working on a variety of Mayan languages, have launched a series of investigations relying on corpora of natural conversation. Eve Danziger has used conversational data (including spontaneous gesture) to examine conceptualization in a variety of semantic domains – especially kinship and spatial cognition (Danziger 1994, 1998, 1999, 2001, 2004). Danziger has also recently joined debates on sociality and intersubjectivity based on evidence from Mopan conversational exchanges (Danziger 2006, 2010, 2013), as has Kevin Groark, in his dissertation and a set of thoughtful papers on interpersonal awareness, empathy, and expressivity among Chamula Tsotsil speakers (Groark 2005, 2008, 2009, 2010, 2013) based on interviews and conversation. Robin Shoaps produced a series of studies of what she calls "moral irony" in Sakapultek (Shoaps 2004, 2007, 2009b), a conversational usage that combines modal particles with an ironic positioning that helps "co-construct [. . .] the evaluative stance" that gives it a moral character (Shoaps 2007:323). Rightly (in my view) insisting on basing her analyses on "naturally-occurring Sakapultek speech events" – data "from indigenous speech events and . . . not the response to elicitation or informal interviews with the researcher" (ibid:298, and fn. 3) – even when she analyzes a scandalous parodic ritual text written in Spanish, Shoaps (2009a) takes pains to link its mechanisms to devices common in quotidian Sakapultek scolding and gossip, as well as in more structured dispute settlement. Olivier Le Guen has brought considerable insight about the workings of everyday Yucatec talk – including systematic uses of gesture – to his varied and growing corpus of cognitively oriented studies, concentrating first on space and deixis, and moving through domains as varied as time, emotion, and the "supernatural" (Le Guen 2006, 2011b, 2012a, b; see also Le Guen and Pool Balam 2012). Conversationally based studies have also begun to appear in the academic productions of young native-speaking Mayan scholars, a point to which I return at the end of the chapter.

Worth special mention in this bibliographic survey are the important contributions to the study of language socialization and acquisition by researchers who have studied spontaneous interaction among children and with their caregivers in different parts of the Maya area. Especially notable for analyzing conversational sequences – sometimes with both audio and video recordings – is the ongoing collaboration by Penny Brown (Tseltal), Lourdes de León (Tsotsil), Barbara Pfeiler (Yucatec), and Cliff Pye (K'ichee'), sometimes joined by Pedro Mateo Pedro (Q'anjob'al, Mam, Chol, and Chuj), and their individual contributions to the study of socialization into Mayan languages – too numerous and varied to characterize here. (See Pye et al. 2007, and Brown et al. 2013 for representative comparative examples; note also the individual bibliography entries for de León and Brown.) Although psychological work on children's interaction tends to rely more on "coding" than "transcription" (see, for example, Chavajay and Rogoff 1999, 2002), an important exception is the extended work by Suzanne Gaskins on Yucatec children (for example, Gaskins 1996, 1999, 2006), along with that of Ashley Maynard on Tsotsil (for example, Maynard 2002; Greenfield et al. 2003; Rabain-Jamin et al. 2003). The role of children in managing information through conversation has also been a theme in Mayan communities (e.g., Berman 2011).

Although one would expect spontaneous conversation to be a fundamental source for understanding bilingual choices, despite ubiquitous bi- (or multi-)lingualism in Mayan communities, rather few conversational studies seem to be based on such empirical material (but see Haviland 1984b; French 2001; Collins 2005; Barrett 2008; Choi 2011).

4 "ORDINARY" CONVERSATION IN TSOTSIL

Mayan languages bring into focus several central issues in recent studies of conversation and interaction. One is the very nature of what constitutes "ordinary talk" as a "general organization of interaction" (Schegloff 2006:72), the main formal characteristic of which Schegloff identifies by the rubric "one speaker at a time." Departures from such a rule are taken to require specific, non-generic organizational or institutional arrangements which

Schegloff characterizes as "unsustainable" (ibid, and see fn. 3) as a default interactional device, by contrast with the general-purpose mechanisms for turn allocation postulated by Sacks et al. (1974). Introducing a comparative study of question-response sequences in ten languages Enfield et al. (2010) are somewhat less noncommittal about the nature of ordinary, "unconstrained" conversation. Their "contributors used only data from max-imally informal social interaction in familiar settings between people who knew each other well. None of the data were institutional or staged. Because of significant cultural variation in terms of when conversation is least constrained, the specific activity con-text varied" (2617). Thus, whereas such "maximally informal" conversation in Italian or American English might take place over a meal, "Tseltal . . . speakers hardly talk while eating" (Enfield et al. 2010:2618).

Tseltal, one of the languages included in the study (Stivers et al. 2009; Enfield et al. 2010; especially Brown 2010; Enfield et al. 2012), is reported to behave like the other languages with respect both to preference patterns for how replies to questions are struc-tured and organized, and to the timing of a response following a question. Here is one area in which further detailed study of Mayan conversation would contribute to a devel-oping research effort. But what sort of "conversation" would be involved? Are Mayans *ever* on the kind of mutual footing that allows them to compete equally for such interac-tive resources as the conversational floor?

Apparently by contrast with their Tseltal neighbors, Tsotsil speakers almost *always* talk while eating – at least in the Zinacantec houses I frequent – and in many other circum-stances as well, whether formal (whatever that might mean [Irvine 1979]) or not. More-over, meals themselves – as well as the talk that occurs within them – are relatively more or less pre-structured depending on what the occasion is (a morning meal in the cornfield shelter vs. a post-baptismal repast in the parents' home, to take two opposing examples) and who is present (for example, a hired laborer from another *municipio* in the former case, vs. wealthy new godparents, who may be either older or younger than the hosts in the latter). There are also social interactions which move smoothly between phases, in some of which control and management of the conversational floor may be explicitly at issue. In Zinacantán for example, meals may begin with an exchange of empty pleasant-ries by those seated at a table, interspersed with side conversations directed at the cooks (sharing the eating space although perhaps clustered around a fire), followed by talk ded-icated to getting the food appropriately served, then a heavily conventionalized series of polite exchanges inviting all assembled to eat, after which there may ensue an apparently more extemporaneous dinner time discussion, usually clearly "led" by a senior male, and ultimately a ritualized exchange of thanks as dishes are removed, water proffered to wash hands, and so on.

Indeed, in Zinacantán, meals often provoke special linguistics registers. Inviting a guest to an impromptu meal, a Zinacantec woman may start by passing a bowl of warmed water, asking "Mi ch-a-'atin?" (Q ICP-B2-wash) "Will you wash?" At a more ritually ele-vated meal, water will be placed on the table, and the most senior male will instead intone to each commensal, in descending order of rank, "*jax j-k'ob-tik, X*" (A1+wash A1-hand-1PL.INCL), "Let us wash, X" where the verb *jax* (which also means brush, or card [wool]) suggests a kind of self-deprecatory "pass our hands through water" and X is whatever address term is appropriate for the particular personal dyad involved. The interlocutor will repeat the formula, substituting the appropriate reciprocal address term.

The point of the example – or of the more general possibility that *all* conversation, at least in places like Zinacantán, is subject to ritual constraints (Haviland 2009) – is not to minimize the importance of a general-purpose turn-taking mechanism, but to point out that a "default" kind of conversation where such a mechanism unproblematically applies will require ethnographic justification, perhaps beginning with an "ethnography of speaking"-style catalogue of "kinds of talk" complemented by analysis of the varieties of speech actually revealed on the ground.

For example, there exists a genre of hyper-polite Zinacantec "small talk" (as I call it – the genre is unlabeled in Tsotsil, as far as I am aware) which is both topically vacant and sequentially constrained. All turns are short. Moreover, the polite conventions of Tsotsil require that an interlocutor produce a spoken, if minimal, response for every few words a speaker utters. The result is a dense stream of more or less equal length utterances between conversationalists.

Consider the following extracts from a conversation between my compadre P and A, the magistrate of his village, which took place at the crack of dawn one morning when I accompanied P who wanted to resolve a land dispute with his sons. As is customary, before launching into the serious business of bringing formal complaints, P began with a variety of this "small talk." Fragment (1) presents the first part of P's conversation with the magistrate, a polite exchange about the weather and the resulting state of the cornfields.[1]

TSOTSIL ZINACANTÁN (transcribed audio conversation recorded 21 July 1993)

(1) P and A begin to talk[2]

1	a;	li	x-Ø-mal		ali.	chabje	le'
		ART	ASP-B3-set(sun)		ART	two.days.ago	there

'Late, uh, day before yesterday there (in my cornfield).'

2		pero	k'un	i-Ø-k'ot
		But	soft	CP-B3-arrive

'Soft (rain) arrived.'

3	p;	k'un	i-Ø-k'ot
		soft	CP_B3_arrive

'Soft (rain) arrived'

4	a;	k'un
		soft

'Soft.'

5	p;	pero . k'u	s-muk'-tikil un
		but what	A3-large-PL CL

'But how big is (your corn)?'

6	a;	lek	y-unen	s-muk'-tikil	une
		good	A3-small	A3-large-PL	CL

'It's got a good little size.'

7	p;	a	yech
		ah	thus

'Is that so?'

      [

8	a;	lek	i-Ø-yal-e
		good	CP-B3-descend-CL

'It (rained) pretty well.'

9	p;	aa
		ah

'Ah.'

      [

10	a;	jii
		yes

'Yes.'

The next part of the same conversation, in (2), displays a characteristic feature of formally polite Zinacantec interaction: a high degree of repetitiveness. Elaborate repetition, where one man echoes exact phrases or close variants of his interlocutor's previous turn, and subsequently is re-echoed by the other, is apparent. Substantively, the two men multiply repeated the observations (a) at lines 12–17 that A's cornfield was not infested by worms, (b) at lines 20–23 that the cornfields now simply needed more rain, (c) at lines 24–28 that they would just have to wait and see if it rained in the next couple of days, and (d) at lines 30–33, again, that the corn needed rain immediately.

TSOTSIL ZINACANTÁN (conversation recorded 21 July 1993)
(2) P and A exchange small talk
11   p;   muk' bu   x-chanul a'a
            NEG where A3-animal EVID
            'It doesn't have any worms, does it?'
12   a;   ch'abal
            NEG
            'No.'
13   p;   ch'abal?
            NEG
            'No?'
14   a;   ch'abal
            NEG
            'No.'
15   p;   aa
            ah.
            'Ah.'
16   a;   ch'abal a'a
            NEG   EVID
            'No, none.'
17   p;   ch'abal une
            NEG   CL
            'None, then.'
                  [
18   a;   jii
                 yes.
                 'Yes.'
19   p;   y-u'un   lek   o
            A3-because good REL
            'Well, that's good.'
20   ja' nox. k'u ora ch-Ø-k'ot   y-a'lel   kik   un
            !   only what hour ICP-B3-arrive A3-water EVID CL
            'It just depends on when it gets some moisture.'
21   ja' to (mi yaxub)
            ! STILL Q   CP+B3+become_green
            'If only it stays moist/green.'

		[
22	a;	ja' nox u:n
		! only CL
		'That's all.'
23	p;	ja' to yu'van
		! still EVID
		It just depends on that.
24	a;	y-u'nan ta k'el-el kik mi x-Ø-k'ot li ok'ob cha'ej=
		A3-cause+EVID PREP see-NMLZ EVID Q ASP-B3-arrive ART tomorrow day_after
		One must just wait and see if perhaps it rains tomorrow or the next day.
26	p;	puta y-u'un ja' ta k'el-el
		EXPL A3-cause ! PREP see-NMLZ
		Damn, one just has to see.
27	a;	y-u'n me un
		A3-cause EVID CL
		That's right.
28	p;	ja' yu'van
		! EVID
		Yes, indeed.
		[
29	a;	jii
		Yes
		Yes.
30	p;	puta y-u'un xa. tz-k'an vo' bi a'a
		EXPL A3-cause already ICP+A3-want water EVID EVID
		Damn, it really does want rain, eh?
31	a;	y-u'n me tz-k'an un
		A3-cause EVID ICP+A3-want CL
		Yes, it really does.
32	p;	tana yu'van
		soon EVID
		Soon, indeed.
33	a;	y-u'un me
		A3-cause EVID
		Indeed.

Contrasting with such a conversational context – where there were pronounced but conflicting asymmetries in age and status between the participants, and where, although the conversation started out with empty pleasantries, a matter of great potential import about land and inheritance was meant to be broached – excerpt (3) is drawn from a much less consequential, casual encounter between two Zinacantec neighbors, shown as M and X on the transcripts. They were gossiping about a truck crash involving hamlet-mates that took place in Mexico City far from the village where they now sat. M asked X who was driving, to determine whether or not the driver was at fault.

TSOTSIL ZINACANTÁN (conversation videotaped 16 July 1990)

| (3) | a. | m; | much'u s-pas manejar |

Who (CP+)A3-do drive
'Who was driving'

b. pero ja' li   pancho   ta   nachij
    but !   ART Francisco PREP Nachij
    'But it (must have) been Francisco from (the village of) Nachij.'

                                        [
c.   x;   ja' li   pancho   ta   nachij une
                                        !   ART Francisco PREP Nachij CL
                                        'It was Francisco from Nachij.'

Fragment (4) shows how the two neighbors went on to identify some of the people injured in the crash.

TSOTSIL ZINACANTÁN (conversation videotaped 16 July 1990)

(4)
a.   x;   ali   jil   chepil b.
             ART EXPL Joey   name
             'It was that whatsisname – Joey B.'
b.   chepil b.   le',   lok'-em j- ch'ul-me'tik-e
             Joey   name there,   exit-PRF AGTV-hold-mother-CL
             'Joey B.   there, the former (Mayordomo) of the Virgen.'

For a final example, contrast with the previous extracts the form and style in excerpt (5) of a quite distinct spoken genre, a fragment of a monologic Tsotsil "prayer" taken from a much longer interaction – a cornfield protection ceremony at the annual *k'in krus* 'Fiesta of the Cross' in May – in which a Zinacantec shaman or *j'ilol* was contracted by a group of farmers to help guarantee a successful crop. He began his prayer by addressing the spirit of the place, known (but not named in these circumstances) as *y-ajval balamil* (A3-owner earth) 'lord of the earth,' and conceived of as a greedy *ladino* or non-Indian, protecting his wealth and always on the lookout for the souls of incautious humans whom he could put to work as slaves. The shaman explained in the formally parallel doublets or triplets of prayer that the cornfield's human owners had come to beg for his intercession to prevent misfortunes: excessive wind, poor rain, falls, accidents, snakes. Here, the shaman knelt at an improvised cross erected at the edge of a recently planted cornfield, to ask various supernatural entities for their intercession.

TSOTSIL ZINACANTÁN (curing ceremony videotaped 12 May 2002)

(5) a.   y-u'un   ch-ul   xa   s-k'an-ik   a-pertonal
          A3-cause ICP-(B3)-arrive already A3-want-PL A2-pardon
          'Because they arrive here to ask for your pardon.'
     b.   o'lol   balamil //³ o'lol   vinajel
          middle earth   middle heaven
          'Center of earth // center of heaven'
     c.   ja' ch-a-s-ta-ik   o ta na'-el //
          ¡   ICP-B2-A3-find-PL REL PREP know-NMLZ //
                   ch-a-s-ta-ik   o ta   k'opon-el
                   ICP-B2-A3-find-PL REL PREP speak-NMLZ

'So they encounter you in thought // they encounter you in speech.'

d. yech'o ch'ul vinajel // ch'ul balamil // ch'ul rey
    thus   holy heaven // holy earth   // holy king
    'So it is, holy heaven, holy earth, holy king.'

e. mu me x-a-maj   // mu me x-av-ut
    NEG CL ASP-A3-beat // NEG CL ASP-A3-scold
    'Do not beat them // do not rebuke them.'
    . . . ((several lines omitted here))

f. komon me ti k'op=e   // komon me ti   rason=e
    common CL ART word=CL // common CL ART reason=CL
    'May your words and reasoning be shared.'

g. san kixtoval j-tot   // san kixtoval   k-ajval
    St. Christopher A1-father // St. Christopher A1-lord
    St. Christopher, my father // St. Christopher, my lord'

h. kalvaryo ch'ul totil // marya ch'ul me'il
    Calvario holy father // Maria holy mother
    'Holy Father Calvario // Holy mother Mary'

i. y-u'un me jun-uk y-o'on k'usi   y-epal
    A3-cause CL one-SUBJ A3-heart what A3-amount
    'May they be content for however much'

j. chanav-ik   // ch-bein-ik
    ICP+(B3)+travel-PL // ICP-(B3)-journey-PL
    'they travel // they journey.'

5 CONVERSATIONAL STRUCTURE

In what follows, I will refer to these examples of Tsotsil talk to illustrate several issues of interest in the study of conversational interaction, to which Mayan languages have contributed significantly – and should contribute more! They include (a) conversational "responses" and repetition, (b) formulation and "recipient design," and (c) "repair" and intersubjectivity.

5.1 Responses

The notion of an "interaction engine" invokes a possibly universal human "response system" (e.g., Brown 2010) and also a "feedback system" (recall Yngve's [1970] original notion of conversational "back-channel"), both linked to the allocation of turns at talk. Tseltal and Tsotsil have been claimed to institutionalize a kind of dyadic ideal even in multiparty conversation, with a single "respondent" serving as a foil – providing feedback – for a main speaker or narrator (Haviland 1986, 1988b, 1997; Brown 2010). The rate and nature of the feedback – what in Tsotsil is labeled with various derivatives of the root *tak'* 'answer (a person)' (Haviland 2010) – is of considerable comparative and theoretical interest. England (1987), for example, speculates that the amount of repetition in narrative may be an index of "language vitality." Students of child language have also found in dialogic repetition a possible source for specific details of Mayan language acquisition (Pye 1986; Brown 1998, 2014; de León 2007).

The applicative form of the Tsotsil root – *tak'* is *-tak'be* 'answer back.' Its syntactic direct object refers to the person to whose words one responds. A social adept knows the proper responses in a wide variety of situations, to many sorts of speakers; he can be almost anyone's interlocutor. By contrast, the socially inept – a child, a fool, a 'leftover'[4] who has never learned the social graces – 'does not know what to answer'[5] when spoken to. Or, 'like a deaf person,' he will 'answer to one side,'[6] saying something inappropriate if he says anything at all. To say of someone that *mu s-tak' lo'il* (NEG A3-answer talk) 'he doesn't answer conversation' is to dismiss him as interactively clumsy and incompetent: someone who can't even defend himself verbally from a joke or an insult. On the other hand, if someone *lek l-i-s-tak'-be* (good CP-B1-A3-answer-BEN) 'answered me well,' she or he has either topped me in a verbal duel (out-answered me, as it were) or acceded to my request.

Explicit Zinacantec etiquette governs responsiveness. Talk requires uptake. Polite behavior typically comes in paired turns. In salutation, the younger person bows, the older releases, touching the first person's forehead. I greet you on the path with a polite "I'm going," and you counter with "Go, then!" When, in a toast, a first part (*k-ich'-b-an* [A1-take-BEN-B2.IRR] 'let me take it (for you)') goes without its matching reply (*ich'-o* [take-IMP] 'take it!') someone will invariably remind the delinquent speaker with *tak'av-an*[7] *la* (answer-IMP EVID) 'answer, they say!' (i.e., "answer, since someone is talking to you"). Indeed, conversation in Tsotsil, no matter how many potential interlocutors may be involved, normally reduces itself to an apparent dialogue between speaker and unique interlocutor: the first saying what there is to say, and the other *tak'be* 'answering him.'

The apparent mechanics of Tsotsil 'answering back' are especially plain in the introductory exchanges between P and A in excerpt (1) above. An interlocutor has available a variety of resources for constructing a responsive turn. Most prominently, he can simply repeat if not the entire previous clause then at least its major parts: verb or other predicate. Thus, in excerpt (1) line 2 is A's observation that recent rains were light: *pero k'un i-Ø-k'ot* (but soft CP-B3-arrive); the next two lines recycle this material: line 3, P's repeat of *k'un i-Ø-k'ot* (soft CP-B3-arrive) 'lit., soft it-arrived,' and A's line 4, *k'un* 'soft.' Lexical variants, such as the alternation between the expression with an explicit negative *muk' bu* (NEG where), i.e., 'there isn't any' and *ch'abal* 'none, not exist,' derived from the 'positional' root of non-existence *ch'ab*, provide raw material for extended sequences of repetition such as that at lines 11–17. A number of evidential particles and clitics are also available for embellishing a repeated phrase. For example, P's turn at line 30, when shorn of various evidentials, has as its heart *tzk'an vo'* 'lit., it wants rain.' A's reply, at line 31, prepends an evidential linkage and appends the otherwise empty phrasal enclitic *un*.[8] Then there are a variety of ready-made responses: 'assent' or 'agreement' markers (*aa* 'oh' and *ji*['] 'yes,' lines 9 and 10, or lines 15 and 18), expressions of 'news receipt' like *a yech* 'oh, is that so?' (line 7), or expressions of emphatic agreement like *yu'un me* 'indeed, that's why' (lines 27 and 33).

For several Tsotsil conversations, I have charted the volume of talk between the various speakers measured crudely in terms of the approximate number of syllables per turn. Such a syllable count, coupled with the alternating structure of utterance and response in Tsotsil, allows one to calculate a ratio of one person's talk to another's. In the opening sections of P's conversation with the magistrate in example (1) above, P has four turns which average 3.25 syllables per turn, while A's five turns average 5.2 syllables each. Figure 16.1 is a graphical representation of this syllable-per-turn measure. Each of P's turns is represented by a small square whose height corresponds to its number of syllables. The corresponding syllable counts for A's turns are shown with small diamonds. The scale of the vertical axis shows syllable counts; the horizontal axis is a time line of successive turns, where the numbers correspond to numbered lines of transcript. The figure

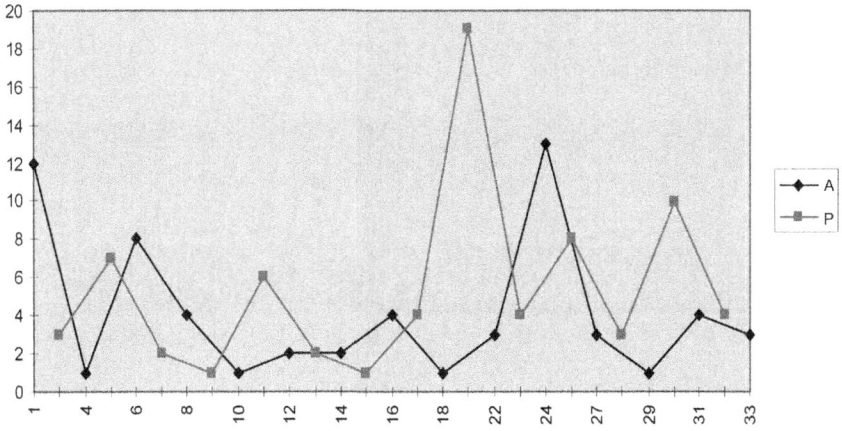

FIGURE 16.1 P AND A MEET, EXCHANGE POLITE PRELIMINARIES

shows the roughly equal distribution of the floor between the two men as they exchange pleasantries.

Such "small talk" only occurs, however, either as a prelude to more serious and purposeful talk (as here), or on those rare occasions when Zinacantecs are brought together with no particular purpose and feel themselves obliged to exchange words. Even in such cases, however, issues of status complicate a neutral allocation of turns, as some interlocutors command more of the conversational floor simply by virtue of age, expertise, or other kinds of micro-political dominance. Moreover, such unconstrained encounters are infrequent compared to other conversational forms, most of which are driven by specific purposes. (In Zinacantán, at least, one never goes to visit just to "shoot the breeze," but always with an errand; and part of the resulting dynamic focuses on interactants' trying to figure out what that errand is.) Divination (Hanks 2006, 2013), curing (e.g., Haviland 2000b), dispute settlement (Haviland 1997), ritual instruction – all specialized conversational venues in Mayan societies, with pronounced status differences between the participants – problematize even more how asymmetries of access, knowledge, and power, as well as shifting access to turns at talk, can (and cannot) be resolved, to facilitate joint action (Clark 1996).

Given what I said earlier about a principal speaker and her or his designated interlocutor in Zinacantec Tsotsil, it should be clear that the admittedly crude measure of speech volume represented in Figure 16.1 suggests who is talking and who is "responding" at any given point in a conversation. It also offers a very approximate measure of "responsiveness" for any given Tsotsil interlocutor. To see this, consider Figure 16.2, which graphically illustrates turn length across the whole of P's conversation with A. The graph shows plainly that the conversation divides itself into three parts. First comes the introductory section – the beginning of which we have already seen – where the two interlocutors trade short turns of roughly equal length. Second comes a section where P's turns are far longer than those of A – indeed, where A rarely utters more than monosyllables. There follows a section where the roles are reversed: A does most of the talking, although P's responsive turns are somewhat longer than were A's when he was "answering."

P's complaint is long, complex, and repetitive, harking back to a history of squabbles, slights, and silence between father and sons over almost ten years. In his litany of woes,

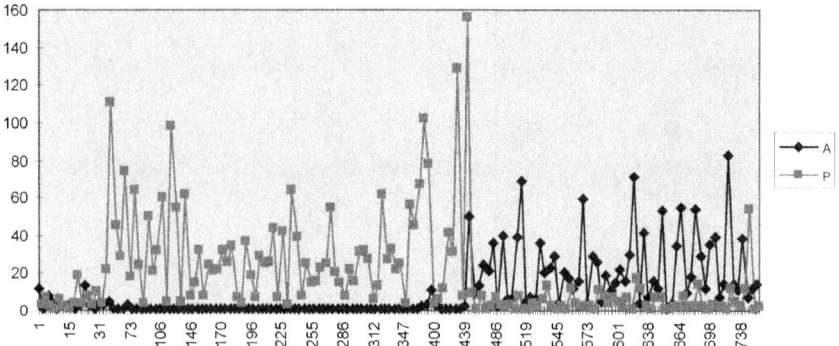

FIGURE 16.2 P VISITS A

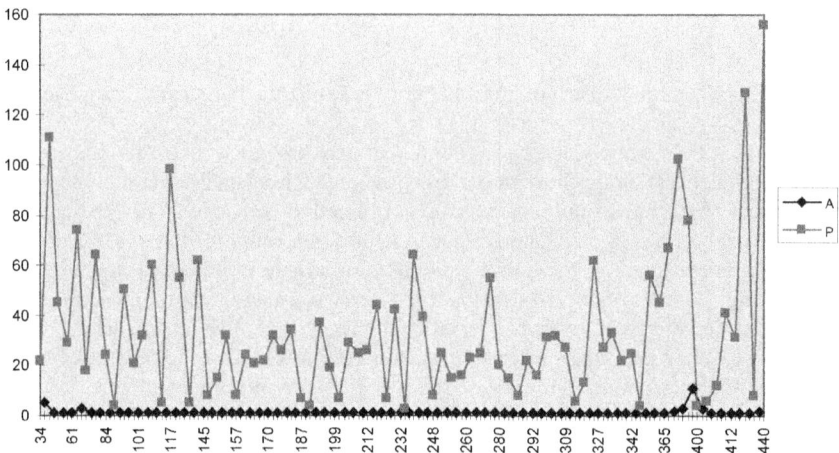

FIGURE 16.3 P TELLS A HIS TROUBLES

P begins by describing how his sons never visit, never speak to him, never offer to help in farming or in the expenses of curing ceremonies. The turn-taking structure in the section of the conversation where P states his complaints is clear in Figure 16.3. Throughout P's long and impassioned speech, the magistrate offers only the barest of responses, rarely venturing more than a monosyllable.

After almost 20 minutes during which P has laid out a complaint against his sons, a drastic shift occurs in the conversation. Up to this point, A has listened to P's whole sorry history virtually without comment, offering responses which closely approximate Yngve's (1970) original notion of "back-channel" – a signal back "up the channel" from listener to speaker that communication is still proceeding. A shows he is listening, comprehending, and that P can continue. However, the notion that P might attempt to disinherit his sons and reclaim the land he has given them – even the plots of land where they have built their own houses – is too extreme for the magistrate to let pass. He steps in with his own optimistically more balanced view, one that might lead to eventual reconciliation instead of total rupture.

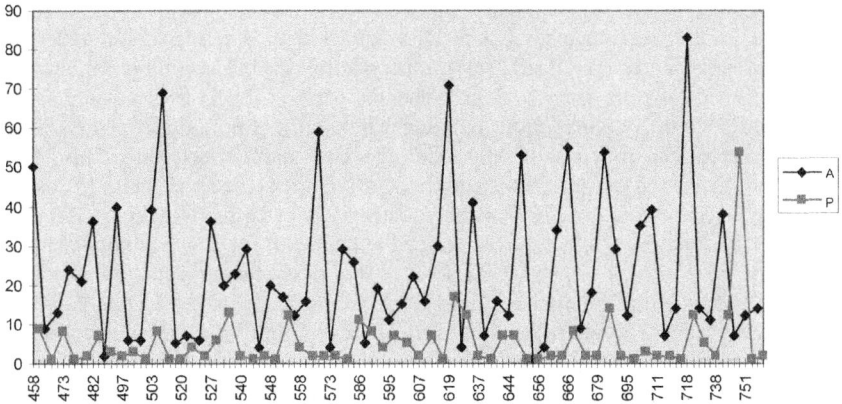

FIGURE 16.4 A GIVES P ADVICE

Once A starts to make substantive remarks, the conversational tables have turned. Abruptly the interchanges shift. A now takes the floor, to explain to P how he thinks matters should proceed. P's contributions recede to mere responses, albeit responses which are on average much longer than those of A in the earlier phase of talk. In the subsequent section of the transcript, for the next 125 turns or so, A averages about 22.2 syllables per turn. P's turns, clearly responsive, average 5.2 syllables. Recall, however, that in the preceding section, A's responsive turns averaged only about 1.3 syllables, which suggests the much more active role P takes in receiving and interpreting A's proffered advice than that taken by A when P was presenting his case. Figure 16.4 graphically depicts this phase of the conversation.

Frequently reported for Mayan conversation is the propensity, amply illustrated in the start of my compadre's conversation above, for "repetition" by which different authors have meant at least three different things.

(a) Mayan languages frequently formulate responses to a turn at talk by recycling or "repeating" some parts of the original (Brown 1979; Brody 1986, 1994; Haviland 1988b). For example, Penelope Brown writes, "during extended turns at talk such as a telling, Tseltal recipients are expected to respond at regular intervals with significant verbal material, repeating parts of the immediately prior utterance" (Brown 1979:ch. 4) (quoted in Rossano et al. 2009:230).

Of considerable interest is how such "repetition" is structurally constrained (see Brown et al. 2009; Brown 2010), and the fact that in multi-party conversations the strings of repetition can extend over many turns (see Haviland 2009), as in excerpt (2) lines 11–17 above. So, too, are the alternatives languages offer to such repetition, through other kinds of non-repetitive, special purpose responsive devices, often with quite specific interactional nuances (Brown 2010).

(b) The rubric of "repetition" is sometimes conflated with a quite different device, often called "parallelism," common throughout Mesoamerica and beyond (e.g., Fox 1974): a special linguistic register that employs exact syntactic parallel constructions often combined with semantically linked lexical doublets or triplets (e.g., Monod-Becquelin 1979, among many others), and characteristic of prayer as well other sorts of discourse genres (Haviland 1994). Such parallelism is clear in the fragments of prayer cited above in excerpt (5). The shaman's talk is almost entirely organized in paired lines (shown with double slashes separating the two parts), in which a single frame is repeated with usually only a simple lexical alternation differentiating them. At lines d and e of (5), the shaman addresses the Lord of the Earth, calling him *ch'ul vinajel // ch'ul balamil // ch'ul rey* (holy heaven // holy earth // holy king). He pleads with this sometimes sinister protector of the fields *mu me x-a-maj//mu me x-av-ut* (NEG CL ASP-A3-beat // NEG CL ASP-A3-scold) 'Do not beat them // do not rebuke them,' i.e., do not mistreat the owners of the cornfield, for example by sending dangerous snakes or causing accidents to befall them as they work. The sometimes euphemistic paired imagery of such parallel talk indexes both the indirectness and the power that characterize such intercessions with the supernatural and the specialized knowledge of the shaman who wields parallel language.

(c) Gossen (1985) also identifies a further, perhaps related, propensity in Chamula Tsotsil conversation for a kind of semantic redundancy in which single ideas are reformulated and repeated, either by a single speaker or by a dialogic partner, but without the strict syntactic parallelism of (b) above. The interactions between these different kinds of repetition in Mayan conversation have direct repercussions for structural analyses of the relevant languages.

5.2 Formulations and repair

A central issue in conversational analysis has been what Schegloff sometimes calls the "formulation problem" (Schegloff 1968, 1972) and its links to "recipient design": the fact that interactants in real time must "formulate" ways of putting things adequate both to their own purposes and to the specifics of the moment, in particular, to whom they are speaking (or intend to speak). How in conversation one refers to another person (Sacks and Schegloff 1979) is a particularly clear case of the constraints on formulations, and as mentioned above it has been studied in some detail for various languages, including three Mayan languages (Enfield and Stivers 2007). For example, if a particular *compadre* P talks to me in Tsotsil about "*l-a-kumpa R*" (lit., 'your compadre R') I must calculate whom he means by virtue of the fact (i) that P knows that R is my compadre, (ii) that P knows that I know he knows it, etc., and (iii) that R must therefore be someone P wants to identify by reference to *my* relationship to R rather than his own; and so on. In excerpt (3) above, the two neighbors seem to be able to agree immediately upon whom they mean by "Francisco from (the village of) Nachij," whereas in excerpt (4) the pause between C's first mention of "Joey B." in line (a) and the expanded formulation "Joey B. there, the former (Mayordomo) of the Virgen" in line (b) suggests an instance of repair (see below) in which the second formulation is intended to help his interlocutor recognize the person he's talking about.

Of course, the formulation problem afflicts all reference in conversation, not just reference to persons. Moreover, much of "recipient design" is not about reference at all, but about appropriately calibrating personal identities, relationships, and social status between interactants. In Mayan conversation, such matters as gender, age, ritual expertise, kinship both real and fictive, and various sorts of social and personal authority, are always indexed in speech, via devices ranging from referential formulations to vocatives, from evidentials to pronominal inflections, or even to the proportion of the conversational floor to which conversational partners are granted access (see bibliographic references to Brown, Brody, Danziger, Hanks, Haviland, Shoaps, inter alia). Arcos López (2009), in a recent MA thesis, argues that something as subtle as omitting the ubiquitous "gender prefixes" on personal names in Ch'ol can index dismissive attitudes towards the names' bearers. Even the existence of marked children's lexicons (Pye 1986), or the special place of children in calculi of respect and privacy (e.g., Reynolds 2008; Berman 2011) speak to the indexical power of linguistic formulations, as do newly emerging forms of, for example, evangelical Protestant discourse (Baron 2004).

The phenomenon of "repair" – mechanisms in talk that allow participants to note and correct various sorts of dysfluencies, mis-speakings, and (at least apparent) misunder-standings – has been proposed as another potentially universal aspect of conversational organization (see Schegloff 2006 for a recent account) which, in recent analyses, has been linked to the distinctly human phenomenon of "intersubjectivity" – the ability of inter-actants to perceive and share one another's thoughts, feelings, and perspectives (Ding-emanse and Floyd 2014; Sidnell 2014). Again, Penelope Brown's work on Tseltal has contributed to a large comparative study of some of the linguistic devices involved in repair sequences, namely the existence in many languages of forms that work (and often sound) like English 'huh?' (Enfield et al. 2013). The very fact that such "repair initiators" seem to signal an interactive realization that what a speaker might have "meant to say" has not been properly "understood" is taken to be evidence for what is often called a "theory of mind" – a characteristically human perspective on mutual access to another's "inner states" (and a conviction that others have such states). Mayan languages have also been drawn up into comparative debates about the extent and depth of such presumed intersubjective access among individuals. (See especially Danziger 2006, 2010, 2013, and Groark 2013. But see Hanks 2013, whose nuanced notion of "co-engagement" gives a cognitively more neutral cast to the issue.) Mayan languages have made important theo-retical contributions to a range of related phenomena, including evidentials (Martin 1998; Haviland 1987, 1989, 2002; Fox 2001; Kockelman 2003a, b, 2004, 2005) which index (and interactively engage) a variety of presumed states of knowledge among interactants, and markers of what is sometimes called "stance" (Haviland 1988; Shoaps 2004, 2007; Danziger 2013, or the contributions of Penelope Brown in Enfield et al. 2012) which expand the range of subjective attitudes in which speakers may be implicated by different linguistic devices.

6 MULTIMODALITY

Conversation most commonly takes place face-to-face (cell phones and iPads not-withstanding), and as a result interaction involves bodies as well as voices. It is thus worth making separate mention of contributions from Mayan linguistics – both past and potential – to the study of multimodality, especially visible aspects of utterance.

Gaze, for example, has been a focus of analysis in face-to-face interaction from the ear-liest studies to the most recent (Kendon 1967; Streeck 2014; see Rossano et al. 2009 for a review). Once again, Tseltal has contributed directly to comparative research: speakers from Tenejapa seemingly employ "gaze avoidance" at moments where mutual eye con-tact routinely occurs in other conversational traditions (Rossano et al. 2009). Brown and Levinson (2005) argue that as a result other sorts of feedback mechanisms must be mar-shaled to compensate for the lack of visual feedback. This may be one of the reasons, on their account, for the repetitiveness of Tseltal responses. Gaze avoidance, in turn, appears partly to result from "observed seating patterns": Tenejapans are said to "prefer" to sit "side to side or at an angle" (Rossano et al. 2009:226) rather than, say, face-to-face, in at least some sorts of dyadic conversation. Patterns of bodily orientation – another early theme in foundational interactional research (Kendon 1990) – are thus linked to patterns of conversational structure.

Gaze is almost a perfect site to observe the contrast between universal claims (how conversational turn-taking as a general mechanism is universal, and how, if at all, gaze orientation may play a role in regulating it) and cultural difference: an interactive style in Tenejapa Tseltal, for instance, where you do *not* gaze at your interlocutor, for reasons both ecological (how your bodies are deployed in space) and "cultural" (where it is polite and appropriate to look, and where it isn't). More detailed studies of comparative bodily engagement in Mayan are required to separate potentially relevant analytic strands: is *all* conversation in Mayan languages similarly constrained, with respect to seating position or gaze? What happens when bodies dispose themselves in other ways – as in conversation when people are seated at a table, or around a fire, or when they move around because of other concurrent activities? Do status differences between interlocutors affect visible, as well as spoken, aspects of utterances? A pattern of bodily and visual interaction quite different from that suggested for Tenejapa Tseltal is described, for example, in Chamula Tsotsil by López Jimenez (2010).

The role of other visible communicative behaviors – especially manual gestures – is still underappreciated for Mayan languages. There are a few exceptions (Haviland 1993, 2000a, 2003, 2005a, 2013b; Danziger 1994, 199, 2004; de León 1998, 2005; López 2010; Le Guen 2011a, b; Pérez González 2012), the authors of all of which have examined the role of pointing gestures in talk about space and time. Some well-known typological features of Mayan – the special classes of what have been called "affective" or "mimetic" verbs (Laughlin 1975; Maffi 1990) or "ideophones" (López 2010; Pérez González 2012), and the class of "positional" roots that elaborate the semantics of anatomies and their configurations – have been suggested to give rise to characteristic patterns of iconic gesturing, as though two complementary semiotic channels are involved in expressing those conceptual domains speakers choose to elaborate (Haviland 2005d).

As an example of how concern with visible and bodily aspects of interaction can complement and enrich ordinary linguistic approaches, consider how Zinacantec talk calls attention to what I have called "referential gestures" – indexical uses of the body that "pick out" referents in discourses of different kinds. Although Zinacantec Tsotsil, unlike many languages of the world, is relatively poor in terms for "cardinal directions" it may come as no surprise that Zinacantecs are extremely well-oriented geographically and make heavy use of that orientation both in talk (where a metaphor of "elevation" is turned to geographic use – *ak'ol* 'high' may conventionally denote East or *lok'eb k'ak'al* 'where the sun rises', and *olon* 'low' may denote West or *maleb k'ak'al* 'where the sun sets' – see de León 1994; Haviland 2005a; contrast Brown and Levinson 1993 for a different convention) and in bodily indications. Zinacantecs know or can calculate where relevant places lie "as the crow flies," and they rely on this knowledge in a variety of ways in conversation, although a large part of the evidence that they do so comes not from their words but from their gestures.

One visible manifestation of such orientation is gaze. Consider how the two conversationalists in the videotaped conversation transcribed in excerpts (3) and (4) above were seated. Figure 16.5 shows how the narrator (on the left in the figure) positioned his body as he said that the accident took place "late, about 2 or 2:30" as the neighbors left Mexico City with a load of freshly bought flowers for sale.

The crucial fact is that the narrator X, seated facing north, was looking up to the west; that is, he looked directly at the place in the afternoon sky where the sun would

FIGURE 16.5 X LOOKS UP AT THE AFTERNOON SKY

FIGURE 16.6 SHAMAN ADDRESSES THE LORD OF THE EARTH AND THE CORNFIELD

have been at the time of the narrated events, a convention of conversation in Zina-cantán but doubtless common for many people living on the land around the world (see Haviland 1993; Floyd 2008). Note that the generalized use of such a referential device requires that conversationalists keep in mind where East and West are, and how the sun travels.

Somewhat more esoteric is the example of the Zinacantec shaman whose prayer is transcribed in excerpt (5) above. Unlike the altars of churches which are normatively arranged so that one prays to the East, the makeshift cross in this case was set up so as to allow the shaman to face the cornfield and its supernatural lord directly. In this case he was facing northwest (Figure 16.6).

Soon the shaman began to enlist less sinister inhabitants of the geography, asking for the joint intercession of the sacred mountains, named for saints, which surround the ceremonial center or *cabecera* of the municipality of Zinacantán as a whole. As he addressed these sacred mountains, he notably turned his body to address them, launching his prayer in the actual directions where they were located, some thirty kilometers away "as the crow flies" (Figure 16.7). That is, his bodily orientation reflected his exact knowledge of where he was *ta s-ba balamil* (PREP A3-face earth) 'on the face of the earth,' and where his distant addressees were, as well.

Geography has a social as well as a spiritual dimension, similarly central in Zinacantec interaction. When knowledge of space is absolute, shared, and highly presupposable, space itself becomes both metonym and mnemonic for social history and biography. The neighbors conversing about the car crash provide several exemplary demonstrations of the use of geocentrically oriented space as an anchored referential map. The two men, X and M, are seated side by side, facing slightly west of north. X, sitting on the viewer's left in the still frames (and thus on the east side) is the narrator, while M, on the right (i.e., to the west) is asking him for more details about the accident.

Their "anchored" uses of direction depend on where they actually sit to locate protagonists mentioned in the ongoing discourse. For example, they discuss whether the driver of the truck was at fault, and their means of identifying the driver are as much gestural as spoken.

In the dialogue transcribed in excerpt (3) above, just as M finished his question at line a, "Who was driving?" he, as it were, answered his own question with a gesture, gazing quickly up to his right (that is to the east of where he and his interlocutor sat), directly in the direction of Nachij, the town where the hired driver for this locally owned truck

FIGURE 16.7 SHAMAN ADDRESSES THE ANCESTRAL MOUNTAINS

lived (Figure 16.8). In fact, he thus identified the driver gesturally before he ventured his name in words.

X confirmed, in overlap, that M was right about the driver, simultaneously pointing with his right hand (Figure 16.9) toward the village of Nachij, about ten kilometers away over steep mountains (Figure 16.10).[9]

And just as X could refer to individuals by indicating where they lived, so could he refer to notable aspects of their biographies (for example religious offices or *cargos* they might have held) in identifying the man injured in the crash in excerpt (4). In fact, naming

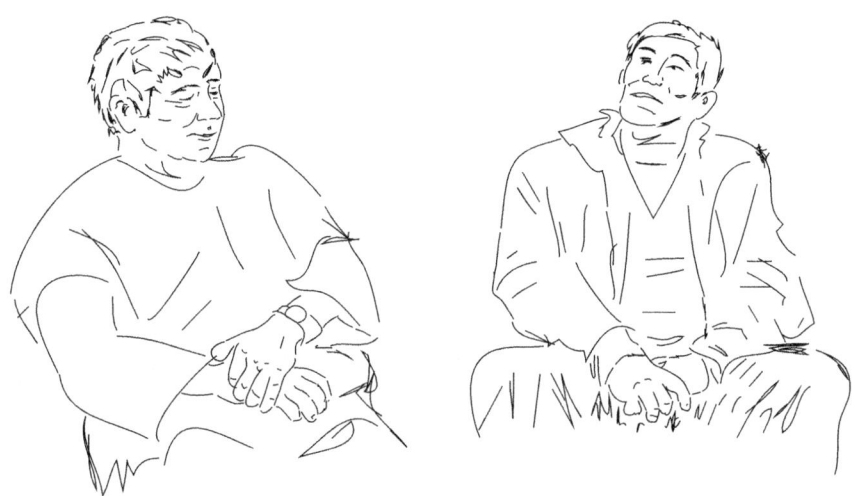

FIGURE 16.8 M GLANCES IN THE DIRECTION OF THE DRIVER'S HAMLET

FIGURE 16.9 X GESTURES TOWARD THE DRIVER'S HAMLET

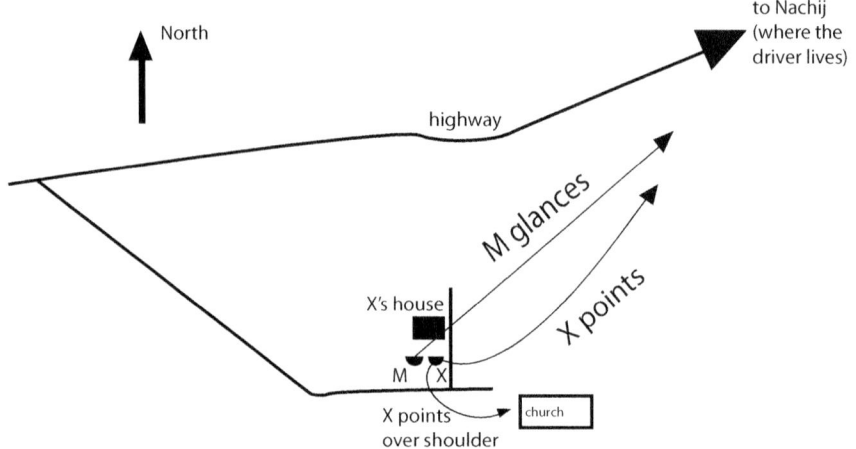

FIGURE 16.10 SIMPLIFIED MAP SHOWING RELATIVE POSITIONS OF INTERLOCUTORS AND THE PLACES MENTIONED

FIGURE 16.11 X INDICATES THE PROTAGONIST'S HOUSE AND NEARBY CHURCH

the individual seems to have been the source of different kinds of interactional "trouble." X himself apparently tried to bring the injured man's name to his mind in part by pointing first in the direction of the man's house from where he sat, even before he pronounced the name (Figure 16.11, left panel). As I noted above in discussing formulations and repair, X's first reference to the injured man met with hesitation from his conversational partner. X continued to point in the direction of the injured man's house as he repeated the man's name (line b of excerpt 4). He then switched the direction of his pointing finger (Figure 16.11, right panel), aiming it instead toward the village church (see the map in

Figure 16.10 again), as he turned to his interlocutor and added that the man in question had performed community service by holding a religious office there. This composite utterance was sufficient to allow M to identify the man.

It is a convention of Zinacantec (Tsotsil) conversation that deictic gestures be "correctly" oriented toward even distant referents, in ways these examples have shown. Such orientation with respect to the place of interaction thus gives interlocutors quite specific information (insofar as their own knowledge of geography allows them to recover it). It is a further convention that the deictic center from which directions are calculated can also be "transposed," that is, moved conceptually to an "origo" other than the actual place where interlocutors find themselves. In such cases a more complex directional precision obtains, and a speaker's pointing gestures are understood to be, as it were, lifted from the present spot and conceptually laminated on top of the new narrated origo, preserving cardinal directions. Such transpositions are extremely common in giving directions or talking about space, and the principles governing them – central for understanding the words involved – are only revealed in natural interaction (see Haviland 2005a).

7 CONCLUDING REMARKS

These topics are only a few among many aspects of ordinary conversation that deserve attention from the new generation of young Mayan linguists and anthropologists who can re-embed the structures of their languages in the ordinary contexts of quotidian use. Deserving special mention, in this context, is the exemplary thesis of José López (2010) on Chamula Tsotsil, which ranges across a broad spectrum of the topics I have mentioned here, from native categories of speech genres to parallelism, from Kendon's (1990) "f-formations" (ways people arrange their bodies in conversation) to iconic gestures and prosody, and from patterns of mutual gaze and attention to participation frames (Goffman 1979). It is only when scholars are able to address the social skills that conversational ability in a language begins to provide that the true genius of Mayan languages as vehicles of social life will begin to be revealed.

NOTES

1   The very first words exchanged, including the formal greetings as we entered the house, are not on my audiotape, as I only asked permission to turn on the tape recorder once we were seated.

2   Square brackets between lines give an approximate location for overlapping turns. Speakers are indicated by single letter pseudonymous prefixes followed by a semicolon. Parentheticals indicate uncertain hearing by the transcriber. In these simplified transcripts I apply a crude notion of "turn" to Zincantec talk, counting as a turn a stretch of a single person's speech sandwiched between the speech of other people. Within a turn so delimited other substructures may be discerned, signaled by pauses, intonation, and various grammatical parsing devices. I indicate these turn-internal divisions on transcripts by dividing a stretch of talk into lines.

3   The double slashes here separate individual subparts of the formally parallel repetitive constructions characteristic of Tsotsil prayer.

4   *kechel* 'leftover, leavings.'

5   *mu s-na'x-tak'av* (NEG A3-know ASP-Ø-answer)

6 *jot o s-tak'be* (side REL [CP+]A3-answer-APPL). The Tsotsil word for deaf person, *uma'*, literally means 'dumb' and is associated with either not speaking at all or with 'answering' inappropriately.

7 The root *tak'* produces a transitive stem *tak'* 'answer [something said],' a ditransitive applicative stem *tak'be* 'answer [someone],' and also an intransitive stem *tak'av* 'respond.'

8 Unhelpfully, Spanish-speaking Zinacantecs ordinarily gloss *un* as *pues*, 'then.' Laughlin's gloss (1975) is "then/participle always occurring at end of phrase/."

9 Reference to individuals by pointing to places associated with them, such as their houses, is widely reported and specifically cited as a naming strategy in LSMY (Lengua de Señas de Maya Yucateco). See Kinil Canche 2015 as well as Haviland 2003 for other Mayan examples.

REFERENCES

Arcos López, Nicolás. 2009. "Los clasificadores numerales y las clases nominales en ch'ol." MA thesis, CIESAS, México.

Baron, Akesha. 2004. "'I'm a woman but I *know* God leads my way: Agency and Tzotzil evangelical discourse." *Language in Society* 33: 249–83.

Barrett, Rusty. 2008. "Linguistic differentiation and Mayan language revitalization in Guatemala." *Journal of Sociolinguistics* 12: 275–305.

Berman, Elise. 2011. "The irony of immaturity: K'iche' children as mediators and buffers in adult social interactions." *Childhood* 18: 274–88.

Brazelton, Thomas Berry. 1972. "Implications of infant development among the Mayan Indians of Mexico." *Human Development* 15: 90–111.

Bricker, Victoria R. 1973a. *Ritual humor in highland Chiapas*. Austin: University of Texas.

Bricker, Victoria R. 1973b. "Three genres of Tzotzil insult." In *Meaning in Mayan languages*, ed. by Munro Edmonson, 184–203. The Hague: Mouton.

Bricker, Victoria R. 1974. "The ethnographic context of some traditional Mayan speech genres." In *Explorations in the ethnography of speaking*, ed. by Richard Bauman and Joel Sherzer, 368–89. Cambridge: Cambridge University Press.

Bricker, Victoria R. 1980. "The function of humor in Zinacantan." *Journal of Anthropological Research* 36: 411–18.

Brody, Jill. 1986. "Repetition as a rhetorical and conversational device in Tojolab'al (Mayan)." *International Journal of American Linguistics* 52: 255–74.

Brody, Jill. 1987. "Particles in Tojolab'al Mayan discourse." *Kansas Working Papers in Linguistics* 12: 1–12.

Brody, Jill. 1991. "Indirection in the negotiation of self in everyday Tojolab'al women's conversation." *Journal of Linguistic Anthropology* 1: 78–96.

Brody, Jill. 1993. "Mayan conversation as interaction." *Proceedings of the First Symposium About Language and Society-Austin: Texas Linguistic Forum* 33: 234–43.

Brody, Jill. 1994. "Multiple repetitions in Tojolab'al conversation." In *Repetition in discourse*, vol. II, ed. by Barbara Johnstone, 3–14. Norwood: Ablex.

Brody, Jill. 1996. "Competition as cooperation: Tojolab'al Maya women's barter." In *Proceedings of the fourth Berkeley women and language conference*, ed. by Natasha Warner, Jocelyn Ahlers, Leela Bilmes, Monica Oliver, Suzanne Wertheim, and Melinda Chen, 99–108. Berkeley: Berkeley Women and Language Group.

Brody, Jill. 2000a. "Co-construction in Tojolab'al conversational narratives: Translating cycles, quotes, evaluations, evidentials and emotions." In *Translating native Latin American verbal art: Ethnopoetics and ethnography of speaking*, ed. by Kay Sammons and Joel Sherzer, 86–103. (Smithsonian Series of Studies in Native American Literatures). Washington: Smithsonian Institution Press.

Brody, Jill. 2000b. "Spatilab'il sk'ujol 'tell them "hey" for me': Traditional Mayan speech genre goes multimedia." *Proceedings of the Seventh Annual Symposium about Language and Society-Austin: Texas Linguistic Forum* 43: 1–14.

Brown, Penelope. 1979. "Language, interaction, and sex roles in a Mayan community: a study of politeness and the position of women." PhD diss., University of California, Berkeley.

Brown, Penelope. 1980. "How and why are women more polite: Some evidence from a Mayan community." In *Women and language in literature and society*, ed. by Sally McConnell Ginet, Ruth Borker, Nelly Furman Praeger, 111–36. Westport: Greenwood Press.

Brown, Penelope. 1990. "Gender, politeness and confrontation in Tenejapa." *Discourse Processes* 13: 121–41.

Brown, Penelope. 1995. "Politeness strategies and the attribution of intentions: the case of Tzeltal irony." In *Social intelligence and interaction: expressions and implications of the social bias in human intelligence*, ed. by Goody, Esther, 153–74. Cambridge: Cambridge University Press.

Brown, Penelope. 1998. "Conversational structure and language acquisition: the role of repetition in Tzeltal adult and child speech." *Journal of Linguistic Anthropology* 8: 197–221.

Brown, Penelope. 2007. "Principles of person reference in Tzeltal conversation." In *Person reference in interaction: Linguistic, cultural, and social perspectives*, ed. by Nick J. Enfield and Tanya Stivers, 172–202. Cambridge: Cambridge University Press.

Brown, Penelope. 2010. "Questions and their responses in Tzeltal." *Journal of Pragmatics* 42: 2627–48.

Brown, Penelope. 2014. "The interactional context of language learning in Tzeltal." In *Language in interaction: studies in honor of Eve V. Clark*, ed. by Inbal Arnon, Marisa Casillas, Chigusa Kurumada, and Bruno Estigarriba, 51–82. Amsterdam: Benjamins.

Brown, Penelope, Olivier Le Guen, and Mark A. Sicoli. 2009. "Dialogic repetition in Tzeltal, Yucatec, and Zapotec conversation." Talk presented at SSILA summer meeting 2009 (Society for the Study of the Indigenous Languages of the Americas). Berkely, CA, July 17, 2009.

Brown, Penelope, and Stephen C. Levinson. 1993. "'Uphill' and 'downhill' in Tzeltal." *Journal of Linguistic Anthropology* 3: 46–74.

Brown, Penelope, and Stephen C. Levinson. 2005. "Comparative response systems." Paper presented to the annual meetings of the American Anthropological Association, San Francisco, November 2005.

Brown, Penelope, Barbara Pfeiler, Lourdes de León, and Clifton Pye. 2013. "The acquisition of agreement in four Mayan languages." In *The acquisition of ergativity*, ed. by Edith Bavin and Sabine Stoll, 271–306. Amsterdam: Benjamins.

Burns, Allen F. 1980. "Interactive features in Yucatec Mayan narratives." *Language in Society* 9: 307–19.

Cancian, Francesca M. 1964. "Interaction patterns in Zinacanteco families." *American Sociological Review* 29: 540–550.

Chavajay, Pablo, and Barbara Rogoff. 1999. "Cultural variation in management of attention by children and their caregivers." *Developmental Psychology* 35: 1–12.

Chavajay, Pablo, and Barbara Rogoff. 2002. "Schooling and traditional collaborative social organization of problem solving by Mayan mothers and children." *Developmental Psychology* 38: 55–66.

Choi, Jinsook. 2011. "El uso de los dos idiomas en Momostenango." In *La Comunidad K'iche'-Maya de Santiago Momostenango: Su Historia, Cultura, Lengua y Arte*, ed. by Robert Carmack and Humberto Ak'ab'al, 115–40. Guatemala: Maya Wuj.

Clark, Herbert H. 1996. *Using language*. New York: Cambridge University Press.

Collier, Jane F. 1968. *Courtship and Marriage in Zinacantan, Chiapas, Mexico*. New Orleans: Middle American Research Institute, Tulane University.

Collier, Jane F. 1973. *Law and social change in Zinacantan*. Palo Alto: Stanford University Press.

Collins, Wesley M. 2005. "Codeswitching avoidance as a strategy for Mam (Maya) linguistic revitalization." *International Journal of American Linguistics* 71: 239–76.

Danziger, Eve. 1994. "Out of sight, out of mind: Person, perception and function in Mopan Maya spatial deixis." *Linguistics: An Interdisciplinary Journal of the Language Sciences* 32: 885–907.

Danziger, Eve. 1998. "Getting here from there: The acquisition of point of view in Mopan Maya." *Ethos: Journal of the Society for Psychological Anthropology* 26: 48–72.

Danziger, Eve. 1999. "Language, space and sociolect: cognitive correlates of gendered speech in Mopan Maya." In *Language diversity and cognitive representations*, ed. by Catherine Fuchs and Stéphane Robert, 85–106. Amsterdam: Benjamins.

Danziger, Eve. 2001. *Relatively speaking: language, thought and Kinship in Mopan Maya*. Oxford Studies in Anthropological Linguistics. New York: Oxford University Press.

Danziger, Eve. 2004. "Deixis, gesture and spatial frame of reference." *Chicago Linguistics Society, Parasession: Body and Mind* 39: 105–22.

Danziger, Eve. 2006. "The thought that counts: understanding variation in cultural theories of interaction." In *The roots of human sociality: culture, cognition and human interaction*, ed. by Stephen Levinson and Nick Enfield, 259–78. (Wenner-Gren Foundation for Anthropological Research). Oxford: Berg Press.

Danziger, Eve. 2010. "On trying and lying: cultural configurations of the Gricean Maxim of quality." *Intercultural Pragmatics* 7: 199–219.

Danziger, Eve. 2013. "Conventional wisdom: Imagination, obedience and intersubjectivity." *Language & Communication* 33: 251–62.

de León, Lourdes. 1994. "Exploration in the acquisition of geocentric location by Tzotzil children." *Linguistics* 32: 857–84.

de León, Lourdes. 1998. "The emergent participant: Interactive patterns in the socialization of Tzotzil (Mayan) infants." *Journal of Linguistic Anthropology* 8: 131–61.

de León, Lourdes. 2007. "Parallelism, metalinguistic play, and the interactive emergence of Zinacantec Mayan siblings' culture." *Research on Language and Social Interaction* 40: 405–36.

de León Pasquel, Lourdes. 2005. *La llegada del alma: lenguaje, infancia y socialización entre los mayas de Zinacantán*. Mexico: CIESAS.

Dingemanse, Mark, and Simeon Floyd. 2014. "Conversation across cultures." In *The Cambridge handbook of linguistic anthropology*, ed. by Nick J. Enfield, Paul Kockelman, and Jack Sidnell, 447–80. Cambridge: Cambridge University Press.

Enfield, Nick J., Penelope Brown, and Jan P. de Ruiter. 2012. "Epistemic dimensions of polar questions: sentence-final particles in comparative perspective." In Questions: formal, functional and interactional perspectives, ed. by Jan P. de Ruiter, 193–221. New York: Cambridge University Press.

Enfield, Nick J., Mark Dingemanse, Julija Baranova, Joe Blythe, Penelope Brown, Tyko Dirksmeyer, Paul Drew, Simeon Floyd, Sonja Gipper, Rósa Gísladóttir, Gertie Hoymann, Kobin H. Kendrick, Stephen C. Levinson, Lilla Magyari, Elizabeth Manrique, Giovanni Rossi, Lila San Roque, and Francisco Torreira. 2013. "Huh? What? – A first survey in 21 languages." In Conversational repair and human understanding, ed. by Makoto Hayashi, Geoffrey Raymond, and Jack Sidnell, 343–80. New York: Cambridge University Press.

Enfield, Nick J., Paul Kockelman, and Jack Sidnell, eds. 2014. The Cambridge handbook of linguistic anthropology. Cambridge: Cambridge University Press.

Enfield, Nick J., and Stephen C. Levinson, eds. 2006. Roots of human sociality. Oxford, New York: Berg.

Enfield, Nick J., and Tanya Stivers, eds. 2007. Person reference in interaction: linguistic, cultural, and social perspectives. Cambridge: Cambridge University Press.

Enfield, Nick J., Tanya Stivers, and Stephen C. Levinson. 2010. "Question – response sequences in conversation across ten languages: An introduction." Journal of Pragmatics 42: 2615–19.

England, Nora C. 1987. "Variation in Mayan narrative." Anthropological Linguistics 1987: 522–32.

Floyd, Simeon. 2008. "Solar iconicity, conventionalized gesture and multimodal meaning in Nheengatú." Paper presented at the Arizona Linguistics and Anthropology Symposium, Tucson, Arizona.

Fox, Barbara A. 2001. "Evidentiality: authority, responsibility, and entitlement in english conversation." Journal of Linguistic Anthropology 11: 167–92. doi:10.1525/jlin.2001.11.2.167

Fox, James J. 1974. "Our ancestors spoke in pairs': Rotinese views of language, dialect, and code." In Explorations in the ethnography of speaking, ed. by Richard Bauman and Joel Sherzer, 65–85. Cambridge: Cambridge University Press.

French, Brigittine. 2001. "Language ideologies and collective identities in post-conflict Guatemala." PhD diss., The University of Iowa.

Gaskins, Suzanne. 1996. "How Mayan parental theories come into play." In Parents' cultural belief systems: their origins, expressions, and consequences, ed. by Sara Harkness and Charles M. Super, 345–63. New York: The Guilford Press.

Gaskins, Suzanne. 1999. "Children's daily lives in a Mayan village: A case study of culturally constructed roles and activities." In Children's engagement in the world: sociocultural perspectives, ed. by Artin Göncü, 25–60. Cambridge: Cambridge University Press.

Gaskins, Suzanne. 2006. "Cultural perspectives on infant–caregiver interaction." In The roots of human sociality: culture, cognition and human interaction, ed. by S. Levinson and N. Enfield, 279–98. (Wenner-Gren Foundation for Anthropological Research). Oxford: Berg Press.

Goffman, Erving. 1957. "Alienation from interaction." Human Relations 10: 47–60.

Goffman, Erving. 1979. "Footing." Semiotica 25: 1–30.

Gossen, Gary H. 1971. "Chamula genres of verbal behavior." Journal of American Folklore 84: 145–67.

Gossen, Gary H. 1973. "Chamula Tzotzil proverbs: neither fish nor fowl." In *Meaning in Mayan languages,* ed. by Munro Edmonson, 207–33. The Hague: Mouton.

Gossen, Gary H. 1974a. *Chamulas in the world of the sun: time and space in a Maya oral tradition.* Cambridge: Harvard University Press.

Gossen, Gary H. 1974b. "To speak with a heated heart: Chamula canons of style and good performance." In *Explorations in the ethnography of speaking,* ed. by Richard Bauman and Joel Sherzer, 389–413. Cambridge: Cambridge University Press.

Gossen, Gary H. 1976. "Verbal dueling in Chamula." In *Speech play: research and resources for studying linguistic creativity,* ed. by Barbara Kishenblatt-Gimblett, 121–46. Philadelphia: University of Pennsylvania Press.

Gossen, Gary H. 1985. "Tzotzil literature." In *Supplement to the handbook of middle American Indians,* vol. 3, ed. by Victoria R. Bricker and Munro Edmonson, 65–106. Austin: University of Texas Press.

Greenfield, Patricia M., Ashley E. Maynard, and Carla P. Childs. (2003). "Historical change, cultural learning, and cognitive representation in Zinacantec Maya children." *Cognitive Development* 18: 455–87.

Groark, Kevin P. 2005. "Vital warmth and well-being: steambathing as household therapy among the Tzeltal and Tzotzil Maya of highland Chiapas, Mexico." *Social Science and Medicine* 61: 785–95.

Groark, Kevin P. 2008. "Social opacity and the dynamics of empathic in-sight among the Tzotzil Maya of Chiapas, Mexico." *Ethos* 36: 427–48.

Groark, Kevin P. 2009. "Discourses of the soul: the negotiation of personal agency in Tzotzil Maya dream narrative." *American Ethnologist* 36: 705–21.

Groark, Kevin P. 2010. "Willful souls: dreaming and the dialectics of self-experience among the tzotzil Maya of Highland Chiapas, Mexico." In *Toward an anthropology of the will,* ed. by Keith M. Murphy and C. Jason Throop, 101–22. Palo Alto: Stanford University Press.

Groark, Kevin P. 2013. "Toward a cultural phenomenology of intersubjectivity: The extended relational field of the Tzotzil Maya of highland Chiapas, Mexico." *Language & Communication* 33: 278–91.

Hanks, William F. 1984. "Sanctification, structure, and experience in a Yucatec ritual event." *Journal of American Folklore* 97: 131–66.

Hanks, William F. 1990. *Referential practice: Language and lived space among the Maya.* Chicago: University of Chicago Press.

Hanks, William F. 1992. "The indexical ground of deictic reference." In *Rethinking context: Language as an interactive phenomenon,* ed. by Alessandro Duranti and Charles Goodwin, 43–77. Cambridge: Cambridge University Press.

Hanks, William F. 1993. "Metalanguage and pragmatics of deixis." In *Reflexive language: reported speech and metapragmatics,* ed. by John Lucy, 127–58. Cambridge: Cambridge University Press.

Hanks, William F. 1996a. "Exorcism and the description of participant roles." In *Natural histories of discourse,* ed. by M. Silverstein and G. Urban, 160–200. Chicago: University of Chicago Press.

Hanks, William F. 1996b. "Language form and communicative practices." In *Rethinking linguistic relativity,* ed. by John J. Gumperz and Stephen C. Levinson, 232–70. Cambridge: Cambridge University Press.

Hanks, William F. 2006. "Joint commitment and common ground in a ritual event." In *Roots of human sociality,* ed. by Nick J. Enfield and Stephen C. Levinson, 299–328. Oxford, New York: Berg.

Hanks, William F. 2007. "Person reference in Yucatec Maya conversation." In *Person reference in interaction: linguistic, cultural, and social perspectives,* ed. by Nick J. Enfield and Tanya Stivers, 149–71. Cambridge: Cambridge University Press.

Hanks, William F. 2013. "Counterparts: co-presence and ritual intersubjectivity." *Language and Communication* 33: 263–77.

Haviland, John B. 1977a. *Gossip, reputation, and knowledge in Zinacantan.* Chicago: University of Chicago Press.

Haviland, John B. 1977b. "Gossip as competition in Zinacantan." *Journal of Communication* 27: 186–91.

Haviland, John B. 1984a. *"Keremcita*: speech relations and social relations in highland Chiapas." *Estudios de Cultura Maya* XV: 329–48.

Haviland, John B. 1984b. "Las máximas mínimas de la conversación natural de Zinacantán." *Anales de Antropología* XX: 221–56.

Haviland, John B. 1986. " '*Con buenos chiles*': Talk, targets and teasing in Zinacantán." *Text* 6: 249–82.

Haviland, John B. 1987. "Fighting words: evidential particles, affect, and argument." *Berkeley Linguistics Society 13*: 343–54. Parasession on grammar and cognition.

Haviland, John B. 1988a. "Minimal maxims: cooperation and natural conversation in Zinacantán." *Mexican Studies/Estudios Mexicanos* IV (1): 79–114.

Haviland, John B. 1988b. "A father-mother talks back: the micro-creation of context in Tzotzil." Paper presented to the conference Interpretive Sociolinguistics III: Contextualization, University of Konstanz, October 2–6, 1988.

Haviland, John B. 1989. "Sure, sure: evidence and affect." *Text* 9: 27–68, special issue on *Discourse and Affect,* edited by Elinor Ochs and Bambi Schieffelin.

Haviland, John B. 1993. "Anchoring, iconicity, and orientation in Guugu Yimidhirr pointing gestures." *Journal of Linguistic Anthropology* 3: 3–45.

Haviland, John B. 1994 [1992]. "Lenguaje ritual sin ritual." *Estudios de Cultura Maya* XIX: 427–42.

Haviland, John B. 1996. " 'We want to borrow your mouth.' Tzotzil marital squabbles." In *Disorderly discourse,* ed. by Charles L. Briggs, 158–203. Oxford: Oxford University Press.

Haviland, John B. 1997. "Shouts, shrieks, and shots: unruly political conversations in indigenous Chiapas." *Pragmatics* 7: 547–73, Special issue on conflict and violence in pragmatic research, edited by Charles Briggs.

Haviland, John B. 1998. *"Mu'nuk jbankil to, mu'nuk kajvaltik*: 'He is not my older brother, he is not Our Lord.' Thirty years of gossip in a Chiapas village." *Etnofoor* 11: 57–82.

Haviland, John B. 2000a. "Early pointing gestures in Zinacantán." *Journal of Linguistic Anthropology* 8: 162–96.

Haviland, John B. 2000b. "Warding off witches: voicing and dialogue in Zinacantec prayer." In *Les rituels du dialogue, promenades ethnolinguistiques en terres amérindiennes,* ed. by Aurore Monod-Becquelin and Philippe Erikson, 367–400. Nanterre: Société d'ethnologie.

Haviland, John B. 2002 [publ. 2004]. "Evidential mastery." Chicago Linguistic Society 38–2: 349–68, The Panels.

Haviland, John B. 2003. "How to point in Zinacantán." In *Pointing: where language, culture, and cognition meet,* ed. by Sotaro Kita, 139–70. Mahwah and London: Lawrence Erlbaum Associates.

Haviland, John B. 2005a. "Directional precision in Zinacantec deictic gestures: (cognitive?) preconditions of talk about space." *Intellectica* 41–42: 25–54.

Haviland, John B. 2005b. 'Whorish old man' and 'one (animal) gentleman': the inter-textual construction of enemies and selves." *Journal of Linguistic Anthropology* 15: 81–94.

Haviland, John B. 2005c. "Dreams of blood: Zinacantecs in Oregon." In *Dislocations/relocations: narratives of displacement*, ed. by Mike Baynham and Anna de Fina, 91–127. Manchester, UK, Northampton: St. Jerome Publishers.

Haviland, John B. 2005d. "Positional roots, semantic typology, and representational gestures." Paper presented to the 2nd ISGS Conference, "Interacting Bodies," Lyon, France, June 17 2005.

Haviland, John B. 2007. "Person reference in Tzotzil gossip: referring dupliciter." In Person reference in interaction, ed. by Nick J. Enfield and Tanya Stivers, 226–52. Cambridge: Cambridge University Press.

Haviland, John B. 2009. "Little rituals." In *Ritual communication*, ed. by Gunter Senft and Ellen B. Basso, 21–50. Oxford, New York: Berg.

Haviland, John B. 2010. "Mu xa xtak'av: 'He doesn't answer'" *Journal of Linguistic Anthropology* 20: 195–213.

Haviland, John B. 2013a. "The emerging grammar of nouns in a first generation sign language: Specification, iconicity, and syntax." *Gesture* 13: 309–53.

Haviland, John B. 2013b. "Xi to vi: 'Over that way, look!' (Meta)spatial representation in an emerging (Mayan?) sign language." In *Space in language and linguistics*, ed. by Peter Auer, Martin Hilpert, Anja Stukenbrock and Benedikt Szmerecsanyi, 334–400. Berlin, Boston: Walter De Gruyter.

Haviland, Leslie K., and John B. Haviland. 1982. "Behind the fence: the social bases of privacy in a Mexican village." *Estudios de Cultura Maya* XIV: 323–52.

Haviland, Leslie K., and John B. Haviland. 1983. "Privacy in a Mexican village." In *Public and private in social life*, ed. by Stanley I. Benn and Gerald F. Gauss, 341–61. London: Croom Helm.

Irvine, Judith T. 1979. "Formality and informality in communicative events." *American Anthropologist* 81: 773–90.

Kendon, Adam. 1967. "Some functions of gaze-direction in social interaction." *Acta psychologica* 26: 22–63.

Kendon, Adam. 1990. *Conducting interaction: patterns of behavior in focused encounters*. Cambridge: Cambridge University Press.

Kinil Canche, Rita. 2015. "Nombres y referencia a persona en la conversación en LSMY." Paper presented at the Primer Coloquio Internacional sobre las lenguas de señas emergentes de las Américas, Mexico, D.F. 11 Sept. 2015.

Kockelman, Paul. 2003a. "Factive and counterfactive clitics in Q'eqchi'-Maya: stance, status, and subjectivity." Paper given at the thirty-eighth annual regional meeting of the Chicago Linguistics Society, *University of Chicago, Chicago*.

Kockelman, Paul. 2003b. "The meanings of interjections in Q'ekchi' Maya." *Current Anthropology* 44: 467–90.

Kockelman, Paul. 2004. "Stance and subjectivity." *Journal of Linguistic Anthropology* 14: 127–50.

Kockelman, Paul. 2005. "The semiotic stance." *Semiotica* 157: 233–304.

Laughlin, Robert M. 1963. "Through the looking glass: reflections on Zinacantan courtship and marriage." PhD diss., Harvard University.

Laughlin, Robert M. 1975. *The great Tzotzil dictionary of San Lorenzo Zinacantan* (Smithsonian Contributions to Anthropology 19). Washington, DC: Smithsonian Institution Press.

Laughlin, Robert M. 1976. *Of wonders wild and new: Dreams from Zinacantán* (Smithsonian Contributions to Anthropology 22). Washington, DC: Smithsonian Institution Press.

Laughlin, Robert M. 1977. *Of cabbages and kings: Tales from Zinacantan* (Smithsonian Contributions to Anthropology 23). Washington, DC: Smithsonian Institution Press.

Le Guen, Olivier. 2006. "L'organisation et l'apprentissage de l'espace chez les Mayas Yucatèques du Quintana Roo, Mexique." PhD diss., Paris 10.

Le Guen, Olivier. 2011a. "Modes of pointing to existing spaces and the use of frames of reference." *Gesture* 11: 271–307.

Le Guen, Olivier. 2011b. "Speech and gesture in spatial language and cognition among the Yucatec Mayas." *Cognitive Science* 35: 905–38.

Le Guen, Olivier. 2012a. "An exploration in the domain of time: From Yucatec Maya time gestures to Yucatec Maya sign language time signs." In *Sign languages in village communities: Anthropological and linguistic insights*, ed. by Ulrike Zeshan and Connie deVos, 209–50. Berlin: Mouton de Gruyter.

Le Guen, Olivier. 2012b. "Socializing with the supernatural: The place of supernatural entities in Yucatec Maya daily life and socialization." In *Maya daily lives: proceedings of the 13th European Maya conference*, ed. by Philippe Nondédéo, and Alain Breton, 151–70. Markt Schwaben: Verlag Anton Saurwein.

Le Guen, Olivier, and Lorena Ildefonsa Pool Balam. 2012. "No metaphorical timeline in gesture and cognition among Yucatec Mayas." *Frontiers in Psychology* 3: 271.

Levinson, Stephen C. 2006. "On the human interaction engine." In *Roots of human sociality*, ed. by Nicholas J. Enfield, and Stephen C. Levinson, 39–69. New York: Berg.

López Jiménez, José Alfredo. 2010. "Estructura, actuacion y multimodalidad en la narrativa personal oral (lo'il a'yej) de la comunidad tsotsil de Romerillo, Chamula, Chiapas." MA thesis, CIESAS, Mexico.

Maffi, Luisa. 1990. "Tzeltal Maya affect verbs: psychological salience and expressive functions of language." *Berkeley Linguistics Society* 16: 61–72.

Martin, Laura. 1998. "Irrealis constructions in Mocho (Mayan)." *Anthropological Linguistics* 40: 198–213.

Maynard, Ashley E. 2002. "Cultural teaching: The development of teaching skills in Maya sibling interactions." *Child Development* 73: 969–82.

Monod-Becquelin, Aurore. 1979. "Examen de quelques paires sémantiques dans les dialogue rituels des Tzelyal de Bachajon (langue maya du Chiapas)." *Journal de la Société des Américanistes* 66: 234–63.

Pérez González, Jaime. 2012. "Predicados expresivos e ideófonos en Tseltal." MA thesis, CIESAS, Mexico.

Pye, Clifton. 1986. "Quiché Mayan speech to children." *The Journal of Child Language* 13: 85–100.

Pye, Clifton, Barbara Pfeiler, Lourdes De León, Penelope Brown, and Pedro Mateo. 2007. "Roots or edges? Explaining variation in children's early verb forms across five Mayan languages." In *Learning indigenous languages: child language acquisition in Mesoamerica*, ed. by Barbara Pfeiler, 15–46. Berlin: Mouton de Gruyter.

Rabain-Jamin, Jacqueline, E. Ashley Maynard, and Patricia Greenfield. 2003. "Implications of sibling caregiving for sibling relations and teaching interactions in two cultures." *Ethos* 31: 204–31.

Reynolds, Jennifer F. 2008. "Socializing puros pericos (little parrots): The negotiation of respect and responsibility in Antonero Mayan sibling and peer networks." *Journal of Linguistic Anthropology* 18: 82–107.

Rossano, Federico, Penelope Brown, and Stephen C. Levinson. 2009. "Gaze, questioning, and culture." In *Comparative studies in conversation analysis*, ed. by Jack Sidnell, 187–249. Cambridge: Cambridge University Press.

Sacks, Harvey, and Emanuel A. Schegloff, 1979. "Two preferences in the organization of reference to persons in conversation and their interaction." In *Everyday language: studies in ethnomethodology*, ed. by George Psathas, 15–21. New York: Irvington Press.

Schegloff, Emanuel A. 1968. "Sequencing in conversational openings." *American Anthropologist* 70: 1075–95.

Schegloff, Emanuel A. 1972. "Notes on a conversational practice: Formulating place." *Studies in Social Interaction* 75: 75–119.

Schegloff, Emanuel A. 1996. "Turn organization: one intersection of grammar and interaction." In *Interaction and grammar*, ed. by Elinor Ochs, Emanuel A. Schegloff, and Sandra A. Thompson, 52–133. Cambridge: Cambridge University Press.

Schegloff, Emanuel A. 2006. "Interaction: The infrastructure for social institutions, the natural ecological niche for language, and the arena in which culture is enacted." In *Roots of human sociality: culture, cognition and interaction*, ed. by Nick J. Enfield and Stephen C. Levinson, 70–96. Oxford, New York: Berg.

Sacks, Harvey, Emanuel A. Schegloff, and Gail Jefferson. 1974. "A simplest systematics for the organization of turn-taking for conversation." *Language* 50: 696–735.

Shoaps, Robin A. 2004. "Morality in grammar and discourse: Stance-taking and the negotiation of moral personhood in Sakapultek (Mayan) wedding counsels." PhD diss., University of California, Santa Barbara.

Shoaps, Robin A. 2007. "'Moral irony': Modal particles, moral persons and indirect stance-taking in Sakapultek discourse." *Pragmatics* 17: 297–335.

Shoaps, Robin A. 2009a. "Ritual and (im)moral voices: locating the testament of Judas in Sakapultek communicative ecology." *American Ethnologist* 36: 459–77.

Shoaps, Robin A. 2009b. "Moral irony and moral personhood in Sakapultek discourse and culture." In *Stance: sociolinguistic perspectives*, ed. by Alexandra Jaffe, 92–118. Oxford, New York: Oxford University Press.

Sidnell, Jack. 2014. "The architecture of intersubjectivity revisited." In *The Cambridge handbook of linguistic anthropology*, ed. by Nick J. Enfield, Paul Kockelman, and Jack Sidnell, 364–99. Cambridge: Cambridge University Press.

Stivers, Tanya, Nick J. Enfield, Penelope Brown, Christina Englert,, Makoto Hayashi, Trine Heinemann, Gertie Hoymann, Federico Rossano, Jan P. de Ruiter, Kyung-Eun Yoon, and Stephen C. Levinson. 2009. "Universals and cultural variation in turn-taking in conversation." *Proceedings of the National Academy of Sciences of the United States of America* 106: 10587–92.

Streeck, Jürgen. 2014. "Mutual gaze and recognition." In *From gesture in conversation to visible action as utterance,* ed. by Mandana Seyfeddinipur and Marianne Gullberg, 35–58. Amsterdam/Philadelphia: John Benjamins.

Yngve, Victor. 1970. "On getting a word in edgewise." *Chicago Linguistic Society* 6: 567–78.

CHAPTER 17

POETICS

Rusty Barrett

1 INTRODUCTION

With a literary tradition spanning two millennia, Maya poetics has received much scholarly attention (e.g. Edmonson 1971, 1982; Tedlock 1983; Sam Colop 1994; Hull and Carrasco 2012). The Mayan languages share a common poetic tradition that is a robust example of cultural continuity between pre-Columbian and contemporary Maya communities. The poetic structures found in Hieroglyphic Maya texts are remarkably similar to those found in contemporary poetry and music. These same poetic structures are a regular part of everyday life in Maya communities, occurring in conversations, narratives, and other speech events. This chapter outlines the primary structures in the Maya poetic tradition, focusing on patterns of grammatical parallelism.

While European poetic traditions typically emphasize phonological parallelism (in the form of rhyme and meter), Native traditions in the Americas generally highlight parallelism in syntax and semantics. The heart of Maya poetics is the use of syntactic couplets. The prototypical couplet structure involves parallel lines that differ only in the substitution of a single syntactic constituent. The constituents that alternate will have some sort of semantic relationship. This pattern can be found in examples (1) and (2). Example (1) is from a pot (K1398) from the city of Naranjo, dating from the Late Classic period (Hull 2003:390):

(1) utz'apil te', utz'apil tuun.
    His planting of the tree, His planting of the stone.

Here, the alternation is between *tree* and *stone*, words that are regularly paired together (a diphrastic kenning, see §3.1). As Hull (2012:91–3) notes, this "sticks and stones" pairing was regularly used in the Classic period in references to the construction of buildings. The combination of the words meaning "wood" and "stone" thus conveys a broader meaning ("architecture" or "construction") than either of the words individually.

Example (2) is from Lintel II in the Temple of the Four Lintels at Chichen Itza (Hull 2003:515)

(2) ta yilil k'in, ta yilil haab'il.
    On the sign of the day, On the sign of the year.

Here again, the substitution is between two nouns that are semantically related: *day* and *year*. Hull (2003:440) discusses Ch'orti' cases in which the combination of the words meaning "day" and "year" serves to evoke the broader meaning of "time". As in example (1), there is a specific semantic relationship between the nouns that alternate within the couplet.

Cases such as these may be seen as the most basic (or "pure") form of Maya parallelism. A number of scholarly analyses of Maya poetics have focused exclusively on the structure of such couplets (e.g. Norman 1980; Lengyel 1988). In his translations of Yucatec and K'iche' colonial texts, Edmonson went so far as to add or delete lines from texts in order to ensure that every line fit into a couplet pattern (see Tedlock 1983; Hanks 1988). As Sam Colop (1994) argues, the scholarly obsession with couplet structure has obscured the full complexity of Maya poetry. Although the couplet may be the central structure in Maya poetics, couplets may vary in their structure. Couplets may involve more than a single alternation and the alternating material may come from different lexical classes (or involve larger syntactic units). Parallelism may also occur in structures larger than the couplet (triplets, quatrains, and even larger units). Similarly, not all forms of parallelism are purely syntactic. For example, Sam Colop (1994) presents cases of parallelism building on patterns in phonology or morphology. While couplet structure is certainly a central component of Maya poetics, couplets are part of a broader pattern of parallelism across all levels of grammar.

After discussing the importance of poetic parallelism within Maya cultures (§2), this chapter outlines the basic forms of parallelism within Maya poetics (§3). Section 4 examines other components of Maya poetics not directly related to parallelism, the use of polysemy and ideophones.

2 MAYA POETICS AND CULTURAL CONTEXTS

2.1 Maya poetics in historical perspective

Because of the ubiquity of parallelism and couplets in Classic Maya texts, poetic structure played an important role in the process of decipherment (see Hanks 1988; Hull and Carrasco 2012). For example, Lounsbury (1980) relied heavily on couplet structure in his interpretation of the inscriptions from the Temple of the Cross at Palenque. Although couplet patterns dominate texts from the Classic Maya period, forms of parallelism can be found throughout Maya history. In addition to carved texts from the Classic period, parallelism is common in the Codices written in the post-Classic period (AD ~900–1500). Example (3) is a triplet from page 24 of the Dresden Codex (Vail 2012:235):

(3) U mu'uk kab   The earth is buried
     U mu'uk ch'e'en   The cave is buried
     U mu'uk winik   The people are buried

Following the Spanish conquest, Maya began writing in the Latin alphabet. Texts from this period are also marked by the same types of couplets and parallelism. Example (4) presents the opening lines of the *Popol Wuj* (Tedlock 2010:310–11):

(4)

1   Are' uxe' ojer tzij,
2   Waral K'iche' ub'i'.
3   Waral xchiqatz'ib'aj wi
4   xchiqatikib'al wi ojer tzij,

1   This is the root of the Ancient Word,
2   Here in this placed called K'iche'.
3   Here we shall inscribe,
4   we shall implant the Ancient Word,

The four opening lines of the *Popol Wuj* demonstrate the ways in which parallelism can be woven into a text without the use of single alternation couplets. The four lines are linked together through repetitions and parallel structures. Line 2 is linked to line 3 through the repetition of *waral* (here), and line 3 is linked to line 4 through parallel verbs, *xchiqatz'ib'aj wi*, *xchiqatikib'al wi* (we shall inscribe, we shall implant). The repetition of *ojer tzij* (Ancient Word) in line 4 links the final line with the first line. The final line contains two parallelisms pointing back to the lines 1 and 3, unifying the quatrain. Of course, the *Popol Wuj* and other texts from the colonial period contain the type of pure couplets given in examples (1) and (2) above. However, colonial texts also demonstrate the broad range or complex interactions involving larger patterns of parallelism.

The Maya poetic tradition continues in the work of contemporary poets and musician. For example, the K'iche' rock group Kab'awil's song "Tyox numam, tyox tat" ("Thank you grandfather, thank you father") opens with a traditional couplet:

(5) Kab'awil, K'iche' (Botto 2008:141)

Inb'enaq pa le b'e jawi xb'in we numam	I have traveled the path where my grandfather walked.
Inb'enaq pa le b'e jawi xb'in we nutat	I have traveled the path where my father walked.

As in the examples from the Classic period, the couplet in (5) involves a single alternation between words that are related semantically. The combination of kinship terms (*numam*, *nutat* "my grandfather, my father") evokes the broader concept of ancestors. Similarly, Yucatec poet Briceida Cuevas Cob's poem "Je'el bix xux eek'" ("Like a bright star") opens with a couplet:

(6) Briceida Cuevas Cob, Yucatec (2008:44, my translation)

Súukchaj in wu'uyik u jóoch'ol in jáak' iik' ti' jáal nak'lik.
Súukchaj in wu'uyik u xúuxub ch'eenaknakil tin tséel.

I have become accustomed to feeling my sighs fade in a corner.
I have become accustomed to hearing the whistling of loneliness beside me.

Although Cuevas Cob employs the traditional couplet form, the alternating constituent is longer and contains more variation compared to the traditional couplet. The tone and topic also mark the poem as belonging to the genre of contemporary lyric poetry. As will be evident from the examples in this chapter, contemporary Maya poets and musicians regularly use parallelism in unconventional and innovative ways.

2.2 Poetics in contemporary communities

Although the majority of examples in this chapter are drawn from literary or musical sources, the use of parallelism and couplets is certainly not restricted to these contexts. Forms of parallelism can occur in almost any Maya speech event. This section describes the use of parallelism in ritual discourse, narrative, conversation, and language acquisition.

2.2.1 Ritual discourse

Ritual discourse is the genre most associated with parallelism, as forms of ritual and religious discourse are constructed almost entirely through the forms of parallelism found in colonial texts. Example (7) contains the opening lines of a curing ceremony from the town of Zinacantán, Mexico.

(7) Curing ceremony, Tzotzil (Vogt 1969:646–51 quoted in Lengyel 1988:100 with updated orthography)

1	en el ch'ul nombre yos jesukristo kajwal	In the divine name of Jesus Christ my lord
2	k'usi yepal un jtot	So much my father
3	k'usi yepal un kajwal	So much my lord
4	ta jk'an ti ch'ul pertonale	I beseech your divine pardon
5	ta jk'an ti ch'ul lesensiae	I beg your divine forgiveness
6	ti ta ch'ul ba mexae	At the holy head of the table
7	ti ta ch'ul chak mexae	At the holy foot of the table

This example contains an opening invocation followed by three consecutive couplets, all involving the substitution of a single noun (see Lengyel 1988). However, the couplets are also linked together through repetitions. The repetition of *ch'ul* "divine" links lines 4–7 together as a quatrain linked back to the invocation (also containing *ch'ul*). The repetition of *kahwal* "my lord" at the ends of lines 1 and 3 also serves to link the invocation to the couplets that follow.

The use of couplet structures in ritual discourse is not simply the maintenance of pre-Columbian poetic genre. Forms of parallelism may be adapted to new contexts. An example of the innovative use of parallelism in ritual discourse can be found in Ixil inhumation ceremonies performed to give proper burials to victims of genocide left in mass graves (García 2012, 2014). While this is certainly not a traditional type of Maya ritual, the language of inhumation ceremonies uses parallelism in highly traditional ways:

(8) Inhumation ceremony, Ixil (García, 2014)

1	Kamal ati pap	Maybe there are those, Lord,
2	ye' tuk lejpoj	who will not be found,
3	kamal ate' pap, sib'lej	maybe there are those, Lord, mercy,
4	kutxutx kub'aal	Our Mother, Our Father,
5	Txi' kat tx'akon vas ikuerpoe'	dogs ate their bodies
6	tulaj tx'akab'e'n	in the mountains.
7	Kamal ate' pap, sib'lej	Maybe there are those, Lord, mercy,
8	tu a' kat b'en kat	who went in the water
9	as kamal ate' pap	and maybe there are those, Lord,
10	tu xamal kat ok kat, sib'lej	who entered into the fire, mercy.
11	kutxutx kub'aal	Our Mother, Our Father.

This example contains four repetitions of a frame beginning with *kamal ati pap* ("maybe there are those, Lord"). The substitutions in this prayer also involve semantic parallelism. The lexical pair of water and fire (lines 8 and 10) is common in Ixil discourse concerning the war (García, 2014). In the case of Ixil inhumation ceremonies, parallelism is used to construct a new genre of Maya ritual discourse.

2.2.2 Narrative

A number of scholars have analyzed the structure of narratives in Maya communities (e.g. England 1987, 2009; Hofling 1987, 2012; Martin 1994; Hopkins and Josserand 2012). In addition to describing patterns involving formulaic openings and closings, syntax, morphology, and discourse structure, these studies have shown that parallelism and couplet structures are a regular part of many Maya narratives. The degree to which a speaker uses these poetic patterns in narrative varies according to contextual factors. For example, England (1987) compared narratives in Mam and Teko and found that the use of parallelism was much lower in Teko. England concluded that the higher rate of language shift among Teko speakers contributed to the loss of traditional poetic forms. Martin (1994) compared two versions of a narrative by a Mocho' speaker, finding more frequent use of parallelism when the story was elaborated in a conscious performance (as opposed to a more basic version intended mainly to convey information).

Parallelism in narratives may include basic couplet forms, as in example (9) from Itzaj:

(9) Itzaj narrative (Hofling 2012:411)

K'in kuman. . .	Days pass,
K'in kutal. . .	days come.
K'in kuman . . .	Days pass,
Kin'kutal. . .	days come.
I a' winikej. . .	And the man,
Te' yan ich a' muknal ket et uyätanej. . .	there he is inside the tomb together with his wife

In this example, the speaker produces a traditional couplet with a single alternation (*kutal/kuman* "come/pass"). The couplet is repeated in lines 3–4 to produce a quatrain. Forms of parallelism in narratives may also involve structures larger than the couplet. In example (10), a Mam speaker combines a couplet and a triplet (see England 1987):

(10) Mam narrative (England 1987:529)

1 entoons ja'la at jun miij awal ook	So there was a bit of cornfield
2 at jun miij cheenq'	some beans
3 per galaan tzaaj jun nimaal cheenq' weena	and the beans developed very well
4 kyee'yx tzaaj	very beautifully,
5 per kyee'yx tzaaj weena	they did very well

In example (10), lines 1 and 2 form a couplet, repeating the frame *at jun miij awal/ cheenq'*, literally "there was one half corn/beans." The pairing of corn and beans follows the traditional pattern of substitutions involving related words (as corn and beans are cultivated beside one another and together form the foundation of Maya cuisine). The couplet is followed by a triplet which involves the repetition of *tzaaj*, literally "it comes." Line 3 serves as a bridge between the two structures, repeating *cheenq'* "beans" from line 2 and introducing *tzaaj*, the central element in the following triplet.

2.2.3 Conversation and language acquisition

In addition to more formal registers such as ritual language or story-telling, parallelism plays a central role in structuring Maya conversations (Brody 1986; Brown 1998).

Parallelism in conversation usually involves forms of repetition. Indeed, the most common form of back-channel in Maya conversation is the repetition of an interlocutor's prior utterance (Brody 1986), as in example (11):

(11) Tojol-ab'al conversation (Brody 1986:260–1)

1	A: b'a aya miša hlahaw ha aktobusi	Then I didn't meet the bus.
2	B: miša alahaw ha aktobusi	You didn't meet the bus.
3	A: miša hlahaw ha aktobusi	Then I didn't meet the bus.
4	B: sk'anaw mas sah ahyi	Should have been earlier.
5	A: sk'anaw mas sah ahyi	Should have been earlier.

In line 2 of this example, speaker B reproduces the previous utterance (line 1) only changing the subject pronoun (from first to second person). Of course, this repetition with a single substitution is the structure found in the traditional Maya couplet (as in examples (1) and (2)). Conversation may also involve exact repetition (without alternation) as in lines 4 and 5 in example (11) above.

The use of repetition and parallelism is also an important part of Mayan language acquisition and socialization (Stross 1972; Brown 1998) as caregivers often respond to children using parallelism. In example (12), a father is talking with his two-year-old daughter:

(12) Tzeltal conversation (Brown 1998:209)

1	Daughter:	t'uxaj k'u'	The shirt fell off [of the clothesline].
2	Father:	ya xt'uxaj sk'u'	The shirt fell off.
3	Daughter:	jo'	Huh
4	Father:	k'iybe me ta k'al i me sk'u' alale.	Spread it out to dry in the sun, the child's shirt.
5	Daughter:	jo. Ya jwoj xi.	Huh. I'll toast it, he/she says.
6	Father:	ya' 'woj	You'll toast it.
7	Daughter:	jo'	Huh.

As in example (11), this example contains a pure repetition (lines 1 and 2) and a couplet with pronoun substitution (lines 5 and 6).

Parallelism is not restricted to formal, literary, or ritual contexts. Maya co-produce couplet patterns regularly in everyday interactions. Maya children learn to interactively produce parallel structures even as they are learning to speak. The poetic structures described in the following section, then, permeate Maya culture across contexts ranging from Classic hieroglyphic texts carved in stone to everyday conversations between children and their parents.

3 FORMS OF PARALLELISM

This section describes the structure of parallelism found in Maya poetic traditions. This includes lexical (or semantic) parallelism involving pairings between words and parallel patterns in syntax, morphology, and phonology. In addition to couplets, poetic structures include triplets, quatrains, and even larger poetic units.

3.1 Lexical parallelism and diphrastic kennings

Diphrastic kennings are pairs of semantically related words that combine to convey a meaning that is more general compared to either of the combined elements (see Knowlton

2002; Hull 2003, 2012). Such kennings are a regular type of morphological compound in Mayan languages. Some examples from K'iche' are given in (13):

(13) Kennings in K'iche'

Compound word	Literal meaning	Compound meaning
qatat qanan	our fathers, our mothers	our ancestors
kaqiq' jab'	wind, rain	thunderstorm
siwan tinamit	canyon, town	public, community

Not all kennings occur as compound words. The two parts of a kenning may also co-occur regularly as the alternating elements in couplets. However, the alternating words in a couplet are not always kenning pairs, but may simply be synonyms or words with closely related meanings. This can be seen in example (14), a segment from the Achi drama *Rabinal Achi*.

(14) *Rabinal Achi*, Achi (Breton 2007:246–7)

1	Keje k'ut mi xpixab chi n[a] ta kan la	So You have left Your recommendations
2	Chi juyubal la	to Your mountains
3	chi taq'ajal la	to Your valleys
4	qatz ku are lal kamel	it is certain that You are going to die
5	lal sachel	that You are going to disappear
6	waral ch(i) uxmut kaj	here, at the navel of the sky
7	ch(i) uxmut ulew	at the navel of the earth.

This example contains three couplet pairs (2–3, 4–5, 6–7). The first and last couplets involve traditional kenning pairs. The pairing in the first couplet, *juyub'/taq'aj* "mountains/valleys," is commonly used to mean "everywhere." Similarly, the pairing of *kaj/ulew* "earth/sky" (in the third couplet) conveys a broader meaning of "the universe." However, the alternation in the second couplet (*kamel/sachel* "one who dies/ one who disappears") is an alternation involving similar meanings. While this pairing adds emphasis, it does not produce a new distinct meaning like that associated with diphrastic kennings.

The elements of a kenning pair always occur in the same order. Thus, the K'iche' pair *siwan/tinamit* (in 13 above) never occurs as *tinamit/siwan*. Norman (1980) proposed that kenning pairs must follow a specific order to be well-formed grammatically. Sam Colop (1994) notes, however, that the order of elements is generally governed by prosody, with longer words coming second in the pair. Similarly, Norman (1980) argued that the elements of a kenning must belong to the same lexical class, while Sam Colop (1994) gives examples of kenning pairs involving adjective-noun pairs. Hull (2012) describes a number of kenning pairs that commonly occur in Hieroglyphic Maya texts. These include categories of kennings, such as those involving calendrical terms or those involving pairs of gendered nouns as well as specific kenning pairs from the Classic period that are maintained in current Mayan languages, such as sky/earth, wood/stone, and wind/rain. However, the formation of kennings is not static and new and innovative kenning pairs may be introduced. As with older kennings, the pairing of words in newer kennings indexes a broader meaning compared to either word in isolation. García (2012) describes a number of innovative Ixil kennings that have emerged in discourse related to genocide. An example from an inhumation ceremony can be seen in (15):

(15) Ixil inhumation ceremony (García 2012:82)

Ati ta', Pap, toq'el kat b'anaxi.   There are those, Lord, cutting was done to them.
Ati ta', Pap, jub'amal kat b'anaxi.   There are those, Lord, shooting was done to them.

In this couplet, *toq'el* "cutting" with *jub'amal* "shooting" are paired in the traditional kenning pattern. The combination of the two terms evokes the broader concept of violence more generally. Innovative kenning pairs play an important role in the description and understanding of the experience of genocide among Ixil speakers (García 2012).

Another example of an innovative kenning associated with cultural revitalization movements pairs the words for "language" and "clothing" to index Maya culture in general. Example (16) comes from an anonymous Tojol-ab'al poet:

(16) Anonymous Tojol-ab'al poem (Lenkersdorf 1979:174)

ja jk'umaltiki ja tojol ab'al   Our language, Tojol-ab'al
ja'xa jk'u'tiki mixa xk'anatik   our authentic clothing, we don't want them anymore

The pairing of language and clothing as a kenning also occurs in the Tz'utujil hip-hop song *Nutzij* ("My words") by Tz'utu Baktun Kan:

(17) Tz'utu Baktun Kan, Tz'utujil (2011)

Pa Chilam B'alam xtz'ijb'ax kan wi   In the Chilam Balam it is written
Jo' Walk'wal   Come my children
Mimestaj li qatzij   Don't forget our words/language
Pa Chilam B'alam xtz'ijb'ax kan wi   In the Chilam Balam it is written
Jo' Walk'wal   Come my children
Mimestaj li qatzyaq   Don't forget our clothing.

Here again, a single alternation (*qatzij* in line 3 and *qatzyaq* in line 6) produces the kenning "our language, our clothing". Wearing traditional clothing and speaking a Mayan language are the two most visible aspects of Maya culture, so the pairing of the concepts readily indexes Maya culture more broadly. Examples (15), (16), and (17) suggest that the creation and use of diphrastic kennings is integrated into contemporary Maya culture in ways that easily adapt to new cultural contexts.

3.2 Syntactic parallelism

The most common poetic form in Maya culture involves syntactic parallelism, where adjacent lines (or members of a couplet) have identical syntactic structure but differ in the specific material within one (or more) constituent. The traditional couplet with a single lexical substitution is the most basic type of syntactic parallelism. Generally, the alternating constituents are also identical in morphological structure and differ only in terms of the root. For example, if verbs alternate, they share person and aspectual marking as in example (18) from the *Popol Wuj*:

(18) *Popol Wuj*, K'iche' (Tedlock 2010:310–11)

Waral xchi-ø-qa-tz'ib'-aj   wi
Here POT-B3SG-A1PL-write-DER   PAR

xchi-ø-qa-tik-ib'al wi ojer   tzij.
POT-B3SG-A1PL-plant-DER   PAR

Here we shall inscribe,
     we shall implant the Ancient Word.

The verbs in example (18) are morphologically identical but contain different roots. Although the prototypical couplet involves a single substitution, syntactic parallelism may involve multiple substitutions while maintaining a uniform syntactic structure. For example, in (19), from the K'iche' rock group Kab'awil:

(19) Kab'awil, K'iche' (Botto 2008:141)

mayaj ri anan,   Don't scold your mother,
mach'ay ri atat.   Don't hit your father.

Here each line in the couplet contains the same syntactic structure: a negative imperative verb followed by an object NP with the determiner *ri* and the second person possessive prefix *a-*. However, the lines alternate both in the verb root and in the possessed noun.

Although most examples of syntactic parallelism involve alternations between pairs of words, it is also possible for alternations to be full syntactic constituents. Example (20) comes from Kaqchikel poet Marcelino Tavila:

(20) Marcelino Tavila, Kaqchikel (quoted in Sam Colop 1994:190–1)

tuxna xtkib'ij,   What they would say,
tuxna xtkinojij   what they would think?
vi xtiwajo niqasaj q'atzun,   If they want to cut it permanently,
vi xtiwajo chi jumul tikäm   if they want to kill it forever.

In the last two lines of example (20), the main clause is identical ("if they want"), but the subordinate clauses are entirely different. In addition to varying in terms of the size of substituted constituents or the number of substitutions, syntactic parallelism may vary in terms of the order of uniform and alternating elements. While it is certainly more common for the latter half of lines to alternate, it is also possible for couplets to be unified through their final elements. Finally, although couplets normally occur in pairs, the lines of a couplet may be separated as a framing device within a larger text, sometimes called enveloping parallelism (Hull 2003:459). In such cases, the two lines of a couplet serve as the opening and closing for a larger unit of text. An illustrative example is given in (21), part of a larger poem by Kaqchikel poet María Elena Nij Nij:

(21) María Elena Nij Nij, Kaqchikel (del Valle Escalante 2010:135)

1 Katamle nata', katok pa wachoch nata',   Come, father, enter my house, father,
2 taponij rij ri wachoch nata',   burn copal around my house, father,
3 taponij ri pa kaji' rutza'n ri wachoch nata'   burn copal in the four corners of my
                                               house, father
4 taponij pa runik'ajal ri wachoch nata',   burn copal in the center of my house,
                                               father
5 katampe nata', kaseqon pa wachoch nata'   come father, smell (the copal) in my
                                               house, father

In this example, lines 1 and 5 form a couplet. The two lines differ only in their verbs ("enter" and "smell"). This couplet is divided and serves as a frame for the intervening triplet (lines 2–4). This poem is also an example of the way in which parallelism may be unified through the final (rather than the beginning) part of a line. Here, all five lines are unified through their final elements (*wachoch nata'*, "my house, father").

3.3 Morphological parallelism

In addition to parallel syntactic structures, parallelism involving morphology is also a basic component of Maya poetics (Sam Colop 1994:182ff). Morphological parallelism involves the repetition of an affix (or set of affixes) added to different stems. An example from the *Popol Wuj* is given in (22):

(22) *Popol Wuj*, K'iche' (Tedlock 2010:312–3)

1 nim upe'o**xik**,	It takes a long performance
2 utzijo**xik** puch ta chi	and account to
k'is tzuk' ronojel kajulew,	complete the lighting of all the sky-earth,
3 ukaj tz'uqu**xik**,	the fourfold siding,
4 ukaj xukuta**xik**	fourfold cornering,
5 reta**xik**	measuring,
6 ukaj che'**xik**	fourfold staking,
7 umej k'ama**xik**,	halving the cord,
8 uyuq k'a'ma**xik** upa kaj,	stretching the cord in the sky,
9 upa ulew	on the earth.

Example (22) contains seven different verb stems each bearing the same affixes: the passive suffix – *x* and the nominalizing suffix – *ik*. Of these, the verbal nouns in lines 1, 2, and 5 also share the 3rd singular possessive prefix (*r-/u-*). Here the primary parallelism is in morphology, as the syntax varies across lines. For example, the verbal noun in line 1 is preceded by an adjective *(nim,* "big"), lines 3, 4, and 6 have *ukaj* ("its four..") before the verbal noun, and nothing precedes the verbal nouns in lines 2 and 5.

A similar pattern of morphological parallelism can be seen in the song "B'atz'" by the group B'alam Ajpu' (which includes Tz'utujil rapper Tz'utu Baktun Kan):

(23) B'alam Ajpu' (2014, my translation), Tz'utujil

B'atz' ruk'amal li qak'aslemal	B'atz' the umbilical cord of our lives
B'atz' ruk'amal li qak'aslemal	B'atz' the umbilical cord of our lives
Xojob'al xojob'al b'atz'al q'ij	The dance, the dance of the day B'atz'

The parallelism in example (23) involves the suffix – *al* which creates an abstract noun from a noun root. The suffix occurs in *k'am-al* (cord-*al* > umbilical cord), *k'aslem-al* (living-al > life), *xojo-b'-al* (dance-INST-*al* > dance), and *b'atz'-al* (from the day of B'atz' in the Maya calendar). Here again, the parallelisms are created through morphology rather than syntax.

3.4 Phonological parallelism

Although Maya poetics generally focuses on syntax and morphology, there are also examples in which parallelism is based in phonology (Sam Colop 1994:195). Phonological parallelism in Maya involves alliteration or assonance, but not rhyme. Meter, rhythm, and line length are also generally irrelevant in Maya poetics. In Maya phonological parallelism, the organization of similar sounding words is not based on their position within lines (as in rhyme). Rather the similar sounding words should be the heads of major syntactic constituents (noun and verb phrases) within lines. Alliteration may also be used to unite words that are semantically related, as in example (24):

(24) *Dresden Codex*, pages 16c and 17c, Hieroglyphic Maya: (Hull 2003:485)

1 8-**MUWAN** u-**mu**-ti U?-IXIK-ki u-**mu**-ka
2 k'u-k'u u-**mu**-ka U?-IXIK-ki OX-WI'
3 mo-o-o u-**mu**-ti SAK-IXIK u-**mu**-ka
4 ya-YAXUN ? U?-IXIK-ki u-**mu**-ti AJAW-le
5 ? u-**mu**-ti U?-IXIK-ki ?-le
6 ku-tzu u-**mu**-wa U?-IXIK-ki UCH'-WE'.

8 Muwan is the omen of the ?-woman, the news,
Quetzal is the omen of the ?-woman, plenty of food,
Macaw is the omen of the White Woman, the omen.
? is the omen of the ?-woman ??,
Turkey is the tidings of the ?-woman, drink and food.

Lacadena (2009) notes that roots *muut* (lines 1, 3, 4, and 5), *mu'k* (lines 1, 2, and 3), and *muwak* (line 6) are all synonyms for "news" or "omen." Lacadena suggests that the author chose these words specifically to produce alliteration (cited in Hull 2003:485). The repetition of *mu* in these words creates parallelism with the opening date of *8 Muwan*.

A contemporary example of phonological parallelism can be found in the Tz'utujil hip-hop song in example (25):

(25) La llama, Tz'utujil (Tz'utu Baktun Kan et al. 2012, my translation)

1	Kin**tzij** le nu**k'otz'i'j**,	I light my candles
2	tik'ama k'a li nu**tzij**	accept my words
3	kinmatyo**xij** chiwe	I thank you
4	juntira le xkan chawe	for all you have left me.

In the first two lines of (25), we find the roots *tzij* (to ignite), *k'otz'i'j* (candle/flower), and *tzij* (word). Although these roots are morphologically unrelated, they have similar phonological shape. In line 3, the repetition of a syllable ending in – *ij* (in *matyoxij*, to thank) links the first two lines to the couplet in lines 3–4 (which is united through the pairing of *chiwe/chawe*, to you/to me).

3.5 Triplets, quatrains, and quintets

In hieroglyphic and colonial texts, the absence of clear divisions between poetic lines leaves the range of quatrains open to debate. Without knowing the author's intentions, a quatrain of four related lines could be also interpreted as two distinct couplets. For example, Tedlock (1983) discusses his disagreement with Edmonson's (1971) over examples of potential quatrains in the *Popol Wuj*, like that shown in example (26):

(26) *Popol Wuj*, K'iche' (Tedlock 1983:224)

ucah tzucuxic,	its fourfold siding,
ucah xucutaxic	its fourfold cornering
retaxic	measuring,
ucah cheexic	its fourfold staking.

While Edmonson (1971) treated this example as two separate couplets, Tedlock (1983:224–5) argues that Edmonson misses the way in which the third line serves as a bridge between the second and fourth lines. This type of quatrain, in which the third line lacks part of the syntactic constituent found in the other four lines (AB, AB, B, AB), occurs elsewhere in the *Popol Wuj*. The poetic use of shortening such as that in the third line of example (26) is common in contemporary K'iche' ritual discourse and narrative. Lengyel (1988) describes similar patterns (which he calls "gapping") in Tzotzil ritual discourse and in Ixil narratives. This type of shortening can also be found in contemporary poetry, as in (27) by the K'iche' poet, Pablo García:

(27) Pablo García, K'iche' (del Valle Escalante 2010:197, my translation)

Le kiparnum taq che'	The sprouts of the trees
ichaj	the plants
je q'ayes	and the grass
ech'uch'uj jer ek'o tura taq raq' q'aq'	are soft like smooth tongues of fire
sib'alaj ke'tze'tzatik kakiterne'j le usaqil Q'ij	they smile as they follow the sunlight
rech kakitzij ri kikotz'i'j chupalaj le kaj.	So they can ignite their flowers in the face of the sky.

Here García plays on the K'iche' word *k'otz'i'j*, meaning both "flower" and "candle," to metaphorically link fire and sprouting plants. The shortening in lines 2 and 3 follows the pattern Tedlock (1983) describes for the *Popol Wuj*. This type of shortening is widely used to construct triplets in texts from the colonial period. Sam Colop (1994:207–8) describes a number of these triplets in the *Popol Wuj*. They can also be found in Yucatec colonial texts. The typical pattern for these triplets is for the first two lines to be complete, while the final line involves shortening of the syntactic frame. A Yucatec example is given in (28) from the colonial manuscript, *Ritual of the Bacabs*:

(28) Ritual of the Bacabs, Yucatec (128 cited in Knowlton 2012:254–6)

Can kin tun bacin lic a zut	It is four days then that you turn
Can kin tun bacin lic a pec	It is four days then that you writhe
lic a sut	you turn

In (28), the truncated line repeats the verb from the first line, unifying the triplet. Another common pattern for constructing couplets involves the extension of a couplet that includes a diphrastic kenning. In such cases, the third line of the triple provides a more general extended meaning (often the broader meaning associated with the kenning itself). The triplet in (29), from a Ch'orti' curing prayer is an example:

(29) Ch'orti' curing prayer (Hull 2003:143)

Tya' matuk'a kamayores,	Where there are none of our older brothers,
Tya' matuk'a kawijtz'inob',	Where there are none of our younger brothers,
*Tya' matuk'a e **pak'ab' e konoj**.*	Where there are no human beings.

In (29), the first two lines involve the pairing of *kamayores/kawijtz'inob'* ("older brothers/ younger brothers"), while the final lines broadens the pairing to include all human beings.

The widespread use of triplets and quatrains by contemporary Maya poets suggests that scholars may have overlooked potential larger structures in earlier Maya literature. Although contemporary poets use couplets and triplets, quatrains are actually more common. The relationships between lines of these quatrains may take a number of forms. It is possible for all four lines of a quatrain may share the same syntactic frame, as in the Q'anjob'al example:

(30) Gaspar Pedro González, Q'anjob'al (2001:12–13)

Elelb'a, kaq ixim,	In the east the red corn,
okelb'a, q'eq ixim,	in the west the black corn,
ajelb'a, saq ixim,	in the north the white corn,
ayelb'a, q'an ixim.	in the south the yellow corn.

In this example, the four lines of the quatrain correspond to the four cardinal directions and the colors and types of corn associated with them. A similar four-line pattern can be seen in example (31) by Bautista Vázquez:

(31) Ruperta Bautista Vázquez, Tzotzil (2008:26, my translation):

Oxp'ej nich k'ok' ch-ak'bat yil sbe,	Three sparks light his path,
oxib manta sta ta ju ju tek'el yab yakan,	Three signs read his footsteps,
oxib yab akanil sta te sbe,	Three signs meet as they walk,
oxib k'ak'al xjoyp'ij yu'un xjambatel sbe.	Three days turn for the door to open.

Here, all four lines of the quatrain have fronted subject NPs beginning with the number three. Quatrains in which all lines share a single form are rare in the work of Bautista Vázquez. *Xchamel ch'ul balamil/Eclipse en la madre tierra*, her 2008 volume of thirty poems is composed almost entirely in quatrains, example (31) is one of only two cases in which the syntactic frame is repeated in all four lines.

A variant of the four-line uniform quatrain is a pattern in which all four lines share some syntactic frame while the alternating constituents in lines 1 and 2 are distinguished from those found in lines 3 and 4. The quatrain in (32) is from Diego Adrián Guarchaj Ajtzalam's poem *Ri loq'olaj q'ij* ("The sacred sun").

(33) Diego Adrián Guarchaj Ajtzalam, K'iche' (Guarchaj 2007, my translation).

Chi uwi' unawal cho	Above the *nawals* of the lakes
Chi uwi' unawal palow	Above the *nawals* of the seas
Chi uwi' le q'an kwa'	Above the yellow well
Chi uwi' ri saq tzampul.	Above the white foam.

In this example, all four lines are prepositional phrases with the same form: *chi u-wi'* (PREP-3SPOS-head), literally "at its top". In lines 1 and 2, the noun constituents that follow this frame ("the nawals of the lakes"/"the nawals of the seas") join the lines into a traditional couplet. Both contain the same syntactic frame (*u-nawal* x) with a single lexical substitution involving semantically related words. The pairing of *cho* with *palow* is a common diphrastic kenning in K'iche' which is sometimes used to mean "all the waters of the earth" (see Sam Colop 1994:66; García 2012:58). Similarly, lines three and four are linked through NPs with identical syntactic structure [determiner, color adjective, noun].

Within quatrains, lines may be paired with one another in various ways. Quatrains that pair the first two lines together and the last two together (as two couplets) are perhaps the most common (as in the previous example). In example (33), the lines are paired in this way, but without the unifying frame across all four lines as in (32).

(33) Diego Adrián Guarchaj Ajtzalam, K'iche' (2007, my translation):

Kojil la	You see us
Kojta la	You hear us
Pa ri qasiwan	In the canyon
Pa ri qatinamit.	In the town.

This quatrain reorganizes the traditional couplet structure to create polysemy in interpreting the relationship between the verbs in the first two lines and the prepositional phrases in the last two lines. This substitutions involve diphrastic kennings (*see/hear* and *canyon/town*) with broader meanings so that the first two lines suggest something like "you have full awareness of us" and the last two lines convey a meaning of "everywhere."

Similarly, a quatrain may be divided so that the first and third lines form a pair which contrasts with another pair formed with lines two and four, as in the following verse from Humberto Ak'abal's poem "Ch'ok" ("Blackbird"):

(34) Humberto Ak'abal, K'iche' (2001:394–5 my translation):

Karil chikaj	He looks at the sky
Are jampa' karaj ri jab'	When he is thirsty for rain
Karil ikim	He looks down
Are chi' jampa' kanumik.	When he is hungry.

Ak'abal's use of an A B A B couplet pattern in example (34) allows him to play with the traditional couplet pattern. Example (34) could be seen either as a pair of couplets or as a single couplet in which each half contains two clauses. The quatrain structure thus highlights the additional parallelisms inside the larger couplet.

Finally, quatrains may be organized so that a single line is distinct. In such cases, the most common pattern is for the third line to be distinct and serve as a bridge between the first two lines and the final line. This is the pattern found in the quatrains involving shortening that Tedlock (1983:223ff) describes in the *Popol Wuj*. A contemporary example also comes from Guarchaj's "Ri loq'olaj q'ij" ("The sacred sun"):

(35) Diego Adrián Guarchaj Ajtzalam (K'iche' 2007, my translation)

Xkaqtarin ri q'ij la	Your sun has reddened,
Xkaqarin ri wach la	Your face has reddened,
Kamul oxmul	Two times, three times,
Xb'an ri atin la.	Your cleaning is done.

Here, the first, second, and fourth lines all have the same form: a verb in completive aspect followed by a subject noun marked with the second person singular formal possessive pronoun *la*. However, the verbs in the first two lines are in the middle voice (marked with the antipassive suffix) while the verb in the fourth line is passive. The distinct third line ("two times, three times") serves as a bridge between the first two antipassive clauses and the final passive clause.

Although less common than quatrains, quintets (stanzas of five lines) also occur. For example, Maxwell (1987) describes a Chuj prayer composed entirely of quintets such as the one in example (36):

(36) Chuj prayer (Maxwell 1987:502)

mato hin-swerte	Might (this be) my fate,
mato x-ʔikoʔ	Might (this be) my lot.
mato tas y-uj ʔixtik	What might (be) its cause.
mato y-ik hinmam hin-nun	Might it (be) from my parents,
mato y-ik hinmam w-ʔicham	Might it (be) from my ancestors.

Although most research on Maya poetics has focused on the couplet, patterns in contemporary poetry suggest that larger units play an equally important role in structuring poetic discourse. The following section examines forms of extended parallelism involving units larger than quatrains and quintets.

3.6 Extended parallelism

The use of extended parallelism in Maya poetics takes three basic forms. In the first, couplets and triplets may be linked together either through shared structure or through overt bracketing within a larger text. Another form involves extended list of parallel constituents. A final form involves exact repetitions of specific lines arranged in symmetric patterns.

The most basic form of extended parallelism involves the combination of couplets into longer series (see Lengyel 1988). This produces a long list of couplet pairs, as in example (7) above. In such cases, there may be no parallelism linking the couplets together (although each couplet contains its own internal unity). The second type of extended parallelism involves lists of parallel constituents. In Hieroglyphic Maya texts, there are numerous examples of this type of list containing titles or names of political figures:

(37) Stela 21, Yaxchilan Structure 44, Hieroglyphic Maya (Hull 2003:397)

ucha'n tajam mo',	His captive, *Tajam Mo',*
ucha'n 9-le ajaw,	His captive, *9-le Ajaw,*
ucha'n a-?-man?,	His captive, *A-? Man?,*
ucha'n ajik'a.	His captive *Ajik'a.*

The use of lists as a poetic device is also common in texts from the colonial period. The *Books of Chilam Balam* and the *Popol Wuj* both contain numerous examples, such as in (38):

(38) *Popol Wuj*, K'iche' (Sam Colop 2001:23, my translation):

Wa'e k'ute nab'e tzij,	These, then, are the first words,
nab'e uchan.	the first speech.

Maja' b'i oq	There had not yet been named
jun winaq	a person,
jun chikop,	an animal,
tz'ikin,	bird,
kar,	fish,
tap,	crab,
che',	tree,
ab'aj,	rock,
jul,	hole,
siwan,	canyon,
k'im,	field,
k'ichelaj,	forest,
xa utukel kaj k'olik.	Only the sky existed, all alone.

As with possible quatrains, translators of colonial literature have also debated whether or not all such lists should be divided into couplets. For example, in his translation of the *Popol Wuj*, Edmonson treated all such lists as groups of couplets, pairing semantically related words together (such as *bird/fish* or *tree/rock* in (38) above). In cases where lists contain odd numbers of items, Edmonson went so far as to add items into the list to ensure that it could be divided into couplets (see Tedlock 1983). In contrast, other scholars of the *Popol Wuj* (Tedlock 1983; Sam Colop 2001) treat lists as larger unified structures (rather than breaking them down into couplets).

The use of lists as a poetic/rhetorical device is another feature of Maya poetics that continues into the present day. Although common in ritual discourse, lists also occur in other contexts. Example (39) is from an 1812 Tzotzil proclamation (*Proclama del duque infantado president*) warning of the dangers posed by Napoleon (cited in Gossen 1985:68). Although it may have been originally written in Spanish, the Tzotzil version is largely written in mostly in couplets and follows traditional Maya poetic structure, including the use of lists:

(39) Proclamation against Napoleon, Tzotzil (Gossen 1985:68)

Bu xtal cux leg cuuntic	Where is our happiness to come from
Te me ja noox ta spu qu'ih	If he [Napoleon] does nothing more than to spread
Chamebal	Sickness
Hilbajinel	Torment
Icti	Anxiety
Huocol	Difficulty
Malchun huaneg	Bearers of false beliefs,
Mean al	Poverty
Huinal	Hunger
Pogh vaneg	Usurpers
Mil huaneg	Murderers
Schiuc yantic pojou xuluan chon	And other snake venoms
Mu ilbiluc ta hom cuuntic	Never seen before in our midst

The use of extended parallelism and lists is also common in contemporary Maya poetry. For example, one of Humberto Ak'abal's most famous poems, "Xirixitem chikop" ("Bird songs"), is an extended list of K'iche' bird names, each repeated three times. An extract is given in (40):

(40) Humberto Ak'abal, K'iche' (2004:49)

Saqk'or, saqk'or, saqk'or. . .	saqk'or = quail
Ch'ik, ch'ik, ch'ik. . .	ch'ik = woodcock
Tukumux, tukumux, tukumux. . .	tukumux = mourning dove
Xperpwaq, xperpwaq, xperpwaq. . .	ixparpwaq = nightingale
Tz'ikin, tz'ikin, tz'ikin. . .	tz'ikin = bird (generic)
Kukuw, kukuw, kukuw. . .	kukuw = type of sparrow

In addition to pure lists, contemporary forms of extended parallelism include multiple repetition of a syntactic frame with alternations. The form of substitution is the same as in traditional couplets only it is repeated more than twice. Examples of extended parallelism are often part of larger structures involving smaller units (such as couplets), as in example (41)

(41) Briceida Cuevas Cob, Yucatec (2008:40, my translation):

	A Táan	Your voice
1	¿Tu'ux ts'o'ok u juum a t'aan?	Where is your voice?
2	¿Tu'ux sa'atij?	Where was it lost?
3	Le ku jalchajal,	This which slips
4	le ku na'akal u ta'akikuba	This which climbs to hide
	[ichil in pool.	[in my hair
5	Le ku k'alkuba ichil in xikin,	This which seals itself in my ears
6	le ku ji'iji'ilkuba tin chi',	This which wallows in my mouth
7	le ku nojk'ajal yóok'ol in tseem,	This which falls head first in my chest
8	le ku yets'tal ichil in puksi'ik'al.	This which sits in my heart
9	Táan in kaxantik u juum a t'aan	I search for it with my teeth
10	yéetel in koj tak yáanal	up to under my nails
	in wíich'ak.	
11	¿Tu'ux u ta'akmajuba?	Where does it hide?
12	¿Ts'o'ok wáaj u tu'ubultech t'aan?	Maybe you have become mute?
13	¿Wa teen ts'o'ok in kóoktal?	Or am I deaf?

In this poem, lines 3–8 contain six repetitions of the same syntactic frame ("le ku X") with alternating predicates (involving positional roots with movement). This extended parallelism is framed by smaller structures. The opening couplet (lines 1–2) is echoed by the final triplet (lines 11–13) with all lines containing questions. The couplet in lines 9–10 serves to bridge the extended parallelism (3–8) with the closing triplet (11–13). The couplet in 9–10 involves shortening in the second half of the pair, a device (discussed above) often used as a bridge between lines. The extended parallelism is embedded in a larger poetic structure and is framed by smaller units (a couplet and a triplet).

The final type of extended parallelism involves exact repetitions of lines arranged to produce specific poetic patterns. In these cases, lines may be repeated in the same order or repeated in inverse order. A case of repetitions following the same order can be found in following example from a carved bone (bone #42) from Tikal:

(42) Carved bone from Tikal, Hieroglyphic Maya (Hull 2003:397):

1.	ub'aak xikuup ajaw ch'ok,	The bone of *Xikuup Ajaw Ch'ok*,
2.	ub'aak ? ajaw ju-?,	The bone of *? Ajaw Hu-?*,
3.	ub'aak ? b'aakal ajaw,	The bone of *B'aakal Ajaw*,

4. ub'aak k'uhul b'aak ajaw tz'ul b'aak,	The bone of *K'uhul B'aak Ajaw Tz'ul B'aak*,
5. ub'aak xukuup ajaw ch'ok,	The bone of *Xukuup Ajaw Ch'ok*,
6. ub'aak ? ajaw hul b'aak	The bone of *? Ajaw Hul B'aak*,
7. ub'aak ??,	The bone of *??*
8. ub'aak k'uhul b'aak ajaw.	The bone of *K'uhul B'aak Ajaw*.

Although part of the text is missing, it is possible to see that the lines in this text repeat in a regular order. Line 1 is identical to line 5 and the preserved elements of line 2 correspond to those found in line 6. Similarly, line 4 and line 8 contain the same elements. If we assume that line 7 must also match with line 3, then we have a repeated quatrain (A B C D A B C D).

The same type of repeated quatrain occurs in the song "Nutzij" ("My words") by Tz'utujil hip-hop artist Tz'utu Baktun Kan:

(43) Nutzij, Tz'utujil (Tz'utu Baktun Kan 2011)

Li wi' numam xepe che ato'ik	your grandchildren have come to help you
ruk'in li qatz'ijb',	with our writing
ruk'in li qab'ix	with our singing
ruk'in li qatzij. . .	with our words
ruk'in li qaxajoj	with our dances
ruk'in li qatz'ijb',	with our writing
ruk'in li qab'ix	with our singing
ruk'in li qatzij	with our words
ruk'in li qaxajoj	with our dances

As with the example from Tikal, the song involves an exact repetition of a quatrain. The repetition of substituted elements produces a cyclic pattern within the text. Another less common pattern involves repetitions in inverted order, a pattern reported for Ch'orti' discourse (see Fought 1985; Hull 2003). In this pattern, lines or couplets are repeated but occur in the reverse order (e.g. A B C D D C B A). Example (44) is from a Ch'orti' healing prayer:

(44) Ch'orti' prayer (Hull 2003:178)

1. *Uyatravesir uyok,*	The inhibiting force of their legs,
2. *Uyatravesir uk'ab'.*	The inhibiting force of their hands.
3. *Uxek'onir yer uyatravesir uyok,*	The stabbing pains of the inhibiting force of their legs,
4. *Uxek'onir yer uyatravesir uk'ab'.*	The stabbing pains of the inhibiting force of their hands,
5. *Ya'syob' tama e gotera,*	There they play in the eaves,
6. *Ya'syob' tama e gotera.*	There they play in the eaves,
7. *Uxek'onir yer uyatravesir uyok,*	The stabbing pains of the inhibiting force of their legs,
8. *Uxek'onir yer uyatravesir uk'ab'.*	The stabbing pains of the inhibiting force of their hands,
9. *Uyatravesir uyok,*	The inhibiting force of their legs
10. *Takar uyatravesir uk'ab'.*	The inhibiting force of their hands.

In the example, the couplets are repeated in reverse order (A1 A2 B1 B2 C1 C1 B1 B2 A1 A2), so that the first and last couplet are the same and the second couplet matches the penultimate. The two lines in the middle couplet (lines 5–6) are identical, marking the center of the inverted pattern.

The various forms of extended parallelism demonstrate some of the ways in which Maya poetic discourse is organized into larger units. Maya poetic patterns are thus not restricted to the couplet. Indeed, couplets themselves may be organized into complex patterns.

3.7 Pragmatics of shifts in parallelism

The construction of structures larger than the couplet is often used to highlight an important discursive shift. In such cases, a pattern of parallelism is established and then broken with a line (or lines) that mark a rhetorical climax or central argument. This poetic device is fairly common in contemporary Maya poetry. Example (45) is from Pablo García's poem "Tat, Nan, kuyu' alaq qamak" ("Father, Mother, forgive us for our sins").

(45) Pablo García, K'iche' (del Valle Escalante 2010:186, my translation)

1	we qapalaj	our faces
2	we qach'akul	our bodies
3	we qariayib'al	our desires
4	we qatzij je we qachak	our words and our works
5	a're' chik uwochib'al ri ch'ob'onel, chomanel awaj.	These are the image of a rational, thinking animal.

The first four lines contain the same syntactic frame of possessed nouns (*we qa-N*, DET 1PL-N). The repetition of the frame in line 4 ("our words and our works") marks the closure of the parallel pattern and, hence, the introduction to the central point given in line 5. The content of line 5 brings the focus of the poem (back) to human rights for the Maya (i.e. "everything about the Maya is human"). The shift in parallelism marks the shift in discourse found in the last line of the verse.

A similar pattern is found in example (46), a poem by Q'anjob'al poet Daniel Caño:

(46) Daniel Caño, Q'anjob'al (del Valle Escalante 2010:275, my translation)

Skuyb'anil Hinchikay	My grandmother's lesson

Kaqchin :
   Watx' b'ay hachik'il.
	Red corn:
	   Good for your blood.

Q'eq nal:
   Watx' b'ay haxil.
	Black corn:
	   Good for your hair.

Saq nal:
   Watz' b'ay hab'aqil, he' k'al hesq'aq.
	White corn:
	   Good for your bones, teeth, and nails.

Q'an nal:
   Watx' b'ay hab'aq'chil.
	Yellow corn:
	   Good for your skin.

Tz'ib' nal:
   Watx' yet chelonteq masanil mamalil
   lana yalay oktoq yullaq hajolom
   b'ay yatutal kuyoj.
	Painted corn:
	   Good when recognizing the dumbasses
	   who are lying to you
	   in school.

In this poem, Caño repeats the same frame five times: a type of corn followed by the health benefits that each type of corn provides. The first four repetitions (eight lines) produce a typical quatrain structure with a distinct third part. In the first, second, and fourth repetitions (lines 2, 4, and 8), the corn is good for one specific body part. Line 6 (the third repetition of the frame) is longer (containing three distinct body parts), producing an AABA quatrain. The quatrain pattern in the first eight lines creates a poetic break before the final (punch)line concerning painted corn (or mixed corn). The first four colors of corn correspond to the four cardinal directions and their co-occurrence reproduces a common quatrain pattern within Maya culture. The painted corn (in which the four colors are mixed together) is not part of the traditional set and serves as a metaphor for the confusion and disorder associated with school education. The disruption of the parallelism in the last line serves to mark the distinct final line as the "punchline" of the poem.

Early studies of Maya poetics (e.g. Edmonson 1971; Norman 1980) tended to view Maya poetry as sequences of syntactic couplets. However, patterns larger than the couplet may be used for pragmatic effect. Parallelism is not purely syntactic, as parallel structures are formed at all levels of grammar. It is only by recognizing the full range of poetic forms that the aesthetic power of Maya literature can be understood.

4 POETICS AND SPEECH PLAY

Although parallelism is the central component of Maya poetics, there are certainly other aspects of Maya poetry that do not directly involve parallelism. This section describes two additional aspects of Maya poetics: the use of polysemy and the use of ideophones.

4.1 Polysemy

Roots with multiple possible meanings are common in Mayan languages. For example, in K'iche', the root *ch'ich'* may refer to metal or objects made of metal, especially buses. Similarly, the verb root *koj* could be translated as *to believe*, *to wear*, or *to use*, depending on contexts. In everyday interactions, this specific meaning of such roots is rarely an issue due to context (e.g. one does not generally "believe" a huipil or "wear" a computer). However, polysemous roots may be used to produce puns in speech play and are a common feature of Maya poetics. For example, Tedlock (1983:312ff) describes the sexual puns that a "divinier" (*aj q'ij*) finds in reading the *Popol Wuj*. In contemporary Maya poetry, polysemy may be used to produce humor as in (47), from Ak'abal's poem "Rayinik" ("Desire"):

(47) Humberto Ak'abal, K'iche' (2004:256, my translation)

Ri tz'ikin	The birds,
ke'**rapapik**, ke'b'ixonik	flap their wings and sing
xuquje ke'kisinik.	and shit.

The root *rap* generally is a positional root referring to the movement of flapping. The form in line 2, *rapapik*, is most commonly used to mean "fly" (for smaller birds). However, *rapapik* may also mean "to fart" (due to the "flapping" of the buttocks when producing a fart). In the poem, Ak'abal writes that his desire is to be like a bird, primarily so that he can fly and shit on people beneath him. The pun between "fart" and "fly" plays with the themes of flight and defecation within the poem (see Barrett 2014).

Polysemy is not always used to produce humor. Indeed, it can produce very somber effects. Example (48) is the opening stanza of a poem by Guarchaj titled "Kinsachik" (either "I am lost" or "I have erred").

(48) Diego Adrián Guarchaj Ajtzalam, K'iche' (unpublished, my translation)

1	Xinsachik nan	I am lost, mother
2	xinsachik tat.	I am lost, father
3	Xinsach ri nub'e	I have lost my way
4	jas che xinsachik.	Why did I err?

In this poem, Guarchaj plays with the multiple meanings associated with the K'iche' verb root *sach*. As a transitive verb, *sach* means to lose or to forget. However, *sach* may also be used as an intransitive verb meaning to get lost, to err, or to sink. The occurrences of *sach* in lines 1 and 2 are ambiguous, meaning either "I am lost" or "I made a mistake". The last two lines of the quatrain play with this ambiguity. In line 3, *sach* is transitive and clearly means "to lose," while the *sach* in line 4 is intransitive with a meaning of "to err." The quatrain as a whole, then, highlights the ambiguity associated with this particular K'iche' verb, linking the experience of being physically lost with the being lost psychologically due to one's own mistakes in life.

4.2 Ideophones

Ideophones are words that depict sensory experiences (Dingemanse 2012:654). In Mayan languages, ideophones may depict sounds (affect roots) or shapes and movements (positional roots). Ideophones are a common component of speech play in Mayan languages and they are frequently used in joking and teasing. They may also be used for rhetorical effect in Maya narratives. For example, England (2009) describes the use of ideophones in a Mam narrative. Ideophone roots may occur in isolation to directly convey a particular sound, usually occurring with a form of the verb meaning "to do/make". In (48), K'iche' poet Pablo García uses ideophonic roots in this way:

(49) Pablo García, K'iche' (del Valle Escalante 2010:201, my translation)

1	Ujkejetal rumal ri k'otol chi'j awaj	Riding the animal inquisitor
2	kaqab'an **puq' puq' puq' puq'**	We go puq' puq' puq' puq'
3	**ruq'uq' ruq'uq' ruq'uq' ruq'uq'**	ruq'uq' ruq'uq' ruq'uq' ruq'uq'
4	pataq we xaq'o'la ja' re we Xib'alb'a.	through the muddy waters of Xib'alb'a
5	Ujkejetal rumal ri k'otol chi'j awa	Riding on the animal inquisitor
6	kaqab'an **chiy chiy chiy chiy**	We go chiy chiy chiy chiy
7	**patz patz patz patz**	patz patz patz patz
8	pataq we xaq'o'la keqiq' re we Xib'alb'a	through the muddy winds of Xib'alb'a

In (49), García uses several ideophones: *puq'* (sound of a rock dropped into water), *ruq'uq'* (sound of splashing), *chiy* (frantic movement of hair or straw), and *patz* (extremely hairy, like a squirrel's tail). The root *patz* may also refer to the process of transporting straw (which sticks out like bushy hair). These ideophones combine to indicate the sounds and movement of an animal trotting through wind and mud on the road to Xib'alb'a.

Ideophonic roots may also be combined with specific suffixes to create nouns, verbs, or adjectives. In example (50), Sabino Esteban Francisco creates parallelism by using the ideophone root *t'uj* (sound of dripping) in different ways:

(50) Sabino Esteban Francisco, Q'anjob'al (del Valle Escalante 2010:367, my translation)

1	Chi tit hintaqintihal	My thirst wakes up
2	yet chi wab'on yay **t'uj**lab'oq ha' a'ej:	to hear the water dripping:
3	**t'uj, t'uj, t'uj**. . .	t'uj, t'uj, t'uj. . .
4	Jujun **t'uj**an chi'	each drop is sweet,
5	Jujun **t'uj**an sik.	each drop is fresh.

In line 2, we have a verb formed with *t'uj* (*t'ujlab'oq*, to drip) with the root repeated in isolation in line 3. In lines 4 and 5, the root is used to form a noun (drop). Here, the repetition of the ideophone root mimics the repetition of the dripping water described in the poem.

K'iche' poet Humberto Ak'abal has written several poems composed entirely of ideophones. These "sound poems" convey the sensory experiences associated with specific context. For example, the poem "Conjuro por la lluvia" ("Rain conjuring") reproduces the sounds associated with a thunderstorm (Example (51)). The ideophones used here are *jin* (sound of thunder), *tz'in* (sound of steady rain), *b'ul* (sound of a waterfall or spring), and *chip* (sound of sprinkling water).

(51) Humberto Ak'abal, K'iche' (Ak'abal 2006:57)

Xxxxxxxxxxxx. . .

JINNNNNNNNN. . .
XXXXXXXXXXXX. . .

Tz'innnnnnnnn. . .
Tz'innnnnnnnn. . .

Bulun, bulun, bulun, bulun, bulun
Bulun, bulun, bulun, bulun, bulun:
chiplaaaaaaaaaaaa. . .

Although Ak'abal typically publishes his poetry in bilingual editions, sound poems like that in (50) never have corresponding Spanish versions (see Barrett 2014). These poems, like ideophones themselves, are meant to directly reproduce experiences of sound (and therefore, cannot be translated).

5 CONCLUSION

The poetic forms described in this chapter are woven throughout Maya literature and culture. They occur in contexts ranging from everyday conversations to lyric poetry. England (1987) found a correlation between language loss and the use of poetic parallelism in Maya narratives, with parallelism being less common as the number of speakers of a language declines. The years since England's study have seen an important revitalization of Maya cultures, sometimes referred to as the "Maya Renaissance" (Montejo 2005). This revitalization includes a resurgence of literature in Mayan languages and new forms of indigenous popular music. These new forms of cultural expression demonstrate that the Maya poetic tradition found in pre-Columbian texts is thriving in the modern world.

REFERENCES

Ak'abal, Humberto. 2001. *Ajkem Tzij/Tejedor de Palabras.* Guatemala City: Cholsamaj. (Corrected edition of Ak'abal 1996. Guatemala: UNESCO.)

Ak'abal, Humberto. 2004. *Chajil Tzaqib'al Ja'/Guardián de la Caída de Agua.* Guatemala City: Cholsamaj.

Ak'abal, Humberto. 2006. *K'ojon che nik'aj ik'/Remiendo de media luna.* Momostenango, Guatemala: Artesanales Tz'ukulik.

B'alam Ajpu'. 2014. "B'atz'" *Jun Winaq Rajawal Q'ij/Tributo a los 20 Nawales.* Spiritual guide, Venancio Morales, Tz'utujil lyrics/Executive producer: Tz´utu Baktun Kan, Spanish lyrics: M.C.H.E., Musical producer, Dr. Nativo, Banco de Sonidos: Sotz'il Jay, Co-Producer: Básico 3.

Barrett, Rusty. 2014. "Ideophones and (non-)arbitrariness in the K'iche' poetry of Humberto Ak'abal." *Pragmatics and Society* 5: 406–18.

Bautista Vázquez, Ruperta. 2008. *Xchamel ch'ul balamil, Eclipse en la madre tierra.* Mexico City: Comisión Nacional para el Desarrollo de los Pueblos Indígenas.

Botto, Malcolm Miguel. 2008. "Music and the modern Maya: a reception study of Rock-Maya music in Guatemala." MA thesis, Brigham Young Univeristy.

Breton, Alain, ed. 2007. *Rabinal achi: A fifteenth-century Maya dynastic drama.* Translated by Robert Schneider and Teresa Lavender Fagan. Boulder: University of Colorado Press.

Brody, Jill. 1986. "Repetition as a rhetorical and conversational device in Tojolobal (Mayan)." *International Journal of American Linguistics* 52: 255–74.

Brown, Penelope. 1998. "Conversational structure and language acquisition: The role of repetition in Tzeltal." *Journal of Linguistic Anthropology* 8: 197–221.

Cuevas Cob, Briceida. 2008. *Ti'u billil in nook' Del dobladillo de mi ropa.* Mexico City: Comisión Nacional para el Desarrollo de los Pueblos Indígenas.

Dingemanse, Mark. 2012. "Advances in the cross-linguistic study of ideophones." *Language and Linguistics Compass* 6/10: 654–72.

Edmonson, Munro. 1971. *The book of counsel: The Popol Vuh of the Quiche Maya of Guatemala.* New Orleans: Middle American Research Institute, Tulane University.

Edmonson, Munro. 1982. *The ancient future of the Itza: The book of Chilam Balam of Tizimin.* Austin: University of Texas Press.

England, Nora. 1987. "Variation in Mayan narrative." *Anthropological Linguistics* 29: 522–32.

England, Nora. 2009. "To tell a tale: The structure of narrated stories in Mam, a Mayan language." *International Journal of American Linguistics* 75: 207–31.

Fought, John. 1985. "Cyclic patterns in Chorti (Mayan) literature." In *Handbook of middle American Indians, supplement 3: Literature*, ed. by Munro Edmonson, 147–80. Austin, TX: University of Texas Press.

García, María Luz. 2012. "Discourse, social cohesion and the politics of historical memory in the Ixhil Maya region of Guatemala." PhD diss., University of Texas, Austin.

García, María Luz. 2014. "The long count of historical memory: Ixhil Maya ceremonial speech in Guatemala." *American Ethnologist* 41: 664–80.

González, Gaspar Pedro. 2001. *The dry season: Q'anjob'al Maya poems.* Translated by R. McKenna Brown. Cleveland: Cleveland State University Poetry Center.

Gossen, Gary H. 1985. "Tzotzil literature." In *Handbook of middle American Indians, supplement 3: Literature*, ed. by Munro Edmonson, 64–106. Austin: University of Texas Press.

Guarchaj Ajtzalam, Diego Adrián. 2007. "Ri loq'olaj q'ij" *No'jmay Wuj*, Santa Cruz del Quiché, Guatemala: K'iche' Mayab' Cholchi' 3(4): 5.

Hanks, William F. 1988. "Grammar, style, and meaning in a Maya manuscript." *International Journal of American Linguistics* 54: 331–65.

Hofling, Charles Andrew. 1987. "Marking space and time in Itzaj Maya narrative." *Journal of Linguistic Anthropology* 3: 164–84.

Hofling, Charles Andrew. 2012. "A comparison of narrative style in Mopan and Itzaj Mayan." In Hull and Carrasco (2012), 401–48.

Hopkins, Nicholas, and J. Kathryn Josserand. 2102. "The narrative structure of Chol folktales: One thousand years of literary tradition." In Hull and Carrasco (2012), 21–44.

Hull, Kerry M. 2003. "Verbal art and performance in Ch'orti' and Maya hieroglyphic writing." PhD diss., University of Texas, Austin.

Hull, Kerry M. 2012. "Poetic tenacity: a diachronic study of kennings in Mayan languages." In Hull and Carrasco (2012), 73–122.

Hull, Kerry M., and Michael Carrasco. 2012. *Parallel worlds: Genre, discourse, and poetics in contemporary, colonial, and classic period Maya literature*. Boulder: University of Colorado Press.

Knowlton, Timothy W. 2002. "Diphrastic kennings in Mayan hieroglyphic literature." *Mexicon* 24: 9–14.

Knowlton, Timothy W. 2012. "Some historical continuities in lowland Maya magical speech genres: Keying shamanic performance." In Hull and Carrasco (2012), 253–70.

Lacadena García-Gallo, Alfonso. 2009. "Apuntes para un Estudio sobre Literatura Maya Antigua." In *Texto y contexto: Perspectivas intraculturales en el análisis de la literatura maya yucateca*, ed. by Antje Gunsenheimer, Tsubasa Okoshi Harada, and John F. Chuchiak, 31–52. Bonn: BAS.

Lengyel, Thomas E. 1988. "On the structure and discourse functions of semantic couplets in Mayan languages." *Anthropological Linguistics* 30: 94–127.

Lenkersdorf, Carlos. 1979. "Poesía contemporánea de los maya tojolabales." *Indiana* 5: 171–76.

Lounsbury, Floyd G. 1980. "Some problems in the interpretation of the mythological portion of the hieroglyphic text of the Temple of the Cross at Palenque." In *Third Palenque Round Table, 1978: Part 2*, ed. by Merle Greene Robertson, 99–115. Austin, TX: University of Texas Press.

Martin, Laura. 1994. "Discourse structure and rhetorical elaboration in Mocho personal narrative." *Journal of Linguistic Anthropology* 4: 131–52.

Maxwell, Judith M. 1987. "Some aspects of Chuj discourse." *Anthropological Linguistics* 29: 489–506.

Montejo, Victor. 2005. *Maya intellectual renaissance: Identity, representation, and leadership*. Austin: University of Texas Press.

Norman, William M. 1980. "Grammatical parallelism in Quiche ritual language." *Proceedings of the Sixth Annual Meeting of the Berkeley Linguistics Society* 6: 387–99.

Sam Colop, Luis Enrique. 1994. "Maya poetics." PhD diss., State University of New York, Buffalo.

Sam Colop, Luis Enrique. 2001. *Popol Wuj: Versión poética del texto en K'iche'*. Guatemala: Cholsamaj.

Stross, Brian. 1972. "Verbal processes in Tzeltal speech socialization." *Anthropological Linguistics* 14: 1–13.

Tedlock, Dennis. 1983. *The spoken word and the work of interpretation*. Philadelphia: University of Pennsylvania Press.

Tedlock, Dennis. 2010. *2000 years of Mayan literature*. Berkeley/Los Angeles: University of California Press.

Tz'utu Baktun Kan. 2011. "Nutzij,." Unpublished recording. Guatemala City: Guatemala.

Tz'utu Baktun Kan. 2012. "Kotzij" *ZOM (Zona música) 2012*. Guatemala: Centro cultural de España y CREA (Ministerio de cultura y deportes de Guatemala).

Vail, Gabrielle. 2012. "Creation narratives in the postclassic Maya codices." In Hull and Carrasco (2012), 223–52.

Valle Escalante, Emilio, del, ed. 2010. *Uk'u'x kaj, uk'u'x ulew: Antología de poesía maya guatemalteca contemporánea*. Pittsburgh: University of Pittsburgh.

Vogt, Evon A. 1969. *Zinacantan: A Maya community in the highlands of Chiapas*. Cambridge: Harvard University Press.

PART 5

GRAMMAR SKETCHES

CHAPTER 18

K'ICHE'

Telma A. Can Pixabaj

This chapter was written while the author was a postdoctoral researcher at UNAM, Programa de Becas Posdoctorales en la UNAM, Becaria del Centro de Investigaciones Multidisciplinarias Sobre Chiapas y la Frontera Sur.

1 BACKGROUND

1.1 Introduction

K'iche' is a language of the Eastern branch of the Mayan family. According to Richards (2003) it had 900,000 speakers in 2001. It is spoken in 78 *municipios* in nine departments of Guatemala. Kaufman (1974) divides K'iche' into four dialect regions: Central, Western, Eastern, and Northern. There can be more than one dialect within each region. Although these regions and dialect divisions are recognized, people usually identify their language more narrowly, by the town (*municipio*) they come from, such as Nahualá, Chichicastenango, etc.

The data used in this study come from bibliographical sources, elicitation (mainly in Santa Lucía Utatlán, Nahualá, and Chichicastenango), and from the database of the project "Documentation of formal and ceremonial discourses in K'ichee'" (Endangered Languages Documentation Programme IGS 0092).

1.2 Data and sources

K'iche' is one of the well-studied Mayan languages. There are documents written in and on K'iche' from the time of the Conquest. Documents written in K'iche' include the *Popol Wuj*, the *Rabinal Achi* (K'iche' is identified as the language in the document itself), and several *Títulos* (land titles, but in essence local histories). Another group of documents corresponds to religious texts, especially the translation of the bible, the missal and some other Christian documents in which these beliefs are translated from Spanish or Latin to K'iche'. There are many documents on K'iche' grammar. Below I make brief reference to the most relevant ones.

López Ixcoy (1997) is the most complete reference grammar up to the present. The most useful PhD dissertations are Larsen (1988), in which he focuses on ergativity and presents a clear and detailed overview of the grammar, and Mondloch (1981), which presents an analysis of voice in K'iche'. Other dissertations include Velleman (2014), which is a detailed study of focus in K'iche'. In this work she shows that focus can be in situ with the exception of focus of the agent (transitive subject); this constitutes a manifestation of syntactic ergativity. Baird's (2014) study is also related to focus, and covers mainly the phonetics of prosody of focus, which had not been well explored until then. Finally, Can Pixabaj (2015) is a study of complement clauses which proposes three structural types of complement clause. Two of them can be used for purpose clauses as well. The third type is superficially similar to a third type of purpose clause but Can Pixabaj shows that it is structurally different.

Among individual articles are a very few on phonology, such as Nielsen (2005) and Henderson (2012). For studies on morphosyntax we have Mondloch (1978), Trechsel (1981, 1993), Larsen (1987), Davis and Sam-Colop (1990), Kaufman (1990), Campbell (2000), Can Pixabaj and England (2011), Yasavul (2011), Aissen (2011), and Velleman (2013). Among works on dialectology we have Par Sapón and Can Pixabaj (2000) and Romero (2006). Acquisition has been studied only by Pye (1980, 1991, and 2001).

Among modern dictionaries and vocabularies the most relevant are Ajpacajá Tum *et al.* (1996), the monolingual dictionary by Edmonson (1965), and Ajpacajá Tum (2001). There are a number of important colonial dictionaries as well, which I will not cover here except to note that they are necessary references for working on the colonial K'iche' literature. There are other contemporary works such as vocabularies, handbooks to learn the language, etc., written by members of various institutions such as OKMA and the ALMG.

Out of the 78 municipalities where K'iche' is spoken, only a few have been the source of the studies that I have listed. These studies are mostly focused on the following towns: Nahualá, Santa Catarina Ixtahuacán, Momostenango, Cantel, Santa María Chiquimula, Santa Cruz del Quiché, Santa Lucía Utatlán, and Chichicastenango (this last only superficially with regard to the vowel system).

1.3 Documentation

Some documentation in the sense of having recorded texts, transcribed and analyzed texts, and an available database of K'iche' exists in AILLA (Archive of the Indigenous Languages of Latin America, University of Texas at Austin). In this archive there are many hours of recorded texts, there are a few transcribed texts, but there are no annotated texts so far. Norman (1976) is the only published text with translation and annotation that I know of. Can Pixabaj is producing a database that will be available in ELAR (Endangered Languages Archive, SOAS, University of London) and AILLA (23 hours of audio files, most of them with video, all of them transcribed and translated into Spanish, and 10 hours of annotated texts).

2 PHONOLOGY

2.1 Consonants

K'iche' has 22 consonants that are phonemic; they are presented in Table 18.1, given in the K'iche' orthography with IPA equivalents in square brackets where different.

TABLE 18.1 K'ICHE' CONSONANTS

	Bilabial	Alveolar	Alveopalatal	Palatal	Velar	Uvular	Glottal
Plosive	p	t			k	q	' [ʔ]
	b' [ɓ]	t'			k'	q' [q', ɢ]	
Nasal	m	n					
Flap		r					
Fricative		s	x [ʃ]			j [χ]	
Affricate		tz [ts]	ch [tʃ]				
		tz' [ts']	ch' [tʃ']				
Lateral		l					
Approximant	w			y [j]			

K'iche' has lost four Proto-Mayan sounds: *ty-ty' (possibly alveolar or post-alveolar sounds), *nh [ŋ], and *h (England 1992). /h/ is preserved in final position in some dialects (e.g., Santa Lucía Utatlán and Nahualá). It is not recognized as part of the inventory of consonants since it is only found in some dialects in a restricted environment.

Allophonic variation in K'iche' includes that of the phoneme /b'/. In onset position it varies between a voiceless implosive [ɓ] and a semi-voiceless implosive [ɓ̥]. In coda position it varies between [ɓ̥] and [ɓ̥']. Examples are from Par Sapón and Can Pixabaj (2000:25–6).

(1) a. [ɓa:qχ] ~   [ɓ̥a:qχ]   'bone'
    b. [kʲeɓ̥'] ~   [kʲeɓ̥]   'two'

There is a pair of changes that are widespread in K'ichean proper languages, including K'iche', and involve occurrence in coda position. The first one is that the simple stops /p, t, k/ are aspirated in coda position, either external as in (2a–c), or internal as in (2d–e), but not in onset position as in (2f).

(2) a. [po:pʰ]   'petate'
    b. [ta:tʰ]   'father'
    c. [kokʰ]   'turtle'
    d. [ʔokʰb'al]   'entry' (in variation with ʔokib'al)
    e. [katakʰtotikʰ]   'walk from one place to another with difficulty'
    f. [tatab'ał]   'stepfather'

The phoneme /q/ is affricated in internal and external coda position.

(3) a. [saqχ]   'white'
    b. [saqχ̥soχ]   'somewhat white'

The second one concerns the lateral and approximant sounds /w/, /r/, /l/, and /y/. These sounds are devoiced in coda position in most dialects.

(4) a. [wah]   'food'
    b. [ʔawaχ]   'domestic animal'
    c. [tew̥toχ] ~ [tewtoχ]   'somehow cold'
    d. [te:w̥]¹   'cold' (environment)

(5) a. [la:ɬ]   'you (honorific)'
    b. [ʔala]   'boy'
    c. [maɬkaʔn]   'widow'

(6) a. [jowa:ɓ̥]   'sick'
    b. [ʔaji:n]   'alligator'
    c. [kamaj̥motikʰ]   'it blinks/it is getting dark'
    d. [k'o:j̥]   'monkey'

The /r/ is voiceless in coda position, but it also varies in other environments; it can be a flap or trill in onset position or between vowels, and in some dialects it can be voiceless in onset position.

(7) a. [r/r/ɹ̝aʃ] [r/r/ɹ̝̥eʃ]   'green'
    b. [ʃupiɾo] [ʃupiɾo]   's/he split it'

   c. [kak'a̠k'otikʰ]   'knock on the door'
   d. [ka̠]   'fish'

As in some other Eastern Mayan languages, the phonemes /k/ and /k'/ are usually palatalized before either a front mid vowel /e/ or a central low vowel /a/ when these are followed by a uvular consonant. The distribution suggests that this allophone has not been phonemicized yet, since the environment for its occurrence is restricted and (mostly) predictable.

(8) a. [kʲaqχ] ~ [kʲeqχ]   'red'
   c. [ʔiʃkʲ'eqχ] ~ [ʔiʃkʲ'aqχ] 'fingernail'
   d. [kʲ'a:qχ]   'flea'

There are exceptions to the rule. In the example [keqach'ab'e:χ] 'we talk to them' the phoneme /k/ is not palatalized, although the environment is suitable for the application of the rule (kʲ /_e + uvular sound). There are also some cases where the phoneme is palatalized, but the vowel is not followed by a uvular sound, such as in [kʲeɓ] 'two', while in others an unpalatalized /k/ occurs before /e:/ as in [ke:m] 'weaving'. This seems to be a lexical rule rather than representing any generalizable pattern. What this shows is that this change is still in progress.

2.2 Vowel system

K'iche' has five simple vowels; most dialects also have phonemic vowel lengthening (which is also the case in related languages, except Kaqchikel). This makes a system of ten vowels, five short and five long. However, there are at least two towns where the distinction is between tense and lax rather than short and long vowels, and some other dialects only have six vowels: five short and one lax vowel (López Ixcoy 1994). Table 18.2 shows the K'iche' vowels.

2.2.1 Long and short vowels

This pattern is found in most dialects of K'iche' (written as double vowels). Minimal pairs can be found for most short-long pairs, but e-ee have no lexical pairs (these are in general infrequent vowels in Mayan languages). Instead, the difference can be illustrated with a grammatically related pair such as the active-passive pair in (10).

	V		vs	VV	
(9)	chaj	'pine'		chaaj	'ash'
(10)	xujek'o	's/he pulled it'		xjeek'ik	'it was pulled'
(11)	k'ix	'shame'		k'iix	'thorn'
(12)	oj	'we'		ooj	'avocado'
(13)	tuɬ	'sprout'		tuuɬ	'kind of mange' (López Ixcoy 1994:20)

TABLE 18.2 K'ICHE' VOWELS

High	i, ii, ɪ		u, uu, ʊ
Mid	e, ee, ɛ		o, oo, ɔ
Low		a, aa, ɔ	

Long vowels occur in most dialects in monosyllabic words and in final syllables of multisyllabic words. However, in some places long vowels can occur in other phonological environments, such as in example (10). The occurrence of long vowels in non-final syllables is due to *CVhC changing to CV:C (for instance in the passive of root transitives as in 10). Long vowels that occur in final syllables shorten when a suffix is added (see examples in (34) and (35) below).

2.2.2 Tense and lax vowels

According to López (1994) this system has been found in only two places: Chichicastenango and Chiché, both in El Quiché. As in the case of short-long vowels, it is difficult to find minimal pairs for the vowel /e/. In this case I have added non-minimal pair examples of /ĕ/ and /e/ in (15) (López Ixcoy 1994:35).

	V̈		V	
		vs		
(14)	chäj	'pine'	chaj	'ash'
(15)	xpëq	'toad'	xpetïk	's/he came'
(16)	k'ïx	'shame'	k'ix	'thorn'
(17)	öj	'us'	oj	'avocado'
(18)	tüx	'sprout'	tux	'kind of mange'

In general, short vowels correspond to lax vowels, and long vowels to tense vowels.

2.2.3 Six vowels

According to López Ixcoy (1994:18), the pattern of six vowels, five short and one lax vowel /ä/, is found in Cantel and parts of Totonicapán. Baird (2014) also reports this vowel system for Cantel; however, Larsen (1988) indicates that in Cantel the distinction between short and long vowel /a/ is sometimes maintained, although he points out that this might be due to variation between speakers. Examples are from Par Sapón and Can Pixabaj (2000:43–4, 82).

(19) nojnäq 'full'
     säq   'white'

Par Sapón and Can Pixabaj (2000:76, 84) also show that Cantel retains long vowels in some words such as *alitoom* 'girls', *alb'omaab'* 'boys', and *wuquub'* 'seven'. The fact that the distinction between short and long vowels persists indicates that the vowel system in Cantel is not yet entirely consistent.

2.3 Stress

Word stress is final in K'iche'; however, there are two exceptions. One is that when a noun phrase contains an adjective, in some dialects a vowel is added after the adjective. In this case, the primary stress remains on the content word, the adjective, and a secondary stress is on the epenthetic vowel. This might be due to the adjective plus noun combination forming a single compound word phonologically.

(20) x-Ø-r-il   le   **sáq-à**   tz'í'
      CP-B3SG-A3SG-see   DET   white-EP   dog
      'S/he saw the white dog.'

The second exception involves the change of this pattern in at least two places, Cunén (El Quiché) and Santa María Chiquimula (Totonicapán). In these places primary stress is on the first syllable, as in the following examples (Par Sapón and Can Pixabaj 2000:54–6):

	Cunén		Santa María Chiquimula	
(21) a.	ínseb'	'my liver'	d. sáqmo'l	'eggs'
b.	xépetik	'they came'	e. xjórb'ik	'it got cold'

3 ROOT AND WORD CLASSES

Major lexical root classes in K'iche' include nouns, adjectives, verbs, and positionals. Minor lexical root classes include prepositions, relational nouns, classifiers, demonstratives, numbers, and directionals. Before discussing the major types of root and word classes, I introduce person marking since it comes up throughout the chapter.

3.1 Person marking

3.1.1 Bound pronouns

In K'iche', there are two sets of affixes for marking person: Set A (with preconsonantal and prevocalic allomorphs) and Set B, as they are called in the Mayan literature. K'iche' makes a distinction between singular and plural, and first, second, and third person. It also makes a distinction between ordinary and honorific second person in singular and plural. The markers for honorific second person do not change regardless of their function – possessor, object or subject. Later, in §3.12, I discuss the grammatical properties of the honorifics, as well as their social use.

Table 18.3 presents the Set B markers. These person markers index the transitive object (O) (22b), the intransitive subject (S) (22a), and the subject of non-verbal predicates (23). Table 18.4 presents the Set A markers. These person markers index the transitive subject (A) (22b). Thus, the functions of Set A and Set B reflect morphological ergativity. In addition, the Set A markers index the possessors of nouns, the arguments of verbal nouns, and the complements of relational nouns.

(22) a. x-**oj**-b'iin-ik
          CP-B1PL-walk-SS
          'We walked.'

      b. x-**oj**-**k**-il-o
          CP-B1PL-A3PL-see-SS
          'They saw us.'

(23) **oj**   matz-al-ik
      B1PL   quiet-PRED-SS
      'We are quiet.'

TABLE 18.3 SET B MARKERS

Number	Person	Markers
Singular	1st	*in-*
	2nd	*at-*
	2nd FOR	*=la*
	3rd	Ø
Plural	1st	*oj-*
	2nd	*ix-*
	2nd FOR	*=alaq*
	3rd	*ee-, e-*

TABLE 18.4 SET A MARKERS

Number	Person	Prevocalic	Preconsonantal
Singular	1st	*w- inw-*	*nu-*
	2nd	*aw-*	*a-*
	2nd FOR	*=la*	*=la*
	3rd	*r-*	*u-*
Plural	1st	*q-*	*qa-*
	2nd	*iw-*	*i-*
	2nd FOR	*=alaq*	*=alaq*
	3rd	*k-*	*ki-*

TABLE 18.5 INDEPENDENT PRONOUNS

Number	Person	Form
Singular	1st	in
	2nd	at
	2nd FOR	laal
	3rd	ri are' (ra're')
Plural	1st	(ri) oj
	2nd	(ri) ix
	2nd FOR	alaq
	3rd	ri e are' (ri a're', ra're')

3.1.2 Independent pronouns

Independent pronouns are formed from the Set B markers, except the third singular and plural. The third person pronouns are usually preceded by a determiner, *ri* or *le*. In some dialects (e.g., Santa Clara la Laguna and Santa María Chiqumula) the independent pronoun in other persons also takes a determiner, especially in the first and second person plurals.

3.2 Nouns

Nouns have different types of morphological structures; some of them are roots, as in (24), but in other cases, they are morphologically derived from other types of words, as in (25), or they are compound nouns, as in (26). The majority of noun roots have a CVC phono-logical structure, but not all of them. There are roots with long vowels (26) and there are also disyllabic roots (24b).

(24) a. tz'i'   'dog'
     b. chikop   'animal'

(25) tz'ib'-a-b'al   'pen/pencil'
     letter-TR-INST

(26) nim-q'iij   'feast'
     big-sun/day

3.2.1 Noun classes and possession

Most nouns can take a Set A marker to indicate possession. Since K'iche' is a head-mark-ing language, the possessor marker is on the possessed noun. According to López Ixcoy (1997) there are six kinds of nouns based on possession, as follows.

1   Invariable nouns: this means that the form of the noun when it is possessed does not change. Most nouns are in this class.

(27) wuuj   'book'   qa-wuuj   'our book'
                                A1PL-book

2   Nouns with a vowel change: in this group, we find nouns that have a short vowel in the last syllable (or only syllable) of the non-possessed form that changes to a long vowel in the possessed form.

(28) kinaq'   'beans'   u-kinaaq'   'her/his beans'
                        A3SG-beans

3   Inalienable nouns: nouns that are ordinarily possessed and the unpossessed form is marked with a suffix. When these nouns are possessed, the suffix is dropped and the vowel of the last syllable is lengthened. Semantically, nouns that indicate body parts, some kinship terms, clothing, and a few others are members of this class.

(29) a. jolom-**aaj**   'head'   nu-joloom   'my head'
        head-UNPOSS   A1SG-head
     b. k'ajol-**axeel**   'son of man' nu-k'ajool   'my son'
        man's.son-UNPOSS   A1SG-man's.son
     c. q'u'-**aaj**   'blanket'   nu-q'uu'   'my blanket'
        blanket-UNPOSS   A1SG-blanket
     d. k'ay-**iij**   'sale'   nu-k'aay   'my sale'
        sale-UNPOSS   A1SG-sale

4   Nouns that add a suffix when possessed: the suffix has the form -V(V)l and is the same as the suffix added to adjectives to form abstract nouns.

(30) a. kik'   'blood'   nu-kik'-eel   'my blood'
                         A1SG-blood-ABST

b. tz'u'uum   'leather'   nu-tz'u'm-aal   'my skin'
                           A1SG-skin-ABST

5   Suppletive nouns: some nouns take a different root when possessed.

(31) a. ja   'house'   w-ochooch   'my house'
                              A1SG-house
     b. k'uul   'blanket'   nu-q'uu'   'my blanket'
                              A1SG-blanket

6   Usually possessed: there is a small group of nouns that are only used as possessed
    forms. These nouns most often refer to a part of a whole.

(32) a. u-xaaq   'its leaf'
        A3SG-leaf
     b. r-iij   'its back/skin/shell'
        A3SG-back

Also, there are some nouns that refer to elements of nature that can be possessed only in
certain contexts (e.g, ceremonial, poetic). López Ixcoy (1997) signals that these nouns
when possessed must be preceded by a kinship term and the Set A marker must be first
person plural as in (33a). However, such nouns can take ordinary possession when they
refer to personal property, as in (33b).

(33) a. **qa-taat**   q'iij   'Our father sun.'   {López Ixcoy 1997:104}
        A1PL-father   sun

     b. q'iij   'sun'   qa-q'iij   'our sun (a toy, a picture, etc.)'
                              A1PL-sun

3.2.2 Plural forms

Some nouns, including most human and some animal referring nouns, can optionally take
a plural suffix -aab'/-iib'.[2] In (34b, d) and (35d) the singular forms have long vowels in
the final syllable, but in their plural forms have short vowels since they are not in word-final position anymore.

Human
(34) a. ixoq   'woman'   ixoq-**iib'**   'women'
     b. ajchaak   'worker'   ajchak-**iib'**   'workers
     c. ajtzala'   'person from Sololá' ajtz'ala'-**iib'** 'people from Sololá'
     d. iyoom   'midwife'   iyom-**aab'**   'midwives'
     e. Tunay   'surname'   Tunay-**iib'**   'members of the Tunay famly'
Animals
(35) a. chikop/chkop   'animal'   chikop-**iib'**   'animals'
     b. amolo   'fly'   amoly-**iib'**   'flies'
     c. koyo't   'coyote'   koyo't-**aab'**   'coyotes'
     d. masaat   'deer'   masat-**iib'**   'deers'

Other nouns are ungrammatical with the plural suffix (body parts, kinship terms, most
animals, some humans, and common nouns).

(36) b. q'ab'   'hand'   *q'ab'iib'   'hands'
     b. naan   'mother' *nan-iib'   'mothers'
     d. teem   'chair'   *temaab'   'chairs'

3.3 Noun classifiers

Proper names in K'iche' can be modified by a determiner, but they can also be modified by a classifier. There are four classifiers; they indicate gender and age or social status. Their absence may be a sign of respect in some dialects. All of them come from common nouns.

Origin		Classifier	
• ali	'girl'	ali/al	'baby girl or young woman'
• ala	'boy'	ala/a	'baby boy or young man'
• taat	'father'	taat	'old/respected man'
• naan	'mother'	naan	'old/respected woman'

(37) a. oj   k'o   r-uk'   le   **taat**   Andres Chávez Zavala
        B1PL EXIST   A3SG-RN DET   CLF   Andrés Chávez Zavala
        'We are with Mr. Andrés Chávez Zavala.'   {R0101001:02}

     b. sin   laj   **al**   Pawola k-e-cha   ch-e,   r-al   **al**   María
        DIM   small CLF   Paola   ICP-B3PL-say PREP-RN   A3SG-daughter   CLF   María
        'The little Paola, they call her, the daughter of María.' {R0111002:98}

3.4 Determiners and demonstratives

According to Larsen (1984:309) in K'iche' the demonstratives form a three-way system along with the definite articles or determiners. The first set are the determiners (Table 18.6). These are like definite articles that precede a noun, including proper names.

(38) **we** junaab' 'this year'
     DET year
(39) **le** nu-xb'aal 'my brother'
     DET A1SG-woman's.brother
(40) **ri** a Xwaan 'John'
     DET CLF John

The second set consists of three demonstratives (Table 18.7) that I call Dem1. This set of demonstratives is used as pronouns.

TABLE 18.6 DETERMINERS

Determiners

we/wa	this	visible and close to the speaker (proximal)
le/la	the	seen by the speaker, but not (necessarily) close to him (medial)
ri	the	not visible, mentioned, far away from the speaker) (distal)

(López 1999:)

TABLE 18.7 DEMONSTRATIVES (DEM1)

Demonstratives	
wa'	this (near speaker, or presented as if it were near speaker)
la'	that (visible, near hearer, or presented as if it were visible or near the hearer)
ri'	that (far away, invisible, or presented as if it were far away or invisible, or mentioned previously in the discourse)

(Larsen 1984:309)

(41) na x-Ø-inw-il   ta **la'**.
      NEG CP-B3SG-A1SG-see IRR DEM1
      'I did not see that.'

Dem1 can be combined with a determiner preceding a noun (Larsen 1984; López 1999). In this case, Dem1 must be paired with its corresponding determiner.

(42) a. wa' we ak'aal 'this child' (this one)
     b. la' le ak'aal 'that child' (that one visible or pointing to him/her)
     c. ri' ri ak'aal 'that child' (that one not visible)

The third set is a second set of demonstratives, Dem2, that is composed of two demonstratives, *lee'* and *rii'*. Notice that this set of demonstratives is only used in postnominal position. Larsen (1984:310) indicates that these demonstratives are usually used "in pointing something out to someone". Also, these demonstratives occur with a noun preceded by a determiner. Interestingly *rii'* which comes from the distal *ri*, is paired with *ri* but also with the proximal *we*, whereas *lee'* only pairs with *le*.

(43) a. ri ak'aal rii' 'that child'
     b. we ak'aal rii' 'this child'
     c. le ak'aal lee' 'that child'

3.4.1 Indefinite article

The indefinite article is *juun/jun*; it is also the number 'one'. This article precedes the noun as in (44a). However, the indefinite article can be combined with a definite noun, where the indefinite article is placed between the determiner and the noun, as in (44b). According to Larsen (1988) and López Ixcoy (1997), (44b) makes reference to a specific man already mentioned in the discourse.

(44) a. x-Ø-pe   jun achi
        CP-B3SG-come ART man
        'A man came.'

     b. x-Ø-pe   **ri** **jun** achi
        CP-B3SG-come   DET ART man
        'That man came.'

Also, an indefinite article can be found in an NP that has a Dem1 and Dem2, as in the example below, or only one of them. This also refers to a specific man already mentioned in the discourse, but more emphatic than in (44b).

(45) x-Ø-pe   **ri'**   ri   **jun**   achi   **rii'**
     CP-B3SG-come   DEM1   DET   ART   man   DEM2
     'That man, that one, came'

3.5 Adjectives

The inventory of adjective roots in Mayan languages is very limited, fewer than 50 items (England 2004). In K'iche' there are about 30 adjective roots and they cover a variety of semantic categories, such as color, size, texture, personal properties and so on. With regard to color, there are five basic underived terms.

(46) a. q'eq   'black'
     b. saq   'white'
     c. keq   'red'
     d. q'an   'yellow'
     e. rex   'green'

Other colors can also be expressed, but either have semantic or morphological derivation:

(47) a. chaaj   'gray (<ashes)'
     b. xaar   'blue (<type of blue bird)'
     c. saqsoj   'cream (<somewhat white)'

Other adjectives refer to various properties (48).

(48) a. nim   'big'
     b. alaaj   'small'
     c. utz   'good'
     d. piim   'thick'
     e. t'or   'deaf'
     f. k'aak'   'new'

3.5.1 Intensifiers

The intensifier is the only element that can modify an adjective. It can be a particle *sib'alaj* or a suffix *-alaj*, and they are in complementary distribution. The particle is used only when the adjective functions as a predicate, as in (49a), whereas the suffix is used only when the adjective is a noun modifier, as in (49b).

(49) a. **Sib'alaj**   nim   le   a-xajab'   ch-aw-e
        INTS   big   DET   A2SG-shoes   PREP-A2SG-RN
        'Your shoes are very big.' (lit: your shoes are very big for you)

     b. X-Ø-ki-loq'   jun   nim-**alaj**   ja
        CP-B3SG-A3PL-buy   one   big-INTS   house
        'They bought a very big house.'

3.5.2 Plural forms

Two root adjectives, the ones in (50a, b), can be pluralized with a suffix -a'q/aq. All adjectives derived from positionals can also take the plural suffix (50c):

(50) a. nim   'big'   nim-**a'q**   'big ones'
         big   big-PL

     b. pim   'thick'   pim-**a'q**   'thick ones'
         thick   thick-PL

     c. set-es-ik 'round'   set-es-**a'q**   'rounded ones'
         round-PRED-SS   round-PRED-PL

-a'q becomes -aq when the adjective is not at the end of the intonational phrase.

(51) a. x-e-pe   e   keb'   nim-**aq** taq   tz'i'
         CP-B3PL-come   B3PL   two   big-PL   PL   dog
         'There came two big dogs.'

Some adjectives can take the nominal plural suffix -aab'/-iib' when they function as human nouns.

(52) a. ch'u'j-**aab'**   'crazy ones'
         crazy-PL

     b. laj-**iib'**   'sick ones'
         sick-PL

     c. yowab'-**iib'**   'small ones'
         small-PL

     d. mem-**aab'**   'mute ones'
         mute-PL

As stated before, when root adjectives (and some derived adjectives) are attributive they take an epenthetic vowel a in some dialects.

(53) X-Ø-ki-loq'   jun   nim-a   ja
         CP-B3SG-A3PL-buy   one   big-EP house
         'They bought a big house.'

3.6 Verbs

A verb in K'iche', as in other Mayan languages, can be either intransitive or transitive. What characterizes a verb is that it takes TAM markers. An intransitive verb, in addition to its stem, has a TAM prefix, a Set B prefix (to index the subject), and a status suffix, and it can optionally include an element of movement (54a). A transitive verb includes the same TAM prefixes, a Set B prefix (to index the object), a Set A prefix (to index the subject), an optional element of movement, and status suffixes that are different from those that occur with intransitive verbs (54b).

(54) a. x-**oj**-e'-b'iin-oq
         CP-B1PL-MOV-walk-DEP
         'We went to walk.'

(54) a. x-**oj**-e'-b'iin-oq
    cp-B1PL-MOV-walk-DEP
    'We went to walk.'

  b. x-**oj**-**k**-il-o
    CP-B1PL-A3PL-see-SS
    'They saw us.'

Another difference between transitive and intransitive verbs, besides the presence or absence of a Set A prefix and different status suffixes, is phonological. All transitive verbs have CVC roots, as in (55a–c). Intransitive verbs, however, permit some other root shapes, as in (55e, f). Below I discuss the morphological elements.

(55) a. chap 'grab'
    b. k'am 'receive'
    c. q'ol 'cut off'
    d. war 'sleep'
    e. atin 'bathe'
    f. peet 'come'

3.6.1 Time, aspect, mood (TAM)

Verbs obligatorily have a TAM marker (morphologically explicit or not because sometimes the marker is dropped). Table 18.8 presents the forms and allomorphs of the TAM markers. Below I exemplify the occurrence of the markers with different types of verbs.

Completive

(56) a. **x**-oj-b'iin-ik
    CP-B1PL-walk-SS
    'We walked.'

  b. **x**-at-q-il-o
    CP-B2SG-A1PL-see-SS
    'We saw you.'

Incompletive

(57) a. **k**-oj-b'iin-ik
    ICP-B1PL-walk-SS
    'We walk.'

  b. **ka**-Ø-qa-tij-o
    ICP-B3SG-A1PL-eat-SS
    'We eat it.'

TABLE 18.8 TAM MARKERS

TAM marker	Category
x-	past completive
k- (/_V) ~ ka- (/_C)	incompletive/habitual
ch-	imperative/potential
j-	imperative with incorporated movement
m- (/_V) ~ ma- (/_C)	negative imperative

Imperative/potential[3] and admonitive (negative imperative), according to Larsen (1988:161).

(58) a. **ch**-at-b'iin-oq
    IMP-B2SG-walk-DEP
    'Walk!'

 b. **j**-∅-a'w-il-a'
    IMP-B3SG-MOV.A2SG-see-DEP
    'Go see it!'

 c. **m**-at-b'iin-ik
    IMP-B2SG-walk-SS
    'Don't walk!'

The progressive is marked by *tajin*, which can be an uninflected particle, as in (59a), or an intransitive verb, as in (59b). It is inflected with third singular and the incompletive marker when it is a verb.

(59) a. ¿Jas u-b'i' la' le chee' **tajin** k-∅-a-koj-o?
     Q   A3SG-name DEM DET tree PROG ICP-B3SG-A2SG-use-SS
    ¿What is the name of that tree that you are using? {R031I002:476}

 b. la're'   ka-∅-tajin   k-∅-u-tzjo-j   la' le
    DET.PRON3SG ICP-B3SG-PROG ICP-B3SG-A3SG-tell-ACT DEM DET
      yoroona
      weeping.woman
    'He was talking about the weeping woman (llorona).' {R022I001:68}

Thus, TAM affixes do not distinguish intransitive verbs from transitives. What makes the difference has to do with person markers and status suffixes, as described below.

3.6.2 Person markers

Arguments of a predicate are marked on the head (verbal or non-verbal predicate). K'iche' is morphologically and syntactically ergative. Transitive subjects (ergatives) are indexed by Set A, while intransitive subjects and transitive objects (absolutives) are marked by Set B. The Set A markers were presented in Table 18.4 and the Set B markers were presented in Table 18.3 in §3.1.

3.6.3 Status suffixes

The status suffixes are another set of affixes that appear on verbal predicates (e.g., Kaufman 1990). Except for positionals, they do not occur on non-verbal predicates. These suffixes convey mood and transitivity. The forms of the status suffixes change depending on the type of verbs, root transitive or intransitive. There are two status categories: independent and dependent. A verb has a dependent status if it is imperative or if it contains movement; otherwise it has an independent status. And finally, when the verb is at the end of an intonational phrase (Henderson 2012) the suffix is dropped or it changes

TABLE 18.9 STATUS SUFFIXES

Status	Root transitive verb	Intransitive verb
Plain	(-o/-u)	(-ik)
Dependent	(-V`)/-V	(-oq)/-a

its form. Table 18.9 gives the forms of the status suffixes on verbs in K'iche'. The suffixes in parentheses appear only when the verb occurs in final position (Can Pixabaj 2015).

Plain or independent status suffixes: this suffix is *-u* on root transitives when the root vowel is *u* and *-o* when the root vowel is not *u*, and it is *-ik* on intransitive verbs and positional predicates. (Note that I do not consider the *-j* suffix on derived transitives to be a status suffix, unlike Kaufman 1990). In (60a) the suffix *-o* appears on the transitive verb *kuch'ob'o* since the verb is the last element in the clause, whereas in (60b) the suffix does not appear since the verb is followed by the subject NP (Can Pixabaj 2015).

(60) a. Jas   nu   k'u   k-Ø-u-ch'ob'-o
       Q   PAR   PAR   ICP-B3SG-A3SG-think-SS
       'Who knows what s/he thinks.'   {R0121002:167 modified}

     b. Jas   nu   k'u   k-Ø-u-ch'ob'-o   [sin   k-aanma . . .] NP
        Q   PAR   PAR   ICP-B3SG-A3SG-think   DIM   A3PL-heart
        'Who knows what their heart wants.'   {R0121002:167}

(61) is an example of the use of the plain status suffix *-ik* on an intransitive verb. The first intransitive verb *xokik* is in clause-final position, therefore it bears the status suffix *-ik*, whereas the status suffix does not appear on the second intransitive verb *xok* since the verb is followed by additional elements that belong to the clause (Can Pixabaj 2015).

(61) we   k'u   x-Ø-ok-ik,   we   k'-na   x-Ø-ok   ta
     COND PAR   CP-B3SG-enter-SS   COND   PAR-NEG   CP-B3SG-enter IRR
     pa   r-sin   ki-joloom
     PREP DET-DIM   A3PL-head
     'Whether they understood it or not.'   {R0361002:082}

Dependent status suffixes occur in two contexts: i) on verbs in the imperative, and ii) on verbs with incorporated movement. Like the plain status suffixes, the form of a dependent suffix varies depending on the conjugation class of the verb and its position in the clause. Dependent status suffixes only *change their form* at the end of the intonational phrase, unlike the plain status suffix that is dropped in this position. On root transitives, this suffix has the form *-V'* at the end of the intonational phrase (*-u'* and *-o'* in harmony with a preceding *u* or *o* and *-a'* in the other cases), as in (62a), and *-V* in other positions, as in (62b).

(62) a. j-Ø-a'w-il-a'
        IMP-B3SG-MOV;A2SG-see-DEP
        'Go see it!'

     b. j-Ø-a'w-il-a   ri   ak'aal
        IMP-B3SG-MOV;A2SG-see-DEP   DET   child
        'Go see the child!'

On intransitive verbs, the suffix is -*oq* at the end of the intonational phrase and -*a* in other positions, although in some dialects it can be dropped.

(63) a. **ch**-at-b'iin-**oq**
         IMP-B2SG-walk-DEP
         'Walk!'

      b. **ch**-at-b'iin-(**a**)   pa   le   b'e
         IMP-B2SG-walk-DEP   PREP   DET   road
         'Walk on the street!'

Derived transitive verbs do not have status suffixes, but there is a phonological effect depending on whether the verb is at the end of an intonational phrase or not. This is reflected in the vowel lengthening of the last syllable of the verb. Thus, the vowel is long when the verb is at the end of the intonational phrase and the vowel is short when the verb is not the last element of the intonational phrase (Can Pixabaj 2015).

(64) a. x-Ø-u-tz'ib'**aa**-j
         CP-B3SG-A3SG-write-ACT
         'S/he wrote it.'

      b. x-Ø-u-tz'ib'**a**-j   jun tziij
         CP-B3SG-A3SG-write-ACT   one word
         'S/he wrote a word.'

In other studies (Larsen 1988; Kaufman 1990; López Ixcoy 1997) the final suffix -*j* has been considered to be the status suffix for derived transitive verbs. However, Aissen (2011) proposed that this suffix indicates that the verb is active. Evidence comes from the fact that when the verb is passive, the passive suffix -*x* takes the slot that in the active form was occupied by the suffix -*j*. The analysis of the suffix -*j* on derived transitive verbs in K'iche' applies to other K'ichean languages. I follow Aissen in this analysis and in Can Pixabaj (2015) I proposed that the reflection of the end of the intonational phrase in derived transitive verbs is vowel lengthening.

3.6.4 Nominalization of verbs

Nominalized verbs in K'iche' are very important since they play significant roles, especially in complex structures such as in complement and purpose clauses. Nominalized verbs are also used as the citation form.

Verbs are nominalized by a number of different derivational suffixes. Table 18.10 shows that there are at least three types of suffixes for intransitive verbs, but only one for passive and transitive verbs and two for antipassive verbs (Can Pixabaj 2015:104). The suffix -*ik* is used to nominalize all types of verbs.

TABLE 18.10 FORMS OF VERBAL NOUNS

Types	Intransitive	Antipassive	Passive	Transitive
suffixes	-iim, -eem, -aam	-ik	-ik	-ik
	– ooj	– eem		
	– ik			

(65a) is an example of a non-finite complement clause where the complement is an intransitive nominalized verb form. (65b) is an example of a passive non-finite purpose clause. (For more details on nominalized verbs see Can Pixabaj 2009, 2015).

(65) a. ch-Ø-qa-chap-a   **[wa'-iim]**
        IMP-B3SG-A1PL-start-DEP   eat-VN
        'Let's start eating.'   {Can Pixabaj 2015:105}

     b. jo   chi   **[r-eta-x-iik]**
        IMP.B1PL.go   PREP A3SG-measure-PSV-VN
        'Let's go to measure it.'

3.7 Directionals and incorporated movement

Directionals are forms that have been grammaticalized from intransitive verbs of motion (Zavala Maldonado 1993). There are seven directionals in K'iche'. The citation form of the directionals includes a status suffix, -*ik* (for *ub'iik*) and -*oq* for the rest, which is only pronounced at the end of an intonational phrase.

	Directional	Intransitive verb of motion	
(66) a.	(u)b'iik	b'ee	'go'
b.	(u)loq	ul	'arrive here'
c.	qajoq/qaaq	qaj	'go down'
d.	(a)q'anoq	aq'an	'go up'
e.	kanoq	kan	'stay'
f.	ukoq/okoq/koq/ko	ok	'enter'
g.	apanoq/opanoq/panoq	opan	'arrive there'

Directionals usually modify verbal predicates and sometimes non-verbal predicates indicating direction or trajectory.

(67) a. e . . .   in   k-Ø-aw-aa-j   ka-tzjo-j   **b'i** la   ch-w-e
        um. . .   PRON1S   ICP-B3SG-A2SG-want-ACT ICP-tell-ACT DIR 2SG.FOR PREP-A1SG-RN
        'um . . . I would like you to tell me.'   {QUC011R007I001:017}

     b. e   nim-'aq   chi **uloq**
        B3PL   big-PL   PAR DIR
        'They came being big already.'

There are also two prefixes which derive from intransitive verbs of motion: -*e'* 'go' (from b'e 'go') and -*ul* 'arrive' (from ul 'come'). These occur after the set B marker either on intransitive or transitive verbs, as in (68a, b). Recall that the use of incorporated movement requires the use of the dependent status suffix.

(68) a. x-in-**e'**-wa'-oq
        CP-B1SG-MOV-eat-DEP
        'I went to eat.'

     b. x-in-**e'**-ki-k'am-a'
        CP-B1SG-MOV-A3PL-receive-DEP
        'They went to take me.'

These prefixes represent the most grammaticalized form of intransitive verbs of motion in K'iche', and is the fifth and last stage of grammaticalization of IVMs that Zavala (1993) proposes. An alternative to the use of prefixes of movement is the use of an intransitive verb of motion in a purpose construction where the main verb is the intransitive verb:

(69) x-Ø-pe   ch-ki-k'am-ar-iik
     CP-B3SG-come   PREP-A3PL-receive-PSV-VN
     'S/he came to take them.'

3.8 Adpositions

Adpositional phrases are headed by prepositions and/or relational nouns. In K'iche' there are two prepositions: *chi* and *pa*. These prepositions mainly introduce locatives, as in (70a), and purpose clauses, as in (70b).

(70) a. x-oj-'e   **pa**   ja
        CP-B1PL-go   PREP   house
        'We went inside (the house).'

     b. ch-Ø-a-ya'-a   kan   **chi**   ja
        IMP-B3SG-A2SG-leave-DEP   DIR   PREP   house
        'Leave it at the door!'

Relational nouns are nouns that are formally possessed; they usually have a Set A marker, which indexes the complement. They can introduce oblique phrases that have thematic roles as shown in the list in (71). They can also introduce certain types of clauses (purpose clauses, for instance) and the comparative of adjectives.

(71) a. -umaal agent ('by'), causative
     b. -eech patient or possessor
     c. -iib' reflexive/reciprocal
     d. -uuk' comitative/intrumental

Examples of some of these uses are shown below:

Finite purpose clauses
(72) ch-Ø-i-tatab'ee-j   [r-eech   na   ka-Ø-sachon   ta   ch-iw-e]
     IMP-B3SG-A2PL-listen-ACT   A3SG-RN   NEG   ICP-B3SG-forget IRR   PREP-A2PL-RN
     'Listen so that you do not forget!'

Comparative construction
(73) le   q'atzu   are   paqal   **ch-och**   le   ti'iij
     DET   mushroom   FOC   expensive   PREP-RN   DET   meat
     'The mushroom is more expensive than the meat.'

Agent Oblique agent phrase
(74) x-Ø-ch'aj-taj   **q-umaal**
     CP-B3SG-wash-PSV   A1PL-RN
     'It was washed by us.'

Instrumental phrase
(75) x-Ø-u-kach'   **r-uk'**   le   u-ware
     CP-B3SG-A3SG-bite   A3SG-RN   DET   A3SG-tooth
     'S/he bit it with his/her teeth.'

In addition to being used alone, prepositions and relational nouns may be combined, as in (76), where they introduce locatives.

(76) a. x-oj-paq-e'   **p-u-wi**   le   ja
        CP-B1PL-go.up   PREP-A3SG-RN   DET   house
        'We went on top of the house (on the roof).'

   b. x-oj-'e   **chi**   **r-ij**   le   ja
        CP-B1PL-go   PREP   A3SG-RN   DET   house
        'We went around the house.'

Following are examples of prepositions and relational nouns introducing an oblique phrase that can indicate a goal as in (77a), and a benefactive as in (77b). In (77b) (also (73)) the relational noun does not have Set A marking; the loss of Set A marking is common in third person singular when the relational noun is used in combination with a preposition.

(77) a. k-Ø-in-tzijo-j   **chi**   **k-e**   konojeel   la'k'alaab'
        ICP-B3SG-B1SG-tell-ACT   PREP   A3PL-RN   all   DET.children
        'I tell it to all children.'   {QUC011R069I001}

   c. x-Ø-u-paqchi-j   le   jun   ixoq   **ch-och**   le   ak'aal
        CP-B3SG-A3SG-push-ACT   DET NUM   woman   PREP-RN   DET   child
        'S/he pushed the woman in front of/instead of the child.'

3.9 Positionals

Positionals constitute a type of root class in Mayan languages and in other Mesoamerican languages. They can indicate position, state, form or physical properties (Martin 1977; England 1983; Haviland 1994, among others). Positional roots in K'iche' have a CVC phonological structure and they share properties with affect words (sound and action symbolic words) (Baronti 2001). This root class needs derivational morphology to form words: non-verbal predicates, as in (78), adjectives, as in (79), and verbs, as in (80). Can Pixabaj and Sis Iboy (2004) report around 300 positional roots in K'iche' and Achi.

(78) **tzay-al**-ik
     hang-PRED-SS
     'hung/hanging'

(79) tak'-at-ik
     stand.up-DER-SS
     'tall'

(80) a. x-Ø-**tzay-e'**-ik
        CP-B3SG-hang-IV-SS
        'it hung'

   b. x-Ø-u-**tzay-ab'aa'**
        CP-B3SG-A3SG-hang-TV
        's/he hung it'

In K'iche' positionals can receive up to 15 derivational affixes specific to positionals, three of which are very productive (they can go with every positional root). They derive the non-verbal predicate, (78), the inchoative, (80a), and the causative (80b). Other derivational suffixes usually derive intransitive verbs with meanings related to manner, as in (81a), and repetitive or continuous events, as in (81b).

(81) a. ka-Ø-**tak'**-ak'-ik
     ICP-B3SG-stand.up-DER-SS
     'stand up precipitously'

   b. ka-Ø-tzay-**ma'y**-ik
     ICP-B3SG-hung-DER-SS
     'go hanging'

3.10 Honorific second person

The honorific or formal second person has a singular form *laal* and a plural form *alaq*. Each form is a clitic and can index any core and peripheral argument as well as function as an independent pronoun. As a possessor marker, the honorific second person functions as an enclitic, as in (82).

	possessee	possessor
(82) x-e-pe	*le aal*	**la**
CP-B3PL-come	DET child.of.woman	2SG.FOR
'Your children came.'		

The intransitive subject and the transitive subject are also enclitics, as in (83a, b). It can be possible to have the honorific second person as a direct object in an active sentence where this object is an enclitic, as in (83c). However, for some speakers, it is necessary to change the verb to antipassive to introduce the honorific second person in an oblique dative phrase as the patient, as in (83d); but for others, the change is only necessary if the subject is third person (Mondloch 1981:35).

(83) a. la   x-wa'   k'u   **la**?
     Q   CP-eat   PAR   2SG.FOR
     'Did you eat?'

   b. x-in-il   kan   **la**
     CP-B1SG-see   DIR   2SG.FOR
     'You saw me.'

   c. ?x-u-ch'ab'e-j   **la**
     CP-A3SG-talk-ACT   2SG.FOR
     'S/he talked to you.'

   d. x-Ø-ch'ab'e-n   **ch-e**   **la**
     CP-B3SG-talk-AP   PREP-RN   2SG.FOR
     'S/he talked to you.'

The honorific second person can be a proclitic or enclitic when it is the subject of a non-verbal predicate. In this case, the proclitic has the form *laal*, as in (84) and the enclitic has the form *la*, as in (83d).

(84) a. **laal**   t'uy-ul-ik
     2SG.FOR sit-PRED-SS
     'You are sitting.'

b. t'uy-ul   **la**
   sit-PRED   2SG.FOR
   'You are sitting.'

While the honorific second person singular varies in form depending on whether it is an enclitic (*la*) or a proclitic or independent pronoun (*laal*), the honorific plural always has the form *alaq*. In (85a) it is an enclitic and in (85b) its first occurrence corresponds to an independent pronoun and the second to an enclitic where it indexes the subject of the antipassive verb.

(85) a. la   x-wa'   k'u   **alaq**?
        Q   CP-eat   PAR   2PL.FOR
        'Did you all eat?'

   b. **alaq**   x-b'i-n   **alaq**   ch-w-e
      PRON2PL.FOR   CP-say-AP   2PL.FOR   PREP-A1SG-RN
      'You (pl) were the ones who told me.'

Socially, the rules for the use of the honorific second person vary, but in general, it is used to address people that have a higher place in a social hierarchy than the speaker or when speaker and hearer are both high in the social hierarchy. This can be due to age, social and political status, family position, or certain achievements. Finally, the honorific second person is not used in all dialects, for instance it does not exist in Chichicastenango.

4 SIMPLE CLAUSE STRUCTURE

A simple clause in K'iche' can include, in addition to the main predicate and its arguments the following elements: topic, focus, negation, interrogation, and secondary predicates. The occurrence of these elements varies depending on the predicate. For instance, secondary predicates can only be found when the primary predicate is a verb. In (86) we exemplify a simple clause where the head of the predicate is a ditransitive verb *ya'* 'give'. This clause includes negation, a direct object, and an indirect object.

Verb and negation		DO				IO	
(86) **na**	**x-Ø-u'-ya'**	**ta**	nim-aq	taq	eqale'n	ch-k-e	kan
NEG	CP-B3SG-A3SG-give	IRR	big-PL	PL	charges	PREP-A3PL-RN	DIR
e	qa-taat	e	qa-naan ...				
PL	A1PL-father	PL	A1PL-mother				

'S/he did not give charges to any of our grandparents.' {Can Pixabaj 2015:42}

I will present examples of each element of the clause as I discuss the types of predicates.

4.1 Word order

Typologically, K'iche' is a verb-initial language – specifically, a VOS language (Kaufman 1990) – although it is rare to find VOS order in discourse, where usually only one argument is expressed by an overt NP. An example of this order taken from a text is in (87).

```
      V                        O       S
(87) x-Ø-u-yup-ub'a           u-wach  ra'chi    ka-Ø-cha',
     CP-B3SG-A3SG-close-TR     A3SG-eye DET;man  ICP-B3SG-say
```
'The man closed his eyes, they say. . .'   {Can Pixabaj and England 2011:17}

However, the order of S and O is flexible and depends on properties of the NPs, mainly definiteness (England 1991; Can Pixabaj and Par Sapón 2000; Par Sapón and Can Pixabaj 2000).

4.2 Non-verbal predicates

In K'iche', as in other Mayan languages, there are two types of predicates, verbal and non-verbal. Recall that the main difference is that verbal predicates have TAM markers, whereas non-verbal predicates do not. At least five word classes can head a non-verbal predicate: positionals, nouns, adjectives, numbers, and relational nouns.

Example (88a) has the positional root *tak'* 'stand' and the derivational suffix *-al* that forms the predicate, and is modified by a directional and a locative adjunct. In (88a, b) the positional carries the Set B first person plural marker *oj* as a proclitic. It indexes the subject. Positionals take a status suffix when they are phrase-final (*-ik* in (88b)) (Can Pixabaj 2015). (88a) has no status suffix because the positional predicate is not phrase-final.

```
      Positional            DIR           Locative adjunct
(88) a. oj  tak'-al         ulo           pa       le    ch'iich'.
        B1PL stand-PRED      DIR:to.here   PREP:in  DET   vehicle
        'We came standing up in the vehicle.'
     b. oj   t'uy-ul-ik
        B1PL  sit-PRED-SS
        'We are sitting down.'
```

Non-verbal predicates headed by nouns, adjectives, and numbers also index their subjects with Set B proclitics.

```
Noun
(89) e    winaq
     B3PL  people
     'They are people.'
```

```
Adjective
(90) e    nim-a'q    chi  le   ak'alaab'
     B3PL  big-PL     PAR  DET  children
     'The children have grown up (got bigger).'
```

```
Number
(91) oj   waqib'    ixoqib'
     B1PL  six       women
     'we women are six' or 'there are six of us women' {Can Pixabaj 2015:45}
```

The relational noun *-eech* which denotes possession can also be a non-verbal predicate. Relational nouns in K'iche' usually have a Set A marker. To form a predicate it is only necessary to add a Set B marker that is indexed to the subject of the non-verbal predicate headed by the relational noun.

(92) e_i   **w-eech**   kan   le   ak'_i
     B3PL   A1SG-RN:possession   DIR   DET   chicken
     'The chickens were mine (when I left them).'

Clauses with non-verbal predicates can have topic and focus positions. In (93) we see an example where the sentence has a topic NP and a focused adjunct; both are preposed to the predicate head (Can Pixabaj 2015:48).

	TOP		FOCUS			Positional		DIR	
(93)	le	winaq	pa	le	ch'iich'	e	t'uy-ul	lo	wi
	DET	people	PREP	DET	vehicle	B3PL	sit-PRED	DIR:to.here	FOC

'As for the people, it was in the vehicle that they came sitting down.'

4.3 Verbal predicates

Verbal predicates have a verb as their head. The verb can be transitive or intransitive. In (94) there is an intransitive verb heading a verbal predicate and in (95) the verb is transitive.

(94) we   k'-na   **x-Ø-ok**   ta   pa   r-sin   ki-joloom
     COND   PAR-NEG   CP-B3SG-enter   IRR   PREP   DET-DIM   A3PL-head
     'And if they did not understand.'   {R0361002:082}

(95) pwes   **x-Ø-u-loq'**   ch-jub'iq'   r-e   waraal
     PAR   CP-B3SG-A3SG-buy   PAR-a.bit   A3SG-RN   here
     'And s/he bought a bit, for himself/herself, here.'   {R1431003:173}

A verbal predicate can include adverbs and directionals. In (96) there is a manner adverb.

(96) **no'jiim**   ta   b'a   ka-Ø-ki-k'oxomaa-j
     slow   IRR   PAR   ICP-B3SG-A3PL-understand-ACT
     no'jiim   ta   b'a   ka-Ø-ki-chama-j   r-iij,
     slow   IRR   PAR   ICP-B3SG-A3PL-think-ACT   A3SG-RN
     'I hope they could understand it slowly, I hope they could think slowly.'
     {R1171010:014}

As stated before, secondary predicates occur only in verbal predicates, as in (97), but not in non-verbal predicates.

	2P			1P	
(97)	we	na	jup-ul-ik	ta	x-e-qaj-ik ...
	COND	NEG	face.down-PRED-SS	IRR	CP-B3PL-go.down-SS

'If they are not born face down.'   {R0561002:090}

4.4 Alignment

Alignment in K'iche' is clearly ergative-absolutive. Thus, the O and S arguments are indexed by Set B and the A argument (transitive subject) is indexed by Set A. (See §3.1.)

There is no split ergativity in K'iche'. In the following sections we will see that the transitive subject cannot undergo some syntactic processes such as interrogation, and focus unless the verb is intransitivized. This is evidence for syntactic ergativity.

4.5 Voice alternation

K'iche' makes a distinction between active, passive, and antipassive voices, although there are also some remnants of the instrumental voice (see Norman 1978; I will not treat it here) (for voice see Mondloch 1981; Larsen 1988, among others).

4.5.1 Passive voice

Passive is the process by which a patient becomes a subject of an intransitive verb through morphological derivation and the agent is demoted to oblique status (Larsen 1988). In K'iche' there are two types of passives (Mondloch 1981; Larsen 1988; López 1997, among others): the syntactic passive and the completive passive or lexical passive. The syntactic passive is marked on root transitive verbs by lengthening the root vowel, as in (98b).

Active verb

(98) a. x-Ø-u-loq'   ri   wuuj ri   ali.
         CP-B3SG-A3SG-buy DET   book DET   girl
         'The girl bought the book.'

     Passive   Agent oblique phrase
   b. x-Ø-looq'   ri   wuuj r-umal   ri   ali
      CP-Ø-buy;PSV   DET   book A3SG-RN DET   girl
      'The book was bought by the girl.'

This passive is marked by the suffix -x on derived transitive verbs, as in (99b). This suffix occupies the same slot as the suffix -j which occurs in the active form of derived transitive verbs.

Derived active transitive verb

(99) a. x-Ø-u-q'aalu-j   ri   nee' ri   ixoq
         CP-B3SG-A3SG-hug-ACT DET   baby DET   woman
         'The woman hugged the baby.'

     Passive form   Agent oblique phrase
   b. ri   nee' x-Ø-q'aalu-x   r-umal   ri   ixoq
      DET   baby CP-B3SG-hug-PSV   A3SG-RN DET   woman
      'The baby was hugged by the woman.'

The subject of a passive verb is indexed on the verb by a Set B marker. The agent, if it is mentioned, is introduced by the relational noun -umaal[4] preceded by a Set A marker, as in (98b) and (99b). Mondloch (1981:138–9) indicates that in this case the oblique agent must be third person.

The lexical passive is indicated by the suffix -Vtaj on root transitive verbs, as in (100a), and by -taj on derived transitive verbs, as in (100b). Larsen (1988) proposes that the lexical passive indicates that the patient changes its state as result of the event; Can Pixabaj

(2007) proposes that this type of passive only occurs with achievement situation types, and indicates the final state of the patient.

(100) a. i   x-Ø-u-min   r-u'-joloom   ri'   r-tz'i'
         and   CP-B3SG-A3PL-introduce   DET-A3SG-head   DEM   DET-dog
      b. i   na   x-Ø-tzoqopi-**taj**   ta   ch-u'loq.
         and   NEG   CP-B3SG-release-PSV   IRR   PREP-DIR
      'And the dog introduced his head, and it was not released anymore.'
                                                     {R030I001:138}

4.5.2 Antipassive voice

The antipassive voice in K'iche' and in other Mayan languages has been addressed not only descriptively but also theoretically in past work (Mondloch 1978, 1981; Trechsel 1981; Larsen 1988; Davies and Sam-Colop 1990; López 1997; Stiebels 2006; Can Pixabaj and England 2011; Aissen 2011, among others). Studies done on the antipassive voice in K'iche' vary in some respects. I will indicate principal variations in my explanation.

According to Larsen (1984:467) an antipassive voice refers to the process of converting a transitive to an intransitive verb where the original subject remains as the subject of the intransitive verb (indicated by set B) and the original object is either demoted to an oblique or not indicated at all. Under this definition, Larsen indicates that in K'iche' there are only two types of antipassive: the absolutive antipassive and the focus (or agentive) antipassive. Mondloch (1981), however, refers to the absolutive antipassive as the absolutive voice; he reserves the term antipassive for the structure that is used for extraction of transitive subjects (equal to Larsen's focus antipassive) or the incorporation of objects (he calls the latter the incorporative antipassive).

The absolutive antipassive is derived by *-Vn* for root transitive verbs, as in (101), and *-n* for derived transitive verbs. The agent, in this type of antipassive, is not necessarily extracted and the patient is not usually realized (Davies and Sam-Colop 1990:525). The patient, if indicated at all, is oblique (101). This is the type of antipassive used to form verbal nouns. Authors agree on this type of antipassive in K'iche'.

(101) k-in-yoq'-on   (ch-ee   lee   in-taat)
      ICP-B1SG-mock-AP   PREP(A3SG)-RN   the   A1SG-father
      'I mock (my father)'   {Mondloch 1981:171}

According to Mondloch (1981:250ff) the incorporative antipassive has an unspecified or generic object and can occur either with finite or non-finite verbs (and he classifies this construction as a subtype of the antipassive voice, along with the agent antipassive). He says it is usually found after a preceding adverb. It is marked by the morphemes *-Vw* for root transitive verbs and *-n* for derived transitive verbs. This type of antipassive is also reported by López Ixcoy (1997:373) although her only example is a finite relative clause.

(102) ch'u'j   k-at-b'i:n-isa-n   ch'iich'
      wrecklessly (sic)   ICP-B2SG-travel-CAUS-AP   car
      'you car-drive wrecklessly (sic)'   {Mondloch 1981:250}

(103) ka-Ø-ki-b'an   b'an-oj   b'ee   lee   winaq
      ICP-B3SG-A3PL-do/make   do/make-AP   road   the   people
      'The people are doing road construction.'   {Mondloch 1981:260}
Mondloch has a few examples without the initial adverbial, as in (104).

(104) k-ix-ok-sa-n   aq'ab'   pa   lee   nimaq'iij
      ICP-B3PL-enter-CAUS-AP   night   in   the   fiesta
      'You will be at the fiesta till after dark.'   {Mondloch 1981:257}

4.5.3 Agent focus

The agent focus construction is used to extract or focus the subject of transitive verbs. For this purpose the verb must be intransitivized by the same suffixes as for the incorporative antipassive: *-ow/-uw* for root transitives and *-n* for derived transitives, and only one argument is marked on the verb by a set B marker. Two different structures are used for this purpose. In one, the verb agrees with the agent and in the other the verb agrees with the patient. In other words, in one case the patient is direct and in the other it is oblique, and this might be the best way to address it (for details, see Aissen 2017). Terminology for these two structures differs. Because of the morphology and the syntactic behavior of this verb, it looks like the antipassive, especially when the agent is the argument marked on the verb. However, it is not like an antipassive when the patient is the argument marked on the verb since it does not fit the definition of the antipassive voice. Since both structures are used to focus the agent regardless of the agreement marking on the verb, I will call it an agent focus or AF construction, with either agent or patient agreement.

Agent agreement/oblique patient: the agent focus construction starts with the extracted subject. The verb becomes intransitive (*-ow/ow* or *-n* suffixes) where the only argument agrees with the agent marked by set B. The patient is obligatorily introduced by a relational noun in some dialects (López Ixcoy 1997); however, in other dialects the relational noun is optional when the patient is an NP (third person) (Mondloch 1981:225).

(105) Aree   ri   jab'   x-Ø-chup-uw   r-eech   ri   q'aaq'
      FOC   DET   rain   CP-B3SG-put.out-AP   A3SG-RN   DET   fire
      'It was the rain that put out the fire.'   {López Ixcoy 1997:368}

(106) ix   x-ix-yoq'-ow   (r-ee)   lee   achi
      PRON2PL   CP-B2PL-mock-AP   A3SG-RN   the   man
      'you are the ones who mocked the man'   {Mondloch 1981:225}

Patient agreement/direct patient: the verb agrees with the patient rather than the agent. All the rest of the structure remains the same as when the verb agrees with the agent (the focused agent is in preverbal position, the verb morphology is the same).

(107) are   ri   achy-aab'   x-**in**-ch'ey-ow-ik
      FOC   DET   man-PL   CP-B1SG-hit-AP-SS
      'he is the one who robbed us'   {Larsen 1984:507}

(Note: I am glossing the suffixes *-on/-un, -n* for absolutive antipassive and *-ow/-uw, -n* for focus antipassive and AF constructions as AP =antipassive to have a consistent gloss for this morpheme.)

The use of these two kinds of agreement in agent focus constructions is based on a person hierarchy as stated by Mondloch (1981) and Larsen (1988:506) for K'iche', and by Dayley (1985) for Tz'utujil.

(108) non-third person > 3pl > 3sg (2formal)

Object agreement in agent focus constructions is used when the patient is higher in the hierarchy than the agent. Thus, in (107) the patient is first person which is higher than third plural, therefore what is marked on the verb is the first person patient. However, agent agreement occurs in examples like (106) where the patient (third singular) is lower than the agent (second plural).

It seems to be the case that in some varieties of K'iche' it is obligatory to follow this hierarchy (Larsen 1984) and (López Ixcoy 1997) when the patient is direct, while in others it is not (Mondloch 1981:225). In Santa Lucía it is not obligatory to follow this hierarchy, but there is a difference in meaning in the use of the two forms (agent and patient agreement), as the following pair of examples show:

(109) are   le   achi   x-Ø-ch'ey-ow   **w-eech**
      FOC   DET   man   CP-B3SG-hit-AP   A1SG-RN
      'it was the man who hit me' (and not somebody else)

(110) are   le   achi   x-**in**-ch'ey-ow-ik
      FOC   DET   man   CP-B1SG-hit-AP-SS
      'it was the man who hit me' (he did it, not me)

For further details, see Mondloch 1981; Larsen 1988; López Ixcoy 1997; Velleman 2014, and Aissen (2017). Thus, in K'iche' the constructions that fit the definition of the antipassive voice are the absolutive antipassive and the incorporative antipassive. However, as discussed, in order to extract the transitive subject it is necessary to use the antipassive verb morphology, but this morphology can be associated with two distinct structures, as explained above. Table 18.11 summarizes passive, antipassive, and AF derivations.

4.6 Topicalization and focus

It is known that topicalization and focus are associated with two syntactic positions before the verb (Norman 1977; Aissen 1992; England 1997; Can Pixabaj and England 2011, and Aissen on information structure, this volume, among others). The topic position comes before the focus position. Thus, if there are two elements before the verb, we can identify the first element as topic and the second as focus.

     TOP   FOC
(111) **q-onojeel**   **wa'**   **pa**   **q'ab'**   **la**   oj   k'o   **wi**   nu-dyoos
      A1PL-everybody   DEM   PREP   hands   2FSG   B1PL   EXIST   FOC   A1SG-God
      'For sure we all are in your hands, God.'   {Can Pixabaj 2015:38}

TABLE 18.11 PASSIVE, ANTIPASSIVE, AND AF DERIVATIONS

	Lexical-Pass	Syntactic-Pass	Absolutive-AP	Incorporative-AP	Agent Focus
Root transitive verbs	-(V₁)taj	vowel lengthening	-on/-un	-ow/-uw	-ow/-uw
Derived transitive verbs	-taj	-x	-n	-n	-n

4.6.4 Focus

Focused elements are fronted to the verb. If these elements are definite NPs they are obligatorily preceded by the particle *are*, otherwise they cannot be preceded by this particle, as the examples in (112) show. (Note, however, that Velleman (2014) indicates that focus can also be in situ except for the A argument).

(112) a. **are ri**   ak'aal   x-Ø-tij-ow   r-eech   ri   wa
         FOC   DET   child   CP-B3SG-eat-AP   A3SG-RN   DET   food
         'it was the child who ate the food'

    b. **ak'al-aab'**   x-e-tij-ow   r-eech   ri   wa
       child-PL   CP-B3PL-eat-AP   A3SG-RN   DET   food
       'it was children who ate the food'

Focused obliques (locative as in (113a), indirect object as in (113b), comitative, and instrument) require the particle *wi* after the verb.

(113) a. **chla'**   x-Ø-ok   **wi**
         there   CP-B3SG-enter   PAR
         'It was there where it entered.'   {R052I001:340}

    b. **jachin   ch-e**   x-Ø-a-b'i-j   **wi**?
       who   PREP-RN   CP-B3SG-A2SG-say-ACT   FOC
       'Who did you tell it to?'

When the agent is focused, the verb must be changed to an antipassive or agent focus form (see (112a,b) and the previous section); there is no change when the focused element is the object.

4.6.5 Topic

Topicalized elements are also found before the verb. If there is only one element preceding the verb, it can be identified as a topic only if it is followed by a pause. Focused elements cannot be followed by a pause (Can Pixabaj and England 2011). In (114–15) the NP in preverbal position is followed by a pause, and so can be identified as a topic.

(114) ... **la'l-tom-aab'**   **le**   **alab'oom**,
         DET.girl-PL-PL   DET   boys
         ya   ka-Ø-ki-k'aq   k-iib'   pa   k'ax-a   taq   jastaq
         ya   ICP-B3SG-A3PL-throw   A3PL-RR   PREP   bad-EP   PL   things
         ' ... girls and boys do bad things.'   {R146I006:039}

Another difference is that transitive subjects can be topicalized without changing the verb form (114) unlike the focus of transitive subjects that requires changing the verb form. Finally, topicalized obliques do not require the particle wi, as in (115), as focused obliques do.

(115) **pa   le   b'e**,   x-Ø-inw-il   kan   jun   kumatz   chi'l   jun   ch'o
       PREP   DET   road   CP-B3SG-A1SG-see   DIR   one   snake   and   one   rat
       'on the road, I saw a snake and a rat'

4.7 Negation and interrogation

Negation is indicated by the irrealis particle *taj/ta* and the particle *ma/man/na* (these forms vary according to dialect (Par Sapón and Can Pixabaj 2000:195). In Santa Lucía Utatlán *na* is the only form that is used, but in Nahualá and Ixtahuacán *ma* can also occur, as well as in other dialects.) The negated element is found between these two particles. The irrealis particle occurs as *taj* if it is the last element of the intonational phrase. It is otherwise shortened to *ta*. To negate a predicate (or sentence) the particles *na* and *ta(j)* surround the verb or non-verbal predicate.

(116) a. **na**   x-Ø-ki-kamsa-j   **taj** x-Ø-ki-k'am   b'i   ch-o-ja
   NEG CP-B3SG-A3PL-kill-ACT   IRR CP-B3SG-A3PL-receive DIR   PREP-RN-house
   'They did not kill it, they took it home.'   {R0521001:067}

   b. Ø   k'o   ne   muul   wa'   xaq   k-e-yakataj   q'anoq
   B3SG   EXIST   PAR   time   DEM   PAR   ICP-B3PL-get.up   DIR
     ma   ka-Ø-k-a'n   **ta**   saqrik,
     NEG   ICP-B3SG-A3PL-make   IRR   good.morning
     'Maybe there are times that they just wake up, and they don't say 'good morning'.'
                {R069I001:135}

For NP or constituent negation the same particles are used; however, the NP has to be moved to focus position and then negation is applied. In (117a) I present the VOS sentence and in (117b) I show the negation of its non-specific NP object, which has been moved to focus position.

(117) a. k-Ø-u-tzuku-j   ixiim   ri   ak'aal
   ICP-B3SG-A3SG-seek-ACT   maize   DET   child
   'The child looks (is looking) for maize.'

   b. **na**   ixiim   **ta**   k-Ø-u-tzuku-j   ri   ak'aal
   NEG maize   IRR   ICP-B3SG-A3SG-seek-ACT   DET   child
   'It is not maize that the child is looking for.'

When the NP is definite, what is surrounded by the negative particles is the focus particle *are*, as in (118), and not the NP itself.

(118) **na**   are   **ta**   le   ixiim   k-Ø-u-tzuku-j   ri   ak'aal
   NEG   FOC   IRR   DET   maize   ICP-B3SG-A3SG-seek-ACT   DET   child
   'It is not the maize that the child is looking for.'

When the original transitive subject is in focus position, the verb changes to an antipassive or agent focus form, and then negation is applied, as in (119).

(119) a. **na**   ak'alaab'   **ta**   k-e-tzuku-n   r-eech   ri   ixiim
   NEG   children   IRR   ICP-B3PL-seek-AP   A3SG-RN   DET   maize
   'It is not children who are looking for the maize.'

   b. **na**   are   **ta**   le   ak'alaab'   k-e-tzuku-n   r-eech   ri   ixiim
   NEG   FOC   IRR   DET   children   ICP-B3PL-seek-AP   A3SG-RN   DET   maize
   'It is not the children who are looking for the maize.'

In some cases the first particle can be dropped, and the second is the only one that indicates the presence of negation. This has been demonstrated by Romero (2012) in Santa María Chiquimula, but it is also possible in other dialects (Par Sapón and Can Pixabaj 2000).

(120) In   k'o-t(a)   k-Ø-im-b'ii-j   chi-r-e
      PRON1SG   EXIST-IRR   ICP-B3SG-A1SG-say-ACT   PREP-A3SG-RN
      'I have nothing to say about it'.   {Romero 2012:91}

Interrogation involves a process similar to negation. The interrogative particles are *la* and *k'u(t)* for yes/no questions. The questioned element appears in between the two particles, as in (121) (Can Pixabaj 2015:80).

(121) **la**   x-at-wa'   **k'ut**?
      Q   CP-B2SG-eat   PAR
      'Did you eat?'

In (122) there is a NP that is being questioned in sentence-initial position. If the questioned NP is the original agent or transitive subject, the verb is in the antipassive or agent focus form, as in (122a). Notice that the NP in (122a) is non-specific. In (122b) the NP is definite; therefore the particle *are* is used, and is the element between the two interrogative particles.

(122) a. **la** ak'alaab'   **k'u** k-e-tzuku-n   r-eech   ri   ixiim?
         Q   children   PAR   ICP-B3PL-seek-AP A3SG-RN   DET   maize
         'Is it children who are looking for maize?'

      b. **la** are   **k'u** le   ak'alaab'   k-e-tzuku-n   r-eech   ri   ixiim?
         Q   FOC   PAR   DET   children   ICP-B3PL-seek-AP A3SG-RN   DET   maize
         'Is it the children who are looking for maize?'

The questioned element in (123) is a locative. It requires the clitic *wi*, like focus of locatives and other obliques (§4.6).

(123) **la**   waraal   **k'u** x-ix-wa'   wi?
      Q   here   PAR   CP-B2PL-eat   PAR
      'Was it here where you ate?'

As in the case of negation, in some cases the first or the second particle used for interrogation can be dropped or sometimes none of them appear, but the rising intonation indicates that it is a question.

(124) a. x-oj-aw-il   **k'ut**?
         CP-B1PL-A2SG-see   PAR
         'Did you see us?'

      b. **la** x-oj-aw-il-o?
         Q   CP-B1PL-A2SG-see-SS
         'Did you see us?'

      c. x-oj-aw-il-o?
         CP-B1PL-A2SG-see-SS
         'Did you see us?'

5 COMPLEX STRUCTURES

5.1 Relative clauses

Relative clauses in K'iche' have not been addressed as thoroughly as other topics, although they are included in some studies. Relative clauses are post-nominal and can be introduced by an overt relativizer or not. López (1997) analyzes the relativizer as a relative pronoun, Larsen (1988) analyzes it as a definite article, and Velleman (2014:81) as a complementizer. The arguments that can be relativized are subjects (except for transitive subjects; for as we have already seen, the extraction of an ergative argument requires the use of the antipassive), objects, indirect objects, instruments, locatives, and benefactives (Can Pixabaj 2015:81–2).

(125) x-Ø-mayamob'   le   achi   [le   x-Ø-tzaaq   pa   xaq'o'l]
      CP-B3SG-collapse   DET   man   REL   CP-B3SG-fall.down   PREP   mud
      'The man who fell down in the mud collapsed.'   {López Ixcoy 1997:415}

What López (1997) describes corresponds to bound relative clauses, but it has been shown that K'iche' also has free (or headless) relative clauses (Henderson 2012; Velleman 2014). In (126) there is no noun head that the relative clause is modifying, but notice that there is a relativizer.

(126) x-Ø-in-tij   [le   x-Ø-a-ya'   kanoq]
      CP-B3SG-A1SG-eat   DET   CP-B3SG-A2SG-give   DIR
      'I ate what you left.'   {Can Pixabaj 2015:82}
Specific studies on relative clauses are needed.

5.2 Complement clauses

K'iche', like most Mayan languages, has finite complements, but K'iche' also has non-finite complements that are not found in all Mayan languages (see Aissen on complement clauses, this volume). These two main types of complement clauses in K'iche' have been recognized by many authors, and some of them have even divided the non-finite complements in particular into various subtypes (Mondloch 1981; Larsen 1988; López Ixcoy 1997). Recently, Can Pixabaj (2015) proposed three structural types of complements: finite complements with complementizers (CP-complements), finite complements without complementizers (S-complements), and non-finite complement clauses (Non-finite complements). This analysis could be applied to the other K'ichean languages such as Kaqchikel, Tz'utujil, Uspanteko, and Sakapulteko since they seem to have the same properties.

Finite complements with complementizers are like any independent clause. Thus, they have topic and focus positions, and they permit negation and secondary predication. Also, they do not display any dependency on the matrix predicate with regard to TAM and arguments. An example is provided below. In (127) the finite complement starts with the complementizer *chi* and is a declarative clause. In (128) the complement includes focus and in (129) it includes secondary predication.

(127) x-Ø-q-il-o   [chi   k-Ø-u-k'am   rajil
      CP-B3SG-A1PL-see-SS   COMP   ICP-B3S-A3SG-receive   money
            le   asosyasyon]
            DET association
      'We realized that the association needs money'   {Can Pixabaj 2015:89}

(128) ... k-Ø-in-b'ii-j   [chi   **are**   **wa'**   sin   x-Ø-i-'an
      ICP-B3SG-A1SG-say-ACT   COMP   FOC   DEM   DIM   CP-B3SG-A1SG-make
      kan in]
      DIR PRO1SG
      'I would say that this is what I have done.' {Can Pixabaj 2015:90}

                                                         2P°

(129) in   Ø-w-eta'-aam   [chi   Ø   **jup-ul-ik**
      PRO1S   B3SG-A1SG-know-PRF   COMP   B3SG   face.down-PRED-SC
      1P°
      x-Ø-qaj-ik]
      CP-B3SG-go.down-SC
      'I do know that s/he was born face down.'   {Can Pixabaj 2015:90}

Finite complements without complementizers are a different type of complement. The verb carries TAM marking and full agreement, but does not allow topic and focus, and some do not allow negation or secondary predication. (130a) is an example of a finite complement without complementizer. (130b) is an ungrammatical example with topicalization in the complement.

(130) a. x-Ø-in-q'i'-o   [x-in-atin   pa   joron]
         CP-B3SG-A1SG-endure-SS   CP-B1SG-take.shower   PREP   cold.water
         'I endured taking a shower in cold water.'   {Can Pixabaj 2015:94}
                               TOP
       b. *x-Ø-r-aaj   [**le**   **u-naan**   ka-Ø-'ee-k]
         CP-B3SG-A3SG-want   DET   A3SG-mother   ICP-B3SG-go-SS
         Intended reading: 'S/he wanted her/his mother to go.'   {Can Pixabaj 2015:98}

Finite complements without complementizers usually show dependence on the matrix clause. TAM marking in the complement usually matches that of the matrix, and the complement subject must be coreferential with the matrix subject (since the complement subject is indexed on the complement verb, this is 'inherent' control in the sense of Stiebels 2007). What all these properties suggest is that finite complements without complementizers are not full CPs.

(131) jawi   **k-Ø-aw-aaj**   [**k-at-wa'** ___ wi]
      where   ICP-B3SG-A2SG-want   ICP-B2SG-eat   FOC
      'Where do you want to eat?'   {Can Pixabaj 2015:96}

Non-finite complements are headed by a verb that carries no TAM marking and shows agreement only with the object, if there is one. This verb form is formally a noun due to its position and its behavior; however, the verb retains its argument structure. Like other nominal arguments, the nominalized verb phrase has no case marking if it is subject or object of the matrix predicate, as in (132); otherwise it is oblique, and marked with *pa* or *chi*, as in (133a).

(132) ch-Ø-qa-chap-a   **[wa'-iim]**
      IMP-B3SG-A1PL-start-DEP   eat-VN
      'Let's start eating.'
                                      {Can Pixabaj 2015:105}

Non-finite complements do not allow the elements that an independent clause does: topic, focus, negation, and secondary predication. This type of complement displays dependence on the matrix predicate in TAM and argument coreference. Thus, the interpretation of TAM comes from the matrix predicate; the complement subject is not syntactically present and is interpreted as coreferent with one argument of the matrix predicate, either subject or object (this is 'structural control' in the sense of Stiebels 2007).

(133) a. x-oj-u-ya'   [pa   kuna-x-ik].
         CP-B1PL-A3SG-give   PREP   cure-PSV-VN
         'He allowed us to be cured.'   {Can Pixabaj 2015:108}

      b. *x-Ø-w-aj   [na kuna-x-ik taj]
         CP-B3SG-A1SG-accept   NEG cure-PSV-VN IRR
         Intended reading: 'I accepted not to be cured.'   {Can Pixabaj 2015:112}

Intransitive and passive verbal nouns are illustrated in (132)–(133). The transitive verbal noun is formed with passive morphology, as in (134). Can Pixabaj (2015) proposes that it is transitive, despite having passive morphology. She gives two arguments in support of this proposal. First, control relations show that the verb in the complement is not passive because the controllee is not the patient (which would be the subject if the complement were passive), but instead is the active agent. Second, the complement allows reflexive, which is only possible in K'iche' with transitive active verbs. Note that the patient is indexed by Set A marker because the complement verb is a nominalized form.

(134) x-Ø$_i$-u$_j$-chap   [$_j$nu$_k$-kuna-x-iik]$_i$
      CP-B3SG-A3SG-begin   A1SG-cure-PSV-VN
      'S/he began to cure me.'   {Can Pixabaj 2015:116}

(135) x-ø-inw-eta'ma-j   [r-iil-ik   w-iib']
      COM-B3SG-A1SG-learn-ACT   A3SG-see.PASS-VN   A1SG-RR
      'I learned to take care of myself.'   {Can Pixabaj 2015:119}

Table 18.12 summarizes the properties of each complement type (Can Pixabaj 2015:135).
Can Pixabaj also shows that non-finite complements can be complements of certain non-verbal predicates with evaluative and manner interpretations. In those cases there are two forms of expressing the controller: oblique (agent or dative), as in (136) or main subject, as in (137).

(136) a. Ø   k'ax [u-keem-ik   le   paas]   aw-umaal
         B3SG   bad   A3SG-weave;PSV-VN   DET   belt   A2SG-RN
         'It is hard for you to weave the belt.'

      b. Ø   utz   [u-keem-ik   le   paas]   ch-aw-e
         B3SG   good A3SG-weave;PSV-VN   DET   belt   PREP-A2SG-RN
         'It is good for you to weave the belt.'   {Can Pixabaj 2015:121–2}

(137) at   no'jiim [ch-u-keem-ik   le   paas]
      B2SG   slow   PREP-A3SG-weave;PSV-VN   DET   belt
      'You are slow at weaving the belt.'   {Can Pixabaj 2015:122}

TABLE 18.12 STRUCTURAL DIFFERENCES BETWEEN COMPLEMENT TYPES

	CP-comp	*S-Complement*	*Non-finite comp*
Negation	allowed	not allowed	not allowed
Focus	allowed	not allowed	not allowed
Secondary predicate	allowed	allowed	not allowed
Agreement	full agreement	full agreement	object agreement (if there is one)
Control	not obligatory	inherent control	structural control
TAM marking	allowed	allowed	not allowed
TAM matching	not obligatory	obligatory	N/A
Category of the comp	**CP**	**S**	**NP**

5.3 Purpose clauses

Purpose clauses can also be finite or non-finite, like complement clauses. However, studies of purpose clauses in K'iche'an languages do not usually include both (attention has been mostly on the finite ones (Larsen 1988; López Ixcoy 1997)). Finite purpose clauses are introduced by the relational noun *-eech* preceded by a Set A third person marker, r-

(138) x-e-pet-ik   [**r-eech**   k-e-wa'   iw-uuk']⁵
      CP-B3PL-come-SS   A3SG-RN   ICP-B3PL-eat   A2PL-RN
      'They came to eat with you.'   {López Ixcoy 1997:440}

Non-finite purpose clauses are like non-finite complement clauses in the sense that they have a nominalized verb form, are introduced by a preposition that can be *chi* or *pa*, and display control relations as well.

(139) k-e-b'ee   [**pa**   wa'-iim]
      ICP-B3PL-go   PREP   eat-VN
      'They are going to eat.'   {Larsen 1988:415}

Can Pixabaj (2015) also presents another construction with a purposive meaning. This construction is composed of two verbs where the first one must be an intransitive verb of motion and the second one can be any verb. Subjects of the two clauses and TAM marking must be identical. Can Pixabaj argues that this a paratactic construction because there is no subordinator.

(140) x-**oj**-peet-ik   [x-Ø-ol-**qa**-k'am-a']
      CP-B1PL-come-SS   CP-B3SG-MOV-A1PL-receive-DEP
      'We came to take her.'   {Can Pixabaj 2015:27}

In summary, Can Pixabaj describes three types of clauses with purposive meanings: (i) finite purpose clauses, (ii) non-finite purpose clauses, and (iii) paratactic constructions (such as (140)). Thus, K'iche' does not display formal differences between canonical purpose clauses and destinative constructions as in Tseltal and Q'anjob'al (Polian *et al.*

2015). I have presented purpose clauses separately from other adverbial clauses since they share the same structural types with complement clauses; however, they function as adverbial clauses.

5.4 Adverbial clauses

In K'iche' various types of adverbial clauses have been identified: purpose, temporal, causal/reason, manner, and conditional clauses (Larsen 1988; López Ixcoy 1997). Aside from purpose clauses, discussed in §5.3. above, adverbial clauses are finite. The examples below illustrate different types of clause: (141) is a temporal clause introduced by *are taq/taq*, or *are chiri'/chri'* and (142) is a reason clause introduced by the relational noun *-umaal* 'because'.

(141) x-oj-ki'kot-ik   [**are.taq** x-at-ul-ik]
      CP-B1PL-be.happy-SS   when   CP-B2SG-come-SS
      'We got happy when you got here.'

(142) Na x-Ø-war   taj   [**rumal** sib'alaj yowaab']
      NEG CP-B3SG-sleep IRR   because   INTS   sick
      'He/she did not sleep because he/she is very sick.'

Manner clauses, as in (143), do not have a subordinator. Also, notice that manner clauses can only occur before the main clause, while the others – temporal and reason clauses – can occur either after or before the main clause (Can Pixabaj 2015).

(143) k-in-xik'ik'-ik   k-in-q'aax-ik
      ICP-B1SG-fly-SS   ICP-B1SG-PSV-SS
      'I pass flying.'

Another restriction of manner clauses is that subjects must be identical, and the TAM on the manner verb must be incompletive, regardless of the TAM on the main verb.

Conditional clauses are usually regarded as adverbial clauses. In K'iche' a conditional clause is introduced by the particle *we* 'if'. The antecedent clause (protasis) can precede or follow the consequent clause (apodosis), as the pairs in (144) and (145) illustrate.

(144) a. [**we** Ø   teew] na   k-in-el   ta   ub'iik
         COND B3SG   cold   NEG   ICP-B1SG-go.out IRR   DIR
         'If it is cold, I will not go out.'

      b. na   k-in-el   ta   ub'iik [**we** Ø   teew]
         NEG   ICP-B1SG-go.out IRR   DIR   COND B3SG   cold
         'I will not go out if it is cold.'

(145) a. [**we** k-at-nuum-ik]   k-at-wa'-oq
         COND ICP-B2SG-be.hungry-SS ICP-B2SG-eat-DEP
         'If you are hungry, eat!'

      b. k-at-wa'-oq   [**we** k-at-nuum-ik]
         ICP-B2SG-eat-DEP COND ICP-B2SG-be.hungry-SS
         'Eat if you are hungry.'

In this type of clause, subjects do not need to be identical. Thus, in (144) there is no coreference between subjects, whereas in (145) subjects are identical.

NOTES

1   Other variations of this sound are [f] also in coda position or [β] between vowels in some dialects such as in: [ʔiβiːr?] 'yesterday'.

2   In Tz'utujiil the vowel of the plural suffix tends to occur in vowel disharmony with the final stem vowel (Dayley 1985), and the same tendency can be seen in K'iche', though with many exceptions. Thus, *-iib'* occurs most often after back vowels and – *aab'* most often after front vowels.

3   It seems that the potential use of the prefix *ch-* is not productive anymore. Thus, it can occur in subordinate clauses, mainly in conditional clauses, but as a variation of the completive prefix *x-*. The following example contains x- in the subordinate clause, but it could be replaced by ch-. [we **x/ch**ink'ayij kanoq] kintzalij aninaq 'If I sell it, I will go back quickly.' However, the most common T/A in this context is the incompletive *k-*.

4   **Umaal** has a long vowel in its last syllable; however, when it is followed by its complement, an NP, the vowel of the last syllable is realized as short. This is the same rule that applies with other elements, such as status suffixes, at the end of the intonational phrase.

5   The grammaticality of this sentence may vary. In the K'iche' of Santa Lucía Utatlán, López's example sounds odd. Speakers change the form of the subordinate verb from finite to non-finite, and this seems to be due to the coreference of subjects:

(i)   x-e-pe   [pa   **wa'-iim**   iw-uuk']
      COM-B3PL-come   PREP   eat-VN   A2PL-RN
      'They came to eat with you.'

REFERENCES

Aissen, Judith. 1992. "Topic and focus in Mayan." *Language* 68: 43–80.

Aissen, Judith. 2011. "On the syntax of agent focus in K'ichee.'" In *Proceedings of formal approaches to Mayan linguistics I,* ed. by Kirill Shklovsky, Pedro Mateo Pedro, and Jessica Coon, 1–16. Cambridge: MIT Working Papers in Linguistics, vol. 63.

Aissen, Judith. 2017. "Correlates of ergativity in Mayan." In *OUP handbook of ergativity,* ed. by Jessica Coon, Diane Massam, and Lisa Travis. Oxford: Oxford University Press.

Ajpacajá Tum, Pedro Florentino. 2001. *K'ichee' Choltziij [K'ichee' Dictionary].* Guatemala City: Cholsamaj.

Ajpacajá Tum, Pedro Florentino, Manuel Isidro Chox Tum, Francisco Lucas Tepaz Raxulew, and Diego Adrian Guarchaj Ajtzalam. 1996. *Diccionario del Idioma K'iche'.* Antigua Guatemala: Proyecto Lingüístico Francisco Marroquín and Cholsamaj.

Baird, Brandon, O. 2014. "An acoustic analysis of Spanish-K'ichee' (Mayan) bilingual intonation." PhD diss., University of Texas.

Baronti, David Scott. 2001. "Sound symbolism use in affect verbs in Santa Catarina Ixtahuacán." PhD diss., University of California, Davis.

Campbell, Lyle. 2000. "Valency-changing derivations in K'iche'." *In Changing valency: case studies in transitivity,* ed. by R.M.W. Dixon and Alexandra Aikhenvald, 236–81. Cambridge, University Press.

Can Pixabaj, Telma Angelina. 2007. "El pasivo completivo en K'ichee.'" Paper given in CILLA III, Austin: University of Texas.

Can Pixabaj, Telma. 2009. "Mophosyntactic features and behaviors of verbal nouns in K'ichee.'" MA thesis, University of Texas, Austin.

Can Pixabaj, Telma Angelina. 2015. "Complement and purpose clauses in K'iche'." PhD diss., The University of Texas, Austin.

Can Pixabaj, Telma Angelina, and María Beatriz Par Sapón. 2000. "Orden de los constituyentes principales en K'ichee'." *Cultura de Guatemala*, Año XXI(2): 47–63.

Can Pixabaj, Telma y Nora England. 2011. "Nominal topic and focus in K'ichee'." In *Representing language: essays in honor of Judith Aissen,* ed. by Rodrígo Gutiérrez-Bravo, Line Mikelson, Eric Potsdam, 15–30. Santa Cruz: Linguistics Research Center, UC Santa Cruz.

Can Pixabaj, Telma Angelina y Nikte' Sis Iboy. 2004. "Contextualizando posicionales K'ichee'-Achi." Paper given at Lengua y mantenimiento cultural en Mesoamérica: Un simposio. Austin: University of Texas.

Davies, William D., and Luis Enrique Sam-Colop. 1990. "K'iche' and the structure of antipassive." *Language* 66: 522–49.

Dayley, Jon P. 1985. *Tz'utujil Grammar*. University of California Publications in Linguistics, vol. 107. Berkeley: University of California Press.

Edmonson, Munro. 1965. *Quiche-English dictionary*. Middle American Research Institute, 30. New Orleans: Tulane University.

England, Nora C. 1983. *A grammar of Mam*, a Mayan language. Austin: University of Texas Press.

England, Nora C. 1991. "Changes in basic word order in Mayan languages." *International Journal of American Linguistics* 57: 446–86.

England, Nora C. 1992. Autonomía de los idiomas Mayas: Historia e identidad. Rukutamil, Ramaq'il, Rutzijob'al: Ri Mayab' Amaq'. Guatemala City: Cholsamaj.

England, Nora C. 1997. "Topicalización, enfoque y énfasis." *Cultura de Guatemala*, año XVIII, vol. II, 273–88.

England, Nora C. 2004. "Adjectives in Mam." In *Adjective classes: a cross-linguistic typology*, ed. by R.M.W. Dixon and Alexandra Y. Aikenvald, 125–46. Oxford: Oxford University Press.

Haviland, John. 1994. "'Te xa setel xulem' (The buzzards were circling): categories of verbal roots in (Zinacantec) Tzotzil." *Linguistics* 32: 691–742.

Henderson, Robert. 2012. "Morphological alternations at the intonational phrase edge." *Natural Language and Linguistics Theory* 30: 741–89.

Kaufman, Terrence. 1974. *Idiomas de Mesoamérica*. Guatemala City: José de Pineda Ibarra.

Kaufman, Terrence. 1990. "Algunos Rasgos Estructurales de los Idiomas Mayances con Referencia Especial al K'iche'." In *Lecturas sobre la Lingüística Maya*, ed. by Nora England and Stephen Elliott, 59–114. Antigua Guatemala: Centro de Investigaciones Regionales de Mesoamérica.

Larsen, Thomas Walter. 1987. "The syntactic status of ergativity in Quiché." *Lingua* 71: 33–59.

Larsen, Thomas Walter. 1988. "*Manifestations of ergativity in Quiché grammar*." PhD diss., University of California, Berkeley.

López Ixcoy, Candelaria Dominga (Saqijiix). 1994. *Las vocales en K'ichee'*. Guatemala: Nawal Wuj.

López Ixcoy, Candelaria Dominga (Saqijix). 1997. *Ri Ukemiik ri K'ichee' Chii': Gramática K'ichee'*. Guatemala City: Cholsamaj.

López Ixcoy, Candelaria Dominga (Saqijiix). 1999. "*Los demonstrativos en K'ichee'*." *Licenciatura* thesis, Universidad Rafael Landívar, Guatemala.

Martin, Laura. 1977. "Positional roots in Kanjobal (Mayan)." PhD diss., University of Florida.

Mondloch, James. 1978. "Differentiating subjects and objects in Quiché." *Journal of Mayan Linguistics* 1: 3–19.

Mondloch, James Lorin. 1981. "Voice in Quiché-Maya." PhD diss., State University of New York, Albany.

Nielsen, K. 2005. "Kiche intonation." *UCLA Working Papers in Phonetics* 104: 45–60.

Norman, William. 1976. "Quiche text." *International Journal of American Linguistics Native American Text Series* 1: 40–60.

Norman, William. 1977. "Topic and focus in Mayan." Presentation at the Mayan Workshop II, San Cristóbal de las Casas, Chiapas, Mexico.

Norman, William. 1978. "Advancement rules and syntactic change: the loss of instrumental voice in Mayan." *Proceedings of the 4th Annual Meeting of the Berkeley Linguistic Society* 4: 458–76.

Par Sapón, María Beatriz, and Telma Angelina Can Pixabaj. 2000. *Ujunamaxiik ri K'ichee' Ch'ab'al: Variación Dialectal en K'ichee'*. Guatemala City: Cholsamaj.

Polian, Gilles, Eladio Mateo Toledo, and Telma Can Pixabaj. 2015. "Construcciones destinativas en lenguas mayas." *Amerindia* 37: 159–88.

Pye, Clifton. 1980. "The acquisition of grammatical morphemes in Quiche Mayan." PhD diss., The University of Pittsburgh.

Pye, Clifton. 1991. "The acquisition of K'iche' (Maya)." In *The crosslinguistic study of language acquisition*, ed. by Dan Isaac Slobin, vol. 3: 221–308. Hillsdale: Erlbaum.

Pye, Clifton. 2001. "The acquisition of finiteness in K'iche' Maya." In *Proceedings of the 25th annual Boston university conference on language development*, 645–56. Somerville: Cascadilla Press.

Richards, Michael. 2003. *Atlas Lingüístico de Guatemala*. Guatemala City: Universidad Rafael Landívar.

Romero, Sergio Francisco. 2006. "Sociolinguistic variation and linguistic history in Mayan: the case of K'ichee'." PhD diss., University of Pennsylvania.

Romero, Sergio Francisco. 2012. "A Maya version of Jespersen's cycle: The diachronic evolution of negative markers in K'iche' maya." *International Journal of American Linguistics* 78: 77–96.

Stiebels, Barbara. 2006. "Agent focus in Mayan languages." *Natural Language and Linguistic Theory* 24: 501–70.

Stiebels, Barbara. 2007. "Towards a typology of complement control." In *Studies in complement control*. ZAS Papers in Linguistics 47: 1–80. Berlin: ZAS.

Trechsel, Frank. 1981. "A categorial treatment of Quichean (Mayan) ergativity." PhD diss., University of Texas, Austin.

Trechsel, Frank. 1993. "Quiche focus constructions." *Lingua* 91: 33–78.

Velleman, Leah (*née* Daniel) Bridges. 2013. "On optional focus movement in K'ichee.'" In *Proceedings of formal approaches to Mayan linguistics 2*, ed. by Lauren Eby Clemens, Robert Henderson, and Pedro Mateo Pedro, 107–18. (*MIT Working Papers in Linguistics 74*). Cambridge: MIT.

Velleman, Leah Bridges. 2014. "Focus and movement in a variety of K'ichee'." PhD diss., The University of Texas, Austin.

Yasavul, Murat. 2011. "Negation in K'iche'." Qualifying paper, The Ohio State University.

Zavala Maldonado, Roberto. 1993. "Clause integration with verbs of motion in Mayan languages." MA thesis, University of Oregon.

CHAPTER 19

MAM*

Nora C. England

Mam belongs to the Mamean branch of the Eastern Division of Mayan languages. It is one of the largest of the Mayan languages (next after K'iche', Yucatec, and Q'eqchi') with over half a million speakers in 2001 (Richards 2003). It is spoken in the Departments of Huehuetenango, Quetzaltenango, and San Marcos in Guatemala in 56 *municipios*, and is bordered on the north by Q'anjob'alan proper languages, on the west by Mocho' and Teko, and on the east by K'iche', Sipakapense, and Awakateko. Mam is characterized by having great internal diversification and can be divided into three major dialect areas (Cojtí and England 1986) – north, south, and west – plus two central subgroups, one in the north and the other in the south.

1 DATA AND SOURCES

Although Mam is one of the largest of the Mayan languages in terms of numbers of speakers, and was the language of an important polity at the time of the arrival of the Spaniards, there is much less colonial written work in Mam than in the other major languages such as K'iche', Yucatec, or Kaqchikel. An early work on the language is Reynoso (1644, re-edited by Carreño in 1916 with a new grammatical introduction). In the 1916 re-edition, it has a little over 34 pages of grammatical sketch and about 100 pages devoted to vocabulary. The principal works on Mam, however, are mostly recent.

Because Mam is the Mayan language with the greatest degree of internal diversity, it is important to document all of the major dialect areas. Unfortunately, the published, available documentation is mostly of the northern dialect area; Southern Mam is more poorly represented and Western Mam is hardly represented at all. The Central Mam subarea is also poorly represented in basic documentation. There are two published full-length reference grammars – England (1983a) on Ixtahuacán (Northern) Mam and Pérez and Jiménez (1997) on Cajolá (Southern) Mam with some information on San Sebastián H. (Northern) Mam as well. A fairly thorough study of dialect differences in Mam arranged like a grammatical sketch also exists (Pérez et al. 2000), as well as another fairly extensive dialect survey (Godfrey and Collins (1987). There is a bilingual dictionary of Ixtahuacán Mam (Maldonado Andrés et al. 1986) and a standardized bilingual dictionary (Pérez Alonzo 2007). Each has about 6,000 entries. A recent thesis (Pérez Vail 2014) on alignment (inverse and obviation) is an important contribution to the morphosyntax of Mam (Cajolá). In addition a dissertation on Todos Santos Mam (the most divergent dialect of Northern Mam) was written in a glossematic framework (Canger 1969), and a grammatical sketch of Southern Mam was the earliest of the recent works (Peck 1951). A dissertation on the grammar of the Mam of Tacaná (Western) was written but unfortunately never filed (Munson 1984) and so is basically unavailable, but a study of spatial reference in Tacaná Mam was made by Godfrey (1981). A study of the intersection of spatial ideas in language and culture also formed the basis for a dissertation on Comitancillo Mam by Collins (2005).

England has published many articles on different aspects of the grammar of Mam, including many on the Mam of Ixtahuacán and several dialect comparative studies. Her articles cover analyses of directionals (1976a), ergativity (1983b), voice (1988), dialect differences (1989 and 1990), adjectives (2004), affect words (2006), narrative structure (2009), plural agreement (2011), non-finite and infinitive clauses (2013a), and aspect and time (2013b).

Mam texts (transcribed recorded oral speech) are available at the Archive of Indigenous Languages of Latin America (AILLA) site (England 2010). The England contributions are fully glossed and translated into Spanish. AILLA has a large number of other recordings of Mam as well, almost none of which have been transcribed.

2 PHONOLOGY

Mam has an extended set of fairly standard Mayan phonemes, having lost only the glottal fricative (*h), velar nasal (*nh), and postalveolar stops (*ty, *ty') from Proto-Mayan. It has, however, added two series of consonants, a retroflex series of stops plus a fricative and a palatal series of stops. In addition, Todos Santos Mam has a series of apico-postalveolar stops plus a fricative (/tch, tch', sh/) that no other dialect of Mam, or indeed any other Mayan language, has as phonemes, although there are phonetically similar sounds in Chajul Ixil and Mazapa Teko. The series of palatal phonemes is the outcome of palatalization rules which are widespread among Eastern Mayan languages but have only resulted in the creation of new phonemes in the Mamean branch (in Mam, Teko, and Awakatek). The series of retroflex phonemes is shared with all other Mamean languages and Q'anjob'alan proper languages (that is, not including Mocho'), and is a major feature of the Q'anjob'alan-Mamean sphere of diffusion.

In addition to losing and adding several consonants or consonant series, Mam has also gone through a shift in consonants whereby *tʃ → tʂ, *t → tʃ, and *r → t (Kaufman 1976:107 and see England and Baird, this volume). Thus although it includes most of the sounds that existed in Proto-Mayan, they often come from different sources.

The Mam consonants are given in Table 19.1, with the IPA equivalent for the base allophone in brackets. Except for the apico-postalveolar series, all the sounds are found in all dialects of Mam.

Mam has the five canonical vowels of Mayan languages plus vowel length. In general the short vowels except for [a] are lower and laxer than the long vowels (Table 19.2).

Stress in Mam follows three different patterns. In Southern Mam stress is penultimate, in Western Mam it falls on the final syllable, and in Northern Mam it falls on the last heavy syllable, where long vowels are the heaviest, vowel + glottal stop is less heavy, and vowels followed by consonants are even less heavy. Most enclitics and two suffixes

TABLE 19.1 MAM CONSONANTS

p [p]	t [t]	tz [ts]	ch [tʃ]	tch [ʈʂ]	tx [tʂ]	ky [kʲ]	k [k]	q [q]	' [ʔ]
b' [ɓ]	t' [d~t']	tz' [ts']	ch' [tʃ']	tch' [ʈʂ']	tx' [tʂ']	ky' [kʲ']	k' [k']	q' [ɢ]	
	s [s]		xh [ʃ]	sh [ʂ]	x [ʂ]			j [χ]	
m [m]	n [n]								
	l [l]								
	r [r]								
w [w]					y [j]				

TABLE 19.2 MAM VOWELS

i [ɪ]	u [ʊ]	ii [iː]	uu [uː]
e [ɛ]	o [ɔ]	ee [eː]	oo [oː]
a [a]		aa [aː]	

(-*b'il* 'instrumental' and -*b'aj* 'inalienable nouns') do not participate in stress assignment in most dialects. Examples follow (England 1983a: 37–8, Munson 1984; Maldonado Andrés et al. 1986; Pérez et al. 2000:54–5). The extra words in Northern Mam show different kinds of heavy syllables.

Gloss	Ixtahuacán (north) heavy syllable	Cajolá (south) penultimate	Tacaná (west) ultimate
'night'	qo'niiky'an	qo'niik'in	qonii'ky'aan
'armadillo'	i'b'ooxh	'ib'ooxh	i'b'ooxh
'two days ago'	kab''jee'	kaa'b'aje	kaab'a'jee
'dipper'	pu''la'		
'clear'	'spiky'a		
'raccoon'	xpi'chaq'		

All dialects of Mam have the same vowels but there is significant variation in rules that pertain to the vowels. For instance, short vowels tend to be dropped in pretonic position, but the precise rules vary from one dialect to another. For example, CVC transitive verb roots in Southern Mam always drop the root vowel when the verb takes a directional and the directional suffix -'*n*. In the west this never occurs and in the north it generally does not (Cojtí and England 1986). In the examples below the suffix -'*n* follows a stem formative vowel, required with various suffixes.

Gloss	north: root + -V-'n	south: root + -V-'n	west: root + -V-'n
'to wash'	tx'ajo'n	tx'jo'n	tx'ajo'n
'to dig'	luku'n	lku'n	luku'n
'to pull'	juk'u'n	jk'u'n	juk'u'n

Another example has to do with the interaction between glottal stops and long vowels. In the west and north, glottal stops are maintained after long vowels at the ends of words, but in the south the glottal stop drops and then the long vowel is shortened (Cojtí and England 1986).

Gloss	Ixtahuacán (north)	Ostuncalco (south)	Tacaná (west)
'tree'	tzee'	tze	tzee'
'grindstone'	kyaa'	ka	kaa'
'firewood'	sii'	si	sii'

Furthermore, nouns of the shape CV'C lengthen their vowels when they are possessed, but with different results in the three major dialect areas. In the north all vowels in roots of this shape are lengthened. In the south the vowels in some words are lengthened, in which case the glottal stop is dropped, while in other words the vowel is not lengthened and the glottal stop remains. In the west, however, the vowel is always lengthened but there is a long copy vowel after the glottal stop as well (Cojtí and England 1986).

Gloss	Ixtahuacán (north)	Ostuncalco (south)	Tacaná (west)
'my squirrel'	n-kuu'k=a	n-ku'k=e'	n-kuu'uuk
'my thorn'	n-ch'ii'x=a	n-ch'i'x=e'	n-tx'ii'iix
'my basket'	n-chii'l=a	n-chiil=e'	n-chii'iil
'my paper'	w-uu'j=a	w-uuj=e'	w-uu'uuj

3 WORDS AND PHRASES

Mam has most of the word classes that have been identified for Mayan languages: nouns with subtypes on the basis of patterns of possession and patterns of compounding; adjectives; demonstratives; numbers; noun classifiers; measures; verbs, both intransitive and transitive; positional predicates; affect words; relational nouns; and adverbs and other particles. Non-verbal predicates can be formed on noun, adjective, positional, demonstrative, and locative/existential bases. Principal phrase types are noun phrases and verb phrases, while minor types are adjective, adverb, and relational noun phrases. Verbs are the most morphologically complex of the word types, while noun phrases are the most complex of the phrase types.

3.1 Inflection

Inflectional categories in Mam include two sets of person markers, Set A and Set B, aspect markers, and a small set of suffixes that mark the irrealis moods on verbs (potential and imperative). Nouns can take Set A markers to indicate the person and number of their possessors. Intransitive verbs inflect for aspect, take Set B markers in agreement with their subjects, and the class-specific mood suffix in the potential. Transitive verbs inflect for aspect, take Set A markers to index their subjects, Set B markers to index their direct objects, and the class-specific mood suffixes in the potential and imperative. Mam is a morphologically ergative language (and syntactically ergative as well, as is shown in §4.1). There are circumstances that trigger split ergativity, and under these circumstances *all* arguments are marked with Set A markers. There are therefore no contexts in which there is a nominative-accusative pattern of agreement in Mam. Non-verbal predicates take Set B markers in agreement with their subjects. Relational nouns, formally a kind of noun, are obligatorily marked with Set A affixes to index their complements. No other word classes take any inflection at all.

The basic person markers include a set of four prefixes. Mam has in all dialects lost the historical markers for second person (both singular and plural) and has extended the historical third person markers to second person as well as third person. It is unique in this regard. To make up the full set of person distinctions it has added a set of enclitics; these additionally mark the difference between inclusive and exclusive first person plural. The enclitics are fairly degraded forms of the Set B markers. Set A markers in Mayan typically have different forms before vowel-initial and consonant-initial stems; in Mam this is true only of first person singular. The Set B markers do not in general make such a distinction (although Mam has added some forms of the third person singular marker before vowel-initial intransitive verbs). In Mam the Set B markers have somewhat different forms with non-verbal predicates and verbs, and have two different forms with verbs depending on the aspect.

The enclitics are different in the different dialect areas. They are most complete in the west, where they have a different form in each use; they maintain the difference between second person singular and all other forms in the south; and they have collapsed into a single form in the north. All of the enclitics are vowel-initial and add an epenthetic *y* if they follow a vowel. They are placed at the very end of the verb word, including after incorporated objects (but before other objects). There is some variation in Sets A and B as well, as can be seen in Table 19.3 (England 1990:229). Note that Set B has long and short forms. The short forms are those without the consonant in parentheses, and the null forms in second-third person singular.

The aspect markers and mood suffixes are given in Table 19.4. The only real variation has to do with the perfective aspect, where northern dialects distinguish between perfective (*o-*) and dependent perfective (Ø), while the other dialect areas use Ø for both functions. The contexts for the use of dependent aspect markers include several different kinds of subordinate clauses and are further explained in §5.2. The proximate aspect, which was formerly called the recent past (England 1983a) or the recent completive (Pérez and Jiménez 1997), indicates that an action is performed in close proximity to a point of reference, which may be the moment of speaking (leading to the recent past/ recent completive interpretation), or may be another action (England 2013b). This point of reference is usually temporally just after or is consequent upon the clause marked with one of the proximate markers.

With the Ø perfective aspect, the short forms of the Set B marker are used. These were the original forms. The short forms of the Set B markers are also the forms used with

TABLE 19.3 MAM PERSON MARKERS

Set A	Ixtahuacán (north)	Ostuncalco (south)	Tacaná (west)
1SG	n- /_C, w-/_V. . .=a	n- /_C, w-/_V. . .=e'	n- /_C, w-/_V
2SG	t-. . .=a	t-. . .=a	t-. . .=a
3SG	t-	t-	t-
1PL EXCL	q-. . .=a	q-. . .=e'	q-~j-. . .=o'
1PL INCL	q-	q-	q-~j-
2PL	ky-. . .=a	k-~ky-. . .=e'	ky-~k-. . .=e'
3PL	*ky-*	*k-~ky-*	*ky-~k-*

Set B	Ixtahuacán (north)	Ostuncalco (south)	Tacaná (west)
1SG	(ch)in . . .=a	(ch)in . . .=e'	(ky)in
2SG	Ø~k-~tz-~tz'-. . .=a	Ø~k-~tz-~tz'-. . .=a	Ø~k-~k'-~tz-~tz'. . .=a
3SG	Ø~k-~tz-~tz'-	Ø~k-~tz-~tz'-	Ø~k-~k'-~tz-~tz'-
1PL EXCL	(q)o . . .=a	(q)o' . . .=e'	(q)o . . .=o'
1PL INCL	(q)o	(q)o'	(q)o
2PL	(ch)i . . .=a	(ch)e' . . .=e'	(ky)e . . .=e'
3PL	*(ch)i*	*(ch)e'*	*(ky)e*

TABLE 19.4 ASPECT MARKERS AND MOOD SUFFIXES

Aspect Proclitics		*Mood Suffixes*	
perfective	Ø (s, w) o- (n)	transitive imperative	-m ~ -n
dependent perfective	Ø	intransitive imperative	Ø
proximate	ma	transitive potential	-a'
dependent proximate	x-	intransitive potential	-(ee)l
imperfective	n-		
potential	(ok)~(k-)		

(the form of the transitive imperative is *-n* before directionals; *-m* with no directional) non-verbal predicates, with some other changes that are specific to non-verbal predicates and differ somewhat from region to region.

3.2 Nouns

Mam has all of the possible subtypes of nouns (England 1983a: 66–75) that have been described for Mayan languages (see Polian, this volume, on morphology). Those that are defined on the basis of changes the stems undergo when possessed follow. Examples are from Cajolá (Southern) (Pérez and Jiménez 1997); a few are from Ixtahuacán (Northern) (England 1983a) and are marked as such.

> *Ordinary nouns*: undergo no changes. Example: *tze'* 'smile', *ttze'ya* 'your smile'.
>
> *Vowel-changing nouns*: a root vowel is lengthened when possessed. Nouns of the shape CV'C obligatorily belong to this class in Northern and Western Mam; other nouns unpredictably belong to the class. In most cases it is the last vowel that is lengthened but there are several disyllabic nouns that lengthen the first vowel of the root (which when not lengthened may be dropped because of vowel dropping rules). Examples: (Ixtahuacán): *b'ech* 'flower', *nb'eecha* 'my flower'; *q'a'j* 'log bench', *nq'aa'ja* 'my bench'; *anup* 'ceiba (silk cotton tree)'; *n'anuupa* 'my ceiba'; *xjab'* 'shoe', *t-xaajab'a* 'your shoes'. (Note that *anup* is one of the few native Mam nouns that maintain the initial glottal stop when possessed. All vowel-initial Spanish borrowings do so as well.)
>
> *Inalienable nouns*: nouns that add a suffix (*-b'aj~-b'j~-j*) in the *un*possessed form. Nouns that belong to the class are most body parts, kin, and clothing, and the hypernyms for the major food classes. Examples: *qanb'aj* 'foot', *nqane'* 'my feet'; *yaab'aj* (Ixtahuacán) 'grandmother', *nyaa'ya* 'my grandmother'; *weexj* 'pants', *nweexe'* 'my pants'; *lo'b'j* 'fruit', *nlo'ye'* 'my fruit'.
>
> *Nouns that add a suffix in the possessed form*. This is a class that has been identified for Mayan languages; however, it is not really distinct from those nouns and adjectives that form an abstract noun with the same suffix, *-il~-eel~-aal* (such as *k'a* 'bitter' > *tk'aayil* 'its bitterness'). The only difference between the nouns that have typically been identified as belonging to this class and abstract nouns is the semantic class of the noun and how different the meaning between the possessed and unpossessed form is judged to be by the linguist. The nouns in Mam that are usually assigned to this class are those for 'bone' (*b'aaq*; *nb'aaqile'* 'my bone (of my body)'), 'blood' (*chik'*; *nchk'eele'* 'my blood (of my body)'), and 'vein' (*ib'otx'*; *wib'otx'ile'* 'my vein (of my body)'). Other nouns that are usually not assigned to this category are nouns such as 'man' (*iichan/xiinaq*), 'woman' (*qyaa'/xu'j*), 'road' (*b'e*). When possessed with the same suffix, however, the semantic change is equally slight: 'my man (husband)', 'my woman (wife)', 'my road (route)'. In conclusion, the nouns that are typically assigned to the category are body parts and occasionally others, but there seems to be little to separate them from other nouns that take the abstract noun suffix, either obligatorily or optionally, when possessed.
>
> *Always possessed nouns*. These are most typically parts of objects, abstract nouns, and relational nouns (see §3.7 on relational nouns). Examples: *t-xaaq* 'its leaf', *tk'aayil* 'its bitterness'.
>
> *Never possessed nouns*: nouns that usually cannot be possessed are mostly nouns referring to natural phenomena. Some of them can be used in a phrase with an

honorific (a kinship term for a parent or grandparent), in which case the honorific takes the possessive marker. For instance, *jb'aal* 'rain' cannot receive ordinary possession, but can be possessed in the phrase *qtxuu jb'aal* 'our mother rain'.

Suppletive nouns: one or two nouns in which there is a complete change of root between the unpossessed and possessed form. Example: *ek'* 'hen', *waaline'* 'my hen'.

The other main group of subclasses of nouns consists of compound nouns with different patterns of compounding. These are:

Compound nouns: single words formed from two roots, usually an adjective plus a noun, which together form a single lexeme. Such words are possessed like single words. Example: *q'antze* 'alder' from *q'an* 'yellow' and *tze* 'tree', *tq'antze* 'his/her alder'.

Complex nouns: formed from two words, usually two nouns, which maintain their separation, but comprise a single lexeme. When possessed, the possessive marker usually accompanies the second word, although in some places it seems to be changing to the first word. Example: *chee'b'l b'utx* 'corn mill' from *chee'b'l* 'instrument for grinding' and *b'utx* 'hominy', *chee'b'l qb'utx* 'our corn mill'.

Nouns of nouns: formed from two words, the first of which is always possessed by the second. To indicate a further lexical possessor, the possessive morphemes must go on the second word, given that the first word already has possessive markers. Example: *tq'ab' tze* 'branch' from *tq'ab'* 'its hand' and *tze* 'tree', *tq'ab' ntzeeye'* 'my branch'.

Nouns plus nouns: formed from two separate related kinship terms. If the term is possessed, both nouns receive possessive markers. Sometimes possession is obligatory. There are very few of these terms in Mam. Example: *itzinb'aj* 'younger brother', *tzikb'aj* 'older brother' form *qiitz'in qtzik* 'our fellows'.

In addition there are proper names and toponyms in Mam. Very few Mayan last names persisted in the Mam area; one of them is *B'aayil* (Vail). First names from Spanish have been used for centuries, but recently Mayan first names are becoming more popular. It was necessary in many places to argue with municipal secretaries to be able to register a child with a Mayan name. Spanish names are phonologically adapted to Mam in speech, for instance *Leexh* for Andrés, *Mal* for María. Toponyms in Mam often make use of the locative relational nouns (§3.7).

3.3 Noun phrases

Word classes that can occur in the noun phrase besides the head noun include adjectives, demonstratives, numbers, measures, classifiers, and possessors.

Mam has relatively few root adjectives (fewer than 50), but many adjectives derived from verbs and positionals. The underived adjectives include terms that describe dimension, value, color, physical property, quantification, and position (England 2004). Adjectives normally precede the noun. In the west and north, however, adjectives may follow the noun if the noun is possessed or is preceded by another word such as a demonstrative, a quantifier, or a number, including the indefinite article *jun* (2a, 2b, 4a).

TACANÁ (west) (Munson 1984)

(1) te   **nuqutxa'n** kuch Ø-Ø-xi t-lo-'n   n-lo'   q'ooq'
DET   long-nosed   pig   PFV-B3SG-DIR   A3SG-eat-DS   A1SG-CLF:fruit squash
'The long-nosed pig ate my squash.'

(2) a. n-ky'aajool **nim**
A1SG-son   big
'my big son'

b. ja   kjo'n   **b'u'ch=u**
DEM   cornfield   small=DEM
'this small cornfield'

c. te   (**xhpu'k**)   xiinq (**xhpu'k**)
DET   hunch-backed   man   hunch-backed
'the hunch-backed man'

IXTAHUACÁN (north): Elicited Examples (ENGLAND 1983A:146)

(3) a. **q'ay-na** lo'j   b. *lo'j q'ayna
rot-PTCP   fruit
'rotten   fruit'

(4) a. juun t-wiixh   **saq**   b. *juun saq twiixh
one   A3SG-cat white
'a white cat of his'

It is unclear if the repositioning of the adjective is optional or obligatory, and this may vary by speaker. Elicitation tends to suggest it is mostly obligatory (but see (2c)); however in Ixtahuacán text examples show both order options. Thus (5) shows the order determiner + adjective + N, while (6) has determiner + N + adjective and (7) has quantifier + N + adjective.

IXTAHUACÁN: Text Examples

(5) qa   tz-uul   xoo-'n   t-uj   t-tzii'   jun   **a'laj**
that B3SG-DIR throw-DS   A3SG-RN:in   A3SG-mouth   one   green
chulal
sapodilla
'. . . that he would throw a green sapodilla in his mouth. . .' {MAM007R006.272}

(6) Txuk   Ø=Ø=xi'   q'i-'n   xjaal   t-witz
directly   DEP.PFV=B3SG=DIR   take-DS   person   A3SG-RN:on
jun   xaq   **matiij**.
one   cliff big
'The person was taken to a big cliff.' {AILLA MAM007R007.38}

(7) t-u'nj   nim   t-xiim-b'il   **b'a'n** ojtxa
A3SG-RN:because   many   A3SG-think-INST   good   before
'. . . because of many good ideas then.' {AILLA MAM007R001.130}

In the south, however, adjectives that follow nouns are interpreted as relative clauses (Pérez and Jiménez 1997:245–6). Thus adjectives can still precede nouns even when there are other modifiers, as in (8), and adjectives after nouns are the base for a non-verbal predicate in a relative clause (9). José Pérez Vail, however (p.c.) says that he thinks this is an overgeneralization – adjectives that follow nouns are not always relative clauses. (In the north the relative clause interpretation may be possible but is generally not given.)

CAJOLÁ (south)

(8) E'ye'   kaaje'   **keq**   xb'aalin   Ø=e'   tzaj   w-i'n=e'.
    DEM   four   red   blanket   PFV=B3PL   DIR   A1SG-bring=1SG
    'I brought the four red blankets.'

(9) Ø=Ø=tzaj   w-i'n=e'   xb'aalin   [**saq**].
    PFV=B3SG=DIR   A1SG-bring=1SG   blanket   white
    'I brought the blanket that is white.'

This analysis cannot be extended to Tacaná, however, because the head nouns that relative clauses modify are obligatorily preceded by *je*, which the examples in (2) above do not have, while that in (10) does (Munson 1984):

TACANÁ

(10) **je**   xhwook'   kaawaay   [Ø=Ø=ok   xajoo-n=te   w-ee]
     DEM   thin   horse   PFV=B3SG=DIR   kick-AP=PAT   A1SG-RN:PAT
     'The skinny horse that kicked me. . .'

Another point of interest with regard to adjectives is that they are used relatively infrequently. In 2,500 clauses only about 20 adjectives were used in noun phrases and a few more were found as the heads of non-verbal predicates. Finally, adjectives can themselves be modified by intensifiers or attenuators as in (11).

IXTAHUACÁN (England 2004:136)

(11) jun   ni   nuxh-**yiin**   b'ix   jun   matiij-**yiin**.
     one   DIM   small-ATT   and   one   big-ATT
     '. . . one a little small and one a little bigger.' {AILLA MAM007R010.104}

Mam has acquired noun classifiers from Q'anjob'alan languages. It has particularly elaborated the set for humans, but has only one for non-humans. There are about a dozen noun classifiers in the north, only a few in the south, and none in the west. In Todos Santos and the south noun classifiers can accompany nouns, as in Q'anjob'alan languages; in Ixtahuacán, however, they can only be used anaphorically, as in (12).

IXTAHUACÁN

(12) 'And I started to talk with Andrés Pérez,'
     n=Ø=xi'=tzan   n-ma-'n=a   t-ee=**ma**
     IPFV=B3SG=DIR=well   A1SG-say-DS=1SG   A3SG-RN:DAT=CLF:M
     'and I said to him. . .' {AILLA MAM007R011.137–138}

Mam, like Teko (Pérez Vail 2007) and Yucatec (Lehmann 1998), but unlike other Mayan languages, has food classifiers. These take the form of what have been called genitive classifiers. One of the hypernyms for food should accompany any specific food item that is mentioned and takes a Set A possessive marker in this structure (Pérez and Jiménez 1997:145–6). These hypernyms take a suffix when used independently in an unpossessed form and are also related to verb roots for 'eating' that similarly classify the thing being eaten. In Ixtahuacán there are five terms: *chib'aj* 'meat, beans, eggs, vegetables', *lo'j* 'fruit', *waa'j* 'corn, corn products, analogous foods like bread', *k'uxb'aj* 'roasting ear of corn and crunchy foods', *k'a'j* 'beverages' (England 1980). An example with a food classifier follows.

IXTAHUACÁN

(13) Toons jaa=tzan   n=∅=tzaaj-a   t-e   weech   **t-waa**
     well   where=well   IPFV=B3SG=come-?   A3SG-RN   fox   A3SG-food
        t-b'an-el   axi'n,
        A3SG-good-ABST   corn
     'So, from where does the fox bring his good corn food. . .' {AILLA
     MAM007R004.11}

Although Mam does not have numeral classifiers, as some other Mayan languages do, it has measure words, which specify quantities of something that is being counted. These words either specify aggregations of that which is to be counted, such as 'bundle' or 'group', or they specify a quantity that is a part that is separated from a larger unit, such as 'bite' or 'drop'. They can also specify an action for the purpose of counting, for instance, a 'wash' or a 'jump' (Pérez and Jiménez 1997:150). The structure of a phrase with a measure word is number + measure + (N), where N can be analyzed as a specifier noun that follows the head noun (the measure word). (14) has a part-of-whole measure term, (15) shows an aggregate measure, and (16) contains an action measure.

IXTAHUACÁN

(14) b'ix at=∅   jun **miij** kjo'n   tok   naqaa'.
     and   EXIST=B3SG   one piece   cornfield   placed   near
     '. . . and there was a piece of the cornfield nearby.' {AILLA MAM007R007.91}

(15) yaa ma   ∅=kyekaj   ky-iyaj-iil   jun **k'loj** xjaal,
     now   PROX   B3SG=stay   A3PL-seed-ABST   one group   person
     '. . . and now the seed of a group of people stayed. . .' {AILLA MAM007R002.132}

CAJOLÁ (Pérez and Jiménez 1997:150)

(16) kab'e **chit**   a'   s=ok   t-chto-'n   w-i'j-e'
     two   splash   water   DEP.PROX;B3SG=DIR   A3SG-put-DS   A1SG-RN:goal-1SG
     'S/he threw two splashes of water at me.'

Mam does not have definite articles, probably the original situation in Mayan languages. It only has the indefinite article *jun* (also the number 'one'). Its absence indicates either a definite or generic NP; which of these it is must be determined from context. Table 19.5 shows the order ot the elements in the noun phrase.

3.4 Verbs

As in all Mayan languages, transitive and intransitive verbs are for the most part quite clearly morphologically differentiated in Mam, both on the grounds of inflection (§3.1) and because some sort of derivation is necessary to convert one to the other. One unusual feature of Mam is that transitive verbs are preferentially, and in the north almost obligatorily, accompanied by directionals. These are phonologically eroded forms that come

TABLE 19.5 ORDER OF ELEMENTS IN THE NP

demonstrative	number	measure	adjective	plural	noun	possessor	(adjective)	relative clause

TABLE 19.6 DIRECTIONALS

Ixtahuacán	Cajolá	Tacaná	
xi'	xi'	xi	'here to there; incipient'
tzaj	tzaj	tza	'there to here'
ul	ul	ul	'hither'
pon	pon	pon	'thither'
kub'	kub'	ku	'downward'
jaw	jaw	ja	'upward'
el	el	e	'outward; to the west'
ok	ok	ok	'inward; to the east'
kyaj	kej	koj	'remaining; complete'
aj	anj	aj	'returning from here; motion behind'
iky'	ik'	ik'	'passing'
b'aj	b'aj	b'a	'complete'

from intransitive verbs of motion and indicate trajectory, deictic categories, or aspectual information. A verb with directionals expresses a single event.

On verbs, and unlike most other Mayan languages, the directionals usually precede the verb and follow Set B markers, except with intransitive verbs of motion themselves, where any of the deictic directionals can follow the verb root, or with all imperatives, where the directionals follow the imperative stem. In this position they are further eroded. The directionals are the same in different dialects of Mam, with very minor phonological adjustments. There are twelve basic directionals, which are given in Table 19.6 in their full forms. (For more information on the phonological changes, see England 1983a for Ixtahuacán and Pérez and Jiménez 1997 for Cajolá. Tacaná data used here comes from Munson 1984.)

The following examples from Ixtahuacán show a transitive verb without a directional (17), one with a directional (18), a transitive verb in the imperative (19), and an imperative transitive verb with a directional (20). (Directionals follow the stem in the imperative, and have phonologically degraded forms.)

IXTAHUACÁN
(17) ma   chi   t-tzeeq'a-ya
     PROX B3PL A2SG-hit-2SG
     'you (sg) hit them' {England 1983a:174}

(18) 'Is it possible that you could'
     xhin   ku'=x   t-iiqa-n   ch'in   wee'
     DEP.PROX;B1SG   DIR=DIR   A2SG-carry-DS   a.little   1SG.PRON
         t-witz   tx'otx'
         A3SG-RN:on   land
     'carry me down onto the land.' {AILLA MAM007R007.80–81}

IXTAHUACÁN

(19) chuux   Ø=ky-yoo-m=a   maajan   t-i'j
     hurry   B3SG=A2PL-look.for-IMP=2SG   worker   A3SG-RN:about
     'hurry, look for some workers for this' {AILLA MAM007R004.55}

(20) Ø=ky-laq'oo-n=x=a! (=x is from xi ')
     B3SG=A2PL-buy-IMP=DIR=2PL
     'buy it!' {AILLA MAM007R001.16}

Those that follow have an intransitive verb without a directional (21), one with a directional (22), an intransitive imperative (23), and an intransitive imperative with directionals (24).

(21) ma   ch=uul   meb'a-yi-l   t-ee   b'eeta-l
     PROX B3PL=come orphan-TR-AGT A3SG-RN:PAT walk-INF
     'When the foster parents came from traveling. . .' {AILLA MAM007R003.51}

(22) b'ix   n=chi   kub'   tzoqpaj   t-uj   b'ee
     and   IPFV-B3PL DIR   flee   A3SG-RN:in road
     '. . . and they fled down the road. . .' {AILLA MAM 007R001.18}

(23) mii'n=ajo   yaa'ya   txi'=ya
     NEG=DEM   grandmother   go=2SG
     'But no, grandmother, go!' {AILLA MAM007R003.214}

(24) chi=mok'-ee=ka=x=a   kyja'w (=ka is from kub'; =x is from xi ')
     B2PL=crouching-INTR=DIR=DIR=2PL thus
     'Crouch down like this! (you pl)' {AILLA MAM007R003.142}

It should be noted that when a transitive verb with directionals is in the potential aspect, it is the directional that takes the potential suffix, which has the intransitive form (25).

(25) qa   Ø=x-el   ky-laq'o-'n=a,
     if   B3SG=DIR-POT   A2PL-buy-DS=2PL
     '. . . if you want to buy it. . .' lit. 'if you will buy it' {AILLA MAM007R001.15}

3.5 Non-verbal predicates

Non-verbal predicates have a base that is a noun (26), adjective (including participles) (27), positional (28), demonstrative (29), the existential predicate (a)t (30), or the negative existential nti' ~ mixhti' ~ tiilo' (31).

IXTAHUACÁN

(26) sinoke   xhii'=Ø=na=qa=jal;
     instead bottle.gourd=B3SG=AFFIRM=PL=CLF:non-human
     '. . . instead they were bottle gourds. . .' {AILLA MAM007R001.110}

(27) li   tx'apo-'n=Ø=qa=kya   nimaal t-jee'   kuch.
     EXCLAM   insert-PTCP=B3SG=PL=3PL.EMPH   AUG   A3SG-tail pig
     '. . . the pig's tails were inserted.' {AILLA MAM 007R001.87}

(28) **xhliky-le**=qe'   t-aa'lan   meeb'a.
     germinated-POS=B3PL   A3SG-animal   orphan
     '. . . the orphan's animals were germinated.' {AILLA MAM007R003.228}

(29) **Aa**=qa=tzan   aj   xmaxh,
     DEM=3PL=well   DEM   monkey
     'These are the monkeys. . .' {AILLA MAM007R003.196}

(30) Jaa=tzan   **t**=e'   q-ryaat,
     where=well   EXIST=B3PL   A1PL-rope
     'Where are our ropes?' {AILLA MAM007R001.54}

(31) per   **nti'**=∅   sii'   b'ix-mo   q'aaq'   t-i'j,
     but   NEG=B3SG   firewood   and-or   fire   A3SG-RN:purpose
     '. . . but there wasn't any firewood or fire for it. . .' {AILLA MAM007R001.7}

Set B markers (with some modifications) are suffixed to the base in agreement with the subject, as in Table 19.7. There are several different forms for person marking depending on whether the base is a demonstrative (*aa*), the existential (*at*), or a noun, adjective, or positional. Some form of a Set B marker (in bold) plus the person enclitics (separated with =) are added to the base. The details differ substantially for each dialect or dialect region.

TABLE 19.7 PERSON MARKING ON NON-VERBAL PREDICATES

Demonstrative (aa)	Ixtahuacán (north)	Ostuncalco (south)	Tacaná (west)
'it is I; I am'	aa **qiin**=a	**aayin**=e'	aa'**iin**
'it is you; you are'	aa=ya	aa=ya	aa=ya
'it is s/he; s/he is'	aa	a	aa
'it is us; we are (excl)'	aa**qo'**=ya	aayo' **qo'**=ye'	aa'**o'**=yo'
'it is us; we are (incl)'	aa**qo'**	aayo' **qo'**	aa'**o'**
'it is you; you (pl) are'	aa**qa**=ya	aaye' **qe'**=ye'	aa'**e'**=ye'
'it is them; they are'	aa**qa**	aaye' **qe'**	*aa'e'*
Existential (**at**)			
'I am (in a place)'	at**iin**=a	atiin **qin**=e'	at**iin**
'you are (in a place)'	at=a	atii=ya	at=a
's/he is (in a place)'	at	ati	at
'we (excl) are. . .'	at**o'**=ya	ato' **qo'**=ye'	at**o'**=yo'
'we (incl) are. . .'	at**o'**	ato' **qo'**	at**o'**
'you (pl) are. . .'	at**e'**=ya	ate' **qe**=ye'	at**e'**=ye'
'they are. . .'	at**e'**	ate' **qe'**	at**e'**
Noun (xu'j or qyaa 'woman')			
'I am a woman'	xu'j **qiin**=a	qya **qin**=e'	xu'j aa'**iin**
'you are a woman'	xu'j=a	qyaa=ya	xu'j aa=ya
's/he is a woman'	xu'j	qya	xu'j
'we are women (excl)'	xu'j **qo'**=ya	qya **qo'**=ye'	xu'j aa'**o'**=yo'
'we are women (incl)'	xu'j **qo'**	qya **qo'**	xu'j aa'**o'**
'you (pl) are women'	xu'j**qa**=ya	qya **qe'**=ye'	xu'je'=ye'
'they are women'	xu'j**qa**	qya **qe'**	xu'j**e'**

(England 1990:235)

The main difference between non-verbal predicates and verbal predicates is that the former do not take aspect markers, although they can take the aspectual enclitic *taq ~ toq* (32). They can also take directionals in the south (33) (Pérez and Jiménez 1997:273–4), but not in the north. It appears from the examples that this is restricted to participle or positional bases, however.

CAJOLÁ (Pérez and Jiménez 1997:274)
(32) Sak'=**toq**   te'   B'ixh.
     diligent=IPRF   B3SG.EMPH   B'ixh
     'B'ixh was diligent.'

(33) Q'ma-'n=Ø=**kj**   q-naa-b'l   k-u'n   q-chman
     say-PTCP=B3SG=DIR   A1PL-think-INST   A3SG-RN:AGT   A1PL-grandfather
     'Our grandfathers have left us advice.'

3.6 Positionals and affect words

Mayan languages have two word classes that are particular to the family. Positionals are a class of roots that describe a combination of position and physical characteristics of an object and must be derived to form words. In Mam the typical derivations that apply to positional roots are *-l/-ch* which forms the positional stative predicate (sometimes called a positional adjective), *-ee'* which forms an intransitive verb meaning 'assume the position described by the root)' and *-b'aa* which derives a transitive verb meaning 'place in the position described by the root'. In Ixtahuacán, for instance, the root *mutz* 'upside down' forms *mutzl* 'upside down', *mutzee'-* 'assume an upside down position', and *mutzb'aa-* 'place upside down'.

The number of positional roots in the language is very large (several hundred), although perhaps not as large as in the Q'anjob'alan languages, which may have more than 600 positionals. (Laura Martin (1977) worked with a database of 270 positional roots in Q'anjob'al, but self-elicitation with Popti' and Q'anjob'al speakers easily yields more than 600 positional roots.) The roots are restricted to CVC shapes in general, although in Mam they can also be of the shape CVnC, for instance *b'onk-* 'a fat person in a standing or sitting position'. Positional *stems* are also (unusually) found in Mam; these consist of positional roots with the *x- ~ xh- ~ s- ~ ch-* prefix that derives words of similar meanings from roots of various classes (with no change in the class). An example is *xhpalch* 'thrown down or placed: long thing' vs. *palch* 'lying down, placed, thrown: something cylindrical' (Maldonado Andrés et al. 1986). The meanings of the root form and the derived form are often the same, and not all derived forms are matched by a root form.

Positional stative predicates can never directly modify nouns. Furthermore, they are always pre-verbal and trigger split ergativity when followed by verbs (§4.1), a Huehuetenango contact area feature. They function as manner adverbs or possibly secondary predicates, although in Mam it has been difficult so far to distinguish these functions.

IXTAHUACÁN
(34) tzin-li=Ø   t-witz
     tight-POS-B3SG   A3SG-RN:over
     '. . . he was tightly (stuck). . .' {AILLA MAM007R006.87}

OSTUNCALCO (South) (England 1990:248)
(35) wa'-l   t-pon
     standing-POS   A3SG-arrive.there
     'S/he arrived standing.'

Affect words are either root or derived forms that name an action, a sound, or an action and its accompanying sound. There are many affect roots, but also many derived forms. In an analysis of the Mam dictionary of about 6,000 entries (Maldonado Andrés et al. 1986), 319 affect words were found, of which 119 were not related to any other forms and the rest were. Of these, many shared roots with words of other classes: 51 with positionals, 25 with transitive verbs, 3 with both, and 15 with nouns. In some cases the affect word seems to be semantically derived from a root of another class, although without any derivational affix, and in others the semantics suggest that the root is basically an affect base and the other forms are derived. However, there are also affixes that derive affect words from other words. Affect words are also often first in a sentence, but unlike positionals, they seem to be more flexible in their position and can occur after a verb or at the end of a clause as well. When they are first in a sentence, they may trigger split ergativity, as in (36), or they may be followed by a dependent aspect marker, as in (37).

IXTAHUACÁN

(36) t'ab'   **t-tzy-eet**   t-u'n   tiiya
    AFF:action.trap.in.mouth   A3SG-grab-PSV   A3SG-RN:AGT   uncle
    '. . . snap! uncle (coyote) grabbed it. . .' {AILLA MAM007R006.251}

(37) t'ab'   **x-Ø-xi'**   waa'j   t-u'n   tal   b'ink   t-uj
    AFF   DEP.PROX-B3SG-go   tortilla   A3SG-RN:AGT   DIM   dog   A3SG-RN:in
    t-q'ab'   tal   k'waal
    A3SG-hand   DIM   child
    'Snap! the small dog snatched the tortilla from the baby's hands.' {Maldonado Andrés et al.: 361}

3.7 Relational nouns

Relational nouns are a closed class of always possessed nouns which introduce locative phrases and clausal participants other than the main arguments, and indicate reflexives/reciprocals. They also are used to mark possessive relations pronominally, to create comparative adjectival structures, and to introduce purpose and reason subordinate clauses. They agree in person and number with their complements through Set A prefixes. Thus structurally a relational noun phrase is similar to a possessed noun phrase, where the relational noun is parallel to the possessed noun and the complement is like the possessor (Table 19.8).

When they are used to introduce subordinate clauses they are always marked in the third person singular; otherwise person and number are open. The relational nouns are very similar in all dialects. In Ixtahuacán they are:

TABLE 19.8 POSSESSED NOUN PHRASES AND RELATIONAL NOUN PHRASES

Possessed noun phrase		*Relational noun phrase*	
t-jaa	xu'j	t-uj	jaa
A3SG-house	woman	A3SG-RN:in	house
Set a-possessed N	*possessor*	*Set A-relational N*	*complement*
'the woman's house'		'in the house'	

Locatives:		Grammatical functions:	
t-witz	'on; in front of'	t-u'n	agent; causative; instrument;
t-i'j	'behind'		purpose clause
t-xeel	'instead of'	t-u'nj	reason clause
t-xool	'between'	t-i'j	patient; malefactive; theme
t-txlaj	'beside'	t-uuk'(al)	instrument; comitative
t-iib'(aj)	'over'	t-ee	possessive; dative; benefactive;
t-wi'	'above'	patient;	topic
t-jaq'	'below'	t-iib'	reflexive/reciprocal
t-xe	'under'	t-witz	comparative
t-uj	'in'		
t-txa'n	'at the edge of'		
t-b'utx'	'at the corner of'		
t-tzii'	'at the entrance of'		

Example (38) shows a locative relational noun, (39) is an agentive, (40) is a reciprocal, (41) shows a comparative adjective introduced by *twitz*, and (42) has a relational noun introducing a purpose clause.

IXTAHUACÁN

(38) nn=Ø=uul   jun   chepaneek   ky-**xool**=q'a.
     IPFV=B3SG=come   one   Chiapaneco   A3PL-RN:among=CLF:M
     '... a Chiapaneco (possibly a deity) came among them.' {AILLA MAM007R002.41}

(39) tii   k=ook-al   q-**u'n**?
     what   B3SG=enter-POT   A1PL-RN:AGT
     '... what are we going to do?' *lit.* 'what will go in by us?' {AILLA MAM007R001.81}

(40) b'ala   ky-tiiya=Ø   ky-**iib'**
     maybe   A3PL-uncle=B3SG   A3PL-RN:RR
     '... maybe they were uncles (reciprocally). . .' {AILLA MAM007R008.78}
     ('uncle' is a term of respect, which is how two individuals can be 'uncles' to each other)

CAJOLÁ (Pérez and Jiménez 1997:227)

(41) b'a'n=Ø=x   ch'i'n=tl   a'q'inl   lu   **t-witz**   jun=tl
     good=B3SG=still   a.little=other   work   DEM   A3SG-RN:compare   one=other
     'This work is a little better than that other.'

IXTAHUACÁN

(42) 'They put a pitcher down by itself on the ground'
     t-u'n   t-tzq'aaj   ky-chi',
     A3SG-RN:PURP   A3SG-cook   A3PL-food
     'for their food to cook. . .' {AILLA MAM007R001.21}

4 SIMPLE CLAUSE STRUCTURE

4.1 Arguments and alignment

Mam, like all Mayan languages, is morphologically an ergative language and is syntactically ergative as well. Nouns are not marked for case, but transitive subjects are cross-referenced on the verb with Set A markers (43), while transitive objects and intransitive subjects are marked on the verb with Set B markers (43) and (44).

IXTAHUACÁN

(43) n=**ch**=iky'   t-ii-'kj   kuch,
     IPFV=B3PL=DIR   A3SG-take-MOV   pig
     '. . . he went and took the pigs. . .' {AILLA MAM007R001.71}

(44) Entoons   n=**chi**   tzaaj   Pich,
     well   IPFV=B3PL   come   Pich
     'So the Piches came' {AILLA MAM007R007.149}

In addition, the subjects of non-verbal predicates are indicated on the predicate with Set B markers (45).

(45) aqaj   xjaal   t=**e'**   maa   Tuj.Ch'yaq
     DEM.PL   person   EXIST=B3PL   there   Tuchiac
     '. . . the people who are there in Tuchiac. . .' {AILLA MAM007R011.154}

Mam shows split-ergative alignment, since under certain conditions the agreement pattern no longer is ergative. Under these conditions all verbal arguments are marked with Set A markers, constituting a kind of super-extended ergative marking. (46) has an intransitive verb marked with Set A, while in (47) both the object and subject of a transitive verb are marked with Set A.

IXTAHUACÁN

(46) ky-aaj=tz   kab'-a   komersyaanta   maax   t-uj   Melaaj
     A3PL-return=DIR   two-?   merchant   there   A3SG-RN:in   Tapachula
     '. . . when two merchants returned from there in Tapachula. . .' {AILLA
     MAM007R002.28}

(47) ok   t-ku'-x   **ky-awa-'n**   xjaal   kjo'n
     when:POT   A3SG-DIR-DIR   A3PL-plant-DS   person   cornfield
     'When the people plant the cornfield . . . ' {England 2013b: 120}

The conditions that trigger non-ergative alignment include temporal clauses, purpose and result clauses, and occurrence after affect words, positional stative predicates, and several adverbs (England 1983a). The clauses with non-ergative alignment are in all instances aspectless (England 2013a).

The question about whether ergativity extends to the syntax arises with any language that is morphologically ergative, and in some it does while in others it does not. Mam is a language which definitely has several syntactic rules that reflect ergative alignment. The first and the most often cited as characteristic of some Mayan languages is that transitive subjects (ergative) cannot be extracted for purposes such as focus or interrogation, while intransitive subjects and transitive objects (absolutive) can (see e.g., England 1983b, 1990). Example (48a) is an intransitive sentence, while (48b) shows the subject extracted for focus.

IXTAHUACÁN

(48) a. ma   chi   b'eet   xiinaq
        PROX   B3PL   walk   man
        'The men walked.'

b. **aa   xiinaq** ma   chi   b'eet
    DEM man   PROX B3PL walk
    'It was the men who walked.'

In (49a) there is a transitive sentence, (49b) shows the object extracted for focus, (49c) shows that it is ungrammatical to extract the subject in the same way, and (49d) shows that the subject can be extracted if the verb is converted to an intransitive verb via the antipassive suffix.

(49) a. ma   chi   kub' ky-tzyu-'n   xiinaq cheej
         PROX B3PL DIR   A3PL-grab-DS man   horse
         'The men grabbed the horses.'

    b. **aa   cheej** ma   chi   kub' ky-tzyu-'n   xiinaq
        DEM horse PROX B3PL DIR   A3PL-grab-DS man
        'It was the horses that the men grabbed.'

    c. *aqaj/aa xiinaq ma chi kub' ky-tzyu-'n cheej
        Intended meaning: 'It was the men who grabbed the horses.'

    d. **aa   xiinaq** ma   chi   tzyuu-**n** ky-i'j   cheej
        DEM man   PROX B3PL grab-AP A3PL-RN:PAT horse
        'It was the men who grabbed the horses.'

Another area in which the effect of ergative alignment is seen is in the control of the subject of an infinitive. Only absolute arguments in the matrix clause (including the subjects of non-verbal predicates) can control the subject of an infinitive, while the ergative argument cannot. Examples (50) through (52) show control on the part of an intransitive subject, a transitive object, and a non-verbal predicate subject, respectively, while (53) shows that transitive subjects do not show control of an infinitive. No transitive verbs whose subjects control an infinitive have been found; (62) below is another example with the verb 'to want' in the matrix clause and a finite verb in the complement.

IXTAHUACÁN
Intransitive Subject
(50) Yaj=xa=tl   n=Ø=xi'   patroon [lo-l   ky-ee
      and=still=another IPFV=B3SG=go boss   see-INF A3PL-RN:PAT
      t-waakxh]
      A3SG-cow
      '. . . and the boss went to see his cows. . .' {AILLA MAM007R001.117}
      Transitive Object

(51) ma   **tz'**=ok   n-q'o-'n=a   [tx'eema-l sii']
      PROX B3SG=DIR A1SG-give-DS=1SG cut-INF   firewood
      'I had him cut firewood.' {England 2013a:287}
      Non-verbal Predicate

(52) **Qiina** [kaana-l   t-i'j   kasamyeent]
      B1SG   meet-INF B3SG-RN:goal wedding
      'I'm going to catch up to the wedding. . .'{AILLA MAM007R006.205}
      Transitive Subject (no control)

(53) a. x=∅=kub'=tzan   q-xii'ma-n=a   t-i'j
    DEP.PROX=B3SG=DIR=well   A1PL-think-DS=1PL.EXCL   A3SG-RN:about
    [t-u'n   t-tzaaj   juun   q-a'=ya]
    A3SG-RN:PURP   A3SG-come   one   A1PL-water=1PL.EXCL
    'Well, we thought of bringing (running) water.' *lit.* 'Well, we thought about it so
    that the water would come.' {AILLA MAM007R011.23–24}

    b. *x=∅=kub'=tzan   q-xii'ma-n=a   [q'ii-l a']
    DEP.PROX=B3SG=DIR=well   A1PL-think-DS=1PL.EXCL   bring-INF water
    Intended meaning: 'We thought to bring water.' {England 2013a:285}

Another complication in the alignment patterns is that Mam, at least in the south, does
not permit active clauses when the object of a transitive verb outranks the subject according to a hierarchy in which local persons (first and second person) are higher than third
person. The usual way to express a situation in which a third person acts on a first or
second person is to use a passive. In (54a) a second person acts on a third person, but
(54b) shows that the reverse is not possible, and (54c) shows that a passive can be used to
express the meaning that was intended in (54b) (Cajolá; Pérez Vail 2014:142). Note that
this particular passive, which is the preferred form for expressing these constructions, is
not morphologically marked. It is also used for an unknown or unspecified agent.

CAJOLÁ
(54) a. ma   **chi**   kub'   **t**-tzyu-'n=a
    PROX   B3PL   DIR   A2SG-grab-DS=2SG
    'you grabbed them'

    b. *ma   ∅=kub'   **k**-tzyu-'n=a
    PROX   B2SG=DIR   A3PL-grab-DS=2SG
    Intended meaning: 'they grabbed you'

    c. ma   ∅=kub'   tzyu-'n=a **k**-u'n
    PROX   B2SG=DIR   grab-DS=2SG A3PL-RN:AGT
    'you were grabbed by them'

The pattern shown by Pérez Vail is a clear case of inverse organization in the person-
marking system. Although there is no inverse morphology, the possibility of expressing
a particular meaning with an active verb, as analyzed by Pérez Vail, is direct, while the
necessity of using a non-active verb such as the passive is the inverse. It is unclear whether
this pattern is as absolute in the north and west. A paradigm in England (1983a:62–83)
shows the possibility of a third person subject with a first person inclusive object in Ixtahuacán, as in (55). However, the same paradigm has gaps for the remaining third person
acting on first or second person forms (i.e., for 3>1SG, 3>1EXCL and 3>2).

IXTAHUACÁN
(55) a. ma   **qo**   ok   **t**-tzeeq'a-n
    PROX   B1PL   DIR   A3SG-hit-DS
    'he/she/it hit us (incl)'

    b. ma   **qo**   ok   **ky**-tzeeq'a-n
    PROX   B1PL   DIR   A3SG-hit-DS
    'they hit us (incl)'

Munson (1984) has an example of an active verb with a third person acting on a first person in Tacaná (56), so at least some of the forms that in Cajolá would be inverse (not active) can be active in the west.

TACANÁ
(56) ma'   **kyin**   ku   **t**-b'uju-'n
     PROX   B1SG   DIR   A3SG-hit-DS
     's/he hit me'

It appears from the very little data at hand that there is a partially similar inverse pattern in the north and that it may not extend to the west. However, since the question of the limitations on third person subjects with local person objects was not further explored by either of these authors, the most that can be said at this time is that the geographical extent and the exact nature of the prohibition in each place needs to be investigated.

In addition to showing that the Mam of Cajolá has an inverse system of organizing local and third person participants, Pérez Vail (2014) has further shown that direct and inverse relations also pertain to third person participants on the basis of obviation. Some participants can be analyzed as proximate and others as obviative on the basis of features such as animacy, definiteness, coreferential genitives, lexical class, and topicality. (This pattern was first noted in terms of animacy only by Eduardo Pérez (Pérez and Jiménez 1997:334–5) and later by his teacher Seth Minkoff, relying on his work (Minkoff 2000), but neither analyzed it in terms of obviation.) For each of these features a hierarchy can be established in which if the third person subject of a transitive verb is higher than the object (for instance higher in animacy, definite rather than indefinite, more topical, etc.) then an active verb can be used, while if the object is higher than the subject in one of these features an active verb cannot be used. Instead of using the active verb (a direct form), a passive, antipassive, or other intransitive form must be used (an inverse form). Thus, for instance, a human noun (proximate) can act on an animal (obviative) with an active (direct) verb, as in (57).

CAJOLÁ
(57) Ma   chi   jaw   t-chle-'n   Wa'n   tx'yan
     PROX   B3PL   DIR   A3SG-hug-DS   Juan   dog
     'Juan hugged the dog.' {Pérez Vail 2014:185}

However, if an animal (obviative) acts on a human (proximate), then a non-active form such as the passive (inverse) is required, as in (58).

(58) a.   Ma   tz'-ok   xjo-'n   tal   k'waal   t-u'n   cheej
           PROX   B3SG-DIR   kick-DS   DIM   child   A3SG-RN:AGT   horse
           'The child was kicked by the horse.'

     b.   *Ma   tz'-ok   t-xjo-'n   cheej   tal   k'waal
            PROX   B3SG-DIR   A3SG-kick-DS   horse   DIM   child
            Intended meaning: 'The horse kicked the child.' {Pérez Vail 2014:186}

Obviation has not been discussed for any other region, so it is unknown how general the system is in Mam. In the texts from Ixtahuacán, all examples of clauses in which the agent is less animate than the patient (usually an animal acting on a human) have either an intransitive verb with an oblique agent (the preferred form) or a passive verb, usually the unmarked passive (see (63) for an example with an intransitive verb). However, no one has ascertained whether these forms are obligatory or not, and the texts also have many examples of the same verb forms being used when the subject is higher than the object in animacy (although active forms are also used when this is the case). It is quite possible that the obviation patterns will be found to extend to the north and may be general in Mam.

4.2 Peripheral arguments

All arguments other than direct subjects and objects are introduced by relational nouns marked for Set A to index their complements. If the participant is third person, it can be expressed nominally as well as by the Set A marker on the relational noun, as in examples (59)–(61). Example (59) shows an indirect object introduced by the relational noun *te*, (60) has a malefactive introduced by *kyi'j*, and (61) shows an instrument marked by *tu'n*.

IXTAHUACÁN

(59) Ø=Ø=ok   q'ama-'n **t-e**   ky'aq.
    DEP.PFV=B3SG=DIR   say-DS   A3SG-RN:DAT pulga
    '. . . when he spoke with the flea . . . ' {AILLA MAM007R004.29}

(60) aj   oo=taq   tz'=ajb'laana-n **ky-i'j**   t'iiw,
    DEM   PFV=PRF B3SG=use-AP   A3PL-RN:MAL eagle
    '. . . that which he had used against the eagles. . .' {AILLA MAM007R007.230}

(61) n=Ø=ku'=tz   t-uub'a-n   **t-u'n**   jun ajlaaj
    IPFV=B3SG=DIR=DIR   A3SG-shoot.with.blowgun-DS   A3SG-RN:INST one reed
    '. . . he shot it with a reed. . .' {AILLA MAM007R003.19}

Agents or patients can be expressed as peripheral arguments when a transitive verb is converted to an intransitive through the antipassive (patient) or one of the passives (agent), when an infinitive is used (patient), or when an intransitive verb is used with an agentive relational noun. The second verb in (62) is antipassive, it agrees with the agent, and the patient is expressed as an oblique with the relational noun *ti'j*. The verb in (63) is intransitive, and an agent is added as an oblique introduced by the relational noun *tu'n*.

IXTAHUACÁN

(62) qapa   t-aj=a   Ø=loq'a-n=a   **t-i'j**   txqan waakxh
    maybe   A2SG-want=2SSG   B2SG=buy-AP=2SG   A3SG-RN:PAT group cow
    '. . . maybe you want to buy some cows. . .' *lit.* '. . . maybe you want you buy
    some cows. . .' {AILLA 007R001.99–100}

(63) juk'   t-jaaw   xjaal   **t-u'n**=jal,
    AFF:pulling   A3SG-go.up   person A3SG-RN:AGT=CLF:non-human
    '. . . whoosh! it (eagle) lifted the person. . .' *lit.* '. . . whoosh! the person went up
    by it. . .' {AILLA MAM007R007.34}

Between direct argument marking on the verb and complement marking on relational nouns, almost every noun phrase is marked for function somewhere. In the example in (64) the subject, *xhoq'*, is marked on the verb with Set B (in this example, zero), *jul* is marked on the locative relational noun *tzi*, *xhooch* is also marked on a second *tzi*, and *xu'j* is marked as the agent with the relational noun *kyu'n*.

IXTAHUACÁN

(64) noq   gaana   n=Ø=toowa-j   xhoq'
      only   in.vain IPFV=B3SG=carry.empty-PSV water.jar

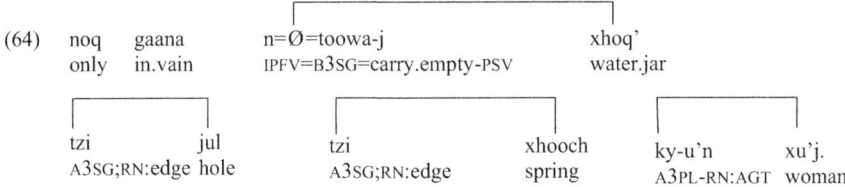

      tzi   jul   tzi   xhooch   ky-u'n   xu'j.
      A3SG;RN:edge hole   A3SG;RN:edge spring   A3PL-RN:AGT   woman

'. . . and it is for nothing that the empty water jars are carried to the edge of the springs by the women.' {AILLA MAM007R011.2}

Like all Mayan languages, Mam uses a relational noun to indicate a reflexive/reciprocal. Also like the other languages, a verb with the reflexive/reciprocal never has an overt form of Set B, while Set A varies with the person and number of the subject. Unlike other Mayan languages, however, the verb in Mam is marked with an *antipassive* suffix while maintaining the Set A marking. Its structure therefore does not quite conform to that of an ordinary transitive verb. Example (65) contains a reflexive; if the verb were not in the antipassive its form would be *tee 'wan*.

IXTAHUACÁN

(65) n=Ø=xi'   **t-eewa-n**   naaj   t-iib'=jal
      IPFV=B3SG=DIR   A3SG-hide-AP   lost   A3SG-RN:RR=CLF:non-human
      t-uj   tzmaal   weech.
      A3SG-RN:in   A3SG;hair   fox
      '. . . it (flea) went to hide itself in the fox's fur.' {AILLA MAM007R004.49}

4.3 Voice

Mam has an antipassive in -*n*, and at least five or more different passives, of which at least two (-*Vt* and Ø) are general syntactic passives. The passives are not quite the same in all dialects (see Pérez Vail 2014 for a detailed discussion of passives in Cajolá and a comparison of some of them with other dialects), but are close. With the possible exceptions of two dialects (Todos Santos (Dayley 1983 from Canger 1969) and Tacaná (Munson 1984), see below), Mam does not ever have an agent focus form of the verb in which the person marker on the verb agrees with the patient; when it needs a special verb form for agent focus the verb agrees with the agent and is in the antipassive. Mam does not have an applicative in any of the functions that have been found in other Mayan languages.

The antipassive is used in all of the functions that have been noted for it in Mayan languages, without any difference in form: the absolutive antipassive for an unknown or unmentioned patient, the object incorporation antipassive, the agent focus antipassive, and a lexical antipassive. The absolutive antipassive is the most frequently used of the different types (66).

IXTAHUACÁN

(66) N=Ø=aq'naa-n   xjaal   t-miij   tx'otx'
      IPFV=B3SG=work-AP   person   A3SG-middle   land
      'The person was working in the middle of the land. . .' {AILLA MAM007R007.31}

An interesting feature of the antipassive of incorporation in Southern Mam is that if there is an enclitic associated with the person marker on the verb, it will occur *after* the incorporated noun (which is always non-specific). Thus in (67) the enclitic =*e'* which is associated with first person singular comes after *kxminch'il.*

CAJOLÁ (Pérez Vail 2014:123)
(67) ex   ma   chin   k'aayi-n   kxminch'il=**e'**
     and   PROX   B1SG   sell-AP   cherry=1SG
     'And I also sold cherries.'

In Northern Mam the enclitic follows the verb, not the incorporated object. Thus in (68) the enclitic =*ya* occurs aftern *k'aanka-*, the verb, and not after *a'*, the object.

IXTAHUACÁN
(68) Baqa   n-chin   k'aa-n=ka=**ya**   a'   chi=chi=tzan   xjaal
     scarcely   IPFV-B1SG   drink-AP=but=1SG   water   B3PL=say=well   people
     kyja'
     like.this
     'But I'm hardly drinking water like this, say the people.' {AILLA
     MAM007R011.35}

The only context in which Northern Mam as well as Southern Mam places the person enclitic after an incorporated object is with the reflexive, where the reflexive relational noun is the incorporated object and always bears the enclitic:

IXTAHUACÁN
(69) aa=tzan   kyee'   mii'n   tz'=ok   ky'q'oo'n
     DEM=well   2PL.PRON   NEG:IRR   B3SG=DIR:enter   A2PL-give-AP
     ky-iib'=**a**   t-i'j,
     A2PL-RN:RR=2PL   A3SG-RN:concerning
     'and you will not include yourselves with respect to this' {AILLA
     MAM007R011.401}

The antipassive in Mam is required for the extraction of transitive subjects. The patient, if expressed, is in a relational noun phrase. This was discussed in §4.1; (70) is another example, from a text. The agent is in preverbal position; it has been extracted for focus, and requires the antipassive. In almost all dialects, the verb agrees with the agent, as in (70).

IXTAHUACÁN
(70) ax   b'a'n   ky-ky'aq   chi=choo-n   q-i'j
     also   good   A3PL-flea   B3PL=eat-AP   A1PL-RN:PAT
     '. . . that the fleas eat us. . .' {AILLA MAM007R004.42}

In Todos Santos, however, the verb appears to index the patient, which is also expressed in a relational noun phrase (71).

TODOS SANTOS (Canger 1969:111)
(71) na'yan   e   Ø-kub'   b'yo-n   **t-e**   n-man
     I   ASP   B3SG-DIR   hit-AP   A3SG-RN:PAT   A1SG-father
     'It was I who hit my father.'

It is possible (but unclear) that in Todos Santos the verb can be marked for a plural patient (*chi*) as well as a singular one (Ø), but the only example in Canger (1969:130) has a plural marker on the verb and a singular relational noun and is translated with a singular patient. Dayley 1983 left off the singular relational noun and translated the example in the plural. It is unclear which is correct; possibly neither.

The pattern in Tacaná is also different from other dialects, in that the verb is always marked with a third person singular Set B marker (usually Ø), no matter what the agent or patient is, and the patient is indicated in a relational noun phrase, as in (72). This suggests a biclausal structure where the verb indexes the first clause. Clearly more data is needed on this structure in Mam dialects.

TACANÁ (Munson 1984)
(72) aa'e'   ma'   **tz'-ok**   **b'ujuu-n=t-e**   **q-ee**
       they   PROX   B3SG-DIR   hit-AP=A3SG-RN:PAT   A1PL-RN:PAT
       'it was they who hit us'

Note that in both of these dialects the verb at least sometimes appears to be in agreement with the patient but the patient is also indicated by a relational noun. It is more likely that the verb is not in fact indexing the patient at all, but as in Tacaná is always third person singular, usually unmarked. Note that in Mam, unlike most other Mayan languages, the third person singular is sometimes indicated by an audible morpheme, as in (72).

Some antipassives derive intransitive verbs from cognate objects. Examples are *aaqan* 'look for hives' from *aaq* 'bee hive', *chuunan* 'play a wind instrument' from *chuun* 'wind instrument', *munula'n* 'give municipal service' from *munulab'il* 'municipal service'. The antipassive also occurs on some intransitive verbs that do not have a corresponding transitive or nominal form. This is a verbal derivational function. Some examples are *aanq'an* 'live', *b'itan* 'beat (heart)' or *qeelan* 'run'.

4.4 Order

Mam has fairly rigid VAO, VS, and NVP S basic constituent orders in all dialects (NVP = non-verbal predicate). Nominal constituents can occur before the predicates, but it is rare for one to do so without some further modification; usually a demonstrative (for focus) or interrogative (for interrogation) accompanies or replaces the NP in this position. Furthermore, if a subject of a transitive verb precedes the verb for focus or interrogation, the verb takes the antipassive suffix and therefore becomes intransitive.

It is quite rare for a transitive clause to have a lexical subject and object, given that the verb has agreement markers for both and that first and second person pronouns are only used for contrastive emphasis. However, in a sample of almost 1,000 clauses in texts, five transitive clauses had both a subject and an object, which was a little over 3 percent of the total transitive clauses. One of these was AVO, the other four were VAO, as in (73).

IXTAHUACÁN
(73) oo=taq   Ø=b'aj   t-qeeta-n   Luuch   t-tzii'.
       PFV=PRF   B3SG=DIR   A3SG-cut-DS   Pedro   A3SG-mouth
       'Pedro had cut their mouths (of bottle gourds).'   {AILLA MAM007R001.111}

In addition to the AVO clause (74), there was one clause in the sample that was AV (75). Examining the context in which these are found, both are examples of a switch in topic. In both texts the participants in previous clauses are other characters and *Luuch* in (74) or *xlitz'* in (75) are being reintroduced as the protagonists. The preverbal NP in (74) is accompanied by *atzan te* 'as for', often used when the protagonist changes. The preverbal NP in (75) is preceded by the negative that is typically used with verbs. The verb in (74) is an ordinary transitive verb, but that in (75) has a dependent aspect marker. Neither, however, is antipassive, which is what would be expected if these were instead examples of contrastive emphasis (§4.1).

IXTAHUACÁN

(74) **A=tzan**   t-e   **Luuch**   nn=∅=ok   t-k'alo-'n
    DEM=well   A3SG-RN   Pedro   IPFV=B3SG=DIR   A3SG-tie-DS
       tzi   saaka   t-u'n   jun   ky'ijaaj
    A3SG;mouth   sack   A3SG-RN:with   one   string
    'So Pedro tied the sack with a string. . .' {AILLA MAM007R001.42}

(75) Nti'=ta   **xlitz'**   ∅=∅=okx   t-b'i-'n
    NEG=3SG.EMPH   wax   DEP.PFV=B3SG=DIR   A3SG-hear-DS
    'The wax didn't pay attention. . .' {AILLA MAM007R006.109}

The contexts that have so far been identified for changes in order such that a noun phrase precedes the predicate are contrastive emphasis, negation with focus on the noun phrase, interrogation of the noun phrase, and changes of topic. A few of the examples encountered seem to simply indicate topic, a function that has not been previously identified for preverbal noun phrases in Mam. (76) provides an example of a subject preceding a non-verbal predicate, (77) shows an object preceding a transitive verb, and (78) has a subject preceding an intransitive verb. This last is the most frequent of the preverbal orders, accounting for 36 of the almost 1,000 clauses that were sampled. In contrast there were only five each of the S NVP and OV orders.

IXTAHUACÁN

(76) yaa   ja'la   aa=tzan aj **alemaj**   t-e'   t-jaq'
    now   now   DEM=well   DEM   animal   EXIST=B3PL   A3SG-RN:under
       montaanya
       mountain
    '. . . and now these animals are in the mountain. . .' {AILLA MAM007R003.46}

(77) aj   ky-ee   **ky-saqb'aaq**   ∅=∅=xi'   ky=xoo-'kj.
    DEM   A3PL-RN:POSS   A3PL-rope   DEP.PFV=B3SG=DIR   A3PL-throw-MOV
    '. . . that it was their own ropes they went and threw. . .' {AILLA
    MAM007R001.47}

(78) **xhiky**   t-poon   sabeer   ni'   oor
    rabbit   A3SG-arrive   who.knows   Q   hour
    '. . . and the rabbit arrived, who knows at what time.' {AILLA MAM007R008.16}

4.5 Negation

Mam is interesting because it has a number of different ways of negating different kinds of constituents. These do not coincide entirely from region to region. Table 19.9 shows the negative words that are used in the three main dialect areas for different kinds of negation (England 1990:241). What is particularly interesting is that if noun phrases are

TABLE 19.9 NEGATION IN MAM

Category of Negation	Ixtahuacán (north)	Ostuncalco (south)	Tacaná (west)
Statives and NPs in focus	miyaa'/nyaa'	mya	nyaa'
Existentials: people	mi'aal		
Existentials: not people		mixhti'	
	miti'/nti'		tiilo'
Verbs: not future/imperative		min	
Verbs: future		mlay	laay/tiilo'
	mii'n		
Verbs: imperative		lan	uun

in focus in any kind of negative structure, they are preceded by the negative marker that is used with statives, no matter what the actual predicate is.

Example (79) shows the negation of a stative, (80) of a noun phrase in focus, (81) of a verb in the non-future, and (82) of a verb in the imperative.

IXTAHUACÁN

(79) **nyaa'** t-baan-al tx'otx'=yiin=tl=t
NEG A3SG-good-ABST land=ATT=other=3SG.EMPH
'. . . and it's not very fertile land.' {AILLA MAM007R004.144}

(80) **nyaa'** chi-b'aj=wa n=∅=b'ant w-u'n
NEG meat-INAL=1SG.EMPH IPFV=B3SG=make A1SG-RN:AGT
'. . . I'm not making meat/it's not meat I'm making. . .' {AILLA MAM007R003.128}

(81) ntii', **nti'** o=∅=t-maa ch'in nee'
NEG NEG PFV=B3SG=A3SG-say a.little small
'. . . no, he didn't say anything.' {AILLA MAM007R004.89}

(82) **mii'n** ku' teen=a t-u n-b'ee=y'
NEG DIR be-2SG A3SG-RN:in A1SG-road=1SG
'. . . don't get in my way!' *lit.* '. . . don't be in my road!' {AILLA MAM007R008.22}

5 COMPLEX STRUCTURES

Mam has the expected subordinate clauses – relative clauses, complement clauses, adverbial clauses, and conditional clauses. There are four different structures that occur in subordinate clauses: (1) the clause has a finite verb and is structurally like an independent clause, other than possibly being introduced by some sort of subordinator (83), (2) the clause has a verbal predicate with normal person marking and dependent aspect marking (this is restricted to proximate marking in the west and south, but extends to perfective marking as well in the north) (84), (3) the clause has an aspectless verbal predicate, in which case it always triggers all-ergative marking (85), or (4) the clause has an infinitive verb, with no aspect or person marking (86). Similar differences have not been shown to occur on clauses that are headed by non-verbal predicates.

In (83) the dependent clause (a relative clause with no relative marker) consists of a fully inflected verb, *kb'ajeel*. Since the potential proclitic is always optional, and the verb has a Set B marker for the subject and a potential suffix, it has the same structure as an independent clause. This example can be compared to (84), where the proximate dependent aspect marker is used in a relative clause. Given that there is no correlate to dependent aspect in the potential, dependent aspect marking is not an option in (83).

IXTAHUACÁN

(83) At=Ø   jun   pyeest   [k=b'aj-eel]
      EXIST=B3SG   one   fiesta   B3SG=finish-POT
      'There's a fiesta that will be celebrated (*lit.* will finish). . .' {AILLA
      MAM007R006.215}

In (84) the proximate dependent aspect marker *x-* fuses with the Set B third person singular marker *tz'=* to produce *s=*. The dependent clause is a relative clause.

(84) mii'n   n-b'aq'=a=Ø   [s=e=tz   w-ii-'n=a]
      NEG   A1SG-testicle=1SG=B3SG   DEP.PROX;B3SG=DIR=DIR   A1SG-take-DS=1SG
      'no, they were my own testicles that I took out' {AILLA MAM007R008.206}

(85) has an aspectless intransitive verb that takes a Set A marker in agreement with the subject. The clause has no subordinator and is interpreted as a temporal clause, as are most clauses with this structure and no explicit subordinator.

(85) n=Ø=jaq'a-n   jun   jooj   [t-iky'   ikyx]
      IPFV=B3SG=scream-AP   one   crow   A3SG-pass   thus
      '. . . the crow was screaming when it passed by.' {AILLA MAM007R007.75–76}

(86) shows one of the most common uses of clauses with infinitives – as purpose clauses after motion verbs. The subject of the motion verb controls the subject of the infinitive, which in this case is an intransitive verb. If the infinitive comes from a semantically transitive verb the object is usually oblique, introduced by the relational noun *-ee* (see England 2013a for details).

(86) n=Ø=xi'   [pasyaa'ra-l   t-uj   tzii'   maar].
      IPFV=B3SG=go   walk.around-INF   A3SG-RN:in   A3SG;RN:edge   sea
      '. . . he went to walk around at the seashore.' {AILLA MAM007R003.10}

These four types of subordinate clauses differ in terms of their structural similarities to independent clauses. From most to least like independent clauses they can be arranged as in Table 19.10.

A great amount of work remains to be done on complex clauses in Mam, especially on the differences among the different dialect areas, which are considerable. An analysis of the dialect differences would contribute to a comprehensive picture of subordination

TABLE 19.10 INDEPENDENCE OF SUBORDINATE CLAUSES

most independent		→	*most dependent*
independent finite	dependent aspect	aspectless	dependent infinitive

in the language. What follows is a very brief introduction to the major structures, taking Ixtahuacán as the model.

5.1 Finite subordinate clauses

The finite subordinate clauses principally function in some relative clauses, such as (83) above, where the aspect is not one of the aspects that has a dependent form; in conditional clauses; and in complements of non-causative transitive verbs. Although the relative clause in (83) has no relative marker, relative clauses can have a demonstrative (*aj* or *aqaj* in the plural) to introduce the clause, which always follows the head noun, as in (87), unless the clause is headless, as in (88). The verb in the relative clause in (87) is intransitive and is marked with both aspect and a Set B marker. That in (88) is also intransitive and is marked with dependent aspect and a Set B marker.

<small>IXTAHUACÁN</small>
(87) B'ix   t-e   xjaal   q'i-'n=x=ta   xjaal   tal   t-k'uuxb'il,
      and   A3SG-RN person   take-DS=still=3SG.EMPH   person   small A3SG-knife
      [aj oo=taq   tz'=ajb'laana-n   ky-i'j   t'iiw]
      DEM PFV=PRF   B3SG=use-INTR   A3PL-RN:MAL   eagle
      'And the person, the person still carried his little knife, which he had used against the eagles. . .' {AILLA MAM007R007.229–230.}

(88) Ky-i   aa=tzan=qa=j   masaat   t=e',   [aqaj
      A3PL-RN   DEM=well=PL=DEM   deer   EXIST=B3PL   DEM.PL
      Ø=i=je'x   oq   t-u   ky-koraal.]
      DEP.PFV=B3PL=DIR   flee A3SG-RN:in   A3PL-corral
      'Those are the deer there are, those that fled from their corrals.' {AILLA MAM007R003.234–236}

In Tacaná the head noun of a relative clause must be preceded by the demonstrative *je*; the same demonstrative can be used optionally to introduce the relative clause, but otherwise the structure is finite and like that of an independent clause (Munson 1984) (87).

<small>TACANÁ</small> (Munson 1984)
(89) je   xhuunk   waakx   [(je)   Ø=Ø=xi   qiituu-n   txoo
      DEM   one-horned   cow   DEM   PFV=B3SG=DIR   run.off-INTR   among
      kjo'n]   Ø=Ø=ku   t-toko-'n   n-b'ii'iixh
      cornfield   PFV=B3SG=DIR   A3SG-knock.over-DS   A1SG-grandmother
      'The one-horned cow that ran off into the cornfield knocked my grandmother over.'

Conditional clauses begin with *qa* 'if' and otherwise have structures that are like independent clauses, as is the result clause (90).

<small>IXTAHUACÁN</small>
(90) [Qa   ma   chiin=x=wa   t-u'n   t'iiw   ja'la]
      if PROX B1SG=go=1SG.EMPH A3SG-RN:AGT   eagle   now
      [aax   milaayx   Ø=aanq'a-n=ta   txkup   w-u'n=a]
      also   NEG   B3SG-live-AP=3SG.EMPH   animal A1SG-RN:AGT=1SG
      'If the eagle takes me today, I'm not going to let the animal live. . .' *lit.* 'If I go by the eagle today, the animal won't live by me. . .' {AILLA MAM007R007.25–26}

The complements of non-causative transitive verbs are close to having the same structure as independent clauses. They are not marked for aspect, but unlike the "aspectless clauses", they also do not take extended ergative marking (§5.3), as in (91) where the complement has an intransitive verb with a Set B marker for the subject. Note however that if the clause begins with the purposive relational noun *tu'n*, as in (53) above, extended ergative marking is used.

(91) Pwes   qa   Ø=ky-aj=a   [**ch**=e'x=a]
     well   if   B3SG=A2PL-want=2PL   B2PL=go=2PL
     'Well, if you (pl) want to go. . .' {AILLA MAM007R003.162–163}

5.2 Dependent aspect

Dependent aspect marking is partial in all dialects of Mam. The proximate aspect *ma* has an allomorph *x-* that is only used in certain subordinate clauses. In the north, but not in the west or south, the perfective Ø has shifted to use in subordinate clauses while a new perfective marker, *o-*, is used in independent clauses. The principal context for use of dependent aspects in Ixtahuacán is after a noun phrase that is in a preverbal position. This includes the head nouns of relative clauses and after focused preverbal noun phrases. Because the dependent aspects are partial, these contexts may also have fully independent clauses if their aspect is not one of the ones that has a dependent form, or they may use aspectless dependent clauses in variation with dependent aspect marking. Other dialects do not use dependent aspect after fronted noun phrases, but there are a number of other contexts for the use of dependent aspect marking, including in some temporal clauses and after certain preverbal adverbs. (92) is an example of a relative clause with dependent aspect marking; (93) is an example of dependent aspect marking after a focused and fronted noun phrase. The form *xi* is fused from the dependent aspect marker *x-* plus the third person singular Set B marker Ø, plus the directional *xi'*.

IXTAHUACÁN

(92) Maas   aax   aj   xhiky=Ø
     rather same   DEM   rabbit=B3SG
         [**Ø**=Ø=ok   t-ma-'n   t-ee   t-tiiya]
         DEP.PFV=B3SG=DIR   A3SG-say-DS   A3SG-RN:DAT   A3SG-uncle
     'Rather it's that same rabbit who said to his uncle. . .' {AILLA
     MAM007R008.248–249}

(93) noq=tzan   kabees   xi   ky-qo-'n
     only=well   head   DEP.PROX;B3SG;DIR   A3PL-give-DS
     '. . . they only put in heads.' {AILLA MAM007R009.47}

The next example (94) shows dependent aspect marking following an adverb, (95) is an example of dependent aspect marking in a temporal clause in Tacaná, and (96) shows dependent aspect marking in a temporal clause in Cajolá.

(94) Iky=san   **Ø**=Ø=b'aj   ky-ma-'n   xjaal
     thus=well   DEP.PFV=B3SG=DIR:complete   A3PL-say-DS   person
     'Thus spoke the people. . .' {AILLA MAM007R011.189}

TACANÁ (Munson 1984)

(95) toq   n=kyin   b'eet   [xh=tz'=ok   nooj   juun
     IPRF   IPFV=B1SG walk   DEP.PROX=B3SG=DIR   meet   one
     xjaal   n-wutz]
     person   A1SG-RN:in.front
     'I was walking when I met a person. . .'

CAJOLÁ (Pérez and Jiménez 1997:404)

(96) Ma   chi   jaw   ik'i-n   [teej   x=qo   poon=e']
     PROX   B3PL   DIR   be.displeased-INTR   when   DEP.PROX=B1PL   arrive=1PL
     'They were displeased when we arrived.'

5.3 Aspectless clauses

Aspectless clauses always take super-extended ergative marking (*all* the principal arguments have ergative agreement markers) and in Ixtahuacán they are used primarily in
temporally subordinate clauses, in purpose, result, and complement clauses introduced
by *tu'n* or *tu'nj*, and after preverbal affect words, affect verbs, and positional predicates.
It is unclear whether these last categories of words are manner adverbials or secondary
predicates. The details of the contexts for the use of aspectless clauses are different in different dialects of Mam. The examples that follow show aspectless clauses in a temporally
subordinate clause (97), in a purpose clause (98), after a preverbal affect word (99), and
a preverbal positional (100). Note that in each the following intransitive verb takes Set
A marking for its subject.

IXTAHUACÁN

(97) aj   t-qoqaax
     when   A3SG-night.falls
     '. . . when night fell.' {AILLA MAM007R001.37}

(98) Tii=tzan   tqal   mooda   k=b'ant-eel   q-u'n
     what=well   what   mode   B3SG=do-POT   A1PL-RN:AGT
     [t-u'n   t-jaq-eet   xaq]
     A3SG-RN:PURP   A3SG-open-PSV   rock
     'What are we going to do in order to open the rock?' {AILLA MAM007R004.59–60}

(99) tillll=tzan   ky-eel   ja'la.
     AFF=well   A3PL-go.out   now
     '. . ."tillll" they left now.' {AILLA MAM007R003.233}

(100) Jop-l   t=kub'   xjaal   t-witz   tx'otx'
      sunken.eyed-POS   A3SG=go.down   person   A3SG-RN:on   ground
      t-u'n   yaab'il
      A3SG-RN:CAUS   illness
      'The person was on the ground sunken-eyed because of the illness.' {Maldonado
      Andrés et al. 1986:108}

A characteristic of relative clauses in Ixtahuacán is that either dependent aspect marking or aspectless clauses can be used in a relative clause to express the difference between
dynamic and static situations respectively (101) (England 1983a: 272–4).

IXTAHUACÁN

(101) a. aj   txkup s=ook=x   t-uj   jaa
       DEM   animal   DEP.PROX;B3SG=enter=DIR   A3SG-RN:in house
       ich'=jal
       mouse=CLF:non-human
       'The animal that went in the house is a mouse.'

      b. aj   txkup   t=ook=x   t-uj   jaa
       DEM   animal   A3SG=enter=DIR   A3SG-RN:in house
       ich'=jal
       mouse=CLF:non-human
       'The animal that is in the house is a mouse.'

5.4 Infinitives

Mam has true infinitives; verb forms that take no aspect or person marking. They are derived from verb stems with the suffix -*l*. The contexts for use of infinitives are in (1) purpose clauses that follow intransitive verbs of motion (102), (2) in complements of causative transitive verbs (103), (3) with the intransitive verb -*teen* 'be in a place', which in this context indicates the beginning of an action (104), and (4) in subordinate clauses of non-verbal predicates (105) (England 2013a:282–3).

IXTAHUACÁN

(102) N=∅=xi'=tzan   [pastoora-l   ja'la]
      IPFV=B3SG=go=well   herd-INF   now
      'So he went to herd. . .'   {AILLA MAM007R001.70}

(103) ma   tz'=ok   n-q'o-'n=a   Kyel   [tx'eema-l   sii']
      PROX   B3SG=DIR   A1SG-give-DS=1SG   Miguel   cut-INF   firewood
      'I had Miguel cut firewood.' {England 2013a:283}

(104) t-u'n   t-ok   teen   [b'iix-l]
      A3SG-RN:PURP   A3SG-DIR   be   dance-INF
      '. . . so that she begins to dance.' {AILLA MAM007R009.89}

(105) qiina   [lo-l   t-ee]
      stative;B1SG   see-INF   A3SG-RN:PAT
      '. . . I (will go) to see (find) him.' {AILLA MAM007R008.167}

6 SUMMATION

Mam has been shown to have a number of unusual or interesting features. These include the addition of a series of back palatal consonants and a series of retroflex consonants. These last, as well as other characteristics like noun classifiers and the behavior of aspect-less clauses, are Huehuetenango areal features, shared between Q'anjob'alan proper and Mamean languages. The loss of historical second person markers is restricted to Mam, and under conditions that lead to split ergativity Mam shows a particular kind of super-extended ergativity that is unique within the family. There is strong evidence for syntactic as well as morphological ergativity. The position of directionals (mostly before the verb root) is unusual, since in most other Mayan languages the directionals come after the verb root. Finally, Mam shows four different levels of finiteness and independence in its subordinate clauses.

NOTE

*   I would like to especially acknowledge the role that José Reginaldo Pérez Vail played in the analysis contained in this chapter. I discussed many issues about the grammar with him, especially complex clauses, but in reality all sorts of points that came up in our many discussions and interactions. All of the material about inverse and obviation is his work and is contained in his master's thesis (Pérez Vail 2014). This was a ground-breaking analysis. All of the discussions of the Mam of Cajolá are due to his work or that of his late brother, Eduardo Pérez Vail.

REFERENCES

Canger, Una. 1969. "Analysis in outline of Mam, a Mayan language." PhD diss., University of California, Berkeley.

Cojtí, Narciso, and Nora C. England. 1986. "Reporte Mam: Análisis dialectal." Unpublished manuscript, Antigua Guatemala: Proyecto Lingüístico Francisco Marroquín.

Collins, Wesley M. 2005. "Centeredness as a cultural and grammatical theme in Maya-Mam." PhD diss., Ohio State University.

Dayley, Jon P. 1983. "Voice and ergativity in Mayan languages." *Survey of California and Other Indian Languages* 4: 5–119.

England, Nora C. 1976a. "Mam directionals and verb semantics." In *Mayan linguistics I*, ed. by Marlys McClaran, 201–11. Los Angeles: University of California American Indian Studies Center.

England, Nora C. 1976b. "Mam text." *International Journal of American Linguistics Native American Text Series* 1(1): 88–97.

England, Nora C. 1980. "Eating in Mam." *Journal of Mayan Linguistics* 1(2): 26–32.

England, Nora C. 1983a. *A grammar of Mam, a Mayan language*. Austin: University of Texas Press.

England, Nora C. 1983b. "Ergativity in Mamean (Mayan) languages." *International Journal of American Linguistics* 49: 1–19.

England, Nora C. 1988. "Mam voice." In *Typological studies in language, 16: passive and voice*, ed. by M. Shibatani, 525–45. Amsterdam: John Benjamins.

England, Nora C. 1989. "Comparing Mam (Mayan) clause structures: subordinate versus main clauses." *International Journal of American Linguistics* 55: 283–308.

England, Nora C. 1990. "El Mam: Semejanzas y diferencias regionales." In *Lecturas sobre la lingüística maya*, ed. by Nora C. England and Stephen R, Elliott, 221–52. Antigua Guatemala: Centro de Investigaciones Regionales de Mesoamérica.

England, Nora C. 2004. "Adjectives in Mam." In *Adjective classes: a cross-linguistic typology*, ed. by R.M.W. Dixon and Alexandra Y. Aikhenvald, 125–46. Oxford: Oxford University Press.

England, Nora C. 2006. "El papel de palabras afectivas en la narración en Mam (Maya)." In *Memorias del VIII Encuentro Internacional de Lingüística en el noroeste*, vol. III, ed. by Zarina Estrada Fernández, Rosa María Ortiz Ciscomani, and María del Carmen Morúa, 157–71. Hermosillo, Sonora: Editorial UniSon.

England, Nora C. 2009. "To tell a tale: the structure of narrated stories in Mam, a Mayan language." *International Journal of American Linguistics* 75: 207–33.

England, Nora C. 2010. Twelve annotated Mam texts published online at the Archive of Indigenous Languages of Latin America. http://www.ailla.utexas.org/search/resource .html?r_id=8103 to http://www.ailla.utexas.org/search/resource.html?r_id=8114

England, Nora C. 2011. "Plurality agreement in some Eastern Mayan languages." *International Journal of American Linguistics* 77: 397–412.

England, Nora C. 2013a. "Cláusulas con flexión reducida en Mam." In *Clases léxicas, posesión y cláusulas complejas en lenguas de Mesoamérica,* ed. by Enrique Palancar and Roberto Zavala, 277–303. Mexico: Centro de Investigación y Estudios Superiores en Antropología Social.

England, Nora C. 2013b. "Marking aspect and mood and inferring time in Mam (Mayan)." *Berkeley Linguistics Society* 33: 119–40.

Godfrey, Thomas. 1981. "Grammatical categories for spatial reference in the Western Mam dialect of Tacana." PhD diss., University of Texas, Austin.

Godfrey, Thomas James, and Wesley M. Collins. 1987. *Una encuesta dialectal en el área mam de Guatemala.* Guatemala: Instituto Lingüístico de Verano.

Kaufman, Terrence. 1976. "Archaeological and linguistic correlations in Mayaland and associated areas of Meso-America." *World Archaeology* 8: 101–18.

Lehmann, Christian. 1998. *Possession in Yucatec Maya.* Munich: LINCOM Europa.

Maldonado Andrés, Juan, Juan Ordóñez Domingo, and Juan Ortiz Domingo. 1986. *Diccionario Mam de San Ildefonso Ixtahuacán Huehuetenango.* Antigua Guatemala: Proyecto Lingüístico Francisco Marroquín.

Martin, Laura. 1977. "Positional roots in Kanjobal (Mayan)." PhD diss., University of Florida.

Minkoff, Seth. 2000. "Animacy hierarchies and sentence processing." In *The syntax of verb initial languages*, ed. by Andrew Carnie and Eithne Guilfoyle, 201–12. Oxford: Oxford University Press.

Munson, Linda. 1984. "To Qyool: a reference grammar of Western Mam." Defense copy of PhD diss., University of California, San Diego.

Peck, Dorothy Miller. 1951. "The formation of utterances in the Mam language." MA thesis, Hartford Seminary Foundation.

Pérez, Eduardo (B'aayil), and Odilio Jiménez (Ajb'ee). 1997. *Ttxoolil Qyool Mam: Gramática Mam.* Guatemala: Cholsamaj.

Pérez, Eduardo, Zoila García Jiménez, Odilio Jiménez. 2000. *Variación Dialectal en Mam.* Guatemala City: Cholsamaj.

Pérez Alonzo, Juventino de Jesús. 2007. *Pujb'il Yol Mam: Diccionario bilingüe estándar Mam ilustrado.* Guatemala: Oxlajuuj Keej Maya' Ajtz'iib' and Cholsamaj.

Pérez Vail, José Reginaldo. 2007. *Xtxolil yool B'a'aj: Gramática Tektiteka.* Guatemala City: Cholsamaj and Oxlajuuj Keej Maya' Ajtz'iib'.

Pérez Vail, José Reginaldo. 2014. "La inversión y obviación en el mam de Cajolá." MA thesis, Centro de Investigaciones y Estudios Superiores en Antropología Social, Mexico.

Reynoso, Fray Diego de. 1644. *Arte y vocabulario en lengua mame.* Printed by Francisco Robledo. Reprinted n.d. France. Republished 1916 with a "note about the Mames and their language" by Alberto María Carreño. Mexico: Sociedad Mexicana de Geografía y Estadística.

Richards, Michael. 2003. *Atlas lingüístico de Guatemala.* Guatemala: SEPAZ, UVG, URL, USAID.

CHAPTER 20

Q'ANJOB'AL

Eladio Mateo Toledo

1 INTRODUCTION

Q'anjob'al along with Popti' and Akateko form the Q'anjob'alan group within the Western division of Mayan languages (Campbell and Kaufman 1985:189). It has all the typological features of Mayan languages. This chapter addresses issues that are characteristic of or occur only in Q'anjob'alan languages. Some of them are explored in previous works (Craig 1977, 1987; Martin 1977; Datz 1980; Zavala 1992, 2000; Raymundo *et al.* 2000; Ross Montejo and Delgado Rojas 2000; and others). A summary of these issues follows.

In the phonology (§2), Q'anjob'alan languages have retroflex phonemes and they retain uvular sounds. At the morphological level (§4), like other Mayan languages, they have positional, affect, and verbal roots, but they unusually have over 500 positional roots, which is double the number of verbal and affect roots together.

Syntactic topics include the following. In the NP (§5), there is no modifying adjective because the noun and adjective form a compound. There are also three systems of nominal classification that co-occur in an NP: a nominal classifier system that classifies non-abstract nouns based on their physical properties or social status, and two numeral classifier systems used in counting. Noun classifiers function as pronouns (§5). As in Mamean languages, Q'anjob'alan languages have a rigid VAO order (§6). In addition to ergative alignment, nominative alignment occurs in nonfinite clauses (§7). Ditransitive alignment is of the indirective type, as in Eastern Mayan (§6.2). Besides marking transitivity, thematic suffixes explicitly mark an intonational boundary (§3). Q'anjob'alan languages have a suffix *-on* that occurs on transitive verbs in three contexts: in an agent focus construction (finite clauses with extracted agent); in a nonfinite subordinate clause; and in finite clauses temporally related to other clauses. The last two uses are unique to the Q'anjob'alan subgroup (§7, §10). In RCs, relative pronouns inflect for person and number (§8). The last feature is complex predicates; while directionals are well known in Maya and the causative in some Eastern languages, Q'anjob'al has at least six complex predicates with a verb-verb frame (§9). This chapter addresses these issues as they occur in Q'anjob'al.

Q'anjob'al is spoken in the northwest of Guatemala in the towns of San Juan Ixcoy, San Pedro Soloma, Santa Eulalia, and Santa Cruz Barillas (Ixcoy, Soloma, Santa, and Barillas, hereafter), as well as in the United States and the South of Mexico by immigrants. The estimated number of speakers in Guatemala varies between 99,112 (Richards 2003:74) and 112,000 (OKMA 1993:12) plus about 10,000 speakers in the US (Peñolosa 1992). Due to disruptions in transmission, Q'anjob'al is somewhat endangered (Richard 2003).

Q'anjob'al is by now a well-studied Mayan language. Well-explored topics include inflectional and derivational morphology, root classes, alignment, clausal dependency, finiteness, complement clauses, complex predicates, and acquisition of verbal morphology (Martin 1977; Mateo Toledo 2004, 2008, 2012a, b, 2013a, b; Mateo Pedro 2005, 2015; Francisco Pascual 2007, 2010). Research on discourse, the NP, verb classes, and the acquisition of the syntax are still lacking, as are a good dictionary and descriptive grammar. There is a corpus of 58 hours of recordings and transcriptions at ELAR (SOAS, University of London) that I use in this chapter and about 15 hours at AILLA (University of Texas at Austin), but a fully annotated corpus and documentation of other dialects and genres are still needed.

Q'anjob'al has little dialectal variation; there are two fairly close dialects: Ixcoy-Soloma and Santa Eulalia-Barillas (Mateo Toledo 1999; Raymundo *et al.* 2000). Variation is mostly in the lexicon and in a few phonological and morphological aspects. This chapter is based on data from Santa Eulalia; but the generalizations apply to other dialects unless explicitly noted. Data without citation are from my own notes and database.

2 PHONOLOGY

2.1 Phonological inventory and relevant issues

Q'anjob'al has 30 phonemes, 25 consonants and 5 vowels. Table 20.1 lists the phonemes in the practical alphabet; their value in the International Phonetic Alphabet (IPA) is included in square brackets if they differ from that of the IPA.[1]

Like all Mayan languages, Q'anjob'al has glottalized stops and affricate phonemes. It has a five-vowel system where *Proto-Mayan *VV, *V', *Vh became short vowels (V) (Kaufman 1990:65). Q'anjob'al is the only Western Mayan language that retains all uvular stops (like Eastern Mayan). Like Mamean languages, Q'anjob'al also has three retroflex phonemes, due to areal diffusion in the Huehuetenango area.

Two phonological issues need to be mentioned. First, the /w/ is becoming a fricative [β] in Ixcoy; it is [β] before front vowels and [β]/[w] in other contexts. It lacks variation in other towns, except in *kanwan* [kanβan] 'four' in Soloma (Raymundo *et al.* 2000:43–5).

IXCOY
(1) k'ixwil   [k'is̞βil]   'embarrassing'
    k'ewex   [k'eβes̞]   'soursop'
    waykan   [βaykan~waykan]   'star'
    lawuxh   [laβuʃ~lawuʃ]   'nail'
    lowoq   [loβoχ~lowoχ]   'eat' {Raymundo *et al.* 2000:43–5}

TABLE 20.1 Q'ANJOB'AL PHONEMES

p	t				k	q	'[ʔ]	i		u
b'[ɓ]	t'				k'	q'		e		o
		tz[t͡s]	ch[t͡ʃ]	tx[t͡ʂ]					a	
		tz'[t͡s']	ch'[t͡ʃ']	tx'[t͡ʂ']						
	s		xh[ʃ]	x[ʂ]	j[x]					
m	n									
	l									
	r									
w				y[j]						

The second issue is the status of the glottal stop. Although it is not orthographically represented before vowel-initial stems, it has consonantal correlates. First, set A prefixes distinguish between vowel- and consonant-initial stems (§4.1), but some speakers use either prefix with these stems as in (2a, b) where *a-* marks the second person before consonants while the absence of glottal stop marks the same person before vowel-initial stems. Second, in reduplications that involve the first consonant, the glottal is reduplicated as in (2c, d) (see Kaufman 2015). Finally, complex codas are unattested, including ones of the form ʔC. Thus, the glottal patterns like a consonant in coda contexts.

(2) a. a+'on   [aʔon~on]   'your avocado'
    b. a+'inat   [aʔinat=~inat=] 'your seed'
    c. lek+lon   [leklon]   'to stand repeatedly'
    d. ak+'on   [ʔak+ʔon]   'to face repeatedly'

2.2 Syllable structure

A syllable can have a (C)(C)V(C) structure where CV is predominant. Complex onsets exist only when C-initial stems occur with consonantal prefixes like *s-* [A3] or the aspect marker *x-* as in (3) or in borrowings with complex onsets like *plato* 'plate'.[2] Complex codas do not exist; they are avoided on verbs by retaining other suffixes (§3).

(3) stxi.tam   'her/his pig'
    xwa.yi   'she/he slept'
    pla.to   'plate'

2.3 Morphophonology

There are two main morphophonological changes. The first case occurs when the third person set A *s-* attaches to a stem beginning with an affricate or retroflex sound as shown by the possessed forms in (4). In Soloma, the resulting clusters surface as fricatives if the second sound is unglottalized and as a fricative plus a glottal stop if the second sound is glottalized (i.e. s+ch >xh, s+tx >x, s+tz >s, s+ch' >xh', s+tx' >x', s+tz' >tz'/s'). There is no change in other dialects, but in Santa-Barillas the prefix is generally dropped. A similar process occurs in Akateko and Popti' (Mateo Toledo 1999; Ross Montejo and Delgado Rojas 2000).

(4) Input	Soloma	Ixcoy	Others	
s+chan	[ʃan]	[st͡ʃan]	[(s)t͡ʃan]	'her skirt'
s+txutx	[ʂut͡ʂ]	[s͡t͡ʂut͡ʂ]	[(s)t͡ʂut͡ʂ]	'his/her mother'
s+tzaq'a'	[saq'aʔ~t͡saq'aʔ]	[t͡saq'aʔ]	[(s)t͡saq'aʔ]	'ember'
s+ch'en	[ʃʔen]	[st͡ʃʼen]	[(s)t͡ʃʼen]	'his rock'
s+tx'otx'	[ʂʔot͡ʂ'~s͡t͡ʂ'ot͡ʂ']	[s͡t͡ʂ'oʔ]	[(s)t͡ʂ'ot͡ʂ']	'his land'
s+tz'ilal	[sʔilal]	[st͡s'ilal]	[(s)t͡s'ilal]	'its dirtiness'

{Raymundo *et al.* 2000:35}

The second process involves the elision of an initial glottal stop and vowel lowering, (5). In all dialects, the absence of glottal stop on V-initial stems marks the second person set A, which is marked by *a*- on C-initial stems. In Santa-Barillas high vowels also become mid-vowels in this context.

(5) Noun   Ix-Sol   San-Bar
    [sek']   'bowl'   [asek']   [asek']   'your bowl'
    [ʔiʂim]   'corn'   [iʂim]   [eʂim]   'your corn'
    [ʔunin]   'child'   [unin]   [onin]   'your child'
    [ʔa͡ts'am]   'salt'   [a͡ts'am]   [a͡ts'am]   'your salt'
    [ʔon]   'avocado'   [on]   [on]   'your avocado'
    [ʔe͡tʃex]   'ax'   [e͡tʃex]   [e͡tʃex]   'your ax' {Raymundo *et al.* 2000:35}

3 INTONATIONAL CONTOUR, STRESS, AND FINAL PHRASE AFFIXES

Q'anjob'al has a stress pattern that relates to prosodic boundaries in intonational phrases. The pattern is that phonological words in phrase-final position or isolation bear main stress on their final syllable and words in nonfinal position bear main stress on the first syllable as in (6). Note that set A affixes like *ha*-do not count for the assignment of stress (i.e. they are opaque). Spaces separate phonological words, slashes indicate intonational boundaries, and acute accent marks the main stress.[3]

(6) /max **tó**.wal ha.**wáj**.b'aj **jáb**'.xa ji.**xím**. . ./
    max-Ø   to-wal   ha-wajb'aj   jab'xa   j-ixim
    CP-B3   still-INTS   A2SG-gather   some   A1PL-corn
    'You still saved some of our corn.'

There are two types of stress: main word stress that falls on the first syllable and sentence stress that is final. The stress pattern in (6) results from the interaction of these stress types; sentence stress overrides word stress in final position and therefore words in final intonational boundaries bear final syllable stress. Furthermore, words in isolation bear final syllable stress because they are treated like intonational phrases.

Q'anjob'al has a set of status suffixes, shown in Table 20.2 (see Polian, this volume, on morphology). With the exception of the thematic suffix -*j* and the infinitival transitive suffix -*oj*, these suffixes occur only in intonational phrase-final position or phrase-medially to avoid a complex coda. These suffixes distinguish transitive and intransitive verbs. They include thematic suffixes for root and derived verbs (§4); irrealis suffix (§4), and infinitival suffix (§7). The suffix -*i* also occurs with the same distribution on particles like the intensifiers =*ton* and *wal*.

The examples in (7) illustrate the intonational phrase-final restriction. Each example shows the same verb in two contexts: in medial position the verb lacks the suffix and in final position it takes the suffix: the thematic suffix -*o'* is shown in (7a), the irrealis -*oq* in (7b), the infinitival -*oq* in (7c), and -*i* on the intensifier *wal* in (7d). The suffix -*j* does not follow this rule as shown in (8).

TABLE 20.2 PHRASE-FINAL SUFFIXES

Suffixes	Intransitive	Transitive
Thematic suffix	*-i*	*-u, -o', -a'* (root)/*-j* (base)
Infinitives	*-oq*	*-oj*
Irrealis	*-oq*	—
Suffix *-i* on particles		

(7) a. Ta   ch-Ø-a-kol   cham,   ch-ach   hin-kol-**o'**
      COND ICP-B3-A2SG-help CLF   ICP-B2SG A1SG-help-TV
      'If you help the old man, I help you.'

     b. q-Ø-q'anjab' ayach   ta   q-ach   q'anjab'-**oq**
        POT-B3-talk to;2SG COND POT-B1PL talk-IRR
        'She/he will talk to you, if you talk.'

     c. X-ach-b'et   xew b'ay-tu   ma   maj   hach b'et   xew-**oq**?
        POT-B2SG-go.return rest PREP-DEM or   NEG;CP B2SG go.return rest-INF
        'You went to rest there or you did not go?'

     d. Hoq-Ø   hel   *wal-i,* chi-Ø xiw   wal   heb'
        POT-B3-GO A2SG;see INTS-FS ICP-B3 be.afraid INTS they
        'You will really see, they really get scared.'

(8) X-Ø-ko-watx'-ne-j   jun-tu
    CP-B3-A1PL-good-CAUS-TV one-DEM
    'We fixed/made that.'

These phrase-final suffixes are retained phrase-medially to avoid complex codas (this does not apply to phrase-final suffixes which attach to CVC roots, as these do not have a complex coda). The examples in (9) show phrase-final suffixes in medial position: the intransitive thematic suffix in (9a), an infinitival suffix in (9b), and the irrealis suffix in (9c). Note that these words have first syllable stress as they occur in medial position. These forms would be ungrammatical without the suffixes since Q'anjob'al does not allow complex coda.

(9) a. Ch-on   tz'in-j-**i**   hon
      ICP-B1PL quiet-INTR-IV EXCL
      'We (exclusive) become quiet.'

     b. X-Ø-toj heb'   aw-j-**oq**   b'ay-tu
        ICP-B3   they voice-INTR-INF PREP-DEM
        'They went to shout there.'

     c. hoq-ach txaj-l-**oq**   yekal
        POT-B2SG prayer-INTR-IRR tomorrow
        'You will pray tomorrow.'

4 MORPHOLOGY

Q'anjob'al is strongly agglutinating. I discuss three topics: inflection, root and word classes, and stem formation.

4.1 Inflectional categories

Q'anjob'al marks three inflectional categories: aspect-mood (AM), person and number, and valence. Person and number are marked by two sets of affixes known respectively as set A and set B. Table 20.3 lists these affixes.

Each set of affixes in Table 20.3 has two variants separated by slashes. The first variant of set A attaches to consonant-initial stems and the second to vowel-initial stems as shown by the first person in (10a, b). The first variant of set B occurs with verbs with an overt AM marker and the second one with verbs without an overt AM marker and with nonverbal predicates (NVPs) as shown by the second person in (10a) and (10c). The 'h' on all affixes signals the lack of initial glottal stop (§2.3).

(10) a. Max-ach   hin-kol-o'
      CP-B2SG   A1SG-help-TV
      'I helped you.'

   b. X-ex   w-il   y-ul   hin-na
      CP-B2PL A1SG-see A3SG-inside A1SG-house
      'I saw you all inside my house.'

   c. Miman   hach   xa   y-et tu?
      big   B2SG   already A3-of DEM
      'Were you already old then?' {txt001}

The first person plural marks three distinctions: exclusive (*hon*), inclusive (*heq*), and unmarked (i.e., without *hon* or *heq* and with either an inclusive or exclusive interpretation). The clitics immediately follow the head that licenses them like *hon* in (11).

(11) Max-on   y-il   hon   heb'
      CP-B1PL A3-see EXCL they
      'They saw us (not you).'

Third person inflection does not make a singular-plural distinction. *Heb'*, which has been analyzed as third person plural clitic (Montejo Esteban 1996; Raymundo *et al.* 2000), is an independent pronoun. Like any NP, in (12) *heb'* marks the object and it follows the basic VAO word order. It also follows a person clitic, (11).

TABLE 20.3 SET A AND B AFFIXES FOR PERSON AND NUMBER

Person	Set A	Set B
1SG	*hin-/w-*	*-in/hin*
2SG	*ha-/h-*	*-ach/hach*
3	*o~s-/y-*	*ø*
1PL (unmarked)	*ko-/j-*	*-on/hon*
1PL (exclusive)	*ko-/j-. . . hon(on)*	*-on. . . hon(on)/honon*
1PL (inclusive)	*ko-/j-. . . (h)eq*	*-on. . .=(h)eq/(h)on=eq*
2PL	*he-/hey-*	*-ex/hex*

(12) X-Ø-y-il   naq unin heb'
      CP-B3-A3-see CLF child they
      'The child saw them.'

As shown in (10)–(12), set A and set B mark various grammatical relations. In finite clauses, set A indexes transitive subjects and set B indexes objects and intransitive subjects (see alignment in §6.2). Set A also indexes possessors and arguments of relational nouns.

The second inflectional category is valence, marked by thematic suffixes. Transitive roots take -*V'* (-*a'*, -*o'*, -*u'*), (10a), and derived ones take -*j*, (8). Intransitive verbs, both derived and root, take -*i*, (13). As shown in §3, the suffixes -*V'* and -*i* occur only at phrase-final boundaries, though -*i* is retained to avoid complex codas like in *tz'inj* 'become quiet' in (13). Person inflection also signals valence; the predicate marks one or two arguments depending on its valence.

(13) Ch-on   tz'in-j-i   y-et   ch-Ø-jay-i
      ICP-B1PL quiet-INTR-IV A3-of ICP-B3-come.here-IV
      'We become quiet when s/he comes.'

The last inflectional category is aspect-mood (AM). Affixes or clitic-like affixes mark AM only on verbs (see NVPs in §6.1).[4] As shown in Table 20.4, the AM system distinguishes between REALIS and IRREALIS. There is an incompletive-completive aspectual opposition in the REALIS and a four-way distinction in the IRREALIS. Each distinction is marked by a prefix and/or by a suffix. The IRREALIS markers may differ for intransitive and transitive verbs. The completive varies with *xk*- without change in meaning, but the form needs more research.

The following intransitive and transitive paradigms illustrate the AM distinctions.

(14) CP   *x-ach way-i*   'you slept'   *x-ach y-il-a'*   's/he saw you'
      ICP   *ch-ach way-i*   'you sleep'   *ch-ach y-il-a'*   's/he sees you'
      POT   *q-ach way-oq*   'you will sleep'   *q-ach y-il-a'*   's/he will see you'
      EXH   *way-oq-on*   'let's sleep'   *j-il-eq (ix)*   'let's see (her)'
      OPT   *way-oq-ab'-i*   's/he may sleep'   *y-il-oq-ab' hach*   's/he may see you'
      IMP   *way-an*   'sleep!'   *il hin!*   'watch me!'

The completive aspect is commonly used to describe past events, but it also occurs in future contexts, as in (15). The incompletive encodes progressive, generic, and habitual meanings. It is commonly used to describe present events, but it also occurs in past contexts as in (16), where it expresses habitual.

TABLE 20.4 THE Q'ANJOB'AL ASPECT/MOOD SYSTEM

ASPECT-	REALIS	Completive	*(ma)x-*
MOOD		Incompletive	*ch(i)-*
	IRREALIS	Potential	*(ho)q-. . .-oq* (IV), *(ho)q-* (TV)
		Exhortative	*-oq* (IV), – – (TV)
		Optative	*-oq-ab'*
		Imperative	– –

(15) Max-ach=mi   kam-i,   hoq-on   meltzoj   hon
     CP-B2SG=DUB   die-IV   POT-B1PL   return   EXCL
     'You might have died, (by) when we will return.'

(16) y-et   x-on   ch'ib'-i,   xol tx'otx'   ch-on   ay   tel-an-oq
     A3-of   CP-B1PL   grow-IV   in land   ICP-B1PL   down   lying-POS-INF
     'When we grew up, we slept on the floor.' {txt003}

The potential is used for possible, planned, and future events. It is marked by *(ho)q-* on all verbs. Intransitive verbs also take the irrealis suffix *-oq* in final contexts or in nonfinal contexts to avoid complex codas (§3). The infinitival *-oq* and the irrealis *-oq* follow the same distribution and they have the same origin, whose details need further research.

(17) Y-et   chuman   aq'b'al   q-ach   apn-oq
     A3-of   middle   night   POT-B2SG   arrive-IRR
     'You will get there at midnight.' {txt204}

The exhortative form occurs only with first person plural. As shown in (14), the irrealis *-oq* (followed by set B) marks the exhortative on intransitive verbs, but there is no marker on transitive verbs and person inflection follows the usual transitive pattern. The optative form is restricted to third person and is marked by the irrealis *-oq* plus the reportative *=ab'*, (14). Optative with other persons is encoded by modal verbs like *je'* 'be possible' that take complement clauses (see §8). As shown in (14), imperative verbs have special forms; intransitive imperatives take *-an* (SG) or *-an=eq* (PL) to index the subject and transitive imperatives do not index the subject, but index the object with set B.

Finally, Q'anjob'al is developing a past tense form. In (18a), the verb lacks an AM marker, it has a past tense interpretation, and it is only compatible with past time adverbs. Unlike the completive aspect, it cannot refer to future events as shown in (18b). The verb in (18a) behaves like verbs with a preverbal AM marker in that person inflection follows an ergative-absolutive alignment. Thus, the verb heads a finite clause (see §7.1).

(18) a. Ø-hach   jay   {junab'i/*yekal}
        PAST-B2SG   come   last.year/tomorrow
        'You came here {last year/*tomorrow}.'

     b. *Ø=hach=mi   way-i,   hoq-Ø   jay-oq
        PAST=B2SG=PAR   sleep-IV   POT-B3   come-IRR
        Intended: 'You might have slept when s/he will come.'

4.2 Root and word classes

Words and roots may belong to different categories. All word classes correspond to root classes but not vice versa. I first discuss word classes and then roots.

Lexical categories differ from grammatical categories in their phonology, morphology, syntax, and lexical-semantics. Lexical categories include nouns, verbs, adjectives, and adverbs; they are illustrated in (19). Grammatical categories include prepositions, relational nouns (RNs), demonstratives, classifiers, articles, particles and clitics; they are illustrated in (20) with information on the number of members.

(19)   Lexical categories
    a. Verbs: *way* 'to sleep', *b'ey* 'to walk', *jay* 'to come', *xoj* 'to wash', *il* 'to see', etc.
    b. Nouns: *na* 'house', *pat* 'tortilla', *lab'aj* 'snake', *ix* 'woman', *wajil* 'hunger', etc.
    c. Adjectives: *saq* 'white', *chi'* 'sweet', *pim* 'thick', *yalixh* 'small', *isaj* 'lazy', etc.
    d. Adverbs: *ewi* 'yesterday', *nani* 'now', *amank'wan* 'quickly', etc.

(20)   Grammatical categories
    a. Preposition (1): *b'ay* 'at'
    b. Relational noun (16): *-intaq* 'behind', *-alan* 'under', *-etoq* 'with', etc.
    c. Demonstrative (2): *tu(')* 'that', *ti(')* 'this'
    d. Noun Classifier (14): *ix* 'female', *naq* 'male', *no(')* 'animals and derived products', etc.
    e. Article (2): *jun* 'indefinite (SG)', *(jun)tzan* 'some'
    f. Quantifier (few): *xiwil* 'many', *jab'* 'some', etc.
    g. Numeral classifier [number+classifier] (many): *b'ulan* 'pile', *suyan* 'rounded' *jilan* 'long', *k'olan* 'ball-like', etc.
    h. Particle and clitic (few): *to* 'still', *wal* 'really', *=ab'* 'reportative', etc.

There is a general correlation between categories, meaning, and function. Lexical categories have lexical content where verbs denote events, adjectives denote properties, nouns denote entities, and adverbs provide information on location, time, and manner. Grammatical categories provide grammatical information about lexical categories like definiteness, deixis, class membership, focus, etc. However, prepositions and RNs have both lexical and grammatical properties as in (21); they introduce adjuncts like the recipient and locative and like lexical categories they stand alone for a phrase. RNs differ from prepositions in that only RNs inflect for set A to cross-reference their complements.

(21) X-Ø-y-al-on   Ø-b'a naq b'ay xal y-ul   na
     CP-B3-A3-say-TCM A3-RR CLF at   CLF A3-inside house
     'And he complained to her in the house.'

A sample of features that distinguish word classes is shown in Table 20.5. They include three morphosyntactic features (take AM affix, allow possession, take the causative *-ne* to form causative verbs), one morphological feature that refers to the attenuative suffix *-taq*, and two syntactic functions (modifier of N/V and clausal argument argument).

Words can be roots or derived forms (see Polian, this volume, on morphology). There are two root classes whose members cannot, however, function as words without

TABLE 20.5 DIFFERENCES BETWEEN LEXICAL CATEGORIES

Features	V	N	Adj	Adv	Others
Aspect-mood	✓	*	*	*	*
Possession	*	✓	*	*	*(RN)
Attenuative suffix *-taq*	*	✓	✓	*	*
Causative *-ne*	*	✓	✓	*	*
Modifier of N/V	*	*	✓(N)	✓(V)	✓
Argument in simple clause	*	✓	*	*	*

derivation: positional and affect (with one exception noted below, (22b)). Positional roots denote states such as posture, form, texture, and brightness (Martin 1977), like *lek* 'standing', *chot* 'sitting', *lok* 'hanging', *jop* 'flashy', and *pan* 'flat'. Affect roots describe actions, movements, sounds, noise, etc. (Kaufman 1971; England 1983a:84), like *weq'* 'shouting', *jor* 'snoring', *juk* 'stand quickly', *k'am* 'greasy', and *kul* 'movement of flame'.

There is some overlap in these two root classes (see below), but they take different derivational affixes. The common derivational affixes for positional roots include *-an* (adjective) 'positional state' as in (22a), *-ay* (intransitive verb) 'change of position', *-b'aj* (transitive verb) 'cause to change position', and reduplications that form verbs with plural meanings (see Martin 1977; Polian, this volume, on morphology). Some affect roots occur in a construction used to refer to a sound as in (22b), but in other usages, they need derivation to function as words, which are mostly intransitive verbs expressing movement and manner like the manner of motion in (22c). Affect and positional roots differ in that only positionals take the derivational suffixes *-an* and *-naj*.

(22) a. ... pak'-an   hin   ay-oq
         face.down-POS B1SG   DIR:down-INF
         '... I am face down.' {txt080}

    b. witz' xhi   jun-tzan pay
       witz' ICP;B3;say   one-PL   skunk
       'Some skunks say *witz'* [sharp noise].' {txt080}

    c. per tol   xuy-uy-i   j-ek'-i
       but INTS   running-INTR-IV   A1PL-pass-IV
       'But we have to run around. . .' {txt047}

Roots are usually monosyllabic with a predominant CVC form. Disyllabic roots are mostly CV(C).CVC. Table 20.6 shows the syllable structure of different root classes based on 1,428 roots: 'few' =less than five, 'some' =about ten, 'many' =more than ten, * =impossible root, ? =possible unattested root. See examples in (19) and the previous paragraphs.

Some observations follow. First, nouns and adjectives are monosyllabic or disyllabic with a predominant CVC and CV.CVC shape. Second, adverbs vary in shape, especially the disyllabic ones. Third, intransitive verbal roots are mostly monosyllabic as only 18 of the 75 intransitive roots in the database are disyllabic. Half of these 18 verbs relate

TABLE 20.6 ROOT CATEGORIES AND THEIR PHONOLOGICAL SHAPE

Syllable form	N	Adj	Adv	IV	TV/Pos/Aff
CV	✓(few)	?	?	*	✓(some)
CVC	✓(many)	✓(many)	✓(many)	✓(most)	✓(most)
CVCC	*	*	*	✓(few)	*
CV.CVC	✓(many)	✓(many)	✓(few)	✓(few)	*
CVC.CVC	?	?	?	✓(some)	*
CV(C).CV	?	?	✓(few)	✓(few)	*
CV.CV.CV	?	*	✓(few)	?	*

to nouns as in *saqchi* 'to play'/*saqach* 'play', *mulnaji* 'to work'/*mulnajil* 'work', and *q'anjab'i* 'to talk'/*q'anej* 'word', but the direction of derivation is unclear. The other half include *meltzoj* 'to return, *ispay* 'to get bored', and *tzaloj* 'to be happy', which seem to be derived forms, but I consider them roots as their synchronic source is unavailable. Finally, all transitive, positional, and affect roots are monosyllabic with a dominant CVC shape.

Transitive and affect roots are fewer than positional roots; in the database of 1,428 roots, there are 8 affect roots, 108 transitive roots, and about 200 positional roots. Martin (1977) reports 270 positional roots, but I identify over 500 roots. Research on Mam (England 2006), Tseltal (Sántiz Gómez 2010; Pérez González 2012), and Tsotsil (Haviland 1994) show that transitive, positional, and affect roots overlap, but in Q'anjob'al, the overlap is mostly between positionals and affect roots. The overlap is illustrated below.

(23)   CVC   TV   Positional   Affect

       a. *ch'ob'*   —   'opened (mouth)'   'noise of opening'

       b. *kul*   —   'form of flame'   'sound of flames'

       c. *xuy*   'to untie'   'untied'   'running'

       d. *b'uq'*   'to swallow'   —   'noise/way of swallowing'

       e. *maq'*   'to hit'   —   —

4.3 Stem formation

Stems are formed mostly through derivation and a limited compounding process. About 69 derivational affixes (excluding voice affixes, see §6.3) are documented. Table 20.7 lists the most productive affixes: the second column specifies the category of the input and output with the general meaning and the third gives an example.

A semi-productive compounding process that involves two roots also forms stems, (24).[5] While the first root can be an adjective, (24a–c), a number, (24d), a positional root, (24e) or a verb, (24f); the second one is always a transitive verb. However, the compound requires the causative affix *-ne* (that derives transitive verbs from N/Adj, see Table 20.7) to receive inflection as in (25); *-lay* passivizes the word derived by the causative *-ne*.

TABLE 20.7 SAMPLE OF DERIVATIONAL AFFIXES

Affix	Input>output (meaning)	Example
-ab'	NUM>ADV (future year)	*ox-ab'* 'in three years'
-ej	NUM>ADV (future day)	*kab'-ej* 'in two days'
-ab'i	NUM>ADV (past years)	*jun-ab'i* 'last year'
-ji	NUM>ADV (past days)	*kab'-ji* 'two days ago'
-el	NUM>ADV (times)	*ox-el* 'three times'
-ne	N>TV (usative)	*chej-ne* 'to use as horse'
-ne	A/N >TV (causative)	*miman-ne* 'to make big', *winaq-ne* 'to make a man'
-b'i	A/N>IV (inchoative)	*kaq-b'i* 'to get hot', *unin-b'i* 'to become child'
-taq	A/N>A (attenuated)	*q'eq-taq* 'blackish', *winaq-taq* 'half man'
-ay	P>IV (asuntive)	*k'ol-ay* 'to become rounded'
-lab'	P>IV (repetitive)	*chot-lab'* 'to sit repeatedly individually'
-C₂on	P>IV (repetitive)	*k'ol-k'on* 'to move in a ball-like form'

(Continued)

TABLE 20.7 (CONTINUED)

Affix	Input>output (meaning)	Example
-b'a	P>TV (causative)	tel-b'a 'to lay someone down'
-kil	P>A (distributive)	k'ol-kil-taq 'rounded things separated'
-VRl	P>A (end-state)	tel-el 'to end lying suddenly'
-xi	P/TV>IV (continuous)	chot-xi 'to sit (continuous)', man-xi 'to buy (continuous)'
-ob'tane	TV>TV (repetitive)	jos-ob'tane 'to scrape repeatedly'
-b'il	TV>A (participle)	maq'-b'il 'bitten', oche-b'il 'liked'
-naq	IV>A (participle)	way-naq 'slept'

(24) Root+V compound
  a. *yax txik-ne-j*   [raw+cook]   'to cook raw (still raw)'
  b. *kok'tzok'-ne-j* [small+cut]   'to cut into small pieces'
  c. *watx'al-ne-j*   [good+say]   'to say clearly/well'
  d. *ka al-ne-j*   [two+say]   'to repeat/reassure'
  e. *b'al tx'aj-ne-j* [round+wash]   'to half wash (not well)'
  f. *tzok'koj*   [cut+grind]   'to cut into pieces'

(25) Max-Ø b'al   tx'aj-ne-lay   an   is
     CP-B3 round wash-TR-PSV   CLF potato
     'The potatoes were half washed.'

5 THE NOUN PHRASE

The elements of the NP have been described in Maya in Berlin's (1968) work on numeral classifiers in Tseltal, in the work of Craig (1987) and Zavala (2000) on noun classifiers, and in descriptive grammars. However, its semantics is still unexplored. In this section I describe the constituents which make up the NP and their ordering. The maximum structure is given in (26). Quantifiers cover measure and numeral classifiers, which I discuss below.

(26) The constituents of an NP in Q'anjob'al
     (IND)+(PL)+ (CLF) + (Qs) + (SET A-) (ADJ) N ⎰+(RC) + (DEM)+(EVID)⎱
                                                  ⎱   (NPGEN)   ⎰

   NPs with all the elements in (26) are rare in natural speech, but they occur in elicitation. The examples in (27a–c) show NPs with different structures. When there is a genitive NP as in (27c), the demonstrative and evidential modify the genitive and they cannot precede the genitive to modify the head. Thus, the genitive occurs in the slot where the demonstrative and evidential occur.

(27) a. [heb' naq ka-wan   yalixh winaq tu   la]
        PL   CLF two-CLF:human   small   man   DEM   EVID:mirative
        'those two small men'

   b. X-Ø-man-lay   [tx'i']
      CP-B3-buy-PSV dog
      'Dogs were bought.'

c. X-Ø-kam [no s-tx'i' [xal ix   tu   (la)]]
   CP-B3-die CLF A3-dog CLF woman DEM EVID:mirative
   'The dog of that woman died (you see).'

Some issues about the NP follow. The plural *heb'* occurs only with human referents. There are only indefinite determiners: *jun* (singular) and *(jun)tzan* (plural). The evidential *la* encodes unexpected information or surprise; it appears on an NP in any position within the clause with a discourse function as in (27c) and (28). The situation in (28) is unexpected in relation to 'the cow' in a possible context where 'the cow was expected to be taken care of by a boy' but something else happened. The speaker also invites the hearer to evaluate the information; I translate this as 'you see'.

(28) A   no   wakax la   x-Ø-y-il   naq winaq ti
     FOC   CLF   cow   EVID:mirative   CP-B3-A3-see   CLF man   DEM
     'It was the cow that this man saw (you see).'

Prenominal adjectives form a compound with the noun and do not constitute phrases (Mateo Toledo 2017). The possessor marker precedes the adjective as in (29a); the compound serves as input to derivation like the causative *-ne* in (29b); multiple prenominal adjectives are marginally possible only with adjectives of size and color as in (29c), and adjectives cannot take modifiers as shown by the intensifiers *kaw* in (29d).

(29) a. naq   hin-jelan   unin
        CLF   A1SG-smart   child
        'my smart kid'

     b. Max-Ø   ko-jelan   unin-ne-j   ix
        CP-B3   A1PL-smart   child-CAUS-TV   CLF
        'We treated her as a smart kid.'

     c. ?no   yal   q'eq   tx'i'
        CLF   small   black   dog
        'the small black dog'

     d. *naq kaw   jelan   unin
        CLF   very   small   child
        Intended: 'the very smart kid'

The final issue involving NPs is classifiers. There are two types of classifiers: numeral and nominal classifiers, which are well documented and understood in Mayan.

Noun classifiers provide information about the noun they classify and about the NP's referent (Craig 1987; Grinevald 2000; Zavala 2000; and others). All non-abstract nouns in Q'anjob'al fall within one of 14 classes that belong to two groups. One group classifies human and personified referents based on gender, age, and social status; the members are *ix* 'female', *naq* 'male', *xal* 'respected female, lady', and *cham* 'respected/old male'. The other group occurs with non-human referents and classifies nouns based on their physical properties, substance, or origin. The members are *te(')* 'trees and their fruits, wooden things', *no(')* 'animals and animal products', *ch'en* 'stone, metal-like things (including ice)', *tx'an* 'fiber (maguey) and products of fiber', *q'a(q')* 'fire', *tz'am* 'salt', *tx'otx'* 'land, objects of clay/soil', *ha* 'water and some liquids', *an* 'plants and their fruits, cotton products', and *(i)xim* 'corn, rice, and rice/corn products.'

Classifiers can substitute for NPs and thereby function as pronouns. In texts, new referents are usually introduced as indefinite or as subjects of existential predicates and once they become given discourse referents, are referred to by a classifier or null pronoun. The fragment on people going hunting in (30) shows the point; *no tx'i'* 'the dog' is introduced as the subject of an existential. Subsequent references to 'the dog' are made with the classifier *no* (*no'* in phrase-final position).

(30) Tay   kax   ta   tol   ay-Ø   *no tx'i' tu*   ch-Ø-yasj-i,
     then   then   COND   INTS   EXIST-B3   CLF dog DEM   ICP-B3-hurt-IV
     '. . . then, if a dog gets hurt',
     tol=hab'   ch'-Ø-iq-lay   *no'*,   ch'-Ø-ay   *no*   y-ul   txim,
     INTS=REP   ICP-B3-carry-PSV   CLF   ICP-B3-go.down   CLF   A3-in   bag
     'it is carried (they say), it is put in a bag of fiber',

     ch'-Ø-ay   *no*   y-ul   pa. . .
     ICP-B3-go.down   CLF   A3-inside   bag
     'it is put in a bag. . .' {txt029}

Numeral classifiers, which are used in counting non-abstract nouns, are of two types in all Q'anjob'al languages: suffixal and sortal (Zavala 2000). Except for the number 'one', suffixal classifiers obligatorily attach to numeral roots as in (31). They divide nouns in three groups: human (*-wan*), animal (*-k'on*), and inanimate (*-eb'*).

(31) a. ox-k'on   tx'i'   b. ox-wan   ix   c. ox-eb'   na
         three-CLF:animal   dog   three-CLF:HUM woman   three- CLF:INAN   house
         'three dogs'   'three women'   'three houses'

As in other Mayan languages (Berlin 1968; Zavala 2000), sortal classifiers come from positional roots and they take the suffix *-an*. They are not obligatory and they group entities according to arrangement, form, organization, etc. As shown by *jilan* 'long' in (32a), they combine directly with a number or number+suffixal classifier. Note that the three classifier systems co-occur in the same NP as they provide different information about the referent. There are about thirty sortal classifiers, a sample appears in (32b).

(32) a. te   {ox-eb'   jilan /ox-jilan}   si'
         CLF   three-CLF:INAN   long /three-long   firewood
         'the three long pieces of firewood'

     b. Sortal classifiers
         suyan   'round like disk'   *xoyan*   'rounded'
         patxan   'flat (table)'   *k'olan*   'rounded ball-like'
         xilan   'rounded small'   *xiqan*   'small elongated'
         kupan   'rolled (string)'   *putzan*   'big ball-like'

6 SIMPLE CLAUSES

Q'anjob'al is a VO language with a fixed VAO/VS order. As it is a head-marking language, lexical arguments are optional and their occurrence depends on syntactic or discourse factors. It has an ergative alignment with restrictions on the extraction of A arguments.

6.1 Predicates

Q'anjob'al has two types of predicates: verbal and nonverbal. All predicates inflect for person and number, but only verbal ones inflect for AM. The predicate may occur with additional elements like directionals, particles, or clitics. Verbal predicates include both intransitive and transitive verbs, as in (33). NVPs are headed by nonverbal words that include positionals, nouns, adjectives, adverbs, and the existential, as in (34).

(33) a. Xan   k'am   ch-ach   uk'-wi   an. . .
      why   NEG   ICP-B2SG   drink-AP   plant
      ' "So, do not drink alcohol . . . ".' {txt062}

    b. k'am xa   b'aq'in   q-in   ha-tayne-j
      NEG already   time   POT-B1SG   A2SG-take.care-TV
      ' "You will never take care of me again".' {txt019}

(34) a. . . . lek-an-Ø   el-teq   cham Ø-ti   y-atut
      standing-POS-B3   DIR:out-DIR:toward   CLF   A3-front   A3-house
      'The old man was standing in front of his house.' {txt017}

    b. Mamej   hach   ok   ko-xol
      father   B2SG   DIR:enter   A1PL-among
      'You are the father among us.'

    c. Kaw   jelan   hach
      INTS   smart   B2SG
      'You are very smart.'

    d. Ay-Ø   ilya
      EXIST-B3   sickness
      'There is sickness.'

NVPs partially differ from verbs in morphosyntax. First, unlike verbs, nonverbal nuclei never take overt AM markers. Without adverbs, their temporal location is determined by context; they overlap with speech time or contextual time as in (34). Second, person markers precede a verb as does -*ach* in (33a), but they follow nonverbal heads as does *hach* in (34c). Third, unlike verbs, NVPs lack imperative forms. Verbs and NVPs also differ in negation (§6.4). Finally, the verbal-nonverbal morphosyntax also reflects an event-stative semantic opposition (Vendler 1957; Smith 1991; and others) without known exceptions: verbs denote events and NVPs denote states. For example, the NVP *ojtaq* denotes the state of 'knowing' as in *wojtaq hach* 'I know you' and the verb *ojtaqnej* the event of 'acquiring knowledge' as in *maxach wojtaqnej* 'I met you'.

6.2 Alignment

In Q'anjob'al, core arguments (A, S, O) follow two alignments: ergative-absolutive in finite clauses and nominative-accusative in nonfinite clauses. In ditransitive clauses, objects follow an indirect alignment. Nominative alignment is addressed in §7.

The ergative-absolutive alignment is shown by the second person in (35) (see all affixes in Table 20.3): while A is indexed by set A in (35a), O and S are indexed by set B in (35b, c), respectively. Furthermore, the S of NVPs is indexed by set B as in (34b) above.

(35) a. xk-in   ha-kol-o'
        CP-B1SG   A2SG-help-TV
        'You helped me.' {txt048}

    b. q-ach   j-ante-j
        POT-B2SG   A1PL-cure-TV
        'We will cure you.' {txt155}

    c. B'aytal x-ach   b'et-i?   xh-i
        where   CP-B2SG   go.return-IV   3;say-FS
        'Where did you go? she/he said.' {txt042}

Core lexical arguments (cross-referenced by set A and set B) lack case and follow a fixed VAO or VS order as in (36); VS stands for intransitive verbs and NVPs. A genitive NP is also a direct argument indexed on the possessed noun, (36b). Non-direct arguments follow the last core argument and are introduced by adpositions like *xol* 'between' in (36a).

(36) a. Max-Ø   y-i-toq   naq ix   ix   [s-xol   te']
        CP-B3   A3-take-DIR:away CLF CLF woman   A3-between   tree
        'He took the woman [into the woods].' {txt095}

    b. ay-Ø   y-uxhtaq   hin-mam
        EXIST-B3 A3-brother   A1SG-father
        'My father had brothers.' {txt003}

Ditransitive clauses show *indirective alignment* in Q'anjob'al. The theme argument (T) in a ditransitive aligns morphosyntactically with O in a simple transitive clause while the recipient/benefactive/goal argument (R) is an oblique (Malchukov *et al.* 2010). As shown in (37), the O and T are indexed by set B and R is introduced by the preposition *b'ay* 'to'.

(37) a. Max-ach   w-il-a'
        CP-B2SG   A1SG-see-TV
        'I saw you.'

    b. Max-ach   ko-sa-toq   b'ay xal
        CP-B2SG   A1PL-give-DIR:away   to   CLF
        'We gave you (as a gift) to the lady.'

The passives in (38) also show indirective alignment. While the O and T become S indexed by set B in the passive, the R is introduced by a preposition.

(38) a. Max-ach   il-lay-i
        CP-B2SG   see-PSV-IV
        'You were seen.'

    b. Max-ach   sa-lay-toq   b'ay xal
        CP-B2SG   give-PSV-DIR:away   to   CLF
        'You were given to the lady.'

6.3 Voice alternations

Q'anjob'al has two voice categories that alternate with transitive voice: passive and anti-passive. In both cases, the verb is intransitive and it indexes one argument. The other argument is an optional oblique or is incorporated. Voice alternations are motivated both by syntactic and pragmatic constraints (Dayley 1990; England 1983b, Zavala 1997; Aissen 1999). Dayley (1990) includes the agent focus under voice, but in §6.5 I show that it is a resource used for extracting an A argument that differs from a canonical voice alternation.

6.3.1 Passive

Q'anjob'al has two passives, formed with the suffixes *-lay* and *-chaj*. They are illustrated in (39). In both passives, the agent is an optional oblique phrase introduced by *yuj* 'by'.

(39) a. Kab'   k'u   max-Ø   kol-chaj   heb'   (y-uj   cham)
        two   day   CP-B3   help-PSV   they   A3-by   CLF
        'They were saved for two days (by the old man).'

     b. Kab'   k'u   max-Ø   kol-lay   heb'   (y-uj   cham)
        two   day   CP-B3   help-PSV   they   A3-by   CLF
        'They were helped for two days (by the old man).'

The passive *-lay* occurs with all transitive verbs without a change in meaning. However, the passive *-chaj* has three special features. First, *-chaj* occurs with roots and some derived verbs that lose the derivational suffix in this passive, but not with the passive *-lay*. These derived verbs include *uk'ej* 'to drink' (*uk'chaj* 'to be drunk/drinkable'), *etz'ej* 'to imitate' (*etz'chaj* 'to be imitated'), *antej* 'to cure' (*anchaj* 'to be cured'), *ab'ej* 'to hear' (*ab'chaj* 'to become heard'), and *iqej* 'to obey' (*iqchaj* 'to be obeyed').

Second, *-chaj* adds a modal meaning of possibility 'the event is doable' or ability 'the unexpressed agent is able to perform the event.' Thus, *tz'ib'chaj* in (40) can mean 'someone was registered and the event was doable' or 'to be registerable'.

(40) To'   [ch]-Ø-tz'ib'-chaj   ok-toq   [heb']
     only   ICP-B3-writing-PSV   DIR:enter-DIR:away they
     'They can only be registered . . . '
     'Someone was able to only register them.' {txt070}

Third and last, *-chaj* contributes to event structure. It adds a change of state meaning that makes an event telic; e.g., *tz'ib'ej* denotes a writing process with an unknown result, but *tz'ib'chaj* 'to be registered' has a result. The examples in (39) also show this aspectual meaning; while *-chaj* adds an endpoint to the event, *-lay* does not. In (39a), *kolchaj* means 'to be saved' and the durative adverb *kab'k'u* specifies how long the result lasted, but in (39b), *kollay* means 'to be helped' and the adverb specifies the duration of the helping process.

6.3.2 Antipassive

There are two antipassives: the absolutive antipassive formed with *-waj* and the incorporating antipassive formed with *-wi*. An antipassive verb indexes the agent and while *-wi* has an incorporated patient, *-waj* may license an oblique goal.

The antipassive of incorporation has a habitual or generic meaning, (41). It occurs with all verbs with an unmarked VS order. The patient is incorporated: it is a bare noun and it forms a morphological word with the verb as it precedes the clitic *hon*.

(41) a. Jun ab'il x-on   waj-wi   sakate hon
        one year   CP-B1PL gather-AP fodder EXCL
        'We gathered fodder for one year.'

   b. ... y-et ch'-Ø-uqte-wi   no   heb'
        A3-of   ICP-B3-chase-AP animal they
        '... when they hunt!' {txt029}

The absolutive antipassive is illustrated in (42). It occurs only with the almost exhaustive list of transitive roots in (43) (those with question mark are marginal with -*waj*) and some of the derived verbs that take the passive -*chaj* (see §6.3.1).

(42) Tol=hab' tol   lan   [s-]toj   maq'-waj y-in   cham...
        INTS=REP   INTS PROG   A3-go   hit-AP   A3-at CLF
        'It is said that he was going to hit at him ... ' {txt222}

(43) Verbs that take -*waj*
        jul   'to shoot'   *tzok'*   'to cut (with machete)'
        maq'   'to hit'   *kol*   'to help, save'
        loq   'to peck'   *b'aj*   'to scold, mistreat verbally'
        tek'   'to kick'   *chip*   'to punch'
        etx'   'to pinch'   *tx'em*   'to bother'
        b'uch 'to despise, reject'   *xiq*   'to cut with machete'
        q'oq   'to throw something at'   *b'al*   'to roll'
        ?pol   'to cut with knife'   *?k'otz* 'to pinch'
        ?iq   'to carry on back'   *?k'up*   'to saw (wood)'

The verbs above denote an event that entails affectedness or change of state. The antipassive -*waj* removes this meaning as shown by the goal-theme alternation in (44), which resembles the English conative construction (Levin 1993:41–2). In the active voice in (44a), the object *heb'* is a theme, but in the antipassive in (44b) the oblique *heb'* is a goal and the verb means 'to shoot at'. Some antipassive verbs cannot even license a goal NP like *polo'* 'to cut' in (45). Thus, the antipassive -*waj* is lexicalized.

(44) a. Max-Ø s-jul   xal   heb'
          CP-B3   A3-shoot CLF they
          'She shot them.'

   b. Max-Ø jul-waj   xal y-in   heb'
        CP-B3   hit-AP   CLF A3-at they
        'She shot at them.'

(45) X-Ø-pol-waj   naq Xhwan *(y-in te')
        CP-B3-cut-AP   CLF Xhwan A3-at CLF
        'Xhwan cut *(at it).'

6.4 Preverbal structure

There are various elements that can precede the predicate in a finite clause. These include a topic phrase, negation, focus, and a secondary predicate. The examples below illustrate these elements: topic and clausal negation in (46a); focus, clausal negation and secondary predicate in (46b). In §10, I show that topic does not constitute a proper element of finite clauses.[6]

(46) a. Ayon,   maj=xa   Ø-j-il-a'
        we   NEG.CP=already B3-A1PL-see-TV
        'As for us, we did not see it anymore.' {txt003}

    b. A   ixim tx'ix   man   tz'ayil-oq s-taj-i
       FOC CLF   tamale NEG   burnt-IRR   A3-cook-IV
       'It is the tamale that cooked and did not result burnt.'

Clausal negation is sensitive to aspect and partially to predicate type (see Mam, this volume, for similarities). *Maj* negates a clause in completive aspect and it fuses with *(ma) x*, (46a); *k'am* negates a clause in incompletive aspect and the existential *ay* that fuses with *k'am* as in (47a, b); and *man* negates clauses in potential mood as well as clauses with NVPs, (47c, d). The irrealis suffix *-oq* occurs on the predicate nucleus in the negation of NVPs and on intransitive verbs in the completive aspect (see §3 on the distribution of *-oq*).

(47) a. K'am ch-ach   low-i
       NEG   ICP-B2SG eat-IV
       'You do not eat.'

    b. K'am-Ø=xa   jun   tu
       NEG.EXIST-B3=already one DEM
       'That one does not exist anymore.'

    c. Man hoq-ach low   yekal
       NEG   POT-B2SG eat   tomorrow
       'You will not eat tomorrow.'

    d. Man anima-oq hach
       NEG   person-IRR B2SG
       'You are not a person.'

Manaq negates a clause with focus, as in (48). This case of narrow focus under the scope of negation differs from the clausal negation in two features: *manaq* does not interact with aspect and *manaq* precedes the focus. This type of negation is open to more research.

(48) Manaq hin-mam   xk-in   kuy-on-kan   y-in. . .
     NEG   A1SG-father CP-B1SG teach-AF-DIR:stay A3-at
     'It was not my father who taught me [that] . . . ' {txt021}

Focus is a pragmatic relation encoded in preverbal position or in situ. I discuss preverbal focus only as it involves a special syntactic position. In (49), the preverbal focus is preceded by the focus particle *a* that is obligatory for third person but is unusual for speech act participants (SAP). When the focus corresponds to the A argument of a transitive clause and is third person, the verb takes the suffix -*n*/-*on*, as in (49a) (more on this suffix below).

(49) a. A   heb'   naq   q-ach   toq   q'ume-*n*-oq
       FOC   PL   CLF   POT-B2SG   go   talk-AF-IRR
      'They are the ones who will go to talk to you.'{txt023}

    b. Ayex   x-in   b'et   hey-a'-kan   nombrar. . .
       you.all   CP-B1SG   go   A2PL-give-DIR:stay   name
       'You were the ones who went to nominate me. . .' {txt015}

Wh-questions also use the preverbal focus position. A wh-question is shown in (50).

(50) Maktxel xk-in   tx'ox-on-i?
    who   CP-B1SG   show-AF-FS
    'Who showed me?'

As shown in (51), preverbal focus and wh-question do not co-occur. This means that they use the same structure. In the meaning, the preverbal focus and wh-word encode new information and the rest of the clause belongs to the presupposition. The next section shows that agent extraction follows the same restrictions.

(51) *Tzetal   a   heb'   x-Ø-jatne-n-i?
    what   FOC   they   CP-B3-make-AF-FS
    Intended: 'What did they do?'

6.5 Agent extraction: agent focus

Some Mayan languages have an agent focus construction (AF) used only when the agent is focused, questioned, or relativized. Its analysis, function and motivation have been the topic of more than two decades of research (on the general Mayan situation, see Stiebels 2006, Aissen to appear, and references in those works). Below I describe the facts on AF in Q'anjob'al (Francisco Pascual 2007).

The example in (52a) illustrates the AF construction in Q'anjob'al. The AF is obligatory when a third person agent is focused. It is not used when the S/O is focused, (52b, c). Furthermore, the AF is used only in the extraction of third person agents and not in the extraction of SAP agents as in (49b). It also allows any kind of object, like the SAP in (49).

(52) a. A   heb'   naq   q-ach   toq   q'ume-n-oq
       FOC   PL   CLF   POT-B2SG   go   talk-AF-IRR
       'They are the ones who will go to talk to you.'{txt023}

    b. A   no   koj   tu   x-Ø-jay   y-in   heb'
       FOC   CLF   lion   DEM   COM-B3-come   A3-at   they
       'It is the lion that came at them.' {txt029}

    c. A   no   kandela   ch-Ø-y-i   heb'
       FOC   CLF   candle   ICP-B3-A3-take   they
       'It is the candles that they take.' {txt129}

The Q'anjob'al AF construction has four features. First, the A argument is extracted from its clause and leaves behind a gap. Except in relative clauses with a gap (§8), the extracted A occurs in preverbal position. Second, the verb takes the suffix *-on/-n* (AF *-on*, hereafter). Third, the verb is formally intransitive (as in other voice alternations): it only inflects for set B that indexes the O and the verb takes intransitive suffixes like the irrealis *-oq* in (52a), see §4.1. Finally, both A and O arguments are present as direct arguments and therefore AF clauses resemble transitive clauses (see Craig 1977; Dayley 1990; Stiebels 2006; Coon *et al.* 2014; Aissen to appear for discussion of AF in relation to issues of transitivity).

The AF is used in focus related constructions that involve the extraction of agents. Like focus, wh-questions involve the extraction of a constituent to the preverbal position. They obey the above restrictions on agent extraction. Relative clauses also use an AF structure in the relativization of agents, but it is not focus (see §8). Wh-questions are shown in (53). As shown in (53), an AF is used only in the interrogation of the agent.[7]

(53) a. Maktxel   ch-on   etz'e-n-i?
        who   ICP-B1PL   imitate-AF
        'Who is imitating us?'

     b. Maktxel   max-Ø   h-aq'-kan   ko-taynomal-oq?
        who   CP-B3   A2SG-give-DIR:stay   A1PL-guard-IRR
        'Who did you leave as our guard?' {txt054}

7 CLAUSE TYPES AND THEIR FUNCTIONS

This section makes two points. First, Q'anjob'al has three clause types: finite, nonfinite and infinitival. Finite clauses have a preverbal structure and inflection for person/number and aspect; nonfinite clauses inflect for person/number and lack both aspect inflection and a preverbal structure; and infinitival clauses lack both inflection and a preverbal structure. According to the grades of finiteness and structure, they follow the hierarchy finite > nonfinite > infinitive. Second, these clause types do not depend on particular constructions since they fulfill functions like complement, adverbial clause, relative clause, etc. I illustrate each type in complement function first, and then show other functions. In the analysis of complements, I discus the morphosyntax of the complement, the syntax of the complex clause, and predicates taking complements.

This section rests on two assumptions. First, a clause consists of three layers (Aissen 1992 and this volume, on complement clauses): the lowest layer, formed by the predicate nucleus and its arguments; an intermediate layer, defined by the categories realized as AM affixes; and the top layer, which includes the previous two plus preverbal positions. Second, finiteness is a gradable property defined by morphosyntactic features and clause structure (Givón 2001:352; Nikolaeva 2007).

7.1 Finite clauses

Finite clauses have all the features discussed in §6. That is, they have a full-fledged morphosyntax and preverbal structure.

Finite clauses function as complements with a declarative or interrogative form. The complementizer *tol* introduces declarative complements as in (54a).[8] Interrogative complements are of two types: those introduced by the conditional *ta* 'if' are like polar questions as in (54b) and those with a wh-word are like wh-questions as in (54c). These complements allow focus and negation as in (54a) and (54c), respectively.

(54) a. X-Ø-ey-ab'e-j   [tol   a   ix   x-Ø-jay-i]
      CP-B3-A2PL-hear-TV   COMP FOC CLF CP-B3-come.here-IV
      'You heard that she is the one who came here.'

   b. Q-Ø-toq   hin-q'anle-j [ta ay-Ø   to   ko-jek]
      POT-B3-go A1SG-ask-TV if   EXIST-B3 still A1PL-debt
      'I will go to ask if we still have debts.' {txt049}

   c. Pero hoq-Ø   ko-q'anle-j   [maktxel k'am ch-Ø-kan-i]
      but   POT-B3 A1PL-ask-TV who   NEG   ICP-B3-stay-IV
      'But we will ask who does not stay.'

7.2 Nonfinite clauses

The material in square brackets in (55) shows nonfinite clauses in complement function.

(55) a. Tom q-Ø-tzaqay   [**ha**-b'ey   w-intaq]. . .
      NEG   POT-B3-be.able A2SG-walk A1SG-behind
      'You will not be able to reach me [walk behind me].' {txt132}

   b. K'am ch-Ø-je   [Ø-**ha**-ten-on   heb' cham]
      NEG   ICP-B3-possible B3-A2SG-move-DM PL   CLF
      'You cannot bother them [old men]'. {txt104}

   c. q-Ø-je   [**hach** j-awte-n-i] . . .
      POT-B3-possible B2SG A1PL-call-DM-FS
      'We might call you.'

Nonfinite clauses have three morphosyntactic features. First, the verb lacks an AM marker as in (55). Second, as shown in (55b, c), transitive verbs take the dependent marker (DM) -on/-n and the suffix -i at final phrase boundaries. Third, person inflection follows a nominative-accusative pattern as shown by the second person: the A and S arguments in (55a, b) are indexed by set A *ha-* and the object is indexed by set B *hach* in (55c). Finally, these nonfinite clauses lack preverbal structure; they are ungrammatical with negation and preverbal focus (see Mateo Toledo 2004, 2013a).

The DM -*on* and AF -*on* are diachronically related, but they differ in their synchronic functions. The AF suffix is triggered by the extraction of a third person agent and derives a finite intransitive verb. The DM suffix occurs in clauses without extraction and is not restricted to third person agents, see (55b, c). It attaches to nonfinite transitive verbs and signals structural dependency (Francisco Pascual 2007; Mateo Toledo 2013a).

7.3 Infinitival clauses

Infinitival clauses are the last clause type. They are illustrated in square brackets below in their complement clause function.

(56) a. X-∅-y-aq'-toq   ix   naq   [ante-lay-oq]
       CP-B3-A3-give-DIR:away   CLF   CLF   cure-PSV-INF
       'She send him to be cured.'

     b. X-∅-s-cheq-toq   ix   naq   [waj-oj   sakate   b'aytu]
       CP-B3-A3-send-DIR:away   CLF   CLF   gather-INF   fodder   there
       'She ordered him (verbally) to gather fodder there.'

Infinitival clauses lack both inflection and preverbal structure. The subject argument is not syntactically realized and must be controlled by an argument in the matrix clause. The infinitive of intransitive verbs is marked by -*oq*, which surfaces only in final contexts as in (56a). The infinitive of notional transitive verbs is marked by -*oj*, which triggers patient incorporation as in (56b). As in the incorporating antipassive (§6.3.2), the O argument (the noun *sakate* 'fodder' in (56b)) is incorporated: it cannot take any modifier and it precedes clitics and arguments. Thus, all infinitives are formally intransitive.

Infinitival complements are of two types. The first type was shown in (56). In this case, the matrix predicate is a verb of manipulation that precedes the complement and the controller is the matrix object. The second type is a focused infinitival clause selected by *unej* 'to do' as in (57) where the controller is the matrix subject. Being focused, the infinitival clause precedes the matrix verb. The construction only permits this order.

(57) [asan uk'-oj   an]   ch-∅-y-une-j
     only drink-INF   alcohol   ICP-B3-A3-do-TV
     'Drink alcohol is the only thing that she/he does.' {txt003}

7.4 Complementation hierarchy

All complement clauses are subordinated: finite ones are introduced by *tol*, wh-words or *ta*; nonfinite ones have dependent morphosyntax; and infinitival ones lack inflection. They are core arguments in the matrix predicate and are placed according to the VAO/VS order.

The alignment between matrix predicates and complement types in Q'anjob'al follows tendencies noted in typological studies. Cristofaro (2003:125) proposes the following hierarchy of semantic matrix predicates: "knowledge, propositional attitude, utterance >perception > desiderative, manipulative >modal, phasal," based on the notion of semantic dependence (with respect to temporal and argument reference). In her proposal, modal and phasal predicates select the most dependent (or least finite) complements, but utterance predicates select the least dependent (or most finite) complements.

Table 20.8 shows the alignment between semantic classes of matrix predicates and complement types in Q'anjob'al. "Few" and "some" refer to the number of predicates of some class that select a complement type. As expected under Cristofaro's hierarchy, predicates of knowledge, utterance, and propositional attitude take finite complements. However, modal/phasal predicates do not follow the proposal as they take nonfinite complements instead of infinitival complements. Furthermore, infinitival complements occur with predicates in the middle of the hierarchy (like those of manipulation) and not with lower ones, which is probably because verbs of manipulation require control and occur in complex predicates (see Mateo Toledo 2008, and §9) or depend on the properties of infinitival clauses.[9]

TABLE 20.8 MATRIX PREDICATES AND COMPLEMENT TYPES

Predicate classes	Finite	Nonfinite	Infinitive
Utterance	x		
Propositional attitude	x	x[few]	
Knowledge/factive	x	x[some]	
Perception		x	
Desiderative	x[some]	x	
Manipulatives		x	x[few]
Predicates of emotion		x	x[few]
Phasal		x	
Modal		x	

In closing this section, I show that NVPs are finite in structure and distribution. As shown in (58), NVPs are selected by predicates that take finite complements and they permit preverbal elements like focus. See §7.5 on other functions.

(58) X-Ø-y-al   heb' [tol   ayach chot-an   hach ay-oq]
     CP-B3-A3-say   they   COMP   you   sitting-POS   B2SG   DIR:down-INF
     'They said that you are the one who was sitting down.'

As shown in (59), NVPs cannot head nonfinite and infinitival clauses as they cannot be embedded under verbs taking such complements.

(59) a. *x-Ø-a-chah-ok   [ha-chot-(an). . .]
        CP-B3-A2SG-receive-DIR:enter A2SG-sitting-POS
        Intended: 'You started to stay sitting down.'

     b. *max-ach   ko-cheq   [chot-an-oq . . .]
        CP-B2SG   A1PL-order.verbally   sitting-POS-INF
        Intended: 'We order you to be sitting down.'

7.5 Non-complement functions of different clauses

The three clause types (finite, nonfinite, infinitive) all have non-complement functions.
   The clauses in square brackets in (60) show that finite clauses also function as adverbial clauses (60a), conditional clauses (60b), and relative clauses (60c).

(60) a. ch-on   xiw   [y-et   ch-Ø-jay-i]
        ICP-B1PL   afraid   A3-of   ICP-B3-come-IV
        'We get afraid when it comes.'

     b. [Ta   man   hoq-ex   meltzoj-oq],   hoq-in   kus-oq
        if   NEG   POT-B2PL   return-IRR   POT-B1SG   sad-IRR
        'If you do not return, I will be sad.'

    c. W-ojtaq-Ø   *jun* [maktxel x-Ø-kam] *tu*
      A1SG-know-B3 one who   CP-B3-die DEM
      'I know that one who died.'

Nonfinite clauses occur in five dependent contexts: complements, periphrastic resultatives, adverbial clauses, preverbal adverbs, and secondary predicates (Mateo Toledo 2013a); aside from complement and adverbial clauses, preverbal elements trigger the use of nonfinite clauses. The non-complement clause functions are shown in square brackets below. The periphrastic resultative is shown in (61a); the second verb is nonfinite and it encodes the cause/manner that brings about the event denoted by the finite verb. In (61b), a nonfinite adverbial clause precedes the main clause. In (61c), a preverbal manner adverb requires a nonfinite main verb. The example in (61d) illustrates a secondary predicate construction where *wahan* 'standing' is the secondary predicate and the main verb is nonfinite (see Mateo Toledo 2012a).

(61) a. X-ach   oq' [hach ko-maq'-on -i]
        CP-B2SG cry B2SG A1PL-hit-DM-FS
        'We made you cry by hitting you.'

      b. [Y-et y-el   yich   tu], ch-Ø=to   wal apn-i
         A3-of A3-go.out bottom that ICP-B3=still INTS arrive.there-IV
        'When it began [and went on], she/he was still going there.' {txt025}

      c. Komo yelk'ulal [s-k'ay-aj   te']. . .
        as   quickly A3-disappear-DIR:up CLF
        'As it is quickly that the trees are disappearing. . .' {txt214}

      d. Wah-an   [ko-tit-a]
        standing-POS A1PL-come-IV
        'We traveled standing up.'

Infinitives function as complement clauses, purpose clauses, and as nominal arguments to verbs which do not select complements.

    A motion-cum-purpose construction is shown in (62); the event denoted by the finite motion verb is carried out to obtain the realization of the event expressed by the infinitive.

(62) ch'-Ø-ul   heb' naq [say-oj   ixim]
     ICP-B3-come PL   CLF look.for-INF corn
     'They come to look for corn [here]. . .' {txt025}

The case of infinitives heading NPs as arguments to predicates which do not select complement clauses is illustrated in (63). The infinitive in (63a) is the nominal argument of the relational noun *xol* and that in (63b) is the subject of the existential. The subject of the infinitive is not controlled by a matrix argument. This infinitive can take nominal elements like the indefinite *jun* or demonstrative *tu* in (63b), but these modifiers are ungrammatical with the infinitival clause in (62). Finally, only notional transitive verbs are documented in this context; infinitives like *saqchoq* 'to play' or *kamoq* 'to die' are ungrammatical as arguments of the existential *ay* or adpositions. In summary, this use of infinitives is a nominal one and differs from infinitival clauses.

(63) a. . . . ah-on   ek'-oq . . .   xol   elq'an,   xol   maq'-oj   anima
      EXIST-B1PL   DIR:pass-INF   between   stealing   between   hit-INF   people
      'We exist [among bad things], among stealing, among killing people.' {txt176}

    b. .. ay-Ø   [jun]   pech-oj   b'e   [tu]. . .
       EXIST-B3   one   clean-INF   road   DEM
       'There is (that) road cleaning . . . ' {txt001}

8 RELATIVE CLAUSES

Following cross-linguistic research (Lehmann 1986; Andrews 2007:206; and others), I discuss four features of relative clauses in Q'anjob'al: the structural relationship between the head and the RC; the syntax of the RC; the form of the head; and the realization of the relativized NP in the RC.

The example in (64) shows a RC in square brackets. It modifies the NP *cham winaq tu* 'that old man' in the main clause. The head is in *italics* in all examples.

(64) X-Ø-kam   *cham winaq*   [max-ach   elaj   y-etoq]   *tu*
    CP-B3-die   CLF man   CP-B2SG   go.away   A3-with   DEM
    'That old man with whom you went away died.'

As shown in (64), the RC is postnominal, it is externally headed, and it is an embedded clause since it follows the noun and precedes postnominal modifiers like the demonstrative.

The RC is finite. When the A is relativized and it is a third person, the RC uses the AF form of the verb as shown by the contrast between (65a) and (65b, c). The parallel structure between AF and RC does not mean that RCs involve focus.

(65) a. Miman-Ø   *jun*   *no'*   [ch-ach   xib'te-n-i]
      big-B3   one   animal   CP-B2SG   frighten-AF-IV
      'An animal that frightens you is big.'

    b. Jelan-Ø   *no*   *ka-k'on*   *tx'i'*   [x-Ø-kam-i]
       smart-B3   CLF   two-CLF:animal   dog   CP-B3-die-IV
       'The two dogs that died are smart.'

    c. Miman-Ø   *jun*   [x-Ø-s-ma'   kam   heb']
       big-B3   one   CP-B3-A3-hit   die   they
       'The one that they killed is big.'

Q'anjob'al employs gap and relative pronoun strategies. While the relativized NP is unrealized in the RC in the gap strategy as in (65), it has a pronominal realization in the relative pronoun strategy like *maktxel* in (66).

(66) X-on   kol-chaj   [maktxel   *hon*   x-on-el-i]
    CP-B1PL   help-PSV   who   B1PL   CP-B1PL-go.away-IV
    'We the ones who left were saved.'

RCs with relative pronouns have the structure of partitive constructions. In partitive constructions, a quantifier, the PART, refers to a proper subset of a whole denoted by an NP (Jackendoff 1977; Ladusaw 1982; de Hoop 1997). The partitive has a [PART+ NP] structure like in (67a). Crucially, the PART inflects for person and number with set B as in (67b). The examples in (67) also have NVP readings that differ from partitives. Cardinal quantification differs from partitives in that the quantifier occurs within the NP like the matrix NP in (65b).The structure of partitives needs research.

(67) a. **ka-k'on**   no   tx'i'
      two-CLF:animal   CLF   dog
      'two of the dogs/The dogs are two.'

    b. **Kan-wan**   **hon**   x-on   way-i
      cuatro-CLF:HUM   B1PL   CP-B1PL   dormir-VI
      'Four of us slept /We are four, the ones who slept.'

Like partitives, the relative pronoun inflects for person indexed by set B as shown in (66) and it can also take a lexical argument like *heb'* 'they' in (68). Note that a SAP can be relativized by restrictive RCs, (66). To the best of my knowledge these facts only occur in Q'anjob'alan languages (see Mateo Toledo 2015).

(68) Ch-Ø-kus   *tzan*   [maktxel-Ø   heb'   x-Ø-kam   y-une']   *tu*
      CP-B3-sad   CLF   who-B3   they   COM-B3-die   A3-child   DEM
      'Those whose children die are sad.'

The heads in RCs have one of three forms: a full NP (65a, b), a determiner head (65c), and a null head (69). Only determiners (demonstrative, indefinite alone as in (65c) or combined as in (68) function as determiner heads.

(69) Mal   Ø-kan   [**tzetal-Ø**   max-Ø   w-al-a']
      already   B3-stay   what-B3   CP-B3   A1SG-say-TV
      'What I said has been saved.'

There is a co-dependency between the form of the head and relativization strategies. Fully headed RCs only occur with a gap, (65a) and headless RCs only occur with relative pronouns, (69); and determiner heads occur with a gap or pronoun, (70).

(70) a. X-Ø-toj   *jun*   [max-Ø   j-al   jun   ab'ix   b'ay]
      CP-B3-go   one   CP-B3   A1PL-say   one   story   at
      'The one to whom we told a story went away.'

    b. X-in-b'et   [b'aytal   kajan   hach]   *tu*
      CP-B1SG-went   where   living   B2SG   DEM
      'I went to where you live.'

Finally, all grammatical relations are accesible to relativization; they can be relativized with a gap or relative pronoun strategy as long as they are combined with the right head. An A, S, and O are relativized in (65), an indirect object in (70a), a comitative in (64), a genitive in (68), and a locative in (70b).

9 COMPLEX PREDICATES

Complex predicates (CP) play a pervasive role in Q'anjob'alan languages, more so than is reported in other Maya languages, but they are not well explored in Mayan.

Following Alsina *et al.* (1997:1) and Butt (2003), among others, I define a CP as a monoclausal construction headed by two or more predicates (usually verbs) whose argument structures merge with the result that the CP predicates as a single unit.

Mateo Toledo (2008) proposes five parameters for the analysis of CPs: three on monoclausality, one on event structure, and another on argument structure. Q'anjob'al has six types of CPs: resultative, positional end-state, causative, monitoring, ditransitive, and directional. These CPs are asymmetric in that the first head (V1) is the primary locus of marking: it bears AM inflection and indexes all arguments to the extent possible. The second head (V2) lacks AM marking and it has an infinitival form when it does not index a third argument. A full description of CPs is beyond this chapter. I only show their monoclausal morphosyntax and the semantic subtypes.

All complex predicates have four monoclausal properties (Mateo Toledo 2008). First, they have one AM marker inflected on V1. Second, person and number inflection is as in simple clauses (§6.2); it depends on the valence of the CP and not of the heads: intransitive CPs have one argument indexed by set B; transitive CPs have two arguments indexed by set A and set B; and ditransitive CPs have three arguments, two indexed by set A and set B and a third one marked as oblique. Third and fourth, like simple (in)transitive predicates, the CPs follow a VAO/VS order and the heads are contiguous. However, ditransitive CPs follow a V1AOV2R order and the heads are not contiguous. Next, I show the details of these features. I organize the CPs in three types based on the valence of the heads.

The first type of CP contains a transitive V1 and an intransitive V2. This results in a transitive CP, (71): on V1, set A indexes the subject and set B the object. V2 lacks all inflection and takes the infinitival suffix *-oq* in final position.

(71) a. Ayach   x-in   ha-nis   *tz'ah-oq* . . .
     you   CP-B1SG   A2SG-put.fire.on   burn-INF
     'You burned me (by putting fire on me).'

    b. q-ach   j-il   *kam*   hon
       POT-B2SG   A1PL-watch   die   EXCL
       'We will take care of you dying [watch die].'

Like transitive clauses, this CP has a VAO order, (72). This order shows that V1 and V2 are contiguous. This is confirmed by the clitic *hon* in (71b); *hon* follows V2 but its associated marker inflects on V1.

(72) X-Ø-Ø-tayne-j   *ch'ib'*   ix   naq   unin
     CP-B3-A3-guard-TV   grow   CLF   CLF   child
     'She raised a boy.'

The template in (71) is used for two semantically different CPs. The one in (71a) involves resultative semantics. It denotes an event with a 'cause-change of state' meaning where V1 (*nis* 'put fire on') denotes the manner and process that causes the change of state denoted by V2 (*tz'ah* 'to burn'). The heads share an argument: in (71a), the first person is understood both as the person on whom fire is put (V1) and the person who burns (V2). Similar examples are listed in (73).

(73) Resultative V1V2s

maq'maloq	[to hit + swell up]	'to make swell up by hitting'
may q'anb'oq	[to move + roast]	'to roast by moving slowly'
pitz'tajoq	[to squash + cook]	'to make ripe by squashing'
tek'kojoq	[to kick + grind]	'to destroy by kicking'
ten koxmojoq	[to move + bend]	'to bend by moving'

The CP in (71b) denotes a monitoring event where 'the agent of the event denoted by V1 is in the position to affect the outcome or development of the event denoted by V2.' In this case, V1 (*il* 'to see, take care of') contributes the subject and V2 (*kam* 'to die') contributes the object; these arguments merge in the CP, which differs from sharing because the argument of V2 is not what the agent of V1 sees. In the monitoring CP, V1 is usually a verb of manipulation or perception (like *ala'* 'to invite, verbally order', *etz'ej* 'to pretend, imitate', *iqej* 'to obey', *jela'* 'to exchange place', *k'exa'* 'to replace, change', and *saya'* 'to search for') and V2 is any intransitive verb that allows monitoring (like *wayi* 'to sleep', *saqchi* 'to play', *kuywi* 'to study', *mulnaji* 'to work', *q'anjab'i* 'to talk', etc.).

The second type of CP contains an intransitive or transitive V1 and an intransitive V2 that is either a positional as in (74) or a verb of motion (known as directional by Mayanists) as in (75). The (a) examples have a transitive V1 that results in transitive CPs and the (b) examples have an intransitive V1 that results in intransitive CPs.

(74) a. [K]ax tol   ch-Ø-ko-pix-ay   *k'ot-an*   no   kalnel
       then INTS ICP-B3-A1PL-tie-DIR:down   thrown-POS CLF sheep
      'And we tie the sheep in a thrown-like position.' {txt213}

    b. Max-in apn-i   *chot-an-oq*
       CP-B1SG arrive-IV sitting-POS-INF
      'I arrived there and end sitting down.'

(75) a. Q-Ø-a-letx-on   *aj-teq*   ja-q   ha-lob'ej. . .
      POT-B3-A2SG-take-TCM   DIR:up-DIR:toward   some-IRR A2SG-food
      'And you will take out some of your food.' {txt019}

    b. Max-Ø q'ajab'-*kan-[ay-teq]*   hin-mam. . .
      CP-B3 t alk-DIR:stay-DIR:down-DIR:toward   A1SG-father
      'My father talked [to me] downwards [and he left].' {txt004}

Similar to the first type, in these CPs person/number are indexed on V1 and V2 has an infinitival form – it takes the suffix *-oq* in final position, (74b). In the intransitive CP, set B indexes the S, (74b) and (75b), and in the transitive CP, (74a) and (75a), set A and set B index the A and O, respectively.

Like the resultative CP, these CPs involve argument sharing. The heads share the S in the intransitive CP, the first person singular in (74b). In the transitive CP, the theme of the event denoted by V1 is also the argument of V2, the object 'some of your food' in (75a).

These CPs are like the first type in word order. The intransitive CP has a VS order, (75b) and the transitive one has a VAO order, (76). In both cases, the heads are contiguous.

(76) X-Ø-s-letx-on   *aj-teq*   naq jab' s-lob'ej. . .
      CP-B3-A3-take-TCM   DIR:up-DIR:toward   CLF some A3-food
      'And he took out some of his food.'

The second type of CP corresponds to two semantic subtypes: an end-state in (74) and a directional construction in (75). The end-state CP encodes a meaning where 'an argument is in the state denoted by the positional V2 after being affected by the event denoted by V1'. In (74a), *k'otan* 'thrown' denotes the state of 'the sheep' after the *pixay* 'to tie' event is over. The verbs in V1 denote a telic motion event encoded by a motion verb (like *aji* 'to go up', *apni* 'to get there', *b'eti* 'to go and return', *ek'i* 'to pass') or verb-directional (like *maq'-aj* 'to hit and move upwards' and *ten-ay* 'to move downwards'). The second head is a positional NVP derived by *-an* or *-naj*.

The directional CP denotes a complex event; V1 denotes the main situation and the directionals add adverbial, trajectory, or aspectual meanings (England 1976; Zavala 1993; and others). In (75a), the V1 is *letx* 'to take out' and the directionals are *aj* 'up' and *teq* 'toward speaker' that indicate an 'upwards toward the speaker' trajectory of 'some of your food'. Note that in adverbial meanings like that of *kan* 'stay' there is no shared argument (see Mateo Toledo 2013b). In general, any predicate can function as V1, but directionals are grammaticized intransitive motion verbs and there can be up to three in a given clause as in (75b). The full list of directionals, organized according to their ordering in the CP, are: DIR1 *kan* 'stay/remain'; DIR2 *ek'/ik'* 'pass by', *ay* 'down', *aj* 'up', *ok* 'in, enter', *el/il* 'out'; and DIR3 *teq* 'toward X' and *toq* 'away from X'.

The third type of CP contains a transitive V1 and a V2 that is usually transitive. This serves as the template for causatives, (77), and ditransitive clauses, (78). Only causative CPs allow intransitive V2s as (77b).

(77) a. Max-ach   j-aq'   *y-achinne-j*   x   Malin
        CP-B2SG   A1PL-give   A3-bathe-TV   CLF   Malin
        'We made you be washed by Malin [we coerced you not Malin].'

   b. Max-ach   j-aq'   *tz'a*   hon
        CP-B2SG   A1PL-give   burn   EXCL
        'We burned you.'

(78) Q-in-a-tx'ox   *y-il-a'*
     POT-B1SG-A2SG-show   A3-see-TV
     'You will show me to him/her.'

A causative CP with an intransitive V2, (77b), is transitive; it is like the first type in its morphosyntax. That is, V2 lacks inflection and V1 marks all arguments: set A and set B index the subject and object, respectively. Lexical arguments follow a VAO order, (79) and V1 and V2 are contiguous as shown by the position of the clitic *hon* in (77b).

(79) Max-Ø   y-aq'   *taj*   naq   an   itaj
     CP-B3   A3-give   cook   CLF   CLF   green
     'He cooked the greens.'

The CPs with a transitive V2 in (77a) and (78) have three arguments. Like other transitive CPs, set A and set B index the subject and object on V1. However, unlike other CPs, V2 indexes the third argument with set A. This CP usually follows a V1AOV2R order as in (80), where the heads are not contiguous, unlike other CPs.

(80) X-Ø-s-tx'ox   cham naq unin y-*il*   naq doktor
     CP-B3-A3-show CLF CLF child A3-see CLF doctor
     'He [old male] showed the child to the doctor.'

The V2 in ditransitive CPs has a special form that differs from that of nonfinite clauses. First, V2 lacks a set B affix for its logical object, the second person in (77a) and first person in (78). Second, V2 lacks AM marking like nonfinite clauses, but it cannot take the DM *-on* of nonfinite clauses (§7.2). Third, V2 takes a transitive thematic suffix like in (78) (see §3, 4.1).

The heads in CPs with three arguments usually share one argument that is understood as the theme of both heads; this is the object indexed by set B *-ach* in (77a). Total sharing is also possible where V1 and V2 share all arguments as in (81). In total sharing, A and R have the same referent and the theme of each head has the same referent. In this case, there are two inflectional patterns. The first case is like that of (80) where set A and set B index the subject and object on V1 and V2 indexes the third argument as in (81a). In the second case, V1 indexes all arguments and V2 lacks inflection, (81b): the subject indexed by set A is interpreted as A and R, and the object indexed by set B is the theme of both heads.

(81) a. . . . tol ch-ach   ul   hin-say   *w-il-a'*
         INTS ICP-B2SG come A1SG-search.for A1SG-see-TV
         'I come to search you (for my benefit).' {txt062}

     b. Tol ch-ach   ul   hin-say   *il-a'*
         INTS ICP-B2SG come A1SG-search.for see-TV
         'I come to search you (for my benefit).' {txt016}

The third type of CP involves two semantic subtypes: causative and ditransitive clauses. The causative CP has a 'cause-effect' meaning where 'the causer/agent acts on an entity, the patient, to bring about an event, of which this entity is itself an argument' (Alsina 1992:521). In (77a), the agent of *aq'* indexed by *j-* acts on the theme argument indexed by *-ach* to bring about the event *tz'a'* 'to burn' denoted by V2 whose argument is also the theme of *aq'*. When V2 is transitive, V1 and V2 share the theme (not the agent) as shown by the translation of (77a). Most verbs that function as V1 are verbs of manipulation (e.g. *aq'* 'to give', *cheqa'* 'to verbally order', *iptzej* 'to encourage, force', *uqtej* 'to urge') and any verb that allow manipulation function as V2 (usually unaccusative verbs).

The ditransitive CP denotes an event with three-participants. It involves a notion of 'purpose' where 'the agent of V1 performs an action on the theme to obtain the realization of the event denoted by V2 that also has that theme as an argument.' Thus, the heads share a theme indexed as object in the CP, the second person in (81). This CP is restricted to about 20 verbal combinations, some of which are listed in (82). They encode three meanings: explication, transfer/giving, and obtaining/receiving.

(82) Ditransitive CPs

al ab'ej	[to say + hear]	'to tell, say'
tx'ox ila'	[to show + see]	'to show, teach'
aq'cha'	[to give + receive]	'to pass, hand in'
aq'jeka'	[to give + owe]	'to give on credit'
say ila'	[to look for + see]	'to search for someone'
taq'wej ab'ej	[to accept + hear]	'to accept to listen'

10 SOME DISCOURSE-RELATED PHENOMENA

In this section, I discuss two discourse related phenomena.

10.1 Temporal coherence marking

As stated in §1, the suffix -*on* in Q'anjob'al occurs on transitive verbs in three contexts (Francisco Pascual 2007). The AF -*on* occurs on finite transitive clauses when a third person agent is extracted, §6.4. The DM -*on* occurs in subordinated nonfinite transitive clauses, §7.2. Both DM -*on* and AF -*on* are subject to syntactic conditions whose violation results in ungrammaticality. The third context relates to temporal cohesion (TCM -*on*) that depends on discourse factors whose violation only results in incoherence.

In texts, finite transitive verbs occur with the TCM -*on*, but they lack focus as in (83). The TCM -*on* specifies a temporal sequence between the clauses that roughly means 'after, and, then'. These clauses cannot be the first ones in texts. The -*on* in (83a) is a TCM (not an effect of the auxiliary verb *ul* 'come').

(83) a. kax   ch'-Ø-ul   y-ih-**on**   ay-toq   heb'   a'ej
          then   ICP-B3-come A3-take-TCM   DIR:down-DIR:away   they   water
          kax   ch-Ø-y-uk'-**on**   heb'
          then   ICP-B3-A3-drink-TCM   they
          'Then they come to take water and then they drink it.' {txt224}

    b. X-on   y-ah-**on**   ok   naq   y-in   tareha,   x'-Ø-elol   ko-libreta,
          CP-B1PL   A3-give-TCM   DIR   CLF   A3-at task   CP-B3-come.out   A1PL-book
          x-Ø-y-ih-**on**   ay-teq   naq   [s]-tojol   k'u. . .
          CP-B3-A3-take-TCM   DIR:down-DIR:toward   CLF   A3-price   day
          'He forced us to work, our notebook came, and he lowered the payday.' {txt001}

Clauses with the TCM can be introduced by sequential markers like *axa* 'as for, then', *kax* 'then', *tay* 'then', etc. as in (83a), but they are not obligatory as in (83b).

The TCM -*on* is not obligatory; it can be omitted as in (84), which is based on (83b). This results in a discourse where the temporal relation between clauses is inferred.

(84) X-on   y-ah- ok   naq   y-in   tareha,   x'-Ø-elol   ko-libreta,
       CP-B1PL A3-give-DIR   CLF   A3-at task   CP-B3-come.out A1PL-book
       x-Ø-y-ih-ay-teq   naq [s]-tojol k'u. . .
       CP-B3-A3-take-DIR:down-DIR:toward   CLF A3-price day
       'He forced us to work, our work record came, and he lowered the payday.'

The TCM and DM overlap in texts. That is, nonfinite clauses can function as main clauses introduced by sequential markers as in (85). Here, all instances of -*on* are DM as they occur on nonfinite clauses (§7.2). These nonfinite clauses are unexpected as they are not triggered by any of the syntactic factors noted in §7.5, an issue which needs more research. However, these -*on* are also interpreted as 'and, then' like the TCM. These data provide evidence for the diachronic evolution of the suffix -*on* (see Francisco Pascual 2007).

(85) a. kax   Ø-hin-xuy-on   el   hin-lasu   kax   Ø-w-oche-n
then   B3-A1SG-untie-DM   DIR:out A1SG-rope   then   B3-A1SG-want-DM
Ø-hin-pixb'a-n   Ø-w-al-on-i. . .
B3-A1SG-tie-DM   B3-A1SG-say-DM-FS
'Then I untied my rope, then thought that I wanted to tie it . . . ' {txt062}

    b. K'am ch-in   ajwan   y-alan. . .   Ø-w-oche-n   wal   ch-Ø-tit-a,
NEG   ICP-B1SG   get.up   A3-under   B3-A1SG-want-DM   INTS   ICP-B3-come-IV
Ø-w-a'-on   wal   hin-pwersa   xin. . .
B3-A1SG-give-DM   INTS   A1SG-strength   INTS
'I was unable to lift it. . . I wanted it to come, I put in all my strength. . .' {txt70}

10.2 External topic

As noted in §6.4, a finite clause can have an external topic in sentence-initial position.[10] The examples in (86) illustrate clauses with external topics: *axa heb'xin* 'as for them' and *axa naq winaq tu* 'as for the man'. The external topic is base-generated in sentence-initial position (Aissen 1992) and precedes other preverbal elements like negation (before focus position) in (86a).

(86) a. A[xa]   heb'   xin,   manaq   jun-tu   ch-Ø-Ø-jatne-j   heb'
as.for   they INTS NEG   one-DEM ICP-B3-A3-make-TV they
'As for them, that is not what they do.' {txt023}

    b. Axa   [naq   winaq   tu],   x-Ø-y-ojtaqne-j   naq . . .
as.for   CLF   man   DEM   CP-B3-A3-know-TV   CLF
'As for the man, he learned . . . ' {txt100}

The examples in (86) show the following properties. First, the particle *axa* (that varies with *ax/a*) 'as for' can introduce the external topic. Second, the external topic belongs to a different intonational unit from that of the rest of the clause as it is followed by a pause (marked with comma). This contrasts with focus where there is only one intonational unit. Third, unlike focus, topics do not require an AF construction when the agent is in topic position as in (86a). Finally, the external topic involves resumptive pronouns when it is a third person; which is *heb'* or a classifier like *naq* in (86). The resumptive pronoun occupies the place of the lexical argument according to the VAO/VS order.

11 SUMMARY

This chapter showed various topics and issues that are interesting or unique to Q'anjob'alan languages. They include the existence of retroflex sounds (like Mamean languages), an unusually large number of positional roots (larger than verbal roots); the use of thematic and mood suffixes to mark phrasal boundaries, the stress pattern that distinguishes between word and sentence stress; three uses of the suffix *-on* on transitive verbs to mark AF, dependency and temporal discourse coherence; the lack of modifying adjectives, three systems of classifiers; a rich set of complex predicates based on a verb-verb frame; the partitive reading and structure of relative clauses with relative pronouns, and the existence of nonfinite clauses functioning as matrix clauses.

NOTES

1 The phoneme /r/ is not productive. It occurs in Spanish borrowings like *roxax* [<rosa] 'rose' and a few native words like *jorori* 'to snore', *t'iran* 'nude', and *turu'* 'to swallow'.

2 There are two known words with a complex onset: *a.man.k'wan* 'quickly', and *tzyap* 'cloak'.

3 In related languages like Popti' (Day 1973:201–21), Tseltal (Polian 2013:85–6), Tsotsil (Laughlin 1975:23), and others, it is proposed that stress falls on the first syllable of roots/stems. In Q'anjob'al, stress is defined on phonological words because particles and clitics like *to* 'still' and *wal* 'intensifier' may form phonological words that bear main stress on the first syllable as in (6).

4 I exclude the progressive because it has a complement clause structure, see §7.

5 I ignore lexical compounds as they involve nonsystematic root/base combinations.

6 The secondary predicate is a special construction in Q'anjob'al that encodes a depictive and end-state meaning as in (i) and (ii). This is finite like in other Mayan languages, but its morphosyntax differs from that of other Mayan languages. I do not describe it here (see Mateo Toledo 2012a).

   (i) **Wah-an**   hach   s-tx'aj-on   naq
       standing-POS B2SG A3-wash-DM CLF
       'He washed you while (he is) standing up.'

   (ii) **Tz'il**   hach   s-tx'aj-on   naq
       dirty   B2SG A3-wash-DM CLF
       'He washed you, but you are still dirty.'

7 In the interrogation of SAP agents no AF is used. The construction has the form of a relative clause whose analysis is open to debate (see Mateo Toledo 2015).

   (i) Mak-ach   x-in-ha-tx'ox   b'ay   heb'?
       who-B2SG   COM-B1SG-A2PL-show to   they
       'Who are you who showed me to them?'

8 There is an exception to the generalization – *tol* is optional with the complements of *je k'ul* 'to be willing to', *aloni* 'to suppose', *yal k'ul* 'to accept', *cha'* 'to opt for', *ochej* 'to want', *q'an k'ul* 'to want (desire)' independent of factors like disjoint/coreference between the subjects, negation, etc.

9 Motion-cum-purpose constructions (analogous to 'to go to eat') are analyzed as complements in other works (Mateo 2013a). I do not follow this tradition as the evidence for it is unclear.

10 Topic is not uniquely encoded in preverbal position. In texts, where series of clauses share the same topic, this may be unrealized.

REFERENCES

Aissen, Judith. 1992. "Topic and focus in Mayan." *Language* 68: 43–80.

Aissen, Judith. 1999. "Agent focus and inverse in Tzotzil." *Language* 75: 451–85.

Alsina, Alex. 1992. "On the argument structure of causatives." *Linguistic Inquiry* 23: 517–55.

Alsina, Alex, Joan Bresnan, and Peter Sells. 1997. "Complex predicates: structure and theory." In *Complex predicates*, ed. by Alex Alsina, Joan Bresnan, and Peter Sells, 1–12. Stanford: CSLI Publications.

Andrews, Avery. 2007. "Relative clauses." In *Language typology and syntactic description*, vol. 2, ed. by Timothy Shopen, 206–36. Cambridge: Cambridge University Press.

Berlin, Brent. 1968. *Tzeltal numeral classifiers: a study in ethnographic semantics*. The Hague: Mouton.

Butt, Miriam. 2003. "The light verb jungle." In *Harvard working papers in linguistics*, vol. 9, ed. by G. Aygen, C. Bowern, and C. Quinn, 1–49. Papers from the GSAS/Dudley House Workshop on Light Verbs.

Campbell, Lyle, and Terrence Kaufman. 1985. "Mayan linguistics: where are we now?" *Annual Review of Anthropology* 14: 187–98.

Coon, Jessica, Pedro Mateo Pedro, and Omer Preminger. 2014. "The role of case in A-bar extraction asymmetries: evidence from Mayan." *Linguistic Variation* 14: 179–242.

Craig, Colette G. 1977. *The structure of Jacaltec*. Austin: University of Texas Press.

Craig, Colette G. 1987. "Jacaltec noun classifiers: a study in grammaticalization." *Lingua* 70: 241–84.

Cristofaro, Sonia. 2003. *Subordination*. Oxford: Oxford University Press.

Datz, Margaret. 1980. "*Jacaltec syntactic structure and the demands of discourse.*" PhD diss., University of Colorado, Boulder.

Day, Christopher. 1973. *The Jacaltec language* (Indiana University Publications, vol. 12). Bloomington: Indiana University Press.

Dayley, Jon P. 1990. "Voz y Ergatividad en Idiomas Mayas." In *Lecturas sobre la Lingüística Maya*, ed. by Nora England and Stephen Elliot, 335–98. Guatemala: CIRMA.

England, Nora. 1976. "Mam directionals and verb semantics." In *Mayan linguistics I*, ed. by Marlys McClaran, 201–11. Los Angeles: University of California American Indian Studies Center.

England, Nora. 1983a. *A grammar of Mam, a Mayan language*. Austin: University of Texas Press.

England, Nora. 1983b. "Ergativity in Mamean (Mayan) languages." *International Journal of American Linguistics* 49: 1–19.

England, Nora. 2006. "El papel de palabras afectivas en la narración en Mam (Maya)." In *Memorias del VIII Encuentro Internacional de Lingüística en el Noreste, Tomo 3*, ed. by María del Carmen Morrúa, 157–71. Hermosillo, Sonora: UNISON.

Francisco Pascual, Adán. 2007. "Transitividad y Dependencia Sintáctica y Discursiva en Q'anjob'al." MA thesis, CIESAS, México.

Francisco Pascual, Adán. 2010. "Predicación Secundaria en Q'anjob'al." In *La Predicación Secundaria en Mesoamérica*, ed. by Judith Aissen and Roberto Zavala, 87–115. Mexico: CIESAS.

Givón, Talmy. 2001. *Syntax: a functional-typological introduction*, vol. II, Rev. editon. Amsterdam: John Benjamins.

Grinevald, Colette. 2000. "A morphosyntactic typology of classifiers." In *Systems of nominal classification, ed. by G. Senft*, 50–92. Cambridge: Cambridge University Press.

Haviland, John B. 1994. "Verbs and shapes in (Zinacantec) Tzotzil: the case of 'insert.'" In *Función 15–16*, ed. by Roberto Zavala Maldonado, 83–117. México: Universidad de Guadalajara.

Hoop de, Helen. 1997. "A semantic reanalysis of the partitive constraint." *Lingua 103*: 151–74.

Jackendoff, Rey. 1977. *X-bar syntax: a study of phrase-structure*. Cambridge: MIT Press.

Kaufman, Terrence. 1971. *Tzeltal phonology and morphology*. Berkeley: University of California Publications.

Kaufman, Terrence. 1990. "Algunos Rasgos Estructurales de los Idiomas Mayances con Referencia Especial al K'iche'." In *Lecturas sobre la Lingüística Maya*, ed. by Nora England and Stephen Elliot, 59–114. Guatemala: CIRMA.

Kaufman, Terrence. 2015. "Initial glottal stop in Mayan languages." Ms.

Ladusaw, Bill. 1982. "Semantic constraint on the English partitive construction." In *Proceedings of the WCCFL 1*, 231–42, Stanford.

Laughlin, Robert. 1975. *The great Tzotzil dictionary of San Lorenzo Zinacantán*. Washington, DC: Smithsonian Institution Press.

Lehmann, Christian. 1986. "On the typology of relative clauses." *Linguistics* 24: 663–80.

Levin, Beth. 1993. *English verb classes and alternations*. Chicago: The University of Chicago Press.

Malchukov, Andrej, Martin Haspelmath, and Bernard Comrie. 2010. "Ditransitive constructions: a typological overview." In *Studies in ditransitive constructions: a comparative handbook*, ed. by Andrej Malchukov, Martin Haspelmath and Bernard Comrie, 1–64. Berlin: De Gruyter Mouton.

Martin, Laura. 1977. "Positional roots in Kanjobal (Mayan)." PhD diss., University of Florida.

Martin, Laura. 1979. "Direction/Location and the Semantics of Kanjobal Positional Roots." In *Papers in Mayan linguistics*, ed. by Laura Martin, 165–84. Columbia, MO: Lucas Brothers.

Mateo Pedro, Pedro. 2005. "Acquisition of the inflectional morphology in Q'anjob'al." MA thesis, University of Kansas.

Mateo Pedro, Pedro. 2015. *The acquisition of inflection in Q'anjob'al Maya*. Amsterdam: John Benjamins.

Mateo Toledo, Eladio. 1999. "La Cuestión Akateko-Q'anjob'al, una Comparación Gramatical." *Licenciatura* thesis, Universidad Mariano Gálvez, Guatemala.

Mateo Toledo, Eladio. 2004. "Revisitando la Ergatividad Mixta en Q'anjob'al (Maya)." *Proceedings of CILLA-I*, Austin, TX. www.ailla.utexas.org/site/cilla1_toc.html.

Mateo Toledo, Eladio. 2008. "The family of complex predicates in Q'anjob'al (Maya); their syntax and meaning." PhD diss., The University of Texas, Austin.

Mateo Toledo, Eladio. 2012a. "Secondary predication in Q'anjob'al (Maya): structure and semantic types." *International Journal of American Linguistics* 78: 139–74.

Mateo Toledo, Eladio. 2012b. "Complex predicates in Q'anjob'al (Maya): the verbal resultative." *International Journal of American Linguistics* 78: 465–95.

Mateo Toledo, Eladio. 2013a. "Clausulas sin aspecto e infinitivas en q'anjob'al." In *Clases léxicas, posesión y cláusulas complejas en lenguas de Mesoamérica*, ed. by Enrique Palancar and Roberto Zavala, 247–76. México: CIESAS.

Mateo Toledo, Eladio. 2013b. "Directional markers in Q'anjob'al: their syntax and meaning." In *Proceedings of the 33rd anual meeting of BLS*, ed. by Zhenya Antic, Charles B. Chang, Clare S. Sandy y Maziar Toosarvandani, 78–89. Berkeley: Sheridan Books.

Mateo Toledo, Eladio. 2015. "Los pronombres relativos y la construcción partitiva en q'anjob'al". *Paper presented at the VII Conference on Indigenous Languages of Latin America*. Austin, Texas.

Mateo Toledo, Eladio. 2017. "Prenominal adjectives in Q'anjob'al and other Mayan languages". Paper presented at the 2017 SSILA Anual Meeting. Austin, Texas.

Montejo Esteban, Ruperto. 1996. *Gramática del Idioma Q'anjob'al*. Guatemala: PLFM.

Nikolaeva, Irina. 2007. "Introduction." In *Finiteness: theoretical and empirical foundation*, ed. by Irina Nikolaeva, 1–19. Oxford: Oxford University Press.

OKMA. 1993. *Maya' chii': Los Idiomas Mayas de Guatemala*. Guatemala: Cholsamaj.

Peñalosa, Fernando. 1992. ¿Cuántos Idiomas Q'anjob'al Existen? *Boletín de Lingüística 5*, 1–15. Guatemala: Universidad Mariano Gálvez de Guatemala.

Pérez González, Jaime. 2012. "Predicados expresivos e ideófonos en tseltal." MA thesis, MLI-CIESAS, México.

Polian, Gilles. 2013. *Gramática del Tseltal de Oxchuc*, vols. 1 & 2. México: CIESAS.

Raymundo González, Sonia, Adán Francisco Pascual, B'alam Mateo Toledo, and Pedro Mateo Pedro. 2000. *Sk'exkixhtaqil Yallay Koq'anej: Variación Dialectal en Q'anjob'al*. Guatemala: Cholsamaj.

Richards, Michael. 2003. *Atlas Lingüístico de Guatemala*. Guatemala: Universidad Rafael Landívar.

Ross Montejo, Antonio, and Patricia Delgado Rojas. 2000. *Variación dialectal en Popti'*. Guatemala City: Cholsamaj.

Sántiz Gómez, Roberto. 2010. "Raíces Posicionales en Tseltal de Oxchuc." MA thesis, MLI-CIESAS, México.

Smith, Carlota. 1991. *The parameters of Aspect*. Dordrecht: Kluwer.

Stiebels, Barbara. 2006. "Agent focus in Mayan languages." *Natural Language and Linguistic Theory* 24: 501–70.

Vendler, Zeno. 1957. "Verbs and times." *The Philosophical Review* 66: 143–60.

Zavala, Roberto. 1992. *El Kanjobal de San Miguel Acatán*. México: UNAM.

Zavala, Roberto. 1993. "Clause integration with verbs of motion in Mayan languages." MA thesis, University of Oregon.

Zavala, Roberto. 1997. "Functional analysis of Akatek voice constructions." *International Journal of American Linguistics* 63: 439–74.

Zavala, Roberto. 2000. "Multiple classifier systems in Akatek." In *Systems of nominal classifiers*, ed. by G. Senft, 114–46. New York: Cambridge University Press.

CHAPTER 21

TOJOLABAL

Alejandro Curiel Ramírez del Prado

1 INTRODUCTION

Tojolabal is spoken by about 50,000 people settled in more than 300 communities in eastern Chiapas, Mexico, in the region between Comitán and Altamirano (INALI 2014). The classification of Tojolabal has been controversial. According to Kaufman (1972), Tojolabal belongs to the Q'anjob'alan branch, although lexical, phonological, morphological, and syntactic evidence has led to several alternative proposals, namely that Tojolabal belongs to Tseltalan (Robertson 1977) or that it is a mixed language (Law 2014).

There is no serious study of Tojolabal dialectology. Partly on the basis of lexical evidence, del Moral (1983) suggested that there are no distinguishable dialectal areas. However, there is subtle microvariation in the morphology and syntax between northern and southern communities.

Language shift has not yet been described. According to INALI (2014), monolingualism is 16.5 percent. Speakers around Las Margaritas and Altamirano strongly maintain Tojolabal as L1, although in the southernmost communities the language is highly endangered.

Descriptive and theoretical work on Tojolabal includes, among others, a reference grammar (Furbee-Losee 1976), an exhaustive bilingual Tojolabal and Spanish dictionary (Lenkersdorf 2008, 2010), several published collections of texts (Furbee-Losee 1981; Gómez Hernández and Ruz 1992; Lenkersdorf and Van Der Haar 1998; Gómez Hernández et al. 1999; Lenkersdorf 1999), a critical edition of nineteenth-century manuscripts (Ruz 1989), and papers and dissertations about syntax and pragmatics (Supple and Douglas 1949; White 1979; Brody 1982, 1986, 1987a, 1987b; Curiel 2007, 2013; Peake 2007a, 2007b; Gómez Cruz 2010).

2 PHONOLOGY

2.1 Phonemes and orthography

Table 21.1 presents the 20 consonants of Tojolabal in their orthographic form (Díaz Cruz et al. 2011).

As in Tseltalan, but not Q'anjob'alan, Tojolabal shifted all Proto-Mayan postvelar stops to velar as in *pak'an* 'flat' (cf. Tseltal *pak'al* and Q'anjob'al *paq'an*). However, the evolution of Proto-Mayan velars to palatoalveolar in Tseltalan is not attested in Tojolabal, e.g. the initial segment in K'ichee' *k'aq* 'flea', Tojolabal *k'ak*, and Tseltalan *ch'ak*.

Tojolabal has five vowels which are distinguished by their height, backness, and roundness.

TABLE 21.1 CONSONANT PHONEMES

		Labial	Alveolar	Alveo-palatal	Velar	Glottal
Nasal		m	n			
Plosive	simple	p	t		k	'
	glottal	b'	t'		k'	
Affricate	simple		ts	ch		
	glottal		ts'	ch'		
Fricative			s	x		j
Tap			r			
Lateral			l			
Approximant		w		y		

(/r/ only occurs in borrowings from Spanish and in expressive predicates (see §7.6)).

2.2 Stress

Tojolabal has fixed stress. In non-interrogative sentences, sentential stress falls on the last syllable of the sentence. The last syllable of the left-dislocated external topic also bears sentential stress. See (1) with the stressed syllables in both positions. Note that there are two external topics in this example, both of which carry sentential stress. Lexical stress is also assigned to verbal roots, shown in italics in (1).[1]

(1) [Ja'xa   jun bwelta **il**   ja=Patrisya] se=*waj*   Chonab'.
    TOP.CHANGE one time   DEM   DET=Patricia perhaps=go Comitan
    'Once upon a time Patricia, perhaps she went to Comitán!' {TEXT}

In polar interrogative sentences like (2), the first phonological word attracts the stress to its first syllable. The root syllable of the verb continues to bear secondary stress.

(2) **Wan**=ma x-a-*sak'*-a   wa-sat-ex   ja=la-k'e'-y-ex
    IPFV=Q   IPFV-A2-clean-SS A2-face/eye-2PL DET=IPFV.SAP-rise-EP-2PL
       way-el=i?
       sleep-NF=TOP
    'Do you guys wash your faces after waking up?' {TEXT}

However, constituent interrogative sentences have the same stress pattern as non-interrogative sentences, with main stress on the final syllable.

(3) Jasuka waw-a'tel-ex   wa=x-ja-*k'ul*-an-ex=i?
    what   A2-work-2PL IPFV=IPFV-B2-make-VRBZ-2PL=TOP
    'What kind of work do you guys do?' {TEXT}

2.3 Phonotactics

Syllable structure in Tojolabal is rather simple. Table 21.2 shows syllable types in Tojolabal. Onsets are generally obligatory and codas are allowed. In two contexts, the syllable onset may be omitted, as shown in (4): first, the second person Set A marker *a*- allows a. V. syllable in word-initial position; second, the determiner *ja*= can suffer phonological erosion as a speech style effect.

(4) [mok.ni **a.,**k'ul.yi? ?en.tre.gar **a.**ga.ra.nyon ha.'wi]
    mok=ni   a-k'ul   y-i'   entregar   ja=garañón   jaw=i
    NEG.IMP=EMPH A2-make A3-DAT deliver   DET=stallion   DEM.DIST=TOP
    'Do not deliver that stallion to him!' {TEXT}

Note that Tojolabal has the same syllable types that are reported in Q'anjob'alan (Zavala 1992:26; Delgado Rojas et al. 2007). Unlike Tseltal, Tojolabal does not have (C)V*h*C syllables. Thus compare Tseltal *k'ahk'* and Tojolabal *k'ak'* 'fire'.

Almost all complex onsets arise only in word-initial position when a consonant-initial stem takes an inflectional prefix such as the incompletive marker *x*- or the Set A prefixes *j*- or *s*-. The only two-segment onset not occurring at word-initial position is the voiceless velar stop [k] followed by the lateral [l] as in [ma.'kla] 'listen to him/her'.

Apart from complex onsets and [.kl.], all consonant sequences are separated by a syllable break and occur in the middle of the word. Further, epenthesis, glide formation, and contraction prevent vowel sequences in underlying representations from occurring on the surface.

2.4 Some phonological processes

> *Geminate consonant reduction.* Identical adjacent consonants (both stops and fricatives) are not allowed and are reduced to a single instance, e.g. *s-sat* 'his/her/its face' {A3-face} > [sat].
>
> *Sibilant assimilation.* The alveolar and palatoalveolar fricatives [s] and [x] assimilate in place of articulation to an immediately following alveolar or palatal sibilant (fricative or affricate), e.g. *wa=x-s-tsik-a* 'he/she/it burns him/her/it' {IPFV=IPFV-A3-burn-SS} > *wa stsika, wa=x-sut-u* 'he/she/it turns him/her/it around' {IPFV=IPFV-A3-turn.around-SS} > *wa sutu, wa=x-ts'inin-i* 'it chimes' {IPFV=IPFV-A3-chime-SS} > *wa sts'inini.* Similarly, [s] becomes palatoalveolar before [ch], [ch'], and [x], e.g. *s-chikin* 'his/her/its ear' {A3-ear} > *xchikin, s-ch'in-il* 'his/her/its smallness'

TABLE 21.2 SYLLABLE TYPES

	Phonetic transcription	*Morphological analysis*	*Gloss*
.V.	a.won	aw-on {A2-avocado}	'your avocado'
.CV.	ˌk'e.'la	k'el-a-Ø {look-TV-B3}	'look at it!'
.CVC.	mis		'cat'
.CCV.	ˌsk'a.'na	s-k'an-a-Ø {A3-want-TV-B3}	'he/she wanted it'
.CCVC.	sts'i'	s-tsi' {A3-dog}	'his/her dog'

TABLE 21.3 CVC ROOT CLASSES

Root Class	Example	Gloss
Intransitive	*cham*	'to die'
Transitive	*mil*	'to kill'
Intransitive/Transitive	*tup*	'to extinguish/to fade'
Noun	*wits*	'mountain'
Adjective	*k'ik'*	'black'
Positional	*nuj*	'prone'
Affective	*wets*	'tinkle'
Numeral	*juk*	'seven'
Noun classifier	*men*	'female'

{A3-small-INAL} > *xch'inil*. Note that when a geminate fricative results, it is reduced by geminate consonant reduction: *s-xux* 'his/her/its callous {A3-callous} > *xux*.

Fricative glottal deletion. When the glottal fricative [j] is preceded by a palatoalveolar, it deletes, e.g. *wa=x-jak-i* 'he/she/it comes here' {IPFV=IPFV-come.here-SS} > *wa xaki*.

Labial approximant fricativization. The labial approximant /w/ fricativizes when it is followed by the palatal approximant /y/ and when it is word-final, e.g. *wa=la-xiw-y-on* 'I'm scared' {IPFV=IPFV.SAP-be.scared-EP-B1} > *wa laxivyon*. Note that [v] is not phonemically distinct from [w].

Some morphological processes involve vowel harmony or disharmony (see § 6.2, 7.5, and §7.6).

3 ROOT TYPES

The most common root shape in Tojolabal is CVC, as in other Mayan languages (Supple and Douglas 1949). Table 21.3 lists root classes. Most root classes can be inflected directly, but most can also undergo further derivation to form stems of other types (or the same type). Positional roots are unique in that they must undergo further derivation before being inflected (see §7.5). All verb and positional roots are CVC. However, noun, numeral and adjective roots may be bisyllabic, e.g. *tsima* 'small bowl', *ta'an* 'lime/ash', *waxak* 'eight', *niwan* 'big'. CV is limited to closed class elements: second position clitics, incompletive marker *wa=*, negation *mi*, and deictic *ti*.

4 PERSON MARKING

4.1 Person markers

As in the other Mayan languages, Tojolabal has two sets of person affixes: Set A, which is used to index the possessor of a noun and the subject of a transitive verb, and Set B, which indexes the subject of an intransitive verb or the object of a transitive verb. Set A is strictly prefixing; Set B is mainly suffixing.

TABLE 21.4 SET A PERSON MARKERS

	/ _ C	/ _ V
1	j-	k-
2	(w)a-/w-	(j)aw-/waw-/w-
3	s-	y-

TABLE 21.5 PLURAL MARKERS FOR SET A

Person	Suffix
1 inc.	-tik, -tikik
1 exc.	-tikon
2	-ex
3	-e'

Table 21.4 shows members of Set A, with their preconsonantal and prevocalic allo-morphs. Note that a stem-initial glottal stop is elided if it is preceded by a Set A prefix, e.g. *k-ʔil-a* 'I saw him/her/it' {A1-see-ss} > *kila*. The same glottal stop does not delete in other morphophonological environments such as after the incompletive prefix *x-*, e.g. *mi x-ʔa'in-i* 'He/she/it doesn't bathe' {NEG IPFV-bathe-ss}. As in Tseltalan and unlike Q'an-job'alan, Set A in Tojolabal marks only person, and not number. Marking of plurality requires a suffix in addition to the person prefix (see Table 21.5).

Table 21.6 shows Set B. Unlike Set A, Set B marks both person and number. Furthe-more, the allomorphy of Set B is conditioned morphologically, not phonologically: 2sg *-Ø* is used only in the incompletive and irrealis, and 2pl *-ik* is restricted to the irrealis. Note that 2pl *-ik* is homophonous to the plural suffix chosen by intransitive verbs in the imperative, as in *nox-an-ik* 'bathe!' {bathe-IMP-2PL}.

Note that Tojolabal makes a distinction between inclusive and exclusive in the first person plural.

4.2 Independent pronouns

Tojolabal has a single series of independent pronouns based on the root *e 'n*. Unlike Q'an-job'alan (Zavala 1992:224) and similar to the second series of Tseltalan's independent pronouns (Polian, this volume), they take Set A prefixes, plus the segment [l] in some

TABLE 21.6 SET B PERSON AND NUMBER MARKERS

	Singular	Plural
1	-on	inc. -otik
		exc. -otikon
2	-a (-Ø)	-ex (-ik)
3	-Ø	-e'

(Note that in the glosses I will not represent B3.)

plural forms: *ke'n* {A1-PRON}, *w-e'n* {A2-PRON}, *ye'n* {A3-PRON}, *k-e'n-tik* {A1-PRON-1PL}, *k-e'n-tikon* {A1-PRON-1PL.EXCL}, *w-e'n-l-ex* {A2-PRON-EP-2PL}, *y-e'n-l-e'* {A3-PRON-EP-3PL}). Independent pronouns in Tojolabal are used for emphasizing the referent as in (5).

(5) Ma   oj   y-il   ja=ixuk-e'   y-e'n   chomajkil=i.
    or   IRR   A3-see   DET=woman-PL   A3-PRON   also=TOP
    'Or she, she would also take care of the women.' {TEXT}

5 NOUNS AND ADJECTIVES

Although nouns and adjectives share many morphosyntactic properties, they constitute two distinguishable word classes. Adjectives and nouns: (1) function as non-verbal predicates if they are suffixed with Set B person markers, e.g. *pal-a-olom-a* 'you're a punk' {tousled-EP-hair/head-B2.SG}, *ch'in-on=to* 'I am still small' {small-B1.SG=still}; (2) partially share derivativational morphology, e.g. verbalizing suffixes -*ax* and -*b'* as in *poko-ax-i* 's/he got older' vs. *Tojolab'al-ax-i* 'he became a Tojolabal'. Unlike nouns, adjectives: (1) cannot be syntactically possessed; (2) take plural marker -*ik* for human referents, e.g. *ch'in-ik=to ja=ixuk-e'=i* 'the women are still small' {small-PL=still DET=woman-PL=TOP}. This is possible for all adjectives in predicate function and for a few in attributive function (see §5.3).

5.1 Noun classes

Possession distinguishes two classes of nouns: alienable nouns, which are unmarked when they are not possessed, and inalienable nouns, whose basic form is possessed.

Alienable nouns may occur unpossessed and require no derivational morphology when they are possessed, e.g. *ich* 'chili', *aw-ich* 'your chili'. At least two alienable nouns have suppletive forms used when the noun is possessed, e.g. *k-o'ot* 'my tortilla' {A1-tortilla.POSS} vs. **j-waj*, and *aw-a'l* 'your water' {A2-water.POSS} vs. **a-ja'*.

Inalienable nouns do not occur unpossessed without further derivation, e.g. *j-nuk'* 'my neck' {A1-neck} vs. **nuk'*, *nuk'-al* 'neck' {neck-NON.POSS}. Note however that at least two inalienable nouns denoting physical and psychological properties (*ip* 'strength' and *nup* 'fit') cannot occur unpossessed at all.

Most alienable nouns can be converted to inalienable nouns by suffixation of -*il*, e.g. *y-ich-il* 'its chili' {A3-chili-INAL}. The resulting noun has a more abstract meaning, as in (6b) where it refers to an inherent quality of the chips.

(6) a. Ay=ma   aw-ich?
        EXIST=Q   A2-chili
        'Do you have chili?' {TEXT}

    b. Ay   y-ich-il   a-sabrita?
        EXIST   A3-chili-INAL   A2-chips
        'Are your chips spicy?' {TEXT}

5.2 Number marking on nouns

Plural marking is not obligatory. In fact, only four nouns can be inflected for plural: *winik* 'man' vs. *winik-e'* 'men', *ixuk* 'woman' vs. *ixuk-e'* 'women', *kerem* 'boy' vs.

kerem-tik 'boys', and *chan* 'animal' vs. *chan-te'* 'animals'. Further plural marking for these nouns is not mandatory if the discourse context makes plurality clear, as in (7). Note that the plural suffixes *-e'* and *-tik* are homophonous with verbal 3pl and 1pl suffixes in Table 21.6.

(7) I   sok   ja=s-luwar   ja=y-il-j-el   ja=ixuk=i
    And   with   DET=A3-RN:for   DET=A3-see-PSV-NF   DET=woman=TOP
       cha=lajan   sok oj   j-neb'-e.
       ITR=like with   IRR   A1-learn-IRR
    'And as for the taking care of women, it is likely that I am once again about to learn it.' {TEXT}

All nouns, including *winik* 'man', *ixuk* 'woman', *kerem* 'boy', and *chan* 'animal', can be optionally marked with the lexical plural marker *=jumasa'*. (8) shows that plural can be marked both lexically and morphologically in the NP. Note that *=jumasa'* follows the noun and cannot occur in isolation.

(8) Lek=to   wa=x-'el   y-uj-il-e'   ja=Tojol-ab'al=i
    good=still   IPFV=IPFV-go.out   A3-AGT-EP-3PL   DET=Tojolabal=TOP
       ja=ixuk-e'=jumasa'.
       DET=woman-3PL=PL
    'Women still speak good Tojolabal.' {TEXT}

5.3 Adjectives

Adjectives in Tojolabal can function as either attributive or predicative. Attributive adjectives occur prenominally within a NP, while predicative adjectives function as non-verbal predicates. Depending on their function, adjectives have somewhat different properties.

First, as in Tseltalan (Polian, this volume) but not Q'anjob'alan (Zavala 1992:107), monosyllabic (root) adjectives require the suffix *-Vl* in attributive function, as in (9).

(9) Puro   **toj-ol**   cha'n-el   wa=la-cha'n-y-ex.
    only   right-ATTR   dance-NF   IPFV=IPFV-dance-EP-B2PL
    'The right dance is the only thing you guys dance.' {TEXT}

Note that in predicate position *toj* does not require derivational morphology, e.g. *toj-ol b'ej* 'straight path' {right-ATTR path} vs. *ja=b'ej=i toj* 'the path is straight' {DET=path=TOP straight}. However, some monosyllabic adjective roots must also be derived to function predicatively. Cf. *najat* 'long (predicative)' vs. *najt-il* (attributive), *ya'ax* 'green/blue' (predicative) vs. *yax-al* 'green/blue' (attributive), *ya'aw* 'tender' (predicative) vs. *yaw-al* (attributive), *tu'uj* 'stinky' (predicative) vs. *tuj-il* (attributive), *tse'ej* 'raw' (predicative) vs. *tse'-il* (attributive) and *che'ej* 'cold' (predicative) vs. *che'-il* (attributive). See Gómez Cruz (2010:164–5) for an exhaustive list.

Second, predicative adjectives can agree in plurality with the subject when it is human-referring. Plural marking can be either *-e'* or *-ik* as in (10a). (10b) shows that only adjectives predicated of a human NP have access to number morphology.

(10) a. Ch'in-e'   /   ch'in-ik.
         small-B3PL   small-PL
         'They are small.' (applying to humans)

     b. *Ch'in-e'=to   ja=yal   mis   jumasa'=i.
         small-B3PL=still DET=DIM   cat   PL=TOP
         Intended meaning: 'The kittens are still small.' (Gómez Cruz 2010:88)

With three exceptions, attributive adjectives do not agree in plurality with the head N. The exceptions are *ch'in* 'small', *nux* 'tiny', and *niwan* 'big', e.g. *ja=ch'in-ik ixuk-e'* 'the small women' {DET=small-PL woman-PL}. Note that plural agreement is obligatory only with nouns that already mark plural (see §5.2) as in (11), where the presence of the lexical pluralizer *jumasa'* forces number agreement on the attributive adjective.

(11) S-kuch-u-w-e'   si'   ja=tsamal(*-ik)/nux-ik   ixuk=jumasa'=i.
     A3-carry-SS-EP-3PL wood   DET=beautiful(-PL)/tiny-PL   woman=PL=TOP
     'The beautiful/tiny women carried wood.' (after Gómez Cruz 2010:89)

5.4 Maximal extension of the noun phrase

The maximal extension of the NP is: determiner + numeral expression + noun classifier + diminutive + adjective + N + pluralizer + demonstrative + possesor NP + relative clause + topic enclitic. Aside from headless relatives, N is obligatory, and it is the only obligatory element.

ja= is Tojolabal's only definite determiner. The numeral *jun* 'one' can be used as an indefinite as in (12).

(12) Ay   jun yal winik sok   jun men   yal   ixuk.
     EXIST   one DIM man   with one CLF.F DIM   woman
     'There was a little man and a little woman.' {TEXT}

But *jun* can also be used in a definite NP as a quantifier as in (13).

(13) Cha-el   ja=**jun**   wo'=i.
     ITR-go.out   DET=one   toad=TOP
     'That very same toad left again.' {TEXT}

Unlike Tseltalan and Q'anjob'alan, numerals do not require a classifier (see §6.3):

(14) Ti   s-le'-a-w-e'   chab' mula.
     DEIC   A3-look.for-SS-EP-3PL   two   mule
     'They looked for two mules.' {TEXT}

Noun classifiers and the diminutive element occupy the position after numeral expressions, as in (12). Noun classifiers are a non-obligatory series with only two members (*me'n/nan* 'FEMININE' and *tan/tat* 'MASCULINE').

If a possessed N is modified by an adjective, the Set A marker usually appears once on the noun as in (15a), but it can also be prefixed to the adjective, as in (15b) or to both adjective and noun, as in (15c). Note that in (15a) the feminine noun classifier applies to *uk'* 'louse'.

(15) a. Cham   ja=men   niwan   y-uk'=i.
        die   DET=CLF.F   big   A3-louse=TOP
        'His/her big louse died.'

   b. Ajn-i   ja=s-k'ik'-il   kawu'   ja=Jwan=i.
      run-EP   DET=black-ATTR   horse   DET=Juan=TOP
      'Juan's black horse ran.'

   c. Ti'   kan   b'a   s-niwan   s-naj   ja=j-tat=i.
      DEIC   stay   PREP A3-big   A3-house   DET=A1-father=TOP
      'He stayed at my father's big house.' (all examples come from Gómez Cruz 2010:152)

The pluralizer *jumasa'* occupies the first post-noun position, as in (8) and (11) It is followed by the demonstratives *it* 'PROXIMAL', *jaw* 'DISTAL', e.g. *ja=winik jaw=i* 'that man' {DET=man DEM=TOP}. The possessor NP and relative clauses occupy the last two post-noun positions.

The final position in the NP is occupied by the enclitic *=i*, which is triggered by the determiner *ja=*. The topic enclitic *=i* can be inhibited in informal speech styles. As in other Mayan languages, this enclitic is restricted to the end of the intonational phrase. That position is also occupied by the discourse continuity enclitic *=a*, which here is triggered by the clause-initial deictic element *ti*. Since only one element can occupy this position, *=a* takes precedence over *=i*, as in (16).

(16) Ti=b'i   wa=x-waj   ja=b'a   y-alaj   ja=winik
     DEM=REP   IPFV=IPFV-go   DET=PREP   A3-maize.field   DET=man
        jaw=a.
        DEM=DCM
     'That man then left to his maize field.' {TEXT}

6 VERBS

As in other Mayan languages, Tojolabal strongly distinguishes intransitive and transitive verbs. Person marking, aspect, mood, and derivational morphology, as well as valency morphemes, make this distinction clear. Within the subclass of transitive verbs, there is a further distinction between derived stems and underived (CVC) transitive stems, as these take different mood and valency suffixes.

Table 21.7 shows full paradigms for an intransitive verb (*cham* 'die'), an underived transitive (*yam* 'grab'), and a derived transitive (*elk'an* 'steal').

6.1 Aspect

Like Tseltalan (Polian, this volume), Tojolabal distinguishes four aspects: perfective, imperfective, perfect, and progressive. Table 21.8 shows that perfective, imperfective,

TABLE 21.7 INFLECTION OF *CHAM* **'DIE',** *YAM* **'GRAB', AND** *ELK'AN* **'STEAL'**

1	cham-y-on	j-yam-a	k-elk'-an
	die-EP-B1	A1-grab-SS	A1-steal-VRBZ
2	cham-y-a	wa-yam-a	waw-elk'-an
	die-EP-B2	A2-grab-SS	A2-steal-VRBZ
3	cham-i	s-yam-a	y-elk'-an
	die-SS	A3-grab-SS	A3-steal-VRBZ

IMPERFECTIVE

1	(wa=)la-cham-y-on	(wa=)x-j-yam-a	(wa=)x-k-elk'-an
	(IPFV=)SAP-die-EP-B1	(IPFV=)IPFV-A1-grab-SS	(IPFV=)IPFV-A1-STEAL-VRBZ
2	(wa=)la-cham-i-Ø	(wa=)x-ja-yam-a	(wa=)x-aw-elk'-an
	(IPFV=)SAP-die-EP-B2	(IPFV=)IPFV-A2-grab-SS	(IPFV=)IPFV-A2-grab-VRBZ
3	(wa=)x-cham-i	(wa=)x-s-yam-a	(wa=)x-y-elk'-an
	(IPFV=)IPFV-die-SS	(IPFV=)IPFV-A3-grab-SS	(IPFV=)IPFV-A3-grab-VRBZ

PERFECT

1	cham-el-on	j-yam-unej	k-elk'-an-unej
	die-PRF-B1	A1-grab-PRF	A1-steal-VRBZ-PRF
2	cham-el-a	wa-yam-unej	waw-elk'-an-unej
	die-PRF-B2	A2-grab-PRF	A2-steal-VRBZ-PRF
3	cham-el	s-yam-unej	y-elk'-an-unej
	die-PRF	A3-grab-PRF	A3-steal-VRBZ-PRF

PROGRESSIVE

1	wan-on cham-el	wan-on s-yam-j-el	wan-on y-elk'-an-j-el
	PROG-B1 die-NF	PROG-B1 A3-grab-PSV-NF	PROG-B1 A3-steal-VRBZPSV-NF
2	wan-a cham-el	wan-a s-yam-j-el	wan-a y-elk'-an-j-el
	PROG-B2 die-NF	PROG-B2 A3-grab-PSV-NF	PROG-B2 A3-steal-VRBZ-PSV-NF
3	wan cham-el	wan s-yam-j-el	wan y-elk'-an-j-el
	PROG die-NF	PROG A3-grab-PSV-NF	PROG A3-steal-VRBZ-PSV-NF

IRREALIS

1	oj cham-k-on	oj j-yam-e	oj k-elk'-an
	IRR die-IRR-B1	IRR A1-grab-IRR.SG	IRR A1-steal-VRBZ
2	oj cham-an-Ø	oj a-yam-e	oj aw-elk'-an
	IRR die-IRR-B2	IRR A2-grab-IRR.SG	IRR A2-steal-VRBZ
3	oj cham-uk	oj s-yam-e	oj y-elk'-an
	IRR die-IRR	IRR A3-grab-IRR.SG	IRR A3-steal-VRBZ

IMPERATIVE

singular	cham-an	yam-a	elk'-an
	die-IMP	grab-SS	steal-VRBZ
plural	cham-an-ik	yam-a-w-ik	elk'-an-ik
	die-IMP-PL	grab-IMP-EP-PL	steal-VRBZ-PL

TABLE 21.8 ASPECTUAL MARKERS

Aspect	Intransitive verbs	Transitive verbs
PERFECTIVE	Ø	
IMPERFECTIVE	la- (+B1/2)	x-
	x- (+B3)	
PERFECT	-el	-unej
PROGRESSIVE	periphrasis (**wan**-B)	

and perfect are morphologically marked, while progressive is expressed through periphrasis (see §9.1).

Verbs inflected in the imperfective usually bear the optional marker *wa=*, e.g. *wa=x-nik-i* 'she moves' {IPFV=IPFV-move-SS}. *Wa=* is a proclitic with a fixed position in clause structure. It cannot be pronounced in isolation or host a second position clitic, unless it is converted into a phonological word by adding a final consonant as in (17). The negation *mi* and deictic element *ti* usually, but not always, inhibit *wa=*, e.g. *ti (wa=)la-jak=a* 'then you get here' {DEIC IPFV=IPFV.SAP-come.here[B2]=DCM}.

(17) **Wan=b'i**   x-s-lap-a.
     IPFV=REP   IPFV-A3-wear-SS
     'They say, she wears it.' {TEXT}

6.2 Mood and valency

Tojolabal distinguishes three moods: indicative, irrealis, and imperative. As in other Mayan languages, aspectual contrasts are neutralized in non-indicative moods. Like Q'anjob'alan and unlike Tseltalan, Tojolabal partially maintains the Proto-Mayan status suffixes that mark valency (transitive vs. intransitive) and mood. See Table 21.9.

Intransitive *-i* appears only in imperfective and perfective, e.g. *wa=la-nox-i* 'you bathe' {IPFV= IPFV.SAP-bathe-SS[B2]}, while transitive *-V* is used in imperfective, perfective, and imperative, e.g. *lut-u-w-ik* 'close it!' {close-SS-EP-PL}. Note that in roots with back vowels, *-V* is copied, while *-a* is selected by roots with front vowels. However, some innovative dialects use *-a* in all cases.

As in other Mayan languages, the status suffix *-i* is inhibited if it does not occur at the right edge of the intonational phrase, as in (18a). In some dialects, this phonological property is also shared by the 3sg intransitive irrealis *-uk* and the singular transitive irrealis *-e* as in (18b) and (18c).

TABLE 21.9 STATUS AND MOOD SUFFIXES

Mood	Intransitive verbs	Transitive verbs
INDICATIVE	-i	-V (only root transitives)
IRREALIS	-k (+B1)	-e (only in sg for underived verbs)
	– an (+B2)	– uk (only derived verbs)
	– uk (+B3)	
IMPERATIVE	-an	-V (only root transitives)

(18) a. Waj(*-i)   Margarita?
     go-ss   Las.Margaritas
     'Did she go to Las Margaritas?' {TEXT}

   b. Jas   ora   oj   jul(*-uk)   b'a?
      what   hour   IRR   come.here-IRR   thus
      'What time will he get here then?' {TEXT}

   c. Oj   k-il(*-e)   ja=j-che'um=i?
      IRR   A1-see-IRR.SG   DET=A1-wife=TOP
      'Would I see my wife?' {TEXT}

As I pointed out, root transitive verbs in the imperative take the status suffix -*V*. In contrast, intransitive verbs in the imperative do not take the status suffix -*i*, but the imperative suffix -*an*, e.g. *chab'-an-an-ik* 'be quiet!' {quiet-VRBZ-IMP-PL}. Note that the plural is marked with -*ik* instead of -*ex* (see Tables 21.6 and 21.7) in both transitive and intransitive verbs.

There are some irregular transitive verbs that take the status suffixes -*an* (*k'ul-an* 'make', *k'u'-an* 'trust/obey') or -*aj* (*i'-aj* 'bring', *u'aj* 'drink') instead of -*V*.

The irrealis mood also has an obligatory pre-verbal marker, *oj*. Like the imperfective marker *wa*=, which occupies the same position, *oj* cannot be pronounced in isolation, unless it changes its phonological shape, in this case to *ojo*. Note that, unlike *wa*=, *oj* can host second position clitics without changing its phonological form, e.g. *oj=xa y-al-e* 'she will already say it' {IRR=already A3-say-IRR.SG}. Note that verbs taking the status suffix -*an* take the irrealis suffix -*uk*, e.g. *mi oj j-k'u'-uk-a* 'I won't obey you' {NEG IRR A1-trust/obey-IRR-B2}.

6.3 Voice

Passive (-*j*), impersonal passive (-*x*), and antipassive (-*wan*) are Tojolabal's only mechanisms for detransitivization. Unlike Tseltalan (Aissen 1999) and Q'anjob'alan (Zavala 1997), there is no productive anticausative and no agent focus voice.

Passive is formed with -*j* for both root and derived transitive stems. The agent is optionally expressed as an oblique introduced by the relational noun *uj* as in (19). Note that *uj* can be omitted under some circumstances. See §8.2 for more on passives.

(19) Nok'-j-i   y-uj   ja=x-chajnul=i.
     cover-PSV-EP   A3-AGT   DET=A3-insect=TOP
     'It was covered by its insects.' {TEXT}

Impersonal passives, formed with -*x*, do not permit the expression of the agent either as a direct argument or as an oblique. However, a non-specific human agent is implied, as in (20).

(20) Ja'xa   inat=i   ta'-x-i.
     TOP.CHANGE   seed=TOP   find-IMPERSONAL-EP
     'As for the seeds, you (indefinite) can find them.' {TEXT}

Note that impersonal passives cannot be inflected either with person or plural marking, e.g. *nok'-x-y-on* {cover-IMPERSONAL-EP-B1}, *nok'-x-y-e'* {cover-IMPERSONAL-EP-B3PL}.

Impersonal passives are not to be confounded with the derivational anticausative infix <j>, which is restricted to a few CVC transitive roots, e.g. *nika* 'move it!' vs. *nijki* 'it moved' or *poko* 'break it' vs. *pojki* 'it broke/he was born'.

The antipassive *-wan* eliminates the object, and therefore does not allow its expression even as an oblique. Unlike Tseltalan (Polian, this volume), Tojolabal's antipassives are not limited to cases where the implicit patient is animate: in (21) the semantic patient refers to eggs that the women were supposed to sell in Comitán.

(21) Ja'xa=ixuk=i   oj=xa=ni   ik'-wan-uk.
      TOP.CHANGE=woman=TOP IRR=already=EMPH   carry-AP-IRR
      'The women, they will definitely carry [them].' {TEXT}

Like other Mayan languages, Tojolabal uses a possessed relational noun *b'aj* for expressing reflexive/reciprocal. The verb remains transitive and *b'aj* fills the position of the object. *B'aj* is morphologically bound to the verbal complex, in the sense that it can be separated from the verb only by second position clitics (see §7.1) and directionals (see §7.2). Further, *b'aj* inhibits plural marking on the verb as in (22).

(22) Wa=x-k-il-a(*-tik)   j-b'aj-tik.
      IPFV=IPFV-A1-see-SS(-1PL)   A1-RR-1PL
      'We see each other' or 'We see ourselves.' {TEXT}

Unlike other Mayan languages, Tojolabal has no inflectional devices for increasing valency such as applicatives and causatives. Causatives are strictly derivational and rather unproductive, e.g. *ajli* 'to flare' vs. *ajles* 'to kindle'. Ditransitive clauses require the dative morpheme *i'* as in (23). *I'* is in a process of grammaticalization (see §7.3 for a more detailed description).

(23) Ja'xa . . .   s-nan=i   a'-j-i   y-i'   s-kuchiyo
      TOP.CHANGE   A3-mother=TOP   give-PSV-EP   A3-DAT   A3-knife
      'As for his mother, a knife was given to her.' {TEXT}

6.4 Nominalizations

As with finite verbal inflection, transitive and intransitive stems have differential access to morphological resources for nominalization. The suffix *-el* attaches directly to intransitive verbs to form nominalizations, e.g. *cha'n-el* 'dancing' {dance-NF}, *cham-el* 'dying' {die-NF}. In order to form a nominalization of a transitive verb, it is necessary to detransitivize it, e.g. through passive morphology. For these reasons, (24a) is ill-formed, but (24b) is not.

(24) a. *Mil-el.
          kill-NF

      b. Mil-j-el.
          kill-PSV-NF

These nominalizations occur in a number of syntactic contexts that are discussed below (see §9.2).

A second way to nominalize transitive stems is by suffixing -*uj*, cognate with Q'anjob'al's -*o*. This suffix forms compound-like action nouns as in (25). Note that these nominalizations take an obligatory bare noun object. They permit definite determiner *ja=* and attributive adjectives as in the example.

(25) A<j>y-i-ta   niwan   mil-uj   chan.
     EXIST<VRBZ>-EP- already big kill-NF bird
     'There was already a big killing of birds.' {TEXT}

These nominalizations also occur in different syntactic contexts which are discussed below (see §9.2).

6.5 Plural marking on verbs and verbal number

As seen earlier (see §4.2), Tojolabal verbs can mark the plurality of its nominal arguments. Since Set B and plural markers for Set A occur in the same structural position, plural morphology can only be marked once in clauses with two semantically plural arguments, as (26a) shows (note that there are dialects where Set B and plural markers for Set A can co-occur and where (26a) is grammatical,). Plural agreement can be either with the agent or the patient as in (26b) and (26c), which leads to ambiguity. Transitive clauses with both arguments in third person raise another puzzle: if -*e'* occurs, it can be interpreted as a 3PL for Set A, as B3.PL, or even as both as in (26d).

(26) a. *J-nuts-u-w-ex-tikon.
       A1-chase-SS-EP-B2PL-1PL.EXCL

    b. J-nuts-u-w-ex.
       A1-chase-SS-EP-B2PL
       'I chased you guys.'/'We chased you guys.'

    c. J-nuts-u-w-a-tikon.
       A1-chase-SS-EP-B2–1PL.EXCL
       'We chased you (sg.).'/'We chased you guys.'

    d. S-nuts-u-w-e'.
       A3-chase-SS-EP-3PL
       'He/she/it chased them.'/'They chased him/her/it.'/'They chased them.'

Tojolabal also has pluractional morphology (see Henderson, this volume). The iterative suffix *cho-* (some dialects use *cha-*) occurs before the stem. In imperfective aspect, *cho-* copies the aspectual prefix *x-*, e.g. *wa=x-cho-x-k-il-a* 'I see it over and over' {IPFV=IPFV-ITR-IPFV-A1-see-SS}. The suffix -*tala('a)n* marks transitive events that are spatially plural (sequentially or simultaneously), e.g. *w=x-jaw-a'-talan a-b'aj-ex* 'You devote yourselves everywhere' {IPFV=IPFV-A2-give-ITR-SS A2-RR-2PL}.

7 OTHER WORD CLASSES

7.1 Second position clitics

Second position clitics in Tojolabal are placed mainly after the first phonological word, e.g. *k'ak'=to ja=j-tat=i* 'My father is still angry' {hot=still DET=A1-father=TOP}. However, some syntactic environments allow them to be placed after the first constituent, e.g. *yaw-al alats=to* 'She is still a tender baby' {tender-ATTR baby=still}. See Curiel (2007:36–43) for a more detailed description. They can form a clitic cluster following the order shown in Table 21.10.

Second position clitics can occur in some types of complement clauses. See §9.1 for more details.

7.2 Directionals and aspectual adverbs

Directionals and aspectual adverbs are a group of thirteen elements that are mostly derived from a set of intransitive motion verbs. They occur with both intransitive and transitive main verbs, and occupy a fixed position in the clause right after the main verb, as in (27).

(27) Jach'   wa=x-waj   j-k'ul-tikon   **k'e'n**   kambyar.
    thus   IPFV=IPFV-go(AUX)   A1-make-1PL.EXCL   DIR   exchange
    'Thus we used to move up here to exchange it.' {TEXT}

Members of this class have a lexically conditioned final vowel that only appears if the directional or aspectual adverb occurs at the end of the intonational phrase. See Table 21.11 for an inventory. Note that, except for *jani*, members of this class are clear grammaticalizations from nominalized intransitive verbs.

The aspectual adverbs *ek'e* 'fixedly' and *kani* 'unchanging' can occur with stative positionals functioning as non-verbal predicates, as in (28a). In contrast, directionals cannot (see §7.5), as (28b) proves.

(28) a. Leb'-an-a   ek'-e
        standing.with.legs.apart-POS-B2   pass-ADV
        'You're standing with the legs apart.' {TEXT}

    b. Waj   y-il-e'   ja=chich   nok'-an
       go(AUX)   A3-see-3PL   DET=rabbit   vertically.stuck-POS
          ek'e   /   *ko'-e.
          fast   go.down-DIR
    'They went to see the rabbit that was fixedly stuck (*down there).' {TEXT}

TABLE 21.10 SECOND POSITION CLITICS

Temporal	Emphatic	Modals/evidential
=xa 'already' =to 'still'	=ni	=ma 'POLAR INTERROGATIVE' =b'i 'HEARSAY' =k'a 'DUBITATIVE'

TABLE 21.11   DIRECTIONALS AND ASPECTUAL ADVERBS (SLIGHTLY MODIFIED FROM PEAKE 2007B:2)

	Gloss	*Source*
		VERTICAL DIRECTIONALS
ko'(e)	'down'	*ko'* 'go down'
k'e'(i)	'up'	*k'e'* 'go up'
		VERTICAL + DEICTIC DIRECTIONALS
ko'n(e)	'down towards the spekaer'	*ko'* + jan(i)
k'e'n(e)	'up towards the speaker'	*k'e'* + jan(i)
		DEICTIC DIRECTIONALS
jan(i)	'towards the speaker'	unknown
jul(e)	'towards the speaker' (+ TELIC)	*jul* 'arrive right here'
k'ot(e)	'away from the speaker'	*k'ot* 'arrive there'
och(e)	'into'	*och* 'enter'
el(e)	'out of sight'	*el* 'leave'
		ASPECTUAL ADVERBS
ek'(e)	'fixedly'	*ek'* 'pass through/happen'
kan(i)	'unchanging'	*kani* 'stay'
ch'ay(i)	'needlessly'	*ch'ay* 'get lost'
waj(i)	'on one's way'	*waj* 'go'

It may be that *jani* and *jule* can be used deictically to index past tense as in (29).

(29) Kada   wa=x-el   jul-e   ja=s-dya   San Migel=i.
       each   IPFV=IPFV-go.out   come.here-DIR   DET=A3-day   Saint Michael=TOP
       'Each time that Saint Michael's day used to come.' {TEXT}

7.3 Auxiliaries

Like Tseltalan, Tojolabal has a number of intransitive verbs that can be used as auxiliaries. Except for *ch'ak* 'finish (intransitive)', these are roughly the same verbs that have been grammaticalized as directionals (see §7.2): *k'e'k* 'go up', *och* 'enter', *ek'* 'pass through', *kan* 'stay', *waj* 'go'. The auxiliary and the lexical verb form a kind of complex predicate, with a repartition of the inflection as follows: aspect is marked on the auxiliary, while person and number are marked on the lexical verb, as in (30) and (31). Note that the lexical verb inflects obligatorily for irrealis.

(30) Och-ta   y-il   yal   k-untikil.
       enter(AUX)-already   A3-see   DIM   A1-sons.and.daughters
       'He already started to take care of our children.' {TEXT}

(31) Waj   a'tn-uk-on.
       go(AUX)   bathe-IRR-B1
       'I went bathing.' {TEXT}

Clauses of purpose (see §9.2) are semantically close to this construction.

7.4 Ditransitive constructions

Tojolabal has a distinctive strategy for introducing the third argument of a transitive verb. This construction, a grammaticalized serial verb construction, involves a morpheme whose position is fixed in the verbal complex. See Curiel (2013) for more discussion.

The dative morpheme *i '*, derived from the verb *i '* 'to carry' introduces the recipient of a ditransitive verb as in (32) and (33). The dative morpheme follows the verb plus any directional or second position clitic. But the dative argument itself follows the object when both are lexically realized.

(32) Oj   wa-le'   jan   **y-i'**   jun   s-k'u'
       IRR   A2-look.for   come.here(DIR)   A3-DAT   one   A3-blouse
       ja=k-ijts'in=i?
       DET=A1-younger.sibling=TOP
       'Will you look for a blouse for my little sister when you come back?' {Curiel 2013:176}

(33) Oj=b'i   y-i'   jan   y-i'   gancho   ja=Karla=i.
       IRR=REP   A3-carry   DIR   A3-DAT   hair-clip   DET=Karla=TOP
       'They say, she's going to bring hair-clips to Karla.' {TEXT}

Note that the dative argument is indexed on the dative morpheme by Set A prefixes.

The reflexive/reciprocal relational noun *b'aj* (see §6.3) can realize the third argument in a ditransitive construction. Note however that it inhibits the dative morpheme, perhaps because they occupy the same position in the verbal complex, as (34) shows.

(34) Jel   s-jip-a   s-b'aj-e'   ton.
       INTS   A3-throw-SS   A3-RR-3PL   stone
       'They used to throw stones at each other.' {TEXT}

The morpheme *ab'* introduces the third argument of two verbs of communication, *ala* 'to say' and *cholo* 'to narrate', as in (35). Note that *ab'* is derived from a verb of perception, *ab'i* 'to hear/feel'.

(35) Jach'   y-al-a   k-ab'-tik   ja=s-ju'un=il   ja=Dyos=i.
       thus   A3-say-SS   A1-ADDRESSEE   DET=A3-paper=INAL   DET=God=TOP
       'Thus the Bible tells us.' {TEXT}

7.5 Existential predicate

The non-verbal predicate *ay* is used for expressing existence, possession, and location, and is also part of a perfect periphrastic construction. (36a) shows a canonical use of existential *ay*. As the language lacks an exact equivalent to English 'have', it uses *ay* plus a possessed NP to convey possession, as in (36b). Some inanimate nouns denoting transient states such as *ojob'* 'flu', *xiwel* 'fright' or *jab'il* 'year/age' cannot be grammatically possessed, and require a periphrastic genitive construction, as in (36c).

(36) a. Ay   k'uts-nuk'!
      EXIST   slice-neck
      'There is a cutthroat!' {TEXT}

    b. Ay=xa   y-al   men=Beta.
       EXIST=already   A3-son.of.a.woman   CLF.F=Beta
       'Beta already has a child.' {TEXT}

    c. Ay   k-i'oj   ek'-lukum.
      EXIST   A1-GENITIVE   go.through-stomach
      'I have diarrhea.' {TEXT}

Ay is also used for expressing location, e.g. *ti ay ja=j-naj=a* 'There is my house' {DEIC EXIST DET=A1-house=DCM}. The locative use of the existential predicate *ay* extends to some adverbs like *lek* 'well', e.g. *lek ay-on* 'I'm doing well' {good EXIST-B1}.
    Ay can also be part of perfect periphrasis as in (37).

(37) Mey   x-k-i'-aj   jun   ala   mispero   il   k'ot-e.
     NEG+EXIST   IPFV-A1-carry-SS   one   DIM   tree_SPECIES   DEIC   arrive.there-ADV
     'I haven't brought a little japanese medlar over there.' {TEXT}

Ay is the only word in the language that can undergo phonological fusion with the demonstrative *ti* and the negative *mi* as in (37). This may be due to its frequency. Further, *ay* can be reduplicated to give a sense of plurality to its subject as in (38).

(38) A-'ay   ja=ason   ta.
     REDUP-EXIST   DET=cloud   indeed
     'There are a lot of clouds indeed.' {TEXT}

7.6 Positionals

Like other Mayan languages, Tojolabal has a set of positional roots with the form CVC. Positional roots are different from other root classes in that they must undergo further derivation before they can be inflected. As in Tseltal (Sántiz Gómez 2010) and Q'anjob'al

TABLE 21.12 SEMANTIC CLASSES OF POSITIONAL ROOTS (AFTER GÓMEZ CRUZ 2010:193–9)

Semantic class	Root	Stative forms
Position	K'AT	k'atan 'crossed'
Containment	CHUP	chupan 'tucked in a pockt/bag'
Blocking movement	LATS'	lats'an 'narrow'
Grouping	TIM	timan 'crowded' [of people or animals]
Shape	TS'IP	ts'ipan 'pointed'
Texture	JIS	jisan, 'thinly furrowed'
Psychological state	MOT'	mot'an 'fearful'

(Martin 1977), positionals in Tojolabal do not necessarily denote position, although this seems to be the core meaning (see Table 21.12). So far 262 positional roots have identified (Gómez Cruz 2010:193–9).

Tojolabal has a very productive morpheme to derive adjective-like stative forms from positional roots, *-an*. The same morpheme is found in Q'anjob'alan (Martin 1977), but not in Tseltalan. There are a number of suffixes that derive transitive and intransitive verbs from positional roots, but these are not productive and are subject to lexical conditioning, e.g. PAK' derives both *pak'a* 'to grind (tr.)' and *pak'tsun* 'to pat (tr.)' while TS'EL derives *ts'elan* 'lie on your side (intr.)', *ts'elpuj* 'slope (intr.)', *ts'elpun* 'lean (tr.)'.

Some roots like JAM 'open' belong simultaneously to two different root classes (transitive and positional). These roots have access both to *-an* and to *-ub'al*, a suffix restricted to transitive roots. Although both suffixes derive stative adjective-like forms, there is a clear semantic difference that involves agentivity (Gómez Cruz 2010:134), e.g. *jam-an* 'open (stative)' vs. *jam-ub'al* 'opened (stative) by somebody'.

Stative positional forms can function as non-verbal predicates as in (39a) or as attributive adjectives as in (39b).

(39) a. Tik'-an-on   il   ja=palabra   it=i.
      limited-POS-B1   DEM   DET=word   DEM=TOP
      'I am limited here with respect to this story.' {TEXT}

    b. Puro   lap-an   s-mojchil   tan-tik   soltero.
       only   dressed-POS   A3-handkerchief   DEM-PL   bachelor
       'Only handkerchief-wearing bachelors.' {TEXT}

7.7 Expressive verbs and quotative predicates

Expressive verbs are a subclass of intransitive verbs derived from CVC roots by a set of characteristic morphological processes. They describe events and states through highly specific and salient perceptual properties. As Table 21.13 shows, reduplication and suffixation are involved in deriving these roots. Some members of this class allow phonemes that do not occur with other major word classes, e.g. /r/, as in *ereri* 'to have a growling stomach'.

Expressive verbs reference semantic dimensions associated with sound (*nilili* 'to make white noise'), movement (*muchuchi* 'to tiptoe'), shape (*xijiji* 'to be straight'), bodily states (*pululi* 'to have cracking teeth'), or natural phenomena (*tiltuni* 'to be a mirage').

In contrast with Tseltal (Pérez González 2009, 2012), expressive verbs in Tojolabal show full paradigms, i.e. they occur in all aspects, moods, and persons.

Quotatives are a closed class of verbs that mark direct speech. The only members of this class are the intransitives *chi'* and *chikan* and the transitive *utaj*. These verbs follow the quotation, as in (40).

(40) "Mi   w-e'n-uk-a?"   x-y-ut-aj-on   kani.
     NEG   A2-PRON-IRR-B2   IPFV-A3-QUOT-SS-B1   unchanging
     '"Wasn't it you?", he yelled definitely at me.' {TEXT}

Note that the quotative verb in (40) inflects in the normal way for person and aspect. In this way they are different from quotatives in Yukatek (Lucy 1993). However, quotative verbs show some morphological idiosyncrasies and paradigmatic gaps: (a) *chi'* and

TABLE 21.13 MORPHOLOGICAL PATTERNS FOR DERIVING EXPRESSIVE PREDICATES

Morphological pattern	Example	Gloss
Partial right-to-left reduplication		
CVC-VC₂	b'alali	'to slip violently'
Partial left-to-right reduplication +		
Suffixation		
CVC-C₁un	b'atb'uni	'to flounder'
CVC-C₁on	josjoni	'to puff and pant'
Suffixation		
CVC-ij	ts'ipiji	'to galumph'
CVC-an	xu'ani	'to whistle'
CVC-tuj	liktuji	'to fall' (only teeth)
CVC-lon	chorloni	'to spin rapidly'
CVC-ulj	pumulji	'to knock on wood'
CVC-olj	wo'olji	'to go shouting'
CV-inaj	b'alinaji	'to roll over and over'

chikan do not take the status vowel *-i* (see §6.2) and *ut* takes *-aj* as status vowel instead of *-V*, (b) the intransitive *chi'* and *chikan* can only be inflected in imperfective and irrealis, and *ut* cannot be inflected in the perfect. Furthemore, quotatives do not occur with directionals (see §7.2) and aspectual adverbs are possible only with *ut* as in (40).

7.8 Numerals and quantifiers

Like adjectives, numerals can function either as predicates or as attributive modifiers, as in (41a) and (41b).

(41) a. Waj-y-e'   ja=chab' winik jaw=i.
     go-EP-B3PL DET=two man   DEM=TOP
     'Those two men went away.' {Gómez Cruz 2010:40}

    b. Kechan-xta   chab'-e ja=yal ch'in burro.
       only-exclusively two-CLF DET=DIM small donkey
       'The small donkeys aren't but two.' {TEXT}

Numerals must co-occur with a numeral classifier. However, Tojolabal's numeral classifying system is one of the simplest in Mayan. Only three classifiers are productively used, *-wan* for humans, *-kot* for four-legged animals, and *-e* by default. However, some very proficient speakers can still produce five additional classifiers under elicitation: *-tuch'* for two-legged animals (i.e. birds), *-k'ol* for round objects, *-ib'* for plants, *-xij* for long objects, and *-b'ak'an* for corncobs (Sántiz Pérez et al. 2012:85–90).

Furthermore, the specific classifiers *-wan* and *-kot* are often replaced by default *-e* as in (41) and in (42), where the speaker is talking about her five sisters.

(42) Sak'-an=to   ja=jo'-e'=i.
     live-PART=still DET=five-CLF=TOP
     'Five of them are still alive.' {TEXT}

TABLE 21.14 MEASURERS

Suffix	Gloss	Source
-lats'	Stacked objects	LATS' 'to stack'
-b'om	Bundles	B'OM 'in bundles'
-lam	Layers	LAM 'clear/calm'
-b'us	Mounds	B'US 'mound'
-tik'	Types	TIK' 'ended up'

Classifiers not only have access to numerals, but to wh-quantifiers, e.g. *jay-wan-ex?* 'how many were you guys?' {how.many-CLF-B2PL}

Measurers are all derived from CVC positional roots and are attached to numerals and wh-quantifiers, e.g. *ox-lam-e k'u'uts* 'three layers of sweater' {three-MEAS-CLF clothes}. Table 21.14 shows an exhaustive list.

There are two subclasses of quantifiers associated with totality and partiality. Totality quantifiers can be morphologically possessed with the domain of quantification functioning as possessor as in (43).

(43) J-petsanil-tikon   ja=Tojol'ab'al-otikon.
      A1-all-1PL.EXCL   DET=Tojolabal-B1PL.EXCL
      'All of us are Tojolabal.' {TEXT}

The totality quantifier *entoril* (borrowed from Spanish *entero* 'whole') can only be used with third person and has to be possessed. Similarly, the native totality quantifier *ib'anal* can only be used with second and third person. Note that this property is shared by some relational nouns (see §7.9). The quantifier *petsanil* (see (43)) does not require morphological possession in the third person, as in (44).

(44) Puro   ajwal-al   petsanil ja=mundo   ta.
      only   landlord-NON.POSS   all   DET=world   indeed
      'The whole world was only landlords indeed.' {TEXT}

Partiality quantifiers are all formed with the suffix *-an* (*jitsan* 'a lot', *t'usan* 'few' and *t'usan yaman* 'some'). *T'usan* can suffer phonological erosion (*t'un*). Partiality quantifiers are not possessed, e.g. *jitsan kristyano* 'a few people'.

7.9 Noun classifiers

Tojolabal has four nominal classifiers that distinguish masculine and feminine in animate nouns, as in (45).

(45) Wa=x-a-na'-a   s-b'aj ja=me'n   (tan)   usej=i'?
      IPFV=IPFV-A2-know-ss   A3-RR   DET=CLF.F (CLF.M) vulture=TOP
      'Do you know the stupid she-(he-)vulture?' {TEXT}

The feminine classifiers *me'n* and *nan* are reductions of *me'jun* 'grandmother' and *nan* 'mother'; the masculine classifiers *tan* and *tat* seem to be related to *tatjun* 'grandfather' and *tat* 'father'. Like adjectives, noun classifiers can be inflected for number (*tan-tik* and *me'n-tik*) if the head of the NP is marked as plural (see §5.3). The use of noun classifiers is subject to dialectal variation: for some speakers they have a pejorative reading, while some others use them in informal speech styles.

Unlike Q'anjob'alan, the nominal classifier system of Tojolabal is rather unstable. Non-pronficient speakers, such as children under 12, extend them to inanimates, and can use feminine classifiers in NPs whose heads are semantically masculine, as in (46).

(46) Ja=me'n   yal   winik   jaw=i   jas   s-b'i'il?
     DET=CLF.F DIM   man   DEM=TOP what   A3-name
     'As for that little man, what's his name?' {TEXT}

At least in some dialects, and unlike Akatek (Zavala 1992:174), noun classifiers require the presence of a noun. This means that classifiers cannot be used as anaphors, as in (47).

(47) *Wa=x-ja-na'-a   s-b'aj ja=me'n=i'?
     IPFV=IPFV-A2-know-SS   A3-RR DET=CLF.F=TOP
     Intended meaning: 'Do you know her?'

7.10 Prepositions and relational nouns

Relations having to do with space, location, and accompaniment in Tojolabal are expressed by prepositions and relational nouns (RNs).

There are two prepositions, spatial *b'a* and sociative *sok*, e.g. *tey b'a j-naj* 'He's in my house' {DEIC+EXIST PREP A1-house}. As in Tseltalan, the preposition *b'a* can introduce a non-finite adverbial clause, e.g. *b'a oj aw-il-e* 'so you see it' {PREP IRR A2-see-IRR}.

The relational nouns are based on nouns and are always possessed. There are two semantic classes, space-oriented and non-space-oriented. Space-oriented RNs are *ts'e'el* 'next to', *oj* 'inside' and *ib'* 'under'. The latter two can only be possessed by third person, as in (48). Although RNs are usually preceded by the preposition *b'a*, this is not mandatory.

(48) Ti   kan-ta   y-oj   ja'.
     DEIC   stay-already   A3-RN:inside   water
     'It remained into the water.' {TEXT}

Non-space-oriented RNs are *mok* and *luwar*. *Mok* is used for expressing the comitative, as in (49a). This noun is actually the origin of preposition *sok* in (49b). The Spanish noun *lugar* 'place' is the source of the RN *luwar~lugar*, which expresses either topic or recipient as in (50c). Note that the possessor marking on *luwar* is optional.

(49) a. Oj   waj-an   ja=CHonab'=i?
        IRR   go-IRR[B2]   A1-COM   DET=Comitán=TOP
        'Are you going to Comitán with me?' {TEXT}

b. Wa=s-jam-a   dulse   ja=j-tat=i   sok   (*s-mok)   ja=kuchiyo.
   IPFV=A3-open-SS   candy   DET=A1-father=TOP   with   A3-SOC   DET=knife
   'My father opens the candy, with a knife.' {TEXT}

(50) Ja=luwar   ja=k-altsil-tik=i   ja'   wa=x-y-ixtalan.
     DET=TOP   DET=A1-soul-1PL=TOP   FOC   IPFV=IPFV-A3-treat.like.a.toy
     'As for our souls, it is him who treat them like a toy.' {TEXT}

It is likely that the origin of RNs are grammaticized meronyms, since other body parts like *ti'* 'mouth' and *sat* 'face/eye' can also be used as meronyms.

8 SIMPLE CLAUSE STRUCTURE

8.1 Arguments, agreement, and alignment

Tojolabal is a strictly head-marking language (Nichols 1986), which means that arguments are cross-referenced on the predicate and NPs do not bear morphological marking for case at all. The language has a rigid ergative-absolutive alignment with no split. (51) shows that the argument of an intransitive verb and the object of a transitive verb are marked with the same morphological resources (Set B), while the agent of a transitive verb needs to be prefixed with ergative morphology (Set A) as in (52).

(51) a. Jak-y-**on**.
        come.here-EP-B1.SG
        'I came here.' {TEXT}

     b. Kechan   k'ul-an-**on**   perton!
        only   make-SS-B1.SG   pardon
        'Just pardon me!' {TEXT}

(52) **K**-il-a   ja=y-a'   k'e'-uk=i.
     A1-see-SS   DET=A3-give   rise-IRR=TOP
     'I saw it when they raised it.' {TEXT}

8.2 Constituent order and changes in order

Tojolabal has all the features reported for VO languages (Dryer 2007): possessum precedes possessor, auxiliaries precede lexical verbs, matrix verbs precede their complement clauses, and relative clauses are always post-nuclear. Although there is a statistically clear preference for just one lexical NP in transitive clauses (Curiel 2007:27–8), unmarked word order is VOA (Furbee-Losee 1976; Brody 1982, 1984; Lenkersdorf 2002), as in (53).

(53) Wa=x-cha-y-i'-aj   s-suprimyento   y-e'n   chajkil
     IPFV=IPFV-ITR-A3-carry-SS   A3-suffering   A3-PRON   as.well
       ja=j-me'xep=i.
       DET=A1-grandmother=TOP
     'My grandmother bears their suffering as well.' {TEXT}

VAO is possible under restricted conditions which remain to be investigated.

Aissen's (1992) proposals for topic and focus in Mayan are fully borne out in the Tojolabal data (see also chapter 12, this volume). Focused NPs may be fronted to the verb, while topics are dislocated to the left edge of the clause yielding the order [TOP] [FOC+V], as in (55). External topics constitute their own intonational phrase (see §2.2) as shown by the topic enclitic =*i* in (54).

(54) [Ja=cham-el   winik=jamasa=i]   puro   toj-ol   k'u'uts
      DET=die-NF   man=PL=TOP   only   right-ATTR   cloth
     wa=x-s-lap-a   y-e'n.
     IPFV=IPFV-A3-wear-SS   A3-PRON
     'Dead people, it was only Tojolabal clothing that they used to wear.' {TEXT}

As for foci, they are usually determinerless, as in (54). If the focus is determined, the focus marker *ja'* is required, as in (55).

(55) Ja'   ja=Patrisya   sema   s-ta'-a.
     FOC   DET=Patricia   maybe   A3-reach-SS
     'Maybe it was Patricia who reached it.' {TEXT}

Clause-initial *ja'* can also be associated with an in situ focus, as in (56). In this case, any NP in the clause can be associated with *ja'* and interpreted as focus.

(56) Ja'   y-a'-a   y-i'   tak'in   ja=j-tat=i.
     FOC   A3-give-SS   A3-DAT   money   DET=A1-father=TOP
     'It was my father to whom he gave the money.' {TEXT}
     Also possible: 'It was money that he gave my father.'
                     'It was he who gave the money to my father.'

See Brody (1982) for a more detailed discussion on topic and focus in Tojolabal.

8.3 Obviation and voice

Because VOA and VAO are both possible (see §8.2) and because NPs are not case-marked, clauses like (57) with two third person arguments are ambiguous.

(57) S-mak'-a-ta   ja=Epra   ja=me'n   Marya.
     A3-hit-SS-already   DET=Efraín   DET=CLF.F   María
     'Efraín just hit María.' {TEXT}
     Also possible: 'María just hit Efraín.'

Note that the two arguments in (57) are both human and definite. If the two arguments differ in animacy and/or definiteness, the more salient argument (i.e. higher in animacy or definiteness) will be interpreted as A and the less salient as O. Therefore, in (58) the human definite NP is the only possible A, while the indefinite non-human is O.

(58) Jel   s-mil-a   chan   ja=tan-tik   untik=i.
     INTS   A3-kill-SS   animal   DET=DEM-PL   children=TOP
     'These kids kill animals all the time.' {TEXT}
     *'Animals kill these kids all the time.'

Likewise, in (59a) only the definite human NP can be interpreted as A. If the indefinite is in fact intended as agent, passive is mandatory as in (59b).

(59) a. Oj   x-ch'ut   jun   kristyano   ja=y-e'n   ta.
        IRR   A3-point.out   one   person   DET=A3-PRON   indeed
        'He is going to point somebody out indeed.' {TEXT}
        *'Somebody is going to point him out indeed.'

    b. Oj   ch'ut-j-uk   sok   kristyano   ja=y-e'n   ta.
        IRR   point.out-PSV-IRR   with   person   DET=A3-PRON   indeed
        'Somebody is going to point him out.'
        *'He is going to point somebody out indeed.'

Thus semantic and pragmatic salience play a central role in the choice of voice in Tojolabal. In this way the language behaves like Tseltal (see Polian 2013), Tsotsil (Aissen 1997, 1999), and Chol (Zavala 2006). See Curiel (2007) for more detailed discussion of Tojolabal.

Semantic and pragmatic salience are also relevant to voice in Tojolabal's ditransitive clauses. However, in this case it is the relative salience of agent and recipient which determines the voice, not the agent and theme. This explains why examples like (60) with an animate agent and an inanimate theme are in fact passive, not active. Passive is required here because the agent is indefinite, while the recipient is definite.

(60) A'-j-i-ta   y-i'   s-waw   jun   nan   xinan
     give-PSV-EP-already   A3-DAT   A3-slap   one   CLF.F   mestiza
       ja=k-ijts'in=i'.
       DET=A1-younger.sibling=TOP
     'My younger sister was slapped by a damn mestiza (literally . . . was given a slap
     by. . .)' {Curiel 2013:193}

The fact that voice selection in Tojolabal's ditransitive clauses reference the agent and recipient, not the agent and theme, is evidence that the recipient, not the theme, is treated as primary object. See Polian (this volume) for related discussion on Tseltalan.

8.4 Negation

Tojolabal distinguishes verbal and non-verbal negation as in (61) and (62) respectively. Verbal negation is marked by the negative marker *mi*, while the scope of non-verbal negation is circumfixed by *mi* plus irrealis *-uk*.

(61) **Mi**=to   x-'el   y-uj   s-k'umal.
     NEG=still IPFV-go.out A3-AGT A3-language
     'He can't speak yet.' {TEXT}

(62) **Mi**   ixuk-**uk**-on.
     NEG   woman-IRR-B1
     'I am not a woman.' {TEXT}

In informal speech styles, progressive and perfect forms (which do not take aspectual prefixes) take the verbal negation *mi*; in formal speech styles, they take the non-verbal circumfix *mi . . .-uk*. See (63).

(63) Mi   och-el(-uk)-on.
     NEG   enter-NF(-IRR)-B1
     'I have not entered.' {TEXT}

Note that the negative in imperatives is *mok*, e.g. *mok mok'-an* 'Do not fall down!' {NEG.IMP fall.down-IMP}.

Negative pronouns are formed with *mi=ni* (NEG=EMPH) plus a wh-word: *mini jas* 'nothing', *mini mach'* 'nobody', *mini b'a* 'not at all'. The Spanish borrowings *nunka* 'never' and *modo* 'way' are also a source for negative constituents: *mini nunka* 'never', *mini modo* 'no way'. Negative pronouns are always fronted as in (64).

(64) a. Mi=ni   jas   x-j-k'an-a.
       NEG=EMPH what IPFV-A1-want-SS
       'I don't want anything.'

     b. *Wa xk'ana mini jas.

     c. *Mini wa xk'ana jas.

The existential predicate *ay* has its own negation (see §7.4).
As answer to a question, *mi* in isolation takes -*uk*, as in (65b).

(65) a. Tseltal-a=ma? Mi-y-uk!
       Tseltal-B2=Q   NEG-EP-IRR
       'Are you a Tseltal?' 'No!'

8.5 Interrogation

Intonation seems to be the favorite strategy for polar questions (see §2.2). However, in formal speech styles, polar interrogatives are usually marked with the second position clitic =*ma* as in (66).

(66) Wan=**ma** x-ja-na'-a   b'ay   j-naj?
     IPFV=Q   IPFV-A2-know-SS PREP+EXIST A1-house
     'Do you know where my house is?' {TEXT}

TABLE 21.15 TOJOL-AB'AL WH-WORDS (PARTIAL LIST)

Human, pro-form	ma'majunuk
	machunuk'ila'
	machunk'ila'
	machuk'a
	mach'a
	ma'
Non-human, pro-form	jasunuk'ila'
	jasunk'ila
	jasuk'a
	jasunka
	ja'sa'
	jas'
Human, determiner (inherent possession morphology is required on the noun)	ma'
Non-human, determiner (inherent possession morphology is required on the noun)	jas
Time, pro-adverb	jas ora
Place, pro-adverb	b'a
Manner, pro-adverb	jastal
Reason, pro-relational noun	jas yuj
Quantity, pro-quantifier	jay-CLASS
	janek'

For polar interrogatives with a verbal predicate, aspect and mood markers serve as echo answers. The answer to (66) could simply be *wan* 'yes'.

Constituent interrogatives are are based on a set of wh-proforms; a partial list is shown in Table 21.15. All expressions listed in the table for human and non-human pro-forms are used both for interrogation and relativization. It is not clear whether their distribution is determined by speech style or by specificity or by both.

Wh-expressions must occur in clause-initial position as in (67) to (70). That is, in situ interrogatives are prohibited, as are multiple wh-questions.

(67) Ma'   jul-i?
     who   come.here-ss
     'Who came here?'

(68) Ma'   oj   s-k'ul-uk?
     who   IRR   A3-make-IRR
     'Who's going to do it?' {TEXT}

(69) Jasunka   wan-a   s-lo'-j-el=i?
     what   PROG-B2   A3-eat-PSV-NF=TOP
     'What is it you are eating?' {TEXT}

(70) Jas   y-uj   mi x-ja-k'an-a   oj a-job' y-i'?
     what A3-REASON NEG IPFV-A2-want-SS IRR A2-ask A3-DAT
     'Why don't you want to ask him it?' {TEXT}

As (67) to (70) show, intransitive subjects, transitive subjects and objects, and adjuncts can all be questioned. Note that Tojolabal requires no special agent focus morphology to question A, as in (68).

Interestingly, wh-proforms are compatible with the interrogative enclitic =*ma* as in (71).

(71) It   ja=nan   trusa   it=i,   ma'=**ma** s-b'aj?
     DEM   DET=CLF.F briefs DEM=TOP who=Q A3-RR
     'Look at these briefs, whose are these?' {TEXT}

Wh-proforms can question NP internal elements, i.e. determiners and possessors. Determiner wh-words trigger marked possession morphology (see §5.1), as in (72).

(72) Ma'   winik-il   jul-i?
     who man-INAL come.here-SS
     'Which man came here?' {ELICITED}

Interrogatives for count nouns and mass nouns are distinguished: *jay* 'how many' vs. *janek* 'how much'.

It is also possible to question the possessor of a NP. When this happens, pied-piping with inversion occurs, as in (73) (recall that non-interrogative possessors follow the possessed noun).

(73) Ma'   s-karro'il   mok'-i?
     who A3-car-INAL fall-SS
     'Whose car crashed?' {TEXT}

The complement of a relational noun can also, at least in some cases, be questioned, e.g. *jas y-uj?* 'why?' {what A3-REASON}.

Arguments and adjuncts can be extracted from complement clauses as in (74). Neither arguments nor adjuncts can be extracted from clausal adjuncts.

(74) Ma'-ma-jun-uk=k'a x-ja-na'-a   w-e'n   ke=s-mil-a
     who-Q-one-IRR-DUB IPFV-A2-know-SS A2-PRON COMP=A3-kill-SS
     ja=j-ts'i-tik=i?
     DET=A1-dog-1PL=TOP
     'Who do you think killed our dog?' {ELICITED}

Finally, note that wh-words can act as non-verbal predicates as in (75).

(75) Machunk'il-on?
     who-B1.SG
     'Who am I?' {ELICITED}

9 COMPLEX STRUCTURES

9.1 Complement clauses

Tojolabal has two basic types of complement clause (henceforth CC), finite and non-finite. The verb in a finite CC is fully inflected for aspect and person. Non-finite CCs do not inflect for aspect but, depending on the type, may inflect for person.

Finite CCs behave like independent clauses with respect to case and aspect marking. They are selected by verbs of communication, mentation, knowledge, emotion, and desire as in (76)–(78). CCs of this type can have access to a complementizer. The Spanish borrowing *ke*= correponds to a factive complementizer, but is not mandatory. The native complementizer *ta*= or hybridized borrowing *si*=*ta*= introduces an embedded polar interrogative CC as in (77). Both complementizers may be used together, in which case *ke*= always precedes *ta*=, as in (78).

(76) Wa=x-jaw-al-a   [**ke**=oj   x-chon-w-e'   tamale]?
      IPFV=IPFV-A2-say-SS   COMP=IRR   A3-sell-EP-3PL   tamale
      'Do you say that they will sell tamales?' {TEXT}

(77) Mi   oj   a-job'   y-i'   [**ta**=oj   waj-an]?
      NEG   IRR   A2-ask   A3-DAT   COMP=IRR   go-IRR.2[B2]
      'Won't you ask her if she's going?' {TEXT}

(78) J-job'-a   y-i'-l-e'
      A1-ask-SS   A3-DAT-EP-3PL
        [**ke**=**si**=**ta**=oj=ma   och   j-je'   ju'un=i].
        COMP=COMP=COMP=IRR=if   enter(AUX)   A1-show   paper=DET
        'I asked them whether I could start teaching how to read and write.' {TEXT}

While a nominal direct object in Tojolabal precedes both the subject and an indirect object (V-O-IO-S), if the direct object is a finite CC, it must follow any other nominal argument, as in (79a) (V-S-O) and (79b) (V-IO-O). Further, such a CC is pronounced as a intonational phrase separate from that of the the matrix clause.

(79) a. Jachuk   x-y-al-a-w-e'   ja=cho   byejo   jumasa'
         thus   IPFV-A3-say-SS-EP-3PL   DET=ITR   elder   PL
            [ke=ja=b'ajtan   ja=j-nan-tik   lu'um-k'inal
            COMP=DET=first   DET=A1-mother-1PL   earth-world/time
            oj   j-k'an-tik   perdon].
            IRR   A1-want-1PL   pardon
         'Also the elders say that it is our mother Earth the first whose pardon we'll ask.' {TEXT}

      b. J-job'-a   y-i'   ja=delegado[2]   [ta=oj   y-a'
         A1-ask-SS   A3-DAT   DET=teacher   COMP=IRR   A3-give
            k-i'-tikon   permiso].
            A1-DAT-1PL.EXCL   permission
         'I asked the teacher, whether he would give us permission.' {TEXT}

Finite CCs have full access to all the preverbal elements of clause structure. Negation is possible in the CC as in (80).

(80) Wa=x-jaw-il-a   [ke=**mi**   x-tse'n-i]?
     IPFV=IPFV-A2-see-SS   COMP=NEG   IPFV-laugh-SS
     'Do you see that he doesn't laugh?' {ELICITED}

In (81) the CC contains an external topic ocurring before a negated existential predicate. Note that the second position clitic =b'i shows that the topic is external.

(81) Wa=x-y-al-a-w-e'
     IPFV=IPFV-A3-say-SS-EP-3PL

     [ke=**ja=kerem-ts'isim=i**   mas=b'i   mey
     COMP=DET=boy-leaf.cutter.ant=TOP   more=QUOT   NEG+EXIST
     s-b'aktel   sok   ja=s-nan=i].
     A3-flesh   with   DET=A3-mother=TOP
     'They say that male leaf cutter ants – it is said – have less flesh than female.'
     {TEXT}

Example (79a) shows focus-fronting withing a CC.

Two verbs in Tojolabal, *ila* 'see' and *ab'i* 'hear/feel', take finite CCs and permit the CC to occur fronted. Compare the examples in (82) with (80). Note that this pattern is reported for Jakaltek (Craig 1977:259) and Tseltal (Polian 2013:752ff).

(82) a. [Ma   mi   x-tse'n-i]   x-jaw-il-a   w-e'n=i?
        or   NEG   IPFV-laugh-SS   IPFV-A2-see-SS   A2-PRON=TOP
        'He's not laughing, don't you see?' {TEXT}

     b. [Mi   x-ajb'an-i]   x-jaw-ab'i?
        NEG   IPFV-be.tasty-SS   IPFV-A2-feel
        'It's not tasty, you think?' {TEXT}

In this case, the complementizer is not possible. Note that the meaning of the main verb shifts and perhaps functions as a kind of evidential.

There are two types of non-finite CCs. The first shows full inflection for person, but does not mark aspect. These are aspectless CCs in the classification of Aissen (this volume). The verb takes the form of the irrealis: intransitive and derived transitive verbs suffix -*uk* in phrase-final position; the pre-verbal element *oj*, which is obligatory in main clauses, is optional here (see §6.2).

(83) a. Ja=k-ajwal-tik   mi   x-s-k'an-a   [oj s-pil-otik].
        DET=A1-landlord-1PL   NEG   IPFV-A3-want-SS   IRR A3-separate-B1PL
        'Our Lord doesn't want to separate us.' {TEXT}

     b. Se=s-k'an-a   [oj   y-u'   trago]   ta=Jwan=i.
        perhaps=A3-want-SS   IRR   A3-drink   trago   CLF.M=Jwan=TOP
        'Perhaps Juan wanted to drink trago!' {TEXT}

c. Mi s-k'an-a   [(oj) el-uk].
   NEG A3-want-ss   IRR   go.out-IRR
   'He doesn't want to leave.'

Aspectless CCs are uttered under the same intonation contour as the matrix clause. (84a) and (84b) show that the matrix subject can occur at one periphery or the other. It cannot intervene between the main verb and the CC.

So far I have identified three verbs that take aspectless CCs: *k'an* 'want', *na'* 'know how/habitual' and the causative *a'* 'give'. With the first two verbs correference between the subject of the main clause and the subject of the CC is mandatory, see the examples above and (84). The causative does not involve control as in (85).

(84) Mi   s-na'-a   [jas   oj   s-k'ul-uk].
     NEG   A3-know-ss   what IRR   A3-make-IRR
     'She doesn't know what to do.' {TEXT}

(85) a. A'=xa   [jak-uk]!
       give=already   come.here-IRR
       'Let her come here!' {TEXT}

   b. Mi   ya'-a   [(oj) el-k-on].
      NEG   A3-do-ss   IRR go.out-IRR-B1
      'He doesn't let me out.' {TEXT}

K'an can also select a finite CC, as in (87). In this case, the verb is interpreted as a verb of propositional attitude. Note also that the subjects in (86) are not coreferential. The same is true of *na'* as in (87).

(86) Wa=x-j-k'an-a
     IPFV=IPFV-A1-want-ss
        [ke=oj kan-an   a'tel   w-e'na=i].
        COMP=IRR   stay-IRR[B2]   work   A2-PRON=TOP
     'I like the fact that you stay at work.' {TEXT}

(87) Wan=ni   x-j-na'-a   [ke=k-e'n   k-a'   kan=a].
     IPFV=EMPH   IPFV-A1-know-ss   COMP=A1-PRON   A1-give stay=DCM
     'I do know that it was me who make him stay.' {TEXT}

The second type of non-finite CCs inflects neither for aspect nor for the person of its subject (or object). I will call these infinitives. The morphology of the infinitives has already been introduced in §6.5. Intransitive verbs suffix *-el* as in (88a). Transitive verbs have access to two suffixes, *-el* and *-uj*, as in (88b) and (88c). Note that *-uj* requires that the object be a bare noun.

(88) a. Mi s-na'-a [cha'n-el].
       NEG   A3-know-ss dance-NF
       'He can't dance.' {TEXT.}

b. Wa=x-ja-na'-a   [s-k'ul-j-el   ja=lima]?
   IPFV=IPFV-A2-know-SS   A3-make-PSV-NF   DET=lime
   'Do you know how to make lime juice?' {TEXT}

c. Jel=xa   x-j-na'-a   [tsil-uj waj].
   INTS=already   IPFV-A1-know-SS   pat-NF tortilla
   'I already know very well how to make tortillas.' {TEXT}

The subject of the infinitive is structurally controlled by the subject of the matrix verb. This is clear in (88a) and (88c). (88b) has two peculiarities. First, as in a number of other Mayan languages (see Aissen, this volume), the transitive infinitive is based on the passive stem. Second, it carries a Set A prefix. It is clear that the prefix does not index the agent, since it can only be third person and the agent in (88b) is second person. Further, it does not appear to index the object since only A3 is possible, not A1 or A2, nor is it possible to index a third person plural argument, as (89a) and (89b) show.

(89) a. *Wa=x-ja-na'-a   [j-k'ul-j-el   apoyar]?
     IPFV=IPFV-A2-know-SS   A1-make-PSV-NF   support
     Intended meaning: 'Can you support me?'

   b. *Wa=x-ja-na'-a   [s-k'ul-j-el-e'   apoyar]?
     IPFV=IPFV-A2-know-SS   A3-make-PSV-NF-3PL   support
     Intended meaning: 'Can you support them?'

Perhaps as suggested by Polian (2013) for Tseltal, the A3 prefix simply marks the transitivity of the infinitive.

Infinitival complements also occur with the aspectual marker *wan* to form a progressive periphrastic construction as in (90). The subject is inflected on *wan* and controls the subject of the infinitive.

(90) a. Wan-on   [cham-el].
     PROG-B1   die-NF
     'I'm dying.' {TEXT}

   b. Wan-otik   [s-makla-j-el   ja=y-ab'al=i].
     PROG-B1PL   A3-listen-PSV-NF   DET=A3-word=TOP
     'We were listening to his word.' {TEXT}

   c. Se=wan-e'   [luk-uj   chay].
     perhaps=PROG-B3PL   lift-NF   fish
     'Perhaps they were fishing.' {TEXT}

Transitive infinitival clauses formed with *-uj* have one property not shared with the other infinitives: they can be fronted to focus position as in (91).

(91) [Puro   tek-uj   wa'in]   wan-on   ek'-e.
     only   endure-NF   hunger   PROG-B1   go.through-ADV
     'I'm just starving.' {TEXT}

Embedded intransitive clauses with a third person argument can undergo clause union, which is the reduction of a complex structure to a simple one. The position of the plural suffix -*tik* proves that *a' + el* and *a' + och* constitute a single complex predicate in (92a) and (92b). This seems to apply only to the verbs *el* 'go out' and *och* 'enter'.

(92) a. Oj=xa   k-a'   el-tik.
       IRR= already A1-give   go.out-1PL
       'We'll take it out.' {TEXT}

   b. Wa=x-k-a'   och-tik   kaj-an.
      IPFV=IPFV-A1-give   enter-1PL   stuck-POS
      'We stuck it.'

9.2 Adverbial and conditional clauses

Temporal clauses are usually marked by the Spanish borrowings *yora* 'its hour' and *kwando* 'when' (the two may co-occur), or by the native complementizers *yaj* and *ja'to*. The definite determiner can also be added to the temporal complementizer, as in (93).

(93) Waj   s-nak'   s-b'aj   [ja=kwando   y-ora
     go(AUX)   A3-hide   A3-RR   DET=when   A3-time
        s-tul-u-w-e'   ton   ja=kristyano].
        A3-collect-SS-EP-3PL   stone   DET=person
     'They went to hide, when people picked up stones.' {TEXT}

Temporal complementizers in Tojolabal do not mark anteriority or posteriority. As in Yucatec (Bohnemeyer 2002), juxtaposition is an efficient way to mark temporal relationships between two clauses. In (94) the event expressed in the second clause follows the event expressed in the first. Juxtaposition is usually reinforced by deictic *ti* plus the discourse continuity enclitic =*a*, or the focus mark *ja'*.

(94) **Ti**   wa=x-y-a'   tiro=**a,**
     DEIC   IPFV=IPFV-A3-give   fight=DCM
     ti   s-kuch-unej   yal   **alats=a.**
     DEIC   A3-carry-PRF   DIM   baby=DCM
     'After having a fight, he managed to carry the little baby.' {TEXT}

Conditional clauses mark the protasis with *ta=*, homophonous with the polar interrogative complementizer (see §9.1). The hybrid complementizer *si=ta=* can also mark the protasis, as in (95). In formal speech styles, the protasis is also marked by the determiner *ja=* plus the final-position topic enclitic =*i*. There is no fixed position in the sentence either for the protasis or for the apodosis.

(95) [**Si=ta=**   mi la-a'tij-i]   mi oj a-ta'   s-ts'akol   a-kosa.
     COMP=COMP=NEG   IPFV.SAP-work-SS[B2]   NEG IRR A2-reach   A3-price   A2-thing
     'If you don't work, you won't be able to pay for your things.' {TEXT}

The dubitative second position clitic =*k'a* distinguishes real from unreal conditionals, as in (96).

(96) [Ta=ay=**k'a**]   oj   j-man-tik.
COMP=EXIST=DUB   IRR   A1-buy-1PL
'If there had been some [fabric], we would have bought it.' {TEXT}

Causal adjunct clauses are introduced by the relational noun *yuj* as in (97) or by the Spanish borrowed complementizer *porke* 'because'. Similar to temporal clauses, causal adjuncts can be expressed by juxtaposition.

(97) Cha-y-i'-aj   xiw-el   ja=s-tat   [**y-uj**]   ja=lom
ITR-A3-carry-SS   be.afraid-NF   DET=A3-father   A3-AGT   DET=in.vain
chab'-e   alats   wa=x-a<j>y-i=i].
two-CLF   baby   IPFV=IPFV-EXIST<VRBZ>-SS=TOP
'His father was afraid too, because there were two babies just like that.' {TEXT}

Clauses of purpose encode a relation between events such that the event coded by the matrix clause is performed with the goal of obtaining the realization of the event coded by the dependent clause. They are non finite. Infinitival clauses of purpose are selected by verbs of motion and involve obligatory control as in (98). Purpose can also be expressed both through an aspectless purpose clause as in (99), or through an auxiliary (see §7.2). Aspectless clauses of purpose are introduced by the Spanish complementizer *para ke* or native *b'a*, homonymous with the preposition. They require the irrealis marker *oj* and do not involve control.

(98) Wan=xa   la-waj   [a'tn-el]?
IPFV=already   IPFV.SAP-go[B2]   bathe-NF
'Did you already go to bathe?' {TEXT}

(99) Ja=k-e'n=i   mi   jak-el-uk-on   [b'a=oj j-toy j-b'aj].
DET=A1-PRON=TOP   NEG   come.here-PRF-IRR-B1   COMP=IRR   A1-praise   A1-RR
'I have not come here in order to praise myself.' {TEXT}

Concessive clauses denote some obstacle which does not prevent the realization of the event of the matrix clause. These clauses choose the complementizer *a'ma*, and are not controlled, as in (100).

(100) [**A'ma**=x-ja-mil-a-w-on]   yujni   mi   oj   jot-uk   b'a.
COMP=IPFV-A2-kill-SS-EP-B1   for.sure   NEG   IRR   break-IRR   thus
'Even if you kill me, for sure it [the boulder] won't break.' {TEXT}

Except for concessive clauses, clausal adjuncts can simply be introduced by the determiner *ja=*, leaving the relation between adjunct clause and the main clause vague as in (101).

(101) Ay=k'a   w-i'oj   boluntar   ma   ay   w-i'oj   ja=balor
EXIST=DUB   A2-GENITIVE   will   or   EXIST   A2-GENITIVE   DET=courage

[ja=oj   aw-il   wa-moj-ixuk-il=i].
DET=IRR   A2-see   A2-partner-woman-INAL=TOP
'You may have the will or the courage, in order to take care of your fellow women.'
'You may have the will or the courage, when you take care of your fellow women.'
'Your may have the will or the courage, if you take care of your fellow women.'
'You may have the will or the courage, because you take care of your fellow women.' {TEXT}

9.3 Relative clauses

Both bound and free relative clauses in Tojolabal are post-nominal, which conforms to the universal prediction of Greenberg for predicate-initial languages. Like sentential adjuncts, a relative clause (italicized in the following examples) can be introduced by a dedicated marker (i.e. a relative pronoun; see Table 21.15), as in (102a), by a definite determiner, as in (102b), or by no marker at all, as in (102c).

(102) a. [Ja'xa   winik   jaw   *ma'   t'uk-an   ek' b'a te'=i*]
          TOP.CHANGE man   DEM   who   perched-POS fixedly PREP   tree=TOP
          ja'=jel ab'ul   s-b'aj=i.
          FOC=INTS wretchedness A3-RR=TOP
'As for that man who was perched on a tree, it was he who was very wretched.' {TEXT}

   b. K-a'-a   kan   y-i'   jun   s-regalo   [ja=winik
      A1-give-ss forever A3-DAT one   A3-present
      ja=mey   s-tak'in=i].
      DET=NEG+EXIST   A3-metal=TOP
'I gave a present to the man who doesn't have money.' {ELICITED}

   c. Ti=b'i   ch'ak   jam-j-uk   kan   y-i'   [ja=tak'in
      DEIC=QUOT finish(AUX) open-PSV-IRR forever A3-DAT DET=metal
      a'-j-i   y-i'].
      give-PSV-EP   A3-DAT
'It is said that all the money that was given to him was forever available to him.' {TEXT}

   Free relative clauses require a relative marker, either a relative pronoun or a determiner as in (103) to (105).

(103) K-il-a   [ja=*it   chak*=xa=i'].
      A1-see-SS DET=REL   red=already=TOP
'I saw the red one.' {Gómez Cruz 2010:107}

(104) Ja=y-altsil=i   [b'a-tik *yaj   wa=x-y-ab'*   ja=waw-untikil=i].
      DET=A3-soul=TOP   PREP-PL pain   IPFV=IPFV-A3-feel DET=A2-son-PL=TOP
'As for their souls, [the places] where your sons feel pain.' {TEXT}

(105) Man-a   [ja=<u>jas</u>   <u>wa=x-ja-k'an-a=i</u>].
     buy-ss   DET=what   IPFV=IPFV-A2-want-ss=TOP
     'Buy whatever you want.'

Relativization in Tojolabal extends to all positions on the NP Accessibility Hierarchy (Keenan and Comrie 1977): subject as in (102a), object as in (106), indirect object as in (107), genitive as in (102b), and oblique as in (108).

(106) Ay   [k-ala   mochila   <u>wa=x-k-i'-a</u>   och-e].
     EXIST   A1-DIM   backpack   IPFV=IPFV-A1-carry-ss   into-DIR
     'I have a dear backpack that I carry there.' {TEXT}

(107) Tey=to   [me'n=ts'i'   <u>a'-j-i</u>   <u>y-i'</u>   <u>patada</u>].
     DEIC+EXIST=still   CLF.F=dog   give-PSV-EP   A3-DAT   kick
     'The dog that was kicked (literally 'was given a kick') is still there.' {TEXT}

(108) Se=ja'   y-a'   kan   y-i'   ja=s-selular   [ja=puta
     perhaps=FOC   A3-give   forever   A3-DAT   DET=A3-cell.phone   DET=prostitute
     <u>waj-ta</u>   <u>sok=i</u>].
     go-already   with=TOP
     'Perhaps he gave his cell phone to the prostitute that he has already gone with!'
     {TEXT}

Tojolabal appears to have non-restrictive relative clauses, as in (109).

(109) Jastal   k-e'n   [ja=<u>winik-on</u>=i].
     like   A1-PRON   DET=man-B1=TOP
     'Like me, who is a man.' {TEXT}

9.4 Coordination

Tojolabal's inventory of coordinators is rather simple: there are only two coordinators, coordinate *sok* and disjunctive *=ma*.

The comitative/instrumental preposition *sok* can be used as a coordinate conjunction between NPs, as in (110), or between clauses, as in (111).

(110) Ja=y-e'n=i   **sok**   ja=k-e'n=i.
     DET=A3-PRON=TOP   with   DET=A1-PRON=TOP
     'He and I.' {TEXT}

(111) [CHa-y-i'-aj   kan   ton   ja=x-choj-il   ja=k-ok=i]
     ITR-A3-carry-ss   forever   stone   DET=A3-cheek-INAL   DET=A1-foot=TOP
     sok   [y-i'-aj   ja=j-xijk'an].
     and   A3-carry-ss   DET=A1-knee
     'A stone hit my calf and it hit my knee.' {TEXT}

=ma is a disjunctive conjunction between NPs as in (112) or VPs as in (113).

(112) Ay   y-i'oj   [tso'yol]   **ma**=[lob'al].
EXIST   A3-GENITIVE   chayote   or=banana
'They used to have chayotes or bananas.' {TEXT}

(113) [Wa=x-makun-i]   **ma**=[wa=x-yam-x-i]   wajab'al.
IPFV=IPFV-be.useful-SS   or=IPFV=IPFV-grab-IMPERSONAL-EP   drum
'Drums, they were useful or they were just played.' {TEXT}

10 SUMMARY

In this chapter I have presented some of the main grammatical features of Tojolabal, but an exhaustive description remains to be done. In particular, its classification needs to be revisited on a detailed comparative basis taking in consideration that the language shares lexical and grammatical features with both Tseltalan and Q'anjob'alan.

Throughout this chapter I have made some observations about this point, comparing Tojolabal with Tseltal (Tseltalan) and with Q'anjob'al (Q'anjob'alan). Tojolabal behaves very similarly to Tseltal (and differently from Q'anjob'al) in that both languages: (1) shifted the Proto-Mayan post-velar to velar (see §2.1); (2) have very similar person-marking patterns (see Tables 21.4–21.6); (3) base their independent pronouns series on Set A (see §4.2); (4) mark the same aspect contrasts (see §6.1); and (5) have the same voice restrictions triggered by obviation (see §8.3).

At the same time, Tojolabal behaves like Q'anjob'al (and unlike Tseltal) in that they both: (1) retained the Proto-Mayan [b'] (see Table 21.1); (2) did not develop (C)VhC syllables (see §2.3); (3) have a paradigm of status suffixes (see §6.2); (4) have noun classifiers (see §7.8); (5) have antipassives that are not limited to cases where the implicit patient is animate (see §6.3); (6) do not have applicative morphology (see §6.3); and (7) can nominalize transitive stems by suffixation in order to form compound-like action nouns (see §6.4).

However, Tojolabal has a number of peculiarities not shared either by Tseltal or by Q'anjob'al, including the following: (1) the status suffixes behave distinctly in intransitive and transitive roots, which has also been reported for other Mayan languages (see §6.2); (2) the noun classifiers in Tojolabal are rather simple and unstable, which suggests that they might be a recent innovation (see §7.8); (3) there is no productive anticausative and no agent focus voice (see §6.3); and (4) there is a dative marker, which seems to be in a process of grammaticalization that might lead to applicative morphology (see §6.3).

It is thus not clear whether the language belongs to Tseltalan or Q'anjob'alan. The evidence suggests merely a deep contact with languages of both branches. Recent work (Law 2014) has suggested that Tojolabal should be treated as a mixed language, although much more work is needed to validate this proposal. A study of the innovations of Tojolabal as well as an exhaustive lexical and grammatical comparison between Tseltalan, Q'anjob'alan, and Tojolabal could shed some light on this point.

NOTES

1 I am following the spelling system proposed by Díaz Cruz et al. (2001) in representing capitalized affricates as {CH} and {TS}.
2 The word *delegado* is used in self-managed communities for volunteer teachers working in schools with no governmental intervention.

REFERENCES

Aissen, Judith. 1992. "Topic and focus in Mayan." *Language* 63: 43–80.

Aissen, Judith. 1997. "On the syntax of obviation." *Language* 73: 705–50.

Aissen, Judith. 1999. "Agent focus and inverse in Tzotzil." *Language* 75: 451–85.

Bohnemeyer, Jürgen. 2002. *The grammar of time reference in Yukatek Maya.* Munich: LINCOM.

Brody, Mary Jill. 1982. "Discourse processes of highlighting in Tojolabal Maya morphosyntax." PhD thesis, Washington University.

Brody, Jill. 1984. "Some problems with the concept of basic word order." *Linguistics* 22: 711–36.

Brody, Mary Jill. 1986. "Repetition as a rhetorical and conversational device in Tojolabal (Mayan)." *International Journal of American Linguistics* 52: 255–74.

Brody, Mary Jill. 1987a. "Creation that endured: three Tojolabal texts on origin." *Latin American Indian Literatures Journal* 3: 40–58.

Brody, Mary Jill. 1987b. "Particles borrowed from Spanish as discourse markers in Mayan languages." *Anthropological Linguistics* 29: 507–21.

Craig, Colette. 1977. *The structure of Jacaltec.* Austin: University of Texas Press.

Curiel, Alejandro. 2013. "Construcciones de verbos seriales gramaticalizadas en tojol'ab'al." In *Clases léxicas, posesión y cláusulas complejas en lenguas de Mesoamérica,* ed. by Enrique L. Palancar and Roberto Zavala, 171–98. Mexico City: Centro de Investigaciones y Estudios Superiores en Antropología Social.

Curiel Ramírez del Prado, Alejandro. 2007. "Clíticos de segunda posición y configuración sintáctica en Tojol-ab'al." MA thesis, Mexico City, Centro de Investigaciones y Estudios Superiores en Antropología Social.

Delgado, Rojas, Edna Patricia, José Aurelio Silveste Sánchez, María Elizabeth Silvestre Díaz, Antonio Benicio Ross Montejo. 2007. *Stz'ib'nheb'anil Ab'xub'al Popti': Gramática Normativa Popti'.* Guatemala City: OKMA.

Del Moral, Raúl. 1983. "Apuntes para una dialectología." In *Los legítimos hombres. Aproximación antropológica al grupo tojolabal,* vol. I, ed. by Mario H. Ruz, 171–8. Mexico City: UNAM.

Díaz Cruz, Alejandro, Antonio Gómez Hernández, Carmelino Méndez Jiménez, Guillermo Pérez Jiménez, María Bertha Sántiz Pérez, María de la Flor Gómez Cruz, Paablo Gómez Jiménez, Ramón Jiménez Jiménez. 2011. Skujlayub'il sts'ijb'ajel k'umal Tojol-ab'al. Norma de escritura de la lengua Tojol-ab'al. Mexico City: INALI.

Dryer, Matthew. 2007. "Word order." In *Clause structure, language typology and syntactic description,* vol. 1, 2nd edition, ed. by Timothy Shopen, 61–131. Cambridge: Cambridge University Press.

Furbee-Losee, Louanna. 1976. *The correct language: Tojolabal. A grammar with ehnographic notes.* New York: Garland.

Furbee-Losee, Louanna. 1981. *Tojolabal text and dictionary: final report to the national endowment for the humanities.* Columbia: University of Missouri.

Gómez Cruz, José. 2010. "Adjetivos en Tojol-ab'al." MA thesis, Mexico City, Centro de Investigaciones y Estudios Superiores en Antropología Social.

Gómez Hernández, Antonio, and Mario H. Ruz. 1992. *Memoria baldía. Los tojolabales y las fincas: Testimonios.* Mexico City, UNAM.

Gómez Hernández, Antonio, Mario H. Ruz, and María Rosa Palazón, 1999. Ja slo'il ja kaltziltikoni'. Palabra de nuestro corazón: Mitos, fábulas y cuentos maravillosos de la narrativa tojolabal. Mexico City: UNAM.

INALI. 2014. *Proyecto de Indicadores Sociolingüísticos de las Lenguas Indígenas Nacionales.* http://www.inali.gob.mx/component/content/article/62-indicadores-basicos

Kaufman, Terrence. 1972. El proto-Tzeltal-Tzotzil. Fonología comparada y diccionario reconstruido. Mexico City: UNAM.

Keenan, Edward, and Bernard Comrie. 1977. "Phrase accessibility and universal grammar." *Linguistic Inquiry* 8: 63–99.

Law, Danny. 2014. *Language contact, inherited similarity and social difference: the story of linguistic interaction in the Maya lowlands.* Amsterdam: John Benjamins.

Lenkersdorf, Carlos. 1999. *Indios somos con orgullo: Poesía maya tojolabal. 'indyo'otik ja jtz'eb'ojtiki.* Mexico City: UNAM.

Lenkersdorf, Carlos. 2002. Tojolabal para principiantes. Lengua y cosmovisión mayas en Chiapas. Mexico City: Plaza y Valdés.

Lenkersdorf, Carlos. 2008. *b'omak'umal kastiya – tojol'ab'al: Diccionario español-tojolabal,* idioma mayense de Chiapas. Mexico City: Plaza y Valdés.

Lenkersdorf, Carlos. 2010. *b'omak'umal tojol'ab'al-kastiya: Diccionario tojolabal-español.* Mexico City: Plaza y Valdés.

Lenkersdorf, Carlos, and Gemma Van der Haar. 1998. San Miguel Chiptic: Testimonios de una comunidad tojolabal. San Migel Ch'ib'tik: Ja jastal aytiki. Mexico City: Siglo XXI.

Lucy, John A. 1993. "Metapragmatic presentationals: reportig speech with quotatives in Yucatec Maya." In *Reflexive language: reported speech and metapragmatics*, 91–125. Cambridge: Cambridge University Press.

Martin, Laura. 1977. "Positional roots in Kanjobal (Mayan)." PhD thesis, University of Florida.

Moral, Raúl del. 1983. "Apuntes para una dialectología." In *Los legítimos hombres: Aproximación antropológica al grupo tojolabal*, vol. 1, ed. by Mario Humberto Ruz, 171–90. Mexico City: UNAM.

Nichols, Johanna. 1986. "Head-marking and dependent-marking grammar." *Language* 62: 56–119.

Peake, Marc. 2007a. "Approche sociolinguistique et linguistique du tojol'ab'al, langue maya du Chiapas." MA thesis, Université de Lyon 2.

Peake, Marc. 2007b. "Directional in Tojol'ab'al, a Mayan language of Mexico." Unpublished manuscript, Lyon: Institut des Sciences de l'Homme.

Pérez González, Jaime. 2009. "Predicados afectivos en lengua tseltal." B.A. thesis, Morelia, Universidad Michoacana de San Nicolás de Hidalgo.

Pérez González, Jaime. 2012. "Predicados afectivos e ideófonos en tseltal." MA thesis, Mexico City, Centro de Investigaciones y Estudios Superiores en Antropología Social.

Polian, Gilles. 2013. *Gramática del tseltal de Oxchuc.* Mexico City: Centro de Investigaciones y Estudios Superiores en Antropología Social.

Robertson, John S. 1977. "A proposed revision in Mayan subgrouping." *International Journal of American Linguistics* 43/2: 105–20.

Ruz, Mario H. 1989. Las lenguas del Chiapas colonial: manuscritos en la Biblioteca Nacional de París. Mexico City: UNAM.

Sántiz Gómez, Roberto. 2010. "Raíces posicionales en tseltal de Oxchuc." MA thesis, Mexico City, Centro de Investigaciones y Estudios Superiores en Antropología Social.

Sántiz Pérez, María Bertha, Gómez Cruz, María de la Flor, Carmelina Méndez Jiménez, and María Guadalupe Gómez Gómez. 2012. *Sju'unil b'a sneb'jel k'umal Tojol-ab'al: Sb'ajtanil swakil ixaw. Lengua originaria tojol-ab'al: Manual para primer semestre.* Mexico City: Universidad Intercultural de Chiapas.

Supple, Julia, and Celia M. Douglas. 1949. "Tojolabal (Mayan): phonemes and verb morphology." *International Journal of American Linguistics* 15: 168–77.

White, John S. 1979. "Lexical and cognitive aspects of Tojolabal semantics." PhD thesis, University of Texas, Austin.

Zavala, Roberto. 1992. *El Kanjobal de San Miguel Acatán*. Mexico City: UNAM.

Zavala, Roberto. 1997. "Functional analysis of Akatek voice constructions." *International Journal of American Linguistics* 63: 439–74.

Zavala, Roberto. 2006. "Inversion and obviation in Mesoamerica." In *Endangered languages: linguistische Berichte Sonderheft 14*, ed. By Peter K. Austin and Andrew Simpson, 267–305. Hamburg: Helmut Buske Verlag.

CHAPTER 22

TSELTAL AND TSOTSIL

Gilles Polian

INTRODUCTION

Tseltal and Tsotsil, previously spelled Tzeltal and Tzotzil, are spoken in a contiguous area in central and eastern Chiapas, Mexico, by more than 400,000 speakers each. According to Kaufman (1972), they split from each other around 1,400 years ago. I will refer jointly to both languages as Tseltalan.

Both Tseltal and Tsotsil are among the best described Mayan languages. Beyond some few early colonial documents, in particular two good dictionaries from the end of the sixteenth century (de Ara 1571 on Copanaguastla Tseltal and an anonymous one on Zinacantán Tsotsil, published as Laughlin 1988), there has been a constant flow of publications since the mid-twentieth century. Published works include general grammatical descriptions (Haviland 1981; Polian 2013a), dictionaries (Laughlin 1975; Berlin and Kaufman 1977; Hurley and Ruiz Sánchez 1978; Slocum et al. 1999; Polian to appear.), syntactic studies (Aissen 1987, 1997, 1999, etc.; Shklovsky 2012), dialectal and diachronic studies (Hopkins 1970; Kaufman 1972; Campbell 1987, 1988; Robertson 1987, 1992; Polian and Léonard 2009), acquisition studies (de León 1994, 1998, 1999; Brown 1998), collections of texts (Laughlin 1977, 1980) and studies of semantic typology on space (Brown 1991, 1994, 2006; Brown and Levinson 1992, 1993; Levinson 1994; Polian and Bohnemeyer 2011), among others. Nevertheless, most studies are concentrated on just a few dialects (for Tsotsil: Zinacantán; for Tseltal: Tenejapa).

Both Tsotsil and Tseltal are moderately dialectalized. Main dialect areas are presented in Table 22.1, with the corresponding dialects explicitly mentioned in this study.

This study presents a panorama of the grammar of both Tseltal and Tsotsil. Examples indicate the language (TSE or TSO); when no indication is given, data are valid for both. Most examples cited from other authors have been adapted in their glosses and orthography.

1 PHONOLOGY

1.1 Phonemes and orthography

Table 22.2 presents in their usual orthographic form[1] the consonants of Bachajón Tseltal, which is the phonologically most conservative dialect of Tseltalan and probably preserves

TABLE 22.1 DIALECT AREAS

Tsotsil	Tseltal
Northern	Northern: Bachajón, Petalcingo, Guaquitepec, Sibacá
Western: San Andrés	Central: Oxchuc, Tenejapa, Cancuc, San Pedro Pedernal
Central: Zinacantán, Chamula, Chenalhó	Southern: Amatenango, Aguacatenango, Villa Las Rosas
Southern: Carranza, Huixtán	Extinct (far South): Copanaguastla (XVIth c.)

TABLE 22.2 CONSONANTS (BACHAJÓN TSELTAL)

	Labial	*Alveo-dental*	*Palato-alveolar*	*Velar*	*Glottal*
Stops simple	p	t		k	
glottal	p'	t'		k'	ʔ
voiced	b				
Affricates simple		ts	ch		
glottal		ts'	ch'		
Fricatives		s	x	j	h
Nasals	m	n			
Laterals		l			
Vibrants		r			
Approximants	w		y		

best the phoneme inventory of Proto-Tseltalan. It stands out in particular because it maintains the opposition between the velar and glottal fricatives /j/ and /h/, inherited from Proto-Mayan but lost in most Mayan languages, opposing for example *jun* 'one' and *hun* 'paper'.[2]

Proto-Tseltalan *h* phoneme has had divergent and complex evolutions in other dialects, depending on the particular phonological context. On the one hand, it was dropped in many cases in V_C contexts: systematically in Tsotsil, and in other Tseltal dialects only before particular sets of consonants (sonorants and /b/, and also before all glottal consonants in Villa Las Rosas). Moreover, Huixtán Tsotsil completely elided it in initial position (non-prefixed roots). For example Bachajón *hun* 'paper' corresponds to Huixtán *un*, without initial glottal stop. On the other hand, it merged with other phonemes: (1) /j/ (here I arbitrarily represent the resulting phoneme as /j/, to conform to the usual orthography); (2) /w/, or more specifically its reflex as /v/ in Tsotsil (see below); (3) /y/ (especially Zinacantán Tsotsil, in initial position before front vowels). Some of these evolutions are represented in Table 22.3, where Bachajón Tseltal matches the original form.

Another phoneme that was lost in two dialects is *p'*, which merged with /b/ in Oxchuc Tseltal and Chamula Tsotsil, thus shifting back to the Proto-Mayan situation where no /p'/ exists as such. As for /b/, it was originally an implosive phoneme /ɓ/, but its actual reflexes are complex. Its implosive feature was lost in most dialects before vowels, but it is usually maintained as prelaryngealization, e.g. Tseltal *chab* [tʃ'aɓ] 'honey'. In coda position, it is commonly nasalized as [m] (and prelaryngealized) in Tsotsil, for example: *tseb* [tsẹm] 'girl' (commonly represented as *tse'm* in the practical orthography). It is also realized as [β] in Northern Tseltal in some contexts (e.g. after /l/).

The labial approximant *w* was another locus of diversification. In all Tsotsil dialects it evolved into some kind of bilabial fricative close to [β], but it is often represented (and identified) as /v/, as in *vaj* 'tortilla'. The evolution [w] > [β] also occurred in Central Tseltal, although the practical orthography still maintains *w*, as in *waj* 'tortilla'. In addition, several dialects of Northern Tseltal (Bachajón, Petalcingo, Sibacá) and Southern Tseltal usually pronounce /w/ as [g] before back vowels, as in *wolol* [golol] 'spherical'.

With respect to Proto-Mayan, the most remarkable evolution of consonants of Tseltalan, together with Cholan languages, was the consonant shift q>k>ch/q'>k'>ch'. Thus compare K'ichee' *k'aq* 'flea' with Tseltalan *ch'ak*.

TABLE 22.3 SOME EVOLUTIONS OF *H

Gloss	Tseltal			Tsotsil		
	Bachajón	Tenejapa	Villa Las Rosas	San Andrés	Zinacantán	Huixtán
'paper'	hun	jun	jun	jun	vun	un
'sand'	hiʔ	jiʔ	jiʔ	jiʔ	yiʔ	iʔ
'this is her/ him/it'	haʔ	jaʔ	jaʔ	jaʔ	jaʔ	aʔ
'skin'	nuhkul	nujkul	nujkul	nukul	nukul	nukul
'dance'	ʔahk'ot	ʔajk'ot	ʔak'ot	ʔak'ot	ʔak'ot	ʔak'ot
'below'	ʔahlan	ʔalan	ʔalan	ʔolon	ʔolon	ʔolon
'smoke'	ch'ahil	ch'ail	ch'ajil	ch'ail	ch'ail	ch'ail

TABLE 22.4 VOWELS

	Front	Central	Back
High	i		u
Mid	e		o
Low		a	

Concerning vowels, Tseltalan keeps the five basic qualities of Proto-Mayan but lost the length correlation, as represented in Table 22.4.

Phonetically, the /u/ tends to be unrounded ([ɯ]) and even further centralized ([ɨ]) in Tsotsil.

Some Central Tseltal dialects are creating a new length correlation by coalescence of hiatus and by evolution of some (C)VhC syllables. Thus, Petalcingo ʔuhul 'traditional therapy' is ʔuul [ʔuːl] in Oxchuc, forming a minimal pair with ʔul 'corn gruel', and Bacha-jón hahb 'steam' is jaab in Oxchuc or Cancuc.

A high-low tonal contrast has been proposed for two dialects. On the one hand, Sarles (1966) and Kaufman (1972) argue for such a contrast in Carranza ("San Bar-tolo") Tsotsil. Specifically, they analyze the emergence of a low tone as a compensa-tion for the loss of an *h in V_C context, as in *ʔihk' > ʔik' 'black', contrasting with *ʔik' > ʔik' 'wind'[3] (the loss of *h in this context is general in Tsotsil, but without compensation in other dialects). On the other hand, Hopkins (1977) states that in Aguacatenango Tseltal an *h in a *VhC context also triggered a tonogenesis but in this case resulting in a high tone, whether *h was lost (before sonorants, fricatives and *b) or maintained (before stops and affricates, the most frequent case among Tseltal dialects). Additionally, this author identifies some cases of high tones before glottal-ized consonants.

Nevertheless, the tonal status of Carranza Tsotsil is rejected by Herrera Zendejas (2014), who shows that no such contrast exists and that vowels before glottal consonants always display a descending contour of F_0, along with a laryngealized final portion (so 'black' and 'wind' are both homophonous and realized as [ɪk' V̰]). No such study is avail-able for Aguacatenango Tseltal yet.

1.2 Stress

Relatively little is known on Tseltalan prosody. At the phrasal level, the dominant pattern is final stress. In Carranza Tsotsil, acoustic correlates of this stress are a rising of F_0 and length (Herrera Zendejas 2014). In isolation, words are therefore stressed on the final syllable, this a reflection of final phrasal stress. However inside intonational phrases, words may bear a root-initial stress, which commonly involves vowel lengthening. This latter stress manifests itself to different degrees according to each dialect and its precise status (as lexical stress or as stress under emphasis, etc.) must still be determined.

1.3 Phonotactics

The most common syllable types are CV and CVC. Many dialects, but not all, allow onsetless syllables V(C). Additionally, Tseltal presents (C)V*h*C~(C)V*j*C syllables, e.g. *k'ahk'*~*k'ajk'* 'fire' (Tsotsil *k'ok'*).

Prefixes create further complex onsets C_1CV, where C_1=/j, s, x/, e.g. *s-me²* 'her/his mother'. Only Petalcingo and Copanaguastla Tseltal display over-complex onsets C_1C_2CV, where C_1=/x/ and C_1=/k/, e.g. *ma²x-k-na²-Ø* 'I don't know' {NEG IPFV-A1-know-B3}.

1.4 Vowel alternation

Tsotsil displays an /a~o/ alternation, where the /o/ of the final syllable of a non-suffixed stem becomes /a/ when a (typically derivative) suffix is added, although not all suffixes trigger the alternation. This is illustrated in Table 22.5.

This alternation is one of the reflexes of the original Proto-Mayan length correlation in vowels (see Campbell, this volume). Oversimplifying, some instances of **a* (whether /a:/ or /a/) became /a/ and others became /o/ in Tsotsil (whereas in Tseltal all remained as /a/). In many cases, the evolution **a>/o/* was conditioned by a word-final position of the vowel. This is how the alternations of Table 22.5 emerged: by adding a suffix, the relevant vowel was not in final position anymore, and thus yielded /a/ instead of /o/. Now, the complete story is much more complex than this and still requires more inquiry (see Brown and Wichmann 2004). I will only highlight the following facts about this alternation: (1) it is highly lexicalized and unpredictable, but it involves many lexical items; (2) some CoC roots whose vowel is a true etymological **o* developed an alternative CaC-form used with certain affixes, by analogy with mutating roots (*tsots* 'hair', marked possessed form: *tsats-al*); (3) it is used non-productively as a derivational device with some verbal and positional CaC roots to produce a CoC noun or a numeral classifier stem, e.g. *mak* 'to close' (transitive) > *mok* 'fence' (noun) (for classifiers, see §7.3).

TABLE 22.5 EXAMPLES OF THE /A-O/ ALTERNATION IN (ZINACANTÁN) TSOTSIL

Unsuffixed form with /o/		Suffixed form with /a/	
tsoj	'red (predicative form)'	tsajal	'red (prenominal attributive form)'
		tsajub	'become red'
me²on	'orphan'	me²anaj	'become an orphan'
mol	'old man'	malal	'husband'

2 ROOT TYPES AND WORD CLASSES

Open lexical root classes are nominal, adjectival, verbal (transitive and intransitive), positional, expressive ("affective") and numeral. Nominal, adjectival and verbal roots function directly as stems of the same name, whereas positional and expressive roots must take derivational material to function as words, typically as positional adjectives and expressive predicates respectively. The same is true of numeral roots, except for 'one' *jun*.

CVC is the most common root form in all open lexical categories, and the only possibility for verbal and positional roots. CV roots exist, but are reconstructable as *CVh with loss of the final *h. Tseltal has CV*h*C~CV*j*C intransitive and nominal roots, some of them probably being historically derived with an <*h*> infix from a CVC root. Nouns, adjectives and numerals also show CVCVC roots and nouns have CVCCVC roots.

Nouns, adjectives and numerals, as word classes, constitute the group of non-verbal predicates, which may function directly as predicates without any verb or copula, but do not take verbal aspect/mood markers. Expressive predicates are intermediate between verbs and non-verbal predicates.

3 PERSON MARKING

3.1 Person markers

As in other Mayan languages, person marking in Tseltalan is distributed between two sets of affixes: Set A (possessive, ergative) and Set B (absolutive). Most common Set A markers are presented in Table 22.6, with their preconsonantal and prevocalic allomorphs (the latter replace initial glottal stops). Dialect variation is commented below.

Petalcingo and (XVIth century) Copanaguastla Tseltal share *j-* and *k-* allomorphs, but with another distribution: *j-* is used only before /k, k'/, *k-* appears everywhere else. This distribution is reminiscent of Chol (see Coon, this volume). Preconsonantal A3 (*s-*) presents an *x-* allomorph by assimilation to a following palatal consonant (/ch, ch', x/). Finally, at least some dialects of Tseltal display other allomorphs of A2 prefix: *ʔa(w)-*, *aʔ(w)-*, *ʔaʔ(w)-* and *ʔ(w)-*.

TABLE 22.6 SET A PERSON MARKERS

Person	/_C	/_V
1	**j-**	**k-**
2	**a-**	**aw-**
3	**s-**	**y-**

TABLE 22.7 PLURAL MARKERS FOR SET A

Person	Suffix
1 inc.	**-tik**
1 exc.	(various markers)
2	**-ik**
3	**-ik**

Set A marks only person in Tseltalan, and not number. Plural person requires a suffix or enclitic in addition to the person prefix: see Table 22.7.

The marking of the first person exclusive is dialectally very polymorphic. It usually is a suffix, as *-kotik*, *-yotik* or *-tikon* in Tseltal and *-kutik*, *-tikótik* or *-tutik* in Tsotsil. Some dialects of Tseltal (Tenejapa, Guaquitepec, etc.) use an enclitic *=joʔtik* (from the 1pl inclusive pronoun *joʔotik*). Finally, some Tseltal dialects (Oxchuc, Amatenango, etc.) do not have an opposition of clusivity, and only have what in other dialects are the inclusive forms.

Set B (absolutive) consists of two subsets: one with only suffixes, one with prefixes, variously combined with plural suffixes. Tseltal only maintains the suffixed subset, shown in Table 22.8, whereas Tsotsil displays both, as in Tables 22.9a and 22.9b. The genesis of this system, too long to develop here, is explained in Kaufman (1972).

The exact distribution of use between the two subsets of set B in Tsotsil is complex and dialectally heterogeneous, but is reducible to the following three principles:

(a) Prefixes can only appear after verbal aspect prefixes (*x-*, *l-* and allomorphs, see §6.1 below). Thus, first person is marked by the prefix *i-* in *l-i-tal* 'I came' {PFV-B1-come} but by the suffix *-on* in *tal-em-on* 'I have come' {come-PRF-B1} (Zinacantán).

TABLE 22.8 SET B PERSON MARKERS IN TSELTAL: SUFFIXES

	Singular		Plural
1	**-on**	inc.	**-otik**
		exc.	**-onkotik, -otikon,** . . .
2	**-at**		**-ex, -atik, -atex**
3	Ø		Ø (**-ik**)

TABLE 22.9A SET B PERSON MARKERS IN TSOTSIL: SUFFIXES

	Singular		Plural
1	**-on, -un**	inc.	**-otik, -utik, -ukutik**
		exc.	**-un-kutik, -otikótik,** . . .
2	**-ot**		**-oxuk**
3	Ø		Ø (**-ik**)

TABLE 22.9B SET B PERSON MARKERS IN TSOTSIL: PREFIXES

	Singular		Plural
1	**i-**	inc.	**ij-, i-** + (varied suffixes)
		exc.	**i-** + (varied suffixes)
2	**a-**		**a-** + **-ik**
3	Ø		Ø (**-ik**)

(b) Prefixes cannot appear before the A2 prefix *a(w)-*. Thus suffix *-on* must be used for a first person object of a transitive verb if the subject is second person, as in *ch-a-mey-on* 'you hug me' {IPFV-A2-hug-B1}. If the subject is changed to third person, prefix *i-* can be used instead: *ch-i-s-mey* 's/he hugs me' {IPFV-B1-A3-hug} (Zinacantán).

(c) Some dialects allow or require double marking (prefix + suffix on the same verb) of transitive objects, others do not. For example, Huixtán Tsotsil would say *ch-i-s-mey-un* for 'she hugs me', with double marking of the first person.

3.2 Independent pronouns

Two series of independent pronouns exist. The first one is based on the root *ha²~ja²*, which functions as a focusing predicate and identifying pseudo-copula, and also as a demonstrative in some Tseltal dialects. It functions as a non-verbal predicate. As such, it takes Set B suffixes, e.g. Tseltal *ha²-at* 'it's you', with irregular forms, for instance in Tsotsil 1sg *vo²on~vu²un~jo²on~o²on*, 2sg *vo²ot~jo²ot~o²ot*; Tseltal 1sg *ho²on~jo²on*. First and second person forms, but not third person, also function as independent pronouns, for example for topicalization as in (1).

TSOTSIL
(1) **O²on**=i   muk'   j-ta-Ø   j-ve²el
    PRON1S=DET   NEG   A1-find-B3   A1-food
    'Me, I didn't find food.' {Huixtán Tsotsil, Martínez Alvarez 2012:59}

The second series of independent pronouns appears as a possessed root *tuk* in Tsotsil, *tukel* in Tseltal. It may mean 'me/you/her/ . . . alone' or just emphasize the referent, typically as contrastive topics, as in (2).

TSELTAL
(2) Yan   te   kaxlan=e,   may-uk-Ø   bi   y-al-Ø=ix   **s-tukel**.
    other ART   ladino=DET   NEG+EXIST-IRR-B3   what A3-say-B3=already   A3-PRON
    'On the other hand the ladinos, *they* don't say anything anymore.'

4 NOUNS AND ADJECTIVES

4.1 Two distinct but similar categories

Nouns and adjectives are morphologically similar, as they share many derivational and inflectional resources, but conform nonetheless to two distinguishable categories. In particular, nouns can be possessed (with Set A markers) without additional suffixes, whereas adjectives receive a possessive prefix only when they derive an "abstract noun" with a -Vl suffix. In turn, nouns can also be possessed with an extra -Vl suffix: this corresponds to a marked possession pattern, whose semantic effect generally is to signal an inanimate possessor or an inalienable possession type, as synthesized in Table 22.10.

Nouns also display unique plural markers: non-possessed nouns take *-etik*, e.g. *na-etik* 'houses', and possessed nouns take *-tak* (also *-Vtak* or *-ab* in most Tseltal dialects); the

TABLE 22.10 PATTERNS OF POSSESSION

	Unmarked	*Marked*
Nouns *na* 'house'	Canonical possession *s-na* 'her/his house'	Inanimate possessor or inalienable possession *s-na-il* 'its sheath or case'
Adjectives *muk'* 'big'	*	Abstract noun, possessed property *s-muk'-ul* 'its/her/his bigness (size)'

latter is generally restricted to human-referring nouns, e.g. *s-bankil-tak* 'his elder brothers', although Tsotsil also allows it with non-human nouns. The suffix *-ik* is possible on nouns, but only as a plural associated with A3 possessive prefix: *s-na-ik* 'their house(s)'.[4] On the other hand, adjectives only pluralize with *-ik*.[5]

As non-verbal predicates, nouns and adjectives function alike: both take personal absolutive suffixes directly, for example in Tseltal with *-at* 'B2SG': *ants* 'woman' > *ants-at* 'you are a woman' and *muk'* 'big' > *muk'-at* 'you are big'.

The similarity between nouns and adjectives is also manifest in the shared derivational morphology. For example, the most common verb-deriving suffix for adjectives is "inchoative" *-ub* (allomorphs: *-ob*, *-ib*), as in *sak* 'white' > *sak-ub* 'turn white', and less commonly *-aj* (or *-Vj*), e.g. *k'ixin* 'hot' > *k'ixnaj* 'become hot'. These two suffixes are shared with nouns, e.g. *me'el* 'old woman' > *me'el-ub* 'grow old (woman)', *elek'* 'theft' > *elk'aj* 'steal'. Nouns also display other verbalizers, not shared with adjectives.

4.2 Alienable versus inalienable nouns

Nouns constitute at least two grammatical subclasses with respect to possession: alienable nouns, which are unmarked when they are not possessed, versus inalienable nouns, whose basic form is possessed. *Chenek'* 'bean' illustrates an alienable noun: it can be non-possessed as in (3a) or possessed as in (3b).

TSELTAL

(3) a. La   j-k'ux-Ø   **chenek'.**
     PFV   A1-eat-B3   bean
     'I ate beans.'

   b. Ay-Ø=to   **x-chenek'**   te   mamal=e.
     EXIST-B3=still   A3-bean   ART   old.man=DET
     'The old man still has beans.'

Most alienable nouns can appear possessed; a few of them seldom or almost never do, but they do not constitute a separate class, as they are not grammatically incompatible with possessive prefixes per se.

Inalienable nouns include kinship and body-parts terms, e.g. (Tseltal) *tat* 'father'. They require a possessor, as in (4a), and by definition cannot appear without one as in (4b). Additionally, many but not all of them derive an "unpossessed form" with a -Vl suffix, as in (4c).

TSELTAL

(4) a. Kuxul-Ø   te   **s-tat**=e.
        alive-B3   ART   A3-father=DET
        'Her/his father is alive.'

   b. *Kuxul-Ø   te   **tat**=e.

   c. Kuxul-Ø   te   **tat-il**=e.
        alive-B3   ART   father-UNPOSS=DET
        'The father is alive.'

The fundamental criterion for the possessive classification lies in the possibility of being unmarked (non-suffixed) when non-possessed: possible for alienable nouns, impossible for inalienable nouns. Note that I use the concept of inalienability only as a convenient label alluding to the prototypical semantics of each class, as those are formal (grammatical) classes, not semantic classes.

4.3 Nominal classes prefixes

Most Tseltalan dialects have maintained the Proto-Mayan gender prefixes *x-* 'feminine' and *j-* 'masculine', from *ʔix- and *ʔaj- respectively. These prefixes are nominal class markers that indicate gender with proper nouns, like *j-Petul* 'Peter' or *x-Mal* 'Mary'. They also appear with some animal and plant species on a rather arbitrary way; most species do not require them. For example in Bachajón Tseltal, *j-ʔechej* 'casquehead lizard (Basiliscus)', *j-ʔib* 'armadillo', *j-xik* 'hawk' and *j-suhm* 'Mexican sunflower' bear the masculine prefix, while *x-ʔahk'* 'small tortoise', *x-kach* 'horsefly' and *x-ʔek'* 'chaya (plant, *Cnidoscolus aconitifolius*)' display the feminine prefix. There is dialect variation in these nominal classes. For example, in Tseltal 'mojarra (fish)' is *j-kokoy* (masculine) in Bachajón and Petalcingo, but *x-kokoy* (feminine) in Cancuc and Tenejapa, and it also exists as *kokoy*, without prefix. In Tsotsil, 'firefly' is *x-kukay* with feminine prefix in Chenalhó, but *kukay* without a prefix in San Andrés. Some dialects have partially lost nominal class prefixes, like Oxchuc Tseltal, which maintains only the feminine prefix.

All nouns with nominal class prefixes belong to the alienable group. They can be possessed only by dropping the prefix, for example *x-Mal* 'Mary' can be possessed as *a-Mal* 'your Mary' {*a-* 'A2'} (Hurley and Ruiz Sanchez 1978:389), or Petalcingo Tseltal *j-kokoy* 'mojarra' as *s-kokoy-il* 'its mojarras (of a river)' {*s-* 'A3', *-il* 'inanimate possessor suffix'}.

4.4 Individualizing ("agentive") prefix

Proto-Mayan masculine prefix *ʔaj- also evolved into another *j-* prefix, homonymous with the masculine class prefix, which combines with nominal stems to derive nouns that denote a particular kind of individual, mostly human; I call those derived nouns "individualized nouns". This prefix is often described as an "agentive prefix", because it typically derives agent nouns from activity nouns, e.g. Tsotsil *ʔabtel* 'work' > *j-ʔabtel* 'worker', and especially from deverbal nominalizations, e.g. Tseltal *mil* 'kill' > *mil-aw* 'murder' > *j-mil-aw* 'murderer'. But this is a misnomer, as it also combines with non-agentive nouns, e.g. *chamel* 'sickness' > *j-chamel* 'sick person', and with toponyms, producing a demonym, e.g. *j-Nachij* 'inhabitant from Nachij'. It also can derive a person-denoting noun from a modifier+noun compound, e.g. from San Andrés Tsotsil *j-tsaj-al-jol* 'red-head person' {INDIV-red-ATTR-head}.

When an individualized noun is possessed, the prefix shifts back to its original full form *ʔaj-*, and then the prevocalic allomorph of the possessive prefix is selected, e.g. Tsotsil *k-aj-ʔabtel* 'my worker', *av-aj-ʔabtel* 'your worker', etc. This confirms that the individualizing prefix *j-* is not to be confused with the masculine class prefix *j-*, which instead drops with possession (see previous section).

4.5 Marked versus unmarked attributive function

Two subclasses of adjectives are distinguished according to their form in the prenominal attributive position: "unmarked adjectives" function without modification as attributive modifiers, whereas "marked adjectives" take a -Vl suffix. Thus, *k'ixin* 'hot' is unmarked as a noun modifier, as in (5a), but *sik* 'cold' must take a suffix *-il*, as in (5b) (Oxchuc Tseltal). The vowel of the attributive -Vl suffix varies with each adjective.[6]

TSELTAL
(5) a. Te   **k'ixin**   jaʔ=e.
       ART   hot   water=DET
       'The hot water.'

    b. Te   **sik-il**   jaʔ=e.
       ART   cold-ATTR   water=DET
       'The cold water.'

I show in (6) that this suffix occurs only in attributive function, as no adjective requires an extra suffix as a predicate.

TSELTAL
(6) a. **K'ixin-Ø**=ix   te   jaʔ=e.
       hot-B3-already   ART   water=DET
       'The water is already hot.'

    b. **Sik-Ø**=ix   te   jaʔ=e.
       cold-B3-already ART   water=DET
       'The water is already cold.'

The distribution of adjectives among the two classes is not semantically motivated. Rather, the explanation is phonological and morphological: most marked adjectives are monosyllabic and/or historically radical, whereas most unmarked adjectives are disyllabic and/or historically derived forms (see Polian 2013a:539 for further discussion). I present in (7) and (8) a short selection of adjectives of both classes from Oxchuc Tseltal.

(7) Marked adjectives
     jay(-il/-al)   'thin'
     kom(-il/-ol)   'short'
     muk'(-ul)   'big'

najt'(-il)   'long'
chi²(-il)   'sweet'
toj(-ol)   'straight'
ch'aj(-il)   'lazy'
Colors: *²ijk'(-al)* 'black', *k'an(-al)* 'yellow', *sak(-il)* 'white', etc.

(8) Unmarked adjectives
   ch'in   'small'
   tsael   'small'
   niwak   'big'
   chopol   'evil'
   bujts'an   'tasty'
   takin   'dry'
   pochan   'idiot'

Some nouns also appear to function as attributive modifiers with a -Vl suffix in a similar way, e.g. *ak-ul na* 'thatched cottage' {straw-ATTR house}, *chenek'-ul vaj* 'bean tamale' {bean-ATTR tortilla}. Those could be cases of compounding rather than attributive modification, or of denominal adjectival derivation (Polian 2013a:545), but no clear criterion has been found up to now to distinguish N-ATTR N construction from Adj-ATTR N.

4.6 Noun phrases

The NP is maximally structured as follows: determiner + numeral expression + attributive adjective(s) + N + possessor NP + relative clause + determiner.

A numeral expression is minimally composed by the numeral 'one' alone: *jun* or by a combination of a numeral root and a numeral classifier (see §7.3), for example *ox-kot* 'three-animal' (Tsotsil).

Attributive adjectives are always prenominal. When a noun modified by adjectives is possessed, the more common situation is that the Set A prefix appears just once on the first adjective, as in (9), but there is dialect variation on this point: some dialects allows the prefix to attach to the noun or else to appear twice on both adjective and noun, as in (10) from Oxchuc Tseltal.

TSOTSIL
(9) l-∅-ch'ay   li   **k**-ik'-al   pixol=e.
    PFV-B3-be.lost   ART   A1-black-ATTR   hat=DET
    'My black hat is lost.' {Haviland 1981:177}

TSELTAL
(10) Ja²-∅   te   **s**-bats'il   **s**-ton   **k**-alak'-tik=e.
     FOC-B3   ART   A3-authentic   A3-egg   A1-chicken-PL1=DET
     'Those are the authentic chicken eggs.'

Determiners, for which there is an initial and a final slot in the NP, include definite articles and demonstratives. Clear definite articles are initial. Some dialects have just one dominant article, which is generally *te* in Tseltal and *ti* in Tsotsil (e.g., Huixtán). Other dialects have up to three articles with distance contrasts, like Zinacantán Tsotsil: *li* (proximate), *ti* (medial) and *taj* (distal). Definite articles frequently come with a final-position enclitic *=e* or *=i*, creating a discontinuous determiner as *li . . . =e* in (9) and *te . . . =e* in (10). I loosely gloss this enclitic as a kind of "determiner", but its precise contribution is difficult to define.[7] In some cases, e.g. in Villa Las Rosas Tseltal, *=e* frequently is the only indication of definiteness in NPs, as in (11). Here, it is properly a definite article.

TSELTAL

(11) Ya   x-kuch-∅   si²   [²ants=**e**]$_{NP}$
      IPFV   A3-carry-B3   firewood   woman=DET
      'The woman carries firewood.'

In Tsotsil, *=e~=i* also appears with locative demonstratives. For example *li²* 'here' commonly takes it, as in (12a), and the two of them can appear discontinuously, as in (12b) and (12c):

TSOTSIL

(12)   a.   Lok'-an **li²=e**.
         exit-IMP here=DET
         'Get out from here.'

      b.   ²Oy-∅   vo² **li²**   ta k'ib=**e**.
         EXIST-B3   water   here PREP   jug=DET
         'There is water here in the jug.' {Zinacantán, Haviland 1981:33}

      c.   **Li²**   ²oy-ot=**e**.
         here   EXIST-B2SG=DET
         'Here you are.' {Hurley and Ruíz Sánchez 1978:77}

In all these examples, *=e~=i* appears at the end of the sentence. Aissen (1992) shows its distribution is restricted to the end of intonational phrases. Concretely, besides sentence-final position, it can also appear in the following contexts: after an initially detached topic (see §8.5 below), and sentence-internally immediately before an adverbial clause or a complement clause of verbs of communication and cognition.

Demonstratives present various combinations of NP-initial and NP-final elements, including definite articles and *=e* or *=i* enclitic, with a considerable dialectal polymorphism. Final demonstrative elements display the same kind of distributional restriction that *=e* does. In (13) from Petalcingo Tseltal, observe the two prenominal demonstratives *me* and *in*, which, in combination with *=e*, function as a distal complex demonstrative. The same *in* appears in post-nominal position in (14) from Guaquitepec Tseltal, with other elements: *ja²*, which is also the focus particle (see §8.5) and *i*, and final *=i*, yielding together a proximate interpretation. Finally, Tsotsil generally combines locative demonstratives in post-nominal position with a prenominal article, as in (15).

TSELTAL

(13) Ya   x-²ahk'otaj-∅   **me**   **in**   ants=**e**.
      IPFV   IPFV-dance-B3   DEM   DEM   woman=DET
      'That woman dances.'

TSELTAL

(14) Bayel   ya   s-k'uban-Ø-ik   **ja⁷**   **i**   biluk   **in=i**
     much   IPFV   A3-order-B3-PL   DEM   DEM   thing   DEM=DET
     'They order a lot this thing.'

TSOTSIL

(15) Ch-a-k-ak'-be   li   tseb   **li⁷=e**.
     IPFV-B2-A1-give-APPL   ART   girl   here=DET
     'I'll give you this girl.' {Zinacantán, Laughlin 1980:38}

5 VERBS

Tseltalan observes the Mayan obsession for distinguishing transitivity in verbs morphologically. Besides person marking, through which transitive verbs are singled out for
bearing ergative prefixes (set A), aspect, mood and derivative morphemes in many cases
contribute to making transitivity evident.

5.1 Aspect

There are four basic verbal aspect categories: perfective, imperfective, perfect and progressive. Aspect marking is complex and variable, both inter- and intra-dialectally. It
involves prefixes, suffixes, auxiliaries, non-finite verbal forms and zero marking, and
it is in some cases dependent on adjacent verbal material, especially person markers.
Tables 22.11 and 22.12 enumerate the main aspectual morphemes reported to date for
intransitive and transitive verbs across dialects, leaving aside part of the allomorphy and
the dialect distribution.

An additional aspectual category has been proposed for Tsotsil: the "neutral aspect",
marked by the prefix x- when it appears as the only TAM marker (e.g. Aissen 1987:41).
This prefix was the original marker of incompletive aspect for Proto-Tseltalan (Robertson 1987), but its functional range was modified when the marking of this aspect was
renewed, especially by the emergence of a preverbal auxiliary (ta in Tsotsil, which produces the contracted form $ta+x->ch$-). Its actual range is typical of a residual category:
it appears in marked (modal, dependent) contexts, fixed expressions and with particular

TABLE 22.11 ASPECTUAL MARKERS FOR INTRANSITIVE VERBS

ASPECT	Tseltal	Tsotsil
PERFECTIVE	Ø **a**	**i-** (+B3) **l-** (+B1/2) **n-** (+B1/2) Ø
IMPERFECTIVE	**ya x-** **x-**	**ta x-** **ch-** [< t(a)+x-] **x-**
PERFECT	**-em**	
PROGRESSIVE	Periphrastic construction	

TABLE 22.12 ASPECTUAL MARKERS FOR TRANSITIVE VERBS

Aspect	Tseltal	Tsotsil
PERFECTIVE	**la(j)** **a**	**i-** (+B3) **l-** (+B1/2) **n-** (+B1/2) ∅ **la(j)**
IMPERFECTIVE	**ya** ∅ **ya k-** (+A2) **k-** (+A2)	**ta (x-)** **ch-** **x-** **ti** (+A1 *j-*) **t-**
PERFECT	**-oj** **-ej** **-bil** (passive)	**-oj** **-bil** (passive)
PROGRESSIVE	Periphrastic construction	

lexical items. In some negative constructions (with *muk'*, a reduction of *mu'yuk*, negation of the existential predicate *oy*; see §8.4 on negation) *x* neutralizes the distinction between perfective and imperfective: compare negation of regular imperfective and perfective in (16a) and (16b), with *ch-* and *l-* prefixes respectively, and negation of the verb with the prefix *x-* in (16c), yielding a neutralized reading (Zinacantán Tsotsil, Haviland 1981:118). Nevertheless, I think it is not correct to analyze all instances of *x-* as a neutral aspect, because in other contexts it maintains its original imperfective value, with an additional modal flavor. This is the case with the simple negation *mu* as in (17). Note this last example cannot be interpreted as 'I didn't go'.

TSOTSIL

(16) a. Muk' **ch**-i-bat.
     NEG   IPFV-B1-go
     'I am not going.'

   b. Muk' **l**-i-bat
     NEG   PFV-B1-go
     'I didn't go.'

   c. Muk' **x**-i-bat
     NEG   NT-B1-go
     'I am not going/I didn't go.'

TSOTSIL

(17) Mu **x**-i-bat.
     NEG   IPFV-B1-go
     'I am not going (I am unwilling or unable).'

Progressive aspect is more common in Tseltal than in Tsotsil; not all dialects of Tsotsil have it (e.g. Zinacantán does not, Haviland 1981:109). It is based on an auxiliary followed by a finite or non-finite form of the verb. The auxiliary is dialectally variable: *yak, yakal, yakil, nok'ol, yipal* are some of the reported forms. Three possible periphrastic constructions exist:

(18) Progressive aspect constructions:
    a. Auxiliary + finite imperfective verb
    b. Auxiliary-{Set B} + preposition + non-finite verb
    c. Auxiliary + aspectless transitive verb

Constructions (18a) and (18b) are illustrated in (19) and (20) (Huixtán Tsotsil, Martínez Alvarez 2012:24); (18a) is common in Tsotsil but present only in two Tseltal dialects (San Pedro Pedernal and Amatenango). Tseltal in general favors (18b). As for (18c), illustrated in (21), it is exclusively found in Northern and Central Tseltal. It requires an aspectless transitive verb, characterized by a *-bel* suffix, no aspect affix and normal personal inflection (see §6.4 below).

TSOTSIL
(19) Yakil   ch-i-ve².
      PROG   IPFV-B1-eat
      'I am eating.'

TSOTSIL
(20) Yakil-un   ti ve²-el.
      PROG-B1SG   PREP eat-NF
      'I am eating.'

TSELTAL
(21) Yak   j-kolta-bel-at
      PROG   A1-help-ASPL-B2SG
      'I am helping you.'

5.2 Mood

Proto-Mayan displayed a system of four suffixes, known as "status suffixes", which marked transitivity (transitive *versus* intransitive) and mood (declarative/independent *versus* optative/dependent) (Kaufman and Norman 1984; Robertson 1992). Tseltalan has completely lost declarative/independent status suffixes, but maintains optative/dependent ones, with important changes: for transitive verbs, it is kept only as an imperative suffix: *-o* in Tsotsil, *-a* in Tseltal. For intransitive verbs, the original **oq* marker expanded its range of use considerably, and now appears as a general irrealis suffix *-uk, -ik, -ok* or *-k* in many constructions, far beyond intransitive verbs (see Polian 2007 for a detailed study of irrealis *-uk* in Tseltal). But it does not mark intransitive imperative, which is *-an* in both Tseltal and Tsotsil.

Exhortative forms exist for first and third persons: intransitive verbs take *-uk* (or allomorphs) and no other aspect marker, (22); transitive verbs with 1pl inclusive subject just appear without an aspect marker, (23). There is also an exhortative marker *ak'o* (Tsotsil)/*ak'a* (Tseltal), the imperative form of *ak'* 'give, put, let', which is used, for example, with transitive verbs with a third person subject, (24).

(22) Lok'-uk-Ø.
　　　go.out-IRR-B3
　　　'Let him go out.'

(23) J-pas-tik-Ø.
　　　A1-do-PL1-B3
　　　'Let's do it.'

(24) Ak'o　s-maj-on.
　　　EXH　　A3-hit-B1SG
　　　'Let him hit me.' {Haviland 1981:327}

Besides imperative and exhortative, other irrealis constructions exist. In Tseltal, an optative category (expression of a wish) is described by Polian (2007, 2013a), in which -*uk* combines with a verb inflected for aspect. In Tsotsil, descriptive work remains to be done on this topic. Haviland (1981:328–42) presents several irrealis constructions, in which the -*uk* suffix is present, including in some cases on transitive verbs.

A "subjunctive" category appears in Tsotsil studies (Haviland 1981; Aissen 1987; etc.), which corresponds to verbs that are not inflected for aspect and with the -*uk* suffix in the case of intransitive verbs; verbs in (22)–(24) are properly subjunctive forms in Tsotsil (Aissen, this volume, prefers to talk about "aspectless verbs" rather than "subjunctive" for those forms). Additionally, transitive subjunctive forms differ from indicative ones by the fact that absolutive person markers are always suffixed, because they can only be prefixed if there is an aspect prefix as well (see §3.1 above): compare indicative *ch-i-s-maj* 's/he hit me' {IPFV-B1-A3-hit} and subjunctive *s-maj-on* {A3-hit-B1SG} from (24). No such distinction exists in Tseltal transitive verbs, since they lost aspect prefixes and absolutive markers are always suffixed.

5.3 Voice

Tseltalan de-transitive voices include passive, antipassive, anticausative and reflexive/reciprocal. All dialects have two or more passive constructions, one of them suffixal (Tseltal -*ot*; Tsotsil -*e* on monosyllabic verbs and unrestricted -*at*), as in (25a). Most dialects also have a periphrastic passive with a transitive auxiliary *ich'* 'get', which takes an infinitival object (see §6.4), as in (25b). Both constructions allow the expression of the agent as an oblique phrase introduced by the relational noun *ʔuʔun*.

(25) a. Ø-ʔIk'-ot-Ø　　　(y-uʔun　Xun).
　　　　PFV-call-PSV-B3　A3-RN　　Xun
　　　　'He was called (by Xun).'

　　　b. La　y-ich'-Ø　　ik'-el　　　(y-uʔun　Xun).
　　　　PFV　A3-get-B3　call-NF.PSV　A3-RN　　Xun
　　　　'He was called (by Xun).'

More on passive is presented in §8.2, along with the agent focus voice (-*on* suffix), which is maintained in a few dialects.

The Tseltalan antipassive totally removes the patient and does not allow its expression even as an oblique, but it is limited to cases where the implicit patient is animate (most typically human). It is marked by a suffix *-(a)wan* (Tseltal)/*-van* (Tsotsil), as in (26).

TSELTAL
(26) Ya   x-ʔik'-awan-on.
     IPFV   IPFV-call-AP-B1SG
     'I call people.'

Other affixes remove the patient, but none is productive. For example, *-olaj* in Tsotsil occurs with verbs such as as *chon* 'sell' > *chon-olaj* 'sell things'. Tseltalan displays no object incorporation antipassive. Instead, transitive roots productively form compounds with notional object nouns, e.g. *man-waj* {buy-tortilla} 'act of buying tortillas', but these are categorically nominal.

Anticausative is restricted to (monosyllabic) transitive roots, and it is marked in Tseltal by an infix <*h*>~<*j*> or by conversion, and in Tsotsil only by conversion. It resembles the passive, because it removes the agent syntactically, but the semantic effect is different: it allows the event to be presented from the viewpoint of the patient – compare (27a) with (27b) (agent semantically removed) – or to yield an abilitative sense when the agent is reintroduced obliquely with the relational noun *ʔuʔun*, as in (27c).

TSELTAL
(27) a. La   j-mak-Ø   te   tiʔnah=e.
        PFV   A1-close-B3   ART   door=DET
        'I closed the door.'

     b. Ø-ma<h>k-Ø   te   tiʔnah=e.
        PFV-close<ANTIC>-B3   ART   door=DET
        'The door closed.'

     c. Ø-ma<h>k-Ø   k-uʔun   te   tiʔnah=e.
        PFV-close<ANTIC>-B3   A1-RN   ART   door=DET
        'I was able to close the door ("the door closed by me").'

Tseltalan anticausative is described as "medio-passive" by Kaufman (1971:5) and by Dayley (1981), but this characterization is not very accurate. In some cases, this voice resembles more a passive. The abilitative construction in Tsotsil was studied in detail by Aissen (1987:229ff), who analyzes it as a case of clause union (see §9.2 for clause union in causative constructions).

Reflexive/reciprocal, like in other Mayan languages, is marked by a possessed relational noun in object position (Tseltal *bah~baj~ba*, Tsotsil *ba*), as in (28).

TSOTSIL
(28) I-Ø-s-maj   s-ba-ik.
     PFV-B3-A3-hit   A3-RR-PL
     'They hit each other.' or: 'They hit themselves.'

Valence increasing concerns mainly the ditransitive applicative, marked by a suffix *-bey* (Tseltal) or *-be~b* (Tsotsil and Tseltal). It combines with any transitive stem, yielding a ditransitive stem (there are no basic ditransitive verbs in Tseltalan). The added argument is typically a recipient, a benefactive or the possessor of the object NP (external possession), and is cross-referenced by the absolutive affix on the verb, as in (29) (see (78) for an example of external possession).

TSELTAL
(29) La   j-pas-**b**-at   ʔul.
    PFV   A1-make-APPL-B2SG   atole
    'I made atole for you.'

The Tseltalan ditransitive construction qualifies as a primary object construction (Dryer 1986, or "secundative alignment", Malchukov et al. 2010), because the recipient/benefactive of the ditransitive verb is treated the same way as the object of monotransitive verbs. For instance, when a ditransitivized verb is passivized, its subject is the recipient/benefactive, as can be seen in (30) by the fact the subject is cross-referenced with the 2SG absolutive affix.

TSELTAL
(30) Ø-Pas-**b**-**ot**-**at**   ʔul.
    PFV-make-APPL-PSV-B2SG   atole
    'You were made atole.'

The Tsotsil ditransitive construction was analyzed in detail by Aissen (1979, 1983, 1987) and Haviland (1981).

Finally, Tseltalan also displays a causative suffix *-tes~-es* (Tseltal) or *-tas~-es* (Tsotsil), that combines with intransitive and nominal stems, but not with transitive verbs, e.g. in Tseltal *lok'* 'exit' > *lok'-es* 'take out', *way* 'sleep' > *way-tes* 'put to sleep'. This is a lexical derivational device more than an inflectional voice.

5.4 Nominalization and infinitives

Tseltalan, and especially Tseltal, stands out in the Mayan family for its development of transitive infinitives and for its many constructions that require non-finite forms in general (see Polian 2013b for a detailed study in Tseltal). Intransitive verbs derive a verbal noun with a suffix *-el*, cognate with *-el* of Chol and *-l* of Mam. This same suffix *-el* attaches also to transitive verbs, but TV-*el* forms have a double identity: they can be used as deverbal nouns or function as infinitives. In this last case, they have a clear passive orientation, as shown in (31), where the infinitive heads a non-finite complement clause (see also (25b)).

TSELTAL
(31) Ma   j-k'an-Ø   **maj-el**.
    NEG   A1-want-B3   hit-NF.PSV
    'I don't want to be hit.' (Not: 'I don't want hitting to be done' or 'I don't want to hit.')

TV-*el* infinitives further evolved in divergent ways across dialects. In many cases, arguments can be indexed onto them in several ways. First, all dialects have an A3-TV-*el* form which originated as a third person possessed passive infinitive, e.g. *s-maj-el* 'its/her/ his being hit', but was reanalyzed as a transitive infinitive with third person object and controlled agent.

TSELTAL

(32) Ya   j-xiʔ-Ø   **s-maj-el.**
     IPFV   A1-fear-B3   A3-hit-NF.PSV
     'I am afraid of hitting it/her/him.'

This construction is straightforward if the A3 prefix cross-references the syntactic object. Indeed, some Tseltal dialects allow changing the person as expected, at least in certain configurations, for example in progressive construction in Villa Las Rosas Tseltal:

TSELTAL

(33) Yak-on   ta   **a-maliy-el.**
     PROG-B1SG   PREP   A2-wait-NF.PSV
     'I am waiting for you.'

Up to this point, the construction with TV-*el* is reminiscent of the transitive infinitive construction of K'ichee' (Can Pixabaj 2015, Can Pixabaj and England, this volume). But other dialects have gone in a completely different direction. For example, Tenejapa Tseltal can index a second person object as a Set B suffix on the A3-TV-*el* form, as in (34). That is, the A3-TV-*el* form has been reanalyzed as an active transitive infinitive, where the A3 prefix does not cross-reference anything anymore. In Polian (2013b), I propose that its function is then only that of activating the agent argument slot for control.

TSELTAL

(34) Ya   j-xiʔ-Ø   **s-maj-el-at.**
     IPFV   A1-fear-B3   A3-hit-NF-B2SG
     'I am afraid of hitting you.'

TV-*el* forms in Tsotsil display similar properties with motion auxiliaries: it is possible to cross-reference the patient through the Set A marker, as in (35), but it is also possible to leave an empty A3 prefix and to cross-reference the patient with a Set B suffix, as in (36). Aissen (1994) demonstrates that the A3 prefix in this last example is not referential and that the construction is truly passive, despite the active impersonal English translation.

TSOTSIL

(35) Tal-em   **k-ik'-el**   t-s-na   a-li   rey
     come-PRF   A1-take-NF.PSV   PREP-A3-house   TOP-ART   king
     'They've come to take us to the King's house.' {Haviland 1993:38}

TSOTSIL

(36) Tal   **s-tsak-el-ot.**
     come   A3-grab-NF.PSV-B2SG
     'They came to arrest you.' {Aissen 1994}

Finally, Southern Tseltal and Carranza Tsotsil have taken further the reanalysis of A3-TV-*el* forms, as these now function as finite passive forms in those dialects. Observe how the verb in (37) takes the perfective auxiliary *la*, properly a characteristic of finite transitive verbs. That is, the combination of A3+-*el* has been reanalyzed as a whole as the regular passive morphology.

(37) La   **s-maj-el-at.**
    PFV   A3-hit-PSV-B2SG
    'You were hit.'

Northern and Central Tseltal have also innovated aspectless transitive forms, characterized by a -*bel* suffix, whose origin is not clear. These forms only lack aspectual marking, but they are regularly inflected for person with ergative prefix and absolutive suffix. Their use is not uniform across dialects, but they appear at least in the progressive construction, as in (38) (repeated from (21)). They also typically appear in several dependent contexts, for example in an oblique complement as in (39) (Oxchuc Tseltal) or after an expressive predicate, as in (40) (Bachajón). In Bachajón, they are also used as a kind of converb in adverbial clauses, as in (41).

(38) Yak   **j-kolta-bel-at**
    PROG   A1-help-ASPL-B2SG
    'I am helping you.'

(39) Ø-k'ax-Ø   k-ot'an   [ta   **j-kuch-bel-at**]
    PFV-pass-B3   A1-heart   PREP   A1-carry-ASPL-B2SG
    'I got tired of carrying you ("my heart exceeded itself from carrying you")'

(40) X-ʔok'ʔon-Ø   **s-k'an-bel-Ø**   y-ixtab.
    IPFV-grizzle   A3-ask.for-ASPL-B3   A3-toy
    'He was whining asking for his toy.'

(41) **S-k'ej-bel-Ø**   s-machit,   Ø-baht-Ø   ta   way-el.
    A3-put.away-ASPL-B3   A3-machete   PFV-go-B3   PREP   sleep-NF
    'Having put away his machete, he went to sleep.'

5.5 Verbal number

Besides nominal number, which manifests itself on verbs through plural agreement with plural arguments, verbs also inflect for number with reference to the plurality of the event (pluractionality; see Henderson, this volume). All Tseltalan dialects display at least an iterative category. The most common iterative suffix across dialects is -*ulan*~-*ilan*, e.g. in Zinacantán Tsotsil *maj-ulan* 'keep beating' and *nuts-ilan* 'keep chasing' (see also Cowan 1969:107). Other alternatives include total or partial reduplicated forms plus an -*an* or -*in* suffix, e.g. *maj* 'hit' > *maj-an-maj-an* 'do a lot of hitting' (Huixtán Tsotsil, Cowan 1969:108) and *kuch* 'carry' > *kuch-uch-an* 'carry over and over' (Cancuc Tseltal).

Tseltal also presents a distributive category, which is marked with a *la(j)*- prefix on intransitive verbs and with a -*tiklan* suffix on transitive verbs (dialect variants: -*tikla*,

-tilay, *-talan*, etc.; see Polian and Léonard 2009). The distributive implies that the event is spatially plural, either that it applies to different participants, sequentially or simultaneously, or that it unfolds through multiple trajectories. For example in (42) it means creating a plural pattern of many scratches.

TSELTAL
(42) La   s-boj-**tiklan**-Ø   te   mesa=e.
    PFV   A3-cut-DIST-B3   ART   table=DET
    'He made many scratches to the table.'

In several dialects, the transitive distributive suffix has been further grammaticalized as a kind of plural marker and has spread onto other predicate types (intransitive, non-verbal), and onto possessed nouns, in a shortened form *-lan* (Polian 2014).

6 OTHER WORD CLASSES

6.1 Positionals

Like other Mayan languages, Tseltalan presents a family of derived words that are described as "positional" because their semantics deals mainly with position ('sit', 'stand'), disposition ('lined up', 'heaped') and/or shape ('long', 'hollow'). Those words are all based on CVC roots and are associated with a dedicated morphology. This typically derives an adjective CV_1C-V_1l, an inchoative verb which means 'adopt the referred position/shape' (Tseltal: CV<h/j>C-aj; Tsotsil: CVC-i) and a causative verb meaning 'put into the referred position/shape' (Tseltal: CV<h/j>C-an; Tsotsil: CVC-an), among other derivations.

In other Mayan languages (e.g. Q'anjob'al, Martin 1977), most roots associated with positional morphology conform a class of pure "positional roots", because they do not appear as such without derivation, while the rest of the roots are "mixed" with other lexical categories, typically transitive roots. Tseltalan is unusual in this respect, because pure positional roots represent less than a half of all roots that receive positional morphology (between 40 percent and 45 percent, according to the dialect),[8] most of the rest consisting of transitive roots, and, in a few cases, intransitive, nominal and adjectival roots. One transitive root and one pure positional root and their positional derivations are illustrated in (42).

(43) Positional derivations (Bachajón Tseltal/Tsotsil when different):

Root	cat.	adjective		inchoative verb		causative verb	
lik	t.v. 'lift'	*likil*	'hanging'	*lihkaj/liki*	'be hung'	*lihkan/likan*	'hang'
ban	pos.	*banal*	'lying (bulky thing)'	*bahnaj/bani*	'lie'	*bahnan/banan*	'set down'

Mayan positional words have drawn linguists' attention for the richness of their semantics and for their lexical abundance. For example, in Polian (to appear), close to 600 positional adjectives have been registered for Tseltal in a multidialectal perspective. Furthermore, authors like Brown (1994, 2006) and Bohnemeyer and Brown (2007) have shown that the favorite way of locating figures in space in Tseltal is with a high degree of semantic specificity about their shape and (dis)position, which is possible thanks to positionals. Haviland (1994), speaking of Tsotsil, called this the "conceptual style" of the language, which speakers seek to master as a sign of verbal virtuosity.

6.2 Expressive predicates

"Expressive" is another name for what is commonly called "affect word" in Mayan linguistics (the latter has the disadvantage of being unknown out of Mesoamerican languages studies). In Tseltalan, expressives are a class of derived predicates, intermediate between verbs and non-verbal predicates, that highlight impacting sensorial properties of events. They are based on CV(C) roots, also CVhC~CVjC in Tseltal, which can be of any other open lexical category (typically verbal or positional) or be properly expressive, often onomatopeic. Additionally, they obligatorily take one of a series of dedicated suffixes that mainly encode information on aspect, pluractionality and degree of emphasis. For example, the onomatopeic root *pum* 'boom' derives the expressive *pum-pon* (suffix -C_1on, where C_1 is a copy of the root's first consonant), which denotes a kind of repetitive sound, as in (44). Note that the expressive predicate takes the imperfective *x*- prefix, typical of verbs, but not the complete verbal marking of imperfective, which would include an auxiliary *ya*.

TSELTAL

(44) X-**pum-pon**-∅   te   k'in=e.
        IPFV-ONOM-EXPR-B3   ART   party=DET
        'The party is resounding (music going *boom-boom*).'

Expressives also function as emphatic forms of other predicates. For example in Tseltal, the positional adjective *sep-el* 'circular (shape)' derives from the positional root *sep*; an emphatic way of describing the same shape is with the expressive *sep-et* 'looking very circular' (-*et* suffix), and even more emphasis is obtained with *sep-ep-et*, with a partial reduplication to the root. In addition to emphasis, expressive derivation often adds a sense of movement or sound to the root's meaning; thus, *sep-et~sep-ep-et* may also describe gyratory movements of circular objects. For studies about the different suffixes and their semantics in Tseltal, see Maffi (1990) and Pérez González (2012), for Tsotsil, see Ringe (1981).

6.3 Numeral classifiers

Tseltal is known for its abundant numeral classifiers ever since Berlin (1968), who documented hundreds of them in Tenejapa (for Tsotsil, see de León 1988). Numeral classifiers combine with numeral roots and specify semantically the counted entity, like *tuhl* 'human' in (45) (Bachajón Tseltal).

TSELTAL

(45) Tal-∅   ox-**tuhl**   ants-etik.
        come-B3   three-NUM.CLF:human   woman-PL
        'Three women came.'

Most numeral classifiers derive from transitive or positional roots by an <h/j> infix in Tseltal or by simple conversion in Tsotsil. In addition, some CaC roots in Tsotsil derive a numeral classifier through a>o mutation, e.g. *vay* (intransitive) 'to sleep' > *voy* 'night spent away from home'. In the absence of a numeral classifier, numerals from 'two' to 'nineteen' take a -Vb suffix (*-eb* in Tseltal, *-ib* or harmonic vowel in Tsotsil). Many nouns (especially abstract and mass nouns) do not have associated classifiers, so they always appear with the general suffixed form of numerals when counted. Nouns with associated classifiers also appear in some cases with a general numeral form without classifier; for example in (45) *ox-tuhl* could be replaced by the general form *ox-eb* without problem. The conditions of this optionality of numeral classifiers are complex and vary according to at least three factors: the dialect, the counted noun and the quantity. For instance, in Bachajón Tseltal the use of *tuhl* is obligatory only with 'one', as *j-tuhl* 'one human' (*jun* 'one' always reduces to *j-* with classifiers in all Tseltalan), whereas in Zinacantán Tsotsil the equivalent classifier *voʔ* 'human' is impossible with 'one' (Haviland 1981).

Many numeral classifiers do not classify nouns but actions. Those typically derive from verbs, like *chuhk* '(number of) knots/acts of tying' from *chuk* 'to tie', and function as adverbs:

TSELTAL
(46) chaʔ-**chu<h>k**   la   x-chuk-Ø   te   x-chihal   s-tep.
     two-tie<NUM.CLF>   PFV   A3-tie-B3   ART   3A-thread   3A-shoe
     'She tied her shoelaces with double knot.'

6.4 Prepositions and relational nouns

Tseltalan shares a unique preposition *ta* (variants: *ti*, *t-*) that takes a NP complement with a locative, instrument or cause reading. This preposition also heads non-finite clauses when they do not function as core arguments of the main predicate (see for instance (12b), (20), (33), (35), (39) and (41) above).

When an instrument relation is questioned, focused or relativized, the preposition *ta* is replaced by a particle *=ʔo* in Tsotsil, *=ʔa* in Tseltal, which cliticizes on the predicate (in Tsotsil) or on the last word before a definite NP (in Tseltal; see Polian 2013a:668ff). The interrogation of an instrument is illustrated in (47a). In the answer to this question, the preposition *ta* reappears as the way to codify an instrument, as in (47b).

TSOTSIL
(47) a. K'usi   l-a-laj=**ʔo**?
        what   PFV-B2-get.hurt=INST
        'What did you hurt yourself with?'

     b. L-i-laj   **ta**   ton.
        PFV-B1-get.hurt   PREP   stone
        'I hurt myself with a stone.' {Haviland 1981:134}

Other oblique relations are signaled by relational nouns. Canonically, relational nouns are stems possessed by the nominal or clausal complement and some of them can be preceded by the preposition *ta*. A subset of them characterizes spatial regions, e.g. *ʔut* 'inside', as in (48).

TSOTSIL

(48) Te   ʔoy-Ø   **ta**   **y-ut**   na.
     there   EXIST-B3   PREP   A3-inside   house
     'There s/he/it is inside the house.'

Body-part terms are also commonly used for specifying spatial locations (for instance, *pat* 'back' in (50)), see Levinson (1994) for a discussion of this phenomenon in Tseltal. For Tsotsil, de León (1992) shows how some meronyms grammaticalize as spatial relators.

One of the most common non-spatial relational nouns is *ʔuʔun*. Its possessor/complement NP is semantically loosely specified and may be an affected or related entity, including agent, cause, benefactive, goal, possessor, etc. (for example, see (25) above). *ʔUʔun* also introduces purpose or cause finite clauses, and may function as a possessive pronoun.

6.5 Directionals

Directionals are a group of around a dozen nominalized forms (-*el* suffix) of basic motion verbs ('come', 'go', 'go down', 'go up', etc.) and at least one phasal verb ('start'), which appear after a predicate or a spatio-temporal localization in order to specify the orientation. (49) illustrates a directional with an intransitive verb in Zinacantán Tsotsil, and (50) the stacking of two directionals after a locative expression ('at its back'='behind'), one of which is phonologically reduced (from *ba-el* {go-NF}), in Oxchuc Tseltal (see Haviland 1993 on Tsotsil directionals).

TSOTSIL

(49) Ch-Ø-jatav   **och-el**.
     IPFV-B3-flee   DIR:enter-NF
     'S/he's going to flee inside.' {Haviland 1981:119}

TSELTAL

(50) Le'   ay-Ø   ta   s-pat   **ko-el**   **bel**   i   wits=to.
     there   EXIST-B3   PREP   A3-back   DIR:go.down-NF   DIR:go+NF   DEM   hill=DEM
     'There it is away down behind this hill.'

7 SIMPLE CLAUSE STRUCTURE

7.1 Arguments and alignment

Arguments are cross-referenced on the predicate. Argumental NPs are not marked for case and need not be explicit. Basic alignment in Tseltalan is ergative-absolutive, without split ergativity: an intransitive subject is marked with an absolutive affix (Set B), (51), as is a transitive object, whereas the transitive subject is cross-referenced by an ergative affix (Set A), (52) (Zinacantán Tsotsil).

TSOTSIL

(51) L-**i**-vay.
     PFV-B1-sleep
     'I slept'

TSOTSIL
(52) L-**i**-**s**-tsak.
      PFV-B1-A3-grab
      'S/he grabbed me'

Nevertheless, alignment in Tsotsil is complicated by the fact there are two sets of abso-lutive markers (see §4.1), whose use is not dialectally homogeneous. For some dialects in certain configurations (e.g. with certain aspects and/or with certain subject-object combi-nations), the prefixed allomorph of Set B cannot be used. For example, for some dialects the perfective aspect with transitive verbs can only be marked by the auxiliary *la(j)* and not with the prefix *l-*; as a consequence, (52) would be replaced by (53) with the suffixed form of B1 -*un* (prefixed absolutive markers require an aspectual prefix on the verb).

TSOTSIL
(53) La   s-tsak-**un**.
      PFV   A3-grab-B1
      'S/he grabbed me'

The comparison of (51) with (53) leads to considering a tripartite alignment for this kind of case. But this tripartite alignment is a product of the particular configuration of aspect and person. For example, in perfect aspect, marked by suffixes on both intransitive and transitive verbs, only the suffixed Set B would be used independently of transitivity, (54), shifting back to an ergative alignment.

TSOTSIL
(54) a. Vay-em-**un**.
          sleep-PRF-B1SG
          'I have slept'

      b. S-tsak-oj-**un**.
          A3-grab-PRF-B1SG
          'S/he has grabbed me.'

Ergativity in Tseltalan is essentially morphological, as the syntax is more clearly nom-inative-accusative. Syntactic ergativity in other Mayan languages (Mam, K'ichee', Q'an-job'al, etc.) concerns principally the existence of agent focus, which is restricted both dialectally and grammatically in Tseltalan, as discussed in the next section.

7.2 Obviation and voice

Passive in Tseltal and Tsotsil functions as a canonical passive voice, totally removing the agent, or as a pragmatic inverse voice, in Givón's (1994) sense, i.e. as a means of showing that the patient is more topical than the agent, but without removing the agent. The latter is especially true of the morphological passive (Tsotsil *-e~-at*, Tseltal *-ot*), but not of the periphrastic passive with *ich'* 'get' (see Polian 2013a:264ff for a comparison between both passives in Tseltal).

Beyond topicality, Aissen (1997, 1999) has shown that the alternation active-(morpho-logical) passive in Tsotsil is governed by obviation. That is, it is a way of disambiguating transitive sentences where both agent and patient are third person. Concretely, active voice is used to signal that the agent is proximate, whereas the passive implies that the agent is obviative, where "proximate" means higher in one of the relevant hierarchies, as animate>inanimate, specific>non-specific, possessor>possessed, etc., and obviative means lower in the same hierarchies. Illustrating this phenomenon with animacy, it means that, if in a transitive clause the agent is human and the patient inanimate, only the active voice is possible, a passive sentence like 'the pot was broken by the man' is ungrammatical. Conversely, an inanimate agent acting on a human patient automatically triggers the passive voice, one cannot say 'the stone killed the man'. This last case is illustrated in (55) (Aissen 1997:725 and 727)

TSOTSIL

(55) a. *I-Ø-s-mil   Xun li   ton=e.
       PFV-B3-A3-kill Xun ART stone=DET
       Intended: 'The stone killed Xun.'

    b. I-Ø-mil-e   ta   ton li   Xun=e.
       PFV-B3-kill-PSV PREP stone ART Xun=DET
       'Xun was killed by the stone.'

Crucially, the restriction disappears when both arguments are equal in animacy (say, both human or both inanimate), because neither of them has priority with regard to proximate status. The same happens whenever any of the arguments is not third person, because obviation is not relevant anymore in that context.

These findings were important, because they showed that obviation, normally associated with Algonquian languages (Hockett 1966; Dahlstrom 1991), may be relevant in languages where no direct morphological marking makes explicit the proximate/obviative status of NPs and the direct/inverse character of verbs, like in Tsotsil. Later on, other studies showed that the same applies for Tseltal (Robinson 1999; Polian 2013a:247ff).

Aissen (1999) added to this panorama the case of the voice marked by -*on* in Zinacantán Tsotsil, which conflates an inverse voice and an "agent focus" voice. Agent focus is the form that verbs obligatorily adopt when transitive subjects are extracted (i.e., focused, questioned or relativized) in some Mayan languages such as K'ichee', Mam, etc. (Stiebels 2006; see also Aissen, this volume). Agent focus in Tsotsil is illustrated by (56) with a questioned agent: the verb is intransitivized, as it no longer bears an ergative prefix, and the only interpretation is that the wh-word corresponds to the agent. The same verbal form would be used with a focused or relativized agent.

TSOTSIL

(56) Buch'u i-Ø-kolta-**on**   li   tseb=e?
     who   PFV-B3-help-AF ART girl=DET
     'Who helped the girl?' (Impossible reading: 'Who did the girl help?') {Aissen 1999:455}

Crucially, Aissen (1999) shows that Tsotsil agent focus differs from the agent focus of other Mayan languages in that it is not obligatory with agent extraction: it is only used, as an inverse voice, if it is required by obviation, that is, if both agent and patient are third person, and if the agent is obviative on some relevant hierarchy. For instance, a questioned agent is compatible with a non-agent focus verb form, as in (57). Note that this sentence is ambiguous, as it is compatible with a reading in which the wh-word corresponds to the patient.

TSOTSIL
(57) Buch'u   i-Ø-s-kolta   li   tseb=e?
     who   PFV-B3-A3-help   ART   girl=DET
     'Who helped the girl?' or: 'Who did the girl help?' {ibid.:459}

Beyond Zinacantán Tsotsil, agent focus inverse voice also exists in Villa Las Rosas Tseltal, as in (58), but this still remains to be studied in detail.

TSELTAL
(58) ʔAy-Ø   mach'a   x-ʔil-**on**-Ø.
     EXIST-B3   who   IPFV-take.care.of-AF-B3
     'Someone takes care of her.'

7.3 Constituent order and changes in order

Tseltalan presents a non-rigid VOA, VS and NVP S basic constituent order (NVP=non-verbal predicate). Previous claims that (Tenejapan) Tseltal had a basic order alternating between VAO and VOA (Smith 1975; Norman and Campbell 1978; Dayley 1981) were correctly discarded by Robinson (2002). VOA order in Tseltal is illustrated in (59).

TSELTAL   O   A
(59) Yakal   y-ik'-bel-Ø   ʔach'ix   te   kerem=e
     PROG   A3-call-ASPL-B3   girl   ART   boy=DET
     'The boy is calling the girl.'

Note that whenever two NPs appear in post-verbal position, there is a frequent asymmetry in determination: the second one, which generally corresponds to the subject/agent, bears the definite determination, whereas the first one is frequently, but not necessarily, devoid of the article. This does not prevent it from getting a definite interpretation, as the translation of (59) indicates.

Departure from VOA order means a marked configuration. Firstly, VAO order obtains when O is slightly more topical than A, but not enough to justify resorting to passive voice, as in (60) (see Polian 2005).

TSOTSIL A O
(60) I-Ø-y-ixtalan   ʔik'   li   j-chob=e.
     PFV-B3-A3-ruin   wind   ART   A1-cornfield=DET
     'The wind ruined my cornfield.' {Aissen 1997:726}

Secondly, as in all Mayan languages, topicalized and focused NPs appear before the verb following a TOP-FOC-V order (Aissen 1992), as in (61). The topic is typically definite as here, in particular ended by the clitic determiner =e. In contrast, the focus is typically determinerless, and may bear one or several of the second-position clitic stock, like here the modal =me.

TSELTAL   TOP   FOC
(61) Melel   te   nujbinel=e   tak'in=me   ya   s-k'an-Ø.
     truth   ART   wedding=DET   money=MOD   IPFV A3-require-B3
     'Really, as for weddings, it's money they require.'

Several particles can head the topic phrase: in Tseltal, we find *in* and *ha²~ja²*; in Tsotsil *²a*, which is a reduction of *ja²*, as in (62).

TSOTSIL
(62) ²A-li   jvabajom=e,   ch-Ø-tal=xa.
     TOP-ART   musician=DET   IPFV-B3-come=already
     'The musician, he's coming already.' {Haviland 1981:14}

Focus of a definite NP normally takes another form: the non-verbal predicate *ha²~ja²* is placed before the verb and the focused NP is in its canonical post-verbal position, as in (63). This same element allows the first and second person to be focused, as in (64) (with irregular forms, see §4.2).

TSELTAL FOC
(63) **Ja²**-Ø=me   ya   x-chon-Ø   te   k'ankujk'=e.
     FOC-B3=MOD   IPFV   IPFV-sell-B3   ART   Cancuc=DET
     'It was the people from Cancuc who sold it.'

TSOTSIL
(64) Mi   **vo²-on**   ch-a-xi²=²o?
     Q   FOC-B1SG   IPFV-B2-be.afraid=INST
     'Is it me you are afraid of?' {Haviland 1981:133}

7.4 Negation

Negative particles always precede the negated element. The basic negation is *ma²~ma* in Tseltal and *mu* in Tsotsil. When the negated element is anything but a perfective or imperfective verb, it may takes the irrealis suffix -*uk* (some obligatorily do, others only optionally). Compare (65a) and (65b).

TSOTSIL
(65) a. Mu   vinik-**uk**-Ø.
        NEG   man-IRR-B3
        'S/he's not a man.'

     b. Mu   x-Ø-tal(*-**uk**).
        NEG   IPFV-B3-come-IRR
        'S/he doesn't come.'

Other lengthened forms of negation exist. Firstly, in many dialects the negation commonly combines with a form of the locative pronoun 'where', e.g. in Tseltal *ma(²) ba*. Secondly, the negated existential predicate *²ay* (Tseltal)/*²oy* (Tsotsil) yields a negative form *ma²yuk* and *mu²yuk* respectively, which is also used as a negation, sometimes in a reduced form: *muk'* in Zinacantán Tsotsil, *muk* in San Andrés Tsotsil, *mak'* in Amatenango Tseltal,

etc. Some forms of negation are restricted in some dialects, for instance to particular verbal aspects (see (16) and (17) on the contrast between *mu* and *muk'* in Tsotsil).

7.5 Interrogation

Polar questions take an initial particle *mi~me* in Tsotsil and *me* in Southern Tseltal, (66).
Central and Northern Tseltal use instead a second-position clitic *=bal*, (67).

TSOTSIL
(66) **Mi**   te-Ø=to   a-me'?
     Q   there-B3=still   A2-mother
     'Is your mother still there?' {Huixtán, Cowan 1969:33}

TSELTAL
(67) Laj=**bal**   aw-il-Ø?
     PFV=Q   A2-see-B3
     'Did you see it?'

Interrogative proforms for content questions always appear at the beginning of the
sentence. If the proform is extracted from inside an NP (interrogation on possessor),
the possessed noun may be extracted along with the proform but must appear after it
(pied-piping with inversion, see Aissen 1996), as in (68).

TSOTSIL
(68) **Buch'u**   **x-ch'amal**   Ø-y-elk'an   chij?
     who   A3-child   B3-A3-steal   sheep
     'Whose child stole sheep?' {Aissen 1996:460}

8 COMPLEX STRUCTURES

8.1 Finite subordinate clauses

Finite subordinate clauses function as relative, complement and adverbial clauses. The
most common subordinators in all structures stem from the definite articles: *te* in Tseltal,
ti in Tsotsil, along with the final enclitic *=e*.
    Relative clauses are always finite and post-nominal, and do not require a subordinator,
although they frequently have one, as in (69). Two interrogative proforms may be used
as relative pronouns: the human one (Tseltal *mach'a*, Tsotsil *much'u~buch'u*), as in (70),
and the locative one (Tseltal *ba~ban~banti*, Tsotsil *bu~buy*).

TSELTAL
(69) Ø-Kol-Ø   beel   te   chij   [te   la   j-nuts-Ø=e]$_{RC}$
     PFV-escape-B3   DIR:go+NF   ART   deer   SUB   PFV   A1-chase-B3=SUB
     'The deer I went chasing escaped.'

TSOTSIL
(70) Ja'-Ø   te   ch-Ø-lok'-ik   ta   barko   li   krixchano-etik
     FOC-B3   there   IPFV-B3-get.off-PL   PREP   boat   ART   people-PL

[**buch'u**-tik x-ba s-k'el-be-Ø s-na li preserente=e]_{RC}.

who-PL IPFV-go A3-see-APPL-B3 A3-house ART president=DET

'The people who went to see the president's house got off the boat there.'

{Laughlin 1980:119}

Complement clauses also may appear with or without a subordinator (see Aissen, this volume). Verbs of the following semantic groups typically take finite complement clauses: communication, knowledge, propositional attitude, desiderative and emotions, although they vary in their tendency to take or not a subordinator (see Polian 2007 and Polian 2013a:813ff). An example of a complement clause with a subordinator is illustrated in (71).

TSOTSIL

(71) Mu Ø-j-k'an [ti ch-a-man-Ø chenek']_{CC}.

 NEG B3-A1-want SUB IPFV-A2-buy-B3 bean

 'I don't want you to buy beans.' {Haviland 1981:355}

Complement clauses also can be non-finite, see examples (31), (32) and (34) above.

Adverbial clauses, as temporal, conditional, purpose and cause clauses, are almost always finite, and headed by subordinators. There can be combinations of subordinators, like the general discontinuous subordinator *te . . . =e* with the conditional/temporal subordinator *me* in Tseltal, as in (72). Some relational nouns also function as subordinators, as the purposive *venta* (from Spanish *cuenta*) in (73).

TSELTAL

(72) Ya [x-]sujt'-on tel [te me la j-ta-Ø=e]

 IPFV IPFV-return-B1SG DIR:come+NF SUB if/when PFV A1-find-B3=SUB

 'I'll come back when I find it.'

TSOTSIL

(73) Ta Ø-j-k'an j-lik jun [s-venta ta Ø-j-ts'iba karta].

 IPFV B3-A1-want one-NUM.CLF:sheet paper [A3-RN IPFV B3-A1-write letter

 'I want a sheet of paper in order to write a letter.' {Hurley and Ruiz Sánchez 1978:338}

8.2 Causative construction

The causative/permissive construction ("causative", for short) is based on the verb *ʔak'* 'to give, to put, let' plus a complement clause, which is typically of reduced finiteness or non-finite. In Tsotsil, reduced finiteness means it is a subjunctive complement (see §6.2): subordinate verbs take no aspect marking, and intransitive verbs take in addition the irrealis suffix *-uk~-ik*, as in (74) and (75).

TSOTSIL

(74) Mu x-Ø-[y-]ak' veʔ-ik-on.

 NEG IPFV-B3-A3-let eat-IRR-B1SG

 'It doesn't let me eat.' {Aissen 1987:214}

TSOTSIL

(75) Ch-Ø-k-ak'   av-il-Ø   li   j-chob=e.
     IPFV-B3-A1-let   A2-see-B3   ART   A1-cornfield=DET
     'I am going to show you ("to let you see") my cornfield.' {Haviland 1981:332}

Aissen (1987) shows that ʔak' and the subordinate verbs in Zinacantán Tsotsil may fuse further together, in what she analyzes as a case of "clause union", that is, the fact that "two clauses reduce to one, a reduction triggered by the predicate of the main clause" (Aissen 1987:212). This leads to several observable phenomena, which confirm that both verbs have merged their argumental structures. For instance, with intransitive verbs, the subordinate subject is treated as the object of the general construction: it is cross-referenced as an object on ʔak', (76), and it becomes a passive subject when the whole construction is passivized, (77).

TSOTSIL

(76) L-i-y-ak'   ʔak'otaj-ik-on.
     PFV-B1-A3-let   dance-IRR-B1SG
     'He let me dance.' {ibid.:215}

TSOTSIL

(77) Ch-i-ʔak'-e   lok'-ik-on.
     IPFV-B1-let-PSV   leave-IRR-B1SG
     'I was allowed to leave.' {ibid.:217)}

A third argument for the clause union analysis comes from external possession: this phenomenon concerns the fact that the possessor of a transitive object (different from the subject) can be indexed as a primary object on the verb, which then bears the ditransitive applicative suffix -be (see §6.3), as the second person in (78). Now, if the subordinate intransitive subject in a causative construction is possessed, its possessor can be treated as an external possessor on ʔak', as in (79).

TSOTSIL

(78) Ch-a-k-il-be   l-a-tseb=e.
     IPFV-B2-A1-see-APPL   ART-A2-daughter=DET
     'I'll see your daughter.'

     TSOTSIL

(79) Ch-a-k-ak'-be   bat-uk-Ø   l-a-tseb=e.
     IPFV-B2-A1-let-APPL   go-IRR-B3   ART-A2-daughter=DET
     'I'll let your daughter go.' {ibid.:218}

Consequently, the whole construction of ʔak'+intransitive verb surfaces as a mono-transitive construction. With a subordinate monotransitive verb, Aissen (1987) shows that the resulting construction is ditransitive, with the subordinate subject surfacing as the primary object of the whole construction. The applicability of this analysis to other dialects is a matter of inquiry. In Polian (2013a), I show that it is not transferable to Oxchuc Tseltal data.

8.3 Motion/phasal auxiliaries

Motion auxiliaries in Mayan, and in Tseltalan in particular, have been the topic of various studies (Haviland 1981:219ff, 330ff; Haviland 1993; Zavala 1993; Aissen 1994; Mateo Toledo 2008). The verbs that function as auxiliaries are about the same as those that were grammaticalized as directionals (§7.5), although auxiliaries include more phasal verbs ('start' and 'finish'). The auxiliary constitutes with the main verb a kind of complex predicate, with a partitioning of the inflection as follows: aspect is marked on the auxiliary and person on the main verb. Additionally, the main verb appears in a dependent form, the one described as subjunctive in Tsotsil (§6.2), as in (80) and (81) (alternative constructions includes combining the auxiliary with a non-finite verb, see for instance (35)–(37) above).

TSELTAL
(80) Ya   x-tal   way-uk-on.
     IPFV   IPFV-come   sleep-IRR-B1SG
     'I come to sleep.'

TSOTSIL
(81) Ch-muy   a-k'el-on.
     IPFV-climb.up   A2-see-B1SG
     'You climb up to see me.'

Aissen (1994) claims that auxiliaries lack an argument structure. One piece of evidence is that, when the whole construction is passivized, as in (82), the omitted agent is still interpreted as the moving entity, so no syntactic argument realizes the notional subject of the motion verb.

TSELTAL
(82) Ya   x-tal   koltay-ot-ok-Ø   te   me'el=e.
     IPFV   IPFV-come   help-PSV-IRR-B3   ART   old.woman=DET
     'Someone/they come(s) to help the old woman.'
     Impossible reading: 'The old woman comes to be helped.'

8.4 Destinative clauses

"Destinative" was a category proposed in Polian *et al.* (2015) for a complex predicate construction V1-V2 in Tseltal and Q'anjob'al, whose semantics is similar to that of the *purpose clause* construction in English (of the type *I got money to buy food*). Its most common expression in Tseltal is with two transitive verbs as in (83), where V1 makes an entity available or implies its availability for a specific use, which is spelled out by V2.

TSELTAL
(83) La   j-man-Ø   mats'   [k-uch'-Ø]
     PFV   A1-buy-B3   corn.dough   A1-drink-B3
     'I bought corn dough to drink.'

Morphosyntactically, V1 is fully finite while V2 appears in a dependent form: it takes only person marking, but neither aspect nor mood or polarity, and appears in a rather fixed position after V1. In Polian *et al.* (2015), it is shown that, minimally, the absolutive argument of V1 (slot in which the "destined" entity is introduced) must be coreferent with some argument of V2. The same construction also exists in Tsotsil, although research remains to be done on this topic.

8.5 Secondary predication and juxtaposition

Depictive secondary predicates (cf. Schultze-Berndt and Himmelmann 2004) are placed just before the main predicate, and share an argument with the latter. They are always intransitive, typically non-verbal but also verbal perfect forms. As a feature of morphosyntactic integration between both predicates, the secondary predicate may appear without its expected personal absolutive affix. This can only be tested with first/second person subjects, as in (84), where the perfect participle *vay-em* optionally lacks the suffix B2SG -*ot*.

TSOTSIL
(84) **Vay-em(-ot)**   l-a-kom   ta   te'tik.
     sleep-PRF-B2SG PFV-B2-remain PREP   forest
     'You remained sleeping in the forest.' {adapted from Haviland 1981:126}

Polian and Sánchez Gómez (2010) claim that the secondary predicate construction in Tseltal appears as a particular case of a more general juxtaposition construction, illustrated in Tsotsil in (85): the bracketed clause is semantically akin to a secondary predicate, but it is a full finite clause and does not necessarily share an argument with the main predicate.

TSOTSIL
(85) [Lek   pim-Ø   s-tsotsil   s-jol]   i-Ø-'ayan.
     well   thick-B3 A3-hair   A3-head   PFV-B3-be.born
     'He was born with a lot of hair ("his hair is very thick he was born").' {Hurley and Ruiz Sánchez 1978:341}

Aissen (2009) describes another construction in Zinacantán Tsotsil related to the depictive secondary predicate construction, which she calls "causative of directed motion", as illustrated in (86). Here, the first verb is a transitive verb of direct contact ('carry', 'wear'), always in the perfect aspect, and the second verb is an unaccusative intransitive verb of motion which expresses caused and accompanied motion. Both verbs necessarily share their absolutive argument, which is only optionally indexed on the first verb (as with canonical secondary predicates, (84)).

(86) S-kuch-oj(-on)   l-i-sut   tal   li   vinik-etik=e.
     A3-carry-PRF-B1SG PFV-B1-return DIR:come ART   man-PL=DET
     'The men carried me back here.' {Aissen 2009:12}

This construction is functionally, lexically and dialectally quite restricted, but it represents an interesting case of an extension of the secondary predicate construction for expressing a particular meaning, associated in other languages with directional serialization.

8.6 Verbal co-compounds

Co-compounds are made up of two lexical items with a relation of natural coordination between them, like 'mother-father' for 'parents' or 'arm-leg' for 'limbs' (Wälchli 2005). Nominal co-compounds are not rare in Mayan languages and Mesoamerica in general, but verbal co-compounds are more uncommon. Tseltalan, especially Tseltal, displays a moderate stock of them, some of which are of frequent use, as the one in (87).

TSELTAL

(87) Ya   **x**-we[7]   **x**-[7]uch'-**on**.
     IPFV   IPFV-eat   IPFV-drink-B1SG
     'I eat and drink (I have a complete meal).'

This construction is noteworthy because of the intermediate stage of fusion between both verbs: they share some inflection markers, as one imperfective auxiliary *ya* and one absolutive suffix, but other affixes are repeated, as the imperfective prefix *x*-.

NOTES

1. The only orthographic convention I don't follow here is the fact I represent the glottal stop in its IPA form /ʔ/, instead of the apostrophe, and that I do represent it at the beginning of words, e.g. *ʔixim* 'corn'.
2. Petalcingo is another phonologically conservative Tseltal dialect very similar to Bachajón, but it is already on its way to neutralizing /j/ and /h/, at least in the initial position.
3. Contrary to Yucatec Mayan, in which an **h* led to a high tone on a preceding vowel.
4. Marginally, some speakers accept *-ik* on predicative nouns, e.g. *ants-Ø-ik* 'they are women'.
5. Marginally, some adjectives can take *-etik*, but only when they function referentially in an NP, as in *te tsaj-etik* {ART red-PL} 'the red ones'. I analyze these cases as a kind of nominalization.
6. In Tsotsil, *muk'* 'big' shows an irregular attributive form *muk'-ta*. This is a unique case, all other attributive forms have a -Vl suffix.
7. Most authors that write on Tseltalan gloss *=e~=i* as a kind of dummy enclitic, but this is an even more imprecise characterization.
8. 42 percent in Zinacantán Tsotsil (Haviland 1994, based on data from Laughlin 1975); 45 percent in Oxchuc Tseltal (Sántiz Gómez 2010).

REFERENCES

Aissen, Judith. 1979. "Possessor ascension in Tzotzil." In *Papers in Mayan linguistics 3*, ed. by Laura Martin, 89–108. Columbia: Lucas Brothers.

Aissen, Judith. 1983. "Indirect object advancement in Tzotzil." In *Studies in relational grammar*, ed. by David M. Perlmutter, 272–302. Chicago: University of Chicago Press.

Aissen, Judith. 1987. *Tzotzil clause structure*. Dordrecht: Reidel.

Aissen, Judith. 1992. "Topic and focus in Mayan." *Language* 68: 43–80.

Aissen, Judith. 1994. "Tzotzil auxiliaries." *Linguistics* 32: 657–90.

Aissen, Judith. 1996. "Pied-piping, abstract agreement, and functional projections in Tzotzil." *Natural Language and Linguistic Theory* 14: 447–91.

Aissen, Judith. 1997. "On the syntax of obviation." *Language* 73: 705–50.

Aissen, Judith. 1999. "Agent focus and inverse in Tzotzil." *Language* 75: 451–85.

Aissen, Judith. 2009. "Depictives and serialization in Tzotzil." In *Hypothesis A/hypothesis B, linguistic explorations in honor of David M. Perlmutter*, ed. by Donna Gerdts, John Moore and Maria Polinsky, 1–17. Cambridge: MIT Press.

Berlin, Brent. 1968. *Tzeltal numeral classifiers: a study in ethnographic semantics*. The Hague: Mouton.

Berlin, Brent, and Terrence Kaufman. 1977. *Diccionario Tzeltal de Tenejapa, Chiapas* (Microfilm Collection of Manuscripts on Cultural Anthropology, Series LIII, 281). Chicago: University of Chicago Library.

Bohnemeyer, Jürgen, and Penelope Brown. 2007. "Standing divided: dispositionals and locative predications in two Mayan languages." *Linguistics* 45: 1105–51.

Brown, Cecil, and Søren Wichmann. 2004. "Proto-Mayan syllable nuclei." *International Journal of American Linguistics* 70: 128–86.

Brown, Penelope. 1991. *Spatial conceptualization in Tzeltal*. Nijmegen: Cognitive Anthropology Research Group, Max Planck Institute for Psycholinguistics.

Brown, Penelope. 1994. "The INs and ONs of Tzeltal locative expressions: the semantics of static descriptions of location." *Linguistics* 32: 743–90.

Brown, Penelope. 1998. "Children's first verbs in Tzeltal: evidence for an early verb category." *Linguistics* 36: 713–53.

Brown, Penelope. 2006. "A sketch of the grammar of space in Tzeltal." In *Grammars of space*, ed. by Stephen Levinson and David P. Wilkins, 230–72. Cambridge: Cambridge University Press.

Brown, Penelope, and Stephen Levinson. 1992. "'Left' and 'right' in Tenejapa: Investigating a linguistic and conceptual gap." *Zeitschrift für Phonetik, Sprachwissenschaft und Kommunikationsforschung* 45: 590–611.

Brown, Penelope, and Stephen Levinson. 1993. "'Uphill' and 'downhill' in Tzeltal." *Journal of Linguistic Anthropology* 3: 46–74.

Campbell, Lyle. 1987. "Tzeltal dialects: new and old." *Anthropological Linguistics* 29: 549–70.

Campbell, Lyle, ed. 1988. *The linguistics of Southeast Chiapas, Mexico*. Provo: Brigham Young University.

Can Pixabaj, Telma Angelina. 2015. "Complement and purpose clauses in K'iche'." PhD diss., University of Texas, Austin.

Cowan, Marion M. 1969. *Tzotzil grammar*. Mexico City: Summer Institute of Linguistics.

Dahlstrom, Amy. 1991. *Plains cree morphosyntax*. New York: Garland Publishing.

Dayley, Jon. 1981. "Voice and ergativity in Mayan languages." *Journal of Mayan Linguistics* 2: 6–82.

De Ara, Fray Domingo. 1571 [1986]. *Bocabulario de lengua tzeldal según el orden de Copanabastla*, ed. by Mario Humberto Ruz. Mexico City: UNAM.

De León, Lourdes. 1988. "Noun and numeral classifiers in Mixtec and Tzotzil: a referential view." PhD diss., Sussex University.

De León, Lourdes. 1992. "Body parts and location in Tzotzil: ongoing grammaticalization." *Working paper* 16, Cognitive Anthropology Research Group, Nijmegen.

De León, Lourdes. 1994. "Exploration in the acquisition of geocentric location by Tzotzil children." *Linguistics* 32: 857–85.

De León, Lourdes. 1998. "The emergent participant: interactive patterns in the socialization of Tzotzil (Mayan) infants." *Journal of Linguistics* 8: 131–61.

De León, Lourdes. 1999. "Verbs in Tzotzil early syntactic development." *International Journal of Bilingualism* 3: 219–40.

Dryer, Matthew. 1986. "Primary objects, secondary objects, and antidative." *Language* 62: 808–45.

Givón, Talmy. 1994. "The pragmatics of de-transitive voice: Functional and typological aspects of inversion." In *Voice and inversion*, ed. by Talmy Givón, 3–44. Amsterdam/ Philadelphia: John Benjamins.

Haviland, John. 1981. *Sk'op sotz'leb: el tzotzil de San Lorenzo Zinacantán*. Mexico City: UNAM.

Haviland, John. 1993. "The syntax of Tzotzil auxiliaries and directionnals: the grammaticalization of 'motion'." *Berkeley Linguistics Society* 19: 35–49.

Haviland, John. 1994. "'Te xa setel xulem' (The buzzards were circling): categories of verbal roots in (Zinacantec) Tzotzil." *Linguistics* 32: 691–742.

Herrera Zendejas, Esther. 2014. *Mapa fónico de las lenguas mexicanas: formas sonoras 1 y 2*. Mexico City: Colmex.

Hockett, Charles. 1966. "What Algonquian is really like." *International Journal of American Linguistics* 32: 59–73.

Hopkins, Nicholas A. 1970. "Estudio preliminar de los dialectos del tzeltal y del tzotzil." In *Ensayos de antropología en la zona central de Chiapas*, ed. by Norman McQuown and Julian Pitt-Rivers, 185–214. Mexico City: Instituto Nacional Indigenista.

Hopkins, Nicholas A. 1977. *Tones in Aguacatenango Tzeltal*. Microfilm collection of manuscripts on Cultural Anthropology No. 183, Series XXXIV, University of Chicago Library, Chicago.

Hurley, Alfa, and Agustín Ruíz Sánchez. 1978. *Diccionario Tzotzil de San Andrés con Variaciones Dialectales*. Mexico City: Instituto Lingüístico de Verano/SEP.

Kaufman, Terrence. 1971. *Tzeltal phonology and morphology*. Berkeley/Los Angeles: University of California Publications.

Kaufman, Terrence. 1972. *El proto-tzeltal-tzotzil: fonología comparada y diccionario reconstruido*. Mexico City: Centro de Estudios Mayas, UNAM.

Kaufman, Terrence, and William Norman. 1984. "An outline of proto-cholan phonology, morphology and vocabulary." In *Phoneticism in Mayan hieroglyphic writing*, ed. by John Justeson and Lyle Campbell, 77–166. Albany: Institute for Mesoamerican Studies.

Laughlin, Robert M. 1975. *The great Tzotzil dictionary of San Lorenzo Zinacantán*. Washington: Smithsonian Institution Press.

Laughlin, Robert M. 1977. *Of cabbages and kings*. Washington: Smithsonian Institution Press.

Laughlin, Robert M. 1980. *Of shoes and ships and sealing wax*. Washington: Smithsonian Institution Press.

Laughlin, Robert M., with John B. Haviland. 1988. *The great Tzotzil dictionary of Santo Domingo Zinacantán: with grammatical analysis and historical commentary*, vols. I and II. Washington: Smithsonian Institution Press.

Levinson, Stephen. 1994. "Vision, shape and linguistic description: Tzeltal body-part terminology and object description." *Linguistics* 32: 791–856.

Maffi, Luisa. 1990. "Tzeltal Maya affect verbs: psychological salience and expressive functions of language." In *Proceedings of the sixteenth annual meeting of the Berkeley linguistics society*, 61–72. Berkeley: Berkeley Linguistics Society.

Malchukov, Andrej, Martin Haspelmath, and Bernard Comrie, eds. 2010. *Studies in ditransitive constructions: A comparative handbook*. Berlin: Mouton De Gruyter.

Martin, Laura Ellen. 1977. "Positional roots in Kanjobal." PhD diss., University of Florida.

Martínez Alvarez, Pedro Rosendo. 2012. "Las manifestaciones sintácticas, semánticas y discursivas de la agentividad en el tsotsil de Huixtán, Chiapas." MA thesis, CIESAS, Mexico City.

Mateo Toledo, Eladio. 2008. "The family of complex predicates in Q'anjob'al (Maya); their syntax and meaning." PhD diss., University of Texas, Austin.

Norman, William M., and Lyle Campbell. 1978. "Toward a Proto-Mayan syntax: a comparative perspective on grammar." In *Papers in Mayan linguistics*, ed. by Nora C. England, 25–54. Columbia: University of Missouri.

Pérez González, Jaime. 2012. "Predicados expresivos e ideófonos en tseltal." MA thesis, CIESAS, Mexico City.

Polian, Gilles. 2005. "Dinámica de la oración tseltal: la topicalidad como un factor determinante del orden lineal." *TRACE* 47: 30–45.

Polian, Gilles. 2007. "El sufijo modal -uk en tseltal." In *Proceedings of the Conference on Indigenous Languages of Latin America-III*, University of Texas, Austin. www.ailla .utexas.org/site/cilla3_toc.html.

Polian, Gilles. 2013a. *Gramática del tseltal de Oxchuc*. Mexico City: CIESAS.

Polian, Gilles. 2013b. "Infinitivos transitivos: innovaciones del tseltal en la familia maya." In *Ensayos de sintaxis en lenguas de Mesoamérica*, ed. by Roberto Zavala and Enrique Palancar, 339–80. Mexico City: CIESAS.

Polian, Gilles. 2014. "Gramaticalización del distributivo verbal como plural en tseltal." In *Issues in Meso-American morphology*, ed. by Jean-Léo Léonard and Alain Kihm, 212–33. Paris: Michel Houdiard.

Polian, Gilles. To appear. *Diccionario multidialectal del tseltal*. Mexico City: INALI.

Polian, Gilles, and Jürgen Bohnemeyer. 2011. "Uniformity and variation in Tseltal reference frame use." *Language Sciences* 33: 868–91.

Polian, Gilles, and Francisco Javier Sánchez Gómez. 2010. "Integración clausal y construcción depictiva en tseltal: la pérdida de la marca de persona como señal de integración." In *Predicados secundarios en lenguas mesoamericanas*, ed. by Judith Aissen and Roberto Zavala, 33–59. Mexico City: CIESAS.

Polian, Gilles, and Jean-Léo Léonard. 2009. "La morphologie dans ALTO (Atlas Linguistique du Tseltal Occidental): Réseau dialectal et systèmes à décideurs multiples." *Géolinguistique* 11: 149–201.

Polian, Gilles, Eladio Mateo Toledo, and Telma Can Pixabaj. 2015. "Construcciones destinativas en lenguas mayas." *Amerindia* 37: 159–88.

Ringe, Donald A. Jr. 1981. "Tzotzil affect verbs." *Journal of Mayan Linguistics* 3: 61–85.

Robertson, John. 1987. "The common beginning and evolution of the Tense-Aspect system of Tzotzil and Tzeltal Mayan." *International Journal of American Linguistics* 53: 432–44.

Robertson, John. 1992. *The history of tense/aspect/mood/voice in the Mayan verbal complex*. Austin: University of Texas Press.

Robinson, Stuart. 1999. "Voice and obviation in greater Tzeltalan." MA thesis, Australian National University.

Robinson, Stuart. 2002. "Constituent order in Tenejapa Tzeltal." *International Journal of American Linguistics* 68: 51–80.

Sántiz Gómez, Roberto. 2010. "Los posicionales en Tseltal." MA thesis, CIESAS, Mexico City.

Sarles, Harvey B. 1966. "A descriptive grammar of the Tzotzil language as spoken in San Bartolome de los Llanos, Chiapas, Mexico." PhD diss., University of Chicago.

Schultze-Berndt, Eva, and Nikolaus Himmelmann. 2004. "Depictive secondary predicates in crosslinguistic perspective." *Linguistic Typology* 8: 59–131.

Shklovsky, Kirill. 2012. "Tseltal clause structure." PhD diss., Massachusetts Institute of Technology.

Slocum, Marianna, Florencia Gerdel, and Manuel Cruz Aguilar. 1999. *Diccionario tzeltal de Bachajón, Chiapas*. Mexico City: Instituto Lingüístico de Verano.

Smith, Joshua Hinman. 1975. "La familia tzeltalana." Paper presented at the Mayan Workshop, Antigua, Guatemala, August 1975.

Stiebels, Barbara. 2006. "Agent focus in Mayan languages." *Natural Language and Linguistic Theory* 24: 501–70.

Wälchli, Bernhard. 2005. *Co-compounds and natural coordination*. Oxford: Oxford University Press.

Zavala, Roberto. 1993. "Clause integration with verbs of motion in Mayan languages." MA thesis, University of Oregon, Eugene.

CHAPTER 23

CH'OL*

Jessica Coon

1 BACKGROUND AND SOURCES

Ch'ol is a language of the greater Tseltalan branch of the Mayan language family, spoken today by around 200,000 people primarily in the northern part of the Mexican state of Chiapas (see Vázquez Álvarez 2011). Ch'ol, Chontal, and Ch'orti' together constitute the Cholan subbranch. Ch'ol is generally divided into two main dialects: Tila and Tumbalá. See López López 2005 and Vázquez Álvarez 2011 on dialect variation. Ch'ol speakers refer to their language as *Lak Ty'añ* ('our words'); Ch'ol is also spelled "Chol", the choice being one largely of dialect (*Ch'ol* in Tumbalá, *Chol* in Tila). Though my own data comes primarily from Tila, I use *Ch'ol* here in keeping with the *Instituto Nacional de Lenguas Indígenas* (INALI).

Older works on Ch'ol grammar include articles on phonology by Warkentin and Brend (1974) and Koob Schick (1979); grammatical descriptions by Schumann (1973) and Warkentin and Scott (1980); a dissertation on morphology by Attinasi (1973); a thesis on nominals by Meneses Méndez (1987); and three dictionaries: Torres Rosales 1974, Aulie and Aulie 1978 and INEA 1992. Montejo López (1999) offers a grammatical sketch written in Ch'ol. This grammar was created for bilingual education programs and offers Ch'ol words for many grammatical and linguistic terms.

More recently, native speakers of Ch'ol have conducted in-depth studies of the language in the masters program at CIESAS (*Centro de Investigaciones y Estudios Superiores en Antropología Social*) in Mexico. These include a detailed overview of Ch'ol verbal morphology in Vázquez Álvarez 2002; a thesis on Ch'ol verb classes by Gutiérrez Sánchez (2004); a thesis on Ch'ol adjectives and property concepts by Martínez Cruz (2007); and a thesis on numeral classifiers by Arcos López (2009). A recent doctoral dissertation by Vázquez Álvarez (2011) provides a clear and comprehensive review of Ch'ol grammar. These works, along with my own work on Ch'ol, will be referenced throughout.

Information on Ch'ol culture and history can be found in a report by Josserand and Hopkins 2001, in the introductions of Attinasi 1973 and Vázquez Álvarez 2002, and to some extent in other works cited above.

2 PHONEMES AND ORTHOGRAPHY

Ch'ol has twenty consonants and six vowels, shown in Tables 23.1 and 23.2 below. The language is written in a Spanish-based practical orthography, which is used throughout this work. Notably, orthographic *j* = IPA [h], *y* = [j], *x* = [ʃ], and Ch'ol's high mid unrounded vowel – IPA [ɨ] – is written as *ä* (some older works use the wedge (ʌ) or schwa (ə) for this vowel). An apostrophe after a consonant indicates an ejective consonant (e.g. *k'ajk'* 'fire'); otherwise, apostrophe represents a glottal stop (e.g. *bu'ul* 'beans').

Ch'ol's consonants are shown in Table 23.1. IPA is shown on the left; in instances where the practical orthography differs from IPA, this is given on the right side of the column. Here I do not include sounds found only in Spanish loanwords, such as [g] and [f]. Previous works (Attinasi 1973; Schumann 1973; Koob Schick 1979) have included [r], noting that it is highly marginal in the system. Vázquez Álvarez (2011) notes that there are no minimal pairs with [r], which is found primarily in Spanish loans and onomato-poetic contexts, and I therefore do not list it here. The non-palatal [t] is also sometimes listed as a separate phoneme.

Initial glottal stop is not represented in the orthography: *ixik* = [ʔiʃik] 'woman'. As in many Mayan languages, the only voiced obstruent in Ch'ol is /b/, a descendant of the Proto-Mayan implosive *[ɓ] (Kaufman and Norman 1984, discussed in Vázquez Álvarez 2011). In Ch'ol, this consonant is typically realized as [ʔ] or [p] word-finally and is pre-glottalized elsewhere (Attinasi 1973; Warkentin and Brend 1974; Vázquez Álvarez 2011). Vázquez Álvarez (2011) notes that Ch'ol /b/ may have an implosive realization in final position, though more detailed phonetic work remains to be done. This consonant, along with the lateral [l], is frequently deleted in word-final position in multisyllabic words (Vázquez Álvarez 2011).

While Ch'ol has palatal consonants [ñ], [ty], and [ty'], it lacks the non-palatal counterparts. Non-palatal [t] is found only in a few forms and never contrasts with [ts]. For example, the perfective marker is realized alternately as *ta'* or *tsa'*.

Ch'ol's vowels are listed in Table 23.2. While close relatives Tseltal and Tsotsil have only five vowels – [a], [e], [i], [o], and [u] (Kaufman 1971; Haviland 1981) – Ch'ol has a sixth: [ɨ] (written as *ä*).

This sixth vowel is contrastive, though it is more limited in its distribution and according to Kaufman and Norman (1984), it derives historically from a contrast in length: a contrast between long and short vowels was lost in Cholan generally, except for *[aa] and *[a], which became [a] and [ä], respectively. Vowel length and height factor into transitivity alternations elsewhere in Ch'ol and the family generally (see e.g. Lois and Vapnarsky 2003). This type of alternation is discussed in Ch'ol passives below (§4.4.1). The six plain vowels from Table 23.2 contrast with vowels or vowel sequences represented orthographically as *Vj*, as in the minimal pair *sak'* 'stinging' and *sajk'* 'grasshopper'. Phonetically, *Vj* vowels begin as modal (voiced) vowels and become breathy (voiceless) during their second half. In addition to static forms like *sajk'*, CVC→CVjC is a productive means of forming an unaccusative (passive) stem from an otherwise transitive-forming root: *mek'* 'hug', *mejk'* 'be hugged' (see §4.4.1). These *Vj* vowels also cause root-final consonants to devoice: [ʈam] 'long' vs. [ʈaʰm̥] '*mecapal*' (a leather strap used for carrying).[1]

In a relatively small number of Ch'ol roots we also find "re-articulated" or "interrupted vowels" – vowels which are interrupted by glottal closure (see Silverman 1997). Examples include *ja'as* 'banana', *si'im* 'mother's brother's wife', and *jo'ox* '*achiote*' (type of tree). There is no general requirement that vowels separated by a glottal stop assimilate (compare the perfective morpheme with a clitic attached, *tsa'-ix*, or the compound *tya'-ek'* 'excrement-star (meteor)'). For more on Ch'ol phonology, see Vázquez Álvarez 2011:ch. 2.4; see Bennett 2016 for a general overview of Mayan phonetics and phonology, as well as England and Baird, this volume.

TABLE 23.1 CH'OL CONSONANTS – IPA AND PRACTICAL ORTHOGRAPHY

	Labial	Alveolar	Post-alveolar	Palatal	Velar	Glottal
Implosive	ɓ (*b*)					
Plosive	p			ʈ (*ty*)	k	ʔ (')
Ejective	p'	ts' (*ts'*)	tʃ' (*ch'*)	ʈ' (*ty'*)	k'	
Affricate		ts (*ts*)	tʃ (*ch*)			
Fricative		s	ʃ (*x*)			h (*j*)
Nasal	m			ɲ (*ñ*)		
Approximant	w	l		j (*y*)		

TABLE 23.2 CH'OL VOWELS – IPA AND PRACTICAL ORTHOGRAPHY

	Front	*Center*	*Back*
High	i	i (*ä*)	u
Mid	e		o
Low		a	

3 WORD FORMATION AND WORD CLASSES

This section discusses word formation and word classes in Ch'ol, as well as basic person, number, and temporal/aspectual inflection. The sub sections below are divided based on *word* class, rather than on *root* class. This type of surface-category division is useful because while some roots may be grouped clearly in one category or another, many roots appear in a variety of surface stem forms, and it is not always clear that one category is more basic than another (see e.g. Haviland 1994 on Tsotsil and Lois and Vapnarsky 2006 on Yucatecan languages). An example of the Ch'ol root *wäy* 'sleep' in different surface stem forms is shown in Table 23.3.[2]

Sections below are thus divided based on distribution of surface stems (nouns, verbs, adjectives, classifiers, relational nouns), with one exception: the class of *positional* roots. As has been previously noted in Mayan linguistics (e.g. England 1983:78), this class of roots does not correspond to a word class. Rather, positional roots always appear with some type of stem-forming morphology, usually entering into surface adjective or verb stems. Section 3.5 is devoted to the inflectional behavior of positional roots.

3.1 Nouns

Bare roots may form nouns in Ch'ol, but they may also be inflected for number and possession, as well as derived from other classes of roots. Full noun phrases and nominal inflection are discussed further in §4.1 below. This section focuses on morphology appearing on the head noun itself.

3.1.1 Possession

Possessed nominals in Ch'ol show person and possibly number agreement with the possessor, marked on the possessum via a "Set A" morpheme. Ch'ol's Set A prefixes – also used to mark transitive subjects, discussed in §3.3 – are provided in Table 23.4. As is common throughout Mayan, there are pre-consonantal and pre-vocalic allomorphs. The first person prefix is realized as *j-* when preceding a velar consonant. Number marking is discussed further in §3.1.3.

Some examples of possessed nouns are shown in (1). The possessor may be dropped, but follows the possessed noun when overt (except interrogative possessors; see Coon 2009).

TABLE 23.3 WORDS FORMED FROM ROOT *WÄY* 'SLEEP'

*wäy-i*ᵥ	*wäy-äl*ₐ𝒹ⱼ	*wäy-el*ₙ	*wäy-ib*ₙ	*wäy*ₙ
sleep-ITV	sleep-STAT	sleep-NML	sleep-INST	spirit.animal
'sleep'	'sleeping'	'sleep'	'bed'	'spirit animal'

(1) a. Tax   k-wuts'-u   **k**-pisl-el.
      PFV.already   A1-wash-TV   A1-clothes-NML
      'I already washed my clothes.'

   b. Chokoch   mi   i-k'ux-b-eñ   **iy**-ak'   **kixtyaño?**
      why   IPFV   A3-eat-APPL-D.NML   A3-tongue   people
      'Why does he eat people's tongues?' {D.20}

While many nouns in Ch'ol are free to appear with or without possessors, some require a possessor. These include body-part and kinship terms like -*ñi'* 'nose' and -*ijts'ijñ* 'younger sibling', as well as relational nouns (discussed in §3.7 below). At least some of these obligatorily possessed nouns may, however, appear without possessors if they take a -*Vl* suffix (-*äl* or -*il*), as discussed in Warkentin and Scott (1980:15) and Vázquez Álvarez (2011:ch. 5.2.1). Examples are given in Table 23.5. The last three rows in this table illustrate that not only does a -*Vl* suffix permit obligatorily possessed nouns to appear without a possessor, it may also mark a contrast in alienability.

3.1.2 Noun class clitics

Many nominals in Ch'ol – most often those referring to humans, animals, and plants – appear with one of two noun class clitics: *x-* and *aj-*. Historically, these marked feminine and masculine noun classes, respectively. In present-day Ch'ol, however, clitic choice does not indicate a distinction in actual gender. Arcos López (2011) provides an analysis of the sociolinguistic factors involved in the use of one clitic over another in Ch'ol; see also Tuz Noh 2011 for analogous facts in Yucatec Maya. The use of these clitics on proper names is discussed in Coon 2010c.

3.1.3 Plural

Bare nominals in Ch'ol are unmarked with respect to number; they may be interpreted as singular or plural, depending on context (see e.g. Arcos López 2009:76). Morphological

TABLE 23.4 CH'OL SET A (ERGATIVE/POSSESSIVE) MORPHEMES

	Pre-C	Pre-V
1st person	k-/j-	k-
2nd person	a-	aw-
3rd person	i-	(i)y-

TABLE 23.5 OBLIGATORILY POSSESSED NOUNS

i-chich	'his older sister'	*chich-äl*	'older sister'
i-pixol	'his hat'	*pixol-äl*	'hat'
i-ñäk'	'his stomach'	*ñäk-äl*	'stomach'
i-bak	'his bone'	*i-bäk-el*	'his bone (e.g. in his soup)'
i-pisil	'his clothes'	*i-pisl-el*	'his cloth'
i-chij	'his vein'	*i-chij-il*	'his cord'

plural marking is also possible for some nouns. The suffix -*ob* (often written -*o'*, see discussion on the behavior of [b] in §2 above) marks plural for humans and some animals. This suffix may show up both on the plural noun itself, as well as on the predicate, shown in (2) and discussed in §3.3.

(2) Tyi   k-il-ä-**yob**   jiñi   wiñik-**ob**.
    PFV   A1-see-TV-PL   DET   man-PL
    'I saw the men.'

An additional plural morpheme, -*tyak*, has been called an "indefinite plural" marker (Vázquez Álvarez 2002; Arcos López 2009) and results in a partitive interpretation. The example in (3) illustrates that -*tyak* is not incompatible with -*ob*, either on the verb, or the nominal.

(3) Ya'-tyo   tyi   i-cha'l-e-y-**ob**   li   ñox-**ob-tyak**.
    there-still   PFV   A3-do-TV-EP-PL   DET   elder-PL-PL.INDF
    'It was clear over there that some of the elders used to have it.' {Vázquez Álvarez 2011:87}

3.1.4 -Vl suffixes and other derived nouns

Suffixes of the form -*Vl*, or ending in -*Vl*, are found on nominals throughout Ch'ol, as already seen in the discussion of possession above. Table 23.6 gives examples of various -*XVl* suffixed nominals (where X is some material before the *Vl*); some are nominals derived from verbal or adjectival roots, while others change the meaning of an already CVC nominal. Those that appear with a possessor in the table are obligatorily possessed. More can be found in Aulie and Aulie 1978 and Warkentin and Scott 1980.

Another productive nominalizing suffix is -*ib*, which appears on intransitive stems to form nominals, most often with a resulting meaning of 'thing used for doing X' (i.e. an instrumental). Examples include *wäy-ib* 'bed' (*wäy* 'sleep') and *jul-oñ-ib* 'rifle' (*jul-oñ* 'arrive-AP'). Roots which form transitive stems may be joined to nominal roots with -*o'* in order to form compounds: *japo'ja'* 'cup' (*jap* 'drink', *ja'* 'water'); *lucho'ja'* 'ladle' (*luch* 'take out', *ja'* 'water'); *k'elo'k'iñ* 'clock' (*k'el* 'look, watch', *k'iñ* 'sun') (Warkentin and Scott 1980:22). There are also many noun-noun compounds in the language, for instance *tyaty-muty* 'father-chicken (=rooster)', *tya'-jol* 'excrement-head (=vulture)', *tyu(ñ)-muty* 'rock-chicken (=egg)'.

TABLE 23.6 -VL NOMINALS

lum	'land'	*i-lum-al*	'his country'
tyaj	'pine'	*tyaj-ol*	'place where pines grow'
ja'as	'banana'	*ja'as-il*	'banana tree'
bäx	'active'	*i-bäx-lel*	'his energy'
jab	'year'	*i-jab-ilel*	'her birthday, age'
k'iñ	'sun, day'	*k'iñ-ijel*	'party'
k'am	'sick'	*k'am-äjel*	'sickness'
mel	'make'	*mel-ojel*	'judge'

(Aulie and Aulie 1978; Warkentin and Scott 1980)

3.2 Adjectives

In his thesis on adjectives and property-denoting words in Ch'ol, Martínez Cruz (2007) argues that Ch'ol, like other Mayan languages, *does* possess a distinct class of adjectives (see also England 2004 on Mam). The number of adjectival roots is given as around 50 (Terrence Kaufman p.c., cited in Martínez Cruz 2007:66). Though many concepts which are expressed in languages like English as adjectives are lexicalized as positionals in Mayan languages (see §3.5), Martínez Cruz (2007) argues that the class of adjectives can be distinguished by their ability to directly modify a nominal head without the addition of special morphology, shown by the bold-faced adjectives in (4).

(4) a. Mi   i-kej   i-lets-el   ili   **tsiji'**   jabil.
        IPFV   A3-PROSP   A3-ascend-NML   DET   new   year
        'It will go up in this new year.'

     b. Juñ-kojty   **kolem   säsäk**   yewa,   che'-bi.
        one-CLF.animal   big   white   mare   SO-REP
        'It's a big white mare, he said.' {Martínez Cruz 2007:70}

Other lexical items must appear with the relative clause marker *-bä* (§4.1) when modifying a noun attributively, as shown by the stative positional form in (5).

(5) Ch'äm-ä   tyäl-el   **wel-el-*(bä)**   tye'!
     grab-IMP   come-NML   flat-STAT-REL   wood
     'Bring me a flat piece of wood.' {Martínez Cruz 2007}

Bare adjectives like those in (4) must precede the head noun, while modifiers with the relative marker may either precede or follow the head. Bare adjectives differ from *-bä*-marked relative clauses in other respects as well. Martínez Cruz notes that while the Set A possessive marker may be prefixed to a bare adjective when marking possession of a nominal phrase (6), it may not directly precede modifiers marked by *-bä*, as shown by the ungrammaticality of (7a). Here the possessive morphology must appear directly on the nominal head; the modifier may either precede or follow the possessed nominal.

(6) Añ   **i**-säsäk   pech.
     EXIST   A3-white   duck
     'He has a white duck.'

(7) a. *Ch'äm-ä   tyäl-el   **k**-wel-el-bä   tye'!
         bring-IMP   come-NML   A1-flat-STAT-REL   wood
         'Bring me my flat piece of wood!'

     b. Ch'äm-ä   tyäl-el   wel-el-bä   **k**-tye'!
        bring-IMP   come-NML   flat-STAT-REL   A1-wood
        'Bring me my flat piece of wood!' {Martínez Cruz 2007:79}

See Martínez Cruz 2007 for details on other properties which distinguish the class of adjectival roots from nominal and verbal roots.

3.3 Verbs

We may distinguish "verbal" (roughly, "eventive") predicates from non-verbal predicates by the requirement that verbal predicates must appear with TAM marking. Ch'ol's three core aspectual markers are provided together with their allomorphs in Table 23.7 (see §4.2). Roots which directly form eventive verbal stems (that is, without the aid of a light verb or derivational morphology) may be divided into two basic classes based on their stem-forming morphology and number of core arguments. These are shown in Table 23.8. We return to non-verbal stative predicates – which may not appear with aspect marking – in §3.4.

Core arguments are cross-referenced on the predicate via two sets of person markers, referred to as "Set A" and "Set B" in Mayan linguistics. Transitive stems always involve both sets of markers (though note that third person Set B is null), while intransitives appear with one or the other, following a split-ergative or agentive alignment; we return to alignment in §4.3 below.

The Set A markers also mark possessors, discussed in 3.1.1 above. They are repeated, together with the Set B markers, in Table 23.9. The glides in the Set B column are part of regular epenthetic insertion (to resolve vowel hiatus), though for simplicity I typically do not parse them out as separate morphemes.

I discuss transitives (root and derived) and intransitives in §§3.3.1–3.3.3 below; the discussion of positional stems is postponed to §3.5. Unergative roots in Ch'ol are encoded as "action nominals" (also called "verbal nouns"); they do not inflect directly as predicates, but appear instead as arguments in light verb constructions, discussed in §3.3.4.

Although the neat divisions in Table 23.8 will be useful to the discussion below, they are in some cases misleading, as noted at the outset of this section. For example, while the Ch'ol root *majl* 'go' listed in Table 23.8 directly forms only intransitive stems, the root *wäy* 'sleep' forms both intransitive stems as well as positional stems (indicating a position

TABLE 23.7 CH'OL ASPECTS

Perfective	*tyi*	*tsa', ta'*
Imperfective	*mi*	*muk', mu'*
Progressive		*choñkol*

TABLE 23.8 CH'OL VERBAL ROOTS

Transitive		Intransitive	
mek'	'hug'	*majl*	'go'
k'ux	'eat'	*wäy*	'sleep'
jats'	'hit'	*uk'*	'cry'
kuch	'carry'	*yajl*	'fall'
choñ	'sell'	*tyijp'*	'jump'
mäñ	'buy'	*lets*	'ascend'
wuts'	'wash'	*wejl*	'fly'
ch'äx	'boil'	*chäm*	'die'
mos	'cover'	*och*	'enter'
boñ	'paint'	*lok'*	'exit'

(Vázquez Álvarez 2002)

**TABLE 23.9 CH'OL SET A (ERGATIVE/POSSESSIVE) AND SET
B (ABSOLUTIVE) MORPHEMES**

| | Set A | | Set B |
	Pre-C	Pre-V	
1st person	k-/j-	k-	-(y)oñ
2nd person	a-	aw-	-(y)ety
3rd person	i-	(i)y-	Ø

of sleeping), without the addition of derivational morphology (i.e. beyond the predi-cate-forming suffixes found on other positional roots, discussed below); see Table 23.3. The root *och* 'enter' appears underived only as an intransitive, while the root *lok'* appears both in intransitive and transitive stems, meaning 'exit' and 'take out' respectively. In the sections below, we focus on the derivation of stems, bearing in mind that a single root may in some cases enter directly into more than one stem form.

3.3.1 Transitives

In the perfective aspect, transitive roots appear in transitive stems with a harmonic vowel suffix, as shown by the examples in (8). As discussed in Vázquez Álvarez 2011, there are a few forms involving a root vowel [a] in which the suffix is not completely identical, but instead appears as the high unrounded vowel *-ä* (IPA [i]). Transitive subjects are co-indexed by Set A prefixes, while transitive objects are marked Set B (null in the third person); see Table 23.9. I gloss the vowel suffix 'TV' for "transitive verb".

(8) a. Tyi i-tyaj-a   k'am-añ.
    PFV A3-find-TV sick-NML
    'They became sick.' (lit.: 'They found sickness.') {C. 21}

   b. Tyi k-päk'-ä   jam.
    PFV A1-plant-TV grass
    'I planted grass.' {C.3}

   c. Ta' k-lu'   choñ-o jiñi wakax.
    PFV A1-all sell-TV DET cow
    'I sold all of the cows.' {C.22}

The same transitive roots do not appear with vowel suffixes in the nonperfective aspects. Instead, transitive roots in the nonperfective aspects form stems either with no suffix, or the suffix *-e'*, glossed 'DEP' for "dependent (embedded) clause suffix". The suffix *-e'*, shown in (9a), is always optional, and only possible with third person objects (i.e. in the absence of overt Set B morphology). The suffix appears on transitives in clear contexts of embedding (§5.3), as well as in the nonperfective aspects, which I have argued are embedded under aspectual predicates (§4.3). Just as in the perfective, transi-tive subjects are marked Set A, objects are marked Set B.

(9) a. Mi   k-päk'(-**e'**)   jam.
     IPFV   A1-plant-DEP grass
     'I plant grass.'

    b. Choñkol k-mek'-ety.
      PROG   A1-hug-B2
      'I'm hugging you.'

3.3.2 Non-root transitives

The *root transitives* from the previous section contrast with *derived* or *non-root* transitives. Derived transitive stems, such as the applicatives in (10), appear with a vowel suffix in the perfective aspect and a *-Vñ* suffix in the nonperfective aspects.[3] Transitives derived via causative and applicative morphology are discussed in the context of other valence-changing morphology in §4.4 below.

(10) a. Tyi k-mel-b-**e**   i-waj   alob.
      PFV   A1-make-APPL-DTV A3-tortilla child
      'I made the child his tortillas.'

    b. Mi   k-mel-b-**eñ**   i-waj   alob.
      IPFV A1-make-APPL-D.NML A3-tortilla child
      'I make the child his tortillas.'

In addition to clearly derived forms like those in (10), there also exists a large class of stems which appear with the same -*V* /-*Vñ* stem suffixes, yet show no overt derivational morphology, as in the forms in (11) and (12). Unlike the root transitives, the vowels in the suffixes are not necessarily harmonic with the root vowel, though the vowels in the perfective/nonperfective -*Vl*/-*Vñ* pair are always identical (modulo the [a]/[ä] alternation in the (c) forms). I gloss these suffixes 'DTV' and 'D.NML' for "derived transitive verb" and "derived transitive nominal" (explained below), respectively.

(11) a. Tyi k-xujch'-**i**   tyak'iñ.
      PFV   A1-steal-DTV money
      'I stole money.'

    b. Tyi i-pi'l-**e**   majl-el iy-ijñam.
      PFV   A3-accompany-DTV go-NML A3-wife
      'He accompanied his wife.'

    c. Tyi i-ts'ijb-**u**   i-k'aba'.
      PFV   A3-write-DTV A3-name
      'He wrote his name.'

    d. Tyi aw-il-**ä**-yoñ.
      PFV   A2-see-DTV-B1
      'You saw me.'

(12) a. Mi   k-xujch'-**iñ**   tyak'iñ.
       IPFV   A1-steal-D.NML   money
       'I steal money.'

   b. Woli   i-pi'l-**eñ**   majl-el   iy-ijñam.
      PROG   A3-accompany-D.NML   go-NML   A3-wife
      'He's accompanying his wife.'[4] {Aulie and Aulie 1978}

   c. Choñkol   i-ts'ijb-**uñ**   i-k'aba'.
      PROG   A3-write-D.NML   A3-name
      'He's writing his name.'

   d. Mi   aw-il-**añ**-oñ.
      IPFV   A2-see-D.NML-B1
      'You see me.'

We will see in §4.4 below that *-V /-Vñ* stems with and without overt derivational morphology behave alike with respect to derivational processes like passivization. We might thus think of forms like those in (11)–(12) as "zero-derived" transitives. Indeed, many (perhaps most) of these forms are clearly *denominal*. The root *xujch'* in (11a) and (12a) appears uninflected as the noun 'thief'; *pi'äl* is 'friend'; and *ts'ijb* is 'scribe' or 'writing'. In other cases, such as with the root *il* in (11d)/(12d), the root is not recognizable from elsewhere in the grammar. There appears to be no phonological rule that can entirely predict the vowel quality based on the root vowel. Additional examples can be found in Aulie and Aulie 1978 or the appendix of Vázquez Álvarez 2002.

At least the suffixes *-i/-iñ* appear to be productive transitivizers in the language. Spanish verbs typically enter Ch'ol in their infinitive forms as *nouns*. In order to inflect as verbs, they appear with *-i/-iñ* suffixes. Unergative "verbal nouns" in Ch'ol, discussed further in §3.3.4, form transitives with the same suffixes. Examples of each are given in Table 23.10.

3.3.3 Intransitives

Ch'ol intransitives appear with the suffix *-i* in the perfective aspect, and the suffix *-el* in the nonperfective aspects, shown in the examples in (13) and (14). The perfective forms in (13) show Set B marking with their subjects resulting in an ergative-absolutive agreement pattern. I gloss the suffix *-i* 'ITV' for "intransitive verb".

TABLE 23.10 DENOMINAL TRANSITIVES

prowal-iñ	'try'	Spanish: *probar*	'to try'
poraj-iñ	'prune'	Spanish: *podar*	'to prune'
pensar-iñ	'worry (about something)'	Spanish: *pensar*	'to think'
k'ay-iñ	'sing (something)'	Ch'ol: *k'ay*	'song'
soñ-iñ	'dance (something)'	Ch'ol: *soñ*	'dance'
alas-iñ	'play (with something)'	Ch'ol: *alas*	'game'

(13) a. Ik'-ix   ta'   jul-**i**-yoñ -loñ.
     late-already   PFV   arrive.here-ITV-B1-PL.EXCL
     'It was already late when we_{EXCL} arrived here.' {E.171}

    b. Pero jiñi   wakax ta'   lajm-**i**.
     but   DET   cow   PFV   die-ITV
     'But the cows died.' {C.18}

Intransitives in the nonperfective aspects mark their subjects via *Set A* morphology. I gloss the suffix *-el* 'NML' for "nominal", discussed further in §4.3.

(14) a. Mi   i-wejl-**el**   aj-loro.
     IPFV   A3-fly-NML   CL-parrot
     'The parrot flies.'

    b. Muk'-äch   k-uch'-**el**.
     IPFV-AFFIRM   A1-eat-NML
     'Yes, I eat.' {B.132}

3.3.4 Unergatives

All of the intransitive roots which appear directly in the forms described in §3.3.3 are *unaccusative*; their subjects pattern with internal arguments, discussed in detail in Coon 2013. Unergative stems are formally nominal and require a light verb construction in order to predicate, discussed in a number of works on Ch'ol (Gutiérrez Sánchez 2004; Gutiérrez Sánchez and Zavala 2005; Vázquez Álvarez 2011; Coon 2012, 2013). While many of these are CVC in shape, some are also -*Vl* nominals, described in §3.1 above; see Table 23.11.

These event-denoting nominals may either appear as complements to the light verb *cha'l*, as in (15a), or subordinated under the preposition *tyi* in what Coon (2013) labels "B constructions", as in (15b). These are discussed again in §4.3.

(15) a. Tyi   i-ch'al-e   **alas**   jiñi   alob.
     PFV   A3-do-DTV   game   DET   child
     'The child played.'

TABLE 23.11   EXAMPLES OF VERBAL NOUNS

Stem	As argument noun	With light verb
soñ	'dance'	'to dance'
alas	'game'	'to play'
ts'ijb	'writing'	'write'
xujch'	'robbery'	'to rob'
chu'	'breast'	'to nurse'
xej	'vomit'	'to vomit'
*naj**al***	'dream'	'to dream'
*tse'ñ**al***	'laughter'	'to laugh'

(see Gutiérrez Sánchez 2004:70)

b. Choñkol-ety   tyi   **k'ay**.
   PROG-B2   PREP   song
   'You're singing.'

3.4 Non-verbal predicate bases

Stative predicates, also known as *non-verbal predicates* within Mayan literature, behave differently from the eventive predicates discussed above in important respects. Some examples of stative predicates are shown in (16).

(16) a. Wiñik-ety.
        man-B2
        'You are a man.'

   b. Ñox-oñ-ix.
      old-B1-already
      'I'm old already.'

   c. Buch-ul   jiñi   x-'ixik.
      seated-STAT   DET   CL-woman
      'The woman is seated.'

   d. Mejk'-em-oñ.
      hug.PSV-PRF-B1
      'I am hugged.'

The stative predicates in (16) differ from the eventive predicates discussed in the previous sections in that stative predicates never appear with aspectual morphology. Temporal relations may instead be expressed via adverbs or recovered from context. With the exception of a limited number of transitive statives, like those shown in (17), stative predicates are generally intransitive (like those in (16)). Intransitive stative predicates always mark their single argument with a Set B morpheme, conforming to the general ergative-absolutive pattern of the language (see §4.3).

(17) a. K-om   waj.
        A1-want   tortilla
        'I want tortillas.'

   b. Y-ujil-ix   k'el   juñ.
      A3-know.how-already   watch   paper
      'He already knows how to read.'

All nominal and adjectival forms can appear directly in stative constructions, shown for instance in (16a, b) above with the noun *wiñik* 'man' and the adjective *ñox* 'old'. Ch'ol does not have an overt equative copula.

Existential and locative constructions in Ch'ol involve the stative predicate *añ*. I gloss this morpheme alternately 'LOC' or 'EXT' while recognizing that these two functions are interconnected (see Freeze 1992). In locative constructions, like the ones in (18a, b), the theme follows the PP when it is a third person DP, and appears as Set B marking on the predicate when it is first or second person. In existential constructions, like the one in (18c), the theme immediately follows the predicate.

(18) a. **Añ** tyi otyoty jiñi ts'i'.
      LOC PREP house DET dog
      'The dog is in the house.'

    b. Kontento **añ**-oñ tyi k-otyoty.
       content LOC-B1 PREP A1-house
       'I'm in my house content.' {B.138}

    c. Wajali **añ**-bi juñ-tyikil x-ñek.
       back.then EXIST-REP one-CLF.people CLF-*ñek*
       'Back then, they say there was a *xñek*.' {D.1}

Ch'ol does not have a lexical verb meaning 'have'. Instead, possessive constructions involve the morpheme *añ* appearing with a possessed nominal, as in the examples in (19). Like other stative predicates, the aspectual morphemes discussed above are impossible in *añ* constructions. Instead, temporal information is inferred from the context, as in the example from a narrative in (19a), or temporal adverbs may be used.

(19) a. **Añ**-tyo k-mama, **añ**-tyo k-e'tyel.
      EXIST-still A1-mother EXIST-still A1-work
      'I still had my mother, I still had my work.' {B.72}

    b. **Añ** i-chup jiñi ts'i'.
       EXIST A3-worm DET dog
       'The dog has worms.'

3.5 Positionals

Positional roots in Mayan languages form a distinct class of roots, distinguishable in part by their semantic content (they usually refer to position, shape, or physical state), but also by the special morphology they use in order to form stems (England 1983, 2001; Haviland 1994; Vázquez Álvarez 2002). Examples of Ch'ol positional roots are shown in Table 23.12.

TABLE 23.12 POSITIONAL ROOTS

buch	'seated'
wa'	'standing on 2 legs'
koty	'standing on 4 legs; crouched'
xity	'standing on head'
jok'	'hanging' (something large)
jich'	'hanging' (something small)
ts'ej	'lying on side'
päk	'lying face down'
xoty	'in a rigid circular form'
soy	'in a non-rigid circular form'

(Vázquez Álvarez 2002)

In Ch'ol, positionals form eventive intransitive verb stems with the suffixes -*li* (also realized as -*le*) in the perfective aspect, and -*tyäl* in the nonperfective aspects, shown in (20a) and (20b). Coon and Preminger (2009) argue for an analysis in which the suffixes -*li* and -*tyäl* are further decomposed and include the -*i* and -*el* suffixes found on the intransitives discussed in §3.3.3 above. These positional forms behave syntactically as the intransitive (unaccusative) predicates from §3.3.3 above. They take a single argument; the perfective marks this argument with the Set B morpheme, while the nonperfective forms show Set A marking.

(20) a. Ta' koty-**li**   jiñi me'.
       PFV   stand.on.4.legs-POS.ITV   DET   deer
       'The deer stood.' {E.55}

    b. Mi   k-wa'-**tyäl**   tyi   karo.
       IPFV A1-stand.on.2.legs-POS.NML   PREP car
       'I stand in the truck.'

In addition to forming eventive intransitive verb stems, positional roots share many inflectional characteristics with transitive roots. For example, both may take a harmonic -*Vl* suffix to form a stative predicate, commonly found in non-verbal predicate (§3.4) and secondary predicate (§5.1) constructions. Both positional and transitive roots may also form numeral classifiers via lengthening and aspiration of the root vowel (§3.6).

3.6 Classifiers

In Ch'ol, numerals must appear with a numeral classifier. Lists of numeral classifiers may be found in Aulie and Aulie 1978 and in the appendix of Warkentin and Scott 1980; see especially Arcos López 2009 for a detailed discussion of classifiers in Ch'ol. The vast majority of classifiers in the language are of the form -CVjC. (Final *l* is often dropped, for instance -*p'ejl*→ -*p'ej*.)

Most of these classifiers are derived from corresponding CVC transitive or positional roots, as shown by the examples in Table 23.13 (a commonly heard exception is the classifier -*tyikil*, used to count people). As the glosses suggest, the thing counted by the classifier corresponds to the internal thematic role assigned by the corresponding transitive root, or to the single thematic role assigned by the positional. We return to the function of numeral classifiers inside the noun phrase in §4.1 below.

TABLE 23.13 NUMERAL CLASSIFIERS

Classifier	For counting. . .	CVC root	Gloss (CATEGORY)
-*xujty'*	pieces	*xuty'*	'divide' (TV)
-*kujch*	loads	*kuch*	'carry' (TV)
-*jojp*	handfuls (of dry granular things)	*jop*	'gather (dry granular things)' (TV)
-*kojty*	animals, 4-legged things	*koty*	'standing on 4 legs' (POS)
-*pajl*	clusters	*pal*	'clustered, bunched' (POS)
-*xejty*	convex objects	*xety*	'in a convex form' (POS)

3.7 Relational nouns and prepositions

Ch'ol has one true preposition: *tyi*. This preposition introduces the oblique argument in passives (§4.4), all locative relations (Vázquez Álvarez 2002:32), some adverbial elements and some non-finite embedded clauses (Coon 2013; Vázquez Álvarez 2013). Examples are given in (21).

(21) a. Mi   a-mos-tyäl   **tyi**   tsuts.
      PFV   A2-cover-PSV.NML   PREP   blanket
      'You are covered by the blanket.'

    b. Añ   waj   **tyi**   mesa.
       EXIST   tortilla   PREP   table
       'There are tortillas on the table.'

    c. Tsajñ-ety   **tyi**   Salto.
      return-B2   PREP   Salto
      'You returned from Salto.'

More specific spatial relations are encoded with possessed body-part terms and other relational nouns, as in the examples in (22).

(22) a. tyi   **i-paty**   otyoty
      PREP   A3-back   house
      'behind the house'

    b. tyi   **i-jol**   otyoty
       PREP   A3-head   house
       'on top of the house'

Relational nouns, described for languages throughout the Mayan family, are also used to express notions of concomitance and possession, as shown with *-ik'oty* and *cha'añ* in (23). Relational nouns appear with possessive (Set A) marking co-indexing the introduced argument. These relational nouns need not be introduced by the preposition *tyi*, and thus differ from other modifiers. The Ch'ol relational noun *-ik'oty* may also show an overt Set B argument, as in (23c).

(23) a. Tyi   majl-i   **y-ik'oty**   k-mama.
      PFV   go-ITV   A3-RN.with   A1-mom
      'He went with my mom.'

    b. Maxki   **i-cha'añ**   ili   pisil?
       who   A3-RN:for/of   DET   clothes
       'Whose clothes are these?'

    c. Mi   ke   k-majl-el   **k-ik'oty-ety**.
      IPFV   PROSP   A1-go-NML   A1-RN.with-B2
      'I'll go with you.'

While relational nouns like *-ik'oty* and *-ebal* are obligatorily possessed, this is not the case with *cha'añ*, which often appears with no Set A marker with readings like 'for', 'because of'. This suggests that the relational noun may be grammatical-izing into a second preposition. *Cha'añ* can also introduce fully finite embedded clauses (§5.3).

(24) a. Mi   i-k'uñ-añ   lum **cha'añ**   ja'al.
       IPFV   A3-soft-INCH land because   rain
       'The land is softening because of the rain.' {Aulie and Aulie 1978}

   b. Tyi   i-mel-e   waj   **cha'añ**   y-alobil.
      PFV   A3-make-TV   tortilla for   A3-child
      'She made tortillas for her children.'

Finally, the preposition *tyi* is also used to introduce certain non-locative/non-temporal adverbial elements, often in a post-predicate position. Some examples are given in (25).

(25) a. . . . cha'añ mi   k-cha'   lok'-el   **tyi**   **libre.**
           so   IPFV A1-again   exit-NML   PREP   free
       '. . . so I come out free again.' {B.158}

   b. Poreso   jiñi   x-ñek   mi   i-sub-eñ-ob,   cha'añ
      that's.why DET   CLF-ñek   IPFV   A3-say-DTV-PL   because
      lu'-i'ik'   **tyi**   **pejtyelel.**
      all-black   PREP   all
      'That's why they call him the *xñek*, because he's all black.' {D.49}

4 PHRASE AND SIMPLE CLAUSE STRUCTURE

This section moves beyond the word to the phrase. We examine the noun phrase in §4.1, before turning to the verb phrase. Relative positions of the main elements in a Ch'ol declarative verbal construction are given in (26), where "object" and "sub-ject" represent free-standing NPs, when present. These elements are discussed in turn below.

(26) topic – focus – negation   [**aspect** – **predicate** – **object** – **subject**]

4.1 Maximal extensions of the noun phrase

Ch'ol nominals are not marked for morphological case. Nominal phrases in Ch'ol can consist of bare nouns, as in (27a), or larger phrases which may include determiners and demonstratives, adjectives, relative clauses, numerals and classifiers, clitics, and plural marking, shown in the examples in (27b, c) and discussed in this section.

(27) a. Y-om   [ja'as].
        A3-want   banana
        'He wants a banana.'

   b. Baki   añ   [iy-alob-il-ob   aj-Maria]?
      where   LOC   A3-child-NML-PL   DET-Maria
      'Where are Maria's children?'

TABLE 23.14 CH'OL NOUN PHRASE

determiners	
demonstratives	
numerals with classifiers or measure/quantifier phrases	
Set A (possessor) agreement	
adjectives and pre-nominal relative clauses	↑ *before N*
NOUN	
possessor	↓ *after N*
post-nominal relative clauses	
prosodic enclitic	

(Martínez Cruz 2007:12)

c. Tyi   k-mäñ-ä   [ili   cha'-p'ej   kolem   alaxax].
   PFV   A1-buy-TV   DET   two-CLF.round   big   orange
   'I bought these two big oranges.'

In his thesis on Ch'ol adjectives and property concepts, Martínez Cruz (2007:21) gives the break-down of Ch'ol noun phrase components shown in Table 23.14, with elements appearing before of the noun at the top, and those after the noun at the bottom. Elements appearing on the head noun itself (noun class clitics, number marking) were discussed in §3.1 above.

4.1.1 Determiners, demonstratives, and pronouns

Bare nominals in Ch'ol may be interpreted as definite or indefinite. Nonetheless, Ch'ol does have determiners and demonstratives. While a definite reading is forced with certain D^0 elements, definite interpretations can also come from context. This can be seen in the sentences in (28) and (29), taken from a narrative about hunters with a dog hunting deer, transcribed in Coon 2004. The dog, which has already been introduced into the narrative, begins to follow some deer tracks:

(28) Che'   tyi   i-säk-l-ä   majl-el   **ts'i'**. . .
     then   PFV   A3-search-STAT-DTV   go-NML   dog
     'Then the dog went to search for it . . . ' {E.20}

The hunters see a deer, but it runs away. The dog chases after the deer but then loses its scent:

(29) Ma'añ   tyi   i-ña'-tyä   baki   tyi   majl-i   **me'** . . .
     NEG   PFV   A3-know-DTV   where   PFV   go-ITV   deer
     'It didn't know where the deer went . . . ' {E.35}

Ch'ol determiners and demonstratives are given in Table 23.15. All of these occupy a prenominal position, and I will gloss all of them 'DET' based on similar restrictions on word order found with these forms (discussed in Coon 2010c and §4.5 below).

As noted in Martínez Cruz 2007, we find an enclitic *=i* – likely related to the final *i* in the forms in Table 23.1. – appearing on the end of the noun phrase, as in (30). Martínez

TABLE 23.15 DETERMINERS AND DEMONSTRATIVES

li, ili, iliyi	definite, 'this'
jiñ, jiñi	definite, 'that'
ixä, ixäyi	definite, 'that over there'

Cruz (2007:42) notes that this clitic is always optional, though its discourse function has not been investigated.

(30) a. Baki   mi   y-ajñ-el   i-mäñ-e'   lembal   **ili**   wiñik=i?
      where   IPFV   A3-be.at-NML   A3-buy-DEP   liquor   DET   man-ENC
      'Where did he buy liquor, this man?' {Martínez Cruz 2007:26}

   b. Pero   **jiñi**   x-ñek=**i**   ma'añ   mi   i-bä'ñ-añ   pañämil.
      but   DET   CL-*ñek*=ENC   NEG.EXIST   IPFV   A3-fear-DTV   world
      'But that *xñek* isn't afraid of anything.' {D.10}

Finally, as noted above the form *jiñ*, and sometimes *jiñi*, is glossed by some as a third person pronoun. This would give us the pronominal forms in Table 23.16. An alternative possibility is that *jiñ* is simply a determiner, and that all pronouns are formed from a combination of the determiner plus the corresponding Set B morpheme. This similarity between Set B morphemes and overt pronouns is found throughout the Mayan family.

4.1.2 Possession

Possession was discussed above in §3.1.1. As the following narrative examples illustrate, possessed NPs may appear preceded by determiners and demonstratives. The noun phrase in (31b) shows a determiner, numeral plus classifier, possession, and an adjective. Here the possessive marking precedes the adjective and noun.

(31) a. Pero   mi   ma'añ   mi   i-tyaj-b-eñ   **jiñi**   **iy**-ak'
      but   if   NEG.EXIST   IPFV   A3-find-APPL-D.NML   DET   A3-tongue
      kixtyaño . . .
      people
      'But if he doesn't find anyone's tongues . . . ' {D.24}

   b. Tyi   k-mäñ-ä   **jiñi**   juñ-kojty   **j**-kolem   ts'i'.
      PFV   A1-buy-TV   DET   one-CLF:animal   A1-big   dog
      'I bought my big dog.' {Martínez Cruz 2007:36}

TABLE 23.16 CH'OL PRONOUNS

	Pronoun	*Set B (absolutive)*
1st person	*joñoñ*	*-oñ*
2nd person	*jatyety*	*-ety*
3rd person	*jiñ*	*-Ø*

4.1.3 Numerals, numeral classifiers, and quantifiers

Like other Mayan languages, Ch'ol has a base-20 numerical system, though Spanish numerals are being increasingly used by younger speakers for numbers larger than four or five. Numerals for 1–20 are given in Table 23.17. A more complete list of numerals is listed in the appendix of Warkentin and Scott 1980.

As the hyphens after the forms in Table 23.17 suggest, numeral-denoting roots may not stand alone. Instead, all numerals in Ch'ol must appear with a classifier (see §3.6 and Arcos López 2009), which varies depending on the nature of what is being counted. Examples are given in (32). The head noun may be omitted in numeral classifier constructions, as shown in (32b).

(32) a. Tyi   j-k'ux-u   ux-**ts'ijty**   ja'as.
     PFV   A1-eat-TV   three-CLF:long.and.skinny   banana
     'I ate three bananas.'

   b. Añ   cha'-k'ej   tyi   mesa.
     LOC   two-CLF:round.and.flat   PREP   table
     'There are two (round flat things) on the table.'

Martínez Cruz (2007, 31) lists two quantifiers: *kabäl* 'many, a lot' and *ts'ity̌a'* 'few, a little'. He also notes that *juñ*-CLF *cha'*-CLF 'one-CLF two-CLF' can be used to convey 'some', as in (33):

(33) Wajali   am-bi   **juñ-tyikil**   **cha'-tyikil**   la-k-pi'äl.
     back.then   EXIST-REP   one-CLF:people   two-CLF:people   PL-A1-friend
     'It's said that back then we had some friends.' {Martínez Cruz 2007:31}

4.2 Aspect

We now turn to a discussion of the core components of verbal predicates, beginning with aspect. Ch'ol distinguishes three basic aspects: perfective, imperfective, and progressive, shown in Table 23.18, repeated from Table 23.7 above. The perfective and imperfective morphemes have two basic forms, a short CV form and a longer CVC form. Ch'ol's minimal word requirement is CVC; the full CVC forms must be used when the aspectual morphemes host clitics. Since the progressive already meets this requirement, it has just one form.

TABLE 23.17 CH'OL NUMERALS

1	juñ-	11	juñlujuñ-
2	cha'-	12	lajchäñ-
3	ux-	13	uxlujuñ-
4	chäñ-	14	chänlujuñ-
5	jo'-	15	jo'lujuñ-
6	wäk-	16	wäklujuñ-
7	wuk-	17	wuklujuñ-
8	waxäk-	18	waxäklujuñ-
9	boloñ-	19	boloñlujuñ-
10	lujuñ-	20	juñk'al

TABLE 23.18 CH'OL ASPECTS

Perfective	*tyi*	*tsa', ta'*
Imperfective	*mi*	*muk', mu'*
Progressive		*choñkol*

In Coon 2010c, 2013 I argued that imperfective and progressive markers *mi/muk'/mu'* and *choñkol* are predicates, while the perfective is not. I refer to Ch'ol's imperfective and progressive aspects jointly as "nonperfective" aspects. In contrast, the perfective aspect marker *tyi* (proposed by Law et al. (2006:442) to be a borrowing from Yucatec) is simply an aspectual particle. I argued in Coon 2010a, b, 2013 that this division is the source of Ch'ol's ergative split, discussed in §4.3 below.

(34) a. **Tyi** wäy-i-yoñ.
  PFV   sleep-ITV-B1
  'I slept.'

    b. **Mi** k-majl-el   tyi   eskwela.
  IPFV   A1-go-NML   PREP   school
  'I go to school.'

    c. **Choñkol** i-mel   waj   aj-Maria.
  PROG   A3-make   tortilla   DET-Maria
  'Maria is making tortillas.'

Like some of the other languages of the Mayan family, for example Popti' (Craig 1977) and Mam (England 1983), Ch'ol does not have dedicated grammaticalized tense morphology. Instead, temporal notions like past and future are marked via adverbs like *wajali* 'back then', *abi* 'yesterday' and *ijk'äl* 'tomorrow'. See Coon (2013:ch. 2) for discussion of the distribution and behavior of these aspect markers.

4.3 Core arguments, agreement, and alignment

As seen above, grammatical relations in Ch'ol are head-marked on the predicate with two sets of morphemes, traditionally labeled "Set A" and "Set B" in Mayan linguistics. Set

TABLE 23.19 CH'OL SET A (ERGATIVE/POSSESSIVE) AND SET B (ABSOLUTIVE) MORPHEMES

	Set A		Set B
	Pre-C	*Pre-V*	
1st person	*k- /j-*	*k-*	*-(y)oñ*
2nd person	*a-*	*aw-*	*-(y)ety*
3rd person	*i-*	*(i)y-*	Ø

A corresponds to *ergative* and *possessive*, while Set B corresponds to *absolutive*. These morphemes are shown in Table 23.19, repeated from Table 23.9 above. Plural marking may appear both on nominals and as agreement on the predicate, and may reflect plural of either the Set A or the Set B argument. Ch'ol's plural morphemes are shown in Table 23.20 and discussed further in Coon 2010a and Vázquez Álvarez 2011.

As nominals in Ch'ol do not show case morphology, constructions with two third person arguments are potentially ambiguous. This ambiguity is resolved either by context or by word order, discussed in §4.5 below. Bare nominals may in some cases be interpreted as singular or plural, definite or indefinite; see appendix 4.1.1 below.

The Set A morphemes co-index transitive subjects (35a), unergative subjects (35b), subjects of intransitives in the *non*-perfective aspects (35c), and possessors of nominals (35d). Unergatives like (35b) are encoded as nominals and require a light verb in order to predicate; see Gutiérrez Sánchez and Zavala 2005; Coon 2012. In (35b), for example, the lexical root is a "verbal noun" (see §3.3) *soñ* 'dance' and appears as the complement of the transitive light verb *cha'l*. The subject – as with subjects of transitive verbs generally – is marked as Set A.

(35) a. Tyi   **k**-wuts'-u   pisil.
         PFV   A1-wash-TV   clothes
         'I washed clothes.'

   b. Tyi   **k**-cha'l-e   soñ.
         PFV   A1-do-DTV   dance
         'I danced.' (lit.: 'I did dance.')

   c. Mi   **k**-wäy-el   tyi   ab.
         IPFV   A1-sleep-NML   PREP   hammock
         'I sleep in a hammock.'

   d. **k**-wakax
         A1-cow
         'my cow'

The Set B markers co-index transitive objects (36a), subjects of *perfective* intransitives, and the theme in predicate nominal and predicate adjectival constructions (36c, d).

(36) a. Tsa'-bi   y-il-ä-**yoñ**.
         PFV-REP   A3-see-DTV-B1
         'She reportedly saw me.'

   b. Tyi   ts'äm-i-**yoñ**.
         PFV   bathe-ITV-B1
         'I bathed.'

TABLE 23.20 CH'OL PLURAL MORPHOLOGY

local [+hearer]	*la*
local [-hearer]	*-lojoñ, loñ*
non-local	*-ob*

c. X-'ixik-**oñ**.
   CL-woman-B1
   'I'm a woman.'

d. Ch'ijyem-**oñ**.
   sad-B1
   'I'm sad.'

Comparing the intransitive verbal forms in (35c) and (36b), we can describe Ch'ol as having aspect-based split ergativity: subjects of intransitives in the perfective aspect trigger Set B marking (an ergative pattern), while subjects of nonperfective intransitives trigger Set A marking (a split pattern). In the terminology of Dixon (1979), this represents a pattern of "extended ergativity" – the marker normally reserved for transitive subjects has been extended to mark certain intransitive subjects; see also Larsen and Norman 1979 on this pattern more generally in Mayan.

(37) ERGATIVE-PATTERNING
    transitive: **A**-stem-**B**
    intransitive: stem-**B**

(38) "EXTENDED ERGATIVE"
    transitive: **A**-stem-**B**
→ *intransitive:* **A**-stem

In addition to the aspectual split, comparing forms like (35b) and (36b, c) illustrates that Ch'ol is also "Split-S": agentive intransitives pattern differently from non-agentive intransitives in requiring a light verb in order to predicate (discussed for Ch'ol in Gutiérrez Sánchez and Zavala 2005; see also Danziger 1996 on Mopan). Note that while the light verb in (35b) is transitive, unergative verbal nouns like *soñ* may appear in other constructions as well. In (39) *soñ* appears under the preposition *tyi*; Set B person marking appears directly on the intransitive aspectual predicate *choñkol*. Robertson (1980) calls constructions like (39) "raising constructions", discussed at length in Coon 2012.

(39) Choñkol-oñ   tyi   soñ.
    PROG-B1   PREP dance
    'I'm dancing.'

Finally, Ch'ol can also be described as having a "Fluid-S" system, since certain intransitives – dubbed "ambivalents" in Vázquez Álvarez 2002 – may appear either directly as predicates (unaccusative) or in a light verb construction (unergative) with a corresponding difference in interpretation, as shown in (40).

(40) a. Tyi   **wäy**-i-yoñ.
       PFV sleep-ITV-B1
       'I slept.' (possibly accidentally)

    b. Tyi   k-cha'l-e   **wäy**-el.
       PFV 1ERG-do-DTV sleep-NML
       'I slept.' (on purpose)

To sum up, with one apparent exception, namely the nonperfective (unaccusative) intransitive in (35c), we may generalize as follows: Set A marks all *external* arguments, while Set B marks all *internal* arguments. Elsewhere I argue that nonperfective unaccusative forms like the one in (35c) do *not* in fact present an exception. I propose that the Set A marking in these forms co-indexes a grammatical *possessor*, which controls the internal argument.

4.4 Voice

4.4.1 Passive

The majority of root (CVC) transitives in Ch'ol form passives by the CVC→CVjC process introduced in §2 above. The resulting form behaves morphologically the same as underived unaccusatives. In (41a), for example, the transitive root *kuch* appears in a transitive stem form: it takes the harmonic vowel suffix *-u* and shows both Set A (subject) and Set B (object) markers. In the passive form in (41b) the root changes from [CVC] to [CVjC] and the agent is left unexpressed. This root now appears with the suffix *-i*, found on underived perfective intransitives.

(41) a. Tyi   i-kuch-**u**-yoñ.
         PFV   A3-carry-TV-B1
         'He carried me.'

    b. Tyi   ku**j**ch-**i**-yoñ.
         PFV   carry.PSV-ITV-B1
         'I was carried.'

Analogous facts are found in nonperfectives, as shown by the progressives in (42). In the passive in (42b) the agent is omitted and the CVjC root now appears with the suffix *-el*, also found on underived nonperfective intransitives. It is worth pointing out that many apparently underived intransitives are also of the form CVjC (see Table 23.8 above). The roots *majl* 'go' and *tyijp'* 'jump' for instance appear in intransitive stems, but there are no transitive counterparts **mal* or **tyip'*. There are no transitive roots of the form CVjC.

(42) a. Choñkol   i-kuch   ñeñe'   jiñi   x-'ixik.
          PROG   A1-carry   baby   DET   CL-woman
          'The woman is carrying a baby.'

    b. Choñkol   i-ku**j**ch-**el**   ñeñe'.
          PROG   A3-carry.PSV-NML   baby
          'The baby is being carried.'

While the majority of CVC roots form passives in this manner, the CVC→CVjC process is unavailable for transitive roots ending in a fricative consonant: *j*, *s*, or *x* (recall that these represent IPA [h], [s], and [ʃ] respectively). While fricative-final transitive roots behave identically to non-fricative-final roots in active stems (i.e. they appear in forms like (41a) and (42a)), fricative-final transitive roots must form passives with the suffix *-li* (perfective) and *-tyäl* (nonperfective), shown in (43).

(43) a. Tyi   k'ux-**li**-yoñ.
          PFV   bite-PSV.ITV-B1
          'I was bitten.'

b. Mi   i-mos-**tyäl**   ñeñe'.
    IPFV   A3-cover-PSV.NML   baby
    'The baby is covered.'

While CVC root transitives passivize either by CVC→CVjC, or with the suffixes -*li*/-*tyäl*, derived or "non-root" transitive stems (see §3.3 above) passivize with the suffix -*tyi* following the -*Vl*-*Vñ* suffixes.[5] In the nonperfective aspects, we then find the suffix -*el*, which also appears on underived intransitives in the nonperfective aspects; vowel deletion results in -*tyel*. Examples are shown in (44)–(45). As noted above, the -*Vl*-*Vñ* stems with and without overt derivational morphology behave alike with respect to passivization.

(44) a. Tyi   yä-s-äñ-**tyi**-yoñ.
      PFV   fall-CAUS-DTV-PSV-B1
      'I was made to fall.'

    b. Mi   k-yä-s-äñ-**tyel**.
      IPFV   A1-fall-CAUS-DTV-PSV.NML
      'I am made to fall.' {Vázquez Álvarez 2002:59}

(45) a. Tyi   koty-äñ-**tyi**-yety.
      PFV   help-DTV-PSV-B2
      'You were helped.'

    b. Mi   a-koty-äñ-**tyel**.
      IPFV   A2-help-DTV-PSV.NML
      'You are helped.' {Vázquez Álvarez 2002:75}

These stems follow the split discussed above: the single argument of the perfective is marked with Set B, while the single argument of the nonperfective is marked Set A.

Finally, the appearance of by-phrases with passives is restricted based on person and animacy. The restriction of voice constructions based on the relative animacy of the verbal arguments in Mayan languages was first noted in Aissen 1997, who connects these facts to *obviation*. See Zavala 2007 for a detailed description of the situation for Ch'ol.

4.4.2 Causative

Ch'ol has one morphological causative, the suffix -*(i)s*, which is possible only on intransitive roots. In the perfective, the suffix is followed by the vowel -*ä* and in nonperfective aspects it is followed by -*añ* (following the general pattern of derived transitives in the language). The appearance of the vowel -*i* does not seem to be phonologically predictable.

(46) a. Tyi   k-wäy-**is**-ä   ñeñe'.
      PFV   A1-sleep-CAUS-DTV   baby
      'I made the baby sleep.'

    b. Mi   k-wäy-**is**-añ   ñeñe'.
      IPFV   A1-sleep-CAUS-D.NML   baby
      'I make the baby sleep.'

The causative suffix often triggers an irregular or reduced form of the root. These forms are not phonologically predictable, and are unique instances of irregularity in a language which is otherwise predictably agglutinating. For instance *yajl* 'fall'→*yä-s* 'make fall'; *lok'* 'exit'→*lo'-s* 'make exit'; The suffix *-(i)s* also triggers regressive anteriority harmony, as in *chäm* 'die'→ *tsäñ-s* 'kill' and *och* 'enter'→*ot(s)-s* 'make enter'. Finally, the causative suffix is impossible with roots denoting directed motion: *majl* 'go', *tyäl* 'come', *jul* 'arrive here' and *k'oty* 'arrive there'. This same set of roots is also unable to appear with imperative morphology.

The morphological causative is possible only with certain intransitive roots. All other causatives in the language are periphrastic. Examples with the verbs *xik'* 'order' and *äk'* 'give' are given in (47). These verbs take non-finite complement clauses, discussed further in §5.3 below.

(47) a. Mi   i-xik'-ety   a-wuts'   pisil.
        IPFV   A3-order-B2   A2-wash   clothes
        'She orders you to wash clothes.'

    b. Tyi   k-äk'-ä-yety   tyi   soñ.
        PFV   A1-give-TV-B2   PREP   dance
        'I made you dance.'

4.4.3 Applicative

Transitive stems (derived or not) appear in double object constructions with the applicative suffix *-b*, followed by *-e* in the perfective and *-eñ* in the nonperfective. The forms in (48) show that a benefactive can be added to a transitive construction as an oblique marked by *cha'añ* 'for' (also a relational noun, described in this context as a preposition by Gutiérrez Sánchez 2004).

(48) a. Tyi   k-ch'äx-ä   ja'.
        PFV   A3-boil-TV   water
        'I boiled water.'

    b. Tyi   k-ch'äx-ä   ja'   **cha'añ   aj-Maria**.
        PFV   A1-boil-TV   water   for   DET-Maria
        'I boiled water for Maria.'

Applicative constructions promote indirect objects, like *ajMaria* in (48b), to primary argument status. That is, in the applicative, the applied argument patterns the same as the object of a mono-transitive construction. The theme is the "secondary object" in the sense of Dryer 1986. If the applied primary object is first or second person, it appears as Set B marking on the stem, as in (49a). When the primary object is an overt third person nominal, the order is V-DO-IO-S, as in (49b). The applicative suffix appears only on transitive stems, never on intransitives. Vázquez Álvarez (2002) notes that the applied object may be a benefactee, as in (48b), a malefactee as in (48a), a recipient, or a target.

(49) a. Mi   k-muk-**b**-eñ-**ety**   waj.
        IPFV   A1-hide-APPL-D.NML-B2   tortilla
        'I hide your tortilla.' {Vázquez Álvarez 2002:304}

b. Tyi i-ch'äx-b-e   ja' **alob** jiñi x-'ixik.
PFV A3-boil-APPL-DTV water boy   DET CL-woman
'The woman boiled the boy water.'

The applicative suffix is also employed in external possession constructions, as shown in (50). Here the possessor of the theme is marked via Set B morphology on the stem (null third person in (50b)).

(50) a. Tyi a-ts'äk-ä-b-**oñ**   **k**-alob-il.
PFV A2-cure-DTV-APPL-B1   A1-child-NML
'You cured my child.' {Vázquez Álvarez 2002:307}

b. Chokoch mi   i-k'ux-b-eñ   **iy**-ak'   **kixtyaño?**
why   IPFV A3-eat-APPL-D.NML A3-tongue   people
'Why does he eat people's tongues?' {D.20}

4.4.4 Antipassive

As with unergatives, discussed in §4.3, antipassive forms in Ch'ol behave distributionally and, in some cases, morphologically with nominals. When used predicatively, they always surface in light verb constructions; see Gutiérrez Sánchez 2004; Vázquez Álvarez 2011; Coon 2013. In Coon 2013 I provide evidence for the generalization that all *predicates* in Ch'ol (i.e. forms which inflect directly for person) require full internal arguments. Thus while unaccusatives and transitives pattern directly as verbs, unergatives and antipassives do not. The transitive in (51a) is provided for contrast with the two antipassives in (51b, c).

(51) a. TRANSITIVE
Tyi k-wuts'-u   (jiñi) pisil.
PFV A1-wash-TV DET   clothes
'I washed (the) clothes.'

b. INCORPORATION ANTIPASSIVE
Tyi k-cha'l-e   wuts' (*jiñi) pisil.
PFV A1-do-DTV wash DET   clothes
'I washed clothes.' (lit.: 'I did clothes-washing.')

c. ABSOLUTIVE ANTIPASSIVE
Tyi k-cha'l-e   wuts'-**oñ**-el.
PFV A1-do-DTV wash-AP-NML
'I washed.' (lit.: 'I did washing.')

The incorporation antipassive in (51b) does not bear any overt antipassive morphology and the verb root and internal argument remain separate words phonologically. Nonetheless, the object must be bare and non-referential, as shown by the ungrammaticality of the determiner *jiñi*. The absolutive antipassive in (51c) appears with the suffix -*oñ* – cognate with antipassive in other Mayan languages – always followed by the nominal suffix -*el*. No internal argument appears. There is no antipassive construction in Ch'ol in which an internal argument is demoted to oblique status.

4.4.5 Reflexives and reciprocals

Both reflexives and reciprocals in Ch'ol involve the relational noun *-bäj* or *-bä*, which can be glosssed as 'self'. This form always appears with possessive (Set A) marking, which is coreferential with the external argument of the verb.

(52) a. Tyi   **k-il-ä**   **k-bä**.
         PFV   A1-see-TV   A1-RN.self
         'I saw myself.'

   b Tyi   **i**-jats'-ä-yob   **i-bä**   jiñi   wiñik-ob.
         PFV   A3-hit-TV-PL   A3-RN.self   DET   man-PL
         'The men hit each other.'
         'The men hit themselves.'

While transitive objects are generally free to undergo fronting for topic or focus, this is impossible with the reflexive, suggesting a very tight relation between the verb stem and the reflexive stem.

4.5 Constituent order

As we have seen above, Ch'ol is a head-marking language: grammatical relations are marked on the predicate via the Set A and Set B morphemes discussed in §4.3 above, and full nominal arguments may be dropped. Full first and second person pronouns are typically used only for emphasis, and generally precede the predicate in topic or focus position. Overt third person nominals follow the basic order of VOS intransitives, VS in intransitives (Vázquez Álvarez 2002). Though transitives with two overt third person post-verbal arguments are rare in naturally occurring discourse, examples are available. A transitive is given in (53a) and an intransitive in (53b).

(53) a. Tyi   i-ña'-tyä   pañämil   kixtyaño.
         PFV   A3-know-DTV   world   people
         'The people understood (lit.: knew the world).' {D.175}

   b. Ta-x   lajm-i   jiñi   x-ñek.
         PFV-already   die-ITV   DET   CL-ñek
         'The *xñek* died.' {D.30}

In Coon 2010c I propose that predicate-initial order in Ch'ol is the result of fronting of the phrasal predicate to a position above the subject. VSO order is also possible for transitives, argued in Coon 2010c to be the result of remnant VP movement. Clemens and Coon (2016), building on Clemens 2014, argue for the possibility of a head movement analysis for VSO, with prosodic incorporation of the object post-syntactically for VOS.

Though predicate-initial order is basic in discourse neutral contexts, both subjects and objects can be fronted to pre-verbal topic and focus positions (see Aissen 1992 for a discussion of topic and focus in Tsotsil, and Coon 2010c for more examples from Ch'ol). All six possible orders of subject, verb, and object are thus possible. Examples in (54) are from naturally occurring text. There is no specific topic or focus morphology in Ch'ol, as there is in some Mayan languages. The enclitic *=i* (discussed above) frequently appears on fronted material, though it is not obligatory, and is also possible on post-verbal nominals.

(54) a. Pero   kome   **joñoñ**   aläl-oñ-tyo . . .
     but   because 1PRON child-B1-still
     'But because I was still a child. . .' {B.25}

   b. Entonses **jiñi me'** ta' y-il-ä-yoñ-lojoñ.
     and.so   DET deer PFV A3-see-DTV-B1-PL.EXCL
     'The deer saw us$_{EXCL}$.' {D.27}

   c. **Yambä** tyi i-tyaj-a   ts'i'.
     other   PFV A3-find-TV dog
     'It was another that the dog had found.' {E.95}

Unlike many other Mayan languages (and many ergative-patterning languages more generally), no special antipassive or agent focus construction is used in contexts in which the external or ergative-marked argument is extracted for focus, relativization, or wh-questions, illustrated by the transitive form in (55); see Coon et al. 2014 on Ch'ol and Aissen 2017 for discussion.

(55) **Aj-Maria** tyi i-juch'-u   ixim.
     CL-Maria PFV A3-grind-TV corn
     '*Maria* ground corn.'

4.6 Negation

Ch'ol has two main negative forms, *mach* and *ma'añ*. In the case of verbal predicates, the former is typically used with stative clauses which do not take one of the aspect markers, while the latter is used when aspect markers appear, as shown in (56).

(56) a. **Mach** k-om   sa'.
     NEG   A1-want *pozol*
     'I don't want *pozol*.'

   b. **Ma'añ**   mi   i-majl-el tyi klase.
     NEG.EXIST IPFV A3-go-NML PREP class
     'She doesn't go to class.'

As the gloss in (56b) suggests, the form *ma'añ* is most likely bimorphemic – a contraction of the negative *mach* and the existential/locative *añ* (see §3.4); see Coon 2006; Vázquez Álvarez 2011.

4.7 Second position clitics

Ch'ol has a number of second position clitics, shown in Table 23.21 (see also Vázquez Álvarez 2002). While Ch'ol -*ix* can be translated into English as 'already', it is more like

TABLE 23.21 SECOND POSITION CLITICS

-ix	'already'
-äch, -ku	affirmative (AFFIRM)
-tyo	'still, yet'
-ba	interrogative (Q)
-bi	reportative (REP)
-ik	irrealis (IRR)
-ka	dubitative (DUB)
-me	"predictive"

(Vázquez Álvarez 2002)

its Spanish counterpart *ya*, which Koike (1996:267) describes as "a reflector of aspect as well as a discourse marker that can serve to transmit an emotional intensity about designated information and to create cohesion in the discourse." I gloss it alternately as 'already' or simply as 'CL'. Textual examples of the clitics *-ix* and *-äch* are given in (57).

(57) a. Porke   jiñ-**ix**   jap-lembal-ob   ñoj   p'umpuñ-ob-**ix**.
        because   DET-CL   drink-liquor-PL   very   poor-PL-CL
        'Because those who drink liquor are very poor indeed.' {B.125}

   b. Pero   solo   dyos   y-ujil   mi   muk'-**äch**   k-cha'   tyaj
      but   only   god   A3-know   if   IPFV-AFFIRM   A1-again   find
         jiñi   k-wakax. . .
         DET   A1-cow
      'But only god knows if I'll again have cows . . . ' {C.63–64}

   c. Añ-**äch-ix**   juñ-kojty   wa'li.
      EXIST-AFFIRM-already   one-CLF.animal   now
      'Now there's already one (animal).' {C.65}

The clitics *-äch* and *-ku* are both used in affirmations. Ch'ol does not have a single word that translates to 'yes'. Instead, the appropriate aspect marker combines with *-ku*: *tsa'-ku*, *mu-ku*, *choñkol-ku* (PRFV-AFFIRM, IMPF-AFFIRM, and PROG-AFFIRM, respectively).

The clitic *-tyo* can be translated fairly straightforwardly to English 'still' or 'yet'. The clitic *-ba* may be used in interrogative constructions, though as noted above the difference between interrogative and declarative sentences is frequently marked only by intonation. The clitic *-bi* is found throughout narratives and indicates reported or non-first-hand information. The irrealis clitic *-ik*, glossed 'subjunctive' in Vázquez Álvarez 2002, is found in various contexts including with counterfactual conditionals and with negation in the Tumbalá dialect. The 'dubitative' *-ka* is used to express uncertainty (Vázquez Álvarez 2002:157). Finally, Vázquez Álvarez lists the clitic *-me* as the 'predictive', which he writes gives information about "warning, exclamation, or surprise".

In a simple declarative sentence, the clitic will attach to the aspect marker in the case of an eventive predicate like (58a), and directly to the predicate in an aspectless stative construction, as in (58b). Recall that the perfective and imperfective aspect markers *mi* and *tyi* have larger CVC allomorphs (see Table 23.7 above), which must be used when clitics are hosted. In some cases these aspect markers are contracted with -VC clitics, for example: *ta'-äch* → *täch*; *ta'-ix* → *tax*; *muk'-ix* → *mux*. The example in (58a) also shows that the clitics do not attach to topicalized or focused NPs. The clitics also do not attach to fronted wh-words.

(58) a. Jiñi   wiñik   mux   i-majl-el   tyi   cholel.
        DET   man   IPFV.already A3-go-NML   PREP   field
        'He's going to the field already.'

    b. Chañ-ety-**ix**.
       tall-B2-already
       'You're tall already.'

5 COMPLEX STRUCTURES

5.1 Complex predicates and adverbial modification

5.1.1 Secondary predicates

Depictive secondary predicates in Ch'ol appear immediately before the main predicate and may contribute meanings related to: physical state or condition; role, function, or stage of life; quantity; and manner (Vázquez Álvarez 2002:229). Secondary predicates (italicized in (59)) are always optional, and give additional information about one of the arguments of the clause. This argument is referred to as the "controller" of the secondary predicate (Schultze-Berndt and Himmelmann 2004). The primary predicate appears in its regular inflected form. As shown in (59b), the secondary predicate may optionally show Set B morphology co-indexing the controlling argument of the primary predicate.

(59) a. *Buch-ul*   tyi   i-juch'-u   ixim.
        seated-STAT   PFV   A3-grind-TV   corn
        'She ground corn seated.'

    b. *Tyij-ik-ña-(yoñ)*   tyi   majl-i-**yoñ**.
       happy-AFFIRM-AFFIRM-B1   PFV   go-ITV-B1
       'I went happily.'

    c. *Ñoty-ñoty-ña*   mi   i-lets-el   majl-el   tyi   tye'   jiñi
       stick-stick-AFFIRM   IPFV   A3-ascend-NML   go-NML   PREP   tree   DET
       x-ch'ejku.
       CL-woodpecker
       'The woodpecker goes up the tree (sticking to it).' {Aulie and Aulie 1978:83}

Vázquez Álvarez (2002) demonstrates that secondary predicates in Ch'ol, like those in (59), belong to the same clause as the primary predicate. First, fronted arguments must appear before the secondary predicate. If they appear between the primary and secondary predicates, as with the first person pronoun in (60a), a biclausal interpretation is forced; Vázquez Álvarez cites prosodic evidence for this. Second, second position clitics, like the irrealis in (60b), attach to the secondary predicate. Finally, negation appears before the secondary predicate, and can have scope over the entire clause, as in (60c).[6]

(60) a. Buch-ul-oñ.   Joñoñ tyi   k'oty-i-yoñ.
      seated-STAT-B1 PRON1 PFV arrive.there-ITV-B1
      'I'm seated. I arrived.' {Vázquez Álvarez 2002:231}

   b. Buch-ul-**ik**   tyi   k'oty-i   aj-Pekro. . .
      seated-STAT-IRR PFV arrive.there-ITV CL-Pedro
      'If Pedro had arrived seated . . . ' {Vázquez Álvarez 2002:235}

   c. **Ma'añ**   buch-ul   tyi   k'oty-i   aj-Pekro.
      NEG.EXIST seated-STAT PFV arrive.there-ITV CL-Pedro
      'Pedro didn't arrive seated.' {Vázquez Álvarez 2002:236}

All core arguments – intransitive subjects and transitive subjects and objects – may control the secondary predicate. As shown by the forms in (61), where the primary predicate has two potential controllers, Set B person marking on the secondary predicate disambiguates. If there is no Set B person marking on the secondary predicate, there seems to be a preference for the internal (Set B) argument to be the controller, though more work is needed here.

(61) a. Buch-ul-**ety**   tyi   k-tyaj-a-**yety**.
      seated-STAT-B2 PFV A1-find-TV-B2
      'I found you (while you were) seated.'

   b. Ch'ijyem-**oñ** tyi   **k**-tyaj-a-yety.
      sad-B1   PFV A1-find-TV-B2
      'I found you (while I was) sad.'

Secondary predicates may consist of any stative predicate. They may include positionals in their stative -*Vl* forms (§3.5); nominal or adjectival predicates; affectives (see Vázquez Álvarez 2011); and other predicates discussed more in Vázquez Álvarez 2002 and in §3.4 above. Like other statives, the secondary predicate never appears with aspect morphology or with the vocalic "theme vowel" suffixes discussed in §3.3.

5.1.2 CVC adverbs

Though likely not a true instance of a complex predicate construction, I nonetheless include a discussion of a certain type of adverbial modification here. A class of CVC roots may appear immediately preceding the root (after the Set A marking, when present), as in (62). Some examples are given in Table 23.22.

TABLE 23.22 ADVERBIAL PARTICLES

lu'	'completely, all'
cha'	'again'
bele	'continuously, always'
weñ	'well, thoroughly, many'
wa'	'quickly'

(62) a. Tyi i-**lu'** k'ux-u i-waj.
PFV A3-all eat-TV A3-tortilla
'She ate all her tortillas.'

b. Nuebamente choñkol k-**cha'** tyech yambä k-e'tyel.
newly PROG A1-again begin other A1-work
'I'm beginning new work again.' {C.37}

Vázquez Álvarez (2002) discusses the fact that many roots which appear in secondary predicate constructions (in their stative forms) can also appear in their bare root forms in this immediately pre-root position. For instance, positional roots may appear here; more work is needed on semantic differences between these two constructions, though it seems that noncompositional meanings may arise when roots appear internal to the stem, as in (63b).

(63) a. **Buch-ul** mi k-wäy-el.
seated-STAT IPFV A1-sleep-NML
'I sleep sitting up.'

b. Mi k-**buch** wäy-el.
PFV A1-seated sleep-NML
'I sleep sitting up.'

5.2 Relative clauses

Ch'ol relative clauses are marked with the morpheme *-bä* (a borrowing from the Mixe-Zoquean language Zoque (Martínez Cruz 2007)), which appears as a second position clitic, attached to the first element of the relative clause. As the forms in (64) illustrate, both ergative (Set A) and absolutive (Set B) arguments may be relativized with no special antipassive or agent focus marking on the predicate (compare discussions in Aissen 1999; Stiebels 2006).

(64) a. Tyi chäm-i abi **jiñi x-'ixik** [ta'-**bä**
PFV die-ITV yesterday DET CL-woman PFV-REL
i-käñ-tyä-yoñ che' x-k'aläl-oñ-tyo].
A3-care.for-DTV-B1 when CL-girl-B1-still
'The woman who took care of me when I was a girl died yesterday.'

b. Tyi chäm-i abi **jiñi x-'ixik** [ta'-**bä**
PFV die-ITV yesterday DET CL-woman PFV-REL
j-käñ-tyä che' x-k'aläl-oñ-tyo].
A1-care.for-DTV when CL-girl-B1-still
'The woman who I took care of when I was a girl died yesterday.'

Because nominals are not marked with morphological case, and third person Set B agreement is null, this results in potential ambiguity in relative clauses with two third person arguments, discussed at length in a processing study by Clemens et al. (2015).

(65) Tyi   och-i   tyi   y-otyoty   aj-Maria   **jiñi**   **lukum**   [ta'-bä
     PFV   enter-ITV   PREP   A3-house   CL-Maria   DET   snake   PFV-REL
           i-k'ux-u   ts'i'].
           A3-bite-TV   dog
     'The snake that bit a dog entered Maria's house.'
     'The snake that a dog bit entered Maria's house.'

While relative clauses most often follow the head noun, they may also precede it, as shown by the textual example from Martínez Cruz 2007. This is unlike most other Mayan languages, where relative clauses obligatorily follow the head. Martínez Cruz 2007 attributes this again to contact with Zoque.

(66) . . . che'   bajche'   [choñkol-**bä**   i-kol-el]   **uj.**
             so   how   PROG-REL   A3-grow-NML   moon
     '. . . like the waxing moon' {T.17/L.51}

5.3 Complement clauses

Embedded declarative clauses in Ch'ol may be introduced with the complementizer *che'* 'that' as in (67). Basic order in the embedded clause is still VOS/VS, though as in main clauses, both subject and object can front within the embedded clause to a preverbal position. Embedded clauses may also be introduced with *cha'añ*, 'because' or 'in order to', and embedded *if*-clauses and conditionals are introduced with the complementizer *mi*.

(67) Tyi   j-k'el-e   [che'   tyi   i-ch'il-i   ja'as   jiñi   x-k'aläl].
     PFV   A1-watch-TV   that   PFV   A3-fry-ITV   banana   DET   CL-girl
     'I saw that the girl fried bananas.'

Aspectless or non-finite embedded clauses are discussed at length in Coon 2013 and Vázquez Álvarez 2013 and for this reason I discuss them only briefly here. Transitive and intransitive embedded clauses are shown in (68). In both embedded clauses, there is a control relationship between the embedded and matrix subjects. Interestingly, the Set A marker is obligatory on the embedded transitive clause in (68a) (what Vázquez Álvarez 2013 terms a "less finite clause", because it appears with person marking, but with no aspect), but impossible on the embedded intransitive in (68b). Coon (2013) argues that aspectless embedded clauses are nominalizations.

(68) a. **K**-om   [**k**-mek'-ety].
        A1-want   A1-hug-B2
        'I want to hug you.'
     b. **K**-om   [wäy-el].
        A1-want   sleep-NML
        'I want to sleep.'

The generalization is that full embedded transitives must appear with Set A marking, which, in an aspectless embedded clause, must be coreferential with the matrix subject (otherwise a fully finite embedded form is used). Apparent embedded transitives with no Set A marking, like the one in (69), are restricted to clauses with bare non-referential objects (cf. incorporation antipassives in §4.4.4 above).

(69) **K**-om   [wuts'   (*jiñi)   pisil].
    A1-want   wash   DET   clothes
    'I want to clothes-wash.'

Finally, note that while absolutive/Set B marking is impossible in non-finite embedded clauses in some Mayan languages (see e.g. England 2013 on Mam), this is not the case for Ch'ol, as shown by examples like (68a). Building on the analysis in Legate 2008, Coon et al. (2014) attribute this difference to a difference in the way that internal arguments are licensed across Mayan languages. Verbs of motion, directionals, and auxiliary constructions are not discussed here for reasons of space, but see Vázquez Álvarez 2011:ch. 13.

NOTES

*   I would like to express my deepest gratitude to the many Ch'ol speakers and scholars with whom I have had the pleasure of working over the past ten years. I am indebted to the entire Vázquez Vázquez family for their hospitality and kindness, and especially Matilde, Irineo, María Asunción, Hermelinda, Dora, and Julio. Many thanks to Morelia and Maria de Jesús Vázquez Martínez and to Doriselma Gutiérrz Gutiérrez. Special thanks are due to Juan Jesús Vázquez Álvarez and Nicolás Arcos López for sharing insights and work with me, and to the volume editors for helpful feedback and questions. Thanks to Cora Lesure and Rebecca Hoff for editorial and formatting help. *Wokox awäläl!*

   Portions of this work appear in the unpublished appendix to my dissertation (Coon 2010a). This work was supported by an FRQSC Nouveaux-Chercheurs grant.

1   Some authors describe the Ch'ol CVjC roots as containing a "*j* infix" (Vázquez Álvarez 2002; Gutiérrez Sánchez 2004), connected to passivizing -*j* suffixes in languages like Tseltal and Tojol-abal (Roberto Zavala, p.c.; see also Campbell 2000). In previous work, I have analyzed this as a vowel quality alternation, rather than an infix (Coon to appear). It is not obvious that competing analyses are relevant to the actual phonetic realization of *Vj* vowels, and I leave this as a topic for future work.

2   In the glosses I include epenthetic glides together with other morphemes (usually the Set B morphemes), and do not parse them out separately. With the exception of phrase-final enclitics, I simply use a dash rather than '=' to indicate clitics, as the status of some elements is less clear. Unless otherwise noted, Ch'ol data comes from fieldnotes collected in Chiapas, Mexico. Citations which include a letter followed by a number (e.g. B.73) are from transcribed narratives, which can be found in Coon 2004.

3   The Proto-Mayan applicative is proposed to be *-*b'e* (see Mora-Marín 2003 and works cited therein). I follow Vázquez Álvarez (2002) in parsing out these forms into an applicative and status suffixes, -*b-e* and -*b-eñ*, to show the uniform morphological behavior of derived/non-root transitives.

4   This example comes from the Tumbalá dialect, in which *woli* (rather than *choñkol*) marks the progressive. *Woli* and *choñkol* appear to have identical syntactic behavior.

5   Note that here we find the -*Vñ* form in both nonperfectives and perfectives. Word-finally and before the Set B morpheme we find simply -*V* in the perfective.

6   The negative morpheme *mach* is also possible in (60c). As discussed in section 4.6 above, *mach* typically negates aspectless stative predicates, while *ma'añ* negates clauses with aspect marking. When *mach* is used in place of *ma'añ* in (60c) the reading becomes 'Pedro arrived not seated' – that is, the negation scopes only over the secondary predicate.

REFERENCES

Aissen, Judith. 1992. "Topic and focus in Mayan." *Language* 68: 43–80.

Aissen, Judith. 1997. "On the syntax of obviation." *Language* 73: 705–69.

Aissen, Judith. 1999. "Agent focus and inverse in Tzotzil." *Language* 75: 451–85.

Aissen, Judith. 2017. "Correlates of ergativity in Mayan." In *Oxford handbook of ergativity*, ed. by Jessica Coon, Diane Massam, and Lisa Travis. New York: Oxford University Press.

Arcos López, Nicolás. 2009. "Los tres sistemas de clasificadores en la lengua ch'ol." Master's thesis, CIESAS, México.

Arcos López, Nicolás. 2011. "Las clases nominales en Ch'ol Tumbalteco." In *Proceedings of formal approaches to Mayan linguistics*, ed. by Kirill Shklovsky, Pedro Mateo Pedro, and Jessica Coon. MIT Working Papers in Linguistics, vol. 63.

Attinasi, John. 1973. "Lak T'an: a grammar of the Chol (Mayan) word." PhD diss., University of Chicago.

Aulie, Wilbur, and Evelin Aulye. 1978. *Diccionario Ch'ol-Español, Español-Ch'ol*. México: Summer Institute of Linguistics.

Bennett, Ryan. 2016. "Mayan phonology." *Language and Linguistic Compass* 10: 469–514.

Campbell, Lyle. 2000. "Valency-changing derivations in K'iche'." In *Changing valency: Case studies in transivity*, ed. R.M.W. Dixon and Alexandra Aikhenvald, 236–81. Cambridge: Cambridge University Press.

Clemens, Lauren Eby and Jessica Coon. 2016. "Deriving verb-initial word order in Mayan." Ms. SUNY Albany and McGill University.

Clemens, Lauren Eby. 2014. "Prosodic noun incorporation and verb-initial syntax." Doctoral diss., Harvard University, Cambidge, MA.

Clemens, Lauren Eby, Jessica Coon, Pedro Mateo Pedro, Adam Morgan, Maria Polinsky, Gabrielle Tandet, and Matt Wagers. 2015. "Ergativity and the complexity of extraction: A view from Mayan." *Natural Language and Linguistic Theory* 33: 417–67.

Coon, Jessica. 2004. "Roots and words in Chol (Mayan): a distributed morphology approach." BA thesis, Reed College.

Coon, Jessica. 2006. "Existentials and negation in Chol (Mayan)." In *CamLing: proceedings of the fourth university of Cambridge postgraduate conference in language research*, ed. by Charles Chang, Esuna Dugarova, Irene Theodoropoulou, Elina Vilar Beltrán, and Edward Wilford, 51–8. Cambridge: Cambridge Institute of Language Research.

Coon, Jessica. 2009. "Interrogative possessors and the problem with pied-piping in Chol." *Linguistic Inquiry* 40: 165–75.

Coon, Jessica. 2010a. "Complementation in Chol (Mayan): a theory of split ergativity." PhD diss., MIT, Cambridge, MA.

Coon, Jessica. 2010b. "Rethinking split ergativity in Chol." *International Journal of American Linguistics* 76: 207–53.

Coon, Jessica. 2010c. "VOS as predicate fronting in Chol." *Lingua* 120: 354–78.

Coon, Jessica. 2012. "Split ergativity and transitivity in Chol." *Lingua* 122: 241–56.

Coon, Jessica. 2013. *Aspects of split ergativity*. Cambridge: Oxford University Press.

Coon, Jessica. To appear. "Little-v agreement and templatic morphology in Chol." *Syntax.*

Coon, Jessica, Pedro Mateo Pedro, and Omer Preminger. 2014. "The role of case in A-bar extraction asymmetries: Evidence from Mayan." *Linguistic Variation* 14: 179–242.

Coon, Jessica, and Omer Preminger. 2009. "Positional roots and case absorption." In *New perspectives in Mayan linguistics: Proceedings of SSILA 2008 (The society for the study of indigenous languages of the Americas)*, ed. by Heriberto Avelino, Jessica Coon, and Elisabeth Norcliffe, 35–58. Cambridge: MIT Working Papers in Linguistics.

Craig, Colette Grinevald. 1977. *The structure of Jacaltec.* Austin: University of Texas Press.

Danziger, Eve. 1996. "Split intransitivity and active-inactive patterning in Mopan Mayan." *International Journal of American Linguistics* 62: 379–414.

Dixon, R.M.W. 1979. "Ergativity." *Language* 55: 59–138.

Dryer, Matthew S. 1986. "Primary objects, secondary objects, and antidatives." *Language* 62: 808–45.

England, Nora C. 1983. *A grammar of Mam, a Mayan language.* Austin: University of Texas Press.

England, Nora C. 2001. *Introducción a la gramática de los idiomas Mayas.* Guatemala: Cholsamaj.

England, Nora C. 2004. "Adjectives in Mam." In *Adjective classes: A cross-linguistic typology*, ed. R.M.W. Dixon and Alexandra Y. Aikhenvald, 125–46. Oxford: Oxford University Press.

England, Nora C. 2013. "Cláusulas con flexión reducida en mam." In *Estudios sintácticos en lenguas de Mesoamérica*, ed. by Enrique L. Palancar and Roberto Zavala, 277–303. Mexico: CIESAS.

Freeze, Ray. 1992. "Existentials and other locatives." *Language* 68: 553–95.

Gutiérrez Sánchez, Pedro. 2004. "Las clases de verbos intransitivos y el alineamiento agentivo en el chol de Tila, Chiapas." MA thesis, CIESAS, México.

Gutiérrez Sánchez, Pedro, and Roberto Zavala. 2005. "Chol and Chontal: Two Mayan languages of the agentive type." Paper presented at *The Typology of Stative-Active Languages*, Max Planck Institute for Evolutionary Anthropology, Leipzig, Germany.

Haviland, John B. 1981. Sk'op sotz'leb: El Tzotzil de San Lorenzo Zinacantán. Mexico City: UNAM.

Haviland, John B. 1994. "Te xa setel xulem" [The buzzards were circling] – categories of verbal roots in (Zinacantec) Tzotzil." *Linguistics* 32: 691–741.

INEA. 1992. Diccionario Español – Ch'ol, Chol – Español. México: INEA.

Josserand, Kathryn J., and Nicholas A. Hopkins. 2001. "Chol ritual language." Technical report, Foundation for the Advancement of Mesoamerican Studies (FAMSI).

Kaufman, Terrence. 1971. "Tzeltal phonology and morphology." In *University of California publications in linguistics, 61.* Berkeley: University of California Press.

Kaufman, Terrence, and William M. Norman. 1984. "An outline of proto-Cholan phonology, morphology, and vocabulary." In *Phoneticism in Mayan hieroglyphic writing*, ed. by John S. Justeson and Lyle Campbell, 77–166. Albany: Institute for Mesoamerican Studies, State University of New York.

Koike, Dale A. 1996. "Functions of the adverbial *ya* in Spanish narrative discourse." *Journal of Pragmatics* 25: 267–79.

Koob Schick, Hildegard María. 1979. "Fonología del Chol de Salto de Agua, Chiapas." *Licenciatura* thesis, Escuela Nacional de Antropología e Historia.

Larsen, Tomas W., and William M. Norman. 1979. "Correlates of ergativity in Mayan grammar." In *Ergativity: towards a theory of grammatical relations*, ed. by Frans Plank, 347–70. London/New York: Academic Press.

Law, Danny, John Robertson, and Stephen Houston. 2006. "Split ergativity in the history of the Ch'olan branch of the Mayan language family." *International Journal of American Linguistics* 72: 415–50.

Legate, Julie Anne. 2008. "Morphological and abstract case." *Linguistic Inquiry* 39: 55–101.

Lois, Ximena, and Valentina Vapnarsky. 2003. Polyvalence and flexibility of root classes in Yukatekan Mayan languages, vol. 47 of LINCOM Studies in Native American Linguistics. Munich: LINCOM EUROPA.

Lois, Ximena, and Valentina Vapnarsky. 2006. "Root indeterminacy and polyvalence in Yukatekan Mayan languages." In *Lexical categories and root classes in Amerindian languages*, ed. by Ximena Lois and Valentina Vapnarsky, 69–115. Bern: Peter Lang.

López López, Rubén. 2005. "Una aproximación al léxico comparativo del chol de los municipios de Sabanilla, Tila, y Tumbalá, Chiapas." MA thesis, CIESAS, México.

Martínez Cruz, Victoriano. 2007. "Los adjetivos y conceptos de propiedad en chol." MA thesis, CIESAS, México.

Meneses Méndez, Domingo. 1987. "Morfología de los elementos del sintagma nominal de Ch'ol." *Licenciatura* thesis, Programa de Formación Profesional de Etnolingüistas.

Montejo López, Bernabé, Rubén López López, Jorge Guzmán Gutiérrez, Enrique Jiménez Jiménez, and Ernesto Martínez López. 1999. *Na'al ty'an Ch'ol*. Chiapas, México: Gobierno del Estado.

Mora-Marín, David F. 2003. "Historical reconstruction of Mayan applicative and antidative constructions." *International Journal of American Linguistics* 69: 186–228.

Robertson, John. 1980. *The structure of pronoun incorporation in the Mayan verbal complex*. New York: Garland.

Schultze-Berndt, Eva, and Nikolaus P. Himmelmann. 2004. "Depictive secondary predicates in cross-linguistic perspective." *Linguistic Typology* 8: 59–131.

Schumann Gálvez, Otto. 1973. *La lengua Chol de Tila (Chiapas)*. México: UNAM.

Silverman, Daniel. 1997. "Laryngeal complexity in Otomanguean vowels." *Phonology* 14: 235–61.

Stiebels, Barbara. 2006. "Agent focus in Mayan languages." *Natural Language and Linguistic Theory* 24: 501–70.

Torres Rosales, Fidel. 1974. *Espa-ch'ol*, 2nd edition. Chiapas, M´exico: Talleres Mimeográficos de la Parroquia de San Mateo: Tila, Chiapas.

Tuz Noh, Narciso. 2011. "La semantica y pragmatica del prefijo x- en el idioma Maya Yucateco." In *Proceedings of formal approaches to Mayan linguistics*, ed. by Kirill Shklovsky, Pedro Mateo Pedro, and Jessica Coon. MIT Working Papers in Linguistics, vol. 63.

Vázquez Álvarez, Juan J. 2002. "Morfología del verbo de la lengua chol de Tila Chiapas." MA thesis, CIESAS, México.

Vázquez Álvarez, Juan J. 2011. "A grammar of Chol, a Mayan language." PhD diss., University of Texas, Austin.

Vázquez Álvarez, Juan J. 2013. "Dos tipos de cláusulas no finitas en chol." In *Clases léxicas, posesión y cláusulas complejas en lenguas de Mesoamérica*, ed. by Enrique L. Palancar and Roberto Zavala, 305–38. México: CIESAS.

Warkentin, Viola, and Ruth Brend. 1974. "Chol phonology." *Linguistics* 132: 87–101.

Warkentin, Viola, and Ruby Scott. 1980. *Gramática Ch'ol*. México: Summer Institute of Linguistics.

Zavala, Roberto. 2007. "Inversion and obviation in Mesoamerica." In *Endangered languages*, ed. by Peter Austin and Andrew Simpson, vol. Linguistische Berichte Sonderheft 14, 267–306. Hamburg: Helmut Buske Verlag.

CHAPTER 24

COMPARATIVE MAYA (YUCATEC, LACANDON, ITZAJ, AND MOPAN MAYA)

Charles Andrew Hofling

1 DATA AND SOURCES

The Yucatecan languages began to diversify perhaps a millennium ago and have had repeated contacts with one another since (Hofling 2006a, 2006b, 2013). The first split in this group was Mopan, followed by Itzaj after 1200, Northern Lacandon and Southern Lacandon after 1700, with Yucatec Maya remaining (Kaufman 1991; Hofling 2006b). Lacandons are refugee groups from the Yucatán Peninsula and Petén, Guatemala, that settled in lowland Chiapas largely after 1700 (Palka 2005; Hofling 2014a).

Yucatec Maya has a long history of documentation and written records beginning in the sixteenth century (see Hanks 2010). Modern general descriptions of Yucatec begin with Andrade's *A Grammar of Modern Yucatec* in 1955. Robert Blair's dissertation (1964) provides a valuable overview of morphosyntax, and Blair and Vermont Salas's pedagogical texts (1965, 1967) provide a wealth of information on phonology and morphosyntax. More recently there have been many studies on more specific topics including word order (Durbin and Ojeda 1978a; Gutiérrez-Bravo and Monforte 2008; Skopeteas and Verhoeven 2011); antipassives (Bricker 1978a); focus constructions (Bricker 1978b; Briceño Chel 2002; Gutiérrez-Bravo and Monforte 2011); split ergativity (Bricker 1981a; Krämer and Wunderlich 1999; Bohnemeyer 2004); negation (Durbin and Ojeda 1978b); transitivity (Durbin and Ojeda 1982); subordinate constructions (Durbin, Hofling and Ojeda 1992); possession (Lehmann 2002); time reference (Bohnemeyer 1998, 2002); and imperatives and related constructions (Hofling and Ojeda 1994). Bricker et al. (1998) provide an extensive dictonary of Yucatec as well as a detailed overview of lexical morphology. Ayres and Pfeiler (1997) provide detailed information on verbs. Hanks (1984) provides a grammatical sketch of Yucatec, as do Kaufman (1991) and Lehmann (2014). Pfeiler (1995) and Blaha Pfeiler and Hofling (2006) also provide information on dialectal variation.

Grammatical information on Lacandon is much more limited. Una Çanger (1970a) compiled a monosyllable dictionary of over 1,400 entries of the Southern Lacandon dialect spoken in San Quintín, Chiapas, Mexico, and provided a brief grammatical sketch (1970b); Bergqvist (2008) wrote a dissertation on Southern Lacandon temporal reference with a grammatical overview; and Hofling (2014a) produced a dictionary of the Southern Lacandon dialect of Lacanjá with an overview of phonology and lexical morphology. Tozzer (1907) provided some lexical and textual documentation of Northern Lacandon; Roberto Bruce (1968) produced a grammatical sketch of Northen Lacandon and recorded extensive collections of texts (1974, 1976, 1979). Davis (1978) provides additional textual and lexical information on Northern Lacandon; and Cook and Carlson (2004) recorded Northern Lacandon terms for flora and fauna. Based on these sources Hofling (2007) produced a lexical database of over 4,000 Northern Lacandon lexical entries.

Regarding Itzaj, Schumann (1971) produced an early sketch and word list of Itzaj of San José, Petén, and an expanded grammar in 2000. Hofling (1991, 1997; with Tesucún 2000) and Hofling and Tesucún (2000) provide extensive documentaton of Itzaj Maya texts, lexicon and grammar. The Itzaj community of the Academia de Lenguas Mayas de Guatemala (ALMG) also produced a descriptive grammar in 2001.

Ulrich and Ulrich (1976) produced a bilingual dictionary of Mopan of San Luís, Petén, and an overview of Mopan verbs (1978). Schumann (1997) produced a grammatical sketch of Mopan, as did the ALMG (2001b), which also published a Mopan vocabulary (2003). Hofling (2011a) produced a trilingual Mopan-Spanish-English dictionary with an overview of phonology and morphology.

Several notable studies of comparative Yucatecan have appeared, including Fisher (1973); Kaufman (1991); the comparative vocabulary of Oxlajuuj Keej Maya' Ajtz'iib' (2003), which includes Mopan and Itzaj; comparative verbal morphology (MacLeod 1983; Bricker 1986; Hofling 2006b); root polyvalency (Lois and Vapnarsky 2006); and comparative historical morphology and lexicon (Hofling 2004, 2006a, 2006b; 2008).

2 PHONOLOGY

2.1 Phonemic inventory

All Yucatecan Mayan languages share essentially the same consonant inventory except that in Southern Lacandon /l/ has changed to /r/.

Consonants

	Labial	Dental	Alveolar	Palatal	Velar	Glottal
Stops						
Voiceless	p	t			k	'
glottal	p'	t'			k'	
voiced	b'	(d')[1]			(g)	
Affricates						
voiceless			tz	ch		
glottal			tz'	ch'		
Fricatives						
voiceless			s	x		j[2]
Vibrants			l, r[3]			
Nasals		m n				
Semivowels	w			y		

The vowel systems are more variable. Yucatec Maya and Southern Lacandon have very similar inventories.

Vowels

Yucatec Maya

	Front	Central	Back
High	i ii íi		u uu úu
Mid	e ee ée		o oo óo
Low		a aa áa	

Southern Lacandon

	Front	Central	Back
High	i ii íi		u uu úu
Mid	e ee ée	ä	o oo óo
Low		a aa áa	

As indicated in the charts, the only difference in the vowel inventories is that Southern Lacandon has a mid central vowel /ä/, which corresponds to Yucatec Maya /a/. Both Yucatec Maya and Southern Lacandon have a tone distinction on long vowels: high tone is marked by an accent, low tone is unmarked. High tone in Yucatec is a reflex of Proto-Yucatecan syllables of the shape CVHC (Justeson 1986; Kaufman 1991), where H represents /h/ or /χ/. In Southern Lacandon short /e/ and /o/ have been undergoing merger with /a/ and now occur in very restricted environments (Hofling 2013; see Tables 24.4 and 24.5; cf. §2.4.10).

In contrast, the vowel system in Northen Lacandon, Itzaj, and Mopan is as follows:

Northern Lacandon, Itzaj, and Mopan Maya

	Front	Central	Back
High	i ii		u uu
		ä (ää)	
Mid	e ee		o oo
Low		a aa	

In these languages there is no tonal distinction. Long vowels generally correspond to long high-tone vowels in Yucatec. Short vowels correspond either to long low vowels or short vowels in Yucatec, with the exception of /ä/, which corresponds to /a/ in Yucatec, while /a/ corresponds to /aa/ in Yucatec. /ää/ is a rare sound that appears in some (mostly) onomatopoeic words in Lacandon and Mopan.

As indicated in Table 24.1, there is generally a correspondence among Yucatecan languages with respect to vowel length. Yucatecan reflexes of the Proto-Yucatecan words of the form CVHC have the form CV́VC with a long high-tone vowel. According to Çanger (1970a), Southern Lacandon of San Quintín also has these forms but there are some exceptions. Southern Lacandon of Lacanjá generally has the same forms as Yucatec among older speakers, but younger speakers lack a tonal distinction and simply have long vowels. Northern Lacandon lacks a tonal distinction and shows variation between long and short vowels. In general, Itzaj and Mopan have long vowels in corresponding forms.[4]

Reflexes of Proto-Yucatecan words with plain long vowels are shown in Table 24.2. They appear with a long low tone vowel in Yucatec and Southern Lacandon, mostly short vowels in Northern Lacandon and almost always short vowels in Itzaj and Mopan.

TABLE 24.1 FLORA AND FAUNA OF PROTO-YUCATECAN WITH THE FORM CVhC

	P Yuc	Yuc	S Lac (S Q)	S Lac (Lac)	N Lac	Itzaj	Mopan	Gloss
	CVHC	CV́VC	CV́VC	CV́VC	CVVC	CVVC	CVVC	
a.	*'ohx	'óox	'oox	'óox	'ox	'oox	'oox	'ramon'
b.	*kehj	kéej	keej	kéej	kej	keej	keej	'deer'
c.	*chuhh	chúuj	chúuj	chúuj	chuj	chuj	chuj	'water gourd'
d.	*k'uhm	k'úum	k'úum	k'úum	k'um	k'uum	k'uum	'squash'

TABLE 24.2 FLORA AND FAUNA OF PROTO-YUCATECAN WITH THE FORM CVVC

	P Yuc	Yuc	S Lac (S Q)	S Lac (Lac)	N Lac	Itzaj	Mopan	Gloss
	CVVC	CVVC	CVVC	CVVC	CVC	CVC	CVC	
a.	*'oom	'oom	'oon	'oon	'oon	'om	'on	'avocado'
b.	*p'aak	p'aak	p'aak	p'aak	p'ak	p'ak	p'ak	'tomato'
c.	*'iis	'iis	'iis	'iis	'is	'is	'is	'yam'
d.	*yuuk	yuuk	yuuk	yuuk	yuk	yuk	yuk	'sprocket deer'

TABLE 24.3 PROTO-YUCATECAN *a

	P Yuc	Yuc	S Lac (S Q)	S Lac (Lac)	N Lac	Itzaj	Mopan	Gloss
	*CaC	CaC	CäC	CäC	CäC	CäC	CäC	
a.	*nal	nal	när	när	näl	näl	näl	'corn'
b.	*makal	makal	mäkär	makär	mäkäl	mäkäl	mäkäl	'macal'
c.	*kay	kay	käy	käy	käy	käy	käy	'fish'
d.	*kan	kan	kän	kän	kän	kän	kän	'snake'

TABLE 24.4 PROTO-YUCATECAN *o > *a* IN LACANDON

	P. Yuc	Yuc	S Lac (S Q)	S Lac (Lac)	N Lac	Itzaj	Mopan	Gloss
a.	*lochik	lochik	rachik	rachik		lochik	lochik	'twist'
b.	*xokik	xokik	xakik	xakik	xakik	xokik	xokik	'count'
c.	*ch'otik	ch'otik	ch'atik	ch'atik	ch'atik	ch'otik	ch'otik	'twist'
d.	*b'onik	b'onik	b'anik	b'anik	b'anik	b'onik	b'onik	'paint'

There are a number of changes in short vowels across the Yucatecan branch. As shown in Table 24.3, the short vowel *a* in Proto-Yucatecan remained /a/ in modern Yucatec, but changed to /ä/ in all other Yucatecan languages.[5]

As shown in Table 24.4, Proto-Yucatecan *o* remains /o/ in Yucatec, Itzaj and Mopan, but changed to /a/ in both Northern and Southern Lacandon. The transitive verb forms are given in the incompletive status with the transitive suffix -*ik*.

As shown in Table 24.5, Proto-Yucatecan *e* has largely shifted to /a/ in Southern Lacandon, but generally remains /e/ in the other Yucatecan languages. Northern Lacandon also has some examples of this shift (e.g., [c]).

The short vowels *i and *u have not changed in the modern languages, as shown in Table 24.6.

For some speakers of Southern Lacandon of Lacanjá there is variation between [e] and [ä] as shown in Table 24.7. This seems more common among young speakers.

2.2 Stress

Generally, lexical stress occurs on the first or second syllable of the root and on alternating light syllables (Blair 1964:2–4: Hofling 1997:3; Hofling 2011a:5). Stress occurs on heavy syllables of the shape CV'C or CVVC in all Yucatecan languages (cf. Blair 1964:2–3; Hanks 1984 1:4). In Itzaj phrasal stress occurs on the last syllable of a phonological phrase (Hofling 2000:6–8). In Yucatec and Southern Lacandon, unstressed vowels may be deleted, e.g., Yucatec *kuyilik ub'áaj > kyilk ub'áaj* 's/he sees her/himself' (Hanks

TABLE 24.5 PROTO-YUCATECAN *e > *a* IN SOUTHERN LACANDON

	P. Yuc	Yuc	S Lac	N Lac	Itzaj	Mopan	Gloss
a.	*mechik	mechik	machik	mechik	mechik	mechik	'bend'
b.	*jek'ik	jek'ik	jak'ik	jek'ik	jek'ik	jek'ik	'break'
c.	*tep'ik	tep'ik	tap'ik	tap'ik	tep'ik	tep'ik	'wrap'
d.	*tzelik	tzelik	tzarik	tzelik	tzelik	tzelik	'tilt'

TABLE 24.6 PROTO-YUCATECAN *i AND *u

	P. Yuc	Yuc	S Lac	N Lac	Itzaj	Mopan	Gloss
a.	*chich	chich	chich	chich	chich	chich	'hard'
b.	*chi'	chi'	chi'	chi'	chi'	chi'	'mouth'
c.	*chukik	chukik	chukik	chukik	chukik	chukik	'catch'
d.	*b'ujik	b'ujik	b'ujik	b'ujik	b'ujik	b'ujik	'split'

TABLE 24.7 [e] ~ [ä] IN LACANDON DE LACANJÁ

a.	*k'e'ik*	~	*k'ä'ik*	**'open'**
b.	*jaarew*	~	*jaaräw*	'tepescuintle'
c.	*ka'-b'ej*	~	*ka'-b'äj*	'yesterday'
d.	*rejik*	~	*räjik*	'lasso'

1984 1:4) or Southern Lacandon *kuk'eeyiken* > *kuk'eeyken* 's/he scolds me' (Hofling 2014a:206). See Kidder (2013) for an extensive examination of stress in Yucatec.

2.3 Phonotactics

CVC, CV'C, CVCVC are common root forms (Lehmann 2014). More details are given below in discussing particular root types.

2.4 Phonological processes

Fisher (1973:4–148) provides a useful overview of phonological processes in Yucatecan languages.

2.4.1 /j/ → Ø/V___V

/j/ may be deleted intervocalically, as in Yucatec /najil/ 'casa de' → [nail] (Fisher 1973:169), Itzaj /mejen/ 'small' → [meen] (Hofling 1997); and Mopan /mejen/ 'small' → [meen] (Hofling 2011a).

2.4.2 Non-glottalized stops → [h]

Non glottalized stops may appear as [h] before stops with the same point of articulation as in Yucatec /'inwéettal/ 'my companion' → [ʔinwéehtal] (Fisher 1973:16–17); Northern Lacandon /k/ → [h]/___ k' or k, as in /chäk k'ek'en/ 'peccary' → [chäh k'ek'enan] (Bruce 1968:36); and Mopan /'ok-k'in/ 'afternoon' → [ʔohk'in]] (Hofling 2011a).

2.4.3 Homorganic assimilation of nasals

Nasals may assimilate to following non-nasal consonants as in /kinb'in/ 'I go' →
[kimb'in]; /kintaal/ → [kintaal]; and /kink'áat/ → [kiŋk'áat] in all Yucatecan languages
(Fisher 1973:98).

2.4.4 Final [l]/[r] ~ [h] ~ [Ø]

Final /l/ (or /r/ in Lacandon) alternates with [h] and Ø], as in Yucatec [xíimb'al] ~
[xíimb'ah] 'walk' (Blair 1964:34); Southern Lacandon /che'ir ya'/ 'chewing gum tree'
→ [che'i ya?] (Hofling 2014a); Itzaj /'unajil tzimin/ 'stable' → [?unaji tzimin] (Hofling
1997); and Mopan /p'eel/ 'inanimate' → [p'ee] (Hofling 2011a:5).

2.4.5 /b'/ → [?]/___#

Final /b'/ reduces to [?] as in /xiib'/ 'male' → [ʃii?] in Yucatec (Bricker et al. 1998);
/k'äb'/ 'hand' → [k'ä?] in Southern Lacandon (Hofling 2014a); /lob'/ 'evil' → [lo?] in
Itzaj (Hofling 1997); and /matzab'/ 'eyelash' → [matza?] in Mopan (Hofling 2011a).

2.4.6 Reduplication $C_1VC_2 > C_1V(C_2)C_1VC_2$

Reduplication may indicate intensity or repetition as in *síis* 'cold' > *síisis* 'frigid', *b'al*
'hide' → *b'a'ab'al* 'hide several times' in Yucatec (Bricker et al. 1998:341,378); *chäk*
'red' > *chäkchäk* 'very red' in Southern Lacandon (Hofling 2014a:5); *k'än* 'yellow' >
k'änk'än 'yellowish', and *ch'o'* 'mouse' > *ch'och'otik* 'gnaw completely' in Northern
Lacandon (Bruce 1968:37); *chäk* 'red' > *chächäk* 'rather red' and *chäkchäk* 'very red' in
Itzaj (Hofling 1997:4); and *chäk* 'red' > *chäkchäk* 'very red' in Mopan (Hofling 2011a:6).

2.4.7 Harmonic -VC

There are a number of harmonic -VC suffixes. For example, root intransitive verbs
take a harmonic -VC suffixes in the incompletive status, as in *'aj-al* 'wake up', *'éem-el*
'descend', *b'íix-il* 'harden', *'ok-ol* 'enter', *k'uch-ul* 'arrive' in Yucatec (Bricker et al.
1998); *b'áax-är* 'play', *b'éech-ar* 'lean', *ríik'-ir* 'fly', *'ook-ar* 'enter', and *'úuk'-ur*
'drink' in Southern Lacandon (Hofling 2014a); *'ach'-äl* 'flatten', *wen-el* 'sleep', *tich-il*
'sprout', *'ok-ol* 'enter' and *'uk'-ul* in Itzaj (Hofling 1997); and *'ach'-äl* 'flatten', *'em-el*
'descend', *tiich-il* 'sprout', *'ok-ol* 'enter' and *'uk'-ul* 'drink' in Mopan (Hofling 2011a).

2.4.8 Disharmony of the causative -k(Ú)Un

The causative suffix *-k(Ú)Un* (capital letters indicate morphophonemic representation),
which derives transitive verbs from inchoative, affective and positional stems appears as
-k(ú)un following /a/, /e/ or /i/, but as *-k(í)in* following stems with /o/ or /u/ in Yucatec
(Bricker et al. 1998:336), as in *'ak-kúun-t-ik*, 'settle firmly'; *ch'eb'-kúun-t-ik* 'tilt to one
side'; *chil-kúun-t-ik* 'make lie down'; *'b'och'-kíin-t-ik* 'pucker'; and *juj-kíin-t-ik* 'pro-
tect'. In Southern Lacandon only *-kin* appears, as in *ta'n-kin-t-ik* 'sprinkle lime on'; *'éek'-
kin-t-ik* 'stain'; *to'ch-kin-t-ik* 'make harden; (Hofling 2014a). In Itzaj, either *-kun* or *-kin*
may follow stems with rounded vowels as in *b'ok-kin-t-ik ~ b'ok-kun-t-ik* 'make it smell';

b'utz'-kin-t-ik ~ b'utz'-kun-t-ik 'makes it smoke' (Hofling 2000:28). In Mopan the dishar-monic pattern is like Yucatec as in *b'ak-kun-t-ik* 'make thin'; *b'is-kun-t-ik* 'perforate'; but *b'ok-kin-t-ik* 'make smell' (Hofling 2011a:6).

2.4.9 *CV'C → CV'VC / ___ C, #*

In all Yucatecan languages syllables of the underlying shape CV'C appear as CV'VC with an echo vowel at the end of a word or before a consonant. Yucatec applies this pro-cess more widely and it may also occur before vowels. For example, Yucatec *ka'an* 'sky', *ko'oxtal* 'become wild'; *lu'um* 'earth' but also *lu'utz'ul* 'be folded'; *lo'olo'ox* 'hit in sev-eral places'; *je'elo'* 'there it is' (Bricker et al. 1998). In Itzaj and Mopan this process is more restricted: *ka'an* 'sky' but *ka'nal* 'high' in Itzaj and Mopan (Hofling 2000, 2011a); *na'at* 'understand' but *na'tik* 'understand it' in Itzaj (Hofling 2000:13).

2.4.10 *Unique phonological processes*

There are also processes unique to particular Yucatecan languages. For example, Yucatec has the rule C' → [ʔ]/___C as in /k'éek'eno'ob'/ 'pigs' → [k'éeʔno'ob'] (Fisher 1973:16). Mopan has a diachronic rule ʔl > d' as indicated by the following examples: *ted'o'* 'there' (vs. *te'lo'* in Itzaj); *'ad'o'* 'that one' (vs: *'a'lo'* in Itzaj); and *jed'a'* 'here it is' vs. (*je'la'* as in Itzaj) (Hofling 1997; Hofling 2011a). Lacandon is particularly innovative. As noted above in §2.1 the change of /o/ → [a] except before a glottal stop is complete and the change of /e/ → [a] is advanced. In Northern Lacandon /l/ → [r]/V___ (Bruce 1968:24) while in Southern Lacandon the shift is complete (Hofling 2014a). In both Northern and Southern Lacandon there is a rule of nasal harmony for //-Vl// or //-Vr// suffixes whereby they occur as /-Vn//N___, as in Northern Lacandon *em-en* 'descend'; *kim-in* 'die' (Bruce 1968:37); or in Southern Lacandon *ráam-än* 'sink'; *ween-an* 'sleep'; *'éem-an*, 'descend'; *chíin-in*, 'bend over'; *kóom-an* 'slip', and *chúun-un* 'begin' (Hofling 2014a). Note that the harmonic vowel is /a/ following stems with /ee/ or /oo/. In the Southern Lacandon the reduction /tz/ → [s] is very common as in *tzo'tzer ~ so'ser* 'hair'; *tzeem ~ seem* 'chest' and *tzuub' ~ suub'* 'agouti' (Hofling 2014a).

3 WORD FORMATION AND WORD CLASSES

3.1 Person markers and pronouns

3.1.1 *Person markers*

In all Yucatecan languages person markers (dependent pronouns) occur on nouns, verbs, and adjectives, and are traditionally divided into two sets: Set A prefixes and Set B suf-fixes. Set A is also referred to as the ergative set and Set B the absolutive set.

3.1.1.1 Set A person markers in Yucatecan languages

The Set A person markers are shown in Table 24.8, based on Hofling (2006b:367 with slight modification of Southern Lacandon based on Hofling (2014a).The forms with the semivowels *w-* and *y-* are prevocalic forms. There is some disagreement on whether some of the forms listed as first person exclusive are actually dual forms (Bricker 1986:21; Bruce 1968:48–9).

TABLE 24.8 SET A PERSON MARKERS

	Yucatec	S Lac	N Lac	Itzaj	Mopan
Singular					
1st	in(w)-	in(w)-	in(w)-	in(w)-	in(w)-
2nd	a(w)-	a(w)-	a(w)-	a(w)-	a(w)-
3rd	u(y)-	u(y)- ~ (y-)	u(y)-	u(y)-	u(y)-
Plural					
1st (excl)	k-	ik- ~ in(w)- . . . -o'b'	äk- ~ in(w)- . . . -o'	ki(w)-	ti(w)-
1st (incl)	k- . . . -e'ex	ik- . . . -e'ex	äk- . . . -eex	ki(w)- . . . -e'ex	ti(w)- . . . -e'ex
2nd (excl)		a(w)- . . . -ech-o'b			
2nd (incl)	a(w) . . . -e'ex	a(w) . . . -ech-e'ex	a(w) . . . eex	a(w) . . . -e'ex	a(w) . . . -e'ex
3rd	u(y)-o'ob'	u(y)-o'ob' ~ (y-o'ob')	u(y) . . . -o'	u(y)-o'ob'	u(y)-o'ob'

TABLE 24.9 PRECONSONANTAL MOPAN INTRANSITIVE *TAL* 'COME', *TAN INTAL* 'I AM COMING'

	Singular		Plural
1st	tan in-tal	excl	tan ti-tal
		incl	tan ti-tal-e'ex
2nd	tan a-tal		tan a-tal-e'ex
3rd	tan u-tal		tan u-tal-oo'

TABLE 24.10 PRECONSONANTAL MOPAN INTRANSITIVE *EMEL* 'DESCEND', *TAN INWEMEL* 'I AM DESCENDING'

	Singular		Plural
1st	tan inw-em-el	excl	tan tiw-em-el
		incl	tan tiw-em-el-e'ex
2nd	tan aw-em-el		tan aw-em-el-e'ex
3rd	tan uy-em-el		tan uy-em-el-oo'

Set A person markers always mark subjects of transitive verbs, indicate subjects on intransitive verbs in the incompletive status, and mark possessors on nouns. Examples of Mopan intransitive verbs are shown in Tables 24.9 and 24.10. Following standard orthographic conventions, word-initial glottal stops preceding vowels are not written, as in *tan in-tal* [tan ?in tal].

Examples of Southern Lacandon possessed forms are shown in Table 24.11.

3.1.1.2 Set B person markers in Yucatecan languages

Set B person markers always mark transitive direct objects, mark subjects of intransitive verbs in the completive and dependent statuses, and mark stative subjects with adjectives and nouns. The examples in Table 24.12 are based on Hofling (2006b:374) with slight modification in Southern Lacandon based on Hofling (2014a:10).

Examples in Yucatec for the intransitive verb *'éem*, 'descend' in the completive status are shown in Table 24.13, based on Bricker et al. (1998:401).

Itzaj examples of Set B stative subjects of the adjective *wi'ij* 'hungry' are as shown in Table 24.14 (Hofling 2000:38).

Examples of a Yucatec transitive verb in the durative aspect with a third person singular subject (*u-*) and variable direct objects are shown in Table 24.15, based on Bricker et al. (1998:386).

TABLE 24.11 SOUTHERN LACANDON POSSESSED NOUN *TUUNICH* 'STONE', *INTUUNICH* 'MY STONE'

	Singular			*Plural*
1st	*in-tuunich*	excl		*ik-tuunich ~ 'in-tuunich-o'b'*
		incl		*ik-tuunich-e'x*
2nd	*a-tuunich*	excl		*a-tuunich-(e)ech-o'b*
		incl		*a-tuunich-(e)ech-e'x*
3rd	*u-tuunich*			*u-tuunich-o'b'*

TABLE 24.12 SET B PERSON MARKERS IN YUCATECAN LANGUAGES

	Yucatec	*S Lac*	*N Lac*	*Itzaj*	*Mopan*
Singular					
1st	*-en*	*-(e)en*	*-en*	*-(e)en*	*-(e)en*
2nd	*-ech*	*-(e)ech*	*-ech*	*-(e)ech*	*-(e)ech*
3d	*-Ø*	*-Ø, (-i[j])*	*-Ø, -i(j)*	*-Ø, -i(j)*	*-Ø, -i(j)*
Plural					
1st (excl)	*-o'on*	*-o'n ~ -(e)en-o'b'*	*-oon ~ -eno'*	*-o'on*	*-o'on*
1st (incl)	*-o'on-e'ex*	*-o'ne'x*	*-oon-eex*	*-o'on-e'ex*	*-o'on-e'ex*
2nd (excl)		*-(e)ech-o'b'*			
2nd (incl)	*-e'ex*	*-(e)ech-e'x*	*-eex*	*-e'ex*	*-e'ex*
3rd	*-o'ob'*	*-o'b'*	*-ij-o'*	*-oo'*	*-oo'*

TABLE 24.13 YUCATEC INTRANSITIVE VERB *ÉEMEL* 'DESCEND' IN THE COMPLETIVE STATUS

	Singular			*Plural*	
1st	*éem-Ø-en*	'I descended'	excl	*éem-Ø-o'on*	'we descended'
2nd	*éem-Ø-ech*	'you descended'		*éem-Ø-e'ex*	'you all descended'
3rd	*éem-ij-Ø*	's/he descended'		*éem-Ø-o'ob'*	'they descended'

TABLE 24.14 ITZAJ STATIVE SUBJECTS WITH THE ADJECTIVE *WI'IJ* 'HUNGRY'

	Singular			*Plural*	
1st	*wi'ij-en*	'I am hungry'	excl	*wi'ij-o'on*	'we are hungry'
			incl	*wi'ij-o'on-e'ex*	'we all are hungry'
2nd	*wi'ij-ech*	'you are hungry'		*wi'ij-e'ex*	'you all are hungry'
3rd	*wi'ij-Ø*	's/he is hungry'		*wi'ij-oo'*	'they are hungry'

TABLE 24.15 YUCATEC TRANSITIVE VERB *MUKIK* 'BURY', E.G., *TÁAN U-MUK-IK-EN*, 'S/ HE IS BURYING ME'.

	Singular DO		Plural DO	
a.	táan u-muk-ik-en	's/he is burying me'	táan u-muk-ik-o'on	s/he is burying us'
b.	táan u-mik-ik-ech	's/he is burying you'	táan u-muk-ik-e'ex	s/he is burying you all'
c.	táan u-mik-ik-Ø	's/he is burying her/him/it'	táan u-muk-ik-o'ob'	s/he is burying them'

TABLE 24.16 INDEPENDENT PRONOUNS IN YUCATECAN LANGUAGES

	Yucatec	S Lac	N Lac	Itzaj	Mopan
Singular					
1st	teen	teen	ten	(in=)ten	in=(n)en
2nd	teech	teech	tech	(in=)tech	in=chech
3d	leti'	raj-i'	lati'	la'ayti'	le'ek
Plural					
1st (excl)	to'on	to'n ~ teen-o'b'	to'on ~ ten-o'	(in=)to'on	in=(n)o'on
1st (incl)	to'on-e'ex	t'o'n-e'x	ton-eex	(in=)to'on-e'ex	in=(n)o'on-e'ex
2nd (excl)		teech-o'b'			
2nd (incl)	te'ex	te'x ~ teech-e'x	te'ex	(in=)te'ex	in=che'ex
3rd	leti'-o'ob'	raj-i'-o'b'	lati'-o'	la'ayti'-oo'	le'ek-oo'

TABLE 24.17 INDIRECT OBJECT PRONOUNS IN YUCATECAN LANGUAGES

	Yucatec	S Lac	N Lac	Itzaj	Mopan
Singular					
1st	(ti') teen	teen	ten	ten	ten
2nd	(ti') teech	teech	tech	tech	tech
3d	ti'leti'	ti'	ti'	ti'ij	ti'ij
Plural					
1st (excl)	(ti') to'on	to'n ~ teen-o'b'	to'on ~ teno'	to'on	to'on
1st (incl)	(ti') to'on-e'ex	t'o'n-e'x	ton-eex	to'on-e'ex	to'on-e'ex
2nd (excl)		teech-o'b'			
2nd (incl)	(ti') te'ex	te'x ~ teeche'x	te'ex	te'ex	te'ex
3rd	ti'leti'-o'ob'	ti'-o'b'	ti'-o'	ti'ij-oo'	ti'ij-oo'

3.1.2 Pronouns

3.1.2.1 Independent pronouns

Independent pronouns occur to indicate discourse highlighting such as topicalization and contrastive focus. The set of Yucatecan independent pronouns is shown in Table 24.16.[6]

3.1.2.2 Indirect object pronouns

In Yucatec, Lacandon, and Itzaj indirect object pronouns are identical to independent pronouns, with the exception of the third person. In Mopan all indirect object pronouns are distinct from independent pronouns as shown in Table 24.17.[7]

3.2 Root types

Roots may be categorized as noun roots (N), numeral roots (Num), adjective roots (A), transitive verb roots (T), intransitive verb roots (I), positional roots (P), affective roots (Af)[8], expletive roots (E) and particle roots (Pt).

3.3 Nouns

Noun roots commonly occur in the shapes CVC, CVVC, CV'VC, CV(V)CVC, and CVCV'VC. In Yucatec and Southern Lacandon long vowels may have high or low tone and Yucatec allows the root form CV'VCVC (cf. Blair 1964:46). I follow Bricker et al. (1998:360–1) in subcategorizing root nouns according to their marking when possessed.

3.3.1 Noun classes

3.3.1.1 Plain nouns

Plain nouns without any modifiers often signal indefinite or generic information. They do not change shape when possessed. Examples are shown in Table 24.18.

3.3.1.2 Active verbal nouns

As in other Mayan languages, there is a substantial class of noun roots that refer to actions, categorized as active verbal nouns. These nouns may also function as active verbs with an antipassive value and transitives may be derived from them, generally with the suffix -*t*. A sample of active verbal nouns is given in Table 24.19.

There is a substantial number of active verbal nouns referring to animal and other natural sounds, as shown Table 24.20.

TABLE 24.18 PLAIN NOUNS IN YUCATECAN LANGUAGES

	Yucatec	S Lac	N Lac	Itzaj	Mopan	Gloss
a.	*nal*	*när*	*näl*	*näl*	*näl*	'ear of corn'
b.	*k'úutz*	*k'úutz*	*k'uutz*	*k'uutz*	*k'uutz*	'tobacco'
c.	*iis*	*iis*	*is*	*is*	*is*	'yam'
d.	*b'a'al*	*b'a'r*	*b'a'al*	*b'a'al*	*b'a'al*	'thing'

TABLE 24.19 ACTIVE VERBAL NOUNS IN YUCATECAN LANGUAGES

	Yucatec	S Lac	N Lac	Itzaj	Mopan	Gloss
a.	*meyaj*	*b'eeyaj*	*meyaj*	*meyaj*	*meyaj*	'work'
b.	*che'ej*	*che'j*	*che'ej*	*che'ej*	*che'ej*	'laughter'
c.	*b'o'ol*	*b'o'r*	*b'o'ol*	*b'o'ol*	*b'o'ol*	'payment'
d.	*míis*	*míis*	*miis*	*miis*	*miis*	'sweeping'

TABLE 24.20 ONOMATOPOEIC ACTIVE VERBAL NOUNS

	Yucatec	S Lac	N Lac	Itzaj	Mopan	Gloss
a.	*jaayab'*	*jaayab'*		*jayaab'*	*jayaam*	'yawn'

(Continued)

TABLE 24.20 (CONTINUED)

	Yucatec	S Lac	N Lac	Itzaj	Mopan	Gloss
b.	tuk'ub'	tuk'ub'	tuk'u'	tuk'uu'		'hiccup'
c.	xóob'	xóob'		xoob'	xoob'	'whistle'
d.	je'esíin	ja'tziim	ja'atz'in	jak'syuum ja'tz'iin	jat'isyaam	'sneeze'

3.3.1.3 Nouns with noun class markers

A set of nouns takes noun class proclitics, either the masculine *(a)j= (äj=* in Northern Lacandon) or the feminine *(i)x=* (the reduced forms appear in Yucatec), as in Table 24.21. Many of these refer to flora and fauna. This class is quite robust in the Southern Yucatecan languages Itzaj, Northern Lacandon and Mopan, but less so in Yucatec and hardly occurs in Southern Lacandon. In Northern Lacandon, only the masculine *äj=* is common. There seems to be a semantic basis for the classifier system historically. In Itzaj, for example, *aj=* is prominent with mammals, large birds, destructive insects and water creatures, while *ix=* prominent with medicinal plants, small birds, small insects and worms (Hofling 1997:22).

Noun class markers may also function to indicate the sex of the referent in Yucatec, Mopan, and Itzaj, shown in Table 24.22. This distinction has largely disappeared in Lacandon.

3.3.2 Derived nouns

3.3.2.1 Agentive nouns

Agentive nouns can be derived from antipassive verb forms with a masculine or feminine noun class marker indicating the referent's gender in Yucatec, Itzaj and Mopan, as in Table 24.23. In Northern and Southern Lacandon no gender distinction is indicated. Note that in Southern Lacandon a possessive suffix generally follows the antipassive stem.

3.3.2.2 Adjectival nouns

Similar forms may be derived from adjectives with the classifiers *(a)j=* and *(i)x=*. These are especially prominent Itzaj and Mopan. Some adjectival noun forms lack noun class markers as in Table 24.24 example (d).

3.3.2.3 Instrumental nouns

Instrumental nouns are derived in a variety of ways and are common in Yucatec, Southern Lacandon, and Mopan, but not in Northern Lacandon or in Itzaj, which tend to use agentive nouns instead. The simplist derivation is with a harmonic *-Vb'* (or *-V'*) suffix, which occurs in all Yucatecan languages. Note that in Yucatec, instrumental nouns occur with the feminine noun class marker *x=*. Southern Lacandon may add an additional *-aar* suffix, while Mopan commonly has forms with the suffixes *-b'-eeb'* with transitive roots Table 24.25 examples (c)–(d) and *-l-eeb'* with positional roots, example (a).

TABLE 24.21 FAUNA WITH *(A)J=* AND *(I)X=* IN YUCATECAN LANGUAGES

	Yucateco	S Lac	N Lac	Itzaj	Mopan	Gloss
a.	ch'omak		äj=ch'ämäk	aj=ch'umak	aj=ch'umak	'fox'
b.	chapáat		äj=chup	aj=chupaat	aj=chupaat	'centipede'
c.	x=chimees	kames		ix=chemes	ix=kames	'centipede'
d.	ch'ejun, ch'ujun	ch'urum	äj=ch'ujum	aj=ch'eje', aj=ch'ejun	aj=ch'eje'	'woodpecker'
e.	j=ch'oom	ch'oom	äj=ch'om	aj=ch'om	aj=ch'om	'zopilote'

TABLE 24.22 NOUN CLASS MARKERS INDICATING SEX OF REFERENT IN YUCATECAN LANGUAGES

	Yucatec	S Lac	N Lac	Itzaj	Mopan	Gloss
a.	j=t'eel	t'eer	ter	aj=t'el	aj=t'el	'rooster'
b.	j=miis	(míix)	äj=mis	aj=mis	aj=mis	'(male) cat'
c.	x=miis	(míix)		ix=mis		'female cat'
d.	x=táab'ay	ix=táab'ay	x=Tab-ay	ix=Tab'ay	ix=Tab'ay	'female ghost'

TABLE 24.23 AGENTIVE NOUNS IN YUCATECAN LANGUAGES

	Yucatec	S Lac	N Lac	Itzaj	Mopan	Gloss
a.	j=meyaj	äj=b'eeyajir		aj=meyaj	aj=meyaj	'worker (male)'
b.	j=tz'iib'	äj=tz'iib'ir		aj=tz'iib'	aj=tz'iib'	'writer (male)'
c.	x=tz'iib'	(äj=tz'iib'ir)		ix=tz'iib'		'female writer'
d.	j=koonol	äj=kanin	äj=kan-b'al=b'äj	aj=kon(ol)	aj=kon(ol)	'seller (male)'
e.	x=koonol	(äj=kanin)		ix=kon(ol)		'female seller'

TABLE 24.24 ADJECTIVAL NOUNS IN YUCATECAN LANGUAGES

	Yucateco	S Lac	N Lac	Itzaj	Mopan	Gloss
a.		äj=tuus		aj=tus	aj=tus	'liar (male)'
b.				ix=tus		'liar (female)'
c.	j=ch'óop			aj=ch'oop	aj=ch'oop	'blind man'
d.	b'oox	b'oox		b'ox	b'ox	'negro' 'dear'

TABLE 24.25 INSTRUMENTAL NOUNS IN YUCATECAN LANGUAGES

	Yucatec	S Lac	N Lac	Itzaj	Mopan	Gloss
a.	x=ch'uy-ub'	ch'uy-ub'		ch'uy-ub'	ch'uy-ub' ch'uy-l-eeb'	'hanger' 'hanger'
b.	x=júuy-ub'	júuy-ub'	juy-u'	juy-u'	juy-ub'	'spoon'
c.	x=b'on-ob'	b'an-ab'-aar			b'on-b'-eeb'	'paint'
d.	x=nat'ab'	nät'-äb'-aar			nät'-b'-eeb'	'tightener'

TABLE 24.26 DERIVED VERBAL NOUNS IN YUCATECAN LANGUAGES

	Yucatec	S Lac	N Lac	Itzaj	Mopan	Gloss
a.	tz'aak	tz'aak	tz'ak	tz'ak	tz'ak	'medicine'
b.	paax	paax	pax	pax	pax	'music'
c.	ok'-ol	ook'-ar	ok'-ol	ok'-ol	ok'-ol	'cry'
d.	b'áax-al	b'aax-äl	b'aax-äl	b'ax-äl	b'ax-äl	'joke', 'toy'
e.	tzik-b'al	tzik-b'aar	(tzik-b'al)	tzik-b'al	tzik-b'al	'chat'
f.	k'ub'-een	k'ub'-een		k'ub'-een	(k'ub'-en)	'comission'
g.		ween-an		wen-el	wäy-äl	'sleep'
h.	kux-tal	kux-taar		kux-tal	kux-tal	'life'

3.3.2.4 Derived verbal nouns

Nouns may be derived from verbs of various kinds, most commonly from antipassive stems. In Table 24.26 examples (a), (b) show active verbal nouns derived from transitive roots. The root vowel lengthens in Yucatec and Southern Lacandon. (c) and (d) are examples of active verbal nouns derived with a -VC suffix; (e) and (f) are examples of other derivations of active verbal nouns; (g) shows a verbal noun derived from an intransitive root; and (h) shows a verbal noun derived from a positional root.

3.3.2.5 Nouns derived with -il

Nouns derived with -il (-ir in Southern Lacandon) may serve a number of overlapping functions involving possession (Hofling 1990; Lehmann 2002) and are very common. For example, it may indicate an inanimate possessor as in Mopan 'u-che'-il (a naja), 'the wood of (the house)' or Northern Lacandon jolo'och-il näl 'husk of ear of corn'. It may also indicate 'place of' or 'part of' as in Itzaj ab'äl-il, 'hogplum grove' and mum-il 'tender part of'; Yucatec x='ab'al-il 'grove of plum trees' and Southern Lacandon u-muun-in u-koj 'the tender part of the tooth'. It may also indicate members of a group, as in Southern Lacandon t'úup-ir 'last child of a group' and Itzaj tz'ul-il, 'patron of a group'. It may also indicate beneficiary or goal, as in Mopan che'-il p'is 'stick for measuring' and Itzaj u-'ak'ä'-il tz'on 'night for hunting'. The -il suffix is also used to derive abstract nouns from adjectives as in Yucatec aal-il 'weight' from aal 'heavy' and Mopan chich-il 'hardness' from chich 'hard'.

3.3.2.6 Nouns derived with -el

A number of body parts have the suffix -el when possessed, indicating inalienable possession of the body part. The same noun may appear without the suffix when the body part is detached. For example, in Itzaj, Mopan, and Northern Lacandon b'ak 'bone' is unattached, but b'ak-el is a part of a body. Additional examples are given in Table 24.27.

3.3.2.7 Nouns derived with -VC

Nouns may also be derived with harmonic -VC suffixes. A number of nouns have a -Vl suffix when possessed, as in Table 24.28 (a)–(d). A variety of other -VC also occur in derived nouns as in (e)–(h). Root values are given for Itzaj.

3.3.2.8 Nouns derived with -al

Nouns may also be derived with -al, often with a sense of a collective possessor, as in Table 24.29.

TABLE 24.27 YUCATECAN INALIENABLY POSSESSED NOUNS WITH -el

	Yucatec	S Lac	N Lac	Itzaj	Mopan	Gloss
a.	tzo'otz-el	tzo'tz-el	tzo'otz-el	tzo'otz-el	tzo'otz-el	'hair of'
b.	chooch-el	chooch-er	choch-el	choch-el	choch-el	'intestine of'
c.	k'i'ik'-el	k'i'k'-er	k'ik'-el	k'ik'-el	k'ik'-el	'blood of'
d.	k'i'ix-el	k'i'x-er	k'i'ix-el	k'i'ix-el	k'i'ix-el	'thorn of'
e.	xiich'-el	xiich'-er	xich'-el	xich'-el	xiche'-el	'nerve of'

TABLE 24.28 NOUNS DERIVED WITH -VC SUFFIXES IN YUCATECAN LANGUAGES

	Root	Yucateco	S Lac	N Lac	Itzaj	Mopan	Gloss
a.	NU'UK (N)	nu'uk-ul		nu'uk-ul	nu'uk-ul		'reason of'
b.	CHOOM (N)		choom-on		chom-ol	chom-oom	'bunch of'
c.	XET' (T)		xeet'-er		xet'-el	xet'-el	'piece of'
d.	XOT' (T)	xóot'-ol	xoot'-or		xot'-ol	xot'-ol	'log of'
e.	TZEL (P, T)	tzel-ek			tzel-ek	tzel-ek	'shin'
f.	CHU'M (I)	chúum-uk	chum-uk	chum-uk	chum-uk	chum-uk	'center'
g.	KIS (N)	kis-in	kis-in	kis-in	kis-in	kis-in	'devil'
h.	PIIK (N)	pik-it		pik-it	pik-it		'fan'

TABLE 24.29 NOUNS DERIVED WITH -al IN YUCATECAN LANGUAGES

	Yucatec	S Lac	N Lac	Itzaj	Mopan	Gloss
a.				k'ewel-al	k'ewel-al	'hide of'
b.	ch'i'ib'-al			ch'ib'-al	ch'ib'al	'lineage of'
c.		paak-ar		paak-al		'stack of'
d.	iik'-al	iik'-ar		ik'-al		'wind of'
e.	paal-al		paal-al	paal-al		'child of'

3.3.3 Tone change with possession in Yucatec and Southern Lacandon

In Yucatec and Southern Lacandon there is a class of nouns whose stem vowels appear as long, low tone under possession. For example in Southern Lacandon chúuj 'bottle gourd' appears as chuujir when possessed and tzíimin 'horse' appears as tziimin when possessed. There are a few differences between the two, such as the categorization of 'cotton', shown in Table 24.30 (d).

3.3.4 Noun compounds

There are noun compounds corresponding to many of the categories outlined above in §3.3.1 and §3.3.2 for simple nouns.

3.3.4.1 Plain noun compounds

Compounds that do not have any prefixes or suffixes may be composed by combining a variety of lexical categories, as shown in Table 24.31. For example, (a) nik=te' (N & N;

TABLE 24.30 VOWEL CHANGES UNDER POSSESSION IN YUCATEC AND SOUTHERN LACANDON

	Yucatec		Southern Lacandon		
	Unpossessed	*Possessed*	*Unpossessed*	*Possessed*	
a.	*chúuk*	*chuuk*	*chúuk*	*chuukir*	'charcoal'
b.	*kib'*	*kiib'*	*kib'*	*kiib'*	'wax'
c.	*k'áak'*	*k'aak'*	*k'áak'*	*k'aak'ir*	'fire'
d.	*taman*	*taman*	*tämän*	*taaman*	'cotton'
e.	*xanab'*	*xaanab'*	*xänäb'*	*xaanab'*	'shoe'

TABLE 24.31 PLAIN NOUN COMPOUNDS IN YUCATECAN LANGUAGES

	Yucatec	S Lac	N Lac	Itzaj	Mopan	
a.	*nik=te'*	*nik=te'*	*nik=te'*	*nik=te'*	*nik=te'*	'frangipani'
b.	*éet=k'aab'a'*	*éet=k'aab'a'*		*et=k'ab'a'*	*et=k'ab'a'*	'namesake'
c.	*b'a'al=che'*		*b'a'al=che'*	*b'a'al=che'*	*b'a'al=che'*	'animal'
d.	*k'áam=b'uul*	*k'áam=b'ur*	*k'am=b'ul*	*k'äm=b'ul*	*k'äm=b'ul*	'great currasow'
e.		*k'uu=che'*	*k'u=che'*	*k'u=che'*	*k'u=che'*	'cedar'

'flower' & 'tree') 'frangipani'; (b) Yucatec and Southern Lacandon *éet=k'aab'a'* (Pt & N; 'with' & 'name') 'namesake'; (c) *b'a'al=che'* (N & N; 'thing' & 'tree') 'animal'; (d) Yucatec *k'áam=b'uul* (Aj & N?; 'yellow' & X) 'great currasow'; and (e) Lacandon, Itzaj and Mopan *k'u(u)=che'* (Aj & N; 'holy' & 'tree') 'cedar'.

3.3.4.2 Noun compounds with noun class markers

Noun compounds with the masculine noun class marker *(a)j=* and the feminine noun class marker *(i)x=* are extremely common in Itzaj and Mopan, particularly in names of flora and fauna. Compounds with *äj=* are common in Northern Lacandon. Compounds with *x=* are prominent in Yucatec, while Southern Lacandon has hardly any. Referents of the terms vary somewhat among languages. Adjective-noun and noun-noun compounds are common. For example, Northern Lacandon *äj=säk=taan* 'white bellied minnow' (a) is made up of the adjective *säk* 'white and the noun *taan* 'front'; Itzaj and Mopan *aj='ek'=xux* 'fer-de-lance' (b) are made up of the adjective *ek'* 'black' and the noun *xux* 'wasp'; Itzaj *ix='is-waj* 'fly (type)' (c) is made up of the adjective *is* 'soft' and the noun *waj* 'tortilla'; Itzaj and Mopan *ix=chäkäl=ja'as* 'mamey' (h) are made up of the adjective *chäkäl* 'red' and the noun *ja'as* 'plantain'; and Yucatec *x=ya'ax=che'* 'ceiba' (j) is composed of the adjective *ya'ax* 'green' and the noun *che'* 'tree' (Table 24.32).

3.3.4.3 Agentive noun compounds

Agentive noun compounds are derived from antipassive compounds, most commonly formed of an antipassive stem and an incorporated object (cf. §3.5.5.1). Like simple agentive nouns, the gender of the agent is indicated by a masculine or feminine noun class marker, except in Lacandon where that distinction is neutralized. Southern Lacandon does not have these forms but, instead, uses possessed-possessor constructions (cf.

TABLE 24.32 COMPOUNDS WITH NOUN CLASS MARKERS IN YUCATECAN LANGUAGES

	Yucatec	S Lac	N Lac	Itzaj	Mopan	Gloss
a.		*(säk=táan)*	*äj=säk=tan*		*aj=säk=taan*	'white minnow'
b.		*(éek'=xuux)*	*äj='ee=xux*	*aj='ek'=xux*	*aj='ek'=xux*	'fer-de-lance'
c.	*x='is=waajil*	*(is=waj)*	*(is waj)*	*ix='is=waj*		'fly (type)'
d.	*(x=)chakal=ja'as*	*(chäk ja's)*		*ix=chäkäl=ja'as*	*ix=chäkäl=ja'as*	'mamey'
e.	*x=ya'ax=che'*	*(ya'x=che')*	*(ya'ax=che')*	*ix=ya'ax=che'*	*ix=ya'ax=che'*	'ceiba'

TABLE 24.33 YUCATECAN AGENTIVE NOUN COMPOUNDS

	Yucatec	N Lac	Itzaj	Mopan	Gloss
a.		*äj=men=puuna'*	*aj=men=che'*	*aj=meyaj=che'*	'carpinter' (male)
b.	*j=tz'ak=yaj*	*äj=men=tz'ak*	*aj=tz'äk=yaj*	*aj=tz'äk=yaj*	'curer' (male)
c.		*äj=ka'ansaj=ju'un*	*ix=ka'ansaj=xok*	*ix=ye'=xok*	'teacher (female)'
d.	*x=meen=janal*		*ix=men=janal*	*ix=chäk=janal*	'cook (female)'

§4.1.2). In Table 24.33 (a), Northern Lacandon *äj=men=puuna'* 'carpenter' is composed of *men* 'make' and *puuna'* 'mahagony'; the similar Itzaj term *aj=men=che'* 'carpenter' has *che'* 'wood' as the object and the Mopan term *ajmeyaj=che'* 'carpenter' is based on *meyaj* 'work'; in (b) Itzaj and Mopan *aj=tz'äk=yaj* 'curer (male)' is composed of the antipassive *tz'äk* 'cure' and *yaj* 'pain', while the similar Northern Lacandon term *äj=men=tz'ak* 'curer' is based on *men* 'make' and *tz'ak* 'medicine'; in (c) Northern Lacandon *äj=ka'ansaj=ju'un* 'teacher' (neutral regarding gender) is based on the antipassive *ka'ansaj* 'teach' and *ju'un* 'paper'; its Itzaj counterpart *ixka'ansaj=xok* 'teacher (female)' has the object *xok* 'reading' and Mopan *ixye'=xok* 'teacher (female)' has the antipassive base *ye'* 'show'; in (d) Itzaj *ix=men=janal* 'cook (female)' is based on *men* 'make' and *janal* 'food' and Mopan *ix=chäk=janal* is based on *chäk* 'cook'.

3.3.4.5 Adjectival noun compounds

Similarly, adjectival noun compounds are formed with noun class markers indicating gender and adjectival compounds, as in Table 24.34 (a) Mopan *aj=chäkäj=pol* 'hot-headed male' based on *chäjäj* 'hot' and *pol* 'head'; (b) Itzaj and Mopan *aj=k'a'=chi* 'drooler' (male)' based on *k'a'* 'drool' and *chi'* 'mouth'; (c) Northern Lacandon *äj=ma'='ich* 'blind man' based on *ma'* 'no' and *ich* 'eye'; and (d) Yucatec *x=ma'=yuum* 'fatherless female' and (e) *j=ma'*=yuum 'fatherless male' based on *ma'* 'no' and *yuum* 'father'.

3.4 Adjectives and participles

3.4.1 Adjectives

Adjective may be expressed by simple adjectival roots or derived from other root types. Adjectives may be partially or completely reduplicated to indicate moderate to high intensity (cf. §2.4.6).

TABLE 24.34 YUCATECAN ADJECTIVAL NOUN COMPOUNDS

	Yucatec	N Lac	Itzaj	Mopan	Gloss
a.	*chokoj-pol*		*aj=chokoj=pol*	*aj=chäkäj=pol*	'hot-headed male'
b.	*j=k'a'=chi'*		*aj=k'a'=chi'*	*aj=k'a'=chi'*	'drooler' (male)
c.		*äj=ma'='ich*	*aj=ma'=ich*		'blind man'
d.	*x=ma'=yuum*			*ix=ma'=yum*	'fatherless female'
e.	*j=ma'=yuum*		*aj=ma'=yum*	*aj=ma'=yum*	'fatherless male'

TABLE 24.35 ADJECTIVE ROOTS IN YUCATECAN LANGUAGES

	Yucatec	*S Lac*	*N Lac*	*Itzaj*	*Mopan*	*Gloss*
a.	*chak*	*chäk*	*chäk*	*chäk*	*chäk*	'red'
b.	*b'oox*	*b'oox*	*b'ox*	*b'ox*	*b'ox*	'black'
c.	*tz'iik*	*tz'iik*	*tz'ik*	*tz'iik*	*tz'iik*	'fierce'
d.	*wi'ij*	*wi'j*	*wij*	*wi'ij*	*wi'ij*	'hungry'
e.	*mejen*	*majan*	*mejen*	*mejen*	*mejen*	'small'

TABLE 24.36 PARTIAL REDUPLICATION OF ROOT ADJECTIVES IN YUCATECAN LANGUAGES

	Yucatec	*S Lac*	*N Lac*	*Itzaj*	*Mopan*	*Gloss*
a.	*k'aa-k'as*	*k'aa-k'as**		*k'a-k'as*	*k'a-k'as*	'rather bad'
b.	*náa-náach*			*na-naach*		'rather far'
c.		*su'-su'tz'*		*su'-suutz'*		'rather astringent'
d.			*ya'-ya'ax*	*ya'-ya'ax*		'greenish'
e.	*muu-mun*	*muu-mun**		*mu-mum*	*mu-mun*	'(rather) tender'

3.4.1.1 Root adjectives

Root adjectives may have the root shapes CVC, CVVC, CV'VC or CVCVC in Northern Lacandon, Itzaj and Mopan as in Table 24.35. Yucatec and Southern Lacandon also have the forms CV́VC and CV(V)CV(V)C.

3.4.1.2 Reduplication

Reduplication of adjectives tends to indicate varying degrees of intensity. In Itzaj there is a consistent iconicity with partial reduplication indicating moderate intensity and complete reduplication indicating high intensity (Hofling 2000:150). In Mopan both partial and complete reduplication may indicate high intensity (Hofling 2011a:21). In Table 24.36 the partially reduplicated forms with an asterisk (a), (e) indicate high intensity. In Yucatec and Southern Lacandon the first vowel tends to lengthen in partially reduplicated forms.

Completely reduplicated forms in Itzaj and Mopan indicate high intensity. In Yucatec and Southen Lacandon reduplicated forms sometimes indicate high intensity, but often this is unclear. In Table 24.37 the fully reduplicated Yucatec forms with an asterisk examples (b) and (c) do not indicate high intensity.

3.4.1.3 Derived adjectives

3.4.1.3.1 ADJECTIVES DERIVED WITH -VC SUFFIXES

Adjectives may be derived with a variety -VC suffixes. Derivation with -*Vl* from transitive verb and positional stems is especially common, as in Table 24.38. In Yucatec and Southern Lacandon the vowel also lengthens or lowers in tone in this derivation (a)–(c) (Bricker et al. 1998:373–4). Adjectives may also be derived from positionals and nouns with a harmonic -*Vl* suffix (d)–(e). The Itzaj example (a) with -*al* is ambiguous as to whether they are adjectives or a participial form to be described below (cf. §3.4.2.5.)

A variety of other harmonic -VC suffixes also appear in derived adjectives in Table 24.39, including -*Vch* (a), (b); -*Vk*, which derives adjectives (or participles) from positional roots (c)–(e); and vowel-nasal suffixes (f). Yucatec and Southern Lacandon consistently derive adjectives (or participles) from positionals with -*Vk-b'al* and -*Vk-b'aar* respectively. Itzaj and Mopan generally derive adjectives from positionals with -*Vk*.

3.4.1.3.2 ADJECTIVES DERIVED FROM AFFECTIVE STEMS

Affective stems indicate sensory information such as sound, color, and texture (Bricker 1999), and a number of adjectival forms derive from them, most commonly with reduplication and the suffix -*kil* (in Yucatec) or -*kij* (in Itzaj and Mopan). No examples were found for Lacandon. There is a considerable range in meaning of these forms across languages. In Table 24.40 roots are given in Itzaj and Mopan forms. Mopan also has an adjectival derivation from affective stems with -*m-en* as in examples (b) and (e).

TABLE 24.37 COMPLETE REDUPLICATION OF ROOT ADJECTIVES IN YUCATECAN LANGUAGES

	Yucatec	S Lac	N Lac	Itzaj	Mopan	Gloss
a.				jay=jay	jay=jay	'very thin'
b.	k'a'an=k'a'an*	k'a'm=k'a'm		k'a'am=k'a'am		'(very) rough'
c.	k'aan=k'an*	k'än=k'än k'aan=k'aan	k'än=k'än	k'än=k'än	k'än=k'än	'yellowish, very yellow'
d.	k'óon=k'óom	kóom=kóom		koom=koom		'very short'

TABLE 24.38 ADJECTIVES DERIVED WITH -*Vl* IN YUCATECAN LANGUAGES

	Root	Yucatec	S Lac	Itzaj	Mopan	Gloss
a.	MAK (T)	maak-al	maak-ar	mak-al?		'capped'
b.	B'UK (T)	b'uuk-ul			b'uk-ul	'knocked down'
c.	B'UL (T)	b'uul-ul	b'uur-ur		b'ul-ul	'submerged'
d.	KUX (P)			kux-ul-	kux-ul	'tender'
e.	CH'UP (N)	xch'up-ul		ch'up-ul	ch'up-ul-	'female'

TABLE 24.39 YUCATECAN ADJECTIVES DERIVED WITH OTHER -VC SUFFIXES

	Root	Yucateco	S Lac	N Lac	Itzaj	Mopan	Gloss
a.	NOJ (A)	noj-och			noj-och	noj-och	'big'
b.	NUK (A)	nuk-uch	nuk-uch	nuk-uch	nuk-uch	nuk-uch	'big', 'old'
c.	CH'EB' (P)	ch'eb'-ek-b'al	ch'ab'-ak-b'aar		ch'eb'-ek	ch'eb-ek	'twisted'
d.	CH'OT (P)	ch'ot-ok-b'al	ch'at-ak-b'aar		ch'ot-ok	ch'ot-ok	'twisted'
e.	TZ'OP (P, T)	(tz'op-okb'al)			tz'op-ot	tz'op-ot	'swampy'
		(tz'oop-ol)					
f.	TAAK' (N)	tak'-an		täk'-än		täk'-an	'ripe'

TABLE 24.40 YUCATECAN ADJECTIVES DERIVED FROM AFFECTIVE STEMS WITH -kil ~ -kij; -men

	Root	Yucatec	Itzaj	Mopan	Gloss
a.	B'ÄJ (Af, T) 'nail'	b'a-baj-kil	b'ä-b'äj-kij	b'ä-b'äj-kij	'planted'
b.	B'OJ (Af, T) 'knock'	b'o-b'oj-kil	b'o-b'oj-kij	b'o-b'oj-kij	'swollen',
				b'oj-m-en	'packed'
c.	B'UJ (Af, T) 'split'	b'u-b'uj-kil	b'u-b'uj-kij	b'u-b'uj-kij	'splittable'
d.	CHOK' (Af, T) 'cram'	cho-cho'-kil	cho'-chok'-kij	cho'-chok'-kij	'crammed'
e.	CH'EEJ (Af, N) 'press'	ch'e-chej-kil	ch'e-ch'ej-kij	ch'e-ch'ej-kij	'packed'
				ch'ej-m-en	

3.4.2 Participles

Participles derived from verbs are used as nominal modifiers and non-verbal predicates. Several participles commonly occur in Yucatecan languages.

3.4.2.1 Participles with -a'an

Participles with -a'an may be derived from transitive and intransitive (including positional) verb stems as in Table 24.41. With intransitive roots a perfect meaning is prominent as in examples (a)–(b), while with transitive roots a passive meaning is prominent (c)–(e).

Positional roots have plain forms with -a'an and forms with -l-aj-a'an (-r-äj-a'n in Southern Lacandon) with a perfect meaning as in Table 24.42.

A variety of other verb stems form participles with -a'an are shown in Table 24.43 including causatives with -s (a); transitives derived with -t, (b) and (c) (with the -t present in Southern Lacandon participial forms); causatives derived with kUn-(t) (d); celeritives (e), agentless passives (f) and antipassives (g) (cf. §3.5).

3.4.2.2 Passive participles with -b'il

Participles may be derived from transitive stems with -b'il shown in Table 24.44, including root transitives (a), (b), active verbal noun roots (c), (d) and causatives (e), (f).

3.4.2.3 Affective participles with -(V)nak

Participles may be derived from affective stems with -(V)nak, as in Table 24.45. In Itzaj the stem is reduplicated as in the affective adjectives described in §3.4.1.2.2. This derivation is rare except in Itzaj and Mopan.

TABLE 24.41 YUCATECAN PARTICIPLES WITH -a'an

	Yucatec	S Lac	N Lac	Itzaj	Mopan	Gloss
a.	bi(n)-(a) j-a'n	b'in-a'n		b'in-a'an		'has gone'
b.		u'r-a'n		u'l-a'an	ud'-a'an	'has arrived'
c.		b'an-a'n	b'an-a'an	b'on-a'an	b'on-a'an	'painted'
d.		ch'a'-a'n	ch'a'an	ch'a'-a'an	ch'a'-a'an	'taken'
e.	t'ab'-a'an		t'äb'a'an	t'äb'-a'an	t'äb'-a'an	'lit'

TABLE 24.42 YUCATECAN POSITIONAL PARTICIPLES WITH (-l-aj)-a'an

	Yucatec	S Lac	N Lac	Itzaj	Mopan	Gloss
a.			käj-än	käj-a'an	käj-a'an	'living'
b.				käj-l-aj-a'an	käj-l-aj-a'an	'has lived'
c.		kux-a'n	kux-a'an	kux-a'an	kux-a'an	'living'
d.				kux-l-aj-a'an		'has lived'

TABLE 24.43 OTHER COMPLEX PARTICIPLES WITH -A'AN IN YUCATECAN LANGUAGES

	Yucatec	S Lac	Itzaj	Mopan	Gloss
a.		kiin-s-a'n	kin-s-äj-a'n	kim-s-aj-a'an	'killed'
b.		miis-t-a'n	miis-a'an	miis-a'an	'swept'
c.	tz'iib'-a'an	tz'iib'-t-a'n	tz'iib'-a'an	tz'iib'-a'an	'written'
d.		k'aas-kin-t-a'n	k'as-kun-a'n	k'as-kun-a'an	'worsened'
				k'as-kun-aj-a'an	'has been ruined'
e.			chin-k'-aj-a'an		'crouched (suddenly)'
f.			litz-p-aj-a'an		'fished'
g.			b'o'ol-n-aj-a'an		'has paid'

TABLE 24.44 YUCATECAN PASIVE PARTICIPLES DERIVED WITH -b'il

	Yucatec	S Lac	N Lac	Itzaj	Mopan	Gloss
a.	tzaj-bil			tzäj-b'il	tzäj-b'il	'fried'
b.	chak-b'il	chäk-b'ir	chäk-b'il	chäk-b'il	chäk-b'il	'boiled'
c.	k'áa'-b'il		k'ak'-b'il	k'aak'-b'il	k'aak'-b'il	'broiled'
d.		che'j-b'ir		che'ej-b'il		'laughed at'
e.		ka'm-sä-b'ir		ka'an-sä-b'il		'taught'
f.		kux-kin-b'ir		kux-kin-b'il		'revived'

TABLE 24.45 YUCATECAN PARTICIPLES DERIVED WITH -(V)nak

	Yucatec	S Lac	N Lac	Itzaj	Mopan	Gloss
a.				chochoj-nak	choj-onak	'coming loose'
b.	chi'ich-nak			chi'chi'-nak	chi'i-nak	'restless'
c.				ch'ech'ej-nak	ch'eej-enak	'compacting'
d.		tz'äm-äknäk		tz'ätz'äm-nak	tz'äm-änak	'soaking'

3.4.2.4 Reduplicated participles

3.4.2.4.1 REDUPLICATION WITH GLOTTAL STOP
In Yucatec and Southern Lacandon participles may be derived from transitive roots with an infixed glottal stop and refer to an action that was repeated several times (Bricker et al. 1998:374; Hofling 2014a) (Table 24.46). Glosses are given for Yucatec. These forms often have corresponding reduplicated verbs (Bricker et al. 1998:374; cf. §3.5.4.).

3.4.2.4.2 REDUPLICATION WITH -Vn-
In Yucatec and Mopan reduplicated participles may be derived from transitive and positional roots with -Vn- as in Table 24.47. In Yucatec there is vowel disharmony with -en- for roots with /a/, /o/ or /u/ as in (a)–(c); with -un- for roots with /e/ as in (d); and with either for roots with /i/ as in (e) (Bricker et al. 1998:374–6). Note too that the vowels are long with high tone in Yucatec. In Mopan the first vowel is short and the second long, while the linking affix is always -in-. Yucatec also has a similar reduplicated participle with -man- (Bricker et al. 1998:376).

3.4.2.5 Other participles

Individual Yucatecan languages have other productive processes for deriving participles. In Itzaj, intransitive participles may be formed with -al as in nak'-al 'risen', ch'eb'-al 'tipped', b'ich-al 'stiff', b'ol-al 'dull', pox-al 'blistered', and b'u'l-al 'filled' (Hofling 1997:19). In Mopan positional participles are derived with -ka'al as in b'itz-ka'al 'bent over on all fours' and jem-ka'al 'hanging' (Hofling 2011a:23). In Yucatec celeritive participles are derived with -alak as in jaj-k'-alak 'slippery' and nix-k'-alak 'wobbly' (Bricker et al. 1998:377).

3.4.3 Adjective color compounds

Adjective compounds referring to color based on a color term, another root, usually transitive, and the suffix -e'en (-en in Northern Lacandon) are found in all Yucatecan languages (Smailus 1989:135–7; Bricker et al. 1998:381–2; Hofling 1997:20; Hofling 2011:23; Hofling 2014a:21), shown in Table 24.48. The meanings of these terms vary somewhat among the languages.

3.5 Verbs

Verbs may be formed from intransitive or transitive verb roots, or derived from other root types. Verbs are marked for aspect, mood, and status, a suffixal category that encodes

TABLE 24.46 REDUPLICATION WITH GLOTTAL STOP IN YUCATEC AND SOUTHERN LACANDON

	Root	Yucatec	S Lac	Gloss
a.	B'UJ (T)	b'u'u-b'u'uj	b'u'-b'u'j	'split several times'
b.	JEK' (T)	je'e-je'ek'	je'-je'k'	'broken in several places'
c.	JOM (T)	jo'on-jo'on	jo'-jo'm	'full of holes'
d.	JAT (T)	ja'a-ja'at	ja'-ja't	'torn in several places'

TABLE 24.47 REDUPLICATION WITH -Vn- IN YUCATEC AND MOPAN

	Root	Yucatec	Mopan	Gloss
a.	K'AX (T)	káax-en-k'áax		
b.	XOT' (T)	xóot'-en-xóot'	xot'-in-xoot'	'cut here and there'
c.	WUTZ' (T)	wúutz'-en-wúutz'	wutz'-in-wuutz'	'folded here and there'
d.	JET (T)	jéet-un-jéet	jet-in-jeet	'split here and there'
e.	CHIL (P)	chíil-en-chíil		'lying here and there'

TABLE 24.48 YUCATECAN COLOR COMPOUNDS

	Yucatec	S Lac	N Lac	Itzaj	Mopan	Gloss
a.			chäk=jal-en	chäk=jal-e'en		'brilliant red'
b.	chak=jatz'-e'en			chäk=jatz'-e'en	chäk=jätz'-e'en	'orange-red'
c.	chak=jep'-e'en			chäk=jep'-e'en	chäk=jep'-e'en	'brownish-red'
d.	chak=pak'-e'en			chäk=pak'-e'en	chäk=päk'-e'en	'bright red'
e.		chäk=pit-e'n		chäk=pit-e'en		'nude'
f.	chäk=til-e'en	chäk=tir-e'n			chäk=til-e'en	'orange-red'
g.		chäk=tz'ar-e'n			chäk=tz'ol-e'en	'nude, bright red'
h.	'ée'=joch'-e'en	eek'=jach'-e'n		'eek'=joch'-e'en	'eek'=joch'-e'en	'very dark'
i.	sak=jatz'-e'en			säk=jatz'-e'en	säk=jätz'-e'en	'bright white'
j.	ya'ax=jatz'-e'en			ya'ax=jatz'-e'en	ya'ax=jätz'-e'en	'dark green'

aspect-mood and transitivity. Aspect-mood (AM) markers may be prefixes, preposed adverbial words, or intransitive auxiliaries. For a general overview see Bricker (1986), MacLeod (1983), Kaufman (1991) and Hofling (2006b). Aspectual, mood and modality markers are shown in Table 24.49.[9]

There is a large set of adverbial aspects that occurs with verbs in the incompletive status shown in Table 24.50 (cf. §3.5.1.1, §3.5.2.2). For example the Itzaj adverb *suk* 'customarily' (a) appears in incompletive constructions like *suk u-b'et-ik* 's/he is accustomed to do it'. These aspectual forms may be inflected like inchoative verbs (cf. §3.5.2.4) for completive and dependent forms, e.g., Itzaj *suk-aj-ij u-wen-el* 's/he was accustomed to sleep' and *ka' suk-ak u-wen-el* 'when she is accustomed to sleep'.

A smaller set of aspectual adverbs appears with verbs in the dependent status, shown in Table 24.51. Note the Mopan aspectual adverb *suk* 'customarily' (a) falls in this class as in *suk u-b'et-e'* 's/he customarily does it', unlike the Itzaj example shown above in

TABLE 24.49 YUCATECAN ASPECTUAL, MOOD, AND MODALITY MARKERS

	Yucatec	S Lac	N Lac	Itzaj	Mopan	Gloss
a.	k-	k-	∅-	k-	walak	'incompletive'
b.	t-	t-	t-	t-	∅	'tran. completive'
c.	(j)-	∅	(j)-	∅	∅	'intran. completive'
d.	ma't-	ma'	ma'	ma'(ta'ax)	ma'(-ta'ach)	'negative'
e.	ka'(aj)	ka'	k(aj)	ka'	ka'	'optative, dependent'
f.					ma'ax-to	'not yet, dependent'

TABLE 24.50 YUCATECAN ASPECTUAL ADVERBS COOCURRING WITH THE INCOMPLETIVE STATUS

	Yucatec	S Lac	N Lac	Itzaj	Mopan	Gloss
a.	suuk	suuk	suk	suk		'customarily'
b.	táan	táan	tan	ta(a)n	tan	'durative'
c.	táan-t . . . e'	táan-t		tan-toj	tan-to(j)	'immediate past'
d.					tan=tun	'immediate future'
e.	chich	chich		chich	chich	'hard'
f.	séeb'	séeb'		seeb'	seeb'	'celeritive'
g.	k'abéet			k'ab'eet		'necessitative'
h.	taak	taak		tak		'desiderative'
i.	yaan	yaan	yan	yaan	yan	'obligative'
j.	ta'ay-tak					'about to'
	óolak			olak		'almost'
k.	ko'ox	kux	ko'ox			'hortative'
l.	je'el . . . -e'	je'r . . . -e'	je'	je'le' . . . -ej	jed'e'ek	'assurative'
m.	páat			pat	paatal	'abilitative'
n.		taab'ar				'immediate future'
o.		b'ik				'abilitative'
p.					tzaj	'necessitative'

TABLE 24.51 YUCATECAN ASPECTUAL ADVERBS CO-OCCURRING WITH THE DEPENDENT STATUS

	Yucatec	S Lac	N Lac	Itzaj	Mopan	Gloss
a.					suk	'customarily'
b.					patal	'abilitative'
c.	kV₂n					'definite future'
d.	sáan, sáam				sam-i	'anterior past'
e.	b'iin					'indefinite future'
f.				ko'ox	ko'ox	'hortative'
g.					(paatal)	'abilitative'
h.					(tan)	'durative'
i.					(tan-toj)	'immediate past'
j.					(tan-tun)	'immediate future'

Table 24.50 (a). In Mopan these markers appear with transitive verbs in the dependent status while intransitives appear as infinitives after *ti*. With the Mopan forms in parentheses, transitive verbs may appear in the incompletive or dependent status, but intransitive verbs appear in the incompletive status or in constructions with *ti* (compare with Table 24.50 above). For example, both *tan inw-uk'-ik* (incompletive status) and *tan-en inw-uk'-u'* (dependent status) mean 'I am drinking it'; both *tan in-tz'iib* and *tan-en ti tz'iib'* mean 'I am writing'. In the transitive dependent status and intransitive *ti* constructions the adverbs are inflected with Set B pronouns. In the Yucatec transitive definite future form kV_2n the vowel copies the vowel of the following Set A person marker as in *kin in-kan-ej* 'I am going to learn it' and *kun uy-a'al-ej* 's/he is going to say it' (Po?ot Yah and Bricker 1981:x)

A number of intransitive verbs function as aspectual auxiliaries with verbs in the incompletive status, except for Mopan, where the dependent status may occur as indicated in Table 24.52 (b), (c). For example, Itzaj *k-u-jop'-ol u-bet-ik* 's/he begins to do it', *jop'-ij u-b'et-ik* 's/he began to do it' and *ka'jop'-ok-Ø u-b'et-ik* 'that s/he begin to do it'. For the future (e), Yucatec has the structure *n-u ka'aj* + incompletive stem for intransitive verbs, e.g., *n-u ka'aj jan-al* 's/he is going to eat' and *n-u-ka'aj u-* + incompletive stem for transitive verbs, e.g., *n-u-ka'aj u-b'eet-ik* 's/he is going to make it' (Hanks 1984 7:5); while Itzaj and Mopan have the corresponding structures *b'el u-ka'a(j) ti jan-al* and *b'el u-ka'a(j) u-b'et-ej* (in the dependent status).

3.5.1 Verb root classes

3.5.1.1 Transitive verbs

Status is a category encoding aspect/mood and transitivity and is marked by verbal suffixes. There are intransitive and transitive forms of the incompletive, completive, dependent (subjunctive), imperative and perfect statuses (Kaufman 1991; Hofling 2006b). Transitive forms are shown in Table 24.53.

TABLE 24.52 YUCATECAN ASPECTUAL AUXILIARIES

	Yucatec	S Lac	Itzaj	Mopan	Gloss
a.	*jo'op'* (inc)		*jop'* (inc)		inceptive
b.	*káaj* (inc)		*kaj* (inc)	*kaj* (dep)	inceptive
c.			*jo'm* (inc)	*job'* (inc/dep)	inceptive
d.	*tz'o'ok* (inc)	*tz'o'kar* (inc)	*tz'o'ok* (inc)		terminative
e.	*n-u ka'aj* (inc)	*b'in u-ka' (ti)* (inc)	*b'el u-ka'aj ti* (inc)	*b'el u-ka'a ti* (inc)	future (intr)
f.	*n-u ka'aj u-* (inc)	*b'in u-ka' u-* (dep)	*b'el-u-ka'aj u-* (dep)	*b'el u-ka'a u-* (dep)	future (tran)

TABLE 24.53 YUCATECAN TRANSITIVE STATUS SUFFIXES

	Yucatec	S Lac	N Lac	Itzaj	Mopan	Gloss
a.	*-ik*	*-ik*	*-ik*	*-ik*	*-ik*	'incompletive'
b.	*-aj*	*-aj*	*-aj*	*-aj*	*-aj*	'completive'
c.	*-ej*	*-ej*	*-ej*	*-V'*	*-V'*	'dependent'
d.	*-ej*	*-ej*	*-ej*	*-V'*	*-V'*	'imperative'
e.	*-m-aj*	*-m-än*	*-m-an ~ m-än*	*-m-aj*	*(-m-aj)*	'perfect'

Transitive verb roots are typically of the shape CVC. Subjects are marked by Set A person markers and direct objects by Set B person markers (cf. §3.1.1.2), as in Table 24.54.

3.5.1.2 Intransitive verbs

Intransitive root verbs may have the shapes CVC, CVVC, CV́VC (in Yucatec and Southern Lacandon) and CV'C (Kaufman 1991:8). The intransitive status suffixes are shown in Table 24.55 (based on Hofling 2006b:374, 377). The historical completive intransitive status marker -ij has been or is being reanalyzed as a third person singular in Lacandon, Itzaj and Mopan (cf. §3.1.1.2).

The intransitive verb jóok' 'go out' is conjugated in Table 24.56. The Southern Lacandon form b'ina'an 's/he has gone' is substituted in the perfect form.

3.5.2 Verbal derivation and voice

3.5.2.1 Reflexive and reciprocal constructions

Transitive verbs may have reflexive and reciprocal constructions with a possessed reflexive pronoun, as in Table 24.57. The reciprocal meaning is expressed with plural morphology. For example, in Itzaj t-u-kin-s-aj u-b'aj-oo' 'they killed one another' (Hofling 1997:351) the reflexive pronoun is pluralized.

TABLE 24.54 YUCATECAN TRANSITIVE VERB CONJUGATION

	Yucatec	S Lac	Itzaj	Mopan	Gloss
INC	k-aw-il-ik-en	k-aw-ir-ik-(e)en	k-aw-il-ik-en	walak 'aw-il-ik-en	'you see me'
COM	t-aw-il-aj-en	t-aw-ir-aj-(e)en	t-aw-il-aj-en	aw-il-aj-en	'you saw me'
DEP	ka'aw-il-Ø-en	ka'aw-ir-Ø-(e)en	ka'aw-il-a'-(e)en	ka'aw-il-a'-een	'that you see me'
	ka'aw-il-ej-Ø	ka'aw-ir-ej-Ø	ka'-aw-il-a'-Ø	ka'-aw-il-a'-Ø	'that you see her/him/it'
IMP	il-ej-Ø	ir-ej-Ø	il-a'-Ø	il-a-Ø	'see it!'
	il-Ø-en	ir-Ø-(e)en	il-a'-en	il-een	'see me!'
PERF	aw-il-m-aj-en		aw-il-m-aj-en		'you have seen me'
	aw-il-m-aj-Ø	aw-il-m-än-Ø	aw-il-m-aj-Ø		'you have seen her/him/it'

TABLE 24.55 YUCATECAN INTRANSITIVE STATUS SUFFIXES

	Yucatec	S Lac	N Lac	Itzaj	Mopan	Gloss
a.	-Vl	-Vr	-Vl	-Vl	-Vl	'incompletive'
b.	-Ø,-ij, -aj	-Ø, (-ij), -äj	-Ø,-äj	-Ø,-aj	-Ø,-aj	'completive'
c.	-Vk	-Vk	-Vk	-Vk	-Vk	'dependent'
d.	-en	-en	-en	-en	-en	'imperative'
e.	-a'an	-a'n	-a'an	-a'an	-a'an	'perfect'

TABLE 24.56 INTRANSITIVE ROOT CONJUGATION IN YUCATECAN LANGUAGES

	Yucatec	S Lac	Itzaj	Mopan	Gloss
ICP	k-a-jóok'-ol	k-a-jóok'-ar	k-a-jok'-ol	walak a-jok'-ol	'you go out'
CP	(j) jóok'-ij-∅	jóok'-i(j)-∅	jok'-∅-ij	jok'-∅-i(j)	's/he went out'
	(j) jóok'-∅-ech	jóok'-∅-ech	jok'-∅-eech	jok'-∅-eech	'you went out'
DEP	ka'jóok'-ok-ech	ka'jóok'-ok-ech	ka'jok'-ok-ech	ka'-jok'-ok-ech	'that you go out'
IMP	jóok'-en	jóok'-en	jok'-en	jok'-en	'go out!'
PRF	jóok'-a'an-ech	(b'in-a'n-∅)	jok'-a'an-ech	jok'-a'an-ech	'you have gone out'

TABLE 24.57 REFLEXIVE CONSTRUCTIONS IN YUCAYTECAN LANGUAGES

	Yucatec	S Lac	Itzaj	Mopan	Gloss
ICP	k-uy-il-ik	k-uy-ir-ik	k-uy-il-ik	tan uy-il-ik	's/he sees her/himself'
	u-b'aj	u-b'äj	u-b'-aj	ub'aj-il	
CP	t-uy-il-aj	t-uy-ir-aj	t-uy-il-aj	uy-il-aj	's/he saw her/himself'
	u-b'aj	u-b'äj	u-b'aj	u-b'aj-il	

3.5.2.2 Intransitive voices of root transitive verbs

In mediopassive (middle) voice constructions the subject is a semantic patient and no agent is mentioned. In Yucatec and Southern Lacandon the mediopassive is marked with a long vowel with high tone; in Itzaj it remains short, and in Mopan it lengthens as in Table 24.58 (based on Hofling 2006b:383).

In the antipassive voice, the subject is the agent and the object is unspecified or indefinite. The antipassive is marked by the suffix -n in all statuses except for the incompletive, except for Mopan, which uses a periphrastic construction (Danziger 1996; Hofling 2006b:386; Hofling 2011b), as in Table 24.59.

The canonical passive construction, where the subject is the patient of the action and the agent may be mentioned obliquely, is shown in Table 24.60, based on Hofling 2006b:384. It is marked by a -b' suffix except for in Yucatec and Southern Lacandon, where it is marked by an infixed glottal stop, except for roots that end in glottal consonates (' and j) such as pa' 'break', where the -b' suffix appears (Bricker et al. 1998:334).[10]

An agentless passive marked by -p-aj occurs in all but Mopan, which has agentless passive forms marked by b'-aan. Celeritive forms marking sudden or unexpected action are marked by -k'-aj in all except Mopan, shown in Table 24.61. The Southern Lacandon incompletive and completive forms are for the verb b'äj 'nail'. The capital J in Itzaj indicates morphophonemic representation and is not pronounced.

3.5.2.3 Positional verbs

Positional verbs are derived from positional roots. As mentioned above, many roots are polyvalent with transitive and positional values. They are marked by an -l suffix (-r in Southern Lacandon) except for in the incompletive status (based on Hofling 2006b:379), as shown in Table 24.62.

TABLE 24.58 MEDIOPASSIVE VOICE FOR ROOT TRANSITIVE VERBS IN YUCATECAN LANGUAGES

	Yucatec	S Lac	Itzaj	Mopan	Gloss
ICP	k-u-lóoch-ol	k-u-róoch-ar	k-u-loch-ol	k-u-looch-ol	'it bends'
CP	lóoch-ij-∅	róoch-ij-∅	loch-ij	looch-i(j)	'it bend'
DEP	lóoch-ok-∅	róoch-ak-∅	loch-ok-∅	looch-ok-∅	'that it bend'
IMP	lóoch-en	róoch-en	loch-en	looch-en	'bend!'

TABLE 24.59 ANTIPASSIVE VOICE FOR ROOT TRANSITIVES IN YUCATECAN LANGUAGES

	Yucatec	S Lac	Itzaj	Mopan	Gloss
ICP	k-u-looch	k-u-rooch	k-u-l(o)och	walak u-loch	's/he bends'
CP	looch-n-aj-ij-∅	rooch-n-äj-∅	l(o)och-n-aj-ij	uch-∅-ij u-loch	's/he bent'
DEP	looch-n-ak ∅	rooch-n-äk-∅	l(o)och-n-ak-∅	uch-uk-∅ u-loch	'that s/he bend'
IMP	looch-n-en	rooch-n-en	l(o)och-n-en	uch-uk a-loch	'bend!'

TABLE 24.60 CANONICAL PASSIVE VOICE FOR ROOT TRANSITIVES IN YUCATECAN LANGUAGES

	Yucatec	S Lac	Itzaj	Mopan	Gloss
ICP	k-u-lo'och-ol	k-u-ro'ch-ar	k-u-loch-b'-ol	k-u-loch-b'ol	'it is bent'
CP	lo'och-ij-∅	ro'ch-i(j)-∅	loch-b'-∅-ij	loch-b'-∅-i(j)	'it was bent'
DEP	lo'och-ok-∅	ro'ch-ok	loch-b'-ok-∅	loch-b'-ok-∅	'that it be bent'
ICP	k-u-pa'a-b'-al	k-u-pa'-b'-är	k-u-pa'-b'-äl	k-u-pa'-b'-äl	'it is broken'
CP	pa'a-b'-ij ∅	pa'-b'-ij-∅	pa'-b'-∅-ij	pa'-b'-∅-ij	'it was broken'
DEP	pa'a-b'-ak-∅	pa'-b'-äk-∅	pa'-b'-äk-∅	pa'-b'-äk-∅	'that it be broken'

TABLE 24.61 AGENTLESS PASSIVES (PASSIVE2) AND CELERITIVES FOR ROOT TRANSITVES IN YUCATECAN LANGUAGES

	Yucatec	S Lac	Itzaj	Mopan	Gloss
Passive2					
ICP	k-u-loch-p-aj-al	(k-u-b'äj-p-äj-är)	k-u-loch-p-aJ-al	k-u-loch-b'-aan-äl	'it is bent'
CP	loch-p-aj-ij-∅	(b'äj-p-äj-ij-∅)	loch-p-aj-ij	loch-b-aan-ij	'it was bent'
Celeritive					
ICP	k-u-b'uj-k'-aj-al	k-u-b'uj-k'-äj-är	k-u-b'uj-k'-aJ-al		'it split'
CP	b'uj-k'-aj-ij-∅	b'uj-k'äj-ij-∅	b'uj-k'-aj-ij		'it was split'

TABLE 24.62 POSITIONAL VERBS IN YUCATECAN LANGUAGES

	Yucatec	S Lac	Itzaj	Mopan	Gloss
ICP	k-u-nak-tal	k-u-näk-taar	k-u-näk-tal	walak u-näk-tal	's/he leans'
CP	nak-l-aj-ij-Ø	näk-r-äj-Ø	näk-l-aj-ij	näk-l-aj-i	's/he leaned'
DEP	nak-l-ak-Ø	näk-r-äk-Ø	näk-l-ak-Ø	näk-l-äk-Ø	'that s/he lean'
IMP	nak-l-en	näk-r-en	näk-l-en	näk-l-en	'lean!'

TABLE 24.63 INCHOATIVE (VERSIVE) VERBS IN YUCATECAN LANGUAGES

	Yucatec	S Lac	Itzaj	Mopan	Gloss
ICP	k-u-sak-tal	k-u-säk-taar	k-u-säk-tal	walak u-säk-tal	'it whitens'
	k-u-sak-ch-aj-al	k-u-säk-ch-äj-är			
CP	sak-ch-aj-ij-Ø	säk-ch-äj-(ij)-Ø	säk-aj-ij	säk-aj-i	'it whitened'
		säk(-ij)-Ø			
DEP	sak-ch-aj-ak-Ø	säk-ch-äj-äk-Ø	säk-ak	säk-ak	'that it whiten'
		säk-ak-Ø			

3.5.2.4 Inchoative (versive) verbs

Inchoative (versive) verbs are derived from adjectives and noun roots and indicate a change of state. Yucatec and Southern Lacandon have two inchoative forms, one with -*ch* (based on Hofling 2006b:381), shown in Table 24.63.

3.5.2.5 Active verbs

Active verbs are derived from active verbal noun roots, have an antipassive voice value, and like other antipassives, are generally marked by the suffix -*n* in statuses other than the incompletive (cf. §3.5.2.2.), as in Table 24.64.

3.5.2.6 Affective verbs

Affective verbs are derived from affective roots and involve the sensory semantics of color, texture, sound and motion. Derivation of affective verbs with -*b'aj* or -*b'al* occurs in all Yucatecan languages, as in Table 24.65. Other derivations are with -*(á)ank* in Yucatec and Southern Lacandon (c), (d), and with -*m* in Mopan (b).

Affective verbs with -*bal/baj* have an antipassive voice value (cf. 3.5.2.2.), as indicated by the -*n* suffix in Table 24.66, with the exception of Mopan.

The Yucatec affective forms with -*(á)ankil* also have an antipassive value, but the corresponding Southern Lacandon forms inflect like regular intransitives, as shown in Table 24.67. Southern Lacandon also has a good number of celeritive affective verbs such as *bär-k'-äráank-är* 'spin', *b'ur-k'-äráank-är* 'sway', *ch'ik-k'-äráank-är* 'stand hopping', and *jir-k'-äráank-är*, 'stretch'.

3.5.3 Deriving transitive verbs

Transitive verbs can be derived from intransitve roots (I), noun roots (N), adjective roots (A) positional roots (P) and affective roots (Af), as shown in Table 24.68. Transitive verbs are derived from intransitive roots and celeritive stems (cf. §3.5.2.2.) with -*(e)s(a)*;

TABLE 24.64 ACTIVE VERBS IN YUCATECAN LANGUAGES

	Yucatec	S Lac	Itzaj	Mopan	Gloss
ICP	k-u-tz'íib'	k-u-tz'iib'	k-u-tz'iib'	walak u-tz'iib'	's/he writes'
CP	tz'íib'-n-aj(-ij)-Ø	tz'iib'-n-äj-Ø	tz'iib'-n-aj-ij	uch-Ø-i u-tz'iib'	's/he wrote'
DEP	tz'íib'-n-ak-Ø	tz'iib'-n-äk-Ø	tz'iib'-n-ak-Ø	uch-uk-Ø u-tz'iib'	'that s/he write'
IMP	tz'íib'-n-en	tz'iib'-n-en	tz'iib'-n-en	uch-uk a-tz'iib'	'write!'

TABLE 24.65 AFFECTIVE VERBS IN YUCATECAN LANGUAGES

	Yucatec	S Lac	Itzaj	Mopan	Gloss
a	(y)úumb'al	yúumb'aj	yuumb'aj	yuumb'aj	'swing'
b.	k-u-b'aj-b'al		b'äjb'aj	b'äjmäl	'plant'
c.	jopk'aláankil	joopáankär	jopb'aj		'light'
d.		rachk'äráankär	lochb'aj	lochb'aj	'bend'

TABLE 24.66 CONJUGATION OF AFFECTIVE VERBS WITH -b'al/baj IN YUCATECAN LANGUAGES

	Yucatec	S Lac	Itzaj	Mopan	Gloss
ICP	k-u-yúum-b'al	k-u-yúum-b'aj	k-u-yuum-b'aj	walak u-yuumb'aj	's/he swings'
CP	yúum-b'al-n-aj-ij-Ø	yúum-b'aj-n-äj-Ø	yúum-b'aj-n-aj-ij	uch-Ø-i u-yuum-b'aj	's/he swung'
DEP	yúum-b'al-n-ak-Ø	yúum-b'aj-n-äk-Ø	yuum-b'aj-n-ak-Ø	uch-uk-Ø u-yuum-b'aj	'that s/he swing'

TABLE 24.67 CONJUGATION OF AFFECTIVE VERBS WITH -ankil/-áankär IN YUCATEC AND SOUTHERN LACANDON

	Yucatec	Southern Lacandon	Gloss
ICP	k-uy-óom-ank-il	k-uy-óom-áank-är	'it foams'
CP	óom-ank-il-n-aj-ij-Ø	óom-áank-i(j)-Ø	'it foamed'
DEP	óom-ank-il-n-ak-Ø	óom-áank-äk-Ø	'that it foam'

TABLE 24.68 DERIVED TRANSITIVES IN THE INCOMPLETIVE STATUS IN YUCATECAN LANGUAGES

	Yucatec	S Lac	Itzaj	Mopan	Gloss
I	k-uy-éen-s-ik-Ø	k-uy-éen-s-ik-Ø	k-uy-en-s-ik-Ø	walak uy-en-s-ik-Ø	's/he lowers it'
N	k-u-tz'íib'-t-ik-Ø	k-u-tz'iib'-t-ik-Ø	k-u-tz'iib'-t-ik-Ø	k-u-tz'iib'-t-ik-Ø	's/he writes it'
A	k-u-saj-kúun-t-ik-Ø	k-u-säk-kin-t-ik-Ø	k-u-säk-kun-t-ik-Ø	k-u-säk-kun-t-ik-Ø	's-he whitens it'
P	k-u-kul-kíin-t-ik-Ø	k-u-kur-kin-t-ik-Ø	k-u-kul-kin-t-ik-Ø	k-u-kul-kin-t-ik-Ø	's/he seats her/him'
Af	k-u-letz'-b'an-kúun-t-ik-Ø		k-u-letz'-b'aj-kun-t-ik-Ø	k-u-leetz'-b'aj-kun-t-ik-Ø	'she makes it shine'

from noun roots with *-t*, *-in-t*, *-t-es*; from adjective, positional roots and *-b'al*, *-b'aj*; and from affectives with *-kun-t* (*b'an-k[ú]un-t* or *-b'an-k[ú]un-s* in Yucatec [Bricker et al. 1998:336]).

In Yucatec and Southern Lacandon, the dependent status is marked by *-ej* for all derived transitives, as in Table 24.69. For Itzaj and Mopan causatives derived from intransitive roots end with the causative *-es* and no status suffix. Imperatives have identical suffixes but no prefixes, e.g., Mopan *emes* 'lower it' and *tz'iib'tej* 'write it!'.

3.5.4 Reduplication

Verbs may be reduplicated to indicate repeated or intense action, as in Table 24.70. Yucatec and Southern Lacandon have reduplicated verbs with glottal stops corresponding to reduplicated adjectives described in §3.4.2.4.1. In Yucatec the basic pattern of the verb stem for verbs with transitive roots is CV'VCVC (a), (b), (e)–(g), while in Southern Lacandon it is CV'CV'C (e), (f). Itzaj and Mopan do not insert a glottal stop, but may copy one for roots of the shape CV'C (b), (c) or CVC' (g).

3.5.5 Verb compounds

3.5.5.1 Object incorporation

Object incorporation is a common process in all Yucatecan languages, shown in Table 24.71. Objects are typically in a patient or instrumental semantic relation to the

TABLE 24.69 YUCATECAN DERIVED TRANSITIVES IN THE DEPENDENT STATUS

	Yucatec and S Lac	*Itzaj and Mopan*	*Gloss*
I	*ka'uy-éen-s-ej-Ø*	*ka'uy-em-es-Ø*	'that s/he lower it'
N	*ka'u-tz'iib'-t-ej-Ø*	*ka'u-tz'iib'-t-ej-Ø*	'that s/he write it'
A	*ka'u-tz'u'utz'-kin-t-ej-Ø*	*ka'u-ya'ax-kun-t-ej-Ø*	'that s/he make it stingy'
P	*ka'u-kul-kin-t-ej-Ø, ka'u-kur-kin-t-ej-Ø*	*ka'u-tz'u'ut-kin-t-ej-Ø*	'that s/he seat her/him'
Af	*ka'u-letz'-b'an-kúun-t-ej-Ø* (Yuc only)	*ka'u l(e)etz'-b'aj-kun-t-ej-Ø*	'that s/he make it shiny'

TABLE 24.70 REDUPLICATED VERBS IN YUCATECAN LANGUAGES

	Yucatec	*S Lac*	*Itzaj*	*Mopan*	*Gloss*
a.	*lo'o-lom-ik-Ø*		*lo-lom(-t-)ik-Ø*	*lo-lom-t-ik-Ø*	'stab repeatedly'
b.	*xi'i-xil-ik-Ø*		*xi'-xi'il-b'aj*	*xi'-xi'il-t-ik-Ø*	'bristle repeatedly'
c.			*xi'-xi'mal*	*xin-xim-b'al*	'walk up and down'
d.	*ch'úu-ch'uyik-Ø*	*ch'u-ch'úuy*	*ch'u-ch'uy-b'aj*	*ch'u-ch'uy*	'swing back and forth'
e.	*ja'a-jap-ik-Ø*	*ja'-ja'p-ik-Ø*			'open mouth repeatedly'
f.	*ja'a-jat-ik-Ø*	*ja'-ja'tik-Ø*			'tear repeadedly'
g.	*ja'a-jatz'-ik-Ø*		*jä'-jätz'-ik-Ø*		'whip repeatedly'

TABLE 24.71 OBJECT-INCORPORATED FORMS IN YUCATECAN LANGUAGES

	Yucatec	S Lac	Itzaj	Mopan	Gloss
a.			*pul=che*	*pul=che'*	'fell trees'
b.		*pur=che'-t-ik*	*pul=che-t-ik'*		'fell trees in'
c.	*mutz'-'ich*	*mutz'-'ich*	*mutz'='ich*	*mutz'='ich*	'blink'
d.			*mutz'='ich-t-ik*	*mutz'-'ich-t-ik*	'blink at'
e.	*níich'=koj*		*nich'=koj*	*nich'=koj*	'bare teeth'
f.	*níich'=koj-t-ik*		*nich'=koj-t-ik*		'bare teeth at'

TABLE 24.72 ADVERBIAL INCORPORATION IN YUCATECAN LANGUAGES

	Yucatec	S Lac	Itzaj	Mopan	Gloss
a.	*ka'aj='a'al-ik*	*ka'='a'rik*	*ka'='a'l-ik*		'say again'
b.	*jáa-jan=jan-al*			*jan=jan-al*	'say rapidly'
c.		*k'aa-k'as='a'r-ik*	*k'a-k'as=t'an-t-ik*	*k'a-k'as=t'an-t-ik*	'speak badly of'
d.			*toj=päk'(-t)-ik*	*toj=päk'-ik*	'plant straight'
e.		*ki'='a'r-ik*	*ki'=ki'=t'än(-t)-ik*	*ki'=ki'=t'an-t-ik*	'say well, bless'

TABLE 24.73 NUMERALS IN YUCATECAN LANGUAGES

	Yucatec	S Lac	N Lac	Itzaj	Mopan	Gloss
a.	*jun=*	*jun=*	*jun=*	*jun=*	*jun=*	'one'
b.	*ka'aj=*	*ka'=*	*ka'=*	*ka'=*	*ka'=*	'two'
c.	*óox=*	*óox=*	*ox=*	*ox=*	*ox=*	'three'
d.	*kan=*			*kän=*	*kän=*	'four'
e.	*jo'oj=*			*job'=*	*jo'=*	'five'

verb, which is in antipassive voice (a), (c), (e). Object-incorporated forms may also be transitivized with *-t* (b), (d), (f).

3.5.5.2 Adverb incorporation

Adverbial modifiers may be incorporated into the verb before the verb stem, shown in Table 24.72. The adverbial modifiers may also be reduplicated (b), (c), (e).

3.6 Numerals and numeral classifiers

Maya numerals over five have largely been replaced by Spanish numerals. Maya numerals for one to five are given in Table 24.73. Numeral classifiers, shown in Table 24.74, specify the category of a noun used in enumerating expressions in the construction:

TABLE 24.74 NUMERAL CLASSIFIERS IN YUCATECAN LANGUAGES

	Yucatec	S Lac	N Lac	Itzaj	Mopan	Gloss
a.	p'éel	p'éej (archaic)	p'el	p'eel	p'eel	'inanimate'
b.	túul	túur (general)	tul	tuul	tuul	'animate'
				teek	teek	'plant'
c.	kóotz'		kotz'	kootz'	kootz'	'roll', 'spool'
d.	b'úuj	b'úuj	b'uj	b'uuj	b'uuj	'half'
e.	cháach		chaach	chaach		'handful'
f.	kúuch		kuch	kuuch	kuch	'load'
g.	kúul ('plant')		kul	kuul	kuul	'round'
h.	xóot'		xot'	xoot'	xoot'	'cut piece'
i.	yáal	yáar	yal	yaal	yaal	'layer'

num & ncl noun, for example, Yucatec *jum=p'éel waaj* 'one (inanimate) tortilla'. Categories involve animacy, shape, and measures. The system of numeral classifiers is quite elaborate in Yucatec, Northen Lacandon, Itzaj and Mopan, but hardly exists in Southern Lacandon. In Yucatec they generally have high tone, in Itzaj and Mopan they have long vowels, but are often reduced to a short vowel in Northern Lacandon.

3.7 Relational nouns and prepositions

The one clear preposition in Yucatecan languages is *ti'* shown in Table 24.75 (a). It may combine with other elements to form complex preposition-like constructions (b)–(e).

Relational nouns are an important class that are formally (possessed) nouns but often function like prepositions. They typically begin with *ti'* prefixed to a possessed nominal form. They are generally inflected for person, e.g., Itzaj *t-inw-ok'ol*, 'over me', *t-aw-ok'ol* 'over you', *t-uy-ok'-ol* 'over her/him'. Shortened forms also occur functioning as prepositions, as in Mopan *et-el* and Itzaj *et(-el)* 'with. The forms in Table 24.76 are inflected for the third person.

3.8 Particles

Particles do not have inflections (Kaufman 1991:74) in contrast to other root classes. They carry grammatical information and include deictics, interrogative/relative markers and a variety of other grammatical markers. Deictic particles, ubiquitous in all Yucatecan languages, are shown in Table 24.77. Many appear in two-part framing particle constructions with a preposed element (a)–(g) and a final element (h)–(l). In Yucatec and Southern Lacandon the proximal and distal markers are *-a'* and *-o'* respectively while the corresponding particle in Itzaj and Mopan are *-la'/-d'a'* and *-lo'/-d'o'*, which only occur with *je'*, *te'* and *a(')*, as in Itzaj *je'-la'* 'this', *je'-lo'* 'that' and *a'-la'* 'this one' *a'-lo'* 'that one'. Yucatec and Mopan also have an auditory particle *-b'e'* as in Yucatec *je'e-b'e'* 'listen there!' and Mopan *je-b'e'* 'listen (to that)!'. See Hanks (1990) for detailed description of deixis in Yucatec, Bergqvist (2008) for detailed description of deixis in Lacandon, and Hofling (2000) for description of Itzaj deixis.

TABLE 24.75 PREPOSITIONS AND PREPOSITION-LIKE CONSTRUCTIONS IN YUCATE-CAN LANGUAGES

	Yucateco	S Lac	N Lac	Itzaj	Mopan	Gloss
a.	ti'	ti'	ti'	ti'	ti'	'in, to, at, from'
b.	chúumuk (ti')	chumuk (ti')	chumuk	chumuk	chumuk	'the middle (of)'
c.	náach (ti')	náach	naach	naach (ti)	naach	'far (from)'
d.	tak (ti')	b'äytäk (ti')	tak	tak (ti)	tak (ti)	'until, up to'
e.	naatz' (ti')		xok'ol ti'	natz' (ti')	natz'	'near (to)'

TABLE 24.76 RELATIONAL NOUNS IN YUCATECAN LANGUAGES

	Yucatec	S Lac	N Lac	Itzaj	Mopan	Gloss
a.	t-u-yáan-al	(u)y-aaram	t-uy-alam	t-uy-alam	t-uy-alam	'below her/him'
b.	y-éet-el	y-ej-er	y-et-el	t-uy-et-el	t-uy-et-el	'with her/him'
c.	t-uy-ik-nal	y-ik-naan	y-ik-nän	t-uy-äk-nal		'facing her/him'
d.	t-u-paach	päch-ir	pach-il	t-u-pach, pach-il	t-u-pach, pach-il	'behind her/him'
e.	t-u-juun-al	t-u-jun-aan	t-u-jun-aan	t-u-jun-al	t-u-jun-al	's/he is alone'
f.	t-u-meen	teen	t-u-men	t-u-men	u-men	'by, because'
g.	ich(-il)	ich	ich(-il)	ich(-il)	ich(-il)	'in(side of)'
h.	t-u-tzeel			t-u-tzeel	t-u-tzeel	'at its side'
i.	t-u-láak-al	t-u-wóor-or	t-o-wol-ol	t-u-lak-al	t-u-lak-al	'all of them'
j.	t-uy-óok'-ol	t-uy-óok'-or	y-ok'-ol	t-uy-ok'-ol	t-uy-ok'-ol	'over her/him'

TABLE 24.77 DEICTIC PARTICLES IN YUCATECAN LANGUAGES

	Yucatec	S Lac	N Lac	Itzaj	Mopan	Gloss
a.	je'(l)	je'(r)	je'	je'	je'	'here'
b	te'(l)	te'(r)	te'	te'	te'	'there'
c.	ti'	ti'	(ti')	(ti')	(ti')	'there'
d.	way	waay	way	wa'ye'	wa'ye'	'here'
e.	tol					'out there'
f.	le(l)	a	la'	a'	a	'the'
g.	b'eey	b'aay	b'ay	b'aay	b'aa	'thus, like'
h.	-a'	-a'	-la'	-la'	-d'a'	'proximal'
i.	-o'	-o'	-lo'	-lo'	-d'o'	'distal'
j.	-i'	-i'		-i'ij	-i(ji)	'scope'
k.	-e'	-e'		-e'	-V	'topic'
l.	-b'e'				-b'e'	'auditory'

Yucatecan languages have similar sets of interrogative/relative particles as shown in Table 24.78. A final *x* is common in these forms, a reflex of an earlier interrogative particle (Hanks 1984 2:3; Kaufman 1991:75).

Indefinite pronouns may also be formed in the frame: *je'(e)*=interrogative *-ak* in Yucatec and Itzaj or simply adding *-ak* in Mopan, as shown in Table 24.79.

TABLE 24.78 INTERROGATIVE/RELATIVE PARTICLES IN YUCATECAN LANGUAGES

	Yucatec	S Lac	N Lac	Itzaj	Mopan	Gloss
a.	b'a'ax	b'a'r	b'a'inkil	b'a'ax	k'u'	'what?'
b.	b'a'ax teen	b'a'u-b'eer		b'a'ax-'o'lal	k'u'b'eel	'why?'
c.	b'a'ax ti'a'al	b'a'kiri'		b'a'ax-ti'a'al		'why?, what for?'
		b'a'u-ka'		b'a'ax u-ka'aj	u-ka'aj	'why?'
d.	b'a'x k'iin	b'éer	b'oon-k'in	b'a'ax k'in-il		'when?'
e.	b'ik'in	b'i-k'iin	tu'-k'in,	b'i-k'in	b'i-k'in	when?'
f.	máax	máak	mak	maax	mak	'who?'
g.	b'ajun, jay	b'oon, múun	b'oon	b'oon	b'oon	'how much?'
h.	tu'ux	tu', tub'aj	tu'	tu'ux	tub'aj	'where?'
i.	b'ix	b'ik	b'ik	b'ix	b'iki'	'how?'

TABLE 24.79 YUCATECAN INDEFINITE PRONOUNS

	Yucatec	S Lac	Itzaj	Mopan	Gloss
a.	je'e=b'a'ax-ak		je=b'a'ax-ak-ej	k'u'-ak	'whatever'
b.	je'e=máax-ak	kaax máak	je'=max-ak-ej	mak-ak	'whoever'
c.	je'e=tu'ux-ak	kaax tub'aj'	je'=tu'ux-ak-ej	tub'aj-ak	'wherever'
d.	je'e=b'ajux-ak		b'oon y-ok'b'oon		'however much'
e.	je'e=bix-ak	kaax b'éer	je=b'ix-ak-ej	b'ikij-ak, ka'ax b'i=k'in	'whenever'

4 PHRASES AND SIMPLE CLAUSE STRUCTURE

4.1 The noun phrase

4.1.1 Modifier-modified noun phrases

Noun phrases may be unmodified, generally with an indefinite meaning, or modified by determiners, numerals and other quantifiers, adjectives and demonstratives. The structure of modifier-modified noun phrases is as follows: DET Possessor Quantity Quality N Deictic (cf. Hanks 1984 3:2).

In Yucatec and Southern Lacandon the determiner precedes the noun and a deictic suffix follows, including nouns with noun class markers in Yucatec, as in Table 24.80 example (d). Southern Lacandon hardly has noun class markers and appears to use the distal marker -o' both as a distal marker (a) and a neutral topic marker as in (c) and (d). In Itzaj and Mopan the distal/proximal distinction requires a full demonstrative, as in (a) and (b), while the topic marker appears suffixed to the noun (c), (d). Itzaj and Mopan nouns with noun class markers do not require a determiner, as in (d).

In more complex definite NPs the terminal deictic occurs at the end of the phrase as in the Yucatec examples in Table 24.81 examples (a)–(d). je'(el) may occur initially in

TABLE 24.80 DETERMINER-NOUN   DEICTIC   CONSTRUCTIONS   IN   YUCATECAN LANGUAGES

	Yucatec	S Lac	Itzaj	Mopan	Gloss
a.	le wíinik-o'	a wiinik-o'	a 'winik je '=lo'	a winik a=d'o'-o	'that man'
b.	le wíinik-a'	a wiinik-a'	a 'winik je '=la'	a winik a=d'a'-a	'this man'
c.	le wíinik-e'	a wiinik-o'	a 'winik-e'	a winik-i	'the man'
d.	le x=kaax-e'	a kaax-o'	aj=kax-e'	aj=kax-a	'the chicken'

TABLE 24.81 DEFINITE NPS IN YUCATEC

	Yucatec	Gloss
a.	le in-k'aan-o'	'that hammock of mine' (Lehmann [L] 2002:96)
b.	le tumb'en máaskab'-o'	'that new machete' (Hanks 1984 2:1)
c.	le x=ch'úupal-o'	'that girl' (Hanks 1990:143)
d.	le óox=túul mejen paal- o'ob'-a'	'these three young children' (Hanks 1984 3:2)
e.	je 'le b'a'al-o'	'there is that thing' (Hanks 1990:257)
f.	je 'el inw-aalak 'kàax-o'b-a'	'here are my chickens' (L 2002:65)
g.	je 'el inw-o 'ch k'eyem-a'	'here's my pozole' (L 2002:67)

ostensive evidential constructions, as in (e)–(g). The Yucatec possessive classifier *aalak'* 'domesticated animal' appears in (f) and the classifier *'o 'och* 'food' in (g).

Definitely marked NPs in Southern Lacandon are formally similar but a default definite marking with -*o'* is more common as shown in Table 24.82 examples (a)–(c). The proximal distinction is apparent in NPs with the frame *a je'. . . . -a'*, as in (d), (e). The possessive classifier *äräk'* 'domesticated animal' appears in (b). In all Yucatecan languages, definite ordinal numeral constructions are formed with an initial 3A- marker, as in (f).

Itzaj definite NPs are similar, but the default topic marking suffix -*e'* is much more common as in Table 24.83. In examples with adjectives, a noun class marker frequently appears instead of the determiner (g). In Itzaj *o 'och* 'ration' does not function as a possessive classifier for food (h).

Mopan definite NPs follow similar patterns with pervasive terminal topic markers. Examples with terminal demonstratives appear in Table 24.84 (a)–(c). With a few adjective-noun constructions the determiner *a* appears as in (d), but with most a noun class marker occurs as in (e)–(g). Constructions with an initial demonstrative are also common as in (f), (g) and enumerated NPs may also occur in the *a . . . -V* frame as in (h).

4.1.2 Possessed (+ possessor) constructions

Constuctions of a possessed noun followed by a possessor noun are common in all Yucatecan languages and indicate a variety of relationships such as part-whole relations, kinship relations, personal property, beneficiary and recipient as well as more marked constructions indicating inalienable possession of body parts, inanimate possessors and members of groups (cf. §3.3.2.5; Hofling 2000:255–87; Lehmann 2002). When the possessor is given information, the possessed noun typically stands alone. Yucatec examples of unmarked possession occur in Table 24.85 indicating relationships such as names (a),

TABLE 24.82 DEFINITE NPS IN SOUTHERN LACANDON

	Southern Lacandon	Gloss
a.	a x=kiik-o'	'the woman' (Hofling [H] 2014a:334)
b.	a inw-äräk' kaax-o'b'-o'	'my/our chickens' (H 2014a:179)
c.	a majan máaskab'-o'	'the little machete' (H 2014a:185)
d.	a je'naj-a'	'this house' (H 2014a:153)
e.	a je'máaskab'-a a=je'r-a'	'this machete' (H 2014a:224)
f.	u-ka'=yaar-ir 'oot'	'the second layer of skin' (H 2014a:175)

TABLE 24.83 DEFINITE NPS IN ITZAJ

	Itzaj	Gloss
a.	(a') ix=ch'up-ej	'the woman' (Hofling [H] 2000:248)
b.	a'in-pek'-ej	'the dog of mine' (H 2000:249)
c.	a'kaj je'-la'-ej	'this town' (H 2000:253)
d.	a'ox=tuul mejen paal-oo'-ej	'the three young children' (H 2000:225)
e.	a'u-ka'=kuul a'naj-ej	'the second house' (H 2000:221)
f.	in-ka'=tuul mejen paal-oo'	'my two small children' (H 2000:225)
g.	aj=polok winik-ej	'the fat man' (H 2000:235)
h.	uy-o'och b'ooyo(j)	'his ration of tamales' (H 1997:489)
i.	je'=lo'in-pek'-ej	'there is my dog' (H 2000:300)

TABLE 24.84 DEFINITE NPS IN MOPAN

	Mopan	Gloss
a.	a pek' a=d'a'-a	'this dog' (H 2011a:296)
b.	ix-chu'a=d'o'-o	'that young lady' (H 2011a:400)
c.	le'ek a ab'äl-il a=d'o'-o	'that plum grove' (H 2011a:77)
d.	a nooch ik'-i	'the big wind' (H 2011a:328)
e	aj=tz'i'ju'um-u	'the little paper' (H 2011a:439)
f.	je=d'a'aj=b'ox sub'ul-u	'here is the black sub'ul tree' (H 2011a:80)
g.	je=d'a'aj=pät-b'il jaay-a	'here is the molded bowl' (H 2011a:346)
h.	a ka'=kuul wolis-i	'the two balls' (H 2011a:253)

TABLE 24.85 UNMARKED POSSESSED (+ POSSESSOR CONSTRUCTIONS) IN YUCATEC

	Yucatec	Gloss
a.	u-k'aaba'le x=ch'up-pàal-a'	'the name of this girl' (L 2002:42)
b.	u-paal-e'x-o'b j=k'áaxil-o'b'	'you are the children of farmers' (L 2002:43)
c.	uy-iitz le che'-o'	'the resin of the tree' (L 2002:61)
d.	inw-o'ch ja'as	'my banana' (L 2002:59)
e.	uy-aalak'peek'	'his dog' (L 2002:109)
f.	u-kib'kili'ch Anton	'the candles for Saint Anthony' (BEN) (L2002:117)
g.	tich in-b'áat-o'!	'pass me my/the ax!' (recipient) (L 2002:117)

kinship (b), part-whole (c), property with possessive classifiers for food (d), and domesticated animals (e), as well as beneficiary and recipient roles for the possessor (f) and (g). Southern Lacandon, Itzaj and Mopan have a similar range of possessed constructions. Mopan examples are given in Table 24.86 with unmarked part-whole constructions (a)–(d), kinship (e), and beneficiary (f).

The Yucatec contrast between unmarked possession and possession marked by -il is shown in Table 24.87 examples (a)–(d) with the unmarked relationship of possessor of property (a) and the marked inanimate possessor in (b); and the unmarked animate possessor in (c) in contrast to the inanimate possessor in (d); and the reversal where the property is in the possessor relationship in (e), (f). Additional examples of possession with -il indicate 'type of' (g), abstract derivation (h), metaphoric usage (i) member of a group (j) and 'painful part of' (k).

Southern Lacandon, Itzaj and Mopan have a similar range of possessed constructions. Mopan examples of marked possession with -il and inanimate possessors occur Table 24.88 including 'of a place' (a)–(c), purpose (d), (e), metaphor (f), abstract derivation (g), and 'member of a group' in (h).

4.2 Core arguments, agreement, and alignment

In all Yucatecan languages the core arguments of transitive subject, transitive direct object, and intransitive subject are marked on the verb by the Set A and Set B person markers (cf. §3.1). Traditionally this agreement system has been described as split-ergative, with ergative marking in the completive and dependent statuses, where the

TABLE 24.86 UNMARKED POSSESSED (+ POSSESSOR CONSTRUCTIONS) IN MOPAN

	Mopan	Gloss
a.	uy-ak'k'aak'	'the flame (tongue) of a fire' (H 2011a:117)
b.	uy-al u-k'ä'	'the fingers of her/his hand' (H 2011a:424)
c.	uy-ich'ak uy-al u-k'ä'	'the nails of his/her fingers' (H 2011a:180)
d.	u-ch'ib'b'äyäl	'the vein of the bayal palm' (H 2011a:167)
e.	u-kik a tz'ub'-u	'the older sister of the boy' (H 2011a:238)
f.	u-jan-al a 'ek'en-e	'the food for the pigs' (H 2011a:218)

TABLE 24.87 MARKED POSSESSED-il (+ POSSESSOR CONSTRUCTIONS) IN YUCATEC

	Yucatec	Gloss
a.	u-x=ba'y Jwaan	'the bag of Juan' (L 2002:43)
b.	u-x=ba'y-il in-nook'	'the bag of clothing' (L 2002:44)
c.	uy-uuk'le paal-o'	'the louse of the child' (L 2002:44)
d.	uy-uuk'-il u-jo'ol le pàal-o'	'the louse of the head of the child' (L 2002:44)
e.	in-yuum	'my lord' (L 2002:44)
f.	u-yuum-il le tziimn-e'	'the owner of the horse' (L 2002:44)
g.	u-che'-il oon	'avocado tree', 'tree of avocado' (L 2002:46)
h.	in-k'oj-a'an-il	'my sickness' (L 2002:52)
i.	u-k'ab'-il in-nook'	'my sleeves', 'the arms of my clothes' (L 2002:84)
j.	u-x-t'uup-il in-paal-e'	'my youngest daughter' (L 2002:96)
k.	u-yaj-il im-pu'uch	'the painful part of my back' (Bricker et al. 1998:310)

TABLE 24.88 MARKED POSSESSED-*IL* (+ POSSESSOR CONSTRUCTIONS) IN MOPAN

	Mopan	Gloss
a.	*uy-ak'-il che'*	'vine of the forest' (H 2011a:118)
b.	*u-kutz-il chäk'an*	'the turkey of the savanah' (H 2011a:251)
c.	*u-pek'-il ja'*	'dog of water', 'otter' (H 2011a:350)
d.	*u-b'en-il k'ik'*	'vein' 'path of blood' (H 2011a:130)
e.	*u-che'-il okom*	'wood for houseposts' (H 2011a:152)
f.	*u-kal-il a koton-o*	'the neck of the shirt' (H 2011a:229)
g.	*u-winik-il u-k'oj-a'an-il*	'the lord of her/his illness' (H 2011a:457)
h.	*u-t'up-il u-mejen*	'the last of his children' (H 2011a:426)

TABLE 24.89 NOMINATIVE-ACCUSATIVE VERB AGREEMENT IN YUCATEC AND MOPAN

	Intransitive	Transitive
Yuc	táan **a**-jóok'-ol	táan **aw**-il-(i)k-en
	DUR A2-go out-IIS	DUR A2-see-ITS-B1SG
	'you go'	'you are seeing me'
Mopan	tan **a**-tal(-el)	tan **aw**-il-ik-en
	DUR A2-come(-IIS)	DUR A2-see-ITS-B1SG
	'you are coming'	'you are seeing me'

transitive subject is marked by a Set A ergative person marker, while the transitive direct object and intransitive subject are marked by Set B absolutive person markers (Bricker 1978a). In contrast, in the incompletive status both the transitive subject and the intransitive subject are marked by Set A person markers while the transitive object is marked by a Set B person marker in a nominative-accusative pattern. In this system, it is the intransitive subject that is marked like a transitive subject or *agent* in the incompletive but like a transitive object or *patient* in the completive and dependent statuses. Other semantic bases for this system have been proposed (e.g., Krämer and Wunderlich 1999; Bohnemeyer 2004). In Mopan the system is further complicated by a loss of the *-n* antipassive voice marker, which has been replaced by periphrastic auxiliary constructions with the auxiliary *uchul* 'happen' in which antipassive subjects are marked by Set A person markers in the completive and dependent statuses, but other intransitive verb subjects are marked by Set B person markers, which has been described as an active-stative alignment system (Danziger 1996).

Yucatecan generally has a split-ergative system and is nominative-accusative in the incompletive status. In this status, transitive and intransitive subjects are marked by Set A person markers, while all direct objects are marked by Set B person markers in a nominative-accusative system. In Table 24.89 the second-person subject of both intransitive and transitive verbs is marked by the 2A- person marker *a(w)-*. Yucatec data are from Bricker et al. (1998:493, 400); Mopan data are from Hofling (2011:11–12).

In contrast, in the completive status intransitive subjects and transitive direct objects are marked by Set B pronouns as shown by the second-person intransitive subject and direct object marked by *-(e)ech* in Table 24.90. As mentioned above, the Mopan pattern described here does not hold for the verbs in the antipassive voice which will described further in §4.4.

TABLE 24.90 ERGATIVE-ABSOLUTIVE VERB AGREEMENT IN SOUTHERN LACANDON AND ITZAJ IN THE COMPLETIVE STATUS

	Intransitive	*Transitive*
S Lac	b'in-Ø-(e)ech	t-in-sut-aj-**ech**
	go-CIS-B2SG	ICP-A1SG-see- DTS-B2SG
	'you went'	'I visited you'
Itzaj	tal-Ø-**eech**	t-inw-il-aj-**ech**
	come-CIS-B2SG	ICP-A1SG-see- DTS-B2SG
	'you went'	'I saw you'

4.3 Peripheral arguments

In addition to the core arguments described in §4.2 are the peripheral arguments of indirect object (IO), oblique passive agents, instruments, locatives and possessors.

4.3.1 Indirect objects

Indirect objects are marked by the preposition *ti'* 'to', 'for' and their unmarked position is after the verb. They also follow direct objects if present in unmarked constructions as in (1).

(1) Unmarked position for indirect objects

YUCATEC

a. Tun-tzol-ik-Ø   wa=b'a'ax **ti'** **(l)e** **x=ch'úupal-o'**.
   DUR;A3-explain-ITS-B3SG Q=thing to DET F=girl-DST
   'He's explaining something to that girl.' (Blair and Vermont Salas [B and VS] 1965:155)

SOUTHERN LACANDON

b. T-in-tz'aj-Ø   a   när   **ti'** **wíinik**.
   CP-A1SG-give;CTS-B3SG DET corn to man.
   'I gave the corn to a man.' (H 2014a:360)

ITZAJ

c. T-in-tz'aj-Ø   ixi'im **t-a'** **winik-ej**.
   CP-A1SG-give;CTS-B3SG corn to-DET man-TOP
   'I gave corn to the man.' (H 2000:191)

MOPAN

d. U-tz'aj-oo'   u-sij='ol-al   **ti'i u-yum-il**   **witz**.
   A3-give;CTS-PL A3-gift=spirit-POSS to A3-lord-POSS hill
   'They gave the offering to the lord of the hill.' (H 2011a:385)

In Yucatec NPs and first and second person (but not third person) indirect object pronouns may also be fronted (Hofling and Ojeda 1994:277) as in (2c). IO pronouns may also be fronted in Southern Lacandon (2d), Itzaj (2e) and Mopan (2f).

(2) Fronted indirect objects

YUCATEC

a. Tun-tzol-ik-∅   **ti'** **(l)e** **x=ch'úupal-o'** wa=b'a'ax.
DUR;A3-explain-ITS-B3SG to DET F=girl-DST Q=thing
'He's explaining something to that girl.' (B and VS 1965:155)

b. Juch-∅-∅   le k'eyem **ten**-o'!
grind-IMPTS-B3SG DET pozole 1SG.IOPR-DST
'Grind the posole for me!' (Hofling and Ojeda 1994:277)

c. Juch-∅-∅   **ten**   le k'eyem-o'!
grind-IMPTS-B3SG 1SG.IOPR DET pozole-DST
'Grind me the pozole!' (Hofling and Ojeda 1994:277)

SOUTHERN LACANDON

d. A   ti'-o'b'-o'   k-u-tz'ik-∅   **teen-o'b'** u-bäk'-er   yuuk.
DET 3PRON-PL-DST ICP-A3-give;ITS-B3SG 1SG.IOPR-PL A3-meat-POSS deer
'They give us venison.' (H 2014a:332)

ITZAJ

e. la'ayti' t-u-k'at-aj-∅   **ten**   ka'=p'e mes   permiisoj
3PRON CP-A3-ask-CTS-B3SG 1SG.IOPR two=INAN month leave
'He asked for two months leave for me.' (H 2000:193)

MOPAN

f. U-tz'iil-t-aj-∅   **ten**   tz'eek a   ja'-a.
A3-take.out-TR-CTS-B3SG 1SG.IOPR little DET water-TOP
'S/he took out a little bit of water for me.' (H 2011a:440).

4.3.2 Possessors

4.3.2.1 Constructions with the existential y(a)an

In addition to marking possession with possessive pronouns, possessors may be indicated in existential constructions with *y(a)an*. In Yucatec, with first and second person possessors the indirect object pronouns follow *yaan*, e.g., *y(a)an ten* possessed, 'I have X' as in (3a), (3c), while with third person possessors the construction is *y(a)an* possessed *ti* (possessor) as in (3d), (3e) (cf. Blair and Vermont Salas 1965:154–5; Hanks 1990:164). As shown in (3b), (3c), when the possessed noun has a Set A prefix, the independent pronoun is optional. In Southern Lacandon the IO pronoun always follows *yaan* regardless of person (3f), (3i) and does not occur with possessed nouns (3g), (3h). In Itzaj the IO pronoun may follow *ya(a)n* regardless of person (3j), (3m) and is optional if the possessed noun is marked by a Set A pronoun (3k), (3l). With the third person the IO pronoun may follow the possessed NP (3n). Mopan seems to have a system where the IO pronoun follows *yan* regardless of person (3o)–(3r), and does not appear with possessed nouns marked by Set A person markers (3p), (3q).

(3) Possession with the existential *y(a)an*

YUCATEC
a. ***Yaan ten*** *tzíimin.*   'I have a horse.' (Hanks 1990:164)
b. ***Yaan in-****tzíimin.*   'I have a horse.' (Hanks 1990:164)

c. **Yaan ten in-***tzíimin.***   'I have a horse.' (B and V 1965:154)
d. **Yaan** *tzíimin* **ti'**   'S/he has a horse.' (Hanks 1990:164)
e. **Yaan** *un=tu tzíimin* **ti'** *im-papa(j) xan.*   'My father too has a horse.' (B and VS 1965:154)

SOUTHERN LACANDON
f. **Yaan teen** *ka'=cháach järär.*   'I have two handfuls of arrows.' (H 2014a:102)

g. **Yaan** *'u-ki'b'ook.*   'It has a good smell.' (H 2014a:71)
h. **Yaan** *'inw-atoch.*   'I have a house' (H 2014a:404)
i. **Yaan ti'** *chäkw-ir.*   'S/he has a fever.' (H 2014a:98)

ITZAJ
j. **Yan-aj-ij ten** *jum=p'e chem.*   'I had a canoe' (H 1997:686)
k. *Ten-ej,* **yan in-***wakax.*   'Me, I have cattle.' (H 2000:286)
l. **Yan (ten) in-***tz'on.*   'I have my gun.' (H 2000:286)
m. *Aj=Jwan* **yan ti'ij** *yaab' tzimin.*   'Juan has a lot of horses.' (H 1997:687)
n. **Yan** *yaab'b'a'axtak* **ti'ij.**   'S/he has a lot of things' (H 1997:687)

MOPAN
o. *Top* **yan ten** *a yaj='ol-al-a.*   'I have much sadness.' (H 2011a:472)
p. *Ma'* **yan in-***laat'.*   'I don't have a crutch' (H 2011a:284)
q. *Top* **yan in-***p'ax.*   'I have a lot of debts.' (H 2011a:364)
r. **Yan ti'i** *aj-p'is aj-B'ex-e.*   'Sebastián 'Sebastian has the ruler.' (H 2011a:473)

4.3.2.2 Constructions with the independent possessive pronoun *ti'-(a')al*

Possessors may also be indicated with independent possessive pronouns based on *ti'(a') al* with Set A person-marking prefixes, e.g., *'in-ti'(a')al* 'mine' as in the Yucatec examples (4a)–(4c). Yucatec also allows first and second person IO pronouns with the *le . . . -a'* frame to serve this function, as in (4d) (Hanks 1990:165). In Southern Lacandon IO pronouns alone can function as possessive pronouns, as in (4e)–(4g). Itzaj uses the *ti'-a'al* form of the independent possessive pronoun, as in (4i)–(4k). While Mopan has the *ti'-al* form of the independent possessive pronoun as in (4m), it more frequently uses ith IO pronouns in this function (4n), (4o).

(4) The independent possessive pronoun *ti'(a')al*

YUCATEC
a. **A-ti(')-(a')al** *le naj-a'*   'This house is yours.' (B and VS 1965:154)
b. **A-ti'-al-e'ex-o'ob'** *le tzíimin-o'.*   'Those horses are yours (pl).' (Hanks 1990:165).

c. *Tz'áaj ten le'* **in-ti'-al-***o'.*   'Give me mine there.' (Hanks 1990:165)
d. *le* **ten-***a'*   'this one mine' (Hanks 1990:165)

SOUTHERN LACANDON
e. **Teen** *in-púutz'.*   'The needle is mine' (H 2014a:271)
f. **teen** *in-p'ookot.*   'The arrow is mine.' (H 2014a:272)
g. *A raay-o'* **teen.**   'That is mine'(H 2014a:330)

ITZAJ
    i. *A' naj-ej **a-ti'-a'al**.*   'The house is yours.' (H 2000:285)
    j. *a' meyaj je'=la'-ej **a-ti'-a'al**.* 'This work is yours.' (H 1997:339)
    k. *Ma' **in-ti'-a'al**-i'ij.*   'It's not mine' (H 1997:606)

MOPAN
    m. ***a-ti'-al***   'yours.' (H 2011a:407)
    n. ***Ten** a k'aan a=d'a'-a.*   'This string is mine.' (H 2011a:267)
    o. ***Tech** wa aj-p'is a=d'a'-a?* 'Is this scale yours?' (H 2011a:103)

4.3.3 Oblique agents

While agents in passive constructions are frequently omitted, they may be mentioned obliquely after the relational noun *tumen* in Yucatec (5a), *teen* or *män* in Southern Lacandon (5b), (5c), *men* in Itzaj (5d) and *(u)men* in Mopan (5e).

(5) Oblique agents

    YUCATEC
    a. Yan   u-xo'ok-ol   ti'   **t-u-men**   **u-láak'**   **máak**.
       OBLIG A3-read;PSV-IIS 3IOPR to-A3-make A3-other person
       'It must be read to her by another person.' (B and VS 1965:454)

    SOUTHERN LACANDON
    b. A   k'áak'-o'   k-uy-us-t-a'r   **teen**   **iik'**.
       DET fire-DST ICP-A3-blow-TR-PSV;IIS by   wind
       'The fire was blown by the wind.' (H 2014a:373)

    c. k-uy-i'r-ir   x=kiik   **män**   **'a**   **wíinik-o'**.
       ICP-A3-see;PSV-IIS F=woman by   DET man-DST
       'The woman is seen by the man.' (H 2014a:221)

    ITZAJ
    d. k-u-tz'on-b'-ol-oo'   **men**   **a'**   **sold'aad'oj**
       ICP-A3-shoot-PSV-IIS-PL by   DET soldier
       'they were shot by the soldiers' (H 2000:387)

    MOPAN
    e. B'ok'-b'-Ø-i   a   je'   **u-men**   **ix=ch'up-u**.
       beat-PSV-CIS-B3SG DET egg A3-by F=woman-TOP
       'The eggs werre beaten by the woman.' (H 2011a:134)

4.3.4 Oblique locatives

Examples with the all-purpose preposition *ti'* are given in (6).

(6) *ti'* 'to', 'on', 'at'

    YUCATEC
    a. T-inw-il-aj-Ø   **ti'**   **b'ej**.
       CP-A1SG-see-CTS-B3SG on   road
       'I saw him on the road.' (ALMY 2003:231)

SOUTHERN LACANDON
b. B'in   in-ka'   **t-in-koor.**
   go   A1SG-go   to-A1SG-milpa
   'I am going to my milpa.' (H 2014a:171)

ITZAJ
c. Je'   in-kin-s-ik-Ø   b'alum   **ti   k'aax-ej.**
   ASSUR   A1SG-die-CAUS-ITS-B3SG   jaguar   in   forest-TOP
   'I am going to kill jaguars in the forest.' (H 2000:320)

MOPAN
d. B'in-Ø-i   b'in   **ti   kol.**
   go-CIS-B3SG   REP   to   milpa
   'They say he went to the milpa.' (H 2011a:133)

4.3.5 Oblique instruments

Oblique instruments/inanimate causes marked by *(é)etel* (*ejer* in Southern Lacandon) are shown in (7).

(7) Instrumental/cause NPs

YUCATEC
a. T-im-b'eet-aj-Ø   **y-éet-el   máaska'.**
   CP-A1SG-make-CTS-B3SG   A3-with-POSS   machete
   'I did it with a machete.' (Hanks 1990 2:1)

SOUTHERN LACANDON
b. K-u-b'an-ik-Ø   pa'=te'   **y-ej-er   ta'n.**
   ICP-A3-paint-ITS-B3SG   split=wood   A3-with-POSS   lime
   'He paints the wall with lime.' (H 2014a:72)

ITZAJ
c. A'   paal-ej   tan   u-jup'-ul   **y-et(-el)   a'   puutz'-ej.**
   DET   child-TOP   DUR   A3-pierce-IIS   A3-with-POSS   DET   needle-TOP
   'The child is sticking himself with a needle.' (H 2000:317)

d. A'   päk'-ej   tan   u-jut-ul   **et-el   a'   ja'-ej.**
   DET   wall-TOP   DUR   A3-collapse-IIS   with-POSS   DET   water-TOP
   'The wall is collapsing because of the water.' (H 2000:317)

MOPAN
e. Tan   u-cho'=chi'   **et-el   nok'.**
   DUR   A3-wipe=mouth   with-POSS   cloth
   'S/he is wiping her/his mouth with a cloth.' (instrument) (H 2011a:158)

f. B'oon-Ø-i   a   nok'   **et-el   itz-i.**
   paint-CIS-B3SG   DET   cloth   with-POSS   rust-TOP
   'The cloth stained with rust.' (inanimate cause) (H 2011a:138)

4.4 Voice

The forms of different voice values of transitive stems were given in §3.5.2. and §3.5.3. In this section examples of the different voices in sentences are provided.

4.4.1 Active transitive

Active transitive verbs have direct objects, which are marked on the verb by Set B person markers.

(8) Active transitive verbs

> YUCATEC
> a. **K-u-jatz'-ik-Ø**   le   wíinik   le   chan   xi'pal-o'.
>   ICP-A3-strike-ITS-B3SG   DET   man   DET   small   boy-DST
>   'That/the man strikes the/that boy.' (Hanks 1984 8:1)

> SOUTHERN LACANDON
> b. Kaax   **k-a-bo'-t-ik-en**   ma'   in-b'eeyaj.
>   Although   ICP-A2-pay-TR-ITS-B1SG   NEG   A1SG-work.
>   'Even if you pay me, I will not work.' (H2014a:179)

> ITZAJ
> c. A'   'o'tzil-il-ej   ma'   tan   **u-p'ät-ik-o'on**.
>   DET   poor-ABST-TOP   NEG   DUR   A3-leave-ITS-B1PL
>   'Poverty doesn't leave us.' (H 1997:492)

> MOPAN
> d. **Tiw-il-aj-ech**   ti   naach.
>   A1PL-see-DTS-B2SG   from   far
>   'We saw you from far away.'

4.4.2 Mediopassive (middle) voice

In the mediopassive voice of root transitive verbs, the subject is the semantic experiencer/ patient of the action and typically no agent is mentioned. The verb has intransitive status marking and the root vowel lengthens in Yucatec, Southern Lacandon, and usually in Mopan, but not in Itzaj. Corripio and Maldonado (2010) provide an extensive discussion of the middle voice in Yucatec.

(9) Mediopassive voice constructions

> YUCATEC
> a. **Ø-k'áal-Ø-Ø**   (l)e   joonaj-o'
>   CP-close/MIDDLE-CIS-B3SG   DET   door-DST
>   'The door shut' (Corripio and Maldonado 2010:150)

> SOUTHERN LACANDON
> b. **K-u-séej-ar**   u-koj.
>   ICP-A3-chip/MIDDLE-IIS   A3-tooth
>   'Her/his tooth chips.' (H 2014a:297)

> ITZAJ
> c. **Toch-Ø-ij**   in-kum-ej.
>   chip-CIS-B3SG   A1SG-pot-TOP
>   'My pot chipped.' (H 1997:595)

MOPAN
d. **P'eej-Ø-i**   a   che'-e.
   break/MIDDLE-CIS-B3SG   DET   wood-TOP
   'The wood broke to pieces.' (H 2011a:367)

4.4.3 Antipassive voice

In the antipassive voice the subject of the verb is the semantic agent. The patient is not mentioned or is incorporated into the verb (10e). For transitive roots, the vowel lengthens in Yucatec and Southern Lacandon, and optionally in Itzaj. Transitives derived with -*t* and -*s* also have antipassive forms. The antipassive marker is -*n* in statuses other than the incompletive, except in Mopan, which generally uses a periphrastic construction with the auxiliary *uch* 'happen' as in (10d), (10e), but does have traces of the -*n* antipassive (10f).

(10) Antipassive voice constructions

YUCATEC
a. Jay   p'e   ja'ab'   **xook-n-ak-ech?**
   how.many   INAN   year   study-AP-DIS-B2SG
   'How many years have you studied?' (B and VS 1967:623)

SOUTHERN LACANDON
b. **B'eeyaj-n-Ø-een**   ich   in-koor.
   work-AP-CIS-B1SG   in   A1SG-milpa
   'I worked in my milpa.' (H 2014a:84)

ITZAJ
c. **Xok-n-aj-ij**   ti   'eskweelaj.
   read-AP-CIS-B3SG   in   school
   'He studied in school.' (H 1997:679)

MOPAN
d. Ma'   **uch-Ø-i**   u-k'ay.
   NEG   happen-CIS-B3SG   A3-sing
   'S/he didn't sing.' (H 2011a:299)

e. A-laaj-oo'-o   **uch-Ø-oo'**   **u-tz'ok-s-aj=t'an.**
   DET-PROX-PL   happen-CIS-B3PL   A3-obey-CAUS-DTR=word
   'They obeyed words.' (H 2011a:441)

f. **Wäy-n-Ø-een**   ti   ak'ä'.
   sleep-AP-CIS-B1SG   at   night
   'I slept at night.' (H 2011a:405)

4.4.4 Passive voice

In the passive voice the subject of the verb is the semantic patient. The semantic agent may be mentioned obliquely (cf. §4.3.3.) but is often omitted.

(11) Passive voice constructions

YUCATEC
a. Yan   **u-xo'ok-ol**   ti'
   OBLIG   A3-read;PSV-IIS   3IOPR
   'It must be read to her.' (B and VS 1965:454)

SOUTHERN LACANDON
b. u-joor-ir   tu'   **k-u-b'a'j-är**   u-xaanab'   tzimin.
   A3-hole-POSS   where   ICP-A3-nail;PSV-IIS   A3-shoe   horse
   'the holes where the shoe of a horse is nailed' (H 2014a:76)

ITZAJ
c. Ti   kaj-ej   **pa(a)k'-b'-Ø-een.**
   in   town-TOP   await-PSV-CIS-B1SG
   'In town I was awaited.' (H 1997:504)

MOPAN
d. **Jul-b'-Ø-een**   u-men jul.
   pierce-PSV-CIS-B1SG   A3-by arrow
   'I was pierced by an arrow.' (H 2011a:224)

4.5 Constituent order and changes in order (topic and focus)

4.5.1 Basic word order

Durbin and Ojeda (1978a) outlined Basic Word Order and the functions of different word orders in Yucatec. Since that time there has been continued debate whether VOS or SVO should be considered Basic word orders (Bricker 1978b; Hofling 1984; Briceño Chel 2002; Gutiérrez-Bravo and Monforte 2008, 2011; Skopeteas and Verhoeven 2011; Verhoeven and Skopeteas 2015). In this regard, I consider VOS as basic word order with SVO as a common and relatively unmarked alternate. Most other orders are the result of fronting topicalized or focused NPs.

(12) Basic VOS order

YUCATEC
a. K-u-kíin-s-ik-Ø   le   wíinik(-Ø)   le   j=chakmo'ol-o'.
   ICP-A3-die-CAUS-ITS-B3SG   DET   man(-DST)   DET   M=jaguar-DST
   'That jaguar kills that man.' (Durbin and Ojeda 1978a:8)

SOUTHERN LACANDON
b. T-u-kuch(-aj)-o'ob'   in-b'a'-tak   tzimin.
   CP-A3-carry(-CTS)-PL   A1SG-thing-PL horse
   'The horse carried my things.' (Bergqvist 2008:67)

NORTHERN LACANDON
c. T-u-kin-s-a-Ø   b'alum K'ak'.
   CP-A3-die-CAUS-CTS-B3SG   jaguar PN
   'K'ak' killed the jaguar.' (Bruce 1974:62)

ITZAJ

d. K-uy-il-ik-Ø   a'   winik   a'   balum-ej.
   ICP-A3-see-ITS-B3SG   DET   man   DET   jaguar-TOP
   'The jaguar sees the man.' (H 2000:191).

MOPAN

e. Walak u-kin-s-ik-Ø   a   winik   a   b'alum-u.
   ICP   A3-die-CAUS-ITS-B3SG   DET   man   DET jaguar-TOP
   'The jaguar kills the man.' (Hofling 1984:40 [adapted])

While SVO may be considered a "Basic" word order in terms of its frequency, it may also be considered an order in which a topicalized subject has been fronted, a common construction.

(13) "Basic" SVO Order

YUCATEC

a. Le   wíinik-o'   k-u-kíin-s-ik-Ø   (le)   j=chakmo'ol(-o').
   DET man-DST   ICP-A3-die-CAUS-ITS-B3SG (DET)   M=jaguar(-DST)
   'That man kills jaguars (/that jaguar).' (Durbin and Ojeda 1978a:8)

SOUTHERN LACANDON

b. A   koor-o'   k-u-tz'ik-Ø   när.
   DET milpa-DST   ICP-A3-give;ITS-B3SG   corn
   'The milpa produces corn.' (H 2014a:360)

NORTHERN LACANDON

c. Hachakyum   t-u-men-t-aj-Ø   jach   winik.
   PN   CP-A3-make-TR-CTS-B3SG   true   man
   'Hachakyum made the real people (Lacandons).' (Bruce 1974:112)

ITZAJ

d. A'   b'alum-ej   k-uy-il-ik-Ø   winik.
   DET jaguar-TOP   ICP-A3-see-ITS-B3SG   man
   'The jaguar sees (a) man.' (H 2000:192)

MOPAN

e. A   winik-i   walak   u-kin-s-ik-Ø   (a)   b'alum(-u).
   DET man-TOP   ICP   A3-die-CAUS-ITS-B3SG   (DET)   jaguar-(TOP)
   'The man kills (the) jaguar.' (Hofling 1984:46)

4.5.2 Topicalization

As noted in §4.5.1., topicalized subjects are frequently fronted in SVO constructions. Other NPs and phrases may also be topicalized and fronted as in the following examples. The topicalized elements appear initially and are marked by the topic marker *-e'* in Yucatec and Itzaj, *-o'* in Southern Lacandon, and *-V* in Mopan.

(14) Topicalization

YUCATEC

a. **T-u-láak'   mees-e',**   u-laak'   gruupoj   k-u-b'in.
   in-A3-other   month-TOP   A3-other   group   ICP-A3-go

'The next month another group would go.' (Bricker 1981b:227.140; cited by Hanks 1984 8:8)

SOUTHERN LACANDON

b. **A   waj-o'**   ta   yaan   ich   uy-aaram   poj=che.
   DET   tortilla-TOP/DST   LOC   EXIST   in   A3-below   table
   'The tortilla, it's there under the table.' (H 2014a:68)

c. **A   áak'b'-ir-o'**   k-in-ween-an.
   DET   night-POSS-TOP/DST   ICP-A1SG-sleep-IIS
   'At night I sleep.' (H 2014a:69)

ITZAJ

d. **U-k'ek'en-ej**   taan   in-kin-s-ik-Ø.
   A3-pig-TOP   DUR   A1SG-die-CAUS-ITS-B3SG
   'His pig, I am butchering it.' (H 2000:194)

e. **A'   noj   winik-ej**   kach-Ø-ij u-k'ab'.
   DET   big   man-TOP   break-IIS-B3SG A3-arm
   'The big man, his arm broke.' (H 2000:194)

MOPAN

f. **U-ab'äl   ek'en-e**   yaab'   u-wich.
   A3-hogplum   pig-TOP   much   A3-fruit
   'The pig's hogplum tree has a lot of fruit.' (H 2011a:77)

g. **A   je'-e**   tan   u-b'ook'-ol.
   DET   egg-TOP   DUR   A3-beat/MIDDLE-IIS
   'The eggs are being beaten.' (H 2011a:138)

4.5.3 Contrastive focus

Another major mechanism of discourse highlighting is contrastive focus, which is marked by the focused NP's position in front of the verb (Verhoeven and Skopeteas 2015). It often has restricted specificity marking (Durbin and Ojeda 1978a) and never has the topic marker. A variety of focused elements in preverbal position are shown in (15) for Yucatec and Southern Lacandon. Yucatec and Southern Lacandon have a distinct construction for agent focus, shown in (15b)–(15d), (15f). It consists of an optional *j-* preceding a verb stem (in Yucatec) without Set A person markers. The verb takes an *-ik* suffix in the incompletive as in (15b); an *-ej* suffix in the completive (15c) (15f) and an *-il* suffix in the perfect (15d).

(15) Contrastive focus in Yucatec and Southern Lacandon

YUCATEC

a. **In-suku'un**   k-u-bin   t-aw-éet-el.
   A1SG-older.brother   ICP-A3-go   to-A2-with-POSS
   'My brother goes with you.' (intransitive subject focus) (Hanks 1984 8:3)

b. **Wíinik**   j=kíin-s-ik-Ø   le   j=chakmo'ol-o'.
   man   M?=die-CAUS-ITS-B3SG   DET   M=jaguar-DST
   'Man (not other animals) kills that jaguar.' (agent focus) (Durbin and Ojeda 1978a:8)

c. **In-suku'un** b'i-s-ej-Ø.
A1SG-older.brother go-CAUS-DTS?-B3SG
'My older brother brought it (away).' (agent focus) (Hanks 1984 8:5)

d. **Leti'** taa-s-m-aj-il-Ø le jaatz' úuch je'ex xan-o'.
3PRON come-CAUS-PRF-DTS-FOC-B3SG DET whip before however also-DST
'He was also the one who used to carry the whip.' (agent focus) (Bricker
1981b:220.25, Hanks 1984 8:4)

SOUTHERN LACANDON

e. A úuch-o' **teen** chichn-een ka' b'in-Ø-een.
DET before-DST 1SG.PRON little-B1SG when go-CIS-B1SG
'At that time, me, I was little when I left.' (intransitive subject focus) (Bergqvist
2008:69)

f. **Raj-i'** räk=b'o't-ej-Ø u-avióon-in in-b'eer.
DEM-FOC all=pay-DTS?-B3SG A3-plane-POSS A1SG-way
'It was he who paid for my fare.' (agent focus) (Bergqvist 2011:250)

g. **A-ro'** ma' a-kuch-ik-Ø!
DET-DST NEG A2-carry-ITS-B3SG
'That, don't carry it!' (object focus) (H 2014a:189)

Itzaj and Mopan similarly allow a wide range of elements to be focused in preverbal
position, but lack a distint agent focus construction. As a result, ambiguity may enter as to
whether it is an agent or a direct object that is focused, as in (16b) and (16e).

(16) Contrastive focus in Itzaj and Mopan

ITZAJ

a. **in=ten** k-im-b'el im-b'en-es-eech
EMPH=1SG.PRON ICP-A1SG-go A1SG-go-CAUS-B2SG
'I am going to take you.' (subject focus) (H 2000:195)

b. **A'** **winik** **(je'-loj)** k-u-kin-s-ik-Ø a' b'alum-ej.
DET man (OST-DST) ICP-A3-die-CAUS-ITS-B3SG DET jaguar-TOP
'The (/That) man kills the jaguar' or 'The jaguar kills the (/that) man.' (agent or
object focus) (Hofling 1984:51)

c. **Y-ok'** **in-b'äk'-el** tan u-jok'-ol ix=chu'chum.
A3-over A1SG-flesh-POSS DUR A3-erupt-IIS F=boil
'Over my body boils came out.' (locative focus) (H 1997:260)

MOPAN

d. **Le'ek** **a** **winik** a jan-Ø-ij-i.
3PRON DET man DET eat-CIS-3SG.B-TOP
'He is the man that ate.' (subject focus) (H 2011a:200)

e. **(A)** **winik** u-kin-s-aj-Ø aj=Jwan-a.
(DET) man A3-die-CAUS-DTS-B3SG M-PN-TOP
'(The) man killed Juan.' or 'Juan killed the man.' (agent or object focus)
(Hofling 1984:51)

f. **Y-alan**   **che'**   top   yan   a   sool-o.
A3-below   tree   much   EXIST   DET   dry.leaves-TOP
'Beneath trees there is a lot of dry leaves.' (locative focus) (H 2011a:390)

4.5.4 Topicalization and contrastive focus

When both topicalization and focus occur in the same sentence, the topicalized element occurs first followed by the focused element and the verb. In Yucatec there are distinct structures for $S_{[topic]}O_{[focus]}V$ and $O_{[topic]}S_{[focus]}V$ disambiguated by agent focus marking (j and the absence of Set A prefixes) as in (1a) and (1b). Itzaj and Mopan lack special agent focus marking and corresponding constructions are ambiguous as to an SOV or an OSV interpretation (1c) and (1d).

(17) Topicalization and Focus: $S_{[topic]}O_{[focus]}V$ and $O_{[topic]}S_{[focus]}V$

YUCATEC

a. Le   wíinik-o'   j=chakmo'ol   k-u-kíin-s-ik-Ø.
DET   man-TOP   M=jaguar   ICP-A3-die-CAUS-ITS-B3SG
'That man kills jaguars (not other animals).' (SOV) (Durbin and Ojeda 1978a:8).

b. Le wíinik-o' j=chakmo'ol j=kíin-s-ik-Ø.
DET man-DIST M=jaguar M?=die-CAUS-ITS-B3SG
'A jaguar (not some other animal) kills that man.' (OSV) (Durbin and Ojeda 1978a:8).

ITZAJ

c. A'   b'alum-ej,   winik   k-u-kin-s-ik-Ø.
DET   jaguar-TOP   man   ICP-A3-die-CAUS-ITS-B3SG
'As for the jaguar, it kills man.' or 'As for the jaguar, man kills it.' (SOV or OSV) (Hofling 1984:55)

MOPAN

d. A   winik-i   b'alum   u-kin-s-aj-Ø-a.
DET   man-TOP   jaguar   A3-die-CAUS-DTS-B3SG-TOP
'The man, it's a jaguar that he killed.' or 'A jaguar killed the man.' (SOV or OSV) Hofling 1984:56).

4.6 Negation

4.6.1 General negative ma'

The general negative marker in Yucatecan languages is *ma'(a)* which may be accompanied by a scope-marking suffix *-i'(ij)* in the frame *ma'. . . -i'(ij)*. In negative clauses the contrast between the incompletive and durative aspects is neutralized and only *t(aan)* occurs (Durbin and Ojeda 1978b; Hanks 1984 5:3). In Itzaj and Mopan the usage of *-i'(ij)* seems to be limited to negative focus constructions (18f), (18h).

(18) Negative constructions with *ma'*

YUCATEC

a. **Ma'**   taan   u-jan-al
NEG   DUR   A3-eat-NML
'He doesn't eat.' (Durbin and Ojeda 1978b:53)

b. **Ma'** in-k'áat   j   taal-**i'**
  NEG   A1SG-want SUB   come-SCOPE
  'I don't want to come.' (Durbin and Ojeda 1978b:55)

c. **Ma'** y-eer   tu'   k-u-b'in.
  NEG   A3-know   where   ICP-A3-go
  'S/he doesn't know where s/he is going.' (H 2014a:244)

d. **Ma'** chich   u-wáat-är-**i'**.
  NEG   hard   A3-break-IIS-SCOPE
  'It is not hard to break.' (H 2014a:378)

e. I   **ma'**   pat-aj-ij   in-mach-ik-Ø.
  and   NEG   ABIL-CIS-B3SG   A1SG-grab-ITS-B3SG
  'And I wasn't able to grab it.' (H 2000:432)

f. **Ma'** in=ten-**i'ij**!
  NEG EMPH=1SG.PRON-FOC
  'It's not me!' (H 2000:443)

g. **Ma'** uch-Ø-i   inw-alka'.
  NEG   happen-CIS-B3SG   A1SG-run
  'I didn't run.' (ALMG 2001b:293)

h. **Ma'** tz'ub'-en-**i'**
  NEG   child-B1SG-FOC
  I am not a child.' (ALMG 2001b:298)

4.6.1.1 Negative perfects

In Yucatecan languages, negative perfects appear in the dependent status (cf. Hofling 1998).

(19) Negative perfect constructions

a. **Ma'** tal-ak-Ø-**i'**.
  NEG   come-DIS-B3-SCOPE
  'He has not come.' (Hanks 1984:5:3)

b. **Ma'** too   y-a'r-ej-Ø.
  NEG   yet   A3-say-DTS-B3SG
  'S/he hasn't said it.' (H 2014a:63)

c. **Ma'** jan-ak-en
  NEG   eat-DIS-B1SG
  'I haven't eaten.' (H 2000:438)

MOPAN

d. **Ma'**   ak'ä'-ak-Ø.
NEG   night-DIS-B3
'It hasn't gotten dark.' (H 2011a:118)

4.6.1.2 Negative imperatives

Negative imperatives are formed in the construction: *ma'* A2-Verb-incompletive status marker.

(20) Negative imperatives

YUCATEC

a. **Ma'**   a-k'al-ik-Ø   (le   naaj-o')!
NEG   A2-close-ITS-B3SG   (DET   house-DIST)
'Don't close it (the house)!' (Hofling and Ojeda 1994:279)

SOUTHERN LACANDON

b. **Ma'**   a-käx-t-ik-Ø   máak!
NEG   A2-seek-TR-ITS-B3SG   person
'Don't look for anyone!' (H 2014a:178)

ITZAJ

c. **Ma'**   a-wa'-tal!
NEG   A2-stand-POS/IIS
'Don't stand!' (H 2000:371)

MOPAN

d. **Ma'**   a-jok'-ol!
NEG   A2-leave-IIS
'Don't leave!' (ALMG 2001b:300)

4.6.2 The negative mix

The negative marker *mix* (*ma'ax* in Mopan) occurs with negative pro-forms, as in Table 24.91.

It also appears independently to mean '(neither) . . . 'nor'. The framing particle *-i'(ij)* may also occur with *mix* in Yucatec and Southern Lacandon, as in (21a) and (21b).

TABLE 24.91 NEGATIVE PROFORMS IN YUCATECAN LANGUAGES

	Yucatec	*S Lac*	*Itzaj*	*Mopan*	*Gloss*
a.	*mix=b'a'al*	*(mäna')*	*mix=b'a'al*	*ma'ax=k'u'i*	'nothing'
b.	*mix b'i'=k'in*	*ma'b'i'=k'iin*	*mix b'i'=k'in*	*ma'ax b'i'=k'in*	'never'
c.	*mix=máak*	*mäna'maak*	*mix=maak*	*ma'ax=mak*	'no one'
d.	*mix=tu'ux*		*mix=tu'ux*	*ma'ax=tub'a*	'nowhere'

(21) *mix* '(neither) . . . nor'

YUCATEC

a. **Mix** chóoch-**i'**   **mix**   chujk-**i'**.
   NEG   salty-SCOPE   NEG   sweet-SCOPE
   'It is neither salty nor sweet.' (Bricker et al. 1998:185)

SOUTHERN LACANDON

b. **Ma'** ti'ar   päk'-ik-Ø-**i'**   kij   **mix**   a-ti'ar
   NEG   child   sow-ITS-B3SG-SCOPE   QUOT   NEG   A2-child
      k-u-räk=pak'-ik-Ø-**i'**   kij
      ICP-A3-all=sow-ITS-B3SG-SCOPE   QUOT
   'The children did not sow it, he said, nor did your children sow it, he said.'
   (Bergqvist 2008:70)

ITZAJ

c. **Ma** tan   in-jan-t-ik-Ø   **mix** ja'as   **mix** 'oop.
   NEG   DUR   A1SG-eat-TR-ITS-B3SG   NEG   plantain   NEG   anona
   'I am not eating either plantain or anona.' (H 2000:441)

MOPAN

d. **Ma'ax** le'ek   a=d'a'   ki'-i   **ma'ax** le'ek   a=d'o-o.
   NEG   3PRON   DET=PROX   good-TOP   NEG   3PRON   DET=DST-TOP
   'Neither this one nor that one is good.' (H 2011a:300)

4.7 Interrogation

4.7.1 Yes/no questions

Questions may be formed with a final rising intonational contour in all Yucatecan languages.

(22) Questions with intonational rise

YUCATEC

a. Jatz'utz aw-il-ik-Ø   le   way-a'?
   good   A2-see-ITS-B3SG   DET   here-PROX
   'Does it look good to you here?' (B and VS 1965:63)

SOUTHERN LACANDON

b. Tzooy   aw-ir-ik-Ø?
   good   A2-see-ITS-B3SG
   'It looks good to you?' (H 2014a:359)

ITZAJ

c. In=tech   nojoch=winik?
   EMPH=2SG.PRON   big=man
   'You are a gentleman?' (H 2000:418)

MOPAN

d. Yan   in-jan-t-ik-Ø?
   OBLIG   A1SG-eat-TR-ITS-B3SG
   'I have to eat it?' (ALMG 2001b:302)

Yes/no questions can also be formed with the interrogative particle *wá(aj)* in Yucatec and Southern Lacandon, *waj* in Itzaj and *wa* in Mopan. The particle follows the element in focus.

(23) Yes/no questions with the interrogative particle

YUCATEC
a. K-u-bin   **wá**   a-suku'un?
   ICP-A3-go   Q   A2-older.brother
   'Does your older brother go?' (Hanks 1984 2:3)

b. K-u-bin   a-suku'un   **wáaj**?
   ICP-A3-go   A2-older brother   Q
   'Does your older brother (and not someone else) go?'
   (Hanks 1984 2:3)

SOUTHERN LACANDON
c. T-aw-ir-aj-Ø   **wáaj**?
   COM-A2-see-CTS-B3SG   Q
   'Did you see it?' (H 2014a:380)

d. T-a-jun-aan   **wa**   yaan-eech?
   to-A2-one-POSS   Q   EXIST-B2SG
   'Are you alone?' (H 2014a:164)

ITZAJ
e. Taan   **waj**   a-jan-t-ik-Ø   b'u'ul?
   DUR   Q   A2-eat-TR-ITS-B3SG   beans
   '*Are* you eating beans?' (H 2000:420)

f. Ma'   **waj**   jan-ak-ech?
   NEG   Q   eat-DIS-B2SG
   'Haven't you eaten?' (H 2000:420)

MOPAN
g. Tan   **wa**   a-jan-al?
   DUR   Q   A2-eat-NML
   '*Are* you eating?' (ALMG 2001b:301)

h. Ak   ti-jan-t-ik-Ø   **wa**?
   already   A1PL-eat-TR-ITS-B3SG   Q
   'Do we eat already?' (ALMG 2001b:301)

4.7.2 Interrogative-word questions

A sampling of interrogative words was presented in §3.8. Examples are given below.

4.7.2.1 'Who'

Who questions may refer to a person in any case role. In Yucatec and Southern Lacandon, when referring to an agent the agent focus construction defined above in §4.5.3. is employed (cf. Bricker 1978b).

(24) 'who' questions in Yucatec and Southern Lacandon

YUCATEC

a. **Máax**   k-u-b'in   y-éet-el?
   who   ICP-A3-go   A3-with-POSS
   'Who's going with (him)?' (intransitive subject) (Hanks 1984 2:3)

b. **Máax**   kíin-s-ik-Ø?
   who   die-CAUS-ITS-B3SG
   'Who is killing him?' (agent focus) (Bricker 1978b:120)

b. **Máax**   ti'   k-a-meyaj?
   who   for ICP-A2-work
   'For whom do you work?' (oblique) (Bricker et al. 1998:181)

SOUTHERN LACANDON

d. **Máak**   y-äräk'   peek'-**i'**?
   who   A3-domestic.animal   dog-FOC
   'Whose dog is it?' (possessor) (H 2014a:65)

d. **Máak**   k'áat-ej-Ø   teech   waj?
   who   ask-DTS-B3SG   2SG.IOPR   tortilla
   'Who asked you for tortillas?' (agent) (H 2014a:205)

e. **Máak**   **y-ej-er**   käj-a'an-(e)ech?
   who   A3-with-POSS   live-PTCP-B2SG
   'With whom do you live?' (comitative) (H 2014a:176)

(25) 'who' questions in Itzaj and Mopan

ITZAJ

a. **Maax**   t-uy-il-aj-Ø?
   who   CP-3A-see-CTS-B3SG
   'Who saw him?' or 'Whom did he see?' (agent/patient) (H 2000:422)

b. **Maax**   t-a-t'an   u-tat-il?
   who   in-2A-thought   3A-father-POSS
   'Who do you think is the father (of the group?)' (possessor) (H 2000:422)

c. **Maax**   **ti'ij**   a'   tz'on-ej?
   who   3IOPR   DET   gun-TOP
   'Whose is the gun?' (possessor/indirect object) (H 2000:423)

MOPAN

d. **Mak**   a   tan   u-kin-s-aj=mutmuch'-u?
   who   DET   DUR   3A-die-CAUS-DTR=fly-TOP
   'Who is killing flies?' (agent) (ALMG 2001b:303)

e. **Mak**   **et-el**   a-b'et-aj-Ø?
   who   with-POS   2A-do-CTS-B3SG
   'With whom did you do it?' (comitative) (H 2011a:296)

f. **Mak**   **ti'i**   a   jan-al-a?
   who   3IO.PRON   DET   food-NML-TOP
   'Whose is the food?' (possessor/indirect object) (H 2011a:296)

4.7.2.2 'What'

'What' questions most commonly refer to direct objects but may refer to other case relations.

(26) 'what' questions

YUCATEC

a. **Ba'ax**   k-a-b'eet-ik-Ø?
   what   ICP-A2-do-ITS-B3SG
   'What are you doing?' (direct object) (Hanks 1984 2:3)

b. **B'a'ax** tz'aak-**il**?
   what   medicine-POSS
   'What (kind of) medicine?' (stative/kind of) (B and VS 1967:764)

SOUTHERN LACANDON

c. Oola,   **b'a'**   k-aw-ir-ik-Ø?
   hi   what   ICP-A2-see-ITS-B3SG
   'Hi, what do you see? How are you?' (direct object) (H 2014a:73)

d. **B'a'**   b'u'r-**ir**   a-k'aat-i'?
   what   bean-POSS   A2-want-FOC
   'What kind of beans do you want?' (object/kind of) (H 2014a:75)

ITZAJ

e. **Ba'ax-tak**   t-u-ta-s-aj-Ø?
   what-PL   CP-A3-come-CAUS-DTS-B3SG
   'What things did you bring?' (direct object) (H 2000:424)

f. **Ba'ax** b'äk'-**il**   t-a-jan-t-aj-Ø.
   what meat-POSS   CP-A2-eat-TR-DTS-B3SG
   'What kind of meat did you eat?' (object/kind of) (H 2000:424)

MOPAN

g. **K'u'-i**   a   tan   a-b'et-ik-Ø-i?
   what-FOC   DET   DUR   A2-do-ITS-B3SG-TOP
   'What is it you are doing?' (direct object) (H 2011a:279)

h. **K'u'**   ti   b'äk'-**il**   a-k'at-ij-i?
   what   to   meat-POSS   A2-want-TR-TOP
   'What kind of meat do you want?' (object/kind of) (H 2011a:127)

5 COMPLEX STRUCTURES

5.1 Complex predicates

When the matrix verb is an intransitive verb of motion, intransitive and transitive subordinate verbs are marked distinctly. In Yucatec subordinate intransitives are marked by a *j* subordination marker and a bare incompletive status stem (27a). Southern Lacandon is the same but there is no overt marker of subordination (most frequently) or it is marked by *ti* like Itzaj and Mopan (27c), (27e), (27g). When the subordinate verb is transitive, it is marked by Set A and Set B person markers in the dependent status in all Yucatecan languages (27b), (27d) (27f) (27h).

(27) Intransitive matrix verb of motion

YUCATEC

a. Xen   **j**   **kim-il**   **t-inw-o'ol-al!**
go;IMPIS   SUB   die-IIS   on-A1SG-behalf-POSS
'Go die for me!' (Hofling and Ojeda 1994:282)

b. Xen   **a-jan-t-e-Ø!**
go;IMPIS   A2-eat-TR-DTS-B3SG
'Go eat it!' (Hofling and Ojeda 1994:285)

SOUTHERN LACANDON

c. B'in-Ø-een   **xíim-b'ar**   or   B'in-Ø-een   **ti'**   **xíim-b'aar**.
go-CIS-B1SG   walk-NML   go-CIS-B1SG   SUB   walk-NML
'I went to walk.' (H 2014a:86, 151)

d. K-u-b'in   **u-jur-ej-Ø**   **b'äk'**.
ICP-A3-go   A3-shoot-DTS-B3SG   meat
'He goes to hunt meat.' (Hofling 2014a:166)

ITZAJ

e. Tal-Ø-oo'   **ti**   **jan-al**   **a'**   **winik-oo'-ej**.
come-CIS-B3PL   SUB   eat-NML   DET   man-PL-TOP
'The men came to eat.' (H 2000:524)

f. porke   wa'ye'   k-i(m-be)l   **im-pak'-t-eech-ej**.
because   here   ICP-1SG.A-go   A1SG-await-TR-DTS;B2SG-TOP
'Because here I am going to await you.' (H 2000:524)

MOPAN

g. Tan   ti-b'eel   **ti**   **xim-b'al**.
DUR   A1PL-go   SUB   walk-NML
'We are going to walk.' (H 2011a:465)

h. Tal-Ø-een   **inw-il-a'-Ø**   **a**   **nooch=winik-i**.
come-CIS-B1SG   A1SG-see-DTS-B3SG   DET   big=man-TOP
'I came to see the gentleman.' (H 2011a:329)

5.2 Relative clauses

5.2.1 Headed relative clause

Headed relative clauses typically have the form: DET head noun [relative clause](-deictic) as in (28). The relativized NP may play any role in the relative clause. In Lacandon a second determiner generally follows the head noun (c), (d), a construction also found in Itzaj (g) and Mopan (i). In the Itzaj (e)–(g) the indirect object and commitative roles are marked by *ti'ij* and *etel* respectively at the end of the relative clauses as stranded prepositions.

(28) Definite head noun relative constructions

YUCATEC

a. T-im-b'eet-aj-Ø   y-éet-el   **le**   **xi'ipal**   [**t-inw-e'es-aj-Ø**
COM-A1SG-do-CTS-B3SG   A3-with-POSS   DET   guy   CP-A1SG-show-CTS-B3SG

tech-o']~RC~·
2SG.IOPR-DST
'I did it with the guy I showed you.' (Hanks 1984 3:4)

b. Utz   t-inw-ich   **le**   **meyaj**   **[k-a-b'eet-ik-Ø-o']**~RC~·
   good   to-A1SG-eye   DET   work   ICP-A2-do-ITS-B3SG-DST
   'I like the work that you do.' (Hanks 1984 3:4)

SOUTHERN LACANDON

c. Ti'   yaan   **a**   **máaskab'**   **[a**   **k-a-sij-ik-Ø**   **teen-e']**~RC~·
   there   EXIST   DET   machete   DET   ICP-A2-give-ITS-B3SG   1SG.IOPR-TOP
   'There is the machete that you gave me.' (H 2014a:309)

d. K-u-chup-ik-Ø   a-k'äb'   **a**   **máak**   **[a**   **yaan**   **u-ti'aar-o']**~RC~·
   ICP-A3-swell-ITS-B3SG   A2-hand   DET   person   DET   EXIST   A3-child-DST
   'The person who is pregnant swells your hand.' (H 2014a:112)

ITZAJ

e. ke   ix-ch'up-ej   b'in-Ø-ij   tulakal   t-a'   **b'ej**   **[k-u-b'el**
   that   F-woman-TOP   go-CIS-B3SG   all   on-DET   road   ICP-A3-go
   ich kaj-ej]~RC~·
   into town-TOP
   'that the woman went all along the road that goes into town.' (H 2000:471)

f. **A'**   **winik**   **[t-in-tz'aj-Ø**   **tak'in**   **ti'ij-ej]**~RC~   b'in-Ø-ij.
   DET   man   CP-A1SG-give;CTS-B3SG   money   3IOPR-TOP   go-CIS-B3SG
   'The man that I gave money to left.' (H 2000:473)

g. **A'**   **winik**   **[a'**   **tal-ij**   **in-kik**   **et-el-ej]**~RC~   b'in-Ø-ij.
   DET   man   DET   come-B3SG   A1SG-older.sister   with-POSS   go-CIS-B3SG
   'The man, the one my older sister came with, went.' (H 2000:474)

MOPAN

h. Saak   ten   **a**   **tz'ub'**   **[inw-il-aj-Ø**   **jod'eej-Ø-ij-i]**~RC~·
   afraid   1SG.IOPR   DET   child   A1SG-see-CTS-B3SG   yesterday-CIS-B3SG-TOP
   'The child that I saw yesterday is afraid of me.' (ALMG 2001b:306)

i. Bek'ech   **a**   **winik**   **[a**   **kana'-a]**~RC~·
   thin   DET   man   DET   there-TOP
   'The man who is there is thin.' (H 2011a:130)

5.2.2 Reduced relative clauses

The head noun may be omitted producing a light headed relative clause: DET [relative clause]-deictic, as in the following examples.

(29) Reduced relative clauses

YUCATEC

a. K-a-b'i-s-ik-Ø   **le**   **[in-tz'áaj-m-aj-Ø**   **tech-o']**~RC~·
   ICP-A2-go-CAUS-ITS-B3SG   DET   A1SG-give-PRF-CTS-B3SG   2SG.IOPR-DST
   'You bring that (which) I gave to you.' (Hanks 1984 3:4)

SOUTHERN LACANDON

b. **A**   **[k-uy-áakab'**   **ich**   **ru'um-o']**_{RC}   k-u-kuch-ik-Ø   ya'b'   máak.
   DET   ICP-A3-run   on   land-DST   ICP-A3-carry-ITS-B3SG   many   person
   'That which runs on the land (the car) carries a lot of people.' (H 2014a:189)

ITZAJ

c. I   aj=Wit'-oo'-ej   b'in-Ø-oo',   **a'**   **[ma'**   **kim-Ø-oo'-ej]**_{RC}   putz'-Ø-oo'.
   and   M=PN-PL-TOP   go-CIS-B3PL   DET   NEG   die-CIS-B3PL-TOP   flee-CIS-B3PL
   'And the Wit's, they went, those that didn't die, fled.' (H 2000:482)

MOPAN

d. Il-a-Ø   ti   ki'   **a**   **[tan u-b'et-ik-Ø-i]**_{RC}.
   see-DTS-B3SG   to   well   DET   DUR A3-do-ITS-B3SG-TOP
   'Look carefully what she is doing.' (H 2011a:182)

5.3 Complement clauses

The structures of object complements vary according to the whether the main verb is modally oriented or not, whether the subordinate verb is transitive or intransitive, and whether or not the subject of the subordinate verb is coreferential with an argument of the main verb.

5.3.1 *Modally oriented main verbs*

Modally oriented verbs include 'want', 'desire', 'tell someone to do something', 'order' and 'demand', among others.

5.3.1.1 Intransitive subordinate verbs

Constructions with intransitive subordinate verbs with coreferential subject have the subordinate structure: *(j)* Vintr-IIS, as in (30).

(30) Intransitive subordinate verb with coreferential subjects

YUCATEC

a. In-k'áat-Ø   **j**   **b'in-Ø**.
   A1SG-want-TS   SUB   go- IIS
   'I want to go.' (Durbin et al. 1992:6)

SOUTHERN LACANDON

b. U-k'áat-Ø   **b'áax-är**   y-ej-er   ma'ax.
   A3-want-TS   play-IIS   A3-with-POS   monkey
   'S/he wants to play with spider monkeys.' (H 2014a:218)

ITZAJ

c. Ii   u-k'a't-ij   **jok'-ol**   t-a'   aktun-ej.
   and   A3-want-TS   leave-IIS   from-DET   cave-TOP
   'And it wants to leave the cave.' (H 2000:488)

MOPAN

d. U-k'at-i   **tal**.
   A3-want-TS   come
   'S/he wants to come.' (H 2011a:258)

Intransitive subjects coreferential to matrix direct objects have the same structures in Yucatec and Southern Lacandon (31a), (31b), but are additionaly marked by *ti* in Itzaj and Lacandon (31c), (31d).

(31) Intransitive subordinate verb subject coreferential to matrix object

> YUCATEC
>
> a. T-u-tab'-s-aj-o'on   j   káal-tal   y-éet-el.
>   CP-A3-tempt-CAUS-DTS-B1PL   SUB   get.drunk-INCH/IIS   A3-with-POSS
>   'He tempted us to get drunk with him.' (Durbin et al. 1992:7)
>
> SOUTHERN LACANDON
>
> b. K-u-tuuchi'-t-ik-Ø   máan-än.
>   ICP-A3-send-TR-ITS-B3SG   shop-IIS
>   'S/he sends him to shop.' (H 2014a:342)
>
> ITZAJ
>
> c. Tan   a-tab'-s-ik-en   ti   uk'-ul.
>   DUR   A2-convince-CAUS-ITS-B1SG   SUB   drink-IIS
>   'You are tempting me to drink.' (H 2000:489)
>
> MOPAN
>
> d. Tan   u-täkaa'-t-ik-Ø   a   tz'ub'   ti   k'ex.
>   DUR   A3-send-TR-ITS-B3SG   DET   child   SUB   shop
>   'S/he is sending the child to shop.' (H 2011a:398)

When the subject of the subordinate verb is not coreferential with an argument of the main verb, the subordinate structure is: *ka'* Vintr-DIS-B, as in (32).

(32) Switch reference with the subordinate subject

> YUCATEC
>
> a. In-k'áat-Ø   ka'   taal-ak-ech.
>   A1SG-want-TS   SUB   come-DIS-B2SG
>   'I want you to come.' (Durbin et al. 1992:5)
>
> SOUTHERN LACANDON
>
> b. K-u-jaatz'=ta'an-t-ik-Ø   ka'   jut-uk-Ø   u-so's-er.
>   ICP-A3-rub=lime-TR-ITS-B3SG   SUB   fall-DIS-B3SG   A3-fur-POSS
>   'S/he rubs it (a hide) with lime so that its fur falls off.' (H 2014a:152)
>
> ITZAJ
>
> c. K-in-tz'ib'ol-t-ik-Ø   ka'   jok'-ok-ech.
>   ICP-A1SG-desire.TR-ITS-B3SG   SUB   leave-DIS-B2SG
>   'I desire that you leave.' H 2000:492)
>
> MOPAN
>
> d. In-k'at-i   ka'   tal-ak-ech.
>   A1SG-want-TS   SUB   come-DIS-B2SG
>   'I want you to come.' (H 2011a:395)

5.3.1.2 Transitive subordinate verbs

Like intransitive subordinate verbs, subordinate transitive verb clauses differ according to switch reference or coreferentiality of arguments in the two clauses. In both constructions, the subordinate verb is in the dependent status.

(33) Coreferentiality on subordinate transitive verb

> YUCATEC
> a. In-k'áat-Ø   **inw-il-Ø-ech**.
> A1SG-want-TS   A1SG-see-DTS-B2SG
> 'I want to see you.' (Durbin et al. 1992:9)

> SOUTHERN LACANDON
> b. Ma'   in-k'áat-Ø   **inw-ir-ej-Ø**   míix.
> NEG   A1SG-want-TS   A1SG-see-DTS-B3SG   cat
> 'I don't want to see a cat.' (H 2014a:205)

> ITZAJ
> c. A-k'a't(-ij)   **a-mäch-ä'-Ø**   a-suku'un-ej.
> A2-want(-TS)   A2-grab-DTS-B3SG   A2-older.brother-TOP
> 'You want to grab your older brother.' (H 2000:490)

> MOPAN
> d. A-k'at-i   **a-k'ex-e'-Ø**.
> A2-want-TS   A2-buy-DTS-B3SG
> 'You want to buy it.' (H 2011a:258)

The subordinator *ka'* occurs when an argument of the matrix verb is not coreferential with the subject of the subordinated clause, as in (34).

(34) Switch reference on subordinate transitive verb

> YUCATEC
> a. T-in-tza'-ik-Ø   tech   **ka' a-k'uch-e-Ø**.
> DUR-A1SG-demand-ITS-B3SG   2SG.IOPR   SUB   A2-load-DTS-B3SG
> 'I am demanding of you that you load it (on your back).' (Durbin et al. 1992:8)

> SOUTHERN LACANDON
> b. Tz'aj-Ø   teen   u-yi'j-ir   när   Tz'íit **ka'**
> give;IMPTS-B3SG   1SG.IOPR   A3-grain-POSS   corn   PN   SUB
>   **in-päk'-ej-Ø**.
> A1SG-plant-DTS-B3SG
> 'Give me the grains of *Tziit* corn to plant.' (H 2014a:364)

> ITZAJ
> c. T-in-t'än-ik-Ø   **ka' aw-il-a'-Ø**.
> DUR-A1SG-call-ITS-B3SG   SUB   A2-see-DTS-B3SG
> 'I am calling him for you to see him.' (H 2000:492)

> MOPAN
> d. Jad'i in-k'at-i   **ka' a-yee'-Ø**   ten   a-jub'
> only   A1SG-want-TS   SUB   A2-show;DTS-B3SG   1SG.IOPR   A2-thigh
> 'I only want that you to show me your thigh.' (H 2011a:223)

5.3.2 Cognitive and sensory matrix verbs

Unlike modally oriented main verbs, the object complements of sensory and some cognitive verbs are generally fully inflected for aspect and may occur in the incompletive or completive statuses, as in (35). (35b) is a non-expectative construction in which the matrix verb is marked by the topic marker and the following clause is its object.

(35) Object complements of sensory and cognitive verbs

YUCATEC

a. T-inw-il-aj-ech   **táan**   **a-jan-t-ik-Ø**   **wáaj**.
CP-A1SG-see-DTS-B2SG   DUR   A2-eat-TR-ITS-B3SG   tortilla
'I saw you eating tortillas.' (Durbin et al. 1992:13).

b. K-inw-il-ik-Ø-e'   **k-a-jan-t-ik-Ø**   **wáaj**.
ICP-A1SG-see-ITS-B3SG-TOP   ICP-A2-eat-TR-ITS-B3SG   tortilla
'Aha! I see that you are eating tortillas.' (Durbin et al. 1992:14).

SOUTHERN LACANDON

c. K-aw-u'y-ik-Ø   **b'a'**   **k-u-juum-áank-är**.
ICP-A2-hear-ITS-B3SG   what   ICP-A3-sound-AFV-IIS
'You hear what makes a noise.' (H 2014a:168)

ITZAJ

d. Ma   inw-oj-el   **bix**   **t-u-b'et-aj-Ø**.
NEG   A1SG-know   how   CP-A3SG-do-CTS-B3SG
'I don't know how he did it.' (H 2000:495)

MOPAN

e. chen   inw-u'y-aj-Ø-a   tan   u-t'up-ik-Ø   inw-ok.
only   A1SG-feel-CTS-B3SG-TOP   DUR   A3-prick-ITS-B3SG   A1SG-foot
'Suddenly I felt something was pricking my foot.' (H 2011a:426)

5.3.3 Verbs of speech

Direct quotation generally has the structure: V (Subject) (IO)-TOP [Quoted Speech] in Yucatec and Itzaj, as in (36a) and (36d), but the topic marker may be absent in Yucatec (Lucy 1993). In indirect quotation the topic marker is generally absent (36b), (36c), (36g), but is optional in Itzaj, which has the additional subordination marker *ke* (36e). The subordinate verbs are fully inflected. Mopan lacks the topic marker in both direct quotation (36h) and indirect quotation (36i).

(36) Direct and indirect quotation

YUCATEC

a. T-inw-a'al-aj-Ø-e':   **"Ten-e'**   **yan**   **in-b'in-Ø."**
CP-A1SG-say-CTS-B3SG-TOP   1SG.PRON-TOP   OBLIG   A1SG-go-IIS
'I said: "I will go."' (Durbin et al. 1992:14)

b. T-inw-a'al-aj-Ø   **yan**   **in-b'in**.
CP-A1SG-say-CTS-B3SG   OBLIG   1SG.A-go
'I said I would go.' (Durbin et al. 1992:14)

SOUTHERN LACANDON

c. T-a-jach='a'r-aj-Ø   teen   **yaan**   **túur-i'**   **u-wich**   **che'**.
CP-A2-truly=say-DTS-B3SG   1SG.IOPR   EXIST   one-FOC   A3-fruit   tree
'You truly told me there was one fruit of the tree.'

ITZAJ

d. ka' t-uy-a'al-aj-Ø   uy-ätan   ti'ij-**ej**:   "**Ma'an   ki-si'.**"
   then CP-say-CTS-B3SG 3A-wife   3IOPR-TOP NEG/EXIST A1PL-firewood
   'Then his wife said to him: "We don't have any firewood."' (H 2000:501)

e. Ka' t-inw-a'al-aj-Ø   ti'ij-e'   **ke   a'   che'-ej   jach   yutzil**
   then CP-1SG.A-say- CTS-B3SG   3IOPR-TOP   SUB   DET   tree-TOP   very   pretty
   'Then I said to him that the tree is very pretty.' (H 2000:505)

MOPAN

f. uy-ad'-aj-Ø   ti'ij: "**B'o'on   u-tool   a   'ek'en-e?**"
   3A-say-CTS-B3SG   3IOPR   how.much   A3-price   DET   pig-TOP
   'She said to him: "How much is the price of the pig?"' (Hofling 2012:410)

g. aal-b'-Ø-i   ti aj-Jwan-a **ka' xi'ik-Ø**   ti   ichkil.
   say-PSV-CIS-B3SG   to M-PN-TOP   SUB   go;DIS-B3SG   SUB   bathe
   'Juan was told to go bathe.' (Hofling 2012:410)

5.4 Adverbial clauses and conditional clauses

5.4.1. Subordinate adverbial clauses

5.4.1.1 Temporal subordinate clauses

Temporal subordinate clauses may precede or follow the main clause in the frame (DET)
Temporal [subordinate clause](-TOP). The punctual temporal marker is *ka'(aj)*. It is typically framed by the derminer and topic marker in Yucatec (37a) and Itzaj (37c), but not in
Southern Lacandon (37b) or Mopan (37d), (37e). In Itzaj the marker *ti* optionally appears
after *ka'* with intransitive completive subordinate verbs (37c), while in Mopan *ti* occurs
alone with intransitive verbs regardless of status (37e).

(37) Subordinate temporal clauses

YUCATEC

a. Peedroj-e'   túun   ki'=ki'=t'aan   **le   káa   j   k'uch-Ø-en-e'.**
   PN-TOP   DUR;A3   good=good=speak   DET   when   CP   arrive-CIS-B1SG-TOP
   'Pedro was praising when I arrived.' (Lehmann 2014)

SOUTHERN LACANDON

b. **Kaj   k'uch-Ø-een   ich   naj,**   t-inw-ir-Ø-Ø   in-na'.
   when   arrive-CIS-B1SG   in   house   CP-A1SG-see-CTS-B3SG   A1SG-mother
   'When I arrived in the house I saw my mother.' (Hofling 2011a: 169)

ITZAJ

c. **I   a'=ka'   (ti')   wak'-Ø-ij   u-tz'on-ej   a'   b'a'alche'-ej   ka'**
   and   DET-when   (CP)   fire-CIS-B3SG   A3-gun-TOP   DET   animal-TOP   then
   jok'-Ø-ij uy-alka'-ej.
   leave-CIS-3SG A3-run-TOP
   'And when his gun fired, the animal, then it left running.' (H 2000:512)

MOPAN

d. Te'-i   **ka'   in-chiit-aj-Ø-a**   naatz'-Ø-i   t-in-tzeel.
   LOC-FOC   when   A1SG-invite-CTS-B3SG-TOP   near-CIS-3SG   to-A1SG-side
   'There, when I invited her/him, s/he neared my side.' (H 2011a:322)

e. Tan-ak-∅   u-jan-al   **ti**   **ud'-uk-en.**
DUR-DIS-B3SG   A3-eat-NML   when   arrive-DIS-B1SG
'She will be eating when I arrive.' (H 2011a:117)

5.4.1.2 Manner subordinate clauses

Subordinate manner adverbial clauses are marked by an initial manner adverb in the frame: manner adverb + [subordinate clause] (+ TOP). In Yucatec, adverbial focus morphology occurs on the verb as well (38a), while in Mopan it may occur on the adverb (38e). (38) includes examples of Yucatec *b'eey* 'like' (38a) and its cognates (38c), (38e); and Yucatec *je-b'ix ~ je-ex* 'just as' (38b) and its cognates (38d), (38f).

(38) Manner subordinate clauses

YUCATEC

a. Óol   **b'eey**   **in-taal**   **in-ch'áaj-∅ a-naj-il-e', b'ey**
sort.of like   A1SG-come   A1SG-take;DTS-B3SG   A2-house-POS-TOP thus
t-u-b'eet-∅-∅-il   **xan-e'.**
CP-A3-do-DTS-B3SG-FOC too-TOP
'Sort of like I come and take your home, thus they did too.' (Hanks 1984 8:6)

Je'ex   **t-u-b'eet-aj-∅**   **le**   **yáax**   **ook-∅-∅**   **espanyool-o',**
OST;how   CP-A3-do-DTS-B3SG   DET   first   enter-CIS-B3SG   DET Spanish-DST
b'ey   **xan**   **t-u-b'eet-aj-∅**   **leti'.**
so   also   CP-A3-do-CTS-B3SG   3PRON
'Just as they did (when) first entered the Spanish, so also he did.'
(Hanks 1984 8:6)

ITZAJ

c. li   **b'ay-lo'**   **ka'**   **ok-∅-ij**   **k'in-ej**   ka'   wen-∅-een.
and   thus-DST   when   enter-CIS-B3SG   sun-TOP   then   sleep-CIS-B1SG
'And thus when the sun set, then I slept.' (H 2000:521)

d. **Je=b'ix**   **u-tz'on-ik-oo'-ej,**   **je=b'ix**   **u-lub'-ul**   **a'**   **b'a'alche'-oo'**
OST-how   A3-shoot-ITS-PL-TOP   OST-how   A3-fall-IIS   DET   animal-PL
t-u-yaam   **a'**   **witz-ej.**
in-A3-clearing   DET   hill-TOP
'Just as they shot them, so the animals fell in the clearing of the hill.'
(H 2000:522)

MOPAN

e. "I   **b'aa=lo'-il-ik**   **a**   **'uj-u,"**   k-u-t'an-oo'.
and   like-DST-FOC-FOC   DET   moon-TOP   ICP-A3-say-PL
'"And the moon is like that too," they say.' (H 2011a:182)

f. **Ja=b'ix**   **ti**   **k'äl-a'an-en**   **ich so'oy-o, b'a=lo'**   **ka'**   **in-k'äx-∅-eech**
OST-how   CP   tie-PTCP-B1SG in   coop-TOP   like=DST   SUB   A1SG-tie-DTS-B2SG
ich so'oy.
in coop
'Just as I was tied in the chicken coop, thus I will I tie you up in the chicken coop.' (H 2011a:198)

5.4.2 *Conditional clauses*

Conditional clauses occur in the frame: *wá(aj)* (or *wa*) + [conditional clause]-TOP.

(39) Conditional clauses

> YUCATEC
> a. **Wáaj** **t'aan-aj-ech** **y-éet-el-e'**, a-ti'a'l le taak'in-o'.
>   COND speak-CIS-B2SG A3-with-POSS-TOP A2-POS DET money-DST
>   'If you talked with him, the money is yours.' (Lehmann 2014)
>
> SOUTHERN LACANDON
> b. **A** **wa** **x=kiik** **yaan** **u-paar-ar-o'** ma' tzooy
>   DET COND F=woman EXIST A3-child-POS-DST NEG good
>   u-päk-t-ik-Ø u-ta'k'-är ik-na'.
>   A3-look.at-TR-ITS-B3SG A3-hide-IIS A1PL-mother
>   'If a woman is pregnant, it is not good for her to look at the eclipse of the moon.' (Hofling 2014a)
>
> ITZAJ
> c. **Wa** **k-aw-an-t-ik-en** **im-p'a'-a'-Ø** **in-si'-ej**
>   COND ICP-A2-help-TR-ITS-1SG.B A1SG-split-DTS-B3SG A1SG-wood-TOP
>   ki-seeb'=b'el.
>   A1PL-quick=go
>   'If you help me split my firewood, we'll go soon.' (H 2000:461)
>
> MOPAN
> d. **Wa** **a-k'at-e'ex-e** in-maan-t-ik-Ø te'ex.
>   COND A2-want-B2PL-TOP A1SG-lend-TR-ITS-B3SG 2PL.IOPR
>   'If you all want, I'll lend it to you.' (H 2011a:303)

5.5 Coordination

5.5.1 *Parataxis*

Clauses are often placed together without overt markers of coordination in paratactic constructions, often with pauses between clauses. It is left to the hearer to interpret the semantic relation between the clauses.

(40) Paratactic constructions

> YUCATEC
> a. Yaan inw-aalak' t'u'ul, t-in-chuk-aj-Ø jo'olje-ak-Ø; ma'
>   EXIST A1SG-pet rabbit CP-A1SG-capture-CTS-B3SG yesterday-DIS-B3SG NEG
>   suuk-ak-Ø-i'.
>   tame-DIS-B3SG-SCOPE
>   'I have a rabbit, I trapped him yesterday (and) it hasn't tamed.' (ALMY 2003:30)
>
> SOUTHERN LACANDON
> b. B'in-Ø-ij, je' u-ka'=suut.
>   go-CIS-B3SG ASSUR A3-REPET=return
>   'S/he went (and) will return again.' (H 2014a:86)

ITZAJ

c. I   t-a'   bej-ej   in=ten-ej   tan   in-tal,   ma'   jach
   and   on-DET   road-TOP   EMPH-1SG.PRON-TOP   DUR   A1SG-come   NEG   very
   ki'   inw-ool.
   good   A1SG-spirit
   'And on the road, I was coming (and) I wasn't feeling very well.' (H 2000:445)

MOPAN

d. In-kiit-i   top   k'as,   walak   u-lox-ik-∅,   u-jätz'-ik-∅
   A1SG-uncle-TOP   very   bad   ICP   A3SG-punch-ITS-B3SG   A3-beat-ITS-B3SG
   u-mejen-oo'.
   A3-child-PL
   'My uncle is very bad; he punches (and) beats his children.' (ALMG 2001b:311)

5.5.2 General conjunctions yéet-el and i(j)

In Yucatec the relational noun *yéetel* may function to conjoin nominals (41a) and larger constituents (41b). In Southern Lacandon the cognate *yejer* conjoins nominals (41c) as does *etel* in Mopan (41e). In both Itzaj and Mopan the conjuction *i(j)* may conjoin various constituents (41d), (41f).

(41) Generalized conjunction

YUCATEC

a. Le=la'   in-múul   kool   **y-éet-el**   in-suku'un-o'ob'.
   DET-PROX   A1SG-common   milpa   A3-with-POS   A1SG-older.brother-PL
   'This is my and my older brothers' milpa.' (ALMY 2003:170)

b. Ka'   t-uy-a'al-aj-∅   le   máak-(e')   **y-éet-el**   tun-púuj-ul
   when   CP-A3-say-CTS-B3SG   DET   man(-TOP)   A3-with-POSS   DUR;A3-complain-IIS
   tun-la'ach-ik-∅   u-pool.
   DUR/A3-pull-ITS-B3SG   3A-hair
   'When the man spoke and he is complaining angrily and pulling his hair . . . '
   (Lucy 1993:112)

SOUTHERN LACANDON

c. A   che'-o'   k-u-ch'ij-ir   chum-uk   inw-atooch   **y-ej-er**
   DET   tree-DST   ICP-A3-grow-IIS   middle-NML   A1SG-home   A3-with-POSS
   kaax.
   chicken
   'The tree is between the house and the chicken (coop).' (H 2014a:112)

ITZAJ

d. Tan   uy-ok-ol   k'in   **i**   to'on-e   ti-kiw-a'al-aj-∅   ti'ij.
   DUR   A3-enter-IIS   sun   and   1PL.PRON-TOP   CP-A1PL-say-CTS-B3SG   3IOPR
   'The sun was setting and we told him.' (H 2000:448)

MOPAN

e. Pom   **et-el**   kib'   u-p'uul-b'-eeb'   u-wich   ix=Kod'eb'il-i.
   incense   with-POSS   candle   A3-cense-PSV-INST   A3-face   F=Virgin-TOP
   'The incense and candles are for censing the Virgin.' (H 2011a:373)

f. Yan   u-xid'-al-il   i   yan   uy-ix=ch'up-il.
    EXIST   3A-male-NML-POSS   and   EXIST   3A-F=female-POSS
    'S/he has her/his males (sons) and s/he has her/his females (daughters).'
    (H 2011a:186)

5.5.3 Temporal coordination with ka'(aj) 'then', 'when', 'and'

A common conjunction in Yucatec is *ka'(aj)* which is used to link events in a temporal
sequence and may be glossed as 'then', 'when' or 'and' (42a), (42b). In Itzaj *ka'* also
serves that function and may occur with *ti'* with completive intransitive verbs (42d). In
Mopan *ka'* or *ti* may serve as a temporal conjunction with intransitives (42e), (42f).

(42) Temporal coordination with *ka'(aj)*

YUCATEC

a. Aaj-en-e'   **ka**   t-in-'aaj-es-aj-Ø   Ped'ro.
    wake-1SG.B-TOP   then   CP-A1SG-wake-CAUS-CTS-B3SG   PN
    'I woke up and I woke up Pedro.' (ALMY 2003:75)

b. B'in-Ø-Ø   t-uy-otoch   **ka'aj**   t-u-kiim-s-aj-Ø   uy-aalak'
    go-CIS-B3SG   to-A3-home   then   CP-A3-die-CAUS-CTS-B3SG   A3-domestic
        x=kaax.
        F=chicken
    'He went to his home and he slaughtered his hen.' (ALMY 2003:115)

ITZAJ

c. t-u-käx-t-aj-Ø   u-xot'-ol   che'   **ka'**   näk-l-aj-ij   **ka'**
    CP-A3-seek.TR-CTS-B3SG   A3-piece-NML   wood   then   sit-POS-CIS-B3SG   then
        kap-Ø-ij   ti   litz.
        begin-CIS-B3SG   SUB   fish
    'He looked for a section of a log, then he sat down, then he began to fish.' (H
    2000:449–50)

d. **Ka'**   ti   näk-l-aj-ij   u-cha'an-t-ej-Ø.
    then   CP   sit-POS-CIS-B3SG   A3-watch-TR-DTS-B3SG
    'Then it sat to watch him.' (H 2000:451)

MOPAN

e. **Ka'**   ka'=b'in-Ø-i.
    when   REPET=go-CIS-B3SG
    'Then s/he went there again.' (H 2011a:231)

f. Jan-Ø-een   **ti**   ud'-Ø-eech.
    eat-CIS-B1SG   when   arrive-CIS-B2SG
    'I ate when you arrived.' (H 2011a:407)

5.5.4 Causal coordination

Causal coordination is marked by the relational noun *tume(e)n* in Yucatec (43a), (43b).
The cognate *teen* occurs in Southern Lacandon (43b). In both Southern Lacandon and

Itzaj the instrumental (*yejer*, *etel*) may signal inanimate causation (43c), (43e) and in both Itzaj and Mopan *(t)umen* functions as a causal coordinator (43d), (43f).

(43) Causal coordination

YUCATEC

a. . . . tun-púuj-ul   tun-la'ach-ik-Ø   u-pool   **t-u-men**   uy-oj-el
    DUR;A3-complain-IIS   DUR;A3-pull-ITS-B3SG   A3-hair   to-A3-do   A3-know-NML
    ti'   u-maama . . .
    about   3A-mother
    'He is complaining angrily and pulling his hair because he knows about his mother . . . ' (Lucy 1993:112)

SOUTHERN LACANDON

    A   naj-o'   rúub'-Ø-Ø   **teen**   ja'.
    DET house-DST   fall-CIS-B3SG   by   water
    'The house fell because of the water.' (H 2014a:297)

c. K-u-b'ées-ar **y-ej-er**   iik'.
    ICP-A3-tip-IIS A3-with-POSS wind
    'It tips over because of the wind.' (H 2014a:72)

ITZAJ

d. i to'on-ej   ti-kiw-a'al-aj-Ø   ti'ij   ke   ma'   u-b'el   **t-u-men**
    and 1PL.PRON-TOP CP-A1PL-say-CTS-B3SG 3IOPR SUB NEG A3-go to-A3-do
    te'   natz'   yan   a'   ayim . . .
    LOC close EXIST DET crocodile
    'And we told him that he shouln't go because there, close, is a crocodile.' (H 2000:453)

e. A   päk'-ej   tan   u-jut-ul   **et-el**   a'   ja'-ej.
    DET wall-TOP   DUR   A3-collapse-IIS with-POSS DET water-TOP
    'The wall is collapsing because of the water.' (H 2000:317)

MOPAN

f. U-p'ek-aj-Ø   u-jan-al   **u-men** ma'   yan   u-'ik-il.
    A3-dislike-CTS-B3SG A3-food-NML A3-do NEG EXIST A3-chile-TOP
    'S/he disliked his/her food because it didn't have chile.' (H 2011a:366)

6 CONCLUDING SUMMARY

The general picture that emerges from this survey of the Yucatecan languages is that they are quite similar and individual languages have had contacts with one another after diversification. Mopan is the most different from Yucatec, reflecting the first split in the family. This is clearly reflected in Mopan's aspect marking, which is most distinctive, lacking the completive aspect marker *t-* and having the incompletive marker *walak*, rather than the *k-* found in the others.

Yucatec and Southern Lacandon are closest in certain respects. They share a tonal distinction on long vowels, have a special agent focus construction, have similar affective verbs, have a distinctive passive marked by a glottal stop, have the reduced deictic suffixes *-a'* and *-o'*, mark negative scope with *i'*, and share dependent transitive status marking with *-ej* among other features.

Northern and Southern Lacandon also share some unique features, probably the result of contact. They both had the shift *o* > *a* and *l* > *r*, nasal harmony with -*Vn* suffixes, and have innovated a first person plural by adding -*o'(b')* to singular forms.

There are also features that contrast Yucatec with the southern dialects, such as the central vowel *ä* in the southern dialects and Yucatec's determiner *le* versus *(l)a(')* in the others and *b'eey* 'thus' versus *b'aay* in the others. Flora and fauna terms are also shared among the southern dialects. The use of the noun clasifers *aj*= and *ix*= is very similar in Northern Lcandon, Itzaj, and Mopan, and especially similar in Itzaj and Mopan. Itzaj and Mopan share passive marking with -*(a)b'*, dependent transitive status marking with -*V'*, marking in transitive subordinate clauses with *ti*, and similar sets of noun compounds and adjective-noun constructions marked with classifiers.

Overall, regional patterns emerge indicating contact after migration, but each language has unique features as well, with the result that languages that are quite close to one another geographically, such as Northern and Southern Lacandon, have differences reflecting different migration and contact histories.

NOTES

1 Parentheses indicate sounds that appear primarily in Spanish loan words.

2 Colonial Yucatec (and Proto-Yucatecan) had a glottal fricative /h/ and a velar fricative /χ/, which Kaufman (1991) and Orie and Bricker (2000) argue can be distinguished phonologically, but not phonetically, in Modern Yucatec. I follow standard practice in representing a single fricative in the modern languages.

3 *r* appears primarily in Spanish loans, except in Northern Lacandon which has partially shifted from *l* > *r* and Southern Lacandon which has completely shifted from *l* > *r*.

4 Here and below, sources for Proto-Yucatecan (p Yuc) forms include Kaufman and Justeson (2003) and Hofling (2014b); sources for Yucatec Maya include Durbin (n.d.); Bricker et al. (1998); and Academia de la Lengua Maya de Yucatán (ALMY) (2003), but Bricker et al. is the standard source; sources for Southern Lacandon are Çanger (1970a) for San Quintín (S Q) Lacandon and Hofling (2014a) for Lacanja (Lac) Lacandon; data for Northern Lacandon are from Hofling (2007); Itzaj sources are Hofling (1997), Hofling and Tesucún (2000); and Mopan data are from Hofling (2011a). Alphabets have been regularized according to the values given in the consonant and vowel charts above.

5 Bricker and Orie (2014) have recently argued that it is Yucatec that has innovated [a] from an earlier [ä].

6 Yucatec data are from Bricker (1986:24); Southern Lacandon are from Hofling (2014a:11); Northern Lacandon are data are from Bruce (1968:51); Itzaj data are from Hofling (1997:11) and Mopan data are from Hofling (2011a:12).

7 Yucatec data are from Hanks (1984 2:5); Southern Lacandon are from Hofling (2014a:11); Northern Lacandon data are from Bruce (1968:51); Itzaj data are from Hofling 1997:11) and Mopan data are from Hofling (2011a:12).

8 I follow Kaufman (1991) in considering affectives as a root class. Some scholars do not consider affectives to be a root class (Bricker et al. 1998:351).

9 Data sources here and below are: Yucatec (Po?ot Yah and Bricker 1981: viii–x, Hanks 1984 3:5; Kaufman 1991:34–5; Bricker et al. 1998:330–32); Southern Lacandon (Hofling 2014a); Northern Lacandon (Bruce 1968; Kaufman 1991:36–7); Itzaj (Hofling 2000; Hofling with Tesucún 1997); Mopan (Kaufman 1991:36; Hofling 2011a).

10 Bricker et al. (1998:334) consider these roots to have an underlying /b'/. Justeson (1989:30) proposes a metathesis of the final consonant of the root with the passive marker -*b'*, which appears as a glottal stop in roots not ending in a glottal consonant, e.g., *loch-b'-ol* > *lo'och-ol*.

REFERENCES

Academia de la Lengua Maya de Yucatán (ALMY). 2003. *Diccionario maya popular*. Merida, Yucatán: Academia de la Lengua Maya de Yucatán, A.C.

Academia de Lenguas Mayas de Guatemala (ALMG). Comunidad Lingüística Itza'. 2001a. *Alb'äl xokna'at t'an. Gramática descriptiva Itza'*. Guatemala: ALMG.

Academia de Lenguas Mayas de Guatemala (ALMG). Comunidad Lingüística Mopan. 2001b. *Tojkinb'eeb't'an Mopan. Gramática descriptiva Mopan*. Guatemala: ALMG.

Academia de Lenguas Mayas de Guatemala (ALMG). 2003. *Much't'an Mopan. Vocabulario Mopan*. Guatemala: ALMG.

Andrade, Manuel J. 1955. A grammar of modern Yucatec. Microfilm Collection of Manuscripts on Middle American Cultural Anthropology. Chicago: University of Chicago Library.

Ayres, Glenn, and Barbara Pfeiler. 1997. *Los verbos Mayas: La conjugación en el maya yucateco moderno*. Mérida, Yucatán, Mexico: Ediciones de la Universidad Autónoma de Yucatán.

Bergqvist, Henrik. 2008. "Temporal reference in Lakandon Maya: speaker and event perspectives." PhD diss., School of Oriental and African Studies, University of London.

Bergqvist, Henrik. 2011. "Agentivity and status in Yukatekan languages." In *New perspectives in Mayan linguistics*, ed. by Heriberto Avelino, 242–56. Newcastle upon Tyne: Cambridge Scholars Publishing.

Blaha Pfeiler, Barbara, and Andrew Hofling. 2006. "Apuntes sobre la variación dialectal en el maya yucateco." *Península* 1: 27–44.

Blair, Robert W. 1964. "Yucatec Maya noun and verb morpho-syntax." PhD diss., Indiana University.

Blair, Robert W., and Refugio Vermont Salas. 1965. *Spoken (Yucatec) Maya, Book 1: Lessons 1–12*. Chicago: Department of Anthropology, University of Chicago.

Blair, Robert W., and Refugio Vermont Salas. 1967. *Spoken (Yucatec) Maya, Book 2: Lessons 13–18*. Chicago: Department of Anthropology, University of Chicago.

Bohnemeyer, Jürgen. 1998. "Time relations in discourse: evidence from a comparative approach to Yucatec Maya." PhD diss., Katholieke Universiteit Brabant.

Bohnemeyer, Jürgen. 2002. *The grammar of time reference in Yukatek Maya*. Munich: Lincom Europa.

Bohnemeyer, Jürgen. 2004. "Split intransitivity, linking, and lexical representation: the case of Yukatek Maya." *Linguistics* 42: 67–107.

Briceño Chel, Fidencio. 2002. "Topicalización, enfoque, énfasis y adelantamiento en el Maya Yukateco. In *La organización social entre los mayas prehispánicos, coloniales y modernos*, ed. by. V. Tiesler Blos, R. Cobos and M Greene Robertson, 374–87. Mexico City/Merida: INAH/UADY.

Bricker, Victoria R. 1978a. "Antipassive constructions in Yucatec Maya." In *Papers in Mayan linguistics*, ed. by Nora England, 3–24. Columbia: Department of Anthropology, University of Missouri-Columbia.

Bricker, Victoria R. 1978b. "Wh-questions, relativization, and clefting in Yucatec Maya." *In Papers in Mayan linguistics*, ed. by Laura Martin, 107–36. Colombia: Lucas Brothers.

Bricker, Victoria R. 1981a. "The source of the ergative split in Yucatec Maya." *Journal of Mayan Linguistics* 2: 83–127.

Bricker, Victoria R. 1981b. *The Indian Christ, the Indian king: the historical substrate of Maya myth and ritual*. Austin: University of Texas Press.

Bricker, Victoria R. 1986. *A grammar of Mayan hieroglyphs*. Publication, 56. New Orleans: Tulane University, Middle American Research Institute.

Bricker, Victoria R. 1999. "Color and texture in the Maya language of Yucatán." *Anthropological Linguistics* 44: 283–307.

Bricker, Victoria R., and Olanike O. Orie. 2014. "Schwa in the modern Yucatecan languages and orthographic evidence of its presence in Colonial Yucatecan Maya, Colonial Chontal, and preColumbian Maya hieroglyphic texts." *International Journal of American Linguistics* 80: 175–207.

Bricker, Victoria R., Eleuterio Po'ot Yah, and Ofelia Dzul de Po'ot. 1998. *A dictionary of the Maya language as spoken in Hocabá, Yucatán*. Salt Lake City: The University of Utah Press.

Bruce, Roberto D. 1968. *Gramática del Lacandón*. Mexico City: Instituto Nacional de Antropología e Historia.

Bruce, Roberto D. 1974. *El libro de Chan K'in*. Mexico: Instituto de Antropología e Historia, Colección Científica Lingüística 12.

Bruce, Roberto D. 1976. *Textos y dibujos Lacandones de Najá Trilingual edition: Lacandón-Spanish-English*. Mexico City: Instituto de Antropología e Historia, Colección Científica Lingüística 45.

Bruce, Roberto D. 1979. *Lacandon dream symbolism*. Mexico: Ediciones Euroamericanas Klaus Thiele.

Çanger, Una. 1970a. "Vocabulary of San Quintín." Unpublished manuscript.

Çanger, Una. 1970b. "Notes on Lacandón structure." Unpublished manuscript.

Cook, Suzanne, and Barry Carlson. 2004. Ethnobiological inventories – birds – fish – mammals – reptiles – insects – plants. http://web.uvic.ca/lacandon/language.htm.

Corripio, Israel Martínez, and Ricardo Maldonado. 2010. "Middles and reflexives in Yucatec Maya: trusting speaker's intuition." In *Language documentation & conservation. Special Publication No. 2: Fieldwork and linguistic analysis in indigenous languages of the Americas*, ed. by Andrea L. Berez, Jean Mulder, and Daisy Rosenblum, 147–71. http://nflrc.hawaii.edu/ldc/ http://hdl.handle.net/10125/6789

Danziger, Eve. 1996. "Split transitivity and active-stative patterning in Mopan Maya." *International Journal of American Linguistics* 62: 379–414.

Davis, Virginia Dale. 1978. "Ritual of the Northern Lacandon Maya." PhD diss., Tulane University.

Durbin, Marshall E. n.d. "Yucatec Maya dictionary." Unpublished manuscript.

Durbin, Marshall, Charles Andrew Hofling, and Fernando Ojeda. 1992. "Subordinate object clauses in Yucatec Maya." Unpublished manuscript.

Durbin, Marshall, and Fernando Ojeda. 1978a. "Basic word order in Yucatec Maya." In *Papers in Mayan linguistics*, ed. by Nora England, 69–77. Columbia: University of Missouri.

Durbin, Marshall, and Fernando Ojeda. 1978b. "Negation in Yucatec Maya." *Journal of Mayan Linguistics* 1: 53–60.

Durbin, Marshall, and Fernando Ojeda. 1982. "Patient deixis in Yucatec Maya." *Journal of Mayan Linguistics* 3: 3–23.

Fisher, William Morrison. 1973. "Towards the reconstruction of Proto-Yucatec." PhD diss., University of Chicago.

Gutiérrez-Bravo, Rodrigo, and Jorge Monforte y Madera. 2008. "La alternancia sujeto-inicial/verbo inicial y la teoría de optimidad." In *Teoría de optimidad: Estudios de sintaxis y fonología*, ed. by Rodrigo Gutierrez-Bravo and Esther Herrera Zendejas, 61–99. Mexico City: El Colegio de México.

Gutiérrez-Bravo, Rodrigo, and Jorge Monforte y Madera. 2011. "Focus, agent focus and relative clauses in Yucatec Maya." In *New perspectives in Mayan linguistics*, ed. by Heriberto Avelino, 257–74. Newcastle upon Tyne: Cambridge Scholars Publishing.

Hanks, William F. 1984. "Outline teaching grammar of Yucatec: 1. Functional structure of Yucatec; 2. General characteristics of Yucatec language; 3. The noun phrase; 4. The verb complex (VC); 5. The verb complex, Part II; 6. The verb complex (Part III); 7. Circumstantial adjuncts: location, time and manner; 8. Word order: scrambling, focus and topicalization; 9. Particles; 10. Complement constructions." Unpublished manuscript.

Hanks, William F. 1990. *Referential practice: Language and lived space among the Maya*. Chicago: The University of Chicago Press.

Hanks, William F. 2010. *Converting words: Maya in the age of the cross*. Berkeley: University of California Press.

Hofling, Charles Andrew. 1984. "On Proto-Yucatecan word order." *Journal of Mayan Linguistics* 4: 35–64.

Hofling, Charles Andrew. 1990. "Possession and ergativity in Itzá Maya." *International Journal of American Linguistics* 56(4): 542–60.

Hofling, Charles Andrew. 1991. *Itzá Maya texts with a grammatical overview*. Salt Lake City: The University of Utah Press.

Hofling, Charles Andrew. 1998. "Irrealis and perfect in Itzaj Maya." *Anthropological Linguistics* 40: 214–27.

Hofling, Charles Andrew. 2004. "Language and cultural contacts among Yukatekan Mayans." *Collegium Antropologicum* 28 (Suppl. 1): 241–48. Zagreb, Croatia.

Hofling, Charles Andrew. 2006a. "La historia lingüística y cultural del maya yucateco durante el último milenio." In *Los Mayas de ayer y hoy: Memorias del primer congreso internacional de la cultura maya*, ed. by Alfredo Barrera Rubio and Ruth Gubler, vol. 2, 1196–216. Mexico City: Solar, Servicios Editoriales, S.A. de C.V.

Hofling, Charles Andrew. 2006b. "A sketch of the history of the verbal complex in Yukatekan Mayan languages." *International Journal of American Linguistics* 72: 367–96.

Hofling, Charles Andrew. 2007. "Lexical database of Northern Lacandon." Unpublished Toolbox file.

Hofling, Charles Andrew. 2008. "Notes on Mopan lexicon and Mopan lexical morphology." In *Proceedings of the congreso de idiomas indígenas de latinoamérica III, Austin, Texas, 2007*. http://www.ailla.utexas.org/site/cilla3_toc.html.

Hofling, Charles Andrew. 2011a. *Mopan Maya-Spanish-English dictionary*. Salt Lake City. The University of Utah Press.

Hofling, Charles Andrew. 2011b. "Voice and auxiliaries in Mopan Maya." In *New perspectives in Mayan linguistics*, ed. by Heriberto Avelino, 144–59. Newcastle upon Tyne: Cambridge Scholars Publishing.

Hofling, Charles Andrew. 2012. "A comparison of Narrative style in Mopan and Itzaj Maya." In *Parallel worlds: Genre, discourse and poetics in contemporary and classic Maya Literature,* ed. by Kerry Hull and Michael Carrasco, 401–48. Boulder: University Press of Colorado.

Hofling, Charles Andrew. 2013. "El Maya Lacandón en el Siglo XXI." Paper presented at the IX Congreso Internacional de Mayistas. Campeche, Mexico.

Hofling, Charles Andrew. 2014a. *Lacandon Maya-Spanish-English diction*ary. Salt Lake City: The University of Utah Press.

Hofling, Charles Andrew. 2014b. "Proto-Yukatekan lexical database." Unpublished Toolbox file.

Hofling, Charles Andrew, and Fernando Ojeda. 1994. "Yucatec Maya imperatives and other manipulative language." *International Journal of American Linguistics* 60: 272–94.

Hofling, Charles Andrew, with Félix Fernando Tesucún. 1997. *Itzaj Maya-Spanish-English dictionary*. Salt Lake City: University of Utah Press.

Hofling, Charles Andrew, and Félix Fernando Tesucún. 2000. *Tojt'an Maya' Itzaj: Diccionario Maya Itzaj-Castellano*. Guatemala: Cholsamaj.

Hofling, Charles Andrew, with Félix Fernando Tesucún. 2000. *Itzaj Maya grammar*. Salt Lake City: The University of Utah Press.

Justeson, John S. 1986. "Yucatecan phonological history." Unpublished manuscript.

Justeson, John S. 1989. "The representational conventions of Mayan hieroglyphic writing." In *Word and image in Maya culture*, ed. by William F. Hanks and Don S. Rice, 25–38. Salt Lake City: University of Utah Press.

Kaufman, Terrence. 1991. "Notes on the structure of Yukateko and other Yukatekan languages." Unpublished manuscript.

Kaufman, Terrence, with John S. Justeson. 2003. A preliminary Mayan etymological dictionary. http://www.famsi.org/reports/01051/pmed.pdf.

Kidder, Emily. 2013. "Prominence in Yucatec Maya: the roll of stress in Yucatec Maya words." PhD diss., University of Arizona.

Krämer, Martin, and Dieter Wunderlich. 1999. "Transitivity alternations in Yucatec, and the correlation between aspect and argument roles." *Linguistics* 37: 431–79.

Lehmann, Christian. 2002. *Possession in Yucatec Maya*. 2nd. revised edition. Erfurt: Seminar für Sprachwissenschaft der Universität (ASSidUE)

Lehmann, Christian. 2014. La lengua maya de Yucatán. http://www.christianlehmann.eu /ling/sprachen/maya/index.php

Lois, Ximena, and Valentina Vapnarsky. 2006. "Root indeterminacy and polyvalence in Yukatekan Mayan languages." In *Lexical categories and root classes in Amerindian languages*, ed. by Ximena Lois and Valentina Vapnarsky, 69–115. Bern: Peter Lang.

Lucy, John. 1993. "Metapragmatic presentationals: reporting speech with quotatives in Yucatec Maya." In *Reflexive language: reported speech and metapragmatics*, ed. by John A. Lucy, 91–125. Cambridge: Cambridge University Press.

MacLeod, Barbara. 1983. *An Eigrapher's annotated index to Cholan and Yucatecan verb morphology*. Austin: University of Texas Press.

Orie, Olanike O., and Victoria R. Bricker. 2000. "Placeless and historical laryngeals in Yucatec Maya." *International Journal of American Linguistics* 66: 283–317.

Oxlajuuj Keej Maya' Ajtz'iib'. 2003. *Vocabulario comparativo*. Guatemala: Cholsamaj.

Palka, Joel W. 2005. *Unconquered Lacandon Maya. Ethnohistory and archaeology of indigenous culture change*. Gainesville: University Press of Florida.

Pfeiler, Barbara. 1995. "Variación fonológica en el maya yucateco." In *Vitalidad e influencia de las lenguas indígenas en Latinoamerica*, ed. by Ramón Arzáplo Marín and Yolanda Lastra, 488–97. Mexico City: UNAM.

Po?ot Yah, Eleuterio, and Victoria R. Bricker. 1981. *Yucatec Maya Verbs (Hocoba dialect)*. New Orleans: Tulane University, Center for Latin American Studies.

Schumann Gálvez, Otto. 1971. *Descripción estructural del maya itzá del Petén, Guatemala C. A., con un diccionario itzá-español*. Mexico City: Universidad Nacional Autónoma de México, Seminario de Estudios de la Escritura Maya.

Schumann Gálvez, Otto. 1997. *Introducción al maya mopán*. Mexico City: Universidad Nacional Autónoma de Mexico.

Schumann Gálvez, Otto. 2000. *Introducción al maya itzá*. Mexico City: Universidad Nacional Autónoma de Mexico.

Skopeteas, Stavros, and Elisabeth Verhoeven. 2011. "Distinctness effects on VOS order: Evidence from Yucatec Maya." In *New perspectives in Mayan linguistics*, ed. by Heriberto Avelino, 276–300. Newcastle upon Tyne: Cambridge Scholars Publishing.

Smailus, Ortwin. 1989. *Gramática maya*. Hamburg: Wayasbah.

Tozzer, Alfred M. 1907. *A comparative study of the Mayas and the Lacandones*. New York: Macmillan.

Ulrich, Mateo, and Rosemary de Ulrich. 1976. *Diccionario bilingüe maya mopán y español, español y maya mopán*. Guatemala: Impreso de los talleres del Instituto Lingüístico de Verano en Guatemala.

Ulrich, Mateo, and Rosemary de Ulrich, with Charles Peck. 1978. "Mopan Maya verbs." Unpublished manuscript.

Verhoeven, Elisabeth, and Stavros Skopeteas. 2015. "Licensing focus constructions in Yucatec Maya." *International Journal of American Linguistics* 81: 1–40.

INDEX

Printed in Great Britain
by Amazon

38565975R00441